PEACE
&WAR

Books by Raymond Aron Published by Transaction

- In Defense of Decadent Europe

- Main Currents in Sociological Thought
  Volume 1: Montesquieu, Comte, Marx, Tocqueville,
  and the Sociologists and the Revolution of 1848

- Main Currents in Sociological Thought
  Volume 2: Durkheim, Pareto, Weber

- The Opium of the Intellectuals

- Peace & War: A Theory of International Relations

- Politics and History

- Thinking Politically: A Liberal in the Age of Ideology

PEACE & WAR

A Theory of
International
Relations

Raymond Aron

With a new introduction by
Daniel J. Mahoney and **Brian C. Anderson**

Transaction Publishers
New Brunswick (U.S.A.) and London (U.K.)

Second printing 2009

New material this edition copyright © 2003 by Transaction Publishers, New Brunswick, New Jersey. Originally published in 1966 by Doubleday & Company, Inc.

This book is printed on acid-free paper that meets the American National Standard for Permanence of Paper for Printed Library Materials.

Library of Congress Catalog Number: 2003048420
ISBN: 978-0-7658-0504-1
Printed in the United States of America

Library of Congress Cataloging-in-Publication Data

Aron, Raymond, 1905-
  [Paix et guerre entre les nations. English]
  Peace and war : a theory of international relations / Raymond Aron ; with a new introduction by Daniel J. Mahoney & Brian C. Anderson.
      p. cm.
  Previously published as: Garden City, N.Y. : Doubleday, 1966. [1st ed.]
  Includes bibliographical references and index.
  ISBN 0-7658-0504-9 (pbk. : alk. paper)
  1. International relations. I. Title.

JZ1305.A7613 2003
327'.1'01—dc21   2003048420

International law is based by nature upon this principle: that the various nations ought to do, in peace, the most good to each other, and, in war, the least harm possible, without detriment to their genuine interests.

—Montesquieu, *L'Esprit des lois*, I, 3

In 1954, in a note on an article entitled "On the Analysis of Diplomatic Constellations" published in the *Revue française de science politique*, I announced a *Sociology of International Relations*. For several years I had been contemplating the book that I now offer. During that time the theme broadened, and the distinctions of *theory*, *sociology*, and *praxiology* came to seem to me fundamental in order to grasp, on the different levels of conceptualization, the intelligible texture of a social universe. Ultimately, although this book deals chiefly with the world today, its deepest aim is not linked to the present. My goal is to comprehend the implicit logic of relations among politically organized collectivities. This effort of comprehension culminates in the question that will determine the future of the human race.

Will the nations henceforth capable of annihilating, without even disarming, each other, discover the meaning of a truly peaceful coexistence? I do not claim to give an answer which only history can afford. But perhaps this book will help readers to reflect on the problem in all its complexity.[1]

Venanson, July 1959
Paris, October 1961

[1] I should like to take this occasion to thank those who have helped me to bring this work to its conclusion: Harvard University, in appointing me Ford Research Professor of Government for a semester of 1960–61, afforded me several months of the student's scholarly leisure; Suzanne Moussouris who indefatigably transcribed and retranscribed manuscripts almost illegible to anyone but herself; Isabelle Nicol who edited the text; Pierre Hassner who translated the English citations; and Stanley Hoffman and Pierre Bourdieu who suggested important corrections.

CONTENTS

PART ONE

THEORY
Concepts and Systems

PART TWO

SOCIOLOGY
Determinants and Constants

PART THREE

HISTORY
The Global System in the Thermonuclear Age

PART FOUR

PRAXEOLOGY
The Antinomies of Diplomatic-Strategic Conduct

Not so long ago, liberal democracy and capitalism seemed on the ascendant. The Soviet Union and its satellite regimes in Eastern and Central Europe had collapsed, the European Union was coming together, democratic institutions were springing up across the globe, and the free market was extending the circle of prosperity and growth ever wider. Political thinkers and pundits began to speak of an "end of history" in a triumphant democratic capitalism, of the obsolescence of the nation-state, of a cosmopolitan "law of peoples." At least for some, it was as if we were entering into a new, post-political era, in which the traditional enmities, passions, and conflicts of human history would give way to the management of success and the staving off of boredom.[1]

The atrocities of September 11, the U.S. defeat of the Taliban in Afghanistan, imminent conflict in Iraq, internal national conflicts within NATO, nuclear brinkmanship between India and Pakistan, the collapse of the dot-com boom, and rising economic protectionism—how different the world appears today. Politics has returned vengefully, making the liberal optimism of the 1990s appear naïve.[2]

The great French liberal Raymond Aron would not have been surprised at the stubborn persistence of politics. In this impressive book, first published in French in 1962, Aron argues that international relations is, and will likely always remain, the realm of independent sovereignties, jealous of their interests and their prestige—their "Power, Glory, and Idea," in *Peace and War*'s formulation.[3] These sovereignties refuse to surrender their right, at least at the limit, to defend their interests and prestige through force of arms. This partial state of nature between states (what Kant famously called the "asocial sociality" of international life) is very different from the civil relations within states. The possibility of war is thus always among the statesman's concerns and therefore should also be central to any attempt to think about international relations.

The political thinker who ignores the problem of war fails two key interrelated duties of his calling: that of advising the statesman (and, in a democratic context, educating the citizen); and that of mirroring as accurately, as "scientifically," as possible, the reality of the political world. *Peace and War* is an ambitious attempt both to describe the permanent aspects of the life of nations and to advise statesmen and democratic citizens. To guide the reader in his reading of this big, complex book, we offer here a brief outline of its principal themes.

Starting from the recognition of the partial state of nature among states, Aron develops in *Peace and War* an array of analytical tools for thinking about international relations. These tools fall under four headings: theory, sociology, history, and "praxeology" (that is, what is right and wrong among states, as distinct from within them).

Under theory, Aron lays out a broad conceptual framework based on power and system. Power concerns the means and ends of foreign policy. As a means, power allows one political unit to impose its will on another, and in Aron's view it has three components—territory, resources, and the collective capacity for action. To understand how territory influences power, simply look at the United States, a vast country, bordered on its eastern and western coasts by enormous oceans. These natural advantages have long protected the United States from invasion, though the threats of intercontinental missiles and of terrorists wielding biological, chemical, and radiological weapons have of course diminished somewhat the importance of territory as a means of power. As for resources, their contribution to a state's power is a function of economic development. America's tremendous wealth, generated from its vibrant open economy, has enabled it to exert its power globally in ways no other nation can match.

It is at least possible to measure both territory and resources as means of power. By contrast, Aron shows, the collective capacity for action of a state depends on spiritual resources that resist all quantification. Who could have anticipated England's fierce resistance to National Socialist Germany during the Second World War?[4] A state can be far more powerful than its territory or level of wealth would suggest.

And what do states use power for? Aron insists on the irreducible complexity of international relations—*pace* those like Kenneth Waltz, who boil them down to the "structural" competition for power and influence, or to neo-Marxists like Antonio Negri who see the machinations of capital behind every state action.[5] Nations pursue many ends, from the dream of autarky to a sacred ideal to the quest for influence or even grandeur.

This irreducible complexity of ends means that we can at best discern probabilities within international relations. No simply predictive theory of state relations is possible. As Aron puts it at the end of *Peace and War*, it is "incontestable" that "political science is not *operational*, in the sense in which physics is, or even in the sense in which economics are."[6] He shares Aristotle's belief that a discussion "will be adequate if its degree of clarity fits the subject matter; for we should not seek the same degree of exactness in all sorts of arguments alike, any more than in the products of different crafts."[7] Conjecture is more art than science.

The notion of diplomatic system is the second part of Aron's "theory" framework. A diplomatic system consists of those political units that maintain relations and that would find themselves inexorably drawn into a generalized war. A system, Aron points out, can consist of "heterogeneous" or "homogeneous" regimes—that is, regimes that pursue similar or dissimilar goals or that have similar or dissimilar constituting principles; a mixed system of heterogeneous and homogeneous regimes is also possible. Today, the Western democracies and Iran or Iraq belong to a heterogeneous system, the democracies themselves a homogenous one. During World War II, the United States and the Soviet Union belonged to a mixed system, dissimilar regimes fighting together against a common enemy. And so on. Though Aron's understanding of the political regime is narrower than Aristotle's, which encompassed an entire way of life, it shares with it a powerful sense of the importance of politics. Aron is a particularly incisive critic of the "realist" delusion that great nations are guided by conceptions of "the national interest" that are more or less immune to fundamental changes of regime and ideology.

These kind of theoretical distinctions allow Aron to grasp international relations from within, in accordance with their inner logic and historical specificity, and the nature of the regimes involved. It is an approach that avoids abstraction and conceptual hubris.

After laying out this broad theoretical framework, Aron next moves to sociological analysis: the study of the myriad factors that influence foreign policy. The sociologist must determine the degree to which such factors influence the life of nations. The sociological causes, in Aron's view, can be material and physical on the one hand, and moral and social on the other.

Physical causes fall under three headings in *Peace and War*. The first is spatial. Like Montesquieu, Aron argues that environment may influence international relations but not determine them. Spatial considerations are also crucial in geopolitics—as the theater of battle and power. Space is also a stake in international relations, though much less so than in the past, given the general awareness that in the modern world wealth no longer depends on land and natural resources but on intelligence and good economics, and that military technology has made distance a diminishing obstacle to lethal force.[8] The second physical factor Aron considers is number. In discerning how number influences peace and war, we can draw no solid inferences, Aron believes. Economic ups and downs do not make war or peace inevitable. As always with Aron, we are in the realm of better or worse conjectures, not deterministic predictions.

Aron pays great attention to the moral and social causes of peace and war. Knowing the nature of a particular political regime or political culture is essential to making a good judgment about how it will act. The foreign policy of the Soviet Union largely took its bearings from ideology, Aron frequently argued. As long as the regime embraced Marxist-Leninist principles, it would seek only tactical peace with liberal democratic societies. Post-communist Russia, for all its difficulties and seemingly endemic corruption, has acted very differently on the world stage than would have a still-communist state. Ignoring such regime differences obscured what political judgment could achieve in international relations.

Nor was it the case that human nature required war. In a powerful passage, Aron writes:

> It is contrary to the nature of man that the danger of violence be definitively dispelled: in every collectivity, misfits will violate the laws and attack persons. It is contrary to the nature of individuals and groups that the conflicts between individuals and groups disappear. But it is not proved that these conflicts must be manifested in the phenomenon of war, as we have known it for thousands of years, with organized combatants, utilizing increasingly destructive weapons.[9]

Different political regimes would allow different articulations of the human propensity to violence, some much more sensible and less destructive than others. Politics matters.

Aron devotes the third section of *Peace and War* to history—specifically, the history of the twentieth century up until the early 1960s. Though its examples might seem dated, in fact the argument is strikingly relevant. He looks both at the technological revolution and the globalization of diplomacy—phenomena Aron believed marked the beginning of "universal history."[10] No one could deny that these two factors continue to play a prominent role in international relations. But as important as technology and universal diplomacy are, Aron rightly emphasized that they have not changed the nature of man or his collective forms of organization. The dramatic features of history—the conflict of men, nations, and regimes—was just as real in 1962—or 2002 for that matter—as it was when Thucydides wrote his great historical narrative. Neither the nuclear bomb nor the global economy has put an end to history. History may have slowed down, as Aron liked to put it, but history would continue "to write its letters in blood"[11] as long as the rivalry of men and regimes persisted.

Theory, sociology, history: a correct comprehension of these categories will inform both a "science" of international relations and the decisions of the prudent statesman. The fourth part of *Peace and War*—in many ways the most profound of the book—concerns "praxeology," Aron's normative theory of international relations. In it, Aron addresses two enduring problems of statecraft.

The first Aron calls the "Machiavellian" problem. Is foreign policy essentially evil? What means may the statesman justifiably use? As the three earlier sections of *Peace and War* have shown, the political leader confronts a world of uncertainty; probabilities are the most he can rely on. He also confronts a diplomatic universe in which states retain their sovereignty and much of their freedom of action.

One possible practical option for the statesman is the idealist "morality of law." Idealist theories attempt to transcend international anarchy by positing a categorical international morality. Aron rejects this approach as foolhardy—and immoral. International "legality" and fairness often conflict. "If, in 1933," Aron writes, "France had heeded Marshal Pilsudski's advice and used force to overthrow Hitler, who had just come to power, she would have violated the *principle* of non-interference in the internal affairs of other states, she would have failed to recognize Germany's *right* of free choice with regard to regime and leader, she would have been denounced with indignation by American public opinion, by moralists and idealists hastening to the rescue, not of National Socialism, but of the will of the people or the rule of non-interference."[12] But would France have been wrong?

This example, Aron maintains, illumines a fundamental truth of international relations. Since states remain "sole judges of what their honor requires," the very existence of a political community can depend on the statesman's willingness to measure the relations of force and, if necessary, to wield force in response to threats. To pretend that "international law" and "collective security" will protect his community in the absence of military might invites disaster. Indeed, such ingenuousness represents a moral failing. As Aron avows, "it is the *duty* of statesmen to be concerned, *first of all*, with the nation whose destiny is entrusted to them."[13] The idealist promotes a vision that reinforces injustice.

But if idealism fails as a morality of international relations, a "morality of struggle"[14] does no better. Its advocates argue that, given the existence of independent sovereignties, the statesman may use all means at his disposal—from the simple ruse to assassination to lethal force—whenever he deems it appropriate. Critics often describe Aron as a realist.[15] But though Aron, like the realists, appreciated the persistence of independent sovereignties, he did not accept that state amorality was legitimate or even necessary. While the statesman owed his paramount moral duties to his own political community, Aron argued, relations between communities were "not...comparable to those of beasts in the jungle."[16]

Aron held that certain *soi-disant* realists took the dark and violent side of human nature—man as a beast of prey—as human nature *tout court*. This was to encourage the very brutality the realist pretended only to explain. "Even in relations between states, respect for ideas, aspirations to higher values and concerns for obligations have been manifested," Aron pointed out. "Rarely have collectivities acted as if they would stop at nothing with regard to one another."[17] The realist might deny it, but morality remained an integral feature of political history.

The realist would even place democratic regimes and totalitarian regimes on the same level—all states indistinguishably pursuing their national interest. But for Aron this was a kind of historical nihilism, treating "Christians" and "barbarians" as if there was no moral difference between them. This was immoral—and unwise even from the standpoint of national interest. For a democracy had more to fear from political marauders than from other democracies, as the twentieth century has proved.

Superior to both the "morality of law" and the "morality of struggle," in Aron's view, was what Aron called the "morality of prudence." Attuned to the rivalrous nature of international relations, yet aware also of a shared human nature and certain moral universals, prudence offered a better sense of reality and morality than its rival approaches. The prudent statesman preferred "the limitation of violence…to so-called absolute justice," and strove to attain "concrete accessible objectives conforming to the secular law of international relations and not to limitless and perhaps meaningless objectives, such as 'a world safe for democracy' or 'a world from which power politics has disappeared.'"[18] It captured what was true in both idealist and realist approaches while correcting their excesses.

The morality of prudence represented political wisdom in the partially Hobbesian world of international relations, where states retained sovereignty but still acknowledged some measure of human universality. Was a different world possible if states surrendered their sovereignty? This, Aron suggested, was the "Kantian" problem of universal peace, *Peace and War*'s second "praxeological" exploration.

There were signs of a world community, but they were for the most part relatively superficial. A transnational society, for example, had emerged from the technological marvels of the twentieth century. Planes and televisions (and today the Internet) brought far-flung corners of the world into regular contact. Yet for every indication of a transnational society, Aron suggested, one could come up with a counter-indication, showing growing conflict between societies and cultures. There might be more talk of human rights in our time, he added, but how could any observer of the age of extremes—an age of mass atrocity and obliterating wars—say that a greater awareness of the human community as a whole had gained much ground? In many ways, humankind remained as divided as ever.

As Aron explained, only law or empire could overcome the "immemorial" order of collectivities. And neither approach was likely to succeed. Even if some super-tribunal or compelling political will came into being, would it not simply amplify the causes of conflict, Aron asked? The in-

equalities and resentments that cause tension within political communities—and that can even lead to revolution—would now be the responsibility of one universal sovereign. Why would such resentments
disappear within a universal state or world federation? This would mean
that man had solved the problem of politics itself.

And would a post-political world be desirable? It would mean the end of
a strong sense of nationhood. Aron saw a sense of political particularity as
something rooted in human nature—and therefore something to treasure.
"The diversity of cultures," he wrote, "is not a curse to be exorcized but a
heritage to be safeguarded."[19] To regret this, the way, say, John Rawls and
other cosmopolitan liberals have done, is to deny that which is common in
the quixotic quest for what is individual and *absolutely* universal. It would
represent an impoverishment of human existence.

One way to address both the need for a community of culture and to
move toward universal peace would be to pursue federation. But could the
world become a giant Switzerland? Turning to the German theorist Carl
Schmitt, Aron said such an outcome was utopian.[20] In Schmitt's view—and
Aron had some sympathy for it—the distinction between friend and enemy
is central to politics. The force that binds a community results in part from
opposition to the other. While Aron did not deduce the impossibility of
world federation from Schmitt's friend-enemy distinction, he did believe
that hostility was natural to man and could only be moderated, not eliminated. And that moderation required a binding of community that in turn
required an outside—if not an enemy, then at least an other. There was a
big difference, Aron felt, between the feasible broadening of world community and the unification of the world, which was a dream at the limits of the
historically possible. At best, the notion of a unified humanity might function as an "idea of reason" that could serve to moderate the bellicose pro-
clivities of human beings and political communities. Here, too, sobriety
and a sense of historical realism are necessary to avoid the twin extremes of
false realism and false idealism.

Peace and War was perhaps Aron's most ambitious book. Aron was justly
proud of this book but was never wholly satisfied with it. He had considerable doubts about whether he had finally succeeded in integrating its theoretical and historical dimensions and he feared that his work contained too
much analysis of the passing events of his day. In any case, *Peace and War* is
by no means Aron's final word on the nature of international relations or
the politics of the twentieth century. It needs to be read in conjunction with
his magisterial book on Clausewitz,[21] the work that Aron considered to be
his great masterpiece, as well as with his writings on the history of the twentieth century, now collected in English as *The Dawn of Universal History:*

Selected Essays from a Witness to the Twentieth Century (Basic Books, 2002). Together, these writings convey the magnitude of Aron's achievement as an authoritative, humane, and trustworthy guide to politics and history in an age unhinged by the ideological temptation. Despite Aron's own lingering doubts, *Peace and War* remains an indispensable book for those who wish to comprehend the place of peace and war in the human order of things. Written with the clear, classically restrained language Aron was noted for, the book stands out as one of the twentieth century's great works of political thought. At a time when history is once again on the move, and the liberal utopianism of recent years appears increasingly shallow, *Peace and War* reminds us of the fallibility of human knowledge, and the limits, but also the grandeur, of human morality in a dangerous and imperfect world.

Daniel J. Mahoney

Brian C. Anderson

Notes

[1] See Francis Fukuyama, *The End of History and the Last Man* (New York: Free Press, 1993); Kenichi Ohmae, *The Borderless World: Power and Strategy in the Interlinked Economy* (New York: HarperCollins, 1991); and John Rawls, "The Law of Peoples," in Stephen Shute and Susan Hurley, eds., *On Human Rights: The Oxford Amnesty Lectures, 1993* (New York: Basic Books, 1993), pp. 41-82.

[2] For Fukuyama's updated, post-September 11 view on whether history has ended or not, see "Has History Started Again?" *Policy*, Winter 2002, pp. 3-7. His answer: no.

[3] This introduction adapts and draws on longer treatments of *Peace and War* published earlier in Brian C. Anderson, *Raymond Aron: The Recovery of the Political* (Lanham, MD: Rowman & Littlefield Publishers, 1997), pp. 121-165 and Daniel J. Mahoney, *The Liberal Political Science of Raymond Aron* (Lanham, MD: Rowman & Littlefield Publishers, 1992), pp. 91-110. See also Bryan-Paul Frost, "Raymond Aron's *Peace and War*, Thirty Years Later," *International Journal*, Vol. 51, Spring 1996, pp. 339-361.

[4] This collective capacity for action can increase or diminish as a consequence of political leadership—another variable of international relations that escapes measurement. Aron underscored this point elsewhere: "Without Churchill, would England have stood firm all alone against the Third Reich?... Traditional history is action, that is to say it is made of decisions taken by men in a precise place and time. These decisions could have been different with another man in the same situation, or with the same man with another disposition. No one can fix, either beforehand or retrospectively, the limits of the consequences that some of these localized and dated decisions generate." Raymond Aron, *In Defense of Political Reason*, edited by Daniel J. Mahoney (Lanham, MD: Rowman & Littlefield Publishers, 1994), p. 138.

[5] See Kenneth Waltz, *Theory of International Politics* (Reading, MA: Addison-Wesley, 1979). For a neo-Marxist vision of the life of nations, see Michael Hardt and Antonio Negri, *Empire* (Cambridge: Harvard University Press, 2001).

[6] See below, p. 768.

[7] Aristotle, *Nichomachean Ethics*, trans. By T. Irwin (Indianapolis: Hackett Publishers, 1995), Bk. I, 1094b.

[8] On military technology, see Raymond Aron, *The Century of Total War* (Lanham, MD: University Press of America, 1985). On knowledge as a source of wealth, see Michael

Novak, *The Catholic Ethic and the Spirit of Capitalism* (New York: Free Press, 1993), pp. 114-43.

[9] See below, p. 366.

[10] See Raymond Aron, *Progress and Disillusion: The Dialectics of Modern Society* (New York: Praeger, 1968).

[11] See Raymond Aron, *Clausewitz: Philosopher of War* (Englewood Cliffs, N.J.: Prentice-Hall, 1985), p. 412.

[12] See below, p. 580.

[13] Ibid.

[14] Ibid., p. 608.

[15] See, for example, Charles R. Beitz, *Political Theory and International Relations* (Princeton: Princeton University Press, 1979), pp. 27-28.

[16] See below, p. 581.

[17] Ibid., p. 609.

[18] Ibid., p. 585.

[19] Ibid., p. 750.

[20] Schmitt, writing during the collapse of Weimer Germany, believed liberalism irreparably doomed by its refusal to recognize the violent core of politics—that politics invariably opposed friend and enemy. See *The Concept of the Political*, trans. By G. Schwab, with comments by Leo Strauss (Chicago: University of Chicago Press, 1996). Schmitt's subsequent involvement with the Nazis has rightly tarnished his reputation, but his work raises pressing questions for liberal democracies, as Aron acknowledged. Philippe Raynaud has sketched out what one could call the "hidden dialogue" between Aron and Schmitt. See "Raymond Aron et le droit international," *Cahiers de philosophie et juridique*, No. 15, 1989, pp. 115-28.

[21] Raymond Aron, *Clausewitz: Philosopher of War* (Englewood Cliffs, N.J.: Prentice-Hall, 1985).

This book, begun several years ago, was completed during the 1960–61 academic year, first at Cambridge, where the author was a Research Professor at Harvard University, then in France during the following spring and summer. It was published in 1962 in Paris, and therefore appears in the United States almost five years after it was written, four years after its first French edition.

If the text, aside from several minor corrections already introduced, for the most part, into the second French edition, has not been modified, the chief reason for this is pre-eminently the character of the book, which is not, in its author's mind, concerned with the present in the sense in which this term is utilized by the press. Of course Part III, entitled "History," offers an analysis of the diplomatic universe in which we live: coextensive with the limits of the planet, dominated by thermonuclear weapons, mainly possessed by two giant states. In a certain sense the first two parts, "Theory" and "Sociology," are also oriented toward the present. But the effort of comprehension, both theoretical and sociological, emphasizes primarily a *conceptual apparatus*, indispensable to a grasp of relations between states, then the scope of the *determinants* which affect these relations, and finally the possible *constants* revealed by the study of the past. Even historical comprehension, beyond the unforeseeable vicissitudes of the cold war or of peaceful coexistence, has for its object the lasting and, so to speak, structural characteristics of the post-1945 world.

Writing at the end of 1965, I should probably be led to formulate or to orient my views differently on one point or another, but the essential thing is that the instruments of analysis remain effective and that the changes that have occurred during these last four years have taken place within an established context. Now, without claiming to summarize the events of the 1961–65 period, I should like to indicate, in a few pages, why the more or less spectacular transformations of the diplomatic scene proceed from tendencies long since visible, and in what direction they tend.

The governing idea by which I interpreted the diplomatic situation was that of the solidarity of the two great powers—the warring brothers—against a total war of which they would be the first victims. Inevitably enemies by position and by the incompatibility of their ideologies, the United States and the Soviet Union have a common interest not in ruling together over the world (of which they would be quite incapable), but in not destroying each other. This politico-strategic doctrine was openly professed in the universities and institutes of the United States; it very nearly became the official doctrine of the Kennedy administration. And the Soviet leaders *acted* as if they in effect acknowledged this same doctrine. But they often spoke as if they were ignorant of it or rejected it. That is why I wondered, before the autumn of 1962, if the asymmetry of strategic conceptions (flexible response on the American side, inevitable escalation on the Russian side), the rejection of even limited agreements (such as relative agreement on the suspension of nuclear tests), was not due to Mr. Khrushchev's conviction or illusion that he was gaining an advantage from the fear such a war inspired—a fear that he felt quite as much as did his rival, but that he affected to ignore.

The Cuban crisis of October–November 1962 seems to have shaken this conviction or dissipated this illusion. Mr. Khrushchev had several times, though in a vague and reticent manner, threatened to utilize thermonuclear rockets to protect Cuba. When he committed the imprudence of constructing a Cuban base for medium-range missiles, an American quasi-ultimatum forced him to choose between a reply in another zone of the planet—where he could benefit from a superiority in conventional weapons comparable to that of the United States off the coast of Florida—a recourse to the apocalyptic weapons, or retreat. It appears that Mr. Khrushchev did not hesitate long: he preferred retreat, at the risk of being accused of "capitulationism" by his Chinese friends.

No shot had been fired, except by the Cubans who had downed an American plane, and yet the American notes, supported by military preparations, had transmitted to Moscow a message whose meaning was clear. For the first time, two states equipped with thermonuclear weapons faced each other in a direct confrontation. Deterrence ceased to be an abstract notion. Discovering, perhaps with surprise, that the American weapons were at the disposal of a man determined, in certain circumstances, to assume all risks, Mr. Khrushchev provisionally drew a lesson from the crisis and from his defeat: henceforth, on the subject of thermonuclear war, he was to use the same language as the American President. Further, insofar as the Soviet leaders continue to affect a certain skepticism toward the subtleties in which American analysts indulge, asserting that local wars, when the nuclear powers are involved in them, will escalate to a general and total war, they must adopt a still more prudent attitude than their enemy. For this reason, the Soviet leaders have officially accepted the American doctrine; they proclaim it on all occasions, and have given two proofs of their adherence in actions: the signing of the Moscow Treaty on the partial suspension of nuclear tests, and the establishment of a direct line between the Kremlin and the White House, a symbol of the enemies' alliance against war.

However incontestable it may be, this change chiefly affects climate and language. The Moscow Treaty allows of no supervision and does not forbid underground tests, lacking as it does an agreement concerning the number of on-site inspections necessary to guarantee respect for the treaty. But it is true that the acceleration phase of the 1961–62 arms race, which I noted at the completion of this book, has been succeeded by a slowdown; both phases are in accord with the logic of that singular hostility that limits the common desire not to perish together for the sole advantage of today's or tomorrow's rivals.

The Russo-American *rapprochement*, though its essential cause and objective was to reduce the danger of nuclear war, is situated in a political context which has, to a degree, provoked it, and which it influences in return. We know better, in 1965, the various episodes of the Sino-Soviet conflict than we knew four years ago. The Chinese have taught us that in 1957 an agreement had been concluded between the two great Communist powers providing for Soviet aid to the Chinese atomic program, and that two years later, after the military operations in the Strait of Formosa in 1958, this agreement had been denounced by Moscow. The desire of the Soviet Union to retain a monopoly of nuclear weapons in the socialist camp has thus been one of the causes of the—subsequently public—break between the Russians and the Chinese. The Russian desire, like the Chinese refusal, was the expression of the normal conflict between two sovereign states, one of which claims to retain the leadership of a common strategy, while the other aspires to independence on the day it can make its own vital decisions.

Perhaps Mr. Khrushchev decided to sign the Moscow agreement, in 1963, only after he had lost all hope of re-establishing the unity of the socialist camp. For in signing with his enemy a treaty whose evident objective was to make the acquisition of nuclear weapons more difficult for his ally, he was consecrating in the eyes of the world a divorce that the publicity of international polemics no longer permitted him to conceal. Of course, the treaty seen from Paris had the same meaning it had for Peking. The three members of the atomic club were trying to keep the other states from doing what they themselves had done, were condemning them in advance to the moral reprobation of the world. Relations between Paris and Washington, as was foreseeable, suffered from a treaty that the American leaders regarded as useful to peace, hence to the protection of humanity, and that General de Gaulle regarded as a manifestation of the age-old egoism, indeed cynicism of national states, "those cold monsters."

However bad relations between Washington and Paris today, however comparable the French or Chinese refusals to subscribe to the Moscow Treaty or to submit to the authority of the leader of their respective camps, the differences are still more marked than the similarities, because the diplomacy of the democratic states obeys different rules from that of the totalitarian states. The split between Moscow and Peking reminds us that a common ideology does not suffice to cement an alliance, but, assuming that conflicting national interests of the Soviet Union and the People's Republic of China were a major cause of the split, the latter would not have had the same character if each of the two rivals had not immediately translated into ideological terms its conception of its own interests or of the opportune strategy, and had not attempted to win over to its cause the other socialist parties throughout the world. In their alliances as in their disputes, the Communist states are neither exclusively governed by their ideologies nor indifferent to the historical philosophy from which they derive. States of the liberal type, such as the United States or France, remain more easily allied, even when they do not manage to agree, because divergence of opinions is a part of the natural process of democracy, and because none of them claims to possess a final truth (nor even imagines that in such matters there is a final truth).

The *rapprochement* of the United States and the Soviet Union in order to prevent war, the Sino-Soviet conflict, the effort of Gaullist France to acquire a purely national nuclear strategic force and even an independent diplomacy —does all this mark the end of the bipolar system and the beginning of a new phase of international relations? Let us remember first of all that bipolarity has never been effective except in the military sphere, and in a limited region of the world. Now, in military terms, bipolarity subsists in the sense that weapons or means of destruction possessed by the Soviet Union and the United States remain overwhelmingly superior to those of all other states, even of Great Britain, which possesses a nuclear force, and of France and China, which are on the way to acquiring one.

But the destructive capacity the giants possess does not correspond to a proportional capacity to impose their wills upon the other states. Never have weapons been so terrifying, never have they inspired so little terror in those who are not equipped with them. Albania defies the Soviet Union, and Cuba the United States. It is as if military strength can be translated into diplomatic power only with great difficulty when the so-called supreme weapons are so monstrously inhuman. Or again, to use another formula, it is as if the Russian and American thermonuclear forces paralyzed each other, preventing the amplification of local conflicts and functioning only in a subsidiary way in relations between great and small powers, particularly in the Southern Hemisphere. At most, the thermonuclear weapons impose on those who do not possess them some moderation in the conduct of their undertakings. In the Siberian north as in southeast Asia, China harasses the "revisionist" ally or the "imperialist enemy." She cannot, without incurring an extreme danger, launch an open aggression.

Outside the two European blocs the so-called non-aligned states, with their many and varying versions of neutrality and neutralism, become more numerous year by year. But in this regard, nothing has changed except at most an accentuation of the tendency to form diplomatic sub-systems, each involving a local balance of forces, national or traditional rivalries between non-aligned states, sub-systems linked to the global system but not merely reflecting it.

Within the two European blocs the symptoms of dissolution have multiplied in the course of recent years. As a result of the Sino-Soviet conflict the states of Eastern Europe have asserted their national interests, some, like Rumania, by opposing the COMECON plans, others, like Hungary or even Czechoslovakia, by internal liberalization, and all, finally, by rejecting the exclusive influence of Russian culture and by re-establishing links with the West. Merchandise, men, and ideas cross what was once the Iron Curtain. Bilateral agreements between the countries of Eastern and Western Europe are increasing. Since the Cuban crisis, Soviet rulers have accommodated themselves to the existing status of Berlin and no longer brandish their weapons to obtain its modification. In this pacified atmosphere, in the absence of a real fear of war, the members of the Atlantic Alliance feel less bound by solidarity. France's veto of Great Britain's membership in the Common Market, Gaullist diplomacy's effort to assure France the greatest possible autonomy in relation to the United States, Bonn's hesitation between the treaty with France and the Atlantic Alliance—all these recent vicissitudes afford an image of the Continent quite different from that available to the observer five years ago. In the light of present events it is not impossible to *imagine*, on the horizon of history, the reunification of Europe "from the Atlantic to the Urals."

But for the moment these are only eventualities possible at an indeterminate date. In military terms the division of Europe exists, as does that of Germany and of Berlin. So long as Germany remains divided, the fundamental stake of the cold war in Europe will remain the same. Only the Soviet Union's abandonment of the so-called German Democratic Republic and her consent to a united Germany would mark the liquidation of the consequences of the Second World War. Now it is on the territory of the German Democratic Republic that the twenty Soviet divisions are stationed threatening Western Europe and effectively guaranteeing a minimum of discipline among the satellite states. The day these divisions withdraw inside the boundaries of the U.S.S.R., what will remain of the Soviet bloc? What will limit the revisionism and nationalism of peoples who have been subjected against their will to a Communist regime but who, after twenty years, have not been converted to the new faith? Communism's historical failure in Eastern Europe is a promise for the future, but at the same time it forbids the Kremlin leaders to make concessions that might involve the complete dissolution of their bloc.

The easing of the political situation in Europe is accompanied by mounting tensions in the third world. Asia in particular is becoming the center of the crisis. But this situation is no longer one of direct confrontation of the two blocs, or the two super powers. The Soviet Union and the People's Republic of China are being drawn into a sort of cold war, the prize of which is leadership in the international communist movement. At the same time, the United States, directly engaged in Vietnam, is endeavoring, by the limited use of military weapons, to contain China and to convert Mao Tse-tung and his men to a policy of peaceful coexistence.

The interrelationship between these two conflicts on occasion results in the convergence of the respective interests of the Soviet Union and of the United States. For example, in September 1965, the two super powers both desired the rapid halting of the Kashmir dispute between India and Pakistan. It is possible that the Soviet Union would look favorably upon a solution reached by negotiation, but she has lost the capability to impose her will upon the Asian communist countries. She is avoiding open intervention, this being susceptible to provoking the emergence of an American republic. Despite everything, she sent a few arms to North Vietnam (ground-to-air missiles) in order not to appear indifferent to the lot of a socialist state; in order not to lose, in the eyes of the third world, the prestige of the revolutionary idea. The Soviet Union cannot ostensibly collaborate with the United States without furnishing some form of argument for her ideological rival.

More than ever before, the distinction between appearances and diplomatic realities is becoming apparent. In the past, the Soviet Union has often concealed the action she has taken with regard to Western Europe. Today, we have reached the stage where she conceals, under veil of invective, an implicit accord with the United States.

Whatever judgment we formulate on the present phase, whatever the optimism with which we envisage the immediate prospects, the fundamental problems of international relations in the thermonuclear age remain today what they were four years ago. Perhaps a change of leaders in Moscow or in Washington would revive the recently allayed anxieties. Certainly, if China became the national enemy of the Soviet Union and no longer merely a rival within the same camp, if the Soviet Union consented to a European settlement acceptable to the West, the situation would become essentially different. Even in this hypothesis, the main uncertainty of our age would still remain. China has already exploded a first atomic bomb. Like the Soviet Union, like the United States, she must seek an answer to the question that dominates the diplomacy of our epoch: how to use the thermonuclear weapons diplomatically so that they will never have to be used militarily?

But how long can a threat be brandished without having to be carried out? Can strategic interaction be indefinitely prolonged in the shadow of the apocalypse? And if the answer is negative, how escape from that interaction? It is reasonable for the great powers not to wage a war to the death, but if the philosophers have often defined man as a *reasonable being,* they have rarely asserted with the same assurance that human history deserved the same epithet.

The Conceptual Levels of Comprehension

Troubled times encourage meditation. The crisis of the Greek city-state has bequeathed us Plato's *Republic* and Aristotle's *Politics*. The religious conflicts that lacerated Europe in the seventeenth century produced, with *Leviathan* and the *Tractatus*, the theory of the neutral state, necessarily absolute according to Hobbes, broadly interpreted, at least philosophically, according to Spinoza. In the century of the English Revolution, Locke defended and elucidated civil liberties. In the period when the French were unconsciously generating their Revolution, Montesquieu and Rousseau defined the essence of the two regimes that were to emerge from the sudden or gradual decomposition of the traditional monarchies: representative governments restrained by the balance of power, and so-called democratic governments invoking the will of the people but rejecting all limits to their authority.

After this century's Second World War, the United States, which throughout its history had dreamed of standing aloof from the affairs of the Old World, found itself responsible for the peace, the prosperity, and the very existence of half the planet. GIs were garrisoned in Tokyo and Seoul in the Orient, in Berlin in Europe. The West had known nothing like it since the Roman Empire. The United States was the first truly world power, since there was no precedent for the global unification of the diplomatic scene. In relation to the Eurasian land mass, the American continent occupied a position comparable to that of the British Isles in relation to Europe: the United States was continuing the tradition of the insular state by attempting to bar the dominant continental state's expansion in central Germany and in Korea.

No great work comparable to those we have mentioned has emerged from the circumstance created by the joint victory of the United States and the Soviet Union. International relations have become the object of an academic discipline. Professorships, whose incumbents are dedicating themselves to the new discipline, have multiplied. The number of books and manuals has swollen proportionately. Have so many efforts come to anything? Before answering, we must specify what the American professors, following statesmen and public opinion itself, propose to discover or elaborate.

Historians did not wait for the accession of the United States to world primacy to study "international relations," but they described or related more than they analyzed or explained. No science, however, limits itself to describing or relating. Further, what profit can statesmen or diplomats derive from the historical knowledge of past centuries? The weapons of mass destruction, the techniques of subversion, the ubiquity of military force because of aviation and electronics, introduce new human and material factors which render the lessons of the past equivocal at best. Or, at least, such lessons cannot be used unless they are assimilated into a theory that includes the like and the unlike, and separates constants in order to elaborate, and not to eliminate, the part played by the unknown.

This was the decisive question. Specialists in international relations were unwilling merely to follow the historians; like all scholars, they wanted to establish axioms, create a body of doctrine. Only geopolitics was concerned with abstraction and explanation in international relations. But German geopolitics had left bad memories, apart from which the spatial framework was insufficient for a theory whose function was to grasp the multiplicity of causes affecting the course of relations among states.

It was easy to characterize the theory of international relations in general terms. "First of all, it makes possible the ordering of data. It is a useful instrument for understanding."[1] Next, "the theory requires that the criteria for selection of problems for intensive analysis be made explicit. It is not always recognized that whenever a particular problem is selected for study and analysis in some context or other, there is practically always a theory underlying the choice." Lastly, "Theory can be an instrument for the comprehension not only of uniformities and regularities, but contingencies and irrationalities as well." Who could object to such formulations? *Ordering of data, selection of problems, determination of constants and variables*—every theory, in the social sciences, must in any case fulfill these three requirements. The problems arise beyond these incontestable propositions.

The theoretician often tends to simplify reality, to interpret behavior by uncovering the implicit logic of the actors. Hans J. Morgenthau writes: "A theory of international relations is a rationally ordered summary of all the rational elements which the observer has found in the subject matter. Such a theory is a kind of rational outline of international relations, a map of the international scene."[2] The difference between an empirical and a theoretical

[1] Kenneth W. Thompson, "Toward a Theory of International Politics," *American Political Science Review*, XLIX, 3, September 1955, pp. 735–36.
[2] These remarks are quoted from a report by Mr. Morgenthau entitled "The Theoretical and Practical Importance of a Theory of International Relations" (p. 5) cited in Thompson, p. 737.

interpretation of international relations is comparable to the difference between a photograph and a painted portrait. "The photograph shows everything that can be seen by the naked eye. The painted portrait does not show everything that can be seen by the naked eye, but it shows something the naked eye cannot see: the human essence of the person who is portrayed."

To which another specialist replies by asking: what are the "rational elements" of international politics? Is it enough to consider merely the rational elements in order to produce a sketch or paint a portrait in accord with the model's essence? If the theoretician replies negatively to these two questions, he must take another path, that of sociology. Granted the goal—to sketch the map of the international scene—the theoretician will attempt to retain *all* the elements instead of fixing his attention on the rational ones alone.

To this dialogue between the advocate of "rational schematics" and the champion of "sociological analysis"—a dialogue whose nature and implications the interlocutors have not always grasped—a traditionally American controversy is often added: the dialogue between idealism and realism. The realism, today baptized Machiavellianism, of European diplomats seemed, from across the Atlantic, typical of the Old World, the symptom of a corruption that men had sought to escape by emigrating to the New World, the land of infinite possibility. But having become the dominant power by the collapse of the European order and the victory of its own weapons, the United States gradually discovered, not without upheavals of conscience, that its diplomacy resembled less and less the old ideal and more and more the practice, once so harshly judged, of its enemies and its allies. Was it moral to buy Soviet intervention in the war against Japan with concessions at China's expense? It was revealed, after the fact, that the venture was not a profitable one; that in rational terms Roosevelt should, in fact, have bought Soviet non-intervention. But would the calculation have been more moral if it had been rational? Was it right or wrong of Roosevelt to abandon Eastern Europe to Soviet domination? To plead the constraint of facts was to return to the argument that Europeans had used and that Americans, mighty in their virtue and their geographical situation, had long dismissed with scorn or indignation. The military leader is accountable to his nation for his actions, his successes or his defeats. What do good intentions and respect for private virtues matter? The law of diplomacy or strategy is a different thing. But under these conditions, what becomes of the dichotomy between realism and idealism, Machiavelli and Kant, corrupt Europe and virtuous America?

This work seeks first to clarify, and subsequently to transcend, these debates. The two concepts of the theory are not contradictory, but complementary: rational schematics and sociological propositions constitute successive moments in the conceptual elaboration of a social universe.

Understanding a realm of action does not permit us to settle the antinomies of action. Only history will perhaps some day curtail the eternal debate between Machiavellianism and moralism. But by proceeding from formal theory

to the determination of causes, and then to the analysis of a specific circumstance, I hope to illustrate a method, applicable to other subjects, which
shows both the limits of our knowledge and the conditions of historical
choices.

In order to explain the structure of the book in this introduction, I must
first define international relations, then specify the characteristics of the four
levels of conceptualization which we call *theory, sociology, history, praxiology.*

[1]

Recently a Dutch historian,[3] appointed to the first chair of international
relations created in his country, at Leyden, attempted in his inaugural lecture
to locate the discipline that it was his task to teach. He concluded with an
admission of failure: he had sought but not found the limits of the field he
proposed to explore.

His failure is instructive because it is definitive and, so to speak, obvious.
"International relations" have no frontiers traced out in reality, they are not
and cannot be materially separable from other social phenomena. But the
same proposition would be valid apropos of economics, or politics. If it is true
that "the proposal for developing the study of international relations as a
self-contained system has failed," the real question lies beyond its failure and
concerns the meaning itself. After all, the attempt to make the study of economics a closed system has also failed; there nevertheless exists, and with
reason, a science of economics, whose own reality and the possibility of
whose isolation are not doubted by anyone. Does the study of international
relations involve a proper focus of interest? Does it aim at collective
phenomena, human behavior whose specificity is recognizable? And does this
specific meaning of international relations lend itself to a theoretical elaboration?

International relations are, by definition it would seem, relations among
nations. But in that case, the term *nation* is not to be taken in the historical
sense it has assumed since the French Revolution; it does not designate a particular kind of political community, one in which large numbers of individuals have a consciousness of citizenship and in which the state seems to be
the expression of a pre-existent nationality. In the expression "international
relations," the nation equals any political collectivity that is territorially organized. Let us say, provisionally, that international relations are relations
among *political units,* the latter concept covering the Greek city-states, and
the Roman or Egyptian empires as well as the European monarchies, the
bourgeois republics or the people's democracies. This definition involves a
double difficulty. Are we to include in the relations among political units the

[3] B. H. N. Vlekke, *On the Study of International Political Science,* the David Davies
Memorial Institute of International Studies, London (undated).

relations among individuals belonging to those units? Where do political units, that is, territorially organized political collectivities, begin or end?

When young Europeans want to spend their vacations beyond the borders of their respective countries, is this a phenomenon that should interest the specialist in international relations? When I buy German merchandise in a French store, when a French importer deals with a manufacturer across the Rhine, do these economic exchanges fall within the realm of "international relations?"

It seems almost as difficult to answer affirmatively as negatively. Relations among states, i.e., strictly inter-state relations, constitute international relations par excellence: treaties are an indisputable example of such relations. Let us suppose that the economic exchanges between one nation and another are entirely regulated by an agreement between the two states: in this hypothesis, such exchanges pertain without reservation to the study of international relations. Let us suppose, on the other hand, that the economic exchanges are withdrawn from strict regulation and that free exchange is the order of the day: in consequence the purchase of German merchandise in France, the sale of French merchandise in Germany will be individual acts not presenting the characteristics of inter-state relations.

This difficulty is a real one, but it would be a mistake, it seems to me, to exaggerate its importance. No scientific discipline possesses distinct boundaries. It is of little importance, in the first instance, to know where international relations end, to specify at what moment inter-individual relations cease to be international relations. We must determine the focus of interest, the proper significance of the phenomenon or of the action that constitutes the nucleus of this specific domain. Now the focus of international relations is on the relations which we have called inter-state, those which bring these entities to grips with one another.

Inter-state relations are expressed in and by specific actions, those of individuals whom I shall call symbolic, the *diplomat* and the *soldier*. Two men, and only two, no longer function as individual members but as *representatives* of the collectivities to which they belong: the *ambassador*, in the exercise of his duties, *is* the political unit in whose name he speaks; the *soldier* on the battlefield *is* the political unit in whose name he kills his opposite number. It is because he struck an ambassador that the blow of the Dey of Algiers' fan assumed the status of a historical event. It is because he wears a uniform and acts out of duty that in war the citizen of a civilized state kills with a clear conscience. The ambassador[4] and the soldier *live* and *symbolize* international relations which, insofar as they are inter-state relations, concern diplomacy and war. Inter-state relations present one original feature which distinguishes

---

[4] It follows that, in this abstract sense, the statesmen, Ministers of Foreign Affairs, Prime Ministers and heads of state are also, in certain of their actions, ambassadors. They represent the political unit as such.

them from all other social relations: they take place within the shadow of war, or, to use a more rigorous expression, relations among states involve, in essence, the alternatives of war and peace. Whereas each state tends to reserve a monopoly on violence for itself, states throughout history, by recognizing each other, have thereby recognized the legitimacy of the wars they waged. In certain circumstances the reciprocal recognition of enemy states has proceeded to its logical conclusion: each state used only its regular army and refused to provoke, within the state it opposed, a rebellion which would have weakened its enemy but would also have shaken the monopoly of legitimate violence which it intended to preserve.

As a science of peace and war, the science of international relations can serve as a basis for the arts of diplomacy and strategy, the complementary and opposed methods by which dealings among states are conducted. "War belongs not to the province of Arts and Sciences, but to the province of social life. It is a conflict of great interests which is settled by bloodshed, and only in that is it different from others. It would be better, instead of comparing it with any Art, to liken it to business competition, which is also a conflict of human interests and activities; and it is still more like State policy, which again, on its part, may be looked upon as a kind of business competition on a great scale. Besides, state policy is the womb in which War is developed, in which its outlines lie hidden in a rudimentary state, like the qualities of living creatures in their germs."[5]

Thus we can readily understand why international relations afford a focus of interest to a particular discipline and why they escape any precise delimitation. Historians have never isolated the account of events which touch on relations among states; such an isolation would have been impossible in practice, so closely are the ups and downs of military campaigns and diplomatic combinations related to the vicissitudes of national destinies, and to the rivalries of royal families or social classes. Like diplomatic history, the science of international relations has to recognize the multiple links between events on the diplomatic and national scenes. Nor can it rigorously separate inter-state relations from inter-individual relations involving several political units. But so long as humanity has not achieved unification into a universal state, an *essential* difference will exist between internal politics and foreign politics. The former tends to reserve the monopoly on violence to those wielding legitimate authority, the latter accepts the plurality of centers of armed force. Politics, insofar as it concerns the internal organization of collectivities, has for its immanent goal the subordination of men to the rule of law. Politics, insofar as it concerns relations among states, seems to signify—in both ideal and objective terms—simply the survival of states confronting the potential threat created by the existence of other states. Hence the common opposition

[5] Karl von Clausewitz, *On War*, Book II, Chap. 3, p. 121. All future references to this work are taken from the translation by J. J. Graham, Barnes and Noble, 1956.

in classical philosophy: the art of politics teaches men to live in peace within collectivities, while it teaches collectivities to live in either peace or war. States have not emerged, in their mutual relations, from the *state of nature*. There would be no further theory of international relations if they had.

It will be objected that this opposition, distinct on the level of ideas, is no longer distinct on the level of facts. It presupposes, indeed, that political units are circumscribed, identifiable. This is the case when the units are represented by diplomats and uniformed soldiers—in other words, when they effectively exercise the monopoly on legitimate violence and recognize each other's existence. In the absence of nations conscious of themselves as such, and of juridically organized states, internal and foreign politics tend to blend, the former not being essentially pacific and the latter not being radically bellicose.

Under what rubric ought one to classify relations between the sovereign and his vassals in the Middle Ages, when the king or emperor scarcely possessed armed forces which unconditionally obeyed him and when the barons swore an oath of fealty but not of discipline? By definition, the phases of diffused sovereignty, of dispersed armament, seem difficult to conceptualize, whereas conceptualization is appropriate to political units limited in space and separated from each other by the consciousness of men and the rigor of ideas.

Occasionally the uncertainty of the distinction between conflicts among political units and conflicts within a political unit appears even in periods of concentrated and legally recognized sovereignty. If a province, an integrated portion of the state's territory or a fraction of the population, refuses to submit to the centralized power and undertake an armed struggle, the conflict, though civil war with regard to international law, will be considered a foreign war by those who see the rebels as the expression of an existing or nascent nation. Had the Confederacy won, the United States would have been divided into two states, and the War of Secession, having begun as a civil war, would have ended as a foreign one.

Let us imagine a future universal state including all of humanity. In theory, there would be no army (the soldier is neither a policeman nor an executioner, since he risks his life against another soldier), only a police force. If a province or a party took arms, the single global state would declare it a rebel and treat it as such. But this civil war, an episode of internal politics, would retrospectively seem a return to foreign politics should the rebel victory involve the dissolution of the universal state.

This ambiguity in "international relations" is not to be imputed to the inadequacy of our concepts: it is an integral part of reality itself. It reminds us once again, should we need reminding, that the course of relations among political units is influenced in many ways by events within those units. It reminds us, too, that the stakes of war are the existence, the creation or the elimination of states. Their study of transactions between organized states often causes specialists to forget that extreme weakness is as dangerous to peace as extreme strength. The zones in which armed conflicts break out are often those in which the political units are decomposing. The states that know or believe themselves condemned awaken rival greeds or, in a desperate attempt to save themselves, provoke the outbreak that will consume them.

Does the study of international relations, if extended to include the birth and the death of states, lose all distinct limits, all originality? Those who begin by assuming that international relations are *concretely separable* will be disappointed by this analysis. But their disappointment is not justified. Having for its central theme inter-state relations in their specific significance, that is, their characteristic alternatives of peace and war, and the alternations between these, the discipline devoted to the study of international relations cannot ignore the various modalities of relations among nations and empires, nor the many determinants operative within world diplomacy, nor the circumstances in which states appear and disappear. A complete science or philosophy of politics would include international relations as one of its chapters, but this chapter would retain its originality *since it would deal with the relations between political units, each of which claims the right to take justice into its own hands and to be the sole arbiter of the decision to fight or not to fight.*

[2]

We shall attempt to consider international relations at three levels of conceptualization, and we shall then examine the ethical and pragmatic problems confronting the man of action. But before characterizing the three levels, we should like to show how two other realms of human action—sport and economics—lend themselves to an analogous distinction with respect to the modes of conceptualization.

Let us consider the game called soccer. For the average spectator, the theory of the game consists of specifying the nature of the plays and the rules to which the player is subject. How many players oppose each other on either side of the central line? What means are the players entitled and not entitled to use? (They have the right to touch the ball with their heads, not with their hands.) How are the players distributed between the different lines (forwards, center, wings)? How do they combine their efforts and thwart those of their opponents? This abstract theory is known by both players and spectators. The coach has no need to remind his players of it. On the other hand, in the framework of the rules, many situations can arise, either without deliberate intention, or conceived in advance by the players. For each side, a coach works out a strategy, specifies each player's role (this wing will cover the opponent's forward), assigns each player responsibilities in certain typical or predictable situations. At this second stage, theory decomposes into various *discourses* addressed to the different players: there is a theory of effective behavior for the wing, for the forward, for the center, simultaneous with an effective behavior for all or part of the team in specific circumstances.

At the next stage the theoretician is no longer coach or teacher, but sociologist. How do the games proceed, not on the blackboard but on the field? What are the characteristics of the methods adopted by the players of this or that country? Is there a Latin American soccer, an English soccer? What is the share of technical virtuosity and moral virtue in the success of the various teams? It is impossible to answer such questions without a historical study; we must observe the succession of games, the development of methods, the diversity of techniques and temperaments. The sociologist of sport might investigate what causes determine national victories, either at a certain period or continually (exceptional gifts, number of participants, state support, etc.).

The sociologist must combine the lessons of both theoretician and historian. If he does not understand the logic of the game, he will follow the players' movements uncomprehendingly. He will not discover the meaning of the various tactics adopted, of zone play, of individual scoring. But general propositions relating to factors of power or causes of victory are not enough to explain the Hungarian defeat in the world championship finals, nor to satisfy our curiosity completely. The outcome of a particular game is never determined by the logic of the sport nor by the general causes of success: certain games, like particular wars, remain worthy of the account that historians devote to the heroes' ordeals.

Following the coach, the sociologist and the historian, a fourth person intervenes, inseparable from the actors: the referee. The rules are given in the text, but how are they to be interpreted? Did the fact warranting sanctions —the hand foul—actually occur in such and such circumstances? The referee's decision is without appeal, but players and spectators inevitably judge the judge, either silently or noisily. Collective sport, or team competition, provokes a series of judgments, laudatory or critical, on the part of players about each other, of teammate about teammate, of one team about the opposing team, of players about the referee, of spectators about the players and the referee. All these judgments oscillate from the appreciation of effectiveness (he has played well), to the appreciation of correctness (he has respected the rules), and the appreciation of team spirit (this team has played according to the spirit of the game). Even in sports, everything not strictly forbidden is not thereby morally permitted. Lastly, the theory of soccer might envision the sport itself in relation to the men who participate in it or to the entire society. Is this sport favorable to the physical health or morality of the players? Should the government support it?

Thus we find the four levels of conceptualization we have distinguished, *the schematic arrangement of concepts and systems, the general causes of events, the development of the sport or of a particular game, and pragmatic or ethical judgments,* bearing on behavior within a particular domain or on the domain itself considered as a whole.

Diplomatic or strategic behavior affords certain analogies with sport. It too involves both cooperation and competition. Every collectivity finds itself among enemies, friends, neutrals or the indifferent. No diplomatic playing field is marked off with lines, but there is a diplomatic field on which all the participants appear, capable of intervening in case of a generalized conflict. The arrangement of the players is not fixed once and for all by rules or customary tactics, but we do find certain characteristic groupings of participants, which constitute so many schematically designed situations.

Cooperative and competitive, the practice of foreign politics also, by its very nature, involves risk. The diplomat and the strategist act—in other words, they make decisions before they have assembled all the knowledge desirable and acquired certainty. Their action is based on probabilities. It would not be reasonable if it rejected risk: it is reasonable insofar as it calculates risk. But we can never eliminate the uncertainty inherent in the unpredictability of human reactions (what will the *other* do, whether a general or a states-man, Hitler or Stalin?), in the secrecy with which states are surrounded, in the impossibility of knowing everything before taking a decisive step. The "glorious uncertainty of sport" has its equivalent in political action, whether violent or non-violent. Let us not imitate the historians who believe that the past has always been inevitable, and thus suppress the human dimension of events.

The expressions we have used to characterize the sociology (causes of suc-cess, national characteristics of play) and the history of sport, or of a single game, also apply to the sociology and history of international relations. It is rational theory and praxiology which differ essentially from one realm to the next. Compared to soccer, foreign policy seems strangely indeterminate. The goal of the participants is not as simple as merely getting a ball across a white line. The rules of diplomatic performance are imperfectly codified, and a player may violate them when he finds it to his advantage to do so. There is no referee, and even when all the participants claim the right to judge as a body (the United Nations), the national actors may not submit to the de-cisions of this collective referee whose impartiality is not indisputable. If the rivalry of nations suggests sport, it is all too often a free-for-all—a catch-as-catch-can—that would be the appropriate image.

More generally, sports have three particular characteristics: the objective and the rules of the game are clearly specified; the game is played within a fixed space, the number of participants is fixed, and the system, delimited in relation to the external world, is structured within itself; action is subject to rules of effectiveness and to the decisions of the referee, so that there are moral or quasi-moral judgments concerning the spirit in which the partici-pants play the game itself. Apropos of each of the social sciences, we might question if or to what degree the goal and rules are defined, if and to what degree the participants are organized into a system, if and to what degree individual action is subject to obligations, either of effectiveness or of morality.

Let us turn from sports to economics: every society, consciously or not, has an economic problem, and solves it in a particular way. Every society must satisfy the needs of its members with limited resources. The disproportion between desires and goods is not always felt as such. Once a way of life is accepted as normal or traditional, a collectivity may aspire to nothing beyond what it already possesses. Such a collectivity is poor in, not for, itself. One may add a paradox only in appearance—that societies have never been so aware of their poverty as in our own day, despite the prodigious increase of their wealth. Desires have advanced even more rapidly than resources. The limitation of resources seems scandalous once the capacity to produce is— mistakenly—regarded as unlimited.

Economics is a fundamental category of thought, a dimension of collective or individual existence. This category is not to be confused with that of scarcity or poverty (disproportion between desires and resources). Economics as *problem* presupposes merely scarcity or poverty: economics as *solution* presupposes that men can master their poverty in various ways, that they have the possibility of choosing among different ways of utilizing their resources; in other words, it presupposes the multiplicity of choices which Robinson Crusoe himself was not unaware of on his island. Crusoe disposed of his own labor time, he could choose a certain distribution of hours of the day between labor and leisure, a certain distribution of labor among consumer goods (food) and investments (house). What is true of the individual is truer still of the collectivity. Labor force being the primary resource of human societies, the multiplicity of possible uses of resources is given from the start. As the economy grows more complex, the possibilities of choice multiply and goods become increasingly interchangeable; the same object can serve several ends and various objects can be used for the same ends.

Poverty and choice—poverty is *the* problem faced by collectivities, and a particular choice is *one* solution effectively adopted. These define the economic dimension of human existence. Men who ignore poverty because they ignore desire are unconscious of the economic dimension. They live as their ancestors have lived, as they themselves have always lived. Custom is so strong that it excludes dreams, dissatisfaction, desire for progress. There would be a post-economic phase if, along with scarcity, the necessity of choice, of painful labor, should disappear. Trotsky says somewhere that abundance is now visible on the horizon of history and that only the *petit bourgeois* will refuse to believe in his radiant future and regard the biblical curse as eternal. A post-economic period is conceivable: capacity for production would become such that each man could consume according to his will and, out of respect for others, would not take more than his fair share from the whole.

The soccer player attempts to send the ball into a space delimited by the two vertical goal posts linked, two yards above the ground, by a horizontal bar. Economic man wants to make the *best* use of insufficient resources, to utilize them so that they supply the *maximum* of satisfactions. Economists have constructed, elaborating various kinds of logic concerning these individual choices, the marginal theory, which is, even today, the most common version of this rational formulation of economic behavior, one that starts with individuals and their ranges of preference.

Although the theory covers the route which proceeds from individual choices to total equilibrium, it seems to me logically as well as philosophically preferable to start from the collectivity. Indeed, the specific characteristics of economic reality are not discernible except on the level of the collectivity. Individual ranges of preference may not differ fundamentally within a given society, since all the individuals more or less adhere to a common system of values. Nonetheless, activities tending to the maximization of individual satisfactions would be ill-defined if money did not introduce the possibility of a rigorous and universally recognizable measurement. African savages rationally preferred glass beads to ivory as long as the objects exchanged did not appear on the same market and did not each have its price in money.

Monetary quantification permits the recognition of accounting standards for the total economy. Such standards, from the physiocratic table down to modern studies of national accounting, do not afford an explanation of changes, but constitute the evidence from which economics attempts to grasp primary and secondary factors, or those which are determining and those which are determined. At the same time, the reciprocity of variables, the interdependence of elements of the economy, becomes evident. To modify one price is indirectly to modify all. To reduce or increase investments, to reduce or increase rates of interest is, step by step, to act on the national product as well as on the distribution of this product among its categories.

All economic theories, whether micro- or macro-theory, whether liberal or socialist in inspiration, emphasize the interdependence of economic variables. The theory of equilibrium, as Walras or Pareto would call it, reconstructs the whole by starting from individual choices, as it defines a point of equilibrium that would also be the point of maximization of production and individual satisfactions (given a certain distribution of income at the start). Keynesian theory or the macro-theories tackle the system directly as a unity, and attempt to isolate the determining factors that must be brought into play to avoid unemployment, raise the national product to its maximum potential, etc.

Hence the purpose of economic activity, at first glance, appears to be defined: maximization of satisfactions for the individual making rational choices, and maximization of monetary resources in the later phase, money being the universal intermediary among goods. But this definition leaves room for uncertainties: at what point, for instance, does the individual prefer leisure to the increase of his income? Further, the uncertainty—or, if one prefers, the indeterminacy—becomes an essential aspect if we consider the collectivity.

The collectivity faces an "economic problem": by a certain organization of production, of exchange and of distribution, the collectivity chooses a solution. This solution involves a degree of cooperation among individuals and a degree of competition. Neither the collectivity as a whole nor individuals as economic subjects are in situations where one and only one decision is rational.

Maximization of the national product as opposed to reduction of inequalities, maximization of growth as opposed to maintenance of a high level of consumption, maximization of cooperation authoritatively imposed by the government as opposed to a laissez-faire attitude toward the machinery of competition—all societies have these three alternatives, but the choice is not a logical consequence that can be deduced from the immanent goal of economic activity. Given the plurality of goals ascribed to societies, every economic solution, up till now, involves a debit account along with a credit one. We need merely invoke duration (what sacrifices must the living accept for the sake of posterity?) and the diversity of social groups (what distribution results from a certain organization of production?) to prevent any solution of an economic problem from being called rationally obligatory under particular circumstances. The immanent goal of economic activity does not unequivocally determine either the choice of individuals or the choice of collectivities as a whole.

According to this analysis, what are the modalities of the theory of the rational economy? Since the economic problem is fundamental, between the phase of unconsciousness and the possible phase of abundance, the theoretician's first obligation is to elaborate the major *concepts* of the economic order as such (production, exchange, distribution, consumption, money).

The theoretician's second and most important task is to analyze, elaborate or construct economic *systems*. Marginal theorists, Keynesians, specialists in econometrics or in game theory, and specialists in national income accounting, whatever their differences, all attempt, with equal success, to isolate the intelligible texture of the economic whole, the reciprocal relations of the variables. Controversies have no bearing on this texture itself, as expressed in uniform standards of measurement: no one doubts the accounting equivalents for saving and investment, but this equivalence is an ex post facto statistical result, and the mechanics by which it is obtained are complex, often obscure. The point is whether and under what circumstances excess savings may be the cause of unemployment, whether and under what circumstances savings do not provoke reactions likely to end unemployment, whether and under what circumstances a balance without full employment is possible.

In other terms, neither the Walrasian design of equilibrium nor the modern designs of national accounting can be refuted *as designs*. On the other hand, the models of unemployment or of crisis drawn from theories are contestable insofar as they imply an explanation or an anticipation of events. The "models of crisis"—relations determined among the diverse variables of the system—are comparable to the "patterns of situation" in a game, with this difference, that individuals as economic subjects are in danger of not knowing the exact situation created by the relations among variables, whereas the soccer players see the exact position of their opponents and their teammates.

Economic theory, as we have just sketched it, attempts to isolate the economic ensemble—the total behavior which actually solves, whether well or badly, the problem of poverty—and to emphasize the rationality of this behavior, that is, choices in the use of limited resources, each of which involves many practices. Every theory, whatever its inspiration, substitutes economic subjects for concrete individuals, whose behavior is simplified and, so to speak, rationalized. It reduces to a small number of determinants the multiple circumstances that influence economic activity. It regards certain causes as *exogenous*, without the distinction between endogenous and exogenous factors being constant from one period to the next or from one author to the next. Sociology is an indispensable intermediary between theory and fact. The passage from theory toward sociology can be achieved in various ways.

The behavior of economic subjects—managers, workers, consumers—is never determined unequivocally by the notion of *one* maximum: the choice of an increase in income or a diminution of effort depends on psychological data that cannot be reduced to a general formula. More generally, the actual behavior of managers or consumers is influenced by the ways of life, the moral or metaphysical conceptions, and the ideologies or values of a collectivity. Hence there exists a sociology or an economic psychosociology whose goal is to comprehend the behavior of economic subjects by comparing it with theoretical schemata or by specifying the choices actually made between the various kinds of maximization elaborated by theory.

Sociology can also attempt to relate the economic system to the whole of society, to follow the reciprocal action which the various realms of action exercise upon each other.

Finally, sociology can take as its goal a historical typology of economies. Theory determines the functions which must be fulfilled in any economy. Measurement of values, conservation of values, distribution of collective resources among the different occupations, matching products with consumer desires—all these functions are always fulfilled in fact, whether well or badly. Each regime is characterized by the mode in which the indispensable functions are fulfilled. In particular, to confine ourselves to our own period, each regime grants a greater or lesser share to central planning or to the mechanisms of the market: the former represents cooperative actions submitted to a superior authority, the latter a form of competitive action (competition, conforming to rules, assures the distribution of income among individuals, and produces results which have not been conceived, determined, or desired by anyone).

The economic historian is indebted to the theoretician who furnishes him the instruments of understanding (concepts, functions, models), and to the sociologist who suggests the framework within which events occur and who helps him to grasp the different social types. As for the experts, the minister of state or the philosopher—that is, those who advise, decide or act—they need to know the rational models, the determinants of the system and the recurrent circumstances. Further, in order to decide for or against a regime, and not for or against a given measure within a regime, we must know first the probable merits and defects of each regime, and next what is required of the economy: what is the good society and what influence do certain economic institutions exert upon life? Praxiology, which necessarily follows theory, sociology and history, again brings into question the premises of this cumulative comprehension: what is the human meaning of the economic dimension?

The goal of economic action is not so simple as the goal of a sport, but although there are several notions of a maximum, the theories can reconstruct the behavior of economic subjects by defining in a certain way the maximum aimed at and, subsequently, the implications of rationality. The economic system is less rigorously structured than the system constituted by a game of soccer: neither the physical limits nor the participants in the economic system are as precisely determined, but the reciprocal solidarity among the variables of the economic system, the standards of measure, permit, once a hypothesis of rationality is admitted, the comprehension of the total texture starting from the elements. As for the precepts of action, they claim to be rational on the level of theory, reasonable on the level of fact. They are devoted to *effectiveness* when an unequivocal goal has been set, to *morality* when it is a question of respecting the rules of competition, and to *ultimate values* when we question ourselves about the economic dimension of life, about work and leisure, abundance and power.

[3]

Let us turn back to foreign policy and inquire how the levels of conceptualization are characterized in this domain.

All human behavior, insofar as it is not a simple reflex or the act of a madman, is comprehensible. But there are manifold modes of intelligibility. The behavior of the student who has just attended a lecture because it is cold outside or because he has nothing else to do between two classes is comprehensible. It can be called either "logical" (Pareto's expression) or "rational" (Max Weber's), if it is a means of avoiding the cold or of whiling away an idle hour pleasantly enough. But it does not present the same characteristics as the behavior of the student who attends a lecture because he thinks he may be asked about the subject in an examination, or the behavior of the manager who makes each of his decisions by referring to the balance-sheet at the end of the year, or the behavior of the forward who keeps back in order to disconcert the opposing center, who is guarding him.

What are the traits common to the behavior of these three actors—student, manager, player? It is not the mode of psychological determination. The manager may be personally greedy or, quite the contrary, indifferent to gain. The student who establishes the courses he will take according to the time at his disposal or the likelihood of the examination questions may like or detest the subjects he is studying, may want a diploma as a matter of conceit, or because he must earn his living. Similarly, the soccer player may be an amateur or a professional, may dream of glory or of wealth, but he is bound by the requirements of effectiveness which result from the game itself. In other words, these actions involve, more or less consciously, a calculation, a combination of means with a view to an end, the acceptance of a risk varying with certain probabilities. This calculation itself is dictated by both a hierarchy of preferences and by circumstances, the latter possessing, in both game and economy, an intelligible texture.

The behavior of the diplomat or the strategist presents certain of these characteristics, although according to the definition given above, this behavior has neither a goal as determined as that of the soccer player's or even an objective, in certain conditions rationally definable by a maximum, like those of economic subjects. The behavior of the diplomat-strategist, in effect, is specifically dominated by the risk of war, confronting adversaries in an incessant rivalry in which each side reserves the right to resort to the *ultima ratio*, that is, to violence. The theory of a sport is worked out starting from the goal (to send the ball across the line). The theory of economics, too, refers to a goal through the intermediary of the notion of maximization (although various modalities of this maximum are conceivable). *The theory of international relations starts from the plurality of autonomous centers of decision, hence from the risk of war, and from this risk it deduces the necessity of the calculation of means.*

Certain theoreticians have tried to find the equivalent of the rational goal of sport or economics for international relations. A single goal, victory, exclaims the naïve general, forgetting that military victory always affords satisfaction for *amour-propre*, but not always political benefits. A single imperative, national interest, solemnly proclaims the theoretician, hardly less naïve than the general, as if adding the adjective *national* to the concept of interest were enough to make it unequivocal. International politics is a struggle for power and security, declares another theoretician, as if there were never any contradiction between the two, as if collective persons, unlike individuals, were rationally obliged to prefer life to the reasons for living.

We shall have occasion to discuss these theoretical endeavors during the course of this work. At the outset, let us confine ourselves to stating that diplomatic-strategic behavior does not have an obvious objective, but that the risk of war obliges it to calculate forces or means. As we shall try to show in the first part of this book, the alternatives of peace and war permit the elaboration of the fundamental concepts of international relations.

The same alternatives permit us to express "the problem of foreign policy" as we have expressed the problem of economics. For thousands of years, men have lived in closed societies which were never entirely subject to a superior authority. Each collectivity had to count chiefly on itself to survive, but it also had—or should have had—to contribute to the task common even to enemy cities, exposed to the risk of perishing together by dint of constantly fighting each other.

The double problem of individual and collective survival has never been lastingly solved by any civilization. It could only be definitively solved by a universal state or by the rule of law. One might call pre-diplomatic the age in which collectivities did not maintain regular relations with each other, and post-diplomatic the age of a universal state which would allow only for internecine combats. As long as each collectivity must think of its own safety at the same time as of that of the diplomatic system or of the human race, diplomatic-strategic behavior will never be rationally determined, even in theory.

This relative indeterminacy does not keep us from elaborating a rational type of theory in Part One, proceeding from fundamental concepts (strategy and diplomacy, means and ends, power and force, power, glory and idea) to systems and types of systems. Diplomatic systems are neither spread out on the map like a playing field nor unified by standards of measure, and by the interdependence of variables like economic systems, but each participant knows roughly in relation to which adversaries and which partners he must situate himself.

Such a theory, producing models of diplomatic systems, distinguishing typical situations on a generalized level, imitates economic theory, which elaborates models of crisis or unemployment. But, lacking a single goal of diplomatic behavior, the rational analysis of international relations cannot be developed into an inclusive theory.

Chapter VI, dedicated to a typology of peace and war, serves as a transition between Part I and Part II, between the interpretation growing out of the conduct of foreign policy and the sociological explanation of the course of events, drawn from material or social causes. Sociology seeks the circumstances which influence the stakes of the conflicts among states, the goals which the participants choose, the fortunes of nations and empires. Theory reveals the intelligible texture of a social ensemble; sociology shows how the determinants (space, number, resources) and the subjects (nations, regimes, civilizations), of international relations vary.

Part III of the book, concerned with present circumstances, aims first at testing the method of analysis elaborated in the first two parts. But in certain respects, because of the worldwide extension of the diplomatic field and the invention of thermonuclear weapons, the present circumstances are unique and unprecedented. They involve situations which lend themselves to analysis by "model." In this sense Part III, at a lower level of abstraction, contains both a rationalizing theory and a sociological theory of diplomacy in the global and thermonuclear age.

At the same time it constitutes a necessary introduction to the last part, which is both normative and philosophical, and in which the initial hypotheses are re-examined.

Economics disappears with the disappearance of scarcity. Under conditions of abundance, the problem becomes one of organization, not of economic calculation. Similarly, war would cease being an instrument of politics the day it involved the mutual suicide of the belligerents. The capacity for industrial production restores some relevance to the utopia of abundance, the destructive capacity of weapons revives the dreams of eternal peace.

All societies have known the "problem of international relations"; and many times cultures have been destroyed because they were unable to limit wars. In our day not only one culture but all of humanity would be threatened by a hyperbolic war. The prevention of such a war becomes for all participants in the diplomatic game a goal as evident as the defense of purely national interests.

According to the profound and perhaps prophetic view of Immanuel Kant, humanity must travel the bloody road of war to have access one day to peace. It is through history that the repression of natural violence is achieved, the education of man to reason.

PART ONE

THEORY
Concepts and Systems

chapter I

Strategy and Diplomacy
or
On the Unity of Foreign Policy

"War . . . is an act of violence intended to compel our opponent to fulfill our will."[1] This famous definition will serve as our point of departure: it is no less valid today than at the moment is was written. War, insofar as it is a social act, presupposes the conflicting wills of politically organized collectivities. Each seeks to prevail over the other. "Physical force . . . is therefore the *means*; the compulsory submission of the enemy to our will is the ultimate object."[2]

I. *Absolute War and Real Wars*

From this definition, Clausewitz deduces the tendency of war to escalate or even to become total. The basic reason for this is what we might call the *dialectics of the contest.*

"War is an act of violence pushed to its utmost bounds; as one side dictates the law to the other, there arises a sort of reciprocal action, which logically must lead to an extreme."[3] Any belligerent that refuses to resort to certain brutalities must fear that the adversary will gain the advantage by abandoning all scruples. Wars among civilized nations are not necessarily less cruel than wars among savage tribes. For the basic cause of war is the hostile intent, not the sentiment of hostility. In general, given the hostile intent on both sides, passion and hatred soon animate the combatants, but in theory a major war without hatred is conceivable. The most one can say apropos of civilized peoples is that "intelligence exercises greater influence on their mode of carrying on War, and has taught them more effectual means of applying force than these rude acts of mere instinct."[4] The fact remains that the desire to destroy the enemy, inherent in the concept of war, has not been hindered or repressed by the progress of civilization.

[1] Clausewitz, I, 1, p. 2.
[2] *Ibid.*
[3] *Ibid.,* p. 4.
[4] *Ibid.*

The goal of military operations, in the abstract, is to disarm the adversary. Yet since "the enemy is to be reduced to submission by an act of War, he must either be positively disarmed or placed in such a position that he is threatened with it." But the adversary is not an "inert mass." War is the impact of two living forces. "As long as the enemy is not defeated, he may defeat me; . . . he will dictate the law to me as I did to him."[5]

War is won only when the adversary submits to our will. If necessary, we measure the means at his disposal and determine our own effort accordingly. But the will to resist cannot be measured. The adversary proceeds in the same fashion, and each side augments its preparations to allow for the hostile intent, so that the competition once again leads to extremes.

This dialectic of the contest is purely abstract; it does not apply to real wars as they unfold in history, but reveals what would happen in an instantaneous duel between adversaries defined solely by reciprocal hostility and by the will to conquer. At the same time, this abstract dialectic reminds us what might actually occur each time passions or circumstances bring a historical struggle close to the ideal model of combat and, thereby, of absolute war.

In the real world "war [does not become] a completely isolated act, which arises suddenly, and is in no way connected with the previous history of the combatant states."[6] The adversaries know each other in advance, they form an approximate idea of their respective resources, even of their respective intent. The forces of each of the adversaries are never entirely mustered. The fate of nations is not staked on a single moment.[7] The intentions of a victorious adversary do not always involve an irreparable disaster for the vanquished. As soon as these various considerations intervene—the substitution of real adversaries for the abstract concept of the enemy, the duration of operations, the apparent intentions of the belligerents, the accumulation and use of every means in order to conquer and disarm the enemy—it becomes a venturesome action, a calculation of probabilities varying with the information accessible to the partner-adversaries in the political game.

For war is a game. It requires both courage and calculation; calculation never excludes risk, and at every level the acceptance of danger is alternately manifested by prudence and audacity. "From the outset there is a play of possibilities, probabilities, good and bad luck, which spreads about with all the coarse and fine threads of its web, and makes War of all branches of human activity the most like a gambling game."[8]

Yet, "War is always a serious means for a serious object." The initial element, animal as much as human, is animosity, which we must consider a natural blind impulse. Belligerent action itself, the second element, involves

---

[5] *Ibid.*, p. 5.
[6] *Ibid.*, p. 7.
[7] Preparation for a single engagement that would decide everything leads to absolute war, Clausewitz says. In the twentieth century, modern weapons risk creating precisely this situation. This has never been the case until the present.
[8] *Ibid.*, p. 20.

an interaction of probabilities and risks which makes war a "work of a free enthusiasm." But a third element must be added to these, one which ultimately dominates them: war is a political action, it rises out of a political situation and results from a political motive. It belongs by nature to pure understanding because it is an instrument of policy. The emotional element involves chiefly the people, the problematical element the commander and his army, and the intellectual element the government; and it is this latter element that is decisive and that must control the whole.

Thus Clausewitz's famous formula—"War is not merely a political act, but also a real political instrument, a continuation of political commerce, a carrying out of the same by other means"[9]—is not the expression of a bellicose philosophy, but a simple observation of fact: war is not an end in itself, military victory is not the goal in itself. Commerce between nations does not cease the day guns begin to speak; the belligerent phase takes its place in a continuity of relations always controlled by the collectivities' intentions toward each other.

The subordination of war to policy as a means to an end, implicit in Clausewitz's formula, establishes and justifies the distinction of absolute war and real wars. Escalation is the more to be feared, and real wars risk coming closer to absolute war, the more violence escapes the control of the chief of state. Policy seems to vanish when it takes the destruction of the enemy army as its single goal. Even in this case, war assumes a form that results from political intentions. Whether or not policy is visible in the belligerent action, the latter remains dominated by policy if we define policy as "the intelligence of the personified State." It is still policy—i.e., the total consideration of all circumstances by statesmen—that rightly or wrongly decides to assume as its sole objective the destruction of the enemy's armed forces, without regard for ulterior objectives, without reflection as to the probable consequences of victory itself.

Clausewitz is a theoretician of absolute war, not a doctrinaire of total war or militarism, just as Walras is a theoretician of equilibrium, not a doctrinaire of liberalism. Conceptual analysis, concerned with isolating the essence of the human act, has been mistakenly confused with the determination of an objective. Clausewitz, it is true, sometimes seems to admire the war that tends to realize its own nature completely, and to reserve his contempt for the imperfect wars of the eighteenth century in which maneuvers and negotiations reduced the combatants' engagements, their brutality and fury, to a minimum. But granted that these sentiments appear on occasion, they express simple emotions. When confronted with war driven to its extreme, Clausewitz feels a kind of sacred horror, a fascination comparable to that wakened by cosmic catastrophes. The war in which each adversary proceeds to the absolute of violence in order to vanquish the enemy's will,

[9] *Ibid.*, p. 23.

which stubbornly resists, is in Clausewitz's eyes both awe-inspiring and horrible. Whenever great interests are at stake, war will approach its absolute form. As a philosopher, he is neither delighted nor indignant. As a theoretician of rational action, he reminds leaders of war and peace of the principle both must respect: the primacy of policy, war being merely an instrument in the service of politically determined goals, a moment or an aspect of relations among states, each of which is obliged to submit to the political realm, i.e., the perception of the collectivity's lasting interests.

Let us agree to call strategy the conduct of military operations as a whole, and diplomacy the conduct of relations with other political units. Strategy and diplomacy will both be subordinate to politics, that is, to the conception on the part of the collectivity or its leaders of the "national interest." In peacetime, politics makes use of diplomatic means, not excluding recourse to arms, at least when threatened. In wartime, politics does not exclude diplomacy, since the latter conducts relations with allies and neutrals, and continues to deal tacitly with the enemy, threatening defeat, or offering a possibility of peace.

Here we are considering the "political unit" as an actor, enlightened by intelligence and prompted by will. Every state has relations with other states; as long as the states remain in peace, they must somehow manage to live together. Unless they resort to violence, they attempt to convince each other. The day they fight, they attempt to constrain each other. In this sense, diplomacy might be called the art of convincing without using force (*convaincre*), and strategy the art of vanquishing at the least cost (*vaincre*). But constraint, too, is a means of convincing. A demonstration of force causes the adversary to yield, symbolizing rather than actually imposing constraint. The side possessing a superiority of weapons in peacetime convinces its ally, rival or adversary without having to make use of such weapons. Conversely, the state which has acquired a reputation for equity or moderation has a better chance of achieving its goals without proceeding to the extremity of military victory. Even in wartime it will convince more than it will constrain.

The distinction between diplomacy and strategy is an entirely relative one. These two terms are complementary aspects of the single art of politics—the art of conducting relations with other states so as to further the "national interest." If, by definition, strategy, the conduct of miliary operations, does not function when the operations do not take place, the military means are an integral part of diplomatic method. Conversely, words, notes, promises, guarantees and threats belong to the chief of state's wartime panoply with regard to allies, neutrals, and even today's enemies, that is, to the allies of yesterday or tomorrow.

The complementary duality of the art of convincing and the art of constraining reflects a still more essential duality which Clausewitz's initial definition reveals: war is a test of will. Human insofar as it is a test of will, war by its nature involves a psychological element best illustrated by the celebrated formula: he is not conquered who dares not admit defeat. Napoleon could only win, Clausewitz writes, if Tsar Alexander admitted he was beaten after the taking of Moscow. If Alexander did not lose courage, Napoleon, though apparently the victor at Moscow, was already virtually defeated. Napoleon's plan of war was the only one possible, but it was based on a gamble which Alexander's steadfastness caused the emperor of the French to lose. The English are beaten, Hitler howled in July 1940, but they're too stupid to realize it. Not to admit they were defeated was indeed the first condition of final success for the English. Whether it was courage or lack of awareness is of little account: what mattered was that the English wanted to resist.

In absolute war, in which extreme violence leads to the disarmament or the destruction of one of the adversaries, the psychological element ultimately disappears. But this operates as a limiting case. All real wars bring into conflict collectivities which are united in expressing one will. In this regard, they are all psychological wars.

2. Strategy and the Goal of War

The relation of strategy and policy is expressed by a double formula: "War is to harmonize entirely with the political views and policy, to accommodate itself to the means available for War."[10] In a sense, the two parts of the formula might seem contradictory, since the first subordinates the conduct of war to political intentions and the second makes political intentions depend on the available means. But Clausewitz's thought and the logic of action leave no room for doubt: policy cannot determine the goals apart from the means at its disposal, and, further, "the political element does not sink deep into the details of War. Vedettes are not planted, patrols do not make their rounds from political considerations; but small as is its influence in this respect, it is great in the formation of a plan for a whole War, or a campaign, and often even for a battle."[11] Examples will illustrate the scope of these abstract propositions.

The conduct of war requires the determination of a strategic plan: "*every War should be viewed above all things according to the probability of its character, and its leading features, as they are to be deduced from the political forces and proportions.*"[12] In 1914 all the belligerents were mistaken as to the nature of the war they were about to wage. On neither side had the general staffs or the ministries conceived or prepared mobilization of industries or populations. Neither the Central Powers nor the Allies had counted on a prolonged conflict whose result would be decided by the superior

[10] *Ibid.*, VIII, 6, p. 127.
[11] *Ibid.*, p. 123.
[12] *Ibid.*, p. 125.

depends on policy.

resources of one of the two camps. The generals had rushed into a "fresh and joyous" war, convinced that the first engagements would be decisive as they had been in 1870. The strategy of annihilation would produce victory, and the statesmen of the winning side would dictate the terms of peace to the vanquished enemy.

When the French victory on the Marne and the stability of the eastern and western fronts had dissipated the illusion of a short war, policy should have reasserted itself, since it is effaced only at that moment of belligerent paroxysm when violence rages without restraint and each of the belligerents is concerned only with being physically the stronger. Of course, policy did not cease to function between 1914 and 1918, but, particularly on the Allied side, it seems to have had no other goal than to sustain the war itself. The victory that the Allies had first sought by a strategy of annihilation they later attempted through a strategy of attrition. But at no time did they seriously consider the goals they might have been able to attain without total victory; disarming the enemy and a dictated rather than negotiated peace became their supreme war goals. The war itself approached its absolute form insofar as the statesmen abdicated in favor of the army chiefs and substituted for political goals, which they were incapable of determining, a strictly military goal, the destruction of the enemy armies.

Perhaps this collapse of policy was inevitable under the circumstances. Would Germany ever have renounced Alsace-Lorraine unless it had been obliged to by the defeat? Could French public opinion ever have been forced to accept a compromise peace, with neither annexation nor indemnities, after so many sacrifices had been imposed upon the people and so many promises lavished by the government? The secret treaties concluded among the Allies sanctioned so many revenges and recorded so many solemn promises that any impulse toward negotiations without victory risked dissolving the fragile coalition of the future victors. Finally, hostilities themselves created a new, ineffaceable fact which upset previous conditions: the status of all Europe seemed jeopardized, and statesmen did not believe that the return to the *status quo ante* afforded a likelihood of stability.

Perhaps major wars are precisely those which, by reason of the passions they release, ultimately escape the men who have the illusion of controlling them. Retrospectively, the observer does not always perceive the conflict of interests that would have justified the passions and excluded the compromise. Perhaps, as I am tempted to believe, it is the very nature of industrialized warfare which ends by communicating hatred and fury to the masses and inspiring statesmen with the desire to disrupt the map of the old continent. The fact is that the first war of the century illustrates the transition toward the absolute form of a war whose political stake the belligerents are incapable of specifying.

The substitution of the military objective—victory—for the objectives of peace is still more strikingly evident in the Second World War. General

Giraud, a soldier who had not given much thought to Clausewitz, repeated in 1942: a single goal, victory. But it was more serious that President Roosevelt, though he did not coin this phrase, acted as though he believed it. The fastest possible destruction of the enemy's armed forces became the supreme imperative to which the conduct of operations was subordinated. By demanding unconditional surrender, a civilian war leader naïvely bore witness to his incomprehension of the relations between strategy and policy.

Unconditional surrender corresponded to the logic of the War of Secession. What had become the stake of the war was the existence of the United States, the prohibition of the states from leaving the Union. The Union victory involved the annihilation of the Confederacy. The demand for unconditional surrender had a rational meaning, whether it concerned the political leaders of the Confederacy or General Lee, commander of the last Southern armies. There was nothing similar in the case of Germany: neither the Soviets nor the Americans intended to suppress the existence of Germany as a state. The temporary suspension of this existence involved as many disadvantages as advantages for the victors. In any case, by assuming the destruction of the German armed forces and the unconditional surrender of the Reich as its sole objective, strategy laid itself open to three criticisms.

It is admitted that it is better to win with as few losses as possible (the formula, in strategy, has a significance analogous to that of the lowest price in economics). The insistence on unconditional surrender incited the German people to a desperate resistance. The American leaders declared they wanted to avoid the repetition of what had occurred in 1918–19, the German protests against the violation of promises contained in President Wilson's "Fourteen Points." As a matter of fact, these protests had counted for little or nothing in the failure of the Versailles Treaty. The Allied victory of 1918 had been sterile because the war itself had released revolutionary forces and because the English and American governments did not want to defend the status they had helped establish. By suggesting the fate that would have been reserved for a conquered Germany, the Americans would not have lost their freedom of maneuver and would have allowed themselves an additional chance of conquering without proceeding to the last extremity of violence.

The manner of achieving military victory inevitably influences the course of events. It was not a matter of indifference in 1944 whether Europe was liberated from the east, the south, or the west. It is no use speculating on what would have happened had the English and American armies landed in the Balkans. Was such a plan even possible? What would have been Stalin's reaction? It remains a mistake, on the theoretical level, that the American decision was dictated by the exclusive concern to destroy the major part of the German army and that consideration of the political consequences of one method or another was regarded by Roosevelt and his advisers as an unwarranted intrusion of politics into the realm of strategy.

Finally, any conduct of a war, within a coalition, must take into account potential rivalries among allies, simultaneous with actual hostilities against the enemy. There is, I believe, a radical distinction between permanent allies and occasional allies. We may consider as permanent allies those states that, whatever the conflict of some of their interests, do not conceive, in the foreseeable future, that they can be in opposite camps. Great Britain and the United States are, in the twentieth century, permanent allies, the English political leaders having wisely decided that once England lost the rule of the sea, the pax Americana was the only acceptable substitute for the pax Britannica. France and Great Britain, after 1914, should also have considered each other as permanent allies. Great Britain should have regarded a temporary and fragile excess of French power with irritation perhaps, but without distress or resentment. The reinforcement of a permanent ally should not arouse jealousy or alarm.

The reinforcement of an occasional ally, on the contrary, is, as such, a long-term threat. Occasional allies, in fact, have no bond other than a common hostility toward an enemy, a hostility capable of inspiring sufficient fear to overcome the rivalries that yesterday opposed and tomorrow will oppose again the temporarily allied states. Moreover, occasional allies, on a deeper level, may be permanent enemies: by this we mean states that are committed to conflict because of their ideology or their position on the diplomatic chessboard. Roosevelt, refusing to conduct the war in relation to the postwar period as well, dreaming of a tripartite (or bipartite) directorate of the universe, denouncing the French and British empires rather than the Soviet Empire, mistook an occasional ally for a permanent one and lost sight of the essential hostility hidden beneath a temporary cooperation.

The disastrous consequences of hyperbolic war were, after the fact, attributed in part to the obsession with military victory at any cost and by any means. Perhaps the West's political defeats, twice following the triumph of arms (a defeat caused the first time by the loser's attempt to gain revenge, and the second time by the excessive reinforcement of the occasional ally but permanent enemy), helped make statesmen aware of the primacy of politics. The war in Korea offers a contrary, almost pure, example of a war waged always as a function of politics and never with a view to military victory alone. When General MacArthur proclaimed: "There is no substitute for victory,"[18] he seemed to be adopting the concept that had been Roosevelt's, assuming as his goal the destruction of the enemy's armed forces and a peace dictated after the latter's disarmament.

President Truman and his advisers hesitated as to their political objective. Was the goal to be only that of repulsing North Korean aggression and re-establishing the status quo ante, that is, the partition of Korea at the 38th Parallel, or the unification of the two Korean states in conformity with a

---

[18] If victory does not mean military victory here, the phrase is no more than a sententious truism.

United Nations decision? Naturally the American leaders would have preferred the second objective to the first, but contrary to what had happened during the two majors wars, they did not start with the imperative of military victory, deducing the logical consequences (total mobilization, recruiting of allies, pitiless combat, etc.); they started with a different imperative (not to transform the local war into a general one), and they sought objectives accessible within the framework of refusal to enlarge the conflict.

After the landing at Inchon and the destruction of the North Korean armies, President Truman, following the advice of General MacArthur, who did not believe the Chinese would intervene, took the risk of crossing the 38th Parallel. The intervention of the Chinese "volunteers" involved the first extension of the hostilities. China became a non-official belligerent, but the American leaders once again took as their goal the limitation of the conflict, with the limitation of the theater of operation being its spatial projection and in a sense its symbol. Again, and finally, the question raised in the spring of 1951 was that of the objectives accessible without the war's amplification. Soon even this question was abandoned and the American leaders, renouncing a local or partial victory, had no ambition beyond obtaining a peace which was virtually equivalent to a return to the *status quo ante*.

Who would the winner be? The Americans, because they had repulsed the North Korean aggression? The Chinese, because they had repulsed the American attempt to liquidate the People's Republic of North Korea? Not having been beaten by the world's first-ranking power, the Chinese had gained in prestige. But the Americans had confirmed the value of the guarantees they had distributed all over the world, and given striking proof that they would not tolerate open aggressions (crossing of frontiers by regular armies). It is not established that the American desire for the conflict's limitation stood in the way of local military successes (with two or three extra divisions, the Eighth Army might have been able, not to disarm Communist China, but to defeat the Chinese "volunteers").

The contrast between the essentially political conduct of the Korean War and the essentially military conduct of both world wars cannot be explained by human fallibility alone. The conduct of the Second World War was essentially political—i.e., dictated by consideration of the consequences remote from the scene of hostilities and of victory—*on the Soviet side*. It is on the American side that no attempt was made to discover whether the world resulting from a total military victory would correspond to the lasting interests of the United States. It is obviously not proved that the adoption of such a line of thought would have sufficed to avoid the deplorable effects of the victory—that is, the excessive reinforcement of the occasional ally but permanent enemy, the excessive weakening of the present enemy but future ally confronting the ally that had become too powerful. The nature of each war depends on many circumstances which the strategist must understand but which he is not always in a position to modify.

It is possible that after 1915 the First World War had to follow its own course to the end, the chiefs of state on either side being unable to formulate and make their peoples accept the terms of a compromise peace. It is possible that with or without unconditional surrender Hitler would have succeeded in sweeping the German people to the twilight of the gods of race and blood. It is possible that with or without the Yalta agreement, the Soviet Union would have intervened in the Far East and reaped the fruits of the victory won by the American forces. The fact remains that neither in Europe nor in Asia did American strategists subordinate the conduct of operations against the enemy and of relations with the occasional ally to a consideration of the objectives they wished to achieve by the war. The strategists did not know *which* Europe, *which* Asia would correspond to American interests. They did not know if Japan or Germany was the enemy, or only a *certain* Japan, a *certain* Germany.

It is not enough to determine the objective, the ally, the enemy, in order to profit by the victory. If the intelligence of the state has not clearly determined its goals, and discerned the true nature of enemy and ally alike, the triumph of weapons will only by accident be an authentic victory, that is, a political one.

3. *To Win or Not to Lose*

The choice of a strategy depends on both the goals of war and the available means. We have just analyzed extreme examples of wars waged with a view to military success alone, or with a view to avoiding the extension of the conflict. But it is within these extremes that we find most of the real wars in which a strategy is chosen with regard to both military possibilities and intentions.

Perhaps the supreme alternative, on the level of strategy, is "to win or not to lose." A strategy can aim at decisively conquering the enemy's armed forces in order to dictate the terms of a victorious peace to the disarmed enemy. But when the relation of forces excludes such an eventuality, the war leaders can still propose *not to lose,* by discouraging the superior coalition's intention of conquering.

German authors like H. Delbrück have found the ideal example of such a strategy in the Seven Years' War. Frederick II nursed no illusions of conquering the Austro-Russian army, but he counted on holding out long enough for his adversaries' morale to disintegrate, and for the Alliance to fall apart. We know how the death of an emperor actually provoked a reversal of Russian policy. The recollection of this piece of luck was so deeply engraved in the German memory that Goebbels, learning of Roosevelt's death, believed that the miracle of Frederick II would be repeated: was not the alliance between the United States and the Soviet Union still more contrary to nature than that of St. Petersburg and Vienna?

Other, more immediate examples will illustrate the problem's lasting nature. Given the relation of forces, what must be the strategist's goal? This was the basic question, by 1915–16, that divided German generals and statesmen. Were the Central Powers to choose as their goal a victory that would permit them to dictate the clauses of the peace treaty? Or, given the superiority of forces that the Allies were acquiring, should the Central Powers renounce victory and limit their ambitions to a compromise peace based on the recognition by each side of its incapacity to prevail over the other decisively?

Contrary to what most Frenchmen believed, the Verdun offensive, in the framework of General von Falkenhayn's strategy, aimed at wearing down, rather than defeating, the French army. The German command intended to weaken the latter until, by the spring and summer of 1916, it would be incapable of any major undertaking. Unconcerned about the west, the German army could take the offensive in the east and score successes there which would convince the Allies to come to terms, even if they were not obliged to.

The Successor group, Hindenburg-Ludendorff, chose, on the contrary, the other alternative. Until the spring of 1918 the German armies tried to force the decision. Russia had been put *hors de combat* in 1917; American troops were flowing into Europe; the balance of forces, still favorable at the beginning of 1918, was becoming increasingly unfavorable. The German general staff tried to win before the intervention of a still intact American army with inexhaustible forces. Historians and theoreticians (in particular H. Delbrück) have speculated whether such a strategy of destruction didn't, by 1917, constitute an error. Shouldn't the generals have economized their means, limited the German losses in order to hold out as long as possible in the hope that the Allies would weary of the struggle and be content with a negotiated peace? Renouncing the effort to force a decision, strategy would have tried, by defensive successes, to convince the enemy as well to renounce his ambition of victory.

Another more striking example of this dialectic of victory and non-defeat is that of Japan in 1941. How could the Japanese Empire, engaged for years in an endless war against China, launch itself into the assault of every European position in southeast Asia, simultaneously challenging Great Britain and the United States, when it produced scarcely seven million tons of steel a year and the United States was producing over ten times as much? What calculation of the war leaders was responsible for this extravagant venture?

The calculation was as follows: by the surprise attack on Pearl Harbor, the Japanese fleet would gain several months' control of the seas, extending at least as far as Australia. Infantry and air force could conquer the Philippines, Malaya, Indonesia, and perhaps the American outposts of the Pacific, such as Guam. Controlling an enormous area rich in stockpiles of raw materials, Japan would be in a position to organize and prepare her defense. None of the highest-ranking generals or admirals conceived of Japanese troops entering Washington and dictating an unconditional peace following a total victory over the United States. The Japanese leaders who took the responsibility of launching the war intended to resist the American counteroffensive long enough to exhaust the enemy will to be victorious (which, they believed, must be weak, since the United States was a democracy).

The calculation turned out to be doubly false: in four years American submarines and planes destroyed virtually the entire Japanese commercial fleet. The latter was already basically defeated even before American bombs set fire to the Japanese cities and Roosevelt purchased Soviet participation in the war (though he should have been ready to purchase Soviet abstention). The calculation was no less false with regard to psychology. Democracies often cultivate pacifist ideologies: they are not always pacifist. In any case, once enraged, the Americans struck hard: the attack on Pearl Harbor gave the Japanese fleet a temporary mastery of Asian waters, but it made United States renunciation of victory very unlikely. The success of the military calculation during the first phase excluded the success of the psychological calculation regarding the final phase. Not that a better strategy[14] was available to the Japanese leaders: none could reasonably promise victory in a showdown between adversaries so unequal.

Pol + Williams

The hope of winning by attrition assumes another meaning in the case of revolution or subversive wars. Insurrections are launched by minorities or by mobs without consideration of the "relation of forces." Usually the rebels have no chance on paper. Those in power command the army, the police: how can men without organization and without arms prevail? For that matter, if the government obtains the obedience of its servants, they do not prevail. But the Parisian rioters in 1830 and 1848 won because neither the soldiers of the regular army nor, in 1848, the *garde nationale* seemed determined to fight and because, abandoned by part of the political elite, the sovereigns themselves lost their courage, quickly abdicated, and went into exile.

The riots which the weak morale of armies transforms into revolutions do not belong in a theory of international relations. We have referred to them because the wars called subversive present certain characteristics of revolutions: above all, the decisive importance of psychological elements. In the Russian civil war between the revolutionary party and the conservative party, between the Bolsheviks, masters of the state, and the generals advocating a restoration, the will of the leading minorities and the state of mind of the masses influenced the outcome no less than the material resources accessible to either camp. (However, in Spain it was Franco's material superiority which determined the outcome still more than the discord in the Republican camp.) The Vendeans did not fight any the less fiercely against the revolutionary

---

[14] Except perhaps Admiral Yamamoto's proposal to carry the initial venture to still greater extremes and attempt the occupation of Pearl Harbor.

power than the Blues for the new world. Let us avoid mythologies. Bare-handed rebels are irresistible when those in power cannot or will not defend themselves. The Russian armies of the nineteenth and twentieth centuries effectively restored *order* in Warsaw and in Budapest.

The wars known today as "subversive," for instance that of a population in a colonial regime against the European power, are intermediary between civil and foreign wars. If the territory has been juridically integrated with that of the metropolitan nation—as is the case with Algeria—the war, in terms of international law, is chiefly civil (the sovereignty of France over Algeria was recognized by all states), although the rebels regard it as a foreign war insofar as they wish to become an independent political unit. In Tonkin, in Annam, in Tunisia, in Morocco, countries that were not colonies but over which France had established a protectorate or suzerainty, the "international conflict" aspect prevails, even in terms of international law, over the "civil war" aspect.

We bring together the problem raised by these subversive wars with that which confronts the strategist who must establish his plan of war because the rebel and the traditional leader must both deal with the alternative: *to win or not to lose*. Yet there is a difference: in 1916, in 1917, even in 1918 the supreme commanders on either side nursed hopes of destroying the enemy's power to resist. Nivelle in the spring of 1917 and Ludendorff in the spring of 1918 counted on forcing the decision by a direct offensive. Both dreamed of an annihilating victory in the Napoleonic style—a victory inaccessible to the efforts of both camps until the end of the war, the attrition of one side, and the reinforcement of the other by American forces deciding the outcome. In the case of a subversive war in which one side controls administration and police, assures order, and mobilizes regular armies, the disproportion of forces is such that only one of the belligerents can dream of a total military success. The conservative party has the desire to conquer, the rebel party the desire not to let itself be eliminated or exterminated. Here again we find the typical dissymmetry: one side wants to win, the other not to lose.

But this dissymmetry, which formally resembles that of the Seven Years' War (Frederick II against an overpowering coalition), has, fundamentally, an entirely different meaning. Frederick hoped to obtain a compromise peace on the day his adversaries recognized, if not the impossibility of beating him, at least the cost and the time victory would have demanded. Not having been defeated, the King of Prussia was in relative terms a victor: he would keep his previous conquests, and his prestige would be increased in proportion to his heroism. Not having been victorious, the coalition of the traditional great powers admitted the newcomer on a basis of equality. But if the rebellious side—the Neo-Destour, the Istiqlal—is not eliminated, but seizes power and obtains independence, it has won a total victory in political terms, since it has achieved its objective, the nation's independence, and since the protecting or colonial power has ultimately abandoned the authority it had arrogated to itself. In this case it would be enough for the rebel side not to lose militarily in order to gain politically. But why does the conservative party accept its defeat politically without having been defeated militarily? Why must it win decisively by eliminating the rebellion if it wants not to lose?

To understand the political outcome of a struggle that is indecisive in military terms, we must recall another dissymmetry of the parties in a colonial conflict. The nationalists who demand the independence of their nation (which has or has not existed in the past, which lives or does not live in the hearts of the people) are more impassioned than the governing powers of the colonial state. At least in our times they believe in the sanctity of their cause more than their adversaries believe in the legitimacy of their domination. Sixty years ago the Frenchman no more doubted France's *mission civilisatrice* than the Englishman questioned the "white man's burden." Today the Frenchman doubts that he has the moral right to refuse the populations of Africa and Asia a *patrie* (which cannot be France), even if this *patrie* is only a dream, even if it should prove to be incapable of any authentic independence.

This dissymmetry is confirmed by the change in the colonial balance-sheet. To administer a territory today is to assume responsibility for its development. Most often, this responsibility costs more than the enlarging of the market or the exploitation of natural resources brings in. It is hardly surprising that the conservative party eventually wearies of paying the price of pacification and of investments for the benefit of the very populations that oppose it. A formally total defeat (the rebel side has finally won the sovereignty it sought) is not necessarily experienced as such by the ex-colonial power.

The apparent simplicity of the stake—independence or not—conceals the complexity of the situation. If the independence of the protectorate or the colony were considered by the imperial state as an absolute evil, an irremediable defeat, we should return to the elementary friend-enemy duality. The nationalist—Tunisian, Moroccan, Algerian—would be the enemy, not *occasional* or even *permanent*, to use the terms defined above, but rather the *absolute enemy*, the one with whom no reconciliation is possible, whose very existence is an aggression, and who consequently must be exterminated. *Delenda est Carthago*: the formula is that of absolute hostility, the hostility of Rome and Carthage; one of the two cities is *de trop*. If Algeria were to have remained *definitively* French, the nationalists seeking an independent Algeria would have had to be pitilessly eliminated. If millions of Moslems were to become French in the middle of the twentieth century, they would have had to be prevented even from dreaming of an Algerian nation, and made to forget the witnesses "who got themselves murdered."

Perhaps some Frenchmen would have preferred this to be the case: reality is less logical, more human. The colonial power conceives of various ways to retreat, whose consequences are not identical; some of these ways to retreat

Underline the power of a system

are in the long run preferable to maintenance by force. The interests of the metropolitan country will be more or less preserved depending on which men wield power in the ex-colony, promoted to the rank of an independent state. Henceforth the imperial power is not in conflict with a single, clearly defined enemy, the *nationalist;* it must choose, delimit its enemy. In Indo-China, Western strategy should and probably could have held the Communist nationalist to be the enemy, but not the nationalist who was hostile or simply indifferent to communism. Such a decision would have implied that France did not regard the independence of the Associated States as fundamentally contrary to her interests. France would have had more opportunities of winning the war by separating Communists and nationalists, granting the latter's chief demands. But to the officers thinking in terms of empire, this so-called rational strategy would have seemed sheer idiocy.

In "subversive" wars since 1945, the conservative power has consistently been confronted by three kinds of adversaries: Communists, intransigent nationalists, and moderate nationalists who would accept progressive steps and sometimes be content with autonomy. Among the intransigents, some sought and others rejected collaboration with the colonial state. Extremists in the immediate present were sometimes moderates in the long run. Depending on the circumstances and the final intentions of the conservative strategy, the three groups constituted a common front, or drew apart. When the imperial power renounced sovereignty, only the Communists and those nationalists desiring a break with the West have remained enemies. King Mohammed V and M. Bourguiba, the Istiqlal and the Neo-Destour, can be the sovereigns or the parties of friendly states. Once again, yesterday's enemy is today's friend. Politics cannot be reasonable without the capacity to forget.

The conviction has spread that the nationalist victory is written in advance in the book of destiny, in accordance with historical determinism. For many reasons the victory of Asian and African revolutionists over the European empires has been assured. But on this level of formal analysis, one observation appears necessary. The inequality of determination among the adversaries was still more marked than the inequality of material forces. The dissymmetry of will, of interest, of animosity in the belligerent dialogue of conservers and rebels was the ultimate origin of what French authors call the defeats of the West.

Is *will* alone enough to stop the nationalist movement? The circumstances in Algeria were, in certain respects, comparable to those in Tunisia and Morocco: here, too, French strategy hesitated over the definition of the enemy, sometimes inclined to include all nationalists in it, sometimes, on the contrary, to limit it to FLN militants, or even to FLN extremists. In Algeria, too, French strategy has learned the difficulty of winning a military victory that must be total to be uncontested, and is prohibited by the very nature of a guerrilla army scattered in the *djebels* and supplied from abroad. But all these classical arguments are opposed by another: the guerrilla forces have still less chance of defeating the regular army. If the men in power are willing to spend hundreds of billions of francs a year as long as is necessary, if the army finds the pursuit of partisans in accord with the normal exercise of the military profession, if public opinion in the metropolitan nation abides by this prolonged conflict and consents to the necessary sacrifices, the impossibility of winning appears—what it actually is—bilateral, as obvious for the rebels as for the forces of order so much do the former's losses exceed the latter's.

The French established in Algeria did not seem any less persistent than the rebels, and they communicated their obstinacy to a portion of the Frenchmen in metropolitan France. That this stubbornness could change the outcome was never likely. That it changed the aspect of events cannot be doubted.

4. Conduct of Engagements and Strategy

Policy does not control merely the conception of the whole conflict. In certain cases it also determines the conduct of a battle, the risks an army leader must accept, the limits the strategists must establish for the tactician's initiatives.

Let us again consider examples to illustrate these formulas. The man who commands an army or a fleet can no longer take "victory as the sole objective" any more than the general in charge of a vast theater of operations. In the famous battle of Jutland, the last in which whole squadrons confronted each other without aircraft, Admiral Jellicoe never forgot for an instant that on that day he could lose not just a battle but the war. On the other hand, there was no need to destroy the German fleet in order to obtain the strategically necessary result. He had to repulse the German fleet's attempt to break the blockade, and still preserve numerical superiority: simultaneously, the only success necessary to final victory would be achieved. In short, to return to the expressions employed above, the English fleet had won as soon as it had not lost. The German fleet had lost by the very fact that it had not won. The relation of forces was not modified: the Allies retained control of the seas.

In relation to the total strategic perspective, Admiral Jellicoe was right not to pursue the German fleet to the point of exposing his own vessels to submarine or torpedo attack. Of course, the destruction of the German fleet would have added to the glory of the Royal Navy and scored a point against German morale, reinforced the confidence of the Allies, and influenced public opinion in the neutral states. But these advantages were marginal, secondary; they were absurd in comparison with the jeopardy of the British fleet, which was indispensable to control of the seas and therefore to the very existence of the Western camp.

Further, this prudence was justified by subsequent events. The German fleet exerted no further influence upon the course of hostilities. It had won prestige because it had fought in an undecided battle, and achieved several technical or tactical successes. But if the chief military leader sometimes takes glory as his supreme objective, the subordinate military leader must not take any objective other than one in accord with the plan of war.

In this case the subordination of local action to the strategic conception is strictly military, without reference to politics. The same is not true of the decision the German military leaders had to make apropos of unrestricted submarine warfare. The memorandum written on this occasion by Max Weber is an admirable illustration of the political-military calculation necessary under such circumstances.

The question was not so much one of knowing if unrestricted submarine warfare—the destruction of merchant vessels without warning—was or was not in accord with international law: as a matter of fact, it was contrary to the rules admitted by the ranking powers before 1914, but Allied behavior in the war at sea (long-distance blockade, camouflaged armament of cargo ships) was not irreproachable either. On the level of strict rationality, the first question was to discover whether the proclamation of unrestricted submarine warfare would provoke the United States to enter the war, or if American intervention would at least be delayed in the absence of such a declaration.

Even supposing this declaration provoked American intervention, it might still be rational if the submarines could insure an effective counterblockade, preventing or delaying the transportation of a great American army to Europe, and if the German army were in a position to win before the weight of this still intact army made itself felt on the battlefields. None of these conditions was realized. The strategic decisions of the Hindenburg-Ludendorff group—unrestricted submarine warfare, offensive on the western front, maintenance of relatively important forces to hold eastern gains—were, if not radically erroneous, at least exaggeratedly reckless. The leaders of the Central Powers played their trump card, not hesitating to defy the United States or to assume offensives which would precipitate irremediable defeat if they did not produce total victory. Let us add, to keep the reader from losing his sense of historical irony, that the American navy practiced what in 1917 was called unrestricted submarine warfare from the first day of hostilities against Japan.

The limitation of military operations as a function of political necessities, objected to by American generals in Korea and French generals in Algeria, is not in itself at all original. It is likely that the bombing of the Manchurian airfields in 1951 or 1952 would not have provoked an extension of the theater of operations or of the number of belligerents. But the bombing would also not have modified the course of hostilities substantially, since the Chinese Migs were not attacking the American positions and were not preventing the American bombers from completing their missions. Further, the Chinese might have replied to the bombing of the Manchurian airfields by bombing Korean ports, if not Japanese bases. The unwritten convention of this limited war involved reciprocal respect of "zones of refuge," of "sanctuaries" outside the theater in which the conflict of the two Koreas was taking place, supported respectively by Chinese and American forces.

Somewhat different is the case of the French decision with regard to Tunisia (between 1955 and 1962). Tunisia was theoretically neutral in a conflict that, in terms of international law, was not a war,[15] between the FLN and French authorities in Algeria. As a matter of fact, Tunisia, on whose territory the FLN stationed troops, did not behave as a neutral state: it gave assistance to the rebels, an action contrary to the international custom of the past but in conformity with the practice of the present. Juridically and morally France was entitled to reply at least by raids on the *fellagha* bases. The point was to discover the consequences, costs and advantage of such raids.

Even a temporary invasion of Tunisia would probably have made the departure of the "French colony" inevitable, and obliged M. Bourguiba's government to break off relations with France and seek support elsewhere. It would have provoked the censure (whether justified or not is of little importance) of Afro-Asian public opinion and of an important share of Western public opinion. These political disadvantages could have been justified only by military advantages of incontestable scope. Yet in order to destroy the FLN's logistic bases in Tunisia effectively, it would have been necessary to occupy the nation over an extended period (which the French general staff, short of forces, was reluctant to do, aside from any political consideration). A temporary occupation of Tunisia, with unforeseeable political countereffects, would have had little effect on the fundamental circumstances of the Algerian conflict.

This analysis aims less at proving a thesis than at recalling a general proposition. Rare in modern history are the circumstances in which the leaders have been free to do *everything* they regarded as effective and useful on the strictly military level. That generals must renounce certain actions out of respect for international legality, for allies or neutrals, is the rule rather than the exception.

Perhaps it would be helpful to consider a final example of a politico-military decision condemned by the outcome, which ministers and generals blame on each other: the decision to defend Laos, then to organize this defense around the entrenched camp of Dien-Bien-Phu. The thesis of the unfortunate general is that the decision to defend Laos against the Viet-minh was taken by the "supreme commander," in this case the government in Paris. This decision, continues the defense, implied the establishment of an entrenched camp at Dien-Bien-Phu, the only position from which Laos could be defended. Once again, it is not our concern to analyze the case in detail, i.e., to determine whether the camp at Dien-Bien-Phu constituted the only possible application of the decision to defend Laos, whether this camp could

[15] Although a certain "belligerence" can be attributed to the FLN.

have been organized so that resistance had a chance of success, or whether this camp, finally, despite appearances, fulfilled at least one of its functions, to preserve the capital of Laos and to keep the strength of the Viet-minh forces out of the Tonkin Delta.

Retrospectively, the polemic between government and military command over Laos or Dien-Bien-Phu is of double interest because it touches on two aspects of the relations between strategy and politics. It was, in fact, politically important to protect Laos, the member of the Associated States whose leaders and population were least hostile to France. The loss of Laos, secondary in military terms, would have dealt a blow to French prestige throughout Indo-China, publicly symbolizing the weakness of French arms. But it would be wrong to conclude as a result that on this occasion political considerations and military considerations were opposed. Anxiety over prestige and the significance of a territory in terms of morale are part of the political order but do not constitute its entirety. In any circumstance, partial political arguments can be opposed by partial military arguments. But the point here is not a conflict between strategy and diplomacy, since arguments *for* and *against* a certain decision occur just as often in the military as in the political order.

The mistake would be to confuse *partial* motives of a political order with the political order itself, which is essentially defined by the total situation, by the unifying overview of the intellect. "That policy unites in itself, and reconciles all the interests of internal administrations, even those of humanity, and whatever else are rational subjects of consideration is presupposed, for it is nothing in itself, except a mere representative and exponent of all these interests towards other states."[16] What the commanders in Paris who were in charge of waging this Far Eastern war lacked was a total view of the war itself, of the interests they wished to safeguard, of the goals they thereby proposed. After the Communist victory in continental China, could they still hope to defeat the Viet-minh? In this hypothesis they entirely misjudged the relation of forces. Did they want to maintain a French demi-authority in the Associated States or else keep the latter outside the Viet-minh zone? If the first alternative was correct, they were subordinating the essential goal—limiting Communist expansion—to a secondary objective, the mode of relations between France and the Associated States. Did they envisage direct negotiation with the Viet-minh or a broadened negotiation with China, the Soviet Union, and the Western powers? In such a strategic perspective, it would have been possible to specify the necessary means and the pledges to be kept at any price. Lacking this total perspective and defined objectives, policy falls into the error indicated by Clausewitz: "That policy makes demands on the War which it cannot respond to, would be contrary to the supposition that it knows the instrument which it is going to use, therefore, contrary to a natural and indispensable supposition."[17] In Indo-China, to use

16 Clausewitz, *op. cit.*, VIII, 6, p. 124.
17 *Ibid.*, p. 125.

Clausewitz's terms again, it is not "the prejudicial influence of policy on the conduct of a War" that was at fault, but policy itself. "It is only when policy promises itself a wrong effect from certain military means and measures" that it exerts a pernicious influence on war by insisting that it follow a certain course. "Just as a person in a language with which he is not conversant sometimes says what he does not intend, so policy, when intending right, may often order things which do not tally with its own views."[18]

It is worse still when politics gives no orders or when a political leader and a military command are each unaware of the other. In Indo-China the military command determined the establishment of the entrenched camp at Dien-Bien-Phu before the Geneva Conference, of whose outcome it was unaware. The International Conference upset the basic conditions of the problem, including the military ones. It incited the Viet-minh to achieve at any price a spectacular success on the eve of negotiations. It should have suggested extreme caution to the French general staff. The Viet-minh *had* to seek a spectacular success, just as the French expeditionary force *had* to refuse it the occasion for such a success at any cost.

5. Diplomacy and Military Means

Let us turn back to one of the Clausewitz formulas we have quoted: policy must know the instrument it is to employ. This formula is no less true in peacetime than in war. Until the Korean War, U.S. foreign policy oscillated from one extreme to the other, obsessed by military victory exclusively in wartime, indifferent to military considerations in peacetime. Alexis de Tocqueville had already noted this inclination to a double extremism —few soldiers in peacetime, little diplomatic subtlety once the guns speak— and had considered it the expression of the democratic spirit.

Rationality, in fact, dictates reflection on peace despite the uproar of the melee, and on war when weapons are silent. The commerce of nations is continuous; diplomacy and war are only complementary modalities, one or the other dominating in turn, without one ever entirely giving way to the other except in the extreme case either of absolute hostility, or of absolute friendship or total federation.

Military indifference, in peacetime, can take two forms: one is characteristic, in our times, of the United States, the other of France. The first consists of taking armament potential for actual power, imagining that diplomatic notes have the same force of conviction whether they are supported by statistics of steel production or by fleets of battleships, aircraft carriers and planes. From 1931 till the summer of 1940 the United States refused to recognize the Japanese conquests and to oppose such ventures by force.

The second modality of diplomacy not in accord with strategy, the French modality, is characterized by the contradiction between the war a nation has

18 *Ibid.*, pp. 126–27.

the military means to wage and the war diplomatic agreements eventually oblige it to wage. Between 1919 and 1936 the occupation or disarmament of the left bank of the Rhine permitted France to impose her will upon Germany, provided she had the determination and the courage to use force. As long as the French army held the Rhine bridgeheads, it had an almost decisive advantage in case of conflict, being in a position from the first days of hostility to strike at the heart of the Reich's industrial arsenal. In this military instance the alliances on the other side of Germany, with the new nations created out of the decomposition of the Austro-Hungarian Empire, supported not French security but French hegemony over Europe. With Germany open to the west, girdled by hostile states to the east and the south, France extended her power to the frontiers of the Soviet Union. But in order to maintain this pre-eminence, she required an army capable of profiting offensively from the demilitarization of the left bank of the Rhine and of forbidding the Reichswehr to reoccupy this zone so vital in military terms. At the crucial moment, in March 1936, the French Minister of War, like the general staff, insisted on complete mobilization before agreeing to a military response. France had no army of intervention and, by digging the Maginot Line, had given evidence of a defensive military attitude which corresponded to the spirit but not to the necessities of a conservative diplomacy: to maintain the Versailles Treaty and the system of alliances in the Balkans and Eastern Europe, France would have had to be capable of military initiatives in order to prevent Germany's violation of the treaty's essential clauses.

Once the Rhineland was reoccupied by the Reichswehr and the latter transformed into a mass army, French pledges to Czechoslovakia, Poland and Rumania changed their meaning. France promised to oppose German aggression by a war which could only be a long one, on the model of that of 1914–18. In such a war the eastern allies represented additional forces, but even this contribution was precarious since these nations, being vulnerable, risked being submerged by the German tide more rapidly than Serbia and Rumania had been swallowed up during the course of the preceding conflict. Further, it was easy to point to the French pledges as involving the risk of a not inevitable war. After all, wouldn't Hitler be satisfied once he had reunited all the Germans into a single Reich, in accordance with his ideology (ein Volk, ein Reich, ein Führer)?

A diplomacy which claims to act without an army in condition to fight, a diplomacy which possesses an army incapable of the missions required by its objectives, these two lapses of rationality are as attributable to the psychology of the leaders and peoples as to intellectual error. Before the age of strategic bombers and ballistic missiles, the United States had never had to fear any neighbor state. It had to win space from the Indians (militias sufficed) and from nature (what was the use of soldiers?). Power politics was an invention of despotisms, one of the aspects of European corruption which had been left behind. The refusal to recognize territorial changes made by force expressed simultaneously a confused legal ideology, the desire not to wage war, and an obscure confidence in the final triumph of morality over force.

The American disarmament of 1945 ("bring the boys back") was the last episode of this traditional policy (or non-policy), the last symbol of the radical break between war and peace. The war had to be won: all other business was broken off, the job had been done, and done well. The moment had come to return to civilian life, to industry, to commerce, to sport, to what concerns the citizens of a free democracy once the wicked or the mad, the fascists or the imperialists, have been rendered harmless.

The French rupture of politico-military unity also had a psychological cause. The status created by the Versailles Treaty was artificial insofar as it did not express the true relation of forces once Great Britain and the United States declared their hostility to it or showed their indifference to it. If the Soviet Union and a rearmed Germany united to destroy it, France, with only her Continental allies, did not have the force to save it. Logically, this precariousness of the European order after 1918 should have incited France to exploit fully, and to conserve as long as possible, the advantages she owed to the victory (Germany disarmed, the Rhineland defenseless). Rationality dictated an active defense supported by the threat of military actions (barring a frank attempt to appease Weimar Germany[19] by offering it satisfaction). But the feeling of potential inferiority prevailed even though there still existed a hegemony in fact. The military organization reflected the desire for security and withdrawal, whereas diplomacy still accorded with hegemony.

The coordination of diplomacy and strategy assumes a new character after 1945 because of the multiplicity of combat techniques. Before the Atomic Age, no one imagined using different weapons according to different circumstances. Today, one does not conceive of using a thermonuclear bomb or even a tactical atomic weapon without regard to the kind of war involved. The nature of the conflict formerly determined the volume of the forces engaged and the degree of mobilization of forces, whether actual or potential. Today it determines the type of weapons used.

From every evidence, the conduct of wars will be still more political than in the past. It is no longer a question of granting the military leaders complete freedom to win the war, no matter how and at no matter what price. The very notion of winning is probably no longer the same and, in any case, the question of the cost, though it has always been asked, now becomes decisive: what good is it to destroy the enemy if the latter simultaneously destroys you?

Let us say, generalizing, that all of yesterday's questions are still asked: What share of the potential forces should be permanently mobilized? What are the strategic eventualities in relation to which military preparation must be organized? What are the missions policy is liable to assign the army in

[19] This theoretical possibility no longer existed after Hitler's accession to power.

various circumstances? But to these classical questions we must henceforth add new questions: How many types of war, distinct according to the weapons used, must be conceived? For how many of these wars can a state prepare? To what degree can the military systems that would see action under various circumstances be administratively separate? Will the same troops intervene in case of total war, of limited war with atomic weapons, of limited war with conventional weapons? A national defense organization has always been the expression of strategic doctrine, but the instruments of combat could be more or less numerous, manipulated according to various methods: the military leaders did not have to choose among panoplies. Henceforth the diversity of panoplies is plainly evident.

At the same time, there reappears in another form a danger present a half-century ago: diplomacy risks becoming a prisoner, at the crucial moment, of military mechanisms which must be prepared in advance, which the government remains free to set off or not, but which it can no longer modify. During the fatal week in July 1914 which preceded the outburst, on two occasions the general staffs—in Russia and Germany—explained to the sovereigns and their advisers that a certain measure was technically impossible. The Tsar desired partial mobilization against Austria, but such a mobilization had not been foreseen; it would have upset all plans and precipitated chaos. Similarly, the only strategy envisaged by the German general staff was that of a war on two fronts with an initial offensive in the west. The Reich, too, could not mobilize against Russia alone nor, after mobilization, remain with guns at the ready: France would have to be attacked and beaten as quickly as possible, before Russia could engage the majority of her forces. At a moment when destiny was still hesitating, the automatic military machinery geared to the war plans was set in motion and men were swept on almost in spite of themselves.

At present the strategy of deterrence requires that the machinery of retaliation be established in advance. Is there a risk that this machinery might be set off by mistake or that it might be set off according to plans established in advance, whereas, for various reasons, the military leaders might hope to modify these plans (partial retaliation and not massive retaliation)? Before 1914 the automatism was that of "administrative machinery," of military bureaucracies in charge of mobilization. In 1960 the automatism to be feared is as much that of electronic devices as of strategic plans. In 1914 statesmen had several days in which to make a decision. In the 1960s they have only several minutes.

It is too simple, actually, to allow for only two actors, oneself and the enemy. Particularly in our times, medium-size states must orient themselves not only in relation to an adverse coalition but also in relation to allies who may desire the enemy's defeat, but who may be hostile or indifferent to the particular objectives of their comrades in arms. The United States or Great Britain, between 1939 and 1945, were not under the obligation to save the

French Empire. Even in the West, the states, united in the effort to defeat the Third Reich, did not otherwise necessarily aim at the same goals.

Curiously, the most serious dissensions among the Americans and the British were not provoked by real contradictions of interest. The United States had as much to gain as Great Britain by limiting Soviet expansion, preventing the Sovietization of Eastern Europe. The strategy of the Western invasion, of attack against the enemy's "fortress," was dictated by strictly military arguments. It is true that at the time Roosevelt and his advisers were not so aware as American leaders today of the Western community and of the irreducible hostility of the Soviet Union.

A different conception of the best way of winning is enough to make the conduct of war by a coalition difficult. But the various ways of winning rarely lead to the same results for all the partners. Logically, each state desires to contribute to the victory, but without weakening itself in relation to its allies. These rivalries fatally diminish the effectiveness of the coalition.

The duality of considerations—defense of one's own interests and contribution to the common cause—combines with the polymorphism of wars to create the present circumstances of the Atlantic Alliance. The generally valid rule for conduct to follow in a coalition is to concentrate forces in the terrain where the nation's particular interests are most important. In this regard, the Indo-Chinese war, even interpreted as one of the fronts of resistance to communism, was an error on France's part which involved a considerable portion of her total resources in a theater secondary for herself as well as for the West.

More justifiable, in this regard, was the transfer to Algeria of the major part of the French army. Of course, the coalition was weakened by this, and the NATO shield became too thin. Insofar as they did not regard Algerian nationalism as a threat, the other Western powers were inclined to criticize France both because she did not furnish the contribution she had promised to the Atlantic forces, and because she compromised relations between the West and the Islamic world. Even if these reproaches were well-founded from the point of view of the Alliance, the French decision was not necessarily erroneous. The weakening of the Atlantic forces did not noticeably increase the danger of war in Europe; the transfer of the French divisions afforded an opportunity of preserving sovereignty south of the Mediterranean. If this sovereignty had a vital importance, it would have justified the engagement of the majority of French forces in Algeria, even if this action displeased other members of the Alliance.

The danger is that all the allies, repeating the same rationale—I am doing little disservice to the common interest but I am doing great service to my own—might end by aiding the enemy's victory. The neutral state, desiring the victory of one camp but judging that the sacrifices required by its intervention would be considerable without adding substantially to the likelihood of victory, is correct—provided it does not set an example. Ultimately there would remain only a single state to assume the burden of indispensable action. Furthermore, the leader of the coalition is the only one inclined to identify the coalition's interests with his own.

The choice, by each ally, of his contribution to the Alliance has been rendered still more difficult in recent years by the alternative of conventional weapons and atomic weapons. Yesterday Great Britain, today France wish to enter the atomic club: what role will be left for conventional weapons if atomic arms and delivery systems obtain their due? The very meaning of the choice remains equivocal: will atomic weapons protect France from possible aggression or possible Soviet blackmail, or will they reinforce France's position within the Alliance?

The unity of policy, including both war and peace, diplomacy and strategy, bars the total solidarity of allies. Only a miracle would insure the coincidence of all the interests of all the states within the coalition. The force of a coalition is always less than the sum of the forces it possesses on paper.

The primacy of policy is a theoretical proposition, not a plan of action. But this theoretical proposition is of a nature to do more good than harm, if the reduction of violence is regarded as desirable.

The primacy of policy, in fact, permits the control of escalation, the avoidance of an explosion of animosity into passionate and unrestricted brutality. The more the leaders calculate in terms of cost and profit and the less they are inclined to relinquish the pen for the sword, the more they will hesitate to abandon themselves to the risk of arms, the more they will be content to limit their successes and renounce the intoxication of dazzling victories. The *reasonable* conduct of politics is the only *rational* one if the goal of the intercourse among states is the survival of all, common prosperity, and the sparing of the peoples' blood.

Of course, the subordination of war to policy has not meant, in fact, the pacification of this intercourse. The nature of war depends on the total historical circumstances. "If policy is grand and powerful, so also will be the War, and this may be carried to the point at which War attains to *its absolute form.*"[20] But if war is in the image of policy, if it varies as a function of the stake the latter determines, pacification ceases to be inconceivable. Calculation can make evident to princes that the cost of the war will in any case be superior to the profits of victory.

Yet this calculation must convince all the participants. Otherwise it would serve no purpose and by provoking inequality of determination would even risk precipitating the very thing it was attempting to avoid. At this level the principle of polarity reappears: a limited war does not depend upon only one of the belligerents. "If . . . one of two belligerents is determined to seek the great decision by arms, then he has a high probability of success, as soon as he is certain his opponent will not take that way, but follows a dif-

[20] Clausewitz, *op. cit.*, VIII, 6, p. 123.

ferent object."[21] The theory of war, in the Atomic Age, would be easier but for the fact that the conduct of one actor is at every moment subject to the other's reaction. No dialogue, peaceful or warlike, can remain reasonable if all participants do not consent to it.

[21] *Ibid.*, I, 2, p. 42.

chapter II

Power and Force

or

On the Means of Foreign Policy

Few concepts are as frequently used and as equivocal as those of *power* (*puissance, Macht*). In English the phrase *power politics,* in German the expression *Macht Politik,* is spoken with an accent of criticism or resignation, of horror or admiration. In French the expression *politique de puissance* sounds as if it were translated from a foreign language. Few French authors have glorified the *politique de puissance* as the German doctrinaires have extolled *Macht Politik,* and few French authors have condemned the *politique de puissance* in the way American moralists have condemned *power politics.*

In a general sense, power is the capacity to do, make or destroy. An explosive has a measurable power, as does the tide, the wind or an earthquake. The power of a person or of a collectivity is not strictly measurable, because of the diversity of the goals chosen and the means employed. The fact that fundamentally men apply their power to their fellow creatures gives the concept its true political significance. An individual's power is his capacity to act, but above all to influence the actions or feelings of other individuals. On the international scene I should define power as the capacity of a political unit to impose its will upon other units. In short, political power is not an absolute; it is a human relationship.

This definition suggests several distinctions: between *defensive power* (or the capacity of a political unit to keep the will of others from being imposed upon it) and *offensive power* (or the capacity of a political unit to impose its will upon others); between *the resources or military force of a collectivity,* which can be evaluated objectively, and *its power,* which, being a human relationship, does not depend on material or instruments alone; between *the politics of force* and *the politics of power.* All international politics involves a constant collision of wills, since it consists of relations among sovereign states which claim to rule themselves independently. So long as these units are not subject to external law or to an arbiter, they are, as such, rivals, for each is affected by the actions of the others and inevitably suspects their intentions. But these interacting wills do not necessarily set up a potential or real military rivalry. Relations among political units are not always bellicose, and peaceful relations are influenced, but not determined, by past or future military accomplishments.

1. Force and the Two Kinds of Power

French, English and German all distinguish between two notions, *power and force* (*strength*), *puissance et force*, *Macht und Kraft*. It does not seem to me contrary to the spirit of these languages to reserve the first term for the human relationship, the action itself, and the second for the means, the individual's muscles or the state's weapons.

In the physical sense a man is strong if his weight or muscles afford him the means of resisting or mastering other men. But such strength is nothing without ingenuity, resolution, nerve. Similarly we propose, apropos of collectivities, to distinguish between military, economic and even moral *forces*, and *power*, which is the functioning of these forces in given circumstances and with a view to particular goals. The forces being susceptible to an approximate evaluation, power can be estimated, with an extended margin for error, by reference to the forces available. But there is such a broad distinction possible between defensive and offensive power, between wartime and peacetime power, between power within a certain geographical zone and power beyond this zone, that the measurement of a power taken as absolute and intrinsic seems to me to do more harm than good. It does harm to the statesman who supposes himself in possession of specific information, whereas he possesses merely a deceptively rigorous measurement of a resultant, of equivocal meaning. It does harm to the political scientist who substitutes for the relation of states—i.e., for human collectivities—the confrontation of masses, thereby depriving the object of study of its true meaning.

The notion of force, in its turn, requires distinctions. At least until the advent of the Atomic Age the end and essence of war was combat. The engagement of soldiers, whatever the distance between the lines imposed by the evolution of weapons, remained the supreme test, comparable to the cash payment in which any credit operations ultimately conclude. On the day of the denouement, that is, of the engagement, only the forces actually mobilized influenced the outcome—the raw materials transformed into cannons and shells, the citizens trained for combat. "The conduct of War is not making powder and cannon out of a given quantity of charcoal, sulphur, and saltpetre, of copper and tin: the given quantities for the conduct of War are arms in a finished state and their effects."[1]

Let us call *potential force* the total human, material and moral resources

---

[1] Clausewitz, *op. cit.*, II, 2, p. 113.

which each unit possesses *on paper,* and let us call *actual force* those of its resources that are mobilized for the conduct of international relations in wartime or peacetime. In wartime, actual force is close to *military force* (without entirely coinciding with it, since the course of operations is, in part, determined by non-military forms of conflict). In peacetime, **actual** force is not to be confused with military force since the divisions, fleets and airplanes in being but- not utilized are only one of the instruments in the service of foreign policy.

Between potential force and actual force the factor of mobilization intervenes. The force available to each political unit in its rivalry with others is proportional not to its potential but to its *potential of mobilization.* The latter, in its turn, depends on many factors which can be reduced to two abstract terms: *capacity* and *will.* The conditions of economic or administrative capacity, and of collective will as affirmed by the leaders and supported by the masses, are not constant throughout history; they vary from period to period.

Is the power of the leaders (the men *in power*) of the same nature as the power of political units?

The link between the two notions[2]—power *within* the political unit (*pouvoir*) and the power of the political unit itself (*puissance*)—is easily perceived. The political unit defines itself through opposition: it becomes itself by becoming capable of external action. Yet it can act as a political unit only by the intermediary of one or of several men. Those who *come to power* (to translate literally the German expression *an die Macht kommen*) are the guides, the representatives of the political unit in relation to the outside world. But they are thereby responsible for mobilizing the unit's forces in order to permit its survival in the jungle where "cold monsters" disport themselves. In other words, when international relations have not emerged from the state of nature, the *men in power,* that is, those responsible for the nation in relation to the outside world, are at the same time *men of power,* possessors of an extended capacity to influence the conduct of their fellow men and the very existence of the collectivity.

This analysis does not lead us to confuse the two kinds of power, *pouvoir* and *puissance.* The statesman's action does not have the same meaning, is not situated within the same universe, but differs according to whether the action is internally or externally oriented. Whether the sovereign is a hereditary monarch or the head of a party, whether he relies upon birth or election, he wishes to be legitimate; the readiness with which he is obeyed depends on how widely his legitimacy is recognized. The conditions under which any man becomes a sovereign tend to be codified, like the methods according to which the sovereign must command. The choice of the chief of state and the means by which his command is exercised are increasingly

[2] Designated by the same word in English (*power*) and in German (*Macht*).

institutionalized. In modern societies, this institutionalization assumes a legal character, expressed in abstract formulas. But in every period, the distinction is at least implicit between the orders of a conqueror and those of a legitimate sovereign. Initially, at least, the conqueror employs or invokes pure force, while the sovereign desires to be the interpreter of the collectivity itself and conform to the tradition or the law that has fixed the rules of succession for the leaders, according to the decree of fortune or popular sentiment.

Yet the confusion of the two kinds of power cannot be explained only by the role played by the possessors of power on the international scene. These latter are often, originally, *men of power* who have succeeded. Political units, constitutional regimes all owe their origin to violence. French school children are taught that in a thousand years the kings made France. The authors of our textbooks have never appeared to be embarrassed by the evocation of the wars against barons or foreign states by which the kings achieved national unification, or by the recollection of the violence with which the revolutionaries overthrew the monarchs in 1789, in 1830 and in 1848. Even in 1958 the vote of the National Assembly camouflaged the new regime's illegality more than it set the seal of legality on its accession. The threat of violence—the landing of parachutists—was also a form of violence.

It is only a step from these incontestable facts to the so-called realist interpretation, of which Pareto's sociology is the expression. In this view, the struggle for power within the collectivity (*pouvoir*) is equivalent to the rivalry of powers (*puissance*), the active minorities being in each instance the actors in this rivalry. The legalization of power does not change the significance of the phenomenon: the ruling classes oppose each other as the political units do, and the victorious class exercises its power in the same manner in which the conqueror rules.

Such an interpretation, to my way of thinking, falsifies the meaning of politics,[3] which is a search for an equitable order, and at the same time a conflict among individuals or groups over positions of command and the sharing of scarce goods. But it remains true that the struggle for power and its exercise within collectivities preserves certain features common to the rivalry for power among autonomous units.

He who commands by virtue of law actually possesses more or less power—that is, capacity to impose his will—according to the *ascendancy* he assumes over his comrades, his partners, his rivals or his subordinates, according to the *prestige* he enjoys among the minority and the majority. Yet this power, whether in relation to the government or pressure groups, is never precisely defined by the legal distribution of privileges or prerogatives. The degree of influence which individuals or groups actually possess, the share each has in the state decisions which concern either relations with foreign states or

[3] Considered as a particular system within the social totality.

relations among the parts of the collectivity, depend on the means of action at the disposal of each, and at the same time on the talent each manifests in the use of these means. A constitution excludes open violence; it sketches a framework within which it specifies the rules by which the struggle for power must abide. It does not suppress the element of "rivalry for power."

The actors in the internal political drama, too, are animated by a desire for power and at the same time by ideological convictions. Those in power satisfy their ambitions, rarely free of all personal concern, even when convinced that they are serving the collectivity. The terms of a constitution, the official practices of parliaments, of administrations, of governments, still do not afford us exact knowledge of the real distribution of power within a country. What is the capacity of men of wealth, men of party, men of ideas or men of intrigue to convince or constrain the governors, to purchase the cooperation of the press or the administration, to provoke disinterested loyalty, to transform the opinions of the elite or of the crowd? There is no general answer to such a question. What is true is that it would be naïve to be influenced by the letter of a constitution or legal proceedings alone. But it would be cynical, without being true, to regard a constitution as a mere fiction and the legal wielders of authority as mere figureheads or mouthpieces. There is no example to warrant the assumption that the rules of the game do not influence the opportunities of the players, or that the legal incumbents consent to do the will of others (even of those to whom they owe their accession to office).

Thereby both the similarity and difference between the conduct of "internal politics" and the conduct of "foreign affairs" are apparent, as well as the reasons for which the theory of the one diverges from that of the other, at least on first analysis. The theory of international relations is entitled to take for granted the participants—the political units—as well as the absence of an arbitrator or laws, and the reference to war as a possibility (hence the calculation of forces, without which the conduct of a participant threatened with aggression would not be rational). On the other hand, political theory is ambivalent, in that the fundamental concepts are not beyond the reach of controversy. To reduce the uncertainty to its basic components, we may perhaps think of politics in terms of permanent competition (who gets what? how? when?); in terms of the need for a peaceful order at any price (civil war is the supreme evil, any kind of order is preferable to it); in terms of a search for the best order; finally, in terms of the reconciliation of complementary and divergent aspirations (equality and hierarchy, authority and reciprocal recognition, etc.).

States recognizing each other's sovereignty and equality have, by definition, no authority over each other. Statesmen controlling administration, army and police are at the apex of a legal hierarchy. The distinction between the two kinds of behavior, diplomatic-strategic and political, seems to me essential, even if the similarities are many. Power on the international scene differs from power on the national scene because it does not use the same means, nor function over the same terrain.

2. The Elements of Power

Many authors have enumerated the elements of either power or force without specifying whether they were discussing military strength or total capacity for action—whether they were referring to peacetime or to wartime. Lacking these distinctions, the enumerations seem arbitrary, heterogeneous, none complete or incontestable.

For instance, the American geographer N. J. Spykman[4] enumerates the following ten factors: 1. surface of the territory; 2. nature of the frontiers; 3. size of the population; 4. absence or presence of raw materials; 5. economic and technological developments; 6. financial power; 7. the ethnic homogeneity; 8. degree of social integration; 9. political stability; 10. national morale.

Professor H. J. Morgenthau[5] lists eight: 1. geography; 2. natural resources; 3. industrial capacity; 4. state of military preparedness; 5. population; 6. national character; 7. national morale; 8. quality of diplomacy.

Rudolph Steinmetz[6] also lists eight: 1. population; 2. dimensions of the territory; 3. wealth; 4. political institutions; 5. quality of the command; 6. national unity and cohesion; 7. respect accorded to and friendship with foreign powers; 8. moral qualities.

Lastly, Guido Fischer, a German author,[7] on the eve of the second major war of the twentieth century, classified the elements of power in three categories:

1. Political factors: geographical position, dimensions of the state, size and density of the population, skill of organization and cultural level, types of frontiers and attitudes of neighboring countries.

2. Psychological factors: economic flexibility and skill in invention, perseverance, and capacity for adaptation.

3. Economic factors: fertility of the soil and mineral wealth, industrial organization and technological level, development of trade and commerce, financial resources.

All these attempts at classification resemble each other, save for the last. All include geographical data (territory) and material data (raw materials), economic data and technological data, and lastly human data such as po-

[4] *America's Strategy in World Politics*, Yale University of International Studies, 1942, p. 19.
[5] *Politics among Nations*, New York, 1949, p. 80.
[6] *Soziologie des Krieges* (2nd ed.), Berlin, 1929, pp. 227–60.
[7] *Der wehrwirtschaftliche Bedarf, Zeitschrift für die gesamte Staatswissenschaft*, Vol. IC (1939), p. 519.

litical organization, the moral unity of the people, and the quality of lead-ership. Doubtless all these elements influence in one way or another the potential or actual strength of political units. But none of these lists seems to me to meet the requirements that theory is entitled to prescribe.

The elements listed must be *homogeneous*—in other words, they must be situated on the same level of generality in relation to history: the number of men, the characteristics of the territory, the quality of arms or organization influence the force of nations in all periods; financial resources signified nothing for the Mongol conquerors and very little for Alexander.

The list must be *complete,* which implies that the elements must be ex-pressed by concepts which cover the concrete diversity of phenomena, vari-able from period to period. Even the military implications of a geographical situation can be modified by the techniques of transportation and combat, but the influence of the geographical situation upon the possibilities of ac-tion of the political units is a constant factor.

Lastly, the classification should be such as to permit us *to comprehend why the factors of power are not the same from century to century and why the measure of power is, in essence, approximate.* This last remark is both ob-vious and, in relation to an abundant literature, paradoxical. Reading the theoreticians one would often suppose they have an infallible scale for measuring the power of political units with great precision. If such measure-ment were possible, wars would not occur, since the results would be known in advance. Or, at least, wars could be accounted for only by human folly. There is no war at sea, Anatole France writes in *Penguin Island,* since the hierarchy of fleets is never subject to doubt. All armies being the Greatest in the World, only trial by combat establishes the true hierarchy.

Let us turn once again to Clausewitz. No one has emphasized more than this rationalist theoretician the part chance plays in war. "War is the prov-ince of chance. In no sphere of human activity is such a margin to be left for this intruder, because none is so much in constant contact with him on all sides. He increases the uncertainty of every circumstance, and deranges the course of events."[8] "The diversity, and undefined limits, of all the cir-cumstances bring a great number of factors into consideration in War, [and] most of these factors can only be estimated according to probability. . . . In this sense, Bonaparte was right when he said that many of the questions which come before a General for decision would make problems for a mathematical calculation not unworthy of the powers of Newton or Euler."[9] And lastly: "The great uncertainty of all data in War is a peculiar difficulty, because all action must, to a certain extent, be planned in a mere twilight, which in addition not unfrequently—like the effect of a fog or moonshine—gives to things exaggerated dimensions and an unnatural appearance. What this feeble light leaves indistinct to the sight talent must discover, or must

[8] Clausewitz *op. cit.,* I, 3, p. 49.
[9] *Ibid.,* p. 69.

be left to chance."[10] By resorting to war, policy surrenders to a high degree of uncertainty, "it troubles itself little about final possibilities, confining its attention to immediate probabilities." Of course, "each Cabinet places its confidence in the belief that in this game it will surpass its neighbor in skill and sharpsightedness."[11] But its confidence is not always confirmed by the event.

Can we imagine that a theoretician of power could eliminate war's uncertainty by adding up the weight of various elements, and announce in advance the result of the combat? Now the power or capacity of a collectivity to impose its will upon another should not be confused with its military capacity. But if the outcome of battle is uncertain, it is because military force cannot be measured exactly, and total power still less than military force.

I propose to distinguish three fundamental elements: first of all the *space* occupied by the political units; second the *available materials* and the techniques by which they can be transformed into weapons, the *number of men* and the art of transforming them into soldiers (or, again, *the quantity and quality of implements and combatants*); and last the *collective capacity for action*, which includes the organization of the army, the discipline of the combatants, the quality of the civil and military command, in war and in peace, and the solidarity of the citizens during the conflict in the face of good or bad luck. These three terms, in their abstract expression, account for the total situation, since they are equivalent to the proposition: the power of a collectivity depends on the theater of its action and on its capacity to use available material and human resources. *Milieu, resources, collective action,* such are, from every evidence, whatever the century and whatever the forms of competition among political units, the determinants of power.

These three terms are equally valid for the analysis of power on all levels, from the tactical level of small units to the strategic level on which armies of millions of men confront each other, and to the diplomatic level on which states continuously compete. The power of a French army company confronting an FLN company depends on the terrain, the troops, the weapons, and lastly on the discipline and command of the two companies. On the superior level of strategy or politics, the capacity to organize the army, to mobilize civilians, to train soldiers is, so to speak, integral with the military strength and seems to appertain to the second term, while the conduct of the military leaders, their strategic and diplomatic talent, and the resolve of the people alone seem to represent the third.

This enumeration suggests not so much universally valid propositions as the means of accounting for historical changes. Only the first term partially escapes the vicissitudes of the techniques of production and destruction.

[10] *Ibid.*, II, 2, p. 105.
[11] *Ibid.*, VIII, 6, p. 122.

Certain situations favor defensive power,[12] in other words, put obstacles in the conqueror's way: mountains, rivers, deserts and distances. Most often, the same terrain that offers relative protection to a collectivity thereby reduces its possibilities of external intervention. "Small states"[13] regard as heaven-sent the barriers created by nature, since they do not claim starring roles and are uninterested in offensive power. Yet the defensive[14] power of a collectivity is a function of the characteristics of the space it occupies.

Mountains account for Switzerland's exceptional capacity for wartime defense, while distance has kept Russia from being entirely occupied ever since the dukes of Moscow first shook off the Mongol yoke. Napoleon could not overcome the resistance of the Tsar and the muzhiks, nor could Hitler, despite more brilliant successes, the Communist state and its people. The capture of Moscow did not weaken Tsar Alexander's resolve; Hitler did not take Moscow. Even in 1941–42 Russia owed her salvation to geography and to the inadequacies of modernization (the mediocre road system), as well as to the factories that were built before the conflict or transferred to the Urals.

The state with great ambitions must be assured of its own territorial barriers while retaining possibilities of intervention outside itself. Until recently, distance deprived Tsarist and Soviet Russia of a large part of her offensive capacity, while it added to her defensive capacity. For centuries England's territory, though far enough from the Continent to make invasion difficult, constituted an ideal base for distant expeditions or even for sending expeditionary forces to the Continent. Neither Venice nor Holland possessed a territorial base enjoying such security. France was obliged to distribute her resources between army and navy and suffered a particular vulnerability because of the relative proximity of her capital to the open northern frontier.

None of these three terms, not even the first, space, is exempt from history. It still remains true that a terrain difficult of access increases the political unit's defensive capacity and diminishes its offensive capacity. Because of the mountains, the populations living in Algeria could resist modern French pacification as well as they resisted Roman pacification seventeen centuries ago. But depending on the techniques of war, England is vulnerable or invulnerable, the Dover Straits are a knot of strategic routes or an insignificant narrowing between two seas equally closed, land and air offering other practicable means of communication.

---

[12] There are two aspects of defensive power: in wartime it is the capacity to stop the invader; in peacetime it depends on this capacity and also on the cohesion of the unit.

[13] We avoid here the common expression "small powers," so as not to introduce a confusion in vocabulary. The use of the word *power* to designate the actors and not merely the capacity of the actors is self-explanatory. The rivalry of power being part and parcel of international life, we identify the actors and their capacity for action, and establish a hierarchy of actors as a function of their capacity.

[14] Military.

Applied to the other two terms, most general propositions would be of little or no interest. It might be said that all other things being equal, number triumphs on the diplomatic field as on the battlefield. But all other things never being equal, this proposition teaches us nothing. We might regard as significant the order of the three elements, the effectiveness of weapons, collective action, number of soldiers: extreme inequality in weapons cannot be offset by either discipline or number of soldiers. Extreme inequality in organization and discipline cannot be offset by number (the principle of the Romans' superiority over the barbarians, of regular armies over militias and mass risings). But it would be desirable—and it is impossible—to specify the degree of inequality which cannot be compensated. Unindustrialized peoples have found, in the twentieth century, a means of combat, guerrilla warfare, which permits them to protect themselves against peoples equipped with every modern weapon. Even in the conflict between political units, if one possesses an overwhelming technical superiority, ingenuity and resolution can inspire the weaker unit with the secret of a lasting if not victorious resistance.

The historical or sociological analysis of the elements of the total force of the units involved has two principal stages: first, to establish what the elements of military strength are. In each period a system of combat proves effective through a combination of certain weapons, a certain organization, and an adequate quantity of weapons and combatants.

The second stage of the analysis concerns the relations between military strength and the collectivity itself. To what degree is superiority in arms and organization the expression of a technical and social superiority (supposing that the latter two kinds of superiority can be determined objectively)? An army is always a social organization, the expression of the entire collectivity. The degree of mobilization—that is, the proportion of fighting men actually mobilized—depends on the structure of the society, the number of citizens in relation to non-citizens (if only citizens are accorded the honor of bearing arms), the number of nobles if the society in question is one in which participation in combat is forbidden to commoners.

In all societies and at all periods there has been a limit to mobilization: enough men must be left at work in order to produce the resources indispensable to the life of the collectivity (the theoretical degree of mobilization rises if there is a peasant overpopulation, if the same harvest can be obtained with a reduced number of workers). But the actual degree has rarely reached or even approached the theoretical degree, the extent of mobilization being determined by social circumstances, the traditional means of combat, or the fear of giving weapons to a portion of the population regarded as inferior or potentially hostile.

Insofar as the organization of the army and the means of combat resulted from custom, it is understandable that the superiority of an army or of a weapon could be extended for decades, even for centuries. The minority that held a monopoly of weapons within the collectivity was in a position to main-

tain its rule almost indefinitely—unless it grew corrupt, that is, lost its cohesion and its determination. The political unit that perfected an effective
combination of various weapons (light and heavy cavalry, light and heavy
infantry, impact weapons and projectiles, lance and armor, etc.), had a chance
of maintaining its superiority for a long time. It was tempting to attribute to
virtue the greatness of the imperial peoples and to regard their superiority of
weapons as proof of a total superiority of customs and culture.

Without proceeding to a detailed study, it is clear that the ratio between
the collectivity's resources and military strength becomes stricter as war itself
becomes more rationalized, and the mobilization of civilians and the means of
production are considered normal and are put into practice. It is in the twentieth century that we have had the misleading illusion that by measuring resources we are measuring military strength and power itself. It is true that
in the age of total mobilization the military system is inevitably related to the
mass of the collectivity. But the *virtue* of the minority can still incline the
balance to one side or the other, and in many ways quality limits the domination of quantity. The conquest of vast empires by a leader and his comrades
belongs to the past,[15] or at least the small troop must begin by conquering
its own country, which will serve as a base. But one must have a weakness
for historical analogies to identify the adventures of Genghis Khan with those
of Lenin and the Bolshevik party. Genghis Khan was chiefly a military
genius, Lenin primarily a political genius. One mustered his armies by imposing himself as their leader and eliminating his rivals, the other was originally a prophet without arms; he avoided forceful means by using the techniques of persuasion.

3. *Power in Peacetime and in Wartime*

The power of a political unit in peacetime can be analyzed by using the
same categories—geographical milieu, resources, capacity for action—but
whereas power in wartime depends primarily on military strength and the use
made of it, power in peacetime—that is, the ability to keep others from imposing their will on the unit in question or to impose that unit's will upon
others—also depends on the various means whose use is admitted as legitimate
by international custom in each period. Instead of considering the military
system, we must consider the non-violent means (or the violent means tolerated in peacetime). As for the capacity for collective action, it is expressed
aggressively by the art of convincing or constraining without recourse to
force, and defensively by the art of not letting oneself be deceived, terrified,
upset or divided.

Between "power in peacetime" and "power in wartime," Europe's traditional diplomacy assumed a vague relationship. The political units considered

---

[15] Even in the twentieth century Ibn Saud relied on swordsmanship in his struggle to
unify the Arab tribes.

to be the great powers were defined, above all, by the volume of their resources (territories and populations) and their military strength. Prussia in
the eighteenth century, Japan at the beginning of the twentieth, were received on a basis of equality by the club of the great powers because they had
proved themselves on the battlefield.

The status of great nation confers certain rights: no matter of importance
can be treated in a system without all the great nations being consulted.
When one great nation had obtained or extorted an advantage somewhere, the
others, whether partners or rivals, insisted on their right to be compensated.

The status of great power was advantageous insofar as peaceful exchanges
and negotiated agreements tended to reflect the relation of forces (supposed
rather than real). A small nation was inclined to yield to a great one because
the latter was stronger. The great nation, when isolated in a conference,
yielded to the will of a coalition whose combined potential was greater than
its own. Nations referred to force in order to conclude a suit peacefully, because this reference seemed to offer a relatively objective criterion and was
a substitute for the test of weapons, whose issue was imagined to be determined in advance by the relation of forces. Gradually, and especially since
the Second World War, this policed intercourse, this wise Machiavellianism,
has vanished.

Between the two wars, diplomats committed such errors—overestimating
Italy's strength to the point of absurdity, underestimating the power of Soviet
Russia—that the very notion of a "great power" has now become suspect. The
great powers of yesterday's Europe, Great Britain and France, seek to remain
the great powers of global diplomacy, and their claims appear to be ratified by
a permanent seat on the Security Council of the United Nations. But the
real status of these great powers is in reality so uncertain that such official
status scarcely affords them any prestige or advantage. Atomic weapons dis-
credit the traditional concepts: weapons become less usable as they become
more monstrous. The politeness and cynicism of good society have vanished
from the chancelleries. Diplomacy, in the traditional sense of the term, functions up to a certain point among allies, but hardly any longer among enemies,
or even between the blocs and the neutral nations. Lastly and above all, no
nation, small or great, considers itself obliged to yield to a nation stronger
than itself once the stronger nation is not in a position to use its strength
effectively. The tactic of the "challenge" ("you won't dare to force me") appears in the ordinary process of international relations.[16] As a matter of fact,
states permanently practice a kind of total diplomacy which involves the use
of economic, political and psychological procedures, of violent and semi-
violent means.

To constrain a state or convince it to yield, another state or coalition of

---

[16] It also includes "misfires." Used by M. Bourguiba in July 1961, this tactic provoked a violent reply on the part of the French troops.

states may resort to economic pressure. By the decision of the League of Nations, sanctions were decreed against Italy: a prohibition against buying and selling certain merchandise. This pseudo-blockade was ineffectual because it was not general. Italy found enough customers to carry out her vital minimum of foreign trade. The prohibition against selling to her was not extended to materials whose scarcity might have dealt her a mortal blow. The blockade by which the Soviet bloc attempted to liquidate the Yugoslav dissidence was not any more effective, the West having come to the support of the state whose very existence bore witness to the possible separation between the Marxist regime and the adherents to the Soviet camp. The United States, in its turn, vainly attempted to destroy Fidel Castro by blockade.

Yet economic means are not always ineffective. The examples just given have a particular character: they all involve, in effect, an attempt at *economic constraint* or even the utilization of economic means as substitutes for military means. The failure is significant, but it has as its cause the impossibility of a universal coalition against a state. The weapon of the blockade could be, in our age, irresistible; however, it would require that the "criminal" state find no external allies. Up to now, such a hypothetical situation has never been realized.

On the other hand, in bilateral relations, economic means are useful, even indispensable, to reaffirm a friendship or cement a coalition. The Marshall Plan led to the Atlantic Alliance. The state that buys a great deal from others is in a position to influence the states of which it is the chief customer (the collapse of the market for raw materials is a catastrophe for the state which derives the greatest share of its trade resources from exporting this product). A state is also capable of influencing those states that expect financial aid from it or that feel dependent on its economic system. Today, particularly, the consent of the so-called underdeveloped nations to remain within a political circuit is a function of the assistance that they find there for their industrialization. Henceforth a state has few chances to maintain its sovereignty over numerous peoples if it is incapable of assuming responsibility for raising their standard of living.

On the economic level as well, the distinction appears between defensive capacity and offensive capacity. An underdeveloped nation often has a great capacity to resist eventual sanctions: only a small fraction of the population would be affected by the interruption of foreign trade. On the other hand, a great state that wants to create and lead a coalition with a minimum reliance on force requires economic resources (technicians, available capital for investment abroad, etc.).

The political means that states have used throughout history in their peace-time intercourse consist of actions affecting either the elite or the masses of the political units. In every century the great states have infiltrated the small states, through agents and money, corrupting consciences or recruiting loyalties. For a long time the presence of "foreign parties" was considered the effect and the symbol of weakness. Those states were "Balkanized" whose foreign policy was the object of dispute among various parties, each of which, reserving its preferences for a great state, could be accused of serving a foreign master.

A new factor, in our century—one implied by our democratic customs—is that the masses are courted just as much as the leading minorities by the words and the spokesmen of the aggressive states. Each of the blocs, each of the giants, attempts to convince the governed, on the other side of the line of demarcation, that they are exploited, oppressed, abused. The war of propaganda, the war of radio, marks the permanence of the conflict among states and the ceaseless recourse to means of pressure. In this interplay, power is not a function of military strength or economic resources. One regime is better suited for export through advertising, another state is better able to recruit disinterested representatives or more willing to supply money for the rape of conscience.

Here, too, the factors of defensive capacity are quite different from those of offensive capacity. The supreme, almost unique condition of defensive power is the cohesion of the collectivity, the adherence of the people to the regime, the agreement among members of the elite concerning the national interest. Switzerland or Sweden, which have virtually no desire or possibility of influencing the thought or action of other nations, are less vulnerable to foreign pressures.

Beyond economic and psycho-political means—and increasingly in our period—states use violence in peacetime. I shall distinguish *symbolic violence* and *clandestine* or *sporadic violence*. Symbolic violence is the kind expressed by what is called *gunboat diplomacy*. The sending of a warship to the harbor of a nation not paying its debts, attempting to deny its commitments or to nationalize a concession granted to a foreign company, symbolized the capacity and the resolution to constrain, if necessary by armed force. The symbol was enough. The transition to the act was never actually necessary. Recalled to order, the "weak nation" had no recourse but to yield. The day the transition to the *act* of violence risks becoming normally necessary, symbolic violence falls into desuetude. The Franco-British expedition to Suez in 1956 might perhaps have been rational if an internal opposition had been ready to overthrow Nasser, if the latter, in the hour of danger, had found himself alone or had suddenly lost his courage. The simulacrum of violence would have been convincing enough.

If symbolic violence appertains to the nineteenth century, sporadic or clandestine violence belongs to the twentieth. Clandestine violence—attacks in the shadows—is always sporadic; the sporadic violence of partisans is often committed out in the open. Terrorist networks in cities are clandestine, partisan forces are scattered, but they eventually wear uniforms and live openly in the *djebels* or *maquis* (underbrush). Some states not at war with each other fight, in peacetime, by means of terrorists and partisans. Egypt trained terrorist teams and sent them into Israeli territory. Algerian partisans were trained in Egypt or Morocco, "the army of liberation" was supplied from Tunisia and Morocco. It is now assumed that the peacetime use of speech and small arms to overthrow a state regime is not contradictory to international law. Here, too, defensive power depends on national unity: revolutionaries do not succeed if they do not find some voluntary complicity among the people. The capacity to use violence for repression is also a determinant of defensive power against subversive efforts. In Hungary the Soviet Union lost on the level of "prestige of morality," but won on the level of "prestige of cruelty." As Machiavelli said, it is sometimes preferable for the sovereign to be feared than to be loved.

The capacity for collective action in peacetime is manifested either by the use of these various means or by the resistance to these same means shown by the rival states. The diplomatic capacity, strictly speaking, has a double aspect: it is either, in the largest sense, the use of all these means and the choice of appropriate ones among them, or, in the more limited sense, it is the quality of action as a result of which a state makes friends and disarms possible adversaries, and the meeting of negotiators ends favorably.

Diplomacy without means of economic or political pressure, without symbolic or clandestine violence, would be pure persuasion. Perhaps it does not exist. Perhaps "pure" diplomacy still suggests, however implicitly, that it would be in a position to intimidate if it resolved to do so. At least pure diplomacy makes every effort to convince both adversary and onlookers that it desires to persuade or convince, not to constrain. The adversary must have the illusion of freedom, even when he is in fact yielding to force.

Diplomacy approaches pure diplomacy when it acts upon neutrals and independents, when its goal is to win sympathy or disarm prejudice. In diplomatic meetings, above all when the negotiators are in each other's presence and exchange arguments, words are paramount, since the interlocutors speak and listen. Thus negotiation is for diplomacy the equivalent of engagement for strategy: it is the cash with which credit operations are made good.

Yet a fundamental difference persists. Diplomatic preparation leads to the conference table as military preparation to a trial by arms. But the negotiators' margin of maneuver is limited by the potential forces of coalitions (when there have been no hostilities), by the *faits accomplis* of battle (when the war has taken place): by manipulating disagreements among the adversaries, a negotiator can occasionally repair the damages wrought by arms. But in this case, it is less the tête-à-tête of negotiation than the adulterated diplomatic interplay—the regrouping of forces—which has transformed the situation. On the other hand, once military action begins, the essentials are in the balance, that is, victory or defeat. Pure diplomatic dialogue confirms the sanction of events, the event judges among rival claims.

4. *The Uncertainties of the Measurement of Power*

It may be useful to consider a particular case in order to specify the less abstract terms in which the three fundamental categories, *milieu, means, and capacity for collective action,* are projected in a given historical period—say the 1919–39 period.

Combat technique and army organization, between the two world wars, were such that total mobilization was both legitimate and possible. All the citizens in condition to fight could be uniformed as soldiers, providing industry was able to equip them. Total mobilization being the rule, the potential of military strength seemed to vary directly with economic potential. Yet this relationship was actually subject to many reservations, both quantitative and qualitative.

It was difficult to determine the economic quantity by which military potential could be measured. Whether one selected the gross national product, total industrial production or certain industrial statistics, any index chosen involved an error. The index of the gross national product was an inexact measurement because agricultural production or services cannot be mobilized for the war effort like the metallurgic or mechanical industries. The same was true for the index of industrial production, for workers and machines cannot be transferred from biscuit factory to aeronautics plant as easily as automobile manufacture can be converted to tanks. Lastly, if only the figures of heavy industry or factory production were used, there was a risk of error in the contrary direction. With sufficient time, transfers of workers and machines can proceed to great lengths. France's industrial war effort between 1914 and 1918, despite the occupation of part of her territory, was remarkable: by the end of hostilities the American army also was utilizing cannons and shells of French manufacture. It is true that at the time, weapons and even planes were relatively simple so far as scientific knowledge and technological potential were concerned.

The transition from economic potential to military strength also depends, in modern times, on the "capacity for collective action" in the form of technical-administrative capacity. A German professor whose name has today fallen into oblivion, J. Plenge, published, in 1916, an interesting work[17] whose central theme is the antithesis between the ideas of 1789 and those of 1914. Ultimately the ideas of 1914 recall one key word: *organization.* For the whole nation to work in terms of the war—some men in uniform, others in factories or offices, others in the fields, all producing what is necessary to nourish population and battle alike—the administration must be capable of redistributing the population among the necessary jobs, reducing to a minimum the number of workers who produce those goods that are not indispensable, and assigning to each man the task to which he is best suited. During

[17] *1789 und 1914. Die symbolischen Jahre in der Geschichte des politischen Geistes,* Berlin, 1916.

the last war it was Great Britain, among the Western powers, which achieved the highest percentage of mobilization. Hitler's Germany started the conflict without having mobilized either all its industry or all its manpower; it had not resolved upon total mobilization after the Polish campaign nor after the French campaign, nor even after the Wehrmacht's invasion of Russia. It was not until Stalingrad that the total mobilization of German resources was undertaken, although millions of workers had been recruited from occupied territories.

In wartime the degree of mobilization is chiefly a function of administrative capacity, but also, in part, of the people's acceptance of sacrifice. Beyond a certain point the war effort cannot be increased except by reducing the level of the standard of living of the civilian population. How far can this reduction go without affecting the level of morale? This question cannot be answered in any general way. It would seem, however, that peoples accustomed to a low standard of living accept privations more easily than those accustomed to a higher standard of living, which tends to reverse the purely theoretical proposition: the margin of mobilization is directly proportional to the standard of living. In the abstract, the gap between the actual condition of the people and the incompressible minimum is greater in rich countries than in poor countries, but the former cannot always do without what the latter classify as superfluous.

Lastly, belligerents wage war with actually mobilized, not potential forces. Now the former depend on space and time, on the map and on the course of hostilities. The total potential may be paralyzed or amputated by the lack of certain raw materials (what would be the use of millions of tanks if they had no gas?). Conversely, mastery of the seas combined with financial reserves or foreign loans can add to the actual potential that of the legally neutral nations (as from the United States, from 1914 to 1917, to the Allies' benefit). But the experience of the First World War had given the Franco-British powers, in 1939, an ill-founded assurance. They assumed in advance the benefit of duration. In the long run the mobilization of the Western world's resources guaranteed them superiority and a victory by attrition. Still, it was essential that defeat in the first phases of the hostilities did not put the industrial potential of a fragment of the coalition into the enemy's hands. Without the victory of the Marne in 1914, there would not have been a total mobilization of the French potential. Without the Battle of Britain, there would not have been, starting in 1940, a total mobilization of the British and later the American potential. In 1939 the Franco-British potential represented only figures on paper if the two democracies did not have available time and freedom of the seas. France had no time, Great Britain, in spite of everything, retained freedom of the seas.

Once military forces are recognized as a function of the human and industrial potential, with the reservations we have just indicated, the question becomes one of quality. In each phase, what would be the relative value of a German, French, English, Italian or American division? The only true measurement is combat itself. Therefore, in peacetime, the evaluation, a problematical one, is made according to the experience of preceding battles. Until the battle of Jena the Prussian army maintained the prestige of the victories of Frederick the Great. Until 1940 the French army still appeared to be that of Verdun (1916) or of Champagne (1918).

Whether it was a question of cannon or army, the same question was raised: to what degree was the quality of weapons the reflection of industrial production? To what degree was the effectiveness of the troops the expression of the martial vigor of the people? In other words, could military force be estimated according to the state of the nation? Or did military force depend primarily on factors peculiar to the military system itself?

Hitler did not believe that the United States could acquire, in the very course of hostilities, an army of the first rank, for by reason of the fundamentally pacificist, commercial attitude of the American people, there was no military tradition or class comparable to the German officers corps. The Führer, to his misfortune and our salvation, was mistaken. A double demonstration has been convincingly presented: providing officers for the troops is no less important in the twentieth than in the nineteenth century, but this no longer requires a social class dedicated to the profession of arms. Many military problems—organization, logistics—resemble the problems of industry or transportation. Technicians rapidly learn the tasks that they must fulfill within the military system, and that resemble those of their civilian profession. But further, the citizens of a prosperous nation furnish soldiers, officers and non-commissioned officers capable of sustaining the rigors and dangers of modern battle.

In other words, the miracle of a leader of men giving his nation, by genius or good luck, an honorable place on the world's stage, the adventure of a Mehemet Ali, though still possible in the last century, is no longer so today. When regular armies are involved, the human and industrial potential assigns narrow limits to the action of the leader. There is no great modern army without a great industry behind it. Any nation provided with a great industry is capable of establishing a great army.

The two propositions, relative to what is and is not possible, being established on the theoretical level, the error would have been to attribute to an incontestable relation a rigor it did not have. Equipped in the same way, two divisions were not equivalent. The role of a dozen German armored divisions, which took a decisive part in the Polish and French campaigns, then in the first victories on the Russian front, would remind us, if necessary, that battle elites exist in the century of quantity. In the last case it seems that training and technical perfection went hand in hand with the passion of the officers and the soldiers to create an instrument which irremediably exhausted itself before Moscow in November–December 1941. The Wehrmacht still won its victories, it had other shock troops, but it never again found the equivalent of that armored force which had been its spearhead in the east, the west, and then again in the east.

That the quality of the military order and the effectiveness of the army are influenced by the political regime and the national psychology cannot be doubted. Depending on the prestige of the profession of arms, depending on the material and moral position of the officers within the nation, the recruiting of military cadres will be more or less good, better minds will be attracted to the study of national defense or will turn from it. It is doubtful that the circumstances to which the German army had owed the quality of its command will be reproduced in the Federal Republic. Neither the aristocracy of public service, nor faith in the country's greatness, nor the prestige of the uniform exist in a Federal Republic without colonized lands to the east, without Junkers, without imperial prospects.

Of these complex and subtle relations, popular phrases, current in certain periods, give us a caricature notion: "There is no discipline in the army when there is no discipline in the nation." The formula is quoted by Renan with praise: as a matter of fact the apparent anarchy within the democracies does not exclude discipline in factories or barracks. From 1945 to 1958 the Fourth Republic sought a stable government: all the officers bore witness to the discipline of the men in their contingents. On the other hand, propagandists of the Fascist Right were finally caught in their own fictions and imagined that the Duce had transformed the Italians into a nation of lions and had given Italy (with neither coal nor steel), a first-rank military force. Spengler had already attributed to Mussolini the empire of North Africa, fallen from the decadent hands of French democracy.

Similarly, an industry on a high technical level will normally furnish effective arms, but Western peacetime industry aims at raising the labor output, hence at producing as cheaply as possible. Cost is not a decisive factor when it is weapons that are being manufactured. A nation which invests a great deal of money and uses its best minds in industries directly oriented toward war production will eventually possess arms as good or better than those of a rival whose industry has nonetheless a superior average productivity (such is the case in the United States and the Soviet Union).

Let us not forget, finally, that with regard to the quality of weapons in our age, nothing is ever established once and for all. The race toward improvement continues during the hostilities themselves. The time necessary for the development of certain weapons was such that the First World War was ended with models used since the beginning of hostilities (long-range naval cannon). But artillery was a traditional weapon which, until the advent of electronics and automatic adjustment, showed only slow improvements during the First World War and the period between the wars. On the other hand, aviation progressed rapidly from 1914 to 1918, then from 1919 to 1939 (especially during the last years before the war), and finally during the course of the Second World War. The side that at the end of the war had machines available or models perfected at the beginning of hostilities would have been immediately outclassed. In 1941 the Japanese possessed the Zero, the best fighter plane in action in the Far East. But they could not stay in the race: in 1945 they were forced to use suicide planes while their fleet was being destroyed. The scientific-technological competition which the rivalry of military forces has henceforth involved can never be won. Qualitatively and quantitatively, the advantage shifts from one camp to the other. French aviation in the last war would have been quite different if it had had another six months—in other words, if industrial mobilization had been undertaken six months earlier, or if the battle had broken out six months later. On the whole, a state with a technologically superior industry has better chances of winning: still, we must not forget that by a greater concentration in one sector, a country's industry can make up for its backwardness as a whole, and that, in peacetime manufactures as well, the palm of victory is not always awarded to the same country.

Beyond these calculations of force, we must take into account the intelligence of the high command and the conduct of the war by the statesmen on either side, and lastly the adherence of the peoples to the regime, their resolution when put to the test. Would the Soviet people be loyal to the state and the party in charge of agrarian collectivization and the great purges? Would the German and Italian people enthusiastically follow their Führer and their Duce? Were the people in the democracies capable of facing the horrors of battle? Whether military leaders or peoples were involved, the answers, formulated in advance, could not be proved, the knowledge on which they were based was not transferable.

The answer given by events themselves was above all a refutation of the relations supposed to exist between the behavior of peoples and the nature of the regime. The Italians were never convinced that the war fought at the side of the Third Reich was really their own and justified supreme sacrifices: the partisans who fought the German troops in northern Italy after the fall of Fascism bore witness to a morale quite different from that of the soldiers (ill-equipped, moreover) in Libya. The German people did not desert their Führer but, in the ruling circles, the conspiracy of July 20 had wide ramifications: the National Socialist regime was basically much less united than the British or American democracy. In the Soviet Union there was no conspiracy in leading circles, but during the first phase of the hostilities, a fraction of the people, particularly the non-Russian groups, received the invaders without hostility, and certain troops showed little ardor. In short, the two nations of Europe in which regime and people stood together, in 1939, were Hitler's Germany and democratic England, with this reservation, that national unity was more capable of resisting defeat in England than in Germany.

In terms of these calculations, what observations are suggested by the *post eventum* analysis of the events of the thirties? The totalitarian nations were in peacetime, with equal forces, more powerful than the democratic nations. They presented a façade of unity, whereas the latter paraded their disputes. France and Great Britain were saturated, conservative nations, whereas Italy and Germany were assertive nations. Regimes in which one man commands, in which the deliberations occur in secret, are more capable of suggesting irresistible force and flawless resolution than those regimes whose press is free and whose parliament debates. In the diplomatic poker game the totalitarian state often bluffs and almost always wins—until the day when another nation calls the bluff.

Italian politics, from 1935 to 1941, consisted of a series of "bluffs" and "bets." When Mussolini proclaimed that he was ready to declare war on Great Britain and France rather than give up the conquest of Ethiopia, according to all probabilities he was bragging of what he would have been incapable of doing. What occurred in 1943 would have probably happened in 1936 had Mussolini been mad enough to involve Italy in a conflict, lost in advance, against the Franco-British alliance. He prevailed because the partisans of sanctions did not want to run the risk of war, and because the ruling circles of France and Great Britain were not unanimous as to the advantage and the consequences of an eventual overthrow of Fascism. In 1940 there was no longer question of a bluff but of a bet—a bet that the war was virtually over and that by intervening, Italy would receive a larger share of the spoils.

The German venture had an entirely different style. It was subdivided into two phases. Between January 1933 and March 1936 Germany would not have had the strength to resist a military response from France. Hitler assumed what at least looked like risks by successively violating all the principal clauses of the Versailles Treaty. His diplomatic technique was that of challenge: he defied France to use force in forbidding Germany decisions which tended simply to suppress the inequalities resulting from the Versailles Treaty. Challenged, France relied on protests—the worst of solutions between the two extremes (equally unacceptable to French public opinion) of frank acceptance and military action.

From 1936 on, the technique of challenge continued, but in another form. Hitler defied France and England to use military means because such means henceforth signified a general war which Germany still had every chance of losing but that constituted, in any case, a catastrophe for the saturated and conservative states. After 1938 Hitler's Germany had a superiority of actual forces, not so great as it tended to claim, as we have since learned, but sufficient to conquer Czechoslovakia in 1938 and Poland in 1939. In case of a general war the Western powers could not win except in the long run, by the mobilization of their superior potential. Hitler had only one last stage to cover in order to acquire an apparently serious possibility of victory, even in case of a general war: to neutralize the principal enemy to the east (the Soviet Union) while he first liquidated the secondary enemy to the east (Poland) and then the Continental enemy to the west.

From this moment on, the calculation of potentials no longer signified anything, since every enterprise was based on the succession of campaigns and bets: to conquer Poland before France intervened, France before Great Britain was mobilized and the Soviet Union belligerent, the Soviet Union before Great Britain was in a position to land on the Continent. All these bets were won, save the last. Protected by the guarantee the Western powers had given Poland, Stalin decided to reserve his forces by signing the pact with Hitler. Poland was eliminated without the French army's moving; France was eliminated from the conflict when Great Britain had only a dozen divisions. But Great Britain was neither invaded in 1940 nor paralyzed by bombings. The Soviet army, despite the disasters suffered in 1941, made a recovery before Moscow. This final lost bet determined all the consequences. In December 1941 the United States was swept into the war by the Japanese aggression. The war on two fronts, a war Germany had already waged and lost, a war the German general staff had not ceased to fear and considered as lost in advance, announced the pitiless ruin of the Führer's hopes. The Germans in opposition, who had foreseen the East-West coalition in case of general war and therefore the defeat of the Third Reich, saw their anticipations confirmed. The bets and successes had merely retarded the fatal outcome.

The Japanese bet, in 1941, was *senseless*, since on paper the Empire of the Rising Sun had no chance of winning and could avoid losing only if the Americans were too lazy or cowardly to conquer. Hitler's bet was *risky* and a legitimate leader would not have made it, since Germany could have obtained more, without fighting, by the mere threat of war, and since the dangers of defeat were so extreme. But the bet was not lost in advance.

Hitler won on all points until the armistice of June 1940. This, to use Clausewitz's terms, was the *culminating point of victory*. From this moment on, he multiplied his mistakes. He could not determine whether to treat France as an irreducible enemy or a recoverable ally; he hesitated to invade England and finally decided to use the unemployed Wehrmacht in a Russian campaign. Directing diplomacy, he himself forged the great alliance which he had so labored to prevent. Directing strategy, he did not have the courage to proceed to that ultimate concentration of forces that might have given him decisive successes. Directing the conduct of the armies themselves, he made on-the-spot resistance into a categorical imperative. As a military leader, he hoped until the end for a disintegration of the enemy coalition and finally died in a Wagnerian catastrophe, having long since lost contact with reality.

Hitler had no monopoly on mistakes. If, in the last analysis, Stalin outwitted him, one dares not attribute the sole merit for this to his genius.

Once Germany was eliminated, there was no obstacle to Russian penetration of Europe. Had the Americans been aware, in 1942, of the contradiction between Soviet and American interests, the master of the Kremlin would have had a difficult role to play. This was not the case. Invited to intervene in order to deliver the *coup de grâce* to Japan and authorized to occupy Eastern Europe as far as central Germany, Stalin accepted, without having to be asked twice, what was so graciously offered.

What is the role of power or of force in international relations? The question is now classical in military schools in the United States. The answer is not unambiguous because the same concept of power designates, as we have seen, *resources, military forces* and *power*.

The status of a political unit within an international system is fixed by the size of material or human resources that it can devote to diplomatic-strategic action. The great powers, in each period, are reputed capable of devoting considerable resources to external action and, in particular, of mobilizing numerous cohorts. International society involves a hierarchy of prestige which approximately reflects the hierarchy established by preceding combats.

Relations of forces also establish, to a large extent, the hierarchy within alliances: but this hierarchy does not necessarily express the relation of power, the highest-ranking state imposing its will on those beneath it. Once the superior state cannot employ military force, it must use means of pressure, indirect and often ineffective, or else methods of persuasion. Alliances are always directed by the great powers, but the small power sometimes takes the great where the latter would not have chosen to go. The small power has the last word in a discussion that concerns its own interests because it forces the great power to choose between concession or the use of force. The tactic of refusal or obstruction, as General de Gaulle practiced it between 1940 and 1944 with regard to Great Britain and the United States, often permitted the weaker entity to impose its will. Once the Free French were established in St. Pierre and Miquelon, the United States could not drive them out except by force and, in the middle of the war, Roosevelt could not give orders to fight Frenchmen who symbolized their country then occupied by the common enemy.

Even relations among rival states are not, in normal times, the pure and simple expression of relations of force. The negotiators make mistakes as to each other's forces and, further, do not consider themselves obliged to conclude the kind of agreement that would emerge from the test of war. So long as men "talk" instead of "fight," reasons of fact and of law are not without influence on the interlocutor. Diplomacy, a substitute for war, is not limited to putting on record, at every moment, the latter's supposed conclusion. "That each receives according to the achievements of his weapons," as General de Gaulle has said,[18] is true only in its vague sense and in the long run. Valid as a counsel of wisdom—states must not assume objectives disproportionate to their resources—this formula implies, if taken literally, an underestimation of the subtlety of relations between independent collectivities.

The disproportion between the potential of nations and the accomplishments of their diplomacy is often caused by the regrouping of units against that power among them that seems about to assume the role of "troublemaker." By definition, sovereign states regard as an enemy any claiming hegemony, that is, any that could deprive them of their own autonomy or their capacity to make their own decisions freely. Therefore, a diplomat of the classical school, like Bismarck, feared an excessive growth of the Reich's powers. He believed that the Reich should limit its ambitions and thereby excuse its ascendency by wisdom and proportion. That his country's power was in the service of justice and European order was, in the eyes of the Iron Chancellor, the necessary condition for German security, the means of avoiding the coalition of rivals whom the Prussian victories must neither humiliate nor disturb. During the first phase after 1870 it was vanquished France, not victorious Germany, that made territorial acquisitions. Rarely, between 1870 and 1914, did the representative of the Reich manifest a capacity to convince commensurate with the armed forces his nation could mobilize for war, either from a lack of diplomatic talent, or as a result of the spontaneous opposition which any virtually hegemonic state faces.

"A universal monarchy," as the eighteenth-century authors called it, or else limited enterprises: the alternative was the unwritten law of the European system, as it is of virtually any system of states. Either the great power will not tolerate equals, and then must proceed to the last degree of empire, or else it consents to stand first among sovereign units, and must win acceptance for such pre-eminence. Whatever the choice, it will live in danger, never having won all the victories necessary, always suspected of aspiring to domination.

If states sought to be great in order to enjoy security, they would be victims of a strange illusion, but, through history, collective greatness has been its own reward.

[18] The formula occurs at the end of the report sent by him in January 1940 to the French High Command.

chapter III

Power, Glory and Idea

or

On the Goals of Foreign Policy

Political units seek to impose their wills upon each other: such is the hypothesis on which Clausewitz's definition of war is based and also the conceptual framework of international relations. At this point, one question arises: why do political units want to impose their wills upon each other? What goals does each of them desire and why are these goals incompatible, or seem to be so?

If we focus on the moment at which a generalized war breaks out, it is easy to indicate, with more or less precision, the goals chosen by each of the states in conflict with the others. In 1914 Austria-Hungary sought to eliminate the threat that the southern Slav claims posed to the dualist monarchy. France, which had consented to the annexation of Alsace-Lorraine without acknowledging the fact morally, discovered intact and ardent, on the day the first cannon thundered, the will to restore her lost provinces to the mother country. The Italians claimed lands that once belonged to the Habsburg empire. The Allies were virtually no less divided than their adversaries. Tsarist Russia wanted possession of Constantinople and the Dardanelles, whereas Great Britain had constantly opposed such ambitions. Only the German danger incited London to agree, secretly and on paper, to what it had stubbornly refused for over a century.

Perhaps the Reich inspired its rivals with even greater alarm because its war goals were not known. At the moment of its first successes, these goals seemed grandiose and vague. Leagues and private groups dreamed of the "African belt" or of *Mittel Europa*. The general staff, as late as 1917–18, demanded the annexation or occupation of a part of Belgian territory for strategic reasons. A dominant power which does not proclaim definite objectives is suspected of unlimited ambitions. Provinces (Alsace-Lorraine, Trieste), strategic positions (the Dardanelles, the coast of Flanders), religious symbols (Constantinople), such were the explicit stakes of the conflicts among the European states. But simultaneously, the result of the conflict would determine the relation of forces, the place of Germany in Europe and of Great Britain in the world. Is it possible to distinguish, in an abstract analysis of general scope, the typical goals which states aim at and which set them in opposition to each other?

1. *Eternal Objectives*

Let us start from the schema of international relations: the political units, proud of their independence, jealous of their capacity to make major decisions on their own, are rivals by the very fact that they are autonomous. Each, in the last analysis, can count only on itself.

What then is the first objective which the political unit may logically seek? The response is furnished by Hobbes in his analysis of the *state of nature.* Each political unit aspires to survive. Leaders and led are interested in and eager to maintain the collectivity they constitute together by virtue of history, race, or fortune.

If we grant that war is not desired for its own sake, the belligerent power that dictates the peace terms at the end of hostilities seeks to create conditions guaranteeing that it need not fight in the immediate future and that it may keep the advantages gained through force. We may say that in the state of nature, every entity, whether individual or political unit, makes *security* a primary objective. The more severe wars become, the more men aspire to security. In Germany, too, from 1914 to 1918, there was speculation as to the best methods to insure the nation's definitive security by disarming certain of its adversaries or occupying certain key positions.

Security, in a world of autonomous political units, can be based either on the weakness of rivals (total or partial disarmament) or on force itself. If we suppose that security is the final goal of state policy, the effective means will be to establish a new relation of forces or to modify the old one so that potential enemies, by reason of their inferiority, will not be tempted to take the initiative of an aggression.

The relation between these two terms—*security* and *force*—raises many problems. On a lower level we may first observe that the maximization of resources does not necessarily involve the maximization of security. In Europe, traditionally, no state could increase its population, its wealth and its soldiers without exciting the fear and jealousy of other states, and thereby provoking the formation of a hostile coalition. In any given system there exists an *optimum of forces*; to exceed it will produce a dialectical reversal. Additional force involves a relative weakening by a shift of allies to neutrality or of neutrals to the enemy camp.

If security were, by evidence or necessity, the preferential objective, it would be possible to determine rational behavior *theoretically*. It would be necessary, in each circumstance, to determine the optimum of force and to act in consequence. A more serious difficulty appears as soon as we raise questions as to the relation between these two objectives, force and security. We concede that man, whether individual or collective, desires to survive. But the individual does not subordinate all his desires to his desire for life alone. There are goals for which the individual accepts a risk of death. The same is true of collective units. The latter do not seek to be strong only in order to discourage aggression and enjoy peace; they seek to be strong in order to be feared, respected or admired. In the last analysis, they seek to be powerful—that is, capable of imposing their wills on their neighbors and rivals, in order to influence the fate of humanity, the future of civilization. The two objectives are connected: the more strength he has, the less risk a man runs of being attacked, but he also finds, in strength as such and in the capacity to impose himself upon others, a satisfaction which needs no other justification. Security can be a final goal: to be without fear is a fate worthy of envy; but power, too, can be a final goal: what does danger matter once one has known the intoxication of ruling?

But on this level of abstraction, the enumeration of objectives still does not seem to me to be complete: I would add a third term, *glory*. In the essay entitled "On the Balance of Power," David Hume[1] explains the behavior of the Greek city-states in terms of the spirit of competition rather than the calculations of prudence: "It is true, that Grecian wars are regarded by historians as wars of emulation rather than of politics; and each State seems to have had more in view the honor of leading the rest, than any well-grounded hopes of authority and dominion." Opposing *jealous emulation* to *cautious politics,* Hume thus formulates the antithesis that we shall call the *struggle for glory* and the *struggle for power*.

When the struggle is joined, there is a danger that military victory in itself will become the goal, causing political objectives to be forgotten. The desire for *absolute victory*, that is, for a peace dictated without appeal by the victor, is often more the expression of a desire for glory than of a desire for force. Dislike of *relative victories*, that is, of a favorable peace negotiated after partial successes, derives from the *amour-propre* that animates men once they measure themselves against each other.

It might be objected that glory is merely another name or another aspect of power: it is, so to speak, power recognized by others, power whose fame spreads across the world. In a sense this objection is valid and the three objectives might be reduced to two: either the political units are in quest of security and of force, or they seek recognition by imposing their wills, by gathering the conqueror's laurels. One of the two goals, force, is material, the other is moral, inseparable from the human dialogue; it is defined by grandeur, consecrated by victory and the enemy's submission.

The ternary division, however, seems to me preferable because each of the three terms corresponds to a concretely defined attitude while it also expresses a specific notion. Clemenceau sought the *security*, Napoleon the

[1] See below, Chapter V, for a fuller analysis of Hume's essay.

power, Louis XIV the *glory* of France (or each his own).[2] In 1918 any rational chief of state would have proposed the same goal: to spare France the recurrence of a war as severe as the one that an immense alliance had just brought to a favorable conclusion. Napoleon, at least after a certain date, dreamed of ruling Europe: he was not content with the honor of being universally celebrated as a great war leader; even Clausewitz's homage—"the God of war himself"—would not have satisfied him. He was ambitious for reality, not for appearances, and he knew that in the long run no state commands others if it does not possess the means of constraining them. Louis XIV probably loved glory as much as power. He wanted to be recognized as the first among monarchs, and he made use of his force in order to seize a city and fortify it, but this half-symbolic exploit was still a way of showing his force. He did not conceive of a disproportionately enlarged France, furnished with resources superior to those of her allied rivals. He dreamed that the names of Louis XIV and of France would be transfigured by the admiration of nations.

This first analysis would be more dangerous than useful if it were not filled out by another. Indeed, if we abide by these abstract notions, we will be inclined to dismiss glory as irrational,[3] to condemn the indefinite accumulation of force as contradictory (the loss of allies more than offsetting, at a certain point, the increase of one's own forces). From this angle, we would arrive at the allegedly unique objective of security. Let us abandon such abstract analyses and consider a political unit—that is, a human collectivity occupying a fragment of space. If we suppose that this collectivity is comparable to a person, with an intelligence and a will of its own, what goals is it liable to choose?

A collectivity occupies a certain territory: it can logically consider the surface of the earth at its disposal as too small. In rivalry among peoples, the possession of space was the original stake. Secondly, sovereigns have often estimated their greatness according to the number of their subjects: what they desired, beyond their frontiers, was not territory, but men. Lastly, the armed prophet is sometimes less anxious to conquer than to convert: indifferent to the wealth of the earth and what it contains, he does not calculate the number of his workers or soldiers; he seeks to spread the true faith, he wants the organization corresponding to his interpretation of life and of history to encompass gradually all of humanity.

Here again, this ternary series seems to me complete. All the goals that states determine for themselves, in historical circumstances, necessarily refer to one of the three terms we have just listed: *space*, *men* and *souls*. Why should societies fight if not to extend the territory they cultivate and whose wealth they exploit, to conquer men who are alien today, slaves or fellow

---

[2] Which does not exclude the fact that each also desired the objectives suggested by the two other terms.

[3] It would be wrong to do so; man does not live by bread alone.

citizens tomorrow, or to insure the triumph of a certain idea, whether religious or social, whose universal truth the collectivity proclaims simultaneously with its own mission?

Concretely, these objectives are difficult to separate. Unless he exterminates or drives out the inhabitants, the conqueror takes possession of both space and the men who occupy it. Unless conversion takes place by the mere force of proselytism, the prophet does not disdain to govern men before administering the salvation of souls. It remains no less true that in certain cases the three terms are distinct: the Crusaders first sought to liberate the Holy Land, not to convert the Moslems. The Israelis wanted to occupy the Palestinian space that had been the Kingdom of David, they were not interested in either conquering or converting the Moslems of Palestine. The sovereigns of monarchical Europe collected provinces—land and men—because the power and prestige of princes was measured by possessions. As for the conversion of the infidel, perhaps it has never been the exclusive goal of any state. Only unarmed prophets dream of pure conversion, but, as Machiavelli said, they perish. Though states are sometimes prophetic, they are always armed. Not that an idea is an instrument or a justification of the desire to conquer space or men. In the minds of religious or ideological leaders, the triumph of the faith, the spread of an idea, may be conceived, in all sincerity, as the true goal of action. It is in the eyes of the unbelievers that this goal seems a camouflage for imperialism: historians and theoreticians, also unbelievers, adhere all too easily to this cynical interpretation.

What are the relations between the abstract series and the concrete series? It would be as arbitrary to subordinate the second to the first as to decree the opposite. The increase of space, the augmentation of material and human resources are, certainly, elements of security and power, sometimes even the objectives of glory. This does not mean that the conquest of a province can never be desired for itself. The French did not regard the return of Alsace-Lorraine to the mother country as a means to some ulterior goal, but as a good in itself, which required no other justification. Without Alsace-Lorraine, France was mutilated: with Strasbourg and Metz, she recovered her integrity. Down through the centuries, regions and cities and the men who populate them have assumed a historical significance, a symbolic value. The question is no longer whether the Moslems of Palestine or the Israelis could have found elsewhere a territory as fertile and resources that would have been equal or superior. It was here, around the Sea of Tiberias and on the plain of Jerusalem, it was here and in no other place on the planet that certain Jews (who no longer believed in God and in the "covenant") wanted to create anew a collectivity that would proclaim itself the heir of a semi-legendary past.

In our times, no guarantee of order and justice suffices to disarm national claims: active minorities leading various populations seek to belong to the political unit of their choice. The Cypriots wanted a fatherland, which could not be Great Britain or the British Empire: fair administration, autonomy, a relatively high standard of living—nothing could compensate for the absence of a political community. Of the two aspirations, not to be uprooted and not to be deprived of a fatherland, it is the first that has ultimately yielded in Europe: transfers of populations have in a sense signified the primacy of the nation over the territory.

In each series, abstract or concrete, the third term, *glory* or *idea*, stands apart. Not that these two terms correspond to each other: on the contrary, glory is an empty notion, and exists only in human consciousness, perhaps especially in the consciousness of the man who desires to possess it. The man "full of glory" is the man who is satisfied with the idea that he believes others have of him. Therefore it is precisely the "vainglorious" man who is a character of ridicule. Even if he is not mistaken as to the sentiments he inspires, the man "full of glory" should be unaware of his fortune or indifferent to it in order to be entirely worthy of it. But thereby, the goal itself retreats progressively as he approaches it. Never will the exploits performed satisfy the doubts of the man who aspires to glory.

An idea—whether it is Christianity or communism, the divinity of Christ or a certain organization of society—is, on the contrary, quite definite. Perhaps the inquisitors will never be sure of the sincerity of conversions. Perhaps the members of the Presidium will never eliminate the "capitalist" tendencies of the peasants, perhaps deviations will always appear, continually renewed upon the expulsion of the preceding deviationists. At least an idea has a specific content, whereas glory cannot be grasped since it is linked to the dialogue of men.

Yet in essence this objective too is situated in infinity. Where truth is concerned, nothing is done so long as something remains to *be* done. The religions of salvation have a universal vocation, they are addressed to humanity since they are addressed to each man. Once a prophet takes arms to propagate them, his enterprise will never know an end unless it covers the entire planet. Wars for glory and wars for an idea are human in a different way from wars for land and its riches. Crusaders are sublime and dangerous. The nobles who fight for prestige can never be through fighting. If the goal is to conquer in order to be recognized as a conqueror or to conquer in order to impose the truth, it suffices that the determination to win be the same on each side for the violence to proceed to extremes. The most humane wars in origin are also, frequently, the most inhumane, because they are the most pitiless.

Hence we are tempted to constitute a third ternary series which, following the Platonic model, would be that of body, heart and mind. Whether it is a question of land or men, of security or force, the stake is ultimately material: the political units seek to enlarge their space or to accumulate resources in order to live free of danger or with the means to avert it. But neither security nor force satisfies the aspirations of communities: each desires to prevail over the others, to be recognized as first among its rivals. Political units have their *amour-propre*, as people do; perhaps they are even more sensitive. Hence they sometimes prefer the intoxication of triumph to the advantages of a negotiated peace. Sometimes the desire for glory will be satisfied only by the diffusion of an idea, of which each community wants to be the unique incarnation. The mind, finally, animates the dialectic of violence and drives it to extremes, once it links its destiny to that of a state, that is, of a human collectivity in arms.

Of course, the demand for security and force also leads to extremes. In the last analysis, a political unit would feel entirely safe only if it had no further enemy, in other words, if it had been enlarged to the dimensions of a universal state. But the desire for security and force does not transform itself into a demand for unlimited power, unless *amour-propre* or faith arouses and finally overwhelms the calculations of interest. Anxious only to live in peace, neither Pyrrhus nor Napoleon nor Hitler would have consented to so many certain sacrifices in the hope of an uncertain gain.

Conquerors have sometimes justified their undertakings in terms of the prosperity their people would enjoy after victory. Such Utopias served as an excuse, not an inspiration. These leaders desired power as an instrument of their glory, with a view to the triumph of an idea for its own sake, never in order that men might know "the good life."

2. Historical Objectives

Like the theory of power, this theory of objectives has a suprahistorical value, while it also permits us to comprehend historical diversity. The objectives of states refer, in every century, to the terms of the two ternary series or even, if one prefers the simplified formula, to the three terms of the last abstract-concrete series. But many circumstances—of military or economic technique, of institutional or ideological origin—intervene to limit and specify the objectives statesmen actually select.

Let us start with the first term, the most constant stake of human conflicts: space. At the dawn of history as on the threshold of the Atomic Age, human groups dispute the territory on which some are established and which others desire. Collectivities distribute territory among their members and legalize individual ownership. But the sovereignty of the collectivity itself over the whole of the territory is not thereby admitted by the other collectivities. During the first millenniums of the historical phase, the tribes retreated before the invaders from the east, to become conquerors in their turn with regard to the populations settled farther west. The horsemen of the steppes established their dominion over the sedentary populations and created hierarchic societies, the warriors constituting a superior class superimposed upon the mass of laborers.

In modern times the struggle for land has lost its primeval simplicity and brutality, but is no less cruel when it breaks out. Israelis and Palestinian Moslems cannot form a single collectivity and cannot occupy the same territory: one or the other is doomed to suffer injustice. In North Africa the French conquest of the nineteenth and twentieth centuries signified partial expropriations from the Berber or Arab populations, the French settlers receiving lands belonging to tribes, villages or families. Tunisian or Moroccan independence brought about a more or less rapid expropriation of French colons. The Algerian War, in a sense, had as its stake the land that both Moslems and French regarded as their own, and upon which they were temporarily obliged to coexist, both demanding sovereignty—the former under the banner of independence, the latter under that of integration.

For the French who were established across the Mediterranean, Algeria was the land on which their fathers lived, and therefore, so to speak, the fatherland. But for France, what has been, what is the significance of Algeria? Why had France[4] desired, since 1830, to extend her sovereignty over a territory which she had never occupied in the course of past centuries? It is difficult to answer, because the very statesmen or military leaders who determined and executed the conquest either did not know why they acted or else were divided as to their motives.

Some emphasized the threat of the Barbary Coast pirates to navigation, and the security that possession of the Algerian coast would assure to Mediterranean shipping. Let us say that they emphasized a *military motive*. Others favored the possibilities of colonization and hinted at a French Empire of a hundred million men on both shores of the Mediterranean. Let us say that they dreamed of an *enlargement of French space* and an *increase of French population*.[5] During the last years Frenchmen cited the many economic advantages of French sovereignty over Algeria, which constituted a reserve of manpower, a customer of and purveyor to the metropolitan economy, a source of raw materials and, particularly since 1956, of petroleum. Let us say that *economic advantages* are invoked here. In other words, this example permits us to discern the three typical arguments in favor of conquest: *military or strategic importance, spatio-demographic advantage, spatio-economic profit.*

Each of these arguments is subject to the law of change. The military, demographic or economic value of a territory varies with the techniques of combat and production, with human relations and institutions. The same positions are or are not strategically important, depending on the state of international relations (with the Russian army established two hundred kilometers from the Rhine, the old frontier between Germany and France is of no significance in military terms), and on armament (the Bosphorus and the

---

[4] When we use such an expression we personify a political unity, we introduce no particular metaphysic: it is clear that men, in the name of France, have taken the decision. But the very object of this book implies that we consider states as endowed with intelligence and will.

[5] "May the day soon come when our fellow citizens, close-pressed in our African France, will overflow into Morocco and Tunisia, and finally establish that Mediterranean empire which will not only be a satisfaction for our pride, but which will certainly, in the future state of the world, be the last resource of our greatness." This text occurs at the end of *La France nouvelle*, by Prévost-Pradol.

Suez Canal have lost most of their value since they are too easily "closed" by atom bombs, too easily "crossed," too, by air transport). With Algeria independent, the security of Mediterranean shipping will not be threatened by the Barbary pirates.

The demographic argument is presented in two radically different forms. Space is still precious when it is empty or sparsely populated. We cannot overestimate the historical influence of the fact that after the sixteenth century Europeans had at their disposal the empty spaces of America. In the nineteenth century, when mortality was diminishing and the old birth rate was being lowered only slowly, millions of Englishmen, Germans and Scandinavians, then Italians and Slavs were able to cross the Atlantic and occupy the immensities of North America. Numbering sixty-five thousand at the period of the Treaty of Paris, there are now over five million French Canadians, less than two centuries later. Even today, if the objective of states is that their populations should "increase and multiply," the occupation of empty space is the ideal means (whence the—truly diabolical—temptation to empty space in order to reserve it for the victors: Hitler would not have resisted the temptation).

On the other hand, the occupation of an already populated space raises problems that vary according to the centuries. Princes once tended to measure their greatness by the number of their provinces and their subjects. When the number of men increased, so did that of laborers and soldiers. In the centuries when underpopulation, a shortage of men, was feared, the extension of sovereignty over inhabited lands passed for advantageous or beneficial. This traditional conception was called into question by the liberal economists, according to whom commerce could and should ignore frontiers. The assumption of sovereignty imposed administrative expenses upon the metropolitan country without affording it any additional profit.[6]

The anti-colonial argument of the liberals, which had wide influence in England in the last century, but did not prevent the expansion of the British Empire, was opposed by the apparent soundness of traditional ideas and several phenomena originating in the industrial era. How could anyone doubt that conquest was profitable, a proof and symbol of greatness, when it was cheap in military terms and when the metropolitan country found in its empire both raw materials at low prices and protected markets? Imperialists and the Marxists were fundamentally in agreement as to the benefits of the colonies: higher rates of profit, guaranteed outlets for manufactured products, insured supply of raw materials. The only difference between the two lay in the judgment of value set upon the enterprise and the goal attributed to it. Marxists denounced an exploitation that was, in their eyes, the cause and goal of imperialism; the imperialists justified by its civilizing mission an enterprise whose advantages for the colonizing state they were not ashamed to proclaim.

The liberal argument again found an audience after the Second World

6 See below, Part II, Chap. IX.

War, following the convergence of political motives and economic motives. Either the colony did not include a European population, in which case the principle of equality of peoples established the right to independence. Or else the colony included a European population, in which case the principle of individual equality forbade treating the natives as inferiors, and led to the power of the greater number—that is, of the indigenous peoples—by means of universal suffrage.

The imperial state discovered, at the same moment, that a "civilizing mission" was expensive when taken seriously. Certain individuals, certain companies benefited from the colonial situation, but the balance-sheet for the collectivity ceased to be positive, insofar as the creation of an administrative and educational infrastructure and the improvement of the standard of living figured among the obligations of the metropolitan country.

Between the *advantage* of possessing the territory and the *cost* of assuming responsibility for its population, the European states, Great Britain first of all, have chosen decolonization (or, more precisely, Great Britain has chosen, France has gradually been forced to choose). The transfer of sovereignty involved diplomatic and military risks: instead of commanding, the ex-imperial state was henceforth obliged to negotiate. The military forces of India were no longer at the service of British interests in the Middle East. But, on the military level too, the abandonment of sovereignty was less costly than a war against nationalism. France has been weakened more by the Indo-Chinese War than it would have been by an agreement with Ho Chi Minh, concluded in 1946. Great Britain would have been weakened more by resistance to Indian nationalism, even had such resistance been victorious over a generation, than it has been by the transfer of sovereignty to the Congress Party and the Arab League.

However summary, these analyses have permitted us to define two of the fundamental factors in the historical transformation of goals: *the techniques of combat and production* change and, thereby, modify the strategic value of positions, at the same time that the economic value of various natural and human resources of the territory, in other words *the modes of organization of collectivities,* authorize or exclude, in every period, certain modes of domination. Conquerors, down through the ages, have rarely acknowledged that victory imposed duties to a greater degree than it conferred rights. Superiority of arms was equivalent to the superiority of a civilization. The conquered were always wrong, and subjection seemed the legitimate sanction of defeat. The chapter in which Montesquieu deals with conquest already belongs to an age in which the judgment of arms no longer passed for the just verdict from the tribunal of history or Providence.[7]

---

[7] "It is a conqueror's responsibility to repair a part of the harm he has done. I therefore define the right of conquest thus: a necessary, legitimate but unhappy power, which leaves the conqueror under a heavy obligation of repairing the injuries done to humanity." (*L'Esprit des lois, X,* 4.)

The doctrine of empires depends on concepts involving relations among governed and governing, and among various populations, even more than on concepts involving war and the privileges of force. When citizenship was limited to a small number within the city-state, when only nobles bore arms and owned laborers as property, no limit could rationally be set on the enterprises of conquest: the number of subjects and slaves could increase without a proportionate increase in the number of citizens. The ruling people remained free to accord or refuse citizenship—the Roman Empire long tolerated a considerable number of populations subject to Rome, but not integrated within the Roman civilization. Similarly, the kings of France and Prussia were persuaded to increase their forces as their territories enlarged and the number of their subjects increased. It was assumed that the desire of men to obey one master rather than another did not count and, most of the time, did not exist. The religious conflicts that had drenched Europe in blood confirmed the merits of the old political wisdom: it is best to keep men from meddling in their own business. In order to re-establish peace in Europe, it had been necessary to order each and every man to believe in the truths of the Church acknowledged by the prince.

The case was altered after the French Revolution, when two new ideas gradually won men's minds: the juridical equality of the members of the collectivity; the aspiration of the governed to belong to a community of their choice, a community of their own.

The first idea, carried to its logical consequences, implied the elimination of the distinction between victors and vanquished within the collectivity, as of the distinction between orders, i.e., between nobles and commoners. "Thus a conqueror who reduces a conquered people to slavery ought always to reserve to himself the means (for means there are without number) of restoring that people to their liberty."[8] In the democratic age, we would say that imperial domination finds its outlet either in accession to independence on the part of the conquered populations, or in the integration of the colonies with the metropolitan country in a multinational (more or less federal or centralized) complex. The choice itself between these two outcomes is determined less by the desires of statesmen than by the nature of the metropolitan country. It is difficult for a strictly national state, like France, to become the nucleus of a multinational community. A state with universal pretensions, like the Soviet State, can attempt a policy of integration on a grand scale.

The second idea, intimately related to the first, is that self-determination of the governed *cannot* be repressed, and *should not* be constrained by force. The national idea, it is true, oscillates between two formulas, that of nationality embedded within the historical, if not the biological, being of populations, and that of the voluntary decision whereby each man (or each group) must determine the political collectivity to which he (or it) will

8 *Ibid.*, X, 3.

belong. According to the first formula, Alsace was more or less German in 1871; according to the second, it was French.

The national ideal is not entirely new, nor did the authentic citizens of the city-states or monarchies obey just any prince. However, even the nobles could pass from the service of one sovereign to that of another without creating the scandal of treason. The extension of citizenship to all members of the collectivity profoundly transformed the meaning of the national idea. If all the subjects became citizens, or if the citizens refused to obey just any master because they sought to participate in the state, political units could no longer take for their objective the conquest of just any territory or just any population. Moreover, the violation of this prohibition was generally "punished" by the difficulty and the cost of governing recalcitrant populations.

In other words, the concrete objectives that political units choose do not evolve with the techniques of combat and production alone, but also with historical ideas associated with the organization and government of the collectivities. In the long run a state does not apply two philosophies, one internally, the other externally. It does not keep both citizens and subjects under its orders indefinitely. If it seeks to keep subjects externally, it will end by turning its own citizens into subjects.

The concrete objectives of states, in a given period, are still not precisely defined by the *state of techniques* (of combat and of production) and *historical ideas*. We must also take into account what we shall call, with the theoreticians of international law, *custom*. The conduct of states with regard to each other, the procedures they consider legitimate, the cunning or the brutality from which they abstain, are not directly determined by the organization of the army or of the economy. Strategic-diplomatic conduct is a matter of custom. Tradition bequeaths, from generation to generation, great or remote goals which statesmen sometimes refuse to forget, against all reason. In 1917, when the government of the Third Republic, in a secret agreement with the Tsar's government, upheld the Russian claims to the Dardanelles as compensation for Russian support of its own claims to the left bank of the Rhine, the *custom of bargaining* and *traditional natural frontiers* prevailed over the techniques and ideas of the period. Perhaps economic and ideological rationality prevail over the habits of the past and the passions of circumstances, but they prevail only in the long run.

3. Offensive and Defensive

The two concepts of *offensive* and *defensive*, Clausewitz writes, are the two principal concepts of strategy. Are they, and in what sense, the key concepts of foreign policy, that is, of diplomatic-strategic conduct?

When the negotiators, in the disarmament conferences, sought to distinguish "offensive weapons" from "defensive weapons," they were unable to surmount the ambiguities: an aggressor nation can utilize defensive weapons, as a state under attack can utilize offensive weapons—supposing that these notions, which have a meaning on the level of tactics or strategy, are valid when applied to weapons.

What political meaning attaches to these notions, which originally concern the conduct of operations or engagements? On the highest level of abstraction I have distinguished *offensive power* and *defensive power*—that is, the capacity of a political unit to impose its will on others and the capacity of a unit not to let the will of others be imposed upon it. In the diplomatic realm, the defensive consists, for a state, in safeguarding its autonomy, maintaining its own manner of life, not accepting subordination of its internal laws or of its external action to the desires or decrees of others. The states called "small powers" generally have—can only have—defensive ambitions. They seek to survive *as such*, as seats of free decisions. On the other hand, the nations called "great powers" desire to possess the capacity that we have called offensive—in other words, the capacity to act on other political units, to convince or constrain them. The great powers must take the initiative, make alliances, stand at the head of coalitions. A state of the first rank which makes use only of its "defensive power" adopts an attitude of "isolationism," it foregoes participating in competition, it refuses to enter the system, it desires to be left in peace. Isolationism—that of Japan in the eighteenth century or that of the United States after the First World War—is not always praiseworthy in itself. That of Japan had no serious consequences for other states, but that of the United States distorted the calculations of force. Twice Germany ignored the potential of the remote state which professed to abstain from world politics.

On a lower level, an offensive is sometimes confused with a demand, a defensive with conservation. In a given circumstance, the satisfied states—generally those that dictated the terms of peace at the end of the last war—desire the maintenance of the status quo, while the unsatisfied states desire its modification. In the West, Germany after 1871 was a conservative state, France a revisionist state, the stake being Alsace-Lorraine. After 1918 France was totally conservative, while Germany pressed its demands on all diplomatic fronts and on all frontiers.

The opposition between revision and conservation does not necessarily determine the distribution of roles and responsibilities at the moment when hostilities break out. In other words, it is conceivable that the conservative state will take the initiative in resorting to arms. For example, seeing that the unsatisfied states are accumulating forces, it foresees the aggression that it fears or judges inevitable. Montesquieu actually attributes some legitimacy to these preventive aggressions or conservative offensives. "With states, the right of natural defense sometimes involves the necessity of attacking; as, for instance, when one nation sees that a continuance of peace will enable another to destroy it, and that to attack that nation is the only way to prevent its own destruction."[9] Israel's operation in the Sinai, in November 1956, might have been justified as "preventive aggression."

The impact of two coalitions brings into conflict, on one side or the other, conservative states and revisionist states: in 1914 Germany, conservative regarding the territorial status in the west, took the initiative of war against revisionist France, but within the framework of a generalized war. Lastly, a state or a camp, without formulating precise demands, may have the sense of some permanent injustice: in proportion to its force, it does not possess its fair share of the wealth. It believes itself capable of conquering, and of holding a great position upon victory. Before 1914 Italy and France made more specific, more assertive demands than Germany. Perhaps Germany was less opposed to a test by arms than these two states, which were both more demanding and less powerful.

Thus the opposition of the revisionist state and the conservative state is often deceptive. The propensity to take the initiative in hostilities also depends first on the relation of forces, then on the chance of success which each state or each side sees for itself. Conservatism is rarely complete, satisfaction rarely total. If the occasion warranted, the "satisfied" state would modify to its advantage the frontiers of enemy or allied territories. It is not always the defeated of the last war who start the next.

Similarly, by another paradox, the unsatisfied and aggressive state may deliberately create the appearance of peaceful intentions. In July 1914 the slogan "localization of the conflict" was bandied by Vienna at the very moment the Austrian cannon were shelling Belgrade. Not that the state drawing the sword is necessarily acting in bad faith when it proclaims its desire to limit the theater of hostilities or the number of belligerents. If it desires not generalized war but political success, it has achieved its goals once other states in the system refrain from entering the conflict. In 1914 Russia could not stop the Austrian action against Serbia without creating at least the probability of a generalized war. Before 1939 the conservative coalition could not stop the unsatisfied Third Reich except by the threat of a generalized war. After the reoccupation of the left bank of the Rhine, France had lost the opportunity (which it owed to the Versailles Treaty) of a limited and effective counterattack.

The objectives sought and the role at the origin of the hostilities do not suffice to determine the character of foreign policy. The final judgment also depends on the consequences that the victory of a state or a side would produce. Did Athens start the Peloponnesian War, and did the Athenians consciously desire hegemony over the Greek city-states? Was the Germany of Wilhelm II responsible (and to what degree) for the explosion of 1914? Whatever the answer given to these questions, it is certain that had Sparta

[9] *Ibid.*, X, 2.

been defeated, Athens would have dominated the whole of the Greek world; had the Western Allies lost, Germany would have possessed, on the Continent, a superiority of forces that would have signified, for the other European nations, the equivalent of a loss of autonomy. Now, since history offers few examples of hegemonic states which do not abuse their force, the state to which victory would give hegemony is regarded as aggressive, whatever the intentions of those governing it.

Still more offensive appears the foreign policy of a state that tends to overthrow not only the relation of forces but the internal status of states. Revolutionary France was not necessarily aggressive on the diplomatic level, she did not have to take the initiative of war; however, she had no choice but to attack kings and princes at the point where they were most vulnerable, on the principle of legitimacy itself. A great deal has been written about the diplomacy of the Republic, and historians have frequently asked how far it prolonged monarchical diplomacy by continuing its objectives, if not its methods. Yet insufficient attention has been paid to one piece of evidence which escaped no contemporary: it was not within the power of men to decide whether the diplomacy of the Republic was or was not in conformity with custom. It was in essence *revolutionary*, insofar as French ideas spread across Europe and toppled thrones. A state's policy is revolutionary if its victory would involve the collapse of traditional states, the ruin of the old principle of legitimacy.

None of these antitheses—conservative-revisionist, attacked-aggressor, traditional-revolutionary—is expressed on the level of strategy by the opposition between defensive and offensive. Even when the state is aggressive or revolutionary, the military leader can order his generals to remain on the defensive, temporarily if forces are not mobilized, permanently if he pins his hopes on the enormous extent of his territory or the patience of his population. Initiating hostilities does not imply the choice of a given strategy. Germany, even if she had been the victim of an aggression in 1914, would have had to apply the Schlieffen Plan—to attack France during the first phase of the conflict in order to put her *hors de combat* before turning against Russia. France, who regarded herself as attacked, launched her troops into Alsace. Strategy, whether offensive or defensive, on the whole or on a given front, is not determined by state policy alone—the initiatives it has taken and the objectives it seeks—it is also a function of the relation of forces, the order of hostilities and the judgments of the military leaders as to the respective merits of the two ways of "using engagements in the service of the war."

We find here the formulas complementary to those we analyzed in the first chapter. On the lowest tactical level the action of the soldier, the company, the battalion, the regiment obeys strictly military considerations. The day a battle is fought, the leader seeks to win it, although he takes greater or less risks, aims at a more or less complete success, depending on the total circumstances and the goals of each side. On the other hand, the establishment of the plan of war depends, in theory and in practice, on both the state's policy and the relation of forces or the geography of the conflict. But if the military leader must *always* take political considerations into account, there is no correspondence between the various meanings of the diplomatic offensive and defensive, as we have just distinguished them, and the two modes of strategy distinguished by Clausewitz.

In the Far East, Japan from 1931 or 1937 clearly pursued an *aggressive* and *revolutionary* policy. She had constituted the Empire of Manchukuo out of Manchuria, which she had cut off from China; she attempted, and made no mystery about it, to create a "new order," which would embrace Asia from Mukden to Djakarta. It was Japan that took the initiative in hostilities against China in 1937, against the United States, Great Britain and the Dutch possessions in 1941. Yet the strategy adopted was offensive-defensive: during the first phase, taking advantage of a local and temporary superiority, Japanese admirals and generals counted on winning brilliant successes and securing territorial stakes; during the second phase, they expected to remain on the defensive and wear down the United States' will to win. This combination of a policy of conquests and an offensive-defensive strategy leading to a negotiated peace had, from the first, little chance of success. A state rarely achieves such grandiose designs if it has not achieved a total victory, in military terms. But it remains true that a revisionist, conquering, revolutionary state may adopt a defensive strategy, relying on attrition, both physical and moral, of its adversaries, without seeking to defeat or disarm them.

On the other hand, a state without ambitions of conquest, without responsibility in the initiation of hostilities, occasionally aims at a victory of annihilation, and prefers, to indirect methods and oblique operations, a brutal onslaught against the enemy's strength. Must we say that the military leader who seeks absolute victory, while he plans limited objectives, acts in an irrational manner? Such a conclusion would be false. It all depends on whether the enemy is prepared to yield before exhausting its means of resistance: Hitler would have continued to the very end of the struggle, even without hope. An absolute victory in military terms, even if it is not indispensable for certain political achievements, adds to the prestige of arms and thereby constitutes a contribution to the victor's diplomacy. Lastly, after the initiation of hostilities, it is natural that the military leaders should try to win an absolute victory, whatever the advantage their nation's foreign policy intends to derive from it.

The choice of an offensive or defensive strategy, the desire for a total or limited victory, the preference for direct assault or for indirect advance— none of these decisions is separated *from*, but none is entirely determined *by*, policy. One can win an absolute victory by wearing the enemy down, one can annihilate the enemy forces in order to dictate the terms of a moderate peace, one can count on the enemy's lassitude to retain one's conquests —which does not alter the fact that, in general, the aggressive state takes the offensive, that the revolutionary state adopts a strategy of annihilation and seeks an absolute victory. The complexity of relations among sovereign states, the many interpretations of offensive or defensive policy, and the combination of the strategic and diplomatic meanings of these terms, had persuaded seventeenth- and eighteenth-century authors not to introduce a *juridical* discrimination between aggressor and victim and to accord all belligerents the advantage of legality. Conceptual analysis shows at least the reasons for this discretion.

The War of 1914 breaks out. The murder at Sarajevo was the *occasion*: to what degree was it the *cause*? Did the historical circumstances, the rivalry of states, the race for arms make the explosion inevitable sooner or later? If the event—assassination, ultimatum—had been merely the occasion, with what right do we attribute to a state and certain men a responsibility that devolves upon the total circumstances?

Apparent cause and underlying causes do not necessarily agree. Many authors have asserted that the commercial rivalry between Great Britain and Germany, of which there was no question in July 1914, was a more active cause of the war than the violation of Belgian neutrality. Should we say that this violation was the *pretext* invoked by the English statesmen or the *motive* of their decision?

It is not enough to have distinguished occasion and cause, pretext and motive, to weigh merits against faults. Once arms speak, the outcome is more important than the origin. What *objectives* do the belligerents seek? What are the probable *results* of the victory of one side or the other? In short, what are the *stakes* of the war?—stake being defined as the divergence between the two worlds, the one that Athens would control or the one Sparta would control, the one the Second or Third Reich would govern, and the one the Russians, the English and the Americans would govern. In this sense the stake is never entirely determined in advance, although what is "at stake" is more or less vaguely perceived by the actors.

The stake itself is not the last word in the analysis. Perhaps peoples do not fight for the motives attributed to them. Perhaps the true causes are buried in the collective unconscious. Perhaps aggressiveness is a function of the number of men or of the number of young men. Perhaps sovereign states are condemned to fight each other because they fear each other.

The doctrinaires of European public law who receive the approbation of Karl Schmitt[10] recommended to the prince moderation and peace, but being aware of the uncertainty of human judgments and the ambiguity of political actions, they urged princes not to confuse law and morality. The aggressor,

[10] *Der Nomos der Erde im Völkerrecht des Jus Europaeum*, Cologne, 1950.

supposing he is known without the shadow of a doubt, would be morally culpable: he would nonetheless remain a legal enemy and not a common-law criminal.

4. *The Indeterminacy of Diplomatic-Strategic Behavior*

Human behavior can always be translated in terms of means and ends, provided that the action is not a simple reflex and that the actor is not insane. What I have said, what I have done cannot fail to have—in my eyes, if not in other people's—certain consequences: nothing keeps us from considering after the fact the consequences as the ends and the steps that have preceded them as the means. The means-ends schema, *zweckrational* according to Max Weber's concept, is nonetheless not the necessary expression of the psychical mechanism or even of the logic of action. If we have referred to means and ends in the course of the two preceding chapters, it is merely to specify the nature of diplomatic-strategic behavior and, thereby, the character and limitations of the theory of international relations.

We started with the opposition between economic behavior and diplomatic-strategic behavior; the former has a relatively determined objective (although it assumes, depending on circumstances and persons, a different content), that is, the maximization of a quantity which, on the highest level of abstraction, would be called *value* or *utility*; the latter has no other initial characteristic than that of occurring in the shadow of war and, consequently, of being thereby obliged to take the relation of forces into account. The plurality of means and ends, which we have analyzed in the course of the preceding chapters, permits us to grasp more clearly the opposition of these two kinds of behavior.

The theoretician of economics is careful not to claim that he imposes or even that he knows from the outside the goals that individuals seek to achieve. He attributes to individuals a scale of preferences or transitive choices: if a person prefers A to B and B to C, he will not prefer C to A. It is by their choice that economic subjects manifest preferences, whose equal rationality (or irrationality) the economist admits by hypothesis. The man who prefers leisure to increased revenue is not more rational than the millionaire who ruins his health to accumulate profits. Theory overcomes the chaos of individual choices by means of money, a measurement of values and a universal means of acquiring goods. The maximization of monetary revenues is regarded as a rational goal since the individual is free to make what use he will of the quantity of money acquired. Money is only a means of buying merchandise, the choice of this merchandise depends on each man: the theoretician, without violating the intimacy of a conscience, while respecting the diversity of tastes, reconstructs the economic system step by step, limiting himself to positing that the subject, in order to maximize his satisfactions, seeks to maximize the monetary means of realizing them. When the behavior of an individual is in question, the economist has no other definition of *interest* than the scale of preferences, variable from individual to individual, or the maximization of the *utility* measured by monetary quantities.

In shifting from *individual interest* to *collective interest,* economists have encountered many difficulties, which have often been discussed. To keep to the major one, any determination of collective interest, if we continue to refer to individual preferences, requires a comparison between the satisfactions of some and the dissatisfactions of others. It is tempting to assume that the poor man whose income increases somewhat derives a satisfaction therefrom which is greater than the dissatisfaction of the rich man whose income somewhat decreases. By such reasoning we justify the transfer of revenues from the richer to the poorer classes, and the tendency to reduce the inequality of income. I myself share this way of thinking and the moral ideas that inspire it, but such reasoning is not rational, in the sense of the evident or the demonstrated, as certain mathematical propositions or even propositions relative to the Walrasian schema of equilibrium are rational. The comparison of one individual's satisfactions or dissatisfactions with another's has no psychological meaning, in that it introduces a mode of consideration radically alien to that which is expressed in the theory of individual economic behavior. Pareto, to my way of thinking, was not wrong in considering that only the point of the *maximum of interest for a collectivity* is the object of a rational determination. As long as it is possible to increase the satisfactions of some without diminishing those of others, it is legitimate to disregard the conflicts between individuals and groups. No one is harmed and some receive benefit. With the condition that he ignores the dissatisfaction occasioned to some by the spectacle of the fortune of others, and that he neglects the consequences of the redistribution of income, the statesman can claim kinship with science so long as he strives to attain the maximum of interest *for* the collectivity.

Pareto himself did not consider that this maximum of interest for the collectivity was, thereby, the maximum of interest *of* the collectivity. Considered as a unit, the collectivity does not necessarily intend to insure the greatest possible number of its members the greatest possible number of satisfactions. It may have power, prestige or glory as its objective. The sum of individual satisfactions is not equivalent to the advantage of the political unit as such. Yet diplomatic-strategic behavior, by definition, acts as a function of the interest *of* the collectivity, to use Pareto's language, or again as a function of the "national interest," to use the language of the theoreticians of international relations. Is this interest, in abstract terms, susceptible of a rational definition which could serve as a criterion or an ideal for a statesman? The three preceding chapters, it seems to me, dictate a negative answer to this question.

To give a "rationalizing interpretation" of diplomatic-strategic behavior, and to elaborate a general theory of international relations comparable to economic theory, many authors have made the concept of *power* or *Macht* a fundamental one, equivalent to the concept of value (or utility). But, as a matter of fact, this concept cannot fulfill this function.

Let us suppose that we understand by power the potential of resources: the latter could not in any way be considered as a rationally imposed objective. Or else we are concerned with resources that can be mobilized for external rivalry: in this case, to take the maximization of potential as the one supreme goal would be equivalent to granting absolute primacy to force or collective power. But a collectivity that extends its territory, increases its population, becomes *different*: it declines or it flourishes. The classical philosophers have always believed that there was an optimum dimension for political units. With what right would the theoretician of foreign policy justify those obsessed by power, or incriminate those whose supreme goal was the coherence or efficacy of the state?

Suppose we meant by power not the potential of resources but *force*, that is, the resources actually mobilized with a view to the conduct of foreign policy? With what right would the maximizing of the degree of mobilization be an obvious or rational objective? In every period, in response to external danger and popular sentiment, the chief of state tries to determine the appropriate degree of mobilization. Here, too, there is no reason for subordinating everything to the exigencies of diplomatic-strategic mobilization.

Might we, finally, define power as the capacity to impose one's will on others? In that case, power is not a final goal, either for the individual or for collectivities. Policy is always ambitious, it aspires to power because political action involves, in essence, a relationship among human beings, an element of power. Yet grand policy wants such power not for itself, but to carry out a mission. Similarly, a collectivity does not desire power for itself, but in order to achieve some other goal—peace, glory—so as to influence the future of humanity, through the pride of propagating an idea.

In other words, for a collectivity to maximize resources or force is to maximize its means of acting on others. One cannot suppose, even in a simplifying hypothesis, that a collectivity has no other objective than to possess the maximum means of acting on others. To maximize effective power is to maximize a reality difficult to grasp (the collectivity that most influences others is not always the one that most consciously attempts to impose itself upon them); it is also to distort the intrinsic meaning of diplomatic-strategic action. Effective power may well constitute the ambition of certain men or of certain peoples: it is not in itself a rational objective.

We may disregard the objection that economic subjects do not seek to maximize utility any more than "diplomatic subjects" seek to maximize power. There is a radical disparity between the two cases. Of course, *homo economicus* exists only in our rationalizing reconstruction, but the relation between *homo economicus* and the concrete economic subject differs fundamentally from the relation between the *ideal-type diplomat* (defined by the search for the maximization of *resources,* of *force* or of *power*), and the historical diplomat. The two "economic men"—one of theory and the other of practice—resemble each other as a retouched photograph resembles a snapshot. The theoretical *economicus* is more true to himself than the practical one; he has perfect information and makes no errors in calculation. But if either seeks the maximization of the same quantity (monetary income, production, long- or short-term profit), the former's perfect calculations help us to understand, and sometimes to correct, the latter's imperfect calculations. The *diplomaticus* of theory, who would have as his goal the maximization of resources, of actual forces, or of power, would not be an idealized portrait of the diplomats of all ages, he would be the caricatured simplification of certain diplomatic personages at certain periods.

The calculation of forces, which the *ideal diplomat* cannot avoid, is neither the first nor the last word of diplomatic-strategic behavior. Sympathies and hostilities at a given moment do not all result from the relation of forces: the *diplomat* attempts to maintain an equilibrium, but certain sympathies or hostilities are *given* as irreducible. He does not *first of all* seek the maximization of his resources, he desires such and such a province, such and such a strategic position, such and such a symbolic city. The eventual subordination of the abstract objective of force to the concrete and immediate objective is contrary neither to the logic of human action nor to the logic of rivalry among states. To drive the infidels out of the Holy Land, for a man who believes in Christ and the Passion, is an enterprise reasonable in a different way than the pursuit of force for its own sake. Even the desire for revenge is not more irrational than the will to power. Political units are in competition: the satisfactions of *amour-propre,* victory or prestige, are no less real than the so-called material satisfactions, such as the gain of a province or a population.

Not only are the historical objectives of political units not deducible from the relation of forces, but the ultimate objectives of such units are legitimately equivocal. Security, power, glory, idea are essentially heterogeneous objectives which can be reduced to a single term only by distorting the human meaning of diplomatic-strategic action. If the rivalry of states is comparable to a game, what is "at stake" cannot be designated by a single concept, valid for all civilizations at all periods. Diplomacy is a game in which the players sometimes risk losing their lives, sometimes prefer victory itself to the advantages that would result from it. Quantitative expression of the stakes is thereby impossible: not only do we not know in advance what the stake is (what the victor would do) but, for the warrior, victory suffices in itself.

The plurality of concrete objectives and of ultimate objectives forbids a rational definition of "national interest," even if the latter did not involve, in itself, the ambiguity that attaches to collective interest in economic science. Collectivities are composed of individuals and groups, each of which seeks its own objectives, seeks to maximize its resources, its share of the national income or its position within the social hierarchy. The interests of these individuals or of these groups, as they express themselves in actual behavior, are not spontaneously in accord with each other, and added together they do not constitute a general interest. Even on the economic level, the general interest is not deduced from private or collective interests by some mysterious calculation of average or compensation. Rate of growth, distribution of resources between consumption and investment, proportion allotted to welfare and proportion devoted to external action are determined by decisions that wisdom may inspire but that science cannot determine.[11]

A fortiori, the national interest is not reducible to private interests or private-collective interests. In a limited sense this concept is useful, it rouses the citizens to an awareness of the political unit of which they are temporary members, which has preceded them and will survive them. It reminds present-day leaders that security and greatness of the state must be the objectives of "diplomatic man," whatever their ideology.

It does not follow from this that national interest might, can or should be defined apart from the internal regime, the aspirations characteristic of the different classes, the political ideal of the state: the collectivity does not always change objectives when it changes its constitution, historical idea or ruling elite. But how can the political units maintain, through revolutions, the same ambitions and the same methods?

Of course, formally, the conduct of all *diplomats* offers similarities. Any statesman seeks to recruit allies or to reduce the number of his enemies. Revolutionists spontaneously resume, after a few years, the projects of the regime they have overthrown. Such incontestable continuity results from the national tradition, imposed by the imperatives of the calculation of forces. It remains to be shown that statesmen, inspired by various philosophers, act the same way in the same circumstances, and that different parties, to be rational as *diplomatic men*, must calculate the national interest in the same manner. Now, such a demonstration seems inconceivable to me, and the hypothesis itself absurd.[12]

How could democrats, fascists and Communists between the two wars have sought the same objectives? Any elite in power hopes for the reinforcement both of its regime and of the state for which it is responsible. But as Hitler's victory would involve the spread of totalitarian regimes, the democrats in any other European country could only have favored the Third Reich by sacrificing themselves on the pretext that their fatherland would

---

[11] The only science that might eventually substitute for wisdom would be that which has been developed in the theory of games; it would formulate the rules according to which a general will is revealed in the contradictions among individual wills.
[12] See below, Chap. X.

be stronger in a National Socialist Europe. Can we characterize the decision of statesmen who accept their own death in the hope that their nation will be stronger under other masters as incontestably rational? Does logic demand setting the strength of the state above the freedom of its citizens?

Should a German of good family have desired the triumph of Hitler's Germany, which in his eyes betrayed the true Germany? When each state or each camp embodies an idea, the individual risks being torn between his allegiance to a community and his commitment to his ideal. Whether he chooses the physical fatherland or the spiritual fatherland, he cannot be approved or condemned by the logic of politics alone. The national interest of political unity as such seems concretely determined only in circumstances where rivalry is reduced to a pure competition whose stake is limited and in which none of the combatants risks his existence or his soul.

If diplomatic behavior is never determined by the relation of forces alone, if power does not serve the same function in diplomacy as utility in economy, then we may legitimately conclude that *there is no general theory of international relations comparable to the general theory of economy.* The theory we are sketching here tends to analyze the meaning of diplomatic behavior, to trace its fundamental notions, to specify the variables that must be reviewed in order to understand any one constellation. But it does not suggest an "eternal diplomacy," it does not claim to be the reconstruction of a closed system.

We have given this first part of our work the title "Concepts and Systems." The elaboration of concepts relative to the behavior of units taken individually leads us to the description of typical situations.

chapter IV

On International Systems

I call an international system the ensemble constituted by political units that maintain regular relations with each other and that are all capable of being implicated in a generalized war. Units taken into account, in their calculation of forces, by those governing the principal states, are full-fledged members of an international system.

I have hesitated to use this term *system* to designate an ensemble whose cohesion is one of competition, which is organized by virtue of a conflict, and which exits most powerfully on the day when it is lacerated by recourse to arms. A political system is defined by an organization, by the reciprocal relations of the parties, by the cooperation of elements, by the rules of government. To what degree do we find the equivalent in the case of an international system?

The following pages will attempt to offer answers to these questions. Let us say, for now, that the term *system* seems useful as it is employed in the expression *party system*. In this case, too, the term designates the ensemble constituted by the collective actors in competition. Party competition, it is true, is subject to the rules of a constitution, for which international law does not offer an exact equivalent. But the number, respective size, and means of action of political parties are not provided for by the legal texts: parties are opposing units par excellence. The difference from international actors remains essential as long as parties regard the vote, and states regard bombs or missiles, as the *ultima ratio*. When parties no longer disdain machine guns, or if states should some day be assimilated into a universal empire, the national and international actors tend, or would tend to become, identified with each other.

An international system, like a party system, involves only a small number of actors. When the number of actors increases (there are more than a hundred states in the United Nations), that of the chief actors does not increase proportionally, and sometimes does not increase at all. We note two superpowers in the world system of 1950, at most five or six great powers, actual or potential. Therefore, the principal actors never have the sense of being subject to the system in the manner in which an average-size firm is subject to the laws of the market. The structure of international systems is always *oligopolistic*. In each period the principal actors have determined the system more than they have been determined by it. A change of regime within one of the chief powers suffices to change the style and sometimes the course of international relations.

1. Configuration of the Relation of Forces

The first characteristic of an international system is the *configuration of the relation of forces*, a notion that itself involves several aspects: what are the limits of the system? what is the distribution of forces among the various actors? how are the actors situated on the map?

Before the present period—more precisely before 1945—no international system included the entire planet. Scarcely more than a century ago, the ambassador of Her Britannic Majesty had difficulty obtaining an audience from the Emperor of China, refused to submit to rites he regarded as humiliating (genuflection), and, to offers of commercial relationships, received this scornful response: What could his remote little country produce which the Middle Empire was not capable of producing as well or better? At the time, there were two reasons that combined to exclude China from the European system: *physical distance* prohibited China from taking military action in Europe, while limiting European military capacity in the Far East; *moral distance* between the cultures made dialogue difficult, reciprocal comprehension impossible.

Which of these two criteria, politico-military participation or communication, is the more important in defining membership in a system? The first, it seems to me. Only the actors performing in the plays belong to a troupe. Performance, for the international troupe, is generalized war, potential or real: it matters little whether one of the actors speaks a somewhat different language. Certainly during the historical periods when a system has existed, in other words, when relations have not been merely occasional and anarchic, the actors belong for the most part to the same zone of culture, worship the same gods, respect the same prohibitions. The Greek city-states, like the European nations, were aware of both their fundamental kinship and the permanence of their rivalry. But the Persian Empire, which the Greeks considered as alien—barbarian—and the Turkish Empire, whose Islamic faith the Christian sovereigns could not ignore, were involved in the conflicts and the calculations of the Greek city-states or the European monarchies. They were an element in the relation of forces, although they were not an integral part of the transnational cultural ensemble.

Uncertainty of limits does not involve merely the duality of the diplomatic or military *participation* and of the *community of culture.* It also involves the enlargement, sometimes rapid and unforeseeable, of the diplomatic field, as a function of technology and of political events. By subjecting the Greek city-states to their law, the Macedonian kings created a political unit whose resources made distant undertakings possible. The international system was extended as the units themselves enlarged, and thereby became capable of including, in thought and in action, a larger historical space.

Before 1914 the European states neglected the eventuality of United States intervention. The United States was not, apparently, a military power, and did not play a part on the European stage. It is not without interest to reflect on this error, which falsified calculations.

Economically, the United States had been, for centuries, inseparable from Europe. European history would have been quite different if, in the nineteenth century, the Old World's surplus population had not found rich and empty lands to cultivate across the Atlantic. Great Britain, because of her mastery of the seas, had possessed, during the great wars of the Revolution and the Empire, at least a share of the resources of the other continents. The European conquests since the sixteenth century should have shown that henceforth distance was no longer an insurmountable obstacle to military action. At the beginning of the nineteenth century, progress in means of transportation seemed limited to maritime services. Great Britain had established herself in India, but it took Napoleon almost as long as Caesar to go from Rome to Paris. In the nineteenth century and at the beginning of the twentieth, on the other hand, the means of land transportation developed to a remarkable degree, due to the railroad, and then to the internal-combustion engine. Such progress made ignorance of the elementary rule of reciprocity still more unjustifiable: if European military forces could be present in India or in Mexico, why should American military force not be present in the Old World?

This unawareness of the possible return to Europe, in uniform, of the European emigrants settled across the Atlantic seems to me to have had many causes. The Spaniards had required few expeditionary forces to conquer Central and South America. The Europeans, at the very period when they ruled the world, reserved for the struggles that retrospectively seem to us quite fratricidal, the majority of their resources. It was difficult for them to imagine transporting mass armies across the Atlantic. Experts tended to overestimate the importance of the officers' corps and still more of the aristocratic class from which this corps was, or was supposed to be, recruited. The stereotyped image, "a commercial state *or* a military state," prevented a recognition of the new fact of the approximate proportionality between industrial potential and military potential. Further, why should the United States, hostile to "entanglement" from the beginning of its existence, eager to keep out of European conflicts, participate in a war whose origin was obscure and whose stake was ambiguous? This latter reasoning was not radically false, but it did not take into account the possibility that the first battles would not decide the results and that the hostilities would extend over several years. In other words, statesmen and generals were wrong to overlook the fact that *materially* the United States could send a great army to Europe. Failing to anticipate the war's amplification due to the draft, to industry, and to the approximate equality of forces, they were surprised when the conflict's dynamism involved the United States in battle and extended the European diplomatic field to America.

This field, whose limits are traced by the techniques of transportation and combat at the same time as by relations among states, is divided into political units and groupings of units (temporary alliances or permanent coalitions). The geography of the diplomatic field is not modified, or is modified only slowly. On the other hand, the strength of each unit and the groupings are modified, sometimes rapidly. Therefore the so-called *constants* imposed by geography are often deceptive. It is not geography, but the projection on a map of a certain relation of forces which suggests the idea of friendship or hostility, original or permanent. Once this relation of forces changes, another policy becomes reasonable. Early in this century, French textbooks of diplomatic history extolled the wisdom of an alliance with a state on the other side of the potential enemy, a tradition that seemed dictated by geography and was actually suggested by a configuration of the relation of forces. A European state would have to be stronger than France to justify this kind of alliance, which aimed at re-establishing equilibrium and creating a threat of war on two fronts. Such an alliance with Poland or the Soviet Union against the Bonn Republic, or tomorrow against a unified Germany (extended to the Oder-Neisse Line), would be senseless. Even a reunified Germany would be weaker than Western Europe (France supported by the Anglo-American nations), or the Soviet bloc. Why should France attempt to weaken further, by surrounding it, a neighbor not to be feared?

Of course, the geographical distribution of alliances exerts an influence on the course of diplomacy. According to the space they occupy, the political units have different resources, different objectives, different dreams. Alliances have a relation to the respective positions of states—the most powerful ally is less alarming if it is remote. If it is not a "permanent ally," a neighboring state easily becomes an enemy. Nevertheless, the essential aspect of a system is the configuration of the relation of forces, space itself assuming a diplomatic significance only as a function of the localization of great and small powers, of stable and unstable states, of sensitive points (in military or political terms), and pacified zones.

To define what we mean by the configuration of relation of forces,[1] it is

---

[1] In German, *Gestaltung der Kraftverhältnisse.*

simplest to contrast two typical configurations, the multipolar configuration and the bipolar configuration. In one case, diplomatic rivalry occurs among several units, which all belong to the same class. Various combinations of equilibrium are possible; reversals of alliance belong to the normal process of diplomacy. In the other, two units outclass all the rest, so that equilibrium is possible only in the form of two coalitions, the majority of medium and small states being obliged to join the camp of one great power or the other.

Whatever the configuration, political units constitute a more or less official hierarchy, essentially determined by the forces that each is supposed capable of mobilizing: at one extreme, the great powers, at the other, the small states, the former claiming the right to intervene in all affairs, including those of states not concerning them directly, the others having no desire to intervene outside their narrow sphere of interest and action, sometimes even resigned to submitting to the decisions, regarding a subject that concerns them directly, taken in concert by the great powers. The latter's ambition is to influence and control circumstances, that of the small states to adapt themselves to circumstances which, essentially, do not depend on them. Such a contrast, of course, is oversimplified and expresses opinions rather than the reality: the manner in which the small states adapt themselves to circumstances contributes to the form circumstances actually assume.

The distribution of forces in the diplomatic field is *one* of the causes that determine the grouping of states. In an extreme case, two states that have no real motive for dispute can become hostile to each other by a "fatality of position." Two dominant states are almost inevitably enemies (unless they are closely united), merely because an equilibrium exists only on condition that each of the two belongs to the opposite camp. When the rivalry itself creates the hostility, the mind or the passions subsequently find countless means of justifying it. In war, too, fury is sometimes the result of the conflict itself, not of the conflict's stake.

This is an extreme case. Alliances are not the mechanical effect of the relation of forces. Simplifying, one might say that some great powers are in conflict because of the divergence or contradiction of their interests or their claims; other powers, great or small, join one side or the other, either out of interest (they hope to gain more from the victory of one camp than from that of the other), or emotional preference (the sympathies of the population incline to one side more than to the other), or a concern for equilibrium. Great Britain had the reputation of taking a position *exclusively* for this last reason. Generally indifferent to details of the map of the Continent, her only aim was to forestall the hegemony or empire of a single power. This pure policy of equilibrium was logical, for Great Britain had sought neither territory nor population on the Continent (since the Hundred Years' War). It was so important to England's security and prosperity to keep Continental forces from uniting against her that British diplomacy could not indulge itself in the luxury of ideological considerations. But to be reasonable, she had to appear both honorable and cynical: to keep her promises to allies during hostilities, and never to regard an alliance as permanent.

If the policies of the Continental states did not seem as detached from ideological or affective contingencies as the policy of the island state, it was not the fault of statesmen, but of circumstances. The European monarchs disputed provinces and positions of vantage. Invasions often left bitter memories. Even in the period of dynastic wars, sovereigns did not switch ally and enemy with complete freedom. After the annexation of Alsace-Lorraine, no French government, however authoritarian, would have agreed to a complete reconciliation with Germany.

Alliances and hostilities are determined, sometimes by the mere relation of forces, sometimes by a dispute with a specific stake, most often by a combination of these two factors. With regard to lasting hostilities or alliances, the opposition of interests or the convergences of aspirations are primary. The long period of wars between France and Great Britain was controlled in part by the inevitable hostility of the island state to the chief state on the Continent, but at the same time, the colonial enterprises of France and England were in conflict on remote territories and on the seas: logically, England's constant goal should have been the destruction of the French fleet or, at least, the incontestable superiority of the English fleet, so that mastery of the seas might guarantee the expansion and security of the British Empire. In the twentieth century the mere calculation of forces does not account for British policy. After all, in the abstract, England could have sought allies on the Continent to forestall American hegemony: yet such a thing was out of the question. To London, American hegemony still seemed to retain something of English hegemony about it, whereas German hegemony would have been felt as alien, humiliating, unacceptable. A change from the *pax Britannica* to the *pax Americana* did not involve a change of universe, and pride, rather than the soul itself, suffered. A *pax Germanica* could not replace the *pax Britannica* without England resisting to the death: only a military catastrophe could have cleared the path from one to the other.

In the last analysis, nations do not fight each other only to maintain a position of strength.

2. Homogeneous and Heterogeneous Systems

The conduct of states towards each other is not controlled by the relation of forces alone: ideas and emotions influence the decisions of the actors. A diplomatic circumstance is not completely understood so long as we limit ourselves to describing the geographical and military structures of the alliances and hostilities, to situating on the map the points of strength, the lasting or occasional coalitions, the neutral powers. We must also grasp the determinants of the behavior of the principal actors—in other words, the nature of the states and the objectives sought by those in power. Thus the distinction between *homogeneous systems* and *heterogeneous systems* seems to me fundamental.[2] *I call homogeneous systems those in which the states belong to the same type, obey the same conception of policy. I call heterogeneous, on the other hand, those systems in which the states are organized according to different principles and appeal to contradictory values.* Between the end of the wars of religion and the French Revolution, the European system was both multipolar and homogeneous. The American-European system, since 1945, is both bipolar and heterogeneous.

Homogeneous systems afford, on first analysis, greater stability. Those in power are not unaware of the dynastic or ideological interests that unite them, despite the national interests that set them against each other. The recognition of homogeneity finds its extreme and formal expression in the formula of the Holy Alliance. Against the revolutionaries, the rulers of the sovereign states promised each other mutual support. The Holy Alliance was denounced by liberals as a conspiracy of kings against peoples. It had no "national justification," since the change of regime did not involve, in the last century, an overthrow of alliances: a victory of the revolution in Spain would perhaps have endangered the Bourbons, not France. At present, each of the two blocs tends to revive, for internal use, a Holy Alliance formula. Soviet intervention in Hungary was equivalent to proclaiming the right of Russian armies to intervene in every Eastern European nation to repress counterrevolution (as a matter of fact, any insurrection against the so-called socialist regime). In the West, too, the regimes are virtually allied against revolution. The Holy Alliance against counterrevolution or revolution is in the end necessary to the survival of each of the two blocs.

The homogeneity of the system favors the limitation of violence. So long as those in power, in the conflicting states, remain aware of their solidarity, they incline to compromise. The revolutionaries are regarded as common enemies of all rulers, and not as the allies of one of the states or alliances. If the revolutionaries were to win in one of the states, the regimes of the other states would also be shaken. The fear of revolution incites military leaders either to resign themselves to defeat or to limit their claims.

A homogeneous system appears stable, too, because it is foreseeable. If all the states have analogous regimes, the latter must be traditional, inherited down through the years, not improvised. In such regimes, statesmen obey time-tested rules or customs: rivals or allies know on the whole what they can expect or fear.

Lastly, by definition, the states and those who speak in their name are led to distinguish between enemy state and political adversary. State hostility does not imply hatred, it does not exclude agreements and reconciliations after battle. Statesmen, whether victors or vanquished, can deal with the enemy

[2] I borrow this distinction from a remarkable work by Panoyis Papaligouras: *Théorie de la société internationale,* a thesis at the University of Geneva, 1941. The book was called to my attention by Mlle. J. Hersch.

without being accused of treason by ideologists reproaching them for having spared the "criminal"[3] or by "extremists" accusing them of sacrificing the national interests to assure the survival of their regime.[4]

Heterogeneity of the system produces the opposite. When the enemy appears also as an adversary, in the sense this term assumes in internal conflicts, defeat affects the interests of the governing class and not only of the nation. Those in power fight for themselves and not only for the state. Far from kings or leaders of the republic being inclined to regard the rebels of the other camp as a threat to the common order of warring states, they consider it normal to provoke discord among the enemy. The adversaries of the faction in power become, whatever their stripe, the allies of the national enemy and consequently, in the eyes of some of their fellow citizens, traitors. The "Holy Alliance" situation encourages those in power to subordinate their conflicts in order to safeguard the common principle of legitimacy. In what we call the situation of ideological conflict, each camp appeals to an idea, and the two camps are divided, with a number of citizens on either side not desiring, or not desiring wholeheartedly, the victory of their own country, if it were to mean the defeat of the idea to which they adhere and which the enemy incarnates.

This crisscrossing of civil and inter-state conflicts aggravates the instability of the system. The commitment of states to one camp or the other is jeopardized as a result of internal rivalries: hence the chief states cannot ignore them. Party struggles *objectively* become episodes of conflict among states. When hostilities break out, a compromise peace is difficult, and the overthrow of the government or of the enemy regime almost inevitably becomes one of the goals of the war. The phases of major wars—wars of religion, wars of revolution and of empire, wars of the twentieth century—have coincided with the challenging of the principle of legitimacy and of the organization of states.

This coincidence is not accidental, but the causal relation can be, abstractly, conceived in two ways: the violence of war *creates* the heterogeneity of the system or else, on the other hand, this heterogeneity is, if not the cause, at least the historical context of great wars. Although we can never categorically retain one of the terms of the alternative and exclude the other, internal struggles and inter-state conflicts do not always combine in the same way. Heterogeneity is not only relative, it can also assume various forms.

In 1914, was the European system homogeneous or heterogeneous? In many respects, homogeneity seemed to prevail. The states *recognized* each other. Even Russia, the least liberal among them, permitted certain opponents the right to exist, to criticize. Nowhere was the truth of an ideology

[3] As Thorstein Veblen reproached the Allied statesmen in 1918.
[4] As Guillemin and other leftist writers accused the peace party that triumphed in 1871. By continuing a revolutionary war, might not the fate of arms have been changed?

decreed by the state or considered indispensable to the latter's solidarity. Citizens readily crossed borders and the requirement of a passport, at Russia's borders, caused scandal. No ruling class regarded the overthrow of the regime of a potentially hostile state as its goal. The French *Republic* did not oppose the German *Empire,* any more than the latter opposed the *empire* of the Tsars. The French Republic was allied with the empire of the Tsars according to the traditional requirements of equilibrium.

This homogeneity, apparent as long as peace prevailed, revealed many flaws which war was to enlarge. Within it the two principles of legitimacy, birth and election, whose conflict had constituted one of the stakes of the wars of revolution and empire, had concluded a precarious truce. Compared to today's fascist or Communist regimes, the Kaiser's and even the Tsar's empires were "liberal." But the supreme power, the sovereignty, continued to belong to the heir of the ruling families. The heterogeneity of the absolutist regimes (the sovereign is designated by birth) and of the democratic regimes (the sovereign is designated by the people) existed potentially. Of course, so long as Tsarist Russia was allied with the Western democracies, neither of the two camps could exploit this opposition to the full. After the Russian Revolution, Allied propaganda did not hesitate to do so.

More seriously, the relationship between peoples and nations had also not been stabilized in the nineteenth century. The German Empire and the Kingdom of Italy had been constituted in the name of the right of nationality. But in Alsace-Lorraine the Reich had given the national idea a meaning that the liberals of France and elsewhere had never accepted: was nationality a destiny that language or history imposed on individuals, or the freedom of each man to choose his state? Further, the territorial status of Europe, based on dynastic heritage and the concern for equilibrium, was not compatible with the national idea, whatever the latter's interpretation. Austria-Hungary was a multinational empire like the Ottoman Empire. The Poles were neither German nor Russian nor Austrian, and they were all subject to an alien law.

Once war was declared, all belligerent states attempted to appeal to the national idea in order to mobilize its dynamism to their advantage. The emperors made solemn and vague promises to the Poles, as though they vaguely realized that the partition of Poland remained Europe's sin. Perhaps, too, the universalization of the profession of arms suggested to those in power that henceforth war must have a meaning for those who risked their lives in it.

This heterogeneity of the principle of legitimacy (how are those in power to be designated? to what state should the populations belong?) did not contradict the fundamental cultural relationship of the members of the European community. It did not inspire any of the states with the desire to destroy the other's regime. In peacetime each state regarded the other's regime as a matter outside its own concern. Out of liberalism, France and Great Britain gave asylum to the Russian revolutionaries, but they gave them neither money nor weapons to organize terrorist groups. On the other hand, after 1916 or 1917, to justify the determination to continue the war to absolute victory, to convince the Allied soldiers that they were defending freedom, to dissociate the German people from their regime, Allied propaganda and diplomacy attacked absolutism as the cause of the war and of the German "crimes," proclaimed the right of peoples to self-determination (hence the dissolution of Austria-Hungary) as the fundamental condition of a just peace, and finally refused to deal with those rulers responsible for igniting the holocaust. Semi-homogeneous in 1914, the European system had become irremediably heterogeneous by 1917 as a result of the fury of the struggle and the Western powers' need to justify their determination to win decisively.

Similarly, on the eve of the Peloponnesian War, the Greek city-states were relatively homogeneous. They had fought together against the Persians, they worshiped the same gods, celebrated the same festivals, competed in the same games. Their economic or political institutions belonged to the same family, were variations on the same theme. When war to the death was launched between Athens and Sparta, each camp recalled that it appealed to the authority of democracy or aristocracy (or oligarchy). The goal was less to encourage the combatants' ardor than to weaken the adversary and to make allies within the opposite camp. This heterogeneity, which concerns only one element of politics, often suffices to transform an inter-state hostility into passionate hostility. The meaning of a common culture is effaced and the belligerents are now aware only of what separates them. Perhaps, in fact, the heterogeneity most inimical to peace or moderation is precisely the kind that stands out against a background of community.

However, heterogeneity of the Greek city-states during the Peloponnesian War, or of the European states in 1917 or in 1939 was less well defined than the heterogeneity of the Greek city-states and the Persian Empire, of the Greek city-states and Macedonia, of the Christian kingdoms and the Ottoman Empire, and a fortiori, of the Spanish conquerors and the Inca or Aztec empires, or of the European conquerors and the African tribes. These examples, in abstract terms, suggest three typical situations: 1. Political units, belonging to the same zone of civilization, have often had regular relations with political units that, outside this zone, were clearly recognized as different or alien. The Greeks, as a consequence of their idea of the free man, regarded the subjects of the Oriental empires with some condescension. Islam distinguished the Christian kingdoms from the Ottoman Empire without prohibiting the alliance of the King of France and the Commander of the Faithful. 2. Spaniards on the one hand, Incas and Aztecs on the other, were *essentially* different. The conquistadors triumphed, despite their smaller numbers, because of the resentment of the tribes subject to the ruling peoples of the empires as well as because of the terrifying effectiveness of their weapons. They destroyed the civilizations that they neither could nor desired to understand, without even being aware of committing a crime. 3. Perhaps the relationship between the Europeans and the African Negroes did not differ, fundamentally, from the foregoing between Spaniards and Incas. Today's anthropologists urge us not to overlook the specific "culture" of those whom our fathers called savages, and not to establish a hierarchy of values too hast-ily. Nonetheless, I think a distinction is justified between the archaic life of the African tribes and the pre-Columbian civilizations.

With regard to cruelties or horror, we cannot establish an order of greater and less, depending on whether we are dealing with wars among related and heterogeneous units, wars among units belonging to different civiliza-tions, wars fought by conquerors against civilizations they were incapable of understanding, or lastly wars between civilized men and savages. All con-querors, whether Mongols or Spaniards, have killed or pillaged. The belliger-ents have no need to be alien to each other in order to be fierce: political heterogeneity, often created or at least amplified by war, is enough. Further, the conflict between units of the same family or civilization is often more intense and furious than any other, because it is also a civil and religious war. Inter-state war becomes civil war once each camp is linked to one of the factions within some of the states; it becomes a war of religion if the in-dividuals are attached to one form of the state more than to the state itself, if they compromise civil peace by insisting on the free choice of their God or their Church.

The international systems that include related and neighboring states are both the theaters of great wars and the space destined to imperial unification. The diplomatic field is enlarged as the units assimilate a greater number of the former elementary units. After the Macedonian conquests, the city-states together constituted one unit. After the conquests of Alexander and of Rome, the Mediterranean basin as a whole was subject to the same laws and a single will. As the Roman Empire developed, the distinction between cul-tural family and state allegiance tended to disappear. The Empire was in conflict, on its frontiers, with the "barbarians," and internally with the rebel populations or non-"civilized" masses. Earlier adversaries had become fellow citizens. Retrospectively, most wars seem to be civil wars, since they set in opposition political units destined to be blended into a superior unit. Before the twentieth century the Japanese had fought major wars only among them-selves, the Chinese had fought among themselves and against barbarians, Mongols and Manchus. Indeed, how could it have been otherwise? Collec-tivities, like persons, are in conflict with their neighbors, who are *other,* even if they are physically or morally quite close. Political units must be huge in order for the neighbor to belong to a civilization that the historian, with the perspective of centuries, considers authentically *other.*

After 1945 the diplomatic field expanded to the limits of the planet, and the diplomatic system, despite all internal heterogeneities, now tends to a juridical homogeneity, of which the United Nations is the expression.

3. *Transnational Society and International Systems*

International systems, as we have said, are comprised of units that have regular diplomatic relations with each other. Now such relations are normally accompanied by relations among individuals, who make up the various units. *International systems are the inter-state aspect of the society to which the populations, subject to distinct sovereignties, belong.* Hellenic society or European society in the fifth century B.C. or in the twentieth century A.D. are realities that we shall call transnational, rather than inter- or supranational.

A transnational society reveals itself by commercial exchange, migration of persons, common beliefs, organizations that cross frontiers and, lastly, ceremonies or competitions open to the members of all these units. A transnational society flourishes in proportion to the freedom of exchange, migration or communication, the strength of common beliefs, the number of non-national organizations, and the solemnity of collective ceremonies.

It is easy to illustrate the vitality of transnational society by examples. Before 1914 economic exchanges throughout Europe enjoyed a freedom that the gold standard and monetary convertibility safeguarded even better than legislation. Labor parties were grouped into an International. The Greek tradition of the Olympic Games had been revived. Despite the plurality of the Christian Churches, religious, moral and even political beliefs were fundamentally analogous on either side of the frontiers. Without many obstacles a Frenchman could choose Germany as his place of residence, just as a German could decide to live in France. This example, like the similar one of Hellenic society in the fifth century, illustrates the relative autonomy of the inter-state order—in peace and in war—in relation to the context of transnational society. It is not enough for individuals to visit and know each other, to exchange merchandise and ideas, for peace to reign among the sovereign units, though such communications are probably indispensable to the ultimate formation of an international or supranational community.

The contrary example is that of Europe and the world between 1946 and 1953 (and even today, although since 1953 a certain transnational society, over the Iron Curtain, is being reconstituted). Commercial exchanges between Communist nations and the nations of Western Europe were reduced to a minimum. Insofar as they existed, they pertained only to states (at least on one side). The "Soviet individual" had no right to deal with a "capitalist individual," except by the intermediary of public administration. He could not communicate with him without becoming suspect. Inter-individual communications were generally forbidden unless they were the express of inter-state communications: officials and diplomats chatted with their Western colleagues, but essentially in the exercise of their functions.

This total rupture of transnational society had a truly pathological character: subsequently the Soviet Union has been represented in scientific congresses as in athletic competitions, receives foreign tourists and allows several thousand Soviet citizens to visit the West each year, and no longer strictly forbids personal contacts with Westerners. Russian wives of English aviators have been able to rejoin their husbands. Commercial exchanges have gradually broadened. Yet it is doubtful if this restoration of transnational society has modified essentials: heterogeneity, with regard to the principle of legitimacy, the form of the state and the social structure, remains fundamental. The Christian community has only a limited scope because political faith is stronger than religious faith, the latter having become a strictly private matter; lastly, no organization, whether political, syndical, or ideological, can unite Soviet and Western citizens unless it is in the open or clandestine service of the Soviet Union. The heterogeneity of the inter-state system irremediably divides transnational society.

In every period, transnational society has been regulated by customs, conventions or a specific code. The relations that the citizens of a nation at war were authorized to maintain with the citizens of the enemy state were controlled by custom rather than by law. Conventions among states specified the status of the citizens of each established on the territory of the other. Legislation made legal or illicit the creation of transnational movements or the participation in those professional or ideological organizations intended to be supranational.

From a sociological viewpoint, I am inclined to call private international law the law that regulates this transnational society as we have just characterized it, that is, the imperfect society made up of individuals who belong to distinct political units and who are, as private persons, in reciprocal relation. It is entirely to be expected that many jurists regard as municipal law all or part of such private international law. Whether in familial or commercial relations, the norms applicable to foreigners or to relations among nationals and foreigners are an integral part of the system of norms of the state involved. Even if these norms result from an agreement with another state, an essential modification does not follow: agreements on double taxation, for instance, guarantee a kind of reciprocity of treatment, by each of the signatory nations, of the other's citizens, at the same time that they protect the taxpayers of each state against a twofold imposition of taxes. The consequences of these inter-state conventions take place within the legal system of each.

On the other hand, the propositions, prohibitions and obligations recorded in the treaties among states constitute elements of public international law. We have, in the two preceding sections, considered the *configuration of the relation of forces*, then *the homogeneity or heterogeneity of the systems*. The control of international relations is located at the meeting point of the two previous studies. To what degree and in what sense are inter-state relations, in peace and in war, subject to law in the same way that individual relations, in the family and in business, are today and in a sense always have been?[5]

Inter-state relations, like other social relations, have never been abandoned

---

[5] There has always been social control; there is not always a juridical elaboration or *a fortiori* a written law.

to the purely arbitrary. All so-called higher civilizations have distinguished between members of the tribe (or the city, or the state) and the foreigner, and between various kinds of foreigners. Treaties were known from earliest antiquity—by the Egyptian Empire as by the Hittites. Every civilization has had an unwritten code that dictated the manner of dealing with ambassadors, prisoners, or even enemy warriors in combat. What new features does public international law provide?

States have concluded many agreements, conventions or treaties, some of which concern *transnational society,* while others concern both that and the *international system.* To the first category belong, for instance, postal conventions, those conventions relative to hygiene, to weights and measures; to the second belong questions of maritime law. In the collective interest of states and not of individuals alone, international conventions control the utilization of seas or rivers, the means of transportation and of communication. The extension of international law expresses the broadening of the collective interests of transnational society or of the international system, the increasing need to submit to law the coexistence of human collectivities, politically organized on a territorial basis, on the same planet, upon the same seas and under the same sky.

Yet does international law thereby modify the essence of inter-state relations? Controversies relating to international law[6] ordinarily occur on an intermediary level between positive law on the one hand and ideologies or philosophies on the other, a theoretical level that might be called, to borrow the expression of F. Perroux, "implicitly normative." The obligations of international law are those which result from treaties signed by states or from custom. On the other hand, "the right of peoples to self-determination," "the principle of nationalities," "collective security" are vague formulas, ideologies that influence statesmen, eventually even the interpretation jurists make of positive law. It cannot be said that they serve as the basis of a system of norms, that they involve, for states, specific privileges or duties. Now the jurist who seeks to define the nature of international law attempts to put positive law in a conceptual form, to discover its specific meaning. But this interpretation is not included in positive law itself. The latter allows various interpretations. Juridical theory, even more than economic theory, conceals an element of doctrine. It brings to light the meaning of juridical reality, but this apparent discovery is also an interpretation, influenced by the theoretician's idea of what international law should be.

In the unanimous opinion of jurists, an important, if not the principal, datum of international law is the treaty. Yet treaties have rarely been signed *freely* by *all* the high contracting parties. They express the relation of forces; they consecrate the victory of one and the defeat of the other.

---

[6] We do not add in each case the word *public.* But it is understood that the international law to which we henceforth refer is what jurists call public international law.

Now the principle of *pacta sunt servanda,* if it is not the originating norm or the moral basis of international law, is nevertheless its condition of existence. But international law thereby tends to assume a conservative quality. It is the victor of the latest war who invokes the principle against the claims of the vanquished, the latter having meanwhile reconstituted his forces. In other words, the stabilization of a juridical order based on the reciprocal commitments of states would be satisfactory in one of the two following hypotheses: either if the states had concluded treaties that were considered equitable by all, or if there existed a claim acknowledged by all and capable of being satisfied by reference to indisputable criteria of justice.

It is true that treaties follow the formula *pacta sunt servanda* with the words *rebus sic stantibus:* it remains to be seen whether subsequent changes justify modification of the treaty. The Western powers have the juridically incontestable right to occupy a part of the former capital of the Reich. But their presence there was related to the project of a united Germany. If this project is abandoned and the division of Germany accepted, is it advisable to modify the treaties because the context has changed? To this question there is no juridical answer.

If treaties are the source for international law, it is because the subjects of the law are states. But by the same token, major historical events, those by which the states are born and die, are external[7] to the juridical order. The Baltic states have ceased to exist, they are no longer subjects of law; nothing the Soviet Union does on the territories that, in 1939, were subject to the Estonian or Lithuanian sovereignty any longer relates to international law, at least in the eyes of those of the states that have ceased to "recognize" Estonia, Lithuania, and Latvia (that is, almost every state). When a state is crossed off the map of the world, it is the victim of a violation of international law. If no one comes to its aid, it will soon be forgotten and the state that has delivered the *coup de grâce* will be no less welcome in the assemblies of so-called peaceful nations. Ideologies scarcely permit us to affirm or deny, in the abstract or even in specific circumstances, that certain peoples have or do not have the right to constitute themselves into a nation. In other words, even the unbiased observer often hesitates to

[7] Or, if one prefers, they are the creators of this order. Certain modern jurists, H. Kelsen for instance, deny that the birth and death of states are metajuridical facts. Granting the theory according to which recognition is more a political than a juridical act, and by no means a formative one, they affirm that international law describes as a "state" those cases that merit this designation. "The juridical existence of the new state does not depend on recognition, but on the objective fulfillment of certain conditions assigned by international law for a state to be recognized." ("Théorie générale du droit international public," *Recueil des cours de l'Académie de droit international,* 42, 1932, p. 287.) If we admit this system, we would say that historical events create conditions of fact which are qualified by international law (and not by the will of existing states), as the birth or death of a state.

assert that a specific violation of the territorial status quo is just or unjust, conforms to or violates, in the long or short run, the interest of the nation directly involved, or of the international community.

The laws of states come into effect, one might say, the day the states themselves are recognized. Non-organized rebels do not benefit from any legal protection. The legitimate authority treats them as criminals and must treat them as such if it wishes to preserve itself. If the rebels are organized and exercise authority over a part of the territory, they obtain certain belligerent rights; the situation becomes that of a civil war and, in practice, the distinction tends to be effaced between "legitimate authority" and "rebels," which appear as two rival governments, the outcome of the war deciding the legality or illegality of the belligerents. International law can merely ratify the fate of arms and the arbitration of force. In a few years the Algerian FLN changed from a band of "rebels" to "a government in exile." In a few more, in the name of national sovereignty, it functioned freely within the frontiers of an independent Algeria.

Jurists have elaborated the rules that are to be imposed upon states or that the latter ought to impose in case of civil war. In fact, practice varies, even in modern times, as a result of many circumstances. There are, as we have seen, two extreme cases: the homogeneous system can lead to the Holy Alliance, to the common defense of the established order, to the repression by the French army of the Spanish Revolution of 1827 or by the Russian army of the Hungarian Revolution of 1848. On the other hand, in a heterogeneous system, each camp supports the rebels opposing a regime favorable to the enemy camp. The rules of "non-intervention" were elaborated and more or less applied during intermediate periods, when neither powers nor revolutionaries had partisans across the frontiers. If there exists neither a popular nor a royal *internationale*, states abstain from siding with the sovereign or the rebels, because in fact the victory of the one or the other does not profoundly affect them.

Juridical norms need to be interpreted. Their meaning is not always evident and their application to a specific case leads to controversy. Now international law does not determine the organ that, in regard to interpretation, holds the supreme power. If states have not promised to submit their cases to the International Court of Justice,[8] each signatory actually reserves the right of interpreting the treaties in its own way. As states have different juridical and political conceptions, the international law to which they subscribe will involve contradictory interpretations, will be split, in fact, into many orders, based on the same texts but leading to incompatible results.

Moreover, states need only fail to "recognize" the same states or the same governments, to reveal the scope of these incompatible interpretations. Supposing that states agree on their conduct with regard to "rebels" or "legal

[8] Or if they remain judges of the application of such a promise.

government," it is enough that a group of men be rebels in the eyes of some and, in the eyes of others, represent the legal authority, for the juridical order, embracing a heterogeneous system, to reveal its internal contradiction. States will not attach the same descriptions to the same situations of fact. The FLN was treated as a "band of rebels" by some, as a legal government by others. The government of the German Democratic Republic is a "so-called government" or an "authentic government." The crossing of the 38th Parallel by the North Korean armies was a "civil-war episode" or an "act of aggression."

It will be objected that such interpretations are not probable to the same degree, and there is no denying the fact. The Korean demarcation line had been drawn by agreement between the Soviet Union and the United States. The FLN "rebels" exerted no regular power over any part of the Algerian territory in 1958. Objectively, to an observer applying traditional criteria unburdened by ideology, one interpretation would be preferable to another. But why should states apply this interpretation if it is not favorable to their undertakings? States are anxious to maintain the juridical order that suits their common interest when they recognize each other's regimes. But this reciprocal recognition is limited, in a heterogeneous system, by ideological rivalry. Each camp seeks not necessarily to destroy the states in the other camp, but to weaken or overthrow their regimes: juridical interpretation, even when it is concretely improbable, is utilized as an instrument of subversive war, a means of diplomatic pressure.

Lastly, supposing that the community of states is in agreement as to the true interpretation (in Hungary, the legal government was that of Imre Nagy, the insurrection was staged by the people and not by foreign agitators or American agents), it is still necessary to punish or constrain the state violating the law. Here, too, international law differs, on an essential point, from municipal law. The only effective sanction against the state that has committed the illicit act is the use of force. The guilty state also possesses arms, it does not agree to submit to the judgment of an arbitrator or to the vote of an assembly. Hence an effort to enforce the law will involve a risk of war. Either Gribouille or Gandhi: to punish the violators of the law, a war is precipitated which it was the law's function to forestall; or else the injustice is merely proclaimed and endured, although the conquerors are usually less sensitive to non-violence than the British of the twentieth century.

Does this international law, which involves neither indisputable interpretation nor effective sanction, which applies to subjects whose birth and death it is limited to certifying, which cannot last indefinitely but which cannot be revised, does this international law belong to the same genre as municipal law? Most jurists reply in the affirmative, and I shall not contradict them. I prefer to show differences between kinds rather than deny membership in the same genre.

4. Legalize War or Outlaw It?

The very title of Grotius' famous work, *De Jure Belli et Pacis*, does not treat the entire substance of international law, but certainly covers its principal objects. Yet this formula suffices to suggest the dilemma confronting jurists and philosophers: Must international law legalize war or, on the contrary, proscribe it? Must it foresee or exclude the possibility of war? Must it limit or outlaw war?

Before 1914 the answer, given by history, was unambiguous. European public international law had never taken the outlawing of war as its object or principle. Quite the contrary, it provided the forms in which war must be declared, it forbade the use of certain means, it regulated the modes of armistice and the signing of peace, it imposed obligations upon the neutral powers with regard to the belligerents, upon the belligerents with regard to civilian populations, prisoners, etc. In short, it legalized and limited war, it did not make it a crime.

War being legal, the belligerents could regard each other as enemies without hating or vituperating each other. States fought, not persons. No doubt a war's legality did not settle the moral question of discovering whether or not it was just. But the belligerent, even when responsible for an unjust war, still remained a legal enemy.[9]

Why did the classical jurists maintain *moral judgments* as to the respective conduct of states in conflict side by side with *juridical judgments* which legalized the conflicts for both sides? The reason was clearly indicated in the works of the seventeenth and above all the eighteenth century: granted that monarchs, if they are wise and virtuous, should not wage war for glory or amusement, covet lands or wealth that do not belong to them, yet how could sovereigns neglect the requirements of their security? If a prince accumulates so many forces that he will soon be in a position to crush his neighbors, will the latter passively suffer the destruction of an equilibrium that is the only guarantee of security in inter-state relations?

The classical jurists were not only aware of the ambiguities we have analyzed above, the necessary distinction between initiating hostilities and aggression, between the responsibility for origins and the responsibility for the stakes; *they admitted the moral legitimacy of action dictated by the requirements of equilibrium, even if this action were aggressive.* They would have subscribed, with varying degrees of reservation, to Montes-

[9] For instance, Emer de Vattel, in *Le Droit des gens ou principes de la loi naturelle appliqués à la conduite et aux affaires des nations et des souverains* (1758), Book III, Chap. 3, paragraph 39: "However, it may happen that the contenders are each acting in good faith; and in a doubtful cause it is still uncertain on which side the right may be. Since, then, the nations are equal and independent and cannot make themselves judges of each other, it follows that in any case susceptible of doubt, the arms of both sides making war must equally pass as legitimate, at least as to external effects and until the cause is decided." Or again, more concisely: "War in form, as to its effects, must be regarded as just on either side." (Book III, Chap. 12, paragraph 190.)

quieu's formula[10] quoted above, according to which "the right of natural defense sometimes involves the necessity of attacking." Hence it became difficult to establish with certainty which was the true aggressor (and not the apparent aggressor). The morality of equilibrium involved a kind of casuistry and did not exclude recourse to arms.

Rousseau and Hegel alike have furnished extreme expressions of the key ideas of this European law of nations. In the *Contrat social*, Rousseau writes: "War is not a relation between man and man, but between state and state, in which individuals are enemies only occasionally, not as men nor even as fellow citizens, but as soldiers. Not as members of their nation, but as its defenders. Lastly, each state may have as its enemy only other states, and not men, since among things of different natures, no true relation can be deduced." In a purely inter-state war, individuals have no motive for hating each other, and a victorious state must cease doing harm to the subjects of the enemy state, once the latter admits defeat. Violence is limited to the clash of armies.

Still more radical are Hegel's texts, in the last part of the *Philosophy of Law*. "International law results from relations of independent states. Its content in and for itself has a prescriptive form because its realization depends on distinct sovereign wills." Such a formula is equivalent to suggesting that because of the plurality of sovereign states, the concrete obligations of international law cannot be enforced by sanctions: they remain prescriptive, like morality.

"The basis of international law as a universal law which must be valid in and for itself among states, insofar as it differs from the specific content of contracts, is that treaties must be respected. *Pacta sunt servanda.* For it is upon them that the obligations of states in relation to each other rest. But since their relation has their sovereignty as its principle, they are, in relation to each other, in the state of nature and do not have their law in a universal will authoritatively established over and above them, but their reciprocal relation has its reality in a particular will." The formula is precisely the one suggested by the analyses of the preceding section. International law consists of commitments made, implicitly or explicitly, by states to each other. Since states do not lose their sovereignty the day they make these commitments, war remains possible either because the parties

[10] Vattel has reservations as to Montesquieu's formula, preferring confederations to preventive war in order to maintain equilibrium, yet he writes (Book III, Chap. 3, paragraph 42): "It is unfortunate for the human race that one can almost always presume the will to oppress where one finds the power to oppress without punishment. . . . It is perhaps unprecedented that a state should receive some notable increase in power without giving others good cause for complaint. . . ." And lastly this formula on the legitimacy of preventive attack: "One is justified in forestalling a danger by reason of both the degree of appearance and the greatness of the evil by which one is threatened."

are not in agreement as to the interpretation of the treaties, or because one or the other desires to modify its terms.

"On the other hand, even in war as a non-juridical situation of violence and contingency, there exists a connection in the fact that states recognize each other as such. In this connection they are valid for each other as existing in and for themselves. So that in war itself, war is determined as necessarily transitory." War is the juridical state, foreseen in advance, that suspends most of the obligations that states contract toward one another in peacetime, but that do not thereby lose all legal character. The belligerents do not employ any and all means, and when violence breaks out they do not forget the future restoration of their juridical relations (a valid proposition, on condition that the very existence of the state is not the stake of the hostilities).

This classical conception had always seemed unsatisfactory to some philosophers; it was scarcely compatible with the obligatory character of law, and it became unacceptable to popular opinion after the First World War. So many dead, so much material destruction, so many horrors could no longer be accepted as in accord with the course of human events. War must no longer be an episode in inter-state relations, it should be outlawed, in the true sense of the word. The victors having decreed that the vanquished were responsible for the outbreak of hostilities, the initiation of hostilities was regarded, retrospectively, as criminal. A League of Nations was established whose task was to maintain the peace. Ten years later, at the instigation of the United States, the Kellogg-Briand peace pact proclaimed still more formally the illegality of war as a political instrument.

The juridical system of the League of Nations and of the Kellogg-Briand peace pact collapsed because the dissatisfied states sought to modify the established order and because the international organ did not have the means either to impose by peaceful methods the changes justice eventually required or to stop the revolutionary states. When Japan transformed Manchuria into Manchukuo and was condemned by the League of Nations, she left Geneva. The aggression was flagrant, but what could the League do if the states with power were determined not to use it? Similarly, Germany left Geneva when it did not obtain satisfaction in the matter of disarmament.

The Italian invasion of Ethiopia did not differ much from other European undertakings in Asia or Africa. But since Ethiopia had been admitted to the League of Nations, since the principle of equality of nations, whether great or small, civilized or barbarian,[11] had been proclaimed, the Italian conquest could not be tolerated without destroying the very foundations of the juridical order born of the First World War and French policy.

[11] Supposing that one can still, according to the ideas of our epoch, distinguish the one from the other.

Sanctions were voted and partially applied, but the League refrained from applying the sanction that had the greatest likelihood of being effective (petroleum). Yet let us recall, the member states of the League of Nations, even the two major ones alone (France and Great Britain), outclassed Italy, which Germany, then rearming, could not support. The risk that Italy would answer the threat of force with force was slight, so striking was the disparity between the aggressor's resources on the one hand, and those of the conservative powers on the other. Either because Paris or London did not wish to upset the Fascist regime, or because they wished to avoid any risk of war whatever, only those sanctions that could neither paralyze Italy nor provoke a military rejoinder from her were applied. Whatever the motives of statesmen, it was apparent that governments and peoples were not accepting the sacrifices of conflict for a cause that would not have been or would not have seemed strictly national. If the international law that forbids aggressions and conquests has its origin in transnational society, the latter did not exist or existed only ineffectually, judging by the emotions and desires of men.

Juridical formalism, seeking to exclude war as a means of settling differences or modifying territorial status, has not been abandoned in the wake of failure, landmarked by the wars in Manchuria, Ethiopia, China, and finally the double, generalized war in Europe and the Far East. In 1945 an attempt was made to use the international law outlawing war to punish the Nazi leaders. During the Nuremberg trials "the conspiracy against peace" was only one of the indictments made against the leaders of the Third Reich, and war crimes do not concern us in the present context. On the other hand, the attempt to shift from aggression, an international crime, to the determination and punishment of the guilty illustrates an aspect of the problem that appears once international law tries to deduce all the consequences of "outlawing war."

Among the belligerents, one—state or bloc—is juridically criminal. What is the result of this "incrimination" of war that was once merely called unjust? Optimistically, let us suppose that the criminal state is defeated. How is it to be punished, and where are the criminals? Suppose we punish the state itself—in other words, amputate its territory, forbid it to arm, and deprive it of a share of its sovereignty. Now what matters most is that the clauses of the peace treaty prevent war's return: is it wise that the desire for punishment, however legitimate, should influence the treatment of the enemy and the clauses of the peace treaty? And we are considering, let us recall, the optimistic hypothesis. It is easy to imagine the use that the victorious Reich would have made of its right to punish the "criminal" states (Poland, France, Great Britain).

If it is a question of punishing not the state or the nation but the persons by whose agency the state has committed the "crime against the peace," a single formula would be quite satisfactory, the one that occurs in several speeches of Sir Winston Churchill: *One man, one man alone.* If one man alone has taken the decisions that have committed a people, if one man alone possessed absolute power and acted in solitude, then this man incarnated the criminal state and deserves to be punished for the nation's crime. But such a hypothesis is never completely fulfilled, the leader's companions have shared in his decision, have conspired with him against peace and for conquest. How far is the search for the guilty to be carried? To what degree are the duties of obedience or national solidarity to be considered as absolving excuses?

Further, even if this search for the criminal individuals, who must pay for the state whose leaders or instruments they chose to be, were juridically satisfactory, it would remain fraught with dangers. Would statesmen yield before having exhausted every means of resistance, if they knew that in the enemy's eyes they are criminals and will be treated as such in case of defeat? It is perhaps immoral, but it is most often wise, to spare the leaders of an enemy state, for otherwise these men will sacrifice the lives and wealth and possessions of their fellow citizens or their subjects in the vain hope of saving themselves. If war as such is criminal, it will be inexpiable.

Further still: even in the case of the last war, for which the major responsibility was manifestly Germany's, it is far from the case that innocent states and guilty states were all on one side or the other. Before 1939 the international system was *heterogeneous.* A complex heterogeneity, moreover, since three regimes were in conflict, profoundly hostile to one another, each of them inclined to put its two adversaries "in the same sack." To the Communists, fascism and parliamentary government were only two modes of capitalism. To the Western powers, communism and fascism represented two versions of totalitarianism. To the fascists, parliamentary government and communism, expressions of democratic and rationalist thought, marked two stages in degeneration, that of plutocracy and that of despotic leveling. But under duress each of these regimes consented to acknowledge elements of relationship with one of its adversaries. During the war Stalin distinguished between the fascisms that destroyed workers' organizations and liberties and the regimes of bourgeois democracy which at least tolerated unions and parties. But at the time of the Russo-German Pact, he hailed the love of the German people for their Führer and the "meeting of two revolutions." The Western democracies, at the time of the anti-fascist coalition or of the Great Alliance, believed they discovered a community of aspiration with the Left, but when the Iron Curtain fell on the demarcation line, they recalled that Red totalitarianism was worth no more than the Brownshirt variety had been. As for the fascists, they were ready, depending on circumstances, to ally themselves with either communism in the interests of the revolution, or with the bourgeois democracies against Soviet barbarism and for the defense of civilization.

This ternary heterogeneity, as it might be called, excluded the formation of blocs depending on the internal regime, a circumstance resulting from ideological dualism. It also gave the advantage to those states, tactically free in their maneuvers, capable of allying themselves with one of their enemies against the other. Now France and Great Britain could ally themselves with the Soviet Union against fascism (though it required imminent aggression for the Right to agree to such a step), but they could not ally themselves with fascism, because of the unshakable opposition of the Left. Finally, the Soviet Union had the most trumps, since it accepted any kind of enemy as a provisional ally and was similarly accepted by any of them.

The Soviet Union and the Western democracies had one interest in common: to prevent the Third Reich from outstripping one or another of the hostile blocs. But forestalling war was to the interest of France and England, not necessarily of the Soviet Union. To turn the first German aggression westward corresponded to Soviet interest, as it would have corresponded to the Western interest that the Soviet Union should receive the first attack. The Russo-German Pact did not extend beyond the framework of traditional Machiavellianism.

But once all the states were participating in this tragic game, the Soviet aggression against Poland, then against Finland and the Baltic countries, however incontestable on the juridical level, could be interpreted as a defensive reply, by anticipation, to the foreseeable Hitlerian aggression. When the intentions of a neighboring and powerful state are obvious, must the designated victim wait passively? The invasion of Germany by French troops in March 1936 would perhaps have been condemned by world opinion; it would have saved the peace. The classical jurists were familiar with the impossibility of resorting to the criterion of "initiative" alone to establish responsibility, and they regarded it as the major reason for legalizing war. As for the Nuremberg judges, who included one Russian, they obviously ignored the aggression of which the Soviet Union, according to the letter of the law, was incontestably guilty with regard to Poland, Finland and the Baltic States. An inevitable discretion, but one that illustrates all too well the formula of injustice: *two weights, two measures.*

In the prewar international system the desire of dissatisfied states to upset the status quo was the primary datum. Among those states threatened by this revolutionary desire, some were more conservative and others less. But all being eager to prevent a German hegemony, each hoped to stop Hitler with a minimum of expense to itself, and to derive a maximum of benefit from the victory. Finally, the expenses were enormous for all, but the benefits were also enormous for the one that had, perhaps out of fear of the coalition of the capitalist nations, given Hitler the occasion to loose the holocaust.

In such a circumstance it is easier for the moralist to blame these maneuvers than for the politician to find a substitute for them.

5. Ambiguities of Recognition and Aggression

The juridical order created after the Second World War and of which the United Nations is the expression is based on the same principles as the Versailles Covenant of the League of Nations. This time the United States has inspired this order and desires to maintain it, instead of suggesting its conception and thereafter withdrawing, as it had done after the First World War.

This juridical order henceforth extends to almost all the world's population (Germany, by reason of its division, and Communist China being the two notable exceptions), and thereby applies to realities historically and politically heterogeneous. The heterogeneity, masked by the principle of equality of nations, is that of the political units themselves: Yemen, Liberia, Haiti are proclaimed sovereign with the same qualification and the same prerogatives as the Soviet Union, Great Britain and the United States. Some regard this as decisive progress in relation to diplomatic circumstances early in the century, when Europeans considered their domination over so many non-Europeans quite natural. Fortunate or not, the development is incontestable: fifty years ago, juridical equality was granted to few states outside the European and American sphere; today it is granted to all, whatever their resources or institutions. International law, which was first that of the Christian nations, then that of the civilized nations, is henceforth applied to the nations of all continents, provided they are peace-loving.[12]

Even more than historical heterogeneity,[13] political heterogeneity burdens the juridical order. Communist states and democratic states are not only different, they are, as such, enemies. The Soviet leaders, according to their doctrine, regard the capitalist states as committed to belligerent expansion and condemned to death. America's leaders, according to their interpretation of Communist ideology, are convinced that the masters of the Kremlin aspire to world domination. In other words, the states in each bloc do not present, in the eyes of the other bloc, that peace-loving character which, according to the Charter,[14] would qualify them for United Nations membership. The liberal states, if they acted according to the logic of their convictions, would not admit the totalitarian ones, which they regard as imperialist, into the international juridical community, and the latter would adopt the same attitude with regard to them.

As a matter of fact, the decision was taken to ignore this political and historical heterogeneity, at least at Lake Success or in New York. NATO and the Warsaw Pact, whose spokesmen exchange Homeric insults and whose member states multiply military preparations, express the real hostilities, implied by facts and ideas. In the United Nations the states, externally hostile,

---

12 Cf. B. V. A. Röling: *International Law in an Expanded World*, Amsterdam, 1960.
13 Cf. below, Chap. XIII.
14 Article 4.

find themselves within the same assembly and, depending on the day, give each other evidence of their good intentions or accuse each other of the worst misdeeds.

As to the historical inequalities of nations, they have been taken into account only with regard to the choice of five permanent members of the Security Council (the United States, the Soviet Union, Great Britain, France, China). In 1961 the Chinese seat remained occupied by the representatives of Chiang Kai-shek—that is, of the so-called Nationalist regime which had taken refuge in Formosa. In the Assembly, one vote is as good as another,[15] although the Great Powers possess, in fact, a clientele.

The circumstance of juridical and historical heterogeneity on the one hand, and the juridical formalism of equality of nations on the other, gives the notion of recognition a decisive importance. Since a state has the right to handle internally everything pertaining to its sovereignty, since it even has the right[16] of appealing to foreign troops, everything depends on what I shall call *the governmental incarnation of the state*. The same facts receive a contrary juridical description depending on whether one government or the other is *recognized* as legal.

The sending of American forces to Lebanon and of British forces to Jordan (1958) was not regarded as contrary to international law and the United Nations Charter because it occurred upon the request of the "legal governments." If the King of Iraq and Nuri Saïd had escaped the conspirators[17] and appealed to English and American troops for help, would the latter's intervention have been illegal? Let us suppose that the Hungarian government, legal in the eyes of the United Nations, had not been that of Imre Nagy but that of the "Stalinists"; the intervention of the Russian divisions, called in by the "legal government," would then have been scarcely more contrary to international juridical formalism than the landing of American troops in Lebanon. Starting from the determination of the "subject of law," the consequences inexorably follow: in some cases one wonders if a certain *de facto* state (the German Democratic Republic, North Korea) will be recognized as a "subject of law," a legal state; in others, one wonders which group of men or which party represents the state, whose existence no one denies (the two blocs do not put the existence of a Hungarian state in doubt, but did Kadar or Nagy preside over the legal government on November 3, 1956?[18]).

Thus we see that the problem of recognition has been at the core of diplomatic discussions since 1945, whether Korea, China or Germany was in

[15] The Soviet Union, of course, possesses three votes, the Ukraine and White Russia being regarded as states.
[16] Which the jurists dispute but which has become a practice.
[17] A further reason, for the latter, to put them to death immediately.
[18] On November 3, 1957, there was no longer any doubt that it was the Kadar government: international law forgets the birth and death of governments.

question. Jurists had elaborated "implicitly normative" theories of recognition, held forth on the distinction between *de facto* and *de jure* recognition, observed the various practices of states. These practices and distinctions are illuminated only by reference to policy.

Let us start from an uncontested proposition: according to custom, states enjoy a certain liberty of recognizing or not recognizing any state which has just been created (Guinea in 1958) or any government which has just assumed power. The United States has employed non-recognition in dealing with the revolutionary governments of South America, and with "territorial modifications imposed by force," non-recognition being a diplomatic instrument. The American leaders hoped to prevent *coups d'état* or conquests by letting it be known in advance that they would not acknowledge the consequences. The United States took years to extend *de jure* recognition to the Soviet Union (sixteen in fact: from 1917 to 1933). Although *de jure* recognition does not constitute an approval of the methods and principles of the regime to which it is granted, the diplomats have added one concept, that of *de facto* recognition, halfway between non-recognition and full and complete recognition.[19]

The weapon of non-recognition has been ultimately ineffectual, against both revolutions and conquests. The leaders of a revolution, like those of the imperialist state, know that in the long run the power of reality is irresistible. It is impossible to ignore the *de facto* authorities indefinitely, on the pretext that their origins are disagreeable and their methods reprehensible. Yet recognition has not thereby become simple and automatic. On the contrary, one might distinguish, sociologically if not juridically, two modes of *de facto recognition* and two modes of *de jure recognition*.

I should call *implicit de facto recognition* the kind that consists in dealing with a *de facto* authority, while denying its legal existence. Such is the case with the relations of the Western states with the German Democratic Republic (Deutsche Demokratische Republik, or D.D.R.). To reduce as much as possible the element of recognition which the contracts contain, the Western powers, in particular the Bonn leaders, have insisted that the economic agreements between the two Germanies be signed by functionaries of inferior rank. There would be *de facto* recognition if agreements in good and due form, on the governmental level, were concluded with the D.D.R.

As for *de jure* recognition, it has, depending on circumstances, two historically different meanings. If the regimes of the states that recognize each other are the same, or different but not opposed, the recognition is valid in

---

[19] The distinction is juridically dubious, since recognition, even *de jure*, could only be the recognition of a fact, the fact that a state or a regime or a government exists. The actual government, by a group of men, of an independent collectivity—such must be the non-ideological meaning of recognition, but, in a heterogeneous system, recognition always has political consequences and ideological implications. Hence governments use the modalities of recognition, or non-recognition, for their own purposes.

all circumstances. The states could fight each other without either one attempting to overthrow the other's regime and instigate or support rebels. On
the other hand, when two states whose regimes are directly contradictory
grant each other *de jure* recognition, neither of the two governments established at the beginning of the hostilities would survive defeat. Even in
peacetime, ideological hostility is expressed in many ways, neither of the states
being capable of completely separating national interests and ideological interests.

Over all the territories liberated by Eastern and Western armies, the dispute of recognition has assumed a harsh character. In Korea, only the Republic of South Korea was recognized by the United Nations, North Korea
having stubbornly refused to apply the U.N. decisions relative to free elections and unification. Further, the crossing of the 38th Parallel was the
action of the North Korean army; responsibility for the aggression (initiation
of hostilities) was therefore unequivocal. But, according to Soviet ideological
interpretation, the North Korean aggression was primarily a civil war, the
attempt of the true (Communist) Korea to free the Koreans established on
the other side of the demarcation line from the imperialist yoke. In appearance, the United Nations succeeded in mobilizing the neutral powers against
the aggressor, a feat the League of Nations had been unable to accomplish
against Italy. In reality, it was the American action that assured resistance to
the aggressor and not a United Nations decision, which was effected only by
the absence of the Soviet Union.[20] Further, the victim suffered no less than
the aggressor, and the United Nations command, far from punishing North
Koreans and Chinese aggressors, dealt with them in the fashion of any
government that was eager to end, by a peace without victory, a secondary
conflict.

In Germany the Western powers refuse to extend *de facto* or *de jure*
recognition to the D.D.R., because in their eyes the Bonn Republic represents
all Germany. The Soviets, on the contrary, recognize the Federal Republic to
the same degree that they recognize the D.D.R.; they have everything to
gain from such a recognition, which serves them as an argument with regard
to the Western powers, who are urged to treat Pankow as they themselves
treat Bonn.

Stranger still is the non-recognition of Communist China by the United
States and most of the Western powers. The Peking regime exhibits the
characteristics of a legal government, at least as much as the regimes of
Eastern Europe. Washington may regard it as illegitimate, but in that case it
should regard the Soviet regime in Russia as illegitimate too. As for the
Chinese aggression in Korea or the treatment of a number of American citizens, these facts do not differ from those that might be invoked against the
Soviet Union. Non-recognition is merely the means of preserving the prestige
of legality for the Chiang Kai-shek government. Similarly, the United States

---

[20] Because of this fact, the legality of the decision is in doubt.

defends Formosa, Quemoy and Matsu against the ventures of the Chinese Communists as the result of an agreement with the legal government of China.

Thus the Peking government is not "recognized" by a number of the Western states, although it presents all the characteristics of *de facto* government (effective control of territory and population), necessary and sufficient, according to most jurists, to justify recognition. Conversely, the FLN, established in Cairo or Tunis, was recognized by most governments of the Arab nations, though it exercised no regular authority over any portion of the Algerian territory. In a heterogeneous system, recognition is a means of diplomatic or military action. It aims at morally reinforcing improvised or revolutionary organizations. The recognition of the FLN was a proclamation of sympathy for the Nationalist Algerian camp, the affirmation that French policy was condemned and the rebel action sanctified by the principle of self-determination. Let us conclude the analysis: for the determination of the subjects of law to be unequivocal, the principle of legitimacy and its interpretation must be unequivocal too, in which case, in what manner must self-determination be applied? By what methods must governments be chosen? But the very heterogeneity that prevents an unequivocal determination of the subjects of law also forbids reaching a definition, unanimously accepted, of aggression.

The reasons why attempts to define aggression have failed are many and complex.[21] The attitudes of the various states on this subject have been, in each circumstance, dictated by considerations of expedience. In 1945 the Americans tried to introduce a definition (one which had been elaborated by the disarmament conference of 1933) into the statute of the Nuremberg tribunal, and the Russians stubbornly opposed it. Ten years later it was the Russians who favored a definition of aggression in the United Nations and the Americans who had meanwhile become hostile to it. A definition of aggression seems to me impossible and, further, useless, whatever the character of the international system. By the term *aggression*, diplomats, jurists and mere citizens designate, more or less vaguely, an *illegitimate* use, direct or indirect, of force. Now relations among states have been and are such that it is not possible to find the general and abstract criteria in the light of which the distinction between legitimate and illegitimate use of force would be automatic and obvious.

If all use of armed force, in every circumstance, is illegitimate, the threat of such use is no less so. But how can a threat be disclosed that has no need of being explicit in order to be effective? What rights should be granted to the state that is, and regards itself as being, threatened? It is true that the United Nations Charter forbids the threat as much as the use of force, but

[21] A detailed study of the attempts to define aggression in the League of Nations and the United Nations will be found in the work of M. Eugene Aroneanu, *La définition de l'agression*, Paris, 1958.

such a formula is pure hypocrisy: lacking a tribunal capable of deciding differences equitably, all states have relied and continue to rely on themselves to obtain justice; none genuinely subscribes to the view that threats in the service of a just cause are, as such, culpable.

Further, it would be an oversimplification to consider armed force and the direct use of this force alone. If we seek to elaborate an international penal code, we must define the delinquencies and the crimes that states are capable of committing outside the extreme crime of "the use of armed force." The various means of constraint or of economic, psychological and political attack must also be condemned. But what procedures of "economic pressure" are culpable? Which propaganda is criminal, and which is tolerable?

In short, in a homogeneous system, it is impossible to define aggression because the recourse to force (or to the threat of force) is intrinsically linked to the relations among states desiring to be independent. In a heterogeneous system, it is impossible to define aggression because the regimes in conflict assail each other continuously and commit, with good conscience, the crime of indirect or ideological aggression.

Futile attempts have been made to overcome the first obstacle by defining, in general terms or by enumeration, the circumstances in which the recourse to force would be either legitimate or illegitimate. But this has merely extended or multiplied the difficulties. If the use of force is legal in the case of legitimate defense, this latter concept requires definition. If we refer to the sequence of events, if the aggressor is the one who initiates the hostility, we are caught in the casuistry of *attack* and *initiative*. We do not always know who started the hostilities. The initiator is not always the disturber of the peace. The state in danger does not always have time to employ the procedures known as peaceful.

Further, must the state that does not receive justice (according to its conception of justice) endure injustice indefinitely? The enumeration of the circumstances in which the recourse to force is not legitimate risks guaranteeing the impunity of those who violate the law, encouraging international anarchy and finally provoking the very thing that it has attempted to prevent.

In a heterogeneous system, only "armed aggression," the crossing of frontiers by regular armies, is clearly identifiable. All forms of indirect aggression are common practice. It is ironic but not surprising that the Soviet representatives serving on the U.N. committees to define aggression have proposed the following formula: "Any state will be recognized as guilty of indirect aggression which:

a) Encourages subversive activities directed against another state (acts of terrorism, sabotage, etc.);

b) Foments civil war in another state;

c) Favors an uprising in another state or political changes favorable to the aggressor."[22]

---

[22] Aroneanu, *op. cit.*, p. 292.

Of course, in the eyes of the Soviets, only the Atlantic bloc knows the "criminal" secrets of subversive war.

In 1933 a committee known as the Politis Committee defined aggression by enumeration of cases. Four of these five cases were readily predictable[23]: "declaration of war against another state; invasion by armed forces, even without declaration of war, of the territory of another state; attack by land, naval or air forces, even without declaration of war, of the territory, ships or airships of another state; naval blockade of the coasts or ports of another state." Providing that the side taking the initiative be regarded as the guilty one, all these cases are simple. But the fifth case assumes, today, a strange relevance. "Support given to armed groups which, formed on its territory, have invaded the territory of another state; or the refusal, despite the demand of the state invaded, to take, on its own territory, all the measures in its power to deprive the said groups of all aid or protection."

Let us consider only this last case: the organization or toleration of armed groups contradicts, in effect, the ancient customs of intercourse among states, but, supposing that a nation becomes guilty of such indirect aggression, what should the corresponding reaction be? Protests are ineffective, military intervention risks returning us to the simpleton's equation: respect for international law equals war by sanctions. It is not certain that the French army would have pursued the groups of Algerian rebels into Tunisian and Moroccan territory, even if the United Nations did not exist.

The Politis definition added an enumeration of the circumstances that did not legitimize the military action of a foreign state: "The interior situation of a state, for instance its political, economic or social structure, the alleged defects of its administration, the disturbances resulting from strikes, revolutions, counterrevolutions or civil wars; the international conduct of a state, for instance a violation or the danger of violation of the rights or material or moral interests of a foreign state or its members, the rupture of diplomatic or economic relations, measures of economic or financial boycott, disputes relative to economic or financial commitments or other commitments to foreign states, frontier incidents not referring to one of the cases of aggression indicated in the first article." The prohibition against intervention in revolution or counterrevolution applies directly to the Soviet action in Hungary, as the prohibition against using force to defend material interests endangered by a foreign state precisely describes the Franco-British action against Egypt. This definition of aggression had been inserted in many pacts concluded by the Soviet Union, in particular those with the Baltic nations and Finland.[24] The latter were not saved thereby. The United Nations has finally abandoned defining aggression and prefers to utilize the other concepts included in the Charter: breaking the peace, the threat to peace or to international security, attack on the territorial integrity or the political independence of states. It

[23] *Ibid.*, p. 281.
[24] *Ibid.*, p. 286.

limits the use of the term *aggression* to a single case, that of the crossing of a state's frontiers by regular troops of another state without the former's consent. Propaganda, agents of subversion, terrorist commandos pass across or through frontiers without being formally condemned by the international organizations or even by the interpreters of international law.

Juridical formalism has yielded to the realities of the cold war.

No juridical system has answered, even theoretically, two basic questions: how can any modification of the status quo be prevented from occurring as a result of a violation of law? Or again, to formulate the same question in different words, in the name of what criteria can an arbitrator or a tribunal dictate those peaceful changes without which any particular international law, based on the will of states, must be conservative? The rights and duties of states being, by hypothesis, precisely defined, how can the *de facto* organic groups be defined that deserve to be regarded as states?

The League of Nations did not answer the first question. The United Nations is seeking an answer to the second, but the historical and juridical heterogeneity of the world system prohibits it from finding it.

chapter V

On Multipolar Systems and Bipolar Systems

Foreign policy, in and of itself, is power politics. Therefore the concept of equilibrium—balance—applies to all international systems up to the Atomic Age (but perhaps not including it).

In the course of the preceding chapters we have distinguished *forces*—the various means of pressure or constraint which states possess—and *power*—the capacity of states, each taken as a unit, to influence the others. Thus we deliberately use the expressions *power politics* and *balance of forces*. The first means that states recognize neither arbitrator nor tribunal nor laws superior to their will and, consequently, owe their existence and their security only to themselves or their allies. If I prefer "balance of forces" to "balance of power," it is because forces are more measurable than power. But if forces are balanced, powers too are balanced, approximately. No state imposes its sovereign will on others unless it possesses resources so decisive that its rivals admit in advance the futility of resistance.

1. The Policy of Equilibrium

It is in Hume's brief essay entitled "On the Balance of Power" that the abstract theory of equilibrium is set forth with the most convincing simplicity.

David Hume takes as his point of departure this question: is the idea of equilibrium a modern one or is the formula alone of recent invention, the idea itself being as old as the world? The second term of the alternative is correct: "In all the politics of Greece, the anxiety with regard to the balance of power is apparent, and is expressly pointed out to us, even by the ancient historians. Thucydides represents the league which was formed against Athens, and which produced the Peloponnesian War, as entirely owing to this principle. And after the decline of Athens, when the Thebans and Lacedaemonians disputed for sovereignty, we find that the Athenians (as well as many other republics) always threw themselves into the lighter scale, and endeavored to preserve the balance."

The Persian Empire behaved in the same way: "The Persian monarch was really, in his force, a petty prince, compared to the Grecian republics; and, therefore, it behooved him, from views of safety more than from emulation, to interest himself in their quarrels, and to support the weaker side in every contest." Alexander's successors followed the same principle: "They showed great jealousy of the balance of power; a jealousy founded on true politics and prudence, and which preserved distinct for several ages the partition made after the death of that famous conqueror." The nations capable of intervening in the war belong to the system: "As the Eastern princes considered the Greeks and Macedonians as the only real military force with whom they had any intercourse, they kept always a watchful eye over that part of the world."

If the ancients seem to have ignored the policy of equilibrium, the reason is the astonishing history of the Roman Empire. It is a fact that Rome was able to conquer her adversaries one after another, for they were unable to conclude in time the alliances which would have saved them. Philip of Macedon remained neutral until the time of Hannibal's victories and then imprudently concluded with the conqueror an alliance "upon terms still more imprudent." The Rhodean and Achaean republics, whose wisdom is celebrated by the historians of antiquity, offered assistance to the Romans in their wars against Philip and Antiochus. "Massinissa, Attalus, Prusias, in gratifying their private passions, were all of them instruments of the Roman greatness, and never seemed to have suspected that they were forging their own chains, while they advanced the conquests of their ally." The only prince who, in the course of Roman history, seems to have understood the principle of equilibrium is Hiero, King of Syracuse: "Nor ought such a force ever to be thrown into one hand as to incapacitate the neighboring states from defending their rights against it." Such is the more simple formula of equilibrium: a state should never possess such strength that neighboring states would be incapable of defending their rights against it. The formula, based as it is on "common sense and obvious reasoning," is too simple to have escaped the ancients.

By virtue of the same principle, Hume then analyzes the European system and the rivalry of France and England. "A new power succeeded, more formidable to the liberties of Europe, possessing all the advantages of the former, and laboring under none of its defects, except a share of that spirit of bigotry and persecution, with which the House of Austria was so long, and still is, so much infatuated." Against the French monarchy, which had been victorious in four wars out of five but which had nonetheless not greatly enlarged its dominion nor acquired a "total ascendancy over Europe," England was in the forefront. We cannot help being amused today by Hume's criticism of English policy. Like the Greeks, he says, "we seem to have been more possessed with the ancient Greek spirit of jealous emulation than actuated by the prudent views of modern politics." England has without profit continued wars begun justifiably and, perhaps more, out of necessity but which might have been concluded sooner under the same conditions. England's hostility to France seems a certainty in any event, and the Allies count on the English forces as on their own and are quite uncompromising in their demands, England being obliged to assume the cost of hostilities. Finally, "we are such true combatants that, when once engaged, we lose all concern for ourselves and our posterity, and consider only how we may best annoy the enemy."

The excesses of belligerent ardor seem to Hume vexing because of the economic sacrifices they involve, but he regards them as particularly dangerous because they risk some day leading England to the opposite extreme: "rendering us totally careless and supine with regard to the fate of Europe. The Athenians, from the most bustling, intriguing, war-like people of Greece, finding their error in thrusting themselves into every quarrel, abandon all attention to foreign affairs; and in no contest ever took part, except by their flatteries and complaisance to the victor."

David Hume favors the policy of equilibrium because he is opposed to huge empires: "Enormous monarchies are probably destructive to human nature in their progress, in their continuance, and even in their downfall, which never can be very distant from their establishment." If the Roman Empire is cited as an objection, Hume answers that though the Roman Empire may have been of some advantage, this was because "mankind were generally in a very disorderly, uncivilized condition before its establishment." The indefinite expansion of a monarchy—and Hume means that of the Bourbons—creates obstacles in and of itself—"thus human nature checks itself in its airy elevation." We would scarcely simplify Hume's thought by offering the antithesis of the *policy of equilibrium* and that of *universal monarchy*. Since universal monarchy seems no less disastrous to Hume than to Montesquieu, the state inevitably losing its virtues with the extension of its territory, the policy of equilibrium is rationally preferable in terms of historical experience and moral values.

The Roman decadence began, Montesquieu said, when the immensity of the Empire made the Republic impossible. Were the Bourbon monarchy to be unduly extended, the nobility would refuse to serve in remote places, in Hungary or in Lithuania, "forgot at court and sacrificed to the intrigue of every minion or mistress who approaches the Prince." The king would have to call in mercenaries "and the melancholy fate of the Roman emperors, from the same cause, is renewed over and over again, till the final dissolution of the monarchy."

The policy of equilibrium obeys a rule of common sense; it issues from the prudence necessary to the states concerned to preserve their independence and not be at the mercy of another state possessing irresistible strength. It seems blameworthy to those statesmen or doctrinaires who regard the clandestine or overt use of force, sometimes leading to violence, as the mark and expression of human wickedness. Yet such censors should devise a juridical or spiritual substitute for the equilibrium of autonomous wills. The same policy of equilibrium will be considered moral, or at least historically justified, by those who fear a universal monarchy and desire the survival of independent states. It will be judged if not immoral, at least anarchic, by those, on the contrary, who, in a given space, at a given time, prefer the unity of an empire to the maintenance of multiple sovereignties. The un-prejudiced observer will decide, according to circumstances, in favor of equilibrium or empire, since it is not likely that the optimum dimension of the state territory (optimum for whom? for what?) will be the same at all periods.

The policy of equilibrium, on the highest level of abstraction, is reduced to maneuvering in order to prevent a state from accumulating forces superior to those of its allied rivals. Every state, if it wishes to safeguard the equilibrium, will take a position against the state or the coalition that seems capable of achieving such a superiority. This general rule is valid for all international systems. But if we seek to elaborate the rules of the policy of equilibrium, we must construct models of systems, according to the *configuration of the relation of forces.*

The two most typical models are the ones I have called multipolar[1] and bipolar: either the chief actors, whose forces are not too unequal, are relatively numerous; or, on the contrary, two actors dominate their rivals to such a degree that both become the center of a coalition and the secondary actors are obliged to situate themselves in relation to the two "blocs," thus joining one or another, unless they have the opportunity to abstain. Intermediary models are possible, depending on the number of chief actors and the degree of equality or inequality of forces among the chief actors.

2. The Policy of Multipolar Equilibrium

Let us posit an international system defined by the plurality of rival states, whose resources, without being equal, do not create a disparity in nature—taking, for instance, France, Germany, Russia, England, Austria, Hungary, Italy in 1910. If these states wish to maintain the equilibrium, they must apply certain rules which stem from the rejection of a universal monarchy.

The enemy being, by definition, that state which ventures to dominate the others, the victor in a war (the side which has gained the most advantages) immediately becomes suspect to its former allies. In other words, alliances and enmities are, in essence, temporary, since they are determined by the relation of forces. By the same token, the state whose forces are increasing must anticipate the dissidence of certain of its allies, who will rejoin the other camp in order to maintain the balance. Anticipating such

[1] Authors generally attach the phrase *balance of power* to the systems I call *multipolar.*

defense reactions, the state whose power is in the ascendant will be wise to limit its ambitions, if it does not aspire to hegemony or empire. If it does aspire to hegemony, it must be prepared, as disruptive force of the system, to face the hostility of all the conservative states.

May we look beyond these generalizations, which are also commonplaces, and enumerate the rules the actors must rationally observe in a multipolar system (again, we are concerned with a hypothetical rationality, based on the postulate that the actors desire to maintain the system)? An American author, Morton A. Kaplan,[2] has formulated the six rules both necessary and sufficient for the functioning of a schematic system which he calls the balance of power and which, it seems to me, corresponds to the one that concerns us.

These six rules are as follows: 1. each actor must act in such a way as to increase his capabilities, but must prefer negotiation to combat; 2. each must fight rather than miss an opportunity to increase his capabilities; 3. each must cease fighting rather than eliminate a "principal national actor"[3]; 4. each must act so as to oppose any coalition or individual actor tending to assume a position of predominance in relation to the rest of the system; 5. each must act so as to constrain the actors subscribing to a supranational principle of organization; 6. each must permit the national actors, whether beaten or constrained, to return to the system as acceptable partners, or must bring a previously non-essential actor into the essential category. All the essential actors must be dealt with as acceptable partners.

Of these six rules, we may immediately detach the fourth, which is the simple expression of the principle of equilibrium, a principle valid for all international systems and already defined in Hume's essay. Not one of the other rules, interpreted literally, is of obvious application, generally speaking.

The first—which enjoins all the actors to increase their capacities (resources, means, forces) to the maximum—is valid for any system defined by the struggle of each against all. Since each state relies upon itself alone, any increase in resources is welcome as such, provided it leaves all other things equal. Now it is rare for a state to increase its resources without modifying either the resources or the attitude of its allies or rivals. That negotiation is preferable to combat may be considered a postulate of rational policy, comparable to that of the least effort for a given economic yield (in production or income). However, this postulate requires that the actors disregard their pride or glory.

The rule of fighting rather than missing an opportunity of increasing capabilities is neither rational nor reasonable. Of course, in the abstract, all other things being equal, any actor on the international stage seeks maxi-

---

[2] *System and Process in International Politics*, New York, 1957, pp. 23 ff.
[3] The principal national actor, in such a system, is what in ordinary terms we call a "Great Power" or a state possessing forces great enough to constitute one of the essential elements of the system of equilibrium.

mum capabilities. But if we attempt to determine in what circumstances it is rational for a state to fight, we shall be reduced to virtually meaningless formulas of the following type: the state must take the initiative in combat if the advantages it anticipates from victory are to exceed the probable cost of the struggle, the gap between advantage and cost widening with the risk of non-victory or defeat. Whatever the specific formula achieved, the possibility of increasing capabilities is not enough to justify recourse to arms.

The classical authors had acknowledged only the threat of hegemony brought about by the growth of a rival as a reasonable and legitimate motive for taking the initiative in hostilities. It is not immoral, but it is imprudent to contemplate passively the rise of a state toward a superiority so great that its neighbors would be at its mercy.

Rules three and six tend to contradict each other or, at least, illustrate the various outcomes possible. In a system of multipolar equilibrium, the wise statesman hesitates to eliminate one of the principal actors. He does not proceed to the extremes of victory if he fears that, by continuing the combat, he will destroy a temporary enemy necessary to the system's equilibrium. But if the elimination of one of the principal actors involves, directly or indirectly, the entrance on stage of an actor of equivalent stature, he will consider whether the old actor or the new is the more favorable to his own interests.

Rule five is equivalent to the following principle: any state which, in a given system, follows a supranational ideology or acts according to a supranational conception is, as such, an enemy. This principle is not strictly implied by the ideal model of a multipolar equilibrium. Of course, so long as this kind of equilibrium is expressed normally in a rivalry of states, each exclusively concerned with its own interests, the state that recruits partisans beyond its borders because it claims a universal doctrine, thereby becomes a threat to the others. But we cannot draw the conclusion from the inevitable hostility between national states and the state appealing to a transnational idea that the former must make war on the latter: it all depends on the relation of forces and on the probability of reducing the attractiveness of the transnational idea by arms.

Again more generally, all these rules presuppose implicitly that the safeguarding of equilibrium and of the system is the sole object or at least the predominant concern of states. Yet nothing of the kind is so. The only state that, more or less consciously, has acted according to this hypothesis is England, which, indeed, had no other interest than safeguarding the system itself and weakening, in each period, the strongest state capable of aspiring to hegemony. None of the continental states was or could have been so disinterested in the modes of equilibrium, even if it did not aspire to domination. Possession of strategic points or provinces, the configuration of frontiers, distribution of resources, such were the stakes of the conflicts which the continental states desired to settle to their advantage. That they were prepared, if necessary in order to achieve their goals, to eliminate a principal actor was not an irrational step, as long as there remained enough actors to reconstitute another system. The elimination of Germany as a principal actor, as a result of division, was not irrational on the part of French policy, which thereby reinforced its own position without dangerously reducing the number of chief actors.

The purely national policy of European states covers only a brief period between the wars of religion and the wars of revolution. The termination of the wars of religion was not due to the outlawing or the irremediable defeat of states appealing to a transnational idea, but to the proclamation of the primacy of the state over the individual; the state determining the church to which individuals would have to belong, if not in which they would have to believe, tolerating dissidents only on condition that the latters' religious choice appeared to be a strictly private matter. The European peace of the seventeenth century was obtained by a complex diplomacy which re-established the equilibrium of states and prevented the disputes of churches or the beliefs of the governed to put this equilibrium to the test. The sovereigns had abandoned the strategy of "ideological war" to return to that of "Holy Alliance": any rebellion against an established power, grievous in itself, was condemned even by those governing rival states. The stability of the powers was given precedence over the weakening by dissidence or rebellion of a state that was a potential enemy.

Perhaps the author whose theses we are discussing would subscribe to the preceding remarks. The six rules he formulates would be those which perfectly rational actors would follow in an ideal typical multipolar (balance-of-power) system. Even granting that these rules are valid for an ideal type, I cannot accept them. The conduct of the *pure diplomat* cannot and must not be held as determined by reference to equilibrium alone, which itself is defined by the rejection of universal monarchy and by the plurality of principal actors. The behavior of economic subjects is determined in a typical ideal market because each member seeks to maximize his interests or his profit. The behavior of diplomatic subjects, in a system of multipolar equilibrium, has no unequivocal objective: all other things being equal, each subject hopes for the maximum resources, but if the increase of resources requires a battle or provokes the reversal of alliances, he will hesitate to take risks. The maintenance of a given system has as its condition the safeguarding of the principal actors, but each of the latter is not rationally obliged to set the maintenance of the system above any of its own interests. To suppose implicitly that states have as their objective the safeguarding or functioning of the system is to return, by a devious route, to the error of certain theoreticians of power politics: to confuse the calculation of means or the context of the decision with the goal itself.

It is possible neither to predict diplomatic events from the analysis of a typical system nor to dictate a line of conduct to princes as a result of the type of system. The model of multipolar equilibrium helps us to understand the systems that have occurred in history, and the rules which we have borrowed from the American author suggest the circumstances favorable to the duration of such a system.

Strictly "national" states regard themselves as rivals, not mortal enemies; the leaders do not regard themselves as personally threatened by those of the neighboring states; each state is a possible ally for every other, today's enemy is spared because he will be tomorrow's partner and because he is indispensable to the system's equilibrium. Diplomacy, in such a system, is realistic, sometimes even cynical, but it is moderate and reasonable. Hence, when the ravages of another kind of diplomacy became tragically evident, this disabused wisdom seemed retrospectively not only an ideal type but an ideal.

The diplomacy called realist, which the system of multipolar equilibrium implies, does not conform to the highest requirements of the philosophers. The state which changes camp the day after victory awakens the bitterness and resentment of its allies, who may have accepted greater sacrifices than that state for the sake of their common victory. A pure diplomacy of equilibrium ignores and must ignore feelings; it has no friends or enemies as such, it does not regard the latter as worse than the former, it does not condemn war as such. It acknowledges the egoism or, if one prefers, the moral corruption (aspiration to power and glory) of states, but such calculating corruption seems in the long run less unforeseeable, less formidable than passions, perhaps idealist but certainly blind.

Until 1945 United States diplomacy was situated at the antipodes of this traditional and prudent immorality. The United States had preserved the memory of the two great wars of its history, that against the Indians, that of the Secession. In neither case was the enemy an accepted state with which, after hostilities were over, a peaceful coexistence would be resumed. Diplomatic relations, alliances and conflicts did not seem inseparable from the normal life-process of states: war was a repellent necessity, to which one was obliged to adapt, a duty of circumstances which had to be performed as well and as fast as possible, but it was not an episode of a sustained history. Thus American public opinion reflected little on the past and the future when the war had begun. The enemy was guilty and deserved punishment, was wicked and must be corrected. Afterward, peace would prevail.

Obliged, in its turn, after 1945, to reverse alliances, America was tempted, following General MacArthur's example, to proclaim that it had assigned roles and merits badly, China having somehow shifted to the wrong side and Japan, simultaneously, to the right side of the barricade. If the enemy is always the incarnation of evil and if reversals of alliances are sometimes inevitable, we must conclude that good and evil change their incarnation.

According to Machiavelli, *virtù* shifted in the course of history from one people to another. According to a moralizing diplomacy, it is virtue, quite different from Machiavelli's *virtù*, which affects such migrations.

Hateful or admirable, baneful or precious, the diplomacy of equilibrium does not result from a deliberate choice on the part of statesmen—it results from circumstances.

The geographical scene, the organization of states and military technique must prevent the concentration of power in one or two states. That there are several states possessing comparable resources is the structural characteristic of the multipolar system. In Greece as in Europe, the geographical scene was not hostile to the independence of cities and kingdoms. As long as the political unit was the city-state, the multiplicity of centers of autonomous decision was the necessary result. To quote Hume, "if we consider, indeed, the small number of inhabitants in any one Republic compared to the whole, the great difficulty of forming sieges in those times, and the extraordinary bravery and discipline of every free man among the noble people," we shall conclude that equilibrium was relatively easy to maintain and empire difficult to impose. In Europe since the end of the diffused sovereignty of the Middle Ages, first Great Britain, then Russia constituted insurmountable obstacles in the path of universal monarchy. The principle of state legitimacy, whether dynastic or national, did not justify unlimited ambitions. European armies, between the sixteenth and twentieth centuries, were not equipped for vast conquests: Napoleon's soldiers advanced on foot from the frontier to Moscow. With distance, they were weakened still more quickly than Alexander's soldiers.

The concern for equilibrium inspires diplomacy in proportion as men— both governing and governed—cling to the independence of their political unit. The Greek citizens did not separate their own freedom from that of their city-state. Together, they had defended the civilization of free men against the Persian Empire, which they regarded as founded on the despotism of a single man. Against each other, they defended the autonomy of city-states. The first French monarchy ardently desired total independence, passionately refused any submission to empire. Peoples have desired independence of which the national state was the expression. This desire for state independence, for absolute sovereignty, checks the tendency to ideological diplomacy, maintaining a kind of inter-state homogeneity despite the conflicts of faith or ideas. It helps to "internalize" the rules of equilibrium that cease to appear as counsels of prudence, becoming moral or traditional imperatives. Safeguarding equilibrium is acknowledged as a common duty of statesmen. The European concert is transformed into an organ of arbitration, of common deliberation, even of collective decision.

Yet changes in the relation of forces must not be too rapid. Whether the people be passive or indifferent, it is better that reversals of alliances not occur from one day to the next. Whatever the intelligence of statesmen, it is better that the shifts of resources not be such that yesterday's calculations are radically false today. The system functions better with known actors and a more or less stabilized relation of forces. None of these conditions, taken in isolation, suffices to guarantee the survival of the multipolar system. The desire for independence will ultimately be swept away by violent transnational passions. The concern for the common system will not resist extreme heterogeneity. All the actors are no longer acceptable partners for each other if the peoples are separated by memories that they refuse to forget or by the suffering of open wounds. (After 1871 France could not have allied herself with Germany even if the calculation of equilibrium had made such an alliance rational.)

Before 1914 the growth of the Reich and the irreducible opposition between France and Germany had contributed to the transformation of the system: alliances tended to become permanent, to crystallize in "blocs." Between the two wars the transnational ideologies of communism, then of fascism, had made the system so heterogeneous that awareness of a common interest in its maintenance had entirely disappeared: partisan hostilities, internal to states, cut through and aggravated inter-state hostilities. The military revolution, a result of the internal-combustion engine, seemed to clear the path for great conquests. At this point theoreticians began to dream nostalgically of the diplomacy of Richelieu, of Mazarin, of Talleyrand.

The system of multipolar equilibrium, as it functioned at the end of the nineteenth century, is a historical compromise between the *state of nature* and the *rule of law*: the state of nature, because the enemy remains the strongest insofar as he is the strongest, because each actor is the sole judge, in the last analysis, of his behavior and retains the right of choosing between peace and war. But this *state of nature* is no longer the struggle of each against all, without rules and without limits. States recognize each other's right to existence; they desire, and know they desire, to preserve equilibrium and even a certain solidarity in confronting the outside world. The Greek city-states were not unaware of their profound kinship and at the same time of the "foreignness" of the barbarians.[4] To Asian eyes, rather than being rivals, the European conquerors gave the impression of being united in a single "aggressive" bloc.

This intermediary solution between the state of nature and the rule of law (or again, between the jungle and universal monarchy) is, in essence,

---

[4] Cf. Vattel, *op. cit.*, Book III, Chap. 3, paragraph 47. "Europe comprises a political system, a body in which everything is linked by the relations and the various interests of the nations which inhabit this part of the world. It is no longer a jumble of isolated parts each of which considered itself unaffected by the fate of the others, and rarely bothered about what did not immediately concern it. The continual attention of sovereigns to everything that happens, ministers in permanent residence and perpetual invitations make modern Europe a kind of republic whose independent members, linked by common interests, gather in order to maintain its order and freedom."

precarious. In theory it leaves the sovereigns free to attack if attack seems indispensable to prevent the rise of a dreaded rival. Equilibrium is the imperative of prudence rather than the common good of the system: yet if the war to weaken the strong is waged frequently, the system becomes sterile, costly and detested. The risk grows greater as it becomes more difficult to distinguish between "weakening the strong" and "humiliating the proud." Was it out of a desire for security or the pride of dominance that the Greek city-states fought each other so often? Was it concern for security or the love of glory which inspired the diplomacy of Louis XIV? There was a time when the diplomacy of cabinets, to which the realist theoreticians show such indulgence today, was harshly judged because the historians blamed the kings and their belligerent dealings for the wars described, whether rightly or wrongly, as wars of prestige. The system of European equilibrium has perhaps limited the violence of wars (at certain periods); it has never reduced their frequency.

A precarious compromise, the system perpetually tends to overstep its bounds, either toward a return to the jungle, or in the direction of a "universal empire" or a "juridical order." The double awareness of a common civilization and of a permanent rivalry is, in essence, contradictory. If the sense of rivalry prevails, war becomes inexpiable and civilized diplomacy is eclipsed. If the sense of the community of culture prevails, the temptation of state unification or of organized peace becomes irresistible. Why did the Greeks, instead of exhausting their military force against each other, not combine to bring down the Persian Empire? Why did the Europeans not choose to rule Africa or Asia together instead of ruining themselves in fratricidal combat?

Let us note: these questions, historically, were raised *after the fact*. Philip, Alexander and their spokesmen have contrasted the city-states' loss of autonomy with the greatness which a united Greece was capable of achieving. It was Valéry, after 1918, who observed that the goal of European policy seemed to be to entrust the government of the Old World to an American committee. Indeed, Europeans have always reserved the major part of their forces for the wars they waged against each other. If the French sent great armies overseas, it was when they vainly disputed the last shreds of their possessions with rising nationalist forces; it was when they were losing, not building, their empire.

Further, it is understandable that this so-called folly be judged as such only after the fact. States fear their rivals, peoples their neighbors, each desiring to dominate those close by rather than aspiring to reign over distant lands and alien populations. The immense empires of Spain and England, whether attributed to the spirit of adventure or of lucre, to the lust or gold or for power, have had as their condition the exceptional military superiority of the conquerors. When such a superiority is not a condition, the wars are most frequently waged within the same sphere of civilization. The Chinese or the Japanese, like the Europeans, have in general fought among themselves.

It is perhaps human but it is futile to cultivate the nostalgia for the amoral and measured diplomacy of equilibrium. Such nostalgia is, in essence, retrospective. Those who regret the days when diplomats were indifferent to ideas are nevertheless living in a heterogeneous system and an age of ideological conflicts. Those who admire the subtle combination of national egoism and respect for equilibrium are contemporaries of the inexpiable struggles between candidates for empire, between faiths both temporal and spiritual, inseparable from the states in conflict. Those who marvel at the subtle combinations permitted by the plurality of actors are now observing a diplomatic field occupied by rigid blocs.

Men, including statesmen, are not free to determine the distribution of forces, the neutral or ideological character of diplomacy. It is wiser to understand the diversity of worlds than to dream of a world which no longer exists because one does not love the world that does.

3. The Policy of Bipolar Equilibrium

I call *bipolar* the configuration of the relation of forces in which the majority of political units are grouped around those two among them whose strength outclasses that of the others. The distinction between the multipolar and the bipolar configuration is evident to the observer because of the consequences, some logical, others historical, which each of these configurations involves.

Whatever the configuration, the most general law of equilibrium applies: the goal of the chief actors is to avoid finding themselves at the mercy of a rival. But since the two great powers call the tune, and since the lesser powers, even by uniting, cannot outweigh one of the great powers, the principle of equilibrium applies to relations among the coalitions, each formed around one of the two influential powers. Each coalition has as its supreme objective prevention of the other from acquiring means superior to its own.

In such a system we distinguish three kinds of actors (and not only "small" and "great"): the two leaders of the coalitions, the states obliged to take part and lend allegiance to one or the other of the leaders, and lastly the states which can and desire to remain outside the conflict. These three kinds of actors behave according to different rules.

The leaders of the coalition must simultaneously be on guard to *prevent* the growth of the other great power or coalition and to *maintain* the cohesion of their own coalition. The two tasks are related to one another in many ways. If an ally changes sides or shifts from commitment to neutrality, the relation of forces is modified. On the most abstract level, the means the leader uses to maintain the coherence of its own coalition fall into two categories, some tending to protect, others tending to punish:

the former assure advantages to allies, the latter hold the threat of sanctions over dissidents or traitors. The rational use of these means depends on many circumstances: to the state which fears the other coalition, the great power gives the guarantee of assistance, that is, of security; to the state which has nothing to fear, it offers financial advantages; it tries to terrify the state which cannot be seduced or convinced.

Thucydides wondered to what degree Athens was responsible for the dissolution of the alliance it led and which did not resist defeat. The league, theoretically composed of city-states equal in rights, had become a kind of empire, directed by a heavy-handed master who required the payment of tribute. The Greek historian suggests that the strongest always tends to abuse his strength. Even without invoking this motive of eternal psychology, today's historian can draw other interpretations from Thucydides' narrative. A league of "insular powers" does not spontaneously keep its cohesion once the external danger is past. A league of equal city-states should have been entirely peaceful and sought no other goal than the security and freedom of its members. By taking the path of imperialism, Athens condemned itself to brutality. The servitudes of power are inescapable.

The political units which, by vocation or necessity, rally around one or other of the two camps, also act as a consequence of two considerations: to a degree, the interest of the coalition is their own interest, yet the interest of the coalition does not exactly coincide with their own interest. Let us consider the alliances within the multipolar system: each of the chief actors, temporarily associated, is alarmed by the growth of its chief ally (or of its chief allies) even when the enemy (or the enemies) is not (or is not yet) conquered. The benefits of a common victory are never equitably distributed: the weight of a state is a function of the strength it possesses at the time of negotiations more than of the merits it has acquired during the hostilities (this "realistic" proposition scandalized France when the British and Americans suggested it in 1918). The rivalry among allies has not the same character in a bipolar system. The more distinct this configuration is, the more the two great powers prevail over their partners and the more the alliances tend to become permanent. As a member of a permanent alliance, opposed to another equally permanent alliance, the secondary state has a major interest in the security or in the victory of the whole of which it is a part[5]; it resigns itself more easily to the growth of its rival-partners. Yet Thucydides' narrative shows over and over that Athens was feared by her allies. The secondary states would feel quite at one with their "bloc" (*its* success is *my* success) if the fate of each, within the alliance, was not affected by the relative forces of the partners; if the leader were purely a protector or an arbitrator: a borderline case, to say the least.

[5] If it is a part voluntarily.

The world being what it is, each political unit tries to influence the policy of the alliance in the direction of its own interests or to reserve the greatest possible amount of its forces for enterprises which directly concern it. In 1959 what the French diplomats understood by the common policy of the Atlantic bloc was Anglo-American support of the pacification of Algeria, a task to which France was dedicating the majority of its army, gradually reducing its contribution to the NATO shield. The difficulties of a diplomacy or a strategy of coalition, though somewhat attenuated within permanent coalitions, cemented by a common ideology or an external threat, still remain fundamentally the same: the various ways of maneuvering, of fighting, of conquering do not benefit the partners equally. Even if the latter were in agreement as to the estimate of risks and opportunities—which is never the case, given the uncertainty of these estimates—they would have rational motives for controversy, for the possible diplomatic or strategic methods largely involve, even for sincere allies, an unequal distribution of immediate sacrifices and eventual gains.

As for the non-engaged, they consist primarily of those political units external to the system which most often have no reason to side with one coalition or the other and which may even have advantages to gain from a generalized warfare weakening both groups of belligerents. The state external to the system is, in both cases, induced by calculation to intervene: either if it expects the victory of one of the two camps to afford it advantages superior to the cost of the aid necessary to insure that victory; or if it fears the victory of one of the two camps because that victory seems likely if it were to remain passive. This latter case illuminates a possible motive of American intervention in 1917 (which does not imply that this intervention had no other causes). Perhaps the Persian intervention at the end of the Peloponnesian War can be classified under the same heading.

As to the choice of states situated within the system—taking sides or remaining neutral—it chiefly depends, assuming each desire neutrality, on the security to be derived from isolation. The small state's geographical situation and actual resources are the two decisive factors: it is no accident that in 1949, when the Atlantic Pact was signed, Switzerland and Sweden, which did not join it, had the two strongest armies on the Continent west of the Iron Curtain. On the other hand, as Thibaudet writes, commenting on Thucydides, a maritime power cannot allow the neutrality of a single island.

The multipolar and bipolar configurations are as radically opposed as they are pure types. At one extreme, each principal actor is the enemy and the possible partner of all the rest. At the other, there are only two principal actors, enemies by position if not by ideology. In the first case alliances are temporary, in the second they are lasting; in the first case the allies do not recognize any leader, in the second all the political units, save the two leaders, are subject to the will of the latter. In the first case several units remain outside the alliance, in the second all units are willy-nilly obliged to lend their allegiance to one or the other of the leaders, to aggregate themselves into one or the other of the blocs.

Intermediate conditions are obviously conceivable and even more often real than the pure types. Even within a homogeneous multipolar system, an actor can rarely ally himself with or oppose just any actor; the stakes (the fate of a province, the contour of a frontier) and popular passions may forbid a reconciliation which a rational calculation would not exclude. Even in a system with many chief actors, one or two of the latter are more important than the rest. If generalized warfare breaks out between two coalitions, each is more influenced by one of the actors than by the other. In other words, if generalized warfare breaks out, a multipolar configuration tends of itself to approach a bipolar configuration. This is why Thibaudet and Toynbee immediately compared the First World War to the Peloponnesian War, although the pre-1914 European system was still multipolar: the comparison involved the generalization of a conflict, gradually embracing all the units in the system and confronting a league directed by the insular power with a league grouped around the continental power, Athens and England, Sparta and Germany. Since then, commentators have alluded to Thucydides to emphasize the bipolar configuration, because the world after 1945 presents such a configuration. But obviously the Greek system differs by nature from the present system, just as the superiority of Athens and Sparta over the other cities was not of the same genre as the superiority of the two giants today.

Thus it is not a question of formulating laws according to which a bipolar system would function or develop. The geometry of diplomatic relations is comparable to the battle plans drawn up by the German strategists (a double flank encirclement: the battle of Cannes; the collapse of one flank: the battle of Leuthen, etc.). The diplomatic configurations, like the battle plans, are few in number, because the modes of distribution of forces within a system or the movements of armies involve only a few typical models. The theory of models, however, permits neither the strategist to know in advance the maneuver he should perform, nor the historian to foresee what a given system, whether multipolar or bipolar, will become.

At best we may note several structural characteristics of a bipolar system. Such a system may not, as such, be more unstable or more belligerent than a multipolar system, but it is more seriously threatened by a generalized and inexorable war. Indeed, if all the political units belong to one camp or the other, any kind of local conflict concerns the whole of the system. The balance between the two camps is affected by the behavior of many small units. Lacking a "third man," whether arbitrator or contributor, the two great powers are perpetually in conflict, directly or through intermediaries. In order to reach an understanding, they would have to trace a demarcation line, distribute zones of influence, forbid dissidence: the client of one would not have the right to shift to the camp of the other, and each would be obliged to desist from inciting the other's allies to dissidence. More or less precise rules of this nature seem to have existed in Greece during the period which preceded the Peloponnesian War. It was difficult for the two ruling city-states to respect these rules, still more difficult to impose respect for them upon their respective allies.

In such a system, indeed, it is the fate of the satellites which is both the occasion and the stake of the conflicts between the great powers. Yet, depending on the rigidity or the flexibility of the coalitions, responsibility for the conflicts rests principally upon the satellites or principally upon the leaders. In the Greece Thucydides describes, the supremacy of Athens at sea and of Sparta on land was not overwhelming. The fleets of Corcyra or of Corinth were enough to modify the relation of forces. The great powers did not exert a sovereign command upon their allies, and the latter could, in their own interests, involve their leaders in a struggle to the death.

Lastly, this system which, by the absence of the "third man," makes a generalized war more likely, also makes it almost inevitable that a generalized war becomes ideological. To avoid fighting, the great powers must prohibit shifts of allegiance. Once they have begun fighting, how could they forego provoking dissidence? The two great powers rarely have the same institutions, particularly when the respective bases of their military forces are not the same. Within the units, factions are formed, some favoring peace, others war, some championing one of the leaders, others another. The preferences for one kind of institution or another govern such assumptions of position, at least in part. All the units are increasingly divided between advocates of one or the other coalition, each coalition exploiting these internal quarrels in order to weaken the enemy units.

The peace of a system having a bipolar configuration requires the stabilization of state clienteles by agreement of state leaders, hence the ban on recruiting partisan clients within states. This ban is dropped once the death-struggle is launched. But peace is warlike or war is cold when this ban does not exist before the death-struggle is launched.

4. The Bipolar System of the Greek City-States

The formal analysis we have just conducted does not afford us a means of forecasting but a kind of outline. Given a bipolar configuration, the historian or the sociologist must traverse these stages if he wishes to gain an understanding of events: 1. Which of the coalitions are in conflict? What degree of rigidity does each exhibit? What are the instruments of power wielded by each of the leader-states? What is the degree of superiority of each of the leader-states over its partners, whether allies or satellites? 2. If the system has provoked a death-struggle, what were the occasions or causes of the explosion? 3. How does the conflict occur, before or during the death-struggle, between the two coalitions, between the leading states, between them and their respective allies? In other words, we must *understand* the nature and structure of each of the coalitions, the occasions and basic reasons for their opposition, and finally the style and modes of their combat.

The first book of *The Peloponnesian War* provides an admirable application of these principles. From it we shall borrow an illustration of these requirements of analysis: "In the face of this great danger, the command of the confederate Hellenes was assumed by the Lacedaemonians in virtue of their superior power; and the Athenians having made up their minds to abandon their city, broke up their homes, threw themselves into their ships, and became a naval people. This coalition, after repulsing the barbarian, soon afterward split into two sections, which included the Hellenes who had revolted from the king, as well as those who had aided him in the war. At the head of one stood Athens, at the head of the other Lacedaemon, one the first naval, the other the first military power in Hellas. For a short time the league held together, till the Lacedaemonians and Athenians quarreled, and made war upon each other with their allies, a duel into which all the Hellenes sooner or later were drawn, though some might at first remain neutral. . . . The policy of Lacedaemon was not to exact tribute from her allies, but merely to secure their subservience to her interests by establishing oligarchies among them; Athens, on the contrary, had by degrees deprived hers of their ships, and imposed instead contributions in money on all except Chios and Lesbos."[6] Two city-states dominate the others, each with a typical element of military force; all the other city-states group around them. The domination of Athens is financial (the allies pay tribute) and maritime (the ships of the allies are "integrated" into the Athenian fleet). The Spartan alliance was founded on the oligarchic character of the regime of the city-states which took her side and also, as Thucydides often says, on the concern of the city-states to preserve their liberties, which the power of Athens endangered.

The case of Corcyra furnishes an example of how the leading states do not respect the treaty which they have concluded in order to avoid war, an example whose significance is apparent as soon as we employ modern concepts. Corcyra and Corinth (the first the colony of the second) began a dispute concerning Epidaurus, claimed by each as a colony. Corcyra was an "uncommitted" city-state, a fact on which both sides, in their contradictory arguments, agree. Why did Corcyra keep out of the pact? According to the Corinthians, because "their geographical situation makes them independent of others" (I, 37); according to Corcyrans seeking the aid of Athens, because Corcyra once believed "in the wise precaution of refusing to involve ourselves in alliances with other powers, lest we should also

[6] Book I, 18. Crawley translation.

involve ourselves in risks of their choosing dangers of a foreign alliance according to the will of our neighbor" (I, 32) only to discover, at the eleventh hour, that this isolation was "folly and weakness." The extension and imbrication of alliances made it increasingly difficult for political units of any importance not to ally themselves with one or the other of the great powers.

Is it consonant with the treaty linking Athens and Sparta in the interest of peace that an uncommitted unit should join one of the two camps? Is the shift from neutrality to alliance contradictory to the pact or not? According to all the orators, the pact forbids defections, the unit that belongs to a coalition must not leave it. The Corinthian advocates say as much to the Athenians: "Do not lay down the principle that defection is to be patronized" (I, 40). If one camp receives the defectors of the other, the adverse camp will do the same. "If you make it your policy to receive and assist all offenders, you will find that just as many of your dependencies will come over to us, and the principle that you establish will press less heavily on us than on yourselves" (I, 40). The supreme principle is "that every power has a right to punish her own allies" (I, 43).

The case of Corcyra, seeking the assistance of Athens, was difficult. Formally Corcyra, having been uncommitted, did not fall under the influence of the ban on receiving defectors. The Corinthians admitted as much: according to the provisions of the treaty "it shall be competent for any state, whose name was not down on the list, to join whichever side it pleases" (I, 40). But the spirit of the treaty excludes, the Corinthians say, those allegiances which in themselves constitute an aggression with regard to the other camp. "But this agreement is not meant for those whose object in joining is the injury of other powers, but for those whose need of support does not arise from the fact of defection, and whose adhesion will not bring to the power that is mad enough to receive them war instead of peace" (I, 40). In modern terms, the treaty involves two ambiguities: its function was to avoid a rupture of the equilibrium of forces, yet the allegiance of certain uncommitted parties, which is not explicitly forbidden, risks provoking this rupture. On the other hand, the uncommitted parties, which retain the right to choose their allegiance, cannot all call upon the treaty as their authority. If Corcyra, which turns against Corinth (whose colony she has been) became the ally of Athens, this commitment would be, in fact and in spirit, an aggression against Corinth and therefore against Sparta. The Athenians are thus aware of the scope of their action when they conclude a simple defensive alliance with Corcyra, involving reciprocal aid in case of attack against Corcyra, Athens or their allies. An offensive alliance would have involved the risk of Athenian participation in an attack against Corinth, hence war with Sparta.

What motive determines the behavior of the Athenians? According to

Thucydides, a calculation of forces in a period when each side anticipates the imminent war. "If any of you imagine that war is far off, he is grievously mistaken, and is blind to the fact that Lacedaemon regards you with jealousy and desires war" (I, 33). That is how the Corcyran ambassadors express themselves before the assembly of Athens. And Thucydides himself: "For it began now to be felt that the coming of the Peloponnesian War was only a question of time, and no one was willing to see the naval power of such magnitude as Corcyra sacrificed to Corinth; though if they could let them weaken each other by mutual conflict, it would be no bad preparation for the struggle which Athens might one day have to wage with Corinth and the other naval powers" (I, 44). There are three navies which count in Greece, that of Athens, of Corcyra and of Corinth. If Athens, out of fear of breaking the truce, lets Corcyra and Corinth unite, would she not lose face by publicizing her fear at the same time as she would sacrifice a considerable military advantage? When the supremacy of the leading states over their partners is not overwhelming, they are led by their allies more than they lead them. They cannot, in effect, abandon their allies without weakening themselves dangerously. Athens did not possess such superiority that she could scorn the Corcyran contribution.

The conflict of Potidaea, which Thucydides presents as the second immediate cause of the great war, was formally of the same type. Potidaea was a colony of Corinth and an ally of Athens. The Athenians decided it was necessary and legitimate to punish a defecting ally. They clashed with the Corinthians, who were desirous to defend their colony. The Lacedaemonians, in violation of the pact, had detached from Athens a tribute-paying city-state "and were openly fighting against her on the side of the Potidaeans" (I, 66). The interlinking of relations among cities—relations between metropolis and colony, between hegemonic city and allies—often made the determination of the just and the unjust uncertain.

But according to Thucydides, these ambiguities of "international law" were not the real cause of the conflict. The historian says as much himself, in a famous formula: "The real cause I consider to be the one which was formally most kept out of sight. The growth of the power of Athens and the fear this inspired in Lacedaemon made war inevitable" (I, 24). The Corinthians, speaking at the Congress of Sparta and her allies, denounced the bad conduct—contrary to justice and to treaties—of the Athenians. But the essential accusation is that Athens was on the point of assuming "the role of tyrant in relation to all without distinction, that she commanded some and dreamed of commanding others" (I, 74). After the vote of the Lacedaemonians deciding that the truce had been broken and that they would have to wage war, Thucydides repeats that the Spartans had been less convinced by their allies; rather "they feared the growth of the power of the Athenians, seeing most of Hellas already subject to them" (I, 88).

Considerations of equilibrium and considerations of equity (justice, conventions) are mingled, at every moment, in the course of the narrative and in the arguments of the first book, which is devoted to the study of what we should call the diplomatic circumstances and the origins of the war. But the historian does not hesitate to regard the first as decisive, and to put in the actors' mouths admissions whose frankness is inconceivable in our day and age, which ideology and the role of the people condemn to hypocrisy. The Athenian delegates declared before the Spartan assembly: "It follows that it was not a very wonderful action, or contrary to the common practice of mankind, if we did accept an empire that was offered to us, and refused to give it up under pressure of three of the strongest motives, fear, honor, and interest. And it was not we who set the example, for it has always been the law that the weaker should be subject to the stronger. Besides, we believed ourselves to be worthy of our position, and so you have thought us up to now, when the calculations of interest have made you take up the cry of justice—a consideration which no one had ever yet brought forward to hinder his ambition when he had a chance of gaining anything by might" (I, 76).

The obsession of equilibrium, the fear the expansion of the Athenian Empire inspired in the Spartans, the resentment of the allies against the Athenian hegemony do not have as their chief cause the material disadvantages of the rule of a single power. Of course, the allies are angered by paying tribute or furnishing ships, Sparta fears for her very existence should Athens become irresistible. But Hume has understood Thucydides precisely when he describes, among the city-states, a conflict of *amour-propre* rather than a concern for security—*jealous emulation rather than cautious politics*. The hegemonic city seeks the honor of ruling as much or more than the commercial or financial benefits of domination. The city-states rebel against subjection, which is as unworthy of a free state as subjection to a tyrant (that is, to an absolute and arbitrary master) is unworthy of a free man. Thus Athens, democratic and insular, appears to the Corinthians and the other allies of Sparta as the major danger to the liberties of the Greek city-states. Thucydides, a citizen of Athens, does not condemn his fatherland for aspiring to empire, since such is the course of human affairs, but he does not deny that the Spartan camp has been that of traditional liberties.

Pericles' oration counseling war gives us another proof that the meaning of the conflict was the protection of autonomy. The supreme argument is "no concession to the Peloponnesians." Yielding to an ultimatum is already accepting servitude: "For all claims from an equal, urged upon a neighbor as commands, before any attempt at legal settlement, be they great or be they small, have only one meaning, and that is slavery" (I, 140). The pretext is of no account. Let it not be imagined that "to die for Megara" would be to die for a small thing: essentials are at stake, safeguarding the autonomy which constitutes freedom.

When Pericles makes this oration, he considers that war is inevitable, which is also what the leaders of the other coalition believe. In the course of this history which Thucydides' narrative presents embroidered throughout by the decisions of actors, men nonetheless have, and communicate to the reader, the sense of fate. Archidamos, King of Sparta, has no more illusions than Pericles as to the duration of the war once it breaks out: both are wise, clear-sighted men, both are resolved or resigned to the struggle, both know that neither of the two camps will win easily. Each is superior on one element, Athens at sea, Sparta on land. Maritime superiority does not suffice to reduce Sparta to subjection any more than the superiority of the hoplites will bring Athens to its knees. Thus the Corinthian ambassador and Pericles proclaim, in turn: *we shall win because we are the stronger,* the historian himself presenting the arguments of each side in such a way that the extension of a hyperbolic war appears fatal in advance and the issue, uncertain at the start, seems to be attributed either to the role of chance, which limits but does not succeed in eliminating human intelligence, or to the faults of the vanquished.

Certain comparisons come to the reader's mind almost of themselves. Of course, the comparison between the Peloponnesian War and certain wars of contemporary history has been sketched by several authors, particularly Thibaudet and Toynbee. Such a comparison is legitimate only provided that it is limited in its significance and its scope. Thibaudet was describing the American Civil War and the European wars since Charles V. The first comparison seems without foundation. The War of Secession had as its stake the very existence of the state, several federated states claiming the right to leave the federation. That this war became "total" and was waged until absolute victory in terms of a strategic erosion still does not justify the historical analogy with a general war which concerns a whole international system, even involving, step by step, marginal or external political units. Of all the European wars, only that of 1914–18 or perhaps the two world wars taken together *formally* present analogous characteristics.

A comparison, we must repeat, that is entirely formal. In Greece, the dominance of a sea power was most feared, because it seemed most capable of exploiting and oppressing, and perhaps, too, because it was wielded by Athens, which outstripped Sparta in her superiority to her allies. Thibaudet observes that in Greece it was the city-state favorable to the freedom of persons which with good reason appeared to be a threat to the freedom of other states. In 1914 a Continental state was at the same time the closest to hegemony and the most authoritarian (Tsarist Russia aside).

In modern Europe as in ancient Greece, it is the hyperbolic amplification of a general war which constitutes, in the eyes of historians inclined to comparisons, the major fact, the one which requires the most explanation and involves the most consequences. Ultimately, in fact, the system of multipolar equilibrium, that of the Greeks or that of the Europeans, is condemned if it provokes excessive and exhausting conflicts. Yet the formation of two coalitions, each around one of the leader-states, has preceded the explosion of the Great War and has marked a transition between the phase of state freedom and imperial unification.

The Peloponnesian War, like the First World War, ended in the victory of the camp which sought to safeguard the freedom of city-states. Sparta's partial hegemony was brief, like that of Thebes which followed. Having rejected the only hegemony which might have been lasting, the Greek city-states were conquered by Macedonia, then by Rome. Having rejected the hegemony of Germany, the European states were subject on one side to the joint domination of Soviet Russia and the Communist doctrine (or practice), on the other to American protection. Perhaps, to quote the Athenian ambassadors, this latter provokes more bitterness in that it dissimulates itself under the principle of equality. "They are so habituated to associate with us as equals, that any defeat whatever that clashes with their notions of justice, whether it proceeds from a legal judgment or from the power which our empire gives us, makes them forget to be grateful for being allowed to retain most of their possessions, and more vexed at a part being taken, than if we had from the first cast law aside and openly gratified our covetousness. If we had done so, not even they would have disputed that the weaker must give way to the stronger" (I, 77).

The victory of the camp of state freedom is not enough to save a system of equilibrium disintegrated by the violence, the duration and the cost of generalized warfare.

We have not even attempted to establish the list of rules of conduct to be deduced from the bipolar configuration of the relation of forces.[7] The reasons such rules are of little significance or arbitrary are the same in either a bipolar or a multipolar configuration. The maintenance of the configuration is not the primary or supreme objective of the actors. It is therefore not legitimate or, if one prefers, not instructive to consider as rules of rational conduct the precepts which must be respected in order to preserve the system. The only universal and formal rule is that of *equilibrium* in the vague sense Hume gave it: each actor (I should add each *principal* actor) tries not to be at the mercy of the others. It increases its resources or its degree of mobilization; it maneuvers in the diplomatic field, forms or breaks

[7] Morton A. Kaplan distinguishes the rigid bipolar system from the loose bipolar systems, but in both cases he introduces into his model certain elements appropriate to the present system (e.g., the international actors). The comparison would be long and, for our purposes, of no use.

alliances in order to avoid that subjection contrary to its idea of itself and perhaps fatal to its security. This desire "not to be at the mercy of others" will be expressed in varying behavior, depending on whether there is a plurality of chief actors of more or less equal capacities or "two giants" overwhelming their rivals. The combination of the desire "not to be at the mercy of others" and of a typical configuration permits us to sketch models of systems. But the models, characterized by only two traits—a desire for equilibrium and the configuration of the relation of forces—remain indeterminate in too many respects for us to be able to discover the laws of their functioning or development.

Is it possible, starting from the preceding analyses, to list the variables which sociological or historical study of a given international system must consider? The concept of a variable seems to me of questionable use, since these data are essentially qualitative and do not even comprise the whole of the distinction of more and less. But if we replace the term *variable* by a neutral term, it seems to me possible to derive from the preceding chapters a list of chief elements of an international system, or, if one prefers, a list of questions which the study of international systems should answer.

Two elements control the systems: *the configuration of the relation of forces, the homogeneity or the heterogeneity of the system.* But each of these two elements is subdivided in its turn. The actors are situated in a geographical-historical space whose limits are more or less clearly defined. On the frontiers, other actors are half-integrated, half-alien to the system. The forces peculiar to each actor depend on his resources and on the degree of mobilization: this latter in its turn depends on the economic, military, political regime. The internal regimes which influence the relation of forces determine the nature and stakes of the conflicts. The same political unit sometimes changes objectives when it changes regimes. The dialogue of political units is a function of the dialogue of classes or men in power: at one extreme, the solidarity of kings against peoples, as was said in the last century (or the solidarity of Communist parties, in Eastern Europe, against the counterrevolution), at the other, the solidarity of the governments of a state (or of a side) with the rebels or the revolutionaries within the rival or enemy state (or side). Between the two is sandwiched the diplomacy of non-intervention, each state inhibiting itself, whatever its ideological sympathies or its national interest, from intervening in favor of either the established power or of the revolution in case of civil war, whether open or latent.

Homogeneity and heterogeneity involve modes and countless nuances. The system is more or less homogeneous or heterogeneous: homogeneous in a certain zone, heterogeneous in another; homogeneous in peacetime, heterogeneous in wartime; homogeneous with partial respect to the diplomatic rule of non-interference, heterogeneous with the diplomatic use of the techniques of revolutionary action. Heterogeneity can be that of social structures or that of political regimes, that of ideas more than that of realities or, conversely, that of realities more than that of ideas. In any case, we do not understand the nature of the rivalry and of the dialogue of political units except by reference to the established power in each of them, to the conception of legitimacy, to the external ambitions, and to the strategy and tactics of the ruling classes.

The configuration of the relation of forces leads, by the intermediary of the degree of mobilization, to the internal regime; the homogeneity or heterogeneity of the systems leads, by the intermediary of the techniques of action, to the relation of forces. The two terms—relation of forces and homogeneity of the system—are not two rigorously circumscribed variables, but two complementary aspects of any historical constellation. The analysis of these two aspects illuminates the system's mode of functioning on the sociological level and the course of international relations on the historical level: calculation of forces and dialectic of regimes or ideas are both indispensable to the interpretation of diplomatic-strategic behavior in any period; neither the goals nor the means, neither the lawful nor the illicit are adequately determined by the calculation of forces alone or by the dialectic of ideas alone. Once we recognize that in the middle of the fifth century B.C. the system of the Greek city-states was bipolar and that the global system in the middle of the twentieth century A.D. is also bipolar, the task of the sociologist and the historian begins: to specify the nature, the structure, the functioning of the two systems.

The distinction of change *in* the system and change *of* the system is entirely relative. The diplomatic groupings may be called systems because an event, at any point within the space considered, has repercussions which extend to the whole grouping. But these systems do not maintain themselves by a self-regulating mechanism, for the simple reason that none of the chief actors subordinates his ambitions to the objective of maintaining the system. Athens desired, or was led to desire, hegemony; she did not have as her goal the crystallization of the bipolar structure or the equilibrium of her own league and the Lacedaemonian league.

The same phenomenon may be considered as a change *in* the system or a change *of* the system depending on the number of characteristics utilized to define a historical system. The French Revolution inaugurated, certainly, a new system, since it introduced fundamental heterogeneity. Does the accession of Napoleon III mark a change *of* the system? The unification of Germany in 1871 opens another phase of European history. Does it radically alter the European system? Such questions seem to me largely a matter of words. It is simplest to distinguish type and case, according to the habits of our old logic. When the configuration of the relation of forces becomes essentially different or when homogeneity yields to heterogeneity, there is a change in type. When heterogeneity or bipolarity are accentuated or attenuated, we speak of either a change in the system or a change of kind. The models or types of international relations serve and must serve only as a preparation for concrete study.

Thucydides has drawn the stylized model of two powers, one based on naval force and the other on territorial force, one with men "addicted to innovation, whose designs are characterized by swiftness alike in conception and execution," the other with men who "have a genius for keeping what they have got, accompanied by a total want of invention" (I, 70), one open, the other closed to foreigners. How many times, in recent years, has de Tocqueville's famous parallel been quoted as to the two peoples destined, by a mysterious decree of Providence, each to dominate one half of the world, the one by the plow and the other by the sword! The comparison of the two types of societies, of the two regimes, of the two ideologies, of the two conceptions of the international world is classical too because it is indispensable to historical and sociological understanding. The system depends on what the two poles, concretely, are, not only on the fact that they are two.

A system which covers the planet differs, *by nature*, from a system of Greek city-states or European states. The Soviet Union and the United States do not run the same risk of being swept into war in spite of themselves by the disputes of their allies or their satellites as Sparta or Athens. The means of destruction which the two protagonists possess change perhaps *the essence* of the diplomatic-strategic competition. On every level, differences of quantity provoke qualitative revolutions.

chapter VI

Dialectics of Peace and War

War is to be found throughout all history and all civilizations. With axes or cannon, arrows or bullets, chemical explosives or atomic chain reactions, remote or immediate, in isolation or en masse, by accident or according to rigorous method, men have killed each other, using the instruments which custom and the communities' knowledge afforded them.

Thus we might regard a "formal typology" of wars and peace as illusory, only a sociological typology[1] retaining the concrete modes of phenomena being valid. Yet, if the following analyses help illuminate the logic of diplomatic and strategic behavior, the formal typology they reveal may be of some use.

1. Types of Peace and Types of War

I have taken war as my point of departure because strategic-diplomatic behavior is related to the eventuality of armed conflict, because the latter is, so to speak, the denouement of operations on trust. This time we shall take peace as our point of departure because peace is rationally the goal to which societies tend.

This proposition does not contradict the principle of the unity of foreign policy, of the continuous relations among nations. The diplomat does not forget the possibility and the requirements of arbitration by arms during the period when he refuses to resort to violent means. Rivalry between political communities does not begin with the breaking of treaties, nor does it end with the signing of a truce. But whatever the goal of foreign policy—possession of territory, domination over men, triumph of an idea—this goal is not war itself. Some men love battle for its own sake; certain peoples engage in war the way others engage in sport. But at the level of the so-called higher civilizations, when states are legally organized, war can no longer be any-

[1] We shall find one in Chapter XII, in Part II of this book.

thing but a means if consciously desired, or a calamity if provoked for a cause unknown to the actors.

Peace has hitherto appeared to be the *more or less lasting suspension of violent modes of rivalry between political units*. Peace is said to prevail when the relations between nations do not involve the military forms of struggle. But since these peaceful relations occur within the shadow of past battles and in the fear or the expectation of future ones, the *principle* of peace, in the sense Montesquieu gives this term in his theory of governments,[2] is not different in nature from that of wars: peace is based on power, that is, on the relation between the capacities of acting upon each other possessed by the political units. Since the relations of power, in peacetime, without being the exact reflections of the actual or potential relation of forces, are a more or less distorted expression of it, the various types of peace can be related to the types of relation of forces. I distinguish three types of peace—*equilibrium, hegemony, empire*: in a given historical space, the forces of the political units are *in balance*, or else they are *dominated by those of one among them*, or else they are *outclassed by those of one among them* to the point where all the units, save one, lose their autonomy and tend to disappear as centers of political decisions. The imperial state, in the end, reserves to itself the monopoly of legitimate violence.

One might object that imperial peace thereby ceases to be, by definition, a "situation of external policy." Imperial peace would not be distinguished from civil peace: it would be the internal order of an empire. This objection might stand were the typology purely abstract, without relation to the data of history. Yet if there are cases in which imperial peace, once established, becomes indistinguishable from peace among nations, reducing imperial peace as such to civil peace would lead us to misunderstand the diversity of the engagements.

The peace within the German Empire after 1871, despite shreds of sovereignty retained by Bavaria, for instance, differed less and less, as the years passed, from the internal peace of the French Republic. On the other hand, the Greek city-states, conquered by Philip and led by Alexander to the conquest of Asia, had not lost all political-administrative autonomy; they were not deprived of all the attributes which we regard as constituting sovereignty; they possessed immediately, in case of revolt, an embryo of armed forces. The Jewish war would remind us, if necessary, of the precariousness of the Roman peace; the conquered peoples were not entirely disarmed, the ancient institutions and sovereigns, henceforth protected by Rome, were overlapped by the imperial order but not eliminated. In other words, *imperial peace* becomes civil peace insofar as the memory of previously independent political units are effaced, insofar as individuals within a paci-

---

[2] That is, the sentiment or, as we should say today, the emotion or impulse necessary to maintain a type of government—virtue, honor, fear.

fied zone feel themselves less united to the traditional or local community and more to the conquering state.

The empire which Bismarck forged with iron and fire became a national state: the Roman Empire remained a pacified zone to the end. The kings of France created the French nation: for a time France caused imperial peace to prevail throughout North Africa.

Between *peace by equilibrium* and *peace by empire* is sandwiched the *peace by hegemony*. The absence of war does not result from the approximate equality of forces prevailing among political units and forbidding any one of them or any coalition to impose its will; it results, on the contrary, from the incontestable superiority of one of the units. This superiority is such that the unsatisfied states despair of modifying the status quo, and yet the hegemonic state does not try to absorb the units reduced to impotence. It does not abuse hegemony, it respects the external forms of state independence, it does not aspire to empire.

In a system of units jealous of their independence, hegemony is a precarious mode of equilibrium. The German Reich, after 1870, possessed the kind of hegemony that Bismarck hoped to make acceptable to the other European states by means of moderation, thus appeasing their fears or resentments. The Chancellor's successors were less fortunate; they could not prevent the formation of alliances re-establishing equilibrium. Perhaps Bismarck's Germany does not deserve to be called hegemonic, since its hegemony was limited to the Continent and the latter did not constitute a closed system. Yet, if we take into account Great Britain and her maritime extensions, the Reich was not frankly hegemonic. It had a preponderance on land as France had before it during the first part of the reign of Louis XIV, or Spain in the sixteenth century. England had always prevented such a preponderance from turning into an empire or even an uncontested hegemony. The German *preponderance* would have become *hegemony* if the Reich, having beaten France and Russia, could have signed a peace of victory or compromise with Great Britain. The Kaiser's Reich would have been content with a hegemonic peace—Hitler's would have dictated an imperial peace.

In North America the hegemonic peace enforced by the United States is not a partial and fugitive aspect of the system of equilibrium: it is the lasting result of the disproportion, indicated on the map and accentuated by history, between the forces of the Republic of the United States and those of Mexico or Canada. During the last century the United States had to fight a great war not to enlarge the space of its sovereignty, but to maintain the federation. The acquisition of Louisiana, Florida, California and Texas required only dollars or very minor military operations. It was the Southern states' claim to the right of secession which caused the shedding of oceans of blood. Once the federation was consolidated and the western and southern lands were conquered and occupied, once the Indians and the other Europeans were dominated or expelled, the United States was too powerful for a system of equilibrium to be constituted on the American continent, too indifferent to the glory of ruling, not needing land to threaten the independence of the neighboring states to the north and south. This combination of hegemony and the good-neighbor policy is called the *pax Americana*. The hegemony of the United States has also contributed to the peace which has prevailed in South America since the Organization of American States (created at the instigation of the United States) forbade open war between states. (Nevertheless, internal disputes, the conflicts of regimes and the repercussions of world diplomacy are generating a kind of cold war there.)

Neither the ancient world nor Asia nor modern Europe has known a lasting phase between equilibrium and empire. The Greco-Latin civilization of the Mediterranean, after long periods of disturbance, evolved toward imperial peace. In Asia the three great civilizations[3] alternated between peace by equilibrium and imperial peace. In Japan, peace by equilibrium was retrospectively considered as a feudal dispersion of sovereignty because the Tokugawa *imperial peace,* thanks to the homogeneity of culture and institutions, turned into *civil peace.* The imperial unity achieved in China over two thousand years ago—as a result of the final victory of one state over its rival— only succeeded through alternate phases of decomposition and restoration, of civil wars, and a peace that was both civil and imperial. In its foreign relations, the empire hesitated between the defensive, behind its great walls, and inclination toward impulses of expansion. Conquered by the Mongols, then by the Manchus, it never entered (before the nineteenth century) into a permanent system of international relations among equals. As for India, before the British domination it had never known as a whole the equivalent of the peace of the *shoguns* or of the peace of the Middle Empire, nor had it developed a system of equilibrium comparable to that of the Greek city-states or of the European states.

Formally, a historical space is either unified by a force or by a single sovereignty, or fragmented into autonomous centers of decision and action. In the first case we shall call it a universal empire, in the second, warring states. The system of equilibrium with a multipolar configuration tends to stabilize relations among units which acknowledge each other and to limit the conflicts that cause one unit to oppose another. As a matter of fact, the conflicts have always, at one period or another, extended and intensified until the partner-rivals within a civilization appear to be warring states, responsible for the common ruin, to the observer who has studied the centuries that have elapsed between the time of the actors and the observer, the future of the former and the latter's past.

The ternary classification of the forms of peace provides at the same time the most formal and the most general classification of wars: "perfect" wars, according to the political notion of war, are *inter-state.* They bring into

---

[3] The word taken in the sense of Spengler's "cultures" or Toynbee's "societies."

conflict political units which recognize each other's existence and legitimacy. We shall call *super-state* or *imperial* the wars that have as their object, origin or consequence the elimination of certain belligerents and the formation of a unit on a higher level. We shall call *infra-state* or *infra-imperial* the wars that have as their stake the maintenance or the decomposition of a political unit, whether national or imperial.

Inter-state wars become imperial when one of the actors in an international system, whether voluntarily or not, is led to establish his hegemony or empire over his rival, in case of victory. Inter-state wars tend to be amplified into hyperbolic war when one of the actors ventures to acquire an overwhelming superiority of forces: such was the case in the Peloponnesian War or in the First World War. The violence of the conflict can be imputed neither to the technique of combat nor to the passions of the belligerents, but to the geometry of the relation of forces. It is the magnitude of the stake—freedom of the Greek city-states or of the European states—that inflames military ardor. Great wars often mark the shift from one configuration to another, from one system to another, and this shift itself has many causes.

In a general way, we cannot attribute to wars of a determined category this or that concrete characteristic. Infra-state or infra-imperial wars such as the war of the Jews against Rome, of the Chouans against the French Revolution, wars of secession such as the war of Algerian liberation, which bring into conflict an organized power and those populations which refuse to obey it, are often among the most cruel; they are, in certain respects, civil wars, especially if the established power wins. Similarly, war becomes imperial when one of the belligerents brandishes a transnational principle, and the inter-state conflict is charged with partisan passions. The enemy is then simultaneously alien and adversary (or heretic or traitor).

It would be just as dangerous to insist on these abstract notions. Men are not always interested in safeguarding the political unit to which they belong or the historical idea their state incarnates. There are units which outlive themselves, and ideas devoid of meaning. Even if these categories determined the violence of the hostility, the former alone determines neither the duration of the combat nor the conduct of the combatants.

2. *Stakes of War and Principles of Peace*

These two formal typologies each require further analysis. If the three kinds of peace—peace by equilibrium, by hegemony, and by empire—have power as their *principle*,[4] the question will be asked: is there no other *principle* of peace except power? If wars are not concretely defined by their *inter-*, *supra-* and *infra-state* character, it will be asked: what other qualifications should be applied to them in order to define them?

[4] This word, may I remind the reader, is used here in the sense Montesquieu gives it.

Let us answer this last question first. Many classifications of wars are possible and have been proposed. Perhaps none of them can be accepted without question; perhaps many classifications have some validity. It is not evident that the different kinds of wars can be organized into a harmonious scheme. It seems to me, however, that the preceding typology, justified by the relation it establishes between the types of peace and the structure of the international system, can be coupled to two other typologies, one based on the *nature of the political units and the historical ideas* which the belligerents incarnate, the other on the *nature of the weapons and the military machinery*. The first of these two typologies implies a reference to ends, the second a reference to means.

It is customary to speak of *feudal* wars, *dynastic* wars, *national* wars, *colonial* wars. All these expressions suggest that the mode of internal organization of collectivities imposes its quality, gives its style to the belligerent behavior of the political units. In reality, the mode of organization helps determine, if it does not exclusively determine, the occasions and stakes of the conflicts, the judgments of statesmen on legitimate and illegitimate action, their conception of diplomacy and of war. The principle of legitimacy,[5] to return to an expression used above, answers two questions at once: who commands within the state? to what unit should a specific territory or population belong? Wars resemble the principle of legitimacy prevailing over the space and in the time within which they are waged.

The principle of legitimacy creates the occasion or the cause of the conflict. The relations of vassal to suzerain are intermingled in such a way that contradictions appear. The desire for power leads to the failure of certain vassals to fulfill their obligations. The limits of legitimate action are difficult to trace when so many inferior powers retain their own military means or claim some freedom of decision. As long as land or men belong to ruling families, the stake of a war is a province which two sovereigns dispute by means of juridical arguments or guns, or a throne which two princes claim. The day the collective consciousness recognizes that men have the right to choose their political unit, wars become national, either because two states claim the same province or because populations divided among traditional units seek to constitute a single state. Finally, if public opinion were to admit tomorrow that the national era has passed and that economic or military requirements of the great *ensembles* should prevail over the preferences of the governed, wars would become imperial as they have never yet been: the Roman conquerors in the Mediterranean, the Europeans in Asia and Africa did not deny the national idea; they were unaware of it or refused its advantages to populations or to classes of men they regarded as inferior and unworthy, either tempo-

[5] Of course, the word *principle* is used here in its ordinary sense, and not in that of Montesquieu.

rarily or permanently, of the dignity of citizenship. This time, the conquerors would deny the idea in the name of material necessities.

Neither Nazis nor Communists invoked such necessities. The true justification of the Third Reich's undertaking, as the doctrinaires of Nazism conceived it, was the racial superiority of the German people. The true justification of world Sovietization, according to the doctrinaires of Marxism-Leninism, is the superiority or the inevitable victory of the regime which they call socialist. In our time, and perhaps in other periods as well, conquerors feel the need of justifying themselves, morally or historically, in their own eyes.

The principles of legitimacy provoke three kinds of conflicts: those which result from the plurality of possible interpretations, those which derive from the contradiction between the existing status and the new principle, and those which result from the actual application of the principle and from the modifications that appear in the relation of forces.

The claims of the King of England to the throne of France belong to the first category, as do the incompatible claims of Germany and France to Alsace, an imperial territory in the Middle Ages, of Germanic dialect and culture, conquered by Louis XIV, and whose population, in 1871, wanted to remain French. In 1914 the territorial status of Europe was a compromise between the national idea and the heritage of dynastic rights. The partition of Poland, the multinational empires of Austria-Hungary and Turkey were the work of past centuries. They did not conform to the ideas of the age. Yet every modification of territorial status risked upsetting the equilibrium. The guardians of European order belonged to the past; perhaps they were working for peace. The champions of the national idea were accounted bellicose in the immediate present, even if they were peace-loving in the long run.

We need not even bring up the countless cases in which a state, absolute monarchy or democratic republic seeks to "round out" its territory, to explain the frequency of inter-state conflicts. The tendency to justification, the desire for recognition, both create more occasions for quarrels than are submitted to arbitration. Even if the permanent instability of the material conditions (economic, political, demographic) did not compel an incessant and precarious adjustment of equilibrium, the evolution of historical ideas would burden the statesman with the heavy task of reconciling the changing imperatives of justice with the constant necessity of equilibrium. It is even easier to understand, in the light of this analysis, why the classical jurists should have distinguished legal wars from just wars, left it to moralists to determine what justice was, and urged princes not to outlaw their enemies.

Yet up to now we have enumerated only the historical ideas which were, as such, ideas of statehood—in other words, which could serve as a basis for the political organization of collectivities. Certain ideas are national, religious or ideological. In certain periods, conflicts of ideas and rivalry for power are inextricably mingled: sometimes the desire for national or state power prevails over religious or ideological faith, sometimes the latter gains ascendancy over the former. The so-called realistic statesman, even if he is a dignitary of the Church, is the man who employs the passions of crowds with a view to the exclusive interest of the political unit which he serves, an interest identified, as far as he is concerned, with the weakening of rival units. But the moralist or the historian should not reproach those who, at whatever point in the scale, set the triumph or at least the safety of their Church, or their truth, above the reinforcement of a state that may be hostile to the supreme values.

The principle of legitimacy is often at the origin of conflicts (which does not mean that it is their *true* cause); it is sometimes consecrated by the result of the combat: the assassination of an Austrian archduke by Serbian nationalists set fire to the powder; national states emerged from the explosion. But Europe, after 1918, even had it not been lacerated by as many national quarrels as Europe before the war, was also less stable. The War of 1939, provoked by a desire for empire, ended in two worlds, each more or less in conformity with the idea of one of the factions of the victorious alliance.

The historical idea is linked to the military force. Down through the ages, political organization and military organization have had a reciprocal relationship. In ancient civilization all citizens—but not the half-castes or the slaves—were combatants. Thus the Greek city-states possessed a military force of which *number*—great numbers and not small, as legend has it—was often the foundation. An empire measured its forces by the number of its nobles who enjoyed the right of bearing arms, and not by that of its subjects. Greece, and not the Persian Empire, was, as H. Delbrück has shown,[6] an almost inexhaustible reservoir of soldiers.

Military force also depended on the available equipment and on the more or less effective use of this equipment. Impact weapons and projectiles determined the distance between the combatants. The influence of gunpowder on the volume of resources necessary to the armies, and hence on the dimensions of the political units, is a commonplace in historical accounts. Conscription and industry, universal military service and the monstrous increase in the degree of mobilization are at the origin of the hyperbolic character assumed by the First World War: a democratic war, since "civilians in uniform" faced each other; a partially ideological war, since these citizens believed they were "defending their souls"[7]; a war of matériel, waged until the nations in conflict were exhausted, since the armies did not win victories of annihilation and since both the physical and human matériel mobilizable on either side was enormous.

The double dependence of the military machine on social and political organization, and on the techniques of destruction, does not permit us, in this

[6] See below, Chap. VIII.
[7] The two expressions are taken from the speech of Paul Valéry when Marshal Pétain was received in the Académie Française.

abstract analysis, to discern pure types than can be characterized by a single word. Each military system is an organization of arms varying with a social hierarchy, or again, by reversing the formula, the deployment of a certain society, taking into account the effectiveness of the weapons and their various combinations. If the men in combat have always been, to a degree, practical —in Auguste Comte's sense of the word *positif*—that is, if they sought to achieve goals and modify their behavior in relation to experience and rationality—they were never, before modern times, exclusively rational, that is, capable of ignoring morality and custom in order to conceive of warfare in terms of pure effectiveness. Further, this rationality, oriented toward an exclusive victory over the enemy as toward a single object, would have been partial and, in certain cases, unreasonable with regard to the privileged class: the structure of the military system is not without influence on the structure of society. Is that ruling class rational which gives weapons to the discontented classes at the risk of weakening its own power? Throughout history it is rare to find a ruling class which, in the manner of the Meiji reformers, took the initiative of a political and social revolution in order to establish the military machine indispensable to their country's independence and strength. More often, the privileged are incapable of overturning the order from which they benefit and which has become incompatible with the requirements of the system of combat: then appears an Ataturk who liquidates the Ottoman Empire and founds a new state.

Only in our times does military technique, following the example of industrial technique, free itself of all shackles and advance indifferent to the human consequences of its progress. Once production or at least the capacity for production becomes (or seems to have become) a goal in itself, how could it be otherwise with destruction or capacity for destruction? Industry and war are related, inseparable. The growth of one, which generous hearts acclaim, furnishes resources to the other, which is cursed by men of good will. Language itself reminds us of this indissoluble alliance, which is symbolized by the resemblance of automobiles and tanks, long files of workmen and columns of soldiers, armored divisions and families fleeing cities: the same word, *power*, designates the capacity to impose one's will on one's kind and to dominate nature.

Of course, a difference exists, although it is often misunderstood. Man's utilization of water and air, the transformation of coal into heat, of heat into energy, the eventual domestication of the phenomena of fusion, spontaneously produced in the sun—all the countless, foreseeable and rigorous methods for the exploitation of natural resources belong to the order of technology. Whether it is a question of substituting *energy* from coal, oil or the atom, for labor, of manufacturing *objects* for which the cosmos offered elements but not models (transformers, automobiles, refrigerators, etc.) or of improving and multiplying the plants or animals by which humanity is fed, the behavior remains essentially technological, in other words, *it leads back to the planned combination of means with a view to ends.* The vagueness of our knowledge and the risks involved in applying to concrete reality laws established in the laboratory create degrees of uncertainty, enforce margins of security; they do not modify the essence of technological behavior, of human power over nature.

Power over men is also characterized by rationality, once the workers, apparently subject to the power of their fellow men, actually obey the imperatives of technology. The authority of the technologists is not so much personal authority as an awareness of the discipline which a humanized nature imposes upon all. On the other hand, diplomatic-strategic action tends to constrain or convince another center of autonomous decisions, in other words a consciousness whose response to external challenge involves an essential unpredictability: any consciousness may prefer death to submission.

The combined progress of the techniques of production and destruction introduces a *principle* of peace, different from power, which usage has already baptized. *Peace by terror is that peace which reigns (or would reign) between political units each of which has (or would have) the capacity to deal mortal blows to the other.* In this sense, peace by terror could be also described as peace by impotence. When traditional peace prevailed among rival political units, the power of each was defined by the capacity to impose its will upon the other by the use or the threat of force. In the ideal peace by terror, there would be no further inequality between rivals, since each would possess thermonuclear bombs which, dropped on the other's cities, would claim millions of victims. Can we still speak of a fairly powerful nation, or of equilibrium or disequilibrium, once the side which has the fewest thermonuclear bombs and the least-perfected launching vehicles still possesses the capacity to inflict upon its enemy losses out of all proportion to the advantages of any victory?

Peace by terror differs fundamentally from any sort of peace by power (equilibrium, hegemony, empire). The balance of forces is still approximate, equivocal, continually threatened either by a secondary unit changing camp or by the unequal development of the leading states. The calculation of forces involves risks: it is only when under fire that the virtues of armies and peoples are revealed. The course of hostilities in relation to diplomatic and strategic combinations adds further uncertainties. It is conceivable that terror could lead to technical certainty. The destruction which the weakest state would have the means of inflicting upon its enemy, without being precisely measurable in advance, would be in any case sufficient for war to be senseless, just as the resistance of a bridge, though not precisely measurable, is in any case sufficient to sustain the maximum weight which it will some day have to bear.

The perfection of this peace by terror has not yet been achieved, even between the United States and the Soviet Union. Perhaps it will never be achieved.[8] In effect, it requires the certain knowledge that none of the belligerents can, in a surprise attack, eliminate the enemy's means of reprisal or reduce them to such a point that the eventual reprisal no longer inflicts upon the aggressor "unacceptable" losses. It has not been proved that this is actually the case. Today or tomorrow, one side or the other may perfect its means of passive defense (shelters for the population) and active defense (rockets against bombardment planes or against ballistic missiles) as well as its means of aggression (number and position of ballistic missiles) to the point where the leaders are tempted by the possibility of a Pearl Harbor on a thermonuclear scale—in other words, of a massive attack on all the enemy's means of reprisal and on several of its cities. Would not, therefore, the victim of the aggression have to capitulate, since retaliation would not noticeably weaken the aggressor, and would involve its own total destruction? Whatever the improbability of such a hypothesis, peace by terror will only be perfected when the advantage possessed today by the one who strikes first is suppressed or reduced to the minimum.

Aside from the vulnerability of the means of reprisal, the uncertainty concerns also the "amount of destruction endurable" or the "threshold of saturation." Initiating war would be absolutely senseless if the aggressor were assured of being also totally destroyed or knew that the number of thermonuclear bombs necessary to eliminate the enemy's means of reprisal was such that its own population or humanity as a whole would be gravely threatened by radioactive fallout. Despite varying opinions among experts, we have not yet reached this point. Here, the question rises: at what point of destruction does war cease to be a justifiable political instrument? By the end of the Thirty Years' War the German population had been diminished by half. In 1941 the first battles cost the Soviet Union tens of millions of inhabitants and more than a third of its industry, which had fallen into German hands. The Soviet Union nonetheless survived and ultimately triumphed.

Of course, losing by occupation and losing by extermination, losing in a few minutes and losing in several years are not equivalent phenomena. Let us be content, provisionally, with noting the original factor which thermonuclear weapons introduce into military calculations: they make possible destruction of such magnitude that the cost of combat would in all rationality seem to be superior to the advantage of victory. In this sense, the effect of weapons of massive destruction could be to jeopardize Clausewitz's formula "war is the continuation of policy by other means."

Between *peace by power* and *peace by impotence* exists a third term, at least on the conceptual level: *peace by satisfaction*. Valéry once said that there can be no true peace except in a world where all the states are satisfied with the status quo. But this status always reflects the relations existing at the end of the preceding trial by force. The status which satisfies some provokes

[8] Cf. a detailed analysis below, Chap. XIV.

claims from others, and this is why there are only truces[9] of a more or less precarious nature.

What are the conditions, in the abstract, of a peace by satisfaction? Perhaps the theory of objectives will permit us to answer such a question. The political units should first seek neither territory external to that under their sovereignty, nor alien populations. This first condition is neither absurd nor even unrealizable. Let us suppose that men are conscious of their nationality —that is, of the political-cultural community to which they wish to belong; why should the leaders seek to integrate by constraint human groups which feel alien, or forbid them to join the nationality of their choice?

Let us suppose the national idea were universally admitted, and honestly applied. Is this enough? Certainly not: it is necessary for political units not to seek to extend themselves, either to increase their material or human resources, to disseminate their institutions, or to enjoy the most vain and intoxicating of victories, the pride of ruling. The satisfaction derived from the respect of *one* principle of legitimacy must be supplemented by the suspension of rivalry for land and men, force and idea, and even for pride.

None of these hypotheses is contradictory or even, as such, unrealizable. But we must proceed with care: nothing is done so long as something remains to be done. Satisfaction will be lasting and assured only on condition that it is general. If one of the actors nourishes ambitions or is suspected of nourishing them, how could the others keep from returning to the infernal cycle of competition? Not to take precautions if he—my neighbor, the evil one, that is—is plotting my death, would be unreasonable and even culpable. But what precaution will replace the superiority of strength, the use of this superiority, while there is still time, the accumulation of resources to guarantee this superiority?

In other words, peace by consent presupposes that confidence is general; it therefore requires a revolution in the procedure of international relations, a revolution which would bring to an end the era of suspicion and inaugurate that of security. But this revolution, unless there is a conversion of souls, must affect institutions. In other words, universal peace by universal consent and mutual confidence does not seem to me effectively possible if the political units do not find a substitute for security by force. Universal empire would furnish this substitute, since it would suppress the autonomy of centers of decisions. The rule of law, in the Kantian sense, would also furnish it, insofar as the states would commit themselves to obeying the decisions of an arbitrator, a tribunal or an assembly and have no doubt that this commitment would be honored by all. But how would this doubt be dissipated if the community was not in the position to constrain the criminal?

The universal state and the rule of law are not like concepts; the one appears at the end of power politics, the other at the end of the evolution of

[9] Paul Valéry: *Regards sur le monde actuel.*

international law. But both ultimately imply the suppression of what has
been the essence of international politics: *the rivalry of states which put their
pride and their duty in taking the law into their own hands.*

Hence there has never been an international system including the whole
of the planet. The partial systems have known only peace by power. If, in
certain areas, at certain periods in time, we divine the premises of a peace by
satisfaction, the relations of power, over a larger area and on a higher level,
do not permit us to state that the *principle* of peace has been satisfaction.
Since 1945 we have seen the beginnings of a peace by terror (between the
Soviet Union and the United States) and a peace by satisfaction (in Western Europe). But the international system tends to become worldwide and,
thereby, the traditional types assume new appearances and are juxtaposed or
combined in a system of singular complexity.

3. Warlike Peace

Peace, whose types we have distinguished in the course of the preceding
pages, was defined strictly by the absence of war and not by a positive faculty: *virtus* (to return to Spinoza's expression). Even peace by consent does
not seem to us distinct from the world of egoism. Does the notion, current
today, of a cold war call into question the distinction between war and peace?
I do not think so. We have said that Clausewitz's formula—war is the continuation of policy by other means—has been replaced by its opposite: policy
is the continuation of war by other means. But these two formulas are, formally, equivalent. They both express the continuity of competition and the
use of alternately violent and non-violent means toward ends which do not
differ in essence. At most we may add that the margin of semi-violent means,
regarded as legitimate in peacetime, has a tendency to broaden, and that
Montesquieu's precept, "nations ought in time of peace to do one another all
the good they can, and in time of war as little injury as possible," is further
from practice now than it has ever been. But it has probably never been very
close.

The situation known as a cold war nonetheless offers certain original features, some of which derive from the *peace by terror,* others from the double
heterogeneity, both *historical* and *ideological,* of a system extended to the
limits of the entire globe. These original features may be summarized, I
believe, by the three words *deterrence, persuasion, subversion,* which designate the three modes of cold-war diplomatic-military strategy.

Peace by terror involves the use of a so-called deterrence strategy. Each of
the two super powers, possessing more or less equivalent means of destruction,
makes a play to the other by threatening to resort to the supreme argument
of weapons of mass destruction. Does peace by terror imply the permanent,
definitive character of cold war (barring a general and controlled disarmament)? This is not certain. But the present phase of the peace by terror has
special characteristics.

First of all, it constitutes the initial phase of peace by terror. Humanity has not yet grown accustomed to the new universe, which it is hesitantly exploring, incapable of foregoing the threat of thermonuclear war, eager not to put this threat into practice, uncertain of the ultimate compatibility between the strategic use of the threat and not carrying it out.

At the time when the United States possessed an atomic monopoly, the Soviet Union had an irresistible superiority of conventional weapons. The inequality of risks taken by the European and American partners in the Atlantic Alliance created a climate of reciprocal suspicion: the desire for peace on the part of the state that has the least to lose in case of war never seems resolute enough for the allies who have nothing to hope for in case of conflict, even in case of victory. It was not the Soviet Union's production of atomic and thermonuclear bombs but the development of strategic bombers and above all of ballistic missiles which put an end to these suspicions and convinced all the Western powers that they were in the same boat.

At this moment there appeared another cause for apprehension: was the peace by terror really secured? At what point was the advantage of either the United States or the Soviet Union in the race for arms, bombs and delivery systems, passive defense for the population and active defense against missiles, likely to compromise the peace by terror? Or again, to substitute another probably better expression, in what measure is the balance of terror as stable or unstable as the balance of forces? If the balance of terror were *perfect*—giving this word the same meaning as above—the notion of the balance of forces would have lost all meaning. But theoreticians and statesmen are not in agreement on this point. Rightly or wrongly, the arms race keeps alive the secret anxiety that the balance of terror is as precarious as the old balance of power.

At the same time, humanity is questioning itself as to the prospects: is it desirable or deplorable that the number of members of the atomic club should increase? There is no lack of argument for both alternatives: could those states not possessing atomic weapons be protected tomorrow by an ally? Will the United States assume the excessive risk of the destruction of its cities in order to save West Berlin today and Western Europe tomorrow? Or rather, will the Russians *believe* that the United States will assume this risk? But on the other hand, is it not terrifying to imagine that within ten or fifteen years states like Egypt or China will possess weapons whose explosive power can be counted in thousands (twenty thousand for the Hiroshima bomb) and millions of tons of TNT (for the thermonuclear bomb)?[10] In short, men have always waged the wars for which they were preparing. The advice *si vis pacem para bellum* justified preparations: it has never, however faithfully

[10] A single thermonuclear bomb has an explosive power superior to that of all the bombs dropped on Germany between 1939 and 1945.

taken, prevented war. Can one use diplomatically the threat of a war which one wants to avoid at *almost* any cost?

Peace by terror is accompanied by ideological rivalry, characteristic of all heterogeneous systems. In the systems which include North America, Europe and northern Asia, the two chief actors are in conflict neither for territory nor for men. The United States and the Soviet Union both occupy an underpopulated space. They have reserves of arable soil and have no reason to fear the growth of their populations. Now, in any bipolar system, the leaders, incapable of ruling together, are doomed to competition, any progress of the one seeming a danger to the other. Today's great powers cannot rule together because of the incompatibility of their institutions and their principles of legitimacy.[11] Therefore they have the entire planet for their theater and all nations and contested frontiers as the stake of a dispute which they are unwilling to decide upon by the sword and which they cannot settle by negotiation.

Not all heterogeneous systems have provoked the equivalent of the present modes of cold war. The origin of the novelty is a combination of industry and conscription, of technology and democracy. During the First World War the belligerents discovered that civilians "in uniform" did not agree, as readily as professional soldiers, to die without knowing for what or for whom. Propaganda, organization of enthusiasm behind the lines as well as at the front, involved, of necessity, an element of ideology, a political and moral justification of the cause to which so many lives and so much wealth was sacrificed. The logic of the justification cut across military necessities. If the Allied cause was just, that of the Central Powers was not. If the conviction that their cause was just sustained the courage of the combatants and constituted an element of strength, it was useful to spread doubt, on the other side of the line of fire, as to the nature of the cause which both soldiers and civilians were defending, or believed they were defending. Thus, inexorably, each side passed from organizing enthusiasm at home to organizing defeatism among the enemy.

Technological means (radio, television) and the establishment of revolutionary parties are enough to make this war of propaganda, newspapers, tracts and sound waves permanent. Allied spokesmen had tried to separate the German people from its regime (and to a certain extent had succeeded): "You are not fighting for yourselves," they insisted by every available means. "You are fighting for your masters, the despots who have deceived you and are leading you to the abyss. We do not make war against the German people but against imperial despotism." Whatever judgment is made about the Versailles

---

[11] The question often asked, do the United States and the Soviet Union ultimately seek security (or power), or on the contrary the diffusion of their ideas, is senseless. Whether statesmen believe they seek one or the other, they cannot fail to seek one *and* the other, since one involves the other.

Treaty, it must have appeared, in the eyes of the conquered, as a sinister mockery of the hopes which the propaganda of the democracies had awakened during the war. It was no different from 1939 to 1945; each side attempted to persuade the enemy masses that they were fighting for and because of a minority of exploiters, capitalists, plutocrats, Nazis, Jews or Communists, not for the fatherland and for a regime that was ultimately just. In the end, all these kinds of propaganda neutralized each other or were neutralized by the faults of statesmen and strategists. Every people followed its leaders to the end: the German armies of occupation revived the various traditional patriotisms; in Russia, the brutality of the occupants forged the unity of the Soviet regime and the population; the Anglo-American insistence on unconditional surrender deprived the adversaries of National Socialism of what would have been their best argument, the chance of escaping absolute defeat.

With Europe divided into a Sovietized zone and a zone of pluralist democracy, with the custom, inherited from the war, of foreign-language broadcasts, the organizing of defeatism abroad, if not of enthusiasm at home, has become a permanent and normal aspect of international relations. Invectives against foreign regimes do not achieve the same violence as during the hostilities. Western broadcasts to the countries of Eastern Europe tend to assume an informative character rather than an openly combative one. But information seeks to be a weapon as soon as it addresses the governed over the heads of the leaders and breaks the monopoly which the state claims to exercise. The minimum result aimed at by the psychological weapon in cold war is to prevent the totalitarian regimes from being alone with their peoples: the *third man*—the stranger, the enemy, the foreigner, the democracies, world opinion—is always present. He does not suppress, but he limits the modern form of the royal prerogative, the right of official lies, of excluding speech and interpretation from the outside.

It is difficult to measure exactly the effectiveness of the strategy of persuasion, but experience suggests that it disturbs neither the Soviet regimes nor the pluralist regimes or, to use the concepts I prefer, the regimes of monopolistic parties and the pluralist-constitutional regimes, provided the former are based on a national party which has effectively accomplished the Revolution, and that the latter reveal a determination and give the people the feeling that they are governed. It is not the Western strategy of persuasion which provoked the Polish and Hungarian revolts of 1956, any more than the Soviet strategy of persuasion was responsible for the collapse of the Fourth Republic.

Things happen quite differently the day persuasion is transformed into subversion—in other words, when action to overturn an established power and substitute for it another is added to the language defining what is extolled and what is not (the regime of the future or the regime of the *other*). We use the expression *technique of subversion* rather than *subversive war* because this latter notion seems equivocal. It tends to identify a juridically defined species of conflict and a means of combat. There is an obvious link between the conflicts in which, at the outset, a single one of the belligerents is internationally recognized and the methods of subversion: that is to say, the revolutionary party which has no or only a few organized troops is obliged to resort to the methods of subversion. But these two notions are nonetheless conceptually separable and sometimes actually separated.

Legally, the wars which French authors have acquired the habit of calling *subversive* or *revolutionary* belong to the genre of conflicts which we have called infra-state or infra-imperial. They can be classified with the civil wars since, initially, only one side is recognized by the international community. But civil wars are not all subversive; the War of Secession in America, although juridically a civil war, was fought by two powers organized from the outset. An undertaking against an established power, like that of General Franco, does not always resort to means which, in the eyes of French theoreticians, are the very essence of subversive war, that is, the conversion and recruiting of the people. Subversion is the weapon used by a national or revolutionary party to strike down the recognized authority in possession of the military and administrative machinery.

If revolutionary parties all belong to the same juridical category, if they almost all resort to the weapon of subversion, it is still proper to outline several cases, depending on the relations between the *established power* and the *revolutionary party*. In China the stake was the regime of an existing, undisputed state. Chiang Kai-shek and Mao Tse-tung both sought to gain leadership over eternal China. Which men, in the name of which ideas, would take over the Middle Empire and adapt it to the requirements of the industrial age, these were the questions which the civil war was to decide. In Indonesia, in Indo-China, in Tunisia, in Morocco, in Algeria, the stake was the independence of a population subject to foreign domination or of a state which had transferred its sovereignty to the advantage of a protecting state. The Algerian War was born from a revolt. The FLN nationalists were rebels and the French government stated that it was dealing with an internal affair. But historically, sociologically, since 1945, all wars called subversive by French authors, from Indonesia and Indo-China to Algeria, have belonged to a category which is not defined by the concept of civil wars: these wars of imperial disintegration, which are defined as subversive in the eyes of the theoreticians of the ex-imperial state, are called wars of liberation in the language of the nationalists. We shall understand nothing of the nature of these conflicts if we insist on the analysis of only the technique of subversion and forget two essential facts: the sympathy of a great part of public opinion for the anti-colonialist cause, and the community of race, language and religion between the revolutionaries and the masses, and not between the masses and the established power.

Abstractly, the goal of subversion is to withdraw a population from the administrative and moral authority of an established power and to integrate

it within other political and military frameworks, sometimes in and by con-
flict. From all evidence, success or failure chiefly depends on the spontaneous
relations between the active minority leading the combat and the mass of the
population.

To Western eyes, what matters most is the relation between the active
minority and communism (local party or Soviet bloc). When this minority
is composed of Communists or directed by them, as was the case in Indo-
China, national liberation brings with it a regime which adheres to the Soviet
bloc. When the minority includes a Communist faction, Western strategy
hesitates between the fear of a Communist advance and the desire to favor
"national liberation" (the moderate nationalists will resist the Communists).
When the minority is anti-Communist, Western strategists (except for
those who belong to the ex-imperial power) tend to favor the nationalist
cause, either by ideological sympathy or by calculation. Still the spokesmen
for the ex-imperial power may contend that the national revolution will turn
to the advantage of the Communists, despite the intentions or convictions of
the nationalists.

Whatever the merits or defects of the two possible Western strategies in
colonial territories, one yielding to and the other resisting the nationalist
claims, events in the territory are chiefly controlled by the relation between
the revolutionaries and the masses, not by the relation between the revolutionaries and the blocs in conflict on the world scene. The outcome of these
wars assumes its historical significance within the framework of global diplomacy; the causes of the victories and defeats are chiefly local.

4. Dialectics of Antagonism

Deterrence, persuasion, subversion—these three concepts designate modes
of action, i.e., behavior oriented to the conduct of other men, neutrals or
objects. Analyses of these three means of action, even on the most abstract
level, are incomplete insofar as they neglect the dialectical essence of politics,
namely the law of antagonism. Each of these procedures is employed by *at
least* two actors: it is the dialogue of the actors which establishes the meaning of the action.

The strategy of deterrence seemed unilateral as long as the Soviet Union
did not have the means of inflicting upon the United States the blows which
the latter would be capable of striking against her. This asymmetry was
more apparent than real, as long as Europe was without protection. Even the
appearance of asymmetry has vanished, thereby producing a doubt as to the
value of deterrence once the latter becomes reciprocal. To what degree is the
threat of killing plausible if the other's death is to be followed by our own?
Is threat of mutual suicide of any use in diplomacy?

In Part III we shall study in detail the problems of diplomacy in the Atomic
Age. Let us confine ourselves here to enumerating the three possibilities
which, in the abstract, the reciprocal capacity for destruction affords. If war

signified mutual suicide, either the great powers would not fight any longer, or they would fight without resorting to weapons too destructive to be used rationally, or else they would fight by means of satellites, interposed allies or neutrals. Peace, non-atomic war, with or without participation of the members of the atomic club, these are the three hypotheses. A limited, non-atomic war between the great powers of the system has not yet occurred, as if the leaders mistrusted each other, fearing that once again the intoxication of battle and the desire for victory at any cost might drown out the voice of reason and the simple instinct of self-preservation.

The reciprocity of deterrence tends, it seems to me, to neutralize a strategy which must be unilateral in order to be completely convincing. The more inhuman the threat, the rarer the circumstances in which it will be taken seriously. When unilateral, the strategy of deterrence holds a death-threat over the enemy. When bilateral, it holds an almost similar threat over all the actors. Reciprocity diminishes the frequency of use and increases the improbabilities of executing the thermonuclear threat.

Asymmetry, in the case of persuasion, derives from the difference between the regimes in conflict. A constitutional-pluralist regime tolerates, in fact, the existence of parties which are in sympathy with another nation and another regime. If it has the right, as a result of its principles, not to tolerate conspiracy, the initial stage of rebellion, it has difficulty distinguishing in practice between persuasion and subversion, propaganda and conspiracy. Also the Western democracies do not forbid the "foreign nationalists" to speak and organize, whereas, in the regimes to which the latter give their adherence, no one is entitled to plead the cause of the West.

Yet it would be a mistake to exaggerate the consequences of this "inequality of opportunity." The West is present in the Soviet Union, despite the radio "jamming." When the Soviet leaders repeat the formula which Stalin launched at the outset of the last Five-Year Plan—overtake the United States—they thereby recognize the American lead in production, productivity and standard of living. Economists, philosophers, propagandists read the Western authors and the dialogue with them continues. Sometimes the excesses of official propaganda ultimately provoke curious reactions. Some men, on the other side of the Iron Curtain, arrive at an excessive idea of the West's standard of living from not believing the caricatured image of capitalism spread by the official spokesmen. A regime based on the state monopoly of political interpretation is perhaps, in the long run, more vulnerable than a (normally functioning) regime which admits dialogue, both interior and exterior.[12]

Reciprocity is still more important in the case of subversion, because reprisal resembles challenge, repression resembles subversion, from which results a striking symmetry of action and reaction, of revolutionaries and conservatives. The former wish to dissolve the existing community, uprooting

[12] See below, Chap. XVII, Sec. 3.

individuals and integrating them into another community. The clandestine organization is the nucleus of this community: when it has managed to gain control of administration and justice, the substitution of the rebel community for the previous community is accomplished. What can be the objective of repression, if not to destroy the clandestine organization, nucleus of the future community, and to restore, both materially and morally, the people to the pre-existing community? This objective is not unreasonable, declare the theoreticians of repression, whatever the sentiments of the people, since only a minority is capable of the energy, courage, and sacrifices which clandestine action requires and since, without the hard core of activists, the masses incline to passivity.

The strategy of persuasion—that is, the methods as a whole which are intended to modify or consolidate the sentiments, opinions or convictions of men—is an element of the strategy of subversion and of repression. The FLN nationalists wanted to make the Algerian Moslem believe that he never was or would be French, that he could have no other country but Algeria. The French officers of "psychological action" wanted to make him believe that if he had never been entirely French, he would be so henceforth, that the Algerian nation proclaimed by the FLN was a deception and would be a disaster for him. The dialogue, addressed to the Moslems, between the adherents of Algerian independence and the partisans of French Algeria, was transformed into a dialectic of subversion and repression the day the revolutionaries used violence in order to break up the existing community and to demonstrate thereby a schism between Moslems and French. At that moment, terror, a decisive element of the strategy of deterrence, became one of the major weapons of subversion.

The word *terror* has been employed, in our era, in at least four contexts: by the Germans to designate the bombing of cities, by those seeking to conserve an established power (German occupation officials in France or French authorities in Algeria) to stigmatize the action of the resistants or nationalists, by all authors to characterize one of the aspects of totalitarian regimes, and lastly by usage to designate the relation of dual impotence between the two great powers armed with thermonuclear bombs. These different uses of the same word reveal certain profound characteristics of our period and the relationship of today's three strategies.

The bombardment of cities, the "raids of terror" as the German communiqués called them, had material objectives. They obliged the enemy to devote important resources to active or passive defense, clearing the ruins, maintaining public services. Directly and indirectly, they reduced production. But the morale of the populations was a further objective; in naming them "raids of terror" the German government denied them a military function, assigning as their sole objective the weakening of the collective desire to resist. Whether true or false, this interpretation constituted a rejoinder to the intention of Allied strategy. The latter may have had as its major objective the morale of the population, but it did not admit the fact. By doing so, it would have reduced the effectiveness of its method: the Germans were meant to believe that the destruction of their cities corresponded to a wartime necessity. The German government, on the contrary, had every reason to denounce the raids of terror, so that the enemy would appear odious and so that the civilians, immediate target of the bombs, would have the desire and the pride to conduct themselves like soldiers at the front.

An action of violence is labeled "terrorist" when its psychological effects are out of proportion to its purely physical result. In this sense, the so-called indiscriminate acts of revolutionaries are terrorist, as were the Anglo-American zone bombings. The lack of discrimination helps spread fear, for if no one in particular is a target, no one can be safe. As a matter of fact, the bombings were effective in a different way when their object was to destroy means of communication or synthetic petroleum factories. Even on the psychological level, non-discrimination was probably an error. The destruction of the factories would have shaken the confidence of the population, whereas the accumulating ruins, apparently without military motive, tended to exasperate rather than to discourage. Perhaps the urban terrorism would have the same effect contrary to revolutionary expectation, were it inflicted on a homogeneous population. Among a mixed population, like that of Algeria, the exasperation of one of the communities provokes the schism which the rebels demand and which the conservative forces wish to prevent. Indeed, the schism between those of French stock and the Algerian Moslems confirms the FLN thesis and denies that of the established power.

In case of "indiscriminate" terrorism, the reaction of those of French stock is to regard all Moslems as suspect, if not to take revenge on any of them who happen to be caught. If terrorism is not selective, the repressive reprisal is not likely to be selective either. As suspects, all the Moslems felt excluded from the existing community. Between them and the French, all confidence vanished. There is no community without confidence: if men do not know what they can expect from each other, they no longer live in society. All are afraid, and each is alone.

The inevitable errors of repression heighten this disintegration. When too many innocents are punished, abstention ceases to seem a protection. The activists have no further difficulty recruiting combatants, once the risks of legally culpable action do not seem so different from the risks of legally innocent passivity.

Hence we understand the transition from the terror created by the dialectics of subversion and repression to the terror erected into a system of government. Let us recall Mr. Khrushchev's speech and its description of the Stalinist universe. Why was none of the members of the Politiburo able to stand against the despot and bring to an end the crimes committed "under the reign of the cult of personality"? Mr. Khrushchev gave as an essential reason the fact that the people would not have understood, but he clearly suggests another reason: the highest state officials dared not trust each other. Never has Montesquieu's theory of fear, the *principle* of despotism, received more striking confirmation or illustration. When one man commands, without law and without rules, fear reduces all men to a common impotence.

The President of the Council of Soviet Ministers also criticized Stalin for having refused to make any distinction between the forms of guilt and for having re-established the practice of collective punishment. The opposition was wrong, Mr. Khrushchev said, yet they were not all traitors or Gestapo agents. Through considering every deviationist as an enemy, honest militants are confused with deviationists. Here, too, the outcome was the typical phenomenon of revolutionary periods, the generalization of suspicion. It is not an accident that the key concept of every phase of terror is that of *suspicion*. Countless are those, guilty or innocent, who feel a vague threat weighing upon them. How could there not be thousands or millions of suspects, since the established power is a new one and knows itself to be surrounded by enemies?

Among the suspects, some groups bring themselves to the attention of the authorities. They justify suspicion by their very being, aside from any action they might take. The *ci-devants* were suspect in the eyes of the Jacobins. Non-Russian citizens had become suspect in the period of the Stalinist madness, and Mr. Khrushchev has described deportation of whole populations, the Ukrainians having escaped such a fate only because of their number. There is no longer any degree in crime since the deviationist does not differ from the traitor, but collective inequalities exist, certain groups being more suspect than others.

Up to a certain point, subversion and repression are both likely to enter the diabolical cycle of strictly political terror. In every war the defeatists are accused of preparing the defeat which they announce, and sometimes they actually contribute to it. How can the established power help but be weakened by those citizens who question its action or its legitimacy? The Frenchman who cast doubt on *Algérie française* objectively gave assistance to the Algerian nationalists. With disregard to his intentions, he was called a traitor, since in fact he *was* aiding the enemy. Similarly, the Moslem who refused to obey the FLN abetted the French cause. He was a traitor to his Algerian fatherland just as for the Ultras the liberal Frenchman was a traitor to France.

Comparing conservatives and revolutionaries, it is the latter who often extend political terror furthest in the so-called subversive war. Whether it is a question of maintaining the clandestine nucleus or of winning enthusiasm, persuasion is not enough. The discouraged must be punished by death, for discouragement is on the watch for combatants who have only rifles with which to face planes and tanks; impulses to negotiate and refusal to obey must be punished severely, for the legitimacy of the political organization, in exile or in hiding, has only uncertain foundations. "Collaborators" must be eliminated, since they tend to refute, by their example, the claims for which so many men are struggling and dying. When the dialectic of subversion and repression is prolonged, the conservative state gradually restrains liberties and the revolutionaries multiply acts of violence in order to forge their own community as much as to dissolve the mixed community upon which they have declared war.

The so-called technique of re-education or brainwashing has developed out of the combined strategy of persuasion and subversion. The effort, characteristic of subversion, to break up an existing community and integrate the uprooted individuals into another, is no longer exerted clandestinely, but in broad daylight, in camps where the captured soldiers are assembled. Here, too, the results were asymmetrical: a few American soldiers were converted, thousands of Chinese soldiers (who however, had previously served in the Nationalist armies) refused repatriation. *The technique is not foolproof.* In Indo-China the captured French soldiers and officers also suffered the ordeals of re-education: the goal was not to induce them to become members of the Vietnamese community, but to interpret their combat and the entire universe in terms of the ideology of their enemies. By imputing to France the sin of imperialism and to the Viet-minh the glory of the struggle for freedom, these Frenchmen would have disavowed their fatherland and admitted that their jailers were right. The effects of this re-education have rarely lasted more than a few weeks, yielding, after liberation, to the influence of the national milieu.

The inspiration of these practices is as old as the attempts at conversion, whether the inquisitors want to save souls, or the conquerors or revolutionaries seek to obtain, from the subjugated or from the *ci-devants,* the homage of a self-styled renunciation. The confessions of the Moscow trials were no more than a grotesque and monstrous semblance of conversion. The majority of *ci-devant* Chinese intellectuals probably do not believe in the version of their own past which they themselves edited, using the concepts of the victorious party. But belief and skepticism are not always distinguished in the soul of militants or prisoners, re-educators or converts. In a sense, Lenin's companions, on the threshold of death, continued to believe that "the party was the proletariat" and that Stalin, who was its leader, did not separate himself from the proletarian cause. Ideological thought proceeds by chain identification. It rationalizes, though it is often irrational. Nothing is easier than to subscribe to rationalizations, reasonable in themselves, although absurd in relation to reality.

Subversion and repression both result in the technique of re-education, since both tend to dissolve a community and forge another one from it. The communities, whether destroyed or broken up, in the case of a civil war, are ideological, and, in the case of a war of liberation, national. Thus the opportunities of either kind of re-education are determined in advance not by the quality of its means but by the nature of the men. A Moroccan nationalist could never, whatever the length of his stay in a camp and the subtlety of the psychotechnicians, be won over to the cause of French greatness. The Algerians, genuinely won over by the nationalist cause, are also no longer recoverable. Ideas are more malleable than souls: nationality is inscribed in souls, not in ideas.

The cold war is located at the meeting point of two historical series, one leading to the development of thermonuclear bombs and ballistic missiles, to the incessant increase of ever more destructive weapons and even swifter carrying vehicles, the other accentuating the psychological element of the conflict at the cost of physical violence. The conjunction of these two series is in itself intelligible: the more the instruments of force exceed the human scale, the less usable they are. Technological excess brings war back to its essence as a trial of wills, either because threat is substituted for action, or because the reciprocal impotence of the great powers forbids direct conflicts and thereby enlarges the spaces in which clandestine or scattered violence flourishes, without too much risk to humanity.

If peace by terror, the triumph of inventive genius applied to the science of destruction, coincides with the age of subversion, historical conjunctions are to some degree the cause. The Second World War precipitated the decline of Europe by undermining the prestige and the force of those who, at the beginning of the century, believed themselves the masters of the universe. It is the Western powers themselves who have returned to the practices which the establishment of regular armies and the international law of war had been intended to suppress or limit: the mobilization of those who have been called soldiers without uniform. From 1914 to 1918, obligatory military service had universalized the duty to bear arms, except for those whose work was considered more useful to the community than their sacrifice. From 1939 to 1945, universality of participation assumed another form, passive under bombing, active in the resistance. Civilians were themselves mobilized to oppose the occupying powers. Civilian resistance, whether effective or not on the military level, bore witness to the stake of the war: to paraphrase Valéry's remark quoted above—man, without being in uniform, was defending his soul. The victory of either side signified, or seemed to signify, a conversion of souls by force.

Peace by terror holds a worldwide and monstrous threat over the mass of humanity. Subversion imposes upon each individual the obligation to choose his fate, his party, his nation. The thermonuclear threat reduces men to a kind of collective passivity. The psychological weapon, manipulated by revolutionaries or conservatives, aims at all men because it aims at each of them.

PART TWO

SOCIOLOGY
Determinants and Constants

The distinction between *theory* and *sociology* is, in the social disciplines, as easy to make in the abstract as it is difficult to respect in practice. Even in the economic sciences, whose theory has been rigorously and systematically constructed, the frontiers are often vague. What data, what causes belong to pure theory? Which data, which causes should be regarded as external to the economic system as such (exogenous)? The answer to these questions varies with the period, even within one and the same period, according to the economists. In any case, theory must be elaborated in terms of its own concepts and of logic for the problems of sociology to become apparent.

The first part of this book has permitted us to grasp the concepts with the help of which we can interpret the logic of the conduct of international relations. In the first three chapters we have analyzed in turn the interconnections of diplomacy and strategy, the factors on which the power of political units depends, and lastly the objectives that statesmen seek to achieve. In the last three chapters we have analyzed not the conduct of international relations considered in isolation, with their means and their ends, but international systems. The analysis of these systems has involved two stages. First the determination of the characteristics proper to any system (homogeneous or heterogeneous, inter-relation of forces and juridical regulation), then the description of the two ideal types of systems (multipolar and bipolar). The analysis of systems leads to the dialectic of peace and war—that is, to the enumeration of types of peace and types of war, including intermediary forms, currently named cold war, or warlike peace, or revolutionary war.

Theory, thus conceived, renders the study of international relations, as they develop, three kinds of service: 1. it indicates to the sociologist and the historian the chief elements which a description of the circumstances should include (limits and nature of the diplomatic system; ends and means of actors, etc.); 2. if the sociologist or historian wants to go beyond description to understand the conduct of international relations of a political unit or of its leaders, he can utilize theory as a criterion of rationality, comparing the action which, according to theory, would have been logical, with that which has actually occurred; 3. the sociologist or the historian can and should seek out the causes, internal or external to diplomatic relations, which determine the formation, the transformation or the disappearance of international systems (just as the sociologist of economics seeks the economic or non-economic causes which determine the birth or death of the regime: feudal, capitalist or socialist).

We have intentionally, in the preceding paragraph, bracketed the sociologist and the historian together. Now the former's task, it seems to me, comes between that of the theoretician and that of the historian. The historian interprets, recounts the events of international affairs; he follows the development of a political unit, of a diplomatic system, of a civilization considered as a singular, unique whole. The sociologist seeks propositions of a certain generality, relative *either to the action which a certain cause produces* upon power or upon the objectives of political units, upon the nature of systems, upon the types of peace and war, *or to regular series or patterns of development* which characterize the situation without the actors necessarily being aware of it.

Thus theory naturally suggests the enumeration of effect-phenomena, the determined factors, for which the sociologist is tempted to seek cause-phenomena, the determinants. These determined factors, following the order of the chapters in the preceding part, are: 1. the *factors of power* (or again, what is the actual weight, in each period, of the factors of power? How do they combine?); 2. the *choice, by any one state or at any one period, of certain objectives, rather than certain others*; 3. the *circumstances necessary or favorable to the constitution of one system* (homogeneous or heterogeneous, multipolar or bipolar) *rather than another*; 4. the *actual character of the various kinds of peace and war*; 5. the *frequency of war*; 6. the *order, if there is one, by which war and peace succeed each other*; the *pattern, if there is one, according to which the fortune—peaceful or warlike—of sovereign units, of civilizations, of humanity itself fluctuates*. These determined factors belong, as we see, to two species: either they are the data by which we understand the logic in the conduct of international affairs, or else they are total processes created by men and perceptible only to the spectator situated at some distance from the event.

To a certain degree, the historian's task is the study of determined factors in the first category, and even of their causes. He alone carries analysis down to the singular case, understood and explained in all its details. But the sociologist is in a position to arrive at facts or relations of some generality, if he succeeds in dividing the material according to determinants and not effect-phenomena. The enumeration of these determinants must be systematic if this sociological essay is to be of any use.

The political units whose peaceful-warlike relations we are analyzing are human collectivities, organized on a territorial basis. Men, living in society within a delimited space—such are the political units, whose sovereignty is identified with collective ownership of a fragment of the globe. A fundamental distinction between the two kinds of causes is suggested by this formulation: the material or physical causes on the one side, the moral or social causes on the other, to use Montesquieu's vocabulary.

The causes in the first category, which we have just called physical or material, are subdivided into three, indicated by the three following questions: what space do these men occupy? how many men occupy this space? what resources are to be found there? *Space, population, resources* or, if one prefers, the names of the disciplines which treat these determinants, *geography, demography, economy*—such would be the titles of the first three chapters.

We may also subdivide the study of the social determinants into three chapters. Not that the latter belong to three species as distinct as the three kinds of physical determinants, but, in the case of the social causes, we are seeking regular relations and above all typical series (if they exist). We are therefore entitled to apportion our inquiry in relation to the historical unities whose development would appear, after the fact, as subject to a general law. Now, I see three such historical unities of paramount importance in the six thousand years of our history: the *nation*, the *civilization, humanity*.

In the first of these three chapters we study the influence which the regime proper to each of the political units exerts upon the conduct of diplomacy or strategy. At the same time, we inquire whether the nation is a major determinant, either by its constancy or by its necessary evolution. In the second we inquire whether the history of each civilization offers a regular and foreseeable series of typical phases, each characterized by a way of conducting international relations, by a determined frequency or style of wars. Finally, in the third chapter, we raise the same question apropos of all humanity. Have nations and civilizations, has humanity itself had until today—will it have tomorrow—an inevitable destiny in peace or in war?

The same distinction can also be presented in the following manner. First, we take the foreign policy of a particular political unit. With the idea in mind of describing the causes, of a social nature, which determine this policy, we first encounter the community organized according to a particular mode, and we must assign appropriate significance to nation and regime. But nation and regime are situated within a larger social milieu which we call a civilization: the Germany of the Third Reich was an integral part of Europe of the twentieth century, itself a temporal period of Western civilization. But this civilization in its turn had dealings with other civilizations. To what degree do these other civilizations differ from the West with regard to the practice of peace and of war? What share must we attribute to the nature of society and to the nature of man? Thus, the questions formulated early in the last three chapters follow each other logically.

It does not seem to me that any of the problems which the sociologist must ask himself can escape this plan. The first three chapters relate to a spatial consideration, the last three to a temporal one. Space, number, and resources define the causes or the material means of a policy. Nations, with their regimes, civilizations, human and social nature constitute the more or less permanent determinants. In the first three chapters the method is analytical, aiming at isolating the action of three causes in which various sociological schools have sought an ultimate explanation. In the last three chapters the method is often synthetic, since it aims at defining institutions created with the participation but without the clear knowledge of the actors.

Whether it is a question of material or social causes, of spatial or of temporal consideration, our inquiry is oriented toward the present. It is to illuminate the distinctive features of our own period that, in each chapter, we interrogate the past.

chapter VII

On Space

Every international order, down to our own day, has been essentially territorial. It represents an agreement among sovereignties, the compartmentalization of space. Thus, international law implies a permanent paradox which in certain circumstances appears shocking: it recognizes political units as subjects of law, as almost the sole subjects of law and, thereby, has to ignore individuals.[1]

The paradox which provoked Pascal's irony is, actually, the least of it: "Truth on one side of the Pyrenees, error on the other." International law, insofar as it seeks to be in the service of stability, *enjoins* the cis-Pyreneans to regard as truth what it is the duty of the trans-Pyreneans to reject as error. The logic of these contradictory obligations is symbolized by the law which put an end to the conflict of Catholics and Protestants in Germany: *cujus regio, hujus religio.* Each man must adhere to the religion of his prince. States recognize each other's rights by denying those of persons.

Even today, too, the United Nations ignores in practice the protests of individuals against the oppression of national powers. However improvised they may be, states, from the day of the proclamation of their independence, act as masters within their own frontiers.[2] They possess a fragment of the earth's crust, with the men and objects thereon. The sea has not been divided up and remains the property of all or of none, but air, in turn, has been made subject—to a height not yet specified—to the authority of states.

The crossing of the line that separates the territories of political units is, par excellence, a *casus belli,* proof of aggression. In wartime, space is open to the movements of soldiers. Strategy is movement; it is influenced by means of transport or communication. The utilization of the terrain is essential to

---

[1] The International Court of the Rights of Man, foreseen in the framework of Europe, would theoretically end this paradox.
[2] In the week that followed the proclamation of independence of the former Belgian Congo, the government of the new state denounced as "aggression" the intervention of Belgian troops trying to protect individuals.

tactics; the occupation of territory has been, down through the centuries, the objective of armies in conflict. The annexation of territories, whether near or remote, has traditionally been regarded as the legitimate ambition of princes and the consecration of victory.

Thus, the two typical conditions of international relations, peace and war, seem both to require a geographical consideration, an analysis in terms of space, of treaties which put an end to the conflicts and combats which have precipitated the collapse of the previously established order. The geographical study of foreign policy is an integral part of what we ordinarily call human geography or political geography: the study of the relations between the environment and human collectivities, the adaptation of the collectivities to the environment, the transformation of the latter by man's hands, tools and mind. But for reasons which we shall indicate, the geographical study of international relations has followed a course peculiar to itself and now constitutes a semi-autonomous discipline.

It is not our intention, in the present chapter, to review the facts accumulated by the geopoliticians or the theories which they have proposed or established, but to specify, by critical or epistemological reflection, the nature and limits of geopolitics.

1. On the Geographical Milieu

Space may be considered in turn as *environment, theater* and *stake* of international relations.

The last of these three concepts is immediately intelligible. Since a state is regarded as the owner of a certain space, any fragment of the latter can be the stake of conflicts between individuals or groups. An Islamic state which has won back its independence, like Tunisia or Morocco, does not willingly leave to French settlers (there by favor of the protectorate) the ownership of the lands they are exploiting. The Moslems fled Palestine (in the hope of returning) at the beginning of the war which the Israelis call a war of liberation. One population has replaced another on a given surface. The event illustrates, if illustration is necessary, the fact that the earth has not ceased in the twentieth century to be a stake of disputes among collectivities.

On the other hand, the distinction between *environment* and *theater*, not common in the literature, requires some explanation. Human geography depicts the societies in a given territory, in a given climate; it attempts to understand and explain the action which the characteristics of the setting have exerted over the life style and social organization at the same time as the modifications wrought in the former by the societies which have established themselves there. The environment which geography studies and defines is both natural and historical. It is concretely defined, involving all the features which specialists in fauna, flora, terrain and climate are in a position to discern and which the scholar considers instructive.

Considered as theater, space is no longer concrete but, so to speak, abstract;

it is simplified, stylized, schematized by the observer's attention. The battle-field, which the strategist must comprehend at a single glance, is no longer the climatic or geological setting whose singularities the geographer has never exhausted, but the framework of a specific activity. The terrain on which a soccer game is played can and must be characterized exclusively by the qualities (dimensions, hardness, bareness, wetness, etc.) which influence the behavior of the players. Similarly, the globe, as a theater of international relations, is only defined by the qualities which the actors in international relations must take into account. It is insofar as planetary space can be conceived as the schematic frame of international politics that geopolitics offers an original and fascinating insight into diplomatic history. Because the framework never entirely determines the playing of the game, the geopolitical perspective, always a partial one, is easily corrupted into a justificatory ideology.

Let us first consider space as a concrete environment. What is the nature of the information which geographical study affords us concerning the life of human collectivities in general, about international relations in particular? One proposition, quite a commonplace one, comes to mind at once. The virtue of geographical study is, first and foremost, to dissipate the illusions or legends of a *determinism* of climate or relief. The deeper and more precise the study, the fewer regular relations of causality it discovers.

Let us remember the boldness of Montesquieu's formulas:

"These fertile provinces are always of a level surface, where the inhabitants are unable to dispute against a stronger power; they are then obliged to submit; and when they have once submitted, the spirit of liberty cannot return; the wealth of the country is a pledge of their fidelity. But in mountainous districts, as they have but little, they may preserve what they have. The liberty they enjoy, or, in other words, the government they are under, is the only blessing worthy of their defense. It reigns, therefore, more in mountainous and rugged countries than in those that nature seems to have favored.[8]

"We have already observed that great heat enervates the strength and courage of men, and that in cold climates they have a certain vigor of body and mind, which renders them patient and intrepid, and qualifies them for arduous enterprises. . . . We ought not, then, to be astonished that the cowardice of people in hot climates has almost always rendered them slaves; and that the bravery of those in cold climates has enabled them to maintain their liberties. This is an effect which springs from a natural cause.[4]

"The barrenness of the Attic soil established there a democracy; and the fertility of that of Lacedaemonia an aristocratic constitution."[5]

[8] *L'Esprit des lois*, XVIII, 2.
[4] *Ibid.*, XVII, 2.
[5] *Ibid.*, XVIII, 1.

Today, no one believes that the courage or cowardice of peoples is a function of the climate, that the political destiny of Sparta and Athens was established in advance upon the soil occupied by each of the two city-states, that notions of good or poor soil, of fertility or sterility suffice to define a territory, that all mountains belong to one and the same category, even all plains. At the risk of being accused of a futile pedantry, let us specify the reasons, both of meaning and of method, which make Montesquieu's propositions unacceptable.

The relations suggested between climate and way of life implicitly suppose a heredity of acquired characteristics. Biologists have made it impossible for us to believe in such a heredity. That climate is favorable or unfavorable to activity in general, or even to a specific activity, is not impossible for us to admit; but the influence which the climate exerts over the mode of expression of hereditary dispositions is never such that whole groups—peoples or races—is forever marked by virtues or vices, whether glorious or detestable. Climate does not make men cowardly or courageous.

The term employed by Montesquieu as causal is never defined with a sufficient rigor for us to be able to attribute to it a constant effect. The further our knowledge advances, the more such crude notions disintegrate. There are too many different kinds of heat and cold, of dryness or humidity, of plains or mountains, for a single type of social organization (or even a single type of habitation) to accompany of necessity a general type of climate or terrain.

Even if we avoid the error of making too vague a definition of the supposed *cause*, we cannot assume a true geographical determinism. However precisely defined the natural situation, we cannot thereby conclude that it will forbid men to live there differently from the way they do now. If the situation is singular, unique, how can we show that the reaction of men could not have been other than it has been in the past? Regularity constitutes the only proof of the necessity of the concomitance. Further, the impossibility of proof confirms the direct observation of the margin of initiative which nature leaves to man. Even when the constraint of nature is most burdensome, for example in the case of the Eskimos, we are disposed to admire the intelligence with which these archaic societies have adapted themselves to difficult circumstances—that is to say, have survived. But we do not conclude that this mode of adaptation was the only one possible.

Furthermore, *non-determination* by the natural environment has nothing in common with *indeterminism*. A geographical determinism (or any other theory which affirms the determination of human societies, or of some aspect of human societies, by *one cause* of a given kind) assumes a philosophy of the object, not the general principle of determinism. This latter principle does not imply at all that, in a given climate or on a given terrain, all societies present certain characteristics. It suffices that the way of life and the modes of organization be a function of history at the same time as of geography, that they be affected by many causes, not by the action of the natural environment alone, for geography itself to contribute to the refutation of what was once called geographical determinism.

These remarks suggest the following formula: it is always possible to *understand* the relationship between a man or a collectivity and the geographical environment. It is rarely (or never) possible to explain it if the explanation requires that the relation established be *necessary*. Understanding is, so to speak, guaranteed *a priori*: whether or not the reaction to the environment has been more or less intelligent, it remains *understandable*, since it has not involved the death of the group. If it had involved the death of the group, it would also have remained *understandable*: the interpreter would attempt to discover the beliefs, obligations or prohibitions which prevented these human beings from taking the measures indispensable to their safety.

Does this mean that the geographical environment, whether physical or historical, is never the cause of social phenomena? Such a deduction would be false. Natural phenomena have been, during the prehistoric phase, the cause —sometimes almost a direct cause—of human events. The migrations of our ancestors were influenced if not determined by modifications of climate. Perhaps, as Toynbee observes,[6] quoting the descriptions of Gordon Childe, geography launched the first challenge taken up by men in creating a civilization:

"While northern Europe was covered in ice as far as the Harz, and the Alps and the Pyrenees were capped with glaciers, the Arctic high pressure deflected southward the Atlantic rainstorms. The cyclones that today traverse Central Europe then passed over the Mediterranean Basin and the Northern Sahara and continued, undrained by Lebanon, across Mesopotamia and Arabia to Persia and India. The parched Sahara enjoyed a regular rainfall, and farther east the showers were not only more bountiful than today but were distributed over the whole year. . . . We should expect in North Africa, Arabia, Persia and the Indus Valley parklands and savannahs, such as flourish today north of the Mediterranean. . . . While the mammoth, the woolly rhinoceros and the reindeer were browsing in France and Southern England, North Africa was supporting a fauna that is found today on the Zambesi in Rhodesia. . . .

"The pleasant grasslands of North Africa and Southern Asia were naturally as thickly populated by man as the frozen steppes of Europe, and it is reasonable to suspect that in this favorable and indeed stimulating environment, man would make greater progress than in the ice-bound north."[7]

But after the close of the Ice Age, the Afro-Asian area began to experience a profound physical change in the direction of aridity; and simultaneously, two or three civilizations arose in an area which had previously, like all the

[6] Cf. Toynbee, *A Study of History*, Vol. I.
[7] V. Gordon Childe, *New Light on the Most Ancient East*, New York, 1934, Chap. II.

rest of the inhabited world, been occupied solely by primitive societies of the paleolithic order. Our archeologists encourage us to look upon the drying-up of Afro-Asia as a challenge. Our response was the genesis of these civilizations.

"Now we are on the brink of the great revolution, and soon we shall encounter men who are masters of their own food supply through possession of domesticated animals and the cultivation of cereals. It seems inevitable to connect that revolution with the crisis produced by the melting of the northern glaciers and the consequent contraction of the Arctic high pressure over Europe and diversion of the Atlantic rainstorms from the South Mediterranean Zone to their present course across Central Europe.

"This event would certainly tax the ingenuity of the inhabitants of the former grassland zone to the utmost.

"Faced with the gradual desiccation consequent upon the re-shift northward of the Atlantic cyclone belt as the European glaciers contracted, three alternatives were open to the hunting populations affected. They might move northward or southward with their prey, following the climatic belt to which they were accustomed; they might remain at home eking out a miserable existence on such game as could withstand the drought; or they might—still without leaving their homeland—emancipate themselves from dependence on the whims of their environment by domesticating animals and taking to agriculture."[8]

Have climatic phenomena, for five or six thousand years—that is, during the so-called historical phase of civilizations—been the immediate cause of events, greatness and decline of peoples, migrations provoked by drought and resulting in vast conquests? This is the opinion of several authors,[9] who believe in the climatic oscillations and in the periods of drought in Central Asia. The Spanish historian Olagüe is also convinced that the diminution of rainfall has been one of the direct and principal causes of the Spanish decadence.[10] Other authors deny the fact with the same assurance:

"The *desertification* of Spain, strictly linked to human intervention," writes M. Roger Heim,[11] "probably originates in the seasonal shifting of sheep pasturage, which Ferdinand and Isabella considerably intensified to increase their personal fortune from profits derived from the European wool market, at the same time that the direct destruction of the forest lands was increased by the repeated cutting of large trees for the invincible Armada. Thus, for five thousand years, no appreciable climatic change, no great natural fluctuations on the surface of the globe, and particularly in the Mediterranean basin, but instead inadequacy of agricultural methods, deforestation, political instability, causing the abandonment of techniques necessary to farming in a

[8] *Ibid.*, Chap. III.
[9] For example, Ellworth Huntington in *The Pulse of Asia*, 1907.
[10] Ignacis Olagüe, *Histoire d'Espagne*, Paris, 1957.
[11] Director of the Muséum national d'histoire naturelle, in *Le Figaro littéraire*, November 21, 1959.

dry country, all of which, today, are continually aggravated in their consequences by the demographic factor."

The uncertainty is related to the primary or secondary character of climatic change. For some interpreters, climatic oscillation is a primary factor, having nothing to do with man, and is the origin of important events. For others, it results from human error or negligence. Exhaustion of lands and deforestation create the geographical environment in which the civilization, incapable of correcting its own faults, will ultimately perish.

Whichever interpretation we choose—we have no qualifications for deciding the controversy—such examples help us to distinguish and to specify the modes of environmental causality. We speak of the historical causality[12] of a natural phenomenon when the latter, without being imputable to human action, brutally modifies the life of a collectivity: the destruction of Lisbon by an earthquake and of Pompeii by an eruption of Mount Vesuvius belong to this category. The same is true if drought, *not imputable to men*, has gradually ruined Spain. But this latter example has quite another bearing because it reminds us of the invisible and permanent influence of environment on human societies.

Mankind is a species which, at least during its historical period, has incessantly transformed its conditions of existence. The environment is different, even when it has not changed, if the collectivities acquire other tools to develop it. The physical data change in relation to scientific knowledge and technological instruments. In this sense the geographical environment, taken concretely, prepared by nature and altered by labor, shares in historical instability.

But, in each period, this environment, as produced by the conjunction of nature and humanity at a certain point in its evolution, influences the destiny of collectivities. It is alternately *inducement* and *limit*, favorable or hostile to the efforts of societies, lenient or merciless to their weaknesses.

Let us suppose that the river civilizations,[13] those of the Nile, the Tigris and Euphrates, and the Yellow River, owed their rise in part to the challenge presented by the necessity of utilizing the spate periods, of regulating the course of the waters, of insuring the irrigation of cultivable lands. The civilizations of hydraulic engineering, as a result of these requirements for collective survival, present specific characteristics, the very ones which define "the Asiatic mode of production," one of the regimes Marx discusses in his introduction to the *Contribution to the Critique of Political Economy*. But such civilizations are more vulnerable than those which prosper under temperate climates and which allow individuals and small groups to survive on their own. The history of France would be less continuous if the political

---

[12] In both the *formal* sense, as a unique sequence, and the *material* sense, as an event relating to the development of human societies.

[13] Cf. Karl A. Wittfogel's very important book, *Oriental Despotism*, New Haven, 1957.

upheavals, not infrequent during the last thousand years, had involved, along with the disorganization of the administration, the wrecking of the apparatus indispensable for agricultural production. When the civilization survives only by annually renewing its victory over a rebellious nature, men accept a stricter discipline and even then the total surrender to a state is sometimes not enough to preserve them from a catastrophe.

The environment, as historically constituted by the conjunction of physical resources and technical means, is far more effective at inducing a determined organization to act than at punishing errors or negligence, and fixes the limit that the number of collectivities cannot exceed. Even today, despite the growing independence which our species is in the process of acquiring in relation to the physical environment, the distribution of the human masses appears not strictly determined, but only influenced, by climatic conditions. The various regions of the globe have not been equally propitious to the development of civilizations. Whatever the state of techniques of production, the number of men capable of living on a given surface remains dependent on physical data, soil, relief, climate. Neither isolable nor specifically determinant, the action of the geographical environment is exerted continually, without our being able to measure its limits. Is it possible to construct, deep in the heart of Africa, societies of the industrial type? Perhaps we are all inclined to underestimate the weight with which nature still weighs, even in our age, upon human societies.

The preceding analysis, valid for political geography as a whole, applies *a fortiori* to environmental explanations of international relations. The *position (die Lage)* is, in effect, essentially historical, since it depends on circumstances which obey the law of change (techniques of movement, transportation, combat, effective circulation of men and merchandise, relation of forces between political units in the same zone, etc.). Once the Islamic conquests closed the Mediterranean to commercial traffic, Marseilles no longer had the same status. The situation of a nation on the physical map is, itself, immutable. But it is at most one cause among others; it suggests certain actions, it offers a framework of possibilities. Perhaps it is subtly present in all centuries, in all aspects of the national destiny. But it is expressed in a position which changes with the rise and ruin of states, in institutions which mark, in each period, the ideas, the dreams, the tools and the weapons of men.

We are sometimes tempted—and even an A. Cournot has not resisted this temptation—to read the destiny of the European nations on the map after the fact. History, in the long run, has effaced the traces of accidents and favored the fulfillment of the law promulgated by geography. Spain, France and Great Britain have definitively assumed the dimensions that corresponded to the natural order. As a matter of fact, Spain has not always been separated from the current of European civilization by the Pyrenees: for a time her armies played the leading role in Europe. Dynastic unions united lands that geography had separated, but geography has not given the provinces of Spain the homogeneity presented by the provinces of France. Was French unity "predetermined" as some today imagine? Such a proposition should be at the least modified by reservations. The frontiers of the *pré carré* were and remain contested. The spread of a single language, the creation of a national community among Flemings, Bretons, Provençals and Béarnais might perhaps have been facilitated by geography: how easy it would be to find the "underlying causes," had this unification not been achieved!

It would be paradoxical to deny that the configuration of Switzerland or France, or the island situation of Great Britain, have constantly *influenced* the diplomacy of these nations down through the centuries. Switzerland owes to its geographical situation a defensive power incommensurate with the number of its inhabitants or the resources of its economy. But it required historical circumstances to create first the confederation, then the Helvetian federation, and then that the latter should adopt the policy of neutrality indispensable to the maintenance of its unity as long as the great neighboring nations were fighting. Still the history of the Swiss cantons—their capacity to stand up to aggressors, to maintain their independence, to constitute a neutral state and to make that neutrality respected—probably owes more to geography than that of any other nation of the Old World.

Similarly, it is easy to speculate on the parallelism between the double vocation—continental and maritime—of France and the hesitation of her diplomacy. With a northern frontier open to invasions and quite close to the capital, France was inevitably obsessed by the concern for an always precarious security. Situated at the western extremity of the small cape of Asia, she could not ignore the call of the sea and the lure of remote expeditions. She divided her forces between a diplomacy of continental hegemony (or of security) and a diplomacy of an overseas empire. She did not succeed completely in either direction.

It is apropos of England that analysis usefully indicates the limits of a geographical interpretation, in itself convincing and apparently irresistible. It is obvious that England's fortune is inconceivable without her island situation. The security from aggression which neither Venice nor Holland had enjoyed to the same degree, the importance of her resources of food, the wheat fields of the south, and subsequently her coal reserves gave English diplomacy a freedom of action unknown to the continental states. To a degree, England owed her defensive power to nature. She could keep apart from the European conflicts, take sides with the momentarily weaker party, decide the issue by the intervention, at the opportune moment, of an expeditionary force, and reserve the bulk of her forces for the demands of naval supremacy and imperial expansion.

This textbook stereotype is not untrue, though it simplifies and schematizes. England has taken advantage of its insular position in order to conduct a policy which would have been forbidden to a state otherwise situated. This policy was not, all the same, *determined* by the situation. The latter left men a marginal autonomy: it offered them a choice among several decisions. The choice was not accidental and it is not unintelligible, but it was not *imposed* by the natural environment.

Abstractly, a collectivity ruling the whole of an island may be tempted either by withdrawal (breaking off relations with the world) or by an active diplomacy. The latter, in its turn, may be oriented in three directions: continental conquest, overseas expeditions, voluntary neutrality. Each of these four policies has been adopted, at various times, by one or another of the two island states, Great Britain and Japan.

When Japan achieved her unity in the seventeenth century, she did not take advantage of it by undertaking conquest elsewhere. On the contrary, during the Tokugawa era, the shoguns' only ambition was to perfect, so to speak, their island isolation. The ideal of a stable society and a refined civilization encouraged them to withdraw their flourishing empire from barbarian contact, from exchanges with the West.

After the Meiji reform, Japan reversed her attitude, but did not cease to vacillate between the two paths accessible to the expansion of an island state: continental or maritime conquest. Lacking the resolution or the capacity to choose, Japan ultimately found herself in a war with China, which the Japanese armies vainly attempted to occupy, and with the United States and Great Britain, maritime powers, protecting the islands (Philippines, Indonesia). England, historically speaking, conducted her enterprises more rationally. The phase of continental ventures ended with the Hundred Years' War. Once the union of the two kingdoms of England and Scotland was achieved, Great Britain acted, in most cases, as if she understood the logic of European equilibrium, and turned her ambition toward the seas, the fleet, commerce and the Empire.

Since 1945 Japan and Great Britain, drawn closer to the continents by technical progress and outclassed by land powers, have both been integrated into the United States system of alliance. Both island states count on American protection, on the support of the dominant naval power in order to insure their security. Great Britain makes this choice virtually without hesitation, by reason of the close relationship of English and American civilizations. Japanese public opinion, on the other hand, is far from being unanimous, so artificial does the rupture of exchanges with China appear. Reduced to secondary rank, could Japan not be neutral without being isolated as in the times of the shoguns, without becoming a satellite of the continental states? Even in England the question has been raised, at least in the indirect form of opposition to the American bases and thermonuclear armament.

The island situation leads to a schematic analysis of diplomatic possibilities; it does not, of itself, establish causal relations. An island state is not constrained to be a naval power. It was in the sixteenth century that the English truly became a nation of sailors. The Japanese have never become such a nation. They have remained to the end a land people, reluctant to emigrate, reluctant to entrust their fortunes to the uncertainty of the waves. The island situation is a challenge, not a constraint.

2. The Mackinder Patterns

In the preceding pages we have gradually shifted from the first term to the second, from *environment* to *theater*. Space, we have said, is regarded as a theater, and no longer as an environment, when the observer takes into account only certain characteristics, namely those that are supposed to influence a specific behavior. For instance, the geopolitician sees the geographical environment as "the terrain of diplomatic and military interplay." The environment is simplified into an abstract framework, the populations transformed into actors, making entrances and exits on the world stage.

How much concrete reality does the geopolitician retain in the designs of the stage and of diplomatic-strategic actors? The conduct of foreign affairs appears *instrumental* to the geopolitician, the use of certain means toward certain ends. Resources—men, tools, weapons—are mobilized by states with a view to security or expansion. Yet lines of expansion, like threats to security, are indicated in advance on the world map if, at least, the geographer can fix his attention on the natural data on which the prosperity and power of nations depend. Geopolitics combines a *geographical schematization of diplomatic-strategic relations with a geographic-economic analysis of resources, with an interpretation of diplomatic attitudes as a result of the way of life and of the environment* (*sedentary, nomadic, agricultural, seafaring*). These too-general formulas will be clarified and illuminated by an example. In our century the Englishman Mackinder has probably contributed more than anyone else to the popularity of geopolitics. He originated several of the ideas which the German school adopted in the service of imperialism. The brief, compact books of Sir Halford Mackinder facilitate epistemological analysis, which is our true object.

In 1904 appeared the essay called "The Geographical Pivot of History."[14] Here Mackinder first explained the central theme of his thought. In 1905 another article, "Manpower as a Measure of National and Imperial Strength" (in the *National Review*), accentuated the decisive influence of productivity (or output of human labor). The principal book which gathers together the essentials of Mackinder's thought appeared in 1919: *Democratic Ideals and Reality*. A quarter of a century later, in 1943, *Foreign Affairs* published an article which assumed the character of a testament, "The Round World and the Winning of Peace." The same geographical designs were employed to

---

[14] Published in the *Geographical Journal* in 1907; the communication to the Royal Geographical Society of London, which served as the basis of the article, dates from 1904.

deal with the problems which would come up at the end of the Second World War, after having been vainly utilized at the end of the First.

Probably the best method of summarizing our author is to start with what I have called the *schématisme géographique*, in other words, to summarize the two concepts of *World Island* and *Heartland*. Ocean covers nine twelfths of the globe. A continent, or the total of the three continents Asia, Europe and Africa, covers two twelfths. The rest, the last twelfth, is represented by smaller islands, North and South America and Australia. In this planetary diagram the Americas occupy, in relation to the World Island, a position comparable to that of the British Isles in relation to Europe.

The second concept, that of the *Heartland* or of the *pivot-region*, has not always been defined in the same terms.[15] The uncertainty as to the exact delimitation of this enormous zone does not extend to the concept itself. The Heartland covers both the northern part and the interior of the Eurasian land mass. It extends from the Arctic Coast to the deserts of Central Asia. It has as its western frontier the isthmus between the Baltic and the Black seas, perhaps between the Baltic and the Adriatic.

The Heartland is characterized by three characteristics of physical geography which have a political bearing and which are combined without coinciding. It constitutes the largest flat area on the surface of the globe: the plain of Asia, the steppes of European Russia which extend across Germany and the Low Countries through the Ile-de-France and Paris, heart of the West. Several of the world's greatest rivers flow through it either to the Arctic Sea or to inland seas (the Caspian, the Aral). Lastly, it is a grassland favorable to the mobility of populations and warriors, whether on camels or horses. The Heartland, at least in its eastern section, has been closed to the intervention of naval power. It opened a way to the incursions of horsemen riding westward.

On the basis of this reading of the simplified map, Mackinder's three famous propositions can be understood. *Anyone controlling Eastern Europe controls the Heartland. Anyone controlling the Heartland controls the World Island. Anyone controlling the World Island controls the world.* These are the three propositions, in a vulgarized form, which have enjoyed most success. Through the German geopoliticians, Hitler learned and was perhaps inspired by them. A theory which claimed to be scientific was transformed into an ideology justifying conquests.

The theory itself is constructed, on the basis of geographical design, by the simultaneous consideration of a *constant element* (the land-sea, continental-seafaring opposition) and of *three variable elements* (the technique of movement on land and on sea, the population and resources utilizable in the rivalry of nations, and the extension of the diplomatic field). Writing at the beginning of this century, when England's fortunes seemed extraordinary

---

[15] I use here the terms of the article published in *Foreign Affairs*.

and invulnerable, Mackinder looked back and ahead, toward past centuries in order to discover the necessary conditions for the victory of the island state, toward the future to discover whether the circumstances to which England owed most of her greatness were destined to disappear.

There is every reason to regard as fundamental, throughout history, the opposition of land and sea, of continental power and seafaring power. The two elements seem to symbolize two ways of life for men, incite in them two typical attitudes. The land belongs to someone, to the *landlord*, individual or collective; the sea belongs to all because it belongs to no one. The empire of continental powers is inspired by the spirit of possession; the empire of maritime powers is inspired by the spirit of commerce. It is not always benevolent (let us recall the domination of Athens, as Thucydides describes it); it is rarely closed.

If land and water represent the two elements in conflict on the global stage, it is because international relations are, in Clausewitz's formula, exchange and communication. Wars create relations between individuals and collectivities, but in a manner different from those of commerce. Nomads, of both land and water, horsemen and sailors, are the builders of the two types of empire, the professionals of the two kinds of combat. Movement and maneuver have not played the same role on land and at sea. The desire to reduce the hazards of battle to the minimum, the strategist's effort to muster his forces on a battlefield and to offer the enemy a continuous front have no equivalent on the ocean. Before the technical discoveries which multiplied the means of communication, to venture upon a maritime career was to accept the uncertainty of fate, to rely on improvisation, on the mastery of the unforeseeable, through the individual's initiative. On the eve of the battle of Salamis the Athenians took the whole city into their vessels; in 1940 the French denied that France could be elsewhere than on the soil of *la patrie*: a double decision symbolic of the state which chose water and the state which will never separate itself from land.

Mackinder is aware of this dualism, but it is the destiny of his country which fosters and orients his inquiry. From one point of view of diplomacy and strategy the insular position exists only after political unification of the island. On the international level a power becomes insular the day when it no longer has any land neighbor. The British Isles are unified, the Continent is divided: such has been the contrast which was chiefly the cause of the United Kingdom's imperial greatness. Yet this contrast is perhaps not an eternal one: not that the unity of the United Kingdom is threatened, but the unity of the Continent is no longer inconceivable.

From his study of the past Mackinder drew two ideas, still valid in twentieth-century circumstances. The first, the most obvious but perhaps the most misunderstood, is that the pitiless law of numbers also functions in the struggle between maritime power and continental power. A maritime power will not survive, despite the qualities of its fleet and its sailors, if it is confronted by a rival possessing material and human resources which are superior to its own. The second lesson, still clearer, is that a maritime power can be conquered on land as well as at sea. When the continental power has seized all the bases, there is no longer any room for the maritime power. The sea becomes a closed sea, subject to a land empire, which no longer needs to maintain a navy: e.g., the Mediterranean under the Roman Empire. The British Empire risks destruction, Mackinder concludes, if a continental state accumulates overwhelming resources or if the network of British bases established on islands and peninsulas around the Eurasian land mass is destroyed or occupied from the land.

For centuries Great Britain has profited by circumstances: Europe was divided, the security of the British Isles guaranteed; the latter possessed resources, in raw materials and in men, on the scale of the resources of the rival states; the other continents were without military force. The English geographer perceives at the beginning of the century that the two variables are shifting in a direction unfavorable to the maritime power.

Between the sixteenth and the nineteenth centuries, maritime mobility was superior to land mobility. Yet Mackinder is struck by two almost contemporary events, the Boer War and the Manchurian War. Russia's capacity to conduct a large-scale war ten thousand kilometers from her bases, at the end of a single railroad, seems to him more striking than England's capacity to supply the South African Expeditionary Corps by sea. The internal-combustion engine was soon added to the contribution of the railroad. Spengler's formula, that the steam horse will reopen the era of great invasions, closed since the days of the Asian cavalcades, might have been utilized by Mackinder who, in two chapters[16] on the seafaring prospect and the land prospect, reviews the empires of past centuries: empires of horsemen, Scythians, Parthians, Huns, Arabs, Mongols, Turks, Cossacks, coming from plateaus, steppes or deserts, and empires of seafaring peoples, from Crete and Athens down to Venice and England.

Now, at the very moment when land mobility prodigiously increases, the Heartland is gaining possession of the material and human resources necessary to world empire. Eastern Europe is the hinge zone where this Heartland touches its marginal regions, open on the ocean, where Slavs and Germans meet and mingle. In 1905 and in 1919, Mackinder feared that the Germans, conquering the Slavs, would be in a position to unify the Heartland into a single sovereign territory and thereby outclass the forces of the United Kingdom. He foresaw the economy of great space which would serve as a base to the land power, certain to prevail, by sheer weight of numbers, over the maritime power. It is in relation to this historical cir-

16 In *Democratic Ideals and Reality*.

cumstance that the three positions reviewed above are explained and assume their partial truth: anyone controlling Eastern Europe controls the Heartland, hence the World Island, hence the universe.

From this analysis the author had drawn consequences, particularly in 1919, which he offered to the attention of those who were writing the peace treaty. As an adviser to kings, Mackinder reread in 1960 seems to have suffered the worst disgrace: he was heeded by statesmen and mocked by events. Since in 1919 the freedom of peoples and the greatness of England were threatened by an eventual unification of the Heartland, it is essential to prevent this unification—that is, the German domination of the Slavs (in 1945, the Slavic domination of the Germans). To this end, the geographer, combining the British tradition with his impersonal (and professional) equation, proposed constituting a belt of independent states between the two great powers, one of which could not subject the other without breaking up global equilibrium. So it was: the small independent states first gave the two great powers the occasion to unite in order to divide the zone of separation, and subsequently become the battlefield on which the Russian and German armies met, and finally fell to the land power which, for the first time, occupied the Heartland with a large garrison and an advanced technology.

Is the history of the last forty years of a nature to disqualify the geographer? One historian, belonging to a traditional school, Jacques Bainville, had more accurately anticipated the consequences of the Versailles Treaty. The independent states between (Soviet) Russia and (so-called eternal) Germany seemed to him, from their origin, incapable of lasting because they were incapable of uniting. Poland, Rumania, Hungary, Czechoslovakia, all so-called national states with, in fact, powerful minorities of dubious loyalty, would never offer a common front to German revisionism and to Slavic revisionism, which were in the last analysis opposed, but if need be prepared, to go part of the way together.

The geographer's answer, it seems to me, might be a double one. No territorial treaty, he might say, is maintained if the conquering states, who have imposed it upon the states now conquered, dissociate themselves from it or weaken it by their disagreement. The Versailles Treaty, it is true, was precarious, the two great continental powers being hostile to it. But the Western nations had been given the means to act if Germany attempted to destroy the established order: Germany was disarmed, the left bank of the Rhine, first occupied by French troops, was subsequently to remain without defense. The authors of the treaty were less responsible for the catastrophes than the statesmen who had to apply it. Germany had been beaten by a coalition which included the maritime states, Great Britain and the United States. American isolationism and English hesitation left to France alone a task which exceeded her forces: if the Versailles Treaty collapsed, it was not because it was intrinsically worse than any other with regard to morality or politics; it was because the states which should have been its guardians deserted their task.

The other answer might be formulated as a question: What should have been done? Destroy the German unity, as one school of French nationalism proposed? None believed in the restoration of *les Allemagnes*. Save the dual monarchy? It no longer resisted when the peace conference convened: the diplomats took cognizance of its utter disintegration. Perhaps a peace, whether separate or general, concluded two years earlier might have given a new lease of life to the anachronistic unity of Central Europe under the Habsburg dynasty. By 1918 it was too late.

In truth, the geopolitical outlook, Mackinder's like the rest, allowed the problem to be expressed, but dictated no solution. To prevent Germany or Russia from achieving the unity of the Heartland from Eastern Europe, such was the first requirement of global equilibrium, the condition of the freedom of peoples. How forestall this unity which German imperialism risked creating either by its victory or defeat? The belt of small states, separating the two great powers, was a method that was not absurd, though it has failed. The failure, even in retrospect, does not definitively condemn the idea, because the British and Americans had, since 1920, forgotten the most obvious lesson of the hostilities: no European order could survive without the active participation of the British and Americans united with the continental democracies.

This is the lesson, in any case, that Mackinder, writing in 1943, drew from the catastrophe. The war was not yet over: the British geographer could not clearly point to today's ally as tomorrow's enemy. But he obviously saw the danger of the unification of the Heartland by Slavs ultimately victorious over the Germans. The Heartland garrison is henceforth numerous. Russia has twenty times the area, four times the population of France. But her open frontier is only four times that of France. This time it would no longer be Mongols or the horsemen of central Asia, but tanks and cannons that would stream westward. The motorized conquerors no longer lack any of the instruments of Western technology. Whether the danger comes from the Germans or the Russians, it comes from the Heartland; it can no longer be warded off by alliances among the peoples who inhabit the marginal zones of the Eurasian land mass and the peoples of the islands, British or Americans. The geographer sees forming before his eyes, on the map, the Atlantic Alliance with a bridgehead in France, an air base outside Europe (the British Isles, comparable to Malta in the Mediterranean), an arsenal and reserves across the Atlantic.

But perhaps the prospect is different from this point on. The objective of the maritime powers is no longer to keep Germans or Slavs from controlling the Heartland by a single domination: the Russian army, established in Berlin, is determined to remain there. The Continental empire covering the Heartland is achieved. Does Mackinder's third proposition, *anyone controlling the Heartland controls the universe,* authorize us to foresee the outcome of the present conflict? We cannot answer such a question without specifying the mode of geopolitical judgments.

3. *From Geographical Design to Ideologies*

Mackinder himself does not hesitate to speak of *geographical causation in universal history.* But in fact, there is no trace of geographical causality, in the strict sense of the word, in his general outlook on universal history.

Of course, he starts from *geographical facts,* that is, the unequal distribution of land and water on the surface of the planet, the allotment of mineral wealth and agricultural resources across the various regions of the globe, the unequal density of population on the various continents, depending on the climate, the relief, and the fertility of the soil. In temperate climates population is concentrated and civilization extended. Only thirty million[17] men live on the twelve million square kilometers of plateau which constitute the southern limit of the plains of the World Island. A billion human beings live in the monsoon countries; only some tens of millions in the tropical forests of Africa or South America. At present humanity is commonly divided into developed and underdeveloped populations, or the Soviet bloc as distinguished from the Western bloc and the rest of the world. Mackinder does try to relate the modalities of human population to the geographical conditions. But he would be the last to suggest a *determination* of the size of populations by environment, since political problems, in his eyes, are precisely altered according to the modifications which intervene in the distribution of human masses over the surface of the planet.

The geographical vision of universal history is instructive, though it is partial and schematic, because it emphasizes facts of enormous consequence: there have been, over the centuries, two kinds of conquerors, two kinds of nomads—the horsemen and the seafarers; many times over, the vicissitudes of diplomacy are controlled by the struggle of land and sea, the victory going to one or the other in turn, depending on whether the continental power or the maritime power possess more resources, and on whether technology favors one or the other. The major facts are *linked* to the geographical framework. The nomadism of the horsemen and the seafarers is a mode of adaptation to the environment, a human way of life which must be situated in a certain kind of space in order to be understood. Mongols or Arabs developed as they were, on the steppes or on the desert. Yet they have not, except in a symbolic sense, been created by the flat spaces, under the enormous immensity of the sky. Genghis Khan and Mohammed are historical persons for whom geography shows at most something of their origin. Hence it would be wrong, though it is tempting, to derive either predictions or ideologies from a *geographical reading of universal history.*

---

[17] All these figures, given by Mackinder, date from about twenty years ago.

Geopoliticians, especially German ones, have not always resisted the temptation. Since the thirties, still more today, one question arises, following the dual consideration of land and sea forces: in a conflict between a continental empire and a maritime empire, which from this point on has the best chances of winning? As a matter of fact, nowhere does Mackinder explicitly answer such a question. The only universally valid rule to be derived from his writings is the reasoning of the man-in-the-street as well: in the long run, the strongest (the most numerous, the richest, the most productive) conquers.

As a theoretician, Mackinder appears in certain respects to be a kind of anti-Mahan. Whereas the theoretician of naval warfare, writing at the end of the nineteenth century, is struck by the decisive role of naval supremacy, the geographer, interrogating the future, fears that the favor of the gods is shifting to the land. Railroads and engines permit man to triumph over solid space as effectively as the steamboats triumph over liquid space. What distressed the English patriot awakens the hopes of the German nationalists. The age of maritime power is ending, that of continental power beginning. The economy of great space will inherit the world market. Whatever the consequence of these general views, it would have been vain, yesterday, to conclude from them the result of the Second World War, and it would be vain, today, to conclude from them the victory of the continental empire. Probably the number of causes which determine the fortune of states or coalitions is too great for any short-term estimate as to the outcome of a political or military crisis to be scientifically possible. But in any case, an estimate of this order should result from a consideration of *all* the data and not from a deliberately partial analysis.

Nor did Mackinder formulate a geographical ideology, if we are to understand by this concept the justification, by an argument of a geographical order, of goals or ambitions of a political order. Yet he nonetheless arrived at the source of many geographical ideologies. The latter, in effect, always return to a fundamental idea: the idea of space itself—by its extension or by its quality—as the stake of the struggle between human collectivities. As a result the ideologies of space-as-stake are divided into two categories, depending on whether the necessity invoked is economic or strategic. *The ideology of vital space (espace vital)* belongs to the first category, *the ideology of natural frontiers* to the second. The ideology of vital space has enjoyed its greatest success in Germany, the ideology of natural frontiers, in France. Mackinder did not subscribe to the German ideology of vital space, but he laid the ground for it, by a curious conception as opposed to Manchester liberalism: the "protection of a predatory type."

He had understood, better than many of his contemporaries, the nature of what we call industrial society, and what he calls a "going concern." A modern nation is comparable to an industrial enterprise: rich in relation to its productive capacity, by the measurement of labor output. The number of men capable of living in a given space increases with the labor output. It is to modern industry that Germany owes the fact that she has been able to double the size of her population in half a century.

From these facts Mackinder did not deduce that the struggle for the earth is losing its violence and its significance, since the growth in intensity makes it unnecessary to enlarge the available surface. He suggests, on the contrary, that the concentration of populations in a confined space feeds new hatreds among the nations by waking the fear of collective famine. The more Germans there are inside the frontiers of the Reich, the more they fear the lack of space, hence someday of bread or raw materials.

The harmonious development of industrial society, during the course of the period previous to the First World War, seemed to Mackinder to have been compromised as much by Manchester liberalism as by protectionism in the German style. In his eyes, both tended to prevent the balanced growth indispensable to each nation or, at least, to each region of the globe. By balanced growth he meant, according to the philosophy of F. List's national economy, the presence in each great economy of all the important industries. Now, free exchange ultimately accorded the advanced nations the possession of certain key industries. The most-favored-nation clause, as Germany had imposed it upon France in the Frankfurt Treaty and, later, upon Russia even in a simple commercial treaty, had comparable consequences.

The Germans, Mackinder wrote, need the Slavs, who must produce a part of their food for them and purchase from them their manufactured products. Thus they are driven by the spirit of panic to ventures of conquest, obliged to maintain a domination indispensable to their existence. But to this end they must first of all eliminate the bridgeheads of island or maritime powers on the Continent. Whereas England doggedly clings to a liberalism that has become anachronistic, Germany, in her anxiety, is ready to fall back into cannibalism, while Bolshevik Russia collapses into the anarchy whose conclusion, the geographer prophecies, will be a pitiless despotism. A balanced development of national economies first of all, a balance among the nations, among the regions of the globe next—such is the sole path to peace.

It was easy to manipulate ideas in order to make them yield a geographical *ideology*. It was enough to insist on the danger incurred by a collectivity whose existence depends on lands, mines or factories situated beyond its frontiers. More simply—more crudely, too—it was enough to attribute to collectivities a natural desire for expansion in order for space to become the *stake* and no longer the *theater* of foreign policy. The German doctrine of vital space and the Japanese doctrine of co-prosperity were both inspired by a naturalist philosophy according to which political units are comparable to living units whose will to live is identified with the will to conquest.

In their propaganda Germans and Japanese were wary of referring to the principles of their metaphysic. They condemned the lack of space from which they suffered (*Volk ohne Raum*), hence the need (that they were obliged to satisfy at any cost) to occupy a more extensive territory, to possess more cultivable land in order to feed their people, more sources of raw materials in order to supply their factories. Imperialism became inevitable and legitimate, since it was a question of life or death. Such an argument is obviously based on the hypothesis that the planet is too small for all the peoples on it to prosper: the lack of space affects all humanity, and the pitiless struggle among states and peoples is the inexorable result.

Such an ideology is contemporaneous not with the great invasions, but with the awareness of what Paul Valéry once called the world finite (*le monde fini*).[18] The great conquerors, from the Mongols to the Spaniards, were not concerned with justifying their enterprises and, insofar as they did so, invoked the superiority of their strength, of their civilization, or of their gods. From the sixteenth century to the twentieth the Europeans have prodigiously enlarged their vital space. It was in the twentieth century, when the planet was or appeared to be entirely occupied, that the Germans, who had come last on the scene, rationalized their bitterness and their ambition by biological-geographic ideology.

In 1960, current opinion, subject to sudden reversals, no longer sees anything but lies and sophisms in the propaganda of yesterday's imperialists. How can one admit that the losers of the last war could not survive without additional space, whereas the hundred million Japanese, crowded within their four islands, enjoy a standard of living previously unknown to the Japanese, lords of the sphere of Asian co-prosperity, and whereas the fifty-five million Germans of the Federal Republic, in the last ten years, show the highest population increase of the Occident? And that this increase seems due, in large part, to the influx of millions of refugees—that is, to the population density which yesterday's propagandists denounced?

Inevitably, today's observers conclude that the imperialist ideology, derived from geopolitics, marks a transition phase. Mackinder and his German disciples clearly confirmed that the industrial system permitted a tremendous increase in the number of men settled on a given surface. But they failed to carry their analysis to its conclusion: they did not appreciate the possibilities of a growth in intensity. Prisoners of old concepts, they supposed those nations were in danger when they were obliged to seek their supplies abroad. Further, they endorsed the old concept according to which farm workers should represent an important percentage of the total population, and suggested that in certain cases only territorial expansion would make it possible to maintain this percentage. Lastly, they did not understand that in our own day, taking possession of a space has a radically different meaning, depending on whether or not that space is empty. By losing Korea, Formosa and Manchuria the Japanese lost their controlling position with respect to the popula-

---

[18] Actually, Valéry was thinking less of the occupation of the entire earth than of the communication of every fraction of mankind, of every region of the planet, with each other.

tions of their colonies and protectorates. But they have thereby evaded the obligation of dispersing their investments. *In the case of Japan* the ruin of the empire has favored rather than compromised, accelerated rather than slackened the development of the national economy.

This interpretation of geographical ideologies and of the Japanese and German empires, created and destroyed by the preceding generation, does not entirely convince the historian. Is it possible that we are so much more intelligent than those who immediately preceded us, than we ourselves were twenty years ago? Was Hitler's undertaking, and Japan's, not only criminal but absurd, since the punishment of defeat is prosperity thereafter?

Things are not so simple. Military strength is not proportional to the volume of production and the level of productivity. Japan, disarmed within her islands, lives better or less badly than yesterday's imperial Japan. But the latter was a great power, the former is not even a second-class power: in military terms, Japan is incapable of defending herself: she is a burden and not a help to her allies. Similarly, the Federal Republic of Germany is richer than the Third Reich: it achieves a per capita production which the latter did not attain. It also assures each man a higher revenue than the revenue of Hitler's subjects. But Hitler's subjects participated in the glory of a great power. The citizen who relied on Chancellor Adenauer owes his security to the strength of the United States. He is a spectator of the great conflicts of history. In other words, the imperial attempts were perhaps not irrational if their goal was collective power, the capacity to affect the course of history.

Even on the economic level, the problems did not appear so clearly twenty years ago as they do today. The danger of dependence on external sources of supply did not seem, at the time, exclusively military; it was regarded as economic too. In 1919 Mackinder wrote that the Germans were obliged to reduce the Slavs to the role of purveyors of food and purchasers of manufactured products. Such a theory incorrectly assumes that the industrialization of one country requires the non-industrialization of another. I believe this proposition is false in general; it was false, in any case, at the beginning of the twentieth century, concerning the relations between Germans and Slavs.

The events of the thirties and the great depression have given an ephemeral probability to these ambiguous conceptions, deduced from an incomplete analysis of the industrial system as well as from the persistence of traditional ideas. Access to raw materials seemed jeopardized by the lack of currency. The barriers raised against the Japanese exports created legitimate anxiety in Japanese public opinion and among the leaders of the Nipponese Empire. The disintegration of world economy, the return to bilateral agreements, the multiplication of protectionist measures, all these consequences of the great depression were indeed of such a nature as to render precarious, in appearance and even in reality, the fate of nations whose existence was subject to the hazards of international exchange. That such, today, is the fate of all or of almost all nations, and that their peoples have grown accustomed to it, does not prevent us from understanding that during the thirties this dependence should have seemed terrifying and caused panic.

Thus the fortune of the geographical ideologies seems linked to three kinds of circumstances. The sedentary peoples, for whom cavalcades and combats are no longer the normal manner of living and who no longer dare invoke the god of battles, were prompted, by a dialectical reversal, to deduce spirit from nature, law from fact and historical legitimacy from physical necessity. Incomplete comprehension of the industrial system emphasized the risks rather than the opportunities of the growth in intensity, of the increase in the number of inhabitants in a given space. Finally, an exceptionally violent crisis suddenly seemed to confirm these fears and revive the specter of famine. Therewith Germans and Japanese believed they were back in the distant ages when populations sought safety in migration.

The ideology of natural frontiers offers, historically, certain features common to the ideology of vital space. The latter supposes that conquests need to be justified and that this justification cannot readily be furnished by spiritual doctrines. Similarly, the ideology of natural frontiers serves to justify the frontier when one does not possess a better argument.

In the age of kings and of the dynastic principle, monarchs determined the possession of cities or provinces among themselves. The will of the populations played virtually no part and would not have sufficed to confirm the legitimacy or illegitimacy of a transfer of sovereignty. The conquests of Louis XIV caused a scandal because they were effected by force, in certain cases without even a declaration of war, not because they ignored the sentiments of populations. The idea of natural frontiers found acceptance in the nineteenth century and appeared all the more convincing to the revolutionaries because it filled a gap in the new ideas. The French Republic could not take or yield provinces in the manner of the kings who actually treated their lands and their subjects as personal property. In its periods of glory and fervor, the Republic did not annex territory, it liberated peoples from tyranny. Still, it was necessary that the peoples be prepared to hail as liberators the soldiers who deposed their kings, to recognize in the French Republic, or in any satellite republic, the consecration of their own liberty (the point had not yet been reached of organizing demonstrations of enthusiasm). Vanquished, France invoked against the German Empire the right of peoples to self-determination. Victorious, she was tempted to appeal to the notion of natural frontiers which authorized her to ignore the will of populations.

A natural frontier, if this formula has any meaning, is a frontier traced in advance on the physical map, indicated by a river or a chain of mountains, hence easy to defend. A natural frontier should be called strategic or military. The military argument is the equivalent of the biological or economic argument of vital space—it is the substitute for a moral argument. The need for security justifies the annexation of a province as vital necessity justifies vast conquests.

The geographical study of frontiers offers virtually no arguments to the doctrine of so-called natural frontiers. In fact, political frontiers, down through the centuries, have diverged from the lines of physical separation (rivers or chains of mountains) as often as they have followed them. The Alps have marked the frontier between Italy and France for only a century. The Pyrenees constitute the political but not the linguistic frontier between Spain and France: on either side of the Pyrenees there are Catalans and particularly Basques. Nor has the Rhine, which does not mark a linguistic frontier, become a political frontier between Germans and French.

Can it be said that a political frontier is stronger, has more chances of being maintained when it consecrates a fiat of geography? This is an illusion. The stability of a frontier depends only to a small degree on physical or strategic conditions. It is a function of the relations between the collectivities which it separates. When in agreement on ideas concerning legitimacy during a particular period, it creates no occasion for conflict. In this sense, a frontier regarded by neighboring states as equitable is, in itself, the best frontier, whether good or bad in military terms. Further, according to the technique of arms and the configuration of alliances, a frontier changes its meaning. In the Europe of 1960, the Rhine has ceased to be a sensitive area. It has always favored contact among people and the exchange of goods and ideas. With the end of Franco-German rivalry, it changes its political-military function, since it henceforth flows not between enemies but partners.

Is the frontier between zones of civilizations more visible, more constant on the map than the frontier between political units? It is along the line extending from the Baltic to the Adriatic, from Stettin to Trieste, that the Asian invasion petered out. It is not impossible to find the causes for this almost natural occurrence: the conqueror's impulse is exhausted with distance. We should be nevertheless wrong to rely on geography alone as a guarantee for the security of Western Europe. If the West were protected only by the Stettin-Trieste line, there would be reason to fear for its future.

No so-called natural fortification is sufficient to repulse the aggressors. The outcome of the struggle between nomads and sedentary peoples has never been predetermined solely by geographical conditions. *A fortiori,* the victory of Communist despotism or of the Western democracies, the coexistence of these two civilizations, the future frontier of two worlds, all are events of which space will be the theater, but not the exclusive or principal determinant.

4. *Space in the Scientific Age*

Is the geographical perspective of history now losing its meaning? Is humanity liberating itself from the constraints of environment as it acquires the mastery of natural forces? Will the collectivities, capable of prospering without conquests, not become more peaceful, once space has ceased to be the preferred stake of the struggle among peoples?

It is difficult to deny that the progress of technology involves a certain liberation of humanity, a reduction of environmental constraint. The number of men capable of living in a given area is no longer rigorously limited in advance. The choices available to a human group settled in a particular territory are increased as the trades and professions accessible to each individual increase. Means of mastering cold or heat permit us to inhabit regions of the globe formerly abandoned. We can foresee the time when scientists will be in a position, without excessive investments, to modify climate itself. More than ever, the earth is the work of mankind, though it has pre-existed and might well survive it.

Yet it would be dangerous to compare this liberation, though it may be gradual and partial, to a total freedom. To take only one example, but the most important, the number of men capable of living upon given surfaces, though no longer rigorously limited in advance, has nonetheless not become unlimited. Thus the judgments of historians or geographers as to the importance of space proceed from one extreme to the other.

One American historian, W. P. Webb,[19] regards that part of the earth's surface which the Europeans possess and have possessed since the sixteenth century as the major factor which has determined and which today explains certain features of their societies (liberalism, mobility, etc.). In 1500, 100 million Europeans lived on a territory of 3.75 million square miles, in other words a density of 7.6 human beings per square mile. With the conquest of America they acquired some 20 million additional square miles, or about five times the surface of Europe. Thereby, each European possessed, so to speak, 148 acres instead of 24, not to mention the natural resources (gold, silver, furs, etc.). The modern period, that which extends from the sixteenth century to the twentieth, was abnormally favorable to the population of Europe. It has enjoyed advantages which no other population has enjoyed in the past, which no other, probably, will enjoy in the future.

In the course of these fortunate centuries, the population of Europe has continually increased. In 1900 the density per square mile had returned to 27; by 1940 it reached 35. Henceforth, space was more nearly filled, the house more crowded than at the dawn of modern times. The American historian thereby concludes that the features peculiar to European societies, especially the liberal institutions, will disappear with the exceptional circumstances that have brought them into being. The European societies will return to the common fate, one like the other.

It is easy to object that Webb exaggerates the significance of his statistics. A density of 27 in 1900 has not the same value as this same density in 1500. Density must be measured in relation to technological means, that is, in rela-

[19] *The Great Frontier*, Boston, 1952.

tion to productivity, either by surface unit or by worker unit. If we adopt this mode of calculation, which is the only valid one, the actual density, even if it were double or triple that of 1500, would be inferior to it in terms of social reality. In this connection, one demographer, M. A. Sauvy, asserts that no portion of the planet today suffers from absolute overpopulation—except perhaps Holland. Everywhere else, the difficulty stems from the inadequacy of development, not the excess of men.

Without discussing this concept at present, which we shall return to in the following chapter, the present distribution of men and resources on the surface of the earth suggests that the struggle for space might not be over, despite the partial independence acquired by the human collectivities with regard to their environment. M. Vermot-Gauchy has published an interesting study of this distribution, from which we borrow the following statistics.[20]

The surface of the earth above water is 52.5 million square miles. The population being 2784 million in 1955, the *average unitary surface* (that is, the available surface per human being) is 12.0 acres. Now let us define two concepts: we shall call a nation's *individual productivity* the quotient of the national revenue divided by the number of inhabitants; we shall call its *spatial productivity* the quotient of the national revenue divided by the number of square miles of its territory.

The United States has a huge area of 3.7 million square miles, a national revenue of $324 billion, a population of 167 million. Its average unitary surface is 14.0 acres, its individual productivity $1940, its spatial productivity $34,100. In the U.S.S.R. the unitary surface is 27.5 acres (for an area of 8.6 million square miles, and a population of 200 million), the individual productivity $600 (for a national revenue of $120 billion), the spatial productivity $5400. In Europe the unitary surface is 2.8 acres (for an area of 10.1 million square miles and a population of 360 million), the individual productivity $650 (for a national revenue of $232 billion), the spatial productivity $58,000.

On the American continent, Canada has a unitary surface of 156.2 acres, an individual productivity of $1320, a spatial productivity of $2100. In Latin America the unitary surface is 28.2 acres, the individual productivity $280, the spatial productivity $2500.

In the Soviet Zone the European satellites have a unitary surface of 6.25 acres, an individual productivity of $600, a spatial productivity of $26,000. China has a unitary surface of 3.75 acres, an individual productivity of $100, a spatial productivity of $6200. Non-Communist Asia has an individual productivity of $100, and a spatial productivity of $5200.

These figures are approximate because of the uncertainty of the calculations of national revenue. Further, they are distorted to a degree because the designated surface does not specify the quality of the land and the nature of

[20] 1955 figures published in the *Bulletin of the S.E.D.E.I.S.*, No. 726, July 1959.

the climate. The northern space which Canada and the Soviet Union possess is not the equivalent of the fertile lands of Western Europe. But these incontestable errors, though difficult to correct (the distinction between cultivable and non-cultivable land is relative), do not eliminate the significance of the major data.

Among the developed nations we perceive two categories: those in which individual productivity exceeds the average (360) more than spatial productivity (this is the case of the United States and even of the Soviet Union); and those, on the other hand, in which the spatial productivity exceeds the average more than individual productivity (the case of Western Europe). Even in absolute figures, the spatial productivity of Western Europe (58,000) exceeds that of the United States (34,000).

Now, on the military level, mediocre unitary surface is a double source of weakness: it prevents the dispersion which, in the age of thermonuclear weapons, offers advantages; and it increases the dependence on the supply of men and factories. Nations with a high spatial productivity—and England, with her $250,000, is the most striking example—are condemned to buy and sell a great deal abroad. During preceding centuries this international commerce took place in the shadow of the Union Jack flying aft on the ships of the Royal Navy. The European population could not do without food and raw materials from overseas, but armies and fleets guaranteed the loyalty of the purveyors. In our century this military guarantee has collapsed. In the name of vital space or the sphere of Asian co-prosperity, Germany and Japan have sought to escape dependence, or rather to escape economic solidarity. Renouncing these ambitions or these illusions, the Europeans have subsequently preached the vanity of conquest, the fruitfulness of exchange: there is room for all. This theory also corresponds to the new situation. Compared to yesterday's imperialist ideologies, it also has the advantage of teaching states the trade of merchants and no longer that of armies.

Similarly, among the so-called underdeveloped nations, two categories are immediately apparent: nations of relatively strong spatial productivity (China: $6200) and nations of relatively weak spatial productivity (Latin America: $2500). China already has a dense population before the process of industrialization begins. Latin America has an individual productivity which is nearly triple China's, and possesses eight times more space per capita. The basic data are much more favorable for Latin America than for China —which does not mean that the latter will not progress more rapidly than the former.

These figures in no way suggest that the people without space will some day resume the forward march that was interrupted by the irreversible defeat of German and Japanese imperialism. On the contrary, everything indicates that in the short run, in terms of decades, unitary surface matters less than the technological capacity of populations. The nations of the Common Market already have a spatial productivity of some $200,000. They have nonetheless experienced since 1950—that is, since the end of the reconstruction period —the highest rate of increase in the free world. In peacetime, purchases abroad of a share of the supplies for men and factories involved dependence (the maintenance of competitive prices is indispensable) but also advantages (the seller of raw materials depends on the purchaser at least as much as the latter on the former: in 1956 Europe was afraid of not having enough oil, the nations which live on royalties are afraid of not finding customers). Similarly, among the underdeveloped nations, it is not those possessing the largest unitary surface that will develop most rapidly in the coming decades, but those likely to establish the most effective industrialization policy. In other words, *during the present historical phase, the ideology of vital space will not be invoked by the imperialist states, and the lack of space will not be the direct cause of possible attempts at conquest.* Yet we cannot thereby conclude that the discrepancies in spatial productivity will always remain without influence. At present, in the race for power, Russians and Americans have the advantage, in relation to Europeans, of a relatively low population density, which permits extensive agriculture, allows a broad margin of demographic and economic growth, guarantees that at the end of one or of several centuries, an increase—however slow—in productivity, combined with a substantial growth of the number of inhabitants, will be expressed by a considerable increase in total resources. In Europe, France remains below the demographic optimum[21] of power and well-being, but Western Germany and Great Britain cannot increase the size of their population without also raising the percentage of externally purchased supplies, for both men and industries. This is not an insurmountable obstacle (the Federal Republic of Germany has shown this for ten years). It is nonetheless, in general, an unfavorable circumstance. More clearly still, the Chinese might some day compare the unitary surface they possess with that of their neighbors. In any case, whether nations tend to modify the distribution of space by force or accommodate themselves to the present distribution, correcting by trade the disparities of density, unitary surface will remain one of the factors which controls the course of demographic advancement. The Frenchmen in Canada, numbering sixty thousand at the time of the Treaty of Paris, today have more than five million descendants. They were not different from those in France, but in the vast spaces of the new country, the majority of their children survived.

The temporary suspension of the struggle for space, as a result of the resources available to peoples by the growth in intensity, coincides with the transformation of what we might call the sense of space (the expression was coined by Professor Carl Schmitt: *Raumsinn*[22]). The sense of space has been, in each period, determined by the image which men have made for

[21] See below, Chap. VIII.
[22] See Carl Schmitt, *Land und Meer, eine weltgeschichtliche Betrachtung*, Leipzig, 1944.

themselves of their habitat, by the style of movement and of combat on land and at sea, by the stake for which societies came into conflict.

Today humanity as a whole conceives its habitat differently from the river civilizations of the Egyptian type, from civilizations of closed seas like those of the Greeks and the Romans, or even from the continental-oceanic civilizations, that is, from Western civilization since the voyages of exploration up to our own period. Lines of communication and thereby those of strategy are no longer those of yesterday. Planes take passengers from Paris to Tokyo via the Pole. The United States and the Soviet Union are no longer separated by Western Europe and the Atlantic: given the speed of strategic bombers or ballistic missiles, they are quite close to each other and they have the Arctic, one might say, as a common frontier.

The opposition of land to sea—the one which symbolized the contrast between the remote control of the ocean and the yard-by-yard occupation of the earth, or even between the possessive and stay-at-home spirit of the territorial power and the adventurous and commercial spirit (pirate or merchant, it matters little) of the maritime power—tends to lessen or to assume a new character. Vessels and their crews are no longer isolated, depending on their own resources for weeks at a time. Corsairs are located by airplanes nowadays, and radio communication permits an orderly regrouping of ships, even when dispersion is required to avoid destruction.

In terms of myth, we might say that earth and water are henceforth subject to the law of air and fire. The same spirit is imposed upon land and sea forces: that of science. In both cases the leader manipulates men, maneuvers units, aircraft carriers or divisions according to a plan coordinating the units. If the spirit of individual initiative, of a surprise attack, of heroic piracy, of terrorism by alternately noble and sordid passion still finds occasions to manifest itself, it is no longer on the desert of sand or waves, where rebels are helplessly hunted down by the air police, but in the mountains and by the *maquis*. Because of the aerial weapon, the sea is no longer the province of adventure. Because of fire, the bases are losing their military importance or, at least, the bases no longer have a fixed site. The protection of the United States against a surprise attack is no longer the passive defense of shelters for the population, nor the active defense of cannons or planes or engines, nor the military system of fortifications, airfields or ports, but the retaliatory force. Yet the latter's security is insured less by the depth of underground protection or by distance in relation to the enemy than by ubiquity. Atomic submarines, armed with Polaris rockets, are everywhere and nowhere, they are somewhere on or under the seas, invulnerable and pacifying. History has decided between the theory of the *res nullius* and the *res omnium*: the sea belongs to all. The air, too, starting from a certain height, will belong to all *because of satellites*. Rockets strike down spy planes of the U-2 type, but satellites photograph the earth and transmit photographs.

Having conquered the oceans, and then the air, European man, subsequently relayed in his race by all humanity, turns his eyes and his ambitions toward interstellar space. Will the closed societies pursue their provincial disputes beyond our planet and our atmosphere, as the English and French fought each other in the snows of Canada? Or will the rulers of industrial society finally bring about the reign of order and peace, leaving to the rebellious no other refuge than secluded caves or the solitude of consciousness?

chapter VIII

On Number

We have often touched on the problem of number in the preceding chapter. Indeed, how can we deal with space without suggesting the number of men who populate each of its pieces? It is the link between the distribution of natural resources and the distribution of population on the earth's surface which suggested to Mackinder the geographical design we have studied above. It is through the intermediary of number that, to a large degree, space affects the course of history and the fortune of nations.

The number of men capable of living on a given surface of the earth obviously varies with their technological means. If we suppose that the latter are constant—and, for long periods of history,[1] this supposition was not far from the truth and even closer to men's awareness of that truth—events and institutions, victories and disasters, the ownership of property and public safety, the attitude of the rulers to trade and wealth, all are justifiably regarded as the direct causes of variations in number.

But this mode of consideration, legitimate in itself, sometimes deceived the most learned authors into making erroneous propositions. Montesquieu believed that the population of Europe, in the eighteenth century, was diminishing.[2] He accused the centralization around Paris of causing this diminution:

"It is the perpetual reunion of many little states that has produced this diminution. Formerly, every village of France was a capital; there is at present only one large one. Every part of the state was a center of power; at present all parts have a relation to one center and this center is in some measure the state itself."

Number is a determinant odious to men and, for this very reason, mysterious. It is anonymous, imperceptible. Men have personified, transfigured

---

[1] Let us repeat, once and for all, that by history we designate the brief period known as that of the higher societies or civilizations, about six thousand years.
[2] *L'Esprit des lois*, XXIII.

into a benevolent or malevolent divinity the land or the sea, fire or air, oil or coal, socialism or capitalism, trusts or the masses. Only a military genius could admit, without being accused of cynicism, that the favors of heaven went by preference to the biggest battalions.

Number is the best explanation of events for the man who prefers to *demystify*. He also risks discouraging or exasperating those who refuse to reduce their ambitions to the measure of their resources.

1. The Uncertainties of Number

The first question number raises is also the one most difficult to answer. To know to what degree number determines the strength of armies, the power of nations, the result of combats, the greatness of states, we would have to establish exactly the size of populations, the strength of troops in conflict. Now the figures given by the chroniclers have often been not only false but foolish. It is as if exactitude, in these matters, filled them with horror.

According to Herodotus, the Persians who besieged the Greek city-states numbered two million (not counting servants or slaves). We need merely calculate the distance between the head and the rear of such an army in columns to perceive at once the absurdity of the estimate.[3] Historians have long been impressed by these assertions from witnesses who in other respects deserved to be believed. Even today, many hesitate to accept Delbrück's demonstration (which I find convincing) that the Athenians at Marathon—an infantry of citizens—outnumbered the Persian cavalry.[4]

Perhaps more moderate in their errors, the chroniclers of the Middle Ages are no more accurate. They count 120,000 Burgundians at the battle of Grandson; Delbrück reduces the number to 14,000.[5] There is no doubt, as can readily be proved by reference to the possibilities of quartermaster service and supply, that the great battles of history, before the eighteenth century, were waged by several thousand combatants. The army with which Alexander set out for the conquest of Asia, more than forty thousand men, was not, as we were taught at school, a small army but an enormous one, by the calculations of the period.

Two psychological mechanisms account for these fantasies in calculation.

[3] In this chapter I am using Hans Delbrück's *Geschichte der Kriegskunst, im Rahmen der politischen Geschichte*, Vol. I, Berlin, 1900, I, p. 10. Herodotus attributes to Xerxes' army a total of 4,200,000, who would have formed a column of 420 miles. When the head of the column had reached Thermopylae, the rear would still have been at Suva, beyond the Tigris.

[4] *Ibid.*, pp. 38 ff. Apropos of Herodotus' figure of two million Persian soldiers, Jean Bérard (*Population*, 2nd year, No. 2, 1947, p. 304) writes that the figure must be at least five times too large, perhaps more. If it were only five times too large, there would still have been four hundred thousand Persian soldiers, which is as improbable as two million.

[5] *Ibid.*, pp. 8–9. The argument summarized by Delbrück is to be found in the lectures published in English, *Number in History*, London, 1913.

I shall call the first *the illusion of multitude*. We can all the more readily understand this mechanism since it continues to function in our own period. In 1940 the French believed that the number of German parachutists, tanks and planes was enormous. As a matter of fact, only several thousand parachutists were engaged in the battle (4500). The tanks which broke the French lines numbered no more than 2580, and there were no more than 3000 airplanes supporting the army; this number was multiplied by the successes they won. Similarly the Normans, the Hussites, and the Mongols who terrorized Europe numbered no more than several thousand.

A somewhat different mechanism accounts for the apparently involuntary errors committed by the British in their count of the German planes shot down in the Battle of England during the summer of 1940. The 185 planes were actually only 46. The same victim was claimed, perhaps justifiably, by several pursuit pilots. By attributing to each of the latter a different victim, the true figure was ultimately multiplied by three or four. The illusion of multitude appears not only when each witness feels he is in the presence of a tremendous host, but also when each witness is supposed to have seen a different enemy.

It is only a step to the second mechanism, which I shall call *interested falsification*. The number of those who paraded in Paris from the Place de la République to the Place de la Bastille in May 1958 varied, according to the political preferences of the newspapers, as much as three times the actual figure. Each camp exaggerates the losses suffered by the enemy and systematically underestimates its own.

Sometimes the illusion of multitude is combined with interested falsification. Did the Greeks believe in the forces they attributed to Xerxes, or did they wish to magnify their own merits? Were hordes of German tanks and planes necessary to excuse defeat, or had the French convinced themselves of the exactitude of the figures which furnished an excuse and, simultaneously, corresponded to the truth of their impressions?

Despite the critical studies of historians, the number of combatants has not been established for every great battle with unquestionable precision. Thus the role of numerical superiority or inferiority remains, by definition, uncertain. Such uncertainty seems to me still greater when the size of populations is in question. It is often difficult to distinguish the *partial depopulation* which affects the privileged classes or, at least, the combatant classes, from total depopulation. The ancient authors leave us no doubt as to the first phenomenon: we know, with great exactitude, the number of citizens in Athens and Sparta at different dates. Yet this does not warrant our drawing conclusions concerning the total population, including foreigners and slaves. And indeed, depending on whether we are concerned with citizens or total population, the phenomenon is not the same. In one case it is a question of *differential fertility* according to class, for which social organization is responsible; in the other it is a question of a kind of exhaustion of vitality.

Even if the first obstacle were surmounted, if we established the numerical data concerning the forces of the combatants and the size of populations, it would not be easy to isolate the influence of number. Let us take a historical example, a well-known one, in which the figures are precise and certain. The Franco-German War of 1870 is subdivided into two phases: during the first the regular armies of the Second Empire, composed of professional soldiers, were defeated by the more numerous armies of Prussia and her allies. During the second phase the armies improvised by the Government of National Defense, despite their numerical superiority, were also defeated. Must we impute the defeat of Napoleon III's armies to numerical inferiority, to the better quality of the Prussian cannon, or to the deficiencies of the French command? To what degree to each of these causes? Rarely, down through the centuries, have authors invoked number in order to explain the fortune of arms, but, even today, it is difficult for us to specify the role such explanations play in a given circumstance or at any one period of history.

As it is not our intention to analyze specific cases in detail—and only such analyses would permit us to reduce the margin of uncertainty—we shall try to develop propositions of a certain generality bearing on two chief problems: the influence of number on strength or power, and the relation between population (or overpopulation) and wars.

Let us first note the changes in the order of size. There were probably three to five thousand Athenian combatants on the battlefield of Marathon. Alexander set out for the conquest of Asia with an army (enormous for the period) of some forty thousand warriors. Napoleon mobilized ten times as many men in order to cross the frontiers of Russia in January 1812. The army which Hitler had amassed in 1941 with a view to the same enterprise numbered in millions and not in hundreds of thousands of men. There were only one hundred million people on earth at the time of the birth of Jesus Christ, about six hundred million at the beginning of the seventeenth century; today there are three billion.

The force and cultural contribution of the collectivities have never been proportional to their respective size. Whether we attribute the miracle of Greece and the creations of Athens to social circumstances or hereditary gifts, the fact remains that one man has never, historically, been "equal to another" on a one-to-one basis. Within political units as in the competition among them, the smaller number has more than once been the artisan of fate.

On the battlefield, number has almost always been an important factor. In particular, within a zone of civilization, when neither arms nor organization were essentially different, it tended to force the decision. Still we may modify or correct the preceding proposition by two remarks. In the case of a conflict between combatants who belong to fundamentally heterogeneous collectivities, a small troop is capable of scoring spectacular successes. The term "conquest à la Cortez" has become classical in the literature. Several dozen Spanish cavaliers represented a force of the first rank, facing the Aztecs of pre-Columbian Mexico. Similarly, in Europe, a few thousand Asian barbarians have more than once spread terror among populations incomparably larger.

Moreover, in antiquity, and even more generally down through the centuries preceding modern times, there did not exist a rigorous ratio between size of population and number of combatants. The most enormous empires could be built on a limited base, as in the case of the Romans, the Arabs or the Mongols. As the result of a high degree of mobilization, a more effective organization and the extension of citizenship to the conquered, a city-state could subject an entire zone of civilization to its rule without ever losing equality or numerical superiority on the battlefield. The capacity to arm a great number of men was a proof of political art, as the capacity to concentrate one's forces is still a proof of strategic art.

To proceed beyond these generalities, we must consider separately two typical periods, antiquity on the one hand, nineteenth- and twentieth-century Europe on the other. In the Greek world Athens was a giant unit because it included, on the eve of the Peloponnesian War, forty thousand citizens and, with foreigners and slaves, over two hundred thousand souls. In nineteenth-century Europe, France seemed doomed to decadence because her population rose only slowly. Turning from the Athens of five centuries before Christ to the France of nineteen centuries after Christ, we substitute for the thousands (or at most the tens of thousands) of the Greek authors the millions of the contemporary demographers and for static consideration (what is the ideal volume of the city-state?) dynamic analysis (what is the preferable rate of increase?).

Further, the relations between the forces of the city-states and the forces of the armies, the size of populations and the number of soldiers, are not the same and cannot be the same in the age of heroism and the age of petroleum or of the atom, to employ the expressions of J. F. C. Fuller.[6] As long as weapons are simple and cheap, the degree of mobilization is a result of the social regime. In our period this degree depends on economic resources and on the solidity of the central power. The number of machines is more important than the number of men.

It is from these two points of view—the way of dealing with the demographic problem, the relation between the size of the population and the number of soldiers, between the strength of the city-states and the strength of the armies—that we shall sketch a comparison between antiquity and modern times.

[6] *The Influence of Weapons on History*, New York, 1945.

2. *Ideal Stability and Demographic and Political Instability*

The Greek philosophers posed the problem of what we shall call the population *optimum*,[7] which can scarcely surprise us, since they were not content with an objective, neutral study of facts and causes, but attempted to grasp the finality of order or of *the good*. The city-state, in their eyes, was the unit in which social life *had to be* organized. Thus Plato and Aristotle both queried not so much the *ideal* as the *natural* size of the city. Ten individuals do not make a city-state, Aristotle writes, nor do ten times ten thousand.[8] Plato, in the *Laws*, suggests the number 5040. "The number 5040 offers remarkable arithmetical properties: it is the product of seven whole prime numbers; therefore it has the advantage over other numbers of being the one which permits the greatest number of divisors. This results in great administrative convenience, when it is a question of subdividing the population, distributing the citizens or recruits, arranging them in columns on public registers, on tax rolls or in the field."[9]

These strange speculations are neither senseless nor even entirely anachronistic. The goal of the city-state, that is, of politics, is not power, but a life according to reason. Since the virtuous life is possible only in society, we must therefore determine the number of citizens that favors or makes possible an order that accords with reason. Two considerations are or risk being in conflict: the necessities of defense against an external enemy require a large number; moral cohesion demands a small number. The compromise must be within a just proportion: the city-state must be neither too small nor too large. An Athens of forty thousand citizens suffers from gigantism.

"The facts prove that it is difficult if not impossible to govern properly a state whose population is too numerous; at least we see that none of those which have the reputation of being well-governed can increase its population without measure. This is evident and confirmed by reason: for the law is a certain order, and good laws necessarily constitute good order; now a too-numerous population cannot lend itself to the establishment of order . . . a city-state that has too many inhabitants cannot be self-sufficient; now the quality of a city-state is to be self-sufficient. The city-state in which the population is too large can no doubt care for all its needs, but then as a tribe, and not as a city-state. It is not easy to organize a political order there. What general can command an excessive multitude? . . . What herald could make himself heard if he had not a stentor's voice? Therefore the city-state is necessarily formed once it is composed of a sufficient multitude to have all the conveniences of life according to the rules of political association. It is possible that the city-state in which the number of inhabitants exceeds this measure is still a city-state on a larger scale; but, as we have said, such excess has

[7] *Nichomachean Ethics*, IX, 10, 1170, b31–32.
[8] Cf. J. Moreau, "Les Théories démographiques dans l'antiquité grecque," *Population*, 4th year, No. 4, October–December 1949, pp. 597–613.
[9] *Laws*, V, 737e–738a.

limits. And what are these limits? The facts themselves readily indicate them. Political acts derive from those who command or from those who obey; and the function of those who govern is to command and to judge. In order to judge the rights of each and to distribute judgments depending on merit, the citizens must know and appreciate each other; when this is impossible, the judgments are necessarily bad. In this regard, it is not just to act without reflection, and yet this is obviously what happens in a very populous city. Further, it then becomes easy for foreigners and slaves to involve themselves in government; for it is not difficult to escape surveillance in an excessive multitude of inhabitants. It is therefore obvious that the most convenient limit to the population of a city-state is that it should include the greatest possible number of inhabitants to suffice for its needs, but without surveillance ceasing to be easy. Let us here end what we have to say on the size of a city-state."[10]

Since the goal is a city-state that conforms to the just measure, neither too large nor too small, large enough to be self-sufficient and capable of defending itself, small enough for the citizens to know each other and for the government to be good, the population policy conceived by Plato or Aristotle tended to avoid overpopulation or depopulation. In other words it aimed at maintaining a stationary population, since the danger, in the classical period, was that of excessive numbers or of insufficient space, *stenochoria*. The Greek idea that beyond a certain size a population can no longer be governed according to reason has today fallen into disuse, but it was long regarded as obvious by Western thinkers. We find an echo of it in the first books of *L'Esprit des lois,* in which the type of government is made to correspond with the dimensions of the territory and where despotism is regarded as inevitable in the vast empires of Asia.

This ideal of stability was, in fact, the counterpart of an extreme instability of number on the one hand, and of the political fortune of collectivities on the other. "One generally thinks of ancient Greece as the country in which Athens and Sparta prevailed. But this simplified image is quite inexact. Athens and Sparta disputed hegemony in the fifth and fourth centuries B.C., and were the great centers of Hellas in the period that marks the apogee of ancient Greek civilization, but they were such centers only at that period. In the Mycenaean period, the greatest centers were the city-states which, like Pylos or Triphylia, had ceased to exist in the classical period or, like Mycenae and Tiryns, had lost all importance. In the archaic period, from the eighth to the seventh centuries B.C., the great metropolitan centers were Chalcis and Eretria in Euboea, or Corinth and Megara in Greece proper. In Asia-Minor, they were Phocaea and Miletus. By the fourth century, the hegemony that Athens and Sparta had disputed in the fifth soon passed to Thebes in Beoetia, whose inhabitants had the reputation of being dull-witted, then to Mace-

[10] Aristotle, *Politics,* IV (vii), 4, 1326 $a17–b24$.

donia, which had hitherto developed on the fringe of the Hellenic world and which to the true Hellenes seemed only half-Greek."[11] How could fortune fail to be fickle when a city-state of ten thousand citizens already passed for a great one?

A "giant" city-state, like Athens, had a future that was still less certain. The population of Athens could live only by importing a great share of its food, at least half, perhaps more. The city-state had begun to perform activities which, in our century, are called industrial. She was selling the products of her mines (silver from Laurium, marble from Pentelica), of her artisans (ceramics, textiles, naval construction); she depended as much on her non-Athenian residents and her slaves as upon her customers and her purveyors. Yet such a dependence, at the time, had a significance entirely different from that of our own period. The maritime empire of Athens, gradually formed in the early stages by alliances among city-states against the Persians, was maintained only by the superiority of the fleet and the tributes paid by allies which had become satellites. Those economic activities which are not based upon the development of the means of production, which are linked to the primary sector (mines) or to the tertiary sector (commerce, services) have been, down through the ages, sensitive to the vicissitudes of military victories and defeats. In the ancient world, imperial greatness and wealth were in fact inseparable.

The ideal of a stationary population was not only a reaction against the fickleness of fortune, but also corresponded to the excess and lack of men from which Greece alternately suffered. The excess of men was the source of the vast movement of colonization of the eighth and seventh centuries B.C. It was also the origin of the surplus of warriors who were ready to serve as mercenaries. This abundance of men dedicated to the profession of arms permits us to explain Alexander's conquests. In the fourth century B.C. Greece was still a vast reservoir of soldiers. The unification of the city-states, even in servitude, created the equivalent of a great power. Independent, the city-states exhausted themselves in sterile conflicts. Subject to one master, they were capable of vast conquests. In the fourth and even more in the third century B.C. the contrary evil, that of *oliganthropy*, was rampant. At the beginning of the fourth century the number of Athenian citizens diminished by one fourth (from forty to thirty thousand). Still more striking is the depopulation of Sparta. According to Herodotus, the hoplites, in 480 B.C., numbered eight thousand. There were no more than two thousand of them in 371, on the eve of the battle of Leuctra. They numbered seven hundred by the middle of the third century B.C. Jean Bérard quotes Polybius, who observes and explains the phenomenon:

"All Greece suffers from a check in procreation and a dearth of men, such that the cities are depopulated because the men of the times, loving luxury,

[11] Jean Bérard, *op. cit.*, p. 309.

money, and idleness as well, no longer wish to marry, or, if they marry, to raise a family, and because they all consented to have two children at most in order to bring them up in luxury and leave them rich when they die."

And, commenting on the ancient historian, the modern one, discussing the first centuries of our era, writes:

"The qualitative and quantitative diminution of the population which successively affects all the provinces of the Empire is particularly manifest in Greece. A disconcerting observation: as if security infallibly softened peoples, as if effort and struggle were necessary to temper them and condition them for a high birth rate."[12]

In the case of Sparta, there is no doubt that the laws were the direct cause of the depopulation. The citizens were warriors all their lives. They had no right to undertake lucrative employment. In order for each man to keep enough funds to pay his share of the common meal, a system of inalienable entail had been established, which naturally exercised a Malthusian influence. Similarly, in all the Greek city-states, the methods conceived to prevent population increase (delayed marriages, exposure of children, infanticide) were put into practice, even in the classical period. They were not abandoned in the following centuries. Malthusianism was implied by the structure of the city-state, by the distinction between slaves and free men, by the essentially political and military vocation of the citizens.

The dimension of political units therefore exerted a major influence on the course of Greek history. The city-state was the typical form of the collective organization (whatever the causes of this organization). The city-states together were capable of resisting the Persian Empire by the simple recourse of temporary alliances. They were capable of setting out for the conquest of Asia once they were subject to the will of a Philip and an Alexander. But when Alexander had subjected to his ambition the forces of Greece, which had remained unrealized in the period of *jealous emulation* (to borrow Hume's expression), the city-states no longer had a future, a *raison d'être*. Deprived of their independence without a Caesar to carry them off on some vast enterprise, they inexorably died out.

How and why did a city-state, located on the fringe of the so-called Hellenic civilization, transcend this final stage and effect a lasting peace not only over the Greek city-states, as Macedonia had done, but over an incomparably more extensive historical space? Admirers of the Roman works, like Arnold Toynbee and Jérôme Carcopino, emphasize characteristically political or moral causes. Toynbee[13] lists five: a favorable geographical situation, generosity toward the peoples who became the allies of Rome and accepted her hegemony, generosity in granting Roman citizenship to allies and subjects, the liberal institution of double citizenship, and finally the practice of es-

---

[12] Jean Bérard, *op. cit.*, p. 312.
[13] *A Study of History*, Vol. XII, Oxford, 1961, pp. 380 ff.

tablishing colonies in newly conquered territories. Simone Weil counters this analysis by another element of Roman policy whose reality is indisputable: the unfortunately indubitable effectiveness of terror: "No one has ever equaled the Romans in the skillful use of cruelty. When cruelty is the effect of a caprice, of a diseased sensibility, of rage, of hatred, it often has fatal consequences to its employer; the cold, calculated cruelty which constitutes a method, the cruelty which no instability of mood, no consideration of prudence, respect or pity can temper, which one can hope to escape by neither courage, dignity and energy, nor by submission, supplications and tears—such cruelty is an incomparable instrument of domination. For being blind and deaf as the forces of nature, yet clearsighted and far-seeing as human intelligence, by this monstrous combination it paralyzes the spirit with the sense of a fatality."[14] Simone Weil does not hesitate to compare the Romans with the Nazis, and, employing modern concepts, she comes to the following conclusion: "The Romans conquered the world by seriousness, discipline, organization, continuity of outlook and method; by the conviction that they were a superior race born to command; by the calculated, methodical use of pitiless cruelty, of cold perfidy, of hypocritical propaganda, employed simultaneously or alternately; by an unshakable resolve always to sacrifice everything to prestige, without ever being sensitive to pity, to peril, nor to any human respect; by the art of decomposing under terror the very soul of their adversaries, or of lulling them by hope before enslaving them by arms; lastly by so skillful a manipulation of the crudest lies that they deceived even posterity and deceive us still."[15]

It would be difficult to deny the share of this psychologico-military technique in the Roman conquests as in the building of all empires. It is nonetheless true that after the terrorist phase, the generosity of the victor granting citizenship to the vanquished and the spread of double citizenship contributed to the strengthening of Rome's power and gave some substance to the eulogy of the Empire intoned by the descendants of those who had lost their freedom.

But, curiously, neither the admirer nor the detractor of the Roman achievement attempts any analysis of what was, and remains, the primary condition of an empire: the fortune of arms. Empire builders, by definition, generally gain it on the battlefield or, in any case, win the last battles. On what did Rome's military superiority depend?

On the whole, we might say that Rome did not possess an incontestable or overpowering superiority in the quality of weapons. Of course, the peoples of antiquity did not all utilize the same weapons. The mode of combat depended on the mode of life and the social organization. Horsemen or foot soldiers, heavily or lightly equipped, using impact weapons or projectiles, the

[14] *Ecrits historiques et politiques*, Paris, 1960, p. 28.
[15] *Ibid.*, p. 24.

warriors of the ancient world were not interchangeable, nor did they do battle according to *one* typical method. But the principal city-states were capable of procuring most kinds of arms, and if their metal was not always of the same quality, the fact remains that the determinant of superiority was not the quality of the weapons.

The superiority of the Roman legions on the battlefield was essentially that of an organization, of a tactic, one might say of the capacity to maneuver.

According to Delbrück, whose authority we accept here as well, it was heavy cavalry that constituted Philip's decisive weapon: the Macedonian horsemen were capable of collective order in the heat of combat. The combination of brutality and discipline was the secret of victory at the time, since neither side's weapons were fundamentally different.

The Romans owed the fusing of their legions into three echelons to the discipline achieved by Philip with his heavy cavalry, thus making the latter's men less vulnerable than the Spartan, Theban and Macedonian phalanx. Whereas the latter was incapable of protecting itself on its flanks or at the rear, the Roman legion, even after the outset of the encounter, could reverse its fronts. Whether it be Philip's cavalry or the legions of Rome, their greatest effectiveness lay in the category of *"capacity for collective action."* This original order of battle generally requires some modification in armament, a new combination of types of combatants and of combat weapons (longer or shorter spears, heavier or lighter body armor, different distribution of infantry and cavalry, etc.). But above all, the superiority based on a *capacity for collective action,* in the realm of military discipline,[16] is not immediately transmissible, for it is linked to the social structure and requires a considerable training. The Romans gradually perfected the legion's organization, tactics and armament; they developed its effectiveness under fire; but they would never have possessed such an instrument of war had the struggle with Carthage not transformed the mobilized citizens into professionals.[17]

The capacity of the Roman legions for maneuver was one necessary condition of its victories; the number of legionnaires was another. In periods of crisis the degree of mobilization was, in Rome, exceptionally high, 10 per cent of the free population, 30 per cent of the adult males, according to this same author.[18] Rome's "generosity" to her conquered enemies permitted her to enlarge her armed forces as the zone of Roman sovereignty increased. No matter how enormous this zone was, the Romans generally equaled or outnumbered their enemies on the battlefield. The Empire was not maintained

---

[16] H. Delbrück, I, 1, p. 239.
[17] *Ibid.,* pp. 277 and 333.
[18] H. Delbrück estimates at a million the free population of Rome at the beginning of the Second Punic War. The mobilization of twenty-two to twenty-three legions, in 212 or 211 B.C., represents a considerable effort.

by the prestige of a small minority, but by the permanent mobilization of the legions.

The power of the Roman legions was nonetheless limited in space. As a result of the immensity of their territory, its forests and sparse population, the Germans escaped, whether for their good or evil fortune, the fate of the Celts of Gaul. The Germans were not Romanized, they continued to speak their *Ursprache,* an original language and not one derived from that of the conquerors. Confronting the Parthian Empire, Rome was content with a peace of coexistence.

Of these elements of the Roman success, that of number (the number of combatants) is almost always omitted, while the maneuverability of the legions is scarcely indicated and intentionally identified with virtue. Now effectiveness in action deserves to be regarded as a political if not a moral virtue, but it implies neither cultural or spiritual values. Since the historians have paid homage to the Roman *virtù* of the imperial edifice, they cannot fail to attribute the decline to corruption. Military force is a function of the number of soldiers the Empire can mobilize, of the discipline of the legions, of their martial ardor. When the legions include more and more barbarians, and are incapable of raising an impenetrable blockade on the frontiers and sometimes even of conquering on the battlefield, it is evident that the system is weakening, a weakness which reflects the decomposition of the state and the loss of civic virtues.[19]

It is difficult for the historians, after having exalted the Roman Empire, not to deplore its fall. But it would be paradoxical, in a period when we denounce the colonial empires under the name of colonialism, still to take the side of the conquerors without reservations.

3. *The French Experience*

According to the Greek philosophers, a sufficient number is a condition of security, but security's goal is friendship among the citizens, impossible in a city-state whose population is too numerous. According to modern authors, number is the condition of power and the latter, in its turn, a condition of *rank.* Since nations are engaged in a permanent rivalry and since some of them grow rapidly, the others must do the same, or risk decadence. The comparison of rates of growth, both demographic and economic, is substituted for the search for the mean.

A century ago, in a book which enjoyed a tremendous success, Prévost-Paradol wrote: "When the present leader of our country declares that a nation's rank is measured by the number of men it can arm, he has only given

[19] For example, Jérôme Carcopino writes in *Les Etapes de l'impérialisme romain,* Paris, 1961: "Rome's military decadence can, on reflection, be reduced to two causes which no longer function in our modern world: the sudden multiplication of enemies whose weapons were virtually equivalent to her own and the specialization of a professional army whose civic ardor would be harmed."

too absolute a form to a true idea, for we must take into account the relative quality of men as well as their number. Xerxes, for example, armed infinitely more men than Greece, and yet the great spirit of Greece conquered him. But in a case of nations equally civilized and of courageous citizens equally sustained by a sense of honor, this maxim becomes strictly true, and political and military ascendancy goes to the most numerous nation, with all the material and moral advantages which derive from it."[20]

It is in France, the first European nation affected by the lowering of the birth rate, that the various problems of number have been looked upon with most anxiety. The first theme is the one which the preceding quotation expresses: to what degree is there a proportion between a nation's size, the strength of its army and its place in the world? The second problem is raised by France's conquests in the nineteenth century: is it possible to compensate by recruiting soldiers in Asia and Africa for the relative decline of metropolitan France?

By the thirties another fear was expressed: did not demographic stagnation involve economic stagnation? Far from small families guaranteeing the fortune of each child, experience proves that in dynamic and not static consideration, in national and not microscopic accounting, the result is entirely different. Demographic growth, at least in certain cases, provokes a more than proportional growth in resources.

Finally, since the Second World War, it is no longer France but the West which apprehensively questions the comparative statistics of populations. Will not the disparity between the standard of living of the privileged white minority and that of the colored masses be increased by a disparity in the opposite direction, numerical growth being faster precisely where poverty makes numerical stabilization desirable?

If we take an inclusive view of France's experience in Europe in the last century, it seems difficult to deny that the law of number has functioned. There were about 28 million Frenchmen in 1800, 41.9 million in 1940. Over the same period the population of the United Kingdom increased from 11 (16 with Ireland) to 46.4 million, that of Germany from 22.5 to 70 million, that of Italy from 18 to 44 million,[21] that of the United States from 5.3 to 131.7 million. The population of Tsarist Russia, known with less exactitude, increased about two and a half times during the nineteenth century.

In 1800 France with 28.2 million represented 15 per cent of the European population; Austria-Hungary, with 28 million, 15 per cent; Italy with 18 million, 9.2 per cent; Germany with 23 million, 13 per cent; the British Isles (including Ireland) 9 per cent; Russia, with 40 million, 21 per cent. In

20 *La France nouvelle*, Paris, 1868, p. 174.
21 These figures do not take emigration into account. The nations whose populations rapidly increased could, at the same time, contribute to the population of America and the Dominions: 17 million people left the United Kingdom between 1825 and 1920, 6 million Germans emigrated to the United States during the same period, and 9 million Italians between 1876 and 1925.

1900 France's percentage had fallen to 10 (40.7 million); Austria's to 12 (50 million); Germany's had risen to 14 (56.4 million); Great Britain's to 10.6 (41.5 million); Russia's to 24 (100 million). In the twentieth century the comparison between France and her European rivals is still more unfavorable. France's population is not increasing at all, that of her rivals continues to do so.

In general, the relation of forces follows fluctuations in size. Yet some reservations immediately come to mind. At the beginning of the nineteenth century, England played a part on the world stage out of proportion to her human resources. Her island position, as long as she had no battle to wage on the Continent, afforded incomparable advantages (which no longer exist today). In the contrary sense, the case of Russia reminds us that the law of number functions, in our times, only in combination with the law of the number of machines. In 1914, lacking adequate industrialization, and lacking too, perhaps, a political regime capable of leading the nation, Russia's strength was far from being proportional to her population statistics.

In France's case, success in war was not directly determined by number in 1870 or in 1939. In 1870, assuming that the major cause of the initial defeats was the numerical inferiority of the imperial armies, this inferiority was attributable to the military system, not to the nation's human resources (which were, at the time, of the same order as the enemy's). Similarly, though the superiority of the Third Reich's human and industrial potential to that of France was enormous, it was not this superiority which determined the overwhelming victory of May–June 1940. The numerical superiority of tanks and above all of planes was one of the causes of the lightning campaign, but the principal cause was a piece of inspired strategy (the plan proposed by General von Manstein to split the Franco-English armies along the Ardennes hinge) and an original tactic, a new combination of firepower and mobility, assault tanks functioning en masse and planes attacking the combatants and the immediate rear lines of the battlefield. It was in 1914–18 and at the end of the 1939–45 conflict that the Second and the Third Reich were finally overwhelmed by number—the preponderance of soldiers and still more of cannon, tanks and planes.

France's European experience reveals the influence of number on the course of diplomatic and military history, but more subtly. Indeed, if France nearly perished from the victory of 1918, she was tragically saved by her defeat of 1940. Of all the belligerents, it was France that, from 1914 to 1918, made, relatively speaking, the most considerable efforts, in both industrial and in human mobilization, and it was also France that suffered proportionally the highest losses (nearly 1.4 million men as opposed to 2 million in Germany). At the peace conference France shone with a glory that was dearly won, but she was also, without a sudden rise in her birth rate, the most weakened of all the European nations. In 1940, with a military establishment adapted to mechanized and motorized war, France—in theory—could have fought for months, perhaps for a year or even two. While the battle continued in the West, the Soviet Union would have played the role of *tertius gaudens* and the Anglo-American forces would have left to France the heaviest burden. Yet German war industry, reinforced by that of central Europe (Czechoslovakia, Austria) outclassed that of France (that of England would not have been mobilized before 1942). In 1941 Germany could have put several dozen additional divisions into the lines. Had the French campaign lasted twelve to eighteen months, material destruction and human losses would have been three or four times greater, perhaps more. Would France have recovered, after a new bloodletting?[22]

The paradox of France's recent history is the coincidence of demographic decline and imperial expansion. It is tempting to resolve this paradox by explaining the latter by the former, France seeking in Africa a reservoir of additional manpower to re-establish equilibrium with her rivals' potential.

Such an interpretation is almost the only one which gives an apparent rationality to France's foreign policy, particularly under the Third Republic. Why did France, which had neither a surplus of men nor of manufactured products to export, why did the opportunist, then radical Republic conquer the second largest colonial empire in the world? Of course, the historians who are content with historical explanations—explanations which philosophers and sociologists delight in heaping with scorn—may recall that once the city of Algiers was taken, it was even more difficult to evacuate Algeria entirely than to complete its occupation.[23] Subsequently, French Algeria could not be secure unless it was shielded by a double protectorate over Tunisia and Morocco. As for the race for equatorial Africa (*Afrique noire*), it was European rather than specifically French. France's originality was the ideology of her civilizing mission, which implied a certain assimilation of the colonies to metropolitan France. Conscription was the first translation of this doctrine, not devoid of a certain abstract generosity.

The reinforcement of the conqueror by his conquests and the mobilization of the conquered are endemic phenomena down through the centuries. Even in 1960, despite the almost universal diffusion of nationalism, thousands of Moslems fought under the French flag, perhaps indifferent to the nation the FLN claimed to be, or animated by resentment against the underground fighters, or simply impelled by poverty. Rarely, in the past, have men known

---

[22] And would the war itself have been won had the British finally lost their expeditionary corps after a year of battle?

[23] In a speech to the Chamber of Deputies on January 15, 1840, General Bugeaud said: "Limited occupation seems to me a chimera and a dangerous chimera." Later in the same speech: "Abandonment: official France, to employ an expression not in my habitual vocabulary, official France does not want it; that is, the writers, the aristocracy of the inkwell, do not want it." And lastly: "Yes, in my opinion, the taking of Algiers is a mistake; but, since you want to take it, since it is impossible for you not to take it, you must do so on a grand scale, for that is the only way to obtain results. Therefore the whole country must be conquered and the power of Abd-el-Kader destroyed. . . ." The speech is published in *Par l'epée et par la charrue*, Bugeaud's writings and speeches, Paris, 1948, pp. 61–71.

(or needed to know) why they were fighting. Loyalty to the leader, submission to the existing order, pure and simple discipline have constituted the cement of armies more often than faith in a nation or in an idea.

In this regard, the European empires, until 1945, have followed the example of their predecessors. The United Kingdom could not have exerted a dominant influence in Asia and in the Near East if it had not had the Indian army with which to complement the Royal Navy. It was with the Indian army, under British command even when the majority of the officers were Indian, that the Crown imposed peace from the Persian Gulf to the Suez Canal and, eastward, to the borders of Indo-China. Similarly, Algerians, Moroccans and Senegalese fought on the battlefields of World War I. Thus Algerians had contributed to the pacification of their own country as they had participated in the remotest conquests of the French Republic.

Does the reinforcement of the metropolitan army by the mobilization of non-native populations have as its condition or limit a specific percentage of non-Romans in the Roman legions, of Vietnamese in the French expeditionary corps in Indo-China, of Africans in the African army? It is obvious that in each period it is dangerous to exceed a certain percentage, yet this percentage is not always the same.

In our period the British Indian army or the French African army on the one hand, the "yellowing" of the French expeditionary corps in Indo-China on the other, differ fundamentally. The British Indian army faithfully served the Crown during World War II, despite the Congress party's refusal to cooperate. Similarly, the Moroccan regiments, of which only the officers and, to a degree, the non-commissioned officers were French, fought for France in 1939–40, in 1943–45 and, even in Indo-China, until 1954. If France had pursued a policy of force in North Africa for a few years more, would the Moroccan troops under French command have remained loyal? Would the more than two hundred Moroccan officers in the regular cadres of the French army have yielded to the nationalism which animated their compatriots? We do not know. In fact, these armies have tended, in our period, to abide by a strictly military discipline—which does not mean that the best-organized troops remain insensitive to the passions of the people from which the soldiers have been recruited.

The integration, in a relatively high proportion though scarcely more than a third, of Vietnamese or Algerians in metropolitan units already represents a half-surrender. The government can no longer trust heterogeneous contingents whose officers alone are recruited from the imperial population. The command accepts a loss of effectiveness, accommodates itself in advance to the anticipated desertions. The method is dangerous: in case of a reverse, the number of desertions rises steeply (as was discovered in Indo-China, after Dien-Bien-Phu).

Is the imperial capacity to mobilize subject populations a function of the numerical relation between the latter and the imperial population? Number, in this crude form, does not decide the fate of empires. If such were the case, the British Empire would never have existed. But the British Empire is, in many respects, exceptional. That a people numerically so inferior could rule so many territories, so many millions of men without even submitting to the demands of obligatory military service, that the sailors, the subjects, and relatively few professionals could maintain the Empire was a miracle requiring abnormal circumstances as well as political genius. This empire, if it was one of the largest history has ever known, was also, in the scale of centuries, one of the briefest. England ruled from afar by the intermediary of her Indian Empire. It was difficult to transform India into a modern state in military and administrative terms without provoking national claims. Ultimately, the relation between conquerors and conquered develops either toward integration into a single community or dissociation into two distinct collectivities. In one way or another the strictly military inequality is forgotten or effaced. Equality tends to be re-established either by enlarging imperial citizenship,[24] or by the autonomy or independence of the non-national populations. The British were numerically too inferior, too conscious of their race, possessed lands too remote and governed populations too heterogeneous to envisage another conclusion than the disintegration of the Empire into many totally sovereign political units (despite a Commonwealth which, in the eyes of the non-British, seems increasingly fictitious).

The numerical disproportion within the French Empire between imperial and non-French populations was less extreme, yet could not produce another result. Integration, another name for assimilation,[25] requires that citizenship, whether Roman or French, be offered to the subject peoples. It raises the latter to the dignity of citizens, but it condemns them to competing for posts with the citizens born in Rome or in France.

The nature of modern economy renders difficult an imperial policy of integration which does not tolerate too great a disparity in the standard of living between parts of the same whole (particularly when men themselves have neither the same language nor customs). But, aside from these reasons of an economic order,[26] citizenship satisfies the non-national populations only on two conditions: it must be desired and received as an honor, and it must offer more opportunities than it retracts. Even in 1936, full French citizenship would have been regarded by the Algerians as an honor. In 1960 it was

[24] The inequality may exist between citizens and non-citizens or, within the single community, between castes whose origin and hierarchy date back to the conquest. Within political units the social inequalities may be, in part, the crystallization of the relations of military forces.
[25] The integration of non-national populations in a metropolitan political unit does not imply the suppression of particularities of language, religion and customs, which assimilation seems to suggest. But these two words imply the uniformity of political citizenship.
[26] Which we shall study in the next chapter.

an honor no longer. How many Algerians, in a French Algeria, competing with those of French stock, could raise themselves to that society's highest positions?

The disintegration of the French Empire, which various events precipitated, was the logical conclusion of conquests which the stagnation of the French population rendered precarious from the start. France could arm the soldiers recruited among the non-French populations; she could not grant French citizenship to the populations themselves, universally and without reservations. She was unwilling to grant that citizenship as long as it was desired. She offered it in vain the day the elites of the formerly subject peoples aspired to the responsibilities and advantages of state sovereignty.

We must observe, with the insight afforded by the knowledge of a future which is now the past, that the hope (cherished by several authors of the last century) of compensating the relative decline of French population by African conquests was illusory. If the declining birth rate had been ascribable to lack of space, the annexation of Algeria would have sufficed to bring this deplored development to an end. But was it enough that Frenchmen should consent to cross the Mediterranean for their fertility to become again what it had been in centuries past and that their children should survive, as in Canada? In French Algeria it was not the European minority but the Moslem majority that multiplied. The French Empire in the Mediterranean, of which Prévost-Paradol dreamed and in which he saw the supreme hope that France, in a universe dominated by the Anglo-Saxons, would avoid a fate comparable to that of Athens in the Roman Empire, disintegrated because it was populated not by citizens but by subjects. We may remark, with a certain sadness, that the conclusion is more in accord with the laws of history than the enterprise itself; a nation with a dwindling population has little likelihood of preserving an empire, even when it finds an occasion to build one.

The fact that colonization temporarily reinforced the power of metropolitan France does not mean that decolonization is always a cause of diminution. It is false, in fact, to compare what the independence of the colonies or protectorates costs the metropolitan country with the profit it derives from these same territories and populations when it exercises a peaceful authority there. In Africa, for instance, France obviously loses military bases, a potential source of soldiers, a vast zone of sovereignty, which afforded both prestige and means of action. But we must compare the cost of a rejected decolonization with that of a decolonization accepted in time. Would France have been more powerful between 1946 and 1954 without the Indo-Chinese War? Would she be more powerful today had she come to terms with Ho Chi Minh in 1946 or in 1947? Was she reinforced or weakened by the Algerian conflict? In 1840 Marshal Bugeaud considered that the maintenance of some hundred thousand soldiers on the other side of the Mediterranean weakened France on the principal terrain, i.e., the Rhine frontier. The same question could have been asked in 1960.

In other words, empires are a source of strength as long as they are cheaply held. In 1961 there were as many soldiers in Algeria as there were adult Europeans to protect. Bugeaud's *colons*, instead of guaranteeing French peace, cannot remain among the Moslem masses except when each is flanked by an armed man from metropolitan France. When an empire requires more troops than it furnishes, what is the most rational policy, by realistic calculation: abandonment or resistance?[27]

French defeatism, nourished in the mid-nineteenth century by little else other than the relative decline in the population, was aggravated, in the twentieth, by the relative slowness of economic growth and by the theory that paired demographic with economic stagnation. States would be doubly weakened if their populations were stationary or decreasing: they would possess fewer soldiers and fewer workers; the labor output or, if one prefers, the per capita income would be less or would rise less quickly than in nations with high birth rates.

To deal with this problem completely, we should have to envisage it from two points of view: What is the influence of the demographic movement on the economic movement? What, inversely, is the influence of the latter on the former? We shall say only a word concerning this second question. The demographers are far from agreed as to the facts and their interpretations, even when they confine themselves to recent centuries.[28] Some believe that the increase in the number of men, from the sixteenth or seventeenth century, has been relatively independent, since we observe it even on the continents which exhibit little or no economic advance. The population of China between 1650 and 1930 rose, according to some, from 70 to 340 million, according to others, from 150 to 450 million. If the demographic movement, in certain cases, does not seem subordinate to the increase of resources (improvement of production techniques, commercial organization, security, etc.),[29] must we attribute it to the changing vitality of populations? Or does the apparently biological formula of vitality conceal many complex phenomena of a social order?

With regard to the contrary influence—of the number of men on the volume of resources—everything depends, of course, on the elasticity of resources (which varies according to the period) and the density of the existing population. We might posit constant technical means (as Montesquieu implicity does): the elasticity of resources, and hence of the number of men, will be a function of social causes such as public order, distribution of

[27] The numerical relation between the metropolitan troops needed to build the empire and the contingents raised within the empire depends on the numerical relation on the battlefield between regular troops and rebels. This question is discussed below.
[28] Cf. E. F. Wagemann, *Menschenzahl und Völkerschicksal, Lehre von den optimalen Dimensionen Gesellschaftlicher Gebilde*, Hamburg, 1948.
[29] The introduction of the potato, according to William Langer, was the principal cause of the European and Asian population increase in the seventeenth century.

property, balance of foreign trade, importance of arts or industry. It would occur to no one, today, to posit constant technical means. Indeed the danger is the converse one. Analysis posits as a possible population the one which could live by the application of known techniques, and not the one defined as a function of the technique which the population under consideration is actually capable of putting into effect.

Abstractly, the economic-demographic potential, like the military potential, depends on three variables: space, tools, capacity for collective action (for production or combat). Traditionally, analysis aimed chiefly at determining at what point the curve of average individual production reversed its direction. Whatever the technical level, a certain population volume is necessary to exploit a territory, to profit from the division of labor, from the addition made to individual productivity by the productive force born of cooperation. The *welfare optimum* occurs at the point where *the law of decreasing returns* begins to function, that is, *when the productivity of the additional worker becomes inferior to the average productivity*. It is easy to conceive of a plurality of points of welfare optimum in terms of the social organization and technological means. Technological and economic progress is defined precisely by the fact that it displaces the point where the curve of average productivity (relation between total production and number of workers) changes direction. The welfare optimum differs from the *power optimum,* if we agree that power is measured by the material and human resources the state possesses to achieve its external goals. *The additional worker who produces less than average, beyond the point of optimum welfare, produces still more than the minimum indispensable for subsistence.* The state is in a position to take a share of this production from the additional worker. The average revenue decreases, the state's resources increase.

These theoretical definitions, which we borrow from Alfred Sauvy,[30] illuminate an idea which is treated by most authors in this realm. Given a technology and a social organization, the preoccupation with political-military power often inspires the desire for a population size superior to that which the mere consideration of welfare would suggest. The "dominant" minority wants as many subjects as possible, not only to recruit soldiers but to levy taxes with which they will maintain state and armies.

In our period, the absolute figures of economic growth, the statistics of the national product—gross or net—simultaneously include the results of the increase in the number of men and the results of individual productivity. A population which grows rapidly may have a national product which also increases rapidly without any consequent improvement in individual productivity. On the other hand, a static population is capable of economic growth insofar as the average productivity increases either because the worker produces more at the same job or because workers shift frrom jobs with low

[30] *Théorie générale la population,* 2 vols., Paris, 1952 and 1954.

productivity to jobs with high productivity. The relation, which French experience has at least made likely, would be as follows: the slowing down of increase in the number of men would contribute (sometimes? often? always?) to slackening the increase in productivity. In an industrial age, military strength depends as much on labor productivity as on the number of men (the higher the productivity, the greater the margin of resources, above the subsistence level, of which the state can take a share). The demographic decline, in this hypothesis, would doubly involve a political-military decline: by the diminution or at least slackened augmentation of the human as well as the economic potential.

There is no doubt that the French national product, between 1850 and 1913, increased less than that of Germany. The former, according to the figures of Colin Clark,[31] shifted, between these two dates, from 16.6 to 36 billion francs, the latter, from 10.6 to 50 billion marks. In the first case it slightly more than doubled, in the second it almost quintupled. The disparity is less if we eliminate the influence of number and consider the real product per employed person. The latter, in France, shifts from 426 in 1850–59 to 627 in 1911 (in international units), in Germany from 406 to 930.

Theoretically, a low birth rate creates circumstances favorable to growth. A family with only two children has greater possibilities for savings. The collectivity has fewer investments to make for the education of the younger generation, and is in a position to invest more for each employed worker. But, in the case of the French, other causes have been of more importance. Growth is not determined by specifically economic causes alone, or at least the latter (volume of savings, encouragement to invest, etc.) are in turn controlled by attitudes adopted by the economic subjects (entrepreneurs, the state). It is conceivable that demographic stagnation encourages attitudes unfavorable to growth.

That this was the case, in France, in the nineteenth century and in the first half of the twentieth, statistics do not permit us to doubt. But the precise action of demographic stagnation on the conservative attitude of the bourgeoisie or of the French state is not easily isolated. Neither the legislation nor the ideology of French society was oriented toward growth. That demographic stagnation *permitted* conservatism cannot be disputed. That it made conservatism *inevitable* cannot be ascertained. That in the absence of demographic growth, nations are doomed to a rate of little or no economic growth has not been proved.

At present the phenomena of expansion are better known than they once were. The authorities responsible, in a planned regime, have the means of determining the increase in investment, which of itself determines, to a degree, the rate of expansion. Even in a regime of the Western type, the state

[31] *Conditions of Economic Progress*, 2nd edition, London, 1951.

has means of intervening to correct, whether rising or falling (more naturally when rising), the rate of expansion which results when the mechanism is left to itself or from the spontaneous behavior of the economic subjects.

In France, where the population was stagnant and the knowledge of the economic phenomena inadequate, expansion was relatively rapid between 1900 and 1910, again between 1920 and 1929. The 1930–39 depression can be attributed to circumstances. Certainly the Japanese and German economic "miracles" after World War II do not gainsay the lesson of the French experience. The return to the Japanese islands of some seven million men after the defeat, and of more than ten million men to Federal Germany, created a population pressure which constituted the equivalent of a high birth rate. Yet, no one dares assert that economic expansion will necessarily slacken once the generations replace each other without numerically increasing. The graph of the number of men, the graph of the average productivity are not independent of each other, but they are not linked to each other by the direct and unconditional causality of numerical increase over that of productivity.

Are the fears of the French, which started in the middle of the last century, now spreading to the West as a whole? Lately, France has advanced less rapidly than her rivals in the Old World. Are the Western powers, taken as a whole, being outstripped in the race for numerical superiority? Before answering this last question, I should like to discuss the so-called demographic theory of wars, according to which societies fight in order to eliminate the surplus of men, this elimination being indispensable.

4. Overpopulation and War

One fact is evident, incontestable: war consists in killing men, or if a more neutral formula is preferred, war has as its constant result the death of men. The hunter kills animals, the warrior kills his own kind. A first version of the theory we are examining is afforded by the shift from the *constant effect* to that of *function*. Since every war reduces the number of living men, may we not say that numerical reduction is the social function of this singular pheomenon that is simultaneously social and antisocial? Then we can formulate another version of the same theory: if war kills, it is because there are too many men alive. All societies have waged war: if there is no other datum than the surplus of men which appears down through the ages with the same regularity as war, must we not conclude that the general cause of the phenomenon of war is quite simply this surplus of men?[32]

The shift from *constant effect* to *function* seems to me, for methodological

---

[32] In France it is Gaston Bouthoul who has most forcefully presented the so-called demographic theory of war. We refer the reader to his principal work, *Les Guerres. Eléments de polémologie*, Paris, 1951.

reasons, either problematical or else meaningless. To assert that a constant effect reveals the goal of the phenomenon under consideration implies a teleological mode of interpretation of a rather crude type. The common character of all wars does not necessarily express the essence of armed conflicts. The death of men can be the inevitable accompaniment of other effects or other functions of wars, the reinforcement of existing collectivities or the constitution of new collectivities.

The numerical reduction of the living is not the only result of armed conflicts between political units. Such conflicts always have an effect on the units: either they consolidate their inner coherence and their separation in relation to others, or else they create a new unit which absorbs the belligerent units. If we observe states and their wars statically, we are inclined to see the latter as a rupture of the social links—as Sorokin says, an example of *anomie*. If we consider wars down through history, we cannot fail to see in them an elasticity of movement, more precisely, of the progressive widening of the zones of sovereignty, hence of the zones of peace.

Let us add finally that wars are not always bloody; they far from effectively fulfill, in every circumstance, the function attributed to them. Epidemics annihilate with far more rapidity. Even in Europe, after the Great War of 1914–18, Spanish influenza cut down about as many men as the machine gun had in four years. The rites or regulations which preside over combats often have the effect of reducing losses—that is to say cost, the concern of the moralist, effectiveness of methods, that of the sociologist, who believes that the function of war is to provoke a "demographic relaxation."

Let us now consider not the function but the cause, first repeating the same reasoning: the surplus of the living (whatever the manner in which this surplus is evaluated) is not the only phenomenon which we observe as regularly as war. The division of humanity into politically distinct units is also present wherever the phenomenon of war occurs. To reason that the final cause of war is the phenomenon which always precedes or accompanies it does not seem to me to be valid: it implies, in effect, that all wars belong to the same species. But even if we regard this reasoning as valid, it does not conform to the so-called demographic theory. There is, in fact, at least one social phenomenon that occurs throughout the history of civilizations as regularly as the surplus of men: namely, the plurality of collectivities, political units being the expression, in the form of military sovereignty, of the plurality of social entities, one might almost say of social humanities.

Going beyond these generalities, how may we demonstrate or refute the thesis which maintains that overpopulation is the cause of war, of the propensity of autonomous collectivities to fight each other? Since the "method of presence" does not afford the desired proof, the cause envisaged not being the only one regularly present whenever the phenomenon to be explained appears, we might turn to the "method of absence." When overpopulation is eliminated, do collectivities cease to wage war? Unfortunately, for humanity as a whole, this is only an intellectual experiment, for, according to the very theory we are discussing, overpopulation is endemic.

Partial experiments have been made by history: Does a bellicose nation become peaceful when the population pressure diminishes? Did imperialist France of the Revolution and the Empire become peaceful in the nineteenth century with the lowering of the birth rate? Did romantic Germany become imperialist as the number of Germans—of young Germans—increased? Let us note first of all that France, supposedly converted to pacifism, certainly fought no fewer wars in the last century than during the preceding ones. She has fought more in the twentieth century. That Germany has replaced France as "troublemaker" is incontestable, but proves nothing more than a kind of imbecile truism: the state which appears to threaten the freedom of others is, in every period, the one whose strength increases fastest. In 1850 France was no longer the "troublemaker" of the European system, just as the Bonn Republic, in 1950, was no longer the troublemaker of the global system. Do the sentiments of men automatically conform to their diplomatic role? This is highly doubtful. Outbursts of aggressive chauvinism have been frequent in France during the last century. Japan after 1945, confined to her islands with a higher population density than in 1938, is as peaceful, even anti-militarist, as it was imperialist twenty years ago.

To transcend the oscillation between a vague and a likely proposition—war, which results in the death of men, must be linked to the facts of demography—and precise and unproved propositions, we must first of all define more rigorously the phenomenon to which we impute a causal action: overpopulation or population pressure. It goes without saying that the number of men does not adequately measure the population pressure. In the eighteenth century France would have been overpopulated by forty million people, today it is underpopulated by the same number. Two centuries ago a figure of forty-five million would have been above the welfare optimum and the power optimum; today it is certainly inferior to the second, and in all probability to the first.

Overpopulation, in a given space, is defined in relation to resources, themselves a function of technological means. But if it is absurd to evaluate population pressure by population figures alone, it would not be any more rational to measure it by referring to the number of men capable of living in that space if they used all the methods that science and industry afford. By this second method we would arrive at Sauvy's conclusion, according to which only Holland experiences absolute overpopulation[33]: the number of people in that country would involve a diminution of per capita income, even using the most advanced methods of production. We must further add "diminution of average income in relation to welfare optimum," that is, in

[33] Moreover, according to Sauvy (*Population*, July 1960), the per capita income, in Holland, continues to increase faster than in the nations of stagnant population.

relation to the income each man might enjoy if there were fewer men. This diminution in relation to a theoretical optimum does not involve an actual diminution: quite the contrary, in the case of Holland, total expansion continues, the per capita production increases. It is the statistician who decrees that this production would increase faster if it were not for the law of diminishing returns—if the investments necessary to win an additional area of cultivable land from the sea did not also increase with the rise in population.

In other words, in order to define the notion of overpopulation we must simultaneously consider space, means of production and social organization. When the geologists or biologists tell us that eight or ten billion human beings could live in comfort on the planet today, provided they applied the knowledge that they have acquired, they are telling us something about science but little about society. The volume of the world harvest of tea or rice which would result from the diffusion of the Japanese methods is interesting in itself. It indicates the margins still available to growth, but leaves us in complete ignorance as to overpopulation as a social fact and the eventual influence of this fact on the frequency or intensity of wars.

Must we no longer define overpopulation in static but in dynamic terms, assuming overpopulation to exist when the number curve rises faster than that of resources?[34] Such a definition would be satisfactory if each society were homogeneous, if all societies were of the same kind. In the past, distribution of income has sometimes been such that the misery of the masses rose with their numerical increase (lowering of wages), while the wealth of the privileged also increased. Do we speak of overpopulation in this case? It is a question, it seems to me, of overpopulation if the latter is characterized by "the impoverishment of the great number" (that is, the impoverishment of the people because the people become increasingly numerous). Yet the comparison of the graph of number and that of resources would not confirm overpopulation, according to the preceding definition. Further, the rapid increase of number, the accumulation of young men, a typical European phenomenon in the nineteenth century, one which Bouthoul considers characteristic of an explosive situation, is not contained within the concept of overpopulation as defined by the comparison between the graph of number and the graph of resources. The European population increased in the nineteenth century more than in any other, though millions of men, as we have seen, emigrated. The increase in the number of men remaining on the soil of the Old World was considerable without the graph of number ever rising faster than that of resources. The German per capita income continued to increase until 1914: hence there was no overpopulation, in the strict sense of the term. Were the Germans warlike out of simple biological vitality?

I myself had envisaged another definition: might we not say that there is a surplus of men once a certain number among them, idle by constraint,

[34] Cf. G. Bouthoul, *op. cit.*

as a result of social circumstances, are available for the profession of arms, because their elimination would not bring about a decrease of production? I must conclude, upon reflection, that the phenomenon thus defined, which I shall henceforth call *surplus of men,* is too frequent to permit a study of all the relations between number and belligerence. The ancient societies had a permanent "surplus of men" of this kind. The very notion refers to a society in which labor is regarded as a primary activity, and combat as a kind of luxury: the opposite being the case for the citizens of the Greek city-states. The obvious fact that labor was necessary to insure existence was not over-looked, but it was to politics and war that the citizen devoted himself. In the European societies which did not know slavery and in which only the nobles had the duty of risking their lives in combat, the rigidity of the social organization, even more than the stagnation of technology, created, in an endemic fashion, a surplus of men. The armies seemed all the more normal in that they mobilized those idle by vocation (the nobles) or by servitude (the unemployed or the vagabonds). The death of the former was regarded as glorious—a state privilege—of the rest, as indifferent. The democratic age and the civilization of labor rejected, in principle, these two categories of the idle.

Surpluses of men have not disappeared with modern society. Agricultural overpopulation, so frequent in the underdeveloped nations, is a phenomenon of the same order. Until we succeed in mobilizing for labor the "useless hands" (as Communist China claims to have done), the majority of the world's agricultural regions will count a surplus of men, since production would not be diminished in the case of the sudden elimination of a part of the rural population. Historians noted that even in France, when she was in the process of modernizing herself during the last century, great numbers of men were idle on account of the slowness of industrialization and the rigidity of the social structure. To explain by the pressure of the unemployed the wars with Spain, Algeria, Italy or Mexico would be absurd. To explain by this fact the government's propensity to wage these wars and the indifference with which public opinion receives them would be impossible.

Three population phenomena, distinct though related, can be connected with the propensity to wage war: *surplus of men, overpopulation* (global or partial),[35] *biological vitality.* None of these can be called, in a general or dogmatic way, the *cause* of wars or of warlike propensity (moreover a causal relation presupposes that all other things are equal; in this case all other things cannot be equal). But each of them has certain links with war, though these links are difficult to determine. *Surplus of men,* in the most general sense of the term, is an endemic phenomenon in all human societies whose technology is virtually stationary and whose organization is crystallized. What

[35] I call partial overpopulation the gap between the curve of number and the curve of resources for a fraction, and not for the whole, of a population.

is called the historical phase is characterized by two so-to-speak negative features: numerical equilibrium is not maintained by a quasi-natural mechanism, as in the small, closed and archaic collectivities[36]; the capacity for initiative, innovation, technological or social adaptation is still weak (not in itself, but in relation to the problems raised). Men of no use to production have of necessity almost always existed. Since, at the same time, conquest, exploitation of the conquered, and pillage constitute sources of enrichment, the transformation of the idle into combatants, who when victorious bring back spoils, is strictly rational. Even if these collectivities had thought in economic terms, they would not have been wrong to set the combatant above the laborer. Not only did the former protect the latter's life, but quite often he *produced* more. In the last century the hierarchy of values was quite different: the economic productivity of wars (particularly the wars waged by Napoleon III in Italy or Mexico) could no longer be compared to that of labor. Only the officers somewhat retained the ancient prestige of heroes. I do not mean that the wars would cease if the surplus of men were eliminated, nor that the wars were determined in their frequency and intensity by the number of idle men. I simply regard the "surplus of men" as a concomitant phenomenon of the phenomenon of war which helps make the latter intelligible. Most societies possessed economically unemployed men who, under arms, *produced* glory or rapine.

Global or partial overpopulation is tantamount to the accentuation of the preceding phenomenon. Under certain circumstances the number of unemployed in rural areas exceeds the norm. The poor, the homeless, the non-integrated grow more numerous. Competition for jobs causes wages to be lowered, even if the worker's productivity is stationary or increasing. Neither experience nor abstract analysis suggests that such a situation necessarily provokes wars or that wars are generally the expression of such a circumstance. Disease eliminates the non-integrated as well as the machine gun. The abundance of manpower tends rather to weaken the claims of the non-privileged. Certain historians, it is true, explain the fluctuation of Chinese history by the fluctuations of number. Even in this hypothesis, overpopulation would be at the source of internal difficulties, revolts, conspiracies, dynastic changes, rather than of wars between sovereign units.

With regard to European history, demographers note a certain population increase from the tenth century to the thirteenth, a falling off in the fourteenth century after the plague, a stagnation in the fifteenth century, a substantial increase in Central Europe in the sixteenth century, a stagnation or falling off in Central Europe in the seventeenth century, an important and general increase in the eighteenth century, a tumultuous increase in the

---

[36] Here, too, equilibrium is not maintained constantly in fact. Certain collectivities contract, others expand. There are societies without writing, there are none without changes. Yet these societies are not historical *for themselves.*

nineteenth century. Now the period that followed the plague should have been less bellicose, and the three periods of wars—the Crusades, the Thirty Years' War, and the wars of the twentieth century—should have been preceded by phases of demographic growth. It is possible that a massive diminution of the population attenuates the violence of the conflict, but, of the three examples, the first two do not exemplify the thesis. It is difficult to measure the intensity of war in the Middle Ages, for it varies with the centuries. The shift from number to the true impulse of the Crusades remains, at the least, obscure. As for the third example, that of Europe in the twentieth century, it brings us to our third phenomenon, *biological vitality*.

In effect, we have said, neither Germany nor Europe suffered in 1913 from overpopulation. The ideology of the people without space (*Volk ohne Raum*) had not yet become common. The Reich's leaders and its public opinion *knew* that total wealth was increasing faster than the number of men. If demographic growth was the cause of German imperialism, a cause of the wars in which the European civilization collapsed, we must seek the essential facts not in mere numbers or comparisons of graphs, but in the unconscious or the obscure life of collectivities.

Germany and Europe had no need to lose tens of millions of men in order to assure their survivors a higher standard of living. No nation had exceeded the welfare optimum. None could even suppose it was staggering under the burden of quantity. In Germany as in every nation with a high birth rate, young men were proportionally more numerous than in the countries where the birth rate permits no more than the replacement of one generation by the next. The potential supply of combatants might have inspired the leaders' ambitions; it could not inspire their anxiety for themselves and their regime. If the European wars of the twentieth century have had a function of "demographic relaxation," to borrow M. Bouthoul's formula, it is because the numerical pressure which creates the fury of combat is not created by either population density or collective impoverishment, but by a kind of vital exuberance, comparable to that which sweeps into fights or games those youths whose blood is too hot for their veins. We do not know enough about the laws which control the development of collectivities to exclude the hypothesis of a link between fertility and aggressiveness. Still, we can assert with certainty that this relation is not always to be found and that, in the case where we suppose we perceive it, other explanations come to mind.

The very author regarded as the theoretician of the explanation of wars by number, explicitly states: "Overpopulation does not necessarily lead to foreign or civil war."[37] Overpopulation, he says, calls into being institutions which result in the elimination of men, war being only one of these institutions among others. Such a formula is obvious, but not instructive. It is equivalent to the proposition that in a given space, with given resources, only

[37] G. Bouthoul, *op. cit.*, pp. 323-24.

a certain number of men survives. Since this number constantly tends to be exceeded, social mechanisms eliminate the surplus.

On several occasions in the past the Japanese have taken deliberate and systematic measures to prevent the surplus from appearing at all. Aside from this rare practice, mortality by epidemics, hunger and labor conditions have regularly eliminated the surplus. Are we to regard war as a complement of or a substitute for elimination by delayed marriages, infanticide or the deliberate and organized special mortality of the young? That wars kill and, especially in the modern period, kill the young, I grant. That we can compare and contrast the "Asiatic solution" (high mortality as a result of labor conditions) and the European solution (relaxation by periodic wars), I do not believe. Until the last century the "European solution" did not differ by nature from the Asiatic one: diseases and high mortality rate among the young performed, in the main, the function of eliminating idle hands. In the last century the function was no longer performed under the same conditions in Europe. But demographic growth did not bring with it an absolute surplus (in relation to the subsistence volume) nor even a relative surplus (in relation to the welfare optimum). If it made Germany imperialist and the Europeans bellicose, *contrary to economic rationality and without necessity,* we should have to conclude that fertility, the accumulation of young people, in certain unspecified circumstances, impelled peoples, leaders and public opinion to wage war. But if the "explosive situation" incites to imperialism, centuries of experience remind us that neither Caesars nor peoples have required this incitement to feed ambition and to believe in their vocation as rulers.

5. *From Petroleum to the Atom and Electronics*

The historical period that begins in 1945 differs profoundly, with regard to the operation of numbers, from both the preceding decades and from the centuries of European expansion.

In modern times, Europeans have benefited from a unique combination of circumstances. The empty spaces of North America were open to them. Between 1840 and 1940 fifty-six million of them left the Old World, thirty-seven million for the United States. At the same time, thanks to the superiority of their means of production and combat, they imposed their rule upon Africa and Asia; they were both rich and powerful, as though to prove once and for all that the so-called alternative of welfare and glory was an anachronism.

The peopling of empty space, the extension of the zone of sovereignty was succeeded, after 1945, by the dissociation from the empires the Europeans had built in Asia and Africa. The "European minorities" left the nations that had become independent and flowed back to the metropolitan countries. It was the non-Europeans' turn to possess the machines with which the little Asian cape has ruled the world. Since the populations of the so-called underdeveloped nations have an average birth rate superior to that of the economically advanced nations, it is easy to spread through Western Europe, through the entire West, the fear of being overwhelmed by numbers which have inspired the French, since 1850, to so many gloomy speculations.

Let us recall, first of all, that in 1700 the Europeans represented about a fifth of the human race (118 million out of 560 million). In 1900 they represented a fourth (400 million out of 1,608,000,000). On the eve of the last world war they still represented approximately a fourth. Were this percentage to diminish and fall from a fourth to a fifth, the decline would still be no more than a return to a numerical relation which already existed scarcely three centuries ago.

Moreover the European–non-European relation means little enough, since the Europeans are divided into two hostile blocs, one of which feels (or acts as if it felt) allied with the revolt of the colored peoples against white domination, the other linked both militarily and morally with the United States. Now the comparison of the rates of demographic increase on either side of the Iron Curtain does not justify the defeatism of those who are obsessed by numbers. It is probable that the population of the United States is increasing today as fast as that of the Soviet Union (the annual rate of increase in the United States has been approximately 1.5 per cent during the last few years). The rate of increase in the Western part of the Old World is lower than that on the other side of the Iron Curtain. But the new advance in the birth rate in France and Great Britain, which were particularly threatened by depopulation, as well as the tendency to a decline in the birth rate in the industrializing nations of Eastern Europe, make it impossible to find this inequality in growth a disturbing characteristic.

Suppose we consider the comparative rates of increase in the United States and in Latin America, taken as characteristic of industrialized nations on one hand and of nations in the process of development on the other. There is no doubt that the rise is more rapid in the latter countries. Between 1940 and 1950 Brazil's population increased at the annual rate of 2.7 per cent, Mexico's at the annual rate of 3.1 per cent. In thirty years the population of Latin America, on an average hypothesis with regard to birth rate, will double. It will probably exceed, between now and the end of this century, the population of English-speaking America, but such fluctuations of numerical relations are not directly dangerous for the peoples that multiply less rapidly and grow rich faster.

The peoples whose per capita income is relatively low, whose farmers are unacquainted with modern methods of agriculture, and whose industry employs only a relatively low percentage of the manpower have a tendency, in our period, to "increase and multiply." Let us concede the fact, which is explained, generally speaking, by the maintenance of a traditional birth rate and the diminution of mortality, this diminution being the consequence of an improved hygiene (an improvement which no longer implies a substantial increase of resources). The rapid numerical increase tends to weaken the new states rather than to reinforce them: it weakens them economically as well as politically.

The abundance of young men, which Bouthoul considers an incitement to war, serves the cause of the nationalists who are eager to drive out the colonists. Ho Chi Minh, before the Indo-Chinese War began, might have said to a French interlocutor: "You will kill ten of our men for every French soldier that we will kill. But in the long run, we will be the winners." In 1960 half the Algerian population was under twenty, and all these Algerian young people were nationalists. Once independence is acquired, however, the situation is reversed and what had been an effective weapon in the struggle against the colonizing power becomes a source of weakness in the struggle against poverty. As long as the cumulative process of economic expansion has not been set moving, the investment indispensable to the education of the young has to be subtracted from investment for raising the productivity of adult labor. The taxes which the state levies for its diplomatic and military purposes curtail either the share of national revenue reserved for consumption or the share set aside for investments. Except for the pitiless regime, military expenses compete with these investments. India would have greater diplomatic possibilities today if her birth rate were cut by half.

Such a proposition does not contradict the lessons of French experience. Once a nation has created the administrative and intellectual infrastructure which modernization of the economy demands, the maintenance of a relatively high birth rate (or, barring this, the immigration of foreign labor) has shown itself to be favorable to the increase of productivity or of the per capita income. Even in the course of the ten years 1950–60, production per active person has increased 5.6 per cent per year in Japan, where, in ten years, manpower has increased 37 per cent; 5.8 per cent in Federal Germany, where manpower has increased 28 per cent; 4.4 per cent in the Low Countries, where manpower has increased 15 per cent; 4.4 per cent in Italy, where manpower has increased 14 per cent. The corresponding percentages are 2.6 and 8 for the United States, 1.9 and 4 for Norway, 2.2 and 4.5 for Great Britain. *At the level of development which the Western nations have reached,* an increase of manpower, which facilitates transfers from job to job and maintains the creative impulse and the conviction of a future, seems then, for the moment, favorable not only to the increase of the national product (which follows as a matter of course), but also of per capita productivity. This is not true for the Asian or Latin American countries nor for rates of demographic increase exceeding 2 per cent. If overrapid numerical increase constitutes a danger to the West, it is because of revolutions and authoritarian regimes which could result from the poverty of the too-numerous masses, the increase of idle hands.

Yet we must not underestimate the present relations between population volume and military strength, between military strength and diplomatic power. The defensive or revolutionary power of high-birth-rate populations has become irresistible. Partisans are incapable of defeating regular armies, but they render maintenance of order costly and pacification impossible. Once the prestige of the conquerors has vanished, the number of the colonized inevitably overwhelms the superior equipment of the colonists, so that by a strange paradox the latter are obliged to mobilize hundreds of thousands of soldiers against several thousand guerrillas. Nine million Moslems against one million Europeans, twenty thousand regular combatants in the army of liberation against four hundred thousand French soldiers, losses in human lives ten or twenty times higher among the Algerian nationalists than among the French, expenses ten to twenty times higher on the French side. Had they reflected on the meaning of these figures, statesmen would have had no doubt as to the outcome.

Prolific and poor populations, impregnable on their own territory, are impotent beyond it, for the concentration of economic resources necessary to manufacture decisive weapons has advanced along with the destructive power of the weapons themselves. It required the administrations of the European monarchies to finance the mobilization of the armies of the seventeenth and eighteenth centuries. Only the states known as great powers were capable, in the First and especially the Second World War, of furnishing millions of men with scientific weapons—artillery, tanks, aviation. In the age of the atom and of electronics, the club of the great powers is still smaller: only those known as super-powers possess, for the moment, the thermonuclear arsenal and the latest-model delivery vehicles, ballistic missiles and strategic bombers.

The influence of number is different, in our times, because the modes of combat are many. The law of number functions differently in daily machine-gun engagements and in a possible combat with weapons of mass destruction. The Arabs are shaking off the yoke of the Western powers, but they are not about to extend their cavalcades as far as Poitiers. The Western powers are not being impoverished as their space of sovereignty shrinks: on the contrary, they will grow richer faster. The instability in the relations of force derives in part from the numerous territories on which the competition between peoples takes place. It derives, too, from the rapidity with which different peoples acquire the industrial weapons of power.

In the Greek world the great powers were based on ten to twenty thousand citizens: it is easy to understand why the great powers did not last long and why, from one century to the next, the virtù, as Machiavelli called it, shifted from Athens to Thebes, or from Macedon to Rome. In the twentieth century it takes only a few decades to create a heavy industry. In 1960 the Soviet Union produced more than twice as much steel as the great German Reich of 1939. And China will perhaps in one generation increase her steel production by some twenty million tons, that is, by an amount exceeding the present production of France. The superiority of certain nations in their industrial career, which they owed in the first place to a head start, is shrinking and tends to disappear as the industrial type of society becomes more widespread.

Relations of force depend on the relative number of men and the relative number of machines: the latter has fluctuated in the last century even more rapidly than the former.

Is it conceivable, beyond the phase of industrialization, and once every nation has achieved a comparable productivity, that the relation may depend exclusively on the number of men? Or, on the other hand, is it henceforth the quality of machines that will be decisive? What can millions of assault tanks do against one thermonuclear bomb? What could dozens of thermonuclear bombs do against a state possessing an invulnerable defense against bombers and ballistic missiles? We shall not play the prophet, confining ourselves to observing that between rivals of the same order of greatness (or of size), it is quality that is likely to gain the decision. What the tactical capacity of the Roman legions did for the ancient world, a defense against ballistic missiles could do for the Northern Hemisphere. But the scientists have replaced the strategists.

chapter IX

On Resources

Space and number generally escape the awareness of the actors: gold, silver, slaves, petroleum have been recognized, down through the ages, as the stakes of conflicts between states. Historians and philosophers have not had to discover that the collectivities in conflict thirsted for precious metals or raw materials: they have more often had to correct cynicism than to unmask hypocrisy. Men, they said, are also animated by the desire for glory or the ambition to conquer. It is in our period that the so-called economic interpretation pretends to originality. Since our civilization grants primacy to labor, scientists and ideologists readily suppose that they are discovering profound and mysterious forces when they explain the course of diplomatic history by economic causes.

I have intentionally chosen the vaguest and most general term, *resources*, in preference to the term *economics*. It is wise, indeed, to leave the latter its precise and limited sense. By resources I mean the sum of material means collectivities can use to assure their subsistence. Men comprise part of resources when they are slaves, in other words when they are treated as objects. In all other cases, they are subjects of the activity by which things are transformed into goods, that is, serve to satisfy men's needs or desires. The concept of resources covers the widest field, from the soil and what lies underneath it to food and manufactured products. It includes in a certain way the realities to which the two notions of space and number refer. The relation between space and number depends on resources, that is, on both the natural milieu (or on material things) and on the capacity for utilization, a capacity itself dependent on the knowledge of men and the efficacy of collective action.

The *economic* concept does not apply to an isolable fragment of the sum of resources, but to an aspect of the activity by which things are transformed into goods. Let us call labor the activity by which men act upon things in order to use them. This activity involves a technological aspect and an economic aspect. The first is logically reduced to the combination of means with a view toward ends. Since the neolithic revolution, societies have been able to cultivate the soil, inciting biological phenomena as a result of which the fruits of the earth ripen and the human race increases and multiplies. But since the dawn of history, the laboring activity has involved another aspect, that of the choice of scarce means with alternative uses and, above all, of the means that are scarce in essence: the time of each laborer and of the laborers taken collectively. It is not impossible to distinguish *technology* and *economics* at the lowest level, that of the individual worker. But consideration of the collectivity is preferable. The disparity between desires (at least in essence) and possibilities of satisfying them is thus explicit, just as the necessity of the choice to which any social existence is subject is also made clear. A collectivity *chooses* a certain *distribution of available labor* among various jobs, a certain *distribution of goods* among classes. We shift from the distribution of labor to the distribution of incomes by the intermediary of a *mode of circulation.* Every economic system, that is, the sum of institutions by which needs are satisfied, involves three characteristics, depending on the systems of division of labor, of circulation of goods, of distribution of incomes.

Hence, if we consider the relationship between resources and foreign policy, it seems that we must distinguish three kinds of data likely to be causes: *raw materials,* afforded by the natural milieu; *knowledge and "know-how,"* which permit the exploitation of these materials; and the *mode of organization* applied to the production and the circulation which determine the economic system, that is, the manner in which the obligations of labor and the incomes from the collective effort are distributed among individuals. It appears that an exhaustive study should constitute types for each of these aspects of the economic system, and determine the action of each one of them upon the behavior and fortune of states. But such a method is likely to lead to virtually endless research. Hence it seems preferable to me—and the experiment will perhaps justify this simplification—to focus our analyses on three problems, analogous to those treated in the preceding chapters: first of all, *resources as means of force,* next *resources as objectives of the belligerents, stakes of rivalries,* or *causes of war. In conclusion we shall briefly compare the influence of various systems of modern economy on the external behavior of states.*

The first theme suggests the classical questions: what is the relation between prosperity, wealth and welfare on the one hand, and political or military force on the other? The second brings us to the eternal question: why do men fight? For gold or for glory? When do they fight for wealth and when for the intoxication of conquest? Lastly, the third theme is oriented toward the future: will labor and war be indefinitely complementary activities, or does a certain kind of labor make the elimination of war inevitable or probable or desirable?

1. *Four Doctrines*

Economists, historians and philosophers have for centuries discussed the problems we have just formulated. But they have not discussed them separately. The answer given to one of these problems almost necessarily involves the answer given to the other. Depending on the meaning the authors assign to labor or trade, they regard wealth as fatal or favorable to the greatness of peoples; commerce and war as one and the same, or not one and the same, in essence; conflicts as either provoked or pacified by trade.

I shall therefore try to present four ideal types which I shall call *mercantilism, liberalism, national economy* and *socialism*. Historically, each of these doctrines has been set forth in various ways. Composite or modified doctrines are more frequent, as a matter of fact, than these pure ones. The following summaries do not aim at reproducing the exact thought of any of the thinkers connected with the four schools I have just listed. I am trying here to set forth the logical framework of four intellectual structures.

The mercantilist doctrine of the relations between economy and international relations has as its initial principle the celebrated formula "money is the sinew of war." Let us quote, among the many possible sources, the following lines from Montchrestien's *Traité de l'économie politique* (1615): "He who first said that money is the sinew of war spoke to the point, for though money is not the only consideration, good soldiers being absolutely necessary along with it, the experience of several centuries teaches us that it is always the principal. Gold is many times more powerful than steel."[1] The inverse relation is asserted by Machiavelli in a celebrated text.[2]

If precious metals are the sinews of war, they are also the measure of the strength of nations, since in the last analysis strength is measurable by what we call "trial by force." The will to power is thus expressed logically by the effort to amass the greatest possible amount of gold and silver. Now there are two methods to achieve this end; one is war, the other commerce. Each state increases its reserve of precious metals by plunder or by exchange. But—and this is the second proposition which dominates mercantilist thought —there is no difference in nature between these two methods. In depth, they are of the same essence.

As Colbert[3] says: "It is only the abundance of money in a state that makes the difference as to its greatness and its power." If this is the case, how could commerce, on which depends the reserve of gold and silver, and thus the power of states, not be a kind of war? "Commerce causes a perpetual

---

[1] Paris, 1889, pp. 141–42. This Montchrestien quotation and the Machiavelli one following are from E. Silberner, *La Guerre dans la pensée économic du XVIe au XVIIIe siècles*, Paris, 1939. Another book by this same author, *La Guerre et la Paix dans l'histoire des doctrines économiques*, Paris, 1957, discusses the nineteenth century.

[2] Machiavelli, *Discourse on the First Decade of Titus Livius*, II, 10.

[3] *Lettres, instructions et mémoires*, Paris, 1862, t. II, 1e partie, p. CCLXIX. Cited by Silberner, *op. cit.*, p. 261.

combat in peace and in war among the nations of Europe as to which will gain the upper hand."[4] And further: "Commerce is a perpetual and peaceful war of spirit and industry among all nations."[5] In the next century Dutot (1738) develops the idea: "To make peace in order to procure for ourselves all the advantages of a great commerce, is to wage war upon our enemies."[6]

Certain British authors echo the continental ones. They, too, refuse to distinguish between commercial supremacy and political hegemony: "Whoever Commands the ocean Commands the Trade of the World, and Whoever Commands the Trade of the World Commands the Riches of the World, and whoever is master of that, Commands the World itself."[7] Consequently, "in no other way can the balance of power be maintained or continued but by the balance of trade."[8]

The identification of trade with war derives from the following reasoning: since a positive balance of trade is necessary in order to accumulate precious metals, and since all the states cannot have a positive balance, trade cannot be profitable to all. He who buys more than he sells loses gold and silver, and is therefore ruined by the exchange or, we would say, *loses in the exchange*. The race for precious metals creates a difference in nature between foreign trade and domestic trade, since the latter does not modify the stock of gold and silver and the former, on the contrary, determines its volume. Even as late as the middle of the eighteenth century a French author expressly formulates the thesis: "The true commerce of a nation consists essentially in the course of exchanges which it makes with foreign nations. On the other hand, exchanges which are made only between the subjects of one and the same state are less a true commerce than a simple displacement of conveniences which facilitates consumption but adds nothing to the total wealth of a nation and in no way extends its advantages."[9]

The search for precious metals attaches an aggressive character to commercial expansion and foreign trade among nations, for the stock of gold and silver is limited, as are the amount of possible exchanges. The mercantilists reason within a finite world, in a static universe. Exchange is not favorable to the buyer as it is to the seller. But, according to the expression of an Italian author, Botero: "The very common means of enriching oneself at the expense of others is commerce."[10] "We lose as much as the foreigner gains."[11]

To depend as little as possible on foreign purveyors, to produce as much

---

[4] *Ibid.*, t. VI, p. 266.
[5] *Ibid.*, t. VI, p. 269.
[6] Quoted by Silberner, p. 53. Dutot, *Réflexions sur la commerce et les finances.*
[7] Quoted by Silberner, p. 106, note 57. John Evelyn, *Navigation and Commerce,* 1674.
[8] Quoted by Silberner, p. 106, note 60. *The Golden Fleece,* 1737.
[9] Quoted by Silberner, p. 109. Goyon de la Plombanie, *La France agricole et marchande,* 1762.
[10] Quoted by Silberner, p. 108. G. Botero, *Raison et gouvernement d'Etat,* 1599.
[11] Quoted by Silberner, p. 108. Montchrestien, *op. cit.*

as possible of what the nation needs, to protect the national artisans against the dangerous rivalry of foreign artisans, such counsels follow, quite strictly, from the effort necessary in order to have a positive balance of trade. "A kingdom that can itself satisfy its own needs is always richer, stronger and more to be feared."[12]

Within this doctrine, the question of the responsibility for conflicts does not arise. Conflict is natural, inevitable, since the interests of states are fundamentally contradictory. "Those who are members of the government of states must have the latter's glory, augmentation, and enrichment for their principal goal."[13] If the French cannot increase their commerce save by crushing the Dutch, why should they hesitate to resort to force in order to realize a legitimate ambition? The mercantilists are not, as such, warmongers. To say that "the advantages of a great commerce" are equivalent to a war against our enemy is in a sense to admit that commerce is a substitute for war. But, if we posit the essential rivalry of states, war is, so to speak, permanent, whether it assumes the open form of combats or the camouflaged form of commerce. For princes, the choice of one or the other is a matter of opportunity and occasion.

Bodin is not a firebrand, but he reduces the choice between peace and war to a rational calculation. A prince, even a powerful one, even if he is wise and magnanimous, "will demand neither war nor peace if necessity, which is not subject to laws of honor, does not force him to do so; and will never wage battle, provided there is no more apparent profit in victory than in loss if the enemies were victorious."[14] Perhaps this formula of Sir William Temple's, in its frankness and its moderation, expresses all the pacifism of which mercantilism is capable: "It is a maxim whose truth I believe one can never deny, that no wise state will ever undertake war save with the intention of making conquests or in the necessity of protecting itself."[15]

The liberal has not only a different objective from the mercantilist, he interprets the facts differently. What I gain, the other loses, affirms the mercantilist. In a free exchange he who profits least still profits, answers the liberal (or at least the liberal type). The demonstration of this formula assumes several more or less refined forms. But the core of the argument is as simple in the liberal doctrine as it was in that of the mercantilist.

According to the latter, commerce is not a means of obtaining the goods one desires by giving up others one is not using, but an apparently peaceful method of enlarging one's own share of a given stock of precious metals. Once the obsession with precious metals disappears, once the development of the means of production dissipates the illusion of a permanently fixed

---

[12] Quoted by Silberner, p. 110. Montchrestien, *op. cit.*
[13] Quoted by Silberner, p. 26. Montchrestien, *op. cit.*
[14] Quoted by Silberner, p. 20. J. Bodin, *De la République,* 1576.
[15] Quoted by Silberner, p. 65. Sir William Temple, 1693.

volume of goods to be distributed or of trade to be shared among the nations, the belligerent character of the exchange disappears of itself and, hitherto unnoticeable, its pacific character appears evident. If each of the parties to the exchange decides of his own will, it cannot be that either of them "loses in the exchange," even if, in monetary values, one party or the other does not make equal gains.

When the obsession with precious metals disappears, so does the idea of an essential difference between foreign trade and domestic trade. Perfect liberalism assumes, by hypothesis, a universal republic of exchanges. Whether or not a province is outside the national borders matters little: buyers will obtain the goods produced in this province only in return for the goods they possess. Ideally, in relation to humanity taken as a whole, there is only a single trade, which the military force of states is impotent to modify. According to Bentham's celebrated formula: "Conquer the whole world, it is impossible you should increase your trade one half-penny."[16]

From this the liberals conclude just as logically that trade is essentially contrary to war. Trade pacifies, whereas political rivalry inflames passions. Already in the eighteenth century, formulas opposed to those of mercantilism are more frequent. Quesnay no longer assumes that foreign trade accounts for the greatness of nations and is, in essence, aggressive. "The reciprocal commerce of nations is mutually sustained by the wealth of the sellers and the buyers."[17] "Custom duties," Dupont de Nemours writes, "are a kind of reciprocal hostility between nations."[18] And in a formula which makes an admirable pendant to those of Colbert a century earlier, the Abbé Baudeau writes in 1771: "The opposition of interests constitutes the essence of the policy of usurpation. The unity of interests constitutes the essence of economic policy."[19]

Once it is assumed, as J. F. Nelson[20] put it, that "the spirit of conquest and the spirit of commerce are mutually exclusive in a nation," the liberals (differing from the mercantilists, for whom international conflicts did not raise any problem because they belonged to the natural order of things) must account for the existence of wars. On the whole, it seems to me, there are three possible answers. The first is to establish that commerce and politics belong to two fundamentally different orders. States are in permanent rivalry not because they have contradictory economic interests but because the princes or the peoples are eager for glory or land. A second answer emphasizes the gap between the true interests of states or nations and the consciousness

16 Quoted by Silberner, p. 260, note 18. Bentham, *Principles of International Law*, 1843.
17 Quoted by Silberner, p. 196. Quesnay, article "Grains" in the *Encyclopédie*.
18 Quoted by Silberner, p. 204. Declaration by Dupont to the Council of Elders (Session of the Fourth Floréal, Year IV). *Moniteur universel* of April 28, 1796.
19 Quoted by Silberner, p. 207. Abbé Baudeau, *Première introduction à la philosophie économique*.
20 Quoted by Silberner, p. 172. *Essai politique sur le commerce*.

governments have of them. Or again, the liberals distinguish between the economy *as it might be* in a republic of exchanges and the economy *as it is*, distorted by private monopolies. Lastly, a final answer is to invoke the factor of overpopulation. Malthus's precursors are numerous. The same author who maintains that the spirit of commerce and the spirit of conquest are mutually exclusive admits that overpopulation is a legitimate motive for conquest.

The first answer is approximately limiting the scope of the economic interpretation of politics. It is unwarranted to conceive of the world as if it resembled a universal republic of exchanges. The political rivalry of states is the first *datum*: advantages and disadvantages of such an economic method must not be judged in relation to the whole of humanity, imagined as one, but in reference to the consequences which this method entails for states which are in fact rivals. (We need merely return to this proposition and to combine it with the relatively new fact of industrialization in order to have the principle of the national-economy school.)

The second interpretation, the more usual one, explains the conflict in terms of the gap between the economy as it should be and the economy as it is. The essential notion, which runs through the entire literature of the last century and which results in books like those of Hobson and Norman Angell, is already to be found under Quesnay's pen: the distinction between merchants and commerce, between the private interests of some and the well-understood interest of the collectivity. "The merchants participate in the wealth of nations but the nations do not participate in the wealth of the merchants . . . all wars and all reservations relating to commerce can only have monopoly as an object, perhaps involuntary on the part of the kingdom's traders, but always fatal to the nations that do not distinguish their interests from those of their merchants and that ruin themselves by undertaking wars in order to assure the national agents of their commerce an exclusive privilege which is prejudicial to themselves."[21]

At the limit, the liberal *à la* Bentham declares that wars always cost more than they achieve, even for the conqueror, that conquests are in essence bad business. What is the use of assuming the expenses of administrating a foreign territory? If the latter were both sovereign and open to commerce, the metropolitan nation would enjoy the benefits which it might derive from its colonies without the expenses which the latter impose upon it.

The events of the twentieth century have not so much refuted this doctrinal optimism as incited the economists of liberal inspiration to become more aware of the gap between nations of a capitalist regime *as they are* and an ideal type of liberal economy. L. Robbins's book on the economic causes of conflicts[22] or J. Schumpeter's on imperialism[23] take their place in the lineage

[21] Quoted by Silberner, p. 197. Quesnay, *op. cit.*
[22] *The Economic Causes of War*, London, 1939.
[23] *Imperialism and Social Classes*, Oxford, 1951.

of Quesnay and Adam Smith, that is, of the economists who impute responsibility for war to the spirit of monopoly and to the residues of mercantilism. Only Thorstein Veblen opens a new chapter by reviving the idea of the similarity between the spirit of commerce and the spirit of war and by locating the seat of the spirit of peace in industry.

The economists of the historical and national school would not subscribe to either of these two themes. They would reject the mercantilist formula that commerce is the continuation of war by other means, but they would also reject the Bentham liberalist formula that "all trade is in its essence advantageous, even to that party to whom it is least so. All wars in essence ruin us." Or again: "Between the interest of nations, there is nowhere any real conflict; if they appear repugnant anywhere, it is only in proportion to their being misunderstood."[24]

The historical school, by definition so to speak, takes historical reality for its point of departure. Now this reality involves the compartmentalization of space, the fractionalization of humanity. The rivalry of states is not reduced to economic competition. The nations do not fight each other merely to gain wealth or to favor trade. The balance-sheet of wars is not to be established in relation to the total number of men and in terms of goods or merchandise. In preserving a nation from invasion, armies are productive to the same degree as the wealth which they save. Victorious, they may afford the state and the people not only spoils but occasions and means for prosperity.

This temperate and reasonable interpretation of the relations between economy (or commerce) and wars (or conquests) would probably have been admitted by most liberals in the last century as corresponding to experience. If we concede the primacy and the fatality of humanity's splitting up into rival states, armies are indispensable to nations, even if they are costly. We may say, with Quesnay, "the statesman regrets the men destined for war as the landowner regrets the land used for the ditch necessary to irrigate the field."[25] If the field is lost when the ditch is filled in, the latter, though representing a loss in relation to the optimum, remains profitable in the real world, if space is no longer compartmentalized. Similarly, the liberal may with some difficulty plead that all war is costly, even for the victor, if he refers to the model of a universal and pacific republic which ignores frontiers and soldiers. But history being what it is, it is difficult to deny that victorious wars have sometimes gained advantages for peoples and increased the possibilities of welfare.

Therefore the new, important idea which dominates the thought of the school I shall call national rather than historical concerns neither the balance-sheet of armed conflicts nor the judgment passed on soldiers. The

[24] Quoted by Silberner, p. 261. Bentham, *op. cit.*
[25] Quoted by Silberner, p. 193. Quesnay, *op. cit.*

originality of the national school lies in its rediscovery of certain arguments of the mercantilists, renewed by the consideration of industrial economy. F. List denies neither that the welfare of individuals is the goal nor that wars in themselves destroy wealth. But the existence of separate political units is a fact. The economist has no right to ignore the fate of the collectivity to which he belongs and to reason in relation to a humanity without frontiers, ideal perhaps but temporarily inaccessible. Now, at the present moment, free exchange does not contribute equally to the prosperity of all nations. It tends, on the contrary, to consecrate, even to reinforce the supremacy of the most advanced nations, that is, those which already possess an industry. How will the less advanced nations manage to progress in their turn in the industrial world if they open their borders to manufactured products? Free trade would condemn them to remaining indefinitely providers of raw materials and primary products. In the century when industry is a condition of power, the suppression of tariff barriers would tend to eternalize the present disparity between agricultural and industrialized nations, and hence the inequalities of power and standard of living, contrary to justice and even perhaps to peace.

List clearly conceived the theory, which we have indicated above,[26] of harmonious development. Since the latter is possible only within a sufficiently extensive framework, it is easy to shift to the notion of great space. The creation of vast economic-political units is the first stage of the republic of exchanges. The partisan of national economy does not deny that this first stage may require the use of violence. For a nation to be able, in essentials, to be self-sufficient, it must first protect its new industries, and always protect its vital ones. It must also on occasion round out the territory of its sovereignty.

Ultimately, F. List does not exclude a peace based on the equilibrium of nations and national economies. Beyond the formation of great wholes, free exchange would reveal itself to be fruitful because it would bring into relation equal partners. Universal peace will not emerge from free exchange, but free exchange will perhaps be the ultimate result of a pacified humanity, as a result of temporary protectionism, as a result of the reinforcement of the political-economic units into which humanity is naturally divided.

Probably the socialist school is the one whose doctrine it is most difficult to summarize in a few propositions relating to conflicts and wars. The Utopian socialist is inclined to believe that peace among states will of itself follow peace within nations. As long as poverty is rampant, as long as injustices are not eliminated, the struggle between individuals and classes will continue. The Utopian socialists have not had, it seems to me, a single and coherent theory of the relations between the class struggle and rivalries among states. But they have postulated, more or less clearly, that the reconciliation of men

[26] Cf. Chap. VII, Sec. 3.

and of groups within an equitable order would lead of itself to the reconciliation of states.

The socialism of Marxist inspiration, on the other hand, professes a few simple and categorical ideas. It regards wars as inevitable in the capitalist system. It borrows from one of the sections of the liberal school the explanation of wars by the rivalry of economic interests. It adds the assertion that with the advent of socialism, the occasions or the causes of armed conflicts would disappear. Simplifying, one is tempted to say that according to the Marxists, the mercantilists faithfully describe the belligerent character of commerce in the *capitalist* regime, the liberals the pacific character of commerce *after the capitalist regime*.

The economy is bellicose in a capitalist system; it will be pacific in a socialist one. The question is: why should this be so? The liberal economists have incriminated the spirit of protection and monopoly, the action of the great corporations or trusts which seek to reserve the domestic markets for themselves and to conquer foreign markets. Lenin summarizes all the accusations formulated by the economists of liberal inspiration against the leaders (private interests, privileged groups) of imperialism. But he transfigures this interpretation by decreeing that imperialism, far from being imputable to minorities, is the necessary expression of capitalism that has reached a certain phase of its evolution (the so-called monopolistic phase). Under the influence of J. A. Hobson and of Rudolf Hilferding,[27] Lenin insists that capitalism is condemned to imperialism and that the peaceful division of the planet among private monopolies or states is impossible. Thus, Leninism reverts to the essential relationship of commerce and war. But the mercantilist dialectic was clearer than that of Leninism: the search for precious metals, whose quantity was not expanding, naturally created rivalries and conflicts. Is the same true of the search for markets, for raw materials, or for opportunities for surplus profit?

Why will the economy be peaceful in a socialist regime? The Marxists have asserted more than demonstrated this proposition, which seemed to them self-evident, because they accepted as obvious the theory according to which conflicts among states have economic causes; but Jaurès' indefinitely repeated phrase, "capitalism bears war within itself as the cloud bears the storm," does not constitute a proof. The question remains: what are the aspects of capitalism—private ownership of the instruments of production, mechanism of the market, concentration of property or power in national or international corporations—which accidentally or inevitably provoke wars among states?

These four schools do not oppose each other on all points. On the question of political conflicts, certain liberals[28] are in agreement with most of the

[27] In *Das Finanzkapital, eine Studie über die jüngste Entwicklung des Kapitalismus* (published in 1909), Vienna, 1920.
[28] Cf. for instance Lionel Robbins, *op. cit.*

mercantilists and the economists of the national school in proclaiming that the rivalry of states is primary and that wars are not always caused by opposed commercial interests. The socialists, like the liberals, have as their final objective, in doctrine, the welfare of individuals. The national school, like the mercantilists, claims to be in the service of the greatness of nations. These schools define themselves and oppose each other by their interpretation of commerce (or of exchange) considered as the essence of economic life. According to the mercantilists, *commerce is war*, according to the liberals *commerce is peace*, on the sole condition that it be free. According to the national economists, *commerce will be peace* when all nations are developed; according to the Marxists *commerce is war* under capitalism, *commerce will be peace* with socialists.

2. Historical Interpretation of the Doctrines

Theories are always partially explained by historical circumstances. Whether the supreme goal is the power of the state or the welfare of the citizens, it suffices that the conditions of power be different for the economists' judgments of men's activities to vary legitimately.

In the age of courage, in antiquity, military force was essentially dependent on number, on the physical vigor of the soldiers, on the organization of the army. Hence the mode of life favorable to the quantity and quality of combatants, that is, the peasant mode of life, was adorned for centuries with all the virtues, both pacific and martial. In 1940 Marshal Pétain still praised the earth "which never lies"; he was ready, under the inspiration of reactionary advisers and age-old beliefs, to prepare France's revenge by a return to the fields. Sully had more justification in assuming, at the end of the sixteenth century, that "strong peoples are peasant peoples because industry causes the citizens to lose the habit of painful and laborious operation in which they need to be trained in order to become good soldiers." Arts and cities seem to be causes of corruption. The industries debilitate the people, luxury softens men. States prosper by simplicity and frugality.

Although these theses, up until the middle of the eighteenth century, were constantly explored by the philosophers, they have been since the dawn of modern times no more than a partial truth. Soldiers using powder and cannon need some instruction. "In the days of courage," as Fuller calls them, the citizens of Rome acquired their tactical mastery only as a result of the Punic Wars: the very length of their service had made professionals out of them. The elite soldiers who in the sixteenth and seventeenth centuries dominated the battlefields on land and even more on sea were no longer amateurs, whether noble or bourgeois. In matters of armament or training, they depended on the political authority—city, principality, state—which possessed enough financial resources to mobilize and equip the troops or crews, to buy or manufacture vessels and cannon.

Machiavelli, at the beginning of the sixteenth century, is reactionary as a military theoretician: he does not believe in the effectiveness of artillery; he is mistaken as to the necessity of the "sinew of war." Out of love for antiquity, by political doctrine, he longs for an army of citizens, and continues to regard the infantry as the queen of battles. In an age when wars of privateering and piracy afforded considerable spoils, when foreign trade required warships as well as cargo vessels, the mercantilists were closer to historical truth, less perverse in their counsel to princes than they seem to us today. Political units did not differ so much from each other by the number of men or the potential of manufactures as by the unequal capacity to mobilize resources. Military force was the primary consequence of this capacity for mobilization. A city enriched by commerce, such as Venice, could become a great military power by buying mercenaries, both soldiers and sailors. A vast kingdom lost its possibilities for action if an empty treasury kept it from mobilizing national troops or recruiting volunteers. Machiavelli's formula: "he who has soldiers finds money," became true, but in a sense which the Florentine had probably not envisaged: the state, which had monopolized police powers, acquired thereby the capacity to draw on an important share of the nation's resources for its own needs. Military force continued to be a function both of the potential and of the capacity for mobilization. But since the latter seemed henceforth to belong to all states, it was the potential which occupied the foreground and represented the differential factor.

At the end of the eighteenth century, the arguments about the respective effectiveness of steel and gold, of infantry and artillery, were exhausted. Whatever the price still attached to precious metals, the wealth of nations (what we now call economic growth or expansion) no longer appeared to be a consequence of the stock of gold and silver possessed and held by each of them. Peace, public order, the activity of merchants and manufacturers, the spirit of initiative—these were the profound causes of the swifter enrichment of some rather than of others. The age of pirates was over. When peace rules, commerce becomes authentically pacific and no one henceforth calls it "camouflaged war." The British authors were all the more inclined to accentuate the peaceful essence of exchange, since their nation had the better share of it.

At the same time, it is enough to open one's eyes to observe that "virtue is always rewarded": by devoting themselves to works of peace, nations guarantee their security, enlarge their power. Adam Smith notes that the conditions of military force are no longer what they were in the past. In the past, the poor peoples were also the strong ones. Arms and weapons were simple, differing little from each other: the differential factor was physical vigor, martial ardor. Arts and luxury were more likely to enervate the combatants than to perfect the instruments of combat. The stereotypes were those of the Roman Republic, which had reached supremacy by frugality and the virtue of its peasant citizens, and which had been precipitated into the abyss by wealth the corruption of the imperial city. It was at Capua that Hannibal's soldiers had discovered their pleasures and prepared their defeat. Henceforth, another image replaces the one which modern authors had borrowed from ancient literature. Civilization, thanks to the arts, henceforth triumphs over barbarism. Wealth and power go hand in hand, since each has industry as its basis.

It is at this point that the "national economists" raise their objection. If industrial development governs both wealth and power, it constitutes the crucial objective. Trade, free trade, is at best only a means. Yet, these economists declare, free trade between political-economic units which have not reached the same phase of development paralyzes or retards those which are behind. The industrialist thesis is maintained, but on the behalf of tariff protection and harmonious growth.

These schools exist in the middle of the twentieth century, as they did in the middle of the nineteenth, although the doctrines have meanwhile assumed subtler forms: one favoring, in principle, freedom of trade, the other emphasizing the necessity of harmonious growth and of industrialization. To a degree, the divergence concerns questions of fact: what is the influence of a liberal policy of foreign trade on industrialization in the case of an underdeveloped nation? No economist would answer such a question by a simple and categorical proposition. The economist of liberal tendency would recognize the necessity for protective measures, at least partial and temporary ones. The economist of protectionist tendency would recognize the utility of certain kinds of trade. But the two orientations exist, either toward the largest possible self-sufficient space, or toward a worldwide solidarity created by the most active commerce possible.

The preference for the formula of great space is generally dictated by political-military considerations as much as by economic ones. The state's power is a function of its dependence on the outside world, at the same time as of its resources and degree of mobilization. An industry, an army can be paralyzed by the lack of a raw material or of a particular product. The problem of productivity leads to an international division of labor that is as extensive as possible. The problem of power forbids the sacrifice of any vital piece of the machinery of production. The reasoning of the "national economists" is convincing in a universe fragmented into rival sovereignties; that of the liberal economists supposes a universal republic or aims at creating its conditions.

Thus, the theories concerned with the relation of resources to military force or to the power of states are readily explained. All contain, for the period in question, a share of truth. None is entirely true because none systematically considers the multiple determinants. If we assume the weapons to be analogous, then number, vigor and organization of the combatants determine the relation of forces. If we except number, there subsists the duality of primitive ardor and organization. *It is the differential factor, characteristic of a period, which the theoretician retains and transforms into a unique cause.*

Yet let us not forget to note that in each period there are marginal, exceptional or aberrant causes. The military power of Athens was based on its mines, commerce, fleet, and its empire. This power was, therefore, precarious and of short duration. It nonetheless dominated the system of the city-states for a time. Similarly Carthage would have subscribed to the mercantilist formula: money is the sinew of war. The citizens of Carthage had fought the Roman soldiers for years before succumbing at the end of the Third Punic War. Yet Hannibal, who made Rome tremble, led an army of mercenaries and foreign units furnished by his allies.

In our own age no one would go so far as to proclaim that the quality of the combatants is the result of the frugality of their mode of life. In piloting planes or driving assault tanks, the level of instruction is much more important than the simplicity of manners. But in the *djebels* of Algeria, the formula of the ancient authors recovers a degree of truth. The Kabyl peasant is much more adept at night fighting, at hand-to-hand combat and ambushes than the young Frenchman of a unit accustomed to cities and electric lights. The French unit remained the master of the terrain thanks to number, organization and certain technical weapons. Yet qualitative superiority, in a particular kind of combat, is not on the side of civilization, even in the age of industry.

There subsists a more general share of truth in the proposition attributing martial superiority to a poor people over a rich one. We agree that the strength of regular armies is a function of their equipment and the latter, in its turn, of industry. Military force would thus be proportional to the human and industrial potential, if the capacity for mobilization were taken to be equal in the various states. But this capacity, as a matter of fact, is never equal. It is controlled by two variables: administrative effectiveness and the people's consent to privation. The volume of resources available for the war effort is measured by the gap between total production and the minimum necessary for subsistence. Habits of frugality reduce the supplies necessary for the army in the field. They permit a lower standard of living for the civilian population and thereby enlarge the gap between total production and the irreducible minimum of civilian consumption.

Lastly the regime, in its turn, is more or less capable of convincing, persuading or obliging the people to accept a lower standard of living. To a degree, the distribution of collective resources, in peacetime and in wartime, is controlled by the mode of government. In the industrial age, the modern alternative of welfare or power reproduces, in a renewed form, the ancient alternative of frugality, the mother of virtue, and luxury, the principle of corruption. It remains to be discovered whether frugality by constraint, which the modern despotisms impose, is morally and politically similar to the virtue praised by the Greek or Roman authors.

If it is relatively easy to explain, by referring to historical data, the theories concerned with the relation between resources and force; the same is not true of the theories concerned with the economic causes of conflicts. The theories of the first type are not a faithful expression of reality, they distort it, simplify it, transform it, but they regularly retain *one* truly essential aspect of it. On the other hand, the economic interpretations of conflict seem to be fashionable to the very degree that they are contestable.

During the ages of stationary or slowly advancing techniques, force was a much more effective method of acquiring goods than trade. The quantity of wealth which the conquerors could seize by arms was enormous compared to the quantity which they created by their labor. Slaves, precious metals, tributes or taxes levied on the foreign populations, the profits of victory, were obvious and rewarding. Yet the classical authors, without ever admitting or denying the economic productivity of empire, almost all asserted that the latter was desired for itself.

On the other hand, in the modern age, the economic profits of victory, however substantial they may be on occasion, have become insignificant or absurd compared to the additional wealth which the yearly progress of technology or organization furnishes the industrialized peoples. Yet it is in our period that the influential authors believe that imperialism remains mysterious as long as the pressure of "trusts" and the appetite for money have not been exposed behind the activity of diplomats and soldiers.

This apparent paradox is, in fact, the best introduction to the problem of economic interpretation of inter-state conflicts. During the millenniums of the historical period, inequality has been extreme between the privileged and the masses within the complex societies, between the various collectivities. The low labor yield did not permit giving the benefits of luxury or leisure to all. Whether he owned land, precious metals, slaves or castles, the property of one man signified the privation of another. Property was, in essence, monopolistic. Abstract economic theory demonstrates that, given a certain distribution of goods, the mechanism of free exchange is the most advantageous for all. It does not demonstrate that the disfavored must passively accept the distribution made at a given moment in history. The use of force by the *have-nots* in order to take from the *haves* was readily intelligible.

The poverty of all known societies from the dawn of civilization, the unequal distribution of wealth within and among collectivities, the extent of the wealth to be seized by violence in comparison with the wealth produced by labor, all these facts have constituted the structural condition of conflict between classes or states, and account in retrospect for the wars of conquest.

Must we conclude that this has always been the motive of the conquerors, down through the centuries? No historian would be so insane or rather so stupid as to say so. The nomads of the deserts or the steppes, the Arabs or the Mongols, lived the kind of life of which combat was the spontaneous expression, the principal activity. They waged war for its own sake, they attacked sedentary populations because battle was their pleasure and empire their vocation. Bonaparte's orders of the day to the Italian army, contrasting the soldiers' poverty with the wealth before their eyes, was not necessary to hurl the Asian horsemen to the assault.

The imperialism of Athens or of Rome would be more consonant with an economic interpretation. Greatness, as we have said, was inseparably political and economic, naval and commercial. Athens could not subsist as a city-state of more than forty thousand citizens, reveling in the splendor of her festivals, without a commercial network and the tribute of her allies. In defeat she saved neither her fortune nor her glory. Yet Thucydides does not consider—and we are tempted to agree with him—that the Athenians were especially greedy for wealth. What animated them was the pride of dominion, which knew no bounds and which swept them into catastrophe.

Roman imperialism, especially starting from the end of the Republic and under the Empire, had many causes of an economic order. The city, having grown huge, needed the African wheat. Without tribute paid by the conquered, handouts to the crowd and public games would have been impossible. Romans of the privileged classes, partisans or knights, went to the provinces to make their money as proconsuls or tax collectors. None would have thought, and none would think today, of applying Bentham's calculus to the Roman Empire: the cost of the colonies to the metropolitan nation. Nor would any have regarded Virgil's advice to the Roman people as merely the camouflage of avarice: *tu regere populos memento*. The Empire had no need for a justification when it was economically profitable.

Why has empire, in the course of modern times, been increasingly interpreted in economic or in philosophical terms, and less and less in frankly political terms, following the example of the Greeks? During a first phase, say from the sixteenth century to the eighteenth, imperial conquests were *obviously* profitable. It would be absurd to claim that explorers or even merchants were animated by the mere desire for profits, by the mere thirst for gold and silver. The psychology of the Spanish conquistadors in America does not lend itself to crude simplification. Perhaps the religious mission was invoked in order to calm consciences which were troubled by the enormity of the profits and the cruel fate inflicted upon the natives. The advent of precious metals, the possession of distant lands covered Spain with power and wealth. Why question the respective share of the various motives in the behavior of the conquerors?

The French and English empires in India or America, different as they were from each other and from the Spanish Empire, were scarcely more problematical. The motives for which Englishmen, Frenchmen, Spaniards or Dutchmen went to settle in America, on the territory of what is today the United States or Canada, were many. Some set out by order of the authorities, others to protect their right to worship according to the imperatives of their conscience, others to find opportunities for a broader, freer life, still others to reap the profits of a distant and speculative commerce. The creation of a new France or a new England in an almost empty territory was self-explanatory, like the attraction of the Indies trade or the creation of military bases by chartered companies whose explicit goal was money.

The errors of judgment committed by contemporaries at the period of the Treaty of Paris and so often repeated by French authors were due to the disparity between the actual importance and the virtual importance of this or that territory. In 1763 Santo Domingo represented for France a more precious possession than Canada, whose icy wastes offered the metropolitan nation little more than furs or a few rare metals. Space for population growth was not yet recognized as the supreme wealth. The link between the spirit of commerce and the spirit of adventure, between curiosity and greed, between the advantages of commerce and the rapine of conquests, between the monopoly of the flag and political sovereignty were sufficiently apparent for a strictly economic theory of European expansion to have had, before the nineteenth century, neither the merit of originality nor that of cynicism. It would have seemed an arbitrary and futile design for explanation.

The intellectual climate changed slowly in the nineteenth century. Philosophers and moralists questioned the legitimacy of wars and conquests just when the liberal economists began to doubt the advantage of empires or colonies for the metropolitan nations. The imperialists found themselves doubly on the defensive. Henceforth they were obliged to justify what had hitherto seemed to correspond to the accepted order of things, to account for empire both on the level of ideas and on that of advantage, against those who denounced it as unjust and against those who denounced it as costly. Which explains the conjunction, in the speeches of Jules Ferry, of phrases about the civilizing mission of France (or of the white man) and of others about the necessity, for the sake of commerce and prestige, of hoisting the tricolor over the four corners of the globe. The interpreters of British imperialism also resorted to two kinds of arguments: Joseph Chamberlain's prosperity by empire and Rudyard Kipling's white man's burden.

Simultaneously the theoreticians of socialism: humanitarians, interpreters of the idealistic hope of the West attack class struggles, inequalities, wars. They attribute armed conflicts to capitalism. And the imperialists as well as the liberals furnish them proofs of capitalism's responsibility. The imperialists pride themselves on the wealth which the colonies afford the metropolitan nation. The liberals, at least those hostile to the colonies and convinced of the pacific character of modern economics, indict the damaging action of the privileged groups. The Marxists use the arguments of both groups in order to demonstrate that "imperialism is the final stage of capitalism."

3. Imperialism and Colonization

Imperialism, according to the simplest and most general definition, is the diplomatic-strategic behavior of a political unit which constructs an empire, that is, subjects foreign populations to its rule. The Romans, the Mongols, the Arabs have been empire-builders whom we properly call imperialists.

Many dubious cases occur in the margins of this phenomenon, which is never absent from the chronicle of the ages. Should we call it imperialism when the populations of the conquering unit and of the subject units share the same culture and, so to speak, the same nationality? (Was Bismarck, as the creator of the German empire, an imperialist?[29]) Should we call it imperialism when the rules of Tsarist Russia or of the Soviet Union seek to maintain a state unity embracing heterogeneous populations? Can we say that the German unification was not imperialistic insofar as it corresponded to the aspirations of the Germans, that the maintenance of the Soviet Empire is not imperialistic insofar as the non-Russian peoples consent to it? It is not easy, even for the unbiased observer, to measure the respective force of popular sentiments favorable or hostile to the construction or conservation of an empire. To trace the limits of imperialism clearly, the frontiers of nations would have to be visible on the map of cultures, of languages or of popular aspirations.

Imperialism is also equivocal in another sense. Does it disappear by the mere fact that state sovereignties are officially respected? Would the peoples of Eastern Europe, liberated by the Soviet army and governed today by Communist parties, be wrong to denounce the imperialism of Moscow? The frontier is vague between the so-called legitimate influence of great powers and the so-called culpable imperialism. Within a heterogeneous system, every ruling power is obliged to exercise an influence on the internal affairs of secondary states, at least to the degree necessary to prevent the victory of the party linked to the rival camp.[30]

Colonization, as practiced by the Greek city-states in the eighth and seventh centuries B.C., by the Europeans in America since the sixteenth century, represents a different phenomenon. The Corinthian colonists who founded Corcyra occupied an available space; the British Puritans from England were less concerned to conquer the Indians than nature. In the long run colonization has more influence on peoples' respective place in the sun than imperialism (unless the latter proceeds to the extermination of the conquered): India could not remain long under the sovereignty of Her Britannic Majesty, but the United States will continue to speak English.

The European empires have been partly the result of imperialism, partly the result of colonization. In North America colonization prevailed over imperialism, in Asia and in Africa imperialism over colonization. The case of the Spanish Empire in South America was intermediary. In both cases men from the metropolitan nation came and settled in the conquered territory. In an extreme case, this minority is reduced to soldiers and administrators who

[29] These questions are not rhetorical, nor do they seek an answer. I am simply concerned to clarify the concepts involved and to reveal the various aspects of the phenomenon.
[30] The dialectic of imperialism, in a heterogeneous diplomatic system, does not exclude discrimination between degrees of interference, influence or domination.

wield the imperial authority. Generally, though, it includes civilians as well, landowners or businessmen who enjoy the privilege of belonging to the ruling power and who derive profit from it. When the imperial minority is definitively established and when it is numerous enough, it takes the initiative in breaking with the metropolitan nation and constituting an independent state. But it does not thereby lose its power and wealth. Imperial domination extends within the new state: in extreme circumstances, there exists one state and two peoples. When the minority from the metropolitan nation is not numerous enough, or when it does not mingle with the native populations, it is at the mercy of a turn of fortune. The "French colonies" of Tunisia or Morocco are in the process of liquidation. They were able to imitate neither the ruling classes of Spanish origin who "liberated" the republics of South America from the metropolitan nation, nor the European immigrants in North America.

Imperialism and colonization involve too many varieties for one and the same interpretation to be applied to all centuries and all nations. It is the Marxist theory of imperialism and the liquidation, by the European states, of their empires in Asia and Africa which have made fashionable the controversies on the nature of the imperial phenomenon. Leaving aside the Greek colonization in the eighth century B.C. and the European colonization in America since the sixteenth century, we should like to raise a single question: is nineteenth-century imperialism attributable to the capitalist regime?

It seems to me preferable to begin with historical considerations, which do not avoid the theoretical question but which afford arguments in favor of this or that interpretation. The three facts which the authors discuss at great length are: the massive exports of European capital during the last decades of the nineteenth and the first decade of the twentieth century, the race for Africa during the same period,[31] and the First World War. The Leninist theory of imperialism demands a relation among these three events. The theory is at least shaken if it does not link them together of *necessity*.

Historical studies of the export of capital and the colonial conquest have been undertaken many times.[32] None confirms a simple and dogmatic interpretation.

The two nations which during the half century before the First World War conquered the largest territories, France and Great Britain, were also the nations which, economically, least needed to acquire new possessions. France had a stationary population, a slow industrial growth, and therefore suffered neither population surplus, lack of raw materials nor dearth of outlets

[31] This period of diplomatic history has been studied by William L. Langer in a work entitled *Diplomacy of Imperialism*, New York, 1935, and also by Parker T. Moon, *Imperialism and World Politics*, New York, 1927.
[32] The classical works are E. Staley, *War and the Private Investor*, New York, 1935; Herbert Feis, *Europe as World Banker*, New Haven, 1930; and A. K. Cairncross, *Home and Foreign Investments*, Cambridge, 1953.

for manufactured products. Population and production increased more rapidly in Great Britain, but the emigration valve remained open and, with the dominions and its sovereignty over India, the United Kingdom was not starved for space. It is true that both France and Great Britain had a surplus of capital, since they had become bankers for the world, but they invested only a slight fraction of this surplus in their colonies.

Out of 40 to 45 billion gold francs[33] invested abroad just before 1914, only 4 billion were invested in the Empire. The majority was invested in Europe (27.5 billion, of which 11.3 was invested in Russia), 6 billion in Latin America, 2 billion in North America, 3.3 billion in Egypt, Suez and South Africa, and 2.2 billion in Asia. Of the British capital invested abroad, half was invested in the Empire, but only a small share in the newly acquired African possessions.

The first question is why France and England had so much capital available for foreign investment. The standard answer is the inequality of the distribution of income, but the figures do not entirely confirm this classical explanation. The French savings[34] have been estimated at 2 billion for the 1875–93 period, at 3.5 billion for the 1900–11 period, and at 5 billion on the eve of the war. Now the national income was on the order of 27 to 28 billion in 1903, 32 to 35 billion in 1913, perhaps higher than 35 billion in 1914: savings did not exceed an average of 10 to 12 per cent of the national income, and the foreign investments represented some 35 per cent of those savings.[35] The total amount of savings not being abnormally high, the incitement to export capital must have been exceptionally strong or else the demand for investments in metropolitan France relatively weak (probably both at the same time).

Similarly in Great Britain, for the year 1907, one British economist[36] arrives at the following figures: the investment of fixed capital rose to £275 million, the addition to stocks rose to £20 million, the addition to the stock of durable goods rose to £30 million; the maintenance of capital representing £175 million, the net domestic investment rose to £150 million and the foreign

[33] The national revenue was on the order of 35 billion gold francs.
[34] Cf. R. Pupin, La Richesse de la France devant la guerre, Paris, 1916, and La Richesse privée et les finances françaises, Paris, 1919; J. Lescure, L'Epargne en France, Paris, 1914.
[35] Furthermore, we must not forget that foreign investments were drawn increasingly from the incomes of previous investments. French investments abroad began again, after the War of 1870, starting in 1886. They reached an average of 450 to 550 million francs between 1886 and 1890, from 519 to 619 million francs between 1891 and 1896, from 1,157,000,000 to 1,257,000,000 francs between 1897 and 1902, from 1,359,000,000 to 1,459,000,000 francs between 1903 and 1908, from 1,239,000,000 to 1,339,000,000 francs between 1909 and 1913 (the figures taken from H. Feis, op. cit., p. 44, referring to H. G. Moulton and C. Lewis, The French Debt Problem, New York, 1925). The income from foreign investments is regularly equal to or higher than the investments during these periods. (Feis, p. 44.)
[36] A. K. Cairncross, Home and Foreign Investment, Cambridge, 1953, p. 121.

investment to £135 million. In short, this latter represented nearly half of the total net investment. "It was also symptomatic that Britain herself had invested abroad about as much as her entire industrial and commercial capital, excluding land, and that one-tenth of her national income came to her as interest on foreign investment."[37]

Of these two causes, one, at least, is sufficiently well known from historical study. French capital was drawn outside the country by excess profits not always paid to the owners of this capital,[38] but to the intermediaries, the bankers. These excess profits would not have been enough to induce the exodus of French capital to Russia or the Balkans had the government not used the nation's financial power as an instrument in its diplomacy. Sometimes the loans served for the construction, in Russia, of strategically important railroads, sometimes they guaranteed projects for national industry, sometimes they insured the loyalty of certain nations in which a party favorable to the Central Powers opposed a party favorable to the Allies.

Investments made outside Great Britain were much less influenced by diplomatic considerations than French investments, and it is not impossible to argue, even today, that on the whole they afforded Great Britain at least as many advantages as disadvantages.[39] The yield from foreign state bonds and from shares in foreign corporations was, on the whole, higher than that from domestic investments. The distribution of this capital among various uses (£1,531 million in railroad stocks) and the various regions of the world (over half in North and South America, almost half in the Empire) confirms the economic motivation of the movement of English capital.

[37] *Ibid.*, p. 3. Perhaps the following indications are even more striking: "In the forty years 1875–1914 capital at home (other than land) increased from about £5,000 m. to about £9,200 m., or by over 80%. Foreign investment rose from £1,100 m. to say £4,000 m. in 1914, or by some 250%. Taking absolute figures, capital investment probably constituted three parts home and two parts foreign investment. Of the investment at home a large part was needed merely to maintain capital per head, for the number of employed persons rose by about 50% between the boom years of 1873 and 1913. Out of a surplus of £4,500 m. beyond what was necessary in order to keep domestic capital per head constant, not far short of £3,000 m. or some 60–65% was actually employed to increase Britain's foreign investments" (p. 4).

[38] Did foreign investments yield the investor more than comparable domestic investments?

Cairncross doubts this in relation to French investments: "It has been estimated that in 1899 the yield on domestic securities at the price of issue averaged 4.28%, while the yield on foreign securities was no more than 3.85%. At the *market* price in 1900, the yields were 2.23 and 3.84% respectively. The difference, whether positive or negative, was trifling" (p. 225).

Feis (p. 36), quoting French authors, states that the yield from foreign investments was higher than that from the corresponding investments in France, 3.13 per cent and 4.20 per cent respectively in 1903; 3.40 per cent and 4.62 per cent in 1911.

In the case of England there is no doubt that the yield from foreign investments was higher. In 1905–9, according to Cairncross (p. 227), the yields were as follows: domestic investments: 3.61 per cent; colonial investments: 3.94 per cent; foreign investments: 4.97 per cent.

[39] Cf. Cairncross, *op. cit.*, pp. 224–35.

During the final period before the First World War, Germany, in its turn, had joined the "club of lenders," impelled both by political ambition and by the desire for economic expansion. The German bankers were sometimes seeking higher profits, sometimes vast enterprises that were expressed by industrial projects. Occasionally, the German government, in its turn, counted on capital to gain political influence or to orient the diplomacy of certain Balkan or Near Eastern countries in its favor. However, the German economy, which was developing more rapidly than that of Great Britain or of France, had higher investment rates but also a greater need of its own capital. German foreign investments were between 22 and 25 billion marks. The annual long-term export of capital, during the twenty years that preceded the war, rose to some 600 million marks; they represented in 1914 only 2 per cent of the national income[40] at most.

It is not without interest to compare the export of European capital, before the First World War, with the aid to the underdeveloped countries since the Second. A double similarity appears. In both cases the export of capital contributes to the development of the nations in the process of modernization: British capital, at the end of the nineteenth century and at the beginning of the twentieth, helped Argentina to construct railroads, the United States to build great industries; similarly, American capital has powerfully contributed to the revival of Western Europe, Russian capital will permit the construction of the Aswan Dam. Today, as yesterday, exports of capital are not entirely disinterested: European loans were seeking a higher return or else were at the service of national diplomacy; American gifts are governed, partially at least, by political considerations. But it would be a mistake, in history, to grow indignant over what Kant called "the radical evil"; let us not insist that men do good for the sake of good, let us be satisfied that their selfishness or their rivalry achieves the good results which might have been sought directly by men of good will.

Both loans of capital in 1900 and aid to underdeveloped countries in 1960 are linked to the strictly political competition of states. France loaned to Russia so that the Russian mobilization might be accelerated in case of a generalized war. It made loans to Rumania with the hope that the latter would side with the Allied camp. The United States has aided Europe with the hope that prosperity would raise a barrier against communism. They were aiding the underdeveloped countries to forestall Soviet aid, with the vague idea that ideas accompany capital and technologists. On the other hand, one difference strikes us: the order of magnitude is not the same. The income from foreign investments represented 6 per cent of the French national income on the eve of the First World War, some 9 per cent of the British national income. France's annual loans on the eve of the war amounted to some 4 per cent of the national income in France; they rose to a still higher per-

[40] Cf. Feis, *op. cit.*, pp. 71–72.

centage in Great Britain. One per cent of the American gross national product would be equivalent, in 1960, to five billion dollars, 3 per cent to fifteen billion dollars. The needs of domestic investments no longer left so large an amount of capital available. The cumulative surpluses in foreign accounts which, before 1914, tended to the continuous increase of foreign investments, have not been repeated since 1945. On the contrary, American surpluses from foreign investments have been gradually balanced and then exceeded by the export of capital, the expenses of maintaining American troops and governmental aid to foreign countries.

Between 1880 and 1914 the volume of available French and English capital prevented neither the growth of production nor the rise of the standard of living.[41] It is not certain that the rich furnished the greatest part of the savings. In France, the *petite bourgeoisie* followed a traditional way of life and made every effort to save as much as possible. Durable consumer goods were only beginning to appear. Occasions for spending did not multiply so rapidly as today. Lastly, and perhaps this is the essential fact, in the pre-1914 capitalist regime, investments resulted chiefly from decisions taken by entrepreneurs. The psychology of the latter is not reducible to the reasoning elaborated by pure theory. The spirit of initiative, of creation, of investment varies with the social context. It is different in 1960 from what it was in 1910.

Whatever the case, surpluses of capital were not the direct cause of either the colonial conquests or the First World War. Why would France have conquered North Africa or Equatorial Africa because of such surpluses since she was not investing them there? (The same reasoning applies to Great Britain.) The rivalry for the profitable investment of surplus capital is not a myth. What is a myth is that the capitalists, bankers or industrialists have, as a class and to increase their excess profits, incited the European governments to conquer colonies, that is, to wage war on each other.

As for the colonies, historical study readily demonstrates three propositions: 1. There is no proportion between the importance of the colonial conquests, accomplished by the various nations of Europe at the end of the nineteenth century, and the need each of these nations would have had for them if the theory[42] which explains colonial imperialism by "capitalist contradictions" were true. 2. The colonies of recent acquisition, that is, essentially, the French, English and German empires in Africa, absorbed only a small fraction of the foreign commerce of the metropolitan nations. Trade between industrialized nations was more important in absolute figures than trade between industrialized nations and non-industrialized nations. Political possession involved neither generally nor immediately an increase of trade with the metropolitan nations. 3. In some cases of armed conflicts or of colonial conquests, private groups, great corporations or adventurers have played a role,

---

[41] The latter, however, seems to have made little progress between 1900 and 1914 in France.

[42] Whether this theory invokes vital outlets or the search for excess-profits.

exerted a pressure on diplomats or statesmen. But, at the origin of the "diplomacy of imperialism" (in the meaning W. L. Langer gives this expression), the strictly political impulse seems stronger than economic motivations. The desire for greatness and glory which animates the leaders of men has had a more lasting effect on the course of events than the more or less camouflaged influence of corporations.

It is impossible to measure precisely the strict efficacy of each cause or the exact motive of each individual. If we consider the case of the French Empire in Africa without postulating an interpretation in advance, the facts do not suggest that the French government intervened in Tunisia to safeguard French interests in secondary companies; quite the contrary, the French government invoked these interests in order to justify an intervention which statesmen saw as a means of preventing Italian colonization, guaranteeing the security of the Algerian borders and providing evidence of French recovery. Similarly, in Morocco, the banks and corporations were attracted by the opportunities offered to them by conquests more than they forced the parliament and ministers to launch the enterprise. South of the Sahara, missionaries, explorers and officers were, originally, more active and more impassioned than big business. The American historian E. Staley, in his book *War and the Private Investor,* has more often remarked on the desire of statesmen than on the intrigues of capitalists as being the source of conquests.

Such an interpretation is not dogmatic. It does not exclude the fact that the Boer War and the British protectorate in Egypt were entirely or largely provoked by the action of private groups. It does not exclude the fact that after taking possession, individuals or societies have profited by French or British sovereignty, either to obtain concessions of territory, or to reserve for themselves a profitable trade, or to insure high profits by the exploitation of rich natural resources and payment of low salaries. To say that the nations of Western Europe were not obliged in order to maintain the capitalist regime or the welfare of the people to take possession of Africa is not to say that once the conquest was made the colonists did not dominate and exploit the vanquished, as all conquerors have done down through the ages.

What makes European imperialism in Africa spuriously mysterious, in the eyes of certain historians, *is that it is not modern if only those phenomena determined by economics are modern.* Even if, following Lenin, we described the capitalist economies as involved in spite of themselves in an endless expansion toward exploitation and the division of the planet, we could not thereby explain the fact that a France without dynamism established her sovereignty over territories to which she sent neither surplus population nor surplus capital nor surplus manufactured products. Imperial conquest remained, in the minds of the European statesmen, the sign of greatness. Europe was at peace, the Western Hemisphere protected by the Monroe Doctrine. One took what remained to be taken, and the unwritten law of compensation, which the diplomacy of cabinets obeyed, obliged the states to claim in turn a share of a continent which all could have safely ignored.

Such imperialism nonetheless created diplomatic conflicts between the great powers: the Reich regarded itself as a kind of victim of the French establishment in Morocco, as though humiliated that the neighboring republic, weakened as it was, should enlarge its territories while Germany remained enclosed within its frontiers. The liberal-minded economists, on their side, stressed that the causes of the conflicts were those encouraging the return of the mercantile spirit. It was not sovereignty, they said, that mattered on the economic level, it was the action of the sovereign. Let the sovereign maintain equal conditions for all rivals and the flags floating over the public buildings will be of no consequence. But the colonial spirit was increasingly marked by the old mercantile spirit. The state, whether colonist or protector, reserved for its nationals the concessions of territories or mines, top administrative posts, and commerce with the metropolitan nation for its own merchant marine. Far from concealing them, the leagues which undertook to popularize the imperial expansion of Great Britain and France (like the *Ligue maritime et coloniale*) tended to exaggerate the profits of imperialism. Public opinion inclined to indifference or to skepticism. Propaganda was not so much directed against the "Marxists" as against the "liberals." Whereas the former could be dealt with by invoking the "civilizing mission," against the latter, it was necessary to prove that the metropolitan nation owed a good share of its prosperity to its colonies.

Were leaders and peoples so convinced by their own ideology that they desired or accepted the First World War, the division of the globe, as necessary (in the double sense of the word)? There is nothing to prove that this was the case. It was not over colonial conflicts that the nations went to war, but over conflicts of nationalities in the Balkans. In Morocco, French and German banks were more disposed to come to terms than the chancelleries. The fate of the southern Slavs jeopardized the existence of Austria-Hungary, thus affecting the whole of the European equilibrium. Were the English determined to conquer Germany in order to eliminate a commercial rival? This legend does not stand up under scrutiny. Certain sectors of the British export trade were affected by German exports. Both nations increased their sales abroad, although German progress was swifter. Shall we say that British public opinion mistakenly believed the national prosperity was threatened? British public opinion was as conscious of the complementarity as of the opposition between the two economies: they were each other's best customer and best purveyor. The voices of the liberals who denounced the futility of conquest carried farther than those backward champions of mercantilism who appealed to arms to save commerce.

Actually the War of 1914, like European imperialism in Africa, was essentially a *traditional phenomenon*. It was, in origin, a general war of a typical character: all the member states of the international system were involved in the struggle because the latter jeopardized the structure of the system. The statesmen discovered too late that industry transformed the nature of war more than there was occasion for conflict.

4. Capitalism and Imperialism

The facts we have discussed in the preceding paragraph *do not refute* any particular theory of imperialism, but they make *plausible* a more complex interpretation than that of the Marxists or of certain liberals. It is not in a period when conquests are less profitable and wars more ruinous than in any other that we should explain either of them by a purely economic mechanism. Does the abstract analysis of the capitalist system permit us to adopt a notion which empirical analysis seems to deny?

Let us first recall that the tendency of the capitalist—that is, progressive and industrial—economy to spread throughout the world is not in question. Every school admits this much. The theory should prove that capitalist economy cannot survive without territories that are not yet capitalist, or, that it is condemned by its internal contradictions to divide up the world into colonial empires and spheres of influence, and that such division cannot be pacific.

Of the first proof—that capitalist economies cannot survive without populations still alien to the capitalist mode of production—we shall say only a few words. It has been attempted by Rosa Luxembourg, and rejected by Lenin and the principal Marxists: it is no more than a historical curiosity.

The proof takes as its point of departure the division of all modern economy into two sectors, one which produces the means of production and one which produces consumer goods. Each of these two sectors produces a value which is subdivided, according to Marxist concepts, into constant capital, variable capital and surplus value. Thus:

$$I = C_1 + V_1 + S_1 \quad \text{(production goods)}$$
$$II = C_2 + V_2 + S_2 \quad \text{(consumer goods)}$$

In a process of simple reproduction, surplus value can be "realized" (in the Marxist sense of the term) only if equality is constantly maintained between the sum of the variable capital and the surplus value in sector I, and the constant capital in sector II.[43]

Now let us consider the process known as that of expanded reproduction. A part of the surplus value of the two sectors is consumed by the capitalist, another part is reinvested so that the constant capital is enlarged. This investment of a part of the surplus value constitutes what Marx called the accumulation of capital.

Let us take as point of departure the accumulation of capital in sector I.

[43] In simple reproduction, variable capital and surplus value are entirely consumed. Now the sum $(C_2 + V_2 + S_2)$ represents the totality of consumer goods available. For V_1 and S_1 to be consumed they must be equal to C_2.

The surplus value is subdivided into two parts: one which will be consumed by the capitalist, the other which will be transformed into capital for the next phase. Henceforth the equation $C_2=V_1+S_1$ is transformed. The total value of consumer goods, that is, the total value of sector II, should be equal to the sum of the variable capital of sector I and sector II, the consumed part of the surplus value of sector I, and the consumed part of the surplus value of sector II ($II=V_1+V_2+S_1C+S_2C$). Or again, the total value of sector I should equal the sum of the constant capital of the two sectors plus the reinvested fraction of the surplus values of the two sectors. Within the system defined by these schemes, the process of expanded reproduction can take place unhampered only if these equations are respected.

Are they? Rosa Luxembourg, her disciples and her critics have played with numerical examples. They have finally concluded that these equations can be maintained on the condition that the rate of accumulation in sector II (consumer goods) be determined by the rate of accumulation in sector I. This conclusion, moreover, has what we might call the quality of evidence. The authors posited the necessary equation between the constant capital of sector II and the sum of the variable capital and the surplus value consumed by the capitalists of sector I. This equation will be respected only in the cases in which the increase of one of the two terms of the equation controls the increase of the other. The Marxists, admitting that the accumulation of capital is the essential phenomenon and the resiliency of the capitalist system, first of all posit the growth of sector I by reinvestment of almost all the surplus value. The value of sector II—in other words, of the consumer goods— should not exceed the value of the consumption of the workers of both sectors (V_1 and V_2), plus the share of the surplus value of each sector consumed by the capitalists. Otherwise, the surplus value could not be "realized," in other words the values, under the physical form in which they present themselves, would not find a corresponding demand. There might exist, for instance, an "unsalable" (or unrealizable) surplus of value, embodied in consumer goods, which would not find a taker within the system.

The idea of an unsalable surplus of consumer goods within the capitalist system (linked to the Marxist notion that capitalism is subject to the law of concentration and that wages are maintained at the lowest possible level) would be reinforced and renewed by the consideration of the relation between the two sectors. As a matter of fact, the accumulation does not really consist of reinvesting an important share of the surplus value in order to produce more goods according to the same organic composition of capital; if this were the case, there would be no insurmountable difficulties about respecting, in the process of expanded reproduction, the equation $C_2=V_1+S_1$. But the essence of technological progress, Rosa Luxembourg and her commentators tell us, consists in modifying the relation of C to V; thus the maintenance of proportionate values between the constant capital of one sector and the variable capital of the other is contradictory and impossible. Or at least, according to the last of these backward disciples of Rosa Luxembourg, "the conditions of equilibrium require, ultimately, a slowing down of the rhythm of technological progress and even of the rhythm of the increase of production in sector II as progress increases in sector I, and this to such a degree that, if we imagined a very intense technological progress in sector I, it might have as its counterpart a requirement for a production halt or even a deferment in sector II."[44]

Is it possible to find factual evidence in order to prove this contradiction? I do not believe so. In the course of the first phase of industrial development, the capitalist nations have perhaps tended to export consumer goods, but these were manufactured products such as textiles. Today, the underdeveloped nations of the world, in the process of industrialization, also desire to sell textile products abroad, not because of a surplus of value in sector II in relation to the domestic purchasing power available for consumer goods, but because such manufactured products are simpler, their technology less difficult than that of most factory-produced goods. At present, the so-called capitalist nations export, in the percentage of their total exports, increasing amounts of manufactured goods, for the simple reason that the nations in the process of development wish to equip themselves and reserve their scarce foreign currency for such equipment. It would be reckless to conclude from this that the relation between the two sectors results in a permanent excess of production goods.

Nor has the transformation of agriculture during the last 150 years tended to confirm the contradiction between the necessary equation of C_2 and V_1[45] on the one hand, or the modification of the relation between C and V on the other. The technological progress in agriculture has been slow or fast, depending on the nations and the periods of capitalism. It has slowed down in the nations where additional production stimulated or risked stimulating the collapse of the market—in any case had to be exported. It has accelerated for some twenty years in the United States for reasons that appear even more technological than social. The complexity of the variables which control technological progress in capitalist agriculture is such that it is impossible to find in the facts the confirmation of the "contradiction" discovered by Rosa Luxembourg.

That the speed of accumulation in sector I tends to slow down the technological progress in sector II might be suggested by a single historical experiment: that of the Soviet Union. Production and productivity have advanced in sector I faster than in sector II. There has not been any surplus of production in sector II but, since the capitalist law of accumulation functions to the full in sector I and since the surplus value, appropriated by the state, was

---

[44] Lucien Goldmann, *Recherches dialectiques*, Paris, 1959, p. 336.
[45] This equation is simplified: developed, it should be $C_2+CA_2=V_1+VA_1$ (CA_2 is the supplementary constant capital of sector II, VA_1 the supplementary variable capital of sector I).

massively reinvested, neither the variable capital of sector I nor the constant capital of sector II increased rapidly. The forced rhythm of accumulation in sector I has not been the only cause, in terms of production and productivity, of the slowness of the progress of Soviet agriculture. The peasant resistance to collectivization has also been responsible. The Soviet case illustrates nonetheless the mechanism, imagined by certain Marxists, which has functioned only in a planned system: if one accelerates the rhythm of accumulation in sector I, the only way of avoiding a surplus of consumer goods is to slow down the rhythm of accumulation and of technological progress in sector II.

We are not concerned with discussing in detail the theoretical schemes of Rosa Luxembourg, which are mainly of historical interest. But it is evident that the increase of the capital intensity per worker—that is, the value of the machines with which the wage-earners work—could not be expressed, without excessive simplification, by the formula of the increase of C in relation to V. The fraction of the value of the constant capital transmitted to each piece of merchandise depends on the duration of the machine, the degree of amortization, the number of products manufactured with the same machine. The detours of production become increasingly long. The share of wages in the national income does not decrease nor does the relation of the value of capital to the annual value of production increase. In the last analysis, all the theories concerning the contradictions in the capitalist regime are based on the hypothesis that the real wages remain at the lowest level.

Hence I am tempted to believe that the best (or the better of two evils) way of transforming into an "economic theory of imperialism" the facts which J. A. Hobson described and which Lenin utilized is that of Mr. John Strachey, in his last book,[46] that is to say, to consider the export of capital and political-economic imperialism as one of the two ways out available to capitalism, while the other is the increase of the purchasing power of the masses by the raising of real wages.

J. A. Hobson described the imperialist movement of the last quarter of the nineteenth century and of the beginning of the twentieth as follows. Within nations, minorities are passionately interested in conquest. Members of the ruling class find, in remote possessions, glamorous and well-paid posts for their sons. Industrial or commercial enterprises accumulate excess profit. Capitalists invest their money around the world and gradually become *rentiers*, parasites of a national economy which, in its turn, becomes a parasite of world economy.

Historical study has not refuted this total view of a kind of symbiosis between *many* individual interests and the imperialist diplomacy of the European nations. It has led to a subtler and more complex interpretation, the initiative of loans of capital or of conquest having often been taken by politicians and not by businessmen, for diplomatic motives and not with a

[46] *The End of Empire*, London, 1959.

view to profits. But it has shown how arbitrary was the "theory" which Lenin attempted to derive from the facts collected by Hobson, a theory which is summed up in three propositions: the export of capital was inevitable, the seizure or creation of zones of influence necessary, and the peaceful division of the planet impossible.

Mr. John Strachey adopts the first proposition in order to save an essential element of the theory. He cites a passage from Lenin on imperialism:

> "It goes without saying that if capitalism could develop agriculture, which today lags far behind industry everywhere, if it could raise the standard of living of the masses, who are everywhere still poverty-stricken and underfed, in spite of the amazing advance in technical knowledge, there could be no talk of a superfluity of capital. This 'argument' the petit bourgeois critics of capitalism advance on every occasion. But if capitalism did these things it would not be capitalism; for uneven development and wretched conditions of the masses are the fundamental and inevitable conditions and premises of this mode of production. As long as capitalism remains what it is, surplus capital will never be used for the purpose of raising the standard of living of the masses, in a given country, for this would mean a decline in profits for the capitalists; it will be used for the purpose of increasing those profits by exporting capital abroad to the backward countries. In these backward countries, profits usually are high, for capital is scarce, the price of land is relatively low, raw materials are cheap. The possibility of exporting capital is created by the entry of numerous backward countries into international capitalist intercourse; main railways have either been built or are being built there; the elementary conditions for industrial developments have been created, etc. The necessity of exporting capital arises from the fact that in a few countries capitalism has become 'over-ripe' and (owing to the backward state of agriculture and the impoverished state of the masses) capital cannot find 'profitable investments.' "[47]

We know today that the capitalist regime—private ownership of the means of production and mechanisms of the market—can, without destroying itself, raise the standard of living of the masses. We even know that this elevation conforms to the properly interpreted interest of the propertied class. The debate henceforth focuses on two points: 1. Does ideal capitalism—as a type analyzed according to a pure model—tend to the accumulation of capital and to the misery of the masses, with only government action, favored by political democracy, reversing the action of spontaneous forces; or on the con-

[47] *Imperialism, The Final Stage of Capitalism,* Chapter IV, quoted in Strachey, *op. cit.,* pp. 110–11.

trary, is the true model that of a simultaneous growth of production, productivity and the level of the masses? 2. Has the immediate and necessary cause of the exports of capital and political-military imperialism at the end of the nineteenth century and the beginning of the twentieth been the distribution of income, the lack of profitable domestic investments?

The determination of a model for capitalism can never avoid some measure of the arbitrary. It is not impossible to construct a model which would involve a tendency to impoverishment. But, as a matter of fact, even omitting the foreseeable interventions of a democratic state, an economic regime such as that of the West at the end of the nineteenth century and the beginning of the twentieth may have stimulated an increased concentration of wealth; it did not bring about the aggravated poverty of the masses. We must assume an enormous industrial reserve army if the progress of productivity (or the reduction of the necessary labor time, in Marxist language) is not expressed by at least a constancy of real wages and generally by a rise in the latter.

It would certainly not be less erroneous to construct a model of market economy which would result in a balanced growth of all nations within the same system, and of all regions or all classes within a single nation. Depending on many circumstances, the cumulative process tends to reduce or enlarge the gaps between the economic collectivities. During the period which we are considering, did the inequality of income among classes *impose* upon European capitalism the export of capital and imperialism? Let us grant that it is difficult to answer categorically yes or no. It would be paradoxical to deny that there was a link between the social structure, the distribution of income and the surplus of capital. It would be risky to assert that these foreign investments were *indispensable* at the same time as being tempting (by reason of superior yield). The interrelation of political and economic motivations, as we have seen, prohibits a simple theory.

Further, even if we subscribe to the relationship of the poverty of the masses and the export of capital, the economic interpretation of imperialism is not thereby established.

The tremendous amount of capital invested by Europeans in the territories over which they did not exercise sovereignty, the insignificance of the sums invested precisely where they did exercise sovereignty, shows the relative independence of the two movements, one of capital, the other of soldiers. Setting aside France, whose conquests in North Africa were long, slow and costly, the European nations intervened in areas where possession did not require great efforts. The Europeans did not guarantee their most important investments by political sovereignty; they seized weak or anarchic nations, either to establish profitable conditions of trade with them, or to acquire strategic positions, or to round out and protect territories already annexed, or finally to serve their glory.

Shall we say, as Lenin occasionally suggests, that the variety of forms—zone of influence, protectorate, colony—in which the European domination

was exercised are of little consequence, that they are merely expressions of
the same profound fact, European domination? This answer is equivalent to
recognizing the distinction between the economic movement and the political
movement. This separation has never been so marked in the modern period
as at the end of the nineteenth century. The conquest of South America by
the Spanish, the exploitation of men and resources by the European masters
in permanent colonies are inseparable. The conquest of India starting from
the commercial activity of a British corporation constitutes another example
of this traditional transition from exploitation to the acquisition of sovereignty. It is at the end of the nineteenth century that, because capitalism
had become industrial at the same time as commercial, in one place the
Europeans chose to conquer without finding wealth on the spot, and in another to invest their capital without conquering.

Thereby, the third proposition—the impossibility of division—is shown for
what it is; purely arbitrary. The impossibility of peaceful division or of
equitable compromise is a vestige of the mercantilist doctrine. Were the great
corporations, the banks, the states animated by such a spirit of monopoly that
they considered war inevitable? Neither the facts nor reasoning afford any
basis to such a proposition. The Europeans had no difficulty finding use for
their capital around the world. At the beginning of the twentieth century,
world economy was in a phase of expansion and rising prices. Monopolistic
exclusion remained a relatively rare practice. The colonizers or moneylenders
were assured of advantages in competition; they did not deprive their rivals
of all opportunities.

Shall we say, with John Strachey, that the unequal development of the
metropolitan states was the insurmountable obstacle to peaceful division?
That the capitalistic nations have had unequal rates of demographic and
economic growth is incontestable, but the phenomenon does not date
from capitalism. The instability of international relations, for centuries and
millenniums, derives precisely from the fluctuation of the relative forces of
states. This fluctuation, for the last two centuries particularly, depends on
the number of men and factories as well as on the authority of the sovereigns.
The rate of development determines directly the configuration of the diplomatic system. At the beginning of the twentieth century the dimensions of
the various colonial empires were not proportional to the (economic or military) forces of the metropolitan states. If this was the cause of the War of
1914, as Lenin suggests, the explanation has nothing to do with Marxism-
Leninism: Germany would have been warlike out of resentment against her
rivals who enjoyed a richer place in the sun. For this interpretation by unequal development to constitute an *economic* theory of the fatal struggle for
the division of the world, the state disfavored in the distribution of colonies
would be obliged by economic necessity to attack its unjustly privileged
rivals. If monopoly—the exclusion of rivals by force—is indispensable to
capitalist economies, the nation whose development has been the swiftest,

Germany, should have been paralyzed by the weakness of its own monopolies or by the exclusion which the monopolies of the others inflicted upon it. Yet in 1913 we find nothing of the kind: Germany's development continued to be swifter than that of the other European nations; foreign trade, export of capital also progressed. Theoretical analysis as well as empirical study lead to a traditional conclusion: perhaps the peaceful division would have been impossible, but it is not modern capitalism, it is the age-old avarice which led to war. If statesmen and peoples had acted according to economic rationality, the War of 1914 would not have taken place. Neither monopolies nor dialectic had made *inevitable* what was irrational.

Modern industrial economy is the first which questions the economic utility of conquest. Slavery was rational, in the economic sense of the term, once the yield of servile labor left a surplus for the master, in other words, when the slave produced more than what he needed to survive. Conquest was rational only when the spoils were higher than the cost of the battle or of dominion. Empire was rational as long as commerce was in essence monopolistic, followed the flag or had as its objective the possession of precious metals, the stock of which was limited. This rationality, for an economy considered as a whole, is no longer evident once wealth depends on free labor, once exchange favors both parties to it, once producers and merchants both gain advantage in accepting competition.

Liberals and socialists are more or less aware of this original feature of the modern economy. But, observing the facts of imperialism, they emphasize other, no less real aspects, of that economy which render imperialism intelligible. An economy of exchanges, to the degree that it is at the same time industrial, is charged with a kind of dynamism. It tends to spread throughout the entire world and to include all of humanity. Marx had said it in the *Communist Manifesto* and he had seen clearly.

We shall not here discuss whether, by some mysterious malformation, a regime of private property is incapable of absorbing its own production. In any case, certain sectors of industry will occasionally be threatened with overproduction. Growth occurs, without a general plan, by a series of creative imbalances. How can we deny that dominion over foreign territories facilitates the sale of manufactured products which do not find buyers in the mother country?

Further, the European or world-wide economy did not conform to Bentham's ideal model. Trusts, cartels, maintenance of high domestic prices, dumping abroad—these practices of the commercial war, contrary to the essence of a free economy, had not disappeared. To these residues of the spirit of monopoly, liberal sociologists and economists imputed the imperialist enterprises of the capitalist and bourgeois nations, while the socialists tried to prove that this spirit of monopoly and conquest was inseparable from capitalism itself.

Both were wrong. Insofar as it was of economic origin and signification, *the imperialism of the end of the nineteenth century was not the last stage of capitalism but the last stage of mercantile imperialism, itself the last stage of millennial imperialism.* Hobson and Schumpeter[48] emphasized in fact the privileged minorities that tended toward imperialism, contrary to the spirit of industry and commerce. But they forgot that men and, still more, states have always desired dominion for its own sake.

It is not enough that empire be economically sterile for the people or for those who speak in their names to renounce the glory of dominion.

5. Capitalism and Socialism

Every modern economy gives states an unprecedented capacity to act abroad, since it enlarges the gap between the minimum indispensable to the life of the population and the available goods. The greater this gap, the higher the maximum degree of state mobilization of collective resources. War is evidently not the only possible use abroad of the resources mobilized: aid is another, but war has been the most frequent. That the capacity for production creates a surplus which men can consume by killing each other is true for any economy of our period, whatever the regime. Stripped of the passions and confusions perpetuated by a century of propaganda and ideological disputes, the question of the influence on the possibility of peace and the risk of war exerted by the choice between a capitalist regime (private ownership and market mechanisms) and a socialist regime (public ownership and planning) leads in the abstract to simple terms: What stakes, occasions, causes of conflicts, inseparable from capitalism, would the socialist regime suppress? What stakes, occasions, or causes would it create? By definition, competition for the investment of capital, the intervention of states in order to protect the interests of their nationals, threatened by expropriation laws, would be eliminated. Similarly, there would be no further private interests to exert pressures on the leaders with a view to obtaining higher tariff rates (which competitors regard as illegitimate or aggressive) or other privileges contrary to the rules of honest competition. Nonetheless, all occasions for conflicts between states in a socialist economy would not thereby disappear.

The conditions of international exchanges, in a world market regime with

---

[48] J. A. Hobson, *Imperialism*, London, 1902, and Joseph Schumpeter, *op. cit.*
Schumpeter's error seems to me to be explained by the confusion between the modern case and the ancient cases. Schumpeter, as we know, explained the imperialism of the Arabs, to take one example, by the persistence, in new conditions, of a traditional way of life. The Arab horsemen continued to conquer because in the desert war was the constant, normal activity adapted to circumstances. But modern societies are differentiated and are not defined by labor as the life of the Arab tribes was defined by horseback raids. The capitalists or the bourgeois do not devote themselves to business as the Arab horsemen devoted themselves to war. According to economic calculations, the bourgeois should be peaceful and anti-imperialist. But they do not apply economic calculations to their entire existence.

relatively free prices, appear often inequitable to one or the other of the parties to the exchange, as a result of the inequality of economic and political weight. The small country which owes almost all its foreign currency to the sale of *one* raw material is often subject to the dictates of the buyer and above all of the chief buyer. In spite of everything, the mechanisms of the market, even international, even imperfect, limit the influence of military force on commercial transactions. The day when these transactions become negotiations between governments, everything depends on men and on regimes. The increasing state control of international commerce enormously increases the possibilities of the exploitation of the weak by the strong. The Russian practices in Stalin's time, the price at which the Poles *had* to sell their coal, illustrate one of the intrinsic risks of this kind of socialism as long as multiple sovereignties subsist.

A regime of private property, as long as it is authentically liberal and as long as states, even hostile ones, respect it, has the advantage of reducing the profits of a military victory. The benefits afforded by rearrangements of borders are limited, once individuals preserve their possessions and their professions. When the Saar was included within the French economic union, the goods the French obtained from it were paid for by those they sent to it. The goods which they no longer sell in the German Saar, they perhaps sell elsewhere just as profitably.

Socialism does not favor the same separation of property and sovereignty. Domestic enterprises and persons are subject to the plan and the will of the state, but foreign buyers and sellers act according to their interest or their preferences. The tracing of borders therefore has a vital importance. Planners do not like to depend on decisions beyond their control and imperfectly predictable. Annexation eliminates unforeseeability, it offers the possibility of putting nationals in positions of command, of transferring to the conquering state the ownership of property taken from citizens of the conquered state. In theory a planned economy reinforces the motives for desiring the enlargement of the space of sovereignty.

Veblen considered that the modern system of production was, in itself, peaceful, that on the other hand the entrepreneurs, industrialists, merchants and corporations animated by the desire for profit were creators of conflicts and responsible for wars. He forgot that the system of production, of itself, determines neither what goods will be produced nor how the collective resources will be distributed among the various uses, nor incomes among classes. These chiefly economic determinations can result either from the mechanisms of the market (more or less controlled or oriented by the state), or from a plan more or less thwarted by the weight of the material aspects of society.

If we adopt the first solution, the stimulus to expansion or to protection comes from ambitious or threatened "private interests." Some of these, in case of failure on the commercial terrain, mobilize public opinion or the state against their competitors. Even if the players accept all the rules of the game, the defeat which involves loss of jobs for workers or of income for capitalists provokes bitterness and resentment, which eventually influence those responsible for diplomatic behavior. Such a regime is all the less dangerous to interstate relations in that the leaders are more likely to act according to long-term considerations and not to confuse with a permanent impoverishment the transitory sacrifices which the commercial struggle inevitably imposes from time to time.

If the second solution is adopted, the chief variable consists of the *political* regime and men. Rates of growth, the share of investments in the national product are by definition the object of decisions taken by the planners, that is, by the leaders of the state. It is to be feared that states, if they consider themselves engaged in a rivalry for power, will extend the traditional competition of military force to the economic sphere. But if all humanity had converted to a socialist regime, we might conceive a planned economy with an eye to welfare and the slowing down of the race for growth.

No regime, then, whether capitalist or socialist, makes war inevitable; none suppresses all occasions for it. It is even difficult to specify, in the abstract, which of these two regimes is more favorable or more contrary to pacification. What is not doubtful is that the conflict of regimes, within an international system, multiplies the causes and amplifies the stakes of conflicts. The Soviet Union has no need to conquer new territories in order to improve the conditions of the life of its people. The Soviet citizens would accommodate themselves easily to the survival of capitalism in other parts of the world: the so-called Marxist-Leninist regime based on the absolute power of a single party and on a state doctrine is nonetheless dedicated to expansion by a necessity which is not economic but political and ideological. It is a necessity in part imputable to circumstances: revolutionaries and rebels the world over experience the attraction of the Soviet technique and model. But this necessity also derives from the way of life and style of thought of the Bolshevik leaders: the political struggle is, in essence, continuous, permanent, and since international relations are conceived in imitation of the struggle between parties, they are also regarded as belligerent until the universal diffusion of redeeming truth.

Every great ideocratic power, whatever its economic regime, is *imperialistic* if the effort to spread an idea and to impose a mode of government abroad, even by force, is specifically considered. In any case, such an effort appears imperialistic to those states that wish to safeguard their own institutions, even when the ideocratic power normally prefers subversion to invasion and refrains from annexing the peoples which it converts to its faith. Crusaders have never been regarded as messengers of peace. It is in our age that they have drawn a dove on their blazon.

chapter X

Nations and Regimes

In the preceding chapters we have analyzed the determinants which directly influence the strength of political units that constitute the elements of the situation, as it is analyzed by the actors. Space, resources and number are possible stakes of the conflict, objectives of those who direct the political units. They may also be the unrecognized causes of collective behavior. The relations of space, number and resources define, in each period, the optimum of well-being or of power; they may govern, in certain circumstances, the warlike impulse of peoples; they provide more or less sincere justifications for the conquerors.

In the next three chapters we shall no longer consider the determinants of the situation, but the actors' styles of being and behaving, that is, the styles of the subjects of diplomatic history which we have called political units. Thus, we shall encounter a second type of explanation of wars. Instead of invoking the inexorable determinism of need, the eternal hunger for gold or wealth, we shall be discussing the arraignment of "eternal Germany," of "the despotic, Communist or democratic regime,"[1] the hypothesis of a fatal development of civilizations or the theory of human nature, the origin and outcome of history. In this chapter we shall proceed from political regimes (Section 1) to national constants (Section 2) to return, by the intermediary of the nation considered as a historical type of political unit (Section 3), and of the diversity of military organizations (Section 4), to the present situation, characterized by the extreme heterogeneity of both states and modes of combat.

1. *On Political Regimes*

I shall take, for my point of departure, the questions which the commenta-

---

[1] In the chapter on Resources, we have already observed a problem of this type apropos of the Marxist-Leninist theory of imperialism.

tors on foreign policy have continually raised since 1945: Is the foreign policy of the Soviet Union Russian or Communist? Is it or is it not influenced by the ideology which the revolutionary state claims as its inspiration? In abstract terms the question is as follows: In a given period, is the behavior of the actors a function (and to what degree) of the political regime?

The political regimes of a given period, which preside over the organization of a certain type of society, inevitably present common characteristics. But they differ at least by the mode of designation of those who wield the sovereign authority, by the manner in which these latter make their decisions, hence by the relations which are established between individuals, public opinion and social groups on the one hand, and those who govern on the other. The same men do not reach power in all regimes, they do not act under the same conditions or under the same pressures. To postulate that the same men in different circumstances or different men in the same circumstances make equivalent decisions leads to a strange philosophy, implies one or the other of the two following theories: either diplomacy is rigorously *determined* by impersonal causes, the individual actors occupying the center of the stage but playing roles learned by heart, or else the conduct of the political units is controlled by a "national interest" capable of a rational definition, vicissitudes of internal struggles and changes of regimes not modifying (nor should they modify) this definition. Each of these philosophies, it seems to me, can be refuted by the facts.

Did Stalin have the same vision of the historical world as Nicholas II? Would the latter's successor have had the same vision as the militant Bolshevik who emerged victorious from the struggle among the diadochi? Did Hitler have the same vision of the future of Germany as Stresemann or Brüning? Would the leader of a democratic party or a Hohenzollern have hurled Germany against the Western democracies and the Soviet Union in the style adopted by the Führer of the Third Reich?

Rhetorical questions, the reader will object. It is obvious that the answer is negative: Hitler's strategy and tactics were quite different from those of Stresemann or of a possible descendant of the King of Prussia. By strategy I mean both the long-term objectives and the representation of the historical universe which makes their choice intelligible; by tactics I mean the day-to-day reactions, the combination of means with a view to previously fixed ends. To claim that the strategy and tactics of a (national or imperial) political unit remain constant whatever the regime is quite simply absurd. In this sense the proposition: the diplomacy of the Soviet Union is Communist and not Russian, cannot be contested. The burden of proof lies, in any case, upon those who seek to deny it.

Beyond this evidence stands the real problem. To what degree do foreign policies change with regimes? Let us note immediately: this is not a question of theory but of fact. The answer may vary according to periods and circumstances. In our era, changes in regimes have involved diplomatic upheavals. The external action of states has not been less influenced by ideologies than the organization of societies.

Let us take the two examples of the Third Reich and the Soviet Union. Hitler's undertaking was inspired by a philosophy in which were mingled theories of various origins: the racist theory of Gobineau or of Houston Chamberlain, the geopolitical theories of Mackinder and of Haushofer, contempt for the Slavs considered as *Untermenschen,* hatred of the Jews—an accursed race to be eliminated like harmful vermin, the need for population space in the direction of Eastern Europe, the detestation of Christianity—that Semitic religion of the weak, etc. . . . . In 1930 none of the politicians of the Weimar Republic would have admitted the possibility of such an enterprise as that which Hitler, quite lucidly, inaugurated in 1933: rearmament, annexation of Austria, liquidation of Czechoslovakia, defeat of France, aggression against the Soviet Union, etc.[2] Certain of these objectives were common to Hitler and to the German conservatives (enlargement of space), others were common to the majority of German public opinion (equality of rights, rearmament, Anschluss). Neither those who were nostalgic for imperial Germany nor the parties of the Weimar Republic nourished such vast ambitions, inspired by such a conception of the world.

The tactics were perhaps more specifically Hitlerian than the strategy. They differed profoundly from traditional or democratic tactics because they applied, on the international scene, the methods tested in the course of domestic and internal struggles. The grand strategy, to adopt the expression fashionable some twenty years ago, involved the constant use of propaganda, that completed and renovated the classic methods of diplomacy. "Defiance" was, during that first period, the instrument of success. In peacetime, instead of yielding to the will of the stronger, according to the polite practices of the chancelleries, Hitler acted as though he were the master, defying his adversaries to use force, to constrain him.

The very act in which superficial observers see the proof that Stalinist or Hitlerian diplomacy was not ideological, the Russo-German Pact of 1939, is, correctly interpreted, the proof if not of the contrary, at least of the influence which regimes exert, in our period, upon the course of events. As a matter of fact, a regime analogous to that of the Weimar Republic, or else a regime derived from Tsarism as it existed in 1900, could not have reversed its propaganda from one day to the next. The Weimar Republic, it is true, had signed the Treaty of Rapallo, and the Reichswehr had undertaken arms tests with the cooperation of the Red army. The kings and emperors had once given the example of the partition of Poland. But, in the twentieth century, the diplomacy of every non-revolutionary regime has lost the capacity for such

[2] I am not asserting that in 1933 Hitler knew the successive stages of his undertaking. But he knew the point at which he wished to emerge: victory over the Soviet Union, enlargement of the Germans' space.

cynicism as that evidenced by Stalin and Hitler in 1939. Obliged to persuade public opinion, to present the allies as good and the enemies as wicked, the diplomacy of the European states, whether conservative or parliamentarian, is modest in its remote objectives, with a limited margin of maneuver at any given moment. Only the regime whose leaders have a short-range but virtually complete liberty with regard to public opinion can, from one moment to the next, burn what they once adored, adore what they once burned, without the people being profoundly disturbed, some believing in no propaganda, others believing in the truth of each moment, still others ready to trust the necessary cunning of their masters.

Following this line of reasoning, we might formulate the following proposition: diplomatic tactics are more flexible as regimes are more authoritarian, that is, the leaders less subject to the pressures of groups or of public opinion; further, the objectives of diplomacies vary with regimes and are more rigorously determined as the regime is more ideological. These two propositions are likely enough but not particularly instructive, and they require several corrections. To say that tactical flexibility is proportional to the leaders' freedom of action is more of a platitude than a law. Moreover, if the leaders sincerely believe in progress, a specific advance in the state's future history, they cannot fail to relate their plans to this prophetic vision. This does not mean that individual decisions are never affected by ideology or that strategy remains rigid in all cases.

Let us take the example of the Soviet conduct of diplomacy. On the whole it is effectively flexible in its tactics and constant in its objectives and its representation of the world. The commentators incline to deny the action of ideology and have an easy time showing that most Soviet decisions can be interpreted in so-called rational terms, that is, in terms of the calculation of forces. The pact with the Third Reich shifted the war toward the West, which was in accord with the national interest of Russia, regardless of regime. Moscow's domination of the Eastern European nations created a protective *glacis* at the same time that it corresponded to a traditional ambition of pan-Slavism. The conflict with the United States conforms to all the precedents, being implied, so to speak, by the geometry of the relations of forces: the two great powers of a bipolar system are enemies by position. This mode of comprehension is not false, but it is partial and may lead to erroneous conclusions.

The contrast between the rigidity of strategy and the flexibility of tactics does not derive exclusively from the ideological character of the former and the non-ideological character of the latter. The ideology of the Soviet state is such that it tolerates, if it does not impel, tactical flexibility. The Marxist-Leninist vision of history is essentially a succession of regimes, socialism following capitalism, socialism being defined as the government of the Communist party identified with the proletariat. But the degree of the development of productive forces does not fix the order in which the different nations achieve socialism. This process may be internal or external, caused by crisis or war, *coup d'état* or intervention of the Red army. Finally, once the first so-called socialist state has been constituted, wars may either set the capitalist states against each other because they are doomed to imperialism, or may set the socialist camp against the capitalist camp because the former's victory is ultimately inevitable.

Whatever the course of events, an explanation or rather a theoretical formulation is possible. Do the United States and Great Britain have a dispute? Nothing is more logical, since the two economies are rivals. Do the Anglo-American powers conclude an alliance? Of course, the contradiction is expressed in an intimate cooperation. Does the Soviet Union sign an expediential pact with the Third Reich? The spokesmen celebrate the meeting of two revolutions. Does the same Soviet Union find itself, by the force of circumstances, associated with the Western democracies? Bolshevism again becomes the brother of social democracy within the great family of the Left. Turn and turn about, wars between imperialist nations, then wars between socialist and capitalist nations will be more likely.

Even the final goal is equivocal. Hitler's strategic goal—a German Empire within an enlarged space—was concretely defined. The strategic goal of the Soviet Union is not defined to the same degree. Is it the universal diffusion of a regime which the leaders in Moscow would agree to call socialist (a single party identified with the proletariat, etc.)? Is it a world empire of the Soviet Union or of the (Bolshevik) Communist party of the U.S.S.R.? The two formulas are equivalent only provided the unity of the socialist camp is maintained outside the struggle with capitalism. Finally, war itself is no longer the inevitable stage before the universal victory of socialism.

Must we agree with those who deny the influence of ideology and impute to institutions alone (to the modes of decisions) the difference in policy according to regime? Even in the case of the Soviet Union this conclusion would be erroneous. The Bolshevik vision of the world did not permit the Soviet leaders during the Second World War to believe in the duration or the authenticity of the alliance with the Western democracies. The awareness of hostility at the very moment of cooperation was dictated by doctrine. The Russo-American rivalry was established within the geometry of the relation of forces: the emotional hostility has been amplified if not created by ideological opposition. But further: doctrinal considerations have, on two occasions, modified the calculation of forces and the determination of national interest.

One policy, called realist, attempts to reduce the resources of its enemies, whether actual or potential; to increase that of its allies and to win to its cause those states that are not committed. Stalin treated Yugoslavia as an enemy the day the latter refused to obey Moscow's directives; can we conceive of the Russo-Yugoslav dispute if the two states did not claim one and the same ideology? Why did Mr. Khrushchev for so many years refuse to show any fear of China, and why did he favor Chinese industrialization when the

West unceasingly pointed out the danger of the "countless and impoverished"[3] yellow masses? According to Marxist philosophy, one socialist state does not endanger another. This philosophy, it is true, has not offered much resistance to experience, and from now on the two metropolitan nations of communism will be rivals, each proclaiming a different interpretation of the same gospel. The conflict, of course, results from opposing national interests, incompatible aspirations to the leadership of the bloc, but it has also been influenced by the faithful adherence of the two states to the same ideology. The Soviet Union and the People's Republic of China would neither have become allies nor have quarreled as they have, without their common adherence to Marxism-Leninism. How could the calculation of national interest help but change with regimes, since each of these, as a result of its own doctrine, gauges affinities and hostilities differently?

As a matter of fact, the Soviet Union seems to me to have behaved with Hitler, with its war allies, with its satellites, with the United States, and today with the United States and China in the manner which only a way of thinking linked to an ideological structure renders intelligible.[4]

Is it possible to formulate some general propositions as to the scope of the changes in diplomacy caused by the substitution of one regime for another? At first glance one is inclined to suppose that a revolution has great diplomatic consequences, insofar as they interest the actors who play the principal roles. In fact, all conduct of foreign policy involves, of necessity, a share of adaptation to circumstances. The share of adaptation is greater, the share of initiative smaller, when the actor plays a smaller role, in other words, has fewer forces at his disposal.

However, this proposition requires modifications. A second-class state, by definition, does not determine major events, the style of diplomatic rivalry. It was Hitler's success, not Mussolini's, which changed the course of European history. But, within a heterogeneous system, the vicissitudes of partisan conflicts within states may cause a shift from one camp to another, or from commitment to neutrality. The "national interest" of small states, far from being alien to ideological considerations, is, in a heterogeneous system, inseparable from such considerations. In 1960 no one could define France's national interest without taking into account the choice between regimes imposed by circumstances.

For the theory of the insignificance of regimes to assume some likelihood, we must imagine a diplomatic system in a space that has been demarked for centuries, a relatively homogeneous system, all the actors following more or less the same unwritten rules of diplomacy and strategy. The geographical constancy of the diplomatic field indicates the lines of expansion of the var-

---

[3] The expression, it will be remembered, was coined by General de Gaulle.
[4] Even in matters of tactics it is not impossible to observe particularities and constants which characterize the Moscow leaders. Cf. N. Leites, *The Operational Code of the Politburo,* New York, 1951.

ious states. At the end of the nineteenth century, when the world's great powers were identified with the European states and the latter, whether republican or Tsarist, formed their alliances according to the moderate Machiavellianism of cabinets, the indifference of chancelleries to ideas and to regimes was considered an ideal, approximately realized with the advances of civilization. It requires a strange blindness in order to transform the model of the diplomacy of one epoch into an eternal model.

2. *The National Constants*

Beyond these observations, on which it would be virtually unnecessary to insist if some authors did not persist in denying them, an authentic question remains, namely, that of *national constants*. Does the "national interest" of a collectivity remain fundamentally the same throughout history?

We have, in an earlier chapter, shown why the "national interest" cannot be the object of a rational determination. If the economist unhesitatingly takes as his objective a certain maximum (of goods, of the national product or profit), it is because economy is a science of means. The economist does not tell men or collectivities what to do with their goods (and the latter are defined in relation to demand). If the sociologist were capable of defining the national interest, he would be in a position to dictate to statesmen, in the name of science, their conduct. Such is not the case. The "maximization" of forces is not obviously imperative, since it implies putting at the state's disposal the largest possible fraction of the collectivity's resources. Why should men be a means to the state's greatness and not conversely? Nor is the "maximization" of power any more obviously imperative, for human quality is not proportional to the capacity of an individual or collectivity to constrain others. In short, the plurality of goals at which a political unit may aim, the essential duality of power in relation to the outside world and the common good (cohesion of the city-state or morality of the citizens) make the national interest an object of study, not a criterion of action.

Without denying this argument, we may ask if these uncertainties are not more theoretical than practical. Strictly speaking, there is no "collective interest" scientifically defined: as a matter of fact, do not the economists more or less agree on the nature of collective interest, even if they do not always agree on the means of attaining it? Similiarly, is not the "national interest" readily understandable in practice, once one abides by the realistic calculations of the diplomats and the strategists? I believe this objection is radically false: the indeterminacy is practical as well as theoretical.

On the economic level the consideration of time adds a further uncertainty to those involved in the shift from an individual to a collective interest. It is no longer so much a question of knowing whether or not the enrichment of some is paid for by the sacrifice of others. Growth, although it involves for certain groups or individuals an impoverishment that is at least temporary, tends, on the whole, toward the amelioration of the lot of all, even toward the diminishing of inequalities. But, if we introduce the consideration of time, the prince and his advisers must, at every moment, establish a balance between the present demands of consumption and the requirements of accumulation. There is no reason why future generations must be preferred to present ones, or conversely. There is no optimum rate of growth as such. The opposition between Soviet economies and Western economies, the controversies within the Western world as to the comparative rates of growth prove that this ambiguity of the collective interest has a political and historical bearing.

If, instead of considering a collectivity as a whole, we concern ourselves with the condition of one group within a political unit, we discover, even on a strictly economic level, another source of uncertainty. Economically, the class hypothetically considered as a cohesive group is concerned about receiving the largest possible share of the national income. But might it not receive, under another regime, a still larger share? Should the interest of a non-privileged class be defined within the framework of the existing regime or by reference to another regime? The alternatives of reform and revolution stand as examples to all those who wish to modify the existing order. No choice is ever gratuitous. In making revolution its goal, the class more often than not loses advantages which would be accessible to it if it accepted the established regime for a frame of action.

These economic uncertainties have an equivalent on the political level. State mobilization of an important fraction of resources (generally) diminishes the sum of resources invested, that is, resources devoted to the increase of the national product. The present mobilization of forces restrains the growth of potential forces. The cost of a great peacetime army, if it is not compensated by the acquisition of territories and resources, is comparable to consumption: it amounts to a deduction from the accumulated income. Armament or investment are forms of the alternative of consumption by present generations: or, investment for the good of future generations.

The increase of forces, by internal development or by conquest, is comparable to the enrichment of one class within the collectivity. It cannot be carried beyond a certain point without provoking reactions which annul it (at least in the framework of a diplomatic system). The other units regard themselves as threatened and try to balance by coalition the disparity of forces created by the disproportionate growth of any one of them. Perhaps there exists an optimum point for a particular collectivity, the point where it possesses the maximum of forces compatible with the tolerance of its rivals. Even if this point exists in theory, statesmen are not rationally obliged to make it their objective: why should they not prefer greatness with its perils to security, if the latter is accompanied by mediocrity?

As the non-privileged class puts its hopes in revolution rather than in accommodation to the fate assigned to it in the established regime, a state accepts in advance the hostility of its rivals which its successes will bring into being. It assigns itself another system as its goal, or a figuration radically different from the present relation of forces. The unification of Germany, the absorption of Austria and the Sudetenland by the unified Reich could not fail to provoke a *rapprochement* of the Russians and the Anglo-American powers: yet was it to Germany's national interest (which Germany, one might ask) to renounce these enormous projects?

Lastly, a collectivity's maximization of forces or of power would still not be a rational imperative for all individuals belonging to that collectivity, even if no unfavorable reaction resulted from this maximization. Were the Germans who hoped for the collapse of the Third Reich insane? These so-called obvious truths, namely, that every patriot must desire for his country the largest area, the most favorable frontiers, and the greatest relative power, have rarely been experienced down through the centuries. Catholics and Protestants have set their Church above their sovereign. *Émigrés* fought with a clear conscience against the armies of the French Revolution. The Third Reich recruited combatants who were authentic volunteers against communism—less numerous, it is true, than the militants who work the world over for the Revolution as incarnated by the Soviet Union.

Why have these uncontested facts often been unrecognized? Why does the primacy of nations over regimes pass for a profound view of historical philosophy when it reappears under the pen of historians (Treitschke), commentators (Walter Lippmann) or statesmen (Charles de Gaulle)? Let us first recall the phenomena that we have noted on several occasions.

A position on the map imposes upon the diplomacy or upon the strategy of a state certain orientations which are likely to be lasting, if not permanent. The more this position is defined in physical terms, the more durable the orientation. The more stable the diplomatic system, the less a change of regime will modify these orientations. Great Britain, to the degree that she exploited her island situation to prevent any hegemony on the Continent and to construct a commercial overseas empire, has given observers and rivals, especially after the event, the notion that she was acting in accord with an immutable doctrine that would not be affected by any vicissitude or internal struggle. Russia must have been tempted by expansion toward the open sea, Germany, without physical frontiers, by expansion alternately to the east, the west, or the south. Yet we may recall that the Soviet Union has never showed Istanbul the interest that the Russian of the Tsars, the heir of Byzantium, paid to Constantinople. Depending on regimes, states do not evaluate the importance of a city or a province in the same way. Depending on military technique, strategic values vary. Finally, it is the relation of forces, not of areas, which dominates realistic calculations. A constant in national policies derives from the constant afforded by the spatial configuration of the relation of forces and the objectives of a political unit. This constant remains immobile within such a configuration.

This constant can nonetheless be variously interpreted. Are not the French still Frenchmen, whether they are Crusaders, Royalist soldiers or *sans-cu-lottes*? Are not the Germans still the same, whether they are the Germanii of Tacitus or Hitler's National Socialists? The national stereotypes, under the form they assume in wartime, do not deserve to be subjected to a scientific analysis. But one question should be asked: To what degree do the particularities of national character determine the diplomatic or strategic conduct of a state? To what degree does the constant nature of this conduct favor the hypothesis of the permanence of the national character?

There is no question of developing here a critical study of the concept of national character. We shall limit ourselves to a few remarks necessary to our problem alone, namely the possible influence of "national character" on diplomatic-strategic conduct.

The concept of character is psychological, not biological. It applies to a mode of reaction, regardless of the innate and the acquired. We call character the manner in which an individual experiences and manifests sentiments, desires, passions. One individual is quick to grow angry, another always calm, one is happy in solitude, another loathes it, one is unsatisfied, always seeking amusement or advancement, another is content with the life circumstances afford him. Character is situated between temperament—the expression of physical and physiological constants—and personality, in part a voluntary construction from a combination of temperament and long experience.

Psychoanalysts regard character—the never-definitive crystallization of an individual mode of reaction—as the joint result of an inherited nature and the first years of existence. Some psychologists reduce the share of heredity, others, the responsiblity of the first years. At the extreme limit those who deny the weight of nature and posit absolute freedom interpret character as the excuse for resignation or of cowardice: this man justifies his negligences by invoking his absent-mindedness, his infidelities by invoking his need for change. Even in this case, character does not altogether vanish: it remains the law of behavior, visible to others, which each of us freely creates by his own choices, constantly renewed.

If we wish to apply this same concept to a collectivity, an immediate ambiguity appears. Is the character of a nation a function of the number of individuals which, within a collectivity, have the same character? Or is it located above individual psychology, on the level of what anthropologists call culture? Each collectivity has a strict hierarchy of values, one or several representations of exemplary life. Each collectivity raises its children in its own manner, teaches them how to behave, within the family, at school, in public. The proprieties change from nation to nation. They change within the same nation from century to century. The expression of eternal desires, love, ambition is marked by culture. Whether the number of choleric or ambitious citizens is constant or varies according to races or peoples, men manifest their wrath or their ambition differently, do not attach the same price to peace or competition, are sensitive or indifferent to the pride of ruling.

Diplomatic-strategic conduct belongs to the area of reactions which can be determined by the psycho-cultural heritage of a human group. A Montesquieu and a Tocqueville, in ordinary language, without the use of so-called scientific methods, seem to me to have offered valid examples of "impressionist" interpretations of national character and of diplomacy by national character.

The "spirit of a nation" which Montesquieu speaks of is a notion as equivocal as that of national character, but is perhaps preferable because it emphasizes the share of culture and the historical heritage. "Mankind is influenced by various causes: by the climate, by the religion, by the laws, by the maxims of government, by precedence, morals, and customs: whence is formed a general spirit of nations."[5] The French nation was not born as it is now, it has become what it is as a result of the events which it has lived through, of the customs which have been slowly established and of the mode of government. A result more than an origin, the spirit of a nation renders a destiny intelligible as a particular act, but it must not constrain investigation; it helps understanding, but it must be explained. When Montesquieu attributes to the national idiosyncrasy a typical diplomacy: "supremely jealous with respect to trade, England binds itself but little by treaties and depends only on her own laws. Other nations have made the interests of commerce yield to those of politics; the English, on the contrary, have ever made their own political interests give way to those of commerce,"[6] character, in the psychological sense of the term, is scarcely involved. Rather it is a question of a habit or custom which geographical position and the experience of centuries have slowly transformed into a second nature.

The portrait of the French nation which figures at the end of Tocqueville's *L'Ancien régime et la Révolution* is a virtuoso passage, but it seems to me to illustrate a typical interpretation of national consistency which is legitimate: "When I observe France from this angle, I find the nation itself far more remarkable than any advance in its long history. It hardly seems possible that there can ever have existed any other people so full of contrasts and so extreme in all their doings, so much guided by their emotions and so little by fixed principles, always behaving better or worse, than one expected of them. At one time they rank above, at another below, the norm of humanity; their base characteristics are so constant that we can recognize the France we know in portraits made of it two or three thousand years ago, and yet so changeful are its moods, so variable its tastes that the nation itself is often quite as much startled as any foreigner by things it did only a few years before. Ordinarily the French are the most routinebound of men, but once

[5] *L'Esprit des lois*, XIX, 4.
[6] *Ibid.*, XX, 7.

they are forced out of the rut and leave their homes, they travel to the ends of the earth and engage in the most reckless ventures. Undisciplined by temperament the Frenchman is always readier to put up with the arbitrary rule, however harsh, of an autocrat than with a free, well-ordered government by his fellow citizens, however worthy of respect they be. At one moment he is up in arms against authority and the next we find him serving the powers-that-be with a zeal such as the most servile races never diplay. So long as no one thinks of resisting, you can lead him on a thread, but once a revolutionary movement is afoot, nothing can restrain him from taking part in it. That is why our rulers are so often taken by surprise; they fear the nation either too much or not enough, for though it is never so free that the possibility of inflaming it is ruled out, its spirit can never be broken so completely as to prevent its shaking off the yoke of an oppressive government. The Frenchman can turn his hand to anything, but he excels in war alone and he prefers fighting against odds, preferring dazzling feats of arms and spectacular successes to achievements of the more solid kind. He is more prone to heroism than to humdrum virtue, apter for genius than for good sense, more inclined to think up grandiose schemes than to carry through great enterprises. Thus the French are at once the most brilliant and the most dangerous of all European nations, and the best qualified to become, in the eyes of other peoples, an object of admiration, of hatred, of compassion, or alarm— never of indifference."[7]

The various propositions relative to the political behavior of the French are not all on the same level of generality. The mixture or alternation of discipline and submission is a characteristic probably more lasting than the preference for Caesarism and the lack of inclination for a "free, well-ordered government by fellow citizens." In any case, the sum total of these characteristics permits a formulation of many an episode in French history, it explains no one episode in particular. Where foreign policy is concerned, Tocqueville emphasizes two tendencies: he prefers fighting against odds, preferring dazzling feats of arms and spectacular successes to achievements of the more solid kind. He is . . . more inclined to think of grandiose schemes than to carry through great enterprises." These propositions are tantamount to attributing actual conduct and events to "tendencies." They reveal what we might call a style of behavior, constant through sudden reversals and the transformations of techniques and beliefs.

A relative consistency in the "style" of foreign policy seems to me to be in fact recognizable. But this style is, depending on the case, related either to rational calculation or to psycho-social tendencies or to the cultural system. The influence of economic considerations on Great Britain's foreign policy is the crystallization of a necessity into a habit. The French ambition for

[7] Alexis de Tocqueville, *The Old Regime and the French Revolution*, Gilbert translation, Doubleday Anchor Books, pp. 210–11.

glory derives from the imprint left on the system of values by the aristocratic heritage, and from the transfer to the collectivity of *amour-propre*, maintained in each man by the spirit of competition cultivated from school days. The diplomacy of the United States, sometimes legalist, sometimes radical to the point of requiring unconditional capitulation, can be explained both by the national past—the refusal of the civilized Machiavellianism of European diplomacy—and by a combination of brutality and repression.

These examples have only an illustrative value. Each is susceptible to long commentary. None of the preceding propositions lays claim to a demonstrated truth. We merely wish to indicate the kind of intelligibility afforded by the reference to national character, the nature of the national constants which we are entitled to assume. We shall sum up our conclusions in the following terms.

Whatever the constants attributed to the French, to the Germans, to the Spanish or to the English as peoples, a psycho-cultural characteristic is never solely responsible for the diplomatic-strategic behavior of a political unit. This behavior is too instrumental; it involves an element of calculation too important for the same "character" or the same "spirit" to be expressed by the same behavior when the data have been transformed. If we observe diplomatic constants, we find they relate to the permanence of the geographical-technological or political circumstances as much as or more than to the immutability of national character. When these circumstances change, it is not the conduct which remains identical, it is, strictly speaking, the style.

Now, in style, we do not include either aggressiveness or pacificism or inhumanity. The national stereotypes have followed the fluctuations of political fortunes. When a state played the role of "disturber," it was said, among its neighbors and in international opinion, to be imperialist by nature. At the time of the Terror, the cruelty of the French was denounced all over Europe. No people has a monopoly of horrors, although the execution of six million Jews constitutes a unique case to this day: as a result of the technological rationalizing of massacres, an ancestral practice finds its issue in the organization of genocide.

Perhaps the culture of *The Chrysanthemum and the Sword*[8] disposes the Japanese nation to seek pre-eminent rank. Such an effort may lead it to isolation under the Tokugawas, to imperialism during the first half of the twentieth century, or in fact to the pacifism which has flourished since 1945. Perhaps France's educational institutions incline the French to the love of glory. This love can be satisfied in other ways than by battles or by the enlargement of geographical zones under the tricolor. The Russians are not committed to an aggressive diplomacy as long as the movements of babies are paralyzed by swaddling-clothes. Its "basic personality" does not permit us to foresee the conduct of a state any more than the "spirit of a nation."

[8] Title of the famous book on Japan by Ruth Benedict (Boston, 1946).

3. *Nations and Nationalisms*

The confusion between method and content, between the permanence of the calculation of forces and the psuedo-constant of objectives and methods is maintained by a philosophy that was explicit at the end of the last century and still influential today, even if it is no longer clearly formulated. According to this philosophy, the nation is the chief actor on the stage of history, in a sense the only authentic one, the one in any case that marks the fulfillment of the work of centuries. "Nazism will pass, the German people will remain' —a formula which seems obvious until the moment it is applied to the neigh boring state. Must we say "Communism will pass, the Russian people will remain or the Russian Empire will remain?" What are the basic characteristics of that people which last while regimes pass? We have hitherto distinguished between political unit and regime, but, taking contemporary examples, we were implicitly assuming the same type of political unit, as Aristotle studied the influence of regimes by taking the Greek city-state as the type of political unit. We must now question the influence of the *types of political unit* as well as the influence of *regimes;* in other words, we must analyze the relation between these two concepts.

The primary phenomenon from which is derived the distinction of internal policy and foreign policy is the plurality of social orders, each being imposed on all the members of *one* collectivity. The obligatory character of the norms which control collective existence, and the diversity of these norms, create the opposition of *compatriot* and *foreigner.* The latter is not always, as such the enemy. Sometimes small closed societies appear to be without hostility curious or not, toward *foreign* customs. The force of the links which attach the individual to *his* group and the incompatibility of the imperatives which govern the conduct of the respective groups merely introduce the opposition of the *same* and the *other,* fragmenting humanity, so to speak, into separate species.

Tocqueville,[9] and many others after him, have observed in certain Indian tribes an institutional separation which heralds those of complex societies The tribes were governed, under normal circumstances, by a kind of heredi tary king, in essence religious, but if war broke out, the tribes designated a chief to lead them into battle. The duality which M. Dumézil finds at the dawn of the history of the Indo-European population, that of the religious chief and the military leader, is already visible in several archaic societies It underlines an essential distinction suggested by analysis. Every collectivity requires a double definition, internally by a system of norms or values, ex ternally by independence or military sovereignty. The foreigner is he against whom it is not criminal to fight to the death.

Over a quarter of a century ago Carl Schmitt published a brochure, en titled *Der Begriff des Politischen,*[10] that posited the opposition of friend and

[9] *Oeuvres complètes,* J. P. Mayer edition, Vol. V, p. 74.
[10] Munich, 1932.

enemy as the origin and essence of politics. This theory, it seems to me, implies that foreign policy is primary, or, at least, that politics should not be defined without reference to the plurality of collectivities. Within one unit, politics does not involve the opposition of friend and enemy; rather, it is the order of command, legitimized by custom or beliefs. Philosophical reflection cannot and must not posit the death-struggle as the basis of order even if, in the so-called phase of civilizations, the collectivities do in fact often separate themselves into parties each of which, in order to create an order in conformity with its preferences, is ready to treat its adversary as if it were the enemy and is sometimes, perhaps, obliged to do so.[11]

The philosopher who in thought and in action attempts to achieve the good society is inclined to regard the plurality of political units as an obstacle. How does one live according to reason if the *other*, the *alien*, the *foreigner*, whether remote or nearby, may burst into one's world at any moment? Plato and Aristotle, as we have seen in reference to the question of number, sought compromises between the requirements of *the good* and the necessities of defense. But, ideally, the good society should be the only one in the world, isolated on an island or by the immensities of the desert. The thinkers who have suggested that the virtuous society was thus rewarded by the favors of fortune no longer distinguished between virtue and political virtue. Sometimes they subscribed to an optimism of convention, according to which the just societies would be, as such, the strong ones.

The distinction between "culture," a collective way of life controlled by customs and belief, and the "military order" in case of conflict with another collectivity, is to be found, down through the millenniums of civilizations (or complex societies), in the form of the distinction between "community of culture" and "political unit." Neither of these two concepts is, in theory, perfectly clear; the frontiers of the "communities of culture" and of the "political units" are rarely delimited with precision. But, in fact, those who fight under the same flag do not always worship the same gods, while those who wage a war to the death against each other sometimes worship the same gods. In other words, relations are constantly fluctuating between the "orders of culture" and the "military orders." Some "orders of culture," related to each other, choose to be politically autonomous and engage in a permanent rivalry of which frequent wars are the expression (for instance, the Greek city-states). Some "military orders," which the governed people accept with indifference, are superimposed upon a diversity of cultures.

What relationship of language or custom is the basis of tribal unity, or of the unity of a people? Probably it would be futile to seek a *single* criterion.

---

[11] It frequently happens that hatred and, consequently, cruelty are worse between adversaries who are members of the same society than between foreigners. Nonetheless, the adversaries regard themselves, even in the heat of combat, as destined to live in one and the same community.

Language created a separation between Celts and Germans, although the dialects of the various tribes, Celtic or Germanic, were not precisely the same. Similarly, today, in the ex-Belgian Congo, languages permit a general distinction of ethnic groups. But the kingdoms or empires of Africa, before the European colonization, were created by military victories, by the crystallization of relations of domination created by these victories: a tribe or a fraction of tribe became the ruling class or the military caste.

The non-coincidence of the community of culture and of the political unit is therefore the rule and not the exception in the course of human history. This non-coincidence has two principal causes: on the one hand, the political unit, such as the Greek city-state, results both from the *domination* exerted by the conquerors upon alien populations and from the fragmentation of a people into military units, each of which is animated by a fierce desire for autonomy. The Spartans were not imperialists with regard to the other Greeks, as the Athenians were, but their own order was dominated by the necessity of maintaining in servitude those who had occupied the soil before them. Slaves and aliens in the city-states were, strictly speaking, neither foreigners nor citizens. Sometimes they participated in the culture of the masters and ultimately received citizenship, sometimes they lived alongside the masters without obtaining from them full recognition of their status.

The Greek city-state was and wanted to be both the military and the political order and, consequently, the community in which man fulfilled his own humanity. Man is man only *with* other men, not just within the family, a group whose root is biological, but in the forum or on the battlefield, discussing or fighting with other men in order to settle the right mode of communal existence. The city-state large enough to defend itself, small enough for all the citizens to know each other, was the natural unit, its regime (*politeia*) the organization conforming to individual and collective nature.

The nation, at the end of the nineteenth century, seemed to European historians or thinkers as natural[12] as the city-state had seemed to the Greek thinkers. In the nation, community of culture and military order met so as to create the political unit, both *in conformity with nature* since all the individuals participated in citizenship, and *ideal* since, on the day when each nation had fulfilled its vocation, peace would rule among the collective beings, free and therefore fraternal. The Greeks were less naïve: they were not unaware that political-military units seeking to be autonomous are thereby rivals, condemned, as a result of the instability of the relations of force, to suspect each other.

Even if the plurality of autonomous units did not create power politics, the optimism of the philosophy of nationalities would still have been based upon a false representation of historical reality. The principle of nationalities multiplied the occasions for conflict as much as the dynastic principle. If we

---

[12] In conformity with the natural order, or with the finality inherent in nature.

define a nationality as a human group, characterized by its own style of life and culture, by the awareness of being unique and the desire to remain so, nationalities are more or less identifiable externally, although the boundaries among "foreign" nationalities are often difficult to distinguish from the boundaries among groups within one and the same nationality. But in what circumstances is this desire for cultural autonomy entitled to claim state independence? If a population which belongs to a zone of language or culture desires to belong to a political unit of another zone, must it decide in favor of the desires of the living or of the heritage of the dead, that is, of those who two centuries before had submitted to the law of the conquerors, accepted henceforth as their fellow citizens?

All nationalities—groups characterized by their own nuance of language and culture—cannot make themselves into a nation, a group seeking to be the vehicle of a state and an autonomous subject on the historical stage. In Central and Eastern Europe, without a transfer of populations, no state could be national. Czechoslovakia was no less multinational than Austria-Hungary. Yugoslavia included Slavic populations whose languages differed somewhat, who had experienced quite different histories, who were not of the same religion and who did not all feel loyally attached to the new state, theoretically the expression of their common will.

The nation, as the ideal type of the political unit, has a triple characteristic: the participation of all those governed in the state under the double form of conscription and universal suffrage, the coincidence of this political will and of a community of culture, and the total independence of the national state with regard to the external world. A nation is always a result of history, a work of centuries. It is born through trials, starting from the sentiments of men but not without the action of force, the force of the political unit which destroys the pre-existing units, or the force of the state which brings into subjection regions or provinces.

Thus defined, the nation passed, at the end of the nineteenth century, for the masterpiece of history, the fulfillment of an age-old effort. Men created a culture together and, by a plebiscite renewed every day, chose to live together. Each nation affirmed its own independence at the same time as its respect for that of others.

Sentiments and ideologies have changed. Today, we burn what we worshiped at the end of the last century. The nation has not liberated men, it has reduced them, according to Renan's expression, to zoological wars. The desire to be a nation has blossomed into a collective pride, into an assertion of superiority: since the sovereign nations are engaged in a competition for power, conquests, far from being pacified by the creating of new states, have assumed an increased intensity. The wars of kings have become the wars of peoples. Men have believed that the fate of cultures was at stake on the battlefields at the same time as the fate of provinces.

The accusation against the nation seems as convincing today as the accusation which the Athenians or the Spartans might have made against the city-states in the second century B.C. We have grown accustomed to apply to wars the adjective which serves to characterize political units. Since the latter were national, wars were national too. If wars have ruined Europe, must we not conclude that nations bear the responsibility for this mutual ruin?

In a sense the reasoning is indisputable. A diplomatic system ultimately destroys itself when it provokes conflicts that are too numerous or too costly. The day when all the units which composed the system have lost their greatness, that is, their independence, the observer readily displays a retrospective wisdom in blaming the warring brothers for having overlooked their cultural fraternity and for having exhausted themselves in sterile struggles. Why did the city-states ignore Hellenic patriotism? Why have the nations ignored European patriotism? Did they not have more in common than they agreed to admit? What separated them did not justify a struggle to the death.[13]

A plausible reasoning and one rather lacking in a sense of history. The zones of civilization have been regularly fragmented into political units, opposed to each other as a consequence of the desire for autonomy which animated each of them. Patriotism, love of the nation, results from the transfer to the political unit of the spontaneous attachment to a territory or to a community. It possesses more effective force than the vague awareness of a Hellenic or European civilization. It is the historian who after the disaster deplores the passions which the living did not regard as mad folly. The Greeks, it will be said, would have occupied quite a different place within the Roman Empire had they been freely united instead of falling under the yoke of Macedonia, then of Rome. The Europeans would have played quite a different role in the global system had they been federated instead of waging pitiless wars by which, alternately and senselessly, Spain, France and Germany attempted to seize hegemony. But was there a possibility of realizing a federation of city-states or nations, each of which insisted on remaining the master of its fate? The French and the English preferred an American hegemony to the empire of the Second or even the Third Reich: were they wrong? The United States is not a part of Europe, in the geographical sense of the term. Nor does it belong to the original zone of Western civilization. Is it closer or further from the authentic meaning of this civilization than Hitler's Germany or Stalin's Russia?

The units, larger than a political unit, to which it is regretted, after the fact, that men have not given their faith and their devotion, are ambiguous, never visible on the map, scarcely real in men's awareness. The Europeans

[13] There is nothing to keep us from following the same reasoning for the two parts of Europe, after 1945, for the two fractions of the white race, or the two versions of industrial society.

occasionally agreed to divide up their colonies or to avenge, in China, the injuries inflicted upon their embassies. Had they obeyed a European will-to-power, and not a French, German or Russian one, they would have been collectively stronger: the Asians and Africans do not consider that this additional force would have been to humanity's benefit. Had the Europeans been united, by definition they no longer would have waged wars among themselves. Would they have lived in peace? During the centuries of the *pax Romana* there was no lack of wars. They were wars of a different kind.

Suppose we assert that the worst wars are national because they are wars of peoples, and therefore regret that men have claimed and obtained the right to constitute themselves into a nation? Both the assertion and the regret are fashionable today: each people, the anti-nationalists tell us, regards itself as invested with a unique mission. Each people yields to a naïve vanity and confuses the greatness of its culture with the power of its state. When this pride is that of a collectivity on a large scale, it sweeps the political unit toward aggressiveness and adventure. When it is that of a small collectivity, it provokes the disintegration of states and the multiplication of units that are too small.

I am not attempting to deny the ravages of nationalism and impure, unstable sentiment, constituted of pride and ambition, and not merely of legitimate attachment to a people and a culture. But the critics of nationalism, who are also the critics of nations, forget too readily the achievements of this type of political unit. The nation has as its principle and its goal the participation of all the governed people in the state. It is in order to participate in the state that the minorities insist that their language be recognized. The historian who admires the time when each of the social functions was fulfilled by men of a certain nationality (in the Ottoman Empire, for instance), forgets that this heterogeneity was the result of military conquests, and that it excluded from politics the major part of the populations. To deny the modern nation is to reject the transfer to politics of the eternal claim for equality.

Citizenship, granted to millions of men, has brought with it conscription. The latter, in its turn, has furnished the apparently inexhaustible human raw material which the war leaders hurled into the furnace between 1914 and 1918. "Reasonable" historians invoke wars that were fought in lace cuffs. Who, indeed, does not regret the time when states mobilized only a limited fraction of their resources to fight each other? The recruiting of professional soldiers among the lower classes assumed a hierarchic structure of society, the restriction of citizenship, the privileges of aristocracy. The nostalgia for the *ancien régime* would be all the more absurd since the monarchic centuries, considered as a whole, were no less bellicose than our own democratic century. The Thirty Years' War in the seventeenth century cost Germany dearer than the thirty years' war (1914-45) in the twentieth.

Further, if we claim to establish the responsibility appropriate to the national type, analytical distinctions are essential. The ideal type of nation (a tendency to make community of culture and political-military sovereignty coincide, absolute sovereignty, participation of all the governed people in political life, that is, in universal suffrage and the honor of arms) was far from being achieved in Europe on the eve of the First World War. The Continent was divided into states which desired to be sovereign but which, for the most part, were national neither in fact nor in idea. The First World War broke out and acquired an extreme intensity during the transitional phase between the traditional and dynastic states and the national states. It is the conflict of principles rather than any principle in itself which provokes the amplification of wars.

Before 1914 the foreign policies of the European states all belonged to a single species. The chancelleries of the parliamentary democracies conformed to the same philosophy of civilized Machiavellianism as that of the dynastic states, the Romanov, Hohenzollern and Habsburg empires. Whatever the responsibility attributed to one or the other in the outbreak of the First World War, it seems to me incontestable that in terms of strategy and tactics, the diplomatic-strategic conduct of the various states did not differ in nature. The secret treaties concluded between the Allies and Italy (to obtain the latter's intervention) or between Tsarist Russia and the French Republic in 1917 involved annexations, detaching of provinces, redistribution of zones of influence.

But the Machiavellianism of all the European states was, in the course of the First World War, civilized in comparison to that of Hitler's Germany or of Stalin's Russia. The technique of defiance, the open violation of formal pledges, the application to international relations of the methods of revolutionary action, the unforeseeable scope, the monstrous cruelty of the means, no longer belong to the realistic tradition of cabinets and still less to the age of nationalities. The diplomatic-strategy of the Third Reich, like that of the Soviet Union, was, between the two wars, *ideological* and *imperial* and no longer essentially national. Nations did not recover, between 1939 and 1945, the cohesion they had known between 1914 and 1918. The number of ideological traitors, of Germans who preferred the defeat of their country to Hitler's victory, of Russians who fought against a regime they regarded as tyrannical, even the number of Frenchmen who preferred Germany's victory out of sympathy for fascist ideas or in revolt against the civil wars of Europe bear witness to the fact that the nation was no longer looked upon by all men as the supreme value and the unique principle of political organization.

Let us conclude: Europe has destroyed itself by wars which we may call national because the constitutive principle of the political units was, at the time, national. The principle has been one of the causes of the hyperbolic character assumed by the wars of the twentieth century. But it would be unreasonable to regard it as solely responsible, in 1914, either for the war's outbreak or for its extention to the whole of the system. It would be still more unreasonable to assume that a supranational principle of political unity

—continental, ideological—would be, as such, more favorable to peace. To believe that a European unity would be peaceful where nations were warlike would be to reproduce the error of those who believed that nations would be peaceful where kings had been warlike. As for those who regard the ideological or imperial units as transitory and only the national units as durable, they are unconsciously putting the seal of eternity upon the historical philosophy of the European nineteenth century.

4. Military Organizations and Regimes

There are three kinds of secular power: economic, political and military. The power that men exert over other men can have three bases: wealth, authority recognized as legitimate and arms. Legitimate authority inevitably derives from or is supported by wealth or arms. Depending on the case, wealth comes to those who command, or the command to those who are wealthy. There is no reason to assume that the causal or chronological relations between these three terms are always the same.

Just as there are three kinds of secular power, there are three kinds of regime in each collectivity: economic, political and military. As we have tried to explain the external conduct of states by political or economic regime, so we may search in military organization for the cause of the diplomatic-strategy of states. After all, is it not natural that those whose profession it is to fight should influence those who choose between war and peace?

A military regime, like an economic one, is defined by the solution of two problems, one technical, the other human. The first is that of arms or tools, of means of destruction or production, the other is that of human relations, in the barracks or in the factory, in combat or at work. The military organization presents, intrinsically, a multitude of aspects, as does the economic organization.

The activity of combat, like that of production, is instrumental and cooperative: it requires the discipline of the combatants in order that the desired goal of victory be achieved. Technological imperatives partially control the relations established among the soldiers and their leaders (or else among the workers and their foremen or engineers); they do not suffice to determine the nature of the social links between enlisted men and officers, between slaves and masters, between farm workers and landowners, in other words, between the various echelons of the hierarchic order of combat or of production.

An economic regime is not identified with a technique of production; it is defined by the social relations between men at work, by a distribution of resources among uses, of ownership and income among individuals and classes, by a mode of exchange of goods and services. Marx has noted, in order to characterize the economic ages of humanity, the specific characteristics of the relations between men at work (slavery, serfdom, wage-earning) and has given a historical justification of the early forms of man's exploitation by man as being the result of the low productivity of labor. Slavery is one of the possible answers to the low productivity of labor, but it is not the only one; it has not been strictly indispensable (one can conceive of the accumulation of surplus value to the advantage of some without recourse to slavery). Similarly, in complex economies, where the context of trade is worldwide, the distribution of resources among uses, of income among classes, the adjustment of supply and demand, can be accomplished by at least two different methods. Technique of production, organization of labor in factory and field, organization of productive and commercial society, these three terms are in reciprocal relation without our being able to call any one of them the cause and the other the effect, without historical changes necessarily having as their origin *one* of these three terms.

Three analogous terms are to be found in the military order. The cooperation of the combatants must be subject to a discipline of efficiency. But the *de facto* discipline is often the expression of the social hierarchy. The effective order of the combatants is a function, in each period, of both the technological requirements and the social structure. Or again, to use another formula, given a technique of combat, the human relations among the combatants or among the individuals of the classes of the society involve a margin of variation. Similarly, the cause of historical changes can just as well be found in one or another of the three terms. A military revolution sets off a social revolution and vice-versa. Powder and cannon assure the superiority of regular armies whose mobilization requires resources inaccessible to feudal principalities: the centralized state becomes technologically indispensable. In the opposite direction, it was the French Revolution which permitted the recruiting of hundreds of thousands of men and thereby revised tactics (deep columns, infantry sharpshooters, levies upon the countryside, etc.).

Still less than the economic order, the military order has been, down through history, the object of free choice and rational calculation. It must not only be effective against the external world, against the possible enemy from without, it must also favor the maintenance of the social structure. South Africa cannot arm the Negroes to whom it refuses civil or economic equality. Rome hesitated to give arms to the slaves. The nobles in the Middle Ages kept a monopoly of heavy weapons. The army of each society has reflected the relations of classes, and these relations depended on the military force of each of the classes as much as on the distribution of property.

Two kinds of questions can be asked apropos of the military regime. If we posit a given type of military organization, what influence is a choice between one or the other variety of this type likely to exert? Further, to what degree is the type of political unit a function of the type of military organization?

In 1870 the Prussian army was based on conscription, the French army was a professional army. Did the choice between professional army and conscription exert an influence on the conduct of foreign policy? Further, the Prussian officers' corps was recruited by preference among the nobility. The style of relations between soldiers and officers was affected by the latter's origin: what were the consequences of this situation on the conduct of foreign policy? It has been a common practice, in certain periods, to impute to the military classes a major responsibility in armed conflicts. J. Schumpeter, among many others, regarded the nobles, whose profession, amusement and justification was to make war (the French nobility, domesticated by Louis XIV, obtained campaigns and glory in compensation), as in opposition to the bourgeois who, accustomed to economic calculations, regarded war as irrational. At the beginning of the twentieth century the militarist philosophy was incriminated, as well as that exaltation of the army and of combat which seemed characteristic of the Prussian aristocracy. The status of the soldier in the Prussian state was the root of German imperialism. In France, after 1918, the hatred of war was expressed in terms of anti-militarism.

We know today that these accusations were superficial and partial. Any ruling class, whether noble or bourgeois, is sensitive to the power of the collectivity. The military is not always warlike. Anti-militarists are not always peaceful. Max Scheler wrote that the French detested military life more than war, that the Germans, on the other hand, preferred the soldier's life to war: there is a degree of truth in this paradox. As for the influence of the general staffs upon statesmen, depending on the circumstances and nations, it has been inspired by the desire for conquest (the French Empire of the Third Republic was to a degree the work of the army) or the fear of war (in France before 1939).

None of the great general staffs, French, German or Russian, directly or consciously desired or provoked the explosion of 1914. None was resolutely hostile to it. All were preparing for the great trial of strength because they foresaw it. Did this anticipation belong to the species of self-fulfilling prophecies? It is always difficult to know precisely to what degree the leaders' expectation is the cause of the events which they anticipate. With regard to the immediate origins of the war, the actual responsibility of the general staffs relates specifically, as we have seen,[14] to the rigidity of their plans. The Russian general staff could not consent to partial mobilization without disorganizing the entire mechanism of general mobilization. Nor had the German general staff envisaged a limited war to any greater degree. In this sense they helped toward the inevitable amplification of the Austro-Serbian conflict into a general war, but this process was less an intention of men than a kind of bureaucratic determinism.

On the eve of the First World War, the military institution of European societies had a double origin: the tradition of the officers' corps, which dated back to the *ancien régime*, and the revolutionary novelty of conscription. The officers were regarded as preservers, in many cases as favorers of the so-called Rightist watchwords (order, authority, etc.). But they were

[14] Cf. Chap. I, pp. 40–41.

preservers in the exercise of their profession as well as in their political opinions. On neither side had they foreseen the duration of the war, the resources necessary for the supplying of millions of soldiers, the vast development of mechanized and motorized weapons on land and in the air. In looking back, they seem less responsible for the conflicts than for the slowness, before 1914, of the race for technological progress. They are to be blamed less for having set off the slaughter than for having disregarded (particularly in the West) firepower and thereby having caused hundreds of thousands of futile deaths. The success of propaganda against the military classes is largely to be accounted for by a historical deception. Many ordinary men, like many sociologists, had believed in the pacific vocation of modern societies, whether bourgeois, industrial or capitalist. Because the type of society was regarded as favorable to peace, the military regime for some, the economic regime for others, had to be at the origin of the slaughter.

It was at the beginning of the nineteenth century that the Saint-Simonian and positivist conception of a fundamental antinomy between war and labor became widespread. The development of the means of production, the multiplication of factories, struck the observers. Jurists, metaphysicians, ideologists, diplomats constituted the privileged class of a social type that was dying out; scientists, engineers, bankers, industrialists, those who accumulated knowledge and directed the activities on which depended the existence and prosperity of all would be the true leaders of the future society. The officers belonged to yesterday's elite, the technologists would take their place.

Auguste Comte offered a theoretical explanation of the antithesis between the essentially feudal society of the *ancien régime* and the essentially industrial society of the future. Every society aims at a single goal. War—first offensive, then defensive—had been the objective of military societies; labor would be the objective of industrial societies. From labor would come the values acknowledged by public opinion. Labor would create the hierarchy of authority and prestige. Herbert Spencer and Karl Marx extended or continued the Saint-Simonian and positivist conception. The former subordinated pacification by industry to free trade, the latter to socialism.

Auguste Comte's major argument—that a society aims at a preferred if not exclusive goal—seems to me, as such, false. Why should collectivities give a kind of unity to their existence when individuals do not succeed in doing so? That the scientific and technological capacity newly acquired by humanity opens a phase of history that is in certain regards original, no one will deny. That this phase ought to be peaceful, that the societies seeking to embrace the entire globe should thereby renounce fighting and oppressing each other, is perhaps a hope, certainly not a certitude.

Doubt is all the more justified since the means of production and the means of destruction have a common origin and, so to speak, a common nature. The manipulation of natural forces cannot help but furnish, as a kind of by-product of technological mastery, increasingly perfected weapons.

Auguste Comte was not unaware of this fact, and he imputed to the fundamental pacifism of modern societies the limited effectiveness of existing weapons, compared to the effectiveness of the weapons whose conception and fabrication science permitted.[15] This disparity has long since vanished.

Auguste Comte hoped that the disappearance of the military class and the character of the new elite would confirm the pacifism of industrial societies. We know today that, at least during the century that has passed since the death of Auguste Comte, the historical development has been quite different. In order to respond to the needs of the war monster, the total mobilization of men and machines produced a different interpretation. Industrial society was not deflected from its peaceful vocation by the superannuated spirit of the military class and by the leaders imbued with the same spirit. Industrial society, as soon as it was no longer bourgeois and liberal but technological and organized, was spontaneously, of itself, a military society. Let us recall the famous decree of the Convention: "The young men will fight. The married men will make weapons, transport artillery, prepare supplies. The women will work in soldier's dress, will make tents and serve as nurses in the hospitals for the wounded. The children will shred cloths for bandages, and the old, resuming the mission which they once had among the ancients, will be carried to public places, where they will inflame the courage of the young warriors, propagate the hatred of kings and love of the Republic." Everything is here, including the organization of enthusiasm (love of the Republic) and ideological propaganda (hatred of kings). Conscription, mass levies, total mobilization of material, human and spiritual resources belong to the essence of modern society, industrial but democratic as well.

The German sociologist J. Plenge[16] proclaimed that the ideas of 1914—ideas of organization—replaced those of 1789—liberty, equality, fraternity—but, by the intermediary of mass conscription, the former derived from the latter. E. Jünger symbolized the new order by the two types, worker and soldier, complementary and related. The army was no longer composed of peasants commanded by nobles, but of workmen directed by technologists. A growing number of men in uniform carried out functions analogous to those performed by civilians in peacetime. The similarity of the two organizations increased in the American army of 1945, staffed with officers who owed their rank to their professional competence, not to a strictly military training. The leader of men in combat is no longer the aristocrat but the engineer—the engineer of arms and the engineer of souls.

By an irony of history, the elimination of the nobles by the engineers, conceived by Auguste Comte, had been in a certain sense fulfilled, but it was industry that had become militaristic, not society that had become peaceful.

---

[15] I have analyzed Auguste Comte's conception in detail in *La Société industrielle et la guerre*, Paris, 1959.

[16] In *1789 und 1914, die symbolischen Jahre in der Geschicht des politischen Geistes*, Berlin, 1916.

Industry was mobilized for war and war impregnated with industrial spirit. In 1949 the nightmare of the "garrison state," of the entire state permanently structured by the requirements of the struggle with is rivals, haunted men's minds.

Subsequently, another reversal has intervened. The production of atomic and thermonuclear weapons suspends the fear of a catastrophe over humanity, but it spares states the servitude of industrial mobilization. The improbability of a war between the great powers, waged with classic weapons, permits the states to limit the share of their economy devoted to preparations for combat. For the societies of the Atomic Age which are not vulnerable to subversion, the image is no longer that of the garrison state but that of bourgeois comfort and millions of automobiles in the shadow of the apocalypse. Similarly, none of the simplistic theories concerning the role of the military classes or the relation between means of combat and types of political unit is any longer valid.

Let us turn back to the ancient world. The political units in which all the citizens bore arms were not any more peaceful than those that reserved that honor to a minority. Athens, a democratic city-state, was regarded as more imperialistic than Sparta, an oligarchic city-state. Rome's first conquest was carried out by legions of citizens. It was in the course of the Punic Wars that the Roman legions, as a result of their length of service, acquired the training of professionals. The military regime changed with the structure of the political unit, without the latter's diplomatic conduct seeming to be directly controlled by the interests of the military class.

The Roman Empire was a different type of society from that of the city-states. It had been constructed by the legions, it was maintained by them. The military regime corresponded to the Empire's needs. But there was no proportionality between the nature of the weapons and the dimension of the political unit. The superiority of the legions was qualitative, due to organization and discipline. Even within the zone of imperial peace, there existed neither a real monopoly of armed forces nor a single and sovereign state. The alien populations retained leaders and weapons. Depending on the provinces and the periods, Roman domination assumed all forms, from total integration to simple protectorate.

The enlargement of the political units in the ancient world seemed to have occurred because of the virtues of the city-state, of its laws, of its customs, of its combatants, or the genius of a soldier. The necessary concentration was that of the military or political authority, in order to raise armies or to maintain their discipline. The development of technological weapons opened a new era. This time the necessary concentration was that of economic resources. Lacking men, factories and money, small units could not afford armed forces of the same type as those possessed by large units. The medieval dispersion of sovereignty became incompatible with the nature of weapons. The formation of the European states resulted logically from the economic requirements of the military regime.

The movement continued until 1914, widening the gap between those states whose soldiers were equipped by industry and those which, on land and even more at sea, had remained at a previous stage of technology. All the European states, small or large, had armies and fleets of the same type, whose forces were proportional to the size of the population. But the populations of Africa and of most Asian states did not have qualitatively analogous forces, except for Japan, as a result of her autonomous modernization, and India under the British Raj. The European system of equilibrium and the European empires expressed, on the diplomatic level, the similarity on the one hand, and the disparity on the other, of the types of military organization.

In 1914 the Belgian army was a small French army, almost the same divisions, infantry, artillery, cavalry, engineering corps, with the same weapons, that were or could all be manufactured in the national factories. In 1939 armored and air forces already introduced a qualitative difference: the small nations could no longer manufacture all their weapons themselves, nor could they put a modern army on a small scale in the field. By 1960 the qualitative disparity had become extreme, since the atomic and thermonuclear weapons were at the disposal of only three states (and even then, possession of thermonuclear weapons did not afford Great Britain effective possession of a retaliatory force). The creating of diplomatic-military blocs, each under the direction of one of the possessors of atomic weapons, is an intelligible if not necessary consequence of this heterogeneity of the means of warfare.

Simultaneously, the superiority of regular armies over improvised combatants has diminished. The effectiveness of guerrilla warfare against the army of occupation, in Russia behind the front, in Yugoslavia or in France, has been the object of divergent evaluations. Partisans are no more capable of conquering a regular army in the twentieth century than they were in the nineteenth, but they are capable, when the terrain is favorable and when they awaken the sympathy of the population, of prolonging their resistance over a period of years. The dissolution of the European empires, which had many other causes, is explained in part by the reduction of the superiority of organized soldiers over partisans.

The heterogeneity of the political units constituting the global system reflects the diversity of the techniques of combat. On the one hand, the European nations desire to unite in order to recover the military autonomy which they have lost in the Atlantic coalition. The coincidence of community of culture and political unit is jeopardized by the economic concentration required by a military force of an industrial type. On the other hand, states consisting of a few millions of men, multiplying in Africa, base their independence on their capacity to resist foreign domination. But they have not yet achieved the coincidence of community, of culture and political unit; nationalism has driven out the colonist, but the nation has not thereby appeared.

The dialectic of community of culture and of political sovereignty, of civil order and military order, far from resulting in a unique and final synthesis, is assuming new forms. Never have such different collectivities participated in one and the same history.

At the end of the preceding chapter I showed that industry furnishes men unprecedented means of enriching themselves without conquest and without exploitation, but also unprecedented means for killing each other. As industry has developed in a world fragmented into rival collectivities, it has been put in the service of national or imperial ambitions. So long as competition between states exists, no economic regime, whether liberal or planned, guarantees that techniques of production will not be corrupted into techniques of destruction.

In this chapter the conclusion is not that a type of unit or political regime, a type of organization or military regime, is, as such, bellicose or peaceful. Or, at least, if there *are* societies or regimes whose vocation is conquest or war, there are none whose vocation is peace. In our times, the major phenomenon is the heterogeneity of state units, of political regimes, of techniques of combat. Multinational states, supranational aggregations, imperial blocs, superpowers, coexist as enemy ideologies coexist, as machine guns, tanks, tactical atomic weapons and ballistic missiles with thermonuclear warheads coexist.

That this coexistence is more peaceful in words than in acts will surprise no one, but, when we think of the possible catastrophe, we are tempted to admire the fact that in spite of everything coexistence remains relatively peaceful.

chapter XI

In Search of a Pattern of Change

The analyses of the preceding chapter afford merely negative precepts. They might warn both actors and historians against systematic and partial perspectives, but suggest no general proposition, law or constant relative to the strategic-diplomatic behavior of a type of political unit or of an economic, social or military regime.

It is not true to say that completely national states are necessarily peaceful: swept on by pride, nations can be, or appear to others, imperialistic. It is not true that a modern market economy is doomed to conquests, nor that a modern economy subject to a central plan is as such peaceful. It is not true to say that peoples remain the same throughout their history, the Germans always cruel, Albion always perfidious, the French always frivolous. It is not true to say that the love of war and the collective desire for power are born with a military class and disappear with it. Neither nations nor regimes are, as such, constants.

These negations have not only the merit of correcting erroneous notions. They remind us of the principal variables which any concrete study must review. Diplomatic-strategic behavior being instrumental, and a matter of risk, a decision cannot be understood except by reference both to the circumstances and to the actor's psycho-sociology. The circumstances are formed by the relations of forces, established within a specific historical area. The collective actor is sometimes intelligible as if he were an individual (the regime of an absolute leader) and sometimes appears to be the resultant of multiple forces. In both cases we must clarify the actor's goals, his conception of the world, and the mode of action he adopts, whether deliberately or under more or less coercive influences.

But this duality—circumstances or relation of forces, strategy, philosophy and tactics of the actor—is artificially simplified. What explains a decision is not so much the real circumstances as the actor's notion of them. Further, the circumstances for each actor are formed not only by a calculable relation of forces, but by the (probable) behavior of other actors, rivals, enemies or allies. Strategists or diplomats do not combine means with a view to ends, like engineers; they take risks, like gamblers.

Any truly historical investigation—that is, one having as its object concrete events or the succession of events—must follow the interplay of causes, the dialectic of situations and actors, the reaction of the actors to each other. The constants upon which it is possible to throw light involve an aspect either of the circumstances or of the actors. These constants are both partial and approximate: when the respective forces of the chief actors within a de-limited system remain virtually the same, the diplomacy of one of the actors presents, in the long run, certain permanent factors (the French tradition of the eastern alliance). When an actor aims at a specific goal, itself sug-gested by a geographical position, he will behave, over the centuries, according to rules which his rivals will discern better than himself (British balance-of-power diplomacy). Further, we must not forget under what conditions these constants become evident, or what transformations would suffice to reduce such constants to variables.

The object of historical investigation is to grasp and distinguish at each moment or within the series of events the durable data and the changing circumstances, without postulating in advance that the changes are always caused by phenomena of one and the same kind. As for sociological investiga-tion, if it is not content with what we have called approximate and partial constants, it must adopt another method. The interplay of causes, the dialectic of states and regimes are incontestable; but it is possible that at a higher level, in a global perspective, we may glimpse either constants or an order of development. Traditional thinkers, who did not question the in-coherence of events in detail, speculated nonetheless on the causes which determined the greatness and decadence of states. In this chapter we shall try to summarize classical considerations on the fortune of arms and peoples.

Two paths, in theory, are open to us. Since vast units are involved, the initial question is that of the nature of these units. Shall we start with a *historical subject,* that is, a nation, a state or a civilization treated as an individual, or with a *historical object,* that is, a century, period or an age taken as a durable set of circumstances?

The first path seems to me preferable to the second. In order to characterize a period, we must specify a variable which we regard as predominant. The choice of this variable is always problematical. Even if we envisage a period from a single point of view—for instance, with regard to the conduct of international relations—it is difficult to isolate *the* ultimate cause, or *the* specific characteristic. Some historians characterize each period by the name of a hegemonic state (Spanish preponderance, French preponderance, etc.), others by the type of political unit and the nature of wars (monarchic states, national states, wars of religions, dynastic wars), still others by the technique of armies and combats (conscription, industry, total mobilization). Was the past century, between 1815 and 1914, with regard to foreign policy, the age of nationalities or the age of industry? Was it characterized predominantly by the constitutive principle of states (nationalities) or by the instruments put at the disposal of soldiers? Does the Atomic Age inaugurate another diplomacy, another strategy? The formation of objective ensembles implies a hypothesis of the relation among the determinants.

Let us follow the other path and start with historical subjects, nations, civilizations, humanity. The analyses in the three following sections will have as their object three problems: What are the causes of the fortune of nations? Do all civilizations meet the same fate? Are there ages of diplomacy within human history?

1. *The Fate of Nations*

I shall consider only the European nations. It is in Europe, as we have seen, that the nation has achieved its final form, that people and state have become so identified that "the will of the French to be a nation" has appeared to be the profound cause of a historical continuity. The state seemed to emanate from the people and no longer the people to result from the age-old action of the state.

The nation, in the sense which this word has assumed since the French Revolution, is of recent date, but it is not unjustified to see in modern France the sequel of monarchic France and to denominate as the French nation the collectivity of the French, united for centuries by an alternately dynastic and democratic state and in a common will. Thus modern historians have reflected on the development of nations no less than did the Greek thinkers on the development of regimes.

Occasionally the problem was raised by experience. The same city-state was subject to various regimes, none of which achieved stability. Revolution, in both senses of the word, seemed the most characteristic phenomenon of political life: one regime was abruptly driven out by another, but these successive crises ultimately led back to the point of departure. The series of regimes organized itself into a cycle, comparable to the cosmic revolutions. On the other hand, the instability not of regimes, but of national fortunes has been the decisive fact about European history. First Spain, then France have meditated upon decadence, the Germans upon the diversity of the historical forms in which they have expressed their own genius. The English until recently have admired the irresistible progress of their destiny.

Historians and philosophers often tended to identify power with greatness, weakness with decadence. Montesquieu's famous lines in the *Considerations sur les causes de la grandeur et de la décadence des Romains*[1] implicitly contains such a confusion: "It is not fortune which dominates the world. We can see this in the Romans who enjoyed a continuous series of successes

---

[1] Chap. XVIII.

when they governed themselves upon a certain level, and an uninterrupted series of reversals when they proceeded upon another. There are general causes, either moral, or physical, which function in each monarchy, raise it, maintain it, or cast it down; all events are subject to these causes, and, if the hazard of a battle, that is, a particular cause, has ruined one state, there was a general cause which obliged this state to perish in a single battle: in a word, the principal notion involves all particular events with itself."

Or further,[2] "It was not the affair of Poltowa that ruined Charles XII: had he not been destroyed at that place, he would have been in another. The casualties of fortune are easily repaired; but who can be guarded against events that incessantly arise from the nature of things?" The action of general causes is affirmed, and simultaneously, the judgment of arms ascribed to the credit or debit of laws, regimes or men.

Neither in theory nor in fact, as we know, can *military* success and reversal pass for an exact measure of the moral merits of a people or of the quality of a culture. Sometimes the flowering of a culture has coincided with the culminating point of victory: thus the brief period of Athenian hegemony, between the exploits of the Median wars and the disasters of the Peloponnesian War, was also that of Phidias, Pericles and Socrates. But the same is not true of the German destiny. The greatest works of German thought were produced in the period of the *Germanies,* of political impotence, and not during the half century of hegemony between the proclamation of the Empire at Versailles and the explosion of 1914. In our own period the creative capacity of peoples is obviously not proportional to the economic or military force of states. Hitler had impoverished German culture at the very moment that his diplomacy was effecting one triumph after another. Bolshevism has smothered Russian literature and thought, paralyzed writers and artists, despite the glory it has given, on the world stage, to the ex-empire of the Tsars as the Soviet Union.

The authors of the past were not unaware of these distinctions. Machiavelli's *virtù,* which shifts from people to people, animates the victors and abandons the declining empires, has always, in the eyes of philosophers, been distinguished from the *virtue* of the moralists. Perhaps certain philosophers have dreamed of a regime in which men achieve a virtue both political and moral, the citizens obeying the sages and the sages the truth. In this ideal city, powerful enough to be safe from aggression, wisdom would possess force and force would submit to wisdom. But the real cities, prisoners of a permanent rivalry, must be strong, even by imposing a pitiless discipline upon the mindless crowd, even by the despotism of the violent.

Authors have not always given an interpretation of political virtue—that of the elite and of the masses—as pessimistic as that of Pareto. Machiavellian thought, having become positivist, having revolted against idealism, defines

[2] *L'Esprit des lois,* X, 13.

the virtue of the masses as blind devotion, the virtue of the leaders as their capacity for violence and cunning, occasionally as the contrary of what the rationalists consider moral virtue. The virtue of the ancient republics, as Montesquieu conceives it, is certainly moral in a different sense, since it implies frugality, patriotism and respect for the law. Nonetheless, even in Montesquieu's thought, it is a soldier's virtue as much as a citizen's. It scarcely seems compatible with well-being or favorable to arts and letters.

Montesquieu has no more illusions than Simone Weil[8] on the methods by which Rome conquered the ancient world. He admires the laws of Rome, the constancy of the Senate in bad days, the rigor of the punishments inflicted upon those who resisted or betrayed, the art of recruiting allies or adherents. Could the man who urged states, in time of war, to do one another as little injury as possible consider this effective use of weapons and of lies as a model of morality? Montesquieu hesitated between two systems of values, one of which stressed the conquerors and the other peaceful activities and productions of the mind. He did not explicitly affirm the incompatibility of the behavior of the victors and the imperatives of morality. Political virtue, based on law and custom, functioned as an intermediate stage between the merit of men and the fortune of states. But this conciliation required that military force essentially depend on the capacity for collective action, and that this capacity, in its turn, be exalted for its own sake, for its effectiveness, whatever the means employed. Today, we refuse to believe that great power is always attributable to virtue, even political virtue, and that the capacity for collective action is the same as the quality of the political civilization.

Theories relative to the destiny of nations inevitably reflect conceptions relative to the determinants of force as well as visions of the future. Meditating upon the fate of states and empires, philosophers and historians have underestimated the role of material factors and of number, have failed to discern the action of military technique proper, that is, of organization, discipline and tactics. They have supposed that political merits were in proportion to military success. Therefore, some attributed the political merits of a city or a people to a man, either legislator or hero. The decadence of a state was due to the exhaustion of a dynasty, to the accession of an heir unworthy of the founder. Others emphasized laws and customs, also doomed to corruption by a mechanism perhaps similar to that of the exhaustion of dynasties: the masses lose their beliefs, the elite, formerly united by the will to power, gradually succumb to frivolity. Thus historical time appears as a force of disintegration: starting from the summit marked by the exploits of the hero, the wisdom of the lawgiver or the virtue of the ancients, how could the sovereigns or the peoples fail to decline? At most the idea of cycles of

[8] See above, Chapter VIII. The study by Simone Weil, of which we have quoted a passage, was written on the eve of the Second World War. It was a comparison of the methods of Rome with those of Hitler.

regimes offers, on the political level, a substitute for the representation of a fatal decadence.

Historical consciousness, the recognition of the diversity, from period to period, of institutions, of types of units, of ideas themselves, have suggested two other mechanisms of decadence to modern authors. Change, and no longer permanence, is henceforth inevitable as well as desirable. Henceforth, conservatism can become a cause of ruin. The Prussian armies, at Jena, were a generation behind. The French armies of Sedan, in 1870 or in 1940, had been, in their turn, bypassed by the progress of weapons or tactics. The capacity to innovate, more than the capacity to maintain, seems to be the expression of collective action.

What is the source of the paralysis of the capacity to innovate? In each nation, in each circumstance, different reasons can be supplied. The tendency to intellectual sloth is common to most individuals; all institutions, all collectivities tend to persevere in their current state. The organization of the army, the recruiting of officers, the *esprit de corps* can explain the qualitative inferiority of the weapons of a nation confronting a nation belonging to the same zone of civilization. The philosophers, Hegel in particular, have suggested an all-inclusive interpretation of what we might call historical conservatism. A human collectivity, organized as a "power state" (*Macht Staat*), derives its vitality from a historical idea. Whether this idea is exhausted or whether it is no longer in conformity with the necessities of the period, the collectivity will gradually appear to be drained of its substance, less and less capable of cultural activity. If the national states belong to the past, can France free herself from the historical idea that is, so to speak, identified with her very being?

It was in the last century that there began, in France, the argument over French decadence. The facts could easily be interpreted according to one or another of the classically recognized mechanisms. Ever since the Revolution, one school said, France no longer had an uncontested sovereign, a legitimacy unanimously acknowledged by her citizens. She could no longer wage war because she no longer had a king.[4] Every national crisis was thereby transformed into a constitutional crisis. A nation divided over the form of the state lost the capacity to act on the world stage. The ultimate victor, among the candidates for empire, was the British people (or the Anglo-Saxon race). The die was cast and the outcome of the struggles between France and England, in the eighteenth century, determined the mastery of the world. No victory of a unified Germany would reverse a final verdict of history. Now the victor is the people of representative institutions, of the Reformation and of Parliament. It was by rejecting liberal institutions that France precipitated her subjection. What made this subjection inevitable, affirmed

---

[4] The little book by M. Sembat, a socialist, has not been forgotten: *Faites un roi ou faites la paix*, Paris, 1914.

still another school, was the decline of the birth rate: ultimately, among nations on the same level of civilization, it is number that determines the
hierarchy. No military genius can gain a victory on the battlefield if the
battle of the cradles has been lost.

These explanations are not mutually exclusive. They can in fact combine,
but do so differently in each concrete case. Division over the form of the state
was incontestably, for France, a cause of weakening throughout the nineteenth century. The unity of the nation—elite and masses—is one of the
determinants of force. The rejection of reforms provoked the collapse of the
monarchy; attachment to customs or beliefs, the resistance of "vested interests" to changes, even those necessary to the common welfare, a certain ob-
scurantism favored by the Church and clericalism, these phenomena of
social inertia were among the causes of decline. As for the influence exercised by the decline of the birth rate, it is obvious. But what is the relation
between laws and customs, between the French Revolution and the lowering
of the birth rate? Are parents who do not want more than two children culpable, and if so, in what sense?

The modern conditions of the problem are such that no one can ignore
the importance of *number* and of *technology*. Virtue can do nothing against
atomic bombs; forty-five million Frenchmen will never equal two hundred
million Russians on the battlefields or in the factories. Hierarchy is pitilessly
dominated by quantity. But beyond such evidence, the traditional uncertainties remain.

The relations between moral causes and material causes, to use Montesquieu's terms, or between laws and customs, the quality of institutions and
that of peoples are as obscure, as equivocal today as in the past. The decline
of the birth rate began in France before the Revolution. Inheritance legislation must have had an unfavorable influence on the size of families, just as
the Family Code contributed to the raising of the birth rate, but laws are
always only one of the circumstances which determine customs. Demographic
growth and economic growth result from a complex of causes, difficult to
disentangle.

More than ever, questions are being asked as to the relationship or the
opposition between political and moral virtue, between historical vitality and
the quality of the culture or of collective existence. One would be overly
pessimistic to assert a radical opposition: the acceptance of sacrifices, a higher
percentage of investments, the rapidity of technological progress require
merit of a moral order on the part of the leaders and the people. But must
we praise the leaders who by constraint wring consent from the people? On
the other hand, the regimes of freedom allow the citizens the opportunity
to refuse the sacrifices which the peoples in authoritarian regimes cannot
avoid. Does a higher rate of growth constitute, in itself, a proof of collective
virtue?

The institutions which, in our eyes, constitute political civilization are not,

as such, contrary to effectiveness, if we measure the latter by the level of
the standard of living or by the productivity of labor. But in the short run,
an authoritarian regime has the means of levying a more considerable sum
from the collective resources for its own purposes. It would be futile to expect peoples always to have access to civilization and to the glory of arms at
the same time. If, lacking a better term, we call the group of qualities that
give the advantage to certain nations in the rivalry for power *historical vitality*, no one would claim that the most vital nations are always the most moral.
Further, it will be asked to what degree collective vitality is compatible with
the respect for persons and liberties.

The question is not a new one, but it has been renewed. It is not new
since virtues that gave power to peoples were never *necessarily* the same as
those recommended by churches and philosophies. It is renewed because the
necessity of number limits the possibilities open to Caesars or to cavaliers.
Thus the exhaustion of dynasties and the corruption of regimes no longer
appear as fatalities. No pattern of change can be constituted out of the chaos
of events, neither one of biological cycles nor even one of disintegration
through time. Retrospectively, the European procession of leading powers
does not seem to have been subject to any law.

Spain and France, more than the United Kingdom and Germany, must
have sought a theory of decadence. The history of the United Kingdom,
since the seventeenth century, appears continuous. That of Germany or of the
Germanies appears to be discontinuous. The geographical situation of the
two peoples offers a partial explanation of this contrast. Protected by their
island situation, the British did not pay for internal struggles by invasion;
they had a better chance of settling their disputes, even religious ones, without involving foreigners. Not since the sixteenth century have they attempted
a continental conquest at the expense of peoples belonging to the same
sphere of civilization. When they lose their Empire, the British preserve their
unity, their independence, the prestige of their institutions. The territory
peopled by the Germans becomes a battlefield when it is not held by a powerful state. The Reformation, with its procession of wars and foreign interventions, brought Germany two centuries of political impotence. Since the
eighteenth century and the establishment in the East of a Russian Empire
whose resources are virtually unlimited and which is capable of borrowing
or acquiring the instruments of force, the central position is both tempting
and exposed. Expansion toward distant lands being forbidden by the English
fleet, the unified Reich was obliged either to content itself with prosperity
and a predominant influence on the Continent, or else to resume the ambition
of what Montesquieu calls universal monarchy, and of what we call hegemony in the case of Wilhelm II's empire and that of Hitler. The attempt
encountered the same obstacle over which the Napoleonic enterprise had
collapsed: the alliance of continental states hostile to the strongest among
them, and the ultimate victory of the maritime state. Still, in the twentieth

century, Germany would have been able to conquer had the European system been closed upon itself. Twice, American intervention determined the outcome.

Today neither the English nor the Germans meditate much on decadence: the first have won the war which marked the end of their reign, the second have won so many battles before losing the last one[5] that it does not occur to them to incriminate the loss of martial qualities. They denounce the pride and madness of yesterday's leader, not the lack of courage or zeal of the people or the soldiers. "Germany, profoundly seduced, followed her Führer ecstatically. Until the very end, she was to serve him slavishly, with greater exertions than any people has ever furnished any leader."[6] "Hitler's attempt was superhuman and inhuman. He maintained it without stint, without respite. Until the final hours of agony in the depths of a Berlin bunker, he remained unquestioned, inflexible, pitiless, as he had been during his days of supreme glory."[7] The inhumanity of the enterprise condemns the master of the undertaking, not those who carried it out. German greatness was slaughtered by the madness of one man. It did not die of consumption, like that of Spain and France.

Unlike Germany, neither Spain nor France fell all at once. They did not remain victorious until the last day in the manner of the United Kingdom. They seemed to decline little by little. Hence the interrogation which Spanish authors constantly renewed in the eighteenth and nineteenth century: why did the Spanish infantry that had made Europe tremble no longer rule the battlefields? Had the afflux of gold and silver constrained the development of the arts and of commerce, created a precarious abundance, a deceptive wealth? Or was the impression of decadence itself, in the eighteenth century, mistaken or excessive, the conjunction of the throne of Spain and the Empire being accidental and temporary? In the nineteenth century, after the ravages of the Napoleonic Wars and the loss of the American Empire, decadence was evident and tragic; civil wars and economic stagnation constantly diminished the state which had been the troublemaker four centuries before.

Still different is the line of French history. After 1815 the drop was brutal, although the France of the Restoration, different from the Germany of 1945, could preserve both unity and independence. But the memory of victories staves off humiliation. France succumbed to an enormous coalition: until the end her leader was inspired and her soldiers were brave. The dream of revenge filled the time of resignation. It was in the middle of the last century that political writers began to draw up the balance sheet. The kingdom of

[5] Like the French, in 1815.
[6] *The War Memoirs of Charles de Gaulle,* Vol. II, *Salvation,* New York, 1960, p. 198.
[7] *Ibid.,* p. 199.

France had been first in Europe during the second half of the seventeenth century and a part of the eighteenth. The armies of the Republic and the Empire had, for several years, outstripped their rivals. What remained, finally, of so many wars, so many dead, and so many victors? Louis XIV had made himself hated by all of Europe. To put his grandson on the throne of Spain, he had waged an endless war and permitted England to gain the advantage in the race for the mastery of the seas and the empires of India and America. Napoleon had repeated, with incomparably superior means, the hegemonic attempt: he ultimately left France smaller than he had found her. Frustrated in her grandiose hopes, France irremediably declined, torn by the conflict of legitimacies, weakened by the declining birth rate.

The circumstances to which Spain, France and Germany owed their accession to first rank are too diverse to be contained by a single pattern. Of course, the troublemaker—that is, the power which, in a diplomatic system, can lay claim to hegemony—must possess superior resources. Spain, in the period when the king of Spain was the emperor in Germany and the sovereign in South America, was also the most prosperous nation in Europe. The France of the seventeenth and eighteenth centuries was the most densely populated and most vigorously administered nation. The Germany of Wilhelm II had the foremost industry on the Continent. In each period the conditions of force were combined in favor of the state with hegemonic pretentions.

Abstractly defined, these conditions are always the same: potential of resources and degree of mobilization. But the respective share of precious metals, of commercial profits, of agriculture and the arts, in the total volume of resources, does not remain constant. The capacity for collective action can be abruptly or gradually increased or diminished by the quality of the central power and the administration, by the accumulation of provinces as a result of dynastic unions, by the dominion exerted over remote lands. Spain could not always keep what she owed to a dynastic union; the dominion exerted over remote lands does not last indefinitely. A nation's qualitative superiority on the battlefields rarely extends longer than one or a few generations (among states of the same nature there are periods when none of them possesses this superiority). The advantage of number and resources shifts from one to another, depending on the vicissitudes of diplomatic history and the changing modes of wealth. If there is one general proposition suggested by the facts, it is that the degree of power, during the past centuries of European history, had little chance of being lasting. The conditions of force were too unstable for fortune to be constant. The circumstances which suffice to reinforce and reduce the capacity for collective action were numerous and accidental (energetic or incapable sovereign, dynastic conjunction or dissociation): the share of the degree of mobilization in relation to the share of the potential (that is, in certain circumstances, of the political conditions in relation to the economic conditions) was, for the centuries previous to the nineteenth, relatively large. Lastly, the advantages from which Spain, France, Germany and England in turn benefited were diverse: how discern a single process, a single style, a single pattern of decadence?

The French and Spanish reflections transmit a single question, insistent and enigmatic. When Renan wrote, in 1871, "Once France is humiliated, there will no longer be such a thing as a French spirit," was he seeking noble excuses for a nostalgia for power? Or is it true that a nation which has known "greatness and glory" cannot accommodate itself to the second or third rank? Is it true that a nation which has played a part on the world stage and which no longer plays one fades away? Is it true that a nation without a historical idea gradually loses its creative vitality in the cultural order as well? In short, is not the power of the state, even when obtained by means contrary to the imperatives of religion or morality, indispensable to the quality of collective existence and the works of the mind?

The experience of European history does not authorize a categorical answer. That the decline of the arts accompanied or followed that of power can be asserted in the case of Spain, and with more difficulty in that of France. There is no question of such a thing in the case of Germany. The question remains, however, no less troublesome. It is immediate and it is eternal. It relates to the mystery of history, it plunges us deep into the heart of present events. Was Hitler right to assert that the earth belongs to the violent? Are the European nations doomed to decadence if they remain nations?

2. *The Fate of Civilizations*

The historical decline of the European nations was precipitated by the two wars of the twentieth century, by the disintegration of the European empires of Asia and Africa, itself accelerated if not provoked by these wars. But the European nations, having exchanged the European framework for the world stage, were, in any case, driven from the first rank and, to follow pessimism to its limit, condemned to impotence and decline. Outside the "minor cape of Asia," the European nations inevitably encountered political units of another "order of magnitude," because they were of another type.

The empire of the Tsars, although the Romanov dynasty had imitated the European monarchies in the eighteenth century, was historically of another species from the nations of the old continent. As a political unit it belonged to the imperial species, the last of the imperial edifices built upon the steppes; but, for the first time, the conquerors had proceeded from west to east and not in the opposite direction. The Tsarist horsemen rediscovered in Central Asia, at Samarkand or at Tiflis, the memories and the tombs of the Mongol emperors. At the same time the Russian state, the work of the grand dukes of Moscow, attempted to unite into one people the European Slavic populations (whose languages differed) with the non-Slavic populations. Finally, the phase, long since completed in Western Europe, of peopling an empty space, continued across the plains of Eastern Europe, as it did toward the western immensities of North America. The establishment of states of a European type in Russian and American space contained the germ of the obsolescence of nations (which the accidents of politics and wars might have delayed). Alone among the states existing today, China and India, perhaps Brazil tomorrow, will be on the scale of the two giants.

Coexistence, within the same system, of states of different types is not an unprecedented phenomenon. In antiquity, the Greek city-states fought the empire of the Medes; the Roman Empire confronted, beyond the marches, tribal populations. Cities, kingdoms, empires and barbarian populations represented political units of different dimensions, and of different constitutive principles. Similarly, free cities, feudal principalities, commercial and wealthy city-states of the Venetian type, monarchies in the process of becoming national were the actors, with little or no homogeneity, in the diplomatic games of Europe. From the point of view of inner structure, of the relations between church and state, then between state and ideology, the European system has never been homogeneous.

The homogeneity of the European system in the nineteenth century was superficial. The political units had all adopted the ideas and the practices of the traditional chancelleries. Parliamentary republics and liberal or authoritarian empires submitted more or less to the unwritten rules of cabinet diplomacy. The dynastic states introduced liberal institutions; the republics preserved certain habits of the dynastic regime; the multinational empires took national claims into account without dissolving in order to do so. All these compromises collapsed in the twentieth century, while a growing technological equality reduced the disproportion between space and resources on the one hand, and mobilizable military force on the other. Hitler still did not believe in the military force of the United States, on the pretext that the latter did not possess a military class. Many observers, before 1939, believed that Mussolini had greatly increased Italy's military force or that the Soviet Union, as a consequence of its technological backwardness or its regime, would be merely a secondary actor in the drama of the Second World War.

The present diversity of the political units which forces the European nations into second rank differs from the various diversities which the European system has experienced in past centuries. The modern monarchies outclassed the feudal principalities, but all peoples were in a position to hope for accession to this historical form. The novelty was of a political order. In a few years or in a few decades, the delay would be made up. The historical ideal is potentially accessible to all, except to the peoples who are prisoners of their history to the point of being unable to escape from it.

The obsolescence of nations assumes, in our period, the appearance of an irrevocable destiny. The approximate proportionality between force and resources, between resources and the number of men and the amount of raw materials, between mobilizable force and power, does not permit any hope that the leader's genius or the people's virtue might reverse the verdict of number. Even if the rate of economic growth is higher in one place than another, even if the nations of small space have a higher birth rate than those of great space, the latter cannot be equaled in terms of resources, hence of power, by the former.

The nations can nourish the hope (or the fear) that political units of vast space will in their turn disintegrate. The possibility is not excluded in the case of India, whose unity is that of a civilization, of a way of life, of thought and belief, and not of a political tradition, a language or a race. Looking even further ahead, the unity of the Soviet Union is also not definitively protected from the vicissitudes of politics, although the unit which withstood the revolutionary phase, between the fall of Tsarism and the establishment of Bolshevism, has a possibility of lasting and seems, moreover, to be reinforcing itself. Neither the unity of the United States nor that of China seems, in the foreseeable future, destined to fragmentation into rival states (although a dissolution by internal struggles is never impossible).

The advantages which fortune has showered upon the four great powers, the United States, the Soviet Union, China and India, are not the same. The United States is a colony of the European nations (in the sense in which we speak of the colonies founded by the Greek city-states). Having arrived with the equipment of European civilization, the immigrants managed to safeguard a single sovereignty over an enormous space. Thus they benefited from the traditions, the ideas, the techniques of the Old World without national barriers, without limitations of territories. The Slavs of Eastern Europe, long at a disadvantage because they were in the path of the Mongol invasions and because the climate was difficult, experienced a change of fortune. They were occupying a space still half empty; the demographic growth of the last century permitted them to extend their culture across vast spaces. Population growth and conquest by arms proceeded on equal footing. Two ages of history were telescoped into one. In the Soviet Union as in the United States, colonization was almost contemporary with accession to first rank in the international system.

The Middle Empire is the oldest and the longest-lasting in the history of humanity. It was even enlarged, in the last century, by the population of the northern regions, outside the Great Wall, which were for a long time the limit and the safeguard of imperial peace. The unity of the Empire was maintained down through the centuries by the administration of the literati, the almost religious authority of the emperor, the permanence of family and local structures, the prestige of a culture accessible to all Chinese by writing, whatever the diversity of the dialect spoken. The Communist regime, having re-established the authority of the central power over the entire Chinese space, builds factories, teaches everyone to read and write: authoritarian, industrial and mass-based, the Communist state makes China a giant.

It is India, among the four powers of gigantic dimensions, which alone has not yet achieved great power and which has the least chances of such an achievement or of preserving it should it succeed. Today, it suffers from the mediocrity of resources mobilizable by the state, as a result of the preponderance in the number of men over the number of machines. The population has grown faster than the productivity of labor; the relatively liberal regime does not permit this disparity to be reduced rapidly. The political and administrative class which controls the state owes its language to yesterday's conqueror and not, as in China's case, to the national heritage. China is becoming a nation in the European sense of the term, if it is not so already; India is and remains a civilization in the European sense of the term.

Must the decline of the European nations, which we impute to the widening of the diplomatic field, be interpreted in the light of historical precedents as a typical moment of Western "civilization"?

We do not choose to undertake here an analysis of the concept of civilization as Toynbee uses it (or of culture in the Spenglerian sense). To what degree are these immense units (of Hellenistic civilization or of Western civilization) *real*? What are their limits? To what cause do they owe their originality? Have they isolable histories? Are these histories the same, the similarity of destiny constituting the best proof of the very reality of these historical subjects?[8] The only problem that concerns us is that of a pattern of change which would impose order upon the apparent chaos of relations between political units. As far as these relations are concerned, do all civilizations pass through the typical phases? Is their succession determined in advance?

Let us consider Toynbee's ideas, as formulated by Quincy Wright.[9] The development of all civilizations can be broken down into four typical phases: *birth, growth, breakdown* and *distintegration*. With regard to relations among political units, the four phases would be that of the warrior states (or *heroic* phase), that of *time of troubles*, succeeded by the *stability of universal empire*, and lastly that of *decline* or disintegration. Leaving aside the initial and heroic phase, varying according to civilizations, the two characteristic moments are the *time of troubles* and the *universal empire*, the first inaugurated by a breakdown (Peloponnesian War) and terminated by the establishment of universal empire (established in 31 B.C. and lasting until A.D. 378).[10]

Reduced to its essentials, this vision may be summarized in the following terms: States dedicated to bellicose activity are born and develop at the same time as the civilization itself; starting from a crucial event, wars become destructive and not creative. They provoke a breakdown in the body of the civilization. The warring states exhaust themselves in their struggles, resign

---

[8] In a work published in Paris in 1961, *L'Histoire et ses interprétations*, discussions concerning Arnold Toynbee, under the direction of Raymond Aron, the reader will find remarks on these problems.
[9] Quincy Wright, *A Study of War*, Chicago, 1942, Vol. I, pp. 117 ff., 462 ff.
[10] I am taking the example of Hellenic civilization because I believe it has suggested to Arnold Toynbee the theory which we are discussing.

themselves to the empire which subjects them to a master but brings them peace. "Empire is peace," to recall a famous remark, but this peace is really a respite before the disintegration it heralds.

The historian who adopts as an intelligible field the study of civilizations necessarily rediscovers the opposition of the two phases, the *time of troubles* and *universal empire*, because these phases are defined in such a manner that they must, in one form or another, appear within all civilizations. At the outset we always find political units that are relatively limited. War being endemic among sovereign units, it is probable, so to speak *a priori*, that these units will exhaust themselves and that one will ultimately triumph over the others. *Time of troubles* and *universal empire* (from the point of view of international relations) add nothing to the two theoretic and formal concepts of *peace by equilibrium* and *peace by empire*. The important questions arise, it seems to me, beyond these resemblances, which are superficial and, one might say, inevitable.

Are these phases of approximately the same duration? Are universal empires all of the same species? It is enough to read Toynbee's work to observe that the empires are either ahead of time or behindhand for their rendezvous, and that it is extremely difficult to compare them.[11] The Ottoman Empire is the *universal empire* of the civilization of eastern Christianity, but several centuries late. The *universal empire* of China lasts well beyond the duration anticipated: it will be "petrified," since it is not on time for its rendezvous with death.[12] Hence it is related to the Japan of the Tokugawas, the phase of political unification of an island population of homogeneous culture, a unification resulting from the action of a shogun (or a palace major-domo) —that is, of a substitute for the emperor, whose sovereignty had never been formally rejected. To include in the same category the Roman Empire, constructed by a unit belonging to the ultimately pacified zone (or, one might say, to one of the marches of the zone); the Ottoman Empire, whose masters did not profess the same religion as those upon whom they imposed peace; the Mongol Empire, the creation of the steppe horsemen, as vast as it was precarious, and the empire which, through a small remote nation, and due to its naval superiority, extended for two centuries over the Indian continent, is rather to compromise than to confirm the method of historical comparisons. The alien conquerors, from steppes or oceans, whether Mongol or British, established themselves within the development of the civilizations to which they were alien. The nomad empires, at the moment of their founding, are

[11] In Vol. XII of *A Study of History* (Oxford University Press, 1961), Toynbee accentuates the heterogeneity of development of the various civilizations even further. Periods of synthesis among civilizations separate the death of one and the birth of the other.
[12] In his *Reconsiderations*, Toynbee suggests that there might be a "Chinese" or rather "Sinesian" model of development different from the Hellenic model, whose generality he had previously recognized (pp. 186 ff.).

not determined by the autonomous development of civilizations. Yet, only the empires which were the result of a *time of troubles* would reveal a kind of fatality in the crisis which they resolve: *imperial peace*, which would be the eventual outcome of *peace by equilibrium*.

Each of these two phases presents well-defined characteristics with regard to international relations, which Quincy Wright, interpreting Toynbee's thought, has attempted to articulate.[13] During the *time of troubles*, the international system belongs to the species of equilibrium: political units of various types (city-states, monarchies, empires) are knit in changing relations, whether peaceful or belligerent. The military systems are not all of the same type, some aristocratic (only the nobles bear arms or at least constitute the decisive force), the others democratic (all citizens, which does not signify all men, being summoned to fight). But by very reason of the duration of the campaigns, amateurs tend to become professionals, war to be considered by the belligerents as a supreme recourse. It constitutes the object of a juridical elaboration which specifies the limits and modes of hostilities, the rights and duties of belligerents and neutrals. It carries on a historical, readily recognizable function: it favors the widening of the diplomatic field and thereby permits the diffusion of a more or less vulgarized culture.

In the age of universal empire, wars no longer bring to grips monarchies or city-states which recognize each other and do not forget their relationship at the very moment they are in conflict, but empires and barbarians, incapable of a duel between equals, sometimes two empires doomed to coexistence because the military force of neither one extends as far as the center of the other, sometimes imperial troops and rebels (the Jews), impatient under the imperial yoke, who seek to preserve both their laws and their gods. Imperial wars against the barbarians, infra-imperial wars against rebels, inter-imperial wars to establish the limits of sovereignty, these three kinds of wars are increasingly waged by professionals, armed and equipped by the state. Philosophy exalts not war, the supreme expression of citizenship, but peace, which affords security and leisure to men of culture. War has a stabilizing function: the day imperial force fails, the uprising of the barbarians within and without the empire precipitates the collapse of the imposing construction.

Using analogous schemes, Spengler and Toynbee arrive at quite different judgments as to present circumstances. Spengler is a pessimist who regards hope (whether historical or religious) as cowardice. Man is a predatory animal; sciences and technologies are instruments of the will to power. Only minorities are authentically creative. Equality among men and democratic institutions herald and precipitate decadence. The creative minority of the West is in the process of being submerged by the double revolt of the white masses and the colored ones. Having transmitted the secrets of its power to the rest of humanity, the West will perish, a victim of the law of

---

[13] *Op. cit.*, I, 7, and Appendix 24, pp. 677–78.

number. We are living through the time of the Caesars: dignity compels us, as individuals, within the Western culture that has degenerated into a civilization,[14] to prepare ourselves for death.

Spengler was an admirer of the Prussian spirit, a spirit of duty, rigor and discipline, an aristocratic spirit. He scorned National Socialism because in it he found vulgarity, lack of decorum and style, characteristics of the democratic age. In the thirties of the twentieth century, he awaited the "decisive years" during which the division of the planet would be accomplished. Swept on by his admiration of the despots and his contempt for parliamentary regimes, he attributed to Mussolini an imperial opportunity in the Mediterranean that events did not confirm. Indubitably, he would denounce the victories of anti-colonialism, the decomposition of the colonial empires of Asia and Africa, as stages in the total disintegration of Western civilization. The United Nations would seem to him the height of hypocrisy, a contemptible and sinister farce: civilized men welcoming the "barbarians" as if they recognized them as equals, letting the "barbarians" decide historical conflicts by their votes.

By reverting to the concepts, vulgarized today, of internal and external proletariat, Toynbee took up the notion of the double revolt. The creative minority—he, too, attributes the initiative of culture to minorities alone—remains always isolated amid the common humanity. Sometimes the latter is ready to follow the example or the appeal of superior personalities, but is never imbued with the values or the significance of the highest works. As the political units are extended, as wars multiply the number of slaves and the conquered, force of arms must substitute for the lack of moral authority. Whether within or beyond the frontiers, the masses have lost their roots. They are within a civilization, but do not belong to it, are not integrated with it; they will listen to the words of a prophet and become the members of a universal Church which develops within the universal empire of the decadent civilization. Toynbee agrees with Spengler as to the facts: the decline of civilization, the revolt of the internal and external proletariat. But the hierarchy of values is contrary: at the summit, the impulse toward divinity and not the exploits of the Caesars. Thus temporal decline is in Toynbee's eyes a promise of a spiritual renewal. The empire is the framework of a Church, and the Church the soul of a nascent civilization.

It is not our intention to discuss these vast interpretations here. We merely wonder what enlightenment they afford us, and if they help us to understand the contemporary period. These comparative studies of civilizations are based on the relationship between the ancient world and the present. Similarities,

---

[14] The vocabulary is Spengler's, not our own. Throughout the rest of the book we use the word *culture* in the sense given to it by American anthropologists, or in the narrower sense of the creation of art or of thought. We employ the term *civilization* in two senses: either the great units of Toynbee, or the quality of existence, as expressed by the term *a civilized man*.

of course, can be found. But do these designs yield the essential? Do they permit us to anticipate our future?

Let us take, for example, one of Spengler's themes: the phase of *civilization* (urban concentration, development of technological means, democratic or demagogic politics, etc.) is also that of great wars, both civil and foreign. The Caesars have their armies, and their empire is the outcome of these chaotic conflicts. In this vision, which seems to have been Spengler's when he was writing *Der Untergang des Abendlandes*, the West had arrived at the wars which had marked the transition from the Roman Republic to the Roman Empire; it would soon reach the end of its millennium, the time period imparted to the living organisms that are cultures. According to Toynbee's chronology, 1914 was equivalent to 431 B.C.—that is, to the beginning of the Peloponnesian War, the moment of the "breakdown."

Is the phase of urban and technological society in itself a decadence? Or does this judgment merely reflect the preferences of the historian? Have not the forces of production, the scientific knowledge available to Western man developed to such a point that the urban civilization of the twentieth century constitutes not the end of a culture, but the beginning of a social type which, in all events, is destined to survive?[15]

Let us consider more particularly the aspect of civilizations which concerns us, international relations, and grant Toynbee's chronology: the War of 1914 is analogous to the Peloponnesian War. The creative center of a civilization —Greece or Western Europe—is involved in a war to the death from which result both the exhaustion of the center and the dimming of the lights. The moral coherence of the social body, in each of the units and in the entire civilization, is definitely impaired. Political sovereignty will be extended over a vaster space, but it will be imposed by arms and will not surmount the inner schism. What point have we reached in 1960?

In 1914 the European nations were the equivalent of the city-states. No pattern, it seems to us, appears in the process of the development of nations; nor does the development of the Greek city-states offer a regular order of change. One after the other, favored by the vicissitudes of civil struggles or by fortune, by their laws or by circumstances, they attained first rank, and rapidly lost it, exhausted by its exploits or betrayed by fate. The Spanish monarchy, united to the Empire by marriages and reinforced by the resources of America; the kingdom of France when political and administrative unity combined with a fertile soil and a favorable climate; Germany, having emerged from chaos, and served by the increase in the number of men and machines: each in turn played the glorious and bitter role of the troublemaker.

Today, are the European nations within the Atlantic Alliance like the Greek city-states under the Roman Empire? Or is the *pax Americana* only a

---

[15] Barring the catastrophe of war.

stage on the way to the *pax Sovietica?* Or is neither one of these hypotheses, suggested by precedents, valid—either because the nation, unlike the city-states or the empire, is a constant reality, or because the weapons of massive destruction are devaluating or revising foreign policy? Whatever the answer, it will be more convincing if it is based upon an analysis of the present rather than upon hazardous and superficial comparisons.

Let us take a position within the framework provided by Spengler and Toynbee. Western civilization presents, in relation to all those of the past, several singular characteristics which affect international relations. The nations have granted political and military citizenship, not only to all free men, but also to all their inhabitants. Nationality is the heritage of centuries; it is registered in the feelings of the people. Can the patriotism of a civilization or of an empire appear in the same manner in which Roman imperial patriotism was formed? Does Soviet patriotism resemble the imperial sentiment of the citizens of Rome? No sentiment of this order exists in European hearts with regard to the Atlantic Alliance. It has not even been shown that a European patriotism is coming into being.

Never before has a civilization been in contact with so many other civilizations; never has a civilization conquered so much land, overthrown so many customs, transmitted so much knowledge and power to the men who were conquered, enslaved, exploited by it. The liberation of India, the reconstitution of the Chinese Empire have nothing to do with the revolt of an external proletariat. No one knows if the equivalent of the Roman Empire is the *pax Americana* or the *pax Sovietica,* if there will be a peace embracing the system which spreads from San Francisco to Moscow, passing through Tokyo or Berlin, or if, even more enormous, it will include the rest of Asia, Africa and South America. How determine such a thing, since such a global system is unprecedented and since the coming phase of human history may create *several* civilizations, different from those of the West, of historical China or of eastern Christianity? Perhaps civilizations also belong to the past, and the history of tomorrow will perhaps be universal.

Lastly, political units have always been a function simultaneously of a historical idea, of international institutions and of the technique of combat. The historical idea in our period favors the nation rather than the empire, since it proclaims the right of peoples to their own destiny and regards as necessary the adherence of the governed to the state. If the power is wielded by means of another color or another race, speaking another language or worshiping other gods, how can the governed regard the state as their own? International institutions have functioned in the same direction, at least to the detriment of European empires. The weakened mother countries possessed no supranational principle to justify their rule. The Soviet Union is strong enough to forestall any interference from the United Nations, to tolerate autonomies of language and culture, to eliminate "bourgeois nationalisms." Finally, military technique, by its duality—weapons of massive destruction, weapons of individual destruction—helps to sustain Lilliputian states, permits the military unification of enormous zones, reduces the capacity of the great powers to oppress the weak ones. We are a long way from the Roman Empire, which was exclusively or almost exclusively maintained by the supremacy that the legions, as the result of discipline and organization maintained down through the centuries over the improvised combatants.

Certain of the phenomena that have marked the development of other civilizations are clearly seen in the course of recent centuries of Western history. But the singularities of these typical phases are more interesting than the characteristics by which the latter suggest the past. In the circumstances, historical comparisons lead to the comprehension of what we will never see twice.

3. Quantitative Inquiry

The search for patterns of change can take another path and follow another method. Hitherto, we have proceeded by direct observation and conceptual comparison; now, the quantitative method recommends itself for one immediately intelligible reason. Patterns of development are, so to speak, the common and unconscious work of men and events. The frequency or the intensity of a phenomenon belongs to that category of works imputable to everyone and to no one. What results does "sociometry" give for that characteristic phenomenon of international relations, war?

Such a study must surmount two difficulties: what definition of war to adopt? in what context is its frequency to be measured, its intensity determined?

The definition which we have adopted in the theoretical section, "armed conflict between political units," though adequate on the conceptual level, does not delimit the phenomenon of war on the level of concrete history. Throughout most centuries, international law was not sufficiently elaborated, the states were not clearly enough delimited, so that all "armed conflicts" were clearly defined, either as *internal* to a sovereign unit or as bringing sovereign units in conflict. Even in our own period, a doubt arises when the theoretical definition of the conflict is transformed between the beginning and the end of hostilities. Juridically, the Algerian War was, in unanimous opinion, a *revolt* in 1954. In the eyes of the governments which had recognized the Algerian provisional government it was a *foreign war*[16] in 1960.

An extreme definition would be the one proposed by a statistician, L. F. Richardson.[17] After all, what is a war if not the putting to death of men by

---

[16] At least a war of liberation.

[17] A summary of Richardson's ideas will be found in the chapter of the anthology published by T. H. Pear, *Psychological Factors of Peace and War*, London, 1950.

Two volumes by L. F. Richardson have recently been published, *Arms and Insecurity*, Quadrangle Books, Chicago, 1960 (published by Nicolas Rashevsky and Ernesto Trucco), and *Statistics of Deadly Quarrels*, Quadrangle Books, Chicago, 1960. The first is devoted to the study of the arms race. A summary and discussion of it will be

other men? A murderer kills one or two men; war is a chain murder or a mass murder. Between murder and war we may set piracy, gangsterism and collective banditry. Intermediary terms offer all the degrees of anarchy or organization. Say that thirty-two people out of a million are murdered every year; the world population being estimated at 1,358,000,000, the number of deaths by murder in a century amounts to millions (5 million between 1820 and 1939). It follows that the objective and quantitative method would be condemned of itself, though the common result is the death of men, if it ignored the fact that the *meaning* of human action is fundamentally different depending on whether murder or combat is involved.

Language offers a great number of different expressions to designate various modes of the more or less organized use of force[18]: internally, we speak of riots, insurrections, revolts and revolutions; externally, of interventions, punitive expeditions, pacification. Qualitatively, it is not difficult to specify the nuances which these expressions are intended to distinguish. Riot seems spontaneous. It concerns a relatively small faction of the population and a relatively narrow space; the rioters oppose law, order, the government; they employ force and are reduced by force, but they do not always have a strictly political organization or objectives (overthrowing the government or regime). Riot becomes insurrection not so much by assuming more extensive directions as by the intervention of leaders, by the presence of a more specifically political will. The insurgents know what they want, at least negatively. Revolution[19] transcends the stage of riot or insurrection when the established power, government or regime collapses. Civil war breaks out when neither the government nor the insurgents immediately gain the victory. A quantitative analysis obviously does not retain these distinctions, which are often vague in reality. These various cases are covered by the concept, utilized by

---

found in A. Rapaport's *Flights, Games, and Debates*, University of Michigan Press, 1960. The second deals more generally with "deadly quarrels." There is no question of undertaking here a detailed discussion of the method and results.

As for the problem which we are examining in this chapter, Richardson's conclusions agree with those of Quincy Wright and with the ideas which we ourselves are developing. For example, Richardson observes no distinct tendency, in the period from 1820 to 1945, either to an augmentation or to a diminution of the frequency of wars. There is perhaps a tendency of great wars to become more frequent and of small wars to become less so.

The various states have not participated so often in wars, but, depending on the periods of history, a given state has taken part in them more or less often. Therefore it is impossible to qualify a state as pacific or warlike as such. States have a tendency to be involved in wars in proportion to the number of states with which they have common frontiers.

Richardson observes, however, that the population increase, from 1810 to 1949, has not been accompanied by a proportional increase in the frequency of wars and the loss in human lives chargeable to the latter. He concludes that this is an indication, not a conclusive proof, that humanity has become less bellicose.

[18] Very often, force is organized on one side alone.

[19] Revolt suggests a more general phenomenon than insurrection, but one which does not result in a revolution.

Sorokin, of "internal disturbances": violent conflicts with the use of available weapons between more or less organized groups within a zone of sovereignty.

The multiplicity of terms serving to designate the methods of the use of force by a state outside its frontiers—intervention, punitive expedition, police operation, pacification—is explained by the heterogeneity of the populations or units in conflict. In the nineteenth century, the French referred to the conquest or the pacification of Algeria because they recognized neither the Algerian state (which perhaps did not exist) nor the human equality of the Algerians. The formula "Algerian War" was already an implicit recognition of the claims of the Algerian nationalists. The latter expressed themselves, moreover, as if the Algerian state had never ceased to exist. On each side, in conformity with the customs of the century, history was being rewritten. On one side we imagine a *tabula rasa* in 1830, on the other we confer a noble lineage upon the Algerian state by according it a past. Interventions or punitive expeditions similarly designated the action of armed force against populations considered as inferior, which the foreign state wished to punish rather than to conquer.

The two most valid attempts to surmount the conceptual difficulties are those of Quincy Wright and of Sorokin. The first combines two criteria, one juridical (distinct sovereignties), the other quantitative (number of combatants above fifty thousand).[20] Thereby, he attenuates the disadvantage resulting from the comparison of heterogeneous phenomena, riots on one side, foreign wars on the other. In fact, the quantitative criterion that he employs —the number of combatants—renders it probable that only civil wars will be confused with foreign wars. And civil wars offer, in the eyes of sociology if not of theory, characteristics which make them comparable to foreign wars.

More satisfactory, it seems to me, is Sorokin's method, which distinguishes, at the outset, internal disturbances and wars between states. As for the intensity of the phenomenon of war, Sorokin[21] combined several criteria, all quantitative: size of armies, number of victims, duration of operations, proportion of combatants to total population. These criteria are acceptable, although they do not permit us to measure either the social cost or the historical importance of wars. The number of dead is less important than the relation of this number to the size of the population and to the latter's capacity for recovery. The several dozen dead at Trafalgar weighed much more heavily in the balance of history than the hundreds of thousands of Frenchmen or Germans dead or wounded at Verdun. Similarly, it is reasonable, in measuring the intensity of the disturbances, to use several criteria: the dimension of the zone involved, the duration of the disturbances, intensity of the violence, the masses affected (each nation is assigned an index propor-

[20] Cf. Quincy Wright, *op. cit.*, Vol. I, Appendix 20, p. 636.
[21] P. A. Sorokin, *Social and Cultural Dynamics*, New York, 1937; particularly Vol. III, Parts 2 and 3. Sorokin's ideas are clearly summarized in F. R. Lowell's *History, Civilization and Culture*, London, 1952.

tional to its weight in the ensemble of the civilizations studied). But, even if this method is rational, it grasps only the quantitative aspect of the internal violence of states. There are creative "disturbances" and others that are historically sterile. The Bolshevik party, according to a famous formula, had no more difficulty seizing power than in picking up a pen. A million Spaniards died in the course of a civil war whose monument, raised by Franco, symbolizes sterile cruelty.

Let us accept the quantitative method, with its inevitable limitations. In what context would it be suitable to apply it and to what result does it lead? Quincy Wright and his collaborators have studied every war (in the sense which they give this word) between 1480 and 1941. They counted 278[22] for modern civilization and established the number of belligerencies for each of the chief nations as follows[23]: England 78, France 71, Spain 64, Russia 61, Austria 52, Turkey 43, Poland 30, Sweden 26, Savoy (Italy) 25, Prussia 23, Holland 23, United States 13, China 11, Japan 9. If we limit ourselves to the 1850–1941 period, the results are as follows: Great Britain 20, France 18, Savoy (Italy) 12, Russia 11, China 10, Spain 10, Turkey 10, Japan 9, Prussia (Germany) 8, United States 7, Austria 6, Poland 5, Holland 2, Denmark 2, Sweden none. The statistician feels an understandable tendency to conclude that the distinction proclaimed by the United Nations Charter between peace-loving nations and the others exists only in the imagination or the hypocrisy of the statesmen of the winning camp.

This conclusion is, in fact, probable. We know, in 1960, how easily "national stereotypes" are transformed according to the vicissitudes of diplomacy. What image did American public opinion have of the Japanese, the Chinese, the Russians, and the Germans in 1941? What image has it today of these same peoples who have inverted their diplomatic role, the Japanese having changed from enemies to allies and the Chinese from allies to enemies, Germans and Russians having also executed the same maneuver? The number of wars in which a nation participates measures the role played by each state on the international stage rather than the aggressiveness of the state or the people involved. If Spain is in the third rank in the classification established for the period 1480–1941, and falls to the sixth rank for the period 1850–1941, the cause is not her conversion to pacifism, but her political decline.

The fact that frequency of participation is proportional to the position occupied by each state in the diplomatic field suggests that common sense is not wrong, despite all propaganda: states are much alike. Not that they are, *at every moment*, equally bellicose, imperialistic, cruel. Certainly, satisfied peoples are less aggressive than revolutionary or demanding peoples. The behavior of peoples is also determined by the relation of forces. But there is not,

[22] *Op. cit.*, pp. 638 ff.
[23] *Ibid.*, p. 650.

in the long run, a nation of the first rank which has been constantly pacific or constantly bellicose.

By another mode of calculation, Sorokin arrives at the same proposition with regard to the propensity to internal disturbances, that is, to violence in internal struggles. The culminating points of violence are not the same, within the same zone of civilization, for the different political units. Each nation has its history, but all national histories resemble each other in the eyes of the statistician or the moralist.

As for the last five centuries of European history, the procession of trouble-makers, the fluctuations in relations of forces, does not seem to have exerted an apparent influence, in one direction or the other. For the period 1500–1715, Quincy Wright noted 143 wars, for the period 1716–1941, 156. It is true that by taking shorter periods of a half century, he observed an unequal frequency of armed conflicts. But he perceived no regularity in these oscillations.

Here the decisive question arises. That the nineteenth century, after 1815, was relatively peaceful in Europe, is acknowledged by all historians, and if the statisticians claimed to refute this impression by statistics, we should venture to contradict them. Historically, there occurred in Europe, between 1860 and 1914, neither a conflict that became general, nor hostilities that overthrew the internal order of states or the movement of ideas and institutions. Granted, the conflicts were all the more numerous in that they were localized, the peoples of Europe multiplied their remote expeditions, during the periods when they were not fighting among themselves. Combativeness is perhaps constant, historical expressions of combativeness are variable.

Many philosophers or scholars would like to discover the law of these variations. It is tempting to imagine cycles, outcroppings, on the surface of history, of biological phenomena. None of the demonstrations which have been attempted seems convincing to me. It is true that after a great war or a prolonged period of wars (1791–1815), it appears as if the nations, like living beings, renewed their forces. Have these formulas of biological resonance more than the value of a comparison or of an image?

The interval between two wars is of one generation, some say, that is, about twenty years: the most striking example is the explosion, twenty years after the 1918 Armistice, of the second European war. Others claim that the interval is of two generations, as was the case between 1870 and 1914. The sons would not forget, but the grandsons would have forgotten the lesson of the preceding massacres and would be swept on by martial ardor toward the fields of glory and horror. Neither hypothesis seems to me to have any general bearing. After the great slaughter, a more or less prolonged phase of alleviation ordinarily intervenes. Those who regard overpopulation as the major cause of men's propensity to kill each other refer to "demographic relaxation." Those who imagine a kind of alternation of expansion and contraction, of belligerent vitality and recuperation, explain the explosions of violence by the mysterious laws of collective life. If events do not correspond precisely to the proposed pattern, there is nothing to prevent taking into account revolutions or internal disturbances under the same heading as wars. With ingenuity, the "crises" of French history in the nineteenth century are organized according to a quasi-regular succession, 1830, 1848, 1870, 1890. I confess I have difficulty giving any precise meaning to such perspectives. How could the losses of men imputable to civil and foreign wars be the immediate origin, the direct cause of a revolution like that of 1830, of a diplomatic conflict like that provoked by the ambitions of Prussia and the weakness of Napoleon III in 1870?[24]

Of all the quantitative studies, Sorokin's seems to me the most constructive. The distinction between internal disturbances and wars prevents us from confusing phenomena essentially different, to follow and evaluate two phenomena, the role of violence in the internal politics of states, the frequency and intensity of armed conflicts between states. That these two phenomena tend to be identified at the birth and death of states, that in certain circumstances they mingle and aggravate each other does not keep their meaning from being different and their role in history divergent.

The merit of Sorokin's statistical study is precisely, it seems to me, that it illuminated the fact that the two curves are not parallel. Applied to the ancient world, the study reveals that wars reach their culminating point in the third century B.C. (the century of the Punic Wars), that on the other hand the curve of internal disturbances continues to rise until the first century B.C. Of course, in the case of Rome, it is not surprising that the Punic Wars, in which the victor was to exert hegemony over the Mediterranean basin, mark the culminating point of the "phenomenon of war," while the centuries of transition between the Republic and the Empire, that is, of armed struggles between the candidates for supreme power, mark the culminating point of the phenomenon of "internal disturbances." Nonetheless, if we grant the validity of the method, the results, at least of a negative order, are not insignificant.

Sorokin denies that we can establish a correlation between wars and internal disturbances, between the intensity of one or the other phenomenon and the prosperity or the decline of collectivities. He denies that we can perceive either a regular movement toward "more" or "less" or a regular alternation of more and less. The internal disturbances of Western civilization have reached three separate peaks, in the eighth century, in the thirteenth and fourteenth centuries, in the nineteenth and twentieth centuries. These three eras would coincide with the periods of transition between two types of culture that Sorokin christens *ideational* and *sensate*.

[24] I refer to the hypotheses of C. Moraze in *Les Français et la République*, Paris, 1956.

It is not our task to discuss the whole of Sorokin's conceptions. We are not convinced that the concepts which he uses to characterize the types of culture are either the only possible ones or the best ones. A typology which must apply to civilizations as remote from each other, in time and in styles of living, as those of antiquity and our own day, is by nature debatable. It would be difficult for me to grant that wars and internal disturbances can be subsumed under the same concept of *breakdown of social relations*. That this is the meaning of internal disturbances, it is easy enough to admit, since every collectivity tends to create an order which tolerates the use of force only for its own maintenance. But the recourse to force to settle conflicts among collectivities has been regarded, down through the centuries, as inevitable, legal and in conformity with the essence of inter-state relations. Thus war is not as such a "breakdown of social relations," since it is linked to the nature of political societies. But since political societies have generally been created by force and since, as they gradually extend themselves, they become more heterogeneous, they sometimes experience internal disturbances which increase in intensity as the intensity of foreign wars decreases. The empire which renounces expansion must still repress rebellions and insure succession to the throne.

Further, the coincidence between the intensity of internal disturbances and the transitional phases between two cultures retains a meaning even for those who do not accept Sorokin's typology. That the intensity of the disturbances is a function of the profundity and the rapidity of social changes is a proposition which will be regarded as commonplace enough. But the quantitative method occasionally permits us to reveal, and not only to confirm, the depth and rapidity of the changes. Above all, the two curves (if we grant their exactitude) rule out the representations of an ordered development, either toward alleviation, or on the contrary toward an increased combativeness, or of an alternation of more or less warlike phases. Yet, the absence of a pattern of change is an indirect proof of a certain interpretation of the phenomenon of war.

The interpretation to which all the preceding analyses led us is, if I may use the expression, historical-sociological. War is a social phenomenon, but unique among all social phenomena; it is both affirmation and negation of *sociality*, of the social relation between the combatants. When the latter belong to the same society and are aware of the fact, they experience armed struggle as a temporary dissolution of their community. When the combatants belong to societies foreign to each other and related, they experience their dispute as significant and legitimate, but the historian is inevitably inclined to judge it as sterile, since it has as its goal a peace which will be precarious as long as the political units insist on the right to take the law into their own hands. In the historical perspective, the wars that are in conformity with their essence, irreducible to internal disturbances, are at most negatively creative (they have avoided the despotism of a conqueror). Imperial and civil wars are fruitful, those which provoke or delimit political units, those which determine the historical idea or regime which will triumph within a constituted unit. Hence, that there is no pattern of change is readily explained: the high points of violence coincide with the phases of fruitful wars,[25] when the structure or principle of the political units is again called into question, when their diplomatic system is decomposed and another appears. The so-called transition periods between two cultures are those during which internal disturbances reach a point of extreme intensity. If the final causes of violence are historical and social, its development is incoherent, according to the image of the destiny of states and values. Space, number and resources are conditions or partial stakes. But men fight because they put ideas in the service of their will to power or the will to power in the service of their ideas, because they live in communities, both related and alien, which consent neither to submit to each other nor to ignore each other. The fundamental causes of wars have been constant down through recorded history. The intensity of the phenomenon of war has been irregular on account of the diversity of the circumstances which increase or reduce it.

4. The Meaning of Human History

There remains, however, one last possibility of discovering a pattern of change: not within the vast groups which we have called civilizations but from one to the other or, at least, from one family of civilizations to another. The hypothesis has no meaning if we refer to Spengler's philosophy since, according to the latter, each civilization[26] is unique in the world, the expression of an individual soul, enclosed within the biological cycle of birth, maturity and death. According to Toynbee, on the other hand, it is possible to distinguish primary, secondary and tertiary civilizations, depending on whether they are born of non-complex societies, of another civilization, itself primary, or finally of a civilization which had already undergone, in its cradle, the influence of another civilization. Western civilization is tertiary because it has emerged from Hellenic civilization (or classical civilization, according to the vocabulary of Quincy Wright), itself the result of Minoan civilization.

The comparison of civilizations taken as a whole, from the viewpoint of international relations or of war, is still more problematical than that of epochs or of city-states. The only attempt we are familiar with is that of Quincy Wright and his collaborators, which seems to me to err in method. The crucial question is simply the following: is it possible to measure *as a whole* the "bellicosity" of a civilization? Quincy Wright employs four criteria[27]: *habits of cruelty* resulting from religious rites, spectacles, sports;

---

[25] Historically fruitful: what is produced may seem to us detestable.
[26] Spengler speaks of culture, not of civilization. According to him, civilization is a culture's phase of decadence. But we shall continue to use our vocabulary and to call civilizations the vast units which he calls cultures.
[27] *Op. cit.*, Vol. I, p. 122.

aggressiveness manifested by frequency of invasions, imperial or inter-state wars; *rigor or influence of military morality* as revealed in the discipline of the armies; and lastly *tendency to despotism or to centralization,* the presence or absence of constitutional limits to the exercise of power.

Utilizing these four criteria simultaneously, Quincy Wright's investigators have established the following classification:

1. The most bellicose civilizations: classical, Tartar, Babylonian, Syrian, Iranian, Japanese, Andean, Mexican.

2. Moderately bellicose: Hittite, Arab, Germanic, Western, Scandinavian, Russian, Yucatanian.

3. The most peaceful: Egyptian, Minoan, Orthodox, Sumerian, Nestorian, Irish, Indian, Hindu, Sinoese, Chinese, Mayan.

The classification does not permit us to discern, from the primary civilizations to the secondary or tertiary ones, the movement toward more or less "bellicosity." Among the most bellicose figure civilizations belonging to the three ages. Nor does any simple correlation with race or geography appear. At most, it is possible to enumerate a few circumstances favorable to the "bellicosity" of civilizations: heterogeneity of populations, facility of communications, the role played by shepherds or nomads. Mountain or plateau civilizations would thus be of a bellicose tendency.

In fact, I doubt that the very notion of a "bellicosity" of civilizations is usable. At best one might employ it with a view to a strictly quantitative study, analogous to Sorokin's. But the documents do not permit the extension of such a method to various civilizations. As for the criteria indicated by Quincy Wright, they are, taken individually, significant, but so heterogeneous that the result obtained by combining them is probably not so.

Let us take criteria two and three, the frequency of invasions and wars and the rigor of military morality, which seem most nearly related. The classical contest of Athens and Sparta reminds us that the aggressiveness of one political unit is not proportional to the rigor of the military order or of the mode of government. During the two hundred years of the Tokugawas, the Japanese order was of a military yet non-aggressive spirit. Similarly, the democratic societies of the West have established a civilian mode of government, but have nonetheless waged great wars. Did they wage these wars because the Prussian Empire and the Tsarist Empire were still impregnated with military morality? Could one say that Soviet despotism in Russia or in China is the cause of aggressiveness and that peace would prevail among the states of the democratic-liberal regime? I confess I am not convinced. Such interpretations were fashionable a generation ago. At present we understand better to what lengths the "cunning of reason" can go. A society of liberal philosophy, such as the American society, does not exalt war for its own sake, it is pacifist in principle, but should the occasion arise it will be impulsive, irascible and seek unconditional victory after having, by negligence, so to speak, invited aggression. It is the heterogeneity of regimes that favors explosions more than any one regime as such.

We would not attempt to deny the difference in "bellicosity" between peoples and between states, whichever of the four criteria—cruelty, aggressiveness, rigor of the military order, mode of government—are used to define it. It is probable, too, that the civilizations seem unequally belligerent—and are so in fact in the quantitative sense[28]—depending on the roles which the warrior groups play in them, depending on their style of living or their way of governing themselves. The important thing is to dissipate the illusion according to which a society whose internal order is civilian, which has eliminated cruel spectacles or sports, which has multiplied constitutional guarantees, would thereby be protected against aggressions or against its own aggressiveness.

It is possible that, in the past, there has been a vague correlation between these various phenomena and that, taken as a whole, the Sinoese and later the Chinese civilization was less belligerent, in several ways at the same time: the populations were less inclined to aggression, they did not experience such frequent wars or invasions, they did not live, in peacetime, according to a military order; but these characteristics, once again, are not always found together. The twentieth century has been bellicose, if we judge it according to the number and the cost of its wars; its political order has nonetheless been detached from the military order and its dominant philosophy has been pacifist. The most ruinous wars are not always waged by the nations for which combat is a national activity.

Must we submit to the gloomy conclusion of one ethnologist at the end of the last century: "There is no evolution of war"? Charles Letourneau devoted a series of books to the evolution of the great social phenomena—commerce, politics, economy, ownership. He also devoted a book to war,[29] in the title of which, however, the word evolution did not figure. All phenomena evolve, he said, except for war.

Certainly the evolutionist representation of the successive forms of commerce, of ownership or of the state were, in many respects, simplistic or illusory. The transformation of politics and of economy are neither so well ordered nor so distinctly oriented. But Letourneau's assertion remains a troublesome question: is war not only endemic in all civilizations or all periods, but constant in its nature and its forms? Is it always the same because it is a negation of everything that man is trying to create within and outside of himself by the age-old effort of culture? Is war the sudden and violent return to savagery, refractory to all evolution because alien to what is properly human in men?

That men in the twentieth century are as capable of cruelty as those of

[28] Frequency and intensity of armed conflicts.
[29] *La Guerre dans les diverses races humaines,* Paris, 1895.

the fifth or tenth centuries B.C., we, as contemporaries of the concentration camps, the gas chambers and the atom bombs, can no longer doubt. That soldiers, swept on by the ardor of battle, commit atrocities worse than those of the men called savages, no one can deny. That police and interrogators have invented refinements of physical and moral torture, we know only too well. If the murder of one's own kind is the essence of the phenomenon of war, if killing as such defines war, then the latter is in fact immutable, defined in its essence by the eternal part of itself.

One fact is indisputable: wars resemble, in many respects, the societies that wage them. The resemblance is *always* that of weapons and tools. The resemblance is *almost always*, whether direct or subtle, that of the social stratification and of the military system. The resemblance of tools and weapons is striking in our own period. The resemblance of the civilian and military order is camouflaged, since the ruling classes are no longer military classes. But this apparent originality of modern societies, organized differently in peacetime and in war, is merely one of the expressions of a more profound originality: international relations have participated in the modern process of rationalization. Analyzed in all its aspects, this rationalization explains both the industrialization of hostilities (the relationship of weapons and tools) and the claim that political power has nothing in common with the military order.

The rationalization involves, in effect, the *differentiation* of activities and functions. In many circumstances the force employed against rebels presents an aspect materially similar to that of the force employed against the enemy. But we designate one or the other by different words because police action has a different meaning from the action of war. This essential duality has even seemed so obvious that we have posited it as a theoretical point of departure. This duality exists in germ in the simplest societies, but, during the course of the historic phase, it was often vague because the political unit created by armed force was maintained by it. Most states did not resist the decomposition of armed force, the supreme recourse and guarantee of the leaders even during the years of peace.

The heterogeneity of the civilian order and the military order is no less in conformity with the historical experience of the last century. The middle class that has taken control of the European nations regards itself as the manager of labor and not as a fighting group. It does not believe that its power is based on force, although force remains at its disposal in order to make its legitimacy respected. Marxism and the American philosophy of politics both emerge from this bourgeois age. The former, enlarging into a general theory the incompletely analyzed experience of capitalism, regards ownership of the means of production as the root of power and privilege, whereas in fact the possession of weapons often precedes that of tools. The American philosophy tends to generalize the experience of immigrants who have triumphed over nature, whose community has emerged from industrial enterprise and not from conquest and who, consequently, have spontaneously recognized the radical antinomy of the military and civilian orders.

International relations being conceived in their specific characteristics, a double rationalization has intervened, that of law and that of theory, formal or sociological. Jurists have elaborated the concepts, specified the consequences of sovereignty, deduced the consequences of the compartmentalization of territorial space and the non-compartmentalization of the sea, established the rights and duties of belligerents and non-belligerents, multiplied international organisms established by convention between sovereign states, and determined rules to which international relations of a private or social and non-state order will be subject. The juridical rationalization left the legitimacy of recourse to war extant up until the League of Nations and the Kellogg-Briand Pact (perhaps even despite the League of Nations and the Kellogg-Briand Pact). Theory, sociological or abstract, thus attempted to elaborate the implications and the conditions of the efficacy of diplomatic-strategic conduct, in the shadow of the threat of war or with a view toward victory. Clausewitz's theory assumes the existence of war as a hypothesis and asks how war should be waged. The theory which this book develops has as its title *Peace and War, A Theory of International Relations* because it tends toward the rational formulation of diplomatic-strategic conduct.

Juridical rationalization and theoretical rationalization are inspired by the same spirit but risk entering into conflict. The more the former aims at resolving conflicts by substituting law for force, the more serious the stake must be in order to justify the rupture of juridical links and the return to age-old brutality. But war, in essence, tends to escalate. Envisaged in terms of its concepts, war leads to the unlimited amplification of violence. Absolute victory is the goal: instrumental rationality enjoins the use of all means in order to achieve it. Since an industrial society lends itself to total mobilization, the same societies that boast of being civilian by belief have perhaps been the only ones, in the event of war, to carry to its conclusion the militarization of society.

Rationalization in its triple form (differentiation, conceptual elaboration, reflection on the essence and effectiveness of diplomatic-strategic conduct) has not yet changed the nature of international relations as they have been observed down through the ages. Means of combat have been in the image of the tools. The contradiction of societies which sought to be peaceful and which have waged total war is expressed in the outburst of propaganda, in the hypocrisy of states, in the conflict of philosophies of foreign policy. Each great power has its doctrine of peace, by international law or by socialism.

War is increasingly divested of every element of peace, until it leads to the extermination of whole peoples and loses its meaning in human terms. Peace is increasingly recognized as alone conforming to the common interest of the belligerents: war is outlawed. Are the instrumental logic of total war and the juridical logic of war-outlawed-as-a-crime doomed to contradict each other?

Does the development of instrumental rationality offer a prospect of salvation? War has imposed total mobilization by application of rational calculation to the conduct of hostilities. Will this same calculation fail to impose peace upon the thermonuclear age?

chapter XII

The Roots of War as an Institution

Is man *by nature* peaceful or belligerent? The question was raised in times when philosophers referred to *nature* in order to establish or explain *social* phenomena. But, depending on the term to which it was opposed, the concept of nature had different meanings.

We have several times, in the first part of this book, alluded to the *state of nature* which subsists among political units and which is opposed to the *civil state*. The latter exists among the members of a collectivity subject to laws, to a legitimate authority. On the other hand, men, before they were in the civil state, recognized neither rule nor master and behaved as their nature impelled or authorized them.

In effect, two ideas are combined in the philosophers' descriptions of the pre-civil state: that of man as he would be outside of all society, as an animal or a being endowed with reason, and that of man as he would be entitled to be if each individual were to rely only on himself. The description of this state of nature by Hobbes and Spinoza has this double character: a psychology of man, conceived as non-social, and the morality of force valid in the absence of the accepted norms.

Is this *natural man* the man he was at the dawn of history? Or, man as he still is today, when government collapses, in revolutions or in the relations among sovereign collectivities? Or as he is defined by the rational or supernatural vocation established within him? In other words, is he *natural* as opposed to *historical*, to *civil*, to *rational* or to *supernatural?* Historical man, certainly, belongs to a collectivity and participates in reason. Is nature contrary to sociability, to reason, or, quite the opposite, does nature tend toward a goal of life in society bound by reason? Depending on whether one admits one hypothesis or the other, the concept of nature has a contrary meaning.

In the expression *natural law,* the adjective suggests universality, that which belongs to man as man, without the particularities which the various *societies* add to him. The law of nations has been inspired by *natural law,* but it has never been able to eliminate the *state of nature.* Precisely because sovereigns do not constitute a civil order, their obligations and prerogatives are those derived from the universal and rational essence of man. But, since none guarantees them the respect of their rights, they must defend them themselves.

The many problems raised by the meanings of the concept of nature are today dissociated. We must question biologists, psychologists, ethnologists and philosophers who give partial and complementary answers to the question as old as history: if war is endemic, is it because man is naturally bellicose? Or, on the contrary, is it possible to conceive of a peaceful humanity whose nature has not changed?

By an apparent paradox, the state of nature, conceived as the war of each against all, does not exclude a theory of eternal peace. Hobbes, having posited that men are by nature at war, relies upon absolute power to constrain them to live in peace. He does not explicitly envisage peace among states because, among the latter, the state of nature has not been surmounted. But, projected into history by Hegelian and Marxist philosophy, the death struggle, having become a struggle for recognition, is at the origin of un-restricted wars; yet it does not condemn the hope of a global peace (or of a universal state). On the contrary, Montesquieu, who writes: "As soon as man enters into a state of society, he loses the sense of his weakness; equality ceases, and then commences the state of war,"[1] counsels limiting tyranny by the balance of power and war by moderation. If man is violent and society peaceful, history leads to peace insofar as it results in a worldwide society. If the roots of warfare are in society itself, wisdom obliges us to adapt our-selves to it.

1. Biological and Psychological Roots

Biologists call *aggressiveness* the propensity of an animal to attack another,[2] of the same species or of a different species.[3] Most animals, but not all, fight within each species. Some are not aggressive—that is, do not take the initiative of attack, but defend themselves when attacked.

According to biologists, fighting, in the animal kingdom, cannot be re-garded as either accidental or abnormal. Aggression is a constant and ap-parently a useful part of the daily behavior of many animals and becomes destructive and harmful only under exceptional circumstances.

Vertebrates of all classes—fish, amphibians, reptiles, birds, mammals—fight. The primates, among which are included the human race, are very unequally combative from the "gibbons in which both sexes fight so vigorously that they can exist only in small family groups to the howling monkeys whose fighting never grows beyond vocalization in either sex."[4] The human race is

---

[1] *L'Esprit des lois*, I, 3.
[2] J. P. Scott, *Aggression*, Chicago, 1958, p. 1: "Used precisely, 'aggression' refers to fighting and means the act of initiating an attack."
[3] As a matter of fact, biologists generally consider aggression among animals of the same species.
[4] *Ibid.*, p. 6.

situated on the upper part of the aggressiveness scale among the primates. Man, as an animal, is relatively combative—in other words, a slight stimulus is enough to release aggression.

The primary stimuli of aggression, in the animal kingdom, are many, and some of them suggest conflicts among human beings. An animal that is made to suffer reacts aggressively; the mouse whose tail is pinched by the experimenter tries to bite him. Many animals, fish and birds fight for the defense of their space, which one is tempted to call a territory. The European sticklebacks fight savagely near their nests, but not elsewhere. Hence they rarely indulge in death struggles unless their nests are near each other. At equal distance from their respective nests, the sticklebacks do not attack, but threaten each other. The outcome of the struggle depends on the distance between the respective nests. The fish closest to its nest is victorious and its adversary flees toward its own place of residence.[5] Similarly, certain mammals live in peace as long as each group does not leave what it appears to regard as "its territory"; on the other hand, an individual belonging to another group is attacked and repulsed if it crosses the line of separation. Food and females are the other frequent stimuli of animal aggressiveness, although the diversity is extreme from one species to the other.

Combativeness or the propensity to aggression varies, within the same species, with sex, age, and often with individuals. Within a species the females are generally less inclined to aggression than the males, but certain females in the upper range of the female aggression scale may be above certain males at the lower range of the masculine aggression scale. Each human individual is endowed by heredity with a certain amount of aggressiveness. We know today that this amount can be increased or diminished by chemical substances. Doctors report that they are now or will be capable of making any man into a lion or a lamb, temporarily or permanently. Whether animal or human, combativity has a strictly biological root.

Combative behavior is modified by the experience of the individual, is learned and is forgotten. Biologists have experimented on mice and shown conditioned reflexes of combat, flight and passivity, in response to one stimulus or another. The learning of combative behavior conforms to the general principles of learning which the Pavlovian school has demonstrated for other kinds of behavior. J. P. Scott insists on a particular characteristic of combative behavior: it disappears slowly. A long time is needed to inhibit the aggressive reaction (as a result of the physiological and emotional phenomena that accompany aggressiveness).

One of the methods of training mice for struggle is particularly striking. An animal that for several days has been allowed apparent victories over adversaries introduced earlier into its cage and then withdrawn . . . will fling

[5] Cf. Konrad Z. Lorenz, *King Solomon's Ring*, London, 1952. Analogous behavior is observed in other species.

itself upon the first rival that resists it. Generally a victor, it becomes still more combative. By easy successes an animal is made capable of fighting, and made into a fierce combatant. A contrary habit either of fleeing battle or of submitting to the stronger without fighting is created among individual mice who have received punishment.

Whether spontaneous or the result of learning, combative behavior, to the human observer, often seems adaptive. Whether the bird drives away the "alien" that approaches it nest, or dogs or baboons fight over a female, aggression tends to remove the cause of the possible danger, to insure something valuable to the victor. Further, animal struggle often leads to a kind of order as war leads to peace.

When two hens meet for the first time, they generally fight; one wins and the other loses. The next time they fight again but the loser gives up more rapidly. After some time, a habit is formed for one of them to threaten combat and for the other to run away. The first is called dominant and the other subordinate. And this hierarchy of force, confirmed by the experience of struggle, is stable, durable, pacified. Experimenters have the greatest difficulty reversing the hierarchy—for example, inciting a dominated mouse to resume the struggle.

Pacification by hierarchy, as a result of the outcome of the struggle, is the contrary of spontaneous pacification among animals raised together, or even among the adults and young living with them. But this primitive socialization also creates, in the animal kingdom, differentiation among family members and aliens, among members of the group and others. The pacification of intra-social relations is often accompanied by the hostility of relations between groups or among individuals of distinct groups.

Among the higher vertebrates, groups or packs often manifest aggressiveness with regard to alien individuals. Thus the wolf differentiates between the members of its own pack and others. More rarely, it is among groups or packs that the aggressiveness is released. In the human race, on the other hand, manifestations of aggressiveness are inseparable from collective life. Even when it is a question of one individual against another, aggressiveness is in many ways influenced by the social context. Aggressiveness of the group toward one of its members, toward an outsider, or toward another group as such—these three phenomena are normally to be found in any society. A group of young boys has its internal hierarchy and sometimes its scapegoat. It offers a united front to the isolated individuals who do not submit to discipline, and sometimes explodes into hostility against a rival group.

The advent of a truly social existence is not the only factor responsible for the new dimensions assumed by the phenomenon of aggressiveness: frustration and non-adaptation resulting from the aggressive reaction constitute the major phenomenon in human relations. Now frustration is a psychic experience; our consciousness reveals it to us. Every human individual experiences frustration from his earliest years. He suffers from being deprived of food, affection, and rarely has the means of adapting himself by aggression to this situation of which he feels himself the victim. He is wounded by the behavior of others, and he cannot cure his wound by fighting against his aggressor, whether the latter is deliberate or not. He does not manifest his aggressiveness externally, but far from being "at peace" internally, he is quite agitated with repressed fury, with contained hostility.

Psychoanalysts have analyzed the mechanisms by which psychic disturbances are produced by such frustrations. Biologists or psychologists with objective leanings have sought the equivalent, in the animal kingdom or by experimental learning, of the frustration-aggression mechanism. Pavlov's disciples have produced, as we know, what might be called neurotic behavior: when two stimuli (a circle and an ellipse), one of which releases a positive reflex and the other a negative reflex, tend to approach each other, there comes a moment when the dog, incapable of distinguishing between the two signals, behaves aggressively, howls and tries to bite. Unable to run away or to adapt himself, he attacks his collar, anything at all. Other experiments of the same type, the connecting of two contradictory reflexes, have yielded the same result, namely, "artificial" neurosis and aggressive, non-adaptive behavior.

There is no contradiction, in fact, between the psychological interpretation of aggression in terms of learning and conditioned reflexes and the Freudian interpretation in terms of frustration. Nonetheless, the facts do not support the assertion that aggression, in the animal kingdom, always has frustration for its cause (easy victories reinforce the tendency to combativeness) or that frustrations are always expressed by aggression. Certain animals fight less when they are deprived of food.[6] Personally, however, I would not wholeheartedly subscribe to the formula according to which *frustration leads to aggression only in a situation in which the individual has the habit of being aggressive,*[7] but it does seem true to me that the frustrated individual is somehow irritable. The threshold of aggressive reaction is lower for him than it would be for another individual.

This, however, is not the essential point. Biologists, from an external viewpoint, can define frustration as the incapacity to make a response that is adapted to the situation. Frustration is first of all, for each of us, the experience of privation, of a goal desired and not obtained, of an oppression suffered. The brother who deprives the newborn baby of a share of his mother's attention provokes the baby's aggression. This aggression will generally be incapable of expressing itself in an "adapted" manner. Often, it will express itself in no manner at all, or will be transferred, by identification, to some innocent person, or will be repressed in the unconscious. If nonadaptation is common to the reaction of the mouse that can neither fight nor

[6] Cf. J. P. Scott, *op. cit.*, p. 34.
[7] *Ibid.*, p. 35 (J. P. Scott's italics).

run away, and to that of the child deprived of a share of his mother's love, what matters to us is not the identity or the similarity of the mechanism, but that men, from their earliest years, live in such a way that they inevitably come into conflict with each other, so to speak attack each other, and invent countless means, verbal and imaginary, to express their hostile sentiments without physical fighting.

A combative animal among the primates, man, according to the psychologists, is moved by impulses—sexuality, the desire for possession, the will to supremacy—which put him in competition with his kind and, almost inevitably, in conflict with some among them. Of course, he does not feel the need for combat as he feels the need for food or sexual satisfaction.[8] The chain of causality which leads to emotions or acts of aggressiveness can always be traced back to an external phenomenon. There is no physiological evidence of a spontaneous impulse to fighting, the origin of which is in the body itself. The human animal happy enough to live in an environment offering no occasion, no motive for fighting, would suffer no damage, either physiological or nervous.

But, without even suggesting the death instinct Freud speaks of, ambivalence of feelings and rivalry among individuals for coveted goals are phenomena of experience, constants which reveal an *element of conflict* in most if not all interpersonal relations. Man does not fight his kind by instinct, but he is, at every moment, the victim and the executioner of his fellow man. Physical aggression and the will to destroy are not the only response to frustration, but they are one of the possible responses and perhaps the spontaneous one. In this sense the philosophers were not mistaken to consider that man is *by nature* dangerous to man.

2. Social Roots

Pride, like the desire for possession, transforms brothers into enemies and partners into rivals. Every society offers countless occasions and stakes for this rivalry, whether absurd or grandiose. The individual occupying first rank is aggressive toward the one who has been demoted to second place when the latter had ambitions for the supreme honor. Any goal which cannot be shared, whether power or glory, is the object of inevitable disputes. When the object of the conflict is a goal that can be shared, compromises are possible, but violence remains tempting. Why come to terms with the other party if, by force, I can obtain everything?

Wars are a specific social phenomenon that probably appeared in a certain moment of human history. They involve the organization of violent action by collectivities in conflict. But we observe conflicts in almost all human collectivities, and conflicts sometimes degenerate into violence—that is, into more or less organized violence, outside of specifically warlike institutions.

[8] *Ibid.*, p. 62.

In the most general sense, two individuals or two groups are in conflict when they attempt to possess the same property or to attain incompatible goals. The conflict becomes violent when one of the adversaries has recourse to physical force in order to oblige the other to submit. We have the expression *moral violence*, of course, and indeed the idea of constraint exercised over a mind or a consciousness is included in the concept of violence. But it is physical force which initiates violence and violates the freedom of persons. Moral violence, of which "brainwashing" is the most repugnant expression, is a subtle and derivative form of violence.[9]

Within modern societies the conflicts are countless, as are the cases of violence. There are eight thousand murders a year in the United States, and two million persons are arrested for serious offenses.[10] I shall formally distinguish these types among cases of violence: brawling, crime or murder, social or political upheavals. Two young people or two groups of young people may brawl as they leave a dance, as two neighbors may dispute over a wall dividing their property. The conflict which the violence provokes is inter-individual although it explodes within a society. The sometimes spontaneous violence of a riot becomes an insurrection or a civil war when it has a cause, or aims at a strictly political object. Depending on the outcome, it will change its adjective. Criminal at the outset, the ultimately victorious insurrection will retrospectively be the source of the new legality. Violence against constitutional law is part of the ambiguity of all historical events, admirable or odious according to preferences. Common-law crimes are those whose qualification does not change, whatever the vicissitudes of the struggles between parties. Murder is not regarded as meritorious except when it has a political meaning. Every year, "resistants" decorate the tomb of the man who killed Admiral Darlan, on the anniversary of the hero-criminal's execution.

As regards conflict, many classifications are possible beyond the context of this analysis. Let us confine ourselves to several elementary distinctions. Conflicts may oppose either individuals or groups, they may be settled by law or by struggle (or by rivalry or by competition), they may conform to

---

[9] The derivation may be schematically summarized as follows. Constraint may be exercised by violence, physical force being effectively employed. Constraint may be exercised by violence, the latter reduced to the threat of the use of force. The individual constrained retains the resource of preferring the punishment with which he is threatened, even death, to submission. Lastly, constraint may be exercised more subtly by acting on the other's will to resist, disintegrating his conscience. At this final stage the victim yields to his executioner. In fact, the final stage is less often achieved than it seems. Most of those accused in the Moscow trials yielded to constraint of the first or second type, they pretended to have been "converted" by the examining judges. Nonetheless, in our era the violence exercised upon populations by the victor is still camouflaged. The Alsatians had protested against annexation in 1871; they did not have the means to do so in 1940. The Baltic peoples voted 99 per cent in favor of entering the U.S.S.R.

[10] J. P. Scott, *op. cit.*, p. 102.

the social order or, quite the contrary, mark its breakdown. What is striking in our period is the number and the gravity of conflicts which are, so to speak, integrated into the functioning of the economy and of politics.

The distribution of the market among sellers, of the national income among individuals and classes depends, to a large degree, on competition—that is, on the results obtained by all in a kind of non-violent combat. Further, conflicts between labor and management are also regarded as the normal expression of a mechanism whose function is the division of property that is scarce (but capable of being shared).

Commercial rivalry and labor-management struggles are two types of normal inter-group conflict whose outcome is determined by competition itself, not by law. They are also characteristic of the conflict-cooperation combination which is from now on the most general model of social relations. Producers of the same merchandise are associates as well as rivals. They are united by a common interest in developing the market, opposed by the desire of each to keep the largest share for himself. Similarly, labor and management have united interests in the prosperity of the business, opposed interests with regard to the distribution of profits. Conversely, apparently cooperative behavior involves an element of conflict, especially among individuals. The two candidates for the leadership of a party are colleagues in the same enterprise, they would collaborate in the same ministry following an electoral victory. Willy-nilly, they restrain the dialectic of their rivalry in order to satisfy the requirements of common action.

The social orders, whose maintenance is based on an organized competition, are all the more fragile in that the rivals forget their solidarity. When the parties are no longer concerned to safeguard the constitution, according to which they are in competition, and when the representatives of the various classes regard themselves as doomed to mortal hostility, the political and social regime is shaken. It is difficult to write a law which prevents a party or syndicates or unions from "sabotaging" or "paralyzing" the regime. It is the parties or the unions themselves which must abstain from doing so out of awareness of the cooperation which precedes competition and which gives it a meaning.

Litigations, rivalry among sellers (in periods of abundance) or among buyers (in periods of scarcity), competition among (individual or collective) political actors do not degenerate into violence if we define the latter as the use of physical force. The strike is often considered as an act of violence, or opposed to dialogue or negotiation. It is, in effect, a means of forcing the adversary to do what the latter, at the outset, refuses to do; a trial of strength, so to speak, between groups which belong to the same political unit and which, by definition, have renounced the use of physical force and, *a fortiori*, armed force to achieve their goals. No society authorizes the use of any weapon in intra-social conflicts. But also no society is definitively assured against the explosion into open violence—that is, into organized violence—of the conflicts which it tolerates.

Socialization, we have said, does not attenuate individual aggressiveness; it tends rather to increase it. The hostility of a group with regard to foreigners and enemies is often stronger than that of one individual with regard to another, because it feeds on noble sentiments, amplified by the number of those who experience it. If the conflicts between groups, within political units, is normally[11] settled without the adversaries resorting to violence, this is not because the hostilities between fellow citizens, rival parties or provinces are rarer or weaker (civil wars are often the fiercest), but because relations among members of the same collectivity are subject to norms, whether customary or legal, because a legitimate authority is recognized by all, because a certain awareness of solidarity unites the adversaries in spite of everything, because a superior force, that of an army or a police force, would be irresistibly imposed in case of need. If a single one of these conditions is lacking, there is a risk of violence. Of course, the awareness of solidarity may be enough to maintain peace or a respect for the laws or legitimacy. But a minority may also feel its interests, ideals or its very existence to be so threatened that nothing except force can restore it to obedience.

If such are the principles of civil peace, nothing is more intelligible than the endemic character of the violent conflicts between the political units. The latter have no—or have only a faint—awareness of their solidarity. They accept neither common law nor legitimate authority. Each having its own army, they cannot be constrained by police action but only by war. Further, down through the centuries, men have exalted the independence of the state as a supreme good, and celebrated the heroes who died to save it. The goal for which the state fought was not always property, the sharing of which by compromise is possible; it was sometimes a goal that cannot be shared, autonomy and glory.

Within states, socialization multiplies the occasions, stakes and motivations of inter-individual and inter-group conflicts, but it also multiplies the instruments of non-violent solutions. Between states, it multiplies the occasions, stakes and motivations of conflict, but without any counterbalance. Quite the contrary, men have thought, acted and spoken down through the centuries as if they regarded the settlement by arms of international conflicts as both reasonable and praiseworthy.

One might object that the aggravation of conflicts does not result from socialization but from certain ways of socialization. Let us refer, for example, to the anthropological studies of the school of Margaret Mead and Ruth Benedict. Psychological at the same time as sociological, these anthropologists

[11] Normally, according to the spirit of the institutions. But, as we have seen in the preceding chapter, internal disturbances are not always less frequent or less serious than wars.

explain societies psychologically and psychic conditions sociologically. They indicate the *drives* subject in their expression to the discipline of institutions and the institutions, in their turn, determined by the mode of expression of the *drives*. According to them, cultures differ profoundly from each other, with regard to competition, war and intra- or inter-social conflicts. Certain collectivities are unaware of war as an important activity, whereas others exalt martial virtues. The competition whose stake is the prestige of force plays a large part in the cultures of the societies which Ruth Benedict calls Dionysiac, almost none in the cultures of Apollonian societies.

Two quotations from Ruth Benedict will illustrate the antinomy of these two types of cultures. "The chief motive that the institutions of the Kwakiutl rely upon and which they share in a great measure with modern society is the motive of rivalry. Rivalry is a struggle that is not centered upon the real objects of the activity but upon outdoing a competitor. The attention is no longer directed toward providing adequately for a family or toward owning goods that can be utilized or enjoyed, but toward outdistancing one's neighbors and owning more than anyone else. Everything else is lost sight of in the one great aim of victory."[12] And, on the other hand, here is a description of the Pueblos. "The ideal man of the Pueblos is another order of being. Personal authority is perhaps the most vigorously disparaged trait in Zuñi. A man who thirsts for power or knowledge, who wishes to be what they disdainfully call a 'leader of his people,' receives nothing but censure and will very likely be persecuted for sorcery, and he often has been. Native authority of manner is a liability in Zuñi, and witchcraft is the ready charge against the person who possesses it. He is hung by the thumbs until he 'confesses.' It is all the Zuñi can do with a man of strong personality. The ideal man in Zuñi is a person of dignity and of affability who has never tried to lead, and who has never called forth comment from his neighbors. Any conflict, even though all right is on his side, is held against him. Even in contests of skill like their foot races, if a man wins habitually he is barred from running. They are interested in a game that a number can play with even chances, and an outstanding runner spoils the game: they will have none of him."[13]

Let us grant the truth of this last description. Let us grant that other peoples, like the Zuñi, may have had or may still have a collective and peaceful existence. This psycho-sociological method emphasizes the important fact that the place accorded by a culture to the spirit of competition varies with the social mode of the expression of human impulses. Certain societies may make the combatant primate peaceful, not because the latter has raised himself to the level of the life of reason, but because the devaluation of concern for prestige and power suppresses the stimuli of aggressiveness. The biologist

[12] *Patterns of Culture*, Boston, 1934.
[13] *Ibid.*

tells us that "aggression, in the strict sense of unprovoked attack, must be learned": perhaps there exist small societies in which men have no occasion for such learning.

In fact, punishment inflicted upon individuals of "powerful personality" suggests rather that despite the cultural devaluation of aggressive behavior, the latter is encountered nonetheless, even among the Zuñi. But all the same—supposing that socialization can, in certain circumstances, reduce the occasions for aggression, eliminate its motivations, disqualify its stakes; supposing that the man who does not fight by instinct or by physiological necessity is capable of living in peace with his kind, in close community—it is impossible to project these irenic images or dreams upon humanity's present or future.

Modern societies are exceptionally competitive. Among their games, those which hold the first rank are competitive ones. Whether the champions seek to overcome the others or themselves, whether they attempt the ascent of virgin peaks or the exploration of interstellar space, the same will to power seeks to triumph over both natural forces and rivals. In this regard the Soviet regimes do not differ from the so-called capitalist regimes. They denounce commercial competition without entirely eliminating it; they substitute for it the many forms of so-called socialist competition.

Even if modern societies were not essentially competitive, they would not permit peace by the devaluation of the concerns of prestige. Every complex society, indeed, involves a more or less differentiated political order. Now, of all of man's social activities, politics is, in essence, the most competitive, since the stake, for each individual, is the place in the hierarchy or the share of the command, which means a goal which cannot be shared and which I cannot achieve without depriving someone else of it. All human relations, as we have said, involve an element of cooperation and an element of conflict. But, in the last analysis, economics, because it has a relation to nature as its origin, is in essence cooperative; politics, because its object and goal is the relation of men among themselves according to command and obedience, is in essence contentious.

Individuals identify themselves with a collectivity to which they belong, they delight in its victories and suffer from its defeats as intensely as from their own failures. They escape from themselves, from their fears, their inner disturbances by participating in the events that effect the collective destiny. They feel injured by the wounds inflicted upon their collectivity, ready to react by aggression and violence. Within nations, group rivalry is, it is true, more or less permanently pacified. Political competition is therefore not *fatally* violent. But it ultimately decides a mode of life in common, hence of the reality of man. Does any group definitively renounce the possibility of defending its ideas or interests by force? Peace, whether national or imperial, is the institutional expression of the peace desired by a community conscious of itself, conscious of being *one* and of desiring to be *one*. Can humanity achieve the same singleness of will as each nation? Can it conform to the monopoly of legitimate violence?

3. Social Types of Wars

Homo sapiens made his appearance some six hundred thousand years ago. The Neolithic revolution, instituting a culture of farming and cattle-rearing, dates back to some ten thousand years. Complex civilizations or societies were inaugurated some six thousand years ago. The so-called historical period, which constitutes our subject, represents only about one hundredth of the total duration of the human past.

I open the group study called *L'Homme avant l'écriture*,[14] recently published in a scientific series: the word *war* does not even occur in the index. Does this mean that men did not fight before the Neolithic period? Were our ancestors, during the Paleolithic ages, different from our immediate ancestors—I mean those of the last six thousand years?

Let us recall the exact meaning of the words: war is the conflict of one form of organized behavior with another, the trial by force between "groups," each of which strives to gain victory over the other by multiplying the vigor of each combatant by discipline. In this precise sense, war cannot be anterior to the formation of groups. A social phenomenon, it implies society by definition. The more we imagine men living in families or packs, like the higher vertebrates, the less we are inclined to attribute to them strictly warlike behavior. Most animals fight, as we have seen, but rare are the species which practice warfare, if the latter implies a collective and organized action. By definition, so to speak, only the so-called social animals wage war, since the latter implies the socialization of the combatants. Bees and ants live in collectivities which involve a differentiation of function. The individuals of one of these collectivities, considered externally, seem to coordinate their behavior and to come in conflict with members of another collectivity, whose behavior is similarly coordinated. The conflict involves the disintegration or destruction of one or other of the groups, with the death of a certain number of individuals.

Did the men of the Paleolithic period fight? How did they fight? Anthropologists have some difficulty in providing a categorical answer. Some believe that the characteristic object of the so-called Acheulean phase (between 400,000 and 200,000 years ago), bifaced stones, were utilized in combats. Others regard them not as weapons but as tools for working or hunting. What served for hunting animals might also serve for hunting men. On the other hand, no anthropologist has found evidence that before the Bronze Age men elaborated a combat organization or tactics.

We are justifiably curious to know how men who did not use metals, and who were not aware of agriculture and writing, behaved toward each other.

[14] Paris, 1959 (editor, André Varagnac).

The answer, whatever its nature, would not be very instructive for the rest of us, contemporaries of the total wars of the twentieth century. The propensity of individuals to brawling or to brutality can and must be measured by direct observation, without reference to hypotheses as to the actions of our remote ancestors. The chances of peace and the risks of war, in the course of the Atomic Age, do not depend on the combativeness of men in the Stone Age.

At no period can weapons be on a different technological level from tools, any more than the organization of the combatants can fundamentally differ from the social organization. Therefore it is not surprising that the first incontestable traces of armies and wars should be contemporaneous with the Bronze Age. "The industry and commerce of the Bronze Age," writes an American anthropologist, Mr. Turney-High, "required a certain degree of political stability. It was at this period that organized war, as distinct from raids and ambushes by family groups, made its appearance. The first proof of the existence of trained troops occurs at Sumer." And, farther on: "If the Iron Age affords man greater security in his struggle with his environment, it also increases the pace and extension of war. In fact, from the beginning of the Age of Metal until today, the greatest threat to man's security has not been nature, but other men. In this regard, human culture in the Age of Metal, although it did not possess writing, assumed a modern aspect."[15]

Between the ages during which man was threatened by wild animals, and those relatively few ages during which the threat has come from other men, did there exist an intermediate, so-to-speak Eden-like phase: man possessing sufficient technology to defend himself against wild beasts without yet being swept into the race for conquest and servitude, class struggle and competition for wealth? Certain ethnologists believe that this kind of golden age may have existed at the dawn of the Neolithic period; some archaic societies, today dying out, transmit to us, despite their poverty, a final echo of it, through their *joie de vivre*.

I am not qualified to decide as to the reality, the duration and the extension of this golden age. Whether it was the privilege of several small societies or a rather general phenomenon at a certain moment of the human past, it offers no lesson either for the prehistoric or historic past or for the future. Small societies, isolated and without metal tools, do not yet afford the characteristic features of warlike societies.

The archaic societies which ethnologists have observed for some centuries, at least in germ, exhibit most of the behavior characteristic of "international relations"; they distinguish between peace and war, diplomats and warriors. The institution of war presents scarcely less diversity than it does in the societies enabled by the existence of writing to accumulate intellectual acquisitions and a conscious tradition.

---

[15] H. H. Turney-High, *General Anthropology*, New York, 1949, pp. 171, 175.

Diversity affects the chief aspects of the phenomenon. The units in conflict are different according to ethnic groups or, within the same ethnic group, according to circumstances. Sometimes it is family groups which are in conflict, sometimes villages, sometimes tribes, sometimes confederations.

The stakes of these armed and organized conflicts do not seem any less varied than those of wars among civilized men. Sometimes the stake is comparable to the object of an instrumental activity: men to be eaten (in the case of cannibalism), heads to be cut off (in the case of religious ceremonies), hunting territories to preserve or slaves to conquer. Sometimes the combat seems a ritual which has no visible goal outside of the rite itself, closely related to a game which is ordinarily not so bloody. In certain tribes all the able-bodied men fight in a war (which sometimes recurs at regular dates); other tribes have warrior castes which alone participate in the combat and which generally exert a dominating influence over the collectivity. Lastly, archaic societies are unequally competitive, unequally aggressive, unequally bellicose. The system of values and beliefs characteristic of each of them places martial virtues at a more or less high rank, exalts either the prestige of victories or, quite the contrary, the peaceful order, and inculcates the glory of combat or the sterility of violence. In other words, although the institutional elaboration of diplomatic and military phenomena remains blurred, the characteristic attitudes are already present and visible.

Is it possible, beyond this perceptible variety, to articulate types? Professor Quincy Wright[16] has distinguished four types of war. Certain archaic societies fight only to defend themselves. Others fight but not to give the appearance of having objectives of a political or economic order. They seek vengeance for an insult suffered, or the death of men outside their group because they need heads or bodies for their own ceremonies. Sometimes they fight out of a desire for competition or sport, or out of a simple desire for prestige. The societies which engage in such kinds of wars rarely have a military caste. Combat, far from being arbitrary, is subject to strict rules. A third category of society wages wars with a view to the acquisition of land, women or slaves. In such wars professional warriors intervene, and a tactical skill is developed. A final kind of war is that which the military classes conduct in order to maintain their own regime or the empire they have built. With the warrior aristocracy and the enlargement of political units by the sword, the so-called archaic societies enter history. The war of the first type is *defensive*, that of the second *social*, that of the third *political-economic*, that of the fourth *aristocratic-imperial*. Archaic societies regard war as a *calamity*, or a *rite*, or a *means of conquest or of enrichment*, or as an *instrument of domination*. So-called civilized societies have not chosen among these four qualifications.

Let us set aside the first type, which applies to societies rather than to wars.

---

[16] *Op. cit.*, Vol. I, pp. 546 and 560–61.

By definition, a war cannot conform entirely to this type, that is, cannot be purely defensive for both adversaries; one or the other must manifest a competitive or aggressive spirit. It is important to know that in the age of archaic collectivities, as during the ages of complex civilizations, certain groups did not attack foreigners, were not tempted to hate them or to drive them away and, consequently, found no sense in battle. But it is no less important to recall that these relatively rare examples of peacefulness are marked by characteristics too singular for us to be able to derive from them any conclusion of a general nature.

The three other types are not, at first glance, similar: the distinction of *social war* from *political-economic* war is based, apparently, upon consideration of the stakes involved, but it is not always easier to discern the stake of the conflicts in archaic societies than in historical societies. Moreover, the cases subsumed under the heading of *social war* do not always appear to be of the same kind. Sometimes the combatants have a goal which, though of a religious nature (vengeance, expiation, skulls), makes no less "rational" that bellicose behavior which has as its objective a so-called political or economic stake. On the other hand, if the combat has no other goal than to designate a victor and to confer upon him the prestige of an acknowledged superiority, then it belongs to another category. It becomes its own objective and is related to game or sport. Encounters of family or village groups often assume this intermediate character between rite and game, controlled like the latter, charged with meaning like the former. Sometimes war is transfigured into a kind of festival, a negation of daily life. As on carnival days before Lent, ordinary interests are suspended, violence is committed against foreigners, all members of the group participate in a collective exaltation, and passions explode: the whole collectivity is nothing but a block of steel.[17]

It seems to me that the characteristic common to all cases of *social war* is the at least apparent predominance of the institution over the objective, and of the rite over the goal. Belligerent behavior in this case would not be explicable in *Zweckrational* terms, to use Max Weber's concepts, but in terms of *value, tradition* or *emotion*. Men fight for glory, in accordance with an established order (i.e., the mode of cooperative-competitive communication among villages) or because of sudden outbreaks of emotion.

The distinction of *social war* and *political-economic* war is liable to the same criticism that is often lodged against the Weberian opposition between *instrumental rationality* (*Zweckrational*) and other types of action: it is less a question of an alternative than of two aspects of human behavior. The war whose stake is the conquest of women or hunting grounds can also be a source of prestige, it can be controlled as competition is controlled or, like festivals, furnish an outlet for impulses. On the other hand, war for heads,

[17] Roger Caillois, *Quatre essais de sociologie contemporaine* (particularly "Le Vertige de la guerre"), Paris, 1951.

territory or slaves sets up, beyond or short of instrumental rationality, a traditional or affective enhancement of the objectives themselves. Also there are many archaic collectivities which practice simultaneously several of these types of wars.

This classification is not uninstructive, all the same. Wars are both a style of relations, a means of regulating conflicts among more or less distinct units, an institution integrated with the system of beliefs and of existence characteristic of collectivities. They may be explained by the actual culture of each of the collectivities and still more by the dialogue of these cultures, sometimes close together, sometimes remote from each other. These propositions are as valid for the societies which are familiar with as well as for those which are ignorant of combat for the conquest of territory, slaves or women. But diplomatic-strategic behavior, having become conscious and consciously instrumental, acquires an apparent autonomy, comparable to that of economic behavior when it is subject to monetary quantification. The autonomy of instrumental diplomatic-strategy is less complete than that of economic action: the desire to conquer for conquest's sake constantly upsets the calculations of diplomats and strategists. War preserves ritual or regulatory aspects, even when it is essentially instrumental, either because obligations and prohibitions continue to weigh upon bellicose behavior, or because the belligerents vaguely attempt to limit the explosion of violence. The Greeks, when they were victorious, set up trophies upon the battlefield instead of pursuing the defeated enemy, as if the glory of having conquered was the warrior's supreme recompense.

Every war within a zone of civilization (or, if one prefers, as long as the enemies have not lost all awareness of their relationship) is a social institution. It is characterized by the meaning which societies attribute to it; it is a human and not an animal violence; it is regulated and not arbitrary. But, as it more clearly involves political and economic stakes external to battle and to the intoxication of victory, war is increasingly subject to considerations of effectiveness. It would be impossible to specify the means which in each period the combatants voluntarily abstain from employing for moral reasons. But the question is not raised in these terms. The means of organization and of combat appear, in each period, as a *traditional* institution which the *rational* search for effectiveness slowly transforms, without its being known for sure whether the continuing use of certain weapons or of customary tactics is due to laziness in thinking or to the respect for prohibitions.

The distinction between the last two types of wars is similarly instructive. *Aristocratic-imperial* war is no less *instrumental* than *political-economic* war, but it determines the course of cumulative history instead of repeating to itself each time that the distinct collectivities should decide to abide by the verdict of arms. Thereby, it is a kind of synthesis of *social war* and *political-economic* war.

This deserves further thought. What is the unconscious function that may be attributed to wars of the first type, in which ritualization, whether religious or competitive, predominates? Manifestly a stabilizing function, a group—clan, village, tribe—arrives at a profounder awareness of its own unity when it opposes other groups. The function of wars of the second type is also suggested by the facts themselves: the tribunal of force is substituted for the authority of custom. Between collectivities each subject to its own customs but thereby rebellious to the customs of the others, only combat can decide. Thus war becomes the supreme recourse, and diplomacy the means of avoiding, waging or concluding war. Rationalizing interpretations single out this instrumental and calculating aspect of the relations between independent groups, of negotiation and the trial by force, of compromise, or of battle.

Wars waged by societies which, enlarged by previous conquests, leave the monopoly of arms to a military class, have both functions: they cement the unity of belligerent collectivities, but they also permit the resolution of the problems of frontiers, the decision as to whom belongs a population or a province. Unlike the two preceding kinds of wars, they have a historical function, and not merely a social or pragmatic one. Without them, the development of civilizations is inconceivable. Because of them empires are born; because of them thrones collapse. Nations have rarely achieved an expression of their will as states without the intercession of force.

Perhaps war is contrary to humanity's destination. It has been inseparable from man's historic destiny.

4. Optimistic and Pessimistic Myths

If the foregoing analyses are correct, war has roots that are simultaneously biological, psychological and social. The aggressive primate man is prompt to respond with violence to pain or frustration. Always deprived of the satisfactions to which he aspires, and in permanent competition with his kind, he is physically and morally combative, tending to resent those, whether familiar or remote, who keep him from money, glory or love. As a member of a collectivity, he shares the tribal coherence which creates the distance between compatriots and foreigners, and forbids the members of one group to ascribe an equal dignity to those belonging to another. Starting from animal aggression, human vanity and tribal coherence, societies develop both production tools and combat weapons; they elaborate the diplomatic-strategic relations which they cannot avoid and which none can lastingly master. Thus is born, it would appear, the historical fatality of war. As uncertain of their limits as of their inner solidarity, the political units cannot help suspecting each other constantly and combating each other occasionally. But if the wise man curses the cruelty of combat, the sociologist replies with a question: without war, would men have transcended the stage of small, closed societies? Most ideologies, those which affirm as well as those which deny the possibility of eliminating war from human history, fail to acknowledge certain elements of the phenomenon of war. They emphasize a certain aspect or phenomenon which justifies resignation to violence or trust in peace. They refuse to admit that war is not only or essentially an animal phenomenon, that it has many roots, and that it is not enough, in order to kill it off, to pull up only one of these roots.

At one extreme we find the biological myths. War remains a manifestation of physical brutality. Is this not the essence of the phenomenon of war, the rising to the surface of the death instincts which civilization temporarily manages to suppress? There have been constant exchanges between social philosophy and biological philosophy. The conception of a struggle for life has been inspired both by the observation of men and by that of plants and animals. Marx and Engels, toward the end of their lives, were tempted to interpret the class struggle in the light of Darwinian thought. What do the facts suggest, consulted without preconceived ideas?

That the living devour each other, that animals eat plants, that big fish eat little fish and wolves lambs, we have been taught at school by our teacher and our books. But they neglect another fact which is no less meaningful: the higher animals do not kill each other within a single species. They do not organize their combats. Thus wolves fight among themselves, but an instinctive inhibition prevents the inflicting of death: the defeated animal that bares its throat is spared.[18] Such inhibitions do not exist in all species; especially in the species considered as peaceful (doves, hares, deer, peacocks) the defeated animal does not save its own life by "capitulating" (baring its throat). If we wished to emphasize man's ferocity by comparing him (as Spengler does) to a beast of prey, we must choose the right beast of prey, and refer to solitary animals such as the jaguar, and not to the wolf.

All inferences of animal data to the human realm are uncertain. I shall refrain from drawing any general conclusion from the phenomena of aggression and struggle between animals and that which concerns the social and human institution of war. All the same, the animals of the species that man considers the most dangerous because their "weapons" are most dangerous for him rarely kill each other and are saved from self-destruction by the instinct to spare the vanquished. The "arms" of men are more dangerous than the teeth or claws of wolves or lions; the victors have not always spared the vanquished. It is economic calculation more than instinct that prevents the infliction of death.

A struggle for life? If this were so, human societies would have the same relations among themselves as animal species: some must disappear so that the others may have the means to survive. One must have a strange imagination to interpret the great conflicts of recorded history according to this design. There was room for Athens and Sparta in the Greek world, for Carthage and Rome in the Mediterranean basin in the third century B.C., for England and Germany in twentieth-century Europe; there is room for Moscow

18 Cf. Konrad Z. Lorenz, op. cit., pp. 195 ff.

and Washington in the global system of the second half of the century. None of these rivalries was made inevitable by lack of a place in the sun. The pride of the states did not permit sharing; the dialectics of the death struggle was human, not animal.

The blind mechanism of the struggle for life functioned (and still functions) in one direction within collectivities. Here the number of men was at every moment limited by the volume of subsistence. The cost of this struggle was excessive, if we add to the children who died in infancy and the victims of epidemics those whom hunger kept from procreating. Scarcity, directly or indirectly, controlled population growth, and the living had, so to speak, triumphed over the dead. But this fundamental poverty has combined, since the dawn of the historical period, with surplus value, the serf or slave producing more than the subsistence indispensable to his upkeep. Thus societies are divided into hierarchic groups, those on top, always a minority, reserving for their leisure and their luxury a share of the surplus value produced by those on the bottom. In this perspective, the privileged classes have constantly benefited by a camouflaged struggle for life of which class struggle appears to the observer in retrospect as an expression.

Such a comparison of civil struggles and the struggle for life has an analogous rather than a philosophical character. The struggle for life, in the strict Darwinian sense, leads to natural selection, the survival of the fittest. Down through the historical ages, the mechanism that selects the survivors is social and no longer biological: it is the armed man, the group strongest in military terms that holds back the surplus value of the labor of others. If a man is better endowed, it is in the art of fighting. The warrior's qualities are neither those which the moralist has tended to exalt nor those which serve humanity best. Further: these qualities belong at best to the victors themselves. Yet conquests are stabilized in an institutional order which the following generations submit to and which does not reflect the gifts of each man. Aristotle did not condemn slavery as such, but he observed that certain slaves had a master's soul, and certain masters a slave's soul. A fortiori, the struggle between two city-states, two nations or two empires does not resemble a "natural selection." Carthage perished, but if Hannibal had seized Rome after Cannae, would the biologist have any reason to claim that the fittest had succumbed? Let us acknowledge the vicissitudes of fortune and avoid supposing that the tribunal of history is always as just as it is pitiless.

In another fashion, Bergson, in his last great book,[19] also developed a biological interpretation of war. Rather in the manner of the classical philosophers, he first attempts to define what belongs to the nature of man and to the nature of human society, stripped of what history may have added. Nature has endowed man with a creative intelligence. Instead of

[19] *The Two Sources of Morality and Religion,* Doubleday Anchor Books, 1956. First published in France in 1932.

providing him with instruments, as is the case for a good number of animal species, nature has preferred that man should construct them himself. Now man necessarily owns his instruments, at least while he is using them. But since they are separate from himself, they can be taken away; to seize them ready-made is easier than making them. A few lines later, Bergson concludes his analysis: "The origin of war is ownership, individual or collective, and since humanity is predestined to ownership by its structure, war is natural. So strong, indeed, is the war instinct that it is the first to appear when we scratch below the surface of civilization in search of nature."[20]

The natural society is the opposite of democracy. Its regime is monarchic or oligarchic. For the world of the insects, the diversity of social functions is linked to a different organization: there is polymorphism. In the natural society of men there is "dimorphism," making from each of us a leader who has the instinct to command and a subject who is made to obey.[21] The formula of this society is "authority, hierarchy, fixity," and each is exclusively a member of his closed society. *Homo homini deus;* when one formulates this maxim, one thinks of some compatriot. The other maxim *homo homini lupus* concerns foreigners.[22]

The natural society is warlike, and the true wars, the decisive wars, were wars of annihilation. "A war-instinct was inevitable, and because it existed to meet the contingency of those savage wars, which we might call natural, a number of incidental wars have occurred, simply to prevent the sword rusting."[23]

Bergson's causal explanations of modern wars are manifestly influenced by the conceptions prevalent in Europe between 1919 and 1939. It is the increasing number of men, he writes, that impels modern societies toward great massacres. If you let Venus do as she will, she will bring Mars upon you. The peoples who fear they will no longer find food or the raw materials they need, who believe themselves threatened by hunger or unemployment, are ready for anything. In order to survive, they fling themselves upon their enemies. Then the true wars break out, in accord with their essence. Waged with the weapons which science puts at the disposal of the combatants, they risk ruining or destroying the entire race tomorrow. "At the pace at which science is moving, that day is not far off when one of the two adversaries, through some secret process which he was holding in reserve, will have the means of annihilating his opponent. The vanquished may vanish off the face of the earth."[24]

Peace, like democracy, is born of a radically different inspiration. In-

[20] *Ibid.,* p. 284. This interpretation is manifestly inspired by Jean-Jacques Rousseau, whom Bergson profoundly admired and reread every year.
[21] *Ibid.,* p. 278.
[22] *Ibid.,* p. 286.
[23] *Ibid.,* p. 285.
[24] *Ibid.,* p. 287.

equality is the law of the collective and differentiated beings which constitute closed societies: democratic equality is proclaimed, asserted by the spiritual impulse which proceeds counter to the impulse of animal and social nature, to instinctive or instrumental behavior. This spiritual impulse is peaceful as it is democratic, it ignores the concern for ownership and enjoyment, it animates a message which, meaningful for each man, is addressed to all. Perhaps man, as an intelligent laborer, will succeed in limiting wars by moderating the causes which provoke them—overpopulation and the frenzy of pleasure. But humanity, incapable of returning to natural societies, will remain warlike so long as the religions of salvation do not unite men beyond their frontiers. And perhaps this unity is impossible if, this side of death, God's word does not manage to transfigure animal and social nature.

Some of Bergson's ideas will be readily accepted. One constant datum without which the phenomenon of war would become unintelligible is the distance created between members of the same species by participation in distinct collectivities. Nonetheless, Bergson enlarges the phenomenon and, it seems to me, distorts its meaning by supposing that the alien is, *by definition,* the enemy. The alien *may* be the enemy because he is not *entirely* of one's own kind.

Rousseau believed that wars are created or, at least, amplified with the enlargement of collectivities, and that inequality of classes and individual ownership are linked to wars of conquest and to the domination of warriors. Ethnologists tend to confirm these notions. How could it have been otherwise, since the political units have been forged by combat and since the goal of victory was inseparably the earth, slaves and precious metals?

The disputable Bergsonian theses are those which interpret man's odyssey as a laborer and a soldier in biological terms. Bergson calls a certain social type *natural* because the latter is declared to be similar to the societies of insects with their functional polymorphism. Historical man, artisan and intellectual, creator of industries and works of culture, remains, in Bergson's eyes, *natural* so long as he is not raised above himself by the call of the divine. Only the impulse of faith answering the Good Word would indicate a break with the laws of life, that is, with the demands of order and the cruelties of the struggle. Bergson is thereby led to ignore the strictly human element in historical conflicts, the rivalries of prestige, a desire for recognition or for instituting a crusade. He regards only wars of extermination as conforming to the essence of the phenomenon of war, in other words he once again reduces human and historical wars to the struggle for life. Demographic and economic interpretations of armed conflicts, fashionable twenty years ago, inclined him to this error, in accord with his metaphysical vision. Since historical man remains an animal, however great the empire, however grandiose the successes of technology and science, wars, too, are natural and, so to speak, animal, whatever their historical stakes, whatever the subtlety of diplomatic and military behavior.

As a matter of fact, historical wars have not been, for the most part, wars of extermination. The barbarians wanted to occupy lands, the civilized state wanted to eliminate a rival: it was rational to enslave the vanquished rather than to put him to death. It is false to reject gentlemen's wars from the category of authentic wars. Historical man aspired to the glory of triumph or to the spoils of victory; he enslaved or he exploited. Extermination was contrary both to the desire for recognition and to economic calculation, alien to the desire for prestige as to the interests of power or wealth. It resulted either from blind fury or from the transformation of historical hostility into inexpiable hatred. War would mean the massacre of the vanquished only when science has both accelerated the multiplication of the species and paralyzed the mechanisms of restraint to the point where, for the first time, in the physical sense of the term, there would no longer be room for everyone on the planet.

The philosophers of biological inspiration are obsessed by the animal origins of the phenomenon of war; the psychologists of good will who hope for peace on earth seek the strictly psychological causes of conflicts between collectivities in order to discover a "therapeutics of bellicosity." Such research has taken various paths.

One leads to the specification of national stereotypes. What image do the American citizens have of other peoples? What image do the various classes of the American people have of the Russians, the Germans, the Japanese, the Chinese, the French? According to the methods known to social psychology, we follow the vicissitudes of these images down through time and simultaneously observe the diversity of these images according to the groups within one and the same society.

Another path leads to the discrimination of psychological types, to the establishment of the frequency of these various types within one nation. A psycho-sociological type is defined by both opinions and attitudes. One believes in the merits of the strong approach, regards war as inevitable to the end of time, capital punishment as indispensable to the social order; another believes that negotiation and compromise must be gradually substituted for force, that the death penalty is a survival of barbarous ages. Verbal reactions correspond more or less to psychic attitudes, to a mode of balance of impulses. The concept of "authoritarian personality" combines and unites a group of opinions and a specific mode of behavior. Political parties, regimes and nations are characterized, more or less distinctly, by the predominance of one type, itself more or less rigorously defined.

It is not important for us to examine in detail these incontestably legitimate studies in social psychology, although the relations between the type of opinion and the type of behavior are often obscure and complex. Let us grant that the percentage of various psychological types is not the same in each party. The membership of the National Socialist party, for instance, would be psychologically, and not only sociologically, specific. Is the same true in the case of the constitutional parties, when we compare the Left and the Right, the working class and the other social milieus?

Whatever answer the facts themselves must give to such questions, the essential thing is not to forget that the psychological causes of combative conduct, in the higher civilizations, are mediated by institutions. The style of life of nomads, living on the steppes or in the desert, led directly to combat, hence to aggression and conquest. Hitler's personality was probably aggressive as a result of frustrations. Among Hitler's partisans, the number of individuals motivated by resentment was probably larger than among the people as a whole; let us grant that. But Hitler's political vision is explained by an ideological universe as the demagogue's accession to power is explained by the events of the century. Psychology adds a dimension to the historical explanation, but does not replace it: psychology subordinates itself to that explanation. The strictly "psychological causes" appear evident only in a historical guise and in historical context. Perhaps Hitler's aggressive character influenced his conduct and, thereby, the course of history. The Führer had drawn his conceptions from books: millions of Germans put their hopes in him or recognized themselves in his dreams.

Have such studies suggested a "psychotherapy of bellicosity?" They have merely indicated three diseases to cure, *tribal egoism, collective aggressiveness* and *the madness of militaristic and heroic morality.*

Non-recognition of one's own kind in the foreigner is one of the social and psychic roots of the distance between the collectivities, hence of wars. It is good to combat the aberrations of national self-esteem, to dissolve the myths of "eternal Germany" or of "cruel Japan." (Moreover, in our century, events come to the doctors' aid: it is difficult to believe in the stereotypes which the reversals of alliances and hostilities oblige us to modify from one year to the next.)

Doctors of the body politic, the American anthropologists had advised the softening of social prohibitions in Japan or in Germany, the relaxation of familial authoritarianism in order that a better balance of impulses in each man might be expressed by the more peaceful conduct of all. If aggressiveness is the effect of the frustrations which a culture inflicts upon those who live within it, it will be attenuated less by speeches or treaties than by the reform of the educational system or the modification of the scales of values.

Lastly, the philosophies that put a high value upon aggressive behavior or warlike institutions can be refuted or unmasked. Peace and no longer victory, negotiated compromise and no longer violence, the wise man and no longer the warrior will be exalted. Thus the Japan of the imperial tradition will become the nation which refuses to rearm.

Let us admire, once more, the cunning of reason. The national stereotypes no longer threaten peace, since yesterday's enemies are today's allies and conversely. To lessen the hostility between today's rivals, the ideological stereotype must be dissolved, that is, the merits of the Western regime must be preached to the Soviets, or the West must be reminded of the merits of the Soviet regime. But an ideocratic state cannot criticize the ideology which served as its own foundation. If one camp is a fanatic, is the other's liberalism favorable to equilibrium? As for easing of repressions and aggressions by an improved technique of education, a more flexible system of obligations, this may contribute to the pacification of the internal order of collectivities, on condition that society provides both the group and the individual with a good life. From such pacification to international peace the road is long, and it is not direct.

The biologists offer no hope: the psychologists and the anthropologists hold out the prospect of a slow re-education of humanity: only the explorers of the collective unconscious interpret war as a *historical invention*, whose initial motivations have been forgotten, and present men with the alternative of awareness or suicide. "As long as the source of our irrational acts remains hidden, the forces that are still driving us to destruction will seem uncontrollable," writes the American sociologist Lewis Mumford. "The worst part about civilized man's original errors and the most threatening aspects of our present situation are that we regard some of our most self-destructive acts as normal and unavoidable."[25] War should have been put on the same level as individual murder, regarded as a collective crime or insane behavior. That it has persisted down through the ages and that it threatens the very existence of humanity—this is the fact, scandalous to the mind as well as to the conscience, which must first be explained, then eliminated.

Lewis Mumford's theory is subdivided into several propositions. It starts with a comparison between the situation of humanity at the dawn of the historical epoch and that of the present. It then attempts to explain by invariable conditions the ubiquity of the institution of warfare. Finally it asserts the radical absurdity of war in the Atomic Age and seeks in irrational impulses the profound cause of the fascination which war continues to exert.

Here, first of all, is the similarity between the dawn of the Neolithic Age and the dawn of the Atomic Age:

"There is a close parallel between our own age, exalted yet stunned by the seemingly limitless expansion of all its powers, and the epoch that marked the emergence of the earliest civilizations in Egypt and Mesopotamia. In his pride over his present accomplishments, it is perhaps natural for modern man to think that such a vast release of physical energy and human potentiality had never taken place before. But on examination this proves a too flattering illusion: the two ages of power, modern and ancient, are bound together by many similar characteristics, both good and evil, which set them apart from other phases of human history.

[25] This quotation, like those that follow, is taken from Lewis Mumford's essay "How War Began," originally published in the *Saturday Evening Post* and republished in *Adventures of the Mind*, ed. Richard Thruelsen and John Kobler, New York, 1959.

"Just as the prelude to the nuclear age came with a large-scale introduction of water, wind and steam power, so the first steps toward civilization were taken in the neolithic domestication of plants and animals. This agricultural revolution gave man food, energy, security and surplus manpower on a scale that no earlier culture had known. Among the achievements that mark the transformation from barbarism to civilization were the beginnings of astronomy and mathematics, the first astronomical calendar, the sailboat, the plow, the potter's wheel, the loom, the irrigation canal, the man-powered machine. Civilized man's emotional and intellectual potentialities were raised further through the introduction of writing, the elaboration of the permanent record in painting, sculpture and monuments, and the building of walled cities.

"This great leap forward came to a climax about 5,000 years ago. A like mobilization and magnification of power did not again take place until our own era."

In these remote times sacred power and secular power were fused in the "all-powerful king, standing at the apex of the social pyramid. The king was both a secular ruler and the chief priest or even, in the case of the Egyptians, a living god. . . . His will was law. Kingship by divine right claimed magic powers and evoked magic collective responses.

"What kingly power could not do solely by intimidation, and what magical rights and orderly astronomical observations could not do alone by successful prediction, the two in combination actually did accomplish. Large assemblages of men moved and acted as if they were one, obedient to the royal command, fulfilling the will of the gods and rulers. . . .

". . . With the growth of an efficient bureaucracy, a trained army, systematic taxation and forced labor, this early totalitarian system showed all the depressing features that similar governments show in our own day. . . .

"Perhaps early civilized man was justifiably frightened by the forces he himself had brought into existence, in the way that many people are frightened now by nuclear power. In neither case was the extension of physical power and political command accompanied by a complementary development of moral direction and humane control. . . .

". . . The king personified the community; he was the indispensable connecting link between ordinary men and the cosmic powers they must propitiate and obey. . . .

"To avert the wrath of the Gods, indicated by any natural mischance, the king himself must be slain as a sacrifice. . . .

"To save the king from this discouraging fate, which might lessen the attractions of the office, a further trick of religious magic came into play. A stand-in would be chosen and temporarily treated with all the honors and privileges of the king, in order to perform the final role of sacrificial victim on the altar. As the demand for such victims increased in times of trouble, these substitutes were sought outside the community, by violent capture. And what began as a one-sided raid for captives in time brought about the collective reprisals and counterraids that became institutionalized as war. Back of war lay this barbarous religious sanction: only by human sacrifice can the community be saved.

"War, then, was a specific product of civilization—the outcome of an organized effort to obtain captives for a magical blood sacrifice. In time, armed might itself took on a seemingly independent existence, and the extension of power became an end in itself, a manifestation of the 'health' of the state. But underneath the heavy overlayers of rationalization, war remained colored by the original infantile misconception that communal life and prosperity could be preserved only by sacrificial expiation. Civilized man's later efforts to impute the origins of war to some primal animal instinct toward murderous aggression against his own kind are empty rationalizing. Here the words of the anthropologist, Bronislaw Malinowski, are decisive, 'If we insist that war is a fight between two independent and politically organized groups, war does not occur at a primitive level.'"

All, or almost all, of this theory seems to me dubious or incompatible with the facts. The explanation of modern warfare by the terrors of Neolithic man points out precisely that irrational thought which the author makes responsible for man's fears today.

Granted that war, defined as a combat between two independent politically organized groups, is of a relatively recent origin, but how could it be otherwise since political organization, too, is not anterior to the Neolithic Age? W. J. Perry's conception, according to which war was an Egyptian invention,[26] accords with neither the historical facts nor the results of observation, in the course of the last three centuries, of archaic societies. The pre-Columbian civilizations practiced war without borrowing anything from the Egyptians. They had no need to receive the lessons of the emperors or priests who built the pyramids and sacrificed expiatory victims. Further, it matters little whether the institution of warfare spread from an original invention or whether it was invented by certain societies. For an institution to be able to spread universally and to persist down through the ages, it must have constant and fundamental causes. Are these causes social, as intelligible to the minds of the actors as to the observers? Or are they radically irrational, unconscious? Lewis Mumford shifts imperceptibly from the first hypothesis to the second. ". . . The original pattern of civilization, as it took form in the walled city and in turn produced the 'walled' state, has remained unaltered until modern times," he writes. The rulers "exalted the sacrifices of war because they wanted to maintain their own power." In this hypothesis, war is a normal element of the relations between political units because the latter are, in their internal order, the stabilized result of violence. We have no need of exposing irrational motivations, transmitted from a remote past and inscribed within the

---

[26] Cf. W. J. Perry, *The Growth of Civilization*, New York, 1923, and Quincy Wright, *op. cit.*, Vol. I, Appendix VI, "Theory of the Unique Origin of War," pp. 471 ff.

collective unconscious, in order to understand the phenomenon of war: the nature of closed societies and their relations suffices as an explanation.

The second hypothesis is quite different, if not contradictory: "The fact that war has persisted and now threatens, at the very peak of our advances in science and technology, to become all-enveloping and all-destructive, points to the deep irrationality that first brought it into existence. This irrationality springs not only from the original aberration but from the unconscious depths of man plagued with repressed guilt and anxiety over the godlike powers he presumptuously has learned to wield. . . .

"The fantasies that governed the ancient founders of civilization have now become fully realizable. Our most decisive recent inventions, the atom bomb and the planetary rocket, came about through a fusion of secular and 'sacred' powers, similar to their ancient union. Without the physical resources of an all-powerful state and the intellectual resources of an all-knowing corps of scientists, that sudden command of cosmic energy in interplanetary space would not have been possible. Powers of total destruction that ancient man dared impute only to his gods, any mere Russian or American air-force general can now command." But, thereby, humanity suffers from an anxiety neurosis in direct proportion to the power of its arms and its guilt complexes.

These fears are all the more irrational in that "the old urban container has in fact exploded, leaving behind only a few citadels of absolute power on the ancient pattern, like the Kremlin and the Pentagon. What is even more important, invisible walls between classes and castes have been breaking down steadily during the last several decades." Economically and politically, thermonuclear war would be madness. "Thus we are back at the very point at which civilization started, but at an even lower depth of savagery and irrationality. Instead of a token sacrifice to appease the gods, there would now be a total sacrifice, merely to bring an end our neurotic anxieties."

That the dreams of our remote ancestors have become realities is true. That humanity feels guilty of its Promethean exploits is possible, although the conscious and rational fear of the scientist facing the risk of thermonuclear war seems to me more real than a collective guilt complex. That the increase of productive capacities must strike down the walls between peoples and classes as the logic of economics takes its course I do not doubt. But that peace is not guaranteed by the simple fact that war must be increasingly irrational according to the calculations of profit and loss will surprise only those who misunderstand the nature of historical man, who is a citizen of one specific state, participating in a particular existence and at the same time in the universal quality of reason. The problem of peace among sovereign and armed collectivities is in itself difficult if not insoluble, without it being necessary to invoke atavistic terrors. Atomic and thermonuclear weapons make war more unreasonable; they also make peace more difficult for the very states that would prefer to be prudent.

The human animal is aggressive, but does not fight by instinct, and war is an expression, it is not a *necessary* expression of human combativity. War has been its constant expression in the course of the historical phase, starting from the moment when societies were organized and armed. It is contrary to the nature of man that the danger of violence be definitively dispelled: in every collectivity, misfits will violate the laws and attack persons. It is contrary to the nature of individuals and groups that the conflicts between individuals or among groups disappear. But it is not proved that these conflicts must be manifested in the phenomenon of war, as we have known it for thousands of years, with organized combatants, utilizing increasingly destructive weapons.

Is peace—that is, the absence of legal wars among sovereign collectivities —possible? Is it probable? We shall raise the question after having analyzed the world today. Let us confine ourselves, at the end of this chapter, to the single conclusion which the biologists suggest.

The difficulty of peace has more to do with man's humanity than his animality. The mouse which has received a beating yields to the stronger, and the hierarchy of domination is stable. The wolf that bares its throat is spared by its victor. Man is a being capable of preferring revolt to humiliation and his own truth to life itself. The hierarchy of master and slave will never be stable. Tomorrow the masters will no longer have need of servants and they will have the power to exterminate.

PART THREE

HISTORY
The Global System in the Thermonuclear Age

In the course of the two preceding sections we have attempted to orient our inquiry toward the present. Whether concepts or determinants were involved, the originality of the present circumstances emerged from the analysis, abstract or historical.

We have raised the question of the weapons of massive destruction, at the beginning of our inquiry, in each of the first three chapters. Do nuclear or thermonuclear explosives modify the relations between strategy and diplomacy (do they oblige us to correct Clausewitz's classical formula: war is the continuation of policy by other means)? In our period, what are the conditions of force or of power? What objectives do the actors propose for themselves on the international scene?

In studying the international systems we have noted the global extension and the bipolar structure of the diplomatic field, the formation of blocs around the two nuclear powers. The dialectics of peace and war results in today's cold war—that is, in the permanent combination of *deterrence, persuasion* and *subversion*.

References to the present were no less numerous in Part II. It is not impossible to interpret the present circumstances in the light of Mackinder's concepts and to regard the rivalry between the Soviet Union and the United States as a new episode in the eternal dialogue of land and sea, of continental empire and maritime empire, both enlarged to the dimensions of the modern world. But the air adds a third dimension to the dialogue, and the scientific mastery of space, by means of transport and still more of communication, attenuates the opposition of maritime and terrestrial styles. The ballistic missile crosses oceans and deserts alike; soon "artificial satellites" will oblige us to define the altitude at which the sovereignty of states ceases.

The relation of number and resources, down through the centuries of history, has governed the fate of nations and the prosperity of peoples. Given a certain technological capacity, the number of men on a certain surface could be less or greater than the optimum of either well-being or force. The authors of the past deplored the disasters of depopulation more often than the risks of overpopulation. The demographic explosion of the twentieth century coincides with an unprecedented elevation of the human density compatible with well-being.

At the same time the nature of the economy radically changes the meaning of conquests. Unless the inhabitants are exterminated, the extension of sovereignty over an additional space rarely corresponds to the real or invoked needs of the conquerors. The Japanese live better within their four islands today than formerly within the sphere of Asian co-prosperity. Provided commercial exchanges are sufficiently free, it is in the interests of an industrialized nation, at least in the short term, not to assume the burden of investments necessary to the initiation of industrialization.

Until 1945 the ambition of Caesars was not affected by the reasoning of liberal economists. The disintegration of the European empires, after the Second World War, accords with the thesis: "Empire doesn't pay." But the British decision to abandon India was imposed by the promises made during the hostilities and by circumstances more than by calculations of profit and loss. The abandonment of India involved that of all the Asian possessions. And the tide of the liberation of peoples swelled irresistibly as it advanced. The resistance of France, in Indo-China and Algeria, would remind us, if there were any need, that the values and passions of peoples do not yet obey the logic (or what is called the logic) of industrial society.

Has Western civilization, in Toynbee's sense of the word, evolved toward universal empire, in the manner of those which have preceded it in time and in the tomb? Is this universal (American) empire the North Atlantic Treaty Organization? Whether or not we admit that the Atlantic zone is an analogue of the universal empires, the originality of the situation is not in doubt, since the Soviet Empire, in the middle of what was the German Reich, confronts the nations of the Atlantic Pact. It is the unification of "civilizations" into a single system which characterizes the period that begins with the so-called Second World War.

Our period must no longer be situated in the national perspective, nor in the perspective of "civilizations," but in that of humanity. War, in the strict sense of bloody conflict between the regular troops of organized states, cannot be traced back further than the very existence of "political organizations" or "regular troops." That war, as an institution, is of recent origin (several thousand years old) is both incontestable and of little interest as a fact: civilization, too—or what we call civilization—is recent. The fact is that men, since they have had metal tools with which to procure the means of subsistence, have become the greatest danger to each other. Not that war seems an essentially biological phenomenon: among the higher animals we do not observe behavior comparable to that of waging war. It is the social animals who fight each other in organized groups. It is the "social units" that create, between animals of the same species, distance, hostility, hatred and pitiless combat.

Both courses end the same way: the circumstances of 1960, dominated by two major facts: the *technological revolution,* origin of both the enormous capacity to destroy (thermonuclear weapons) and to produce (the futility of conquests), the *global extension of the diplomatic field,* origin of both real heterogeneity (diversity of the principles of state legitimacy, dimensions of the political units) and of juridical homogeneity (United Nations, equality and sovereignty of states).

The more detailed study, which we shall now undertake, of international relations in the Atomic Age has two chief objectives. It seeks first to define the new characteristics of strategy and diplomacy in the age of the thermonuclear bomb. It also seeks to present a description, enlightened by the previous study of concepts and determinants, of a concrete situation. Now these two objectives can only be achieved simultaneously.

What are called weapons of mass destruction have changed *something* in the course of relations between what are called sovereign states. They have changed neither the nature of men nor that of political units. Thus it is a question of determining what has changed, first on a higher level of abstraction and, so to speak, in theory, then returning by stages to concrete reality. We shall first consider the *heterogeneity of the global system,* resulting from the extension to the whole of the planet of the diplomatic system, of which the industrialized states are the chief protagonists. In every period, international relations occur among "political units," among "military sovereignties," among "centers of autonomous decisions." Which are the actors today, the states recognized by the United Nations, the blocs formed by the military alliances or ideological bonds? Or rather, to what degree and in what direction are the actors states or blocs?

We shall then consider the most truly revolutionary of the two original features of the present circumstances: thermonuclear weapons; and we shall analyze their significance and their effect by a method resembling that of models. For the first time, men are preparing a war they do not want, a war they hope not to wage. What is the meaning of the strategy of deterrence or a strategy which aims to prevent a virtual enemy from taking certain actions by threatening him with what one would detest doing?[1]

The answers to the questions formulated in the first two chapters should appear in Chapters XV and XVI. The formation of blocs owes little or nothing to the introduction of atomic weapons. It has been a mechanical effect of the situation created by the Second World War. Two states had emerged reinforced from the turmoil: the Soviet Union, despite the devastations suffered, because it alone possessed a great army after the Anglo-American demo-

---

[1] The formula "what one would detest doing" is deliberately vague. The analysis in Chapter XIV will specify its meaning.

bilization of 1945–46; the United States because its territory had been spared, its industrial plant increased, and because it possessed a monopoly of the atomic weapon. The constitution of a Soviet zone of influence in Eastern Europe provoked a regrouping in the West which, in its turn, provoked a reply in the form of a tightening of the links between the People's Democracies and the Soviet Union. The dialectic of the blocs is, as such, classical, in accord with the predictable logic of a bipolar equilibrium. The problem is to know to what degree this dialectic is, has been and will be affected by the new strategy of deterrence.

In the next stage the analysis will deal with the non-committed powers which are also, to a degree, the undeveloped ones. The blocs, in Europe, in North America, group the majority of the developed nations. If they wage war on each other, they assure the victory of those remaining outside the hostilities. But if they are concerned not to destroy each other, they are inevitable competitors outside the zone of direct conflict. Each of them, in fact, wants the non-committed powers to come over to its side, or to rally to its flag, or to become industrialized according to its own model. In other words, the rest of the world reinforces the paradoxical character of the relation between the blocs *which in all reason must not fight each other to the death and which cannot come to agreement.*

It will then be possible for us, in conclusion, in Chapter XVIII, to analyze the meaning of the major conflict of our time in relation to the two great powers. To what degree do they resemble each other? To what degree are they brothers at the same time that they are enemies? What interpretation does each of them give to their rivalry? What interpretation is given by others, allies of one or the other bloc, or the non-committed?

chapter XIII

Le monde fini
or
The Heterogeneity of the Global System

Since 1945 the international system has included the five continents, the whole of humanity.

There is no event, in Korea or Laos, which does not make itself felt in the Soviet Union or in the United States. The diplomatic universe is like an echo chamber: the noises of men and events are amplified and reverberated to infinity. The disturbance occurring at one point of the planet communicates itself, step by step, to the opposite side of the globe.

The role played by the two super powers confirms the unity of the system. The presence of American soldiers or advisers at the 38th Parallel, on the coastal islands of Quemoy and Matsu or in West Berlin, symbolizes the ubiquity of the United States military forces as well as the solidarity of the European and Asian theaters of operations. It suggests drawing up the map of the diplomatic field according to the Mackinder design: the American Republic is located on an island in relation to the Eurasian land mass, comparable to the British Isles in relation to the mass of Europe. It tends to protect the coastal fringe of the Eurasian land mass, Western Europe and Eastern Asia. The infiltration of Communist ideas or institutions into Africa and Latin America constitutes a reply to the American bases established on the periphery of Soviet territory. The continental power, by its propaganda or the circulation of its doctrines, forces the blockades raised by its rival and disturbs the latter even in those zones whose very distance seemed to protect them from such enterprises.

Finally the United Nations, whatever one's judgment as to its effectiveness, attempts to be a universal society, to which all states belong by right. The absence of continental China is imputable to the obstinacy of American diplomacy, the absence of Germany to the consequences of the last war.

The global ensemble thus presents the characteristic features of an international system: all the events, wherever they occur, react upon each other. Political units, from one end of the earth to the other, are organized into a single hierarchy, two among them playing on the world stage the role played by the great powers on the European stage; all the states forming juridical-diplomatic relations. Some transnational institutions are open to individuals of all races. Today's Olympic Games are born of an anachronistic imitation of the Greek games, which never prevented wars among the city-states but bore witness to a community among the city-states or better still among their citizens. The community which the Olympic Games (on the level of relations among individuals) and the United Nations (on the level of relations among states) claim to represent is that of the human race.

The global extension of the international system has nothing to do, on a first analysis, with the weapons of mass destruction and the thermonuclear duopoly. The United Nations would be in a position to act in military terms in Korea and in Vietnam, on the Elbe and in the Arctic, even if its bombers only carried conventional weapons. Similarly, ideological infiltration and subversion would penetrate as far as the Republic of Panama and Cuba even if the Soviet Union possessed neither ballistic missiles nor thermonuclear bombs.

Historically, the global extension of international systems has had the Second World War as its cause. The combination of German and Japanese moves obliged Great Britain and especially the United States to distribute forces between the two theaters of operations. The American war leaders faced problems analogous to those confronting the German leaders between 1914 and 1918. The two fronts of the Kaiser's empire were in Europe. The two fronts of the United States were on the Rhine and in the Philippines. The collapse of the German and Japanese empires made inevitable the extension if not the permanence of the American presence on the frontiers of the Soviet Empire.

But the global extension of the system was inevitable, one day or another, because of the constant factors in the situation. The modern means of transport and communication strike down the barriers once raised by distance. The Soviet Union has two faces, one turned toward Europe, the other toward Asia, just as the United States faces the Atlantic and Europe in one direction, and the Pacific and Asia in the other. Once the Soviet Union and the United States assumed the leading roles on the international stage, they extended that stage to the limits of the planet. Finally, the *dimensions* of the diplomatic stage are on the whole, down through history, proportional to the *stature* of the actors. The distance affected by the power of one state depends on the latter's resources. Given a constant technology, it is the nature of political units and the size of forces concentrated in each of them which determine the extension of the diplomatic field. The Greek city-states were doomed to a provincial policy unless they united or submitted to a single master. The disproportion between the dimensions of the European states and the enormity of their empires is due to exceptional circumstances. On the other hand, the international system is logically worldwide when each of the two super powers is capable of mobilizing and arming some ten or twelve million men, of producing tens of millions of tons of steel.

The weapons, the character of the possible war affect the course of diplomacy, but the latter is first of all a function of the actors, of their interests, their ideas, their practices. Just as a system of democratic policy is understood in terms of the actors, that is, of the parties, so an international system is understood in terms of *its* actors, that is, in terms of the states. In both cases the semi-clandestine actors, or those that do not conform to the dominant type, act on the stage or behind the scenes. Pressure groups or professional syndicates in one case, transnational, supranational or international groups in the other.

The United States and Gabon (a half-million inhabitants), the Soviet Union and Libya are all members of the United Nations, thus all members of the international society, all states with regard to law. The important thing is not so much to emphasize this *diversity*, known to all the observers, but rather to specify its nature, that is, to analyze the heterogeneity characteristic of the global system.

1. Community and Heterogeneity

Let us take as a point of departure the fact that all political units derive more or less clearly from one and the same conception of the state, to which lip-service is paid everywhere. This concept synthesizes three historical ideas: legitimacy is *democratic*, the state is *neutral* in relation to the beliefs which relate to individual conscience, authority is exercised through the intermediary of a *bureaucracy*.

The democratic character of legitimacy has two meanings. The peoples no longer belong to princes, they belong to themselves. They themselves are sovereigns. Exchanges of provinces among monarchs are inconceivable in our century. Compromises or trades—two territories of analogous value, passing simultaneously from one state allegiance to another—are as forbidden, at least in an official form, to the democratic regimes as to the Soviet ones. All those who govern claim to express the will, at least the ultimate will, of those who are governed.

Democratic legitimacy constitutes not only the basis of political regimes, but also the basis of national existence. In other words, it is implicitly admitted, though not always without hypocrisy, that the individuals, tribes, inhabitants of one province have the right to choose their nationality, to break with the state which they do not regard as their own in order to constitute an independent state or to join another. The so-called principle of self-determination or the right of a people to choose its own political status is an apparently logical consequence of democratic legitimacy. This principle does not raise excessive difficulties where centuries of history have made peoples aware of their identity, have made possible the plebiscite of citizens daily renewing their loyalty to the state. Where Europeans had imposed colonial domination, this principle has justified so-called nationalist revolts and contributed to the victory of parties or men who had led these revolts. But once the colonial masters had left, the same principle may favor the breakup of the new state or prevent the formation of a national body. In Europe the nations have not been formed without princes employing force. It is probably illusory to hope that the African states will manage without violence to found *one* nation out of those tribes (or ethnic groups) which have not forgotten their past wars.

More generally still, the right of peoples to self-determination presupposes that they have the desire to be a nation, and have raised themselves to a state of political awareness. When a threshold of political awareness is achieved, this right functions first of all against the historical empires (none of which were based on the will of populations): thus the Austro-Hungarian and Turkish empires perished but not the empire of the Tsars—which would suffice to remind us, if this banal lesson were necessary, that there are compromises with principles, and that the state structures sometimes survive the ruin of their principle by finding a principle of replacement. When a threshold of political consciousness is not achieved, the right of any ethnic group to self-determination may justify the relapse into tribal anarchy.

Democratic legitimacy and the right to self-determination have not prevented the submission of Eastern Europe to regimes of the Soviet model, themselves subject to the Moscow government. One cannot conclude from this that the historical ideas have been or are futile and ineffectual. The Soviet Union has not formally suppressed the sovereignty of the states of Eastern Europe. The juridical maintenance of the states reserves for the future the possibility of liberation, the opportunity of an increasing autonomy, both internal and external. Further, the conqueror cannot be content with invoking the rights of conquest, but enters into discussion with the Western powers, with the elite groups of the satellite states. The conqueror wishes to prove to the West that the constraint temporarily imposed on the desires of peoples responds to a historical necessity, to the mission of the class which is to save humanity. To the brother parties, the Moscow leaders explain that the equality of the socialist nations must be combined with the primacy of the Soviet Union, the vanguard of the Soviet camp, just as the Communist party is the vanguard of the proletariat. Historical ideas are *one* of the causes which determine the course of events. They are neither the only cause nor a simple epiphenomenon: men do not willingly sacrifice their interests to their ideas, but even when they violate their ideas, they are not entirely unaware of them. Utter cynicism is more frequent among theoreticians reacting against their intimate feelings than among men of action who need to believe in what they are doing and who seek reassurance in a clear conscience.

The neutral or secular state has been, in Europe, the consequence of the wars of religion. In theory, there were and still are two means of preventing civil conflicts between Churches and believers: one is to impose the religion of the prince or the territory upon the subject, the other to regard religion as a private matter. The first method, applied in Germany to end bloody anarchy, gradually led to the second insofar as the members of a Church which was not that of the state were tolerated, provided they obeyed the laws and were prudent in the exercise of their worship. When the Germanies became the Kaiser's Germany, the diversity of confessions left no other issue than *Kulturkampf,* or equality among the Churches. The age of the conflict between Churches and between Church and State ends at the beginning of the twentieth century in Europe, but the recognition of various confessions, the individual's right to have or not have a religion, and the state's neutrality involved many institutional translations, and these translations have provoked conflicts, not all of which have been resolved today.

Does the state derive the sums necessary for the upkeep of the Churches by taxation (as in the case of Germany)? Or does it ignore the financial needs of the Churches, as in the case of France, where the faithful are organized to meet the financial needs of the Church? Is education to be Catholic, Protestant, or secular in the primary schools, depending upon the desires of the parents? Does the state consent to distribute the available funds among the Catholic schools and the secular schools depending on their relative importance? Or does the state recognize only the secular schools, without prohibiting but without subsidizing the religious schools? None of the three solutions, German, Belgian or French, is incompatible with state neutrality or with the formula "religion is a private matter." The choice of one or the other leads to endless discussions of principles and opportunities, and is explained, in each case, by the circumstances of both yesterday and today. Today, peoples are not always capable of achieving a neutral state, either because religion appears to constitute their nationality (Pakistan) or because tradition makes a radical separation of civil power and faith inconceivable. In this regard Israel offers a curious example. The Jews who emigrated to Palestine are not all racially the descendants of the people of Solomon and David. They have only their religion in common, and yet, because some among them were unbelievers or because the historical idea of the neutral state dominates their minds, they have decreed that the Israeli state would be a secular one.

State secularity raises a problem of a general order: on what is the loyalty of the citizens based to whom we hypothetically attribute various religious beliefs? The modern state presupposes a differentiation of the political order, a specific awareness of nationality, above family or local attachments, below that of a transcendental faith. This awareness scarcely exists among the Moslem populations, divided into sects or tribes, who have difficulty in identifying themselves with an Iraqi or Jordanian state. It exists still less in the populations of equatorial Africa, suddenly promoted to independence within frontiers inherited from the colonial regimes.

In Europe the national awareness, separated from the religious consciousness, has been given a political content, the idea of the nation, of the values which it incarnates and of the regime suitable to it. The state cannot be neutral with regard to all values without being degraded into a purely administrative instrument. It passes for the expression and the servant of the single vocation the nation must fulfill in the world. More or less clearly, a certain concept of the regime, if not of the government, is implied by "national vocation." Thus the citizens feel authorized to violate their oath of allegiance when a revolution upsets institutions to the point where the national vocation changes its direction or meaning. The German patriot "betrays" the Third Reich in order not to "betray" the values to which he chooses to be loyal.

The totalitarian state does not differ from the liberal state in the sense that the latter is a "night watchman" and the former a "guardian of the faith." The argument between ideologies and parties which the liberal state tolerates must occur, ideally, in a context accepted by all the citizens: respect for the same national values, respect for democratic legitimacy, the basis and guarantee of the debate itself. Soviet totalitarianism should not, ideally, exclude discussion as to the effective administration of the economy, the distribution of the sacrifices and conquests of industrial growth, the application of the socialist ideal. But the Bolsheviks have gradually identified the national vocation and the legitimacy of their state with Marxism-Leninism in such a manner that the citizens no longer have the right to question the doctrine itself, or its interpretation, by those in power.

One might be tempted to say that the state has become neutral in religious terms because the political-economic ideologies henceforth constitute the stake of the historical controversies. To a degree, this formula is valid: the liberal state is that state which accepts ideological debate, whereas the totalitarian state is that state which does not separate itself from an ideology. But the liberal state is not devoid of ideas: it permits debate among citizens hypothetically devoted to the national vocation, respectful of the democratic legitimacy and consequently of the rules of honest discussion. When this national unity, and this unanimity concerning the principle of legitimacy, do not exist, the liberal state and the community itself are threatened with disintegration.

Outside the zone of Western civilization, nations (in the sense of populations having achieved the differentiated consciousness of the national vocation) are not numerous. The peoples of the new states are less nations than they are, more or less, heterogeneous populations. The African states are for the most part small (aside from Nigeria), but they have neither ethnic nor linguistic unity. India is an enormous country of over four hundred million inhabitants. It is possible that the Indians have an "awareness of a common civilization" which can be expressed in "a political awareness of the national vocation," but this awareness of a civilization does not contain several of the elements of a national awareness: language, regime, legitimacy, etc.

Thus, throughout most of the world, the task of creating nations is incumbent upon the state. The latter, in Africa as in Europe or in Asia, is first of all an administration: functionaries manage the public services, represent the state in foreign capitals, maintain order. Tax collectors, diplomats and policemen fulfill three of the functions of every state, three functions which the modern state entrusts to men recruited and supported for this purpose.

The functionaries participate, according to theory, in the state's neutrality, while the politicians in a one-party state are interpreters or servants of doctrine, and in a liberal state are chosen by discussion and competition to manage public affairs according to the ideology temporarily prevalent in the context of common convictions. But neither the totalitarian formula nor the liberal formula exactly corresponds to the needs of those states whose people lack coherence, awareness of a common vocation. The totalitarian formula would give the political awareness a content more ideological than national. The liberal formula would give free rein to all centrifugal forces. The more or less unique party, without ideological content or with a content more national than ideological, is an intermediary formula increasingly popular in Africa and the Near East.

The party which has waged the struggle for independence, or whose leader has been the hero in the anti-colonialist struggle, quite naturally becomes the state party, from which are chosen administrators and politicians (a distinction between the former and the latter is not yet clearly made, for lack of a sufficiently numerous qualified personnel). The state party does not declare itself legitimately unique, it does not impose an ideology, but it restrains the rights of the opposition and prevents the formation of a party which would attempt to compete for the exercise of power.

That in our century, so proud of its democratic professions of faith, the representative institutions and liberal values are as manifestly in retreat would astonish only those who, to quote Montesquieu, identify the power of the people with the freedom of the people or, to put it better, those who misinterpret the paradoxes of our time. The ideas, or at least the words of politics, tend to proceed around the world: the heterogeneity of populations, whether in terms of degree of development, historical traditions, religions or national coherence, remain extreme. According to the philosophy dominant in the United Nations, the actors on the international stage are sovereign states, whose principles and ideals are those of the national state of European, democratic, secular, administrative origin. But the façade of the national state is sometimes reduced to a flag, a few ambassadors, a delegation to the United Nations and a few hundred persons educated in the universities. The global or worldwide extension of the system is simultaneously manifested by the diffusion of the same words and the diversity of situations.

If we consult the lists of the states represented in the international organization, we are immediately impressed by the heterogeneity of the historical realities that positive law calls nations and proclaims sovereign and equal. China numbers hundreds of millions of inhabitants, whereas Luxembourg or Gabon number only hundreds of thousands. Four states (China, India, the U.S.S.R., the United States) include more than half of the world's population.

This heterogeneity in regard to space and number is the most striking, but perhaps the least significant, aspect of international relations, at least for anyone wishing to understand their *meaning*. Most often this quantitative heterogeneity, as we may call it, expresses the diversity of social bodies, that is, of populations subject to a single sovereignty. Not that the social bodies of the great states are always incohesive and the social bodies of the small ones always cohesive. Quite the contrary, the social body of Libya is incohesive and that of Japan or even of China is cohesive. But the diversity of ethnic groups within an African state of several million souls as well as the cultural uniformity of the hundred million Japanese, are the heritage of centuries. That one or the other should refer, in ideas or in words, to the national state of European origin symbolizes in itself the diffusion throughout all of humanity of a single political concept, inevitably applied to radically different societies, some of which had, in a broad or narrow context, reached national awareness, while others had known only a tribal community and submission to an imperial law.

World opinion, or what is conventionally called world opinion, thus tends to forget that the hundred or so states of the United Nations have behind them divergent pasts and are not governed by political bodies of the same type. On the other hand, it continues to recall and deplore the fact that "societies" are unequal in terms of "development," that is, in terms of industrialization, of per capita production, hence of standard of living. The obsession with *inequalities of development* combined with the misunderstanding of the diversity of political bodies expresses and explains the unfortunately illusory conviction that development, and the principal institutions of an industrial society, are transferable at will and on short terms, as machines or even factories are transferable. In fact, to transfer to equatorial Africa the collective behavior which permits each individual to produce a high value, one must evidently completely overthrow customs and provoke a social and human revolution.

This social revolution, inevitable in any case, is today conceived in the manner of one or the other of two political-economic regimes, Soviet and Western, between which the developed fraction of humanity is divided. Not that these two regimes, as represented by the United States and the Soviet Union, are the only possible ones (at most they suggest two ideal types), nor, still less, that they indicate the two roads between which the underdeveloped countries must choose (indeed the underdeveloped countries, in most cases, cannot and should not take the road followed by the United States in the last century, nor that which the Soviet Union has followed in this one).

But the global unity of humanity, combined with the concentration of the

military-economic power in two gigantic states, gives the opposition of regimes and ideologies, Soviet and American, the character of a fundamental
alternative. The dialogue of Washington and Moscow, of single party and
legitimized conflicts, of plan and market place, falsely assumes, with regard
to actors and spectators, the meaning of a death struggle.

Hence the unity of the diplomatic field is not simply material, imputable
to the force of the continent-states and to techniques of destruction, transport
and communication; it is sustained by a community of political vocabularies
which express a partial community of historical ideas. But since this partial
community covers an extreme diversity of social bodies, the inequality of
economic development appears scandalous, and the community is rent by the
contradictions between regimes and ideologies. The global system is more
heterogeneous than the systems of the past if we judge it by the realities of
nations: it tends to a greater homogeneity if we judge it by the juridical
formalism of the United Nations, by the protests against underdevelopment,
by the universalist ambitions of social doctrines. For the first time, humanity
is living one and the same history, tempted to ignore in turn what prevents
and what commands it to unite.

2. European Blocs and Alliances

A description of the international system according to the method of
diplomatic history would begin with one observation: never have there been
so many alliances concluded in peacetime, never have there been so many
organizations, either inter-state (postal union) or transnational (churches,
parties of universal vocation) or super-state (European High Commission);
never so many military groupings, despite the United Nations, theoretically
destined to bring power politics to an end. The United States, long opposed
to any external commitment, has become a collector of pacts.

Two coalitions, often called *blocs*, dominate the situation, one led by the
United States, the other by the Soviet Union, one officially instituted by
the North Atlantic Treaty, and the other by the Warsaw Pact. Everything
occurs as if each of the two super powers had grouped protected or satellite
states around itself.

It hardly matters "who started it." The origin of the formation of blocs was
the misunderstanding between Stalin and Franklin D. Roosevelt as to the
meaning which should be given to the formula of "governments friendly to
the Soviet Union." According to Marxist-Leninist theory, only a government
dominated by members of the Communist party could be authentically
friendly. Every man, every party opposed to the power of the Communist
was, or could be treated as, fascist. Thus, as we know today, reasoned Stalin
and those around him. Roosevelt and Churchill, as a result of the Western
notion of democracy, conceived of free elections, representative institutions,
multiple parties. Sir Winston probably had fewer illusions than Roosevelt
concerning the Soviet leader, but he maintained the hope that the resistance

and the hostility of the peoples would render Russian domination in Eastern Europe precarious.

There is no need to review the stages of the establishment, in Eastern Europe, of the regimes imitating and subject to the Soviet regime. It is enough to indicate that the Sovietization of Eastern Europe has occurred *in the Atomic Age*, but that it is not at all connected with the latter. Whatever respective share one attributes to the strictly Communist ambitions, to the concern for security and to the aspirations of pan-Slavism, the fact is that the Sovietization of Eastern Europe has not been a cautionary measure against the atomic danger, but a procedure in accord with the practices of imperialist or ideological expansion.

The Atlantic Pact is a classical reply to a classical *démarche*. Just as France, after the First World War, had hoped for an Anglo-American guarantee because the participation of the two Anglo-Saxon powers had been necessary to the victory, similarly the states of Western Europe hoped for an American peacetime commitment, because the United States had contributed decisively to the liberation of the Continent. The North Atlantic Pact, it is true, no longer envisaged aggression from the enemy, but from yesterday's ally. It was nonetheless the expression of a concept in accord with precedent. Henceforth the American Republic was an integral part of the European system. It had a vital interest, manifested twice over, in preventing the establishment, throughout Europe, of a hegemony or an empire, whether the Caesar was brown or red. Walking backward into the future, statesmen were inclined to believe that the North Atlantic Pact would prevent the next war since, had it existed, it would probably have prevented the previous one.

The constitution, after the outbreak of the Korean War, of the NATO Supreme Command marked a new stage in the formation of blocs. The fear of the extension to Europe of the "local hot war" at the same time as the military necessity, recognized in the course of two world wars, of integrating Allied forces under a single command, incited Europeans and Americans to perfect, in peacetime, what would be, in any case, indispensable on the first day of hostilities. Thus the Atlantic Treaty was gradually developed into a political-military community closer than that which could have existed between France and Great Britain between 1914 and 1918, comparable only to the Anglo-American cooperation between 1941 and 1945. The Warsaw Pact, concluded in 1954, scarcely modified the previous state of things: the authority of the Russian command over the armies of the satellite states had not waited for the Warsaw Pact to make itself felt (and there was no integrated general staff).

The military communities of both blocs are due to circumstances, to certain unique considerations, yet do not constitute a break with the ordinary process of international relations. The constitution of the NATO Supreme Command was logical as the result of the risk of general war, as the result of an evident goal (to preserve Western Europe from invasion in case of war), as the result of the military conditions, some temporary (the weakness of the European states), others lasting (the impossibility of the operational autonomy of national armies due to the limitations of terrain and the rapidity of movements, on land and in the air). Risk, goal and military conditions are linked to the major fact that is the direct cause of military blocs: the direct impact of the two super powers in the center of Europe, the latter being simultaneously the *site* and the *stake* of their encounter.

Situated in another geographical zone, medium-sized states such as Great Britain and France would possess military forces—conventional today, atomic tomorrow—not inferior to the task of national defense. They could deter an aggressor (not armed with thermonuclear weapons) by their capacity to defend themselves against an attack made with conventional weapons. What reduces the autonomy of the European states, for the moment, is that they are close to the dominant continental power, that they constitute a stake of considerable value, and that they are incapable of uniting, if not under the direction of the United States.

After the war, the partition of Germany and the Sovietization of Eastern Europe created a climate of permanent conflict. The victors could not reach an agreement on a territorial settlement, and ideological competition with its wild propaganda gave a violent style to the opposition of the two worlds. In 1949–50 statesmen and peoples had not yet fully understood and acknowledged that the absence of peace, in the nineteenth-century sense of the word *peace,* does not signify the probability of war. The Atlantic Pact and the Warsaw Pact were concluded, *the Atlantic bloc and the Soviet bloc were formed with a view to waging the cold war in a period when a hot one was feared. The two blocs continue to be instruments of the cold war while having as their objective the avoidance of a hot one.*

The conditions peculiar to the European blocs are not duplicated in any other part of the world. The states of the Southeast Asia Pact (South East Asia Treaty Organization) or of the old Baghdad Pact (Central Treaty Organization) lack a community of civilization or of political institutions. This community exists between the United States, Australia and New Zealand, but the British dominions are not threatened with invasion, and are separated by the seas from any aggressor: a mutual-assistance treaty suffices, without a permanent military organization. As for the treaties concluded by the United States with the Nationalist Chinese government on Formosa, with South Korea and Japan, they are of a classical type: whatever the terms employed by their authors, the fact is that the protected state puts bases at the disposal of the protecting state. The alliance affords an advantage of each of the contracting parties as long as the bases granted to the protecting states seem to afford the protected state more guarantees against a possible attack than risks of being involved, by the military presence of its ally, in a conflict that does not concern it.

Nor are the conditions in which the Soviet bloc has been formed to be found outside of Europe. The Soviet Union does not impose its will upon the states of Eastern Europe merely by the acknowledged prestige of the nation which took the initiative of the revolution of salvation, and which remains the center of the new faith. The Soviet army is present or nearby. It intervened in Hungary, it was ready to do so in Poland, it could still do so in case of need. The inequality of forces between the Big Brother on one side and each of the little brothers on the other is such that the Soviet bloc in Europe, if not monolithic, is certainly monocephalic. The Soviet bloc in Asia is bicephalic.

This proposition teaches us nothing as to the degree of coordination, the solidity and duration of the alliance between the Soviet Union and China. It is limited to recognizing the fact, in itself incontestable, that in Europe the Soviet leaders keep the possibility of resorting to military force in order to maintain the unity of the bloc, but that they are not in the same position in Asia. China is too large, too strong, too arrogant to submit to the wishes of the Big Brother. The Kremlin must conduct a dialogue with the Forbidden City. The Russian leaders lack neither arguments nor material means for persuasion, but they do not possess the age-old instrument of constraint. In Asia the Soviet Union has an ally, not satellites.[1] The United States has allies, it has not constructed a political-military community, and the relations among its allies are sometimes bad (South Korea and Japan).

The confrontation of the two super powers in Asia has the character of the eternal struggle of the bear and the whale, of the sea and the land. The United States figures there as an essentially maritime power, established on a belt of island bases from Japan to Taiwan, passing through Okinawa and the Philippines. On the continent, the United States kept no more than a bridgehead, South Korea, until it became engaged in South Vietnam.

If we refer to the texts, the treaties concluded by the American leaders fall into three categories, according to the precision and the extent of the commitments made. To the first category belong the North Atlantic Treaty, signed April 4, 1949, and valid on August 24, 1949,[2] and the Inter-American Treaty of Reciprocal Assistance, signed September 2, 1947, and valid on December 3, 1948.[3] In Article 5 of the first of these two treaties, as in Article 3 of the second, we find the decisive formula: the contracting parties "agree that

[1] North Korea and North Vietnam are not satellites because they have two Big Brothers. The Soviet Union and the People's Republic of China both concluded a mutual assistance pact with North Korea in the spring of 1961.
[2] The signers were twelve in number: the United States, Canada, Iceland, Norway, Great Britain, Holland, Denmark, Belgium, Luxembourg, France, Italy; the German Federal Republic, Turkey and Greece were subsequently admitted.
[3] The members are: the United States, Mexico, Cuba, Haiti, the Dominican Republic, Honduras, Guatemala, Salvador, Nicaragua, Costa Rica, Panama, Colombia, Venezuela, Ecuador, Peru, Brazil, Bolivia, Paraguay, Chile, Argentina, Uruguay.

an armed attack against one or more of them in Europe or North America shall be considered an attack against them all."[4] The formula does not imply, strictly, that such an attack would be a *casus belli* for each of the contracting parties. The North Atlantic Treaty adds: "And consequently they agree that if such an armed attack occurs, each of them, in the exercise of the right of individual or collective self-defense recognized by article 51 of the Charter of the United Nations, will assist the party or parties so attacked by taking forthwith, individually and in concert with the other parties, such action as it deems necessary, including the use of armed force, to restore and maintain the security of the North Atlantic area."[5] Obliged to come to the aid of the Atlantic or American state attacked, the United States is not, according to the strict terms of the treaty, obliged to declare war on the aggressor and to engage all its forces. But in fact, the two treaties have received this meaning, especially the North Atlantic one, consolidated by the establishment of a common general staff and of an army integrated in peacetime.

To a second category belong the treaties with the Philippines (signed on August 30, 1951, valid on August 27, 1952), with Australia and New Zealand (signed on September 1, 1951, valid on April 29, 1952), and the collective defense pact of southeast Asia (United States, France, Great Britain, Australia, New Zealand, the Philippines, Thailand, Pakistan, signed on September 8, 1954, valid on February 19, 1955). The decisive formula that recurs in each of these three documents is less categorical than that of the treaties of the first category. Instead of proclaiming that an attack against one of the member states would be an attack against all, what is said is that the contracting parties recognize that an attack in the region covered by the pact would endanger their own security. For instance, in the Southeast Asia Treaty:

"Each party recognizes that aggression by means of armed attack in the treaty area against any of the parties or against any state or territory which the parties by unanimous agreement may hereafter designate, would endanger its own peace and safety, and agrees that it will in that event act to meet the common danger in accordance with its constitutional processes."[6] In other words, each state remains, in all circumstances, free to choose the measures with which to deal with aggression.

To a third category belong the mutual defense treaties with Japan, South

---

[4] The formula of the inter-American treaty is the same: "an armed attack by any state against an American state shall be considered as an attack against all the American states."

[5] The text of the inter-American treaty is the same, except that the expression "including the use of armed force" does not figure in it.

[6] Article 4 of the treaties with the Philippines and with Australia and New Zealand contain an equivalent formula, except that they mention only the attack against the contracting parties.

Korea and the Republic of China (Formosa). The decisive formula is the same: an attack against the territory of one of the contracting parties would be dangerous for the peace and security of the other.[7] But further, the partners of the United States put bases at the disposal of the American armed forces.

With regard to the texts, these three categories of treaties can be classified in two different ways: the North Atlantic Treaty, like the mutual assistance pacts with South Korea, Japan and the Republic of China, involve military cooperation between the contracting parties, the establishment of American armed forces on the bases put at their disposal by the allied states. On the other hand, the treaties of the second category (for example, the SEATO Pact) involve military consultations, not an integrated general staff or the stationing of American armed forces on foreign bases. But categories two and three can be combined and opposed to the first category, since only the treaties of the first category employ the categorical expression: an armed attack against one of the contracting parties will be considered as an attack against all.

Beyond this formal analysis, is it possible to distinguish the functions of these various alliances? In a general way, in our period, these alliances can fulfill two quite different functions: either they aim at deterring a possible aggressor, or they aim at influencing the internal policy of the allied states (of course, these two functions are not exclusive of each other). Secondarily, their goal is to facilitate the coordination of diplomacies and to present a common front to the enemy.

Since these two functions differ radically and since each of them is linked to the particular features of the present system, it is easy to criticize the American alliances either by reference to the traditional conception of alliances, or by misunderstanding the specific function each of them has.

Let us first consider the alliances of the first type, those which aim essentially at deterring the aggressor, for example the mutual security pact with Japan. They can be criticized either by the protector (the United States) or by the protected nation (Japan). In the age of the thermonuclear duopoly the alliances represent a risk as well as an advantage for the wielder of the monstrous weapons. An alliance, according to the interpretation still most common, is solid on condition that it is advantageous to both parties. The great power promises to defend the small one; the latter will join its forces to those of the great power. Frenchmen and Englishmen promise to come to the aid of Belgium, and the latter sends a dozen divisions into the field. In our period, if we refer only to the possibility of thermonuclear war, the small power offers the great power no contribution of a military order

[7] In the Japanese treaty the formula is slightly different: there is no mutual defense, Japan being constitutionally barred from having an army. The only attack envisaged is against the Japanese territory, not against the American possessions in the Pacific.

(outside of bases, which are less and less necessary as the technology of ballistic missiles advances). Thus the commentators who know no other basis for alliances than the reciprocity of military aid fear that the protector will be less interested in his protégés the day he no longer needs bases, whether for planes or for ballistic missiles.

This reasoning is false. The objective of the mutual assistance treaty with Japan or South Korea has always been to convince enemy states that they could not attack with impunity a territory protected by a solemn commitment of the United States and on which American troops were stationed. The function of deterrence remains even when the protector no longer needs the bases which the protégé puts at his disposal.

On the other hand, protector and protégé question themselves as to the risks which their solidarity involves for each other. Certain parties in Japan argue that an armed aggression, on the part of the Soviet Union or China, is not to be feared, and that consequently the pact is no longer necessary and has no results other than to nourish anti-American sentiments. Let Japan be neutral, they say, and the Japanese people will have only friendship for the American people. On their side, the Americans, from the day their territory, too, is vulnerable, wonder to what degree a deterrence that is not based on an equilibrium of local forces creates useless risks for them, the possible choice between capitulation and the carrying out of a threat mortal for all. Even in the case of its "deterrence alliances," the influence of the pact on the internal policy of the state protected is perhaps the principal consideration. Would the withdrawal of American troops from Japan reinforce the pro-American parties because it would deprive the opposition of an argument, or would it reinforce the neutralist and leftist parties, because it would seem to signify a diplomatic defeat for Washington and announce a change of allegiance? *A fortiori*, these arguments are decisive in the case of alliances which have less a military function of defense or deterrence than a diplomatic (to constitute an imposing coalition) and political one (to sustain, within the allied countries, the parties favorable to the United States or to the West).

The SEATO Pact still has both functions. It would serve as a context for common, possibly military action against Communist penetration. It would permit the President of the United States to make decisions without seeking the authorization of Congress. But at the same time and above all, it is intended to convince the threatened governments that the United States will not abandon them. In Africa or in Latin America, where the nations are not exposed to a direct aggression of the Communist powers, the treaties concluded by the United States can have only a psycho-diplomatic function: to prevent states from sliding toward neutrality or toward the Soviet camp, to reinforce parties or men favoring the West.

The cost and advantage of these treaties (mutual assistance pacts or agreements on military aid) between the United States and any Asian or Middle

Eastern state today or African state tomorrow depend on many circumstances. The arms furnished to the pro-Western government, in certain cases, reinforce the latter's authority. In others, the unpopularity that the alliance with the West costs the government more than balances the material support, so that the final accounting is unfavorable to the very interests the West had intended to support.

Local circumstances, in the sub-system, also determine the meaning which is given to American intervention. Will the latter be interpreted as legitimate in the global context or illegitimate in the regional one? Did Nehru regard the Southeast Asia Treaty as likely to reinforce the defense of the free world, or to introduce the cold war into a zone which could and should remain outside the world conflict? Are the American weapons provided to Pakistan being turned against the Soviet bloc or against Afghanistan or against India, since the Kashmir question has not yet been solved?

Lastly, these alliances or pacts of military aid are effective or deplorable depending on the political circumstances within the nation. Is the government, whose power is confirmed by the alliance or by American aid, the only possible one, outside the Communist party? Is it the most popular of the non-Communist parties? The danger is that American intervention will make the opposition parties increasingly anti-American, including those preferring neutrality to commitment without inclining to the Communist camp. Would the best method of avoiding the Sovietization of Laos have been to support the groups on the Western side or the partisans of neutrality?

The Soviet Union's policy of alliances is much simpler. Before 1939 Moscow had concluded non-aggression pacts with the neighboring nations, the very ones it was to absorb in the course of the Second World War. Its mutual assistance agreement with France became null and void when the non-aggression treaty with the Third Reich was signed in 1939. The mutual assistance treaties with Great Britain and France, signed in 1943 and 1944, rapidly fell into desuetude and were denounced by Moscow following the Paris agreements which provided for the Federal German Republic's entry into NATO.

Since the war, the Soviet Union has signed mutual assistance treaties against Germany (or the nations allied to Germany) and against Japan (or the nations allied to Japan) and only with states of Communist regime, states of Eastern Europe, Communist China, North Korea, and North Vietnam. These mutual assistance treaties have all confirmed, not created, a situation of fact. At the time of the Korean campaign the Soviet Union had no mutual assistance pact with the Pyong-Yang regime. The German Democratic Republic was not established within the network of mutual assistance pacts until 1954, when the Warsaw Treaty was signed. Before 1939 the Soviet Union, isolated and on the defensive, sought non-aggression and mutual assistance pacts in order to ameliorate its diplomatic position. Since 1945 it has concluded treaties only to confirm existing links with the brother states.

3. *System and Sub-systems*

The analysis of political units has revealed the plurality of classifications possible according to the criterion adopted. The description of the groupings which the actors compose has, on the contrary, revealed *one* essential distinction visible on the map. The global system involves two zones, one which extends from Vladivostok to San Francisco by way of Moscow, Berlin, Paris and New York, divided into two blocs, each around the thermonuclear monopolists. In the other zone the states are either committed or non-committed (commitment and non-commitment involving various nuances) but they are not grouped in blocs.

The current formula of the bipolar system is valid if we keep within the zone covered by the two blocs: the Soviet Union and the United States are the two super powers around which are grouped the medium-size and small states situated in the intermediate space. It is certainly not valid applied to the whole planet considered as *one* system.

At first glance it seems as if the two blocs of industrialized nations—though not all equally advanced—were opposed in a double rivalry: a direct one in Europe, whose principal stake is the fate of Germany and the tracing of the line of partition; and an indirect one whose stake is the economic and political regime of the rest of the world, especially the economically underdeveloped states. The absurdity of a hot war between the two blocs immediately appears in such an analysis, however summary: the two groupings between which the rich fraction of humanity is divided would destroy each other merely to determine which method the other fraction of humanity would employ to surmount its ancestral poverty. The common interest in thermonuclear non-war not only creates a subtle cooperation between the United States and the Soviet Union; it also marks the relations of the two blocs.

Apart from the British dominions, which despite their geographical situation belong to the zone of Western civilization, the other continents, Asia, Africa, and America were, in 1945, the object rather than the subject of history. Fifteen years later, three events had revolutionized the international situation: the victory of the Communist party in China, the disintegration of the European empires in Asia and Africa, and the spread of Soviet influence throughout the world, including those regions which were the "game preserves" of the West or of the United States (the Near East, South Africa) after World War II. In a sense it remains true that the "third world" constitutes the principal stake of the rivalry between the two blocs. But the action of the two super powers must be adapted to the situations which are largely defined by the very nations that are the stake of the competition. In short, the third world has become history's subject, at the same time being its object.

There is no rigorous correlation between the diplomatic attitude and the internal regime of each state of the world outside the blocs. The nations which go beyond neutrality and draw closer to the Soviet bloc tend to adopt institutions or to resort to practices imitating those of the Soviet Union and China. Even this tendency is not clearly affirmed, at least as long as a party professing allegiance to Moscow or Peking has not seized power. The United Arab Republic utilizes Soviet weapons, but it imprisons leftists or extreme-left militants, including Communists, indeed Communists first of all.

The nations of the world outside the blocs which join the Western cause are characterized neither by degree of development nor by type of regime, whether liberal or democratic. Geopolitical situations, weakness of the faction in power, external threat, local conflict, desire to receive military or economic aid seem the most frequent causes of the alliances concluded by the Asian states with the United States. Verbal or diplomatic friendship with the Soviet Union is explained, according to cases and in various proportions, by resentment against the West, a blackmail tactic (any state threatening to go over to the other camp will sell a mere neutrality at a higher price), or a desire to disarm the extreme-left opposition by outstripping it in diplomatic words and gestures.

Analyses, at this level of abstraction, neglect one dimension of reality. The two super powers or the two blocs encounter each other, oppose each other, compete in the four corners of the world, but the regional circumstances are various. The system is global, but it is fragmented into sub-systems. The two super powers are present in Europe, in Asia, and in South America as in the Near East; the United Arab Republic is not present in southern Asia, even if President Nasser pays a visit to President Sukarno. Certainly the concept of *presence* is not a precise one. In a sense, thanks to the United Nations, all states, however small, are present everywhere, in relation with all others. On the level of propaganda or diplomatic tourism it is not impossible to evoke a "bloc of non-committed powers," although the formula is contradictory and politically meaningless. The non-committed powers would be committed if they constituted a bloc; a common interest in the non-war of the super powers and in anti-colonialism does not suffice to dictate a common policy.

However ambiguous the notion of sub-system, however uncertain the limits of these sub-systems, one example will show what the term designates. In the Near East, despite the armistice signed by Israel and its neighbors, a state of war officially subsists. The Arab states have not "recognized" the state created by the Jews, and in all probability, they would not hesitate to destroy it if they had a military superiority which would permit them to achieve their goal in a few days. The equilibrium of local forces is a decisive factor in the situation. Yet this regional equilibrium cannot be envisaged without considering global conditions. Israel, despite its victories in the course of the Sinai campaign, has kept no piece of occupied territory (but Elath is today open to navigation, and the frontiers, symbolically guarded by blue helmets, are calm).

The super powers, to avoid a war which they fear, the United Nations, out of loyalty to its principles, forbid regular armies to cross the frontiers, rapidly put to an end the combat of uniformed soldiers (for various reasons, guerrilla fighters are ignored or tolerated). But neither the super powers nor the United Nations can bring the dead to life nor refuse for long to accept a *fait accompli*. The Nagy government has disappeared, its leader has been shot, and the "traitor" Kadar, received in the United Nations with the honors due his rank, expresses himself there unrestrainedly on the principles of the Charter. The equilibrium of local forces remains, for Israel, the indispensable condition of safety: it excludes the creation of the *fait accompli*, the elimination of the state-stake by surprise attack.

In other regions, what one would call sub-systems, the characteristic feature of the Near East—a state of war and the equilibrium of local forces—are not to be found. But another example illustrates the meaning of the regional system or sub-system. The Cuban revolution immediately modified the situation throughout the Western Hemisphere. China's conversion to communism, the achievement of a thermonuclear weapon by the Soviet Union, the launching of the Sputniks—none of these *weltgeschichtlich* events, as the Germans say, has not so much impressed the leaders and peoples of South America, nor so profoundly shaken the prestige and authority of the United States, as the Castro revolution and the challenge to the super power launched by the revolutionary regime of the small one. The anti-Yankee sentiments latent in South America have had an opportunity to manifest themselves, and the leaders, despite the hostility which the Cuban leader's excesses and demagoguery inspire, fear contradicting the sentiments of the masses, exalted by the exploit of this bearded David standing up to a Goliath armed with dollars.

Why did the earth shake, in Latin America, after the Cuban revolution and not after the Chinese one? The reasons are simple, eternal: neither the means of transport nor the means of destruction have suppressed the human significance of distance, the mutual reinforcements of historical relationship and spatial proximity. What Fidel Castro has done, other men in Brazil or Peru may also dream of doing. In any case, all the peoples of Latin America feel that the Cuban experiment is instructive, that it suggests a possible path. Revolutions accomplished far away, by people of other races, do not provoke the same passions. Humanity is perhaps one, but the peoples have not a clear awareness of their unity. Regional communities remain stronger than the human one.

In abstract terms a sub-system acquires a reality since, even in the absence of a local equilibrium of military forces, states or peoples spontaneously experience the solidarity of their destiny and observe a difference between what is happening inside and what is happening outside their geographic-historical zone.

This second criterion is not easy to use, for in certain regions the geographical, racial and historical solidarity seems less powerful than the remote solidarities of an economic or ideological order. In Japan, for instance, in the early 1950s, Tokyo seemed closer to Washington, to London or even to Paris than to Peking. Established within the network of alliances and bases woven by the maritime power, Japan communicated more readily with the Anglo-Saxon world than with nearby China, the hearth of the culture it had received, enriched, and finally transformed according to its own genius. This paradox seems to be in the process of attenuation, if not of disappearing. It is explained by the direct impact of the two super powers (or more exactly, by the impact of one of the super powers and the Soviet-Chinese alliance): in Europe, this impact has created the blocs; in northern Asia, it has caused a temporary rupture between the allies of the whale and those of the bear.

A third criterion of the sub-system results from the very rivalry of the two super powers, from the stake which it constitutes in each part of the world, and from the manner in which it is carried on by each power. Europe does not constitute a sub-system merely on account of the equilibrium between the two coalitions or on account of the awareness of a common civilization: the direct impact of the two super powers and the constitution of military blocs make Europe a sub-system or, if one prefers, a theater of diplomatic operations with a certain autonomy. The actors feel more vitally affected by what happens inside than by what happens outside the regional ensemble.

In northern Asia, similarly, it is the direct impact of the maritime power and the continental power which gives the situation its true character. In southeast Asia, on the contrary, it is the absence of this direct impact which is the primary datum. The external threat is Chinese, not Russian. The United States has linked itself to certain states (Pakistan, Thailand) at the risk of alienating others which prefer to be neutral (India, Indonesia, Ceylon). The United States, directly or by the intermediary of SEATO, is attempting to reinforce Laos and South Vietnam against Communist infiltration. In this case the situation involves both local rivalries (India-Pakistan), American alliances with weaker states, perhaps a rivalry of historic scope (India-China), and a potential tension between the committed states and non-committed ones.

Still different is the situation emerging in Africa. It is still too soon to formulate a categorical judgment as to the strength of the rational sentiments of the Westernized elites (the example of the Congo suggests that on the whole, a tribal consciousness still prevails over a national one). Reconciliations and hostilities among new states are just beginning to appear. Mali and Senegal are hostile to each other because they have tried to unite and because the former is more "leftist" than the latter. French-speaking states and English-speaking states do not constitute two groupings, but the education received by the men in government, in both places, will probably be manifest in the ways they act and still more in the ways they speak. Part of the present diplomacy is essentially verbal and breaks down into a kind of permanent discussion.

Neither the United States nor the Soviet Union is, in military terms, present in Africa. The United States does not aim at the same goal there as in Asia or in South America: the neutrality of the states is enough, and the commitment of the Western side seems futile or dangerous. The Soviet Union applies its usual techniques: propaganda, education of militants in special schools, invitations to students, moral or material aid to the governments regarded as sympathizers or as merely in conflict with the West, etc. But even when it achieves its goals and one of the African republics declares itself a "people's republic," the result is not the equivalent of the Sovietization of a European nation. The African republic may be converted to the new faith when it is governed by converts. But it is not subject to the same pressure, exposed to the same sanctions as the satellites near the temporal and spiritual capital. The states which become "people's republics" or "socialist democracies" in Africa or in South America have not been constrained by the Soviet Union as Poland and Hungary have been and are still. They are not alienated, to the same degree, from their own autonomy. If the Communist elite attempts a reconciliation with the West, if it is overthrown by another group, the change of allegiance does not meet with the same resistance as that which broke the heroic attempt of the Hungarians.

In Africa each of the super powers has as its main objective to keep out the other. The United States hopes to preserve the greatest possible number of the new republics from communism, not to establish bases there, nor even to retain markets or sources of raw materials, but simply to channel a tidal wave which would otherwise end by covering the earth. A nation of several million inhabitants is in itself of little interest to either one of the two super powers. But each change of allegiance marks a gain in prestige for the one, a loss of prestige for the other. And prestige augments strength as strength augments prestige.

Matters proceed differently in the last sub-system we may discern, that of the two Americas. Only a few years ago, the United States could regard the Western Hemisphere as its private "game preserve," outside the disputed zones of the cold war. A good-neighbor policy and the Organization of the American States seemed to guarantee its security and prevailing influence. Certainly Communist propaganda was at work within most of the Latin American republics, even when the Communist party was forbidden and reduced to a clandestine existence. But the governments, whether democratic or despotic, and whatever the color of the despotism involved, ordinarily followed Washington's guidance in the United Nations. Not one of them was Communist or sympathetic to Communism, not one of them, whether relations with the United States were good or bad, practiced "active neutralism" and the "blackmail of the strong by the weak."

The sign, in effect, that a region of the world is becoming a theater or a stake of the cold war is that the ordinary relation between strong and weak is reversed. "Help me or I will succumb to communism" is how the argument runs, endlessly repeated in various forms, by which the so-called pro-Western leaders ask the help of the super power. "What you refuse me I will obtain from the other side," so runs the formula by which a government that declares itself to be neutral blackmails the West. "I want your aid, but I will consent to no concession in order to obtain it. So much the worse for me and for you if the masses go over to communism," so runs the argument of a neutral state in the style of India.

The United States has presented 500 million dollars to the states of Latin America since Castro's success in 1959. The lesson cannot be missed: Castroism risks setting an example. In any case, if it is granted that the fear of Castroism compels the United States to such generosity, who would not be tempted to keep that fear alive?

One could claim that the Soviet threat of using intercontinental ballistic missiles in case of American aggression against Cuba is the cause and the symbol of the cold war's extension into the Western Hemisphere. It is impossible, in effect, as long as the experiment has not been made, to be certain that the Soviet Union would not risk intervening in military terms,[8] even in retaliation for an American action. But in any case, the fact that the relation of global forces is henceforth such that the Soviet Union can, at least in diplomatic terms, establish itself near the shores of the United States as the latter has, for years, established itself quite close to the Soviet frontiers, is neither the sole nor the chief cause of the new character of inter-American relations.

The social crisis is no less serious in Latin America than elsewhere, the governments there are no more solid, the grievances against the United States are more virulent by very reason of the latter's proximity and supremacy, and by reason, too, of the action of the great corporations. In order to obtain increased aid, Latin America lacked only one argument, but a decisive one, the Communist or "leftist" peril. This Castro has furnished, and in good measure.

The disappearance of the private "game reserves" is, one might say, an aspect of the unification of the diplomatic field. Each of the super powers leads one bloc; outside the blocs, both compete freely, not without respecting certain rules of moderation and prudence. This is an indisputable unification which nonetheless does not efface the approximate limits between the subsystems suggested by geography and which history, inscribed in the hearts of man, confirms or effaces.

---

[8] Personally, I do not believe that this intervention would have occurred if United States Marines had landed after or with the *émigrés*. The events of October 1962 rather confirm this proposition, written in 1960, at the time of Khrushchev's saber rattling.

4. Destiny of the National Territorial State

The type of state which constitutes the historically dominant idea of our period, we were saying, is the national state: a people, expressing its will to independence, becomes a nation organized into a state. Yet a number of authors suggest the decline or the end of the national state.

The apparent contradiction disappears in the light of an analysis of what those who announce its decline call a national state. For example, J. H. Herz refers to a territorial state rather than to a national one. The territorial state, characteristic of the classical age in Europe, between the end of the wars of religion and the Second World War, is chiefly defined by the unity of action of a political unit, sovereign within the limits drawn on the map. The modern state is a "centralized area unit whose sovereignty, independence and power all resulted from its territoriality."[9] The sovereign—the king or his bourgeois successor—has the capacity to impose his will over the entire surface of the territory. In other words, he has assured himself a monopoly of the internal military force. Thereby he appears, externally, as the representative of the collectivity in whose name he has the right and the duty to speak, since he protects its independence by an irresistible military force against rebels and is capable of withstanding enemies. "For throughout history, we notice that the basic political unit has been that which actually was in a position to afford protection and security to human beings, peace within, through the pacification of individual and group relationships and security from outside interference or control."[10]

In military terms the state's primary object, in case of war, is the *defense* of the territory: fortifications were built to prevent or halt invasion. In peacetime there were no other armed forces on the national territory than those belonging to the nation. The sovereigns had neither the right nor the capacity to interfere in the internal affairs of other states. The distinction between diplomacy and internal politics was confirmed by the compartmentalization of space. It is clear that today's state has lost certain characteristics which it possessed at the dawn of modern times and which gave a full meaning to the formula of territoriality.

In peacetime today, satellites fly over the air space of states. The U-2 flight was illegal, the flight of the satellite is not: at what altitude does sovereignty cease? In case of atomic war the state would be incapable of protecting its nationals, its space, its cities. In peacetime it accepts the stationing of allied troops and symbolizes thereby the loss of military autonomy. In a cold-war period, ideas, militants, even guerrilla fighters, pass the frontiers that are as permeable to transnational movements as to ballistic missiles.

All these incontestable facts can be subsumed under three headings: devaluation of the national states by military technique, confusion between in-

[9] John H. Herz, *International Relations in the Atomic Age*, New York, 1959, p. 58.
[10] *Ibid.*, pp. 40–41.

ternal affairs and external affairs by the very fact of transnational ideas and
parties, constitution of inter- or super-national organizations, whether economic, political or military (NATO, Common Market).

The national state is devalued by ballistic missiles; so be it. But is it devalued because it is national? In reality every territorial state is devalued
because the thermonuclear bomb gives its possessor the capacity to destroy
his enemy before or without disarming him. It is the traditional notion of
defense which the weapons of mass destruction fundamentally modify. Whatever the dimensions of the territory, whatever the constituted principle of
the political community, a thermonuclear bomb could claim two or three
million victims by exploding over a great city; ballistic missiles or bombers
carry these weapons of extermination from one end of the planet to the
other. In other words, the devaluation of national states by military techniques is an incontestable fact, which it would be nonetheless erroneous to
invoke with a view to justify any supranational organization, federated Europe or Atlantic unity, for these greater organizations would also be incapable of protecting territories or citizens.

The permeability of frontiers to ideas and to transnational parties is also incontestable, but it does not represent a radical novelty: it is, as we have seen,
the consequence of the expression of the system's heterogeneity. The territorial state of an absolute monarchy, after the wars of religion and before
the wars of revolution, repressed heterogeneity by forbidding individuals to
choose their religion, by forbidding sovereigns to concern themselves with
the relations between the other princes and their subjects, by forbidding
Churches to pursue their proselytism and their disputes across frontiers. Each
state settled the problem in its own way: provided it established peace at
home and did not trouble that of its neighbors, the settlement was recognized
as legitimate. Peace was well worth the sacrifice of the individual's right to
choose his Church, a sacrifice difficult as long as men considered that the
salvation of their souls depended on this choice.

The French Revolution compromised the homogeneity of the European
system. For twenty-five years the Europeans know treason, shifts of allegiance, Prussian officers in the Tsar's service while the King of Prussia
"collaborated" with Napoleon, émigrés fighting the armies of France, a republican general, having become king of Sweden, waging war against the
nation of his birth, another republican general mortally wounded by a French
bullet while fighting on the side of the monarchs allied against his fatherland,
some Germans tempted by "liberty" and "Jacobinism," like some Frenchmen
nostalgic for the ancien régime. The impenetrability of the frontiers, the
cohesion of the body politic have as their condition the states' general consent to the legitimacy of regimes and the legality of governments. In the
nineteenth century, potential heterogeneity did not develop all its consequences. The Holy Alliance against the revolutionaries was not of long
duration (however, as late as 1848 the Tsar applied the principle of the Holy

Alliance and came to the aid of his Austrian brother in order to repress the Hungarian revolt). The combination of traditional diplomacy and transnational movements contributed curiously to the limitation of conflicts. The kings contented themselves with military machinery inferior to the available resources and to the possibilities of technology. The transnational movements —liberalism, socialism, nationalism—were either weak (the First International did not assume a historical meaning except retrospectively) or led by men more conservative than revolutionary (it was Bismarck who achieved the German unity for and through Prussia). Nationalism waged an ideological war against the states which it wished to absorb in a higher unity; it could not aim at as grandiose a goal as did the movements with a universal calling.

The heterogeneity of the global system today carries to their extreme the implications of the rivalry between the state ideologies, each state being linked to a conception of the just order of things (economic, social, political) and thereby denying the historical or human legitimacy of the regimes based on the opposing principle. The global extension of the system prevents adoption of the method of pacification applied at the end of the wars of religion: to confirm the ideological division by the compartmentalization of space, to render the frontiers as impermeable to ideas as to enemy soldiers. At best, this might have been the case if the two blocs were alone in the world. Today, the ideological conflict cannot be contained or resolved by a compartmentalization of space, for the simple reason that, even by deliberate accord, the two super powers are incapable of giving each other guarantees against the diffusion of their respective ideas.

In the zone of the two blocs, heterogeneity is above all that of *regime*, nations and states deriving from the same principle of legitimacy, the degrees of development not being too unequal. Of course, the Soviet Union was, in origin, a multinational empire and it continues to maintain a distinction between nationality (Ukrainian, Georgian, Armenian) and common Soviet citizenship. This difference is a real one; it involves the gap in dimension between the multinational empire and the national states. But in theory,[11] the nationalities of the Soviet Union have the right of dissidence and belong to the Union only of their own free will. The original nationalities of the American citizens tend to melt into a "nationality of adoption." In spite of everything the dimensions of the territory and the diversities of origin bring the United States closer to the Soviet model than to the European one.

Outside the zone of these two blocs, heterogeneity is deeper because it affects the *body politic* itself. The newborn African republics are, as we have indicated, too small to have the means of a modern economy or a national defense, and are without cohesiveness because of tribal multiplicity. The African states are prenational or subnational, one might say, since the

[11] It goes without saying that we are dealing here with a fiction, which simply signifies that the Soviet leaders recognize the right of self-determination.

state is not confronting a unified nation, while the truly national states of Europe feel outclassed by the super powers and are attempting to unite in inter- or supranational organizations.[12] Between these two extremes—the Republic of Guinea, with three and a half million inhabitants, which aspires to total independence on the basis of territoriality, and the states of Western Europe which, with some fifty million souls, consider themselves outclassed —are situated the dozens of states of Latin America and Asia, some as small as those of Africa, others as vast as the super powers, some as cohesive as France or Germany (Japan), others as diverse in their races, religions, languages as the Soviet Union (India). Up until now, the diversity of the Indian population has not seemed to weaken loyalty to the federal state. But the Communists have already provoked several linguistic quarrels, with the manifest desire to compromise the unity of the "multinational nation" and the solidity of the federal state. Other states, like Burma, Thailand and Ceylon are of small dimensions yet include "national minorities" (the equivalent of what we call by this name in Europe).

Ideological heterogeneity of the system appears in every state in a different form: sometimes the rivalry of the two super powers is directly and brutally expressed in two parties—that is, two governments, each attached to one of the super powers, each imitating the regime of its protector or inspiration.[13] But more often than not, the parties express tribal, social or national realities appropriate to the state or to the zone of civilization, some of these parties seeking and obtaining, or obtaining without having sought, the support of one of the super powers.[14] The heterogeneity of two states within a subsystem (Mali and Senegal) is a function both of the national (or tribal) realities and of the ideological (regional or global) realities. The new states are threatened both by action against their regime and by action against their national unity. Everything occurs as if they were living through the national conflicts of the nineteenth century in Europe at the same time as through the social conflicts of the twentieth.

Must we conclude from this that the territorial-national state is dead before being born in the zones of civilization outside the West? Yes and no. The territorial state is permeable to ideologies and to guerrilla fighters, and it has not known the era of fortifications, of ideological neutrality and of non-interference in internal affairs. It participates in the disputes of the super powers—*volens nolens*—without having enjoyed the advantages of the closed state that has reached the age of maturity. But despite or through internal quarrels, whether regional or imported, it attempts to realize itself.

---

[12] The supranational organizations imply transfers of sovereignty, the internal organizations a simple cooperation of states. In fact, the limit between these two kinds is a vague one.
[13] In fact, if the Communist party readily imitates its inspiration, the pro-American party cannot, if only because of the presence of a strong party of Soviet inspiration.
[14] We should add, seeking to imitate, or imitating without having intended to do so, one of the models of political or economic institutions.

The type of state that all the new states wish in fact to become is a *territorial and national* state: territorial in the sense that within its frontiers the sovereign has the right to do what he wishes, national in the sense that the sovereign wishes to be not the possessor of the soil, not the master of those who occupy it, but the expression of the people. In May 1961 the representatives of twenty African states met in Monrovia and undertook to elaborate a code of good-neighborliness, as though to find a mode of relations intermediate between the Holy Alliance and the cold war.

Far from the national state being historically out of date, it is, for a great part of humanity, an objective on the horizon, a goal to achieve. The new states have been created by nationalisms, that is, by the refusal of one or several groups of human beings to be governed by men of other races, from other continents. Nationalisms do not always emanate from nations, if the latter suppose either a community of culture or a collective will to political existence or even both at the same time.

Are those of the new state, numbering only several million inhabitants, doomed from the start, incapable of surviving juridical fictions rather than historical realities? I should avoid any hasty conclusion on this subject. The United Nations remains based on certain ideas of the national-territorial state. Those governing the state, however feeble they may be, maintain, in the present situation, the capacity to make legal or illegal, with regard to international law, a military intervention of one of the super powers on their territory, to hand over or to refuse a strategically important position to one of the super powers. It is true that the price of this double capacity is precisely the psycho-political interference of the super powers in the internal affairs of small states. But since international law forbids and prudence shuns the use of military force (of regular armies), a resolutely united elite, a cohesive people, have a certain power in relation to the super powers, insofar as they can avoid rallying to either of the two camps and, thereby, keep territory they occupy outside the cold war. In other words, a state incapable of protecting itself in military terms is not incapable of surviving, because of the bipolar structure of the international system and because of the ideas granted, not without some hypocrisy, by the United Nations and world opinion.

Is the incapacity of the small states to exist related to economics? Doubtless there is an optimum dimension for states in every period. Yet it is not established that this optimum has a general character; that, at a given period, over the entire surface of the earth, a certain dimension can be regarded as the most advantageous with regard to production, growth, standard of living. Furthermore, we know that the notion of the economic advantage is not unequivocal. The optimum well-being at a given moment does not coincide with the highest rate of growth. The same standard of living can be obtained with a different distribution of labor among sectors. Let us limit ourselves to offering or to recalling several apparently incontestable propositions.

There is a minimum dimension less than which the general, strictly political expenses of the state are too high in proportion to the population total. Nations of less than a million inhabitants are, in this regard, evidently irrational, although, in certain cases, a local resource (the petroleum of Gabon, the iron of Luxembourg) gives a population the means and the desire to affirm its independence. In western Africa the general expenses of administration and government would be reduced in case of a fusion of several of the republics. But those whom nature has more richly endowed would lose by their integration into a larger group, even if the latter led to a raising of the available revenues for each of the citizens of the greater state (the taxes raised in the Ivory Coast would be partially expended in other regions of the West African state).

Let us leave aside the problem, important but not decisive from a certain point, of the general expenses of the state in relation to the population. The essential question is to know what is the most favorable context for development. The dissolution of Central Europe's economic unity had deplorable consequences between the two wars because it provoked the breakdown of links long in existence. But the economic progress made by all the nations of Europe, including the small countries such as Austria, which were not long ago declared to be incapable of surviving, manifest the extreme flexibility of the industrial system and the danger of attributing a permanent meaning to lessons drawn from singular circumstances.

Let us observe the new states of Africa and America. Two kinds of considerations determine the most favorable context for development: political considerations and economic ones. Often, these considerations are not in agreement with each other. The cohesion of the nation, the authority of the state are indispensable to modernization. In Africa, where the mass of the population has a stronger awareness of ethnic solidarity than of national or state solidarity, it is not established that the Balkanization of Africa is worse than imperialism. Certainly the small countries are not thereby cohesive. Tribal diversity exists, even in a population of a million.

At least the Westernized elite, which takes the responsibility for the state, is relatively cohesive and, being closer to those governed, has a better chance of maintaining the government's authority without excessive violence. Even Senegal and the Sudan have not managed to federate themselves. Perhaps the phase of small states was inevitable in order to surmount the tribal tradition and to create a state loyalty (that is, the sentiment of allegiance to a remote and abstract reality, the nation or the state).

On the other hand, one might raise two arguments: the national interests, with their series of passions and prejudices, soon become ineradicable. Perhaps it would have been better to pass immediately from the tribes to the major groupings. The answer to this objection, it seems to me, is that it might have been desirable to skip the stage of the small states but that it was probably not possible to do so, at least in a period when the use of force passes for immoral. The other objection is economic: what development will be possible within such narrow contexts? Certainly a larger context would be preferable in theory. But whether it is a question of improvement of the soil or agriculture, of the means of communication or even of the exploitation of raw materials, the first stages of the development are not forbidden to the dwarf states. It is at the final stages that obstacles are in danger of accumulating.

The smaller the state, the more specialization its development demands. The more the planners must make a choice between industries, the more the industries finally decided upon will depend upon foreign markets. Many new states entrust to functionaries the task of instituting and orienting industrialization. The narrowness of the context adds to the intrinsic difficulties of development in African conditions and of planning by often improvised administrations. Incontestably, on the economic level, it would have been preferable to limit the "Balkanization of Africa."

This point made, national cohesion remains, for the present phase, the first requirement. The small country, whose leaders are obeyed, is worth more than the great state threatened at every moment with disintegration (especially since a common market or inter-African agreements may attenuate the disadvantages of numerous and small states).

From these considerations it would be only superficially paradoxical to conclude that a small state is sometimes—in Africa—more viable than a large one. Traditionally, a state was regarded as viable only if it was capable of a certain defense. Still, this formula involves many reservations. When the small states were not capable of resisting the large ones, the latter often agreed, for various reasons, to let them exist (the most frequent reason being the impossibility of reaching an agreement as to the distribution of territories). The small state, which held an important strategic position, deprived all the great states of the advantages which one of them would be assured of upon occupying its territory; or again the small state created a neutral buffer zone between the frontiers of the great ones. Often, then, the small state owed its existence less to its own capacity for defense than to the interests of the great powers. The military capacity for defense was merely a secondary instrument of national independence.

Today more than ever, the great powers have the means of destroying the small ones; they even have the means of destroying them, their cities and their populations without disarming them. But, so long as a military thermonuclear monopoly has not been established and perhaps even granting the hypothesis of a thermonuclear monopoly, excessively powerful weapons cannot be used in secondary conflicts. None of the great powers[15] has tried to intimidate a small power by rattling the "thermonuclear saber." It is by subversion that the great powers attempt to overpower the small ones rather

[15] Khrushchev began to do so in 1960 but without much success.

than by atomic intimidation or invasion. Yet the capacity for resistance to subversion is a function of national cohesion or of government authority, and not of the volume of resources. The solidarity of the nation and its leaders is the best defense against the most likely type of aggression in our period. In this sense the new state's defensive power in peacetime is on more than one occasion inversely proportional to its dimensions.

Further, in a global system, the reasons which persuade the European great powers to respect the independence of the small state function to the advantage of multiple states, even of vast regions. The great powers can reach an implicit agreement on an uncommitted Africa, as Great Britain, France and Germany reached agreement on Belgium's neutrality. The rivalry of the great powers constitutes the fortune of the small ones when the latter are favored by geography.

Even the declining status of the European states, at the very moment when the Lilliputian states are multiplied, assumes a certain logic in the light of this analysis. The Lilliputian states are not subjects of "grand politics"; the European states, on the other hand, cannot cease to be subjects of it, because they are rich, and potentially strong. They do not adopt gestures of resignation and refuge in neutrality, they hesitate to create, once and for all, a supranational unit which alone would attain full autonomy. Oscillating between the nostalgia of greatness, the temptation of non-commitment and the desire for a supranational integration, the ex-great powers of Europe lack the resources necessary to a protagonist of the first order but retain too many resources to find security in renunciation.

Probably the arms race will exert a decisive influence on the final status of these states, too small for their greatness, too great for their smallness.

The global extension of the diplomatic system, the universality of industrial society, the triumph of the American philosophy of international legal order result in the strange situation we are in the process of describing. The ex-great powers of Europe are medium-size, in terms of this century, and only the continent-states cross the threshold of greatness. Only those who have sufficiently advanced in their industrial career possess strength: enemies have a common interest in not fighting, confronting each other at every point of the planet and yet allied against war. Outside the zone of civilization, the source of modern society, all peoples aspire to the same means of wealth and power. The underdeveloped nations do not, however, constitute a unit, even a negative one. Some are small, others great; some adhere to the Soviet ideology, others to the Western; some are neutral, others committed one way or the other, without these three alternatives corresponding term for term. Whether it is a question of race, culture or standard of living, the differences among the underdeveloped nations are evident and striking. The heterogeneity of civilizations henceforth included within the same system may in the long run have greater consequences than the opposition of two regimes or two doctrines to which most people profess to adhere, but it is temporarily concealed by the establishment of two blocs, each one invoking an idea (a mode of industrial society), and by the formal equality of states, represented in the United Nations.

The two blocs, equally desirous of winning the sympathy of the ex-colonial peoples, fiercely compete in the denunciation of racism and, except for some European states, of colonialism. The "barbarians," recently subject to Europeans, do not emerge from empires to return to their traditions or to carve themselves kingdoms with great strokes of the sword; they attempt to organize their political life according to the models offered by their former masters, and they are immediately recognized as equals on the juridical level, of the old states and of today's giants. No one dares to suggest that the equality of states in the General Assembly of the United Nations implies the equal value of civilizations any more than the equality of souls before God effaces the inequality of persons with regard to intelligence or wisdom.

chapter XIV

On the Strategy of Deterrence

Deterrence, a mode of relation between two persons or two collectivities, is as old as humanity. The possibility of a slap deters the child from tearing up the books in his father's library, as the possibility of a ticket deters the driver from parking in front of the meter longer than the hours marked on the dial. If the father has threatened the slap, then deterrence has been practiced explicitly. The threat of the ticket is implied by the law, effective in proportion to the number of policemen assigned to checking the meters. The risk of an accident deters the driver, however indifferent he may be to administrative sanctions, from going through red lights. In other words, in social life, an individual is deterred from performing an act by fear of the possible *consequences*, by *legal* punishments, or by a *threat* made by someone else.

Between two political units, each sovereign and armed, the mechanism of deterrence is also capable of functioning in the absence of an explicit threat. No one has doubted, in the twentieth century, that Switzerland would defend itself if attacked. Switzerland has multiplied the proofs of its determination by the sacrifices it has made in order to arm and train its army. Switzerland's military force sufficed to render the occupation of its territory costly for a possible aggressor. The Swiss capacity to deter aggression depended both on the material means accumulated by the government and on the courage and unity which foreign leaders attributed to the people.

A neutral state, by definition, counts on deterrence: it does not plan to impose its own will upon other states, save to convince them to leave it in peace. The power of deterrence is situated between defensive and offensive power, in the sense in which we have taken these two concepts.[1] It is not strictly defensive, since the state which deters another can intervene in a geographically remote zone. It is not strictly offensive, since it tends to prevent, not to provoke the action of another state.

The power of deterrence becomes purely defensive when a state aims ex-

[1] Cf. Part I, Chap. II.

clusively at preventing the aggression directed against it. The neutral state exerts deterrence only for its own benefit. A military force entirely oriented toward defensive warfare corresponds to the requirements of this diplomacy, which is also defensive. The chances of success, for such a diplomacy, vary directly with the estimated military capacity of the neutral state and inversely with the profits which the aggressor might derive from his conquest.

The military means which deterrence required in the past were defensive for a neutral state; they were not so for the great powers. The Maginot Line did not deter Germany from attacking Czechoslovakia or from annexing Danzig. Of course, it was not without effect in the trial of wills that precede armed conflict. Let us suppose that the Maginot Line had been considered, in Berlin and Paris, as the point of departure for a French army offensive, and also as a guarantee that the battles would not be waged on French soil. Insofar as the fortifications added to France's resources and favorably modified the possible map of hostilities, the threat of general war by which Great Britain and France attempted to deter Hitler's Germany from attacking Poland might have made more of an impression on the leaders of the Third Reich. It remains true nonetheless that a great power, to deter another from attacking one of its allies, often requires an army capable of taking the offensive. A defensive diplomacy, i.e., one concerned to maintain the status quo, as we have seen, does not imply an army reduced to the defensive.

In 1938 France tried to deter Hitler from attacking Czechoslovakia: Hitler was not impressed, and Frenchmen and Englishmen preferred Czech capitulation to the risk of having to carry out their commitments, i.e., their threat. In 1939 Great Britain took the initiative of signing a mutual assistance treaty with Poland in the hope of deterring Hitler by the striking demonstration of a resolution which could no longer be doubted. England did not go back on her word: by signing the pact with Poland, she had burned her ships and left herself no other choice, in case of a German aggression against Poland, than that between dishonor and war. The choice was war.

These historical evocations, however summary, remind us, if there is any need, that the mechanism of deterrence does not date from the Atomic Age. The deterrence which the British authors call passive—to deter an attack directed against the possessor of the instrument of deterrence—is comparable to that of the neutral nations: the subject of the deterrence is also its only beneficiary. Active deterrence is comparable to that which France and Great Britain attempted to exercise for Poland's sake in 1939. Today as yesterday, deterrence depends on both the *material means* at the disposal of the state that wishes to stop another, and on the *resolution* that the state which is the object of deterrence attributes to the state that threatens it with punishment. Today as yesterday, the essential problem of deterrence is both psychological and technological. How can the state diplomatically on the defensive convince a state diplomatically on the offensive that it will carry out its threat? Today as yesterday, the two most common procedures are those that symbolize the English guarantee to Poland in 1939 and the Swiss defense preparations: a solemn commitment that makes retreat almost impossible, and proof of the resolution by action.

Where does the novelty of deterrence lie in the nuclear age? The answer comes to mind of itself: the novelty lies in the material consequences of carrying out the threat. Hitler knew that France and Great Britain passionately desired to avoid a second world war which, even if they emerged from it victorious, would further weaken France and would involve the disintegration of the British Empire. *The threat is less convincing in proportion as its execution is contrary to the interests of those who make it.* Nonetheless, in 1939, execution was neither absurd nor improbable, because war itself was manifestly preferable, in the eyes of the leaders and probably of the majority of citizens of both countries, to a capitulation which involved the triumph of Hitler's empire. The war appeared costly in advance, not catastrophic. It did not exclude the possibility that one side would emerge the victor. The leaders in London and Paris regarded peace without war preferable, in any case, to a victorious war—in other words, they considered that the situation, after a victorious war, would be worse than the situation on the eve of war, but they also considered that the situation, if they did not resist Hitler, would be worse than that which would result from armed resistance. Hitler had reasons not to believe in the threat, but Frenchmen and Englishmen could execute that threat without irrationality. But what is the situation when the weapons available are first atomic bombs, then thermonuclear ones?

That the so-called weapons of mass destruction are incommensurable with those that humanity has used in the course of history is probably not unknown to the reader, but he may not comprehend the ultimate degree of the military revolution. "The individual weapons against cities and population masses are thousands of times more powerful than they were only ten years ago, and millions of times more powerful than twenty years ago. One single bomb can harbor a force greater than all the explosives used by all the belligerents in World War II or even greater than all the energy ever used in any form in all previous wars of mankind put together. Yet this form is concentrated in a device which can be transported in a conventional aircraft of which there exists thousands. And, in the world as a whole, there are dozens, probably hundreds, if not thousands, of such bombs."[2] Never has the banal formula—the difference in quantity creates a difference in quality—been illustrated so strikingly. Never has the acceleration of history been made so arresting. Less than ten years passed between the kiloton bombs (thousands of tons of TNT) and the megaton bombs (millions of tons of TNT). Comparable progress in delivery vehicles, after the age of the bombers, has opened the age of ballistic missiles. Speed per hour is no longer reckoned in hundreds but in thousands of kilometers. The time necessary for missiles to cross

[2] Morgenstern, *The Question of National Defense,* New York, 1959, pp. 9-10.

the space separating continents is no longer reckoned in hours but in minutes (about thirty between the U.S.S.R. and the United States). How could humanity fail to have had the conviction of a new era? The simplest interpretation, the one which corresponded to the needs of hope, was expressed by President Eisenhower: "There is no alternative to peace," or again: "War is impossible."

Both phrases are obviously inexact and, in a sense, contradictory. If thermonuclear war were impossible, in the material sense of the word, how could anyone be deterred by a threat whose execution is impossible? Such is, in effect, the paradox of the "thermonuclear deterrence"[3]: if the threat cannot be executed, how can it be used as a means of deterrence? If the threat is used, then it is because its execution is considered possible by both the subject and the object of deterrence.

It will be objected that the impossibility is not material but moral. Of course, it will be said, the execution of the threat is conceivable, otherwise deterrence would not function. But all the states possessing the monstrous weapons have the passionate desire not to use them. For the first time in history, they are preparing for a war that they do not wish to wage. At no moment are they forgetting that their common interest in not fighting—that is, in not destroying each other—greatly prevails over the stakes of the conflicts in which they are opposed all over the world. The possessors of "thermonuclear systems"[4] have become increasingly prudent as they have acquired greater capacity for destruction. Everything has occurred, since the Hiroshima and Nagasaki explosions, as if humanity had sworn to resort only to yesterday's weapons and to stockpile tomorrow's.

Doubtless the most evident effect of the thermonuclear armament has been to deter the two super powers from total war, to incite both of them to moderation, to dissuade each of them from aiming a blow at the vital interests of the other. The optimistic theory of peace by fear (or at least, of the limitation of wars by fear of the thermonuclear apocalypse) may be based on the experience of the last fifteen years.

But this experience is too brief to confirm or invalidate a theory, especially since the Soviet Union, during the greater part of this period, was in a manifest state of inferiority, at least in the atomic or thermonuclear competition with the United States. During the first phase the United States possessed a monopoly of the atomic weapon (until 1950-51). During the second phase the Soviet Union possessed atomic bombs and, after 1955, thermonuclear bombs, but its only carrying vehicles were strategic bombers, less numerous than those of the United States and, more important, based on fields located

---

[3] We use this simplified phrase in order not to repeat, on each occasion, the more developed one: deterrence by the threat of thermonuclear attack or retaliation.

[4] As we call the entire group constituted by thermonuclear weapons and carrying vehicles, as well as the additional services and essentials of detection communication and command.

at a greater distance from the objective. It was only with the development of intercontinental ballistic missiles—i.e., in 1959 or 1960—that a parity for the capacity of destruction was perhaps established between the Soviet Union and the United States. *The balance of terror,* which has been discussed for so many years, if real, is quite recent.[5]

Authors, especially American ones, have elaborated a theory of the *thermonuclear strategy of deterrence,* but this theory is speculative, for lack of experience. No one knows for sure in what cases the threat would be regarded as plausible by the state to which it was addressed. Further, progress in armaments is so rapid that the reasoning valid for a certain state of thermonuclear development ceases to be so a few months or years later. Theories risk being outdated as fast as weapons. Hence it seems to me indispensable, in order to distinguish the propositions whose truth is lasting from those subordinate to a transitory state of armaments, to analyze first the *typical situations* conceivable between two states possessing thermonuclear systems.

There is no need to refer to games theory in order to justify the method of models. The theoreticians of tactics had spontaneously drawn models of battles (Cannae, Leuthen). The theoreticians of thermonuclear strategy must, similarly, draw models of relations between duopolists.[6]

1. The Three Models

A thermonuclear bomb falling in the heart of Moscow or New York or Paris would claim two or three million victims, would destroy the greater part of the city, and radioactive fallout would affect the territory within a radius of hundreds of kilometers. The immediate reaction of every individual to such propositions is to assert: thermonuclear war will not take place. Never has old Herodotus' formula seemed so obvious: no man is so bereft of reason as to prefer war to peace.

But this "obviousness" supposes that the victim of a thermonuclear attack is still capable, after having endured the first blow, of inflicting upon his enemy retaliation of the same degree as the destructions he himself has endured. In other words, if we grant that two states possess thermonuclear systems, two extreme situations are possible: either the state which strikes first kills its rival and escapes unharmed, or the state which strikes second retains the means of a revenge proportional to the damages caused by the aggression. Let us call the first situation that of *impunity from the crime* as in the case of two gangsters confronting each other, and the second that of *equality of the crime and the punishment which* becomes, eventually, that of mutual suicide. What circumstances suggest the realization of either model?

[5] This balance has existed for years, if one takes into account the Europe-United States solidarity. Europe served as a hostage, and could have been as effectively destroyed as the Soviet Union.
[6] The situations will become even more complex when there are a half-dozen and not just two possessors of the thermonuclear apparatus.

When do the duopolists confront each other, like two gangsters, with impunity? When, on the contrary, can we count on the equivalence of attack and reprisal, of first and second strike? In a simplified analysis, two data are decisive: the vulnerability or invulnerability of the thermonuclear system, and the physical and human characteristics (dimensions, urban concentration) of the territory of each of the two states.

The meaning of the first condition is readily intelligible. Assuming that one of the duopolists takes the initiative of using the thermonuclear system, he will take into consideration, if he acts according to reason, the opposing thermonuclear system. In fact, if he destroys this system, his rival will be at his mercy. On the other hand, if the latter retains his thermonuclear system —that is, his means of reprisal—the aggressor will in his turn be exposed to destruction similar to that he himself inflicted. The vulnerability of the thermonuclear system creates the situation of impunity of the two gangsters. As the vulnerability of the system diminishes, the situation approaches that of the equivalence of crime and punishment.

Yet it does not suffice for the thermonuclear system to be invulnerable for the victim of aggression to inflict a revenge proportional to the outrage. Even if Israel or France possessed an invulnerable thermonuclear system of the same order of size[7] as that of either of the two super powers, the punishment would be equal to the crime in absolute terms, not in relative ones. France and Israel would have ceased to exist once they had suffered the first strike, and their vengeance would be a posthumous one. The vengeance would be terrible, but it would not cost the aggressor's life, while the victim of the aggressors would not survive.

Some may answer, it is true, that given a certain volume of destruction, men no longer weigh the difference between more and less. The mind no longer distinguishes between the death in a few minutes of a third, a half, four fifths or nine tenths of the population. For the statesman as for the man in the street, it is a question, in all these cases, of an "absolute catastrophe," an Armageddon no one would have the courage to look beyond.

I do not know whether, in fact, statesmen weigh or will weigh the difference between more or less, given a certain threshold of intolerable destruction. On the other hand, I am sure that in an abstract analysis, it is incorrect to assert in principle that the relative amplitude of destruction does not count beyond a certain point. Someone has attributed, gratuitously I hope, to Mr. Chou En-lai the expectation that after a thermonuclear war there would remain some million Englishmen, some tens of millions of Russians or Americans, and some hundreds of millions of Chinese. It is easy to modify these figures to express an even more obvious notion: given equal destructions, a population of fifty million on a small territory would be exterminated, while

---

[7] Need we explain that this hypothesis cannot be realized?

a population of nine hundred million on a vast one would recover in a few years or a few decades, however terrible the ordeal.

Abstract models of a thermonuclear duel express two concepts of victory which do not fundamentally differ from the concepts elaborated by traditional theory. Absolute victory supposes that one of the parties, having disarmed the other, is in a position to dictate in sovereign terms the conditions of peace. The novelty is that henceforth disarmament requires nothing more than the destruction of the means of retaliation, that is, of the thermonuclear system. It is unimportant that the disarmed duopolist maintains fleets or armies, fortifications and warships. In theory the duopolist without retaliatory capacity would be forced to capitulate since he could be entirely destroyed without means of protecting himself or taking revenge. As for relative victory, it would not necessarily result from negotiations or from a treaty favorable to one of the belligerents. It would be defined, in fact, by the inequality of losses endured by each. They would eventually be acquired in the course of hostilities, although it is not inconceivable that after indecisive thermonuclear exchanges, the duelist in an inferior position would attempt to limit his losses by resigning himself to a peace of defeat.

Neither of the two abstract models has much chance of being realized, at least so long as the duopolists we envisage are the two super powers of the global system. It is, in fact, improbable that the first strike would *entirely* eliminate the other power's means of retaliation. But it is also improbable that the super power on whose territory several dozen thermonuclear bombs of five or six megatons have fallen would be in a position to inflict a punishment in proportion to the crime. In short, the most likely model, intermediate between these two abstract ones, might be called "*the inequality of the crime and the punishment.*"

Optimistic theoreticians[8] of thermonuclear deterrence are those who either know no other model than that of the *equivalence of the crime and the punishment* or else profess the meaninglessness of "more" and "less" above a certain threshold. The pessimistic theoreticians[9] are those who do not exclude the possibility of a situation close to that of the impunity from the crime or who, in any case, attach an extreme importance to the inequality of the crime and the punishment.

Let us suppose, in effect, that each of the duopolists[10] knows that if he strikes first, he will endure three times less damage than if he had left the initiative to his adversary. In other words, relative victory would go to the power dealing the first blow, and neither of the two powers is unaware that this is the case. Of course, even the victor would be severely damaged and would prefer non-war to relative victory, if he had the choice. But he would

---

[8] Those who believe in "peace by fear."
[9] Those who believe in a serious risk of thermonuclear war.
[10] We assume, to simplify matters, a symmetrical situation. But asymmetry is obviously possible, the thermonuclear system of only one power being invulnerable.

also prefer relative victory to relative defeat. If he suspected his adversary of preferring relative victory to non-war, he would hasten to take the initiative since, contrary to the legend of Fontenoy, victory would belong to the side that strikes first. In other words, in abstract terms, every situation of inequality of the crime and the punishment, particularly if this inequality is imputable to the vulnerability of the thermonuclear system, creates the risk of what the American authors call the *pre-emptive strike*, the blow dealt in anticipation of the blow one side suspects the other to be on the point of dealing. "Pre-emptive" war is not "preventive" war. The latter is waged in cold blood, at a moment regarded as favorable, in order to avoid a deterioration of the relation of forces or in order to profit by favorable circumstances. The former is waged in a period of crisis, not because victory is preferred to peace, but because there is a continual expectation of imminent attack.

The pessimistic theoreticians would concede at most that the inequality of the crime and the punishment does not prevent one of the super powers from deterring the other from a direct attack. The destruction caused by the reprisal, even if inferior to that caused by the attack, still exceeds the amount which the leaders of the aggressor state consider tolerable. Or at least, they are not assured that the retaliation would not exceed the threshold of tolerability. But the great power capable only of deterring a direct attack against itself would have fallen back to the level of the medium-size or small states of the past. If the United States could deter the Soviet Union from attacking itself but not from attacking Western Europe, it is logically driven back to adopt the strategy of "fortress America." The state whose deterrence force protects only itself would be comparable, in the age of thermonuclear strategy, to the neutral states in the age of gunpowder.

Abstractly, the decisive question occurs at this point in the analysis, in other words when we inquire about the influence of the relation of thermonuclear forces on the capability of deterrence. The verb *deter* involves two complements: deter *whom* and *from what?* Can the United States deter the Soviet Union from an attack against itself? Against Western Europe? Against South Korea? In case of direct attack, the American determination to respond is not in doubt, but what portion of the thermonuclear system will have been spared by the enemy bombs? On the other hand, let us suppose that the Soviet troops seize Berlin and that simultaneously the Soviet government formally commits itself not to engage in actions against the United States—what would happen? What President of the United States would give the retaliation order to the Strategic Air Command, knowing that this order would involve the death of tens of millions of Americans? The same question may be formulated by imagining an attack with conventional weapons against one of the nations of Western Europe or against Western Europe as a whole. In case of an attack that is not directed against the possessor of the thermonuclear weapon—let us say in case of an extreme provocation—the response depends on the resolution of the state possessing the instrument of deterrence. But what is the state of armaments which renders this determination both reasonable and likely?

The current theory consists of combining the three models (impunity from the crime, equality of the crime and the punishment, inequality of the crime and the punishment)[11] and the three methods of deterrence (direct attack, extreme provocation, attenuated provocation). The situation likened to the two gangsters is, by definition, the most unstable. If it were perfectly symmetrical,[12] it would be of such an instability that it could not last. One of the two powers would rapidly take the initiative of eliminating its rival in order to rid itself of an intolerable threat. Why live under the obsession of an impossible catastrophe when by striking first the danger could be averted forever? Fortunately, this "ideal" situation, though it is perfectly possible on paper, will never be realized. Neither of the two super powers, the United States and the Soviet Union, will ever have at the same time the capability —and the certitude of possessing the capability—of destroying all of the other's means of retaliation. Further, let us consider two states of the future, Israel and Egypt. Supposing they were to find themselves in the impunity situation in relation to each other, they would still have to take into account the reaction of the other thermonuclear powers.

It is also possible that only one of the super powers may appreciably weaken the other's thermonuclear system, or again that both may, if they take the initiative, appreciably weaken the other's thermonuclear system. In all these hypotheses we abandon the model of impunity from the crime for the real world of inequality of the crime and the punishment. This inequality can have two causes: either each of the two powers is capable of attacking the enemy's thermonuclear system (counterforce strategy) on condition it takes the initiative, or else the inequality derives less from the weakening of the thermonuclear system of the side striking second than from the general disorganization of the nation in general, and of the thermonuclear system in particular, after a massive attack by the enemy.

What conclusions may we legitimately draw from this situation of inequality? Let us consider first of all the symmetrical situation. We say that the instability will be greater as the inequality is more evident, and will approach the situation of the two gangsters. On the other hand, as we move away from the situation of impunity, the temptation to strike first will weaken. The inequality of the crime and the punishment weighs less heavily than the very enormity of a punishment inferior to the crime. The day when each thermonuclear system is invulnerable to the other and when the retaliation is not

[11] Not that these concepts are classical: I merely think that these three phrases summarize the essential points of the current analyses.

[12] The instability is still greater if we assume an asymmetrical situation. If A possesses only a *force de frappe*, B is tempted to strike since by striking first, it can destroy the enemy striking force. But A is also tempted to strike first in order to take revenge in advance on what the other might do to him.

attenuated in relation to the attack except by social disorganization, the certainty of possessing a retaliatory capability liberates the duopolists from the fear of a thermonuclear Pearl Harbor and hands them over to the rational fear of total war.

But if the temptation of taking the initiative is weakened, if deterrence from a direct attack is reinforced, deterrence from a provocation, even from an extreme one, may be shaken. What, in effect, deters each of the duopolists from provoking the other is the fear that a conflict, even a secondary one, might gradually be enlarged and escalate a thermonuclear exchange. Now, the vulnerability of the thermonuclear system would increase the risk of escalation. In a case of a grave crisis, the duopolists would be all the more inclined to a pre-emptive strike since they would be more aware of the inferiority of the punishment in relation to the crime. On the other hand, if neither duopolist had the means to attack the enemy's thermonuclear system, if both had no other recourse than to attack each other's cities (counter-cities strategy), then the obsession that the other side would take the initiative disappears. Each power, assured of its own means of retaliation, doubts that the other would risk a crime leading to an equal punishment. But, at the same time, escalation becomes more unlikely and the effective deterrence which the thermonuclear system, even when it is not made explicit, exercises over minor provocations disappears. In other words, the stability toward which relations between the duopolists tend, as the punishment approaches equality with the crime, excludes the extension of the secondary conflicts and simultaneously renders the thermonuclear apocalypse more unlikely and limited wars more likely. Monstrous war and the effectiveness of the threat of such a war against any provocation occurring *at the same time* is inconceivable.

Does this mean that once the thermonuclear system is safe—in other words, that once a strategy against the adverse apparatus (counterforce strategy) is rendered impossible—the only deterrence of which even the super powers are still capable is that of the first type, that is, deterrence from direct attack against the possessor of the retaliatory instrument? I do not believe so for two reasons. Even in the absence of a strategy against the opposing force, there would exist an advantage in striking first, even if only to disorganize the opposing system of communications and command, and to perfect one's own defense network. Further, each of the super powers can signify to the other that certain territories, certain stakes count no less for itself than its own territory, its own existence.

It is legitimate to assert, in the abstract, that the relative invulnerability of the thermonuclear system, the approximate equality of the crime and the punishment increase the improbability of total war and, thereby, the risks of limited wars. It would not be legitimate to conclude that the super powers can no longer protect their allies or that the diffusion of thermonuclear weapons is called for. The strategy of deterrence is a test of wills, in which the technique of arms and delivery vehicles determines the conditions but not the outcome.

2. *The Meaning of "More" and "Less"*

To be deterred is to prefer the situation which will result from inaction to that which would result from action, when the latter would produce the anticipated consequences—that is, on the level of international relations—the carrying out of implicit or explicit threats. A state is more liable to be deterred the more it believes the threat would be carried out (in case it should persist), the more frightful the effects on the state if the threat is executed, or the more tolerable the prospect if the state should abstain from the action to be deterred. The success of deterrence therefore depends on three factors, one *psychological* (does the side which deters succeed in convincing the possible aggressor that its threat is serious?), one *technological* (what would happen if the threat was executed?), and the third *political* (what gains and what losses would result, for the state which is the object of deterrence, from action on the one hand, or abstention on the other?).

The technological factor varies with the progress of armaments; the political factor depends on diplomatic circumstances at the same time as on weapons; the psychological factor, finally, is a function of the two preceding ones and of the result, often undetermined in advance, of a test of wills. The interrelation of the three factors is such that concrete studies of strategy run the risk of following the fate of the arms to which they refer and to be out of date just as rapidly. That is why we have separated the analysis of models and the abstractly valid propositions from the studies that claim to apply to the real world and which are triply uncertain (because the technological data change, because the political circumstances are never precisely the same, because the behavior of men is unpredictable).

What is the content of the thermonuclear threat? In other words, supposing that the war no one wishes to wage, but with which one state threatens the aggressor in order to deter him, occurs—what would happen? The effects of the atomic explosions have been described in the official work published by the U. S. State Department and the Atomic Energy Commission.[13] The most impressive figures are assembled in the following chart:

	Hiroshima	Nagasaki
Total population	255,000	195,000
Square miles destroyed	4.7	1.8
Killed or missing	70,000	36,000
Wounded	70,000	40,000

The authors also indicate the normal rate of losses (killed or wounded) for an urban population whose density is one per one thousand square feet. This rate would be 40 for a large chemical-explosion bomb (one ton), 260,000 for the Hiroshima bomb, 130,000 for the Nagasaki bomb.

The work does not give the probable losses if a one- to five-megaton thermonuclear bomb were dropped on one of the world's great cities. Probably

[13] *The Effects of Nuclear Weapons,* Washington, D.C., 1962.

the number of victims, as well as that of survivors, would depend on many factors (type of bomb used—whether "dirty" or "clean," the height at which the explosion occurred, point of impact, the state of civil defense, the nature of the shelters, the possibility of survivors remaining in the shelters several days or weeks, etc.). Lacking an organization of civil defense which, for the moment, exists nowhere, the city struck by a thermonuclear bomb would be largely destroyed and entirely paralyzed.

The surface destroyed by the twenty-kiloton Hiroshima bomb is estimated at 4.7 square miles. A chart published in the same book[14] suggests something of the area destroyed by a thermonuclear (megaton) bomb. The damages caused at 1.2 miles from the zero point by a twenty-kiloton bomb would now be caused at a distance of 5 to 6 miles from zero point. The area of complete destruction would thus be twenty to thirty times greater. Further, immediate and persistent radioactivity would raise problems of a much more serious order.

Perhaps even these estimates are still far less than the truth: if, we are told by M. Camille Rougeron, we take as our basis Khrushchev's declaration that one thermonuclear bomb would be enough to devastate a country like Denmark or the Netherlands, we would have to multiply by ten the American estimates of the area devastated by a twenty-megaton bomb: "For the American explosions of 1954, produced at the top of a pylon and even for those made some thousand meters above the ground, the damages are chiefly due to the effect of the blast, their radius increasing according to the cubic root of the power. The incendiary effect which, at a distance of several kilometers, remains more important than the blast effect, diminishes under the influence of the absorption by the atmosphere, according to an 'exponential' law—that is, when distance figures as an exponent in the term this absorption represents, the radius of the incendiary damages for bombs of great power falls far below that of the damages due to the blast. The conclusion is reversed if the explosion is produced at a high altitude, 25 or 30 kilometers for instance, for a power of 20 megatons. We believe we were the first to indicate this, in December 1954, in an article where we anticipated this mode of bomb attack against agricultural objectives. Instead of passing through tens of kilometers of air at a density close to that of the soil, the extremely oblique rays which would be released even at a great distance from the explosion would pass through the layers where absorption was negligible. The only factor of attenuation of the incendiary effect with distance would derive from the fundamental law of photometry, according to which the same luminous or thermic flux emanating from one source is distributed over an area which increases as the square of the distance. Thus the radius of incendiary damages increases for an explosion as high as the square root of the power, whereas the radius of the damages due to the effect of the blast increases

14 *Ibid.*, p. 195.

only as its cubic root. Such is the essential factor of superiority of high-altitude explosion. Taking into account a number of other factors which we have discussed several times: the rise in energy which appears in thermic form in a quasi-vacuum, in which the shock wave carries off only a negligible amount of energy in mechanical form, the possibility of the accumulation of thermic effects not reaching the incendiary threshold if simultaneous explosions are produced, the radius of 'severe' damages by fire (instantaneous inflammation of combustible dry materials) would attain more than 200 kilometers for an explosion of 20 megatons—in other words, more than ten times that of the 'severe damages' by blast effect. Lacking precise confirmation, the increase in high-altitude explosions sufficiently indicates that this is the path which has been followed."[15]

Texts of this kind run the risk of paralyzing reflection. The uninitiated reader feels a sense of incredulity and horror: "Such a war will not take place." He is quite ready to believe alternately the speech of the scientist that makes him fear the end of the world in case of thermonuclear war, and that of the strategist which makes him hope for the universal peace based on the fear which the possible catastrophe inspires in all.

Each of these alternatives is not in itself without meaning. If a thermonuclear bomb of several megatons (and perhaps, today, of some tens of megatons) were to cause several million deaths by falling on a city and were to contaminate an extensive zone, it is not inconceivable that a great power, at no very remote date, might succeed in making weapons whose use would be equivalent to genocide (extermination of the active population of the enemy state) or even, according to the hypothesis of Herman Kahn, in producing a doomsday machine, an apocalypse-maker, whose use would bring an end to human existence altogether. But this talk is premature. Today no state possesses such a machine. No state has the means, if it wages the war it is preparing, to exterminate the population of the enemy state. Of course, each of the two powers possesses enough atomic or thermonuclear bombs to kill three billion human beings if the bombs were distributed solely for this purpose. As a matter of fact, thermonuclear attacks on both sides, whether they aim at the enemy's nuclear force or his cities, would bring about material damages and human losses which would be incommensurable with the cost of past wars but which would constitute in material terms neither the "annihilation of the enemy" nor "mutual suicide" nor the "end of history."

It was the physicist of the Rand Corporation, Herman Kahn,[16] who

15 *Revue de défense nationale*, May 1958. Monsieur Rougeron's ideas have been subsequently confirmed. In a press conference on October 1, 1961, a spokesman for the Atomic Energy Commission, discussing the destruction produced by a 100-megaton charge, attributed for the first time to the incendiary effect of high-altitude explosion destruction over 30,000 square kilometers, twelve times more extensive than those of the blast effect. Cf. New York *Times*, October 2, 1961.
16 *On Thermonuclear War*, Princeton, 1961, p. 20.

violated the taboo and obliged statesmen, professional or amateur strategists, and citizens themselves to face what all refuse to consider: what would happen if "it," "the monstrous war," "the impossible war," "the thermonuclear apocalypse" occurred? To this question, employing studies produced by a team of scientists, he has given an answer which, it seems to me, first confuses, then convinces and finally leaves the mind uncertain. Thermonuclear war, as it would be if it took place in 1967, even in 1970, would constitute a tragedy whose horror would be unprecedented, but it would not seal the destiny of humanity.

This first chart illustrates Kahn's thesis:

No. of Dead	Years Necessary for Economic Reconstruction
2 million	1 year
5 million	2 years
10 million	5 years
20 million	10 years
40 million	20 years
80 million	50 years
160 million	100 years

Another proposition completes this chart: "Despite a widespread belief to the contrary, objective studies indicate that even though the amount of human tragedy would be greatly increased in a postwar world, the increase would not preclude normal and happy lives for the majority of survivors and their descendants."[17] In other words, the consequences of the increase of radioactivity would be lamentable, not mortal.

The demonstration of this first chart depends on a distinction, introduced by the author, between Zone A and Zone B in the United States. Zone A is made up of the fifty-three urban agglomerations which contain virtually a third of the population, half of the "wealth" (capital), more than half the industrial potential, and virtually three quarters of the war industry. Zone B contains virtually all the agriculture and a fraction—in most branches between a fifth and a third—of the industrial potential. Supposing Zone A were completely destroyed, experts have attempted to discover how long it would take Zone B to reconstruct what had been destroyed. They have concluded that if several precautions had been taken in advance and circumstances were favorable, this task could be accomplished in a relatively few number of years.

The number of years would obviously depend on the number of losses in terms of human lives. Now, according to the same author,[18] the number of dead could be greatly modified by the measures taken for active and passive defense. Whereas in the case of attack against the Strategic Air Com-

[17] Ibid., p. 21.
[18] Ibid., p. 113.

mand and the first fifty urban agglomerations the number of dead might reach ninety million in the absence of any passive defense measures (civil defense), it might be lowered to a figure between thirty and seventy million if some precaution were taken against radioactive fallout, and to a figure between five and twenty-five million if these same measures were combined with a 70 per cent evacuation of the cities.

These analyses suggest a simple conclusion: once it is granted that even thermonuclear war is not the "end of the world," it becomes unreasonable to risk everything on deterrence and to be unconcerned about what would happen if the latter should fail. This indifference is all the more senseless since the amplitude of destruction and the loss of human life can be substantially reduced by measures of active or passive defense.

This common-sense argument is opposed only by a feeling which we ourselves share: the horror of a thermonuclear war would be such that it would matter little what came afterward—would matter little whether there were several million bodies, more or less. This emotional reaction to the calculations of the experts can be justified, in a pseudo-rational manner, by arguing that above a certain volume of destruction men make no difference or no longer feel the meaning of the difference. It is this argument which is the common element in all the optimistic theories of peace by fear; it is this argument which serves as a final basis for the theory of "minimum deterrence," which sustains confidence in the balance of terror, which encourages the proliferation of thermonuclear weapons, which discourages the efforts of passive and active defense, and which leads to the alternatives of *deterrence or defense*. All these attitudes, in effect, become at least relatively rational if one admits what we are all tempted to admit not with our head but with our heart: beyond a certain threshold, the inequality of the crime and the punishment does not count.

Let us turn again to the model of the duopolists, each armed with a thermonuclear system. The current theory is that of "mutual suicide": whatever the advantage one might gain from having taken the initiative, the retaliation inflicted upon the aggressor would be "intolerable" to the latter and thereby equivalent to the damages endured by the victim of the first strike. By the notion of "unacceptable retaliation," the psycho-political importance of the inequality between the crime and the punishment is effaced.

Similarly, let us suppose not the confrontation of today's super powers, the Soviet Union and the United States, but that of one of the super powers and another nation or group of nations possessing a thermonuclear system and an incomparably smaller area (for instance France, or France and Germany together). Would the balance of terror be identical to that which exists today between the two continent-states? The first answer is that the balance would inevitably be different because, by reason of the enemy's proximity, the instruments of European reprisal would be more vulnerable than those of the United States. But let us, as a hypothesis, eliminate this increased vulnerability. The European lack of space would suffice to create a major difference: by striking first, the possessor of the thermonuclear system could cause the retaliation to be posthumous. Let us say, in abstract terms, that the approximate equality between attack and reprisal supposes a similar capacity to endure destruction on both sides. Whatever its armament, France or France-and-Germany would always be inferior to the Soviet Union because of the difference in area of the two territories.

It is not that we choose to dismiss altogether the so-called theory of minimum deterrence.[19] It may be that with the increasing invulnerability of the thermonuclear system, no power has any further need of destroying or even of appreciably weakening its rival's thermonuclear system, and that consequently it can inflict but not avoid punishment, or that it can take revenge but not escape the first strike. In this hypothesis, logically, the margin of limited wars not involving the use of thermonuclear (or atomic) weapons would be considerably enlarged. But in this hypothesis, the minimum deterrent would only be symmetrical if the double capacity of striking (first or second) and enduring destruction were identical or at least similar.

The partisans of proliferation of atomic or thermonuclear weapons often commit the error of hypothetically considering only the model of equality of the crime and punishment. But they commit this error by confusing all punishment with a mortal one, by regarding any reprisal as intolerable. Eventually, they give this conception of the effective equality of the crime and the punishment a kind of rationality by substituting proportionality for equality. Any state possessing a "small" atomic capacity also represents a "small" stake. If it is capable of inflicting "small" retaliation upon an enemy, it will be protected since the proportionality of reprisal to stake will be the equivalent of the equality of the crime and the punishment. Of course, this reasoning overlooks many circumstances: the small state cannot take the initiative in an exchange which would involve its destruction, and the great power can wrest concessions from a threat which it will not have to carry out.

The notion of "unacceptable losses," which inspires a feeling of security (no one will employ such weapons), also helps spread a kind of indifference about so-called passive or civil defense as well as about all measures destined to facilitate reconstruction after an eventual thermonuclear war. The argument—there is no possible civil defense—is debatable.

---

[19] By minimum deterrence is meant the capacity of states to prevent an aggression by inflicting a certain volume of destruction on the enemy without any capacity to absorb the destruction which the enemy, on his side, would be capable of inflicting. At the limit, in case of the perfect invulnerability of the thermonuclear system on each side, even the two super powers would be reduced to "minimum deterrence." Medium-size states, such as France or Great Britain, have no other prospect than to possess a minimum deterrent. Whence the temptation of the theoreticians of national forces (General Gallois, for instance) to assert that all states, even the great ones, possess no more than a minimum deterrent—in other words, to deny that a counterforce strategy is still possible.

The same argument could be employed against active defense (fighter aircraft, ground-to-air or air-to-air missiles). The first, in the course of the last war, was regarded as effective when it knocked 5 to 10 per cent of the enemy bombers out of the sky. Since each of these planes had to perform many missions, aircraft were unable to endure a 10 per cent rate of losses on each raid. But if each thermonuclear bomb destroys one city, each bomber has accomplished its task as soon as it has reached its target once. Yet, on both sides, the authorities are reluctant to be convinced by such arguments that active defense against air attacks is futile. Quite reasonably, they insist on the necessity and the utility of even an imperfect defense. Ground-to-air rockets may not insure Russian air space against bombers, but they oblige, and will perhaps oblige in the future, substituting ballistic missiles for bombers, or even installing, on the bombers, launching apparatus for rockets of such a nature that the thermonuclear system has no need to approach its target and can strike from a distance. Further, an active defense, though not effective against an intact thermonuclear system operating according to plans established in advance, might be effective against the same system weakened and disorganized, attempting to deliver a retaliatory strike. The bombers are heavy, and thus deprived of part of their range or their load by the electronic apparatus destined to paralyze the "homing" mechanism of the missiles or the enemy shells. In any case, the function and consequence of active defense is to oblige the rival state to make additional expenditures, every defensive innovation requiring an offensive innovation.

Why should it be otherwise with civil defense? Merely because an *entire* population cannot be sheltered does not mean that possible losses cannot be reduced. At first glance it appears madness, on the part of a state which stakes almost everything on deterrence, not to devote more resources to protecting the inhabitants of cities or of the countryside, even if only to add to the "credibility" of the thermonuclear threat. I believed, some years ago, that this apparently irrational attitude could only be explained by a kind of irrational and organic refusal to entertain the possibility avowedly being prepared for.

Without abandoning this explanation, which seems to me to involve a degree of truth, I perceive other interpretations today. The cost of urban shelters, whose effectiveness will never be guaranteed, is enormous, almost prohibitive, even for the richest state in the world and in history. Yet the hundreds of millions spent on the development of these underground, rein-forced-concrete shelters furnished with the equipment necessary for a long stay, would probably not suffice to save the mass of the urban population in case of a surprise attack: between the alert and the explosion, millions of people would not have time to reach the shelters. The enemy's temptation to strike by surprise would have increased more than the security of the civilians.

Further, the state which decided to construct such shelters (or to prepare evacuation plans for its cities) would offer its rival a dilemma: either to take analogous measures or else to resign itself to a lasting inferiority (not to

mention the not inconceivable possibility that such a program would be regarded by the other power as a provocation, even as the proof of a distinct
and determined desire for war). If, after many years and the expenditure of
millions, the duopolists reach an approximate equality of respective capacities
for passive defense, neither will have gained anything in terms of power to
deter the other. At most each will have reduced the number of hostages left
to the other's discretion. But both will have improved their chance of survival
in case of war and somewhat diminished the size of material and human
losses. The fear of escalation in the national defense budgets, without altering
the balance of terror, affords one partially rational explanation of the indifference manifested toward measures of passive defense which would be
relatively cheap and effective (light shelters against radioactive fallout, stockpiling of the machines and materials most indispensable to reconstruction,
evacuation plans for cities, education of the population, etc.). In this regard
the leaders, particularly in the West, behave as if they regarded thermonuclear
war as so monstrous that it would be futile to attenuate its horror and absurd
to show concern for the postwar period.

Thus the theory of the insignificance of "more" and "less" seems to determine, to a degree, the conduct of states. Both super powers are engaged in
a race for arms and technological progress with regard to active defense. Both
are almost entirely neglecting the possibilities of civil defense. It is not
impossible to discover the psychological motives for these apparently contradictory attitudes, though it does not seem to me possible to regard this
contradiction as a reasonable one.

3. The Stages of the Dialectic of Deterrence

Once we abandon the sophism which justifies a lack of differentiation between "more" and "less," two kinds of questions arise: What is the effective
degree of inequality between the crime and the punishment in various abstract or actual circumstances? On the other hand, in accord with which
theories have the duopolists acted during recent years, or will they be led to
act in the course of the coming years?

The most celebrated example of the first kind of question is the polemic
provoked by the already famous article by A. J. Wohlstetter, "The Delicate
Balance of Terror."[20] The author, studying a situation of fact, that of the
Strategic Air Command in 1957–58, considering the number of bases used
(approximately twenty-five), the number of ballistic missiles necessary to
attain a high probability of eliminating each of these bases given the acknowledged precision of the missiles, concluded that the retaliation of which
the American thermonuclear system would be capable after a massive surprise
attack would not necessarily be "unacceptable" and would even, in certain
circumstances, be far from equaling the losses sustained by the Soviet Union

[20] *Foreign Affairs*, January 1959.

in the course of the 1939–45 War or even in the course of the first year of that war.

We are not qualified to continue the technological argument and to inquire, in our turn, to what degree the balance of terror is "delicate" or "precarious." A. J. Wohlstetter considered only the bases of the SAC. He assumed that the air bases at the disposal of American aircraft in Europe, in Asia or in Africa were either destroyed, or else, not serving for the stationing of the strategic bombers, did not noticeably add to the retaliatory potential. Further, he did not take into account the aircraft carriers whose bombers also carry atomic or thermonuclear bombs.

In any case, the situation analyzed by the article (published in January 1959) no longer exists at the present writing; it will exist still less at the moment when these lines will be published and read. The SAC bases have been multiplied, they have been reinforced. The precision of the ballistic missiles increases, but the precision necessary to destroy a base is also increasing. The traditional dialectic of shell and armor is nowadays extended and renewed in the rivalry between striking force and retaliatory force, between the effort to acquire strategic means against the adverse thermonuclear system and the effort to insure the invulnerability of that system. On one side the number of missiles, the explosive power of the thermonuclear warheads, the precision of firing increases, and on the other the bases become more numerous, more dispersed, and eventually more mobile and better protected.

Were the Rand Corporation experts, in 1960, too alarmist, as I am tempted to believe? The simultaneous destruction of twenty-five SAC bases in the United States, three or four hundred bases used by the B-47 bombers and attack bombers carrying atomic bombs, and finally of the aircraft carriers, even though theoretically conceivable, represents a masterpiece of organization and technological coordination whose probability neither the Soviet leader nor his advisers would readily admit in advance.

Further, it would be senseless to conclude that the Soviet leaders will be tempted to do everything they have the capacity to do. Of course, at first glance, one is inclined to agree with Mr. Oskar Morgenstern's assertion that we should base our conduct on the enemy's objective capacities and not on the intentions we may attribute to him. We cannot know whether or not the Moscow leaders are preparing or envisaging a thermonuclear Pearl Harbor, but we can and must act in such a way that they do not have the means to do so. The counsel is a prudent one, but the reasons adduced are not convincing.

The distinction between the enemy's *capacity* and his *intention* would of course be inevitable if we were in a position to know the nature of this capacity, and if the enemy himself were able to evaluate it with certainty and exactitude. But even the number of missiles necessary to destroy a base results from a calculation of probabilities. The probability of as complex an operation as the simultaneous attack on fifty bases occurring to a predetermined plan is itself highly unlikely. If we add that the information of one of the super powers concerning the state of its rival's armament is by no means exact, we will conclude that neither of the duopolists is sure of having a precise knowledge of either its own capacity or that of its enemy.

None of the Western experts, even the most pessimistic, suggests that at any given moment the Soviet Union has been capable of eliminating *all* of the American retaliatory force. Some merely declare that the first strike had the chance of reducing the American force to such a point that the Soviet Union would suffer less from the response than it had suffered in June–July 1941 from the Hitler attack. But there is a distinct difference between millions of dead in four years or even in four weeks and millions of dead in four hours. Further, when a technological failure or a human error can cost the lives of millions of men, the uncertainty attached to such enterprises weighs heavily upon the minds which must take this decision. I cannot conceive of the leaders who, in cold blood, relying on highly provisional and uncertain calculations, would run such a risk. I can conceive still less that the leaders educated by Bolshevik doctrine would ever consent to run it, unless virtually obliged to do so by circumstances.

The leaders of the Soviet Union do not conceive of history in biological terms. They are not fighting the American people, they are not seeking to exterminate it or to reduce it to slavery. They believe in the gradual and inevitable diffusion of the regime whose first model they have created. They are convinced that the wind of history blows in the direction of their anticipations and their hopes. Why would they endanger all that they have created for the mere purpose of accelerating an evolution that is inevitable in any case? Why would they do so, above all, at the moment when China's rise doubtless inspires anxieties, though such apprehensions have no place within the intellectual universe of Marxism-Leninism? The Politburo's code of behavior has always condemned a policy of useless risks as *adventurism*. Thermonuclear adventurism would be more unjustifiable than any other.

Thus the American authors who insisted most on the precariousness of the balance of terror never derived from it the conclusion that the leaders of the Kremlin were preparing a thermonuclear Pearl Harbor in cold blood. They had a chiefly pedagogic and pragmatic objective. They wanted to persuade those responsible for American defense to take measures to reduce the vulnerability of the means of retaliation (multiplication, dispersion, hardening of the bases). They wanted to dissipate the complacent illusion that the balance of terror is acquired without difficulty and without danger and that, once established, it endures by itself. Above all, they wanted to make evident to all eyes the difference in nature between first strike and second strike. In the first case, strategic aircraft is intact, it operates according to established plans, and each group knows its mission in advance; the enemy's defenses are not in a state of alert or else they have only been warned at the last moment. Let us suppose, on the other hand, that half or two thirds of the bases are destroyed by the enemy's ballistic missiles, the nation itself having received two hundred ballistic missiles, each carrying a thermonuclear warhead of a power of several megatons. How would communications function? What targets would the surviving thermonuclear system attack? How many would penetrate the alerted enemy defenses? The inequality of the crime and the punishment would be far more likely than their equality. At most, if one assumed on one side the SAC concentrated on a small number of non-reinforced bases, and on the other two or three hundred intercontinental missiles, it was not unreasonable to evoke, not the situation of impunity, but circumstances in which, given a disparity between attack and retaliation, action, which had the advantage of the initative, would be preferable to abstention, which would allow the enemy the chance to strike first.

That this situation in fact ever existed seems to me dubious at the very least. At the period when the SAC was concentrated on some twenty bases, the Soviet Union did not possess, it appears, the hundred intercontinental ballistic missiles necessary to attain a sufficient probability of disabling bases and system. The simultaneous destruction of medium bombers and fighter bombers dispersed on the bases near the Soviet Union as well as on aircraft carriers, if it did not raise an insoluble problem on paper, involved difficulties and enormous risks in case of a significant difference between calculation and actual effects.

If we set aside the 1957–58 period—that to which A. J. Wohlstetter's studies applied—what has been, in fact, the relation of deterrence between the Soviet Union and the United States? This relation has not ceased to be asymmetrical—*in favor of the United States*—up to the moment when the Soviet Union developed intercontinental ballistic missiles. Before 1949 the United States alone possessed atomic bombs (though the American stockpile was a small one). Toward 1955 both super powers had thermonuclear bombs, but the United States' strategic air force was more numerous, technologically superior, and better trained than that of the Soviet Union, and above all it possessed more numerous, more dispersed bases closer to their objectives than did its rival. By striking first American aviation had the capacity to ravage the majority of the Soviet cities; even by striking first, Soviet aircraft did not have a capacity of the same degree.

The result of this was not necessarily some inequality in the respective capacities for deterrence. For the Soviet Union, thanks to the superiority of its armies, could, in case of a generalized conflict, invade Western Europe and seize the strategic points of the Near East. Did the threat of occupying Western Europe re-establish the balance of terror, despite the disparity between the American atomic or thermonuclear apparatus and the Russian? On paper, we would have replied no. As to what had in fact happened, it is more difficult to formulate a categorical judgment. In spite of everything, at no moment between 1945 and 1957 did the Soviet Union seem paralyzed or terrified by the capacity which American strategic aircraft certainly possessed to devastate its cities. The course of the Chinese civil war was not affected by it. The atomic threat neither halted North Korean aggression nor prevented the Chinese intervention nor hastened the conclusion of an armistice. The changes in style of Soviet diplomatic-strategy after 1953 are manifestly attributable to Stalin's death, to the disputes and personalities of his successors, not to modification in the relations of atomic or thermonuclear forces.

It is true that during the years 1950–60 the world situation, in certain regions of the planet, has been profoundly transformed. The French and British empires in Asia have completely dissolved; the French, English and Belgian colonies in Africa have become independent. In the Near East, where Western influence prevailed almost exclusively in 1950, the Arab nations now play off one bloc against the other. The failure of the Franco-British expedition in 1956 symbolically marked the end of an era. In the Western Hemisphere itself, under Uncle Sam's beard, Czech machine guns and Soviet assault tanks have landed in Havana to equip the "rebel army" of the socialist Republic of Cuba.

That the Soviet Union, in the course of the last six years, has extended its action into regions which seemed private "game reserves" of the West cannot be disputed. What, on the other hand, escapes us is the link between the modification of the relation of nuclear forces in favor of the Soviet Union and the boldness of the Soviet undertakings. Personally, I doubt if this link has been a very close one. The first agreement Moscow made to deliver weapons to Cairo dates from 1955: the American strategic air force had never been so powerful. Soviet strategic airpower had probably, at this date, put an end to the invulnerability of the American territory; it had not, if we consider only the super powers, re-established the balance of terror (if the latter requires the equality of capacities of destruction).

When only one of the two super powers had the means of laying waste the other's cities, it was that state which determined the circumstances in which atomic (or thermonuclear) deterrence functioned. Between 1945 and 1958 the United States, if it had had the clairvoyance or the resolution to do so, could have determined by itself the cases of atomic war, have established the limits outside which the threat would be carried out. Once the two super powers have equivalent capacities, each attempts to determine the cases of atomic war and to establish the limits outside which the threat would be executed. It remains to be seen how each state reacts if the other exceeds the limits, implicit or explicit. If the President of the United States sent the Marines against Cuba, despite Mr. Khrushchev's promise of support to Fidel Castro, what would be the Kremlin's reply?

In a general way, it seems that the logic of mutual deterrence must result in the paralysis of the thermonuclear system, hence in the non-involvement of regular armies (particularly those of the super powers) in the case of limited conflicts and in the predominant role of infiltration and subversion throughout the rest of the world. Such, at least, seems to have been the doctrine of Mr. Khrushchev himself. He intended, in his turn, to impose by thermonuclear threat the non-intervention of American armed forces in the contested territories and the nation torn by civil war. This non-intervention would suffice, according to the Communist conception of the world, to guarantee the victory of the "armies of national liberation" and of the parties allied to the socialist camp.

As for thermonuclear war itself, according to the declarations of the leaders and the studies published by the military reviews, official theory seems to offer the following ideas, widespread in the West as well. A massive attack, even when launched by surprise, would not destroy a sufficient fraction of the adverse thermonuclear system for the aggressor to escape punishment. A thermonuclear war would be horrible and would inflict unspeakable suffering upon humanity, but it would not mark the end of the world. The exchanges of ballistic missiles would not even end the war: despite the losses sustained, states would continue the struggle with the means of combat they had preserved.[21] The distinction between limited atomic war and total atomic war would be artificial; if one of the super powers resorts to nuclear explosives, escalation is inevitable.[22] Finally, assured that history is naturally evolving in the direction of communism, the Soviet Union declares itself ready for a general disarmament and, in the absence of such a disarmament, resolved to utilize its thermonuclear capacity only to neutralize the American thermonuclear capacity and to forestall Western aggression.[23]

What is the doctrine by which the United States national defense is organized? The first objective is obviously to insure as complete an invulnerability as possible to the thermonuclear system. Since 1960 and the discussions about the precariousness of the balance of terror, measures have been taken in three directions: dispersal and hardening of air bases, development of atomic submarines with Polaris missiles and activation of a huge program of such submarines (forty-one), and development of solid-fuel (Minuteman) missiles which require only a few minutes to fire and which can be launched from moving bases.

In 1960–61, discussions centered around two points, one of fact, the other theoretical. The first question concerned the number of ballistic missiles that the Soviet Union and the United States would have at their disposal in 1963 or in 1965. The theoretical question was a much larger one: assuming the

[21] Do the Soviet authors really believe in this "broken-back war," or merely write as if they do? It is difficult to determine.
[22] Again we may wonder whether the Soviet authors are convinced of this. They may consider it to their interest to suggest that they would not tolerate a limited atomic war. If the question actually came up, would they in fact do so?
[23] From the Soviet viewpoint, interventions against an anti-capitalist or anti-imperialist revolution are "aggressions."

invulnerability, at least relative invulnerability, of thermonuclear weapons, and assuming that this invulnerability would be maintained by both sides in spite of the qualitative arms race and technical innovations, then what diplomatic strategy should the West adopt?

The missile gap has not only been one of the themes of journalistic speculation, but it was also an issue in the American electoral campaign of 1960. The controversy is only of historical interest today, since all the American experts maintain that this gap (even when referring to intercontinental missiles alone) only existed in the public imagination. In fact, in 1962 Mr. McNamara estimated that American superiority was so great as to allow for counterforce strategy, even in the case of a second strike (at least for several years). The observer is inclined to ask why, in 1960, the American leaders did not succeed in informing the United States and the world of the exact balance of forces then prevailing. Or had the American leaders themselves overestimated the Soviets' capacity or determination to produce a large number of intercontinental missiles?

On the other hand, the theoretical discussion continues. Even while affirming that today [1966] the United States is still able to destroy a part of the Soviets' thermonuclear power, the American Secretary of Defense recognizes that this counterforce capability will diminish in the coming years. When that happens, what should be the objectives of a defense policy? What combination of conventional weapons, tactical nuclear weapons, strategic nuclear weapons and civil defense will permit the United States not only to discourage a direct attack against its own territory, which is relatively easy, but also to fill its role as a great power, that is, to protect its allies scattered throughout the world?

In order to maintain a "plausible first strike" capacity, should not the United States maintain a certain counterforce capability and improve its civil defense? Lacking this plausible first-strike capacity, ought not the United States to acquire more weapons applicable in limited wars, either conventional weapons or tactical atomic weapons? Should the objective be the stabilization of mutual deterrence at the strategic level, even though this entails reinforcement with weapons adapted to limited warfare, or, on the contrary, should it be the maintenance of an effective threat at the higher level? The speculations of American analysts center on questions such as these.

4. How Deterrence Works

Let us consider the present situation, insofar as published information permits us to reconstruct it, at least in a probable form. The United States had a genuine opportunity to destroy the majority of the Soviet Union's means of retaliation[24] until the development of ballistic missiles. Today, even

[24] Those that would have "punished" the United States, not those that would have "punished" Western Europe.

by taking the initiative, the American striking force would not save American cities from massive destruction.

The Soviet Union, if it took the initiative, might have been able to destroy the launching bases for intermediate-range missiles in Great Britain, in Italy, in Turkey (before they were removed), and most of the airfields in Western Europe. But the surviving fraction of the American system would certainly still have been capable of inflicting retaliation which Moscow regards as "unacceptable." The present situation—absence of war and presence of the United States, with an intact thermonuclear force—seems to Moscow preferable to the situation resulting from aggression, this situation being defined both by the intensity of the probable retaliation and by the likelihood of its execution.

In these circumstances, neither rival will intentionally launch a total war, unless it is bereft of reason or mistakenly believes itself capable of reducing the enemy's force of retaliation more than it is actually capable of doing. Rational conduct obviously supposes exact knowledge of the data. Inexact information can provoke irrational conduct against the side that knows the truth. But, in the present circumstances, the uncertainty of the results of a thermonuclear exchange helps prevent the apocalypse: it is difficult to imagine a situation in which either super power would judge the likelihood of escaping retaliation sufficient to justify the decision of war.

In a thermonuclear duopoly the super powers have a double interest in common: not to destroy each other (and thereby assure the victory of *third powers*), not to favor and, if possible, to prevent the dissemination of the decisive and terrifying weapons. For ten years it has seemed as if the two super powers (especially the United States) were at every moment conscious that their common interest in avoiding war prevailed over their opposed interests, however important; as if they were equally concerned to delay the moment when the accession of France and China to the thermonuclear club would put an end to the duopoly. The Soviet Union, despite socialist solidarity, has not helped China any more than the United States, despite the Atlantic Pact, has helped France. Neither alliances nor hostilities have ever been total, down through history. Solidarities among enemies, oppositions among allies assume an original form in the thermonuclear age.

If we imagine two states, essentially friendly, both possessing a thermonuclear system, what would they do? The problem is not gratuitous: perhaps it will soon be raised by the Russo-Chinese dialogue. These two states could not simultaneously renounce their thermonuclear capacities without losing their power with regard to other states. They could not subject their two capacities to a single command without losing their respective military sovereignty. They could not brandish their arms against each other without belying their protestations of friendship. They could not continue the race for technological innovations without wakening anxieties which, gradually amplified by the dialectic of suspicion, would ultimately risk creating hostility by fear. In this case, terror, provoked by armaments, would transform friend-ship into hostility. The only solution, outside of a fusion of sovereignties, would be an agreement on the stabilization of the systems and the reduction of secrecy—in other words, the equivalent of the agreement to which the United States, if not the Soviet Union, aspires.

It is not the case, however, from all evidence, that the thermonuclear duopoly involves the same consequences, whatever the degree of hostility be-tween the two protagonists. The two super powers today have different political-economic regimes, each of which implies historical or moral condem-nation of the other. They are not in agreement as to the frontier between their spheres of influence, and they observe that the rest of the world—hundreds of millions of men who belong to states not affiliated with either bloc—can, depending on the circumstances, join one camp or the other. They have, whatever they do, many occasions for conflict. What influence does the thermonuclear duopoly exert on the functioning of the bipolar system, and on limited conflicts?

It is wise, above all, to avoid a false rigor in our reasoning. Some plead that the horror of a total war is such that no one will launch it. They conclude from this, with an apparent logic, that geographically limited hostilities are possible and even probable. Others utilize the same argument of the horror of a total war to conclude that even limited wars have become unlikely because of the risk of escalation: there is no longer a break in continuity between conventional weapons and atomic weapons. Certain of the latter may have less power than certain of the former. The shadow of the apocalypse will suffice to prevent any use of force at all precisely because, on the ladder of violence, the rungs occur at intervals so regular that no one can be certain, once he steps on the first, that he will not be obliged to climb, one at a time, to the very top.

These two lines of reasoning, literally interpreted, are incompatible with each other, and the authors who employ them simultaneously contradict themselves without even realizing it. He who emphasizes the monstrous horror of thermonuclear war is not entitled to invoke the risk of constant escalation. Of course, it is legitimate to maintain that a danger, even very slight, of escalation incites the protagonists to prudence, deters them from even a limited use of military force (which is true). But it is not legitimate to combine the senseless excess of total war with the risk of escalation, tri-umphantly assuming the reign of peace by fear.

The risk of escalation depends on three factors: first of all, as we have seen, on the relation of the forces of deterrence between the duopolists; then on the nature of the limited conflict (geographic localization, explicit or latent stake of the conflict, etc.); lastly on the conduct of diplomatic strategy by statesmen. The first factor, which we have analyzed at the level of models, is essentially concerned with the degree of advantage which the duopolist draws from striking first. The greater this advantage, the more each super power will be inclined to suspect the other's intentions in a period of crisis. On the other hand, the more each of the duopolists relies on the invulnerability of its own system, the less it will be tempted to rely on the dialectic of suspicion and to take the initiative because it fears (or believes) that the other is doing so.

It seems to me that the progress made on both sides in the direction of the invulnerability of the thermonuclear apparatus already attenuates the danger created by the reciprocity of suspicions amplifying each other to the point of a fatal decision. As of today, escalation becomes either supremely unlikely or at most only conceivable, depending on whether the hostilities occur in Laos or Berlin, whether the stake is the internal regime of a poor and thinly populated kingdom in southeast Asia, or, potentially, the destiny of Western Europe, cradle of Western civilization, which is realizing for the first time the historical unity of humanity and which remains one of the three great industrial concentrations of the planet.

Neither the relation of the forces of deterrence nor the location and stake of the conflict mechanically determine the course of a crisis and permit us to estimate in advance the probability of escalation. Each diplomatic crisis is a series of events—that is, of human actions—for which several individuals assume responsibility. Each crisis is a test of wills in which bluff plays an inevitable role. The duel of deterrence does not always involve a foreseeable conclusion. As soon as a possessor of the thermonuclear apparatus wants to protect another territory besides his own, he is obliged to make likely, in the eyes of the possible aggressor, a decision which would probably not be reasonable. If we suppose each thermonuclear system to be relatively invulnerable, *it would probably be unreasonable in all circumstances, as much for the Soviet Union as for the United States, to launch a thermonuclear war.*

This situation provokes endless speculation, for it suggests many circumstances in which the worst might happen, be it a war by which one threatens the enemy in the hope of not waging it, or be it the loss of the stake by capitulation, which the threat had as goal to prevent. Let us imagine a massive attack by the Soviet armies, in France or in Western Europe, combined with the evacuation of the Soviet cities and a blackmail maneuver with regard to the United States (the latter will be spared if it does not intervene, ravaged if it honors its commitments). Would the President of the United States give the order to the SAC that would mean death for millions, for tens of millions of Americans? Or again: for how many millions of (probable) dead would the President of the United States regard himself as bound to come to the aid of his allies? The "credibility" of the threat is weaker as the state that brandishes and eventually executes it would be more seriously hurt by the other state's reprisal. With reasonings of this kind, it is easy to demonstrate in appearance to the Europeans that the Americans will never again be able to protect them, since New York, Washington and

Chicago would be the price to pay if London, Paris or Bonn were not abandoned to its fate.

Such reasoning does not convince me, and I regard it as little more than sophistry. If a thermonuclear war must claim millions or tens of millions of victims, it is probably reasonable for neither of the super powers in any circumstance. If we start from the hypothesis that the aggression has taken place (Paris is bombed, but the Soviets have promised to spare Washington), we may justifiably conclude that there will be no American intervention, but if we start from the hypothesis that the American threat has been made with the necessary solemnity, we may conclude that the aggression will not take place. The whole question is to know which point of departure one must choose.

Now, personally, it seems to me that the point of departure unavoidable for "common sense" is the situation as it in fact presents itself to the two super powers: so long as neither of them takes the initiative of provoking its rival, it is sure of avoiding the horrors of thermonuclear war. Since these horrors are out of all proportion, it is enough to create a risk, even a slight one, of incurring them, for the super power, however ambitious for conquests we suppose it to be, to choose to abstain (when abstention does not endanger the state itself). We grant that aggression is too irrational to take place, hence that the defensive side will not have to consider retaliation, or the choice between capitulation and the execution of the thermonuclear threat, because the rival will not take the initiative of a major provocation. The basic hypothesis is as follows: in case of a dialogue between the two super powers, the thermonuclear weapon is employed only defensively; each brandishes it to prevent the other from taking certain initiatives, neither brandishes it to "cover" an aggression and prevent the other from defending first-order positions.

What are the initiatives which defensive deterrence prevents? What are the territories for whose protection the thermonuclear threat is brandished? These questions do not always allow of a categorical answer. The strategy of deterrence involves a certain ambiguity. The super power's responses are not, and must not be, rigorously predictable. For certain second-order stakes, it is wise not to commit oneself in advance, but it is not wise to parade an indifference which might not resist the shock of the event itself. In any case, when the subject of deterrence attaches a vital importance to a territory, he sets up a political-military system that renders the monstrous decision plausible, that obliges him, so to speak, to execute his threat if the other power transgresses.

The system, intended to make plausible to a possible aggressor a decision monstrous in itself, has a double character, technological and psychological. Technology permits the creation of a means of retaliation which, in certain circumstances, would function *almost* automatically. Automatism need not be total; otherwise, there would be a risk of an accidental war because of some technical error. The order to launch the thermonuclear system must be in the hands of men, perhaps of a single man, situated at the summit of the political-military hierarchy. But the organization of aircraft and missiles must also make reprisal extremely probable in case of massive attack, whatever the destruction inflicted on any element of the system.

Simultaneously, the subject of deterrence attempts to convince the other side of the value attached to the stake of the conflict. To this end, he multiplies his words and acts, signs treaties, garrisons troops on the territory he seeks to protect, installs launchers there for intermediate-range ballistic missiles. Parchments, troops and launchers symbolize the super power's commitment, a pledge of honor which cannot fail to appear, to the other power, as an irrevocable commitment, more imperative than any calculation of rationality.

To manifest the importance of the *stake*, to form ties of *honor*, to insure popular *emotion* in case of aggression (the American garrisons would share the fate of the Europeans)—all these measures refer to the category of *commitment*. The subject of deterrence in a sense forces him not to retreat. The more solemn the promise, the more humiliating capitulation would be. Who would still believe in the word of the United States if Europe were abandoned at the moment of danger? The question is no longer to know whether the game is worth the candle. The fact is that the aggressor can no longer take his rival's retreat for granted. The decision, perhaps irrational theoretically, has become virtually certain and rational, with regard to the state, the commitments, and the emotion.

This does not mean that a super power could, at will, protect any position by making solemn promises. The value of the stake remains the necessary but not sufficient condition for an excessive threat to appear plausible. The Soviet threat of a possible recourse to missiles to prevent the United States from undertaking a military operation against Cuba was scarcely plausible (which does not mean that it made *no* impression on the occupant of the White House). An American threat of the same kind apropos of Laos would be still less plausible. In general, territories of secondary value, outside the zone where the two blocs are directly confronted, can be defended only by the weapons utilizable in the context of limited wars. At most, the thermonuclear threat functions implicitly, from the fact that any hostilities involve a risk, however slight, of escalation.

The super power to be deterred possesses two tactics by which it hopes to break down its rival's commitment: that of the *artichoke* and that of the *fait accompli*. The first, a military version of the method applied by the Communists in Eastern Europe to seize total power, consists of *dividing aggression into as many parts as necessary so that no one step justifies a violent rejoinder*. The day the Soviet Union concludes a peace treaty with the German Democratic Republic, the only change will be that of the official authority: who will wage war for a seal on the official papers? This first tactic can be combined with the second, that of the *fait accompli*: let us suppose that the Western nations wake up one Monday morning and learn that Denmark has been occupied during the night. The initial situation would be reversed: the aggressor would henceforth be on the defensive and the side initially on the defensive would have to force the other to retreat.

To deal with these two tactics, the defensive side must possess conventional weapons which permit it first to avoid the creation of *faits accomplis*, then to oppose each of the aggressor's movements with a show of force of the same nature and of comparable violence. When deterrence has become bilateral, recourse to thermonuclear weapons inevitably becomes a *supreme recourse*. Not that the threat is not implicit at the first echelon of the use of force. But it is not, so to speak, physically possible to launch the thermonuclear system except in reply to a massive attack. Thus the two camps add to the nuclear weapons, which function diplomatically insofar as they are not actually used, conventional weapons which, by making possible the use of the thermonuclear system, increase the probability of their non-use.

The dialogue of deterrence has appeared asymmetrical in favor of the defensive side because we have presumed that the latter was committed and the other side not. However, the aggressor must not have engaged a part of his prestige in the action, for the loss of face that would result for the side that "fails to gain" would be no less than that which would result from a defensive incapacity to maintain the status quo.

The situation of double commitment is conceivable; indeed it is partially realized in the Berlin dispute. The Soviet semi-commitment in favor of change is a way of denouncing as a bluff the West's anterior commitment in favor of the status quo. Defense of a locally indefensible position by the threat of thermonuclear retaliation was logical when the threatening power was not itself subject to counterthreat. It is no longer logical to the same degree once deterrence is mutual.

When commitments, and spectacular ones, have been made on both sides, it is as if two automobiles were driving at top speed toward each other, each driver hoping that the other will swerve or stop at the last moment. It is likely, indeed, that one of the two will prefer to lose his nerve rather than his life. But in this game called "chicken," it is not necessarily the best, but the most determined who wins.

In fact, the Berlin crisis is the first to suggest the situation of the double commitment. Everywhere else, the distinction was clear between the subject and the object of deterrence, between the side on the defensive and the side suspected of offensive intentions, which had only to abstain from any initiative to enjoy security. Thus the theoreticians, to make apparent the dangers of the diplomatic duel in the thermonuclear age, have imagined an element which we have eliminated in the course of the preceding pages: non-action, which according to our hypotheses guaranteed security, can, in certain circumstances, also be fraught with danger.

Let us look back to the Hungarian crisis of October–November 1956. The repression of the Hungarian Revolution was merely a tragic diplomatic episode within the Soviet bloc, as long as the United States did not intervene. But if the latter had taken steps toward a possible intervention, Moscow would have had to choose, or would have feared being forced to choose, between a defeat of the first order (and possibly the disintegration of the Soviet bloc) or war. In this situation the determination of roles was equivocal: with regard to morality and international legality the Soviet Union was playing the aggressor's role. With regard to power politics United States intervention in relations between a super power and a satellite state could be regarded as aggressive. Who would have been the subject, who the object of deterrence? Who would have been obliged to retreat?

Hitherto the two super powers had been careful not to take useless risks. The United States abandoned the Hungarians to their misfortune and their master. Some years have passed since Mr. Khrushchev "committed" himself to modifying the status of Berlin. By and large, implicit agreements exist between the two powers concerning the legitimate means to be employed in each area and in each type of situation. But cases of a double commitment remain possible, and depending on the degree to which thermonuclear systems are vulnerable, statesmen and doctrinaires must acknowledge either the temptation of an initiative, by reason of the inequality of the crime and the punishment, or the possibility of relatively large limited wars and the consequent necessity of conventional armaments, because the exchange of ballistic missiles would be senseless for all.

5. The Impossibility of Rigorous Calculation

Does deterrence, regarded as the supreme concept of diplomatic-strategy in the thermonuclear age, belong to the traditional theoretical and practical categories of international politics?

States, in our age as during the preceding centuries, reserve the right to make autonomous decisions, including the decisions of peace and war. They continue to aim at incompatible objectives, to regard their interests as opposed, to suspect each other of the darkest plots. Inter-state relations are more than ever a test of wills. If we call power politics the peaceful or belligerent relations between states which acknowledge neither law nor arbitrator and attempt to constrain, seduce and convince each other, the politics of our period conforms more than ever to this age-old model.

The competition for moral and material superiority, inseparable from power politics, is more constant, more intense today than yesterday. Rates of economic growth, armaments, Sputnik and Lunik, quality of institutions and men—all achievements, all ideas are interpreted as instruments of the struggle or as arguments in the debate between the Western and the Communist worlds.

The difficulty of integrating the realities of the thermonuclear age into classical theory exists only for those who fail to distinguish resources, military strength and power, and identify power politics with the politics of military action. Such commentators ask whether a diplomatic-strategy whose final objective is not to use military force, or only to threaten it, is of the same nature as the diplomacy which regards war as the denouement of operations "on credit."

The effort not to execute the threat brandished—an effort which is explained by the monstrous excessiveness of the available weapons—inevitably modifies the diplomatic performance. There is less than ever a proportionality between a state's means of force and its capacity to impose its will on others. (Such at least is the situation as long as the thermonuclear duopoly lasts: even in the case of a monopoly, it is doubtful that a state would prevail by carrying out the threat to exterminate the recalcitrant populations.) There is less than ever a proportionality between strength and security. Never has the United States been so strong, never has it known such insecurity. Never has the course of diplomacy been in such striking contradiction with the theory according to which the single and supreme goal of states is the accumulation of maximum resources, by themselves or by alliances. There would not be so many alliances if these were all based on the calculation of military forces. The United States risks losing more by promising to protect the states bordering the Eurasian land mass than it would gain in additional means in the event of a trial by strength.

The essential difference between the thermonuclear age and the pre-Atomic Age, as we know, is the difference in the cost of a total war, that is, a war waged with all available weapons until absolute victory. Henceforth a state can be destroyed, a population exterminated in the very course of hostilities without having been previously disarmed. It has become true, in a sense, that the only possible defense against an enemy armed with thermonuclear bombs is the capacity for reprisal. Without this capacity, active or passive defense is too imperfect for a state to be able to resist thermonuclear intimidation. A state which has no retaliatory capacity must accept any ultimatum presented by a state possessing a thermonuclear system.

Not that humanity has definitively emerged from the *age of defense* to enter into the *age of retaliation*. The means of defense, weapons or fortifications, have always been instruments of deterrence, and active and passive defense against atomic or thermonuclear attacks remains an element of deterrence. Shelters for the population, like counterforce strategy, are elements of the strategy of deterrence. But it is true that henceforth the two super powers will devote more resources to the preparation of retaliation than to that of defense (in the largest sense of the concept) and that the gradual disappearance of defense to the advantage of retaliation (even posthumous retaliation) is becoming conceivable. (For the moment, the development is in the opposite direction.)

The conduct of a strategy of thermonuclear deterrence obviously presents certain original features in relation to the conduct of a conventional strategy. But the pattern of deliberation, preceding the diplomatic decision, remains formally the same.

Let us imagine a head of state considering the possibility of launching or not launching a war, for example Napoleon before the Russian campaign. He must consider, if he wants to act rationally: 1. the value of the objective; 2. the cost of the war according to the latter's possible developments; 3. the respective probability of these various developments; 4. the probability of finally achieving his goal. The chief uncertainty, in this deliberation, refers to the probability of the various possible courses of the operations. What chance had Napoleon of convincing Tsar Alexander to acknowledge that he was defeated? Napoleon may have hoped that at the moment of danger, the Tsar's will would weaken and that he would come to terms without being constrained to do so. The calculation was not a rigorous one because of the unpredictability of the campaign and the role of chance in the course of the battles, and also because there was no quantitative evaluation of the benefit of victory and the consequences of defeat.

Let us now imagine two states, both provided with thermonuclear systems, one of which seeks to conquer a position belonging to the other's sphere of influence but not territory. What is the aggressor's calculation? He must consider: 1. the value of the objective; 2. the cost of the operation according to the other side's various responses; 3. the likelihood of the various responses; 4. the likelihood of achieving the objective in the various eventualities created by the other side's responses. How does this calculation—that of Mr. Khrushchev with regard to Berlin—differ from the preceding one—that of Napoleon before crossing the Russian frontier?

Mr. Khrushchev was no more able than Napoleon to evaluate quantitatively the value of the elimination of the American troops garrisoned in West Berlin. He could probably not even be precise about the relation which existed, in his system of preferences, between the three terms: elimination of the troops, non-elimination of the troops after a crisis, non-elimination of the troops without a crisis. He obviously preferred the third term to the second, but he would be unable to specify whether the relation between the first and the second is greater or smaller than the relation between the third and the second. Nor could he strictly determine the probability of the cost according to the various answers, though he scarcely doubted being able to achieve his objective.[25] What is in doubt is his rival's response. Napoleon knew that the war would be launched by crossing the Russian border, but he did not know if the Grande Armée would manage to conquer the Tsar's will. The aggressor of the thermonuclear age does not know what war would

---

[25] Local superiority is not always acquired by the aggressor, but in a situation of thermonuclear duopoly, it is in this circumstance that aggression is most to be feared. If he does not have even local superiority, the aggressor will not attack.

be launched by a local initiative. The uncertainty bears less on the development of the campaign than on the psychology of the enemy, who also, in this hypothesis, possesses a thermonuclear system.

The aggressor, in order to reach a "rational" decision, must be capable of determining what his enemy's "rational" response will be. Before reaching a decision, he tries to reconstruct his enemy's deliberation. The latter will consider: 1. the value he attaches to the objective sought by the aggressor; 2. the cost of the various responses; 3. their probable results, direct or indirect. If we attribute numerical values to the gains and losses of the aggressor and of his victim, as well as to the probabilities of the various responses,[26] we can determine the moment when aggression will be "rational," that is, profitable. Similarly, the super power in a defensive position can calculate the probable effectiveness of its deterrence by attempting to reconstruct the calculations of gains and losses the aggressor makes as a result of the possible responses. But the mathematical expression does not prove that the actors in the real world are capable of determining these values and probabilities.

Let us take an aggressor A, a defensive side D, and certain contested territories B. A has a choice between a massive attack with conventional forces on B, or inaction; D, in case of aggression, has a choice between *massive retaliation* and *passivity*. Further, we suppose that B's value for A and D is equal to 20, the cost of total war equal to —100 for both. We then obtain the following results:

		A	
		Attack	*Non-attack*
	Retaliation . . . . $\frac{10}{100}$	—100	—
D		+20	o
	Non-retaliation . . . . . $\frac{90}{100}$		
	Expected value	+8	o

If we grant that in case of attack there are ten chances out of a hundred that D will reply by massive retaliation, the difference between 90 chances out of 100 of gaining 20, and 10 chances out of 100 of losing 100 is positive and equal to 8.[27] A has evaluated the probability of the response by calculating his rival's "expected values." But two calculations are possible. Either he tries to calculate the probability which D attributes to A's attack, or else he

[26] Cf. Glenn H. Snyder, "Deterrence and Power," *Journal of Conflict Resolution*, Vol. IV, No. 2. The author has also employed this analysis in his book *Deterrence and Defense*, Princeton, 1961, pp. 17 ff.

[27] $-100 \times \frac{1}{10} = -10$; $+20 \times \frac{9}{10} = +18$.

calculates the gap between the cost of retaliation and the cost of inaction. Since this latter gap is considerable, the aggressor can reason that the defensive side, faced with the *fait accompli* of aggression, doomed to lose the stake in any case (—20) and suffering considerable losses if it replies by massive reprisal (—100), will be resigned to limiting its losses. The defensive side, if it considers the future, will conclude that aggression is likely, although it can hope that the aggressor will nonetheless be stopped by the eventuality, however faint, of the execution of the threat.[28]

The numerical examples which we have borrowed from the American author have the eminent merit of showing one of the reasons why calculations of deterrence cannot be rigorous, that is, expressed in numerical values. The relation between the advantage of a local aggression and the cost of a total war is incommensurable with the relation of —100 to +20. The essence of deterrence by thermonuclear threat is the possibly excessive cost of the highly unlikely eventuality (highly unlikely by definition, because the cost of retaliation is considerable even for the side that strikes first). If we assume the aggression has already taken place, it is easy to show that the defensive side should prefer a limited loss to the cost of retaliation (cost for the enemy as for itself). The error is to forget that it is the aggressor who first creates the risk of this catastrophe for himself and that, consequently, he will be deterred from it by even a light probability of massive reprisal. If, instead of assuming —100 as the cost of a response in the case of aggression, we assumed —100,000, we could lower to 1 chance out of 1000 the probability of response without reaching a "rational" decision to engage in aggression.

As a matter of fact, the super powers have abandoned the strategy expressed by the simplified scheme we have just utilized. The aggressor is not reduced to the choice between the two procedures—massive attack or inaction—any more than the defensive side between massive retaliation and passivity. The two super powers have *reasonably* judged these two alternatives intolerable precisely because of the nature of these calculations (enormous cost, very slight probability). By maintaining these all-or-nothing alternatives, the rivals risked involuntarily provoking what they both sought to avoid. Hence the calculation would become more complex: the possible responses are five in number (local defense with conventional weapons, local defense with atomic weapons, limited atomic retaliation, massive retaliation, passivity). Passivity becomes almost as improbable as in the pre-Atomic Age, once the defensive side has several recourses. But from this moment on, calculation becomes too complex to be possible, even in theory. What is the cost of the various kinds of war for the aggressor and for the defensive side? How would such wars develop? What would be the probability of escalation? To what degree would the losses of one side differ from the losses of the other?

The diversity of the possible replies reduces the probability of massive

28 I have simplified Snyder's analysis considerably.

retaliation. It deprives the aggressor of the certainty of winning the stake, and augments the cost of the local operation. On his side, the defender modifies the data of rational calculation by committing himself in a spectacular manner and forcing himself to do what at the last moment he would perhaps prefer not to do.

Must we conclude that in the thermonuclear age Clausewitz's famous formula "war is the continuation of policy by other means," which we have taken as a principle at the outset of this book, is no longer true? The argument of those who believe that Clausewitz's formula is no longer meaningful, once a single thermonuclear bomb is enough to raze a city, runs as follows in its rigorous form: no stake can be worth the destruction of a thermonuclear war, even for the victor. If the losses exceed the gains for *all* the belligerents, war becomes irrational for both camps, and cannot be said, in a rationalizing interpretation, to be the continuation of policy.

Unfortunately this argument is not entirely true, at least at the present time. First of all, the cost and gain of a war are not susceptible of rigorous evaluation. One can calculate the losses and the advantages, in lives and material resources, of the belligerents. According to this calculation, most wars between thermonuclear powers are and will be irrational. But what value can either of the super powers attribute to the fact of being rid of the threat embodied by the other? What price can a people without space set on the fact of doubling or tripling its territory? The irrationality of war in relation to expenditure and gain results from a true but vague sentiment or else from the substitution of an economic calculation for a political one.

Further, even this sentiment and this calculation are not always in accord with reality. If the situation of impunity, of "the two gangsters," between the super powers is unlikely (unlikely but not impossible), it is not so between a great power and a small state, or between two small states. A great power can eliminate a small state's means of retaliation entirely or nearly so: the threat brandished by the great power to obtain the small state's capitulation, or even the execution of this threat, is not at all contrary to the traditional rationality of diplomatic strategy. It is possible that even the absolute victory of the great power over the small state will be less costly, hence more rational, than such victories in the past.

It remains true that for the super powers, the exchange of thermonuclear bombs would not be, strictly speaking, the "continuation of policy by other means." But the threat of this war that no one wants to fight is an integral part of the strategic-diplomatic conduct of the two super powers and even of all states (insofar as the latter take into account the reciprocal paralysis of the thermonuclear system). Thus we do not leave the context, set up by Clausewitz, of the permanent rivalry of states, of their alternatively peaceful and belligerent dealings, of the reference to the possible use of force in peacetime, and the reference to political goals in wartime. Further, this inevitable and rational solidarity of strategy and diplomacy has never been so indissoluble as today, when the thermonuclear system on each side is almost continually in a state of alert, aimed at the opposing system even while the leaders of the enemy states are deliberating.[29]

Nonetheless the weapons of mass destruction open the prospect of a historical revolution at the end of which the very essence of the relations between states will be different. Let us imagine each of them possessing an invulnerable capacity for retaliation so that in any circumstances each will be in a position to inflict a mortal punishment upon any aggressor. Let us even imagine, taking a further step, that each state is in a position to exterminate all humanity, to render the planet uninhabitable. At this moment there will no longer be any difference between "more" and "less," between crime and punishment, between great power and small state. Each state would possess a veto right over the existence of all the others.[30] It is legitimate to presume that the rivalry of political units might continue. But I do not think that this rivalry would remain psychologically or socially possible. No member of the system would agree to be permanently at the mercy of all the others. As humanity approached this system, it would realize that it must renounce either the diplomatic-strategic performance or life itself. Yet the choice it would make between these two alternatives is not predictable.

[29] The reader will recall the alerting of the entire American system at the time of the presence of the four heads of state or government in Paris for the summit conference which did not take place (May 1960).
[30] This hypothesis corresponds to one of the six systems described by Morton A. Kaplan, in his book already cited.

chapter XV

Les grands Frères
or
Diplomacy within the Blocs

The thermonuclear duopoly and the universal extension of the diplomatic system establish the uniqueness of the present situation. These two facts determine the hierarchy of the actors and the relations they maintain. The duopolists have a privileged position, for they alone possess the status of great powers, in the traditional sense of the term—that is, they alone are capable of choosing in a sovereign way between war and peace. But this capacity tends to become increasingly illusory, since the choice of a general or total war would obviously involve unacceptable destruction for both. Excessive force ceases to be rationally utilizable.

The distinction between great, middle-size and small powers does not, however, disappear. In a sense, it is more pronounced than ever, but its relevance has diminished. It has never been so difficult for the strong to impose his will upon the weak. To paraphrase the poet: is the force which does not act a true force? Neither between each of the super powers and its allies (or satellites), nor between the blocs and the non-aligned states, do negotiations conclude in results equivalent to those which a military test of force would reveal. In the past the weaker side logically made concessions to the stronger, either because this civility obeyed the unwritten rules of the game or because, in the background, a second power revealed its intention and capacity to resort, in case of need, to another language. Diplomacy has renounced civility since Lenin and Hitler, but in general today the threat of the other language would not be taken seriously.

On the whole it seems to me legitimate to distinguish three categories of relations: those between the members of the bloc, those between the blocs, and those between the blocs and the rest of the world. These three categories can also be called: relations between allies, between rivals (or potential enemies), between the two opposed camps and the rest of humanity (this "rest" not being homogeneous). The role of force is different in each of these categories of relations. In simplified theory, allies convince rather than constrain each other; enemies keep the means of constraint in reserve; those who are not directly involved in the hostility between the two blocs attempt both to reduce the risks to themselves and to derive the maximum advantage from the situation. But these formulas can only serve as an introduction: historical reality is much more complex.

1. *The Atlantic Bloc*

The two blocs are not homogeneous. Relations among states depend, to a degree, on their internal systems: the collective organization of democratic states cannot help being different from the collective organization of the Soviet states (whatever order of succession we acknowledge in the formation of the two blocs).

Since the criterion of the bloc is the military community, hence the loss, by each of its members, of all or part of its military sovereignty, the structure of the bloc is determined by the answer given to the following questions: 1. What military autonomy do the member states retain? 2. What autonomy do the member states retain in the use of their military force outside the zone of collective organization? 3. What part do the member states play in the determination of policy—diplomacy or strategy—with regard to the other bloc? 4. What autonomy do the member states retain with regard to the determination of their own policy in the zones external to the bloc? 5. What autonomy do the member states retain in their relations within the blocs, particularly in the regional groupings without the participation of the leading state? 6. What autonomy do the member states retain with regard to the determination of their internal policy, that is, their government and regular decisions?

The Atlantic bloc consists of a Supreme Command and a partial integration of armies which remain national in their recruiting, their administration and their officers, their spirit and their weapons. The standardization of weapons, often proclaimed to be necessary, has not been accomplished: none of the principal countries wishes to sacrifice its industries; the selection of a prototype weapon depends upon, or seems to depend upon, considerations which are not all strictly technical (at least in the eyes of the representative of the state whose prototype has not been chosen). The ministries of war and the careers of officers remain strictly national. Perhaps in the general staffs, at the NATO Defense College, an Atlantic spirit is being created; it does not yet seem to be dominant.

What does this collective organization permit, what does it forbid? It permits the member states to withdraw their troops that are under the Supreme Command when their policy, in zones external to the bloc, requires it. France employed this freedom in order to counter the Algerian rebellion. The military community is thus limited to Europe. If the Franco-English expedition to Suez failed, the fault was neither that of the Atlantic Pact nor of the abandonment of the military autonomy which the latter implies, but the opposition of the two super powers.

On the other hand, it would appear that the military community prevents the use of armed force in possible conflicts between member states. The German army's bases and maneuver areas are partly in France. Collective exercises, plans and mutual preparations exclude, both materially and morally, the likelihood of battles between the armies of partners. But in any case, the states are no longer in conflict or, at least, the secondary conflicts which might set them in opposition are insignificant compared with the Soviet threat. With or without the Atlantic Pact, the states of Western Europe would feel united as long as government and the majority of public opinion feared the expansion of the Soviet power, by invasion or by infiltration.

Available in Africa or in Asia, the armed force of the member nations is also available in case of civil war. In 1958, 1959, 1960 and 1961 many Frenchmen believed in the possibility of a military *coup d'état*. Whether or not troops and ships were integrated in peacetime, whether or not their integration in wartime was anticipated, the alliance does not suffice to guarantee the civil power against a possible rebellion of its generals or admirals.

Of course, the presence of American divisions in Europe, of an American fleet in the Mediterranean, is likely to "impress" (a little less than to "intimidate") rebels in uniform. The American government could offer its aid to restore the military leaders to discipline. The Atlantic community creates a context that is scarcely favorable to *pronunciamentos*. It does not forbid them *de jure*, and does not prevent them *de facto*.

In spite of this the relative autonomy, the national armies of the Atlantic Pact have been obliged to renounce many privileges which the equality of partners theoretically implies. Since only the Americans possess the decisive weapon—strategic air force, thermonuclear bombs, nuclear warheads and short-range missiles—only they have elaborated the bomb targeting programs. There exists in Washington a Standing Group which studies the military problems of the Alliance and which includes representatives of three of the principal powers. As a matter of fact, the disproportion of forces between the United States on the one hand, and each of the European nations on the other, is such that the decisions are inevitably made by the American leaders and the plans resulting from these decisions are established by the general staffs in which the American influence dominates or, on occasion, the Anglo-American influence (special relations continue, in spite of everything, between the United States and Great Britain).

The policy of the Atlantic community with regard to the other bloc is formally discussed in the plenary sessions of the Atlantic Alliance. It is discussed regularly, by diplomatic means, among the four principal members of the Alliance. When the question of Berlin comes up, the chancelleries in Bonn, London, Paris and Washington remain in constant contact. When a crisis occurs, who decides? The United States, of course, answers the "realist." Yes, perhaps, if it is a question of a strictly military measure, involving the risk of hostility; even in this case the theoretical right of veto—the Alliance is supposed to act according to the principle of unanimity—is not without importance. Federal Germany or France could paralyze initiatives designed by Washington. With regard to diplomatic-strategic behavior when confronted with an attempt to blockade Berlin, the four great Western powers would have their word to say, would exercise their influence without one's being able to anticipate the opinion which would prevail or even to know after the fact what opinion would have been decisive: it is not unprecedented that the American leaders should secretly desire to be "held back" by their allies. If the latter satisfy their desire, if the British Prime Minister entreats the President not to run a risk, who will ever establish the division of responsibilities between them?

It is not possible, in such a matter, to formulate general and categorical propositions. The relationship between the United States and its allies is, in a sense, analogous to the relationship which existed between civil and military authority between 1914 and 1918. The primacy of the former is not theoretically jeopardized; the latter's stronger will often prevailed (Joffre prevailed over the government leaders). The United States, which has no legal authority over its partners, possesses means of force, but it cannot employ them without the consent and cooperation of its allies. Finally, the personalities of the heads of state or government will influence, on each occasion, the distribution of influence and responsibility. The United States, at the supreme moment, will retain the last word because it alone possesses the ultimate weapon. There are not many "supreme moments" in diplomacy: the Atlantic Alliance has not yet experienced a single one.

It goes without saying that the United States, and the United States alone, would be in a position to negotiate a tête-à-tête with the Soviet Union. The invitation which President Eisenhower sent to Mr. Khrushchev without consulting either General de Gaulle or Mr. Macmillan reminds us—as is obvious—that the United States retains the means to act on its own. But the conversation produced no result. In a summit conference the nay-sayer is in a position to prevent what his allies desire. An alliance among democratic nations is a Polish parliament in which the *liberum veto* functions (within certain limits).

Which benefits more from the Atlantic Pact, the European nations or the United States? France, Federal Germany, Great Britain, in isolation or in common, do not constitute a weight equivalent to that of the Soviet Union. By uniting with the United States they increase their capacity for opposing the Soviet Union and, potentially, influencing it. It is not the Atlantic Pact, it is their weakness which deprives them of their past independence. On its side, the United States has an advantage in an instrument of this kind: an advantage on the level of discussion or of propaganda insofar as the entire West becomes a bloc, the free world confronting the Soviet Union; an advantage on the level of action or the legal justification of action. On what would the presence of American troops in Europe be based without the mutual assistance treaty which provides its principle and its context? In other words, even discarding the military arguments which the evolution of technology could null and void at any moment, both European and American partners find it an advantage to form an alliance and organize into a community, the Europeans because they need the American guarantee and because the pact permits them to influence the Washington leaders, the United States because it needs European cooperation in order to deploy its forces and confirm its "commitment."[1]

The Atlantic Pact is more than a traditional alliance within the zone of the blocs. It is less than a traditional alliance outside that zone. The French government repeatedly insists on an extension of the pact to the entire world. General de Gaulle has given a new form to this claim by proposing a tripartite directorate responsible for the diplomatic conduct of the Atlantic Alliance throughout the world. Such a concept would tend to transform the Atlantic bloc, a bloc within a limited zone, into an "actor" on the world stage. The United States has never accepted such an interpretation of the pact, and the very ones who seem to demand it—the French—do not accept its implications. Collective action on the world stage would require a kind of diplomatic fusion which General de Gaulle, concerned with questions of absolute independence—"We depend on no one," "to bind myself to no one" —would be the first to reject. Yet, since Great Britain and France also desire to maintain their autonomy of action in Africa or in Asia, why should the United States regard itself obliged to take the advice of its European allies? The Atlantic Pact applies to a limited space.

An Atlantic directorate could function—supposing that the other partners of the pact consented—only if there was agreement concerning objectives and means among the members of the directorate. A directorate would not have sufficed to surmount the divergences between Washington, London and Paris following the nationalization of the Suez Canal (although such a directorate would probably have avoided the explosion of hostilities). The American leaders who, in 1955–60, evidently did not approve of French policy in Algeria, would not have convinced the leaders of the Fourth or those of the Fifth Republic. And the latter would not have yielded with good grace to an "Anglo-American majority." Since there is no agreement, the independence of the partners of the Atlantic Pact, outside the zone of confrontation of the blocs, is of mutual advantage.

Autonomous outside the zone of confrontation of the blocs, the partners of the Atlantic Pact remain equally autonomous in questions of internal action and of regional groups. This means that the struggle among parties is, in part, controlled by the rivalry of the super powers, by the influence

---

[1] In the sense given to this word in Chap. XIII.

which the "protector" and the "enemy" exert over public opinion. These phenomena necessarily derive from the system's bipolar structure, and the opposition between the ideologies of the two powers multiplies the effects of this bipolarity. But a people invulnerable to propaganda, situated outside the range of the Soviet army, would have nothing to fear from the American force. America's capacity to influence the course of the internal policy of her allies and of the neutral powers is in proportion to the homogeneity of the elites or of the nations. This influence is zero or virtually zero in the case of Switzerland. Where democratic governments are threatened by the Communist party or a leftist public opinion, the appeal to money, to propaganda or to American aid becomes inevitable.

Are the leaders who depend on American support obliged or gradually led to execute decisions made in Washington? The facts are more complex. Leaders who confess the weakness of their government and unpopularity of their regime often receive more support than the leaders who are permitted by the nation's homogeneity to resist both subversion and blackmail. The leaders of the Fourth Republic sometimes obtained, by invoking the dangers they faced, what the leaders of the Fifth would not obtain by parading their security. Further, since the European economy has been restored by the Marshall Plan, the American representatives are no longer concerned and are generally incapable of applying pressure, at any given time on the leaders of the allied nations.

As to the groups within the bloc, they have been favored, not paralyzed, by the United States. The latter does not consciously elaborate its relations with Europe in terms of domination or hegemony. On the economic level Europe's recovery has already diminished America's relative power. The federation of the Six powers would constitute virtually a first-class state, capable of competing with the two super powers economically, perhaps politically and, ultimately, even in military terms. Whether or not certain Americans have developed a liking for power, or Washington is attempting to retain leadership, the capacity to direct if not command has been eliminated. Empire—the monopoly of authority by means of the monopoly of military force —is neither the object of deliberate action nor the content of America's secret ambition. The American republic, following the Second World War, assumed responsibility, willy-nilly, for both vanquished powers and allies, all of which lacked military or economic resources. It has given this responsibility the character of a commitment due to the Soviet threat (whether real or illusory). It has formulated this commitment in the traditional language of alliances. It has hoped that its allies would soon acquire, by following its example, the means of doing without its help. Would the United States— the leaders, the citizens themselves—regret having to pull out of Europe, were the latter one day to become strong enough to defend itself? The support given to the Europe of the Six demands a categorical negative response, unless we presume an extreme cynicism. But perhaps the question is a futile one. Why should we or the Americans wonder if they would regret a power they are not about to lose? It is enough to say that the Atlantic Pact is not an empire in the traditional sense of the word, because military unification has not been developed into a political unity and because the possessors of force are more ashamed than proud of a monopoly they are not at all sure how to use.

2. The Soviet Bloc

Parallel analysis of the other bloc immediately reveals contrasts and similarities. The Soviet Union, after an initial hesitation, has been radically hostile to regional groupings within the European bloc. In 1947 Dimitrov and Tito[2] had envisaged a Balkan federation, with the approval—perhaps even at the suggestion—of Stalin. The two men passed for the most resolute, the most orthodox of Communists. The regional organization probably appeared useful to Moscow for reinforcing the Soviet hold over the nation whose subjugation was as yet imperfect. In January 1948 the project of federation was publicly condemned by Pravda and the two men responsible were, it appears, severely disciplined. During the Stalin period "bilateralism" was de rigueur. Treaties linked the Soviet Union to one or the other of the Eastern European states or two Eastern European states to each other. Treaties of friendship or mutual assistance followed the classic model. They specifically provided for common resistance against a rearmed Germany or against any state associating itself with German aggression. The only exception was East Germany, which signed with the other states of the bloc only treaties of friendship and sometimes of cultural cooperation (with Poland on August 1, 1952, with Rumania on October 9, 1950, with Bulgaria on May 5, 1952). As for the Soviet Union, it signed treaties of friendship and mutual assistance with all the states of Eastern Europe except for East Germany, treaties of cultural cooperation with none. There was no need for cultural cooperation with the Soviet Union, imposed upon all the states of Eastern Europe, to be confirmed by a diplomatic instrument.

The Warsaw Pact, signed on May 14, 1955, marks the shift from bilateral to multilateral technique. It provides for a common military organization under the command of a Soviet general. It gives a kind of legality to the presence of Soviet troops on foreign soil (although this legalization received its definitive juridical form only after the events of 1956[3]). Finally, for the first time, the German Democratic Republic figured in a mutual-assistance treaty on the same level as the other states of Eastern Europe. The Warsaw Pact imitates the North Atlantic Pact, but the Soviet Union, up till now, would not tolerate the equivalent of the Rome Treaty.

The formal similarity of the two pacts, creating two blocs, should not con-

[2] Cf. Z. K. Brzezinski, The Soviet Bloc, Cambridge, 1959, pp. 55–56, for the Balkan conflict of Dimitrov and Tito.
[3] Cf. Z. K Brzezinski, ibid., pp. 170–71.

ceal a second difference. The military policy of the Soviet bloc with regard to
the other bloc is determined in a sovereign way by the Soviet Union. There
is no general staff of the Warsaw Pact equivalent to the NATO general
staff. Against the West, the Soviet Union possesses not only the monopoly
of the thermonuclear system; it also possesses the quasi-monopoly of immediately utilizable conventional weapons. The threat which weighs upon
Western Europe is that created by some twenty-five motorized and mechanized divisions of the Red army stationed in Eastern Germany.

Not that the autonomy of the national armies of Eastern Europe has
been entirely eliminated. The role of the Hungarian army in October–
November 1956, and the role the Polish army was prepared to play, had the
Soviet divisions continued their march on Warsaw, proved that the states of
Eastern Europe, a few years ago, still existed as such in the souls of the
soldiers. If these armies, according to the Soviet plan, do not seem to have an
offensive function in case of a conflict with the other bloc, it is because their
loyalty is uncertain. The authority of the Big Brother is more rigorous because
the sincerity of consent—the consent of the populations above all—is more
dubious. In the West the Communist parties (especially their clandestine
apparatus) constitute known fifth columns. Behind the Iron Curtain an open
fifth column does not exist. Yet no one concludes from this that there are
no enemies on the spot.

Diplomacy with regard to the other bloc is determined by the Soviet
Union in almost as sovereign a way as strategy. In the United Nations, representatives of the Eastern European states faithfully follow the line laid
down by the Moscow leaders. Whether it is a question of establishing or re-
laxing the Berlin blockade, it does not seem that Stalin yesterday or Khrushchev tomorrow need take anyone's advice or listen to anyone's opinions. Yet
let us not go too far! It is impossible to leave the administrative apparatus
and the juridical appearance of sovereignty to states without the leaders of
these states being tempted to act and sometimes being capable of doing so. It
is obvious that the leaders of the German Democratic Republic would not
take the *initiative* of interrupting communications between Western Germany
and West Berlin or even of firing on Allied tanks or planes trying to force
the blockade. But the satellite-princes[4] can apply their instructions in one
sense or another and thereby influence the course of a crisis.

Further, the Soviet bloc is *ideocratic*. It claims to be inspired by a common
ideology and its leaders seek an essential accord deriving from the nature of
the regime that is based on, and constructed according to, a sacred doctrine.
Now, policy—diplomacy or strategy—with regard to the other bloc should

---

[4] During the war Father Gaston Fessard suggested the concept of slave-prince to
designate the Vichy government, administrator of French affairs but a prisoner of the
Germans. The governments of Eastern Europe are not slaves, but they are satellites,
whether voluntary or not.

logically be deduced from doctrine. So long as the true interpretation of the doctrine, at a given moment, was decreed by the Soviet Union alone, or even by one man alone, the ideocratic character of the Soviet regimes and bloc reinforced the monopoly of the decisions Moscow had reserved as its own. But the moment the interpretation of the doctrine constitutes the object of public debate, because divergent interpretations occur within the Soviet Union or within the bloc, the satellites recover a certain capacity for autonomous action by the simple fact that they are liberated from the discipline of language to which Stalin had subjected them. We are unable to say to what degree Khrushchev and his colleagues were "impressed" by the "extremist"[5] or "moderate"[6] language adopted by the satellite elites of Tirana, Warsaw or Bucharest. We are not certain to what divergences of interest or of method the theological controversies correspond. All those entitled to take part in the theological controversies become interlocutors in a dialogue of which the "line" of the bloc is the conclusion. Yet the decisions in each circumstance are related to the strategy of the moment, hence to the doctrinal line which the bloc, by the intermediary of its leader or leaders, has established.

For the nations of Eastern Europe, the problems of diplomacy and strategy with regard to external regions scarcely come up. It is through their colonial possessions that the nations of Western Europe have a diplomacy distinct from that of the bloc. Nonetheless, Gomulka's Poland, while maintaining total solidarity with the Soviet Union in the United Nations and in (written or spoken) words, has retained a certain margin of maneuver with regard to cultural and economic relations with the other bloc. It receives aid from the United States and permits its students, professors and writers to travel and study in the West.

Finally, the decisive question, with regard to the states of Eastern Europe, is that of the freedom they are allowed in the application of the doctrine and the conduct of everyday affairs. Between 1945 and 1956 four phases appear quite distinctly in this regard. The first, from the arrival of the Soviet troops to the condemnation of Yugoslavia in 1948, involves the double distinction between the popular democracies and the Soviet Union (already a socialist state), and between the various popular democracies, each adapting the universal truth to local circumstances. During this first phase Tito's Yugoslavia is situated at the extreme left. It severely criticizes the non-violence of the Western (Italian and French) parties, the repugnance of certain Eastern parties to commit themselves utterly to the construction of socialism, and the insistence of these same parties on underlining the diversity of the national situation. During this period, the Yugoslav party, ready to take risks to attain its external objectives (Trieste), confident, because of the role it

[5] Individualist or sectarian in case of condemnation.
[6] Opportunist in case of condemnation.

played during the war, of popular support, does not acknowledge a lasting cooling-off of its relations with the Big Brother or a dalliance with the equivocal zone of popular democracy.

The second phase is that of the integral Stalinization between 1948 and 1953, symbolized by the spectacular trials against Rajk, Kostov and Slanski. Under the double pressure of the Yugoslav schism and the cold war, a double process of subjugation occurs. The Communist parties in each country finish liquidating the vestiges of pluralist democracy and, simultaneously, eliminate the Communist leaders suspected or likely to be suspected of nationalist deviation (or even likely to symbolize nationalist deviation). Entirely in control of the government, the Communist parties are entirely subject to Moscow; the Polish army is under the orders of a Soviet marshal, police systems are infiltrated and supervised by the Soviet secret police, the ambassador of the Soviet Union supervises, from day to day, the conduct of affairs while the U.S.S.R. Bolshevik party exercises a doctrinal and fanatical authority over the satellite parties. Everything occurs as if the satellite-princes were completing both their tyranny and their servitude.[7]

The third phase extends from Stalin's death to the Polish and Hungarian rebellions. The man who ruled by terror but to whom the satellite chiefs were linked by a certain kind of fidelity is no more. The successors agree, while struggling for power, to restore a certain flexibility to the regime, within and without. The discipline of language, which attained, on the eve of Stalin's death, a kind of grotesque and terrifying perfection, is officially broken. In the Twentieth Party Congress, the comrades who have become his heirs reveal the backstage manipulations, the pointless cruelties of the man they had feared and flattered. The trials of the thirties were denounced, as were, implicitly, the trials of the postwar years. Disputes between factions in the Soviet Union are projected into analogous quarrels within the people's democracies. The crisscrossing of rivalries among the leaders of the Soviet Union on the one hand, among the leaders of the national party on the other, produces the incoherences (Nagy's return, then his second disgrace) which contributed to the Hungarian explosion of 1956.

The last phase, which is still in effect at the present writing, does not mark a return to Stalinism but an effort to maintain both the cohesion of the bloc and certain benefits of the "thaw." The Moscow leaders, none of whom inspires in his followers or in his comrades the same respect and horror that Stalin inspired, are unwilling to renounce either the doctrinal homogeneity of the socialist camp or the primacy of the Soviet Union. But these two principles involve nuances of interpretation and application.

The dogmas that socialism implies a single party, that the Communist party is the representative of the working class, are not subject to discussion.

---

[7] The trials were merely a spectacular episode of the purges practiced by all the Communist parties (Brzezinski, *op. cit.*, p. 97).

But, in the legitimate margin of adaptation to circumstances, in the urgency of agrarian collectivization, in the rate of growth, in the percentage of investments, in the distribution of investments between heavy industry and light industry, there is room for political-theological controversy, each of the interlocutors justifying his position by reference to the sacred text. Partisans of agrarian collectivization, of a higher rate of growth, of the primacy of heavy industry are regarded as the "tough guys" and are often called the "left." But in Poland in 1957 the Natolin group—that is, the nostalgic survivors of Stalinism—were classified as the right. Further, a certain leader is both "tough" with regard to political economy (heavy industry) and relatively liberal with regard to culture; Mr. Khrushchev denounced Mr. Malenkov for his economic policy without renouncing the "thaw." Lastly, there is no rigorous correspondence between Big Brother and little brother among the factions. Mr. Khrushchev ultimately supported in Poland a Gomulka whose line he would not have tolerated (with regard to agriculture, for instance) in the Soviet Union or in any other state of Eastern Europe.

The relaxation of Stalinist centralization corresponds to several intentions on the part of the Moscow leaders, and also to a historical quasi-necessity that is both political and psychological. None of the heirs could assume Stalin's role because none possessed the charisma conferred upon despots by deeds and crimes, bloodshed, and lofty monuments of stone, concrete and steel. The Kremlin's absolute power had a meaning only as a result of the divinity of the Pope-Emperor. It was irrational in the long run because it was based on a permanent constraint upon human nature. And once the satellite elites were solidly established, once the representatives of the past were eliminated, the governments of the Eastern states could not help but feel the desire to exercise for themselves the power accorded them by the juridical formula of national independence and the socialist principle of the equality of states. Nowadays, unless it is obsessed by power for power's sake, in other words unless it seeks the servitude of others in order to enjoy its own omnipotence, the Soviet elite has no constraining reason to intervene in the conduct of daily affairs or in the rivalries among individuals within the satellite states (providing these individuals are equally devoted to the common interest of the bloc).

The autonomy left to the satellite elites eventually attenuates the unpopularity of the regime and reinforces its national character. Mr. Gomulka has more authority over the Poles than Mr. Cyrankiewicz had during the years when the present Secretary-General of the party was in prison. The relaxation of relations between the Big Brother and his protégés conforms to the properly understood interest of the latter as well as of the former. Once the leader of the bloc does not doubt the loyalty of the satellite-princes, he must logically grant them all that contributes to their popularity among nations more resigned than converted to communism. The Gomulka regime would be the best solution both for the Soviet Union and for the Polish people, but it may also be so for the United States as well. It stabilizes the Polish-Soviet relations and it leaves the future open. Poland does not become a province of the Soviet Empire.

Mr. Khrushchev's method is, however, not without risks. In the West, the United States has no need to impose an ideological discipline. As long as the leaders of the allied nations are neither Communist nor neutralist, the Atlantic bloc is maintained, since it involves nothing more than the military community and the diplomatic coordination resulting from it with regard to the Eastern bloc. Behind the Iron Curtain the Soviet leaders cannot renounce a certain ideological discipline without compromising or reforming their own regime. The Communist party derives its legitimacy from its doctrine: the primacy that it claims entitles it to interpret that doctrine. The divergences of national interpretation must keep within rather narrow limits. What are these limits? Probably no one can answer such a question with any certainty. What is, in the long run, the objective of the Communists? What is their image of a future and ultimate world? What would be the structure of international relations if there were no capitalist states? Such questions are not idle because on the answer to them depends the *goal* actually sought by the Communist leaders. The Soviet Empire would not be, like Hitler's, based on the supremacy of a master race and on the extermination or servitude of inferior peoples. The Soviet Union, a multinational empire, extends over a vast space which it has no need to enlarge further. Beyond the conflict between the two blocs, would all states wither away simultaneously or would they be consolidated into a single state? Would the socialist regimes increasingly resemble each other or would nations impress upon regimes the increasingly accentuated stamp of their original culture?

Meanwhile, the concern of the Kremlin during the present phase—that of the conflict between the two blocs—must be less remote, more pressing. The unity of action of the Soviet bloc in Europe can be *imposed* in case of need (the Hungarian repression dealt a blow to Moscow's humanitarian propaganda; it gave an unprecedented force to the propaganda of terror; henceforth it was understood that the satellites would be, if necessary, subjugated by force). Unity of action between the Soviet Union and China must be *negotiated* without even implicit recourse to military threat. Already before the open break of 1962 it was not impossible to discern some objects of conflict: for instance, should the Soviet bloc distribute its aid to all Afro-Asiatic states alike, provided they act *objectively* against the West, or must it reserve its favors, at least in priority, for leftist regimes which are rallying to popular democracy? Should it or should it not take into account the fact that President Nasser persecutes or liquidates Communists? Is or is not an international *détente* to the interest of the Soviet bloc? Should it emphasize the possibility of peaceful coexistence or the inevitability of war? But whatever the stakes, and even if the Chinese and Soviets resolve or camouflage their oppositions, together they restore, within the Soviet universe, a certain freedom of political-theological controversy, a freedom which was passionately utilized in Lenin's time but was gradually smothered under Stalin's regime, and which the latter's successors have been gradually obliged to tolerate while disputing his legacy, and which the Chinese, by their mere existence, are in the process of imposing upon the Soviet bloc. The juxtaposition of a Russo-Soviet bloc in Europe and of three Communist regimes in Asia (China, North Korea, North Vietnam), one in the world's most populated states, modifies relations within the European bloc. In words at least, East Germans and Albanians can adopt the so-called Chinese language whereas the Czechs stick close to the formulas of the Kremlin leaders, and the Poles shift away from Russian orthodoxy, but in a direction opposed to that of the Chinese.

We are not in a position to know with any precision how the negotiations between the Communist great powers take place, how decisions are made—by one or the other, or by both—nor the influence which the theological controversies exert on the conduct of strategy. The fact remains that the autonomy granted to the satellite-princes has introduced a diversity into the style and even into the content of socialist construction, just as the existence of a second Communist great power restores a certain freedom of ideological discussion to all the states of the bloc. Such a freedom, which the *grand frère* in the West would consider with indifference, the Eastern *grand frère* cannot observe without anxiety, because the Kremlin is no longer (or is not yet) accustomed to it and because it takes ideas seriously.[8]

3. *Economic Organization*

The blocs have been created by the collapse of the European states, by the encounter, in the center of the old world, of the two "liberating" armies. They are political in origin and military rather than political in content. But our society is industrial; and the ideology in whose name the Soviet Union constructed the regimes imitating its own is historic-economic. It announces an irresistible and foreseeable movement of humanity toward an economic regime, called socialist at first, Communist later on. The states in each of the blocs all have economic regimes appropriate to the dominant ideology on each side, the margin of variation being evidently larger in the West than in the East, although since 1953 the states of Eastern Europe increasingly differ from each other, even in economic procedure, which is theoretically subject to the exigencies of orthodoxy.

The formation of the blocs has had as its chief result, in the economic order, the breakdown of the unity of the world market (the expression is the one used by Communist authors). In the years following the end of the war, commercial relations of the satellite states were modified as a result of the international situation. To a degree, the changes were implied by the

[8] Or what it calls ideas.

regime itself: it is difficult to establish a planned economy without simultaneously making a perspective evaluation of exports, and this planning is uncertain when the purchasers belong to countries of a free economy, in other words are firms which, in the last analysis, depend on consumers. But the reorientation of foreign trade[9] also expressed a Soviet desire. The socialist states were to organize an international market according to the law of planned economy, as they were to construct an internal economy according to the Soviet norm.

Theoretically we conceive two models of international socialist markets. Either priority would be given to a supranational plan of which the national plans would be the chapters, just as the regional plans are the chapters of the national plan. Or else the national plans are established first, bilateral accords concluded between the governments of the bloc, and the international market constituted in a network of bilateral agreements. The first model is preferable on paper, but it is inapplicable in any strict way. The second model involves intrinsic defects which Stalinism exaggerated to an insane degree.

Priority being granted to the national plans, the latter could be, in each case, adapted to the national circumstances. But, as a matter of fact, the tendency of the years 1948-53 was to multiply Soviet Unions on a reduced scale, each emphasizing heavy industry, each having its own steel production and its metallurgical and mechanical enterprises. Hungary was the symbol of this folly: metallurgy was sustained by imported coal and iron; the cost of these imports was itself higher than the external purchasing price of the finished or semi-finished products which emerged from the Hungarian factories.

Although the priority of the national plans has not been abandoned, and although these plans are still marked by the concept of "miniature Soviet Unions," the multiplication of bilateral agreements and the work accomplished by the COMECON (created in imitation of the Marshall Plan and the Organization for European Economic Cooperation but long inactive) have increased the division of labor within the Soviet bloc. All the Eastern European states have produced a heavy industry—industry of means of production, metallurgy, chemistry, tool manufacturing—that is relatively important in relation to their total production. European organization of economic cooperation, in the East, has managed, in the course of these last years, to impose a certain specialization upon these industries. *All* of them no longer manufacture *all* types of machines.

This specialization was also required by the common or coordinated in-

[9] In 1951 the share of the Soviet bloc in the foreign trade of the peoples' democracies (imports and exports) rose to 92 per cent for Bulgaira (12 per cent before the war), 67 per cent for Hungary (13 per cent), 58 per cent for Poland (7 per cent), 79 per cent for Rumania (18 per cent), 60 per cent for Czechoslovakia (11 per cent).

fluence of the Soviet bloc on the extra-European fields of operation. Loans or gifts henceforth constitute one of the cards in the Soviet hand with regard to underdeveloped nations. Eastern Germany, Czechoslovakia and even Poland are henceforth not negligible exporters of the means of production. Each of these nations has new or traditional relations with certain nations, certain zones of the globe. All participate in the commercial offensive, in political objectives which tend to compete with the Western bloc for the markets of the rest of the world.

This inter-state economic organization, within a bloc, does not proceed without negotiations and controversies. We know that the prices of the products exchanged by the socialist states were objects of dispute. Poland obtained retroactively, in 1956, an increase in the price of coal which it had sold to the Soviet Union. Other arguments seem to be continuing even while the socialists claim to abide by world prices. Do not the latter favor certain socialist countries at the expense of certain others?

The redistribution of labor among nations within the bloc does not proceed without difficulties either. Not one of them wishes to sacrifice any of its so-called essential manufactures. None consents to depend too narrowly on another, although all depend, for their supply of raw materials, on the Soviet Union. Indeed it seems that, the context being established by the Soviet Union, the satellite states, among themselves and with the Big Brother, maintain relations subject to the law of *negotiations*. The representatives of these states meet, discuss and seek to convince each other. They do not jeopardize their community—the bloc constituted by the economies of the same regime, independent of the capitalist world market—but each seeks to assure himself of advantages by the traditional interplay of claims and concessions. Poland has even succeeded, since 1956, in obtaining credit both from the Soviet Union and from the United States, the ambiguous character of Mr. Gomulka's regime affording an additional capacity for negotiations *with regard to either of the two super powers*: a somewhat liberalized communism appears to both super powers preferable to a regression, perhaps a bloody one, to Stalinism.

Between the Soviet Union and the satellite states, economic relations have evolved in two opposite directions. Between 1945 and 1953 Soviet control was reinforced and the exploitation of the satellites, even of those which could not be considered as ex-enemies, increased. Planned economy on the bloc level, division of labor among the partners remained projects or themes of propaganda. Since 1953 the Soviet Union has relaxed its control, granted a margin of maneuver to national policies, tolerated in Poland the slowness of agrarian collectivization, encourgaed the COMECON enterprises, shifted from exploitation (mixed corporations with Soviet predominance, demands for reparations, underevaluation of merchandise delivered by satellites) to aid (long-term loans). In the East as in the West the *grand frère* has come to the aid of the satellite-princes endangered by popular discontent. To a degree, the Soviet Union has combated revisionism by rubles, just as the United States has combated communism and neutralism by dollars.

In the West the first phase has been the opposite of the first phase in the East. The United States helped the European nations to recovery and in 1948 established the Marshall Plan, which was meant to accelerate reconstruction and also to prevent Communist expansion. The American conception was at this time exactly the opposite of the Soviet one. The Marshall Plan incited the European nations to organize themselves into a group, it even encouraged this group, of which the OEEC was the expression, to practice "commercial discrimination" with regard to American merchandise. The European nations granted each other the advantages which they did not grant to the *grand frère*, even as adverse propaganda accused the latter of imperialism and neo-colonialism. To fill the "dollar gap," the United States obliged its allies to cooperate and they were supplied a valid interpreter in the European community. In the same period, from 1948 to 1953, Stalin allowed nothing but bilateral relations with each of his satellites, taken individually.

The United States reasoned in economic terms: the restoration of Europe is impossible if the nations again commit the fault of the thirties and return to the practices of national economies, the administrative management of foreign trade, each trying to sell as much and to buy as little as possible. *Each satellite state was to resemble, economically, a microscopic Soviet Union, while the whole of Europe was to model itself on the United States.* America's goal was to make its own aid unnecessary, thus restoring to the nations of Europe their lost independence (economic, not military); the Soviet policy tended to make definitive the economic dependence of the satellites, whose supply of raw materials could be assured only by the Soviet Union.

The American policy has been a success, and a success which has probably exceeded its initiators' hopes. The proof of this success is double: in the course of the fifties Europe's rate of growth has been higher than that of the United States; in particular, Continental Europe has advanced faster than the Anglo-Saxon world, Great Britain and the United States. The Continent is experiencing the mass-production phase of durable consumer goods, the excitement of the automobile, the refrigerator, the television set. Even more striking is the proof afforded by the accumulation of gold and dollars in Western Germany and Italy. The deficit has crossed the Atlantic: dollars are no longer rare, they are too abundant. In ten years the United States lost over six billion dollars in gold. The result of the Marshall Plan and the American policy has been the reconstitution of a world market, even as the result of the Soviet policy has been the constitution of a socialist world market. But the latter links the states to their Big Brother, the former granted an increasing autonomy with regard to the dominant economy.

Economic relations among the Western states have provoked multiple and incessant negotiations. Commercial diplomacy has become an almost isolated universe of specialized officials, the ministers of state following only from a distance arguments which are conducted in a language virtually incomprehensible to the uninitiated.

During the first phase, that of the Marshall Plan, negotiations between Europeans had as their principal object the distribution of dollars and the gradual elaboration of the code of free exchange under the European Payments Union. The governments re-created, through an inter-state organization, a system of multilateral payments, even as they dismantled the administrative management of imports. Simultaneously, the missions of the Marshall Plan, in each nation, encouraged the governments to combat inflation, liberalize exchanges, increase investments. Such negotiations belonged to a traditional type. Each of the negotiators sought to win the favors of the *grand frère* or of certain of his partners. Each emphasized alternately his weaknesses and his merits, the strength of his enemies and the services he had rendered to the common cause. Each sought to convince his interlocutors, none could constrain either his small brothers or his *grand frère*. The only paradox of these negotiations was that since the distribution of aid was, in theory, proportional to need, a reward ran the risk of being granted to a poor administration, the needs of currency inevitably increasing with inflationist pressure.

An additional complication was introduced by the French proposal, in the spring of 1950, of a "European Coal and Steel Community." Henceforth negotiations with a view to supranational organizations of a specific character were combined with negotiations as to the modes of commercial exchanges and international payments. The partners of the European Community of the Six have formed relations of a particular type. The High Authority holds certain powers that are supranational on paper, but it is composed of men who have not renounced their nationality of origin and who are sensitive both to the interests of their nation of origin and to those of the supranational institution. Further, the latter is subject to the influence which the national governments exert upon it from within or from without.

The Rome Treaty presented additional dimensions. The European nations not belonging to the Six were, to different degrees, hostile to the Common Market which, by definition, involves discrimination between participants and non-participants. Both attempted to assure the favors of the *grand frère* while the non-participants tried, more or less discreetly, to tempt one or another of the participants whose loyalty to the Common Market was known to be fragile.

What were the features characteristic of economic diplomacy, within the Atlantic bloc, during the fifties? Military force scarcely influences the capacity of a state to impose its will on others in negotiations whose stake is strictly economic. The states no longer respond to the seizure of their nationals' property, on the territory of a foreign state, by sending warships: the latter would be repulsed by the fire of coastal batteries, and it would be necessary to launch an expedition. Between allied nations this eventuality is out of the question. No doubt the state powerful in military terms ordinarily possesses considerable resources whose size must normally affect the course of all negotiations. But in these matters, too, the relation between force and power is more subtle than a shortsighted realism imagines.

Of course, when a state derives the greatest part of the currency necessary to finance its imports from the sale of *one* product (tin, cotton or coffee), it depends on its principal customer more than the latter depends on it. But the negotiations we are analyzing occurred between industrialized nations, with a diversified economy. None depended on a single or even a chief customer, none was obliged by a deficit to solicit a loan from the *grand frère*. Negotiations concerned tariff concessions, establishment of an international system of payments and the formation of regional groupings. Negotiations over the lowering of tariffs are, in essence, bargainings in which the great power has a broader margin of maneuver because concessions equivalent to those of the small power have a lesser significance for it. But thereby, the small power can reach an advantageous position because advantages considerable for itself are almost meaningless for a nation twenty times more populous.

The small power, it is true, is not in a position to respond by reprisals to a measure, which it regards as unjust, taken by a great power or by a community of medium ones. The closing of the Swiss capital market to the Six provoked more smiles than anxieties. When the President of the United States attempts to limit the entry of Swiss watches by recourse to the so-called "escape clause," Switzerland has no other weapon than protest, the reminder of the liberal principles which the West's *grand frère* claims to honor. Moral weapons are not always without effect.

The diplomatic battle, of which the Rome Treaty was the origin and France and England the two chief protagonists, is intermediate between the two kinds of relations—economic and political—which we are distinguishing within the blocs. The Six had elaborated a treaty which foresaw, in some fifteen years, the formation of a Common Market, with a common foreign tariff and a harmonization of laws. The free circulation of goods, capital and persons—the ultimate result of the enterprise—was subordinate to the respect for common laws, the establishment of common institutions. Certain architects of European unity did not conceal the fact that the Common Market itself was a means more than an end—a means to economic integration, itself the means to a political federation.

Great Britain and some small nations of Europe (Sweden, Norway, Denmark, Switzerland, Austria, Portugal) were unsympathetic to the economic means, if not the political objective of the enterprise. The latter, seen from London, involved the following disadvantages: in the first phase it established, according to international law,[10] a tariff discrimination: at the end

[10] The text of GATT (the General Agreement on Tariffs and Trade).

of the transitional period, German merchandise would enter France free while English merchandise would pay rates provided for by the common foreign tariff. This discrimination, slight in the course of the first years, would immediately exert an influence, consumers and importers adapting themselves to the discrimination even before the latter was substantial enough to create a difference in prices effective in itself.

In the second place the continental nations have been those whose rate of growth has been highest during the fifties. Competition would be intensified by the opening of frontiers, and perhaps the progress of continental economies would thereby receive additional encouragement. Would not British industry, protected by a low tariff or none for raw materials and by a high tariff for manufactured products and production goods, be outpaced in a productivity race?

In any case, the Six would constitute an economic unit of the first order, the greatest world importer of raw materials, in the process of becoming the prime exporter of manufactured products. If they negotiated together, in the manner of a single state, their weight would soon be, on the level of economic diplomacy, incomparably superior to that of Great Britain and at least equal to that of the Commonwealth as a whole.

Among the Six, Germany possesses the most developed, the most advanced industry, and would inevitably be the strongest, the most dynamic partner. Would it not, tomorrow, have a preponderant influence over the organs and functioning of the European community? If the latter were to be transformed into a federation, would the way not be open to a German preponderance in Western Europe? This peaceful preponderance would not, of course, resemble the hegemony which the Kaiser's Germany would have exercised, or the empire which Hitler had constructed: nonetheless it awakened memories and resentments.

The hostility to the Common Market of some small nations of Europe was readily explicable. Neither the neutral nations (Sweden, Switzerland, Austria) nor the nations politically committed but traditionally oriented toward the oceanic world sought to become full-fledged members of an essentially continental structure whose political implications might seem, to Moscow, incompatible with neutrality. Now Switzerland and Austria are continental nations which trade chiefly with the Six. Between the *tariff discrimination* which non-participation inflicted upon them and the *consent to the demands of integration*, the inevitable consequence of participation, they refused to choose, since either term of the alternative seemed scarcely less disagreeable than the other.

Incontestably, European unification in the form of the Common Market and in the context of the Six powers involved, at the outset, divisions among those who cooperated within the OEEC, in the shadow of the Marshall Plan. "On the pretext of uniting, you divide," said the British with bitterness and irony. "How unite," answered the Six powers, "without separating those who have determined to commit themselves from those satisfied with the status quo and the various modes of intergovernmental cooperation?"

Great Britain and the small nations of Europe were legitimately hostile to the Common Market. France was legitimately hostile to the project of the European Free Trade Area. Within the latter, manufactured products would have benefited from the same freedom of circulation as within the Common Market, but the members of this area would have been held neither to the establishment of a common foreign tariff, nor to the integration of economies (or harmonization of codes), nor to a common agricultural policy, nor to some common laws.

Of course, negotiations were possible which would have involved the exchange of concessions. Great Britain's initial project was a point of departure, it represented the ideal formula for London, but Her Majesty's government would have consented to several steps in the direction of the French proposals if Paris had, on its side, envisaged subscribing to the principle of an area of free exchange.

Now, Paris did not[11] and could not accept this principle, for two chief reasons. The French industrialists, though they did not envisage the rivalry within the Common Market without apprehension, wanted to make the experiment. On the other hand, they feared and refused its immediate extension. Rivalry within the context of the Six represented a calculable risk, a limited uncertainty: the free trade area appeared to them charged with unforeseeable dangers. As for the French government, it had another, still more pressing reason for opposing the simultaneous establishment of the two organizations. In case a free trade area was constituted *at the same time* as the Common Market, it was the area that would become the major reality, demanding the concentrated efforts of the best and most ambitious leaders. The economic integration—a common agricultural policy, harmonization of codes —which the Six had already had so much difficulty in achieving, would be paralyzed and gradually abandoned. To consent to a free trade area at the very moment when the Common Market was going into operation would ultimately reduce European unification to a free trade area for manufactured products, develop intergovernmental cooperation of OEEC in the direction of the free trade area, discriminatory with regard to the rest of the world, without political objective.

It was certainly a question of an authentic conflict of interests among allies. The Six on one side, Great Britain and the small nations of the Continent[12] on the other, continued to be united by the Atlantic Alliance: for both sides, the Soviet enemy remained the supreme threat, NATO the expression of their solidarity and the American deterrent their common protection. But, according to the political-economic groupings among the little brothers, the

[11]Although at the beginning of negotiations it had subscribed to the principle.
[12] Neutral countries excepted, of course.

position of each of them would be more or less advantageous, and the relation of forces within the bloc more or less favorable to Great Britain or to the Continent.

Having summarized the conditions of the controversy, we now ask: what was the course of diplomatic debate? It involved two chief elements: negotiations proper on one side, and on the other the efforts to convince public opinion among the partners, of the adversaries and of the *grand frère*. Efforts of persuasion accompanied the course of negotiations. The French efforts aimed above all at the *grand frère* and the partners; the British efforts, at the *grand frère* and, among France's partners, Germany and Holland, both with a strong party which preferred the free trade area to the Common Market.

Negotiations and persuasions presented certain similarities: on both sides the interlocutors (negotiators and propagandists) had to *debate*. They addressed themselves not to ignorant crowds but to officials or to competent politicians. They were obliged to advance meaningful arguments, to answer valid objections. The French representatives, even if they had known from the beginning that their final response would be negative, could not say *no* immediately without upsetting their partners among the Six and perhaps the *grand frère*, for the British thesis was based on a proposition that was incontestable as such. The Common Market *divided* the Europe of the OEEC into two groups. The French refusal was acceptable to Washington, to Bonn, and to the Hague only after proof that the free trade area was incompatible with the Common Market.

The British effort of persuasion utilized three chief arguments: with regard to the United States, the London spokesmen denounced the tariff discrimination, the pejorative term which is applied to advantages accorded to one nation or another contrary to the most-favored-nation clause and by which an attempt is made to provoke hostile feelings with regard to tariff differentiation, inseparable by definition from any free trade area or any Common Market. With regard to the United States again, they evoked the ruin of European unification, of which the Marshall Plan had been the opportunity and the OEEC the instrument. With regard to the "liberals" of Germany and Holland, they underlined the irrationality, for nations whose trade is worldwide, of binding themselves to a traditionally protectionist country such as France. (In a round-about manner, whispered propaganda suggested to the French the folly of a close link with the Federal Republic, yesterday an enemy, tomorrow hegemonic.)

The French effort of persuasion with regard to the United States was similar and opposed. To the argument of discrimination, the reply was easy: the free trade area was no less discriminatory than the Common Market with regard to American merchandise. It permitted thirteen nations the same discrimination with regard to American merchandise which the British blamed on the Six. Every commercial grouping is created in terms of discrimination with regard to the outside world. For the United States, a zone encompassing all of Europe is more embarrassing, *on the economic level,* than a Common Market limited to the Six. To the argument of the division of Europe, the Six replied with the argument of the unification of Continental Europe. How could the United States, after having supported the European army with all its forces, contradict itself by withdrawing its support of the Common Market which aims at the same goal by other means? With regard to the partners, and in particular to the Germans, the French propagandists pointed out that Germany would never be anything but a brilliant second (or third) in a worldwide economy dominated by the Anglo-Americans, not divided into regional groups. On the other hand, by means of the Six the Germans would recover access to a major world policy. The Common Market would be capable, by the volume of its trade and the surpluses of its external accounts, to intervene, as an independent subject, in the developing markets of Africa, Asia and South America. Temporarily and on the military level the Six would be a simple partner in the Atlantic bloc. On the economic level they would be capable of holding their own with the United States. They would appear in any case as a subject, to the same degree and with the same dignity as the United States.

The conversations continued over some eighteen months. The experts discovered the difficulties, one after the other: certificates of origin, made necessary by the differences of external tariffs, relations between Great Britain and the Commonwealth, agricultural policy, common institutions, harmonization of codes, tariff sovereignty (would each nation retain the right of modifying external tariffs without having to solicit its partners' approval?). But strictly speaking, the conversations never assumed the character of true negotiations, with bargaining and exchanges of concessions. The French tactic, consciously or not, tended to emphasize the impossibility of the area concept without assuming responsibility for the break. By the end of 1958 the British themselves took the initiative of the break: they had succeeded neither in reducing France's partners nor in rallying the United States to their proposals.

What is the nature of such a diplomatic battle? Manifestly, it resembles a conflict of internal policy more than a dispute between sovereign states. By the fact of being allied for better or worse, the adversaries were deprived of the supreme recourse. The British could not forbid the Six to constitute a Common Market conforming to the international law of the GATT. They had to convince the American leaders that the Common Market was contrary to the true interests of Europe and the United States. They had to persuade either public opinion or the governments of Holland and Germany that the Common Market would be dominated by French protectionism; or French public opinion that the Common Market would lead to German hegemony. Unable to convince the former or to persuade the latter, the British had to accept the fact of the Common Market, that is, the separation between the Six and the other nations, and perhaps seek another means of organizing the unity of Continental Europe. The formation of the small free trade area indicated one way,[13] the pure and simple adherence of Great Britain to the Common Market would mark another.[14]

The pattern we have just suggested is not radically different from that of the conflicts among multiple parties, each of the two principal parties being unable to prevail unless it rallies the neutral parties or seduces the partners of the rival party. The exact equivalent of the configuration we have analyzed is perhaps not easily found within states. The stake and the final result of the battle of the Common Market was the separation or non-separation of the Six and the non-Six. The final result of a battle among political parties is always, by definition, a governmental coalition, a majority decision, unless there is a breakdown of constitutional procedure. The parties must live together, whereas, in a sense, the Six demanded the right to divorce.

The resemblance is still closer with regard to methods and style: the interlocutors in these diplomatic conversations were, like political parties, engaged in a dialogue, both intellectual debate and a test of skill, conducted according to unwritten rules imposed by the circumstances. None was in a position to employ military force; none could employ the threat of a commercial war: such threats were resented by public opinion because the reprisals would not be in accord with the spirit of the fundamental alliance among the adversaries and because no violation of the GATT charter by the Six would have justified it. The foils had to remain buttoned. The fencers were debaters, the winners more skillful and more determined. If Minister Erhard's side had prevailed over Chancellor Adenauer's, if the Six had not managed to elaborate a common agricultural policy, if the American administration had ceased to support the Six, the battle would have changed its nature, and fortune would have changed camps.

4. Intra-Bloc Conflicts

Political battles among the partners of the Atlantic bloc fall into four categories: a conflict between partners who are also ex-enemies (the stake being a territory, the Saar); a conflict between partners over the organization of the bloc of interest to an ex-enemy (rearmament of the Federal Republic); a conflict between partners over measures relating to the initiative of the other bloc; a conflict over regions outside the bloc, in which the partners do not follow a joint policy. The word conflict may not always be the mot juste: sometimes it is only a question of differing opinions concerning the best

---

[13] It is essentially a means of exerting pressure on France's partners, especially upon a Germany threatened with commercial discrimination in the Scandinavian markets.
[14] The British government tried to join the Common Market in 1962. After long drawn-out negotiations, similar to the free trade area negotiations, General de Gaulle in his famous press conference of January 1963 decided to put an end to the discussions. This time the initiative for the break came from France.

solution, comparable to divergences between the various administrations or parties in one and the same country.

I shall leave aside conflicts of the third type, which derive as much from diplomacy between the blocs as from diplomacy within the blocs. For the three other types, without proceeding to a detailed analysis, I shall attempt to discuss the nature, rules and modes of the peaceful battle.

The conflict over the Saar after the Second World War was, so to speak, a repeat performance. The Versailles Treaty had assigned France to administer the Saar and to exploit its mines in compensation for the destruction caused by the Germans in the mines of the north. After fifteen years a plebiscite would decide the fate of this territory rich in coal and industrial resources.

After the Second World War, while an extreme coal shortage prevailed, French negotiators demanded and obtained[15] the provisional separation of the Saar. The material condition of the population during the first years after the German capitulation was noticeably better than that of their compatriots in the Federal Republic. At the same time the French administration found a way to introduce a democratic form of government: the parties entered into competition according to the Western rules, with the reservation that the establishment of a state, that is, the Saar's autonomy, was not in question.

From the outset, the precariousness of the enterprise was evident. The dominant ideology of the Western world did not permit France to annex the Saar or to impose an authoritarian regime. Not only was the government to be composed of Saarlanders, but the latter were to be free to debate every issue except rejoining West Germany. As long as the contrast between victors and vanquished, between the poverty of occupied Germany and the relative comfort of the oppressed Saarlanders was marked, the combined regime of democracy and proconsulate was maintained without too much difficulty. Matters altered as soon as the "German miracle" became a fact, and France and the Federal Republic, in the course of reconciliation, experienced the same desire to liquidate this dispute.

Perhaps the Saarlanders would have approved of a European status if the latter had been linked to the European Defense Community. It is likely, though, that they would have voted in favor of a return to Germany the day such a choice was explicitly offered them. A population living on the frontier, conscious of its nationality, can scarcely, in ordinary circumstances, fail to declare itself in favor of its national state. The democracy-detachment combination did not resist the referendum in good and due form. Even the threat, formulated in the Franco-German agreement of 1955, according to which, in case of a rejection of European status, the status quo would be maintained, did not prevent the Saarlanders from voting for Germany. They sensibly

---

[15] The Soviet Union rejected this demand, which was the origin of the break between the Soviet Union and France at the Moscow Conference in January 1947.

decided that the agreement itself could not be applied against the formal expression of the will of the Saarlanders. And such proved to be the case.

The Saar conflict is not a typical example of international conflict. It resembles conflicts among allies more than conflicts among enemies, although it was the repetition of a conflict which had already occurred in time of hostility between the two countries. Above all, it offers an instructive illustration of the authority of unwritten rules. France could not, without reneging, without violating the ideas to which she and the Atlantic bloc subscribed, refuse the Saarlanders the advantage of freedom, hence of the primary freedom of choosing their own nationality. The outlawing of propaganda and of parties favorable to attachment to the Bonn Republic collapsed of its own accord when the referendum was organized. Perhaps, if the French had assumed this risk, a referendum organized before 1950 would have produced different results. I doubt, though, that these results would have been regarded as definitive. In the historical context, with the procedures which it was in a position to employ, French policy would logically have had to fail: the failure was ultimately honorable in that it did not compromise the Franco-German reconciliation and in that France yielded without bitterness to the will of the people.

The dispute—shall we say conflict or controversy—over the rearmament of the Federal Republic also has a mixed character. In a sense it is only a question of a divergence of opinion over the defense or reinforcement of the bloc. At the time of the Korean War, and encouraged by the United States, the partners in the Atlantic Alliance decided to make, individually and together, an effort to rearm. What would be the status of Germany? Would the Bonn Republic continue to be merely the object, the theater of the possible battle? Or would it become, in its turn, a partner of the bloc?

According to the traditional mode of reasoning, the answer is not at all doubtful. To rearm the Bonn Republic, to treat it as an ally and no longer as an enemy, was to reinforce the bloc, to add German contingents to those now guarding the frontier of the Western world. But this decision to rearm provoked a tempest in France.

Germany is yesterday's enemy. The war launched by the Third Reich is still close at hand. Memories have not yet crumbled into oblivion, and resentments are scarcely appeased. The French ministers indicated that the time had not yet come when Frenchmen and Germans could serve, side by side, under the same flag. German rearmament can also be discussed with rational arguments, ignoring these legitimate emotions. What would be the Soviet Union's reaction to such a decision? Would the Russians not regard it as evidence of an aggressive intent? In any case, would arming West Germany raise an insuperable barrier between the Federal Republic and the Democratic Republic? Would it not increase tension still further? In other words, the French diplomats could dispute with their American colleagues as partners in good faith, trying to measure advantages and disadvantages, probable consequences and possible risks of a measure effecting the entire bloc. Finally, the French representatives could be concerned over the effect, on the relation of forces within the bloc, of the German rearmament, that is, of the Bonn Republic's accession to the status of an ally. Before 1950 France was, on the Continent, the only medium-sized power belonging to the bloc. After 1950 if the American plan were accepted, France would have to reckon with another power of the same dimensions as herself. In other words, was rearmament *acceptable* to French public opinion? Was it *opportune* with regard to the Soviet Union? Was it *favorable* to the French position within the bloc?

It is not possible to measure precisely the influence of each of these three arguments on public opinion or on the minds of the leaders. Nor is it a question of following in detail the long controversy between the French government on one side and the government of the United States on the other. The latter had brought all the partners of the bloc to accept, without too much difficulty, the *principle* of German rearmament. France, too, had finally subscribed to the principle, not without hesitations and protests, but the method remained indeterminate. The project of a European army, launched by Paris at the instigation of the "European party," provided an additional dimension to the dispute in France and abroad.

The North Atlantic Treaty reserved for each of the signers a veto right as to the decisions of the bloc, in particular the decision to rearm Germany. Legally as well as practically, the United States would have had difficulty overriding France's opposition. Certainly France would have had difficulty using her veto power against the common desire of all the partners of the bloc, but this will was more official than authentic. The other partners had accepted the American project, but they did not all share Washington's impatience and were not outraged by the French obstruction. In this test of wills, what were the grand *frère's* means and those of the recalcitrant little brother?

The former, obviously could not employ military force. In theory it could have suspended or reduced the aid which it was granting through the Marshall Plan, but this attempt at *coercion* would have provoked violent reactions not only in France but in the United States and the other nations of the bloc: the United States is constrained by the ideology of equality among allies, the official ideology of the Western world. It could use a threat: either the threat of an "agonizing reappraisal" of the American presence in Europe, or of overriding the French veto by signing a bilateral agreement with Bonn outside the framework of the Atlantic Alliance. The threat of an "agonizing reappraisal" was not taken seriously by French public opinion: the latter estimated, not without reason, that the United States would defend Europe out of enlightened self-interest, in other words that the threat of abandonment was blackmail. The eventuality of a bilateral agreement with Bonn, however, was taken seriously and contributed to the French Parliament's acceptance of the Federal Republic's entrance into the Atlantic Alliance.

The various French governments possessed many arguments. They multiplied affirmations of good will, but approval of German rearmament required a parliamentary vote. The ministers were not able to impose upon the assembly the ratification of a European Defense Community or any other formula permitting rearmament of the Bonn Republic. The project of a European army, with German rearmament providing a further step on the road to European unification, had obtained the almost enthusiastic support of the American administration. The latter was ready to wait in order not to compromise the chances of a European organization, whose significance exceeded the military requirements of the occasion. At the same time Paris suggested that it was still assuming the responsibility for a remote and unpopular campaign in Indo-China. Its very weakness constituted its strength. When it reminded the American leaders of the danger of "collapse" if the grand frère applied too strong a pressure on the crumbling edifice, it was not bluffing, or was not regarded by its interlocutors as bluffing. Paris did not threaten to do what its interlocutors knew it preferred not to do (like John Foster Dulles evoking the "agonizing reappraisal"); it announced the misfortunes which would beset it and which its interlocutors believed it was in fact incapable of preventing. The blackmail of the strong by the weak was, in this circumstance, more effective than the blackmail in the opposite direction because the weak power did not threaten to take a fatal decision: it announced the unhappy fate which would overwhelm it.

Ultimately, however, the United States nonetheless obtained the French Parliament's approval of the Bonn Republic's rearmament and entrance into NATO. It could not be otherwise, since there was nothing that permitted any hope of German reunification. The British government feared both the economic and commercial advantages which Western Germany derived from its low military budget and the American reactions to an obstinately maintained French veto. A bloc which integrates the liberum veto principle into its juridical status functions only if the partners finally submit to unwritten rules; in particular, the weak powers must not make an abusive use either of their veto right or of the blackmail possibilities they derive from their very weakness.

The differences of opinion between the British and Americans concerning the ways of dealing with the Berlin crisis or the Korean campaign do not deserve to be called conflicts, at least if it is essentially a question of opposition as to effective measures in given circumstances. At the time of the Berlin blockade or of the Chinese intervention, it could not be said that the British and Americans had an essentially different conception of the objectives to be achieved. Both wanted to save West Berlin without launching military operations. In Korea the Americans were perhaps more eager than the British to reach a unification of the entire country by a military victory, but fundamentally, both sides had the same immediate goal: to repulse the North Korean aggression, and both insisted on the same refusal of a total war with Communist China. What decisions would they have to take, what risks would they have to accept? The answers to these two questions were not necessarily the same in London and in Washington.

These controversies were not sustained by considerations of pride and by the desire for glory which, in the course of hostilities, provoke so many quarrels among generals. They did not differ in nature from those which arise among the various services, the various parties, or even the various individuals within a political unit. I should be tempted to say that in the Atlantic bloc the British have the tendency to reduce their controversies with the Americans to discussions of opportunity. The French have the opposite tendency to present those controversies in terms of divergences among states.

The British governments, since December 1941, have all been convinced that the American alliance was indispensable in order first of all to win the war, then to assure the security of Great Britain. They accepted the American leadership as inevitable. As the result of this resolution (or resignation), British tactics always involved the same procedure: first to attempt to convince the American leaders to adopt the policy London regarded as best, subsequently to influence public opinion and the organs of public opinion. And once the American leaders have taken a decision, even contrary to London's preferences, London will "follow the leader" without losing hope that events or criticism will open his eyes. It is by discussion, loyalty and presence that the British attempt to influence the United States in a direction favorable to their own interests or concepts.

The French have neither the same means nor the same methods. The governments of the Fourth and the Fifth Republics have maneuvered according to quite different styles. They have had in common the rare use of *discussion* and the frequent use of *obstruction*. The Fourth Republic's obstruction was often founded on the blackmail of the weak. The Fifth Republic's obstruction was based on claims to greatness. But the adversaries of German rearmament among the leaders of the Fourth Republic rarely tried to convince their American interlocutors that the bloc should or could adopt a different policy (unification of a neutralized Germany, negotiation with the other bloc). General de Gaulle demanded, with the memorandum of September 1958, a tripartite directorate of the Atlantic Alliance and consultations before the use of atomic weapons in any part of the world by the United States; he indicated that his cooperation in the Atlantic Alliance would depend on the satisfaction of these claims, but he made no particular effort to convince his interlocutors of the legitimacy of his claims, or to suggest a course, acceptable to all, of implementing the principles raised. He has formulated demands and supported them, subsequently, by the diplomatic equivalent of a "sitdown strike." During the war, in London, lacking material forces but strong because he incarnated the nation and symbolized an idea,

General de Gaulle had got into the habit of imposing his will upon his partners not by negotiations and bargaining, but by *faits accomplis* (St. Pierre and Miquelon), by threat of resignation or retreat to Brazzaville or Moscow, by defiance of the ally-adversary (Syria, Stuttgart). Once General de Gaulle was leader of a real and weakened France, and no longer of an absent and ideal one, the ally-adversaries did not hesitate, on various occasions, to accept the challenge. The French were obliged to evacuate Syria, not without a humiliation which a voluntarily effected departure, anticipating the inevitable, would have avoided.

The two tactics, English and French, tend on the one hand to accentuate, on the other to blur the difference between the bloc (or the alliance) and a political unit. In a sense the English attempt to discuss and negotiate with the Americans as the English or American parties debate among themselves (or as the Army, Navy and Air Force pursue their disputes in the United States, in the wings and in public). But the two tactics are also characteristic of the two parliamentary styles: the French parties practice obstruction, that is, the rejection of a policy without offering a policy to replace it, with a complete indifference, whether affected or real, to the consequences of the paralysis, in other words, of the absence of any policy.

Not that the French interests have been more abused by the bloc's conduct than those of any other partner. Once the Soviet bloc became the enemy and created the only threat to the existence of a non-Communist Europe, France had the same higher interest as her partners in the solidity of the Atlantic bloc, in the Bonn Republic's entrance into this bloc, in the United States' victory in Korea, a victory which, by increasing the *grand frère*'s prestige, contributed to the security of all the allies. The difference between France and the other states of the bloc, a difference more marked under the Fifth than the Fourth Republic, is that France is more concerned not to be identified with the coalition. If we reason in pragmatic terms, two kinds of considerations seem pre-eminent: is the bloc's decision favorable to the bloc as such? How does it affect the interests of the various members? The leaders of the Fourth Republic could plead that the rearmament of the Bonn Republic created a risk of a Soviet attack or weakened the French position within the alliance. But the concern of Paris also seemed to be for the maintenance or the appearance of a diplomacy independent of that of Washington or of the bloc as a whole.

Today, this latter concern, under General de Gaulle's regime, is dominant and virtually obsessive. In the matter of the summit conference of 1960, the chief of state apparently conditioned his consent on a previous visit by Mr. Khrushchev to Paris. To make manifest that he controlled the date of the conference constituted in his eyes a valid reason for accepting or preferring a delay of several months. Autonomy of decision thus becomes not a means to attain certain objectives, but an end in itself.

General de Gaulle has never indicated what advantages he expected for

France from the Atlantic directorate, nor in what direction he would orient the bloc's action in Africa or in Asia. On Berlin, he supported the policy of firmness defended by Chancellor Adenauer and some in the American administration. Hitherto, General de Gaulle had not opposed his partners in the bloc and the *grand frère* on concrete problems, nor the decisions to be taken. He did protest against the distribution of command posts, against the integration of the troops under the Atlantic command, against the Anglo-Saxon leadership. He has not defined an original policy; he has claimed, for France, a less dependent military capacity for action and an increased participation in the conduct of the bloc.[16]

The British prefer to influence the *grand frère* and regard with even more irony than surprise a chief of state who presents claims which cannot be satisfied. Had they read it, they would certainly quote the report by Colonel de Gaulle which we have already quoted: "As always, it is from the crucible of battles that the new order will emerge, and each nation will finally achieve its deserts according to its achievements in arms." It would be better to say, in peacetime "according to its achievements," arms being merely one of them. No obstruction will force the *grand frère* to grant what it is not free to concede. As for political-military autonomy, it exists or it does not exist *de facto*. Diplomacy can create fictions but not transform them into realities.

5. Conflicts between Partners Outside the Bloc

The Atlantic Alliance is more than an alliance in Europe, less than an alliance in the rest of the world. This paradoxical, unprecedented combination is the logical consequence of the global extension of the diplomatic field.

The same idea can be expressed in another form. In Europe the Atlantic community has attempted to act as a bloc. In Asia, in Africa and in South America the nations of the Atlantic Alliance act each for its own account, although in certain circumstances they combine their action. SEATO involved the participation of the two principal allies of the United States— Great Britain and France. But the latter's participation is scarcely more than symbolic.

The American refusal to give a worldwide application to the Atlantic Alliance is explained, in any case, by the disproportion between America's resources and obligations on the one hand, and those of its allies on the other. But, in 1949, there was a further reason: the European allies remained the metropolitan nations of the so-called colonial empires. American public opinion was spontaneously hostile to the colonial empires, which both diplomacy and propaganda condemned under the name of colonialism. Between 1945 and 1960 the British, Dutch, French, Belgian and Portuguese empires in

---

[16] In the last years, General de Gaulle went further: he recognized Communist China, recommended neutralization of Vietnam, and insisted on nuclear autonomy.

Asia and Africa disintegrated. The Atlantic Alliance has been shaken on several occasions, but only once seriously threatened by the various attitudes adopted by the United States on one side, and the metropolitan possessors of colonial empires on the other.

During the war, under the inspiration of Franklin Delano Roosevelt, the United States deliberately assumed a liberal stance. The President's remarks on the British Empire, his conversations with the Sultan of Morocco were known at the period by initiates and published subsequently. In the course of the first years after the war, without openly siding with the colonial powers, the United States, chiefly concerned to reconstruct Western Europe, exercised an extreme prudence each time a so-called colonial problem was submitted to the United Nations.[17] From 1945 to 1948 the Americans were favorable to mediation between Indonesia and Holland. It was only at the end of 1948 that they reacted violently to the second "police action" undertaken by the Dutch army. In the United Nations the American representatives sided openly against Holland, which had resorted to force and violated the decisions of the Security Council. In the Senate, Senator Vandenberg sponsored a resolution which forbade giving financial assistance to any state condemned by the United Nations and against whom the international organization had taken measures of sanction. Indonesia acquired its independence and Holland abandoned her possessions, the United States having finally rallied to the camp composed of the anti-colonialist and Soviet states.

During the fifties it was North Africa which was on the agenda, in the United Nations as on the stage of history; Tunisia and Morocco first, Algeria after 1955. Discussions turned first of all on the question of competence: could the conflict between France and Tunisia (or Morocco) be referred to the United Nations, or since France assured diplomatic representation of the protected nations by the protectorate treaty, had the latter lost the right to appeal to an organization consisting exclusively of sovereign states? With regard to Algeria the French argument of incompetence acquired increased force, since the departments of this territory had ceased, for over a century, to constitute a state and had been internationally recognized as an integral part of the domain subject to French sovereignty.

In general, the American delegation, without taking sides in the juridical debate, without approving the colonialist theses, did not vote with the anti-colonialist bloc. The balance sheet, drawn up by Mr. Robert Good, is as follows: "Of thirteen key votes on substantive resolutions concerning French North Africa from 1951 through 1957, the United States has abstained but once, voted with the colonial powers ten times (in all ten cases, the anti-colonial powers went the other way), and voted with the anti-colonial bloc but twice. These two votes involved the support of mild Latin American

[17] Cf. Arnold Wolfers, ed., *Alliance Policy in the Cold War*, Baltimore, 1959, especially the chapter "The United States and the Colonial Debate."

resolutions on Morocco and Tunisia, which were passed only after severe Afro-Asian resolutions had been defeated. Many of the Afro-Asian powers voted for the mild resolutions only under protest, and in each case Britain and the Netherlands abstained."[18] In 1959 the United States, at the last moment, abstained instead of voting against the motion hostile to French policy in Algeria. This abstention provoked clamors of indignation in France.

In other words, the United States managed not to oppose France directly and openly in the course of the years 1952–60, despite the United Nations debate on North Africa each year. Tunisia's independence, then that of Morocco were imposed, on the spot, by the weight of circumstances and by French mistakes, without the French government or French public opinion being able to regard the United States as the chief element responsible for events.

The United States was nonetheless a target for the reproaches of both sides. Even if it had not voted with the anti-colonialist bloc, it had not espoused the French cause with conviction. It had expressed its sympathy to the nationalists with moderation. It had pronounced itself for a "liberal" solution, and had opposed putting a problem on the agenda or an Afro-Asian motion merely for motives of expedience, because it relied on France to achieve her noble objectives. Of course America's semi-solidarity with its European allies did not fail to outrage the Afro-Asian nations, but did not seem unpardonable to the former or the latter.[19]

There are two contrary exceptions to this course of half-measures, of voting with the Europeans and sympathizing with the Afro-Asians: the virtually all-out commitment, starting in 1950–51, in favor of the French in Indo-China and against the Franco-British forces at the time of the Suez expedition. The first decision can be explained by reference to the Communist threat, the second, although its result was a Soviet-American combination, is also explained by considering the rivalry of the blocs.

In 1945 the United States had shown itself hostile at first, subsequently reticent, with regard to a restoration of French authority in Indo-China. When the war broke out, at the end of 1946, between Viet-minh troops and those of France, neither public opinion nor Washington subscribed to the thesis French representatives were already defending: France's combat did not figure on the honor roll of the free world as long as Ho Chi Minh, a national hero, claimed freedom for all Vietnam. The arrival of the Chinese Communists on the frontiers of Vietnam and the launching of the Korean conflict changed the "objective" meaning of events: Ho Chi Minh, allied with Mao

---

[18] *Ibid.*, p. 250.
[19] The position taken against Holland at the end of 1948 can be explained in part by Holland's recourse to armed force, and also by Holland's weakness and the means of pressure Washington possessed. The United States had to take more account of French susceptibilities: first because France was indispensable to the Atlantic Alliance; second because until 1954 France was fighting in Indo-China; third because the French governments were unstable and threatened.

Tse-tung and Stalin, became an instrument of Communist imperialism, bent upon the conquest of the entire universe. But since Ho Chi Minh owed his prestige and popularity to the nationalism which he had symbolized for so many years, any successful resistance must deprive the Communist enemy of the monopoly of nationalism. If one refused to deal with the Viet-minh because it was Communist, one must grant another man what one denied the former militant of the Comintern. France, even before being certain of American support, had hesitantly inaugurated such a policy. Between 1951 and 1954 the United States, while paying for the war, brought pressure on the French government to grant true independence to the Associated States.

This joint Franco-American policy suffered from internal contradictions which prevented its success. Those who were anti-colonialist in France were not sufficiently anti-Communist to countenance a war whose sole objective was to grant independence to a non-Communist Vietnam. Those who found a meaning in this war were the French nationalists, the defenders of empire. The officers with whom I was able to speak in Indo-China were impatient of the supervision of the American mission. None would have agreed to fight merely to make way for the Vietnamese non-Communists, i.e., probably pro-American and anti-French forces. Indeed M. Bidault would have argued that the abandonment of Indo-China would involve the ruin of the entire empire and that by blocking the path of communism in Vietnam, France was at the same time preserving her heritage.

Another grave contradiction undermined the enterprise: it is difficult in the middle of a war to create, on command, a substitute nationalism. When a party or a man is the incarnation of a national will (this will becoming aware of itself only in a minority of the population), it is almost impossible for another party or another man to take over the monopoly of popular feeling. In any case, even if Bao Dai had been more eager to succeed, more ardent, more ambitious than he was, he represented a traditional legitimacy in a revolutionary century.

After the Geneva agreements Ngo Dinh Diem managed to establish a national semi-authoritarian and anti-Communist regime in the south. If France had favored his accession to power during the war, perhaps the military effort of an independent and anti-Viet-minh Vietnam would have some effect. While the French government did not resign itself to the complete independence of the Associated States, it did not treat the nationalists (i.e., the adversaries of French domination) as true allies. Had there been an opportunity, however faint, of disputing the Viet-minh's monopoly of nationalism, the French government's refusal to accept the honorable liquidation of the empire as a war goal sacrificed that opportunity. In any case the Viet-minh, assured of the support of Communist China, had means of conquering at least half the country by weapons and negotiations.

The other exception to the rule of mediation—the American response to the Franco-English expedition in the Suez—is at first glance quite different.

There is no question of an attempt to reconcile support of a colonial power, sympathy with the aspiration of peoples to national independence, and resistance to Soviet imperialism: obliged to choose between the Franco-English forces and Israel on the one side, and Egypt, supported by the Afro-Asian powers and the Communist bloc on the other, the United States resolutely chose the camp of its enemies and the neutral powers.

The reasons for this position were many, pragmatic and idealist, spontaneous and deliberate, personal and national. President Eisenhower, engaged in an electoral campaign for his re-election, reacted to the Anglo-French initiative as being an attack against him personally. Perhaps he was inclined to attribute to the ministers of Paris and London malevolent intentions with regard to his own candidacy. American diplomacy is based, in theory and even to a large degree in practice, on denouncing resort to force, force being defined as armed force, regular troops of one nation crossing the frontiers of another. The United States, on many occasions, has not replied to the nationalization of American enterprises by military sanctions (Mexico nationalized the branches of the American petroleum companies with impunity). Whatever the uncertainties relative to the concept of aggression itself, the Franco-British ultimatum and the bombing of the Egyptian airfields could scarcely be justified by any argument in the Security Council or the General Assembly. A secret entente between Paris and Jerusalem was more than probable. Even if this Franco-Israeli conspiracy, this "collusion" did not exist, nothing authorized the Franco-British forces to arrogate to themselves the role of administrator of justice, to intervene in order to separate the combatants and, of the two states involved, to attack the one whose territory had been invaded.

Israel, it is true, could reply that the crossing of the frontier by *fedayins*, commandos specializing in the minor war of raids and destruction, was also an aggression. Doubtless Egypt was guilty, with regard to Israel, of acts which constituted indirect or clandestine aggression, a notion contained in certain non-aggression treaties between the two wars and carefully analyzed by jurists.[20] But as a matter of fact, since 1945 international practice has tolerated the organization of guerrilla forces on the territory of a neighboring state, either because the partisans passed for the defenders of a noble cause (the independence of oppressed peoples) or because the leaders resign themselves to this anarchic violence out of fear of the excesses of legalized violence.

The dilemma which the American leaders found themselves facing was both clear and dramatic. To support or excuse the Franco-British forces was to alienate Afro-Asian public opinion and to renounce a tradition of non-recourse to force. To condemn the Franco-British powers was to give a

---

[20] Tunisia and Morocco were also guilty of this kind of aggression with regard to France and Algeria; cf. above, Chap. IV, Sec. 5.

gratuitous victory to the Communist bloc, to jeopardize the Atlantic Alliance, perhaps to favor the Soviet hold on the Near East. Between these two decisions, both deplorable in certain respects, President Eisenhower chose the second, without much hesitation it appears. He was approved by an immense majority of public opinion, only a "realistic" minority offering reservations or objections. Many Americans were seized by the same idealist enthusiasm as on June 25, 1950. On that day the United States had taken arms with the sole purpose of enforcing international law. In November 1956 it once again set respect for the law above its friendships. But, at the same time, in relation to Hungary, it set concern for peace above justice.

The Suez episode is, in many regards, pathological. It would not have occurred if relations between the American Secretary of State and the British Prime Minister had been more trusting, if wrongly interpreted memories of 1936 and 1938 had not misled a French *Président du Conseil*, impatient to find abroad the means of ending an endless war in Algeria. The British rapidly liquidated, then forgot about this adventure, which contradicted the wisdom or the resignation they have manifested since 1945. Those nostalgic for empire were delighted with the sudden reawakening of the diplomacy of another era, but soon fell back into their vacuum; the best of them were welcomed back by the Conservative party under the leadership of the man who had approved of the expedition and understood the lesson of failure.

Henceforth, the advances of decolonization promise an easier cooperation among the partners of the Western bloc in Asia and in Africa. The economic recovery of Western Europe, the deficit in the United States external account, the new Vietnam war obliged that great power to demand the cooperation of its partners in order to manage its policy of aid to the non-aligned nations. It is even possible that in South America, it will be the Europeans who will dissociate themselves from Yankee imperialism, as the United States dissociated itself, in Asia, from European imperialism.

chapter XVI

Stalemate in Europe

or

Diplomacy between the Blocs

The diplomatic situation in Europe is the direct result of the world war. Neither the rivalry of the two super powers nor of the thermonuclear duopoly implied the constitution of two military blocs or the division of Europe, the demarcation line passing through the middle of the territory of the former Reich and the city which was the capital of modern Germany. Since 1946 the Continent has been the theater of a cold war because it had been the principal battlefield of a hot one. The destruction of Hitler's empire left the Soviet Union and the United States, once united against the conquered power, inevitably antagonistic as soon as it was a question of filling the void.

In 1945–46 it was clear that every country liberated by the Red army would be taken over by the Communist party. Seizing power, the latter effected a revolution-from-above, liquidated men and parties favorable to the West, introduced institutions and methods imitating those of the *grand frère*, yesterday's "liberator," today's "protector."

Could the Soviet Union have acted otherwise—that is, given free rein to party competition and respected the independence of trade unions in the Western sense of the term? Certainly it was not physically or politically constrained to Sovietize Eastern Europe by the intermediary of parties derived from it and under the threat of its army. The best proof that Sovietization was not inevitable, was not automatically set in action on the day the Hammer and Sickle was hoisted over the public buildings, is the example of Austria. Occupied for nearly ten years by the four powers, Austria retained a social structure and political institutions of the Western type. Even in the Soviet zone of occupation the pro-Western parties split the votes, only a small minority voting for the Communist party. It could have been the same in the Soviet zone in Germany, but since 1946 the fusion of the Communist party and the Social Democratic party heralded the decision to Sovietize the Eastern part of the Reich.

If no constraint weighed upon the Moscow leaders or the Russian occupation authorities, the temptation was strong and in a certain sense irresistible. Was not the establishment of a Communist regime, for a "true believer," the crowning achievement of military liberation, even if the masses, corrupted by capitalism and unconscious of their destiny, did not desire the liberation which brought them a party government?

The Leninist conception does not forbid the avant-garde (the party) to use violence in carrying along the rest of the body politic. The Stalinist conception grants no less dignity and efficiency to revolutions-from-above than to popular insurrections. Would the Soviet Union have been loyal to its faith if it had not seized the opportunity presented by events, not so much for security's sake as to spread abroad the brand of socialism made in the U.S.S.R.?

The decision—what regime to establish in the country liberated by the Red army—could only be a general one. A Communist Hungary or a Communist Czechoslovakia could not be separated from the *grand frère* by a capitalist state. East Germany itself had to be converted to the new faith. Cut off from the territories east of the Oder-Neisse Line, all Germany which would not be Sovietized would inevitably be anti-Soviet. What better guarantee against the reawakening of German imperialism than the Democratic Republic, whose leaders would, the less they enjoyed popular support, be all the more loyal to the Big Brother?

The constitution of a group of states in Eastern Europe all governed according to methods imported from the Soviet Union, and by parties subject to orders from the Kremlin, could not fail to appear, in the eyes of the West, to be imperialistic. That Stalin and his leaders had never intended to launch the Red army against Western Europe and to present the United States with the *fait accompli* of the arrival of the Russian soldiers on the Atlantic coast was possible and even, up to a certain point, probable. But on the other hand, it is certain that Stalin, both to consolidate his conquests and to weaken the resistance of the nations west of the Iron Curtain, did not cease to dangle over the West a threat which his own prudence obliged him not to carry out. Whereas the Anglo-American powers had demobilized, the Russian divisions, established in the heart of Europe two hundred kilometers from the Rhine, remained armed, with constantly improved equipment, ready, at a signal from Moscow, to occupy the free zone of the minor cape of Asia in a few days.

From 1946 to 1949 the two blocs had only a political character, and one of the two was disarmed. The signing of the North Atlantic Treaty explicitly confirmed an American guarantee that the Soviets had doubtless already regarded as valid. The events in Korea provided the turning point. They precipitated the transformation of the two European groups into military blocs. After 1950 the Western powers undertook to organize a defense system which the arms race and technological progress obliged them to reform several times. Fifteen years after the constitution of NATO, territorial status has not changed. The free world has survived, which means that the Atlantic Alliance may have achieved its defensive objective (to prevent aggression). But the dialectic of military preparations has not facilitated—it has made even more difficult—an agreement as to the modification or even the acceptance of the status quo.

1. *From Unilateral Deterrence to the Balance of Terror*

The two European blocs are asymmetrical. The Soviet bloc, with regard to the Atlantic bloc, acts as a unit. If war broke out, this unit might fall to pieces. In 1956 the Polish army and the Hungarian army remained loyal to their national leaders and not to the leaders of the Kremlin, or to international communism. As long as the peace lasts, diplomacy (the Berlin blockade) and strategy (the maintenance of several divisions in East Germany) are determined in Moscow and in Moscow alone. The diversity of institutions (agriculture) and of ideological positions (the "leftists," Bulgaria and East Germany, opposed the "moderates," Hungary, or the "quasi-revisionists," Poland) may exert an indirect influence on the leaders of the Soviet Union, but the latter are not obliged to consult or to listen to the satellite-princes before taking a decision. The United States is obliged to consult and to listen to the leaders in Paris, London and Bonn. In Europe the Atlantic bloc functions as an alliance despite the military community which makes it an unprecedented coalition.

This asymmetry is all the more apparent in that the Soviet bloc has, on the military level, adopted offensive tactics (which does not mean that it intends to attack). From 1949 to 1950 the Soviet army in East Germany consisted of some twenty-five divisions whose forces were complete and whose armaments were regularly modernized. The Western powers opposed this army by only a few incomplete divisions without collective organization or unified command. When hostilities broke out in Korea and the fear of war spread, the Western powers decided to put Europe in a position to defend itself.

In 1950 the United States possessed an atomic monopoly (the first Soviet bomb having been exploded in 1949). The planners anticipated the moment—1953-54—when a duopoly would replace the monopoly. They had as their objective an Atlantic force capable, according to some, of offsetting the Soviet forces available outside the frontiers of the Soviet Union, according to others, of holding in check the Red army in case of a general war. Not that military plans, even the most ambitious of all, those of the ninety-six divisions provided for in Lisbon in 1951, were based on the hypothesis of a general war waged with only conventional weapons on both sides. Statesmen, if not military leaders, combine memories of the last war with a simplified vision of the next. What was involved, this time, was sparing Europe an invasion—otherwise one risked liberating only a corpse—hence what was necessary was an Atlantic army sufficiently numerous and well-equipped to "stop" a possible aggression as far east as possible (forward strategy).

Some years later, in 1954, despite the progress made, the forces of the Atlantic army remained largely inferior to the requirements of the experts. The reduced objective of thirty divisions had not been achieved. The rearmament of the Federal Republic had not begun. The heads of state authorized the military leaders to provide for the use of tactical atomic weapons in case of Soviet aggression, even if the latter were to be carried out with conventional weapons alone.

At this time each of the two super powers possessed an atomic system and knew how thermonuclear bombs could be manufactured, but mutual deterrence remained asymmetrical in favor of the United States. The latter, because of the numerical and technological superiority of its strategic air force, because of the number, dispersion and proximity of its bases in relation to the Soviet centers, was capable of inflicting destruction incomparably superior to that which its rival would have been able to inflict upon it in return. The United States, regarding itself as more or less invulnerable, practiced, at least in words, the diplomacy of brinkmanship; it formulated the theory of massive retaliation.

Global disequilibrium was less than the Russo-American inequality suggested in terms of destructive capacity. For European vulnerability was total, both to an attack by troops armed with conventional weapons and to air attack with TNT bombs or with atomic bombs. In the event of total war Europe would be ravaged and/or occupied. It was, logically, terrified each time the American leaders spoke of massive retaliation. Europe was serving as a hostage. The Atlantic bloc could not be stronger than the weakest link in the chain. It could not take more risks than the least determined or most vulnerable allies were ready to take. Between 1950 and 1953 British influence on Washington still appeared to favor moderation. Inequality of danger was the common origin of European pacifism and of American brinkmanship.

Two or three years later there was no longer a question of massive retaliation: each of the two super powers henceforth possessed a thermonuclear force. The reciprocal neutralization of weapons of massive destruction, which the European planners had envisaged since 1950, seemed to have occurred. But the political-military consequence was radically different from what had been anticipated. No longer can we claim that the two super powers, equally capable of inflicting intolerable destructions upon each other, could fight with yesterday's weapons without resorting to those of today. But some lose interest in the land shield, others seek to reinforce it.

In 1957, after the fiasco of the Suez expedition, Mr. Duncan Sandys, British Minister of Defense, drew up—or had his advisers draw up—a white paper which expressed, with a maximum of clarity and simplicity, one of the doctrines possible. In Europe at least, the white paper said in substance, there cannot be an intermediary state between peace (the non-use of armed force) and total war. All doctrines of "limited reprisal" or of "graduated deterrence" are dangerous. They reduce the "credibility" of the threat of thermonuclear reprisal, whereas, in fact, if hostilities began in Europe, they would inevitably escalate. Hence one increases the likelihood of the very thing one claims to avoid by fictively creating a hypothesis intermediate between the two terms of the alternative, peace or total war, since this hypothesis would necessarily lead to the second of the two alternatives. As a result of this doctrine of all or nothing—the official doctrine of the British in 1959 —the abolition of obligatory military service was envisaged and the reduction of forces from 690,000 to 375,000 announced for 1962. British forces on the Rhine were immediately diminished from 77,000 to 64,000, and were later diminished still further.

This reasoning was opposed by the spontaneous feeling of the public at the same time as by the reasoning of many experts. No military preparation, no officially proclaimed peace will, in the last analysis, accurately express what is manifestly contrary to good sense, or to the instinct of self-preservation. Great Britain and the United States would not launch the apocalypse over a minor incident, before being assured that the enemy envisaged a total attack or sought to obtain advantages to which the Atlantic powers could not concede without disaster. The horror of thermonuclear war, even for the power which launches it, is such that a decision of this kind can be taken at a considerable stake, if the power is involved under irresistible pressure. The Atlantic bloc must therefore liquidate the absurd fiction of the alternative (peace or total war) and provide means, in case of provocation or limited aggression, of avoiding both capitulation (or passivity) and the apocalypse.

As a matter of fact, hesitation or oscillation between these two extreme doctrines has hitherto remained verbal and "abstract," theoretical; no aggression, even a minor one, having occurred in the zone occupied by the blocs. This absence of aggression is, moreover, not mysterious. Aside from Berlin (and the former capital of the Reich will be, one day or another, the occasion and the stake of a crisis of the first order), one does not see where and why the Soviet Union would set its armed forces in motion. The military situation —whichever of the two extreme doctrines was adopted—helped deter any aggression (the crossing of frontiers by regular armies). It is not the weakness of NATO's armies nor the white paper of Her Majesty's government which constituted the most effective instrument of deterrence with regard to minor aggressions, but the advantage of striking first. As long as the United States was or considered itself exposed to the danger of a serious weakening of its thermonuclear system in case of surprise attack, as long as it could be incited to strike first by the anticipated inequality of crime and punishment, the doctrine of the white paper of 1957 had a serious chance of being true, although for motives different from those it advanced. As the blocs moved toward the balance of terror, the strategy of deterrence seemed no less unsatisfactory. Essentially psychological, it leaves some uncertainty in the minds of both protector and protégé.

The former wonders which territories it can and must protect outside its own—in other words, in what circumstances the aggressor will take the retaliation threat seriously; it wonders what various means of reprisal, from conventional weapons to the thermonuclear force, it must possess in order not to be forced into the alternatives of capitulation and apocalypse. As for the protégé, he is torn between two fears. He wonders if the enemy will be deterred by the protector's commitment and is therefore inclined to seek an increasingly formal commitment, an increasingly automatic retaliation. But he also fears that the horror of total war is such that skepticism will resist the most eloquent proclamations and his protector will finally be forced into doing what all fear most of all. In short, the protégés want the enemy to be convinced of the seriousness of the threat but also want the protector to reserve all the freedom of not carrying out his threat.

The very nature of the uncertainty provokes endless polemics, each expert triumphing over the other so long as he does not specify his own solution, the latter being just as susceptible to criticism as the one he has refuted. The threat of massive retaliation is only a bluff, repeat certain of the most eminent military writers (Liddell Hart for instance). The enemy does not believe in such threats if he knows he can inflict damages approximately equal to those which he himself would suffer. It would be difficult for a President of the United States to give the fatal order to the Strategic Air Command[1] so long as the United States itself has not been attacked, if this order would involve the death of tens of millions of Americans. But the day the Soviet divisions crossed the demarcation line in force, United States soldiers, aircraft and ballistic missiles would go into action. The Strategic Air Command would be in a state of alert, ready to forestall the enemy's blow. Who can say that the war would remain a limited one? The threat of a massive retaliation on the occasion of any minor incident is a bluff, but the same persons who denounce this bluff are also among those who often doubt the possibility of limiting a war that would break out in Europe. If they doubt the possibility of limiting a war in Europe, why shouldn't the Soviet leaders doubt it as well? Which means that the thermonuclear threat is "plausible."

In Europe the stake is considerable, the conventional forces available on both sides important: What would a limited war mean if it left matters as they are? How would one of the sides accept the shifting of the demarcation line? By such reasoning, one concludes that in all probability a war in Europe would irresistibly be magnified. But in that case, why not return to the initial

[1] Before the Senate committee, at the time of his nomination, Mr. Christian Herter said: "I cannot conceive of any President involving us in an all-out nuclear war unless the facts showed clearly we are in danger of all-out devastation ourselves, or that actual moves have been made toward devastating ourselves."

formula of massive retaliation, which dissipates the illusion that hostilities on the Continent might not involve an escalation and consequently presents a better chance of deterring any aggression, even a secondary one carried out with conventional weapons?

All these reasonings seem plausible and create the troubled security of a Europe today. It is true that the West cannot launch the apocalypse over a minor incident; hence the West must possess troops and an air force capable both of preventing the creation of *faits accomplis* and of increasing the importance of the state in case the aggressor pursues his offensive. But it is also true that the thread of massive retaliation *which is not brandished* helps deter secondary or local aggressions because the aggressor cannot avoid fearing the expansion of hostilities, especially given the present vulnerability of the thermonuclear system. The day there is an explicit agreement over the limitation of war (for instance, concerning the non-use of atomic and thermonuclear weapons), limited conflict will recover a greater probability in that the signers of the agreement will have more confidence in each other.

In such a circumstance the Europeans will always have cause for anxiety (and the Americans as well). If they ultimately accept the limitation of conflicts, they will fear being the battlefield while the super powers square themselves. If they doubt the limitation of conflicts, they will fear that the super power may finally be responsible for the destruction of those it had promised to protect (but not to defend, since protection was based on deterrence and the failure of deterrence involves the destruction of the protégés). According to hypotheses or speculations, the Europeans want the Americans to be either calmer or more combative, either resolved to keep their promises or not to keep them.

As a result of these uncertainties, what have been the measures actually adopted by NATO? The United States has acted as if it wanted to reassure its allies and to convince the Soviet Union of its resolution; it has multiplied proofs of *commitment*; in particular it has added to the atomic armament of its divisions (atomic artillery, ground-to-ground rockets) launching pads for medium-range ballistic missiles. These pads were established in sites known to the enemy. They were vulnerable to air attack or to medium-range ballistic missiles; none of them were hardened. If they therefore added little to the total deterrence capacity of the United States or of the Atlantic Alliance, they had, *de facto,* a double function: they symbolized commitment, they rendered a limited aggression more difficult. How could the Soviet troops cross the demarcation line before having eliminated these retaliatory instruments (a reprisal which could be limited, not total)?

Simultaneously the Atlantic command would like to reinforce the "shield," in other words, the army. But the obstacle is the majority of the European nations which refuse expenditures and sacrifices, probably because their incontestable dependence on the American deterrence instrument makes the European leaders and public opinion feel that their own efforts, in any case, would be futile. The Atlantic bloc, in recent years, has thus not adapted itself to the change in the military situation. Convinced that American vulnerability reduced the credibility of the thermonuclear threat, it should have both reinforced the proofs of American commitment and enlarged the margin of possible actions. It has done the former (to a degree), but not the latter—the chief reason for the deficiency being that the Atlantic military community is a coalition, not a bloc.

Among the European states, three deserve to be considered separately, Great Britain, France and Western Germany.[2] Great Britain had participated, during hostilities, in the research which led to the first atomic bombs. It was the first nation to dedicate important resources to the acquisition of knowledge and technology necessary to both peaceful and military use of atomic energy. By the end of the fifties it possessed a strategic air force consisting of V-bombers capable of flying at high altitude and subsonic speed, and also of carrying thermonuclear bombs. Did Great Britain thereby possess a true deterrent capacity? At best, it possessed what the British authors call a "passive deterrence": in case of direct attack, a part of the thermonuclear instrument would have a *chance* to survive and to inflict reprisals upon the aggressor (the effectiveness of the reprisal would depend on the fraction of the thermonuclear force surviving the blow struck by the aggressor). But this passive deterrence, itself dubious, has only a slight value on the diplomatic level. American commitment in favor of Great Britain is such that the Kremlin leaders cannot launch a massive attack on the British Isles without attacking the United States at the same time. Granted the *probability* of an American reprisal, the only rational procedure, in the case of a Soviet desire for aggression, would be an all-out attack on the entire Western thermonuclear system. In other words, it is not the British thermonuclear force which deters the enemy from making a direct attack on the British Isles, but the entirety of Western—especially American—means of retaliation. On the other hand, if Great Britain were to find itself isolated diplomatically, its thermonuclear system would be of no avail against Soviet blackmail because there is no common measure between the losses which Great Britain would suffer and those to which the Soviet Union would be exposed in case of a limited war between these two nations. If Great Britain and the Soviet Union were to come to grips, the latter would perhaps be deterred from a direct attack involving the risk of some kind of retaliation, but the former should logically make enormous concessions in order to avoid the total destruction which a posthumous vengeance, carried out by the remains of British strategic airpower, would not suffice to compensate.

Great Britain's possession of a thermonuclear system contributes more to

---

[2] Among the others the only interesting case is that of Norway, which is both a loyal and determined member of the Atlantic Alliance and which does not accept, in peacetime, the stationing of allied troops in its territory.

its influence within the coalition internally and to its prestige on the world stage than to the effectiveness of its deterrence. Actually, the defense policy adopted by Her Majesty's government is part of the worldwide policy which the metropolitan nation of the former Empire has, since 1945, resolutely adopted (the Suez expedition is the exception which confirms the rule: it divided the nation). This policy's basis is, first and foremost, the American alliance. Since the British fleet no longer rules the waves, Her Majesty's government must be the constant and irreproachable ally of the leading sea power. Not that it resigns itself to a satellite status; the conception is quite different; it is by fully accepting the obligations of the alliance that Great Britain acquires the best chance of influencing the course of history and convincing the American leaders. The Atlantic community inevitably being led by the United States, the middle-size allies, as we have seen, have a choice between two tactics which express and symbolize two strategies: either to influence events by means of the leader, or else to reserve a field of autonomous decisions. Her Majesty's government is indifferent to its margin of autonomy bcause it does not despair of making the American decisions conform to its advice and its preferences.

The thermonuclear system is a rational element of this alliance. It guarantees the British scientists the cooperation of the American Atomic Energy Commission, the communication of at least a part of the latter's scientific and technological "secrets," and the cooperation of the general staffs for the permanent improvement and potential activation of the instruments of deterrence. Thereby Great Britain obtains in its favor an American commitment more indubitable than that of any other nation at the same time as an implicit promise of consultation[3] in any serious circumstance. Whether or not the British thermonuclear force would survive the first enemy attack becomes, in the light of this analysis, less important than it seems at first sight.

The case of France, especially of Gaullist France, is quite different. No French government can have[4] the same capacity as the British government of influencing the American administration, directly or through the intermediary of public opinion. Further, the objective of General de Gaulle (more categorical than his predecessors, but not fundamentally different) is less to influence the United States to take the decisions which he regards as best for the bloc and for France than to reserve the right and the means of acting as he sees fit, independently of the bloc, even in the zones covered by the Alliance. If such is the goal, the French deterrent, in order to come up to the national ambitions, should be effective against a possible threat of Soviet intimidation or aggression. The striking force called for by the program-bill was to consist, around 1965, of some fifty Mirage IVs capable of carrying atomic bombs to Moscow. These planes are fighter-bombers flying at a speed

[3] "No annihilation without representation."
[4] Perhaps one should say, *believes it can have.*

twice that of sound and apparently capable of penetrating the enemy defenses. But how many would survive a massive thermonuclear attack by a great power? How many planes surviving such a blow would manage to reach their targets?

The case of Germany is still different. Germany is committed, by the Paris Treaty, not to manufacture atomic weapons and the Bonn government does not seek to withdraw, for the moment, from the restrictions imposed upon it by the treaty. The space of the Federal Republic is narrow, and it is in immediate contact with the potential enemy. Federal army training camps and depots are in France; it would be irrational to establish in West Germany factories manufacturing atomic or thermonuclear bombs. When the Bonn leaders want their own deterrent, they will attempt to buy it, and if they find no seller, they will attempt to manufacture it in agreement with their European allies and by utilizing the latter's territory.

The case is different with tactical atomic weapons: if the Atlantic force is provided with such weapons, why should the German divisions which today constitute the bulk of this army not have them as well? The Americans have reserved control over the thermonuclear deterrent and cannot allow their allies free use of atomic warheads or even of tactical weapons, on account of the legislation voted and maintained by Congress. Nor can they discriminate between the German divisions and the other Atlantic divisions. All must be in a position to utilize atomic weapons, if hostilities, even limited ones, in Europe inevitably imply recourse to nuclear warheads. But will this be the case? Is it to the advantage of the Western powers to anticipate the use of tactical atomic weapons in every case?

The preceding analyses have sought only to clarify the problems which the Atlantic community must solve in order to maintain itself, facing the Soviet Union, in the present arms situation.

The first problem is that of the independence or non-independence of the instruments of deterrence. Is it to the advantage of the Western powers to commit themselves to a collective deterrent force or to several national deterrent forces? If the former, what arguments will convince the Europeans and what concessions should the latter demand and can they obtain in return for the provisional renunciation of national striking forces?

The second problem is that of the military organization of the Alliance as the result of a political-strategic concept. Must an army be prepared which will wage important battles without recourse to tactical atomic weapons? In this hypothesis, what arguments will convince the Europeans and what common strategy should be prepared in advance?

2. National Deterrent Forces or Collective Deterrent Force?

Granted that the American threat is now less convincing, the thesis of national deterrents becomes rational only when these instruments inspire the enemy's respect. At present and for the next few years, this condition will not be satisfied. Let us consider, in the abstract, the duel of a small and a great power, supposedly confronting each other. The former will not take the initiative of a recourse to atomic weapons, since this eventuality would involve a total catastrophe for itself whatever the course of events. It must therefore possess a retaliatory force, that is, an atomic or thermonuclear system capable of surviving a blow struck by the great power and of penetrating the enemy defenses in a state of alert. It would be excessive to assert that no French bomber could perform such an exploit, but it is evident that the inequality of crime and punishment would be so enormous as to make grotesque the application, in this case, of the thesis of "irrelevance of degree."

The so-called proportional-deterrence theory is an attempt to validate this thesis in the case of a duel between a small and a great power. Of course the theoreticians of proportional deterrence say that there will be no common measure between the losses France would sustain as the victim of a Soviet attack and those it would inflict in return. But as a stake, France itself is limited. The great power will rationally assume only the risks proportionate to the stakes. The risk of receiving several atomic bombs on several cities is disproportionate to France as a stake.

As a general theory, this argument is open to many objections. First of all, the super power could find itself, vis-à-vis the small power, in the situation of a gangster toward a policeman whose revolver has the safety catch on. If the great power strikes first, it eliminates the small power and withdraws from the episode unharmed. Let us suppose that the small power has a certain capacity for reprisal, that is, that its atomic system is not entirely destroyed by the first blow. Will the risk of reprisal still be higher, for the great power, than the stake the small power represents? This relation cannot be calculated abstractly. The great power's capacity to employ its thermonuclear force offensively would be substantially increased once it had proved in action that it did not hesitate to carry out its threat. Circumstances are conceivable in which it would be worth the trouble, in order to punish audacity and to spread terror, to run the risk of absorbing the small power's posthumous vengeance.

Finally, it is false to suppose that the great power must choose between inaction and massive attack. A super power cannot blackmail another super power because it would leave its rival the advantage of initiative. But a super power can blackmail a small power (assuming that the latter is isolated). What concessions would the latter refuse to make, knowing that resistance would mean the destruction of the state and near-extermination of the people?

But, it will be objected, the duel of the great and the small power cannot take place under such conditions. I would not dream of denying it. The small power, Great Britain or France, will never confront the Soviet Union alone: the United States, even if it has withdrawn from Europe, will remain one of the elements which the Soviet strategy must take into account in its relations with Europe. In order to reduce a small power, one super power cannot run the risk of weakening itself in relation to the other super power. The value of the British or French atomic capacity must not be measured in the unreal hypothesis of a tête-à-tête with the Soviet Union, but in the bipolar circumstance of our time.

One might suppose that national deterrents are necessary to prevent a blackmail which the Soviet Union might exercise upon any one European state. But the danger, it seems to me, does not exist. The Soviet Union can initiate a diplomatic play against one or another member of the Atlantic Pact but it cannot practice a blackmail by atomic attack, as long as American troops are stationed in the Federal Republic and as long as the national contingents are integrated into a peacetime Atlantic army.

The Soviet Premier could offer the West German Chancellor a prospect of German unification, promise him a peace treaty on condition that the existence of the two Germanies is officially recognized. He could, simultaneously, offer the President of the French Republic the resumption of a historical alliance against a revival of German imperialism. The member states of the Atlantic Pact are not protected against such attempts at seduction because they have not renounced their diplomatic independence. They seem to be protected against military blackmail because they *have* renounced their *military* independence. To demand of the Federal Republic, under threat of thermonuclear attack, that it leave the Atlantic Pact or renounce a certain kind of armaments, would be to run the risk of receiving the first blow.

In other words, provisionally, the European states cannot individually guarantee their own security, in the particular sense in which a deterrent is supposed to guarantee security. They retain the choice between two paths, one of which leads to the modern version of neutrality, the other to the modern form of coalition (the latter not excluding national atomic forces of a secondary rank).

The intellectual and political movement which was expressed in the Party Conference of 1960 by the passage of a motion in favor of unilateral atomic disarmament indicates one of the possible paths. The American "guarantee," symbolized and confirmed by air bases used by American squadrons, or by launching pads for medium-range ballistic missiles, soon appeared to be a two-edged sword: did it attract Soviet bombs or repel them? It is generally admitted that in case of war the American bases would "attract" Soviet bombs. The question is whether they "repel" war. Supposing they do not, would it not be possible for the secondary power to remain outside potential hostilities?

It is easy to denounce such an argument as cynical: it is in accord with the mode of conduct which history reveals to be characteristic of states. Why should a small country not seek its security by deriving advantage from the conflict between the great powers, assuring itself both the guarantee of one of the super powers (or of both) so long as peace lasts and there is a chance of

being spared on the day when the bombs explode? It is not the moral mediocrity of this argument which discourages states from accepting it. Its penalty
would be the danger of neutrality and, in part, too, the loss of prestige.

The problem does not come up in precisely the same terms for Japan and
Great Britain. Japan was the enemy of the United States in the period of its
imperial greatness. Today, with a population of about 110 million concentrated in a small territory, it no longer has the means of a major power, but
it retains the resources necessary to a prosperous economy and a high standard of living. The leaders, condemned to a diplomacy of peace, can, without
absurdity, without excessive illusion, assume that the security the American
guarantee affords would be forthcoming in any case and that, rid of the
American bases, Japan, less provocative in Soviet and Chinese eyes, would
entertain better relations with the Communist states. It was the socialists,
more or less close to "fellow travelers," who have been leading the campaign
against the pact with the United States. But one could imagine that the
conservative politicians, without any sympathy for communism, might prefer
neutrality to the American alliance insofar as the former gives them the same
advantages as the latter at lower cost.[5]

In Great Britain it is less the comparison of cost and the return (of the
Atlantic community and the American bases) which inspires the debate
within the Labour party and also among intellectuals. It is, it seems to me,
pacifism, the moral rebellion against the possible horrors of thermonuclear
war, against the diplomatic use of such a threat. The majority of British
public opinion remains loyal to the Atlantic Alliance out of tradition, without strict calculation of the risks and benefits involved. But this immediate
loyalty is sustained by a reasonable conviction: there is no longer any defense—whether it is deterrence or defense in the old sense of the term—for
Great Britain confronting the Soviet Union by itself. Great Britain must be
allied to the power which rules the seas; it can no longer count, as it has done
down through the centuries, on the reciprocal weakening of the European
states, engaged in permanent competition and intermittent wars.

The U-2 incident afforded additional arguments to the partisans of neutrality throughout the world. For the first time it appeared, if Mr. Khrushchev's remarks were to be taken seriously, that a state could be the victim,
even in the absence of general war, of an alliance with the United States.
The Kremlin leader threatened to reply to the spy-plane overflight of Soviet
territory with "limited reprisals" against the plane's bases of departure and
landing. In this eventuality, either the United States would tolerate the reprisals and an allied state would have nothing to do but bandage its wounds,
or the United States, in its turn, would inflict a limited punishment upon the
Soviet Union, with the possible risk of a gradual enlarging of hostilities. In

[5] We are here leaving aside the influence of either the treaty or neutrality on the
development of internal policy.

both cases the ally would be implicated in a conflict which would not concern it and by which it would have nothing to gain. If these considerations have hitherto remained discreetly in the background, it is because the leaders in Pakistan or elsewhere have not believed that Mr. Khrushchev would take action or that the United States would repeat the U-2 experiment.

As for the continental states of Europe, they do not even know the temptation of neutrality without weapons. The essential reason for this is the division of Germany and Berlin. The Bonn Republic, despite its economic miracle, leads a politically precarious existence: on the other side of the demarcation line a so-called Democratic Republic has been formed, dominated by the Communist party. Of course, the Democratic Republic's regime remains unpopular, even today. According to all probability, this regime would not survive the departure of those who inspired and established it. But as long as twenty-five modern Russian divisions are established on the territory of the Democratic Republic, as long as the Soviet Union maintains its pressure on Western Europe by demanding the definitive recognition of the status quo, the Federal Republic feels threatened, and with reason. It exists and can survive only by the guarantee and the will of the United States.

Since the Federal Republic chooses the path of a reinforced American commitment, the other continental states must take the same path, all moreover, except Gaullist France, being resolved upon an identical choice, even if they had the freedom to make another. The only question is to know what changes in military tactics are suggested or required by the increasing vulnerability of the United States. Until now, neither of the two kinds of measures which might have seemed rational has been taken: neither the reinforcement of the land shield nor the formation, in Europe, of a retaliatory deterrent capable of surviving a Soviet attack. The reinforcement of the land shield would have been the implicit confession that the threshold of atomic reply inevitably rises once the threatener cannot destroy the enemy nuclear force, hence cannot avoid massive destruction. The constitution of a retaliatory deterrent in Europe and under NATO or European command would have symbolized at least the relative military autonomy of the Continent, an autonomy which would have been the answer to the so-called French argument (in the thermonuclear age, the nations can no longer protect each other; each must protect itself).

As a matter of fact, Continental Europe itself so far has been unable to acquire an adequate and autonomous deterrence capacity (this capacity being defined by the probability, in case of an enemy surprise attack, that the second strike force would still inflict "intolerable" destruction upon the aggressor[6]). Launching pads and airfields are close to the Soviet Union and consequently vulnerable. Bombers and intermediate-range ballistic missiles,

[6] It goes without saying that this classic definition, speaking rigorously, leaves a margin of guesswork: what is intolerable destruction?

effective for striking the first blow, are not effective as means of reprisal (except in a minor sense). They were not, however, useless. Multiplication and dispersal of bases make an all-out surprise attack more difficult. On-the-spot accumulation of atomic weapons helps prevent local aggression by conventional weapons.

Yet the Atlantic bloc has not yet found the means of reconciling the necessity of a rational division of tasks within the Alliance, and the desire, English or French, for a national deterrent. Yet, in the long run, the cohesion of the coalition requires a doctrine adopted in common and this, in turn, will require reciprocal concessions.

At present both American and French spokesmen refuse to acknowledge the partial truth of the thesis each side is opposing. The American experts are correct in asserting that France will be incapable of possessing an independent retaliatory force, hence a deterrent, for another ten years. They are wrong to forget that the possession of even a minor atomic or thermonuclear apparatus confers some authority within the context of the Alliance, some prestige on the world stage, some diplomatic autonomy. The French are not alone in thinking that there will be no great power tomorrow without thermonuclear weapons, as there was no great power yesterday without heavy industry and armored divisions. Even if this thermonuclear force is not utilizable diplomatically against either a great power or a small power, it establishes the status of states, their rank in the hierarchy of the actors on the diplomatic-strategic stage. Henceforth, if it wants to coordinate military programs, the United States will be led to grant concessions to France, with regard to atomic secrets, delivery means or the leadership of the Alliance.

European participation in the disposition of the system of deterrence and retaliation has at least a psychological function. So long as the United States alone possesses the decisive weapons, establishes plans and makes decisions, the Europeans are not interested in their own defense because they have the feeling that it does not depend upon themselves. In the long run this has unfortunate consequences for both protector and protégés. The latter do not even make the contribution of conventional weapons which mutual security requires. The former ultimately finds the burden of deterrence and defense unendurable, economically and morally. A European or Atlantic nuclear force involves the double necessity of interesting the Europeans in their own destiny and of not dispersing the instruments of deterrence and retaliation.

Two methods for this sharing in the deterrent have been envisaged and even, to a degree, applied: the bilateral agreement whose essential clause is that of the "two keys," and the multilateral agreement granting the Atlantic Alliance itself possession and deployment of the thermonuclear force.

The so-called "two-key system" requires the agreement of two governments —that of the nation on whose soil the launching platforms are installed and the United States—for the right to fire the ballistic missiles. Thereby, the government of the European nation obtains the promise of consultation in case of international crisis, but it does not obtain the guarantee that it will be consulted before *any use* of atomic weapons in *any part of the world*. The explicit promise of consultation does not guarantee the members of the Atlantic Pact against the extension to Europe of a conflict starting in some other part of the world, for which American policy would be in part responsible. But this objection, however valid, must not be taken as tragic: no solution is fully satisfactory. The choice for the European nation is between solitude without a deterrent and a compromising solidarity with the United States. If it chooses the second alternative, then by definition the European nation risks being involved in a conflict which does not concern it. But this risk is attenuated by the interest common to both super powers of not expanding a local conflict, and also by the veto-right granted the allied nations over the use of retaliatory weapons installed on their own territory. The two-key system was not perfect, but it was for the time being the best of the systems on the path of commitment.[7] In the current state of technology, launching pads for liquid-fuel ballistic missiles would not have survived a general surprise attack. They did not assure the protégé the free deployment of these weapons in order to resist the blackmail of the enemy super power. Nor did they oblige the allied great power to grant consultations in case of crisis, but they did create an additional—not decisive but not insignificant —reason for the protector to consider the protégé's interests, for the aggressor to regard the small state as inseparable from the bloc.

The establishment of a deterrent subject to the directives of the Atlantic general staff appears to represent a further step on the way to sharing. The atomic or thermonuclear force—according to the plan of ships armed with Polaris missiles—would be under the commander-in-chief of the Alliance. The formula itself immediately reveals difficulties. This commander is an American general. The day such a question comes up, whom would he obey if not the President of the United States, even if he is obliged by signed agreements to consult the representatives of the allied nations and in certain circumstances to make the decision himself?

Once again, the critic can win easy successes here. The general in command of NATO *cannot* be subject to the veto of fifteen governments. Nor can he be at the orders of only the President of the United States; nor is he qualified to assume strictly political responsibilities, above all to choose between peace and war. If we insist on a formula without either disadvantages or obscurities, we must obviously renounce the proposal of a deterrence force to be controlled by the Atlantic general staff. But flexible formulas would have been conceivable had the Europeans been seeking only a further security, an even more formal and incontestable American commitment. Such is not the situation.

[7] The path of non-commitment is one of non-alliance, of "denuclearization." The commitment is that of both protector and protégé.

General de Gaulle would not accept the atomic monopoly of the United States, even if someone managed to convince him that the latter constitutes the most effective guarantee for France and for the entire Continent. He refuses the status of a protégé state, which in his eyes is equivalent to a satellite status. He aspires to a national defense that is at least partially autonomous. He has therefore shown no interest in the suggestion of a NATO atomic force. As the British government was also hostile to this "Atlantic force" because it feared a dissemination of nuclear weapons and because it, too, wished to retain a national force, the project was abandoned even before being elaborated. In 1962 President Kennedy, as a result of the Mc-Namara Doctrine,[8] emphasized the necessity of the American monopoly, although neither France nor England renounced their respective national forces.

3. Conventional Weapons and Tactical Atomic Weapons

Debate over the advisability of resorting to tactical atomic weapons in case of limited war has continued indefatigably in the course of recent years, the arguments for or against being modified as time passes to accord with technological progress, depending on whether the latter favors one side or the other, suggests one conception or the other. I do not propose to summarize the entire controversy here,[9] but to focus on the ideas which to me seem decisive and which are not without consequences on the level of strategic-diplomatic conceptions.

What authors today call *limited war* is both a non-general war (actually a non-global war insofar as the system today is planetary and in which, consequently, a general war including the entire system would involve the entire planet) and a war in which the belligerents employ only a fraction of their forces. These two characteristics of limited wars are not original: Great Britain did not engage its entire army in South Africa, any more than Russia engaged its entire army in Manchuria. Even if distance and problems of transportation and supply had not imposed this restraint, the consideration of other enemies, actual and potential, would have imposed it upon the two empires, maritime and continental. What is new in the Atomic Age is that the same weapons are not employed in the various kinds of wars.

The Korean War furnishes the model of the campaign fought in a geographically limited space, during which both sides used only chemical ex-

---

[8] This doctrine involves numerous intermediate steps, in case of crisis, between the "nothing" of capitulation and the "all" of thermonuclear apocalypse. Hence the insistence on the necessity of increasing conventional forces, or not resorting immediately to tactical atomic weapons, of adapting to circumstances the blows delivered by the nuclear weapons, the latter aiming first at the enemy's military installations, the enemy cities being spared as long as the enemy does not take the initiative of attacking cities.
[9] A summary will be found in the article by Henry A. Kissinger, published in the special number of *Daedalus*, 1960: "Limited War: Conventional or Nuclear; an Appraisal," and reprinted in the book *Necessity for Choice*, New York, 1961.

plosives. We need only evoke the thermonuclear apocalypse—one of the super powers launching its bombers and ballistic missiles against the enemy retaliatory force, the other replying by the destruction of the aggressor's cities—to indicate the other extreme. On one hand, a three-year campaign with millions of tons of steel[10] transformed into shells projected at the adversary and occasioning tens of thousands of deaths, on the other an exchange of blows lasting only several hours, with tens of millions of deaths caused by weapons whose cost in dollars does not exceed several billion and which in raw materials, directly or indirectly employed, represent only several thousand tons of steel. The exchange of thermonuclear bombs has become the present-day representation of what Clausewitz called *"Steigerung bis zum äussersten."*

But the absurd horror of this escalation does not permit the theoreticians of strategy or diplomacy to consider merely this summary opposition. Between the exchange of thermonuclear blows and the Korean campaign, many intermediate steps are possible. The search for graduated means has concentrated on one question: what weapons can be employed in a conflict which must not become general? It is not certain that such a formulation of the question is the best one: compatibility of particular means with the limitation of hostilities depends on many circumstances. By considering weapons alone we are perhaps preventing ourselves from giving a satisfactory answer, any answer to an ill-defined eventuality being uncertain or equivocal.

Let us keep to the general formulation of the problem: is it opportune to resort to tactical atomic weapons in case of a secondary conflict? The answer depends on the answer given to two other questions: What is the probability that the tactical use of atomic weapons will provoke escalation? Does one of the sides gain an advantage by this tactical use, and if so, which one? Now to these two questions, the specialists, whether military or civilian, give contradictory, equally unproved answers.

All agree on one simple idea: the non-use of atomic explosives is the best protection against escalation. The truth of this proposition is based on psychological probability. Rightly or wrongly, men, at all ranges of the social scale, establish a radical discrimination between conventional weapons and atomic weapons.[11] So long as only the first are in action, opinion—that of the leaders of governments as well as of the governed—correctly assumes that the desire for moderation exists on both sides. This discrimination between the two types of weapons remains valid despite today's re-established continuity between chemical explosives and atomic explosives (the least powerful of the latter category being perhaps less powerful than the most powerful of the former). The reason this discrimination remains rational is that it is the

---

[10] From the 1939-45 war to the Korean conflict, the intensity of firepower increased by as much as it had from the 1914-18 war to that of 1939-45.
[11] More specifically, between chemical and atomic weapons.

simplest, one that enemies can simultaneously acknowledge without needing communication or explicit agreement. Now, the limitation of a conflict in which one or the other of the super powers, or both, would be implicated could only result from an implicit understanding. Even if the heads of state whose armies are at grips are on speaking terms materially and morally, their words are always less convincing than their acts. It is by acts that one of the sides must convince the other of its restraint.

Hence it is *evident* that escalation is less to be feared if neither of the belligerents possessing atomic weapons takes the risk of using them. But it would be erroneous to deduce from this *evident* proposition the false or dubious proposition that it would be *impossible* to prevent escalation in a conflict, even a geographically limited one, if one or the other belligerent used nuclear explosives. The probability of escalation is first of all a function of the vulnerability of the retaliatory system. The more vulnerable the latter, and the more anxious one of the super powers is about the security of its means of reprisal, the more inclined it will be to interpret an enemy action as the proof of an aggressive intention; the more tempted it will be to take the initiative. But, outside of this general relation between the stability of reciprocal deterrence and the probability of limitation of local hostilities, many circumstances intervene. What is the stake of this conflict? What nations are involved in it—the two super powers directly, or one of them through its allies or satellites? What is the course of the combat? What advantage is the side taking the initiative on the battlefield seeking to secure? What objectives is it aiming at?

That the non-use of atomic weapons improves the chances of avoiding escalation (which corresponds to the interest of both sides) still does not signify that the violation of the atomic taboo would be irrational in every circumstance. One of the belligerents might regard the non-use of atomic weapons as disadvantageous and their use as not likely to create the danger of expanding hostilities. Non-use might have become impossible, either because one of the belligerents had no other local means permitting him to avoid defeat, or else because the use of these weapons by the other power seemed inevitable (or simply likely), so that initiative by pre-emption acquired a virtually rational character (the dialectic of pre-emption can, in effect, function for the tactical as well as for the strategic use of nuclear weapons).

In other words, the answer to the first question would be: the use of tactical atomic weapons increases the danger of escalation, without our being justified in formulating a general proposition with regard to the exact degree of this danger: too many circumstances intervene in each concrete case which are likely to influence the course of the crisis and the conduct of the adversaries. Similarly, the second question—which of the two super powers or of the two blocs would derive an advantage from the tactical use of nuclear explosives?—does not seem to me to invite a specific answer. The essential reason is that a combat between armies utilizing atomic bombs has never yet taken place and that we have all military history to remind us of the weakness and the errors of the imagination. In the past, technical or tactical innovations which in retrospect seem of modest scope have sufficed to give battles an unexpected turn. No general staff before 1914 had prepared industrial mobilization. Imagine, then, the risk of error when the expert attempts to represent the action of armored detachments over more or less enormous zones devastated or contaminated by atomic explosions.

Would more forces be needed because of increased losses, or less, because of increased firepower? Granted that concentration would be forbidden, how would the defenders protect the nation against both bomb damage and infiltration or occupation by enemy detachments? Does the use of conventional weapons alone favor the United States, whose industry is superior, or the Soviet Union, which can recruit more soldiers? How can the observer risk a categorical prediction when, according to Mr. Kissinger,[12] each of the three American armed services professes a different doctrine of limited atomic war? "The Air Force thinks of it as control over a defined air space. The Army considers it vital to destroy tactical objectives which can affect ground operations, including centers of communication. The Navy is primarily concerned with eliminating port installations."

The only conclusions we can deduce with certainty from these speculations are quite banal: the tactical use of nuclear explosives tends to efface the distinction between limitation and non-limitation of weapons, of destruction and hence of the hostilities themselves. That the limitation of hostilities should be obtained by the non-use of certain weapons is without precedent, but this originality is in accord with tradition. Down through history the victor generally did not eliminate the vanquished state, did not exterminate its population, though in the case of absolute victory (disarmament of the vanquished power), he would have been physically capable of doing so. Henceforth, atomic weapons permit the extermination of enemy populations even before they are vanquished or disarmed. It is natural that states should seek combat without destroying each other: the non-use of thermonuclear weapons is the equivalent, in our period, of the relative moderation which civilized states imposed upon themselves after victory.

But, it will be asked, is it true that the use of atomic weapons would step up the ravages of so-called limited war? I am not unaware that certain authors question even this proposition. What is the use of violating the "atomic taboo" if one does not use weapons more powerful than conventional weapons? To justify violating the taboo, one must resort to shells or bombs whose power is superior to that of the chemical explosives, without doing what is incompatible with the proximity of populations or allied soldiers to the explosion area. There remains the argument according to which a prolonged

[12] *Daedalus*, 1960, p. 806.

campaign, like that of Korea, may ultimately cost more than a rapidly terminated campaign waged with atomic weapons. This hypothesis is not inconceivable. It supposes that the belligerents discover their misunderstanding or that the aggressor, instructed by a brutal rejoinder, renounces his enterprise, without there having been either victor or vanquished. On the whole, it remains likely that the tactical use of atomic weapons[13] increases both the risk of enlarging the conflict and the human or material cost of operations.

Have these propositions a direct application to the problem of European defense? Can we refuse atomic weapons to the German army?[14] The NATO general staff was authorized, in 1954, to take atomic weapons into account in establishing defense plans for Europe, a decision determined both by the inadequacy of forces and by atomic plenty. Since the "Miniaturization" of bombs and the increase of stockpiles permit employing the nuclear explosives on the battlefield, why not replace men by machines and fill the gaps by firepower? But the same dialectic which has inspired doubt concerning the doctrine of massive retaliation now inspires doubt as to the tactical use of atomic weapons. The enemy, too, can threaten with massive retaliation; the enemy, too, can employ atomic weapons tactically. Is the measure which seemed favorable as long as it was unilateral still favorable when the other side replies with an equivalent threat? The tactical use of atomic weapons compensated for the lack of forces, as long as the West alone had recourse to these weapons. Would this be the case on the day both camps possessed these weapons?

Many military writers do not hesitate to derive from equality acquired by tactical use of atomic weapons the same lesson they derive from equality acquired by strategic use. The threat of massive retaliation is inoperative once it is reciprocal. Similarly, the threat of using atomic weapons in localized land battles would be inoperative once the potential enemy had the same capacity. An independent expert, Liddell Hart,[15] returns to his favorite doctrines: the defensive side, given a qualitative equality, can stop an offensive waged with very superior forces. A superiority of three-to-one is indispensable to the aggressor in order to force the lines of resistance held by a mobile and well-equipped army. The Western powers are mistaken to count on a threat that is, in fact, a bluff and that will eventually force NATO into a humiliating situation or an absurd catastrophe.

The plea in favor of the reinforcement of the Atlantic army is convincing.

[13] If the tactical use involves the destruction of naval and air bases, from what distance from the battlefield will these bases be attacked? And at that moment, how distinguish strategic from tactical use?
[14] The German divisions possess tactical atomic weapons as do the other contingents of NATO, according to the two-key system. Atomic warheads cannot be used without the agreement of the American authorities.
[15] *Deterrence or Defence?*, London, 1960.

Western Europe, today enjoying great prosperity, should be capable of permanently maintaining several dozen major units in combat condition. It is unprecedented that one of the centers of human civilizations should, so to speak, renounce its own protection, that nations which are among the richest in the world should declare themselves unable to afford, even by a collective effort, an army strong enough to face a *fraction* of the Soviet army operating two or three thousand kilometers from its bases.

The obstacles in the path of rational organization of Western defense are many, psychological and political more than technical. The incitement to an arms effort, especially a conventional arms effort, is weak because a limited war in Europe is not impossible but improbable, and because this improbability derives from the existence of thermonuclear forces. The reinforcement of land armies would give the diplomacy and strategy of the bloc an increased flexibility. An Atlantic army of some dozens of divisions could have intervened in Hungary. But if the availability of a range of choices for the Western powers reduces the risk of the fatal alternatives of capitulation or disaster, it may[16] increase the risk of minor aggressions and halfway hostilities. As long as the all-or-nothing doctrine (total peace or total war) of the British White Paper of 1957 succeeds, a strange feeling of anxious security will persist—muffled anxiety, repressed by the (well-founded) conviction that no one desires the apocalypse.

Since, in any case, European security is based first of all on the American thermonuclear force and since, in any case, the Soviet Union is seeking to avoid useless risks, military preparation, the reinforcement of the land shield, is relevant to diplomatic functions or to horrible but very unlikely eventualities. The arguments of the experts do not affect public opinion because they are complex and because they do not manage to dissipate the illusion of security created by the alternative: peace or mutual suicide.

The day one of the European states is once again animated by national ambition, tensions will appear within the bloc. Gaullist France no longer is willing to depend entirely upon American protection. The army of the Federal Republic, which became the strongest on the Continent when the bulk of the French army was transferred to Algeria, demands and receives the same weapons possessed by both allies and enemies. The possession of tactical atomic weapons corresponds not only to a military necessity but to a

---

[16] "May" because the reasoning is not evident, though it seems convincing at first glance. Actually, it is not impossible to argue that the reinforcement of conventional weapons deprives the enemy of the hope of gaining certain advantages by minor aggressions, and thereby tends to deter him from even these. Atomic retaliation would be made more likely if the means were given to reply on lower levels. I do not believe that we can choose dogmatically between these reasonings, all more or less likely. Let us not forget that the event depends on what is happening in the minds of the leaders of the other side, and that we can arrive at hypotheses, not possess certitudes, with regard to the mental processes and strategic calculations of the enemy leaders.

necessity of moral equality as well. How could the German soldiers have the heart to fight if they were deprived of weapons used by the neighboring divisions? The distinction between divisions trained to use conventional weapons alone and divisions trained to use atomic weapons would be unacceptable to the partners of the Atlantic Alliance. Divisions of the second category would all have been American.

On the other hand, if all the divisions of all the Atlantic nations are trained to use atomic weapons, the command has, so to speak, alienated its freedom of choice in advance. In the Atomic Age more than ever, military arrangements adopted in peacetime control the decisions which statesmen take when the crisis comes. The mechanism of mobilization, as of July 30, 1914, prevailed over the peaceful impulses of statesmen. If the Atlantic divisions are all equipped with atomic weapons and if the Soviet divisions in East Germany are equipped with the same weapons, if both armies are deployed in relation to a use regarded as inevitable, the event will indeed fulfill the anticipation. The decision will have been imposed upon the statesmen by the general staffs, acting, it is true, within the framework created by the statesmen.

For the moment, everything occurs as if the Atlantic bloc hoped to enjoy simultaneously the benefits of both doctrines: to forestall even minor aggressions by making the enemy believe that atomic weapons will be employed in any circumstances, and at the same time to reserve freedom of choice if aggressions nonetheless occur. Up to a certain point these advantages are not strictly incompatible with each other. To maintain doubt as to one's intentions has always been a part of rational strategy. The adversary cannot and must not know with certainty what the reaction would be in certain eventualities. Further, the military system must not suppress the strategist's freedom. If atomic weapons are in the hands of all, all will use them. Further, we must consent to pay the price of this uncertainty, i.e., the risk of a misunderstanding. If the enemy does not know what our answer to certain initiatives will be, he may be wrong in counting on our passivity or, on the contrary, on an atomic rejoinder. If he is mistaken in one direction he will provoke a violent reply on our part. If he is mistaken in the other, he himself will take a violent initiative by pre-emption.

Down through the centuries, conventional weapons have never effectively exercised the function of deterrence, but they have often managed to protect the territory from foreign invasion and the population from the horrors of war. To imagine a campaign waged with conventional weapons is to return to a strategy of defense. To threaten a thermonuclear response is to renounce defense and to count on the effectiveness of deterrence. To prepare for a limited atomic war is to count on deterrence without entirely renouncing defense. The theater of operations would be ravaged, the cities of the principal belligerents would be spared. By definition, the threat of a local campaign waged with atomic weapons has a deterrent value somewhere between the threat of a conventional response and the threat of a thermonuclear response, as well as a defense value somewhere between the two extreme threats. Does this intermediate formula combine the advantages or the disadvantages of the two extreme formulas?

4. The Military Crystallization

The theme of this chapter is diplomacy *between* the blocs and we apparently have continued to discuss diplomacy *within* the blocs. The explanation of this paradox is simple: during the postwar period, diplomacy between the blocs has been reduced to the minimum and, the territorial status being unsatisfactory but tolerable for both, the action of each of the super powers with regard to the other has chiefly consisted of measures taken on one side of the demarcation line. The Allied (U.S., U.K., Fr.) monetary reform of 1948, and subsequent establishment of the tripartite zone and of the Bonn Republic confirmed the existence of two Germanies, hence the division of Europe. The Atlantic bloc reacted to the North Korean aggression by the formation of the integrated general staff and rearmament. The Soviet bloc has created, on paper, an equivalent general staff following the signing of the Warsaw Treaty in 1954. The rearmament of the Federal Republic, a partner in the Atlantic community, at the end of 1954, was a spectacular moment of the same process, that meant the integration of West Germany into the European community of the Six and the Atlantic Alliance.

At no point during the first decade after the war did the Soviet Union engage in negotiations with the United States or the West in order to settle the German problem or modify the status quo. The leaders of the United States and Great Britain, convinced in 1947 that Moscow was determined to keep East Germany under a Soviet regime, had as their objective to prevent the extension of Communist ideas and institutions to West Germany. The law of competition between the two blocs made it necessary to treat West Germany according to the principles proclaimed by the democracies of the Western type, just as East Germany was gradually transformed into a "people's democracy." The German Democratic Republic nonetheless continued to pay reparations, and it was not until 1954 that it was covered by a mutual-assistance treaty as a signatory of the Warsaw Pact. The Federal Republic, too, did not achieve equal status for several years. In 1950 when the idea of German rearmament was launched by President Truman and Dean Acheson, the period of discrimination was reaching its close. It was no longer a question of reducing the industrial potential, dismantling installations or even of demanding reparations. The Federal Republic was a member of the OEEC, it received its share of the Marshall Plan aid, in addition to the direct aid granted by the American occupying forces. The difficulty, seen from Washington, was to win over France and, secondarily, the other nations of Europe to this policy which the British and American leaders regarded as the indispensable rejoinder to the Sovietization of Eastern Europe. Moscow could not prevent the Western powers from acting within their own zone, but it could paralyze their action by exploiting the inevitable divergences among democratic and sovereign states. A major obstacle to the rearmament of the Federal Republic was the resistance of an important part of French public opinion and consequently the opposition of the Paris government. The long dispute of the EDC was one of the episodes of the cold war, of the diplomacy between blocs. The United States sought to acquire an additional card, not so much in order to play it as to keep it in reserve. The Soviet Union did its best to prevent that acquisition by multiplying threats and promises, by mobilizing its followers and by impressing the non-aligned nations. The United States applied pressure by evoking an "agonizing reappraisal," Soviet Russia by evoking a terrifying reprisal.

There is no need to analyze in detail the means employed by the U.S.S.R. to prevent the parliamentary ratification of the EDC. On the whole, one might say that the spokesmen—whether conscious or not—for the Moscow thesis employed simultaneously the traditional arguments of anti-Germanism and the new arguments adapted to and suggested by the situation (what would be the Soviet reaction to a German rearmament? What would the Federal Republic do, once rearmed? Can one give arms to an unsatisfied government which seeks first of all to reunite the two Germanies, then to recover all or part of the territories annexed by Poland?). But it is interesting to note that in private the official Soviet representatives suggested that Germany's neutrality, negotiated between the two blocs, might constitute a substitute for the rearmament of the two Germanies.

Personally, I have never believed in the possibility of this intermediate solution. The West would have accepted Germany's neutralization only on condition of obtaining first or in return free elections in the Democratic Republic, in other words the latter's de-Sovietization. The more time that passed, the more deeply Soviet institutions were rooted in East Germany and the more unlikely this exchange became. A regime which regards itself as destined for universal victory, which invokes its connection with a historical destiny, does not willingly consent to a spectacular retreat. What would have been the repercussion, in Czechoslovakia or in Hungary, of the elimination of Ulbricht and his henchmen? What guarantee would the West have been able to give the Soviet Union that Germany, unified under a regime of the Western type, would maintain a position of diplomatic and military neutrality after having abandoned ideological neutrality? In Central Europe, on the line of direct confrontation of the two powers, intermediate solutions—the regime of the single party not subject to Moscow, the regime halfway between the single party and multiple parties—are equally difficult, not to conceive, but to achieve.

Further, the United States, too, envisaged with anxiety the formula of a neutral and unified Germany which, in its eyes, offered two major disadvantages: it made almost impossible the organization of a local defense on the Continent; it introduced an additional unknown quantity into a complex equation. What would be the policy of a unified Germany, potentially endowed with the resources of a great power and condemned to neutrality by the decision of allied conquerors hostile to each other—in other words, by the will of the enemy *grands frères?* Partition is the substitute for neutrality in the age of ideological conflicts. At the same time it guarantees to both super powers the suppression of one variable: there cannot be a German will so long as two regimes claim to embody it.

Not without difficulty, all the obstacles were surmounted on the path taken by the Western powers in 1947. In 1960 the Federal Republic was becoming the most prosperous nation of the free world. It is this Republic which has the most important financial reserves (over seven billion dollars). It is this Republic which is called upon to support the flagging dollar as well as to take its part in aiding underdeveloped nations, which has the largest and best-equipped army on the Continent, whose regime appears to be firmest, with a majority party (the Christian Democrats) and a Chancellor in power for over ten years. Had not the policy inaugurated in 1947, renewed in 1950, confirmed in 1954, achieved its goal by 1960? Western Germany has been saved from poverty and resentment, preserved from the temptation of communism, integrated into Europe and the West. It is in East Germany that troubles have broken out, it is in East Berlin that the workers have rebelled, it is in Hungary that the Soviet army has had to intervene in order to crush the first anti-totalitarian revolution of the century, victorious after street battles because of the defection of the army and an important fraction of the Communist party. Since 1946 the West has won every political battle in Europe: the Berlin blockade failed; Franco-German reconciliation has become a *fait accompli;* the democratic regimes have presided over the European miracle of prosperity during the decade 1950–60; Yugoslavia defected in 1948 and has not resumed its place in the family of socialist states despite the regrets expressed by Mr. Khrushchev. Neither in Poland nor in Hungary has the Communist regime taken root; the peoples endure it without recognizing themselves within it. It is only in Poland that I have completely understood what the Marxist notion of alienation can mean: men foreign to the social relations they experience, to the authority they support, to the collective undertakings of which they are the involuntary artisans.

Yet, despite these victories, observers of the European scene are certainly not exalted by a sense of success. The spectacular and in certain regards sensational progress made by the economies of Italy and France have not seriously weakened the Communist parties of these two nations. Prosperity is striking west of the demarcation line but economic progress in the East is also not below average. Certainly, for the moment, indications of growth are more impressive than the standard of living. The number of Germans who left the Democratic Republic for the Federal Republic was several times higher than that of the Germans who, seeking work or fortune, moved from West to East. If they had the choice, the great majority of workers, intellectuals, and mere citizens, in Eastern Europe, would still prefer Western democracy to popular democracy. But—and this is ultimately the decisive fact—*they know that they will not be free to choose in the foreseeable future.*

Western non-intervention in October–November 1956, as well as the pitiless Soviet repression, has definitively and tragically confirmed the Soviet capacity and resolution to maintain, against any and all opposition, the authority of Moscow over Eastern Europe. The dialectic of military preparations leads to the reinforcement of the global balance of terror by a local balance of armies and armaments, both conventional and atomic. Atlantic diplomacy attempted the offensive, refused to accept the Sovietization of Eastern Europe, proclaimed the right of Europeans subject to the Communist regime to choose their destiny freely, encouraged the captive peoples to resist. But simultaneously the Atlantic bloc adopted a diplomacy-strategy that was essentially defensive. The Atlantic army, the Strategic Air Command had no other object than to deter aggression: and in fact, there has been no aggression.[17] But if this policy aimed at creating conditions for a favorable settlement of the German and European problem, it has manifestly failed. Could it succeed as long as the United States and the Europeans refused to take any risk?

Thereby, the debate has resumed within the Atlantic bloc: Is there a substitute for the dialectic of military preparations, each bloc responding to the measures taken by the other in such a way that the balance is established at an even higher level of weapons or of nuclearization of weapons without either bloc using them, exploiting a temporary superiority, of one kind or another, to achieve its goal? Could the risk of explosion be diminished by renouncing the use of nuclear weapons in certain zones? Could a territorial settlement acceptable to both sides be prepared by an agreement over armaments?

The formula of "denuclearized zones" was conceived and proposed to the East as well as to the West. In 1955 Sir Anthony Eden had envisaged a zone in the center of Europe where the density of troops would be reduced, where no atomic armament would be established, a zone of separation between the armies which would be subject to rigorous inspection and which would permit the experiment of a cooperation between the blocs. The Polish Minister of Foreign Affairs also launched a plan, which in the diplomatic annals bears his name—Rapacki—a plan that involved the denuclearization of the center of Europe.

Negotiations have never been seriously undertaken on behalf of either of these plans, the Western powers, particularly the Bonn government, fearing that such a formula, however attenuated, might contain in germ the neutralization of Germany as a whole. Now this neutralization is evidently inac-

---

[17] It goes without saying that there might possibly have been no aggression in any case, even without all the preparations.

ceptable to the West, by very reason of the unequal depth of the two blocs. The Soviet bloc can withdraw its line of defense some hundreds of kilometers without serious disadvantage. The Atlantic bloc cannot sacrifice several hundred kilometers without being obliged to abandon all military organization.

More generally, it would be somewhat naïve to believe that the presence of mechanisms capable of launching projectiles with atomic warheads creates a danger of war in and of itself. The race for strategic weapons is, as such, dangerous insofar as it involves the establishment of automatic retaliatory mechanisms or the reduction of the time in which the President of the United States could make a decision in certain circumstances. Tactical atomic weapons do not go off of their own accord, any more than conventional ones.

Further, the direct contact of the armies tends to forestall incidents, accidents and misunderstandings: it was in the void created by the retreat of the American troops that the North Korean aggression occurred. A military void is more dangerous than a presence. I am aware that certain observers fear and evoke the possibility of a rebellion in East Germany and the impossibility of a West Germany possessing a national army remaining passive in such a situation. These speculations seem to me highly unlikely: living conditions in East Germany have improved, they are not so bad as to provoke rebellion, and the leaders of the Communist party are united with the Big Brother, incapable of finding salvation in treason or rallying to the opposite camp.

Further still: supposing that there were a risk of popular insurrection in Europe. This risk would be unduly increased should a sizable denuclearized or demilitarized zone be set up. As a matter of fact, the meaning of such measures would be to put an end to the reciprocal paralysis of the two blocs by reducing the military significance of the potential political transformations. In 1956 the Soviet Union was not ready to tolerate in Hungary either the establishment of multiple parties or the proclamation of a neutrality of the Austrian type. But if the two blocs were no longer in direct contact, if there were no danger that a popular democracy, disloyal to the Big Brother, were to change camp, perhaps the Soviet Union would tolerate certain transformations which it would brutally repress today.

Such speculations suggest the advantages and the disadvantages of the policy which the West might gradually substitute for the present policy. The line of demarcation being clearly drawn, the American troops being present in force to the west of this line, the Moscow leaders have no illusions as to the dangers of an aggression and the "captive peoples" also have no illusions as to the help they can expect. Aside from the former capital of the Reich, nothing happens, nothing can happen on one side or the other because political agitation, which persists in depth, is repressed and concealed by the military carapace. To favor the political thaw, the risk must be taken of eliminating the artificial freeze spread by the military organizations of both blocs.

If this analysis is correct, the military stabilization of the two blocs represents, contrary to common opinion, the policy of prudence and the status quo. The neutral zone, the denuclearized zone, the various modes of disengagement, *unless they lead to the neutralization of Western Germany without a counterpart on the Soviet Union's side,* are so many risky operations intended to restore a certain fluidity to events. Such would be *a fortiori* the meaning of the evacuation of Europe by the Russian and American armies.

This simultaneous evacuation, object of a concerted negotiation, would not necessarily involve the re-establishment of a military void, comparable to that which existed in 1945. The hundred million Franco-Germans west of the demarcation line are normally capable of mobilizing together the thirty divisions demanded by the experts. They are even capable, with the cooperation of their European partners (and of the British, eventually) of acquiring a certain deterrent force.[18] Yet Europe without the presence of American troops would not be without protection. The American commitment to Western Europe would lose a degree of formality, of obviousness, it would not be eliminated. And, if we suppose the Soviet troops also withdrawn within the frontiers of the Soviet Union, the possibility of a massive aggression against democratic Europe becomes extremely unlikely.

What keeps the European statesman from seriously envisaging this conversion—renouncing the crystallization of the military fronts in order to favor the political thaw—is that this new diplomatic-strategy would be charged with uncertainties. Would the peoples of Eastern Europe convert the popular-democratic regimes without overthrowing them? In case of a popular rebellion, would the Soviet Union invoke, as in Hungary, the revolutionary holy alliance against the counterrevolution? What would be the relation of the two Germanies? What would be the diplomacy of a peacefully unified Germany? Everything becomes possible once again, including a Russo-German agreement at Poland's expense, as soon as we speculatively eliminate the military crystallization of the two blocs and the tête-à-tête of the two powers in the middle of Europe. In their present mood the Europeans are not inclined to take risks. The dialogue of military measures, actual or envisaged, will probably continue.

Not without a crisis whose course is uncertain. For the Russian leaders and not the West have *one* means of starting the game again: Berlin. The Western garrisons in West Berlin are the symbol of the common victory over the Third Reich, a symbol of the German unity which the victors had solemnly proclaimed, a symbol of the juridical non-recognition of the

---

[18] Another formula has been suggested by George F. Kennan: Europe would rely on militia, on passive resistance in case of occupation. This is a great deal to ask of the Europeans.

Sovietization of East Germany and Eastern Europe. It is this symbol which the Western powers desire to and must maintain. It is this symbol which the Soviets desire to and must eliminate.

The result of the Berlin crisis will determine the conditions in which the next phase of the European tournament will open. But the dilemma could certainly remain exactly the same tomorrow as it is today: the Western powers must choose between *military crystallization* and *political changes.* If they do not renounce the former, they cannot hope for the latter. All diplomatic negotiation of the classical type will afford only the *possibility of political changes* at the cost of an *increased insecurity.* Have the Europeans enough confidence in themselves and in the Germans to desire and not to fear political changes, to count more on their own defense capacity and less on American protection?

To these questions, the answer, for the moment, is negative. But it is not impossible that some day, Europeans will be obliged by events to assume the risks they are refusing to take thus far.

The analysis of the "draw in Europe" has led us to an apparently paradoxical result. The competition of arms is a guarantee of security to the extent that it guarantees the status quo and excludes a misunderstanding. Yet in general the observers wonder if the arms competition does not create the danger of a war which neither camp desires and which the opposition of interests does not justify. As a matter of fact, these two apparently contradictory interpretations are not incompatible with each other.

A risk of war is perhaps created in the course of technological progress; it is not created by the constitution of NATO and the Warsaw Pact. The military crystallization assures the duopolists mastery of events, whereas a restored Europe would perhaps again become tumultuous and unpredictable.

The military crystallization which, locally, avoids graver dangers, seems—when considered from a global point of view—to be an aspect of an arms rivalry that could provoke what both camps wish to avoid. A part of the world-wide interplay, it feeds anxieties to the same degree as the other modes of stockpiling nuclear weapons.

Is there a third path? Of course, the military crystallization without an arms race or the official acceptance by both blocs of the status quo would seem to combine the advantages of the two conceivable attitudes. But Europe cannot escape the arms race once each of the two halves is committed to a military system. Nor can Western Europe any longer willingly subscribe to a status to which it resigns itself. It temporarily prefers security-in-impotence to the dangers and anxieties of a regained autonomy.

chapter XVII

Persuasion and Subversion
or
The Blocs and the Non-Aligned Nations

Among the hundred or so states represented in the United Nations, three quarters belong neither to NATO nor to the Warsaw Pact. The concept of non-alignment now belongs to the vocabulary of diplomacy. The General Assembly of the United Nations, if not all humanity, may be considered as divided into three groups: the Western bloc and the Soviet bloc confront each other on the Old Continent like two goats face to face on a narrow bridge, each as incapable of moving forward as the other, but the states—whether old or new, large or small, African, Asian or South American—outside this direct confrontation may be seen as the true stakes in the debate or the historical conflict between Washington and Moscow, between the Western world and the Soviet world.

The concept of non-alignment is not without ambiguity. Does it apply to all the nations that make up the third world? Is it sufficient merely not to belong either to the Soviet bloc or the Western bloc in order to earn membership in this third bloc, curiously defined by its members' freedom of action? Our first task will be to analyze the different terms—non-alignment neutrality, neutralism—so that we may go on to distinguish the various attitudes adopted by the nations of the third world.[1]

The nations of Africa or Asia are experiencing local conflicts comparable to those waged down through the centuries by the European nations. The United States has never succeeded in reconciling South Korea and Japan, even though both these ex-enemies are linked to America by treaties. South Vietnam and Cambodia, since they became independent, have had disputes of a purely local origin whose stakes are of little interest to the super powers.

---

[1] The term third world (*tiers monde*) has a cultural rather than a diplomatic meaning. It covers that part of humanity outside the two blocs. But there are Western nations (Sweden, Switzerland) which are outside the Western bloc without belonging to the "rest of the world."

The tension between India and Pakistan can be imputed to Kashmir: at least at the outset, in 1948, it had nothing to do with the preferences on a world level of the two states which had replaced the British Raj, or with either Soviet or American action.

The diplomacy of these extra-bloc nations is of interest to us insofar as it is an integral part of the international system. Now the nations of Africa, Asia and Latin America are rapidly becoming, in effect, a part of the international system, and also of the United Nations, some voluntarily, some against their wishes. Each of the two super powers takes at least a negative interest in *Ruritania*: they are anxious not so much to obtain its allegiance as to prevent its allegiance to the other camp. The rivalry of the two blocs causes the world to become an object of permanent competition, the stake of which is a choice, both diplomatic and moral, which the non-aligned nations cannot elude.

An object of competition, the third world becomes a subject of the historical drama by the very fact that the two blocs hold each other in a state of paralysis and do not dare, for the most part, to resort to forceful means. Consequently the powerful nations today aid the weak ones instead of exploiting them. They try to persuade them and make no attempt at coercion. Not that the diplomacy of the super powers with regard to the non-aligned nations can be compared to a contest of generosity or to a debate between economists, in which the victory goes to the one who gives the most or produces the best arguments. Beyond the "aid to underdeveloped countries," beyond the controversies over the rate of growth, beyond the speeches or the resolutions of the United Nations, it is by subversion, even by guerrilla warfare, that the revolutionaries succeed in changing the political map of the world.

1. *Non-alignment, Neutrality, Neutralism*

Even in Europe, three different categories of states can be said to be neutral. Switzerland and Sweden practice the traditional type of armed neutrality, Finland and Austria practice unarmed neutrality, Yugoslavia practices a certain variety of neutralism.

Switzerland and Sweden have institutions which are fully Western and democratic. They belong to the international organizations for economic cooperation, and they make no mystery of their sympathies. They differ from Norway or Belgium in their non-adherence to the military alliance constituted by the North Atlantic Treaty. But on the other hand, they possess armaments which are quite considerable in relation to their populations. Sweden has developed the organization of passive civil defense, preparations for urban evacuation and construction of underground shelters further than any other country, including the two super powers.

Austria committed herself to permanent neutrality at the signing of the peace treaty, but unlike Switzerland and Sweden, she possesses only a small army whose function is to maintain order within the country, not to oppose any possible aggression by a super power. Her institutions and sympathies place Austria on the side of the West. Finland, too, is governed by a regime of the constitutional pluralist type and does not belong to any military bloc, but, because of her proximity to the Soviet Big Brother, enjoys only a semi-independence; any important diplomatic decision (for example, economic involvement in the small free trade area) is always subject to Moscow's approval; Finland is resigned to the concessions necessary in order to be tolerated by her powerful neighbor.

Yugoslavia is, in Europe, or even in the world, a unique case; a dissident from the Soviet camp, she still continues to claim that she is a Marxist-Leninist state. The regime belongs to the type of "one-party state," although it is perceptibly less rigorous now than it was at one time. Excommunicated by Stalin, Yugoslavia received American aid at a time when it was blockaded by the Soviet camp. Since 1954 she has also received aid from Russia. Even if he felt the desire to do so, Marshal Tito is unable to abjure his schismatic convictions and become once more the satellite-prince of a state forming part of the Soviet bloc. He is therefore in no position to threaten either of the super powers by any openly hostile action. He can no more become a "good Western state" than he can return to being a "good Soviet state." Nonetheless, the United States draws a double advantage from the aid it unconditionally extends to a dissident Yugoslavia: it is consolidating a regime preferable, in its eyes, to an orthodox Moscow-guided regime, and it is advertising American good will toward other satellite-princes who may be tempted to follow Marshal Tito's example.

Outside Europe there exists no equivalent to the traditional type of neutrality practiced by Switzerland and Sweden. The principal distinction is between neutrality (India) and a more or less positive neutralism (Nasser); almost all new states declare themselves non-aligned, and seek to escape involvement in the cold war between the blocs. But the spectrum of non-alignment runs from the Tunisian sympathy for the West to Cuba's adhesion to the Soviet bloc.

India's Prime Minister, Mr. Jawaharlal Nehru, was hostile to all military alliances on principle, regarding them as a source of increased tension rather than as a guarantee of security. In particular, and for obvious reasons, he deplored and disapproved of SEATO and America's military aid to Pakistan. Seen from New Delhi, this aid only altered the balance of local forces in the Kashmir quarrel and not Pakistan's capacity to resist communism.

Economically and politically, in institutions and ideology, India is nearer to the Western bloc than to the Soviet bloc. The greater part of her trade is with the Western nations. Most Indian students pursue their studies in the universities of the West and it is from the West that India receives most of her economic aid.

The language adopted by the spokesmen of the Indian Republic has varied, approaching the language of the left when Mr. Krishna Menon was the orator, coming closer to a moderate kind of socialism and to a moralism of principle when the orator was the Prime Minister himself. India's condemnation of the Anglo-French Suez expedition was more severe than her condemnation of the Soviet repression of the Hungarian revolt or the Chinese repression of the Tibetan rebellion. But this injustice is perhaps less attributable to sympathy than to the fear inspired by the totalitarian world.

The United Arab Republic, under the government of Colonel Nasser, affords another kind of neutralism. Within the Republic, Communists and leftists are ruthlessly hunted down, imprisoned and often executed. Externally, the state and the regime appear to be linked to the Soviet Union, which provides armaments, buys Arab cotton (which is then resold in the world market) and constructs dams and factories. However, the United Arab Republic and the Soviet Union have no *formal* alliance, and Moscow does not have any monopoly on economic aid or technical assistance in the country. By eliminating European influence in Egypt and nationalizing the Suez Canal, the U.A.R. has *objectively* aided Soviet strategy, insofar as the Soviet Union's primary objective in all parts of the world is to set peoples and governments against the West. Yet President Nasser has not alienated his freedom of action, he is not a prisoner of revolutionary forces within his state or outside the Soviet bloc. He could increase his Soviet aid with American aid tomorrow and still not betray his principles or depart from the line he has laid down for himself. Nasser's blackmail of the West is not expressed by the threat: "Give me aid or I shall turn to communism," but by a different threat, in which Mr. Khrushchev was a willing accomplice: "Give me aid, for if you do not, the Soviet bloc will provide it without asking anything in return." Nehru got aid from both sides without blackmailing either one. President Nasser achieves the same result by explicitly blackmailing the West and implicitly blackmailing the Soviets ("the West would welcome me back like a prodigal son").

Mr. Sekou Touré's Guinea and Mr. Fidel Castro's Cuba are "active neutralists" of a different sort. The regime in Guinea is in fact a one-party regime. All the African republics, it is true, tend toward the one-party regime, and all the African political leaders are inclined to use a more or less leftist language (at least when it is a question of the relations between Europeans and colored peoples). But Guinea's political party has the structure and methods of a Communist party, and Guinea's representatives in the U.N. supported Mr. Lumumba in the Congo with an ardor in no way inferior to that displayed by Moscow's loyal flock. This does not mean that Mr. Sekou Touré would enter into complete solidarity with the Soviet bloc. It is greatly to his interest not to break with the West in order to receive eventual aid and to preserve the recourse to blackmail: in order to be able to wield the threat of becoming Communist, a nation must not be entirely Communist already.

The case of Cuba is still different: the establishment of a regime modeled fairly closely on Soviet example in close proximity to the United States, in a geographical zone which had always been thought to be entirely subject to Yankee influence, obviously has a historical significance far greater than Guinea's decision to vote *no* in the referendum of September 1958. Fidel Castro, having come to power backed by the sympathy of a majority of world opinion and by material aid from certain quarters in the United States, has risen, in the space of two years, to the rank of enemy number one of the United States. As Tito defied Stalin, so is Castro defying Uncle Sam. Cuba combines all three chief criteria of alignment: a regime similar to the one-party regimes of the Soviet bloc; language hostile to the United States and favorable to the socialist bloc; the voluntary support, on the diplomatic level, of all Soviet actions. In one sense Fidel Castro has gone further than any other state outside the zone of direct confrontation between the two blocs, since he is now no longer to reserve his commitment.

The Castro revolution probably marks a turning point in the history of the Western Hemisphere. The countries of Latin America, close to the United States but living in the giant's shadow, had allowed their actions to be governed by habit, accepting the hegemony of the stronger, with ill will fundamentally constant though intermittent in its expression. They had not yet seized the opportunities offered by the competition of the blocs to non-aligned nations or understood the impotence of the stronger who lacks the right or rejects the occasion to resort to force. Other South American countries may follow the example of Fidel Castro, who himself learned his lesson from Nasser: a zone ceases to be a "private hunting ground" and develops the status of "theater of the cold war" as soon as the super power's proximity and resources cease to impress the small power and the latter becomes convinced that the other duopolist will protect it from armed intervention and grant it, in case of need, economic aid.

If we review the diplomatic attitudes symbolized by the names of Nehru, Nasser, Tito and Fidel Castro, it becomes immediately apparent that between India's *neutrality* and Cuba's alignment with the *neutralism* of Egypt and Yugoslavia lying somewhere in between, the differences are at least as significant as the similarities. India's neutrality reflects the personality of Nehru, loyal to the values of the West as well as to the fight against colonialism; Egyptian neutrality reflects the anti-Western but not pro-Soviet nationalism of the Arab world; that of Yugoslavia the history of a left-wing Communist unable to accept Big Brother's stifling protection; that of Cuba, the revolt of leftist intellectuals and of a Latin American country against capitalist exploitation. All the countries that claim to be neutral, and almost all the states of the third world, would agree in denouncing colonialism. But when it comes to their institutions, to the meaning they assign to the world conflict and to their own non-alignment, to the real sympathies they feel for Moscow or for Washington, they are divided by much more than mere nuances, even if they all express a unanimous desire for an "international *détente*" and for "disarmament."

The choice of a certain sort of neutrality or neutralism is not a function of the degree or of the nature of a country's underdevelopment: it is political circumstances, the psychology of the elite groups and of the peoples that determine the form of non-alignment or alignment in favor of one bloc or another. The cases of the neutralist countries we have just discussed illustrate this proposition, which is further confirmed by an examination of the attitude adopted by the new states in their relations with the former metropolitan states, on a diplomatic level as well as on that of fundamental values.

The British colonies in Asia attained independence after the Second World War without, at least after 1945, having to fight for it. India and Ceylon have preserved British-inspired institutions which, especially in India and in spite of extreme difficulties, function respectfully. Burma, though its population is thought of as peace-loving, suffered long years of civil war. Pakistan has never managed to organize free elections, competitive parties or the genuine methods of deliberation that characterize a true parliament. For the time being, a British-formed army took charge of a neutral administration. There was no manifest correlation between the nature of the institutions and the diplomatic positions assumed. Pakistan, ruled by a marshal, is bound to the West by SEATO; India, proud of her parliamentary government, seeks to be at one and the same time a member of the Commonwealth and a non-aligned nation. The electoral victory of the left-wing parties in Ceylon resulted in the British evacuation of their military bases there, a language more or less resembling that of the leftists, but not the renunciation of non-alignment.

Of the French colonies in Asia, only Cambodia has achieved any sort of unity within an authentic neutrality in the Indian style. The government of South Vietnam has taken anti-communism as its password and carries on a constant struggle with guerrilla forces organized and supplied by the Communist regime at Hanoi. As for Laos, it is divided into three groups, each of which adopts, in word and deed, one of the three attitudes which have divided French intellectuals since 1945: the Pathet Lao is Communist, a portion of the army recommends a resolutely anti-Communist policy, Prince Souvanna Phouma,[2] half-brother of the Communist leader (Souvannouvong), is trying to reconcile the nation by means of a neutral policy in foreign affairs and a conciliatory domestic regime.

In Africa the Negro republics have all achieved independence without going through the "War of Liberation" phase. The diplomatic line followed by the governments of these new states depends almost exclusively on the preferences of the man (or at the very most, of the few men) in control of

---

[2] He seemed, at the end of 1960, to have thrown in his lot with his Communist half-brother. Two years later he was taken on the other side.

the majority party or the single party. The preferences of this man, or of these men, are not out of line with the economy of the country or the wishes of its people, but no one can doubt that the leader, whether he be called Sekou Touré or Houphouët-Boigny, who was free yesterday to decide between *yes* or *no* in the constitutional referendum of September 1958, is free today to choose between the preservation of present ties with other nations and complete independence, to speak the language of the Western democracies, of the more or less active neutralists, or of the leftists close to the Communists. The French-speaking states of black Africa, all underdeveloped in the general sense of that term, are not, at least in the near future, condemned to shift from independence to a leftist position via neutrality or neutralism: the political leaders who presided over the "liberation" are able to refuse a break with the metropolitan state and, without siding with either bloc in the international arena, remain economically and intellectually linked with the West.

Neither Tunisia nor Morocco broke with France, despite the prolongation of the Algerian dispute. In 1961 secondary education was conducted in French, and the future University of Tunis was to be for the most part French-speaking. The situation is not much different in Morocco. It is true that the French "colonies" in the ex-protectorates have melted away since the accession to independence. By April 1960, 114,000 French people, or 63 per cent of the total number, had left the Republic of Tunisia. The rate of departure has been slower in Morocco where, on the same date, 200,000 French people remained out of 315,000 to 330,000 (between 35 and 40 per cent). Despite the rapid liquidation of "French society" settled on Islamic territory, Tunisia and Morocco continue to trade for the most part within the franc zone. Over 50 per cent of Moroccan imports come from France (51 per cent in 1959), over 50 per cent of Moroccan exports go to France (62 per cent in 1958, 56 per cent in 1959).

Let us recapitulate the three zones of French colonization: Indo-Chinese states, African Negro republics and North Africa. The fundamental point in the present situation in Indo-China is the fact that the leaders of the nationalist movement—the Viet-minh—were also Communists. The successive French governments were incapable of choosing between a compromise with the Viet-minh—despite the allegiance of its leaders to Moscow—an agreement with the non-Communist nationalists (Ngo Dinh Diem) and an opposition to both communism and nationalism. The results were the partition of Vietnam and the tearing apart of Laos, only Cambodia, thanks to the intelligence of Prince Norodom Sihanouk, having managed to preserve both the unity of its people and diplomatic neutrality.

In Tunisia and Morocco the essential fact has been the bourgeois composition and leadership of the nationalist movements. The *combattant suprême* is an orator who can speak French as well as Arabic. Far removed from communism, his desire[3] is a Tunisia independent but still linked with the West as much as with the Arab world. There are fewer middle-class people of French education in Morocco than in Tunisia, and many of the political and labor leaders, since they do not speak French, have, only to a negligible extent, come under the intellectual influence of their ex-protector. Independent Morocco will probably be closer to Arab or Islamic nationalism than Tunisia. But here again, the diplomatic attitudes assumed depend on essentially political circumstances—method of achieving independence, composition of the party which conducted the struggle for liberation, relations with the metropolitan state, sentiments of the people and, even more, of the leaders with regard to transnational movements (Arabism, communism) and to the blocs.

Let us summarize the conclusions of these analyses. If we call those states which do not explicitly belong to one of the military blocs *non-aligned*, and those countries which do not form a part of either the Western or the Soviet worlds the third world, then neither the non-aligned countries nor the third world presents any unity in political institutions, values or diplomatic attitudes. The choice between the two camps, the various nuances of neutrality and neutralism are determined by multiple causes, much more political than economic, among which the formation of elite groups is the most important. In the present century the masses are everywhere potentially active. It is the minorities which realize the revolutionary potential. If these minorities, regardless of geographical location, rally to communism and to Moscow, then all the rest—party organization, mass leadership, nationalization of private property, an authoritarian planned economy—will follow.

2. Dollar Diplomacy and Ruble Diplomacy

For the first time in history the rich peoples are or seem to be aiding the poorer peoples without expectation of return. For the first time in history it is now accepted as consistent with the interests of the strong to aid the weak. For the first time in history the beneficiaries of these gifts are formulating demands of their own and rejecting those of their benefactors. For the first time in history each of the latter seems to fear a greater generosity on the part of its rival. Yet the nature of men and of states has not changed.

In the preceding chapter we analyzed the economic organization of the blocs. Devastated by the war, the European countries west of the Iron Curtain were subjected to pressure from the nascent Soviet bloc. The United States invested in those countries, in the form of gifts and loans, some twenty billion dollars in several years. Original in the vastness of its scope, the Marshall Plan was easily accounted for by the *new* conditions introduced into the *traditional* rivalry between states: a state's allegiance is a function of its

[3] Or what he desired, before the Bizerte crisis.

regime, and the American *grand frère* by his gifts favored those men and those parties devoted to his cause.

During the first postwar period, as we have seen, the experience of the other half of Europe offered a perfect contrast with the experience of Western Europe. Stalin's empire was triply pathological: *it lowered iron curtains between its own satellites*, each being thus imprisoned within itself and condemned to reproduce the Soviet model on a Lilliputian scale; *it disregarded economic division of labor among provinces*, the agreements between socialist countries being all bilateral without any apparent effort toward a rational integration of those agreements into a coherent whole; *it kept the lion's share for the conqueror*, thus invalidating the claims of the *grand frère* to being the missionary of the new faith. Everything that has happened since 1956 seems to indicate that the Soviet Union has recognized the incompatibility between economic exploitation and ideological conversion. Russia now behaves like a real *grand frère*, egotistic but enlightened.

The mixed corporations have been liquidated, the reparation levies have come to an end, the terms of trade (which still give occasion for public controversy from time to time) no longer seem intentionally unjust, further, both Hungary and Poland, after their revolutions, have received aid from Moscow. Ruble diplomacy, in Europe, has had neither the same purpose nor the same scope as dollar diplomacy. Total credits to the satellite countries, between 1945 and 1956, amounted to no more than 727 million dollars. Between February 1956 and May 1958, the total credits to these same countries reached 966.5 million dollars,[4] to which we should add 1,770,500 dollars in canceled debts. Two billion dollars' worth of credit to the countries of the Soviet bloc between 1945 and 1960 are insignificant compared to the twenty billion of the Marshall Plan; but the gap in resources and standards of living between the *grand frère* and his siblings is not the same in the East as it is in the West. Today, relations within the blocs, on the economic level, are comparable: by planning or by free exchange, the two blocs are attempting to organize production and exchange on a rational basis, each bloc creating a potentially worldwide market inside which the principle of the division of labor may be applied.

The argument by which the generosity of the Marshall Plan was justified, in realistic terms, is valid, even more obviously, in the case of the underdeveloped countries. The poorer a country is and the further it is from the threshold of self-sustained growth, the more it needs help from an outside source. In fact, economic aid is all the more useful if the beneficiaries already possess the administrative material, political and intellectual capital necessary to economic progress, as was the case in Western Europe, which for several years was short of foreign currency. American aid provided foreign exchange and, at the same time, the counterpart funds proceeded to in-

[4] J. J. Berliner, *Soviet Economic Aid*, New York, 1958, pp. 50 ff.

crease investments. Since 1950–51, Europe has been able to continue its progress alone. When the *social* conditions of growth are not already present, aid seems *economically* necessary and is often fruitless.

Until recently, economic aid was thought of as the monopoly of the United States. Since Stalin's death and above all during the past few years the Soviet Union has, in its turn, entered the lists. Sometimes even, paradoxically, the same country receives aid from both camps at once. How can the two camps both have an interest in supporting the same regime? This paradox is not inexplicable once it is placed in its world context.

To understand the use to which, in recent years, Soviet strategy has put its economic weapons, two propositions, both of a very general nature, must be established from the very start. A foreign trade entirely conducted by the state is normally controlled by political considerations far more than a foreign trade conducted by private companies or persons. This does not mean that *all* foreign credit offers (Soviet aid normally takes the form of long-term loans at a low rate of interest, 2 or 2.5 per cent) are inspired by more or less sinister designs of infiltration or subversion, but the observer is inclined to give a subtle interpretation to *all* the agreements concluded between the Soviet Union and underdeveloped countries, since a political advantage *might always* result from these agreements even if such was not their objective.

Further, the Soviet leaders seem to have recognized the importance, at least the psychological importance, of economic aid as an argument in the debate or a weapon in the contest whose stake is the future allegiance of the underdeveloped countries. They have manifestly attempted to give the Soviet Union, in its role as super power, the reputation of a lender whose means are not inferior and whose generosity is superior to that of the Western super power. To aid a non-aligned country is to prove by actions that one possesses a surplus, that the sacrifices willingly accepted by the Russian people for forty years now enable them to contribute to the amelioration of the lot of less fortunate peoples. The Soviet Union, by this very action, claims its place among the rich nations and, by the way in which it gives aid, abstaining from the imposition of any conditions, prides itself on its disinterestedness. Economic aid in such cases is an instrument of *persuasion*, not a means of subversion.

In this light the Soviet Union's contribution to India's development becomes intelligible. If the West is convinced that it is helping to maintain liberal institutions by the development of metallurgical industries, why is the Soviet Union doing likewise when, according to all observers, its aim is entirely the opposite? There is a double explanation, it seems to me: the development of metallurgical industries by Soviet technicians puts the homeland of socialism on the same level as the homelands of capitalism. The operation is profitable in terms of prestige, and it is not costly on the other levels. The Soviet leaders, according to their own philosophy, must believe that economic development leads no less surely to socialism than stagnation.

In addition, the sums advanced to India by the Soviet Union are quite small: 200 million dollars more or less will scarcely make any great difference to the present experiment (credits granted up till the end of 1957 amount to 362 million dollars).

Another interpretation[5] also comes to mind: this economic aid might be a means of infiltration. It might make it possible to introduce ideas and spies on the spot. This explanation seems to me unlikely: why should Soviet capital achieve what American capital has never been able to achieve? In any country the most efficient propagandists are always the Communist nationals. The spy network is always separate from the party's official organization. It is possible that certain Soviet engineers belong to an information network, just as many diplomats supplement their public duties with clandestine activities. But the Soviet Union's economic diplomacy does not permit itself to become entangled in such secondary considerations. The development of metallurgical industries on credit is not a means of supplementing a secret organization for collecting information and initiating political action.

The case of India is almost unique among the countries which have received Soviet aid. This is because Soviet aid has been concentrated on only a few countries, for openly political reasons. This aid has been aimed either at *preventing* the country from entering an alliance with the West and at *linking* it with the Soviet bloc, or else at rendering it, first economically and afterward politically, *dependent* on the Soviet bloc; it is a preparation for eventual *subversion* and either accession or the *reinforcement* of a pro-Communist regime.

Syria and Egypt have been among the principal beneficiaries of Soviet aid (397 million dollars out of a total of 1.581 billion to the end of 1957[6]). Supplying arms to Egypt, whatever the means of payment, was a profitable operation for both parties. Egypt was asserting her autonomy as Yugoslavia had asserted hers: the former by accepting arms from the Soviet Union, the latter by accepting them from America. The Soviet Union won a spectacular victory by demonstrating that the Near East was no longer a Western "game preserve." The small power acquired the possibility of blackmailing the great one.

The diplomatic use of trade agreements, even if the latter include the granting of credit, is no novelty in international relations. All capitalist countries, at one time or another, have oriented their trade relations with a view to political objectives, or to put their capital at the service of their alliances. Before 1914 the capital market, in Paris, was open or closed to

[5] I have not, it may be remarked, discussed the interpretation based on disinterestedness. According to this explanation, the Soviet Union has given aid to India for purely humanitarian reasons. It is not out of hostility to the Soviet Union that I dismiss such an interpretation, but because the leaders of any state, and above all those of an ideocratic state, are forced to consider their own interests by their very function, by the laws of politics.

[6] To the end of 1960, 670 million dollars, apparently excluding the sale of arms.

states according to their likelihood of becoming allies, according to their submission to directives issued from the Quai d'Orsay. The French loans to Tsarist Russia were used for the construction of strategic transport routes, in order to facilitate Allied action in case of war against Germany. The Third Reich, only able to buy certain exports from the Balkan and Danube countries, tried to link those countries to its own fortunes. Neither the experiment of France nor that of the Third Reich confirms the effectiveness of these methods unconditionally.

Before 1914, as before 1939, trade and financial agreements were used to ratify rather than to create solidarities and oppositions. At the crucial moment it is the geographical position, the sentiments of the people, the national objectives, the anticipation of the result of a struggle which determine the allegiance of each nation. The network of agreements woven by Dr. Schacht did not prevent Yugoslavia from fighting against the Third Reich. Rumania yielded only when Hitler's armies were in command of Europe. Hungary counted on German revisionism to satisfy her own ambitions.

There is no proof that matters will turn out differently today. The first offers of Soviet aid caused a certain stir because they were the inauguration of a new phase and took people by surprise. But Burma has not been won over morally because the Soviet Union has offered to buy her rice harvest in a year when there were no takers in the capitalist market. The Soviet technique—loan rather than gift, entire freedom of the beneficiary to choose what the loan shall be used for—is probably better received than certain features of the Western technique (examination by experts of the projects for which the aid has been requested). Other elements in the comparison may reverse or modify these preferences. The Soviet products which the countries receive, whether merchandise sold or exchanged or secured through credit, do not always give satisfaction.

Economic aid by itself is a successful means of assuring the allegiance of a small power only on one condition: the aid must be equivalent to an important part of the assisted country's national income. This condition has been fulfilled in two cases, Afghanistan and Syria. The 115 million dollars advanced to the former was equivalent to 23 per cent of its 500 million-dollar national income; the 184 million dollars advanced to Syria was equivalent to 46 per cent[7] of national income estimated at 400 million dollars. In this case the resultant state of political-economic dependence risks leading to Sovietization. When the United Arab Republic was created, Syria was in the process of being conquered from within by the Communist party there. It is possible that Afghanistan will henceforth belong to the Soviet sphere of influence, although nothing can be thought of as irrevocable as long as the leaders have not lost the power to break with their "benefactor" and turn to the other super power.

[7] This percentage is valid for the total credit granted from 1953 to 1957, but not necessarily for the credit used.

During the last few years the formation of regimes ideologically favorable to the Soviet bloc without being composed of militant Communists has offered the Soviet Union the opportunity for another category of aid. Once Guinea or Cuba suddenly loses its usual customers and suppliers, the other super power comes to the assistance of the victim of the blockade (the United States did exactly the same thing for Yugoslavia when she was cut off from the Soviet bloc to which she had belonged). But above all, the Soviet bloc buys Cuban sugar and provides the island with petroleum and machinery. We should add that these exchanges operate in the form of a barter: only 20 per cent of the first million tons of Cuban sugar have been paid for by Moscow in negotiable currency.

In what ways does the Soviet practice with regard to economic aid differ from that of the West? The last kind we have considered—aid to dissidents from the other bloc—is common to both blocs: the only question is to know which of the two will have more opportunities to offer aid to such dissidents. Spectacular offers of aid, for reasons of prestige, are more typically Soviet than Western because the United States has no need to advertise its wealth: the non-aligned countries are perfectly aware of the wealth of the American Republic. The United States has two ways of giving aid which have no equivalents on the other side: *defense support programs,* or dollars given to South Korea, to Chiang Kai-shek in Formosa, or to South Vietnam in order to maintain armies for which local resources would be insufficient, and still more important, *strictly economic aid* to non-aligned countries, comparable to that which the Soviet Union grants to countries within its own bloc, but whose aim is not to provide a spectacular manifestation of generosity (India is, as it were, a beneficiary of a *potlatch* between the United States and the Soviet Union) but to accelerate economic growth, this being considered an indispensable safeguard for more or less liberal institutions analogous to those of the West and, at the same time, favorable to genuine neutrality.

In the case of "defense support aid" the contrast between the two camps concerns how it is financed: the Soviet Union does not even provide arms for nothing,[8] whereas the United States pays for the arms of a regime threatened internally and externally at the same time. In the case of economic aid, the difference, apart from the question of amount, seems to be a matter of strategic-political conceptions; the Soviet Union, outside its own bloc, has aimed mostly at nearby objectives, the seduction of hesitant countries or the reinforcement of countries already won over to a positive neutralism, while the American strategy sometimes takes its inspiration from an elementary Marxism: the progress of underdeveloped countries would in itself favor the cause of the West. According to this theory, developing countries are less vulnerable to Communist subversion. The Western powers,

[8] Indications suggest that the arms supplied to Cuba in 1960 were free.

and above all the Americans, have spent billions in territories which Soviet leaders refer to as "colonial or semi-colonial," these investments, whether public or private, often producing neither gratitude nor friendship. It is possible, moreover, that tomorrow's historian will view with similar irony the aid the Soviet Union has granted to the People's Republic of China: is there room for two *grands frères* within one and the same bloc? Will not one of them, as George Orwell says, want to be a little more equal than the other?

Is there an aspect of the economic expansion of the Soviet bloc which we have failed to consider? Are the credits granted by one or another Soviet state not intended, like the credits granted by Great Britain or by the Federal Republic of Germany, for the immediate purpose of winning a market but also for the long-range aim of reducing the zone of the "capitalist world market" and, at the same time, precipitating the "final crisis" of capitalism?

The Soviet Union and its partners are now producing large quantities of the merchandise which the underdeveloped parts of the world eagerly absorb. The extension of commercial trade between the Soviet bloc and the non-aligned countries is not, in itself, either an instrument of the cold war or an element of economic aid: it is an expression of the progress achieved by the Soviet bloc. As the latter gradually advances along the path of industrialization and exhausts its richest deposits of primary raw materials, it imports either more raw materials which are cheaper outside the bloc or else more manufactured goods complementary to those which it produces itself. The real question centers on the intentions of the Soviet economists: have they given up their old conception of reducing to a minimum the dependence of the socialist bloc on the capitalist world, or, in order to hasten the latter's decay, are they hoping to deprive it, by means of a strictly commercial competition, of its suppliers and customers?

We should note first of all that, apart from the countries which have received major Soviet credits in proportion to their national income (Afghanistan, Egypt, Yugoslavia),[9] the underdeveloped countries conduct over 90 per cent of their foreign trade with non-Soviet countries. Only Egypt, in 1956, was selling over 30 per cent (34 per cent) of its exports to the Soviet bloc, followed by Yugoslavia with 24 per cent. Only Yugoslavia and Afghanistan received over 20 per cent of their imports from the Soviet bloc.

Furthermore, the so-called underdeveloped countries represent only a modest fraction of the Soviet Union's foreign trade, which in its turn is very modest considered as a function of the gross national product of the Soviet Union or of the Soviet bloc as a whole. In 1948 the underdeveloped countries[10] were absorbing 20 per cent, in 1953, 8 per cent, in 1956, 23 per cent of

---

[9] These figures are several years old. Only Guinea and Cuba should perhaps be added to the countries just mentioned.

[10] J. J. Berliner, whose figures I have borrowed, places the following nations in this category: Egypt, Ghana, Iran, Iraq, Israel, Lebanon, Morocco, Nigeria, the Sudan, Syria, Turkey, Yugoslavia, Burma, Ceylon, India, Indonesia, Malaya, Pakistan, Vietnam, Argentina, Brazil, Cuba, Uruguay.

the Soviet Union's total exports to countries outside the Soviet bloc. Compared to the Soviet Union's total imports from countries outside the Soviet bloc, imports from underdeveloped countries amounted to 35 per cent in 1948, 13 per cent in 1953, 21 per cent in 1956.[11] For the European countries within the Soviet bloc, the fluctuations were the same but less marked; in 1948 the underdeveloped countries received 22 per cent of the exports of these countries, and the percentage was again the same in 1956, after a drop to 16 per cent in 1953; for imports, the 1948 percentage was 28, falling to 17 in 1953 and returning to 25 in 1956. For the *economic* competition of the Soviet bloc to endanger the West, the Soviet economists would have to convert to a doctrine they have never subscribed to thus far—they would have to allow the supplies and trade outlets of the Soviet bloc to be largely dependent on economies that were not state-controlled. The economists cannot propose as their objective *both* a *relative autarchy* within the Soviet bloc and the *stifling of the capitalist bloc*,[12] deprived of its customers and its suppliers in the underdeveloped zones. And, of these two objectives, it is the first they prefer to the second.

Of course, this does not mean that the Soviet leaders could not exert a very successful pressure on prices in a given market, say petroleum or tin, or even "break" the market by a sudden massive offer. I do not say that such considerations may not sometimes dictate the conduct of those in charge of Russian foreign trade. But I believe such considerations are less familiar to the minds of Bolsheviks than to the minds of capitalists. Only an American businessman could possibly believe that the leaders in the Kremlin are attempting to ruin the United States by lowering world prices or by forcing up American prices to inflationary effect.

The same situation of fact which prevents us from believing that the Soviet Union seeks to drive the capitalist bloc out of the underdeveloped countries by economic competition also permits us to understand why Soviet aid is, or appears to be, more effective than Western aid. Soviet intervention is, for the moment, almost always welcome because it breaks the American or Western monopoly. Suddenly, the rulers of the countries of Asia, Africa or Latin America find another card thrust into their hand which they can play against the capitalist states: what they cannot obtain from the West, they let it be understood, they will ask for and obtain from the East. Of course, economic aid does not automatically entail political allegiance, and Soviet generosity is limited. The Western powers might very well fail to be impressed by this threat: yet they cannot help taking it seriously, either because the leaders who brandish it are capable of going over to Moscow without destroying themselves, or because they declare themselves unable to oppose the Com-

---

[11] The absolute figures for 1956 are as follows: for exports, 183.6 million dollars out of a total of 806.3 million; for imports, 166.1 million out of a total of 780 million.
[12] These two objectives would become compatible, it is true, if the majority of the third world joined the Soviet camp.

munist peril on their own. In both these cases the leaders of the underdeveloped countries have a strong argument, whose vulgar expression would be: "If the Communists win, it will be worse for you than it will for me."

Quantitatively, the superiority of the West appears overwhelming. Sixteen countries[13] (Yugoslavia, India, Egypt, Syria, Afghanistan, Paraguay, Nepal, Indonesia, Ceylon, Cambodia, Burma, Turkey, Argentina, the Sudan, Lebanon, Yemen) received 1.581 billion dollars in credits from the Soviet bloc, 342 million of which had been spent at the end of 1957; these same countries received 781 million dollars in credits from the United States between 1945 and 1947 and 1.816 billion dollars in gifts, or 2.597 billion dollars in all. In 1956 and 1957 the total of American gifts and credits was greater than the total credit granted by the Soviet bloc, although it was during those very years that the latter inaugurated its new policy.[14]

It would not be impossible to make the generosity of the Americans look even more impressive by the use of different statistics.[15] The total of gifts and credits approved for the underdeveloped countries by the United States since 1945 would then reach the figure of 12.815 billion dollars: 835 million to Yugoslavia, 3.404 billion to the Near East, 925 million to southeast Asia, 5.706 billion to the other Pacific and Asian areas (excluding Japan), 1.945 billion to the Latin American republics. For the single year 1957 the total amounts to 1.628 billion (the regional breakdown is: 45,343,145,847,-248). But such figures call for explanations and commentaries. A considerable portion of the gifts is the counterpart of the agricultural surpluses which the governments of India and Yugoslavia pay in their national currency, the United States then giving these governments the freedom to use the counterpart for the needs of their economies. A large part of the economic aid to the Asian countries turns out to be "defense support." In 1956, out of a total of 763 million dollars spent in the Far East, 724 million consisted of "defense support." In the Near East, in Africa and in southeast Asia, "defense support" represented 287 million dollars out of a total of 449 million.

Even eliminating the figures coming under the heading of "defense support," it would still be easy to swell the total amount of Western aid still more by including in it the private long-term American investments (1.268

---

[13] J. J. Berliner, op. cit., pp. 32–34.

[14] According to statistics published by the New York Times, June 19, 1961, the credits granted by the Soviet bloc as a whole amounted to a total of 5 billion dollars at the end of 1960. Credits granted during 1960 were alleged to amount to 1 billion dollars. If this figure is accurate, it represents a substantial increase over the 1955 figures (189 million dollars in credits granted by the U.S.S.R.) and the 1957 figures (411 million dollars), but scarcely any over the 1956 figures (960 million dollars). On the other hand, the credits are spent at the slower rate of some 200 million dollars per year. A study of the C.N.P.F. indicates a figure of 3 billion dollars in economic credits (not including armaments) up to the end of 1960 for the U.S.S.R. alone, which corresponds fairly well to the estimate given by the New York Times. According to the French study, on the other hand, the "aligned" spending already amounts to 2.8 billion dollars.

[15] Ibid., p. 267.

billion dollars in 1956), the loans from the International Bank for Reconstruction and Development (183.7 million dollars in 1957, 1.530 billion dollars from 1954 to 1957). Finally, adding together the statistics we have just quoted, the share of the technical-assistance program of the United Nations financed by the United States, the governmental programs of economic aid presented by other governments of the free world (750 million dollars) and finally the private investments originating within the Atlantic bloc, we reach a total of nearly 5 billion dollars (4,800,000–4,900,000) against a total of 120 million to 200 million for the Soviet bloc.

I shall not say that the 200 million dollars of Soviet aid have been psychopolitically more effective than the 5 billion dollars of Western aid. But the truth is that for one thing these 5 billion dollars are an abstraction, a total arrived at by a computer. Nobody knows this total, it is not proclaimed by any propaganda agency. In matters of publicity and propaganda, what is not known does not exist: only appearances are real. But that is not all: even if this total were publicized, public opinion in the non-aligned countries would deduct from it the defense loans, the private investments (inspired by the desire for profit) and the loans or gifts to colonial or ex-colonial countries (tainted with colonialism). These deductions would cause a massive reduction in the original 5-billion-dollar total, a reduction of at least two thirds and possibly of four fifths. However, even for the year 1957–a year in which Soviet aid was substantial—the strictly economic aid given by the United States alone and by the Atlantic world was still several times greater than that of their rival (leaving aside private investments and the aid given to colonies or ex-colonies). But Soviet aid is concentrated and spectacular, Western aid is not. And above all, a fact that cannot be repeated too often, peaceful competition is not a contest of generosity in which sumptuary expenditure guarantees the victory. If the competition were in the nature of an Indian *potlatch* or a meeting of kings on the Field of the Cloth of Gold, then the West could be certain of success. But it is neither a contest of giving nor a debate between economists.

3. The Dialectic of Subversion

In 1815, after twenty-five years of wars, the European princes, members of a homogeneous system, concluded a Holy Alliance. They were more concerned to weaken the Revolution than to weaken each other. The solidarity of sovereigns outweighed the rivalry of states. The cold war is the same situation reversed. Each bloc wishes to rouse the people against the system established in the enemy bloc. The democratic states and the Soviet states cannot and will not agree, in the manner of the Catholic and Protestant princes, to delimit their respective zones of influence and preserve peace by abandoning the attempt to convert the subjects on the other side of the demarcation line. In the absence of a common desire for stability, the constant effort of persuasion and subversion derives from the heterogeneity of the system.

In Europe this effort is so deeply ingrained in custom that we are no longer even conscious of it. Radio propaganda addressed to whole peoples, which played a spectacular and successful role against the Third Reich, has become a normal institution. Every country talks to listeners in other countries in the same way that the BBC talked to occupied Europe and *les Français aux Français*. The BBC, Voice of America, *Radio-Liberté* all seek to spread or to consolidate feelings hostile to Communist power, to preserve the hope of liberation, or simply to make known what life is like in the West; in every case their minimum objective is to prevent the satellite-princes from being the exclusive sources of information, from keeping a monopoly of ideology and historical interpretation. Now, since the Soviet regimes claim the right to such exclusiveness and to such a monopoly, they regard Western radio propaganda as a subversive activity and treat it as such (by jamming). The West, on the other hand, since it does not lay claim to this exclusiveness or to this monopoly, does not attempt to jam the "Voice of the Soviet Union," because such jamming would contradict its doctrine, and because the *other*, in any case, is expressing its opinions through the intermediary of those who, quite disinterestedly, are dedicated to its cause.

The heterogeneity of the system seems, at first glance, to favor the West on this point: the latter readily accepts the loss of a monopoly which it has never needed and which does not accord with the logic of its institutions, while the Soviet state is vainly trying to stifle the voice of the "third man" interposed between itself and the masses. The West does not forbid the victims of capitalism to seek refuge in those regions where there is no "exploitation of man by man," yet the flood of emigrants continues to flow from East to West.

It is true that if, as the result of a "contest of ideas," a Soviet regime is shaken or destroyed, the *grand frère* retains the supreme recourse to military force (the Western *grand frère* would not have this supreme recourse, at least in Western Europe). Outside of such extreme situations, Communist propaganda is only one of the weapons, and one of the least effective, in the Soviet arsenal, just as the strictly Communist organizations form only one, and not always the most important one, of the organizations dependent on Moscow. The campaigns against German rearmament, against the atom bomb, in favor of Franco-Soviet friendship, are only three of the innumerable examples of the technique—let us call it infiltration—by which Soviet policy attempts to win sympathizers or adherents to its cause in milieus which would not subscribe to the Communist cause presented as such. The profit gained from these subsidiary actions and from these "parallel organizations" is double: the opposition which would have manifested itself, in any case, against a measure desired or taken by a Western government is amplified; non-Communist are thus induced, without even realizing it, to militate in an association whose leaders are all either Communists or pawns in a game directed by Communists.

Despite these advantages, the balance-sheet of heterogeneity in Europe is more even than most observers are inclined to believe, at least in the sphere of psycho-political warfare. In fact, the presence of the West between the Kremlin and the Soviet citizen is quite as real and perhaps more effective than the presence of the Soviet Union between the White House or Westminster on the one hand and the American or British citizen on the other. The influence of the *third man* is not proportionate to the freedom with which his voice is allowed to be heard. The voice of the West carries all the farther for being three quarters muffled. If the voice of the Soviet Union has achieved such renown in France, it is because there are millions of French people who think they are, or wish to be, hostile to the established order. That they are being mobilized or manipulated by the Communist party affords certain disadvantages, but it also has its advantages as long as they are not in a position to seize power. The adherence of millions of French voters to the Communist party in the elections falsifies the functioning of democracy because that party is, as it were, excluded from the community, untouchable. But this exclusion also makes possible a pro-Western policy which these same electors, by choosing "neutralist" or "socialist" representatives would threaten with paralysis.

For the time being, after fifteen years of the cold war and of the dialectic of persuasion-subversion, the Soviet citizen appears to be quite as little inclined to revolt against the so-called Communist regime as the American citizen against the so-called capitalist-democratic regime. In Europe the Soviet bloc has, on the whole, lost the battle of ideas. No one seriously doubts that if free elections with more than one party were to be held today, all the countries of Eastern Europe would return to a constitutional-pluralist system of government. But the peoples of Europe on both sides of the demarcation line have even less doubt that such elections will not be held. The events of 1956, which have not been forgotten, confirm that in those places where the proletariat has been "liberated," rebellions, which must by definition be counterrevolutionary, are not tolerated. Communism on the Continent appears less as the hope of men than as the inexorable law of history.

The balance-sheet of heterogeneity and the dialectic of subversion are different in the relations of the two blocs with the third world, which lies open to the propaganda of the two blocs, to the infiltrations of men and ideas coming from both (as long, that is, as the Communists are not in control). It is not the *arbiter* (the best political system for highly developed nations may not be the best for the underdeveloped nations), but it contributes to *historical arbitration*, since neither of the two blocs can gain a victory over the other without war, unless they win the non-aligned countries to their cause. Nor is it the *tertius gaudens*, who assists ironically at the debate or of the struggle between the two super powers, but the very *object* of this dialogue that sometimes has the appearance of a debate (which is the better method of industrialization?) and sometimes that of a death struggle. It is the object, but it is also the *subject*, since the super powers cannot, for the most part, admit the use of force. Now, at least at first glance, one of the two debate-combatants would seem better adapted to the nature and rules of this conflict, which is more political than military, more clandestine than open, more violent than peaceful.

Subversion consists in planting the spark or fanning the flame of discontent in a people, in inciting the masses against their governments, in provoking or exploiting riots, rebellions or revolts in order to weaken rival states and to facilitate the spread of certain institutions even more than certain ideas. For complete success it needs certain definite conditions: in the state attacked, the masses must be dissatisfied and the minorities ready to take action in sympathy with the ideological themes propagated by the revolutionaries both at home and abroad. As for the state effecting the subversion, it must possess agents or an organization capable of transforming rebellion into revolt or revolt into revolution, of directing the revolution in the path most consistent with its interests or with its ambitions. Now, whether it is a matter of ideology or of organization, the Soviet camp is equipped for subversion, and the circumstances favorable to subversion may be found in most of the (third world).

The Soviet ideology is admirably adapted to the needs and desires of those who have received a semi-education from the West (a subtle version of the ideology can be elaborated by great minds eager to render their faith intelligible, if not intelligent). The resentments many Asian, African and Latin American revolutionaries spontaneously feel are in pre-established harmony with the vision of the world presented by Marxist-Leninist propaganda. In Cuba the Communist party played almost no part in the revolution which deposed Batista, but revolutionary dynamism swept Fidel Castro and his men to the place where the men in Moscow wanted to lead them.

Before seizing power the Communist party, whether a clandestine sect or a mass party, takes great pains to paralyze the regimes of freedom and to eliminate liberals and socialists capable of promoting economic development. After seizing power it becomes the single party which, armed with an ideology, directing the masses, imposing an intellectual orthodoxy, gives the government stability, ardor and the appearance, if not the reality, of effectiveness.[16]

The Americans, too, through the intermediary of the Central Intelligence Agency, have tried their hand at subversion. It was the CIA which undermined the regime, in Guatemala, of Colonel Arbenz, who was thought to

---

[16] The political effectiveness is unquestionable. The economic effectiveness, when one considers the results of Soviet agriculture after forty years, is at least disputable or variable according to the region.

be a Communist or a Communist sympathizer. It was the CIA which encouraged the Cuban refugees and organized the lamentable Bay of Pigs invasion attempt But subversive actions controlled by secret services differ in nature from the same actions utilizing the believers of a faith and the militants of a party.

A simplified interpretation would be that the American anti-subversive strategy has banked mainly on economic aid (and has been, in this respect, Marxist in inspiration). It has been paralyzed in many countries by the absence of effective administrators or leaders, without whom dollars corrupt persons more than they favor economic progress.

Occasionally it is subversion itself which prevents recourse to the economic instruments of resistance. Once guerrilla warfare breaks out, as in Laos and South Vietnam, American aid will go for the most part toward maintaining the army, and the resources available for investment will be diminished by that amount. Furthermore, hostilities between Communists and non-Communists will almost inevitably produce a conflict in the latter group between the partisans of national reconciliation or of neutralism and the partisans of "absolute victory." Those in power invoke the state of military emergency in order to curtail liberties. Put another way, the subversive activity, whether indigenous or implanted from without, is an obstacle to the realization of the political-economic conditions of development and favors the paternalistic or traditional despotisms which, in their turn, encourage, against their own wishes, the revolt of the modernizers and the liberals.

I do not wish to discuss propositions raised today to the dignity of dogma. It is true that the peoples of non-aligned nations are more or less conscious of their poverty and of the wealth of a privileged section of the human race. It is true that there is an immense discrepancy between the aspirations of hundreds of millions of men and the actual conditions in which they live. It is true that this discrepancy favors subversive activity and that it is in the interests of the West to reduce it as far as possible. It is true, finally, that the method of industrializing the non-aligned nations is the stake in the debate between the two blocs. But, *to the very extent to which one subscribes to this economic interpretation there results an inevitable primacy of politics.* For, in order to resist subversion by means of economic growth, one must also establish and maintain regimes capable of assuring that growth.

Nowhere, or almost nowhere, in the world is power still founded on tradition, on the past. Kings and princes still exist here and there, the sons of kings or the sons of princes, whose titles go back through the centuries. But these heirs of tradition are either now losing their prestige and authority little by little, or renewing them by redefining themselves with a view to the future. The descendants of emperors, in Mali and Ghana, are today at the head of the leftist parties. Prince Sihanouk, in Cambodia, heads the neutralist party; he supplies the unity for his people in relation to the two blocs, while at the same time the memory of his ancestors probably affords him a sort of respect rarely granted to men who owe everything to themselves and to circumstances.

Power being essentially turned toward the future, aggressively revolutionary parties and regimes often have an advantage, at least at first glance. They present an internal logic, carrying the consequences of their principles to a logical conclusion. Since all the experts admit the necessity of a semi-planned economy in order to reach the economic "take-off point" more quickly, they propose a totally planned economy. Since no one questions the necessity for the people's acceptance of, or even enthusiasm for, sacrifices, they are able to mobilize the masses better and more thoroughly than all the other parties. The Communists are the great simplifiers. If political effectiveness is defined as the minority's art of imposing its will on the majority, inducing the majority to act according to the will of the minority while believing that it is obeying only its own wishes, then the technique of Communist action may truly be called supremely effective.

On the other hand, despotisms like those of Syngman Rhee or Diem, or semi-despotisms like that of Menderes in Turkey, constitute mere expedients. They alienate the moderate left-wing, the modernizers concerned to preserve the liberal heritage of the West; they force democrats of good will toward communism, without even insuring order and administrative competence as a compensation. It is difficult to make any general judgment of the comparative performances of the liberal regimes and the despotic regimes in South America, but on the whole, it does not appear that the violation of constitutional law has favored development, or that military leaders in power have done better work in the cause of economic progress than representatives elected by the people or in assemblies.

Not that one cannot discern, during the last hundred years, the figures of several despots belonging to the type, already defined by Aristotle, of the "progressive tyrant," acclaimed by the poor and vilified by the privileged, or of the tyrant who erects impressive monuments. Perón was for a long while supported by the trade-unions, and still retains millions of loyal followers. Vargas, in Brazil, was constitutionally elected after having held power illegally some years before and then re-establishing a constitutional regime himself. But conservative or reactionary despots are more numerous than the progressive ones. Perón was a "demagogue" rather than a "modernizer."

Despotism without a single-party system does not guarantee a regime capable of carrying out the initial tasks of industrialization. A despotism with a non-Communist single party would risk taking the path followed by the Fascist parties between the two world wars. In nations where there is a relatively numerous political class and a modern culture, a single party needs an ideology in order to prevail. It is not possible to direct the masses, to recruit militants, to maintain discipline inside the organization, without some forceful ideas capable of awakening enthusiasm for a great undertaking or for a set of sacred values. What could the basic content of an ideology for a non-Communist single party be, if not nationalism? Perhaps a certain nationalism is necessary to attain the "economic take-off point" to achieve the moral cohesion of peoples who have been given the status of states, before the individuals have acquired the sense of their community. But the fervor of nationalism always runs the risk of degenerating into frenzy and, in Latin America at least, might it not rise in opposition to the West?

Diversity of its political systems will be the mark of the non-Communist third world during the coming decades, and it would be ridiculous as well as unreasonable to carry on a crusade for democratic orthodoxy as though the West were betraying itself by abandoning the attempt to impose throughout the world the political system which it considers the best in or for itself. The Soviet bloc, in the battles waged within states, has a constant objective: to help the party which follows the Kremlin line and aspires to a regime derived from the Communist model. Despite this constant objective, the diplomacy of the Soviet Union, if not that of China, does not hesitate to support, in certain countries, a nationalist party hostile to the West but also hostile to a regime of the so-called Marxist-Leninist type. The Western bloc has no constant objective equivalent to that of the Soviets because no one party in power is a guarantee of a "pluralist democracy," in the same way that a Communist party guarantees the elaboration of a "people's or socialist democracy."

To the tactical opportunism thus imposed on both camps we must add, for the Western bloc, the obligation to adapt its own institutions to the various demands of other nations, an adaptation that the Soviet bloc legitimately postpones until after seizing power. A Communist party that imitates the organization of the Bolshevik party and, after its conquest of the state, introduces the same monopoly of propaganda, education and authority, is in fact adopting the substance of the Russian political system. The wigs worn by judges in Ghana, the mace of the Speaker of the House, are merely symbols: the adoptions of these symbols illustrates, without confirming, the intention of prolonging a Western tradition. But parliamentary debate and representation are only institutional forms: it is practice alone that constitutes the substance of a system. Will the parties play the game as it should be played?

This does not mean that Communist parties or parties applying Communist methods are indispensable or inevitable during the "take-off" phase or during the present historical phase. It only means that the Western powers cannot be certain of finding in every country a solution that will be acceptable in their eyes—in other words, a party, group or individual capable of effecting the modernizing process without rallying to the Soviet bloc. The support given to "non-progressive despots" cannot always be excused by the absence of other candidates fit to wield power. But it is still true that the choice sometimes seems to be restricted to alternatives of which one is immediately deplorable and the other deplorable in a remoter future, one being a Communist or leftist regime, the other a despotic regime unable to meet the requirements of modernization. Inevitably, American and even Western diplomacy prefers the second alternative—a preference as inevitable as it is disagreeable.

The Soviet camp possesses three indisputable advantages in the battle of subversion. The single-party totalitarian regimes violate the rules of peaceful competition since they refuse their adversaries the liberties they themselves benefit from elsewhere. The quasi-revolutionary situation of a great part of the third world favors those parties which re-establish order, at whatever price, over the parties concerned with the equilibrium between state authority and the rights of the citizens. Finally, the elites of the majority of non-aligned nations, if they are forced into making a choice, prefer economic development to representative institutions, factories to freedom; they accept despotism provided it is a modernizing force.

During the initial phases of growth, very few of the third-world nations will practice a pluralist-constitutional democracy in accord with British or American orthodoxy. But the White House and the Kremlin are the symbols of two worlds, not the two terms of an inexorable choice. Even in Europe there is no rigorous correspondence between internal institutions and the position taken in world affairs. *A fortiori* we must dissipate the fear that all the third-world countries, governed by methods we regard as despotic, belong, morally or diplomatically, to the Soviet bloc. Even the countries whose regimes may be classified as "single-party systems" present a spectrum that runs from pro-Western Tunisia to Guinea. Cuba became the most pro-Soviet of the third-world republics before it acquired a single-party regime.

4. The Dialectic of Neutrality

The fifteen years of the cold war between 1945 and 1960 may be divided into two particularly clear-cut phases with regard to the relations between the blocs and the non-aligned nations. During the first, the blocs, after having been crystallized in Europe, apparently strove to recruit clienteles in the other parts of the world, as if both had decided their objective ways to create in every zone of the planet a situation equivalent to the one bequeathed to the Continent by the Second World War. On the one hand, American diplomacy, after 1947–48, took pains to make alliances with all the peoples who would agree to do so and to supply them with arms theoretically intended as a defense against external aggression, actually often used (especially in Latin America) to keep the rulers of the countries in power. On the other, the ideological-diplomatic line followed by the Soviet Union permitted only two alternatives to exist, not three: two camps, two kinds of nation and regime were at grips during the present phase of the world revolution and of the transition from capitalism to socialism. The new so-called liberated states, which did not join the socialist camp, remained in reality, according to Moscow's interpretation, under the yoke of neo-colonialism, voluntary or involuntary agents of imperialism. India's neutrality at the beginning of 1953, before Stalin's death, was "immoral" in the eyes of John Foster Dulles, while according to the Kremlin spokesmen it was a form of subjection to or alliance with the West.

No one attained the goal he sought in this strange competition in which each bloc seemed to be doing its best to present the other with unearned successes. The refusal of India or of the Arab countries in the Near East to form diplomatic ties with the West constituted a success for the Soviet Union, but the Kremlin hastened to deny the substance of that success by attributing to the West the capacity (which it did not in fact possess) of gaining by clandestine manipulation whatever it failed to achieve by open diplomacy. Moreover, neither of the Big Two succeeded in pushing into the arms of the other those whose allegiance was being sought and whose abstention was being denounced. Once again Nehru's India is symbolic, standing by her neutrality despite contradictory and convergent accusations of "immorality" and "submission to imperialism."

From 1953 on, the ideological-diplomatic line of the Soviet Union gradually changed. Stalin's successors made it their immediate aim to break up the West's system of alliance or influence. Far from denouncing those countries that declared themselves neutral and unwilling to enter the conflict between the two blocs, they openly approved of this course and declared themselves ready to grant such countries economic aid. The travels of Mr. Bulganin and Mr. Khrushchev in Asia were the proof and symbol of this conversion. Not that the theses of Soviet dogma relative to the two blocs, their inexpiable struggle and the ultimate commitment of all countries to one or the other, had been abandoned. But neutrality had been recognized as legitimate and potentially authentic during the present phase. This interpretation was manifestly in keeping with Soviet interests and favorable to the bloc's undertakings as a whole, since it offered all the countries linked to the West the opportunity of detaching themselves from their friend, their protector or their master without taking the risk of being forced into a new liaison.

The Western powers hesitated a long while before accomplishing a comparable conversion. In 1954, after the disaster of Dien-Bien-Phu, the southeast Asian defense treaty was concluded—a pact which the Soviet Union denounced as aggressive, and which the neutral countries (India in particular) deplored because it was likely, they claimed, to introduce the cold war into southeast Asia. In the Near East, it was, again, after Stalin's death that the so-called Baghdad Pact was signed, a treaty in which Jordon was unable to participate because of internal disturbances and which the United States approved without entering. After the revolution which cost the King of Iraq and Noury Saïd their lives, this pact was comprised of only the non-Arab Moslem countries (Turkey, Iran, Pakistan).

It would be difficult, even if it were our intention, to gauge the advantages and disadvantages of these "multilateral agreements." In the Near East they are unpopular (as was proved by the disturbances in Jordan and Iraq); they annoy the neighboring countries that wish to remain neutral, and they make it difficult to maintain good relations with the pro-Western and non-aligned nations, the former clamoring for the reward of their fidelity and the latter threatening to seek from the other side what they are denied by the West. But the regimes that are weak internally are often strengthened by a regional alliance, by the proof that they command the interest of a world power. And the latter obtains, in return, military bases.

In southeast Asia, according to a joke current in Washington, the treaty was signed as much between the President and Congress as between the United States and its allies in Europe and Asia. The commitment, vague in any case, which the United States assumed toward Thailand, Pakistan, South Vietnam, Laos and Cambodia (the last three protected by the treaty, which they did not sign) permits the President to present and justify, before Congress and public opinion, an intervention in this part of the world as a supreme military recourse, at the same time as it perhaps consolidates regimes threatened internally, and provides a means of associating France and Great Britain in the collective action. It remains to be seen whether the presence of European allies, indispensable to the action's collective character, will not entail, in case of crisis, the probability of inaction. It also remains to be seen whether the United States can flatter or help the neutral countries without incurring the displeasure of its allies, whether it can arm the latter without alienating the former.

Despite this persistence, inevitable in any case, of the method of military alliances, the United States was gradually obliged by the dialectic of the competition to adapt its answer to the challenge, to cease demanding commitment to the West as a counterpart to the Soviet offer of non-alignment. The American conversion, posterior to the Soviet conversion, was effected gradually by the force of circumstances.[17] In 1956, after the crisis of the Israeli expedition to Sinai and the Franco-British landing on the Canal, the United States tried, according to its own expression, to "fill the gap" opened by the retreat of the European powers. But this gap could not be filled by military alliances, which all the Arab countries—Egypt, Syria, Jordan— passionately rejected and which public opinion condemned even in Iraq. In those countries where the populations—elites and masses—harbor too many resentments against the Western nations to tolerate any kind of solidarity with them, the best the latter can hope for is that these countries will not shift from one camp to the other, but will stop at some intermediate position, without slipping from neutrality or neutralism into pro-Sovietism. In other words, the disintegration of the "empires" and the disappearance of the "private hunting grounds," hastened but not provoked by the diplomacy of

[17] The conversion is still not general. The United States would be very disturbed by a Latin American declaration of non-alignment or neutralism.

Stalin's successors, put the Western powers in a position where they were forced to accept, in their turn, the neutrality of certain countries.

The dialectic of competition implies the adoption by one camp of the other's watchword. When a country is linked to the West, Soviet diplomacy attempts to convince it of the advantages of neutrality. When that same country seems on the point of joining the Soviet bloc, then it is the West's turn to undertake the defense and illustration of neutrality. Of course, neutrality covers many different realities, and the two camps often use the same word without having the same thing in mind. But once it has been understood that each camp prefers one kind of neutrality to another, it is not impossible for both of them to reach agreement, in certain circumstances, on a precisely defined neutrality, even though this may better suit the ideology and interests of one more than it might of the other.

In Europe the Soviet Union signed a treaty which entailed its evacuation of Austrian territory and insured the neutrality of an Austria whose internal regime was liberal and sympathetic to the West. In 1958 the Western powers directed their efforts in Lebanon toward maintaining the internal equilibrium of the communities at the same time as the country's diplomatic neutrality. The West, resigned to aim at the possible rather than the desirable, sought first to prevent an Islamic-Christian Lebanon from rallying to a positive neutralism, and second to prevent an Egypt already won over to positive neutralism from rallying to the Soviet bloc.

The case of Laos, in 1960–61, marked a further stage, or perhaps simply an original example of neutrality. This was at the same time an aspect of the world conflict and a means of escaping it, a result of the competition between the blocs and an effort to escape from the dialectic of competition. According to the terms of the treaty which ended the war in Indo-China, Laos was not to enter into any military alliance. France still retained two bases there and a military mission whose task it was to train the Laotian army. As two of the northern provinces were in fact occupied and administered by the Pathet Lao movement, under Communist orders, since 1954 there existed the alternative either of civil war or partition, or else of the integration of this movement into a coalition regime, the "partisans" being integrated into the royal army and the principal leader, Prince Souvannouvong, becoming a member of the coalition government. The attempt to create a coalition regime continued from 1954 till 1958; Prince Souvanna Phouma, half-brother of the "Red" Prince Souvannouvong, was the symbol of national reconciliation and the head of the so-called neutralist faction. According to him, the neutrality of Laos could only exist on condition that all the factions within the country had a share of governmental power.

In 1958 American diplomacy, fearing that under cover of a national reconciliation, whether genuine or faked, the Communists might succeed in infiltrating the state and seizing all the key positions, instigated the formation of a resolutely pro-Western government. The partisans of the Pathet Lao returned to the bush, while Prince Souvannouvong was jailed.

In 1960, tired of civil war and the corruption in government circles well oiled with American dollars, a parachutist commander named Khong Lee effected a *coup d'état* in favor of Prince Souvanna Phouma and a neutralist government (national reconciliation at home and neutrality abroad), to which the reply, several weeks later, was another *coup d'état* led by General Phoumi Nosavan in favor of a pro-Western government led by Prince Boun Oum. The Pathet Lao and the neutralists fought side by side against the pro-Western part of the royal army. At the Geneva conference in 1961 all the participants—Soviets, Western powers, non-aligned nations—declared themselves in favor of neutrality and a coalition government. The Western powers had abandoned the idea of military intervention. They did not dare declare themselves in favor of partition (they had not the means to do so in any case) and viewed a diplomatically recognized neutrality as a lesser evil than the possibility of a total military victory by the Pathet Lao and the neutralists.[18]

The coalition of the three groups—Communist, pro-Western and neutralist —was to serve for the first time as an internal basis for what was referred to as a diplomacy of neutrality. Such a neutrality would be far different from that of India or Cambodia, even supposing it lasted (which was fairly improbable, the Communist and neutralist groups having the capacity to eliminate the third group, or at least reduce it to impotence). The example of Laos has, nevertheless, a double significance: it illustrates one of the possible solutions for civil wars within a country that is a member of a heterogeneous international system, and it represents one of the first applications of the *troika* principle defined by Mr. Khrushchev in 1960, the principle of the necessary representation of the three groups (the two blocs and the non-aligned nations).

Most countries that contain factions favorable to both blocs and both ideologies are governed by one of these factions by democratic or authoritarian methods, according to the allegiance of the governing faction. France is governed by the national parties, India by the Congress party. In France, as in India, the Communist party is legal; it participates in elections, it has representatives in both local and national assemblies, but it holds no key positions, it wields no influence over the course of diplomacy. Whatever the nature, ideology and practice of the parties or men ruling the United Arab Republic, Cambodia, Yugoslavia or Mali, the neutrality or neutralism of these various countries is not the result of an equilibrium between pro- and anti-Communists, but of a *single* desire, common to all the men and all parties, for non-alignment or for a particular form of non-alignment. Up till the

---

[18] Perhaps the agreement with the Soviet Union was also a means of preventing the intervention of China, in almost open conflict with Moscow.

present time the result of any open and violent conflict between pro- and anti-Communists has always been partition. If it should turn out to be the case—improbable though it seems—that the authentic neutrality of Laos has been safeguarded by a government established according to the *troika* principle, a third solution between those of partition and victory for one of the factions would appear to be possible.

The *troika* principle, equal representation of the three factions (the two blocs and the non-aligned) has a manifestly different meaning according to whether it is applied to the Secretariat of the international organization or to the coalition destined to take over the reins of the little kingdom of Laos. But whether it is a question of Laos or of the United Nations, the same question arises: does the third group really exist as such? Does it have a unity? Is it an impartial arbiter, an equitable judge? Do the different members of the group give the same meaning to an attitude which bears (or may bear) the same name?

Our previous analyses allow us to answer these questions. Among the non-aligned nations (whatever the extension given to the concept) there exists no community either regarding institutions, or the third world ideological preferences or diplomatic action on the world stage. If we apply the term non-aligned nations to all those states that have not contracted a written alliance with either bloc (or with a state which is a member of one of the blocs), Tunisia and Guinea, India and Cuba all figure equally on the list of non-aligned nations. The meanings these states give to non-alignment —whether moral or diplomatic—obviously manifest profound differences.

Mr. Nehru believed in the values and the political institutions of the West, though he often doubted whether the West was being true to itself. Non-alignment, in his eyes, was both a contribution to the *détente* or to peace and an affirmation of freedom of action and mind, each problem having to be assessed on its own, according to the given situation in each case, without this assessment being in any way determined or affected by any position taken up in advance. In this sense Indian neutrality claims a position of impartiality between the two conflicting blocs.

Things are quite different in the case of Yugoslavia, the United Arab Republic, Guinea or Cuba. None of these four countries admits any affinity with the values and the institutions of the West, three of them claim to be Marxist-Leninist, one of them, Yugoslavia, denouncing with intermittent vigor the use made of Marxism-Leninism by Stalin and his successors in the Soviet Union, the other two accepting with the same enthusiasm both doctrine and practice. The fourth, the U.A.R., has so far kept all its invectives for use against the West, but without displaying any internal indulgence of the partisans of leftist or Soviet ideas.

The non-alignment of these four nations expresses a desire not to participate in a conflict in which they are not directly concerned, but not a desire for moral detachment or impartiality. Neither the United Arab Republic, nor

Guinea, nor Cuba, nor Mali, to judge from the speeches of their representatives, can be said to lie halfway between the two blocs and equally open to arguments from both sides, equally anxious to take into account the interests of both camps. Positive neutralism is a commitment in favor of a policy that does not coincide precisely with that of any bloc, but which does not pretend to be, and is not, impartial.

Besides which, even would-be impartial non-alignment is far from being so in effect. For easily understandable reasons, Africans, Asians and Arabs are more sensitive to the misdeeds, whether real or imagined, of colonialism than to those of Soviet imperialism. The war in Algeria made them far more indignant than the forceful repression of the Hungarian Revolution. The fact that the Soviet bloc, with the help of the war, imposed on all the countries of Eastern Europe and on a third of the German nation a regime that those populations would not themselves have chosen and that they would still throw off today if they were free to do so, is of little concern to non-Europeans and above all to the colored peoples. In the eyes of the latter, colonialism begins when ruled and rulers do not have the same color skin. It is not enough to denounce racism in order to be free of it.

The non-aligned nations cannot therefore be considered as a bloc, for they cannot act collectively, and they cannot assume the role of arbiter. When they were forced to choose between the candidates for government in the Congo chaos, they split into two and perhaps three groups, one unreservedly—or nearly so—supporting the Soviet Union in its quarrel with the Secretary-General of the United Nations, the others, on the contrary, approving, more or less with conviction, Mr. Hammarskjöld and the Secretariat of the United Nations. The diplomacy of each non-aligned nation is a function at one and the same time of its local situation, its internal regime, its ideological preferences, and its fears and preferences. The zone of non-alignment will probably grow larger, since in every region of the world at least one of the super powers is passionately declaring itself in favor of neutrality. The United States seeks to "keep Africa out of the cold war"; it would probably have somewhat more mixed feelings if Latin America were to leave that war by a proclamation of neutrality.

The dialectic of neutrality rarely leads to peace, but it controls the ideological and diplomatic modes of peaceful competition, of persuasion and of subversion.

chapter XVIII

The Enemy Partners

The idea that the two great powers of an international system are brothers at the same time as being enemies should be accepted as banal rather than paradoxical. By definition each would reign alone if the other did not exist. And candidates for the same throne always have something in common. The units of an international system belong to a single zone of civilization. Inevitably they both claim, to some extent, the same principles and conduct a debate at the same time that they carry on a combat.

The debate between Washington and Moscow is no less constant than the combat. Both present original features which fundamentally seem to me reducible to the following propositions: the two powers regard themselves as more unlike each other than the observers—the third men—are inclined to admit. The third men regard them as enemies despite their kinship—a conclusion which is not false but which tends to ignore the degree of unconscious or implicit solidarity that tinges their hostility. Each prefers to preserve the thermonuclear duopoly rather than allow the dissemination of weapons of massive destruction, and both fear total war more than the limited advances of their rival.

1. *The Dialogue of the Two and the Others*

Alexis de Tocqueville was the first, a century ago, to give a classic form to the antithesis *Washington or Moscow*. We shall not quote the text, worn out by its own celebrity, but we shall review in everyday language the data—visible at the beginning of the last century—already preparing, without making inevitable, the present duopoly.

The two possessed space and resources before possessing numbers and the modern instruments of force. They had, and still have, a reserve of growth in space. The cultivation of the virgin lands of central Asia is a symbol of the conquest which the peoples of Western Europe or of the Far East had already completed long before. In the course of the nineteenth century the surplus population of Western Europe was absorbed by towns and factories; the growing population in Russia and in the United States spread itself out in space, advanced to the West or to the East, colonized the still empty land. The armies of the Tsar also seized the lands of the old civilization, and the Westerners drove out the Indians, while Washington bought or wrested from France, Spain or Mexico the states of Louisiana, Florida, Texas and California. The historical luck of the two great powers, in this simplifying perspective, was to have achieved their formation in the century of the birth of industrial society, to have extended their sovereignty over a vast territory which had not yet been cultivated, at an epoch when other peoples were exhausting their strength merely to subjugate remote populations or to advance frontiers one or two miles. We have pointed this out in a preceding chapter[1]; the Soviet Union and the United States both have reserves of space, as is indicated by their low agricultural or, more generally, economic productivity per acre.

The coincidence of the scientific-technological revolution and the taking possession of the land explains the primacy accorded to practical tasks, the exploitation of soil and mines and the quest for effective methods of production or profit. Tocqueville attributed the predominating concern for commercial and industrial activities which he observed in the America of 1830 to the original way in which the country had been settled by European immigrants of Puritan tendency now in contact with virgin nature, which to them was a setting for adventure and also a means toward a permanent establishment. The traditional culture inherited by the Russians of today did not stimulate the same desire for economic-technological progress. But it was in order to borrow from the West the instruments of wealth and the weapons of power that Peter the Great undertook the modernization of his country. The ambition to catch up with America in order to build socialism has resulted today with the spread of the cult of machines and an obsession with science and scientific progress. It is possible that the Russians are more conscious than the Western countries, even more conscious than America, of the scientific character of our era: because of their past, the Americans are inclined to link commerce and industry, to identify technological yield and economic yield, to regard the market, competition and profit as elements characteristic of any economic system. In the eyes of the Russians it is production alone that counts, hence technological progress, itself conditioned by scientific progress. In the United States increasing production and productivity are, or seem to be, a by-product of the race for profit; in the Soviet Union they are the direct object of both state planning and the collective ideal.

We have thus suggested the basis for both kinship and hostility. Reduced to ideal types, a modern economy may be regulated in one of two different ways, by planning or by the market. Either the distribution of resources among their various uses, and hence the composition of the national product

1 See Part II, Chap. VII.

and the distribution of incomes are determined by a plan, itself established by the political leaders of the state with the aid of economists or administrators; or else the citizens, by their individual and innumerable purchasing decisions, control the distribution of the collective resources among the sectors, each man's income being determined either by directors or firms or by success or failure in the market. These are, of course, vastly simplified images of the facts. In the West the state also takes upon itself certain tasks which are in the public interest and which cannot be accomplished according to the laws of competition for profit, and by means of the budget, by means of its fiscal and financial policy, indirectly influences the circumstances; volume and even the distribution of investments. The antithesis of the two methods of regulation nevertheless does contain an approximate but incontestable truth, as is evidenced by certain facts, almost symbolic. In 1960 Soviet consumers possessed television sets in abundance while the factories were turning out only two or three hundred thousand pleasure cars a year. It is the state which decides—and its judgment brooks no contradictions—that television sets should be available to the majority of Soviet citizens, but that automobiles should not.

Similarly, the antithesis of private property and public property can be expressed in terms of ideology and propaganda. Either the means of production belong to private persons and to corporations, or else they belong to the state. Here again, the facts are susceptible of a more subtle interpretation. The great American corporations are legally the property of tens of thousands of shareholders, but the power of organization is in the hands of experts and administrators, the supreme authority being granted to a few men who, in fact, co-opt one another far more than they are elected by the assembled shareholders. In this sense one might argue that the concentrations of the means of production no longer belong to anyone anywhere—in the sense that the castle belonged to the baron and the field belonged to the peasant. The right to use or to abuse no longer applies to anything except consumer goods. The administration of the means of production is a generalized social function, fulfilled by one or more individuals in the service of a collectivity. In spite of everything, and whatever the partial truth of this subtle interpretation, the cult of private property and free enterprise, the denunciation of capitalism and the exploitation of man by man, leading to the nationalization of all enterprise, represent the two equally possible and contradictory versions of industrial organization, related because the means of production are in both cases technically the same, hostile because legal relations between private persons and the state are radically different.

An analogous stylized antithesis may be set up at the political level. On one side, two parties carry on a permanent rivalry for the sovereign's favor and participate every four years in a spectacular tournament of which the Presidency is the prize. Numberless pressure groups, workers' unions, management associations, religious communities, voluntary groups of citizens with a local or worldwide aim—the construction of a school or world peace —demonstrate, protest, recommend, endeavor to promote this (the advancement of the rights of the Negro) or to prevent that (discrimination against racial or religious minorities). On the other side, a single party erects a historical-social doctrine into a state truth, and rules in the name of the proletariat which it embodies and in the name of the historical mission it has assigned itself. Diversity of religion or of "national cultures" is recognized, the equality of races and peoples is formally proclaimed, but all questioning of the single party is forbidden.

Here again, the contrast does not exclude similarities. Political life in the United States resembles a carnival, but, beneath the tumultuous surface, social conformism reigns. The majority of citizens obey the same rules and subscribe to the same values. On the other hand, below the smooth surface of the monolithic party, quarrels between factions or personalities—conflicts over what action should be taken and/or over the orthodox interpretation of any event—persist, amplified further by the rivalries between the socialist states, quarrels which to us seem theological in their expression and in which the stakes are both theological and practical.

The kinship-hostility of the two super powers obviously lends itself to two interpretations, one of which insists on the depth of the relation and the other on their inexpiable hostility. At first glance, the *third men* are inclined to choose the former and the duopolists the latter. To devalue the meaning of the conflict is thereby to give oneself a clear conscience in neutrality. To speak of the two barbarians is to exalt, implicitly, the virtues of the third group, of the non-aligned nations, of the recalcitrant allies, of Europe the cradle of civilizations whose flowering has been made possible only by the vast spaces of America and Russia.

But the opposition between the interpretation of relation, characteristic of the spectators, and the interpretation by hostility, characteristic of the actors, is false, because it is a simplification. In certain respects it may be reversed. It is true that on a first analysis each of the super powers understands itself differently from the way in which the other understands it, and that it can no more give up its own interpretation than it can subscribe to the heterointerpretation of its rival. Soviet propaganda denounces American pluralism and the rites of democracy as "illusions" or "hoaxes": the "monopolists," the leaders of capitalism who reserve real power for themselves, exploit the masses and orient American diplomacy in the direction of imperialism. The Russians, by their propaganda, are attempting to "unmask" American democracy, to unveil a reality which will give the lie to its surface appearance. To which the Americans reply that the decisions evidently taken by one man or a few men (how could it be otherwise?) are influenced by the desires or the opinions of the vast majority. It is the dictatorship of the proletariat, adds the American propagandist, which is in reality the dictatorship of the party (in other words, of the minority) *over* the proletariat. The formula was coined by Karl Kautsky at the dawn of the Bolshevik regime; it remains, forty years afterward, the central theme of the accusatory-interpretation of the Soviet regime by its liberal and socialist enemies. How is it possible to call "democracy" or "liberation" the obedience of the masses to a party which is very few in number and itself controlled from above by one man or a few, a party which reserves for itself the monopoly of power, forbids citizens to discuss its right to that power or to choose freely those who will be responsible, in theory, for representing them?

In other words, the dialogue of the propaganda-makers has as its basic theme the question: who is authentically democratic? We are democratic, reply the Soviets, because we have done away with exploiters, monopolists and capitalists, and because among us it is the proletariat that rules. We are democratic, reply the Americans, because our citizens are free to vote, our newspapers free to criticize, our workers free to strike, our generals free to protest. The same dialogue continues on the subject of the classless society; both countries boast that all careers are henceforth open to anyone with talent, but the differences in standard of living and prestige have not been eliminated on one side or the other.

Neither of the two powers, on the level of the dialogue of propaganda, can renounce the attempt to justify itself and unmask its rival. But, on a higher level of subtlety, no American or Russian propagandist keeps to the official version of self-justification and accusation of the other. Upon a moment's reflection one realizes that the merits of the two systems are, in certain respects, the opposite of those which the official spokesmen attribute to them. Authoritarian planning obviously provides the rulers with great facilities, whether it is to accelerate growth by augmenting the percentage of investments or to concentrate resources in such and such a sector of the economic machinery. The sovereignty of the consumers (insofar as it exists) limits and checks the authority of the state. What the one loses in democracy the other loses in economic efficiency or in historical achievement. The open debate on fidelity to the democratic concept masks another half-secret debate, conducted by speakers of a different sort, more sensitive to facts than to ideas, more concerned with knowing to whom the future belongs than who is entitled to lay claim to the highest values.

This dialogue, whose theme is the relative efficiency of the two regimes, does not always assume the character of an exchange of invectives. Half in secret, the economists meet in order to compare their solutions, identical, similar or different, of the same problems; they ask each other objectively what advantages and what disadvantages are implied in the solutions adopted by each of the super powers. Sometimes they even try to discover if a combination of the two techniques would not be best. Similarly the scientists, and in particular the atomic scientists, have discovered in recent years that they have arrived, along similar paths, at similar conclusions. As regards the dialogue of the scientists on the political implications of their knowledge, it is more difficult to measure the exact degree of authenticity.[2]

The paradox of this objective confrontation of the two regimes is that Marxism provides a workable ideological framework that makes it possible. There are two versions of Marxism which can equally well claim to be legitimately descended from Marx himself, one which puts the emphasis on the forces of production, in the technical and social sense of that term, and the other which puts the emphasis on the relations of production and, more particularly, on the relations of property. The first version brings the two regimes *closer,* because they both have, in effect, the same forces of production. The second version forces them *apart* because the relations of production and the status of property are different in the two systems. The former is semi-clandestine in the East but affirmed with a greater or lesser degree of hesitation by numerous sociologists and economists in the West; the latter is officially accepted in the East, and answers all the desires of the economists who are adherents of liberal orthodoxy, despite the fact that the latter make the reverse value judgment in this regard (collective ownership is beneficent according to the Marxists and diabolical according to the liberals).

Of these three dialogues—democracy, effectiveness, forces and relations of production—which is the one which most interests the *third men?* The mistake which must not be made (and which is often made) is to imagine that this question necessarily entails a single answer and that that answer will be defined by the primacy of the debate on the respective *morality* of the two regimes. According to which part of the world they are in, the peoples outside the two blocs have different images of the two super powers, and the interpretation that each people gives of them and of their conflict is controlled first and foremost by the actual situation.

Let us review the reactions of the European nations during the first postwar years. The old states of Europe, yesterday still great powers and now suddenly fallen to the rank of protégé states, hesitated between the obvious fact that American hegemony was preferable to Soviet domination and a nostalgia for their lost autonomy, a dream of non-alignment. The result was a curious distribution of tasks: the statesmen, supported by the majority of voters, were creating, maintaining and reinforcing Atlantic solidarity. On the other hand, many intellectuals, including some true liberals, amused themselves by evoking an image of the two super powers equal in strength and lack of culture.

In Europe the recognition of the enemies' fraternity remained verbal; it was useful as a moral alibi for a commitment that was inevitable and generally accepted, if not desired. Only a very few sought to draw consequences from the situation that were genuinely political. Neither Communists nor

[2] We refer to the conferences of scientists on the question of armaments (called Pugwash conferences).

anti-Communists could subscribe to any *rapprochement* between the two powers. The Communists were obliged to maintain their doctrinal orthodoxy with an intransigence all the greater because the opinion of the majority was hostile to the typical institutions of Sovietism. If the single party, the suppression of electoral, personal and intellectual freedom were not *at the same time* the liberation of the proletariat and the end of the exploitation of man by man, then the similarities between the two versions of industrial society, however real they were, provided a stimulus not toward either neutrality or neutralism but rather toward an alliance with America. For the United States offered the advantages of wealth without the rigors of the lock step. As for the anti-Communists, without denying the similarities between the two super powers, they too rejected the thesis of the "Fraternity of the Giants": by restricting political or intellectual liberties, the democratic parties would have endangered the very values for which they were professing to fight.

There were only a few partisans of a non-aligned Europe who sought to draw political conclusions from the comparisons they chose to make between the Two. If, when all was said and done, Sovietism and Americanism had no reason to envy each other and both arrived at the same results, why should Europe take sides—if, that is, there was a possibility of her being allowed to abstain? But the crusaders for neutralism came up against a brutal, a massive fact: the Russian army was stationed some two hundred kilometers from the Rhine. Would Europe be any more secure if, unable to defend itself, it based its future on nothing more than the supposed Bolshevik repugnance to progress by invasion? The increased vulnerability of the United States and the thermonuclear capacity of the Soviet Union have brought the neutralist faction back into topical prominence, and in Great Britain it expresses itself by propaganda favoring unilateral disarmament.[3] I do not believe that this faction will achieve any historical importance during the next phase.

The circumstances peculiar to Europe are not to be found reproduced in any other region of the world. No other continent is divided between two military blocs. In no place is the contrast between democracy and totalitarianism, between the multiple-party system and the single-party system so clearly marked. Europe was the cradle of the type of society of which the Two are henceforth the representatives par excellence. The situation that comes closest to the European one is that of Japan. Japan is loyal to its American alliance for realistic reasons, is capable of an exceptionally high rate of economic growth with representative institutions, but is not without ideological sympathies, among the intellectuals, with the Left, if not with communism, and also has the secret pride of a culture threatened by barbarians.

In Asia the two super powers, first and foremost, look similar; the similarity is, moreover, obvious if we merely look at the facts: the same ambitions of

[3] Cf. above, Chap. XVI, pp. 488 ff.

production and productivity, the same diffusion over the vast spaces of both the United States and the Soviet Union, the same typical phenomena, urbanization and industrialization; comparable factories and skyscrapers, the same thermonuclear bombs and similar ballistic weapons. By contrast with the traditional societies of Asia and Europe, the Russian and American enemies are brothers.

This way of interpreting the rivalry of the Two leads, in Asia, though not in Europe, to neutrality. Moreover, it is neither the major cause nor the necessary expression of neutrality; it is the ideological-philosophic justification of an attitude adopted as a result of the historical context. Nehru's India, so long as it did not feel threatened by Communist, i.e., Chinese, expansion, had no motive constraining it to take sides. Morally, the most satisfying justification of this refusal is to consider both adversaries in the wrong or to attribute equal merits or failings to both.

In Africa the rulers of the new states already use the language of one or another of the three interlocutors—democratic, Soviet or neutral. But this language, whichever it may be, is a result of the world debate, it does not spring from any local reality. Almost all of the African republics south of the Sahara are orienting themselves in the direction of a single-party system. This party probably differs slightly according to whether the rulers use the language of the East or that of the West. But the language used is an expression of the rulers' ideological preferences, of the bonds they hope to create with one or another of the super powers or worlds, of their diplomatic orientation rather than their internal practice. The African countries have not yet reached the stage of insisting on the "brotherhood of the enemies," even though the differences and oppositions of the Western and Soviet regimes may well seem insignificant in African eyes.

Finally, in South America, the role of imperialist power has been attributed once and for all to the United States, which holds a dominating position in the Western Hemisphere, which is wealthier and stronger than all the states of Central and South America put together.[4] It is the American corporations that invest capital in Latin America, that exploit natural resources, that appear to prevent the construction of factories and the development of processing industries where the governments and the ruling classes have been incapable of promoting harmonious growth. Prejudice in favor of socialism and hostile to capitalism is reinforced by experiences peculiar to South America and it runs the risk of provoking an acute awareness of the misdeeds of the capitalists together with an almost total indifference to the cruelties of the Soviets. The same phenomenon has probably been produced, in an inverse direction, in the regions where Soviet domination is exercised with most rigor, as for instance in Eastern Europe between 1945 and 1956: the Vice President of the United States was welcomed with acclamations in

---

[4] But which, by the century's end, will be less densely populated.

Poland, and in Latin America with riots and tomatoes. One is tempted to conclude with cynical resignation that the popularity of a super power is in inverse proportion to its proximity. The morality tournament engaged in by the spokesmen of the two camps rarely determines the preferences of the *third men*.

2. Hostility and Fraternity

Why, if they are brothers, are they enemies, and enemies to the death, the two super powers who face each other from opposite sides of the Potsdamer Platz, and in the frozen wastes of the great north, who exchange Homeric challenges and brandish huge weapons as terrifying for their possessors as for those at whom they are aimed?

The United States and the Soviet Union are attached to each other first by a *hostility of position*. In every international system, relations—alliance or hostility—are to some extent determined by the calculation of forces and the demands of equilibrium, aside from all considerations of friendship and enmity between sovereigns, rulers or peoples. The choice of opposition to the Kaiser's Germany made at the beginning of this century by Great Britain and Russia conformed to this logic of the rivalry of powers despite the bonds of kinship between the ruling families of all three countries: it was the Kaiser's Germany which was cast in the role of troublemaker, and which Great Britain was obliged to fight. In the same way, the United States and the Soviet Union have, as it were, discovered their hostility now that the Third Reich, which temporarily united them, has disappeared from the scene. For two great powers in one system not to be hostile to one another, it would be necessary for them to reign together. History presents us with no example of such a miracle.

This "hostility of position" is amplified, almost spontaneously, in diverse ways. Each international unit, as we know, legitimately suspects the others' intentions. Security can only be founded on power or on a balance of power. The larger a political unit, the more it is threatened and the more it feels threatened, for, in case of defeat, it would risk punishment proportionate to the sacrifices its enemies had had to accept in order to conquer it. The Treaty of Versailles reflected the fear Germany had inspired and the cost of the victory far more than it corresponded to the "crimes" of the vanquished nation. Each of the great powers can not help fearing the conditions its enemy would impose on the ultimate day of reckoning.

The traditional paradox of international politics—the search for security through a balance of power engenders or maintains universal anxiety, reciprocal suspicion, anguish in the weak and pride in the strong—is modified but not profoundly transformed by the appearance of weapons of massive destructive power. In the past, the security of one nation implied the insecurity of the other, since such a security implied a superiority which the other interpreted as a threat. If Germany felt secure with regard to France because she was the stronger of the two, then France ought to have felt in danger, since, incapable of resisting a potential aggression, she was reduced to relying on her enemy's moderation.

Even if the objective of security through equilibrium was not, as such, inaccessible, it was always precarious simply because of the inconstancy of human affairs. The law of "unequal development" applies to all ages: it makes the search for security through equilibrium a labor of Sisyphus.

The strategy of deterrence, as it is commonly understood, seems to offer a way out of this dilemma. It is enough, in effect, to admit that the weaker side still retains, even in the case of a surprise attack, the capacity to inflict "unbearable" destruction on the aggressor, for the traditional danger of inequality to be removed. The weapons of deterrence appear to permit Sisyphus to get his rock to the top of the mountain. What does unequal development matter, when the weaker side is still able to strike a mortal blow at the stronger?

In fact, this has not turned out to be the case. The leaders of the Soviet Union could not consider themselves secure, in the recent past, so long as their own cities were vulnerable while the United States still had a chance of limiting the damage that could be inflicted on American cities. The leaders of the United States may consider that their country will not be secure so long as the Soviet Union is in a position to destroy by surprise attack a part, and perhaps a considerable part, of the American thermonuclear system. In other words, the search for stability through mutual deterrence has been no more successful than the search for security through the balance of power. Sisyphus is still pushing his rock. Reciprocal deterrence has not yet attained, even supposing it will ever attain, the final phase of stability. If one of the super powers has thermonuclear bombs and the other has only atomic bombs, if one of them has shelters for three quarters of its population and the other has not, if one of them has intercontinental ballistic missiles and the other only bombers, if one of them becomes able to use space craft for military purposes and the other does not, any such inequality will compromise the balance of terror. The latter condition does not require that the probable destruction the aggressor would suffer as a reprisal from its victim be equal to that which it is itself able to inflict. But the inequality must still not be excessive.

The instability has been, it is true, more psychological than political. There has been no great war and, in this sense, deterrence has been effective. But both sides have suffered from insecurity, sometimes, perhaps, both at once. How can the future be in any way secure when one side possesses, and knows that the other side also possesses, weapons of such a nature that a single one could destroy an entire city and kill two or three million people? Hostility of position has been aggravated by the technological race that the two super powers have been drawn into, almost in spite of themselves; by the logic of a rivalry from which neither side was able to withdraw.

Certain manifestations of hostility are clearly linked to the technique of reciprocal deterrence. U-2s had flown over Soviet territory regularly, and other craft have approached the frontiers of Soviet air space in order to collect the information indispensable to what is termed "counterforce strategy," whose eventual objective would be the enemy's thermonuclear system. (This information ceases to be necessary the moment one abandons the attempt to discover the location of airfields and launching pads in order to concentrate one's threat on the cities.) It is in order to prevent the chance of being destroyed on the ground by surprise attack that the bombers carrying thermonuclear bombs maintain more or less permanent patrols. When suspicious spots appear on the radar screens, the bombers fly toward the Soviet Union.[5]

But, on the other hand, by a paradox in accord with the theory of deterrence, the same armaments that oblige the duopolists to adopt attitudes of hostility also force them not to allow these attitudes completely free play, but to "limit" their expression. In case of war the duopolists would have to engage each other directly. (The allies of the United States would be affected because part of the American thermonuclear force is installed on their soil. Otherwise the Soviet Union would have no interest in laying waste the cities of Europe.) Each of the two duopolists being the other's chosen target, the two super powers are inclined to expend their hatred for each other in evocations of the damage they could inflict if they did fight, but they are in fact yielding precisely to those reasons which compel them not to fight. They have a common and vital interest *not* to resort to the use of the weapons they brandish.

It is not only because they both risk being defeated together by their conflict, but because the victor—absolute or relative—might not receive any benefit from the victory. For the only benefit that could equal the risk or the sacrifices involved would have to be the elimination of *all* enemies, domination over the whole of the contested territory. The United States cannot even hope that the eventual elimination of the Soviet Union would assure its security for any extended period: lacking both collective resolution and the appropriate institutions, it would not be able to forbid other states to acquire in their turn the weapons and delivery means which constitute a deterrent force. The Soviet Union would be less ill-equipped, in theory, than the United States for maintaining the disarmament of humanity after the elimination of its rival. But despite this, it seems to me that the time is past when a victorious Soviet Union could enjoy a thermonuclear monopoly without difficulty. China has entered the race in its turn, and communism has proved to be too weak to overcome nationalisms and form the cement of a universal empire. The global system is still bipolar and, in military terms, it is probably

---

[5] The American air force has perfected a security system ("fail safe") which permits them to recall craft on their way to the Soviet Union, provided those craft have not received in flight an explicit order to attack.

more bipolar in the 1960s than at any time since 1945 (the technologists not yet having perfected a deterrent for poor nations). But in Washington as in Moscow—in Washington more than in Moscow—there is no longer a refusal to envisage a future, perhaps one not too remote, in which the *enemy* will be officially a *brother* against another great power.

Even if this possibility did not remind the enemies of their brotherhood, the super powers would still have another reason to reject a war to the death: in our time, the most totalitarian state manages only with the greatest difficulty to combine *domination* and *exploitation* lastingly. Twentieth-century conquerors upset the living conditions of the subject peoples much more than the conquerors of the past. But they are unable to reserve for themselves an honorable life of combat and leisure in the way that the "masters" of the ancient world did: workers and warriors are also technologists. The only way in which it is possible to perpetuate the subjugation of the conquered is to forbid them entry into the qualified professions, to insure the representatives of the master-race a monopoly of the functions of scientific and administrative leadership. This is how the whites proceed in the Union of South Africa. It is what the Nazis would probably have done in Eastern Europe, drawing the logical conclusions from the doctrine according to which the *Slavs* are a subhuman race born into slavery and destined to permanent servitude. The doctrine of the essential inequality of men, a doctrine condemned by industrial society within homogeneous communities, can be applied by racists to the relations between communities: the races, and no longer the classes, would thus be unequal as such and the incontestable inequality[6] of the social and intellectual development of human groups at the present time would furnish striking though fragile arguments to these doctrinaires.

Neither Russians nor Americans are tempted to renew the ancient practices of slavery. The former first pillaged the countries they "liberated."[7] The latter are accused of exploitation when they buy raw materials at prices considered too low, or when they prevent (or seem to prevent) the creation of local industries. But, on the whole, as long as they lack neither space nor raw materials, the super powers do not employ racist reasoning. Each of them would be rid, by victory, not only of an enemy but also of a cooperator. The survivor of the duel would remain solely responsible for the impoverished half of humanity. The two powers almost openly recognize their common interest in not fighting each other. They also recognize, though not without hesitation, their common interest in contributing to the development of the rest of the world. And they act, to some extent, as though they admit the reality of this solidarity at the same time as the reality of the hostility of their principles.

[6] The anthropologist may argue that tribal life is not inferior to civilized life, but whatever the value of such affirmations, the "primitive" or "undeveloped" peoples are inferior with regard to the activities our age holds to be the highest expression of humanity.

[7] Cf. Chap. XV, Sec. 3.

The economic aid which each of the super powers provides to certain countries of the rest of the world can *always* be explained, and often is explained as we have seen,[8] by the strategy of the cold war. The United States, in accelerating the reconstruction of Western Europe, was raising a dam against Communist expansion. It was reinforcing its system of alliances, and the military bloc of the West. The construction of a steelworks in India with the aid of Soviet technicians and Soviet credit was intended to testify to the power and generosity of the land of socialism. The credits granted to Egypt, Mali or Guinea are intended to support countries taking the road to a people's democracy or countries that in the recent past were still dependent on Western capitalism. It is not false to say that the generosity of the super powers is a by-product of their hostility.

Adversaries, rivals, contradictory models, incompatible protectors, the two super powers, in relation to the third world, are enemies, not brothers —except in the rare circumstances when they agree to accept, at least provisionally, a state's neutrality (in the double sense of diplomatic and ideological non-alignment). The two powers are enemies—even if they resemble each other—because the presence of one involves the elimination of the other (once again, except for neutral countries). It is of virtually no importance to know whether the representatives of the two camps are doing the same thing (they are not doing the same thing). It suffices for them to drive each other out for their hostility to be inevitable.

It would have been even more accurate to speak of enemy brothers with reference to the Fascist and Communist movements in the thirties. Those movements used procedures analogous to each other, recruited militants inclined to the same brutality, pledged to a fanaticism of a similar sort, sometimes quick to shift from one extremism to the other. Communists and Fascists readily denounced the same men or the same political targets (capitalism, plutocracy, formal democracy). Of course, they were ideologically antipodal to each other, one proclaiming a universal ideal, the other a racial ideal, each accusing the other of being in league with its enemies, communism accusing fascism of being the agent of big capital, fascism accusing communism of being the agent of "Jewry" or of "world democracy." But whatever the sincerity, whatever the truth of these invectives, both were violent and revolutionary, both liquidated other parties, representative institutions, free discussion and personal liberties. The *third man* could not appease the hostility between Communists and fascists by reminding these enemies that they were brothers. Supposing that the conflict had no moral significance, it was still true that the Communists were always in prison when the fascists were in power (and vice versa). The similarity of their methods did not at all attenuate a hostility nourished by such a dialectic.

In the sense in which fascists and Communists were brothers, Russians

---

[8] Cf. Chap. XVII, Sec. 2.

and Americans are not: they do not use the same methods and they do not have the same style of life and government as their objective. This difference involves a radical asymmetry. As soon as the Communists gain power, the leaders of the Western parties vanish into death, prison, exile, at any rate into political liquidation. The Communists keep their freedom, for the most part, and carry on their political existence under the regimes typical of the West.[9] The hostility, in this case, reveals no element of fraternity, whether in the form of similar practices with a view to contradictory ends or in the name of contradictory ideas.

Nevertheless, even in relation to the third world, the hostility of the super powers is not total. In other words, both proclaim that the economic development of the third world corresponds to their own aspirations, to their own interests and to the interest of all humanity. In this respect they are in agreement as to the proper objective of rich nations with regard to poor ones. Thus the aid the super powers grant no longer appears to be merely a by-product of the cold war, a means of persuasion, infiltration or subversion.

Is it true that the economic development of the poor nations is in accord with the self-interest of both super powers? Whatever the answer, it is a good thing that the powers themselves should be so convinced, or at least that they should pretend to be so convinced. Are they right to believe that it is true? Yes, without a doubt, as long as there is an abundance for all, of land to cultivate and of raw materials to transform. In theory, the economic progress of the third world could threaten either the supply of raw materials or the military superiority of the individualized peoples. But, for the moment, the latter do not take these two threats seriously.

Finally, in political terms the super powers may reasonably believe that they both have more to gain than to lose by the diffusion of industrial society and a general amelioration of living conditions. The Russians, despite the fact that they have won their first and most outstanding successes in countries scarcely embarked upon the path of industrialization, have nevertheless remained faithful to the Marxist dogma of the inevitability of capitalism's evolution toward socialism. They do not admit, as a general rule, that communism attains supremacy only in those countries where capitalism is deficient. The Americans, for their part, readily subscribe to an inverted and simplified Marxism: economic progress, on its own, is the best antidote to communism.

Such an agreement appears to be based inevitably on an illusion on one side or the other, if not on both. But the semi-clandestine thesis of the fraternity of the enemies—and of a fraternity that grows with economic progress—gives this agreement a less illusory basis. The Russians think that

[9] This proposition is not valid, even in Europe, for every country. In West Germany the Communist party is illegal.

as it grows older capitalism will come closer to socialism. The Americans think that as it grows older socialism (or Sovietism) will become more liberal. If they were both right, would they not discover a fraternity beneath this hostility? If they were to leave to the future the task of deciding between these two theses, or of determining to what degree each of them is true, would they not then find themselves once more united by the conviction that they are unable to agree but that they must not destroy each other?

Must we say, given these conditions, that the hostility between Washington and Moscow is determined by ideological conflict? Or must we, on the contrary, say that it is determined by the respective situations of the two powers in the international arena, by their incompatible ambitions, by the inevitable course of the arms race? Our preceding analyses are sufficient to show that both these extreme theses are indefensible. The ideological conflict is an integral factor within the total conflict—which does not mean that on the day the Two recognize their fraternity they will cease to regard each other as enemies.

Whatever the degree of similarity between the institutions of the super powers, they must, in their roles as heads of coalitions, give full weight to those factors which divide them. The bipolarity of the world situation does not create the ideological rivalry, but it accentuates it. Since 1945 the ideological bipolarity has no more provoked the hostility of position than it has resulted from it. But the coincidence of "hostility of position" and "ideological hostility" is a major fact in the situation, which explains certain of its characteristics. The ideological conflict prevents bargaining in the classical or cynical style. The Western leaders cannot abandon two million Berliners without losing face. The Russians cannot accept free elections in East Germany without losing face. Each of the super powers is a prisoner of its own propaganda or its own convictions, unable, short of betraying itself, to exchange one territory for another, a concession here for a concession there. Kings used to exchange provinces. Washington and Moscow do not surrender portions of the "free world" or the "socialist world" to "Communist tyranny" or "capitalist slavery."

The ideological character of the conflict also explains the role of persuasion and subversion in the battle being waged in or over the third world. One of the best methods of rallying an African or Asian country to the Soviet cause is to persuade its rulers or its future rulers that the Soviet cause is superior, which can mean "morally noble" or "certain of victory" or "in accord with the interests of that country" ("alliance with the Soviets is more profitable than alliance with America, since Soviet institutions are better adapted to local needs than American ones"). Not that intellectuals or political leaders normally act "by ideology," if this means taking decisions with exclusive reference to ideas and without regard to either possible advantages to be gained or to the forces present in the situation. Political ideologies, in the twentieth century, determine the ways of thinking, of believing and of acting. A left-wing intellectual in Japan, in France, in Cuba, in Brazil—and I mean a non-Communist left-wing intellectual, not even a *fellow traveler*, simply a "progressive"—has an identifiable language and thought-structure, a prejudice in favor of techniques of planned economy, a prejudice hostile to capitalism and "corporations"; he will defend freedom vigorously against a conservative government and sacrifice it gladly as long as the despotism which demands his sacrifices proclaims itself to be leftist or revolutionary, etc. This way of thinking must correspond to profound needs, since even superior minds manifest its naïvetés or its contradictions. In this sense the ideological battle is one of the essential elements in the polymorphous war between the two blocs—at least, provided we understand the deeper meaning of this ideological battle.

It includes oratorical and statistical jousts, the comparison of the rates of growth, economic institutions or democratic methods proper to each of the super powers. Such debates, conducted by the spokesmen of the two powers before the tribunal of the third world, are not without consequence. Slowly, the advantage gained by the one or the other in one or another aspect of their rivalry helps attract sympathies or affect expectations—and the latter have no less an influence on the non-aligned nations than the former. But these debates are only one element in the real competition of which the prize is the minds of the ruling minorities rather than of the masses. Now the minds of these minorities are conditioned by ideology in the widest sense of the term: after a few minutes' conversation in any country of the world, one can tell what family one's interlocutor belongs to—Communist, leftist, democratic idealist or conservative. Each of these terms denotes a mental attitude which includes both a way of interpreting facts and a way of judging values. It would be childish to imagine that it is "Washington agents" or the "Moscow agents" who create the conflicts or determine the outcome. But the outcome of these conflicts can in fact be determined by the mental attitude of the militants and of the leaders, a mental attitude formed at the University of Moscow or at Harvard.

If we analyze these "mental attitudes," it is not impossible to add a further illustration to the thesis of the fraternity of the enemies. The partisans of Moscow emphasize the effectiveness of the Soviet technique of industrialization; the partisans of Washington reply by denouncing the suppression of intellectual and personal liberties. To which the first group retorts that those liberties are no more than a sinister mockery in an underdeveloped country which is actually dominated and exploited by foreign corporations allied to a local and servile capitalism. The competition, formulated in terms of accusation and defense, rests on the question of which is the most effective method of achieving an economic and social transformation that both sides regard as necessary.

But this way of defining the competition, although it is valid in the abstract (everyone wonders whether it is possible to industrialize the underdeveloped countries without sacrificing representative institutions, and if a planned economy is not superior to the market economy during the initial phases of economic development), remains, in this case, superficial, secondary: the heterogeneity of the mental structures characteristic of the militant Communist (or leftist) and of the militant pro-Westerner or pro-American is predominant. The simplest way of expressing this heterogeneity is to say that the former *has an ideology* and that the latter *has not*.

Of course, both of them have a certain mental structure. The American citizen is no less circumscribed by his ways of thinking, believing and acting than the Soviet citizen. The difference nevertheless remains, and it is decisive. The Communist interprets the historical world, if not the entire cosmos, humanity included, according to a global view which embraces the past, the present and the future. This interpretation claims to be both a way of knowing reality and judging values, the lines of action to be undertaken being sketched out by the interpretation itself. The conception of the Communist, and to a lesser degree of the leftist, is articulated into a system that offers an appearance of coherence. The militant pro-Westerner has no equivalent for such a system: he distinguishes facts and values, the general conditions of development and the particular circumstances that render one method more desirable than another, isolates the similarities of the growth phenomena in any given phase of the process and decides on the possibilities of recourse to the various techniques available according to the period and to the continent. At his best he is a sociologist rather than an ideologist, at his worst he is an ideologist without a system, bound to provincial institutions (parliament, political parties) which, detached from their social context, risk becoming a farce. In Europe representative institutions and, *a fortiori,* the rejection of a state orthodoxy are rooted in tradition, in the sentiments of the people. The Soviet regime, imposed on the countries of Eastern Europe in 1945 by the Russian Big Brother, broke those countries' historical links with the West, forced them into often quite useless sacrifices, and created the logical delirium of the new Faith. We may wonder whether the regimes of Western democracy would or would not have functioned effectively in Eastern Europe. But there is no doubt that the Soviet Union, in creating its bloc, coerced men, and that the United States, on the contrary, helped Europeans to safeguard their liberty and to preserve the mode of government that they preferred to that which would have been established by the minority adherents of Sovietism if they were victorious.

In Asia, in the Near East, in Africa and in South America matters did not follow the same course. For the most part, the Soviet Union was absent or a long way off, the United States or the Europeans were present or near at hand. The task that the elites regarded as primary was not the establishment or restoration of a representative regime, but economic growth. The Soviet Union has colonies in central Asia, but these colonies are in the interior of the continental mass and contiguous, under the direct sovereignty of Moscow. Cultural autonomy, imperial citizenship (Tsarist or Soviet), and the repression of bourgeois nationalism maintain the cohesion of the Union, and the rumor of revolts, if there are revolts, never escapes to the outside world. It is the Europeans who, in Asia, ruled over hundreds of millions of men; it was they who, in the Near East, exercised a dominant influence through the intermediary of rulers in their pay; it was they who, in Africa, hacked out colonial empires for themselves.

With regard to the nationalist movements in the European colonies, the two super powers could manifest their fraternity more or less discreetly. Born of a revolution against the British mother country, the American Republic felt a moral solidarity with the rebellions against the European empires, provided it forgot the difference between European settlers established overseas and the populations of Africa and Asia which other Europeans had subjected to their laws when they had been unable to find unpopulated territory. Because of the Atlantic Alliance, the United States did not dare to side too spectacularly with the nationalists against Dutch, British or French sovereignty. They manifested some sympathy toward them, not enough to satisfy them, but enough to convince the European powers of the anti-colonialist brotherhood of the two super powers.

The disappearance of the European empires, which will soon be total, is modifying ideological relations on the world stage. In relation to the dominant ideas of the age, the European empires, whatever they had accomplished in the past, were open to condemnation, and were unflaggingly condemned by Soviet propaganda, by the representatives of the third world in the United Nations, and by an important section of public opinion within the European powers themselves. The United States felt in a position of inferiority compared with the Soviet Union, because its alliance with Europe restricted it to a moderate expression of anti-colonialism, while Soviet anti-colonialism was free to be extremist. In the propaganda battle, moderation is supposed to be less effective than violence. The majority of American diplomats are experiencing a sort of relief as they observe the course of events: at last they will no longer have to justify what in their hearts they thought unjustifiable, they will no longer have to ask for delays so that "France may execute the liberal projects her representatives have announced. . . ." Thus, as Kant wrote, the bird imagines it would fly faster if it were not impeded by the resistance of the air which supports it.

It is true that, on the level of the propaganda battle, the disintegration of the European empires deprives the Soviets of a sledge-hammer argument and frees the Americans from a weight which they were finding increasingly burdensome. It is not forbidden to envisage as genuine progress the creation of fifty or so independent nations in Asia and Africa, and even the substitution of neutralist regimes, in Iraq and Egypt for example, for the pro-Western regimes of the recent past or of before the war. This mode of interpretation, familiar to the Americans as long as it concerned a zone hitherto subjected to European domination or influence, will tomorrow be adopted by Europeans without much difficulty with regard to South America. Authoritarian as it is, is not Fidel Castro's regime superior to Batista's? Why grow indignant over the desire expressed by the states of Latin America to remain outside the cold war, to commit themselves neither to one side nor the other?

The impoverished masses or the intellectuals in revolt against the alliance of the great landowners, the army and the American corporations (whether the alliance is real or not is of little importance here) consider themselves victims of a "colonialism" to which they impute misdeeds comparable to those imputed to French or English colonialism in Asia or Africa. It would be mere self-deception to expect propaganda against imperialism to cease the day there are no more empires (outside the Soviet Empire, naturally). Foreign investments, the possession of land or of factories by individuals or companies of another nationality are considered, by left-wing opinion and by intellectuals, as a form of imperialism.

If any influence whatever exercised by a capitalist country is imperialist— and that is how Communist propaganda understands the matter—the West will only cease to be "imperialist" the day it loses all ability to act outside its own zone of civilization. The disintegration of the European empires will not enhance the fraternity of the super powers; it will give their hostility new occasions to reveal itself. Apparently paradoxical ideological regroupings, such as an alliance of the West and the Moslem world against the Soviet Empire, are not inconceivable, but they are not yet visible today, even on the horizon.

Equally conceivable, and unfortunately less improbable, would be a halfway complicity of the Soviet bloc and the Europeans against the "Yankee Empire" in Latin America.

3. The United Nations

We have analyzed diplomacy within the blocs, between the blocs, between the blocs and the non-aligned nations, without explicit reference to the United Nations. There can be no doubt that the international organization plays a role here, but what role?

The blocs were constituted without violating the Charter, insofar as the latter contains no restriction on the "natural right of self-defense" and authorizes defensive regional alliances. But the imposition of regimes of the Soviet type on the countries of Eastern Europe was contrary to the spirit of the Charter, in any case as it is understood by the Western nations. Revolutions from above have been the result of the occupation (or liberation) of these nations by the Russian army. They are an example of what once used to be called "indirect aggression": taking advantage of the presence of its troops, a great power puts into power, in a small country, a group of men or a party that is entirely devoted to its cause. One could perhaps compare this procedure to the Quisling technique, if the bipolar structure of the system did not constrain the two super powers gradually to imitate each other even as they oppose each other.

Not that there is an equivalence, with regard to the peoples, between the regimes. If the Red army had not occupied Poland and Hungary, those two countries would not have chosen a regime of the Soviet type, and the Communist party would not, in all probability, have succeeded, either by cunning or by violence, in conquering the state. In the West, on the other hand, although the military presence of Great Britain and the United States did have some influence, Western democracy—plurality of parties, free elections, personal liberties—corresponded to the expectations of the great majority of the people and of political class. It was legitimate *de jure* because it conformed to the dominant concept of legitimacy, and it was legitimate *de facto* because that concept was honestly applied.

Heterogeneity with regard to peoples and ideas is not, however, the last word of the analysis. The regimes in Eastern Europe conformed, despite popular resistance, to the Marxist-Leninist concept of legitimacy. In a vague sense this concept is democratic: the Communist party is supposed to be the avant-garde of the proletariat; it interprets and represents the masses, it expresses the will of the proletariat, because it is accomplishing a historic mission, even when the members of the proletariat are opposed to it. Finally, on the basis of this philosophy, these Eastern European regimes claim a legitimacy comparable[10] to that which the Western regimes derive from free elections and the assent of the citizens.

The process of creating the two blocs occurred outside the United Nations for the good reason that at the moment when the latter was created the Iron Curtain had already been lowered. The United Nations could do nothing to protect the peoples of Eastern Europe, since their rulers, recognized as legal by the governments of the West, were under Communist domination and had returned with, or were supported by, the Red army. Any action on the part of the international organization would have been evidently contrary to the letter of its Charter, since the latter, in the name of state sovereignty, forbids "all interference in internal affairs." Once in power, a regime, however oppressive, whatever the feelings of the masses, is protected by the principle of international law—respect for state sovereignty and a radical distinction between internal affairs and diplomatic questions.

The United Nations did have one occasion to deliberate a problem of intra-bloc diplomacy. In Hungary, when the rebels had succeeded in seizing power and constituting a legal government (the latter having taken over from the government formerly recognized as legal by the international organization), it was the Kadar government and the action of the Red army which were rightly considered as illegal by the General Assembly of the United

---

[10] Which does not mean that we assign them an equal value.

Nations. The Soviet Union was guilty of aggression insofar as the Kadar government and the appeal it made to the Red army were held to be the effect of a conspiracy or of a manipulation on the part of Soviet Russia. On the other hand, within the historical Communist system, the counterrevolutionary government of Imre Nagy being illegitimate, as well as illegal by reason of the conditions of its advent to power, Kadar's "workers' and peasants'" government was automatically, by definition, legitimate, and, secondarily, legal.

The lesson of these events is clear. The United Nations cannot come to the aid of a people subjected, against its will, to a government of the Soviet type established by, or under the protection of, the Red army. Usually the legal government is protected by international law against outside intervention. Even if a popular insurrection should happen to overthrow that despotism, nothing has been gained: the Soviet Union can resort to military intervention, at the request of the "workers' and peasants'" government, and this intervention, illegal in the eyes of the international organization, legitimate within the ideological system of the Soviet world, can easily stand against a vote of the General Assembly. To *coerce* the Soviet Union, one would have to be resolved to do so, eventually, by open warfare. Even the wildest idealists do not entertain such a notion.

The most spectacular example of United Nations intervention in an episode in the relations between the two blocs (although it did not occur in the European theater) was the Korean crisis. When the North Korean armies crossed the 38th Parallel, the Security Council, on the request of the American representative, immediately ordered the North Korean government to withdraw its troops and upon the latter's refusal, invited its member states to come to the aid of the victim, the government of South Korea. The circumstances were exceptionally favorable for this first attempt of the United Nations to induce an aggressor state, by the use of force, to respect international law. Against Italy, economic sanctions had been powerless to make right prevail; the military sanctions, in 1950, launched a limited war in which there was neither victor nor vanquished. Can the non-defeat of the aggressor be a victory for justice?

The absence of the Soviet Union[11] permitted the Security Council to legalize this military action, which the United States would have initiated in any case, even if the United Nations had not existed or if it had been paralyzed by the veto. Not that the actual events were exactly those that would have occurred if Roosevelt's dream of an international organization had not been realized. It was easy to convince both Congress and American

[11] Various explanations have been given for this absence, the most likely of which seems to be that it was the result of a miscalculation. The North Korean attempt being known in Moscow, the Soviet delegate intended to return to the Security Council, once South Korea had been completely occupied, to present a solution that would save everyone's face.

public opinion by invoking respect for international law. Enthusiasm would have been less lively if President Truman or Secretary of State Acheson had been forced to give the valid but prosaic motives which dictated their decision: an imperious necessity to confirm, in the eyes of the world and above all in the eyes of Europe, the value of an American assurance, and the fatal loss of prestige if South Korea—the only Korean government recognized by the United Nations—were to be eliminated by a North Korean government which had defied the decisions of the United Nations (refusal of entry to observers appointed to assure free elections, etc.). Perhaps unconsciously, perhaps misled by the declarations of American statesmen, who did not list Korea among the American defense positions in Asia, the Kremlin, on June 25, 1950, hurled a challenge at the United States which the latter could not fail to accept without disastrous consequences.

The fact that the armies, composed essentially of American and South Korean divisions, were called armies of the United Nations and were, in theory, in the service of the policies determined by the General Assembly, was not without secondary consequences. The British, Turkish and French contingents gave the troops fighting on behalf of South Korea the aspect of an international legion. To the eye of a propagandist, the United States, mobilizing world opinion and a world organization, had "the advantage and almost the victory." But the major decisions were taken by the belligerents, in councils of war and on the battlefields, not by the United Nations. The order to cross the 38th Parallel was given by President Truman, shortly after the landing at Inchon, after an interview between the President and General MacArthur: the decision was ratified by a vote of the General Assembly. The offensive to the Yalu was, in large part, attributable to General MacArthur himself.[12] The government of the Chinese People's Republic was not checked by any fear of being condemned as an aggressor by the United Nations. The fiction according to which its regular divisions were "volunteers" had its origin in the desire, common to both camps, to prevent the conflict from becoming general and thus forcing an official declaration of war. When the United States relinquished the idea of an absolute victory, it forgot that North Korea and China were the aggressors, or at least did not take this into account. It negotiated a compromise peace as it would have done with any other state. The idea that aggression is a crime in the eyes of international law was not sufficient to inspire the United States with the resolution to wage the war to its very end. It was on the battlefields and not in the tribunal of the Assembly that the fate of Korea was decided. The United Nations had an influence on the style and on the moral significance of the event and its outcome, but not on the origin, the development or the results of the campaign.

[12] Dean Acheson told me that the President himself and the chiefs-of-staff were hostile to this offensive.

It is difficult to envisage a repetition of the Korean crisis: most of the member states of the United Nations would hesitate to engage in an armed conflict against even a minor satellite of the Soviet Union and China. The two Communist states, on their side, tend more to infiltration than to aggression in the classical sense, that is, the crossing of frontiers with regular armies.

The coincidence of the Hungarian crisis and the Suez crisis, the impotence of the United Nations in the face of the Soviet Union, the secondary but useful role played by the United Nations in the liquidation of the Suez crisis illustrate the possibilities and the limits of the "universal actor" in the world today. A vote of the General Assembly of the United Nations cannot, quite obviously, force one of the super powers to capitulate. Furthermore, Great Britain and France could not have withstood a combination of both super powers and the third world, even in the absence of the international organization. By the time Mr. Bulganin brandished his rockets, the United States had already taken up its position against its allies. The moment the Soviet power of intimidation was not balanced by the power of the American deterrent, France and Britain were forced to yield.

Not that the vote of the General Assembly was completely without consequence: democratic states are more sensitive to the judgments of world opinion and of their friends than are states of the Soviet type, which are always able to justify their actions, however cruel they may be, by a metaphysics of history. The existence of the United Nations also constituted, for the United States, an additional reason for not tolerating the Israeli campaign in the Sinai and the Franco-British landing. Finally, and above all, sending the "blue helmets" both morally and materially facilitated the evacuation of Egyptian territory by foreign troops; the international armed force helped re-establish peace and at the same time paralyzed any activity on the part of the Soviet bloc. Even while French opinion was heaping curses on the United Nations, Mr. Khrushchev was beginning to feel toward it, especially toward its Secretary-General, the hostile sentiments he did not dissimulate for long.

But it is on the relations between the blocs and the third world, especially between the European colonial powers and their protectorates or colonies, that the United Nations has had the most influence. It would be absurd to say that the European empires were lost in New York. Whatever term one employs, whether "liberation of the colonial peoples" or "dismemberment of the European empires," this historical process has manifestly been brought about by multiple and profound causes (weakening of the colonial powers, aspirations of the colonial peoples to independence, effectiveness of partisan warfare, anti-colonialism of the super powers), but the United Nations did provide a tribunal for the representatives of those countries who belonged to the anti-colonialist cause, it did echo and amplify the propaganda against imperialism, and it did influence the style and probably the speed of decolonization.

The organization also continues to give the states of Africa and Asia, and tomorrow the states of Latin America, an opportunity to play at world politics (*die grosse Politik*). In fact, it is not in New York that history is written; it is within the states, by the ruses of infiltration and subversion, that the regimes recognized, one after another, by international legality are born and die. Neither the plan of partition elaborated by the United Nations, nor the cease-fire order, could have assured the existence of the state of Israel or even the continuing presence of the Jews in Palestine without the victories won by the troops of the Haganah. But history is also written to a degree in New York, and the delegates of the small states find it difficult to avoid the illusion that this degree is a large one.

Since a motion of the General Assembly requires a two-thirds majority, the super powers are obliged to court the small powers in order to gain the promise of a favorable vote. Equals of the super powers according to the law of the Assembly, the small powers can pride themselves on using their votes to make historical decisions. Without the United Nations, what chance would the Presidents of the African states have to leave their own capitals, whose names the schoolboys of Europe have not even learned yet, and see the world and participate in global diplomacy? The international organization embraces virtually the whole of humanity, and it aims at creating a universal community, whose present divisions it expresses and whose call to unity it symbolizes.

In the course of the last few years, as a result of decolonization and the "Balkanization" of Africa, the so-called Afro-Asian group of nations has swollen to such a point that some people are already envisaging a bloc of non-aligned nations which would hold the two hostile blocs in equilibrium, serve as a mediator, arbiter or judge between them, and be able to release a region or a country from the rending of the cold war. But that is not possible. The third world is a geographical rather than a political notion. As for non-alignment, the term includes many different modes. Those who claim to be non-aligned do not necessarily have the same opinions or the same interests in all circumstances, whether or not the problem in question is concerned with the rivalry of the super powers.[18]

The Congo crisis confirmed the importance but also the division of the non-aligned countries in the deliberations of the international organization. The United States, fearing a direct confrontation with the Soviet Union, transmitted to the United Nations the ungrateful task of preventing both chaos and Sovietization, and to the Secretary-General the even more ungrateful task of applying the decisions or recommendations, expressed in vague terms, of the Security Council or the General Assembly. The intention was good, and the desire that the Congolese state should remain outside the cold

[18] Cf. Chap. XVII, Sec. 4.

war was reasonable. But, insofar as the aims of the Soviet Union were entirely opposed, the substitution of the United Nations for the United States merely resulted in precipitating a conflict between Moscow and the Secretariat instead of the expected collision between Moscow and Washington.

The Congolese state did not, in fact, exist. There was no man and no party in a position to impose a single authority on the country as a whole, or to assure the continued functioning of public services. The real choice was between a sort of United Nations trusteeship, a return of Belgian technicians under a Congolese government disposed to use them, or else the control of the country by technicians sent from the East. As we know, the weaker and more divided a new state, the more difficulty it has attaining neutrality. The fact that the state did not exist made the neutralization of the Congo all the more desirable, but it also made it impossible for the very same reason that made it desirable. The United Nations and Mr. Hammarskjöld could find no way around this paradox.

According to its Charter, the United Nations must not interfere in the internal affairs of a country once its sovereignty has been recognized. It was the organization's mission to guarantee the security of private persons and to facilitate the retreat of the Belgian troops. But this was a self-contradictory task. If the Congo government was incapable of guaranteeing the security of private persons, it was unworthy of the international recognition which had been so lightly accorded it. If the duty of the United Nations was to maintain public order, then it was ineluctably compelled to intervene in the "internal affairs of the country." By their very presence, the multinational contingents were influencing the course of the disputes between the Congolese politicians and the respective chances of the pro-Soviet faction and the Westerners, the "federalists" and the advocates of a centralized state. The day the Prime Minister of the central government, legal when the United Nations went into action, was deposed and put under arrest by those who could claim a certain amount of both *de jure* and *de facto* power (the President of the Republic and Colonel Mobutu), the Soviet states, upheld by the leftist states of Africa and the other continents, denounced the United Nations, that is, ultimately, the Secretary-General. A crisis comparable to the one in Korea threatened: the Communist bloc was attacking the international organization because it had, in fact, favored one camp against the other.

During the crisis some of the non-aligned nations favored Mr. Kasavubu, some of them favored Mr. Lumumba, and some of them favored a reconciliation between the two men. If this reconciliation had taken place with the blessing of the two super powers, probably all the non-aligned nations would have found that they, too, were miraculously in agreement—an agreement which would have been all the easier because it would no longer have been necessary. In fact, the positive neutralists, the United Arab Republic, Guinea, Mali, joined by Ghana and Morocco (the latter because of Mauritania and also, probably, for reasons to do with its internal politics)[14] supported Mr. Lumumba to the end and violently criticized the Secretary-General. The latter retained, nevertheless, the support of a majority of the non-aligned nations and of the General Assembly.

Being composed of the two blocs and the non-aligned nations, the United Nations could not have a "general will." The minority yields to the "majority will" only on condition that its vital interests are not affected. On the frontiers of Israel and Egypt the "blue helmets" maintained the peace and separated the combatants who, for various reasons, wanted to be separated. It was convenient for the United States to leave the task of putting pressure on Holland and France to the Afro-Asian countries, and to keep for itself the role of mediator between the anti-colonialist and the colonial states of Europe. Which is to say that neither the blocs nor the non-aligned nations, neither the great nor the small powers behave any differently within the United Nations than they do elsewhere. Each actor expresses ideas or passions there and tries to serve his own interests. The international organization has not modified, though it has somewhat complicated, the course of international diplomacy. Original as an institution, it is not so in its principles, which are contradictory, nor in its language, which is more hypocritical than idealist, nor in its action, which is effective in proportion to the remove at which it remains from the major conflict of our time.

4. Conflicts and Appeasement

Has the international situation evolved during the past twenty or so years toward a sort of stabilization, or has it, on the contrary, evolved in the direction of an intensification of the cold war? Or is it simply stationary, with alternating periods of tension and détente, punctuated by more or less acute crises regularly liquidated by the two super powers with a limited use of force?

Let us take the last hypothesis as a point of departure. The fact is that the two super powers, or the two blocs, have coexisted for about twenty years, their relations marked by a succession of crises—Berlin (1948–49), Korea (1950–53), Indo-China (1953–54), Suez and Hungary (1956), Iraq, Jordan and Lebanon (1958), a second Berlin crisis initiated at the end of 1958 but maintained in a latent state. The behavior of the two super powers, in the course of each of these crises has been manifestly dictated by the firm resolve not to engage in an unlimited war. Controversy in the West at the time of the Berlin blockade or the Korean campaign centered not on the objective (to limit the conflict) but on the risks that could be run without creating a serious danger of widening the sphere of hostilities. Was it unwise to bomb the Manchurian airfields? Would the North Koreans or the Chinese retaliate

---

[14] The government, being conservative, diverted the leftist opposition to the least dangerous ground, that of verbal and international diplomacy.

by bombing the South Korean ports or the American bases in Japan? Would it be unwise to force the Berlin blockade with an armed convoy? Would it be unwise to land several thousand Marines on the shores of Lebanon or to drop several thousand English parachutists into Jordan? If one looks back on the decisions actually taken on both sides, one has the impression that—apart from the American decision to cross the 38th Parallel and the decision, made by MacArthur rather than by Truman, to advance the Eighth Army to the Yalu—it is the United States which has shown most restraint. It was the Soviet Union which took the initiative in the Berlin blockade and which tolerated, even if it did not provoke, the North Korean offensive in June of 1950. It was the Chinese who trained and provisioned the Viet-minh divisions victorious at Dien-Bien-Phu. It was the Soviet Union that threatened France and Great Britain with "rockets" and "volunteers" at the time of the Suez crisis. It was the Soviet Union, once more, that vaguely promised to come to Cuba's aid in case of military aggression by the United States, despite the fact that Cuba can be considered as situated within the American zone in much the same way as Hungary was within the Soviet zone.

Even though, to my mind, the Soviet bloc has most often been the more offensive and daring of the two, even during the period from 1945–55 in which the superiority of the American atomic force was beyond dispute,[15] it has nevertheless always left itself an emergency exit. The Soviet bloc has never burned its bridges behind itself. For example, it never officially proclaimed the blockade of Berlin. It pleaded technical difficulties first on the waterways, then on the railways, then on the roads. At any given moment it had, in the event of a violent reaction on the part of the Western powers, the possibility of retreating without losing face. It never attempted to interrupt air traffic by force—which, technically, would have been easy enough to do. The rule of the game which, in this case, was respected by both camps was the ban on recourse to armed force. The Soviet pursuit planes did not attack the heavy transport planes, which would have been unable to defend themselves, and the Western powers, on their side, did not attempt to force a way through the ground blockade. The rule had probably not been conceived clearly in advance by either camp. It was elaborated by the interaction of local circumstances and the desire, common to both adversaries, not to relinquish their control over events. If the Western powers had sent an armed convoy through, the Russians would probably not have fired. But if they had fired, then the Western bloc would have had to double its bet. Similarly, if the Russians had stopped all air traffic, they would have been forcing the Western bloc to choose between a defeat too spectacular to be tolerable and

---

[15] It is possible that American superiority was never greater than between 1955 and 1959. The SAC was at the height of its power. The Soviet strategic air force was mediocre, and it is also possible that the ICBMs were not available in great numbers.

recourse to arms. The airlift represented a middle solution acceptable to both protagonists.

The same common desire to limit the conflict was expressed by a different set of rules in Korea. The Americans refrained from carrying hostilities beyond the Korean frontier, and the Sino-Koreans or the Soviets did the same. Neither the Chinese bases in Manchuria nor the American bases in Japan were bombed. The Soviet submarines made no attempt to sever relations between Japan and Korea. Thus Korea was transformed, by an implicit agreement, into a closed lists in which the representatives of the two super powers settled a quarrel. The application of this rule—which one might call the geographic localization of hostilities—resulted in a draw, without such a result having been inevitable (two or three more American divisions in the spring of 1951 or even the spring of 1952 would have been enough to guarantee a local victory without any enlargement of the theater of hostilities or the employment of atomic weapons). Here again, the rule was invented and respected by both parties during the actual course of events. It had less the merit of rationality than of simplicity: it was identifiable by both adversaries without explicit communication.

The war in Indo-China was of another sort, since neither the Soviet Union nor China was directly involved, and the United States limited itself to supporting France and the anti-Viet-minh government of Vietnam by financial contributions and deliveries of arms. The decisive moment came in the spring of 1954, when the French garrison of Dien-Bien-Phu lost its first battle and appeared to be doomed. Without American intervention France would have had to abandon the struggle, and the price of an armistice would have been, at the very least, the Sovietization of half of the country. The United States decided in favor of non-intervention, and the Sino-Soviet bloc imposed conditions that were not significantly different from those it would have been able to obtain before, or without, the victory at Dien-Bien-Phu.

In fact, the crisis in the spring of 1954 was accidental rather than intentional. After Stalin's death the members of the Presidium, concerned with internal conflicts of succession, wanted to reduce international tension. In Korea they urged the Chinese not to persist in demanding the repatriation of all prisoners, and would probably have consented to the negotiation of an armistice in Indo-China at the same time as the one in Korea. It was the obstinacy of the French government, encouraged by the blind will of the American government, that caused the prolongation of hostilities and gave the Viet-minh, with the help of Mao's China, the opportunity for such a spectacular success—a success which transformed the meaning and the consequences of the peace, even if it did not substantially modify its terms.

The crisis of 1956—Hungary and Suez—was not provoked by the super powers themselves. The nationalization of the Suez Canal was an episode in the Arab revolt against the influence or the presence of the West in the Near East. There is no need to impute its initiation to Moscow: any Egyptian government could have conceived the project, especially since the concession was due to expire some dozen years later in any case. The British reaction was surprising, unpredictable: why did Her Majesty's government make an attempt at military reoccupation of the zone it had just evacuated? The French reaction is more easily explicable, insofar as the French leaders were seeking, yet again, the solution to the Algerian problem.

Despite armed force being generally utilized by the Soviet Union, by France and by Great Britain, the meaning of the crisis, with regard to the two super powers,[16] lay rather in the twofold refusal of the Americans: the refusal to intervene in order to "liberate" a satellite, and the refusal to allow its allies to take military action against a country belonging to the third world. These two refusals had one thing in common: the fear of an unlimited war. Both can be explained in realistic terms, the one was prudent but morally mediocre, the other was possibly justified by prudence but also by an ideal.

It was doubtless prudent, perhaps reasonable, certainly not glorious, to have stood by and watched the Hungarian Revolution be snuffed out. It was doubtless prudent on the part of the United States to forbid the French and the British to occupy the Suez Canal Zone. It was perhaps reasonable to consider the position taken against the two ex-great European powers as more "profitable" with regard to the cohesion of the Atlantic bloc. But the formula used by Eisenhower on the day of the Anglo-French ultimatum and on the eve of the Soviet intervention in Budapest—there cannot be two laws, one for our friends and one for our enemies—was, ironically, to be turned against the American President: with the help of its enemy, the United States applied to its allies a severe law and tolerated, with no more than a verbal protest, an open aggression on the part of its enemy. One American author[17] has suggested an entirely cynical interpretation of the Suez-Budapest crisis. The *grands frères* in the hour of peril discovered—in both senses of the word—their fraternity.[18] Each decided that it would be to its own interest if the other super power were to re-establish discipline within its own bloc. The United States could not tolerate France and Great Britain initiating actions of a nature likely to provoke unlimited hostilities. Despite their sympathy for the Hungarian rebels, the American leaders, in a confused manner, blamed them for being forced to choose between a not very honorable abstention and an imprudent intervention. They chose, without visible hesitation, the first alternative.

The forceful measures employed two years later, at the time of the Iraqi

---

[16] We analyzed this same crisis, in the preceding chapter, with regard to the relations between the partners of the Western bloc. Cf. Chap. XV, Sec. 5.
[17] C. A. McClelland, in a report to a conference organized by the Center of International Studies, Princeton. The title of the report is *Acute International Crisis in the Cold War: A System Theoretical Note.*
[18] They discovered it themselves, and showed it to the world.

Revolution and the troubles in Lebanon and Jordan, were even more reduced. This time, it was the United States that sent its Marines. But it sent them at the request of a legal government recognized by all states and by the United Nations. Furthermore, the Marines did not fight; they were careful to keep out of the civil war, which continued, intermittently, for several weeks. Their intervention consisted of their presence, of the proof they gave by being there, of the American determination to act if the need should arise, and of the moral support they afforded the legal authorities of Beirut. Even if the Kadar government which, according to the Soviet version, asked the Big Brother to help in order to re-establish a "workers' and peasants'" government, had been legal in the eyes of either internal or international law—which was not the case—there would still have been a major difference between the two interventions: the one was bellicose—it had both the aim and the result of crushing the revolutionaries, while the other helped effect without bloodshed the reconciliation of the two camps, a reconciliation which was indispensable to Lebanon's very existence.

From this review of the various crises it is not impossible to draw an optimistic conclusion. The use of armed force, at least by one of the super powers against the other, has been increasingly restricted. The length of each crisis has been growing shorter. The Berlin blockade lasted for months, as though the Two did not know how to escape unscathed from the trial of strength which they had launched. The Korean War went on for three years, and during the last two years negotiations repeatedly broke down, according to official declarations, over the single obstacle of the repatriation of prisoners (the plenipotentiaries of Communist China refused their subjects captured by the Americans the right to choose freedom). The Suez-Budapest crisis was liquidated within a few days, the Iraq-Lebanon-Jordan crisis within a few weeks. The number and caliber of weapons used diminished from crisis to crisis.

To this optimistic interpretation it will justifiably be objected that the principle of the *trend toward the diminution of the force used* can only be applied to direct relations between the two super powers or between the two blocs. Against Hungary the Soviet Union employed a dozen divisions—more than the effective force necessary for the repression, but brutal and massive as it was, it made the latter correspondingly shorter and less costly. In the Near East the American intervention was symbolic. It was the equivalent of gunboat diplomacy, its aim being not to make a government yield by means of an act symbolizing the use of force, but to reinforce a legal government by an act symbolizing support by means of force.

What prevents us from subscribing unreservedly to this thesis—the tendency toward decreasing the use of force—is first that the crises each have the character of an event, and that a comparison of the crises seen as single events creates the appearance of a tendency, although that appearance may well be created in the eye of the observer. The Russians sent a large army into action in Hungary because the military circumstances demanded it. The American Marines in Lebanon did not fire a shot because such restraint corresponded to circumstances. The real question is whether the two super powers have learned to settle their quarrels as cheaply as possible and are determined to limit the volume of violence to the minimum.

I think, in fact, that the United States and the Soviet Union, despite the ravings of their propagandists and their Homeric challenges, have learned to know each other and no longer lightly impute bellicose intentions to each other. Even supposing that the members of the Presidium feared in the past that the United States might launch a preventive war,[19] they have been reassured on this point for some time now. The war would not be preventive: to take the first step today would be to throw oneself into the water for fear of getting wet. No longer disposed to doubt each other's desire to limit the conflicts, the two super powers are less inclined to hysteria and panic when, through the fault of an ally or a neutral, a crisis arises in which a country or a regime runs the risk of changing allegiance.[20]

The changes of allegiance all take the same direction, it is true; an ex-colonial country becomes independent, neutral at first, then neutralist, sometimes leftist. How many times will the United States submit to the rules of the game it has imposed on its allies if these changes of allegiance grow more frequent and, above all, if they occur in the United States own zone (Latin America) instead of in the zones that were formerly under the influence of European states?

The rules of the game are at first glance those suggested by the Charter of the United Nations: non-recourse to force. But since no definition of aggression has been arrived at, either in theory or in practice, only direct aggression, the crossing of frontiers by regular armies, is excluded by these rules. This has meant that all other forms of aggression have been legalized, because they have been tolerated. The recruiting and training of partisans destined to combat the government of a foreign country—which the Soviet bloc considered as a typical example of aggression when they feared such practices instead of indulging in them—is henceforth legal tender. Tunisia made no pretense of concealing the fact that she harbored Algerian *fellagha*, and a French complaint against Tunisian aggression on this score would have been futile. The transnational organization of the war of partisans against the European empires has received the blessing of both the United Nations and the United States. (The latter has attempted this kind of sport itself, successfully in Guatemala, unsuccessfully in Cuba.)

The only thing that can be placed in the scales to balance the illegality

[19] I do not believe Stalin ever feared such a thing: at the time when Stalin feared a German attack, from 1933 to 1941, he behaved quite differently from the way he did from 1945 to 1953.
[20] The book was written before the Cuban crisis of 1962, which I have analyzed in *The Great Debate* (1965) and which does not contradict the general thesis.

of intervention by regular armies and the legality of the transnational organization of partisans is the legality of an appeal for foreign assistance made by a recognized government. The Egyptian *fedayins* were tolerated by the United Nations, the Israeli campaign in the Sinai condemned, as was the Anglo-French ultimatum to Egypt. On the other hand, the American intervention in Lebanon and the British intervention in Jordan were legal because the foreign troops arrived at the request of legal governments. Since, in the eyes of international law, foreign intervention is legal when it is solicited by the legal power within a state, the rivalry of the super powers takes its course within states, the aim of both being to favor those men who will call for their help, should the occasion arise.

Since international law, as we have seen, is based on the sovereignty and the equality of states, it is not a reflection but a negation of the present reality. Conceived for the European states that, in a sense, were reciprocally recognizing their right to existence, international law was then extended to the world as a whole, at a time when, even in Europe, the ideological conflicts from which the heterogeneity of the system resulted were already bringing it into disrepute. At the present time, international law is a permanent incitement to hypocrisy. It creates an obligation for the super powers to dissimulate what they cannot avoid doing, that is, interfering in the internal affairs of member states of the United Nations. No one refrains from intervening, but each tries to intervene in such a manner that the role of non-intervention will remain officially unbroken: the chief condition of success is for each camp to "possess" a government which is an adherent of its cause. When the two camps attain their goal, the third country is either divided, like Germany, or in a state of civil war. Occasionally the country is divided and the section not won over to communism is in a state of civil war (South Korea, South Vietnam).

It goes without saying that the rules of the game concerning the third world—the legalization of the transnational organization of partisans, obligation to camouflage intervention in the internal affairs of states, competition between the super powers to help a legal government devoted to its cause—have not been established by decrees on either side, or by any agreement between the Two. These rules have, as it were, been crystallized by the diplomatic history of the past twenty years. Juridical formalism is the extension to the entire globe of a law elaborated by and for a homogeneous system. The heterogeneity of the system in Europe itself has already changed its character, since the Soviet Union, even as it was proclaiming the principles of state sovereignty and equality,[21] was ignoring its spirit, since the U.S.S.R. was and intended to be a revolutionary state whose concept is destined for universal diffusion. As a state, the U.S.S.R. adopted

[21] Cf. Jean-Yves Calvez, *Droit international et souveraineté en U.R.S.S.*, Paris, 1953.

the most traditional and the most uncompromising theory of sovereignty. Insofar as the government of the U.S.S.R. was composed of the members of the Politburo of the Communist party and actually controlled the actions of the Comintern, it organized subversion within the states with which it maintained diplomatic relations, according to the customs of the *jus gentium Europaeum*. The non-Communist states had the choice between tolerating this duplicity or breaking off diplomatic relations. They have all, for obvious reasons, preferred the first alternative.

The growing strength of the Soviet Union after the Second World War and the multiplication of new states immeasurably increased the scope and opportunities for this duplicity. Roosevelt, prolonging the Wilsonian tradition, expected the United Nations to provide a decisive contribution to the maintenance of peace. He also saw the international organization as a means of preventing the United States from returning to isolationism. The combination of an international law, tending to "outlaw" war, and of a civil war on an international scale (or of a transnational organization of subversion) finds its logical expression in the present practice: regular armies no longer cross frontiers, but are stationed in foreign countries where they are summoned by an appeal from the legal governments. Such legal governments therefore do enjoy, within their own frontiers, a sovereignty which is not futile, since it permits the rulers of a small power to seize with impunity the property of the citizens of a great power. But as a necessary concomitant to this freedom of action, they must expect a constant effort on the part of the great powers to bring pressure to bear on their decisions.

Are not these rules, it will be asked, more favorable to the Soviet camp than to the Western camp? Should not the latter have constantly denounced the transnational organization of partisan warfare instead of emphasizing non-recourse to force (which is, in fact, only non-recourse to force by regular armies)? The industrialized states and the liberal regimes are constrained to employ only their regular armies, whereas the underdeveloped countries and the revolutionary parties resort spontaneously to terrorism or guerrilla warfare.

This objection is indisputable, but it is difficult to see how it could have been otherwise. Could the United Nations have recognized the legitimacy of using punitive expeditions as a retaliation against partisans supplied from abroad? If it had recognized the legitimacy of such retaliation (the Greek army entering Bulgaria or Yugoslavia, before that country's break with the Soviet Union), would the course of events have been changed? One can argue that the threat of reprisals by regular armies against the partisan's logistic bases might, in certain cases, have had some effect. It would at least have prevented what is now a kind of international confirmation of the right to indirect aggression. But in China, in Indonesia, in Indo-China and in North Africa the partisans were an expression of a revolutionary situation that another interpretation of international law would not have been sufficient to contain.

The fact remains that the tendency to the diminution of the use of force can be applied only to the use of organized force, the use of regular armies. The countries in which partisans maintain a state of insecurity are not perhaps more numerous than they were twenty years ago. But, meanwhile, the Communist order has been established in a number of countries which, in 1945, were suffering the ravages of war: elsewhere, nationalist revolts have won independence from colonial powers, and the regimes established are more or less precarious; finally, other countries, which were once "private hunting grounds" of the West, now have regimes threatened by rebels and inclined to neutrality or neutralism.

An over-all judgment on the evolution of the past twenty years—appeasement, intensification of the conflict, intermittence—is not simple. Nor can it be categorical. There has been a series of more or less violent crises alternating with periods of calm: nothing suggests that the end of this alternation is in sight. The crises of the last few years have been less prolonged, they have involved a reduction in the amount of violence, they have revealed that men have in a way become accustomed to conflict, as if the adversaries were beginning to perceive their reciprocal intentions more clearly and were acting in consequence.

Humanity is nonetheless still far from being a new order: on the contrary, revolutionary agitation provoked or exploited by the Communist parties, and sometimes independent of them, is spreading throughout the rest of the world. Perhaps the United States will no longer submit to the rule of not employing regular armies which it has hitherto imposed on its allies. This was suggested in the Cuban crisis in 1962.

Even if it does submit to such a rule, there will be no appeasement as long as the three principal causes of what it has been agreed to call the cold war remain: *the partition of Europe, the arms race, the fate of the third world.* Now these three causes are the effect of what the two super powers or the two camps *are* as much as or more than of what they *do.* Allaying hostility would necessitate an accepted delimitation of zones of influence incompatible with the universal pretensions of both ideologies. The socialist bloc, by its very being, aside from all subversive action, offers the third world a model of development. The West cannot avoid fearing the influence of the Soviet example, since those converted to it automatically become its enemies.

It is only on the level of the arms race that any progress is conceivable. It would appear that each of the duopolists has become increasingly reassured as to the other's intentions while each is at the same time terrified by the means of destruction which it possesses and which the other therefore possesses or will possess. The major fact in the circumstances of the sixties remains the balance of terror, the desire of the two super powers not to start the war for which they are preparing. A major but a negative fact: the giants

are paralyzed but *paralyzed in relation to each other*. Provided they do not
come to grips directly or use their most destructive weapons, they are free to
consider the entire globe as the field of their activity and to ignore the
frontiers that their silent missiles might cross, frontiers that are being continually crossed by propaganda and the agents of subversion.

The goal of the West is not to destroy the Soviet-dominated regimes, but
to persuade the Communists that there is room for different regimes that need
not consider each other as enemies. The goal of the Soviet bloc is to eliminate
the capitalist regimes and to utilize the revolutionary movements, movements
of national or social liberation, to this end. One of the super powers aims at a
victory that is to be total in political if not military terms, the other aims at
peaceful coexistence as an end, and not, in the manner of its rival, merely as
a means.

Do the Soviet rulers think or act in terms of their official doctrine of
inexpiable hostility, or in terms of the clandestine doctrine of the growing
resemblance between the two worlds? It would appear to me, speaking
personally, that, *for the moment* it has been the official doctrine that was
dominant, even during the Khrushchev era, and not the clandestine one.

It is true that the fear of total war may be imputed to a sort of *embourgeoisement*. The Russian Revolution is fifty years old. The privileged members of the regime, and even the mass of the people, have found a place
in the sun. Sufferings have been commensurate with accomplishments. The
Russian people as a whole are as hostile to adventure as the American people.
In this sense the attitudes of the super powers toward each other resemble
each other more than they resemble that of Communist China toward the
United States. Similarly, the Soviet Union often acts in the third world as
an enemy of the United States rather than as a revolutionary state. It still
continues to grant aid to the United Arab Republic, though President
Nasser's regime is ruthless in its treatment of Communists.

We do not deny the possible influence of a Soviet *embourgeoisement* on
the conduct of foreign policy. We merely think that this influence is for
the time being a secondary one. Thermonuclear war is too horrible for the
Kremlin to risk, either voluntarily or through imprudence. The chances of
socialist advances in the rest of the world are too favorable for the Soviet
leaders to accept any formula for stabilizing it. The Soviet leaders and
even the ruling classes are too much in need of Marxist categories for giving
a moral foundation to their power; they have been thinking too long in those
categories to give way to skepticism so soon. They continue to believe in the
irreducible hostility of the two blocs as firmly as in the inevitability of their
own victory. Once again, each super power acts externally according to its
own being. The United States exports more capital than ideas, the Soviet
Union exports more ideas, and above all more ideologists, than capital.
The Americans dream of an agreement between the Two. The Soviet
leaders declare a reconciliation to be impossible. Reconciliation becomes all

the more impossible because one side wants to believe in it and the other side does not.

Only one possible event, and one that is even probable in the indeterminate future, would be likely to modify the present situation profoundly: the Soviet realization of a danger created by China. For those who regard *nations* and *races* as the actors in the historical drama, this eventuality is not only possible, it is certain, inscribed in advance in the great book of history. China, which already has a population of 700 to 800 million, will one day seek to extend itself either southward or northward. Russia, possessing immense and almost empty tracts of land, is already potentially threatened by an overpopulated China, *if the stake of great conflicts is the possession of space.* The Russian people belong to the white race and to the Christian zone of civilization. The yellow masses are "miserable and innumerable."[22] How then could the Russians remain indefinitely the enemies of those of their race or of their religion?

In fact, down through history, neither race nor religion has cemented political units together or prevented war. Those cities or states that fought each other most ruthlessly were almost always members of the same civilization. Possibly China and the Soviet Union will become enemies tomorrow: I doubt that the color of their inhabitants' skins will be the cause of this potential hostility. The regrouping of races into continent-states is beyond our historical horizon.

Nevertheless, the disintegration of the Soviet world is already perceptible. The quarrel between the Kremlin and the Forbidden City, between Mr. Khrushchev and his followers on one side and Mao Tse-tung and his followers on the other, became apparent at the Twenty-second Congress of the Soviet Communist party. The Russian invectives against Albania were aimed at the Chinese giant; the Chinese invectives against revisionist Yugoslavia were aimed at the Russian Big Brother.

According to the arguments of those interlocutors, the great powers of communism have different conceptions of the correct strategy with regard to the West and the third world: the Chinese would recommend a more active diplomacy against imperialism, and would accept with a light heart the increased risks of war. They would also reserve their support of countries in the third world for the Communist parties, instead of supporting, as Mr. Khrushchev does, any governments that are *objectively* hostile to the West.

Is this controversy the cause or the effect of the tension between Moscow and Peking? Are the Russians and the Chinese belaboring each other with conflicting ideological theses because the national interests of the two states are different? Because Mr. Khrushchev wanted to maintain his authority and Mao Tse-tung wanted to reject it? Because the two nations are not at the same stage of socialist development and therefore the attitude of each is

[22] The expression is General de Gaulle's.

determined by the internal exigencies of its regime? It is not possible, and it is probably not necessary, to choose among these hypotheses. They are more complementary than contradictory in an ideocratic world.

Let us confine ourselves to the statement that the United States has done nothing to provoke this quasi-rupture (any more than the Soviet Union is responsible for the Cuban Revolution). The two great Communist powers continue to outdo each other in the ardor of their denunciations of capitalism and their solemn proclamations of loyalty to Marxist-Leninism: on this point the West would be mistaken not to take them at their word.

PART FOUR

PRAXEOLOGY
The Antinomies of Diplomatic-Strategic Conduct

Normative implications are inherent in every *theory*.[1] But depending upon the nature of the human action of which the theory is a systematic comprehension, the transition from *de facto* propositions to imperatives assumes a different character, and the imperatives are more or less vague *counsels* or *precepts* based on regularities or evidence.

Clausewitz observes somewhere that strategy can have no basis in theory, as can tactics, because the problems faced by strategists are more complex and do not offer the same regularities as those faced by tacticians. How could Napoleon have vanquished Alexander? Was the former right or wrong in seeking the key to victory in Moscow? Granted that he failed, was another method, giving him a better chance, available? Such questions never prevent unequivocal answers. No commander-in-chief before Napoleon had ever undertaken a campaign against Russia under similar circumstances. Thus, strategic theory has long been limited to the enumeration of a few principles which are little more than vague formulas: *the principle of the concentration of forces* (avoid dispersion); *of the objective* (choose a plan and stick to it, adverse pressures notwithstanding); *of persistence* (pursue any advantage gained); *of the offensive* (take the initiative at the opportune moment, and exploit it fully in order to force the issue); *of security* (protect one's forces and lines of communication against surprise attack); *of surprise* (deceive the enemy as to one's intentions); *of economy of forces* (exploit all the available forces fully).

Obviously these rules do not permit determining, in a particular situation, which is the best strategy. For one thing, they are contradictory: it is difficult to obey both the principle of pursuit and that of security, both the principle of the concentration and that of the economy of forces, at the same time. The Cartesian imperative—once committed to a line of action, to pursue it to the end, rather than to retrace one's steps—would appear to be, according to

---

[1] We have in mind here only those theories relating to the social sciences.

previous cases, the height of absurd obstinacy or the expression of sagacious determination.

Is the contrast between strategic indeterminacy and tactical constants always present? It seems to me, as a matter of fact, that strategic indeterminacy has not been reduced (at least until the Atomic Age), but that many tactical regularities have been challenged by technological advances. Which precepts, among those the nineteenth-century theoreticians formulated with regard to engagements and fortifications, remained valid for the motorized armies of 1940–45? The answer could be given only by detailed analyses which, in any case, would not have affected two commonplace propositions: certain precepts are dependent upon a particular state of firepower and mobility, others survive the prodigious development of means of transportation and destruction.

Strategic indeterminacy persists to this day because it can be attributed to two irreducible causes: the decisions to be made are profoundly influenced by the total situation, consequently by the unique elements resulting from a combination of factors; furthermore the decision is oriented toward an end less clearly defined than that envisaged by the tactician.

Napoleon's decision to attack Russia and the same decision taken by Hitler were each made in a singular constellation of circumstances; and in spite of the fact that the theater of action was unchanged, the events of 1811, like those of 1941, had to depend as much, or more, on historical circumstances as on geographic milieu (relation of forces, possibilities of British action, Russian resistance, etc.). The more an action concerns a total situation or is inscribed within it, the less it can refer to those elements of the situation which are recurrent. Churchill's decision to send an armored division to the Suez Canal at the very hour of the Battle of Britain was governed by what, in the constellation, was unprecedented.

The second and less obvious cause has still more considerable consequences. Tactical precepts refer to an objective generally not open to dispute: the aim of the engagement is to prevail over the enemy; in other words, not to be taken by surprise, to maintain one's lines of communication, to break through the enemy's front line, to exploit every success, etc. These various formulas show that even for the initiator of the new tactic, the objective is not always unique and defined once and for all. But as one gradually rises from squadron commander to the general staff, orders are more influenced by political considerations and by the plurality of objectives, determined not only by local engagements and military operations, but by the campaign and the war itself.

Many observers might be inclined, at first glance, to reverse the foregoing propositions and claim the indeterminacy of tactics (local circumstances must be considered) and the determinacy of strategy (one sole objective: victory).[2]

---

[2] This formula is General Giraud's. The Americans have an analogous one, that of General MacArthur: there is no substitute for victory.

The history of the twentieth century suffices to remind us that there are many ways to win a war, that the various ways are not equivalent, and that the final victory does not necessarily belong to the side that dictates the conditions of peace.

Strategic-diplomatic conduct—or that of foreign policy—cannot be more determinate than strategic conduct itself. It involves the two causes of indeterminacy just mentioned, the reference to the singular and unique elements of the situation, and the plurality of objectives. But it involves—or seems to involve—still others. First of all, the moment one shifts from observation to precept, the paradox of international relations is clearly revealed: relations between states are social relations controlled by the *possible and legitimate* recourse to force. Now, the use of force is not of itself immoral (might in the service of right has always been considered moral). But each of the actors, if he be the judge, and the sole judge, of the legitimacy of his cause, must feel threatened by the others, and the international game becomes a struggle in which the player who abides by the rules runs the risk of being victimized by his (relative) morality. At this point two sorts of questions arise: Is foreign policy in and of itself diabolic? What means may be legitimately employed, it is being understood that the states are jealous of their independence? Further, is it conceivable, and if so is it practicable, to go beyond foreign policy? To subject states to one law, that of collective security or of a universal empire? Can we put an end to what we call international anarchy, that is, the claim of states to take the law into their own hands? In other words, the essence of inter-state relations raises two praxeological problems that I will call the *Machiavellian problem* and the *Kantian problem*: that of legitimate means and that of universal peace.

In the first chapter of this section (XIX), I examine the problem, a classic one especially in American literature, raised by the antinomy of realism and idealism. In a world where law does not prevail, what is moral behavior? In the following chapter I discuss the question of whether the development of atomic weapons modifies traditional diplomatic-strategic action, whether the so-called idealistic doctrines of absolute pacifism have not become the only form of prudence. I conclude that fortunately or not, this is not at all the case: in the shadow of the thermonuclear apocalypse, as yesterday in the shadow of armored divisions, or the day before yesterday in the shadow of the legions or the phalanxes, statesmen or simple citizens must act according to prudence, without the illusion or the hope of absolute security.

Granted that the rivalry between the two blocs remains temporarily irreducible, the two following chapters attempt to sketch the strategy which would give the West the best chances to achieve the aims it has in view: not to wage a total war, not to succumb. Chapter XXI considers the strictly military aspect, Chapter XXII the political aspect of the strategy. In these two chapters I try to draw the conclusions which emerge from the formal analyses of Part I as well as from the sociological constants of Part II and from the historical descriptions of Part III.

Finally, in the two last chapters, I return to the question, in the light of our present experience, of the very foundations of international order, or rather disorder: Is it possible to subject the states to the rule of law? What national "sovereignty," what "independence," would the states retain in a universal federation or universal empire? Would states survive at all? Would a universal state still deserve the name of state?

In other words, the first two chapters are devoted to the problem of means in the world as it is, the last two to the problem of the ultimate goal, peace. The two intermediate chapters attempt to specify the conduct suitable to today's needs without being contrary to our hopes for the future. But there are limits to such desired reconciliations: the situation of the diplomat-strategist, that is, all of us, is antinomic if history is violent and our ideal peaceful.

chapter XIX

In Search of a Morality

I: *Idealism and Realism*

We have tried to make the analysis of international relations independent of moral judgments and metaphysical concepts, taking as our point of departure the plurality of states, the shadow of a possible war hovering over the decisions of governments, the customary or legal rules more or less respected by the sovereigns but never interpreted by them as excluding a recourse to force in order to safeguard "vital interests" and "national honor." This analysis was neutral, as we see it, because it was a discernment of the *facts* (such has been, down through the centuries, the course of relations between states) and of the *subjective meanings* (statesmen, citizens, philosophers have always recognized a *difference in nature* between the internal order of states and the order between states).

Diplomatic-strategic conduct *has appeared* to us in the past to be a kind of mixture. It is social behavior; the actors—except in extreme cases—acknowledge each other's humanity, even their kinship, and do not believe they are entitled to abuse each other, whatever the pretext might be. But it is also anti-social behavior insofar as force decides the issue in case of conflict and constitutes the basis of what treaties might confirm as the norm. Now, insofar as diplomatic-strategic conduct is governed by the risk of or the preparation for war, it obeys, and cannot help but obey, the logic of rivalry; it ignores —and must ignore—the Christian virtues insofar as these are opposed to the needs of the competition.

The double character of the relations between political units is the origin of praxeological and philosophical disputes. The actors—the political units or those who represent them—always try to justify themselves. But are they, should they feel obliged to stand by the juridical or ethical reasons they invoke, or should they act according to a calculation of forces or of opportunity? What role do nations and statesmen accord, or should they accord to principles, ideas, morality, necessity?

1. *From Idealist Illusions to Prudence*

In March 1936, on Chancellor Hitler's orders, German troops entered the Rhineland. The event constituted, without a doubt, a violation of the Versailles Treaty as well as the Treaty of Locarno. But the spokesmen of the Third Reich could plead that the disarmament of the left bank of the Rhine was unjust since France had fortified her own frontier. Equality of rights,[1] an ideology agreed upon by all, gave an appearance of equity to an action contrary to existing norms. Should the statesman or the moralist not party to the dispute have raised his voice in favor of legality or equity? Or else, observing that the reoccupation of the left bank of the Rhine would compromise the French system of alliances and put Czechoslovakia and Poland at the mercy of the Third Reich, should he have championed a military countermove in order to maintain a demilitarized zone, indispensable to the security of Europe?

Today's historian has no hesitation in answering these questions. We know that the German troops were ordered to withdraw if the French troops advanced. The attempt to punish by force the violation of a norm, regardless of the equality of rights, would have been justified because it might have prevented and, in any case, did delay the war of 1939; because it is morally legitimate to deny equality of rights to anyone who would make use of this same equality to deny it to others.

If, in 1933, France had heeded Marshal Pilsudski's advice and used force to overthrow Hitler, who had just come to power, she would have violated the *principle* of non-interference in the internal affairs of other states, she would have failed to recognize Germany's *right* of free choice with regard to regime and leader, she would have been denounced with indignation by American public opinion, by moralists and idealists hastening to the rescue, not of National Socialism, but of the will of the people or the rule of non-interference. The violence done to the German nation would have been stamped with the seal of infamy, and historians would never know from what miseries Hitler's disappearance would have saved humanity.

These ironic remarks about a past which did not come to pass are not intended surreptitiously to point a moral, but to bring to light some consequences of the true nature of relations between states. Since states have not renounced taking the law into their own hands and remaining sole judges of what their honor requires, the survival of political units depends, in the final analysis, on the balance of forces, and it is the *duty* of statesmen to be concerned, *first of all*, with the nation whose destiny is entrusted to them. The necessity of national egoism derives logically from what philosophers called the *state of nature* which rules among states.

---

[1] It is, in fact, difficult to define equality of rights in a strict sense. In concrete terms, the rights of each, individual or collectivity, are different.

Relations between states are not, for all that, comparable to those of beasts in the jungle. Political history is not purely natural. Diplomatic-strategic conduct tends to justify itself by ideas; it claims to obey *norms,* to submit to *principles.* We call *cynics* those who regard ideas, norms and principles as mere disguises of the desire for power, without real effectiveness. Those who repudiate the fact that all international order must be maintained by force are accused of *idealistic illusions.* The idealistic illusion assumes diverse forms, depending upon the character of the imperatives and the values invoked. *Ideological idealism* consists in considering a historical idea as the exclusive and sufficient criterion of the just and the unjust—for example, the right of peoples to self-determination, or the idea of nationalities. We use, with good reason, two different concepts, *right* and *idea,* because, in actual fact, both were and are used, and because the fluctuating vocabulary expresses the inevitable uncertainty of the thought.

The Germans did not bother to deny in 1871 that the majority of Alsatians wanted to remain French, but answered (when they did not confine themselves to brandishing the victorious sword) that violence had been done to the Alsatians by Louis XIV, two centuries before, and that belonging to German culture was more important than the accidental and transitory desires of one generation. In 1919 the Czechs did not claim that the Sudeten Germans wanted to be part of Czechoslovakia, but they asserted that, deprived of the territory inhabited by the Sudetens, they were doomed to subjection. Inevitably, the liberty of one or the other would have to be sacrificed, and the Czechs outnumbered the Sudetens.

The translation of a historical idea into territorial status does not proceed without uncertainty, either because the idea is open to several interpretations (what should be the fate of Alsatians of German culture and French preference?) or because the requirements of security prohibit its honest application (Bohemia, without the periphery inhabited by the Sudetens, is indefensible). The cynic will be tempted to conclude that in this case the idea serves only to mask appetites or interests, but he will not be right. Ideological idealism has little to do with reality: no state holds to *one* idea as an absolute to which all else must be sacrificed. That would be dangerous. Failure to appreciate strategic or economic necessity adds to the precariousness of a given status, even one allegedly consistent with the idea. But most states are reluctant to reject overtly an idea by which they justify, in the twentieth century, the annexation of peoples manifestly accustomed to and desirous of constituting independent nations.[2]

Juridical idealism consists in making decisions or carrying out strategy as a consequence of a more or less well-defined rule. George F. Kennan has

---

[2] The victors nonetheless retain three possibilities: extermination, deportation, establishing the fifth column or a satellite state in power. The *historical idea* exerts a certain influence on the conduct of states; it does not guarantee survival.

often denounced this "legal idealism," and recent authors, even those who concede an important role to international law, are beginning to take into account the arguments formulated by the realists.

"The authors recognize the merits of criticisms that distinguished observers such as George Kennan have made regarding too great a reliance upon legal processes. American foreign policy has often been formulated without sufficient attention to the role of force and of national interests. We do not wish to encourage naïveté of the sort he describes as 'legal idealism,' a reliance upon abstract rules that are institutionally unsupported. We concede that nations often do act in partisan ways in support of immediate political objectives." But the writers are quick to add: "But we contend that much of international conduct is doctrinally consonant with normative standards, even though inconsistent with particular immediate interests, and that long-term self-interest can and does provide political support for internationally lawful conduct."[3]

Legal or semi-legal formulas by which American diplomats have expressed a given policy or concealed the absence of one are numerous and, in fact, well known: the Open-Door Policy in China, non-recognition of changes effected by force, outlawing of war as a political instrument, collective security. The first two formulas do not claim to modify the essential features of politics among nations, while the last two tend to do so. But all four have the same character: they are abstract propositions, offered as normative, but stripped of all authority because they do not express needs genuinely felt by men, and because they are supported neither by force nor by institutions. Such formulas, then, do not constitute valid answers, effective solutions to immediate or eternal problems.

The Open-Door Policy was intended to protect China's independence and territorial integrity, an objective held to conform with the national interest and the ideal of the United States. However, the difficulty resulted not only from the imperialist ambitions of the European powers, but also from the disintegration of China's old regime and the absence of a central government in Peking capable of prevailing upon the provinces and being respected by foreign states. So long as a new dynasty had not received an indisputable mandate from heaven, European interference, with a view to gaining privileges or spheres of influence, easily overcame the obstacle of the Open-Door Policy.

Still more futile is the principle of the non-recognition of changes effected by force. Populations annexed against their will receive no help from the refusal of the government of the United States to accept a *fait accompli*. Men know that in the long run international law must bow to fact. A territorial status invariably ends up being legalized, provided it lasts. A great power

---

[3] Morton A. Kaplan and Nicholas de B. Katzenbach, *The Political Foundations of International Law*, New York, 1961, p. 10.

that wants to forbid a rival from making conquests must arm and not proclaim in advance its moral disapproval and its abstention from force (such is the meaning of the non-recognition of changes affected by force).

The outlawing of war, in the Kellogg-Briand Pact, and the principle of collective security pose a basic problem which we shall consider in another chapter, namely: is it possible to devise and bring into being a juridical system which effectively assures the security of states and deprives them of the right to take the law into their own hands? But one thing is certain: between the two world wars such a system did not exist and had no chance of existing.

The authors cited above write: "The efforts to outlaw war eventuated in the supreme monument to human futility, the Kellogg-Briand Pact."[4] And elsewhere: "The presence or absence of institutional means of enforcement of legal principles determines whether a system of law exists or not. Municipal courts are able to call upon the assistance of sheriffs, or, if necessary, the total armed force of the state, to aid in the execution of sentence. The political arm of government is obligated to sustain legal process. And a municipal system of law that is not sustained by the cooperation of the body politic will not persist. The assertion that the Covenant and the Pact of Paris outlawed wars of aggression seems excessive when measured against the realities of the international society of the time. These were the statements of wishful thinking, not law."[5]

It would not be easy, as a result of the criterion established here, to determine the norms of international law which deserve to be considered as strictly juridical. But, on the subject of the Kellogg-Briand Pact, the conclusion seems to me indisputable: neither the moral state of the community of nations nor international institutions offered a basis for outlawing war. Anyone imagining he was guaranteeing peace by outlawing war was like a doctor imagining he was curing diseases by declaring them contrary to the aspirations of humanity.

Considering the background of international politics, the condemnation of wars of aggression as such would involve the traditional difficulties of application. If, in order to maintain the status quo and prevent the foreseeable attack of the Third Reich, France had taken the initiative in 1933, she would perhaps have been formally guilty of aggression (in 1936 this initiative would have been viewed as a juridical punishment of the violation of the Locarno Treaty), but this aggression would have had a limited and conservative objective. On the other hand, the day a rearmed Germany took the initiative, she sought to modify the status quo, but violating the treaties, she was not thereby morally guilty if the status quo were unjust. In other words, it is

[4] *Ibid.*, p. 43.
[5] *Ibid.*, p. 291.

difficult to condemn, morally or historically, the initiative of a recourse to force for two reasons: this initiative may be the only means of preventing an attack that will ultimately be mortal; no tribunal, judging equitably, is in a position to say what peaceful changes are imperative and to compel respect for these decisions.

Likewise, if one postulates a system of militarily autonomous states, one must make many assumptions for the principle of collective security to be applicable. First of all, the states must agree on the definition of an aggressor. Hence they must be either disposed to subscribe to the status quo as such or else bring the same judgment in equity to bear on the acts of the states in conflict. A state having been unanimously recognized as an aggressor, legally and in equity (Italy, for example), the other states must feel sufficiently interested in safeguarding the juridical order to accept possible risks and sacrifices in view of an interest that is not strictly national and that is *their* interest at most in the long run (if we assume that all states not party to the conflict are interested in safeguarding the juridical order). Finally, one must assume that the coalition of states united against aggression is so superior in force to the state guilty of aggression that it has no other recourse but capitulation or a hopeless combat. If the aggressor state is, by itself, as strong as the coalition of states defending the law, collective security involves the generalization of a war, or localized, it runs the risk of leading to a general and total war. If several states refuse to accept the responsibilities involving sanctions against the aggressor, collective security paralyzes the defensive alliances without replacing them by a universal alliance.

The criticism of idealist illusion is not only pragmatic, it is also moral. Idealistic diplomacy slips too often into fanaticism; it divides states into good and evil, into peace-loving and bellicose. It envisions a permanent peace by the punishment of the latter and the triumph of the former. The idealist, believing he has broken with power politics, exaggerates its crimes. Sometimes states obey their principles and, with the excuse of punishing aggressors, go to the extreme of war and victory; sometimes, when their interests are at stake or circumstances oblige them to do so, they follow their opportunities. The United States did not hesitate to "interfere in Colombia's internal affairs" to provoke or favor the creation of a state of Panama, ready to concede it a perpetual sovereignty over the Canal Zone. To obtain (wrongly) a Russian intervention against Japan, Roosevelt yielded to Stalin's demands, even to those that could be satisfied only at the expense of the Chinese ally (whose government, it is true, was not hostile to these concessions).

States, engaged in incessant competition whose stake is their existence, do not all behave in the same manner at all times, but they are not divided, once and for all, into good and evil. It is rare that all the wrongs are committed by one side, that one camp is faultless. The first duty—political, but also moral—is to see international relations for what they are, so that each state, legitimately preoccupied with its own interests, will not be entirely

blind to the interests of others. In this uncertain battle, in which the qualifications of the participants are not equivalent but in which it is rare that one
of them has done absolutely no wrong, the best conduct—the best with regard
to the values which the idealist himself wishes to achieve—is that dictated
by *prudence*. To be prudent is to act in accordance with the particular situation and the concrete data, and not in accordance with some system or out of
passive obedience to a norm or pseudo-norm; it is to prefer the limitation of
violence to the punishment of the presumably guilty party or to a so-called
absolute justice; it is to establish concrete accessible objectives conforming to
the secular law of international relations and not to limitless and perhaps
meaningless objectives, such as "a world safe for democracy" or "a world from
which power politics will have disappeared."

Two quotations, borrowed from George F. Kennan, illustrate an analogous
conception of the attitude at the same time most favorable to peace (or to
the limitation of war) and to the relative morality of which states are capable:

"We must be gardeners and not mechanics in our approach to world
affairs." And elsewhere: "This task will be best approached not through the
establishment of rigid legal norms but rather by the traditional devices of
political expediency. The sources of international tension are always specific,
never general. They are always devoid of exact precedents or exact parallels.
They are always in part unpredictable. If the resulting conflicts are to be
effectively isolated and composed, they must be handled partly as matter of
historical equity but partly, also, with an eye to the given relationships of
power. Such conflicts, let us remember, usually touch people at the neuralgic
points of their most violent political emotions. Few people are ever going to
have an abstract devotion to the principles of international legality capable of
competing with the impulses from which wars are apt to arise."[6]

2. *The Idealism of Power Politics*

The conclusion of the preceding section—prudence is the statesman's supreme virtue—seems to me obvious because it is based upon two incontestable facts: the particular character of each situation (which condemns the
spirit of system or principle to irrelevance) and the frequency of a recourse to
force by states in conflict,[7] a recourse which, despite attempts to "outlaw"
war, still conforms to written and traditional international law. Hence we
have not contrasted *prudence* and *idealism*, but prudence and *idealist illusion*,
whether that illusion is juridical or ideological.

[6] *Realities of American Foreign Policy*, Princeton, 1954, p. 92, quoted by Kenneth W.
Thompson, *Political Realism and the Crisis of World Politics*, Princeton, 1960, pp. 55
and 60–61. Kennan has expressed similar ideas in *American Diplomacy* (1900–1950),
Chicago, 1951.
[7] The Kellogg-Briand Pact made not just any war, but "wars of aggression" a crime.
And the non-aggressor states did not rely upon the pact to protect them.

But by the same token it appears that we have hardly touched on the philosophical and moral problems. What meaning do we assign to the competition among states? Is power politics bestial or human, ignoble or magnificent? Is the desire of states to take the law into their own hands unpardonable or, quite the contrary, admirable? Is perpetual peace a perhaps unrealizable ideal, or is it not even an ideal? Or again, should one attibute a positive or negative value to the sovereignty of states, to their permanent rivalry, to their occasional wars?

The ideas of the German historian Heinrich von Treitschke, as expressed in the lectures delivered at the University of Berlin at the end of the last century, and published under the title *Politik*,[8] illustrate one of the two possible attitudes toward *power politics*. According to Treitschke, power politics is not a bondage but an authentic expression of Providence: *Man fulfills his moral vocation only in and through the state, states realize their essence only when they come to grips with each other, war, in fact, is not barbarism but a holy ordeal which rightly determines the destiny of peoples.*

Let us illustrate by quotations the three propositions we have just formulated.

"The state is the people, legally united as an independent power. By the people we mean a certain number of families living together over a long period of time. Consequently, the state is primordial and necessary, and will continue to exist as long as there is history, and is as essential as language."[9] Man, according to Aristotle's formula, is a political animal. The political impulse in man is identical with the tendency to create a state. The idea of humanity is not given to men immediately: it is Christianity which taught them they were brothers. Even today, "man feels himself to be, first of all, German or French, and then only man as man [*Mensch überhaupt*]." "It is not true, physiologically or historically, that men come into the world first as men and only afterward as compatriots."[10] If the political capacity is innate in man and must be developed, it is not suitable to consider the state as a necessary evil; quite the contrary, it is a lofty necessity of nature (*höhe Naturnotwendigkeit*).

The state is a personality, first in the juridical, then in the moral and historical sense. As a personality, it has a will (*Wille*), the most authentic of all wills, even if this will does not always accord with that of the living. For the state exists only in duration, by the transmission of the heritage accumulated by the generations. "There are circumstances in which the shadows of the

---

[8] Published by Max Correlius, Leipzig, 1897.

[9] "Der Staat ist das als unabhnägige Macht rechtlich geeinte Volk. Unter Volk kurzweg verstehen wir eine Mehrheit auf die Dauer zusammenlebender Familien. Mit dieser Erkenntnis ist gegeben, das der Staat uranfänglich und notwendig ist, dass er besteht, solange es eine Geschichte gibt, und der menschheit so wesentlich ist wie die Sprache" (Vol. I, p. 13).

[10] *Ibid.*, Vol. I, p. 19.

past are invoked against the misguided will of the present [*gegen den verirrten Willen der Gegenwart*] and assert themselves more forcibly than the latter. In Alsace, we appeal to Geiler von Kaisersberg against the misguided will of the Francillons, and trust that his spirit will be resurrected."[11]

If the state is a personality, a plurality that is both necessary and in accord with reason (*Vernunft-gemasse*) results from it. "Just as in human life the ego supposes the presence of a non-ego, so it is in the life of the state. The state is a power [*Macht*] only in order to maintain itself side by side with other equally independent powers. War and the administration of justice [*Rechtspflege*] are the foremost tasks of even the crudest barbarian state. Now, these tasks are conceivable only in a plurality of coexisting states. This is why the idea of a universal empire [*Weltreich*] is odious [*hassenswert*]; the ideal of a state of mankind [*Menschheitsstaat*] is no ideal at all."[12]

The plurality of states is not only the necessary consequence of the essence of the state, it is also an expression of human richness, evidence of a design of Providence. No one people realizes the whole content of culture, every people is in some way partial, limited. "The rays of the divine light appear limitlessly refracted among the different peoples; each manifests another image and another idea of the divinity."[13]

The nations which give an individualized expression to culture exchange their riches: the coexistence of the peoples of culture rests upon the Christian law "give and it shall be given unto you." Because they have recognized and apply this law, the peoples of modern times will not vanish like those of antiquity. Yet they will not thereby renounce their respective vocations and their sovereignty. "Sovereignty in the juridical sense, the complete independence of the state in relation to every other power [*Gewalt*] on earth is so much the essence of the state that one might say it constitutes the criterion of its nature. Where there exists a human collectivity which has won sovereignty, there is the state."[14]

"Sovereignty does not admit of division, neither more nor less. It is ridiculous to speak of a superior state [*Oberstaat*] or an inferior state [*Unterstaat*]. Gustavus Adolphus once said: 'I recognize no one above me, except God and the sword of the conqueror.' Once again, the future of humanity cannot be to unite under the authority of a single state, the ideal is to constitute a society of peoples [*Volkergesellschaft*] which, by means of treaties freely concluded, limit their sovereignty without relinquishing it."[15] But this society of peoples, as long as states survive and history continues, will have no higher tribunal than that of arms. Treaties limit the sovereignty of states, but the

[11] *Ibid.*, Vol. I, p. 24.
[12] *Ibid.*, Vol. I, p. 29.
[13] *Ibid.*, Vol. I, p. 29.
[14] *Ibid.*, Vol. I, p. 35.
[15] *Ibid.*, Vol. I, p. 37.

states themselves have imposed these limitations and they are not permanently committed. They have always maintained an implicit reservation: *rebus sic stantibus*. The moment war is declared, all treaties cease to exist among the belligerents. Now a state, as sovereign, has the incontestable right (*unzweifelhaft*) to declare war when it wishes (*wann er will*), and by the same token to tear up the treaties.

How could it be otherwise: to be sovereign is to determine the extent of one's power oneself, to choose between war or peace oneself. When a vital question is raised, no impartial arbiter exists. Such a situation is not even conceivable. "Were we to commit the folly of treating the question of Alsace as though it had not been settled (*offene Frage*), and to confide it to an arbiter, who seriously believes that the latter would be impartial? Hence it is a matter of honor for a state to settle such a question itself."[16]

If authentic sovereignty is defined by the effective right of a recourse to arms, only the powerful state is authentically sovereign, is authentically a state. "If the state is power, only the state which is truly powerful corresponds to its idea."[17] And Treitschke, in a style quite alien to our ways of thinking today, adds: "Hence there is something undeniably ludicrous in the small state. Weakness is not ludicrous in itself, only when it seeks to assume the style of power." In a Germany divided between the school that retained a nostalgia for small states and that which extolled the work of Bismarck, the historian sided with the latter, without hesitation or qualification: it is in the great power that the highest values are realized.

The justification of the great power, in the last analysis, is that it alone is able to retain first place in the ordeals of war. Now, only war keeps individuals from being entirely absorbed in their private economic pursuits, only war reminds men of their political vocation and re-establishes the primacy of the state over society, only war checks mounting materialism and inspires a new concern for noble values. "War is politics $\mu\alpha\tau$ $\dot{\epsilon}\xi o\chi\dot{\eta}\nu$. The truth that a people becomes a people only in a war will always be confirmed."[18] "The state is not only in itself a high moral good, it is also the condition of a stable existence of peoples. It is only within the state that man's moral [*sittlich*] evolution reaches its fulfillment."[19] Now, "without war, there would be no state."[20] All the states known to us are born of war. The protection of citizens by arms remains the state's first and most essential task. If perpetual peace is an ideal no more valid than universal empire, we must not deplore this, for wars have been, are, and will be fruitful. "The great advance of culture must be achieved against the resistance of barbarism and unreason [*Unvernunft*] and only by the sword. Among the peoples of culture [*Kulturvölker*], therefore, war remains the form of the test whereby the claims of the

---

[16] *Ibid.*, Vol. I, p. 38.
[17] *Ibid.*, Vol. I, p. 43.
[18] *Ibid.*, Vol. I, p. 60.
[19] *Ibid.*, Vol. I, p. 63.
[20] *Ibid.*, Vol. I, p. 72.

states are decided."[21] It was futile for Prussia to try to convince the small states that she should take command in Germany: the argument became convincing only on the battlefield, in Bohemia or on the Main.

Is judgment by arms the final judgment? Is the history of the world the tribunal of the world? Treitschke answers affirmatively, but not without reservations and nuances. "No people has been more deservedly destroyed than Poland."[22] Broadly, the state's evolution is the external and necessary form taken by the inner life of a people: hence, the peoples achieve the form of state commensurate with their own moral substance. But this historical justice is imperfect because those who execute its decrees are also guilty. And the law of numbers, and not moral force alone, decides the destiny of states.

Likewise, it is only in the course of time that the judgments pronounced by the god of war appear as the judgments of God. "A state like the Prussian state which, according to the character of its poeple, was inwardly more free and reasonable than the French state, could, under the influence of a temporary lethargy, come very close to annihilation."[23]

Having justified power politics, with its symbolic expression, war, as a necessary condition of the higher virtues and heroism, the German historian does not subscribe to a vulgar Machiavellianism. Honest and legal policies are also, ordinarily, the most effective and profitable. They inspire the confidence of other states. The lie is by no means the typical characteristic or the indispensable means of diplomacy. The requirement that politics submit to the universally valid moral law is also recognized in practice.[24] Hence there is no ordinary justification for evoking the contradiction between politics and morality as if it were inevitable.

Not that on occasion politics may not counter positive law: treaties cannot constitute an absolute imperative. But the essential idea, beyond the possible conflicts between the obligations of law and the necessities of action, is that the moral law (*sittliches Gesetz*) of Christian inspiration compels the states to fulfill their vocation, that is, to concern themselves with their power. "Let us remember that the essence of these great collective personalities is power and that, as a consequence, the moral duty of the state is to care [*sorgen*] for its power."[25]

"The individual can and must sacrifice himself for his country. But a state which sacrifices itself for a foreign people is not only not moral, but contradicts the ideal of self-affirmation [*Selbstbehauptung*], that which is what is highest in the state." Of all the sins of the state, the most unpardonable is

---

21 *Ibid.*, Vol. I, p. 73.
22 *Ibid.*, Vol. I, p. 22.
23 *Ibid.*, Vol. I, p. 73.
24 *Ibid.*, Vol. I, p. 97.
25 *Ibid.*, Vol. I, p. 100.

weakness, "a sin against the Holy Ghost of politics."[26] It is because lawyers would like conflicts between states to be decided by tribunals, because jurists place respect for treaties above the public good, that the theory of an antinomy between politics and morality has found credence. Let morality become more political and politics more moral, both recognizing that judgments on the conduct of states should refer to the nature and goals of these collective personalities.

Such a form of power politics cannot always use the means that the Christian catechism recommends or tolerates. Especially with regard to barbaric or inferior peoples, the means are occasionally forcibly cruel, just as cunning plays a legitimate role in diplomatic maneuvers. But a moderate and intelligent power politics does not plunge, in the manner of Napoleon, into ventures of unlimited conquest, ventures which, incompatible with the relation of forces, are both immoral and doomed to failure.

The conclusions of Treitschke's philosophy are not cynical, at least if we take them literally. In the last chapter of the work, the so-called naturalist doctrine of power is explicitly refuted: "The goal of the state is to maintain internal order: how could it do so if, in external relations, it refused to be bound by any legality?"[27] A state which, in principle, despises fidelity and faith (*Treue und Glauben*), would be permanently threatened by its enemies. The state is power, not for itself but in order to protect and promote the highest good. Law is not based on war alone. The state must have a touchy sense of honor. "If its flag has been offended, it should demand redress and, failing to get it, declare war."[28] "The respect to which it is entitled in the society of states should not be renounced at any price."[29]

In spite of this concern with honor and prestige (notions rather alien to the American philosophy), the German historian's last word resembles that of the American diplomat. "It is a question of understanding how the divine reason has been gradually revealed in this diversity of real life, not of controlling history. The greatness of the statesman is to know how to interpret the signs of the times and to be able to recognize, approximately, how the history of the world unfolds at a given moment in the process. Nothing is more suitable to the politician than modesty. Granted the multiplicity and the complexity of the relations with which he comes to grips, he must not permit himself to be led into dark and uncertain ways. He should seek only attainable ends and keep his objective clearly and steadfastly in view."

Modesty, limitation of objectives, balance of various possibilities before taking a decision—are not these counsels of prudence much like those we borrowed from George F. Kennan at the end of the preceding section? To understand one's times, to resolve conflicts as they present themselves, to take

[26] *Ibid.*, Vol. I, p. 27.
[27] *Ibid.*, Vol. II, p. 544.
[28] *Ibid.*, Vol. II, p. 551.
[29] *Ibid.*, Vol. II, p. 551.

into account the relation of forces, not to try to convert states and international politics, such is the task of the diplomat-gardener according to the former ambassador to Moscow. The German historian and the American diplomat, inspired by altogether different philosophies, arrive at certain similar precepts.

A *rapprochement* more significant than paradoxical, provided we do not forget that Treitschke claims his inspiration from idealism and that Kennan does not reject the epithet "realist" which commentators assign to him with various sentiments. Both counsel prudence, but the one starts from power politics exalted as conforming to the vocation of men and states, the other from power politics accepted with resignation to avoid greater evils.

3. From Machtpolitik to Power Politics

It would have been easy, choosing other texts, to lay more emphasis on Treitschke's nationalism or cynicism.

For example, the idea of various peoples all illuminated by a ray of the divine light might have laid the foundations of a philosophy of modesty or tolerance. But, in fact, the German historian draws a lesson of pride from it. "Every people has the right to believe that in itself certain forces of the divine reason find their highest expression. A people does not achieve self-awareness without overestimating itself." Treitschke adds that the Germans lack this massive pride. Elsewhere he evokes the case of conquerors who, in spite of their cultural superiority, are not numerous enough to convert the conquered peasantry. Such, for example, is the case of the Germans in Lithuania and Latvia. He does not hesitate to conclude: "No other solution remained than to keep the subjects in a state of the greatest possible *Unkultur* so that they would not become a threat to the less numerous masters."[30]

The German historian does not doubt that the European nations will always be the leading actors of history, those who have and will have the right to draw the sword in order to fulfill their vocation and create the superior values of culture. He does not conceive that a type of superior state could appear tomorrow, or that on other continents a culture could flourish equal to that of Europe. "Europe is always the heart of the world and, since we are now familiar with the entire planet, we can predict that it will be so in the future."[31]

Today it is no longer necessary to dispel the illusions of European and Germanic vanity. The quasi-cynicism to which power politics of idealist inspiration sometimes led seems almost naïve in the light of the experience of our century. What still interests us in Treitschke's thought is the joint justification and almost the exaltation of the sovereignty of the state, of the rivalry of powers, or war. In other chapters we will take up certain

[30] *Ibid.*, Vol. I, p. 127.
[31] *Ibid.*, Vol. II, p. 534.

problems raised by this defense and illustration of power politics: the indivisibility of sovereignty, the impossibility of a superior state (*Oberstaat*). It was important for us to look back at the German philosophy of the last century in order to understand at what point it differs from the American philosophy of today.

In crossing the Atlantic, in becoming *power politics*, Treitschke's *Machtpolitik* underwent a chiefly spiritual mutation. It became fact, not value. The American authors who are commonly regarded as belonging to the realist school declare that states, animated by a will to power, are in permanent rivalry, but that they are not self-congratulatory about the situation and do not regard it as a part of the divine plan. The refusal of states to submit to a common law or arbitration seems to them incontestable, intelligible, but not sublime, for they hold neither war nor the right to draw the sword as sublime. "The rational task of a people constituted in a state and aware of itself as such is to keep its rank in the society of peoples and thus to make its contribution to the great task of human culture."[32] Thus Treitschke, by the vocation of culture, justified the political duty of every people. I do not believe that the American realists, the theologian Reinhold Niebuhr any more than the diplomat George F. Kennan or the professor Hans Morgenthau, have ever established so close a link between the will to power and the work of culture. I would be tempted to summarize the opposition between the German doctrinaires of *Machtpolitik* and the American theoreticians of *power politics* by citing the celebrated formula invented by Max Weber to illustrate the contrast between the Puritans at the dawn of capitalism and the men of today: "The Puritan willed to be the vocational man that we have to be."[33] The German nationalists desired power politics for itself. The American realists believe they are obliged to acknowledge its existence and accept its laws.

It is a theologian, Reinhold Niebuhr, who is considered the ideologist of the so-called realist school. Now, his criticism of the liberal, optimistic, individualistic philosophy of foreign policy has as its origin and basis a certain conception of human nature. Man is corrupted by sin. He is selfish and violent. The collective beings that constitute states are worse than individual beings. The former occasionally practice the Christian virtues, the latter never. The immorality of states in conflict with one another is all the greater in that the citizens can have the legitimate feeling of acting morally when they dedicate and occasionally even sacrifice themselves to the state. But since the latter is fundamentally immoral,[34] self-seeking, violent, the citizens

[32] *Ibid.*, Vol. II, p. 32.
[33] H. H. Gerth and C. Wright Mills, tr. and ed., *From Max Weber*, New York, 1958, p. 50.
[34] These are the qualities he attributes to it: lust for power, pride, contempt toward the other, hypocrisy, moral autonomy.

remain prisoners of a sort of tribal egoism, even when they serve the collectivity. Taking as a term of reference and as a criterion of ethical values the conduct of Christ, Niebuhr insists on the radical antinomy between the Christian virtues and political action, in particular that of the diplomat. There is no state that has been created or which maintains itself without the use of force. It is the corruption of man by sin which is manifest in the violent course of history and which the philosophers of the contract, those who believe in a peace by law or those who condemn all recourse to force, persist in ignoring.

Of course, it would not be impossible to find, from the pens of the German doctrinaires, texts which relate war and sin, and from the pens of the American theoreticians texts which put a high value on the statesman's prudence. In fact, Treitschke wrote: "So long as the human race remains sinful and passionate as it is, war cannot disappear from the face of the earth."[35] For his part, Robert E. Osgood, in his book *Limited War*,[36] went so far as to declare immoral any war whose objects are or seek to be transcendent. "But military force is not only ineffective as an instrument for attaining transcendent moral ends: it is morally dangerous as well. It is dangerous because the use of force with a view to such grandiose ends tends to become an end in itself, no longer subject either to moral or practical restrictions, but merely to the intoxication with abstract ideals."[37] To use force to make the world safe for democracy or to substitute the rule of law for that of power politics by the punishment of the guilty and the organization of a League of Nations is to engage in an enterprise which runs the risk of being all the more violent in that it professes its ultimate objective to be the elimination of violence and in that reality will never yield to these sublime dreams. Whence, the author's conclusion: "In this sense, nations would do better to renounce the use of war as an instrument of all politics other than national."[38] Thus national selfishness, without thereby becoming sacred, appears to be the more moral attitude and not only the more prudent.

These texts—others could be added—do not affect, it seems to me, the opposition of intellectual climate, of metaphysics, even of theology between the nineteenth-century German doctrinaire and today's American theoretician. The banal formula (war will not disappear from the face of the earth so long as man is corrupted by sin) that Treitschke, who was a Christian, used in passing, explains neither the profound meaning of the doctrine nor the conclusions his audience was to draw from the master's lectures. Much more instructive, eloquent and persuasive are the long passages in which the educational value of war is proclaimed, the ideal of perpetual peace denounced. Tomorrow, when war will return, it is God who will have sent it

[35] *Op. cit.*, Vol. II, p. 554.
[36] Chicago, 1957.
[37] *Ibid.*, p. 17.
[38] *Ibid.*, p. 21.

to cure men of their blindness, of their surrender to pleasure, to instruct them in the superior virtues of devotion and sacrifice which they were about to forget. No American realist uses such language. At most they are seeking "the moral equivalent of war"[39] if they expect the victory of the pacifists.

As for the justification of national interest, it remains of contrary significance for each side. Reinhold Niebuhr, Hans Morgenthau, George F. Kennan, Robert E. Osgood do not exalt the "sacred selfishness" of states. They fear that this selfishness will become even worse, more brutal, less reasonable, if it hides behind words of a vague and grandiose kind. On the pretext of punishing the aggressor, the state carries war to extremes, to the destruction of the enemy state, all the more immoral as it believes itself moral, all the more egotistical as it supposes itself obedient to a transcendent principle. In other words, if the realists come to the conclusion of Robert E. Osgood— force should not be used *except* in the service of national politics—it is not because they intend to confer a sacred value on collective selfishness (as Treitschke was inclined to do), it is because the so-called idealism, in their eyes, either conceals a will to power that is even more dangerous because it is unconscious of itself, or else leads to disaster because it is incompatible with the essence of international politics. The teachings of a theologian like Niebuhr or of professors like Osgood or Morgenthau are inseparably *pragmatic* and *ethical*: statesmen *should* be concerned with the interest of the collectivity for which they are responsible, but they *should not* ignore the interest of the other collectivities. Now *realism*—the recognition of national selfishness—is more conducive to an awareness, on everyone's part, of the interests and ideas of the others than idealism or the cult of abstract principles. Yet Niebuhr, and even Morgenthau, adds that realism should not be cynical and that "the remedy for a pretentious idealism which claims to know more about the future and about humanity than is given to mortals to know is not egotism. It is a concern, at one and the same time, with oneself and with the other, a concern in which the self maintains a proper respect for the opinions of humanity, derived from a modest awareness of the limits of its own knowledge and its own power."[40] And again, nations are egotistical, but "the sense of justice should keep prudence from becoming too prudent, in other words, too opportunistic in its manner of defining interest."[41]

The formula "the ego, individual or collective" suggests a second mutation in *Machtpolitik*, that is, the neglect or, at least, the lack of emphasis upon the *primacy of foreign policy*. The state, Treitschke tells us, is the scale (of justice) and the sword (of war). But it is above all the sword, since it can only impose justice once the state is assured, by the sword, that

---

[39] The title, it will be recalled, of a book by William James.
[40] I have borrowed this text from a collection of excerpts entitled *Reinhold Niebuhr on Politics*, edited by Harry Davis and Robert C. Good, New York, 1960, p. 332.
[41] *Ibid.*, p. 334.

it can enforce obedience. The American realists, arguing against a false idealism but imbued with the individualistic and moralistic philosophy of their country, take as their point of departure either the nature of man (self-seeking, violent) or the nature of politics, which inevitably implies power, means or end of the rivalry between the individual or collective egos.

The word *power*, in English, has a very broad (or very vague) meaning, since, depending on cases, it translates the three French words *pouvoir*, *puissance*, *force*. Power is first of all, in the broadest sense, the capacity to act, to produce, to destroy, to influence; then it is the capacity to command legally (to come to power, exercise power); it is also the capacity of a person (individual or collective) to impose his will, his example, his ideas, upon others; finally it is the sum of material, moral, military, psychological means (or one or the other of these means) possessed by the three capacities we have just enumerated.

It is not unjustifiable to regard the concept of *power* as the fundamental, original concept of all political order, that is, of the organized coexistence among individuals. It is true in fact that within states as on the international scene, autonomous wills confront one another, each seeking its own objectives. These wills, which are not spontaneously reconciled, seek to check each other. Bismarck wanted to achieve a unified Germany under Prussia's leadership despite the opposition of Napoleon III, as John F. Kennedy wanted to become President of the United States despite the opposition of Richard Nixon. But this comparison, as I see it, conceals the essential point, namely that the members of a collectivity obey laws and submit their conflicts to rules, while states, which limit their freedom of action by the obligations to which they subscribe, have hitherto always reserved the right to resort to armed force and to define for themselves what they mean by "honor," "vital interests" and "legitimate defense." On this point the American realist school seems to me backward compared with traditional European thought. Obsessed with a concern to refute the philosophy of the contract, the version of liberalism according to which respect for law and morality is enough to impose obedience on *homo politicus*, the realists set one anthropology against another and power against law (or morality). They define politics as power and not international politics as the absence of an umpire or of police. It is another Christian, British this time, who returns to the tradition when he writes: "In international relations, it is the situation of Hobbesian fear which, so far as I can see, has hitherto defeated all the endeavour of the human intellect."[42] Neither Reinhold Niebuhr nor Hans Morgenthau is unaware— we scarcely need add?—that conflicts among citizens within a collectivity take their course according to rules (the highest of which is called a constitution in modern societies) or are settled by tribunals. The opposition between "the monopoly of legitimate violence" and "plurality of military sovereignties"

[42] Herbert Butterfield, *Christianity and History*, London, 1949, p. 90.

is evidently not unknown to them. The insistence with which Hans Morgenthau reminds us that survival constitutes and must constitute the primary objective of states, amounts to an implicit admission of the Hobbesian situation among states, hence the essential difference between international and national politics. Nonetheless, the fact remains that this avowal is implicit rather than explicit.

It is not impossible, it seems to me, to understand this irresolution of analysis if not of thought. The American realists, we have said, are located on the margin of the idealist situation and come later in time. They think *against*, they criticize the picture the idealists present of the world or the precepts they formulate. They are led, without being fully aware of it, to follow the example of those whom they oppose. Now, the idealists accept the whole or almost the whole postulate that there is not and should not be an essential difference between international and national politics. States are at the service of individuals and not vice versa. They must obey the law as citizens have learned to do. Once international law has been established, all legal recourse to force will be police action, as it is within states today.

Further, on the level of sociology or history, one would search in vain to find a clear limit between the use of armed force by states in order to establish authority and the use of this same force against external enemies. The establishment and distintegration of empires or even nations assumes that an enemy, external at the beginning of hostilities, becomes a compatriot at their end, or conversely that compatriots fight each other because some want to secede and organize an independent unit in their turn. This *de facto* continuity does not in essence contradict the distinction, but in order to demonstrate this distinction, it would have been necessary to use methods alien to the American school: either the analysis of the intrinsic meaning of a human activity, or else a reflection upon history itself. The vision of humanity, progressing from tribes to a universal empire by way of national states, is distorted by an unjustifiable extrapolation. The widening of the zones of sovereignty is only a change in scale, within a history whose nature remains the same; the unification of humanity into a single state would signify a conversion *of* history and not *within* history.

As long as the realist school limits itself to criticizing moral or juridical illusions, these conceptual ambiguities have no serious drawbacks. But when the realist attempts to be a theoretician, when he claims to offer not an approximate image but a finished portrait, a rational blueprint of international politics, he will need strictly defined notions.

Hans Morgenthau's two fundamental concepts are those of *power* and *national interest*. But is power regarded here as the necessary means to any undertaking whatever? Or the objective to which individual or collective egos cling? Or again, is it the primary objective of states, since they can count only on themselves in order to survive? It would be easy to cite texts in favor of each of these interpretations.

The oscillation between these three interpretations is striking in the first pages of *Politics among Nations.*[43] Here Morgenthau writes that "international politics, like all politics, is a struggle for power. Whatever the ultimate aims of international politics, power is always the immediate aim." The notion of the immediate aim is ambiguous: if power is not the ultimate aim, the immediate aim can be considered only as a means. Elsewhere Morgenthau writes: "The aspiration for power being the distinguishing element of international politics, as of all politics, international politics is of necessity power politics."[44] But if it should be true that the aspiration for power plays the same role in international politics as in all politics, the specific nature of power politics among nations would disappear. The moment the essence of international politics is identical "with the essence of politics, with *its domestic counterpart*," why could war not be eliminated from one as from the other?

Finally, if one compares the Crusaders who wanted to liberate the Holy Land, Woodrow Wilson who wanted to make the world safe for democracy, the National Socialists who wanted to open Eastern Europe to German colonization, dominate Europe and conquer the world, if one asserts that all are actors on the stage of international politics because they have chosen power to gain their ends, then power is only a means and defines neither the nature of international politics nor that of the goals the actors strove to attain. This last interpretation would be confirmed by a text borrowed from another work. "The interests to which power attaches itself and which it serves are as varied and manifold as are the possible social objectives of the members of a given society."[45]

But if power is only a means, the propositions which serve as a basis for Hans Morgenthau's theory are open to doubt. According to Morgenthau, every regime tends to have the same kind of foreign policy. The content of national interest is constant over long periods of history. Why this constancy? Because all the elements, ideals and materials which form the content of national interest are subordinated at the very least to requirements which are not susceptible of rapid change, "on which depend the survival of the nation and the preservation of its identity."

Is it true that states, whatever their regime, pursue "the same kind of foreign policy"?[46] This statement is admirably ambiguous. Are the foreign policies of Napoleon, Hitler and Stalin of the same kind as those of Louis

[43] New York, 1949, p. 13.
[44] *Ibid.*, p. 15.
[45] In *The Theoretical Aspects of International Relations,* edited by W. R. T. Fox, University of Notre Dame, 1959, p. 26.
[46] "They assume that the kind of foreign policy which a nation pursues is determined by the kind of domestic institutions it possesses and the kind of political philosophy to which it adheres. All of recorded history militates against the assumption." In *Diplomacy in a Changing World,* edited by Stephen D. Kertesz and M. A. Fitzsimons, University of Notre Dame, 1959, p. 12.

XVI, Adenauer or Nicholas II? If one answers *yes,* then the proposition is incontestable, but not very instructive. The features which all diplomatic-strategic behavior have in common are formal, they come down to selfishness, to the calculation of forces, to a variable mixture of hypocrisy and cynicism. But the differences in degree are such that a Napoleon or a Hitler suffices with the help of revolutionary circumstances to change the course of history.

By the same token the falsity of the second proposition is evident: national interest would not change rapidly because the state's requirements for survival are relatively constant. Even if one assigns a narrow and as it were a material sense to survival—non-massacre of the population and independence of the state—national interest can, as everyone knows, require a complete reversal of alliances in several years, friends becoming enemies (the Soviet Union, best of allies in 1942, embodies a mortal threat in 1946) and enemies becoming friends (friendship with Adenauer's Germany replaces hostility toward the Third Reich). Further, in a heterogeneous system, the opposition party favoring the ideology of the enemy camp obviously does not have the same conception of national interest as the party in power, and would pursue a different diplomacy if they came to power.

Could one say, at least, that the elements involved in the definition of national interest are subordinate to the needs of survival? If this is to be a *de facto* proposition, it is obviously false. Let us grant all states, large and small, the will to survive as they are, even if this will is peculiarly uneven according to place and time (the German principalities, in the middle of the last century, had only a feeble will to survive such as they were: neither the rulers nor the people considered the loss of independence as a catastrophe). But let us assume this will: it is not defined by a final objective or a chosen criterion. All great states have jeopardized their survival to gain ulterior objectives. Hitler preferred, for himself and for Germany, the possibility of empire to the security of survival. Nor did he want empire—or an accumulation of power—as a means to security. It would be useless to define the objectives of states by exclusive reference to power, to security, or to both. What life does not serve a higher goal? What good is security accompanied by mediocrity?

Moreover, the very idea of survival lends itself to many interpretations. In 1960 the France seeking to survive is Western, with institutions of the constitutional-pluralistic type. Absorbed in the Soviet world, she would lose her Western "identity" but probably conserve a substantial part of her historical culture. Neither in one camp nor the other can she regain a total "independence," in the sense of the ability to make major decisions on her own, but she would be less autonomous within the East than she is with the West. Finally, with one side as with the other, if she participates in the great game of strategy in the thermonuclear age, she exposes her population to the risk of cruel and perhaps fatal losses. Granting that survival is defined by independence, the identity of the political regime, of the historical culture, or finally, the preservation of the life of individuals, diplomats will make different decisions. Even if they all pursued "the same kind of foreign policy," even if they all had as their final goal, or accepted as the first requirement, the security of the state in their charge, they still, in many circumstances, would have to choose between the safety of the regime and the defense of independence.

Hans Morgenthau has not devoted more time and effort to the analysis of these basic concepts because he, too, is more concerned with praxeology than with theory. He, too, is a crusader, but a crusader of realism. To invoke national interest is a way of defining not a policy but an attitude, of polemicizing against ideologies of perpetual peace, international law, Christian or Kantian morality, against the representatives of special groups who confuse their own interests with those of the collectivity as a whole and in time. If statesmen did not listen to Utopians, if they strove to forestall wars or limit hostilities, if they preferred a compromise to a quarrel, if they negotiated with all states and took less interest in the regimes of their allies or enemies, how much less would humanity suffer from the inevitable rivalry for power among collective wills!

Perhaps, in fact, it is good to tell the Wilsons and the Roosevelts that they are mistaken about themselves and the world, that they, too, are motivated by an obscure and hardly conscious sense of the national interest of the United States, that their actions would be more effective if their thoughts emerged from the idealistic fog and submitted to the harsh law of equilibrium. Perhaps a lesson of a certain realism is not entirely useless when it is addressed to men of good will who run the risk of sinning by overzealousness and not out of a lack of illusions. Perhaps the realist school has marked a necessary reaction against the naïve conception of an international order which would stand of its own accord, without any other basis than respect for the law, against the false idea that it suffices to apply principles (the right of peoples to self-determination) in order to settle conflicts peacefully. Unfortunately, by mixing theory and praxeology, and by lacking a rigorous distinction between the permanent characteristics and the historical particulars of international politics, the realist school has arrived at an ideology comparable to that which it took for the target of its criticisms.

What is true in all epochs is that the necessary reference to the calculation of forces and the endless diversity of circumstances requires statesmen to be *prudent*. But prudence does not always require either moderation or peace by compromise, or negotiations, or indifference to the internal regimes of enemy states or allies. Roman diplomacy was not moderate, the peace imposed by the Union on the Confederacy rejected all compromise. Negotiations with Hitler were most often fruitless or harmful. In a heterogeneous system, it is hardly possible for a statesman to model himself upon François I making an alliance with the Grand Turk, or upon Richelieu supporting the Protestant princes. True realism today consists in recognizing the action of ideologies upon diplomatic-strategic conduct. In our epoch, instead of repeating that all states, no matter what their institutions, have "the same kind of foreign policy," we should insist upon the truth that is more complementary than contradictory: no one understands the diplomatic strategy of a state if he does not understand its regime, if he has not studied the philosophy of those who govern it. To lay down as a rule that the heads of the Bolshevik party conceive the national interests of their state as did all other rulers of Russia is to doom oneself to misunderstanding the practices and ambitions of the Soviet Union.

The invitation made to the West today not to mix ideology and diplomacy assumes a paradoxical character in our epoch. The Soviet Union promises perpetual peace at the end of the world crisis, when socialism will have prevailed over capitalism permanently and universally. Can the West promise nothing? Can it not champion a type of institution within states, a type of relation among states? Must it resign itself to an inevitable war while the Communist world proclaims glorious tomorrows?

A true realism takes into account the whole of reality, dictates diplomatic-strategic conduct adapted not to the finished portrait of what international politics would be if statesmen were wise in their selfishness, but to the nature of the passions, the follies, the ideas and the violences of the century.

4. Proudhon and the Right of Force

The victorious pride of the Second Reich, at the end of the last century, explains the exaltation of power politics by the German historian. "Only courageous peoples have an assured existence, a future, an evolution; weak or cowardly peoples are destroyed, and deservedly. It is in the endless rivalry of the different States that the beauty of history resides."[47] The tragic experience of the two great wars, and the national philosophy of the contract prompt the American authors to resign themselves to power politics, but to emphasize its horror rather than its beauty. Historical circumstances account for the reversal of terms; the German historian invoked idealism, the American theologian or sociologist speaks of realism. This reversal has still another and more profound significance: is power politics, as such, contrary to morality? The dialogue of German idealism and American realism is an expression of an *intrinsic antinomy of diplomatic-strategic action*.

To condemn power politics is to condemn the whole course of political history. And how justify it without recognizing a certain right—anterior to the right based on consent—of force?

The philosophy of the German historian shocks more than it convinces us because it is based upon the inequality of individuals and peoples. Now, after the excesses of Hitlerian racism, we are tempted to subscribe without hesita-

[47] Treitschke, *op. cit.*, Vol. I, p. 30.

tion to the opposite dogma, the equality of individuals, peoples and races. Let us beware, though, not to offer our own hostages to fashion.

Individuals are born unequally gifted, peoples are different. The inequality of personal gifts is known to every educator, and biology confirms the fact and explains it. Moreover, this natural inequality does not contradict either the equality of rights and obligations or the equality of opportunity. Treitschke's mistake lies not in having pointed out this natural inequality, but in having underestimated the contributions of technological progress and in supposing that the majority of men would never receive more than the necessary minimum for the satisfaction of elementary needs: "The masses will always be the masses; no culture without servants [*Diensboten*]."[48] It is to material labor, he assumes, that almost all men will always dedicate most of their time. Led by a traditional conception of society to exaggerate the irreducible share of economic and social inequality in whatever regime, he is also inclined, by nationalism, to celebrate German greatness and to deprecate other peoples of culture. He also shifts from the historical diversity of nations (which is incontestable) to the natural inequality of peoples, without our knowing whether, in his eyes, this inequality is established by heredity or is only the result of circumstances.

I am not certain whether science today is in a position to give an unequivocal answer to the problem. The diversity of cultures, in the sense anthropologists give to this expression, is at one and the same time the least disputable and most mysterious fact. Closed, so-called archaic and illiterate societies, those anterior to six thousand years of historical societies (or civilizations) and those still extant, present hundreds of varieties. Ethnologists have distinguished more than six hundred, each characterized by original features that constitute its way of life and thought. The behavior of individuals, in each society, is influenced by a system of values and education so that the human psychic structure seems to vary from society to society, which does not rule out the possibility that the basic impulses are the same.

Have predispositions, fixed in the genes of individuals, originated the specificities of culture, or, on the contrary, have the specificities of culture, the result of a combination of circumstances, given individuals a kind of second nature, not transmitted by heredity but reproduced in every generation by education? The fact that even primary education contributes to the formation of the personality of members of each group is not open to doubt; that this personality, down through the ages and even today reflects genetic predispositions of the majority of the members of a group, cannot, it seems to me, be either affirmed or denied with incontestable proof.

If we turn from archaic societies to the European nations (French, German, Italian), then to the races defined by the anthropologists, then to the still larger human aggregates characterized by skin color, the diversity is evident,

[48] *Ibid.*, Vol. I, p. 50.

the influence of historical circumstances incontestable, the role of genetic predisposition more mysterious still. In a population numbering millions of individuals, the diverse kinds of gifts, temperaments, characters (whatever the exact definition of these terms) are certainly present, but not necessarily with the same frequency. That such a population—of a nation or race—has a higher or lower percentage of certain gifts, genetically transmitted, is not inconceivable but neither is it demonstrable. In any case, the manifestation of these genetic predispositions will be colored, if not determined, by the social milieu, itself subject to historical change.

It is rare that such possibilities are considered with regard to the largest aggregates, those characterized by skin color. Granted that belief in the equality of human races also transcends scientifically established truths, at least it has consequences preferable to the excesses of the contrary belief. It is also based on recognized facts: the accomplishments, in the course of history, of all races, the dependence of existence, individual and collective, on an understanding of external conditions, the extreme, apparently natural inequality that created domination and enslavement. The young Germans who triumphantly swept down the roads of France in June 1940 did in actual fact seem to be a race of supermen; the same Germans, prisoners, herded together on the Russian steppes, seemed, just as effectively, a race of slaves. It is victory which creates the masters, not mastery which leads to victory. Before postulating the hereditary inequality of human groups, let us grant them all approximately similar opportunities.

But let us also beware of confusing two philosophically distinct theses: one according to which the diversities of culture cannot be ascribed to dispositions transmitted by biological heredity, the other according to which this diversity resists any hierarchy, an archaic society being as perfect as the so-called civilized societies, a *de jure* state being worth neither more nor less than a despotic one, Christians deserving no privilege in relation to cannibals. The appraisal superior and inferior, with regard to human accomplishments, never attains the certitude of scientific propositions. But if humanity has gained nothing by emerging from the structure of closed societies, if the manipulation of natural forces and the accumulation of knowledge signify nothing, then power politics would have no meaning, and all of history would share the same fate. Retrospectively, we declare absurd the course of the human adventure and prospectively run the risk of inflicting the same disgrace on the centuries to come.

If we leave aside this kind of historical nihilism, if we accord a meaning to the procession of states and empires, we are not thereby obliged to applaud all the judgments of the tribunal of history and proclaim that the best ones always prevail, as though there were no other virtues but martial ones, as though the struggle of states was the instrument of a pitiless but necessary selection.

Quite simply, it is a fact that for thousands of years states and empires have been made and unmade in and by war. It is as impossible to reconstruct a history in which men did not kill one another as to imagine literature if men and women were coupled at the whim of their desires and were ignorant of love. The struggle of peoples and states has been an integral part of the movement of ideas and civilization. It has been destructive as much as it has been creative. States belonging to the same zone of civilization fought each other in vain to the point of mutual exhaustion. The victors sacked cities, and reduced to slavery thousands of men who represented a unique culture. No one is in a position to draw up a total and honest balance-sheet. Yet the fact remains that war has not always been meaningless or criminal; it has had meaning and function.

In the United Nations the spokesmen of states profess to reject the use of force. Yet the states that are the successors to colonial administrations often discover that it is impossible to unite the tribes of a nation without using coercion. All these states aspire to the modernity the conquerors brought them in the last century. The elite whom we call Westernized are witnesses of the violence done to the traditional culture, and they will do violence to their compatriots who are still attached to tribal customs. Colonialism always involves a burden of danger and cruelty. History being what it is, should we deplore the fact that the Europeans have imposed their civilization and destroyed the archaic cultures for which the ethnologists nurse a certain nostalgia?

Among peoples of like civilization, the purpose of war can only be political in order to determine frontiers, establish states, distribute power and prestige among the political units, celebrate and impose the triumph of an idea. In the last century, how could the Germans and Italians have achieved their unity if not through war? In this century, how many peoples owe their national liberty only to their resolve to resort to arms! When it is a question of the very existence of states, I fear that Proudhon is right: "What is the evidence of citizens dropping their votes in a ballot-box against that of soldiers spilling their blood?"[49]

If we quote Proudhon, it is because the French socialist and moralist, starting from a philosophy altogether different from that of the German historian, also recognized, within certain limits, the right[50] of force. The worker has the right to the product of his labor, the brain has the right to "reject what seems to it to be false, to debate probable opinions, to publish its findings," "love, by its very nature, involves certain reciprocal obligations between the lovers." Similarly, there is "a right of force by virtue of which the stronger, in certain circumstances, has been preferred to the weaker, rewarded at the higher price."[51] All these rights are the manifestation "of the most constant and

[49] P. J. Proudhon, *La Guerre et la paix. Recherches sur le principe et la constitution du droit des gens,* Paris, 1861, Vol. II, p. 398.
[50] This right is what is called a "subjective right": "force has the right to . . . ," etc.
[51] *Op. cit.,* Vol. I, pp. 189–200.

fundamental of our affections, the respect for humanity in our person and in that of our fellow men."[52]

And, as though to exasperate his reader, Proudhon adopts in support of his thesis the argument usually used against it: "Wolves, lions do not war among themselves any more than sheep and beavers: for ages, this observation has been employed in satirizing our species. How, on the contrary, can we fail to see this phenomenon as the very sign of our greatness; if by some impossibility, nature had created man an animal exclusively industrious and sociable, and not at all warlike, he would have fallen, from the very first day, to the level of the beasts whose herd is their entire destiny; he would have lost, along with the pride of his heroism, his revolutionary faculty, the most marvelous and fruitful of all!"[53]

If we leave aside these eloquent tirades, at the core of Proudhon's demonstration is a simple argument. All international jurists set law in opposition to force. Might, they say, cannot make right. But the law resulting from agreements between states is based upon force, since without it the states would not exist. To declare that force is intrinsically unjust is to decree the original injustice of all juridical norms, inconceivable without the existence of states. Hence the ultimate alternative: either there is a right of force, or the whole of history is a web of injustice.

To the objection that the phase of the formation of states, during which the right of force inevitably prevailed, is henceforth over, Proudhon answers that the war that is just on both sides, political war in the pure state, remains the only way of solving four kinds of problems[54]: "1) the incorporation of one nation into another, of one state into another; the absorption or fusion of two political societies . . . ; 2) the reconstitution of nationalities . . . ; 3) religious incompatibility . . . ; 4) international equilibrium, the delimitation of states. . . ." Since religion is no longer, in our period, the principle of states, the third case—"war between two segments of the same people divided in its religion and in which tolerance is impracticable"—no longer arises, at least in this form (though an ideological sect may forcefully impose its belief upon the rest of the people). On the other hand, formation of nations or of empires, and organization of systems with a view to maintaining equilibrium, remain stakes of conflicts that do not all allow for a peaceful solution.

Yet let it not be supposed that Proudhon, or the right of force as he conceives it, justifies any kind of conquest whatever. Quite the contrary, Napoleon was beaten, and deservedly so, because his enterprise of conquest was unjust, contrary to the right of force. "The wars of pure ambition undertaken by Louis XIV were fruitless, the war against his normally constituted monarchy

[52] *Ibid.*, Vol. I, p. 197.
[53] *Ibid.*, Vol. I, p. 39.
[54] *Ibid.*, Vol. I, p. 225.

also had to remain sterile."[55] And not without lucidity Proudhon sets against the *rectification of frontiers* (Nice and Savoy), accepted by Europe, the Algerian War: "Algeria alone has become our conquest; but this conquest, after thirty years as after the first day, is no more than a military occupation. Nothing is so difficult for civilized men to assimilate as barbarism and the desert. France, in an average year, has expended fifty million francs and twenty-five thousand men."[56]

We are not concerned to maintain or to jettison Proudhon's vocabulary. The reference to the philosopher of justice was to help us recall certain propositions, basically incontestable but easily forgotten. No great state has been established without recourse to coercion, without absorbing smaller collectivities. If the use of force is absolutely culpable, all states are branded by a brand of original sin. Hence, without being unaware of the horrors of war— and Proudhon has not failed to denounce them—anyone seeking to understand history must not stop at the antinomy of force and juridical norms. He must distinguish between the various modes according to which force has been employed, must acknowledge the historical, if not the juridical, legitimacy of the use of force in certain circumstances, even of certain violations of existing law (international law is conservative in essence; it obliges states to yield to each other and, occasionally, it is the very existence of a state which is in question). Bismarck did not achieve German unity without coercing the German principalities: he does not, however, merit the same moral judgment as a Hitler attempting to subjugate all Europe. In short, the *ethical* judgment of diplomatic-strategic conduct is not separable from the *historical* judgment of the goals of the actors and the consequences of their success or failure. To stop at the alternative of law and force is to lump together and condemn all revolutionary attempts *en bloc*. That this historical judgment is uncertain (no one knows the future), often partisan, there is no doubt. This is not a valid reason for abandoning all discrimination.

We do not mean to suggest that the process of formation and dissolution of states by war must last as long as the human race: we reserve the problem of the future for a later investigation. Nor do we assert that it is good in itself and for peoples that the states have a jealous awareness of their sovereignty. We confine ourselves to declaring that force has, to a large degree, determined the birth and the death of states. Therefore, unless we hold all historical creations equally guilty (or innocent), we must, in order to make an assessment, even a moral one, take into account both interests and ideas, principles and security. As long as the survival of nations is not guaranteed by the omnipotence of a tribunal or of an impartial arbiter, the consideration of the relation of forces must enter into the ethical-historical judgment of the causes of the sides in conflict.

[55] *Ibid.*, Vol. I, p. 328.
[56] *Ibid.*, Vol. II, pp. 329–30.

The counterproof of this demonstration is afforded by an author of the so-called idealist school, F. S. C. Northrop. He would revive the Locke-Jefferson-Lincoln tradition against the Machiavelli-Hobbes-Austin tradition, but he acknowledged that humanity is divided with regard to the conception of law and morality. How impose an international law upon a divided humanity? A text from one of Northrop's books summarizes the principles of the compromise between metaphysical pluralism and the unity of international law:

"1) All men, and not only Americans or those physically strongest, have received from God the natural right to be free; 2) the United States will be negatively neutral in wars between nations guided by a foreign policy of power, but positively so—even in affording physical aid, as it did in Cuba's war against Spain—on the side of peoples struggling for their independence against nations guided by power politics; 3) a legal system or a nation obtains lasting influence and effectiveness not by the policeman's stick which it must on occasion use as well, but by the freely accepted moral principles, which fill the heart and mind of its people, and of the peoples of the entire world. Hence, 4) it is not, as Machiavelli, Hobbes, Austin and their contemporaries suppose, physical power which renders morality and law effective, but law freely accepted which renders the use of force by a legal system or a nation just and effective. Consequently, 5) no use of force outside its borders by any nation is justified or can avoid, in the long run, opposing its own goal, if it is not subordinate to principles and to democratically established moral and juridical methods dedicated to the following mission: to guarantee to another people, here again only with its free consent, its natural and contractually legal and political right to conduct its own affairs."[57]

Ideology or long-range vision of what the world of relations among states should be, perhaps such a philosophy is inseparable from the United States, necessary to its action on the world stage. Does it solve the problems of decision? Can it be applied?

The first proposition—all men have the right to be free—can be admitted by all those who subscribe to a conception, however vague, of natural law. But it does not permit us to define the content of that freedom or the relation between the freedom of the individual within the community and the independence of the community itself. What populations have the right to constitute themselves into sovereign nations? Must the rights of man be sacrifices to national independence, or conversely? Such a choice can become inevitable: it has happened so many times in our epoch.

The second proposition—neutrality in the case of a conflict provoked by the collision of wills-to-power, support of peoples fighting for their independence—condemns the United States to a fatal oscillation between the spirit of isolation and the spirit of crusade. The politics of states is rarely either one or

[57] *Philosophical Anthropology and Practical Politics*, New York, 1961, p. 182.

the other, either power politics or the struggle of a people for freedom. International politics is a mixture that can be understood only in its ambiguous complexity. Every international crisis has a "power politics" dimension. The Hungarian rebellion of 1956—a rebellion of a people against foreign oppression—cannot be understood by a statesman without consideration of the repercussions which the dissidence of Hungary, leaving the Warsaw Pact, would have had on the equilibrium between the blocs. If the American leaders had blindly obeyed the principle of supporting the peoples struggling for their freedom, they ran the risk of provoking a war.

F. S. C. Northrop proudly evokes President Eisenhower's decision, at the hour of the Franco-British Suez expedition. "Forced to choose between siding with his best friends or putting his nation unequivocally against the unilateral use of force and on the side of the world community's international law, he chose the latter course, as did the majority of nations in the United Nations."[58] With the naïveté of a clear conscience, Northrop does not even mention that at that same moment the United States was abandoning the Hungarians to their fate "fighting for their independence against nations guided by power politics." The Europeans, at the time, preferred to quote La Fontaine: "*Selon que vous serez puissant ou misérable . . .*" (depending on whether you are powerful or poor).

Propositions three and four—it is not force which makes a legal or moral system effective, but rather the convictions of men—involve a degree of truth. The norms cannot survive without popular adherence; they must be rooted in the minds and hearts of men. Neither the policeman's stick nor bayonets establish a solid and respected order. But it is also true that laws can be imposed by force and that peoples ultimately adopt the ideas of the conqueror or of the party which has seized power. The Russian people, in 1917, did not adhere to the legal or moral system of the Bolsheviks. Within states, many norms are obeyed without being sustained by force. The state (or the government) which obeys the verdict of a tribunal that has condemned it, thereby demonstrates that law is sometimes imposed without being based on force. But such phenomena occur within communities. The President of the United States respects the decision of the Supreme Court, the French Prime Minister the decree of the Conseil d'Etat (sometimes). It would be imprudent to conclude from this that states will submit to the decisions of an international court without being obliged to do so.

Hence the last proposition, which condemns the use of force outside the nation's boundaries and decrees its sterility unless it is in the service of the freedom of peoples, seems to us both equivocal and optimistic. The Communists, within their legal and moral system, consider the use of force to promote regimes based on their own to be fully justified. It has not been proved that such a use of force is condemned to failure. Unless we consider—

<hr/>

[58] *Ibid.*, p. 205.

as Northrop certainly does not—that the constitution of the peoples' democracies is a form of liberation, it is hard to see how it could be maintained
that "the submission to democratically established moral and juridical methods" is indispensable to the effectiveness of force, at least in the long run.

In order to reconcile moral pluralism with the juridical unity of the international community, the American philosopher finally recommends the peaceful coexistence of the various worlds, each with its own moral or legal system.
International law would guarantee respect for the various living laws: "It
would guarantee to each ideology and nation of the world protection of its
particular norms in its own living law geographical area."[59] What Northrop forgets is that the non-use of force belongs to one moral-legal system,
that of the United States, and to one philosophy, that of the contract and of
consent, not to the Soviet system or to Marxist philosophy. Hence it is not
respect for an international law whose authority they do not acknowledge
which will incite the Kremlin leaders not to use force outside their borders,
but prudence. And prudence will not forbid them all uses of force, but only
open war, the crossing of frontiers by regular armies. By the same token we
leave the universe where peace by law prevails, and re-enter the real world
where the absence of war is due to fear rather than to a common will, and in
which the secret games of subversion are played.

States constitute a society of a unique type which imposes norms on its
members and yet tolerates recourse to armed force. As long as international
society preserves this mixed and, in a sense, contradictory character, the
morality of international action will also be equivocal.

Relations between states are a test of wills, peaceful or bloody depending
on the occasion. Peoples therefore cannot ignore the morality of struggle
which enjoins individuals in collectivities to be courageous, disciplined and
devoted, and urges them to respect promises and have a concern for honor.
Why have the French passionately debated—and why do they continue to
debate—the armistice of June 1940, both in and beyond its political and
military consequences? Because the armistice raised a question: Did France,
by leaving the war, break her word on honor? Was she violating the supreme
rule that binds allied combatants? When the United States sided, in the
United Nations, against the Franco-British Suez expedition, many Frenchmen and Englishmen felt that they had been "betrayed" by their ally. The
United States, on the other hand, considered itself doubly innocent: it had
not been forewarned; even if it had been, it would have subordinated the
morality of struggle to the morality of law.

The morality of struggle is easily corrupted to a gang morality. Those who
scorn the laws of society are not thereby "faithless and lawless." Obedience

[59] *The Taming of Nations. A Study of the Cultural Bases of International Policy.*
New York, 1952, p. 272.

to the leader, gang solidarity, testify to a crude sense of discipline and honor which do not forbid the use of any means against other gangs and the orientation of collective behavior toward inadmissible goals. States are not always delicate in their choice of means; nor always faithful to the promises they make. The morality of struggle will have some meaning as long as war remains the final sanction of international relations, but it will never afford a prospect of lasting peace or universality.

The morality of law is the antithesis of the morality of struggle, because the law is valid for all, without consideration of persons, whereas the promises made by states or by gangsters are essentially linked to persons. But since international law is conservative, since states have never fully accepted its obligations, since, further, no tribunal, judging in equity, recommends the necessary changes, the states that invoke the morality of law often pass for hypocrites rather than heroes. A rare event in itself, respect for the law is too readily explained by national interest. If acted upon more frequently, this same respect would multiply wars and make them inexpiable.

The ambiguity of international society makes it impossible for a partial logic to be followed to its end, be it one of law or one of force. The only morality which transcends the morality of struggle and the morality of law is what I would call the morality of prudence, which attempts not only to consider each case in its concrete particularities, but also not to ignore any of the arguments of principle and opportunity, to forget neither the relation of forces nor the wills of peoples. Because it is complex, the judgment of prudence is never incontestable, and it satisfies completely neither the moralists nor the vulgar disciples of Machiavelli.

He who attempts to play the angel plays the beast. The statesman *ought* not forget that an international order is maintained only on condition that it is supported by forces capable of balancing those of dissatisfied or revolutionary states. If he neglects to calculate forces, he fails the obligations of his responsibility, hence the morality of his job and his vocation. He makes an error, since he compromises the security of the persons and values whose fate has been entrusted to him. Selfishness is no virtue, but it nonetheless prevails among states, whose survival is guaranteed by no one. But anyone who would play the beast does not play the angel. The Spenglerian realist, who asserts that man is a beast of prey and urges him to behave as such, ignores a whole side of human nature. Even in the relations between states, respect for ideas, aspiration to higher values and concern for obligations have been manifested. Rarely have collectivities acted as if they would stop at nothing with regard to one another.

The morality of prudence, the best on both the level of facts and that of values, does not resolve the antinomies of strategic-diplomatic conduct, but it does attempt to find in each case the most acceptable compromise. However, if the procession of states and empires continues endlessly, are the historical compromises between violence and moral aspiration little more than expedients? In the thermonuclear age, is a policy enough which reduces the frequency and the amount of violence? Proudhon proclaimed the right of force but also heralded an age of peace. Now that humanity possesses the means of destroying itself, have wars a meaning if they do not lead to peace?

chapter XX

In Search of a Morality

II: *Conviction and Responsibility*

"Before the turn of the century, either human life will have ceased on our planet, or the population will have been catastrophically reduced and relapsed into savagery, or humanity will be subject to a single government, having a monopoly of all decisive weapons." So wrote Lord Russell in the first issue of the German review *Der Monat*, in 1948. There are less than forty years left for us and our children, if we credit the distinguished philosopher, to choose between these three prospects. But if these are the alternatives, is it reasonable to play the game of deterrence? Is it reasonable for the small nations to imitate the great ones? Is it reasonable for the great powers to prolong power politics when available weapons have rendered this senseless?

At the end of the previous chapter we concluded that the morality of prudence, a compromise between rather than a synthesis of the morality of struggle and the morality of law, was the best. Is this consistently true in the thermonuclear age?

1. *Atomic Weapons and Morality*

Does thermonuclear war present the moralist with a problem qualitatively different from the one presented by so-called conventional wars? An affirmative answer generally rests on two arguments: the character which the hostilities would assume, and the latter's long-term consequences for the whole human race. War retains a human character only when it is a test of strength, of will, of intelligence. Men confront other men, each risking his life in order to render his enemy powerless. To be sure, wars have not, throughout history, respected the rules of honor. Guile has always passed for lawful, even when it revealed more villainy than ingenuity. Wars between "civilized peoples" and "barbarians," when technical superiority guaranteed the victory of the former or physical vigor that of the latter, the countless wars between heterogeneous populations, did not always have the quality of a test and confirmed neither the judgment of God nor the triumph of the worthiest side. It requires a certain retrospective confidence in historical Providence to maintain that the "barbarians" have prevailed when the "civilized peoples" needed new blood, or that the latter have subdued barbarian populations when these needed—albeit against their will—to be civilized.

It is nevertheless true that between states belonging to the same zone of civilization, it has been possible to consider wars just or unjust with reference to the various belligerents, according to the part taken by each in the *launching of hostilities*, the *objectives* held by each, and the *probable results* of the victory of each side. Do such distinctions, however ambiguous they may have been in the past, still have meaning in the thermonuclear age? Could a thermonuclear war ever be just?

Such a war would accentuate the tendency, perceptible between 1940 and 1945, not to regard the combatants alone as targets. The extension of zones of bombardment was provoked and in part justified by two arguments: it is no more immoral, and perhaps more effective, to destroy the factories in which weapons are produced than the weapons themselves. The entire war potential can and must be eliminated in order to weaken the enemy's will to resist. Places of work as well as workers are part of this potential. They must be attacked according to the necessities of war, which the moralist has a right to reject altogether but whose consequences he cannot refuse if he has accepted their principle. This first argument—the whole nation participates in the conflict, all of it is therefore the legitimate object of hostilities—combines with a second. Since the will to resist characterizes the entire population, and neither the leaders nor the army can continue to fight once the masses have lost courage and confidence, it becomes rational to attack the non-combatants, even if the war potential is not physically damaged. The morale of the enemy population becomes a target in its turn: what the British called "area bombing" and the Germans "terrorist attacks" proceeded logically from this consideration of collective psychology.

In practice this method has been found ineffective, but its *ethical* condemnation nevertheless remains uncertain: where do we stop in the extension of objectives? If the war is waged by the entire nation, why would it not be legitimate to regard the entire nation as the target? Rather, the practice of indiscriminate bombing must be condemned for motives of prudence. Does it not compromise the aftermath of the war more than it hastens victory? If both sides resort to it, they increase the cost of the war without either being sure of a substantial advantage. Would the same be true of atomic or thermonuclear bombing?

Thermonuclear bombing, if it were no longer a threat but a reality, might be of several types. In the abstract, I shall distinguish the following: 1. *Rotterdam*: a power, armed with thermonuclear weapons, would destroy a city of a state not possessing similar weapons, either to punish the latter for a previous action, or to obtain its capitulation and at the same time to spread terror. 2. *Limited reprisals:* a great power might try to check aggression or to punish an aggressor by attacking a city of the guilty state (after or before evacuation of the population). 3. *Traditional war:* if we assume the two super powers to be in conflict, logically each would have to attack the other's thermonuclear force. The populations would suffer as a result of the extension of the zone affected by explosions but they would not be the direct targets. 4. *Execution of the threat not taken seriously:* a small nation can play the game of deterrence by threatening a great power with thermonuclear retaliation in certain circumstances. If the great power does not believe in the execution of the threat, the small nation may be driven to reprisal before or after the punishment it will bring upon itself. 5. *Free-for-all:* the super powers, once war has broken out, may abandon all moderation and simply seek to do each other the most harm possible, each trying to destroy the enemy's cities with the idea that hostilities will cease not by negotiation or by explicit agreement but by exhaustion of one or the other of the belligerents, the victor being the survivor or the state capable of the fastest recovery. 6. *Extermination:* If one of the super powers still has weapons and delivery systems and the other does not, the first can seize the opportunity to exterminate its rival, even if the latter surrenders unconditionally.

Some will object that these distinctions have no meaning, since the explosive power of thermonuclear weapons is such that destruction will be considerable in any case. I do not believe this objection is valid: destruction will indeed be considerable, but it will vary greatly according to the political-strategic intentions of the belligerents.

In 1962, in his speech at Ann Arbor, Secretary of Defense McNamara brought up the possibility of waging war according to the methods of the past, that is, essentially against military installations. These distinctions, however abstract they may seem, are not therefore devoid of meaning.

Let us consider these six types and ask ourselves whether and why they would be, as such, more immoral than the area bombing practiced by the British and Americans with a clean conscience during the last war. The "Rotterdam" type is ordinarily regarded as moral or immoral depending on whether the subject is the aggressor or the victim, in other words, depending on the cause of the belligerent who takes the initiative. I am well aware that other moralists will feel that such a means, even in the service of justice, is wrong: the method of terror degrades its user to the level of the aggressor state. I am not overlooking the risks of this method, but there is no ethical judgment possible, no abstractions to be made of historical circumstances. Since all warlike action is destructive in our age, a brutal action that would bring about the swift capitulation of an aggressor would be potentially justifiable.

The next two types—limited retaliation, traditional war by mutual attack on the thermonuclear force—would not necessarily be more ruinous for societies than operations practiced for years with conventional weapons. If we face these grim comparisons resolutely, it is not evident that a supreme authority would accept as consistent with morality the death of twenty million Russians between 1941 and 1945 and condemn as incompatible with the law of God and man the death of five million men, scattered victims of limited reprisals, the price of a successful termination of hostilities.

Indeed, the deep and irrational feeling that there is a fundamental difference between nuclear weapons and conventional weapons—a feeling that I share and that I feel it desirable to entertain—has, it seems to me, three sources. First of all, men are reacting to this unprecedented weapon just as they have reacted to other innovations, beginning with gunpowder (it is *immoral* to kill someone at a distance: a knight would not resort to such an unfair weapon) or poison gases. This reaction has never prevented the spread of the so-called diabolical weapons in the past, but in the present case, the reaction seems healthy to me: the human race has realized that the atom bomb and even more so the thermonuclear bomb raised political and moral problems *qualitatively* different from TNT bombs. The qualitative difference is first the result of the quantitative difference: a ton of TNT bombs dropped on Germany between 1940 and 1945 caused on the average a certain number of deaths (around 0.2 per ton, if we accept the approximate figures of 300,000 dead and 1.5 million tons). An atom bomb of 20 kilotons (20,000 tons of TNT) caused tens of thousands of deaths at Hiroshima; a thermonuclear bomb of several megatons, falling on the center of Paris, would cause millions of deaths. Per ton of explosive, the "yield" is already increased tenfold but, as we have seen, one thermonuclear bomb possesses an explosive power greater than that of all the bombs used during the last war. The difference in scale, in terms of explosive power, also entails a difference of scale in terms of destruction and loss of human life. If this difference of scale did not appear in the first three types, it is because we offset it by the strategic intention we assumed: hostilities would be short, limited to a small number of exchanges, the belligerents would not aim at the cities. These hypotheses are not absurd and suggest that any use of these weapons does not amount to the apocalypse, but they also explain mankind's instinctive horror. The difference in the scale of explosive power and of destruction is such that henceforth escalation would certainly be fatal for one side and often for both.

The last three types we have listed—execution of a threat that was rational only if it were not carried out, unlimited thermonuclear warfare, extermination of the state now without means of reprisal—are horrible in a different way from the first three, for they are absurd as well (at least types four and five). What revolts and outrages an observer like Bertrand Russell is that states use a threat against one another that they would have to be truly desperate to translate into action. According to a comparison repeatedly used in the Anglo-American literature, everything proceeds as in the game of "chicken": the drivers of two automobiles speed right at one another, each one sure that at the last moment the other will swerve aside in order to avoid smashing both vehicles at once, and the driver who swerves first loses the game. But if neither swerves, each counting on the other to avoid the catastrophe, the latter may occur in spite of the drivers' common intentions. Let us leave aside the question of whether there is a diplomacy that would avoid this double bluff or double blackmail, and merely observe that the power of thermonuclear weapons is such that in changing the scale of destruction it also potentially changes the moral nature of war. Is there a single reason that justifies killing millions of human beings, even if the state that claimed to act on behalf of these millions of people has been guilty of aggression?

Practical-moral reflection seems to lead to perfectly contradictory conclusions, according to whether it concerns itself with the first three types or the last three. This apparent contradiction is easily resolved, since the novelty of the thermonuclear weapon is *qualitative* as a result of a quantitative change. We need only eliminate the influence of this quantitative change by an appropriate strategy in order for the originality of the moral problem to disappear. The moment the instruments of retaliation are dispersed on the high seas and war would assume the form of submarines pursuing one another, then the war waged by thermonuclear vessels upon one another might be less costly than yesterday's wars waged by industrial societies of coal, steel and oil. However compatible they may be in the abstract, these two kinds of conclusions nevertheless raise a further question. The possible justification of the first three types presupposed a limited use of these monstrous weapons. But the skeptic will be inclined to doubt even the possibility of this limitation. Is not escalation inevitable once atom or thermonuclear bombs begin to explode?

Let us concede that, lacking experience, we have no way of knowing. Two opposing arguments are convincing and current. If war breaks out, some say, statesmen will lose their *sang-froid* and let themselves be carried away by fury (escalation is inevitable). Even if war breaks out, others say, statesmen (assuming they are not themselves victims of the first attacks) will try to stop the homicidal madness as fast as possible. In short, a nuclear explosion makes escalation less probable given the so-called rational conduct of the leaders, but more probable if we consider the leaders as incapable of so-called rational action once the atomic weapons are unloosed. Personally I am inclined to believe in the persistence of fear, hence of caution, but too many circumstances will determine the event for us to be able to prophesy with confidence.

The result of these analyses might also be expressed as follows: since thermonuclear weapons make the complete destruction of the enemy nation —territory and population—possible, the use of these weapons remains admissible, in terms of the traditional rules of international relations, only provided Rousseau's formula that "we wage war on states, not on peoples" still retains a minimum of meaning, or again provided there is a limited use of these weapons: whether it is a case of the "Rotterdam" type, of the "limited reprisals" type, or of the "attacks upon the thermonuclear system" type, the aim is to obtain the capitulation of the state itself or to punish it, not to wipe out cities and their inhabitants. The next three types might be termed *vengeance, homicidal madness* or *extermination*. The case of the potentially posthumous vengeance of a small nation which preferred death to capitulation provides philosophers with an eternal theme for meditation: can or should a state—that is, the few men who decide for all—choose, like the commander of a fort, a heroic death over capitulation, if this death is that of the population itself?

The question, which is both a moral and a political one, has shifted: to what degree is this limited use possible? Up to what point is it conceivable that the threat of an unlimited use of these weapons may not someday lead to the execution of the threat? The problem seems no longer to be whether the use of these weapons is justifiable in certain circumstances and according to a certain strategy, but whether the possession of these weapons by several states and their diplomatic use (in the strategy of deterrence) do not create an intolerable, morally culpable *risk* of this total catastrophe which so many philosophers and scientists have evoked?

This brings us to the second argument underlying the thesis that in our time the unconditional rejection of this kind of war is the only reasonable and realistic policy, given the consequences of a thermonuclear war for the human race: the genetic heritage of humanity itself would be affected. Generation after generation of children would be born abnormal, a tragedy ascribable to the war mania of their ancestors.

Is it *morally* worse to compromise the health of human beings as yet unborn than that of the living? I do not know, but I am inclined to believe that the difference is above all quantitative and material, as it were. However considerable the destruction caused by a war, reconstruction—as we know from the experience of these last fifteen years—is possible and relatively swift as long as men have survived in sufficient numbers and with their technical capacity intact. Whatever the losses occasioned by a war waged with nuclear weapons, the recovery of nations remains at least conceivable —provided the health of the generations to come has not been irremediably compromised. A thermonuclear war would indeed be incomparable to any other if it damaged the genetic endowment of humanity. Tomorrow's men are predetermined, as it were, by the trillions of genes which three million living persons carry in their chromosomes. Most of the genetic mutations caused by radiation are, according to biologists, teratological. Would not a thermonuclear war increase the frequency of such mutations in a truly catastrophic manner?

Biologists do not all give the same answer to such a query. But the majority of them would, I believe, subscribe to a statement which I borrow from

Herman Kahn: *any kind of thermonuclear war* would not *necessarily* amount to the suicide of the human race:

"I once mentioned in an unclassified lecture that I could easily imagine a war in which the average survivor received about 250 roentgens. Now 250 roentgens is 25 times greater than the 10 roentgens we have talked about [the limit of safety recommended in a report of the National Academy of Sciences]. . . . Ten roentgens produces about .04 per cent defectives. According to the widely accepted theory of a linear relationship between dose and damage, 250 roentgens would produce 25 times as much damage as 10 roentgens. This would mean that about 1 per cent of the children who could have been healthy would be defective; in short, the number of children born seriously defective would increase, because of war, to about 25 per cent above the current rate. This would be a large penalty to pay for a war. More horrible still, we might have to continue to pay a similar though smaller price for 20 or 30 or 40 generations. But even this is a long way from annihilation. It might well turn out, for example, that U. S. decision makers would be willing, among other things, to accept the high risk of an additional 1 per cent of our children being born deformed *if that meant not giving up Europe to Soviet Russia.* Or it might be that under certain circumstances the Russians would be willing to accept even higher risks than this, if by doing so they could eliminate the United States.

"At this point in the lecture a lady in the audience got up and said in a very accusing voice, 'I don't want to live in your world in which 1 per cent of the children are born defective.' My answer was rather brutal, I fear. 'It is not *my* world,' I observed, and then pointed out that if she did not want to live in a world in which 1 per cent of the children were born defective she had a real problem, since 4 per cent of the children are born defective *now.* This story illustrates that peace also has its tragedies, and that we tend in our day-to-day life to ignore the existence of this continuing risk. Unless their own family or close friends or relatives have been affected, most people just ignore these kinds of risks in the environment in which we live and raise families.

"I can easily imagine that if we lived in a world in which no children had ever been born defective and we were told that as a result of some new contingencies 4 per cent of the children would be born seriously defective we would consider such a world to be intolerable. We might not believe that people would be willing to bear and raise children if the risk were about 1 in 25 that these children would have a serious congenital defect. However, we live in that world now. We not only bear this relatively high rate of tragedy; we come close to ignoring it."[1]

Bertrand Russell urges us to realize that it is better to capitulate than to wage a thermonuclear war which would seal the fate of civilization, that is,

---

[1] H. Kahn, *op. cit.,* pp. 46–47.

of humanity itself. But he does not distinguish clearly between various counsels: the counsel to capitulate rather than *run the risk* of a war that *would be*
the death of the human race, the counsel to capitulate rather than *run the
risk* of a war that *might be* the death of the human race, the counsel to
capitulate rather than *wage* the war that *might be* the death of the human
race, and finally the counsel to capitulate rather than *wage* the war that
would be the death of the human race. One often has the impression that
Bertrand Russell and most of those who think as he does confuse these four
counsels or reduce them all to the forth. For the *risk* of a war that *might be*
the suicide of all belligerents they substitute the certainty of such a war.
But if the war necessarily entailed the disappearance of the human race, what
state, unless insane or courting self-annihilation, would force another to
choose between capitulation or war?

The questions which arise are as stirring but more complex; they are
formulated in terms of *risks* and objective possibilities. Should a great state,
if it has the means, manufacture weapons capable of utterly devastating vast
areas, in other words of making life on the planet impossible or of exterminating all human beings? Should the medium-size states, which do not have
the necessary resources to acquire airplanes or ballistic missiles capable of
dropping the bomb or the nuclear warhead near the target, compensate for
this inferiority by manufacturing bombs as "dirty" as possible, which when
exploded at high altitudes would spead fire or radioactive contamination
over vast areas? How must deterrence be handled in order to reduce the risk
that the threat will be executed: by which alternative—that of the arms race
or that of Russian-American agreements—will the risk be reduced to the
minimum?

2. *The Two Alternatives and the Nuclear Test Ban*

In late 1960 the distinguished physicist, high official and novelist Sir
Charles P. Snow, addressing his learned colleagues,[2] expressed himself along
the following lines:

"We are faced with an either-or, and we haven't much time. The *either* is
acceptance of a restriction of nuclear armaments. This would begin, just as
a token, with an agreement on the stopping of nuclear tests. The United
States is not going to get the 99.9 per cent 'security' that it has been asking
for. This is unobtainable, though there are other bargains that the United
States could probably secure. I am not going to conceal from you that this
course involves certain risks. They are quite obvious, and no honest man is
going to blink them. That is the *either*. The *or* is not a risk but a certainty.
It is this: No agreement on tests. The nuclear arms race between the United
States and the U.S.S.R. not only continues but accelerates. Other countries

[2] At a meeting of the American Association for the Advancement of Science in New
York. See New York *Times*, December 28, 1960.

join in. Within, at the most, six years, China and several other states will have a stock of nuclear bombs. Within, at the most, ten years, some of those bombs are going off. I am saying this as responsibly as I can. *That* is the certainty. On the one side, therefore, we have a finite risk. On the other side we have a certainty of disaster. Between a risk and a certainty, a sane man does not hesitate."

Is this presentation of the problem—a choice in which one of the alternatives involves limited risks and the other implies the certainty of disaster—accurate, is it complete, is it fair? To these three questions I find myself reluctantly forced to answer *no*. The fact that Sir Charles is a physicist and invokes knowledge which the humanist does not possess makes the distortion of the facts even more serious. One argument underlies the reasoning I have just quoted. "We most of us are familiar with statistics and the nature of odds. We know, with the certainty of statistical truth, that if enough of these weapons are made—by enough different states—some of them are going to blow up. Through accident, or folly, or madness—but the motives don't matter. What does matter is the nature of the statistical fact." How many states, how many bombs, how much time is required for the statistical fact to be incontestable? I do not think it is so easy to calculate the statistical probability of "accident, folly, or madness." But let us accept the fact, since the scientist declares it to be incontestable. Is he right to conclude that by the alternative of disarmament the risk is limited, while by the alternative of the arms race the disaster is certain? This conclusion is doubly erroneous.

What Sir Charles has demonstrated or at least declared, is that some bombs will explode. It is possible, in literary language, to term a few explosions a "disaster." (The bombs which were dropped on Hiroshima and Nagasaki caused a disaster, but an American attempt to land on Japan would, in terms of material destruction and loss of human life, also have been a disaster.) In contrasting "limited risks" and "certain disaster" Sir Charles is implying that without disarmament *the* disaster is certain. In other words, he is confusing the explosion of some bombs (an explosion declared to be certain) with total thermonuclear war. But it is neither established nor even probable (although it is possible) that the explosion of some bombs will release the "homicidal madness."[3]

As for the potential consequences of a disarmament treaty which one of the two super powers might violate, they are not necessarily slighter than the consequences of the explosion of *several bombs*. Furthermore, if we are talking not about *a* disaster but *the* disaster, not about the explosion of a few bombs but about total thermonuclear war, it remains to be established by what means we have the best chance of reducing the probability. The risk of a thermonuclear war will not be radically eliminated either by a policy of

---

[3] In a subsequent discussion published by *Commentary* (October 1961), Sir Charles himself recognized the validity of this distinction.

armament or by a policy of disarmament. In theory, it would be eliminated only by the establishment of a universal state: such a state could not be established *today* by agreement between the rival powers; it could result only from the victory of one or the other.[4] The two super powers, whatever agreements they may sign, will retain their military sovereignty and, if they should come into conflict, would be tempted to resort to thermonuclear weapons, even if they had previously signed a treaty forbidding their use.

The comparison of the two alternatives does not amount to the comparison of *certainty* with *risk,* or the comparison of *disaster* with *limited risk.* There is a more or less considerable risk of the disaster of total thermonuclear war, whatever alternative is chosen. If the spread of atomic weapons involves, according to Sir Charles, the *certainty* of *some* explosions, it remains to be seen what risks would attend the alternative of disarmament. This is not the place to specify the nature and extent of these risks. Let us merely consider the nuclear test ban treaty, which Sir Charles's speech tends to present as indispensable by making it the symbol of the alternative leading to the limitation of armaments and to salvation, while the other alternative leads to "certain disaster."[5] The nuclear test ban treaty that was signed in 1963 was a public acknowledgment by the two super powers of their mutual advantage in avoiding war and still retaining possession of the decisive weapons. We know that insofar as it is possible they have abstained from helping their allies, China on the one hand, and Western Europe on the other. *Communist solidarity, like Western solidarity, stops just short of atomic weapons.* The study of the advantages and disadvantages of such an agreement thus involved, for each of the two super powers, at least three kinds of considerations. What would be the effect of secret testing (that is, of violations of the treaty), by the other super power, on the balance of power, and what is the probability of such violation? What would be the effect of such an agreement on the relations of each super power with its allies (the relations

---

[4] Unless by demanding that the United States capitulate at once in order to eliminate this risk; but such a demand is Utopian. In terms of our values it would be entirely unjustified. We would accept a *great and certain* evil in order to avoid the *risk* of an evil *perhaps* greater still.

[5] Sir Charles presents another case of "certain knowledge" which arouses some doubt. "For scientists know, and again with the certainty of scientific knowledge, that we possess every scientific fact we need to transform the physical life of half the world. And transform it within the space of people now living. I mean, we have all resources to help half the world live as we do, and eat enough. All that is missing is the will." One must give the word *will* an extremely broad meaning for this statement to assume not the character of truth (which it never will) but a kind of credibility. If it is a case of the *technical* means for prolonging human life and increasing the production of food, of course men do possess them. If it is a case of the political-economic-social possibility of transforming the hygienic and nutritional conditions of half the human race, I marvel that Sir Charles should display a certainty which scientists who are occupied with these problems have never exhibited.

Let me add that we are dealing with a public speech in which the desire to convince prevails over the scruples of the scientist, and the invocation of scientific certainty is merely a rhetorical device, in this case a dangerous one.

of the Soviet Union with China, of the United States with France)? Thirdly, what would be the effect of such an agreement on relations between the two super powers, and the prospects of further disarmament?

The experts have agreed on two points which are of fundamental importance to the practical-moral analysis we are making here. Underground tests in mines or caverns, whether natural or created with this end in mind, cannot, at the present stage of thermonuclear development, be definitely detected. The upper limit of presently undetectable experiments can be raised by various muffling devices. Underground testing would aid in the improvement of small-caliber weapons, in the reduction of the weight of the warhead for a given explosive power (in other words, in reducing the weight-yield ratio),[6] and eventually in the creation of other weapons (a neutron bomb or anti-missile missiles). Since instruments often register apparently suspicious seismic movements, which are difficult to distinguish from nuclear experiments, groups of scientists must be on the spot to observe the nature of the phenomenon. The risk that a secret and illegal test might be detected increases with the number of inspections called for. The probability of a violation by one of the signatory states depends upon the anticipated advantage of these secret tests, the probability that the check system is effective, and the political disadvantages in the event of a proved violation. Of all these various considerations, the most important may be reduced to a naïve question: what military advantages can a state expect today from the continuation (or resumption) of nuclear testing which by common consent is indetectable? Which amounts to saying that the treaty is without great danger precisely to the extent that it is technically without great significance. If secret testing allows for advances of substantial or decisive importance, one of the states[7] will be tempted to "cheat." Which leads to the somewhat discouraging conclusion that such an agreement would have a more psychological than military significance. It would be a gamble on the good faith of the states that sign it, undertaken less out of confidence in the worth of the signature than out of indifference to possible violation.

What influence would a test ban have on the international situation, that is (in a simplified analysis), on the relation of the two super powers with their respective allies and with one another?

We do know that a great many Chinese physicists have worked in the atomic laboratories of the Soviet Union and have signed scientific publications along with Russian physicists, but that China itself has received from the Soviet Union only a reactor of an old type. On the Western side, the United States has furnished only limited aid to the atomic programs of its European allies, and none at all to the military elements of the French program. It has cooperated quite closely with Great Britain and given it the

[6] To increase the explosive power for a given weight.
[7] The probability that this state would be the Soviet Union need not be explained by the superior virtue of the United States. It is enough to consider the difficulty, for the United States, of keeping secrets.

advantages of the clause in the legislation which authorizes the exchange of information with sufficiently advanced countries. There seems, therefore, to be an approximate symmetry; each super power willingly contributes to the training of scientists in allied countries, that is, to progress in the area of the peaceful utilization of atomic energy, and tries, without violating the rule of solidarity within the bloc too openly, to delay if not to prevent the independent acquisition of atomic or thermonuclear weapons by its partners.

In one respect, however, an asymmetry exists between the Soviet Union and the United States, or perhaps one would have to say between Europe and Asia. The Soviet Union has not given China the atomic means to deter American provocation. It has declared, once and for all, by means of the treaty of mutual assistance, that in the event of war between Communist China and the United States it would intervene on behalf of the former against the latter. This alliance is enough to "protect" China from American aggression or again to deter the United States from any open aggression. But it does not enable Communist China to take the initiative in any large-scale hostilities, even against Quemoy and Matsu. The Soviet Union, in keeping atomic arms for itself, deters both its ally and its enemy from settling their differences by force. But obviously it gives China additional reasons for developing its own nuclear arms program as rapidly as possible.

In Europe, the United States, as we have seen,[8] has tried to attain two objectives at the same time: to retain control of nuclear weapons and to give its allies the advantages which would result from the possession of such weapons. For the past ten years, the means employed have varied according to technical advances.

With respect to the allies, the test ban treaty could have been effective, but on one condition: that the two super powers promised formally or secretly to impose respect for it by non-signatories. But such a promise, in turn, was difficult to make and even more difficult to keep. The Soviet Union cannot openly acknowledge, even in a secret negotiation with the United States, that it fears Communist China's acquisition of an independent atomic capacity. Similarly, the United States is ready if necessary to oppose the acquisition of an independent atomic force by any state, even an ally, but even so it does not foresee resorting to force or threats in order to discourage France from manufacturing atomic bombs. In other words, the nuclear test ban treaty would reveal a desire to apply a policy that is conceivable in the abstract and perhaps reasonable: the intended prohibition by the two super powers of the manufacture of atomic arms by all states. But this policy remains paralyzed by the hostility between the two blocs and the insoluble paradox of an *open* alliance of the enemies against their respective allies.

Thus we come to the ultimate questions: What would be the effect of such a treaty upon relations between the two super powers? Would the creation of a system of inspection, even an imperfect one, have marked the beginning of

---

[8] See above, Chap. XVI.

a new era, the opening of the Soviet Union to international officials, the lessening of the age-old and obsessional concern for secrecy, a first step, however hesitant, toward a free world?

These questions cannot be answered with certainty. Some of the experts, especially the physicists, argue that a first agreement, however limited, would have a significance and importance that would greatly exceed the material results or guarantees obtained. Others mercilessly expose the hidden meaning of the treaty. In the last analysis, the two super powers would have promised one another to be content with the weapons now available, in order to prevent the other states from acquiring equivalent ones. The treaty would be respected insofar as, on both sides, the experts did not believe in the importance of the advances that could be made through new tests. What would the positive argument be against these limitations and uncertainties? Humanity would regard this treaty, symbolic as it was, as proof that the two super powers had the desire and capacity to agree. But this argument—the clinching argument of the optimists—is reversed by the pessimists: the feeling that an important step had been taken toward disarmament or peace would be illusory. The West would tend to rely on a false security. In fact, there would have been no essential change.

It is not the purpose of these analyses to suggest that the United States should have signed the nuclear test ban treaty at whatever price, even by subscribing to the *troika* principle (the Secretariat, responsible for supervising and insuring respect for the treaty, would be directed by a committee of three members, one Soviet, one Western, the other non-engaged). They are intended to illuminate the nature of diplomatic-strategic deliberation in our time and lead, like those in the previous section, to a conclusion which some will find commonplace and others misleading: deliberation has not become fundamentally different because destruction, in the event of war, might prove to be excessive.[9]

Bertrand Russell makes capitulation appear to be the obvious rational course to take by presenting it as one of the alternatives of a choice, of which the other would be the certainty of a total thermonuclear war. Sir Charles changes the meaning of the nuclear test ban treaty by presenting it as one of the two alternatives open to humanity, the other leading to *certain disaster*.

In fact, the originality of the deliberations we have analyzed is not that the only way to be a realist is henceforth to obey the arguments of morality. Neither of the two super powers, short of capitulation, can renounce its deterrent, the monstrous threat of devastating cities or killing millions of innocent human beings. But this threat is morally justifiable only if it is a

---

[9] The test ban treaty of 1963 does not require on-the-spot inspection because underground tests have not been included. I have not changed the text written in 1961, before the new testing by the Soviet Union and then by the United States, because the aim of the analysis is to show the nature of the deliberation, not to suggest any political conclusion.

supreme threat, each trying to create conditions such that it will never have to be executed. Now in this respect, the objective of the Machiavellian coincides with that of the moralist: both seek to reduce the risk of thermonuclear war and, in the event that thermonuclear weapons are used, to prevent escalation. But let us note that if the advocates of pragmatism and those of morality tend to agree, it is not because prudence as such has become a guarantee of justice, it is because we place the lives of millions of people above justice itself. We dare not repeat *fiat justitia, pereat mundus* because today the danger that the *world might perish* is no longer mere rhetoric.

3. *The Choice of the Small Powers*

The nuclear test ban treaty concerned all the other countries. By subscribing to it, they prohibited themselves from joining the atomic club. Was such a decision *incumbent* on the rulers of France or India, and if so, for what reasons?

Hostile to the production of atomic bombs for reasons of morality, the French should also, logically, denounce alliances concluded with one or the other of the powers possessing an atomic force, hence the Atlantic Alliance. If they regard the diplomatic use of the thermonuclear threat as morally unjustifiable, then they should also refuse to base the security of their country upon this threat brandished by an allied state. Still further, Britons and Frenchmen who *for ethical motives* seek to withdraw from partnership in deterrence strategy must not only renounce the manufacture of bombs or the stationing on their territory of planes or ballistic missiles, they must, insofar as possible, give up the advantages of this strategy. Perhaps they cannot help retaining, at least in part, the advantages, even if they withdraw from such alliances. Before risking aggression, each of the two super powers would *in any event* wonder about the reactions of *the other*. The dissolution of alliances concluded in the shadow of deterrence strategy would nevertheless be the symbol of a will transcending the political order: to accept all risks rather than resort to the threat of a "massacre of the innocents."

It is possible, by arguments of another type, to advocate a club of non-atomic states, or the definitive closing of the atomic club on another level. But in this case we are dealing with a "politics of responsibility," with the preference for assured protection by a greater power, not with the refusal of all protection and the reliance on the "pacifism" of nations and empires. Let us analyze the conditions of the choice for France, as we have analyzed the conditions of the choice for the United States.[10]

---

[10] We have avoided concluding that the United States should or should not have signed the nuclear test ban treaty; similarly we shall avoid concluding that France should or should not pursue its program. Here we are merely examining the *nature* of the problems facing statesmen and trying to clarify the character of the decisions they must make.

The government of a medium-size state, France, for example, is assailed by three kinds of advisers: realists, usually the British and Americans, beseech it *on behalf of the welfare of the human race* not to increase the number of states possessing the terrifying weapon; other realists, Frenchmen, beg it to give France the means of deterring aggression and of taking her place among the great powers; finally, realists and moralists beg it not to spend a considerable sum of money for a weapon which would be both useless to France and dangerous for humanity.

The statesman will first be inclined to question the British and American realists. To what extent does France's acquisition of atomic and thermonuclear armaments increase the risk of general or total war? It is easy to say that the greater the number of bombs, the greater the chances of "accident." But if accident means technical accident, this can also occur in the case of a peaceful utilization of nuclear energy. In any case, the number of bombs manufactured by the two super powers is already in the thousands. Statistically, a few hundred bombs manufactured in France will not perceptibly increase the risk of a "technical accident"—unless it can be proved that the French will take fewer precautions or be less competent than the Russians, Americans and British. Very likely the accident so frequently alluded to by the advisers of the first school is political rather than technical. But actually, as long as France belongs to the Atlantic Alliance and the latter's armies are deployed in West Germany, in what way do the French bombs increase the risk of a "political accident"?

The least one can say is that the proposition that France's accession to the atomic club substantially increases the risk of a "political or technical accident" has yet to be proved. It even seems on first sight scarcely probable.[11] Therefore the advisers of the first school will be inclined to assure the President of the Republic that the danger derives less from the bombs manufactured than from the example afforded by France. A small atomic force in a country geographically and politically integrated in one of the blocs does not perceptibly alter either the strength of the alliance nor the risk of "accident, folly, or madness." But what will happen if West Germany and Italy, then Egypt and Israel move in the same direction? To which the French statesman will be inclined to reply that the example of Great Britain is no less "blameworthy" in this respect than the example of France. Why is it France rather than Great Britain which we choose to indict? Either one advocates maintaining the duopoly, in which case the United States and Great Britain are guilty of the major offense, the latter in acquiring thermonuclear power, the former in practicing a close collaboration on the scientific

11 Does it increase the risk of a war "through folly or madness," in Sir Charles's words? Yes, on the principle that the more men there are whose mental health is necessary to peace, the more peace will be jeopardized. We are permitted to doubt the quantitative measure of this threat.

level with the third member of the club. In setting up a hierarchy within the Atlantic Alliance—the leader of the bloc, the privileged ally, the protected states—the United States is itself provoking France to the very quest for *rank* which it deplores and condemns.

Furthermore, if the United States regards the proliferation of atomic states as contrary to the interest of the Atlantic Alliance and of humanity, it must convince its allies or at least do everything it can to convince them. Now, the attempt to convince involves two kinds of elements, *arguments* and *means of exerting pressure* (promises or threats, and since in this particular case threats are difficult to use, especially promises). The arguments are essentially those of the third school, the one that asserts the futility of the "small striking force." But, as we shall see in a moment, these arguments are not decisive. They need to be supported by "promises." Implicitly, in the present state of intra-Atlantic diplomacy,[12] the United States "advises" France "in the name of the higher cause of humanity" to renounce her atomic program. What does it offer as compensation? Not even more advanced scientific cooperation in the area of the peaceful utilization of atomic energy. I am well aware that American statesmen might reply that they do not ask for an advantage for themselves, but for the Alliance and for humanity. But, even assuming they are right, their interlocutors are not convinced of it. In renouncing their own atomic program French statesmen would have the feeling that they were sacrificing "national interest," in the narrow and traditional sense of the word, to the Atlantic or human community. The state whose strength affords it the role of leader is called upon to offer a compensation for this sacrifice, a compensation which may be scientific (aid in the construction of a submarine) or political (promises of consultation, commitments in the event of a withdrawal of American troops).

The American negotiators still might reply: why should we pay the French in order to convince them to follow a policy consistent *with their own interest?* Consequently, it is the arguments of the third school, which is fundamentally realistic even if it includes many moralists, which are or should be decisive: the national striking force would be useless. But, as we have seen, the problem is curiously complex.[13]

To simplify, one can say that a striking force, to be an instrument of deterrence, must have a second strike capability, that is, must not be too vulnerable to the enemy's first strike. Moreover, the delivery vehicles and the organization of atomic or thermonuclear equipment must be such that the communications necessary to action are maintained even after a possible attack. Finally, the potential for retaliation must be sufficient to "give pause" to the leaders of the state possessing the atomic force of the first order. To

---

[12] In 1962 President Kennedy outspokenly condemned French efforts to establish a national force as inimical to the interest of the Atlantic Alliance, but apparently he did not even try to "deter" General de Gaulle, except by arguments.

[13] See above, Chap. XVI, Sec. 2.

these surely indispensable conditions, certain analysts add a fourth: that the destruction which the small nation would suffer in case of war not be equivalent to extermination.

It is easy to show that France will not, in 1965–70, possess an independent retaliatory force; will she possess one in 1975–80? Will a striking force ineffective with regard to the Soviet Union have no utility at all for France? The French program of 1960 consists of two parts: one, the scientific part, is indispensable if France is ever to possess the technical and industrial basis for an atomic force; the other seeks to create a striking force as soon as possible. Admitting that this second part is irrational, it is still true that France must put the scientific part of her program into execution immediately if she is to possess, fifteen years from now, a certain autonomous capacity for thermonuclear and ballistic missile production.

Can she acquire such a force? Certain experts hold that she can, others deny it. If we consider the amount of money spent by the United States in developing and producing ballistic missiles and H-bombs, the answer will be negative. But this kind of calculation is open to objection. The time and expenditure necessary to scientific and technical progress may be reduced for those who come second, who know the objective to be attained and have accumulated much information on what path to follow. Nor is it out of the question that the same military problem—to be capable of inflicting significant destruction on the enemy—may be solved by different technical procedures, some more costly, others less costly.

American scientists have taken great pains to produce "clean" bombs, that is, bombs having a minimum radioactive fallout. A small state which seeks, come what may, to gain a certain military autonomy may have an advantage in manufacturing and letting it be known that it is manufacturing "dirty" bombs, even if its own population were to be victims of radioactive fallout (since in any case it will be helplessly exposed to the attacks of the super power). Moreover, French technicians, once they abandon accuracy of fire and resolutely adopt a counter-city and not a counter-force strategy, may produce delivery systems of reduced cost and vulnerability. In the event that the objective is merely to devastate a certain surface of enemy territory by exploding "dirty" bombs at high altitudes, it is perhaps not impossible that a country like France might succeed in acquiring the means to do so without excessive expenditure.

For all that, will France have a deterrent force? Everything depends on what is required in order to call a "striking force" a "deterrent." If the requirement is a capacity to neutralize enemy attack either by attacking the enemy's thermonuclear system or by guaranteeing the protection of her own population, France will not have a deterrent in the foreseeable future; the French territory is too small, the nation's vital organs are too concentrated. The day the Soviet Union lays down an ultimatum, the French government, left to itself, would in the majority of cases be obliged to capitulate, for the physical survival of the French people would be at stake. Nevertheless, France could potentially answer an extreme provocation with a desperate move, and perhaps even respond to a surprise attack.

The next stage of reflection for the French President is a comparison of the advantages and disadvantages of this semi-deterrent for the nation, for the Atlantic bloc, for the community of peoples. The argument against efforts now under way runs as follows: if France pursues this path, other states will follow her; she will be exposed because of the multiplicity of atomic forces to graver dangers than those she will avoid or mitigate by her own armament. In any case the resources utilized for thermonuclear armament would have a higher "yield" if they were devoted to conventional weapons.

The opposing thesis is based primarily on two arguments. It is impossible to know what, as a result of technological development, the Soviet Union's strategic and diplomatic policy will be. The creation of a thermonuclear force is at least insurance and, since it is a matter of life and death, a necessary insurance. Moreover, even if an equivalent security could be acquired by agreement with one of the super powers, there will be no lack of Frenchmen who feel that no state should abandon its own defense as long as it has the means to do otherwise. The possession of atomic bombs can be considered as an advantage in itself, whatever its actual utility, insofar as the state's autonomy is regarded as an end and not as a means. General de Gaulle's decisions are clearly determined less by an assessment of costs and yield, less by a comparison between the security provided by one's own deterrent force and the security provided by an Atlantic organization, than by the doctrine revealed in the speech at the Ecole Militaire: a state which does not assume responsibility for its national defense is no longer a state.

Put this way, the doctrine is anachronistic, for in this case there would remain only two authentic states, the United States and the Soviet Union, since the others are defended only by the mutual paralysis of the super powers. Moreover, carried to its logical conclusion, this doctrine would encourage all heads of state to aspire to the autonomy conferred by an atomic force.

When all these reservations have been stated, there remain, at the end of this analysis, two insoluble doubts, one of which has to do with the unpredictability of the technological and political future, the other with the plurality of legitimate objectives.

On the level of defense, efforts toward the establishment of a quasi-autonomous retaliatory force and hence of deterrence will seem rational or senseless according to 1) the technological results obtained and 2) the diplomatic situation ten to twenty years from now. If this situation is approximately the same as today in its fundamental features, it would probably be preferable not to spend billions of francs each year in order to acquire a deterrent that will be effective only within the thermonuclear system of the Atlantic Treaty.

On the other hand, it is impossible to overlook completely such eventualities as the withdrawal of American troops from Europe or an even more radical change in the relations between the three truly great powers (Russia, China, the United States)—eventualities in which a semi-deterrent would have strategic-diplomatic significance.

This is not all. French efforts constitute a new phenomenon which the United States and Great Britain cannot ignore. If Great Britain eventually joins the Common Market, it will become increasingly difficult for it to retain its position of privileged ally, the only one permitted to cooperate with the American Atomic Energy Commission. It will be almost inevitably led to cooperate with France and its partners in the European Community. In this connection, the possibility, indeed the probability arises of a "European deterrent" which would encourage political unity and be an expression of it —a force which would be coordinated with the American deterrent. Such a formula—a strong American deterrent, a less powerful European one—creates scarcely any additional dangers and involves obvious advantages, since it reduces the disparity between the great power on the other side of the Atlantic and the small states of the Old World.

States, like individuals, desire not only life but honor, not only security but dignity. Often they prefer danger in autonomy to peace under the protection of a stronger power. Are they "irrational"? Was the captain who went down with his ship irrational? If so, let us hope that human beings will not cease being irrational!

4. The Choice of the Super Power

Max Weber used to cite as an example of the morality of conviction the pacifist or the attitude of the revolutionary trade-unionist. Today he would point to the "unilateralists," the partisans of unilateral atomic disarmament. The latter do seem to me to represent in fact a modern version of unconditional pacifism.

The case of the English unilateralists is different from that of American unilateralists. The first actually lends itself, as we have seen,[14] to an interpretation which deprives it of any moral merit but makes it more acceptable in political terms. Let us suppose, for instance, that Great Britain decides to renounce its nuclear armament and to leave NATO. If this were to happen, Great Britain would not be abandoned to the mercy of her enemies. Neutral or non-aligned nations have often in the course of history been protected by the great powers without having made any explicit alliance with them. As long as there are two states in possession of thermonuclear arms, neither of the two prevails and all members of the non-atomic club can have the illusion that their security does not require recourse to the use, even the diplomatic use, of this terrible weapon.

14 Cf. above, Chap. XV.

It is not surprising that once deterrence has become bilateral, all allies of the United States wonder whether the "American commitment" exposes them to more danger than it provides security. Or, to put the same matter differently, they wonder whether they might not obtain the same or almost the same security against aggression while retaining a better chance of surviving in case of war. Europeans favor American commitment in proportion as they are convinced that deterrence will prevent war and aggression. The day this conviction is shaken, they will begin to reconsider.

Is this diplomacy of neutrality the best policy for Great Britain or for Continental Europe? There is no lack of arguments[15] against it, arguments which consist in reversing the preceding ones: breaking the Alliance increases the danger of an explosion without substantially increasing the probability of remaining outside the conflict, if the latter develops into total war. No one can measure accurately the likelihood of these various possibilities. Then too, these possibilities vary according to the advances in military technique and the international situation. As long as Berlin and Germany are divided and American troops are stationed in Europe, an official split between the Old and the New World would hardly alter the historic solidarity which would manifest itself, in wartime, by the impossibility of one remaining neutral when the other had begun to fight.

However this may be—and once again, it is the logic of these choices which concerns us rather than the content of the choices themselves—neutrality of this type, justified by these kinds of reasons, would be a policy of responsibility, not a policy of conviction. Those individuals would be moralists of conviction who would ask the United States or the Soviet Union to disarm unilaterally, or who, in Great Britain, would ask the British to prefer occupation to an atomic war or, since any war between regular armies in our time risks provoking the use of atomic bombs, to prefer occupation to any war.

Even this last choice—to prefer occupation to war—lends itself to a realistic interpretation such as that which Commander Stephen King-Hall, for example, has given. Revolts against colonial authorities throughout the world have shown just how effective civil disobedience, non-violent resistance, terrorism and guerrilla tactics can be—costly for the imperial power which, incapable of re-establishing order, is doomed to spend on this endless task sums greater than those yielded by the exploitation of the subjugated people. It is enough that a population, even without arms, be resolved to make a conqueror's life

---

[15] Even if the argument for neutrality were stronger in terms of probability, many Englishmen would nevertheless choose the opposite side for various reasons, reasons related to the very nature of diplomatic-strategic activity: weakening of Western capacity for negotiation with the Soviet Union, renunciation of an active role on the international scene, dishonorable or at any rate inglorious character of the decision to depend on another for one's own defense, etc.

impossible for the latter to discover, little by little, the vanity of conquest.[16]

This theory, *insofar as it claims to be realistic,* is open to decisive objections because it envisages certain facts and overlooks others. First of all, it assumes that the day of massacres or exterminations is definitively over, that a people which lays down its arms will be neither deported nor reduced to slavery nor simply exterminated. Unhappily, there is no reason for subscribing to this act of faith. The Russians had interned ten thousand Polish officers in camps: they massacred them before withdrawing. Stalin had proposed to Roosevelt and Churchill to shoot some tens of thousands of Wehrmacht officers. The Germans had closed all the Polish universities and effectively suppressed even secondary education. The educated classes of the Inca and Aztec empires were decimated by the Spanish invaders, and the Indian masses, robbed of their traditional culture, vegetated for centuries, with no reason to live, treated as subhuman by the victors who had become the privileged class of colonial society. There is no need to evoke the wholesale execution of six million Jews in order to conclude that *the cost of enslavement, for a people and a culture, can be higher than the cost of war, even atomic war.*

In the second place, the effectiveness of passive resistance, as practiced by the Indians under the leadership of Mahatma Gandhi, is subordinate to the respect, on the part of armed men, for certain rules. During the war, when the British resolved upon an unrestrained use of the means of force, they mobilized India for war in spite of the decision of the Congress party and a show of semi-active resistance. The execution of nationalist leaders at the opportune moment would not have stopped but perceptibly retarded the movements of national liberation throughout the world.

In French North Africa the movement was accelerated because the French law was too tyrannical for its liberal aspects, and too liberal for its tyrannical ones. It was not possible to maintain a foreign domination in the name of democracy while tolerating nationalist agitation. A half-repressive regime only aggravated passions and further nourished revolt. But in Hungary, the Soviets proved that provided one pays the price by making full use of military force, it is not impossible, in the twentieth century, to crush an almost unanimous popular desire for resistance or liberation. The success of Gandhi or of anti-European revolts in our time has other causes than the cost of maintaining order against partisans.

It is true that in Hungary the Soviets, after taking over the repression themselves, did not exercise power directly, but turned it over to the Hungarian Communist party. Indeed, if we imagine that Great Britain or France were occupied tomorrow by that army called Red in memory of its past, the Soviet leaders would create a government called "worker and peasant" in

[16] George F. Kennan, in his *Reith Lectures* (London, 1958), has outlined a theory of this kind.

memory of 1917, composed of Communists and collaborators, leftists or realists who would rightfully regard their action as indispensable to the physical survival of the French or British people. In this eventuality, against a national Communist government, without the prospect of outside help, armed resistance would quickly cease and the conqueror would not have to carry on costly and interminable operations against the partisans.

It will be objected that one cannot *simultaneously fear massacres, enslavement and conversions.*[17] For the vanquished to be *converted,* they must not be *enslaved* or *massacred* in great numbers. Actually the Spanish conquerors in the past did not scorn to combine these three practices: people dispossessed of their culture were simultaneously evangelized. In our time the combination is more difficult because the religion is secular; it promises happiness in this world and not in the next, and proclaims the equality of individuals and of peoples. It is therefore true that, in the short run, the risk is above all that of *conversion,* which implies the loss of national independence and of those liberties that are incompatible with Sovietism. Massacre and enslavement in the traditional manner of Europeans in America and Africa would be less likely in the short run, though not permanently out of the question.

It would be more difficult for an American to argue the cause of unilateral disarmament in realistic terms.[18] First of all, the partial protection that the U.S. thermonuclear force confers on all states, allied or neutral, would disappear. As sole possessor of a nuclear force, the Soviet Union would be in a position to threaten without risk. No state would then be able to oppose the Soviet force with an equivalent one. Soviet Russia would have the physical means to destroy states, peoples and cultures without being exposed to the danger of retaliation. Whoever proposes unilateral disarmament must, if he wants to be moral, decide honestly for his part whether this *certain* omnipotence of the Soviet Union would be preferable to the permanent *risk* created by the thermonuclear duopoly.

This duopoly does not lead *inevitably* to total war; this possible war would not *inevitably* mean the extinction of one or both belligerents, or of the human race. The question is to compare the certain evils of a thermonuclear monopoly with the possible disasters involved in the duopoly. Once again, the comparison does not provide us with findings that are either precise or beyond question. No one knows the probability of a nuclear war in the course of the next ten or twenty years, nor the probability that in the absence of unilateral disarmament the two super powers may reach an agreement either

[17] Submission to a regime modeled on that of the victor.
[18] It may be asked why we consider the problem for the United States, and not for the Soviet Union. The reason is that the ideological unanimity imposed by the Soviet regime makes the question entirely academic in the East. No one there can argue the cause of unilateral disarmament. Moreover, the training received by Soviet citizens renders them impervious to propaganda for non-violence.

on mutual disarmament or on the transfer of decisive weapons to a neutral international authority. In short, acceptance of the nuclear duopoly need not be definitive and may lead to a monopoly less fearful than that of a state armed with a secular religion.

Let us leave aside these remote possibilities. Must we prefer the immediate certainty of a Soviet nuclear monopoly to the constant risks of the nuclear duopoly or of the arms race? Personally, I do not hesitate to answer *no* to such a question. The choice of unilateral disarmament has not become a responsible choice because of technological innovations; it remains a rejection of the political order, an individual moral decision, a decision that cannot be translated into a state decision.

The uncertainty of the future, which it is claimed would be eliminated by capitulation,[19] would persist in other forms. The people of the United States would no longer be exposed to nuclear bombardment because the Soviet Union would have other means of massacring, enslaving or converting. Incapable of defending itself, the United States would retain neither its standard of living nor its way of life (or at any rate, it would no longer be sure of retaining them). The future would not cease to be uncertain, but the present would become so. If a reader objects that the other states would respect the one which had thrown itself upon their mercy, he must prove that states will have a change of heart the day one of them provides the example of an abdication not contemptible but sublime. There is no need to endow states with any special perversity; it is enough to assume that they have remained what they have always been throughout history. Without arms, the people of the United States would be sure neither of the land they have cultivated nor the cities they have built, nor the wealth they now enjoy. Even if it is true that this wealth means nothing without the men who have accumulated it and who now maintain it, it requires a curious optimism to suppose that men of other races and other continents would not have illusions of an enormous booty offered to the conqueror.

Once again, the comparison between certainty and risk is a false one. The only certainty unilateral disarmament provides[20] would be the certainty of helplessness. Now helplessness, for a collectivity, means the greatest uncertainty. The slave who depends upon the whim of his master has no security. The state without arms, at the mercy of an armed state, has no security.

The only difference is that the day the nuclear monopoly was established in favor of a single power, mankind itself would no longer, in theory, be threatened with extinction. Still, it would remain to be proved that this

---

[19] Unilateral disarmament amounts to capitulation. Anyone who imagines that all states would follow the example provided by the first great power to disarm is a fool and not worth arguing with.

[20] It goes without saying that what we have in mind is total unilateral disarmament. Certain unilateral initiatives may be useful, in the area of disarmament, because they may provoke, without a formal agreement, analogous responses on the part of the other super power.

monopoly is definitive and that scientists will not create other means of destruction, presently unknown, capable of restoring the danger averted by capitulation. But assuming that this monopoly were lasting, even definitive: the risk of an extinction of the human race is for the moment minute, and if it increases, so will the efforts of princes to avoid war and to elaborate another kind of international relations. To accept the Kremlin's omnipotence *today* in order to eliminate *immediately* the infinitesimal chance of the extinction of mankind in a yet unforeseeable future is to make ourselves guilty of what Julien Benda called the ultimate *trahison des clers*: stupidity.

Only the path of disarmament offers a chance of salvation, according to Sir Charles Snow. Occupation rather than war, declares Commander King-Hall. Rather the triumph of the Soviet Union than recourse to thermonuclear weapons, proclaims Lord Russell. And yet not one of these three distinguished men would accept the label *moralist of conviction*. Two are scientists and claim to demonstrate that the policy they recommend is the most reasonable, even the only rational one. I have tried in the preceding pages to reveal the sophistries or distortion of facts by means of which they present as self-evident, irresistible, a line of reasoning to which it is easy to offer objections of at least equal weight. Their attitude is inspired by revolt against the horrors of the possible war: even if this attitude does not cause them to choose the worst solution, it does blind them to the arguments of those who choose differently.

This, I think, is the lesson to be learned from the controversies of our age. The relation between morality of conviction and morality of responsibility are no different today from what they have been down through the ages. The politician who obeys his heart without concerning himself with the consequences of his acts is failing the duties of his trust and is for this very reason immoral. The non-violent individual who refuses unconditionally to bear arms, indifferent to the consequences of his refusal for himself and for his country if his example is followed, may have a clear conscience, but he leaves the political world and must recognize the legitimacy of the sanctions he incurs. The morality of the citizen or of the leader of men can never be anything but a morality of responsibility, even if convictions that transcend the order of utility inspire this quest for something higher and determine its goals.

The original aspect of our age of thermonuclear bombs is the propensity to give an air of responsibility to decisions made for motives of conscience and without calculating the risks and advantages. For that matter, why should this be so surprising? Never has the statement "none of the evils men claim to avoid by war is as great an evil as war itself" seemed so true as it does today: and yet it is not true. Thermonuclear weapons make it possible to exterminate the enemy population in the course of hostilities. But extermination after capitulation has always been one of the possible expressions of victory. The capitulation of one of the duopolists would not necessarily mark the end of the danger. This capitulation being out of the question, it is futile to transfigure a partial measure which may be opportune or which may be more dangerous than useful, and to pretend that it alone opens a path to salvation.

Mankind has not been able to gain mastery of cosmic forces without becoming master of its own life and death. Diplomatic-strategic action, like technological action, can be reasonable only on condition that it is calculating. But what it calculates is the reaction of another intelligent being, not the resistance of metals. Lacking rigorous criteria, it cannot define what the other's rational reaction would be. It can and must hope that this reaction will be reasonable.

chapter XXI

In Search of a Strategy

I: *To Arm or Disarm?*

The existence of thermonuclear weapons does not change the nature of the morality of diplomatic-strategic action: such is the conclusion of the foregoing chapters.

To be sure, it ridicules the traditional rhetoric concerning the regenerative influence of war or the courage of peoples. It makes clear the dissociation between the conditions of military force and the conditions of creative vitality or of the harmonious community. A state which, by virtue of its possession of thermonuclear arms and ballistic missiles, possesses the means to terrorize and even to exterminate the rest of the human race has not therefore given proof of the merits that would single it out as fit to rule the world. Perhaps it was too optimistic, but it was not absurd to have stated, as Proudhon did, that a people had no right to form an independent state unless they were capable of defending themselves. The same reasoning would suggest today that only a few giant states have a legitimate claim to independence.

If thermonuclear weapons have perhaps changed the meaning of war, of martial virtues and of the independence of states, if the texts we borrowed from Treitschke manifestly belong to another age and not to the century of Hiroshima and Nagasaki, the practical-moral problems facing politicians are not fundamentally different; contrary to appearances, they have become more complex rather than simpler. All those who act, individuals and collectivities, have always had a tendency to consider the short rather than the long run, their own interests rather than those of the collectivity to which they belong, i.e., the advantages afforded by a certain action rather than the repercussions which this action will inevitably provoke. In the thermonuclear age this propensity on the part of the actors runs the risk of being fatal. The statesman who makes the decision, in France, to manufacture atomic bombs must, if he wants to be genuinely realistic, consider the consequences of the expansion of the atomic club and not only the advantage France might derive from being its fourth member. The statesman who, in the United States, wants Congress to approve a vast program of civil defense should consider the countermeasures which the Soviet Union would not fail to take. Finally—and this is both the simplest and the most important idea— *the aim of each of the super powers is to conquer the other without war and not to conquer "so oder so."*

The common interest of the two super powers, the common interest of mankind that there be no thermonuclear war,[1] is as great a consideration, and should be a greater one, than the limited stakes of each conflict. No statesman can define the national interest for which he is responsible without including in it the advantage of peace. Unfortunately, any statesman of the two super powers who was constantly aware of the disproportion between the stake and the cost of a potential war would condemn himself to beating a retreat each time there was or seemed to be a risk of explosion; thus he would condemn himself for losing, one after another, the stakes of all partial conflicts. But if each of these stakes is modest, are they still so all together?

The only way to resolve this antinomy—either to accept risks disproportionate to the particular stake or else to risk losing all the individual stakes— is for the two super powers[2] to create conditions such that they do not need to brandish the thermonuclear threat or, at least, that neither need brandish it except in circumstances so rare, for stakes so considerable, that the other cannot commit an error in judgment and has no temptation to risk its execution. How are such conditions to be created? I see two means: that of disarmament (in a broad sense which we shall specify), and that of a strategy-diplomacy reducing the role of deterrence and reinforcing that of defense. These two means intersect, and it is not easy to follow one or the other to its end.

1. Peace by Fear

The development of weapons of massive destruction has suggested a concept of possible if not eternal peace, which I have already referred to in passing and which a great many writers, in the course of the last few years, have entertained more or less seriously: the concept of peace by fear.

The idea is not new. It is over a century since the statement "war will kill itself" was advanced and found occasional acceptance, actually during periods of relative peace. Belied by a fresh outbreak of the monster of war, hope was soon rekindled by the development of a method of killing more men more quickly: the thermonuclear bomb, which amounted to a qualitative revolution so great was the quantitative increase in explosive power, gave this classic theme an actuality it had never had before. Friedrich Engels was

---

[1] It is not entirely true that this is the interest of the *whole* human race. Perhaps the Chinese would not be sorry to see a Russo-American war.
[2] Or for whichever one is inclined to give in.

mistaken when he thought that the development of military technique was nearly complete; the writers of the last century were mistaken when they counted on the machine gun and the cannon to prevent killing; the theorists of the period between the wars were mistaken when they prophesied the end of civilization in the event of a second world war: all these mistakes still do not prove that we are wrong to count on thermonuclear deterrence to prevent a third world war.

The thesis of "peace by fear" has three different versions, which are not always clearly distinguished but which are logically and historically separable. The extreme thesis would be that of *the possible generalization and duration* of peace by fear: the spread of atomic or thermonuclear arms would create by degrees the same kind of peace between all states as the peace that reigns today between the United States and the Soviet Union. A second version would be that of the peace between "nuclear" states which refuse to fight one another even with conventional weapons alone, for fear of escalation. Finally, a third, more modest version would merely hold that a thermonuclear war is impossible since the belligerents, even if they have access to these weapons, refuse to use them for fear of reprisal.

Of these three versions it is the first which is the most improbable, and it is also the only one that presents itself as a doctrine of peace. The other two amount to hypotheses concerning the possible course of events, given the present situation. They indicate the objectives of a conceivable strategy as much as they formulate hypotheses concerning the future. In any case, they operate within the context of the existing diplomatic strategy.

The extreme version of peace by fear can hardly be taken seriously, but it exercises a kind of fascination over a certain type of mind, it possesses a pseudo-logical probability, it lends itself to an allegedly rational formulation. Hence it is not entirely pointless to indicate why it cannot be accepted.

If it is enough for two states to have the means of "atomizing" one another for them to lay down their arms, why not give such means to all states? In this way eternal peace would presumably be established. The skeptics find themselves accused of the grim desire to "save war" by humanizing it (i.e., de-atomizing it). The error in this argument is twofold: peace between the possessors of thermonuclear forces *is not* assured. Assuming that it is at least probable, it is impossible to generalize it by promoting the spread of atomic arms.

Let us begin with the second proposition. The probability of peace between the possessors of thermonuclear arms is based on the hypothesis that reality resembles the model of "equality of crime and punishment," and not the two other possible models (the two gangsters, the disproportion of punishment to crime). But between two small states, at least during the coming phase, atomic arms are more likely to create the temptations and anxieties of "the two gangsters" than the security of justice. A state whose territory is small would be devastated before it exercised a posthumous vengeance (again, provided the means of retaliation are not destroyed by the attack which would have struck the peoples and their cities).

An increase in the number of states belonging to the atomic club would add two other factors of instability: the possibility of launching a war, whether intentional or not, between the super powers as a result of a small state's voluntary or involuntary action, and the greater probability of a war provoked by a statesman's so-called irrational decision.

The hypothesis of peace by fear between the super powers breaks down into a series of propositions. None of the advantages that might be brought about by victory could be compared to the calculated cost of a thermonuclear exchange. Each of the duopolists reasons in this way and knows that the other does so too. Neither lives with the obsession that the other is going to attack it. Neither one has its finger on the trigger. Each relies on both its capacity for reprisal and on what it calls the enemy's rationality. This kind of security would not withstand the indefinite expansion of the atomic club. The member of a bloc in possession of a small striking force would be in a position, under certain circumstances and by certain initiatives, to set off hostilities between the super powers against their will. In other words, the international structure of a duopoly involves fewer unknown factors than a structure characterized by an increasing number of military sovereignties. Two actors have a better chance of conducting a duel according to their intentions than four or five actors in conflict, with several possible groupings.

If an event which is not consistent with the desires of the super powers is rendered less probable by polyarchy, it renders the so-called irrational or irresponsible conduct of a diplomat-strategist more likely. We have not succeeded at any point in this book in giving an unambiguous definition of rational conduct, and on occasion we have even shown why the definitions that have been attempted failed in their purpose. We shall later muster[3] the various arguments we have encountered in the course of our discussion. But, to avoid a pseudo-precision and to return to popular terminology, we shall merely say: the fear that future possessors of atomic or thermonuclear weapons will not conduct themselves in a "rational" manner is well founded.

It is not easy to determine whether the diplomatic use of the thermonuclear threat is ever "rational." Perhaps it would be irrational to execute this threat when the first blow struck by the enemy has destroyed the greater part of our thermonuclear forces. But at least let us assume that those in charge of the two major states and of the two thermonuclear forces are calm, reflective, that they do not act on impulse, that up to the last moment they will weigh the alternatives before giving orders the result of which might be millions of deaths. Let us also assume that on both sides such orders cannot be given on a lower level of the hierarchy, that the chain of command, like the network of communications, would stand the test of an international crisis. Such as-

[3] See below, Final Note.

sumptions have less chance of being true for five states than for two, for states less precisely organized, less accustomed to the handling of modern technology than the duopolists.

The preceding remarks have a strictly limited meaning and objective. Between the two antinomic theses, each of which has its partisans—peace through the generalization of thermonuclear deterrence and the dangers created by enlargement of the atomic club—I do not hesitate to choose: the first is illusory, deceptively seductive, it has the characteristic appeal of sophistries. In short, *it is war which must be saved,* in other words, the possibility of tests of armed strength between states rather than eternal peace, which would have to be established by the constant threat of the thermonuclear holocaust.

We might go further still and consider whether a generalized peace by terror is actually a possible model for eternal peace (or even merely a lasting peace). Among the four models of international systems not yet realized but conceivable, Morton A. Kaplan has advanced what he calls the unit veto system, the system of the *liberum veto.* Just as a single dissenting voice paralyzed the Polish Diet, each actor—and not just each principal actor—would have not the right but the capacity to paralyze any other actor by actually threatening him with death. Every state would have the capacity to deter any other because it would have the means either to exercise mortal retaliation against the aggressor or to effect the extinction of the entire human race. The first hypothesis would require the small states to be in a position to render their thermonuclear force invulnerable, that is, in general, to locate it outside their territory, to bury it in the earth or disperse it in the depths of the ocean. The second hypothesis—that of a Doomsday device—will long, if not forever, exceed the resources of small or medium-size states. Even the super powers will probably not decide to construct a machine which, in the event of a "technical error," would seal the fate of mankind along with that of whichever state had constructed it.

The outclassing of the small states by the great does not therefore seem to be a phenomenon of short duration. We do not yet perceive on the historical horizon a reversal favorable to the small states. To be sure, it is conceivable that the latter may acquire weapons which, even in responding to aggression, would cause serious damage to the great power. But they would still be vulnerable to a strategy of intimidation, so great would be the disparity of dangers, and the smallness of their territory being a further cause of inferiority. It is true that other techniques—chemical, bacteriological—could be used for the mass extermination of human beings. It is not entirely impossible that these techniques might be less costly than thermonuclear and especially ballistic-missile technique, and that consequently they might offer the small states a chance to possess arms qualitatively similar to those of the great powers. But these do not seem to be immediate prospects.

Let us add that the international system of *liberum veto,* in all probability, would not be lasting. The great powers would rightfully regard it as intolerable. Well before it was put into effect, the great powers would have agreed to prevent the small states from jeopardizing their superiority. *No international system has ever been, or ever can be, equalitarian.* In the absence of a single authority, a reduction of the number of principal actors is indispensable to a minimum of order and predictability.

If the doctrinal version of peace by fear is, upon reflection, indefensible, the same is not true of the two moderate versions, the one whereby possessors of thermonuclear arms will not attack one another directly, even with conventional weapons, or at most will fight with conventional weapons. This is a hypothesis based on limited experience, and concerned with objectives which the duopolists can accept. The best method of estimating the degree of stability of peace by fear is to consider the circumstances under which the duopolists, by the desire of one or without the intention of either, might use against each other the weapons with which they threaten each other but which they do not intend to launch.

American writers have made up a list of the typical cases in which the "war nobody wants" would occur in spite of the fear it inspires. In one form or another, they arrive at approximately the following list:

1. The stability of peace by fear presupposes the approximate equality of crime and of punishment. But this stability is not definitively acquired. It is constantly being threatened as a result of the "qualitative arms race." One of the super powers may acquire a superiority such that it considers itself in a position to eliminate its rival at a cost acceptable to itself or again may believe it can impose its will on its rival without the latter's daring to resist. In the first case it would take the initiative; in the second, it is the duopolist in an inferior position which would reply to an extreme provocation by an initiative motivated by fear but fatal to both. Let us say that the breaking of the balance of terror by a technical breakthrough would create a risk—difficult to evaluate but real—of the war for which men are preparing but which they do not want to wage.

2. Even if one of the super powers is not sure of a distinct superiority over its rival, it may happen that both imagine they are reduced to the situation of the two gangsters, each believing that the advantage of attacking first is enormous and constitutes the difference between (relative) victory and defeat, between survival and disappearance. The magnitude of the retaliation to be feared is still too great for either to launch its thermonuclear force in cold blood. But each will be tempted if it suspects its rival is about to do so. Hence all that is required is a misunderstanding concerning the other's intentions for either one of the duopolists to have a so-called rational motive for doing what fear presumably forbids. This second case, usually called *war by misunderstanding,* requires a certain instability in the balance, hence places a premium on initiative.

3. Finally, even assuming that the balance of terror persists, an "accident" may occur; the inaccurate reading of an instrument, the explosion of a bomb, may give the impression of an attack; a break in the system of communications or the hierarchy of command may enable an officer of lower rank to give an order on his own responsibility that will provoke the explosion, etc. In other words, the "accident" can be either technical or social.

4. A fourth case is that of an escalation as a result of an armed conflict in which one or both of the super powers would be implicated. This escalation is obviously more to be feared in proportion to the advantage of striking first, and to the fear each of the duopolists entertains of its enemy's initiative. Escalation would therefore involve a certain element of misunderstanding or of *rage*.

5. A final eventuality is the one in which the explosion would be provoked by a third state, whether or not it possesses thermonuclear weapons. If it does possess them it may, voluntarily or not, involve the super powers in an inexpiable war which the latter do not desire but which would be consistent with the interest of the *tertius gaudens*. If it does not possess nuclear weapons, one of the duopolists may use or threaten to use its thermonuclear force against it and thereby provoke its rival's intervention.

No one can claim that this list is exhaustive, and the cases enumerated, though conceptually distinct, may be more or less mingled in reality. What is the probability of each of these eventualities? What is the probability of all these eventualities together? I am not sure that any observer, mathematician or political analyst is in a position to give a precise and sure answer. What we are dealing with is, in fact, neither a purely mathematical probability (if we increase the number of thermonuclear bombs, one day or another a bomb will explode by accident) nor a purely political probability (in the event of a duel between two states armed with thermonuclear forces, it is inevitable that one or the other or both will eventually decide to settle their differences by war). The probability is of a mixed character, it depends on technological factors (the results of the race for technological progress) and psycho-political factors. It differs in kind from all known arms races.

For the time being let us waive this perhaps futile question: are these illusory fears, since the real fear inspired by thermonuclear war assures an effective protection against it? Let us merely confront the conclusions of the two analyses, one devoted to the doctrinal version of peace by fear, and the other to the two pragmatic versions. The first has led us to the following proposition: it is impossible to imagine a general and lasting peace by the spread of thermonuclear weapons to all states. The second has led us to the following proposition: even between two states that are the sole possessors of a thermonuclear force, fear does not guarantee peace. But obviously we have not disproved the self-evident proposition that the fear of thermonuclear war urges moderation upon diplomats. We shall add the proposition complementary to this: if atomic or thermonuclear weapons could be eliminated, given the international system as it is, a general war would be more rather than less likely. There is every reason to think that a general war, waged with ballistic missiles and thermonuclear bombs, would be more horrible than all those of the past, but there is no reason to think that the global system would be more peaceful than the partial systems of bygone millenniums if the great powers did not possess these terrifying weapons.

This fundamental antinomy obliges those who, like the author of this book, desire to reduce the role of force in international relations, to consider the function of disarmament in a stategy whose goal is peace or, at least, the diminution of the volume of historical violence.

2. Peace by Disarmament

We have examined and, if possible, dissipated the illusion of *peace by fear*. Now, going to the other extreme, we should like to examine and dissipate the analogous illusion of *peace by disarmament*.

Traditionally, three expressions have been used: *disarmament, reduction of arms* and *arms control*. The first evokes the idea of a world in which states have renounced the means of fighting one another, that is, have put their battleships and airplane carriers on the scrap heap, have blown up their cannon and their fortifications, disbanded their regiments and kept only those police forces necessary, as they say, for the maintenance of order. Auguste Comte, always an extremist, did not hesitate to predict the transformation of standing armies into constabularies. This vision of the future, whether probable or possible, has always been Utopian in the pejorative sense of the word, in that it was a representation of a world different from the real one, incompatible with the nature of man and societies, and did not even indicate the path toward an accessible objective.

There is scarcely any need to prove at length that states, such as we know them in the 1960s, divided as to good and evil (or, to put it differently, as to the notion of the good society), convinced of their mutually hostile intentions, are neither capable nor desirous of renouncing the means of war, or in other words their capacity to defend their interests and to impose their wills by threats or arms. The hierarchy of the great and small powers would disappear in this imaginary universe; still, the inequality of the "police forces" necessary to "maintain order" would run the risk of re-establishing a hierarchy and provoking interminable debate over the matter of the "police forces" tolerated by the general and total disarmament treaty. A system without a hierarchy of power, without a supreme tribunal, without a monopoly of strength, is truly inconceivable. It is an ideal type, if you will, but one that is misconceived because it cannot be realized.

Fundamentally, the theory of peace by disarmament, for the millenniums preceding the development of weapons of massive destruction, was inapplicable for the following reasons: politicians have never regarded peace—or, if you prefer, the non-use of force—as more important for them than certain interests (territory, natural resources, booty). Only those who despaired in advance of surviving or emerging victorious from the test of war would therefore have subscribed to a peace by disarmament. Assuming that the princes would have agreed to submit their differences to a judgment other than that of arms, what could have been the nature of the tribunal of justice replacing the tribunal of war? Finally, the distinction between the force necessary to support the throne and the force necessary to conquer provinces was not sufficiently clear for even the idea of transforming all armies into police forces to have a meaning. The pacification of relations between states presupposes the pacification of relations between citizens (or parties, or provinces) within states. To some extent, all politics were violent, not only international politics.

Does intra-state or intra-bloc pacification make it possible to imagine, if not to achieve, a pacification of inter-state or inter-bloc relations? It seems to me that we must reluctantly but resolutely answer *no* to such a question. Within the nations longest established, like the French nation, no social group or political party has definitively renounced the use of force to defend either its assets or its ideals. The "police forces" necessary to "maintain order" against peasant uprisings or a Communist revolution should not be insignificant. But above all a large portion of humanity has not yet achieved national consciousness, either because individuals remain the prisoners of tribal customs, on this side of the state and the nation, or because the political units established today are unsure of themselves and of their future (either large and non-cohesive like India, or small and weak like Gabon or Mauritania). In both cases it is just as difficult to imagine the indefinite continuation of the status quo as the latter's non-violent transformation. Can nations grow without opposing one another, can they assert their existence without finding an enemy?

Let us grant for the moment that a tribunal of justice can theoretically, according to men's desires and economic-social circumstances, pronounce verdicts which may prevent or check bloodshed, which may enable nations to appear and to become aware of themselves without combating enemies within and without. Such a tribunal would presuppose an agreement among the great powers as to both a ratio of forces and the definition of just and unjust. Given the conflict between the duopolists, on the plane of force and on the plane of ideas, the third world is itself condemned to follow the path of violence with the sole hope that in their mutual interest, that of avoiding a total war, the two super powers will try to limit the hostilities which might break out in one place or another.

Finally, since the super powers are obliged, in order to maintain their positions, to retain a substantial quantity of conventional weapons, that disarmament which is held to be the prerequisite of peace would be concerned first and foremost with atomic and thermonuclear bombs on the one hand and with delivery systems on the other. But at this point a contradiction arises which is created by technology but which reveals a fundamental perplexity in the policy.

The elimination of atomic or thermonuclear weapons is all the more difficult as the verification of an eventual agreement is more uncertain and as the violation of the treaty would be likely to produce higher dividends. Let us remember the Washington Treaty on the limitations of naval armaments: no measure was provided to insure respect for the promises made. The five states—the United States, Great Britain, Japan, France, Italy—had less confidence in one another than they did in the ability of news to travel. It was considered impossible to build a battleship in secret. The commissions for control of German disarmament were not entirely effective. Nevertheless, until the time when the rearmament of the Third Reich was openly begun, Germany remained militarily weak and France, alone or with her network of alliances, would have been in a position to impose her will on Germany, if she had had a will.

Whether in the case of atomic bombs or of means of delivery, it is impossible to have a reasonable assurance that the agreement by which the two super powers promised to eliminate them would be respected. No one knows where, in the Soviet Union and the United States, the thermonuclear bombs are stockpiled. Even if officials were authorized to travel freely through the immense territory of the two super powers, they would have no chance of discovering all the places where such weapons were concealed, if we assume that one or the other power was firmly resolved to preserve a certain stock of thermonuclear bombs in violation of the treaty. The resources of concealment are, in the present state of affairs, greater than the resources of inspection.

Nor is it any more possible to eliminate the means of delivery. Underground launching platforms have become difficult to detect. In the event of the elimination of ballistic missiles, any commercial airplane would suffice, with or without modifications, to transport an atomic or thermonuclear bomb. Finally, preparations for chemical and bacteriological warfare can be camouflaged even more easily. The principal states possess stockpiles of gas bombs which attack the nerves and cause either almost instantaneous death or a more or less temporary paralysis. In the absence of atomic, thermonuclear or radiological means, chemical weapons of mass destruction would still be available.

Now, the advantages of fraud have not increased less rapidly than the difficulties of control. Let us suppose that one of the two super powers, after having signed a treaty providing for the destruction of all atomic and thermonuclear bombs, has managed to conceal several hundred of these weapons: this power could terrorize the rest of the world. The treaty limiting naval armaments was signed because it was almost sure to be respected by all and because marginal violations had only mediocre consequences. A treaty calling for wholesale atomic disarmament will never be signed because its control would be impossible and because the possible consequences of fraud would be beyond measure. No one trusts a rival's honesty if the reward for breaking one's word can be world dominion.

Reasoning of this kind has seemed so convincing to almost all who have reflected on these problems that the thesis of peace by disarmament has scarcely any more partisans than the thesis of (general and lasting) peace by fear. It is just as bizarre to imagine that industrial societies will live in peace because they will no longer have the means to fight as it is to imagine that they will live in peace because they will all have the means to destroy each other in a few moments. The seemingly opposite intellectual error is actually the same in both cases. The doctrinaire of peace by fear imagines an equality between states by the capacity of the weakest to deal the strongest a mortal blow. The doctrinaire of peace by disarmament imagines the equality to consist in the inability of the strongest to coerce the weakest. Neither equality is attainable. Neither equality is or would be acceptable to the super powers.

These two doctrines have yet another point in common: they are based on a conception of an international system in which peace would be insured automatically, as it were, without the intervention of men and their free decisions. In order that the world of a thermonuclear *liberum veto* might not seem infernal, one presupposes a rational *Homo diplomaticus,* in a certain number of examples. That the world of states without weapons might seem secure, one presupposes citizens and states who are resolved never to resort to force on the pretext that they have flung traditional or modern weapons on the scrap heap or to the bottom of the sea. It is unjustifiable and absurd to put politicians, individuals or groups, citizens or diplomats between parentheses. There is no infallible "gimmick"—armament or disarmament—which will guarantee definitive peace to a violent and divided humanity.

If general and total disarmament is no more the secret of eternal peace than the generalization of the balance of terror, the policy of armament, like the fear of a thermonuclear war, has a certain influence upon the risk of a conflict and the character the latter would assume. Just as after having dissipated the illusion of peace by fear we advanced the idea that the fear of war could be the beginning of wisdom, similarly, after having dissipated the illusion of peace by disarmament, we do not exclude the possibility that the policy of armament may be one of the factors of peace and of war.

So long as there remains a plurality of military sovereignties, it is impossible to assert that in and of itself the reduction of arms is favorable or unfavorable to the maintenance of peace. The limitation of one type of arms (battleships) shifts rather than abolishes the rivalry. If one of the great powers (the United States, for example) reduces its peacetime arms level below its potential, it encourages rival states to underrate the force it is capable of mobilizing or the resolution it will evince in the course of the hostilities. Similarly, if one side does not rearm or does not arm quickly enough, whereas the opposing side rushes into an extensive arms program, this acceptance of inferiority is often of a nature to precipitate rather than prevent the explosion. In the international system of which history provides examples, the balance of power has never, in the long run, prevented wars, but the acceptance of imbalance has sometimes hastened or provoked a particular conflict which was not inevitable, at least at the time when it occurred.

Historically, the arms policies which seem to have been most favorable to the reduction of violence are policies of limitation, not the result of a unilateral decision or a negotiated agreement, but the object of an implicit agreement between the principal actors. The Washington naval treaty or the one Great Britain signed with Hitler in 1935 had, by the most generous interpretation, no effect—either favorable or unfavorable—on the course of events. The two wars which it was hoped could be avoided by preventing an arms race—the war between the United States and Japan, the war between Great Britain and the Third Reich—both took place, without even their dates having been affected, probably, by the treaties. On the other hand, during the nineteenth century the European states more or less deliberately avoided mobilizing, either in peacetime or in wartime, all the resources theoretically available.

That these implicit and half-conscious agreements of arms control have contributed most effectively to what we might call the "reduction of the volume of historical violence" is almost self-explanatory. When states can or will mobilize only a fraction of their theoretically available resources, it is either because internal regimes are restraining this mobilization, or because the people do not believe in an immediate danger, or because they do not attribute great significance to any foreseeable conflicts. In all cases, hostilities will be less frequent, and less costly in lives and in wealth.

On the other hand, the disparity of forces created by disarmament or even the slightest unilateral rearmament encourages the unsatisfied state or the side which has taken the initiative in rearmament. As for arms-control treaties, they are the symptom of the fears of peoples or governments. Disarmament conferences multiply when nations fear war and vaguely perceive the seriousness of conflicts on the international plane. Whether or not these conferences come to anything, they do not cure the evil, that is, the not artificial but real and justified hostility between states.

An arms policy, whether it involves increase or decrease, should not be judged in the abstract, but in terms of the situation.[4] It cannot be called good or bad in itself, but only in relation to circumstances, to the existing territorial status, to the ambitions of certain persons, to the comparative

---

[4] It goes without saying that this statement presupposes that we judge an arms policy in terms of the probability of war or peace and of the volume of violence. Economically or morally, the reduction of arms may be considered good in itself.

strength of revisionist and conservative states. What happens to this principle in the age of thermonuclear bombs and ballistic missiles? Actually, it remains valid but its application becomes more complex and involves certain new aspects.

The traditional arms policy sometimes sought to prevent war, but it always sought to win that war if it broke out in spite of everything. For the moment, the arms policy adopted by the two super powers seems virtually to overlook the concern for victory and to have no other object than the perpetuation of non-war (or at any rate non-thermonuclear war). To the extent that deterrence completely replaces defense, everything proceeds as if the actors were identifying peace with victory and were unconcerned with the future in the event that deterrence should fail. But no one would say that this strategy is reasonable; in fact, the arms policy should tend to reduce the volume of violence, even or especially if war breaks out.

Formerly, one would have said that the formula "to reduce the volume of violence" means to reduce the frequency and intensity of war. But already, throughout history, the intensity of wars has sometimes been all the greater when they were less frequent. Before 1914 European societies had lived in peace, at least on the Continent, for almost half a century. The security of individuals within the states was better insured than it had ever been before. Party rivalry occurred without or almost without recourse to physical force. Even strikes, the traditional means by which one social group seeks to force its will on another, rarely gave rise to violence and still more rarely to casualties. Living conditions, the stability of the administration, which had favored the pacification of social existence, favored the mobilization of human and material resources, once the call to arms was sounded. A government which acquires ways of imposing peace upon citizens thereby acquires the means of fighting abroad.

The classical antithesis between frequency and intensity is henceforth transformed by the availability of thermonuclear weapons. The strategy of deterrence, as expounded in the British white paper of 1957, presupposes the *possibility* that a thermonuclear war will never take place and the *probability* that this war, if it does break out, will be fought with all available weapons.

But almost without exception,[5] observers have realized that the threat of a war that would mean unlimited destruction could not be brandished on every occasion. The greater the horror of thermonuclear war, the less plausible the threat to resort to it, and the less improbable the eventuality of armed conflicts in which atomic or thermonuclear weapons would not be used.

---

[5] The most notable exception is General Gallois who, for that matter, holds that all wars can be prevented by providing all states with atomic or thermonuclear arms. He proves this thesis by the argument of proportional deterrence.

Such, in effect, is the first dilemma confronting statesmen in our age: do they wish to save war or save humanity from a certain war (thermonuclear war)? Do they seek to erase the distinction between conventional and atomic weapons in the hope that, if the latter are used in any conflict, no one will resort to *any* weapon at all? Or, convinced that states are not yet ready to settle their differences peacefully, do they anticipate the possibility of hostilities in which the belligerents would fight with conventional weapons for limited stakes? Up to now, the West has accepted the first alternative in Europe, the second in the rest of the world. Generally speaking, it is the second alternative which strikes me as the more reasonable. The first suffers from a fundamental contradiction: *one cannot maintain that the thermonuclear holocaust is too horrible for anyone to launch it and at the same time count on the effectiveness of this threat in most circumstances.* If the first assertion is true, there will rise a statesman who does not believe in a threat that the other party nonetheless made in earnest.

Let us restate the two propositions which we have tried to establish in this section: it is impossible to imagine, the international system being what it is, a controlled disarmament which would deprive the two super powers of their weapons of mass destruction. It is impossible to imagine the definitive abolition of armed conflict, even among members of the atomic club, by the strategy of deterrence, that is, the threat of using thermonuclear weapons. The translation into action of the traditional objective of "reducing the volume of violence" presupposes a difficult pursuit of a *political-military conduct according to which the two super powers would reduce to a minimum the risk of being involved in spite of themselves in a war they do not want to wage, without either of the two being favored in the prosecution of the cold war.* American writers have invented the new concept, *arms control,* to designate the military aspect of this proceeding that would correspond to the enemies' mutual interest by preserving them both from a war they fear without condemning either one to defeat.

The French expression *contrôle des armements* is ambiguous, suggesting the control of the agreements concluded between states, whereas the American writers have in mind the whole group of unilateral or coordinated measures, the ensemble of implicit or explicit agreements by which states are trying to reduce the volume of violence in the thermonuclear age, hence primarily but not exclusively to prevent thermonuclear war. But to prevent thermonuclear war is to reduce as much as possible the risks of a thermonuclear war by pre-emption, by misunderstanding, by technical or human accident, by escalation, by the diabolical ruse of a small power. The risks are a function of the total situation, of the relation between the forces and arms systems available to both sides. This is not all: the procedures implied by "arms control" also aim at reducing the volume of violence in the case of a limited war, whether tactical atomic weapons are employed or not. They aim, in short, at "limiting the volume of violence," even assuming ballistic missiles armed with thermonuclear warheads had been exchanged—that is, they seek to maintain communications between the enemies with a view to ending hostilities either by agreement between the two, or by the capitulation of one of them.

Thus conceived, arms control would be better designated by the terms *arms policy* or *policy of armament and disarmament*. The main idea is, in fact, that of the inevitable solidarity between what is done in peacetime and what will happen in wartime, between military preparations and diplomacy, between what I do and what my enemy does, between measures of national defense and the probability of war (or of a certain war). This main idea may be deduced from Clausewitz's two principles which we recalled in the first chapter of this work, namely the continuity of peaceful or warlike relations between states, the consequences of reciprocity of action[6] and the danger, as one reprisal leads to another, of escalation. But these two principles assume a more tragic meaning in our age than in the past, because the value of time and the destructive capacity of weapons have changed qualitatively. States have always waged war with weapons accumulated in time of peace. But from 1914 to 1918 they had time to continue their mobilization after the beginning of hostilities, and the intervention of neutral states tipped the scale. Even if the weapons are conventional or atomic tomorrow, time will be short. To avoid escalation, the hostilities must be brief: the troublemaker must create a *fait accompli* in order to assume a defensive position immediately and to force the conservative party or side to take the offensive or resign itself to losing the stake. With strategic bombers it required hours to reach Moscow from Washington (or Washington from Moscow). With ballistic missiles the duration of the trajectory is reckoned in minutes (thirty). As for the probable destruction, it was already great before 1939 but the progression is of kind, not of degree, since we have leaped from several tons to several million tons.

Arms control involves or may involve measures to reduce armaments, but it can also involve, on the rational level, measures to increase armaments: three hundred invulnerable ballistic missiles on both sides contribute more "stability" to the balance of terror than one hundred such missiles. Arms control is therefore the pursuit of a national defense adopted by one or several friendly or rival states, with a view to insuring each state and all together the maximum security of each with respect to a possible aggression. In short, this is a case of a combined policy of armament and disarmament whose objective would be the control of the instruments of death by all mankind. If there existed only a single military sovereignty, mankind, at least in theory, would easily attain this control. Is this control attainable by mankind taken as a whole, as long as each sovereign power considers the measures proposed in relation to its *own* advantage in competition rather than in relation to the

---

[6] Or the dialectic of antagonism.

common interest of the system, that is, in the interest of avoiding thermo-nuclear violence?

3. In Search Of Stability

To the problem posed in this way—What defense policy offers the greatest chance of waging the cold war without permitting its degeneration into a thermonuclear war?—American writers have almost unanimously offered two principal answers: limit the number of members in the atomic club and in-sure the invulnerability of retaliatory weapons, while curing both major powers of any illusions regarding such invulnerability.

When I was writing this book, in 1960–61, negotiations for the suspension of nuclear testing had been under way for several years, and I predicted their temporary breakdown. In fact, the Soviet Union instituted a new series of tests at the end of 1961, and in turn the United States started a new series of tests. The qualitative arms race was speeded up, but after the Cuban crisis in the fall of 1962, negotiations were resumed in 1963, and led very quickly to a test ban treaty. This treaty, however, is incomplete for two reasons: underground tests are not prohibited, because an agreement on this point would have necessitated on-site inspections, which the Soviets have steadfastly refused to permit; and on the other hand, any signatory can abro-gate the treaty with three months' notice. The course of events—long and sterile negotiations from 1958–61, a moratorium on testing unilaterally an-nounced by each of the Big Two, the sudden resumption of testing by the U.S.S.R., and the rapid agreement on a partial test ban treaty when the leaders in Moscow decided to cooperate—this course of events is significant and carries a lesson.

I will not review the reasons for which President Kennedy and his ad-visers wanted a test ban treaty (to prevent or delay increased membership in the atomic club, to perfect a new system of inspection, or to create a favorable climate for wider agreements). It has also been explained why the French leaders, even though they recognized their obligations toward the world community, could decide with a clear conscience that the advantages for France (in developing an independent French deterrent) outweighed the disadvantages *for the system* from a global point of view. Why close the door of the club after the entrance of the third member, and not after that of the fourth?

The theory of limiting membership in the atomic club, despite its apparent logic, is basically unrealistic within the context of the present situation. In any case, this theory presupposes that states are able to adopt, because of the hard facts of the Atomic Age, a behavior *basically different* from that which they have displayed throughout the course of history. In 1963, the two states which were determined to acquire nuclear arms, France and China, did not sign the Moscow treaty. The first Chinese bomb was exploded in 1963, and several nations of the "third world" sent their congratulations to Mao Tse-tung, in spite of their customary hostility to atomic arms.

In the extent to which only France and China intended to continue testing, the diplomatic marathon in Geneva from 1958–61 was an attempt at a treaty between enemies against their respective allies: a logical attempt, since the enemies had in fact a common interest in closing the doors of the atomic club, but could neither admit their objectives nor force other nations to abide by their decision. Why did this attempt fail in 1961, and partially succeed in 1963?

In 1961, I discerned three probable reasons for the failure.

A test ban treaty could not have been enforced without the consent of China. I have always wondered why the new dynasty of the Middle Kingdom, or if one objects to this irreverent reference to the past, why the Communist party, having through its own efforts won the Civil War, should agree to renounce today's decisive weapon, the weapon that, whether one likes it or not, determines or seems to determine the hierarchy of actors on the international scene. Moscow, since 1951, had a stake in protecting China against the risk of American aggression, by means of a mutual aid treaty. It had no interest in giving China the means to institute an offensive strategy in the Formosa Strait, a strategy that, for strictly Chinese objectives, could have exposed the Soviet Union to a conflict with the United States.

Since 1961, the Chinese have revealed to the world their quarrels with the men in the Kremlin on the subject of atomic weapons, the treaty of 1957, and the unilateral denunciation of that treaty by Moscow in 1959 (one year after the military operations in the Formosa Strait). The arguments advanced by the American and Russian leaders to their respective allies, France and China, are peculiarly, or rather inevitably, similar. "How could the Soviet Union withhold its support of Chinese objectives, if I supported yours? Besides, my deterrent force is entirely sufficient to insure your security," asserts one camp. "The Soviet deterrent force is sufficient to protect the entire socialist camp, and the United States would have difficulty in resisting the demands of the German *revanchards*, if we offered them any pretext or justification," repeats the other camp. Each of the Big Two pleads the cause of limiting the spread of atomic weapons by invoking the eventual reaction of its brother-enemy if this cause were ignored. A perfectly logical and even reasonable policy if you will, but reasonable or not, the response of France and China is equally logical. I have never been able to believe that a nation as powerful and as proud as China could permanently resign herself to such a fundamental inferiority.

Between 1961 and 1963, the Chinese attitude did not change, but the Sino-Soviet conflict became more violent. The leaders of both countries dropped even a façade of unity. The invectives of the Kremlin no longer fell on Albania, but on the "Chinese adventurists." And, in the same way, Yugoslavia no longer served as a scapegoat in Peking's pronouncements. A test ban treaty between Washington and Moscow could only be regarded by Mao Tse-tung and his followers as an unfriendly act. The men in the Kremlin hesitated to sign such a treaty as long as they hoped for a reconciliation with China. In 1963, that hope no longer existed, and as a result, they had no further reason for hesitation.

In 1961 a second explanation was frequently given for the failure of negotiations, namely, the technological "lag" of the Soviet Union. The 1961 test series prove, in effect, that Soviet engineers and scientists wanted to improve certain weapons, and in particular to perfect bombs of several tens of megatons. These improvements necessitated atmospheric testing, which is impossible to disguise. The situation was identical in the United States. A number of scientists, generals, and members of Congress criticized the moratorium without a treaty and without inspections, favoring a resumption of testing both to improve existing weapons and to develop new ones (anti-missile missiles). In 1963, not without serious debates in the Congressional committees, the Moscow treaty was approved by a large majority. The point in question is whether the Big Two have simply agreed not to do what they no longer have any interest in doing, or whether the ban on testing in the atmosphere, in the ocean, and in outer space marks a new phase in relations between the United States and the Soviet Union.

On the one hand, neither power has renounced the right to develop its weapons, and neither power has definitively renounced its freedom to test in the atmosphere if and when it should see fit to do so. Both are continuing underground tests. Probably the treaty neither prevents nor inhibits any of the innovations on which the technicians are working: vertical take-off planes, a perfected anti-missile missile, observation and communications satellites, more powerful bombs per a given weight, etc. Technically, the treaty hardly seems to affect the qualitative arms race as it is developing between the Big Two.

In addition, Russian hostility toward any system of territorial inspection—the third reason frequently invoked by commentators hoping to explain the refusal of the Soviet representatives in 1960–61 to grant the concessions required by the treaty—has not softened. When the Kremlin leaders finally decided to sign the treaty, they preferred to return to their position often taken previously and "legalize" underground testing, rather than accept on-site inspections.

Here again the events are full of significance. At the beginning of negotiations the inspection system envisioned by the Americans for a limited treaty (providing only for a ban on nuclear testing) included the recruiting of highly qualified personnel, the construction of technical stations, and annual expenditures of several hundred million dollars. The observer is tempted to wonder, if this were the case for such an agreement, what requirements would be made in the hypothetical case of a general and universal treaty (referring to all weapons and all nations!). Perhaps not without irony, one

American writer, Professor Oscar Morgenstern, has stated that effectively controlled disarmament would cost almost as much as the arms themselves. The layman may react to such a statement by wondering why we should have disarmament at all. When analyzed, this is an unreasonable reaction. Why shouldn't we spend as much money to protect ourselves against war as to protect ourselves against each other?

This reaction is also typical of the general public, which fails to distinguish between disarmament and the reduction of military budgets. Statesmen themselves see a sort of contradiction between an international treaty limiting armaments and the billions of dollars necessary to guarantee to all signatories that the treaty will be respected. The Soviet dislike of all complex inspection systems is perhaps not only based on a fear of spying and an obsession for secrecy; it may also have originated in a feeling of contradiction between the goal and the means, between a treaty symbolizing agreement, and a system of inspection inevitably symbolizing enmity and suspicion.

In any case, the Moscow treaty affects only those tests that do not require an international system of enforcement. Technology came to the rescue of the diplomats. The Moscow treaty of 1963, like the naval treaty of 1921, cannot be secretly violated. Thus nothing proves that the opposition between the Russians and the Americans on the decisive point of the enforcement of treaties has been overcome. According to the time-worn joke, Americans prefer inspection to disarmament, while the Russians loudly advocate general disarmament, but reject all effective means of enforcement. Their opposition to such enforcement is understandable, moreover, in terms of their own interests: the Soviets fear inspection because they benefit from the secrecy with which they surround themselves. The Americans, less able or anxious to dissimulate their activities, can only imagine a disarmament plan that simultaneously pierces the wall of Soviet secrecy. The Moscow treaty was signed only when it permitted underground tests, the prohibition of which would have required an inspection system.

Thus, on a technological level, this treaty signifies nothing, or very little. It does not even permit, as President Kennedy and his advisers would have wished, experimentation with a pilot system of international inspection. The situation is different on the political level, since the treaty simultaneously establishes cooperation between two enemies (the Soviet Union and the United States), and creates a rupture between two allies (the Soviet Union and the People's Republic of China). It was one of the American leaders' express intentions, in their unceasing efforts to establish a test ban treaty, to give a concrete example of two enemies united against the common danger of war, to stabilize the balance of terror, and to check the qualitative arms race. The question was: to what extent would the men in the Kremlin adhere to the subtle doctrine of the "control of armaments through cooperation among enemies"?

The basis of the American thesis, as we have seen, is that war, which no one wants, can nevertheless occur through a technical, bureaucratic, political, or psychological blunder. Do Marxist-Leninists accept the possibility of an accident of such magnitude? They are obliged to fear, according to their doctrine, that the capitalists will launch the war, but that if such a war should break out, it had to be required by the capitalists at bay; without this, history would lack the rationality that Marxist-Leninists have attributed to it. It is legitimate to wonder whether the Soviet leaders fear the "great war" as much as the leaders in Washington do.

Another question arises regarding the qualitative arms race. Are the Soviets anxious to reduce the economic burden of this race? Do they consider it dangerous in itself? Are they reasoning in the same way as some American writers, who can see no possible outcome of such competition other than a final catastrophe?

Finally, and this is the most important question, have the Kremlin leaders been taking advantage of man's fear of a thermonuclear war, even though they are themselves only mildly frightened by such a prospect? When Mr. Khrushchev bragged of preventing American aggression against Cuba through the threat of ballistic missiles, he was obviously counting on the American President's retreat before a direct confrontation. Being unable to aid Cuba in the Caribbean, the Soviet Union would have been forced to react either through limited reprisals on the United States and its allies, or through massive retaliation. Either eventuality was improbable. However, if the balance of terror were to be entirely stabilized, by an explicit agreement, this type of blackmail, or bluff, would be out of the question. Did the Soviet leaders hope that neither of the big powers would any longer be in a position to threaten something which in effect they were determined not to do? In 1961, it was Moscow that did not hesitate to take up the doctrine of massive retaliation, already fallen into disuse in the West.

Everything seems to point to a change of thinking among Soviet leaders between 1961 and 1963. The Cuban crisis of 1962 apparently convinced them both that war was more to be feared than they had thought and that the Americans were capable of assuming its risk. From then on, instead of *dissimulating* their solidarity with the enemy against war, as they previously did, they have *publicly demonstrated* such solidarity by two symbolic acts (the Moscow treaty and the hot line between the Kremlin and the White House). The Cuban crisis, more than the Sino-Soviet split, seems to me to be at the root of this conversion, or rather this change in attitude.

This development, whatever its significance, is still only a vicissitude. The Big Two, although they oppose war, continue to interpret history according to different philosophies, and to give unequal attention to eventualities that are in any event improbable; one power seems to prefer a public in a state of anxiety, while the other may attempt to promote a feeling of security among its citizens.

For a long time technical and psychological difficulties will in all probability continue to prevent a solid treaty stabilizing reciprocal retaliatory capacity. A certain equilibrium will exist, but the asymmetry of political systems, geographical positions, and diplomatic relations encourages the United States to maintain a margin of superiority over the Russians (through the increased number, dispersion, mobility and protection of retaliatory weapons). Theoretically, the balance of terror can be stabilized through the defense policies adopted unilaterally by each of the big powers, without any bilateral agreement. However, in the absence of such an agreement the two enemies cannot be sure that this balance is, in effect, a stable one; in any case, they are obliged to leave no stone unturned, less in an effort to upset this balance in their own favor than to insure that it will not be tipped in the other's favor through negligence or a relaxation of efforts.

4. The Limits of Agreement between Enemies

Two schools confront each other in the United States, one favoring general and above all nuclear disarmament, the other favoring "arms control" in the sense we have given this expression, control which does not imply total or general disarmament and which, in the eyes of advocates of the other school, sometimes looks like the maintenance of arms rather than their abolition or reduction.

The foregoing sections are inspired, with an increased pessimism, by ideas of the second school. For, unless we subscribe to unilateral disarmament no matter what the cost, or unless we imagine an international system radically different from the one we know, in which states would live in security without arms and without conflicts, these ideas are convincing and I should say almost self-evident. They may be summarized, actually, in the following statements. Disarmament or the reduction of arms is not an end in itself but a means—a means of reducing the risk of war without increasing the danger of defeat if war were to occur. Since this formula applies to both sides or both super powers, an agreement limiting arms has a chance of being signed only if it does not alter the balance of power, if it offers neither one nor the other marked advantages. Moreover, since it is inconceivable, at least in the immediate future, that peace will result from the disappearance of arms and the consequent impossibility of fighting, agreements reducing or limiting arms should not allay the fear of thermonuclear war, which contributes temporarily to the state of non-war. Finally, these potential agreements do not differ in kind from the decisions made unilaterally by states in order to reduce the danger of a war by accident or by misunderstanding, without relinquishing their capacity to use force or threats to attain their own ends or to discourage the enemy.

The reasoning of the school of "arms control"—treaties of reduction, limitation or inspection are only one aspect of the general policy of armament and should be put in the total context to be judged objectively—is, in my opinion, irrefutable, in terms of the requirements of the policy of responsibility. But—this concession must be made to the other school—it has so far not resulted in any disarmament measure, and as of this writing nothing suggests that it might do so.

In the course of events the discussion of the control of a test ban had assumed a symbolic value. The failure of the negotiations also has a symbolic value. The minimum of inspection required by the United States exceeded the maximum to which the Soviet Union was prepared to consent. The latter did not want to exceed the three on-the-spot inspections per year intended to determine the nature of the "suspicious phenomena" registered by the instruments. The United States at first demanded twenty and did not want to settle for less than a dozen. The Secretariat which would have been entrusted with organizing the inspection system, by common consent in 1960, was to have a neutral director. In 1961, after the Congo affair, Soviet diplomats reconsidered the agreement which had been made and obstinately proposed a *troika* Secretariat (one Soviet, one Western, one non-aligned member)—which amounted, in the eyes of the Americans, to introducing a veto power into the inspection system. Whatever interpretation one accepts of the Soviet attitude from 1959 to 1961, the harsh fact remains that in the last analysis the Kremlin leaders did not feel that the advantages of a "gentlemen's agreement" on the limitation of the arms race outweighed the drawbacks, from the viewpoint of their own immediate interest and advantage (disadvantages of an inspection system established on Russian territory or of tension with their Chinese ally). For their part, the Americans felt that an agreement which would not offer a sufficient guarantee of being respected—an agreement based on confidence[7] in the other party and not on strictness of inspection—would be more dangerous than useful. Unless there occurs an event altering the psychology either of the Russian or of the American leaders, one cannot see why negotiation involving a partial limitation of armaments would not come up against the same kind of obstacles. One cannot even see what would be the point of starting any negotiation at the present time.

Let us consider, for example, the problem of mutual deterrence. The point is to reassure each side as to the other's intentions, without giving either of them an advantage in terms of the present situation. The hypothesis, usually unstated, is that both sides are equally interested in easing tension, that both take seriously enough the risk of a war by accident, pre-emption or misunderstanding to relinquish the possible advantages which either may derive in certain cases from the fear of escalation. This hypothesis strikes me as anything but proved. Generally speaking, it is the Soviet Union which would lose most by the "end of fear," but even the United States would at times regret not being in a position to discourage its adversary by a vague threat.

---

[7] It is not just a matter of confidence in the other party's promise. One has to be confident that the other will make the same judgment concerning his real interest, will refrain from cheating out of regard for his interest clearly understood.

Let us admit, however, that the two super powers agree in preferring a stable to an unstable deterrence. Each knows that the other possesses an invulnerable nuclear force, each knows that this enemy force is aimed at its own cities and not at its striking force, hence that its enemy has no more aggressive intentions than itself. Perhaps this situation does exist to a certain extent, but to be sure that it does and will not be altered, it would be necessary to develop a system of inspection so complex, so subtle that another diplomatic marathon comparable to the one at Geneva on the nuclear test ban would probably end in the same fiasco.

The ban on the qualitative arms race is more difficult to imagine, negotiate or insure than the nuclear test ban. The exploration of space, of course, opens unprecedented possibilities of a military nature. It is already known that the job of the U-2's—observation vehicles flying at very high altitudes—has been taken over by the Samos and Midas satellites. Other utilizations of the satellites have been or will be conceived. To consolidate mutual deterrence in the technical form it assumes today, an agreement on cooperation in space matters or a ban on military use of interplanetary space would be indispensable.

Let us suppose that we wish to stabilize deterrence by limiting the number of ballistic missiles available to both sides. I admire those American experts who ask in all seriousness whether the best figure would be three hundred, five hundred or one thousand. These theoretical controversies have one purpose and one only: they oblige advocates of disarmament to recognize that maximum security does not necessarily coincide with minimum arms. But, aside from this educational value, these controversies are mere intellectual games without any conceivable relation to any negotiation whatever. It is true that the aggressive state which proposed to destroy the other's retaliatory force would have to be certain of a considerable numerical superiority (at least three to one, probably more). If the number of ballistic missiles to which each of the super powers would be entitled were too small, a certain amount of cheating would be enough to endanger the balance. On the other hand, if each of the super powers were entitled by treaty to five hundred missiles, only a major fraud in the realm of one thousand missiles, at least, would give it a chance of decisively weakening the opposing thermonuclear retaliatory force. But anyone imagining American and Soviet delegates gravely discussing whether each super power will have two hundred, three hundred or five hundred missiles, whether each will promise not to build underground shelters for its population, not to place thermonuclear bombs in satellites, will end up, for all this subtlety, being just as naïve as the partisans of disarmament at any price and under any condition.

Who will know a few years from now how many ballistic missiles the United States and the Soviet Union each possess? Where are the launching pads set up? If the object of the inspection were to insure disarmament, it would still be possible, but if the point is simply to perpetuate a situation which, in the eyes of statesmen, has a strong likelihood of already existing, such efforts will seem excessive and absurd. There are in addition some difficulties (probably not insurmountable ones) in combining mutual knowledge of the instrument of deterrence with that secrecy which, for at least one of the two super powers, is a factor in its invulnerability.

In short, I do not see that any of the elements which affect the balance of mutual deterrence promises to be the subject of a negotiated agreement, insured by a system of inspection. Inspection of laboratories to prevent the improvement of existing weapons (better weight-yield ratio, cheaper manufacture) or the development of new weapons (neutron bomb, chemical or bacteriological weapons), and inspection of territory to locate launching sites for ballistic missiles are not perhaps physically or technologically impossible, but they are unacceptable to the Soviet Union and moreover contrary to the principle of the equality of advantages or disadvantages. The loss of secrecy would cost the Soviet Union a great deal, the United States almost nothing.

Would there be a better chance of success by attempting to prepare a general plan encompassing all weapons and providing for all successive stages until the so-called final stage (minimum armament compatible with the domestic security of states)? In theory, the all-embracing method would present one advantage compared to the analytic method: the stake—if the leaders really want disarmament—would not be unworthy of the efforts made and the sacrifices accepted.

However, up until now, it does not seem that the negotiations regarding general disarmament have ever been taken seriously by either of the super powers, that they have been anything but one aspect, and a secondary one, of the war of propaganda, of the competition to convince public opinion that the *other* was responsible for the arms race. But such skepticism might have circumstantial rather than permanent causes.

There were reasons to believe that the United States and the Soviet Union were or thought they were in a situation of approximate equality with respect to strategic and retaliatory forces.[8] On the other hand, the Soviet Union and its allies have a substantial superiority in Europe and an enormous one in Asia with respect to conventional forces (a quantitative, not a qualitative superiority). This latter superiority is neither irresistible nor inevitable, at least on the Continent. The Soviet Union has reduced its forces. It cannot be sure of the loyalty of the Polish and Hungarian armies, not to mention the army of East Germany. The European countries are by no means incapable of mobilizing from thirty to forty divisions, which would balance whatever di-

[8] This statement was no longer true by 1962. The American leaders, Mr. McNamara in particular, affirm American superiority in the matter of ballistic missiles, since they declare themselves capable, even if the Soviet Union strikes first, of carrying out an anti-nuclear strategy—which implies that after having covered the enemy force, the United States would still have enough missiles or bombers to respond by an attack on the enemy cities in the event that the enemy attacked American cities.

visions the Soviet Union would be in a position to engage immediately at hundreds of kilometers from its bases. But the states of Western Europe do not manifest the slightest inclination to pursue those efforts of conventional armament for which they have the physical capacity.

Let us assume that even this difficulty were resolved, that the Soviet Union agreed to reduce its own armies to a level such that the balance between the two sides would be restored. The day the objective became a grandiose one—a worldwide plan of successive disarmament—would the obstacles that stood in the way of partial agreements yield by some miracle? Such was the sense of Mr. Khrushchev's repeated declarations to the effect that on the day the West accepts the principle of total disarmament, he would agree to any inspection—inspection which, in an armed world, would amount to espionage. What prevents the West from answering in the same style and declaring itself likewise a partisan of total disarmament?

The answer is first of all that the style of Western propaganda differs from the Soviet style. Western heads of state dislike "enormous" lies or statements which are obviously inapplicable. Time and again they have betrayed the same bad faith as the Soviets, and have introduced into their plans certain clauses unacceptable to the other bloc. But they will not make up their minds to subscribe to the principle of total disarmament, whose realization they regard as out of the question. In Mr. Khrushchev's insistence on obtaining Western acceptance of this principle, they believed they detected indifference to agreement and exclusive concern with propaganda.

In other words, what up to now has revealed itself as impossible in detail does not strike me as probable as a whole. In the case of each stage, it will be necessary to determine what sort of inspection will bring about the reduction or limitation of armaments, to be sure that the balance of international forces is maintained and the balance of deterrence safeguarded. The inspection system that had been conceived for the nuclear test ban treaty gives an idea of the system that would combine aerial observations (to determine the location of launching sites), and ground inspection of factories, laboratories and garrisons, not to mention inspection of submarine fleets. In all honesty, I must confess that the monumental work done by American writers on the subject of "control, reduction or limitation of armaments" has convinced me (contrary to their intention) of the extreme improbability of any treaty—except for the treaty regarding the nuclear test ban. To this conclusion, which will be called pessimistic, I should like nevertheless to append three reservations.

Measures which reduce armaments may be taken by unilateral decision. It is conceivable, for example, that one or the other of the Big Two, the day it has a firm resolve to diminish the accumulated stock of atomic or thermonuclear weapons, might offer to transfer a certain fraction of them each month or each year to an international body, provided its rival did the same. The inequality of reserves at the outset would not prevent disarmament by the "dialectic of unilateral decisions." Each would retain—and openly—an adequate reserve so that it would still possess a substantial retaliatory capacity, hence would not be at the mercy of its rival.

I do not think that this dialectic of disarmament, which is comparable to and the reverse of the arms race, is about to be adopted tomorrow and to lead the human race to a world without arms. But—and this is the second reservation I should like to make—the present situation involves a combination of two reciprocities, a reciprocity of armament and a reciprocity of disarmament. The first is very much in evidence in the laboratories, the second in the refusal to build shelters; the two together determine the military budgets of the two super powers.

If we agree to characterize as arms control all those measures taken on both sides to prevent thermonuclear war and avoid escalation in a local conflict, then all states practice "arms control," whether they realize it or not, in the same way as M. Jourdain was talking prose. For the purpose of the West's strategic diplomacy, like that of the Soviet Union, is to avoid a great war, yet not to lose the cold war and not to allow local wars to develop. Such being the objectives of strategic diplomacy, arms policies are determined not only by the desire to prevent *the* war, or to *win* it should it occur, but by the more complex desire to reduce the volume of violence and hence, depending on circumstances, to prevent any recourse to force by the threat of thermonuclear reprisal and to prevent the expansion of a war by means of the balance of deterrence.

A great many considerations relative to arms control are inseparable from controversies among Western states concerning the best arms policy. For example, one of the goals of arms control, one of the applications of the idea of the reduction of violence, is the localization and limitation of possible armed conflicts. But this limitation, insofar as the desire for it is expressed in advance, may increase the risk of conflicts. Moreover, the desire for limitation is demonstrated in the enemy's eyes only by the acquisition of conventional weapons in sufficient quantities. In other words, it is by the distribution of expenditure between conventional and thermonuclear weapons—a distribution that was and must be decided unilaterally—that each side influences the probability either of local conflicts or of the limitation of local conflicts.

Of course, all the objectives of arms control cannot be attained merely by unilateral decision, in the absence of a negotiated agreement. But, insofar as the desire exists to eliminate as much as possible the risks of war by technical accident, or by human accident, or by pre-emption and misunderstanding, unilateral measures, combined with the logic of reciprocal action, offer greater possibilities than any negotiation. It is up to the experts to select arms systems which reduce to a minimum the risk of a bomb exploding without the mechanism having been released by human intention or without the indications furnished by the instruments having permitted a false interpretation. It is up to the state leaders to reflect in advance about the ways of reassuring one another concerning their intentions, of maintaining communications in time of crisis, or of retaining a chance of ending, before available stocks are exhausted, a war in which thermonuclear bombs would be used. It is not unreasonable, as the American writers keep telling us, to imagine circumstances in which capitulation would be necessary in order to save a part of the population. But here again, an excess of rational subtlety is hard to distinguish from a kind of naïveté. The limitation of conflicts requires a fear that they will spread: it is impossible for one side to reassure the other of its intentions without creating another danger. It would be useful, but it may not be possible, to know in advance how responsible leaders in Moscow and Washington would manage to resist "homicidal madness" and to limit the use of weapons each of which contains a force beyond measure.

Finally—and this is the third reservation—the probability that arms control involves little or no formal agreement on the reduction of armaments is not presented as definitive. The technical difficulties of inspection are enormous, but they are not definitive and inherently insoluble. Inspection will never provide an absolute security against undetected violation and war, but neither will armament. Here, as always, the decision comes down to a comparison of risks. For the moment, the leaders of the two super powers are more afraid of the risks of disarmament and inspection than of the risks of the present peace by the balance of fear. The motives for this evaluation of risks are multiple, but they can be reduced, I think, to some simple statements: the Soviets have a horror of inspection-espionage, the Americans are extremely suspicious of the Soviets and their intentions. Neither greatly fears thermonuclear war, in spite of the reiterated warnings of the experts. In any case, this fear is vague and remote. The immediate fear of inspection or of cheating outweighs it.

It may be that a crisis would reverse this hierarchy of dangers and this choice of risks in the minds of the American and Russian leaders.[9]

Is the arms race the cause of the political conflict or is the political conflict the cause of the arms race? This classic question, as we have said, admits of no categorical answer. The arms race is the result of the pursuit of security by force, it symbolizes the dialectic of hostility in peacetime, it is the non-warlike form of escalation. It is therefore capable, under certain circumstances, of intensifying the hostility from which it proceeds, of aggravating the insecurity felt by each of the rivals. Each rival arms because the other arms, and neither is capable of arresting this progression. This situation, obviously absurd for anyone who refuses to enter into the logic of the actors, may actually be created less by the suspicions each entertains toward the other than by the arms the latter acquires, less by the intentions

[9] The Cuban crisis of 1962 seems to have had a certain influence on the Russian way of thinking.

each attributes to his rival than by the means of destruction he knows him to possess. Such, perhaps, is the present situation.

Advocates of "disarmament" or of "arms control" do not necessarily subscribe to the thesis that the sole or principal source of the danger is thermonuclear weapons. Indeed, some merely hold that these weapons do not eliminate the danger of war and that they would give war the character of an unprecedented catastrophe. Others maintain that the antagonism of position, power or ideology between the two super powers would not justify a major war and that the United States and the Soviet Union hate each other primarily because of the thought of the harm they might do each other. Yet others do not hold the weapons responsible either for the violence of the conflict or the hostile passions, but feel that the development of the weapons constitutes a supplementary and independent cause of a war which, as a result of this very development, would exceed in horror all the evils which men have inflicted upon one another throughout the ages.

The three arguments all contain at least an element of truth. Even if the weapons of mass destruction do not increase the risks of war, they obviously increase the cost of a potential war. They provide another dimension to the conflict, a greater bitterness to the passions, they may even give rise to real risks of explosion (misunderstanding, accident, etc.). The uncertainty has to do with *quantity*: does the fear inspired by war balance and outweigh the danger created by weapons and innovations? To this question I feel personally incapable of giving a categorical answer, but I am impressed by the fact that most American scientists incline toward pessimism. Even though thermonuclear war may be improbable at each moment, in each crisis, is it not probable in the long run if states continue both to multiply innovations and to brandish this threat?

Whatever the magnitude of the danger, I do not see how mankind, for the moment, can escape it. The inspection system earlier discussed for the nuclear test ban makes it possible to imagine the system required by an agreement on total disarmament and to explain why such an agreement will not be signed in the course of the next few years. Neither of the super powers will promise not to take the initiative in resorting to atomic or thermonuclear weapons: such a promise would require, on the part of the West, an effort at conventional rearmament which—wrongly, I suspect—they would refuse to make.

Not that the Big Two are acting as if the danger did not exist. On the contrary, they are acting partly as if they had listened to the partisans of "arms control"; they are trying to defend their interests by reducing the volume of violence, to prevent the enlargement of conflicts, to use only conventional weapons when recourse to force becomes inevitable, to reassure each other in time of crisis as to their peaceful intentions. But all these agreements, if agreement there be, are implicit, the measures taken are unilateral, and they do not eliminate what most experts regard as the most serious aspect of the present global rivalry: the qualitative arms race.

I do not underestimate the gravity, at once tragic and absurd, of this race. But I ask the question: short of a revolution in the heart of man and the nature of states, by what miracle could interplanetary space be preserved from military use? How could the United States and the Soviet Union each agree to relinquish their own plans and henceforth to have no more satellites except those they possessed in common? Why should the super powers agree not to proceed from bombs of a few megatons to bombs of several dozen megations?[10] Why should they not perfect fusion bombs whose detonator would not consist of a fission bomb and which would kill men without destroying buildings?

To be sure, the two super powers would experience a sense of security if the balance of mutual deterrence were stabilized with a known number of missiles. The balance of deterrence would no longer deserve the name of balance of terror. Why should we be surprised that this balance has not been the subject of a formal agreement, when the United States has not even been able to convince its allies to abandon these weapons?

In the course of the next few years perhaps technological progress will in fact stabilize mutual deterrence. We must not count on the diplomats to achieve this stabilization.

[10] Unless the experts declare 100-megaton bombs to be "useless."

chapter XXII

In Search of a Strategy

II: *To Survive Is to Conquer*

The goal of the West is not only to avoid thermonuclear war, but also to be victorious or not to be vanquished. If the sole goal were to avoid thermonuclear war, the rational decision, the one that gives the best chance of attaining the goal, would be capitulation. If the West is not capitulating, despite the thermonuclear bombs and ballistic missiles which were brandished by Mr. Khrushchev, it is because the stake of the struggle is worth the risks of resistance.

This last proposition, applied to a particular case, will perhaps seem paradoxical, and even absurd. Is the freedom of two million Berliners *worth* the risk of a thermonuclear war? No particular stake, in fact, will be comparable to the "lost wager" or to the "bluff." But once we consent to yield everything, each particular stake increases its desirability, more than itself, since it involves, in a sense, the fate of the whole. It is not just the fate of two million Berliners which is at stake, but virtually the choice of the West Germans (between unity under Soviet protection and freedom for the favored two thirds), hence the destiny of Western Europe as a whole, hence, in the last analysis, of the West itself and all it represents.

But, the skeptic or cynic will object, does the "salvation of the West" ever deserve to be defended at the price of millions, of tens of millions of victims? This objection is spuriously rational. It is true that the West will not be saved if the thermonuclear war takes place. In the age of the strategy of defense, it was possible to save a nation or a civilization by war. In the age of the strategy of deterrence, it is not possible to save a nation or a civilization by war, *but neither is it possible to save them by capitulation.* The point therefore is to convince ourselves and others that the values which would perish along with the regime and the civilization of the West justify the danger which we are creating for tens of millions of people, a danger which capitulation would dissipate *temporarily*.

1. *The Stake*

It is not easy, in the age in which we live, to justify that which in other times would have seemed obvious. The difficulty springs not only from the enormity of the losses which would be entailed by a thermonuclear war and which has provoked numerous dignitaries of the Catholic Church to declarations that such traditional concepts as that of a righteous war are henceforth inapplicable. To "atomize" a population of "innocents"—men, women and children—because their leaders were guilty of aggression would be a wicked mockery. The (political) justice of the cause does not justify the use of such horrible means. Once again, the only answer to an objection of this kind consists, for the West, in not placing itself in a situation where it would have to take the initiative in resorting to such weapons. The problem we are raising is different: have we something to save in order to justify sacrifices and dangers?

Some will answer immediately that the mere fact of raising such a question is in itself a confession. If a "crusader for the cold war" resorts to expressing his doubts and cross-examining himself publicly, is this not one more proof among countless others that a declining civilization no longer believes in itself? The mere fact that we raise the question signifies, in my opinion, just the reverse. Only the fanatic and the barbarian cannot question themselves regarding the justification of war in an age when a single thermonuclear bomb can kill more people than all the Frenchmen killed by German shells, bombs and bullets in several years of fighting. He who, confronted by the dangers of thermonuclear war, has not asked himself at some time: does there exist a single cause that is comparable to the danger involved, does not deserve to be called a man.

That we cross-examine ourselves in public and that on the other side of the Iron Curtain people do not have the right to do so is the best introduction to the "defense and illustration of the West," our present theme. In Chapter XVIII, I analyzed *the enemy partners* by extending to its limit the effort of *neutrality*. I did not write as a committed Westerner; in fact, I adopted no viewpoint at all, neither that of the European who is critical of the United States, of which he knows himself to be an ally in spite of everything, nor that of the Indian who prefers the West to the Soviet world but fears the latter more than the former, nor any of the multiple and complex attitudes of the various types of non-aligned nations. In fact, with a pretension all the greater because it was well concealed, I posed as the "pure spectator" who understands and judges the whole composed of all points of view. But I am not really this "pure spectator," and in the last analysis the latter does not grasp a part of what is essential, the meaning that men and states assign to their existence.

As long as we are comparing the structure and function of the political and economic regime on each side of the Iron Curtain, nothing is easier and, in a certain sense, more necessary than to note advantages and drawbacks of either authoritarian planning or market regulation imposed by state intervention; either a monopolistic and ideological party, or a plurality of parties competing according to constitutional law. Personally I hold that, even on the sociological level, with regard to the ideals both sides profess to cherish, the Western regime is, as a whole, preferable to a regime of the Soviet type, the advantages of the latter being characterized primarily by their relation to power (the capacity to maintain a higher rate of investment, to concentrate investment in certain vital sectors, etc.). But I am also prepared to recognize that this judgment as to which is preferable may be influenced by my prejudices or passions. I admit, in short, that the regime which is preferable in general or in the abstract is not always possible *hic et nunc*. It is not out of the question that the regime preferable in a given situation may be other than the one preferable if we were to compare two ideal types. When entrepreneurs and credit mechanisms are lacking, when only the state and its bureaucracy are capable of promoting industrialization, the regime of the monopolistic ideocratic party is potentially the least deplorable means of performing a historically necessary task.

But this way of looking at things which, even when applied to economic regimes, arouses some anxiety (after all, it is also the lives of men as well as of economic subjects which are determined by the regime), ignores the essential dimension of the phenomenon when it is applied to political regimes. A one-party regime and a multi-party regime may, of course, be analyzed and understood as the two typical solutions to a single problem, as the two logically acceptable interpretations of democratic legitimacy, as two methods of performing the same functions. Since authority derives from the people, either they choose from among the candidates those who will govern and the plurality of possible choices will be the proof of liberty, or they ratify, by acclamation, the power of a party which knows, interprets and executes the true will of the masses (or of the class whose will is historically decisive). In both ideal cases the dialogue is maintained between government and governed; in both cases, the governed can feel that they are obeying their own representatives, while those who govern can be conscious of the legitimacy of their office; in both cases, political class is recruited from the party or parties.

Let us go further. Neither of the two regimes, in the abstract, guarantees the dialogue between government and governed, neither radically prevents the breakdown of communications, the despotism of minorities, the omnipotence of a charismatic leader, the reciprocal alienation of people and power. Below a certain threshold of popular participation, elections, even genuinely free ones, reinforce the oligarchy. Above a certain threshold of hostility between people and the monopolistic party, nothing of the democratic fiction remains.

This way of reducing the two current modes of democratic legitimacy to a common denominator for the sake of impartiality does not, however, overlook the reasons for which we commit ourselves to or against certain political institutions. Even more than economic institutions, political institutions are merely one aspect or one sector of existence itself. But, as individual or collective existences, these two kinds of regimes are radically heterogeneous. They are not distributed along a scale that ranges from less to more; they are opposed, as positive and negative.

Democratic legitimacy, which both blocs claim to represent, cannot and should not be realized in all collectivities by the same institutions, but institutions cannot honestly say that they exemplify this legitimacy unless they are characterized by one or another of the ideas of *constitutionality, representation* or *personal liberty.* The choice of rulers or the exercise of authority proceeds according to rules—not just anyone can assume power, and whoever has power cannot do whatever he likes; the people feel that they are represented by the rulers and the latter seek to be the representatives of the former; each citizen, within the limits prescribed by law, is entitled to think and act according to his desires—these, I think, are the three ideas (complementary in an ideal democracy but separable in any real democracy) which constitute democratic legitimacy. If any of the three is not even approximately realized, a regime that calls itself democratic is lying. That it is lying with or without realizing it matters little; the hoax still exists.

The one-party regime of the Soviet type remains unconstitutional in its country of origin. There is no mechanism that provides for the transmission of power in the event of the death of the chief. There is no visible relation between what happens and what is provided for by the Constitution which, enacted at the time of the great purge, guaranteed respect for all intellectual and personal liberties. Even today, the members of the Presidium are hardly the representatives of the Central Committee, and the latter represents the members of the party only in a very vague sense. I do not mean that the members of the party are hostile to the Central Committee and do not feel that they are in touch with them: I mean simply that for the moment the leaders of the party choose those who are then said to represent the millions of members instead of the latter choosing their representatives. Finally, the Soviets are deprived of a great many concrete liberties—to travel freely outside their country, to listen to any foreign radio station, to write novels or paint pictures in their own way, liberties formerly enjoyed by a great many subjects of more or less enlightened despots and denied to members of the proletariat "liberated" by the victory of socialism.

To call the so-called regimes of popular democracy democratic is therefore to abuse the meaning of words or, to speak more cautiously for the time being, to admit that the same words do not have the same meaning in the East that they do in the West. But is this really true? In 1956 the Hungarians and the Poles strikingly demonstrated that they still gave what Mallarmé called "a pure meaning to the words of the tribe." As a matter of fact, neither in public nor in private, neither officially nor secretly do the Soviets regard as liberty what we regard as non-liberty.

Regimes of the Soviet type justify themselves first of all by the formula "for the people" if not "by the people." The absolute power of the party or, if one prefers, the leading role played by the avant-garde of the proletariat, is not presented as the expression of democratic orthodoxy, but as a historical necessity. Between the heterogeneous class society[1] and the homogeneous society of the future, dictatorship is exercised by the party in the name of the proletariat. Similarly, non-constitutionality of succession or of decisions and non-choice of representatives are by no means exalted as symbols of a superior legality or purpose. The best proof of this is the tribute paid by vice to virtue in the form of the Stalinist Constitution of 1936, the elections-by-acclamation or party Congresses. Will it be objected that these are concessions to propaganda or to bourgeois ideology? But such concessions, if that is the purpose of the Constitution or elections, would once again prove that the Soviet leaders have no doubt about the meaning that their people, like other peoples, attach to democratic legitimacy. The Russians do not identify the omnipotence of the party with liberty any more than the Americans do: police terror was terror and not the fulfillment of humanism. Socialist realism, as Zhdanov imposed it, was tyrannical and not liberating.

The theory which, it seems to me, partisans and leaders believe, the true theory of this system of lies, is the historical theory. If plurality of parties and free elections are dismissed as bourgeois and denounced, it is not because the single party and phony elections are regarded as a higher form of democracy as such. But plurality of parties in the West, according to the historical vision of Marxism-Leninism, conceal the despotism of monopolistic capitalism, and only the Communist party is capable of overcoming this despotism and of opening the way for a classless society.

But the philosophy of history which serves as a foundation for these categorical condemnations and these confused justifications is false. Because their philosophy does not agree with the facts, the Soviets have been forced gradually to construct an extraordinary system of lies and to oblige conquered or converted peoples to live in a perpetual lie. Necessary progression from a capitalism defined by private ownership of the means of production to a socialism defined by planning and the power of the party identified with the proletariat, disappearance of all alienation with the disappearance of private ownership of the instruments of production and of capitalism, a classless and stateless society upon the accession of socialism—these are the major propositions which constitute the framework of the ideological construction. But these propositions are almost absurd. The party is not the

[1] We are using the words *homogeneous* and *heterogeneous* here in the popular sense given them by the current idiom, not in the precise sense of a homogeneous or heterogeneous system.

proletariat, except in a mythology; the abolition of private ownership does not bring about the abolition of economic and social inequalities. However effective the organization of the economy, it will not eliminate the political order, the necessity for a state. Because they have done something different from what they believed they would do, because they pursued inaccessible goals, goals contrary to the nature of men and societies, the Communists lie as perhaps no other great historical movement before them has ever lied. The rejection of communism is for me above all the rejection of the enforced lie.

I can picture the smile of the skeptic, the scorn of the "leftist intellectual," who is convinced that the Soviet side, because it calls itself socialist, sustains and embodies the hopes of mankind. To make matters worse, I shall therefore carry my idea to its conclusion: those intellectuals who seek to be "humanitarians," who claim an association with the tradition of the Enlightenment and who either reserve their sympathy for the Soviet side or else refuse to distinguish between the two giants (or barbarians) seem to me to be suffering from a perversion of the moral sense. Between a society that is essentially totalitarian and a society that is essentially liberal, a man who, without being converted to the so-called new faith, chooses the former or sees no real difference between the two has become blind to fundamental values.

I would not be misunderstood: Western societies are imperfect and, in certain regards, perhaps more imperfect than Soviet societies. In particular, if one compares the United States and the Soviet Union, perhaps the former has more trouble putting into effect the principle of racial equality than the latter. Nothing prevents an observer from hating the commercialized radio and television from across the Atlantic more than the politicized radio and television from behind the Iron Curtain. But criticism of American civilization is an integral part of that civilization itself—which is not the case with Soviet civilization—and above all the negative aspect of the regime is not transformed into a positive one by dialectical jugglery. One may debate the share of power in the hands of monopolies (or large corporations). But it would never occur to any American theorist to claim that the more power such monopolies have, the more completely democracy is realized. *On the Soviet side, such an inversion of values is the foundation of the regime, since party is identified with class and the rule of the party with the realization of liberty.* From this point on, the deification of the party (or of the few or the one man incarnating it) corresponds to a necessity which is both psychological and logical. The party must be transfigured so that in obeying it the individual may feel he is obeying the highest reason. Why would the dictatorship of the party be indispensable to the liberation of the proletariat if history had not transferred to the party the mission which Marx and the first Marxists attributed to class? But, having become sacred, the party is entitled to extend its lawmaking indefinitely. Social man is total man, and the party is master and possessor of social man. A regime which claims to mold the totality of man is "totalitarian"; it is tyrannical by nature and not by accident because it is based on a false philosophy.

Once again I hear the skeptical reader countering with historical precedents. The French Revolution was also "totalitarian" at certain moments or in certain of its representatives. It, too, opposed the Church because it was of religious (in the broad sense of the word) inspiration. It, too, was denounced by the Church as incompatible with its traditional teachings. It withered away like all historical movements. The institutions which it finally resulted in—equal rights, individual freedoms, universal citizenship, representative government—far from contradicting the dogmas of Catholicism, have turned out to be consistent with Christian inspiration (at least with certain tendencies of that inspiration). Why should the same not be true of the Soviet Revolution? In the long run the latter will have contributed certain institutions—planned economy, accelerated industrialization, social rights of individuals—from which all the regimes of our time will borrow something. As for the Marxist-Leninist ideology, it will gradually fall into desuetude. The Soviets will salute the statue of Karl Marx with as much indifference as the Christian who has lost his faith continues to make the sign of the Cross when he enters a church.

This way of thinking—in the future perfect—has virtually become the rule among the intelligentsia of the West. It consists in putting oneself today in the place of those who will judge as *past* the events we are living through in the present. It adds to this a kind of popularized Marxism by devaluing the underlying *intention* of a historical movement and regarding as real only those institutions which emerge from it. In other words, we are asked not to regard Soviet totalitarianism as a tragedy, because it is merely the "ideological point of honor" of economic planning and because it will have disappeared by the time our grandchildren are grown up.

That the totalitarian faith or purpose will eventually wither away it would be ungracious to deny, especially if one feels that totalitarianism is contrary to the eternal springs of human nature. But one would not be justified in deducing from this that the dogmatism of immanence, the claim to create a total man and a new man are merely superstructures or myths. Soviet society is indissolubly a group of institutions *and* the metaphysical intention of those who build it. That certain of these institutions may survive although emptied of the intention that inspires and distorts them is possible. But one cannot today consider this dissociation as already achieved. Our duty is to combat what we condemn and not to assume in advance the privileges of the pure spectator, as if our immediate future were already our distant past. I am the one who is deliberating and not my grandchildren. If they do not take the totalitarian threat as a tragedy, perhaps I may have helped to make their detachment possible by the very fact that I will have averted the danger. But to invoke a future detachment is really to seek an excuse for cowardice or abstention.

2. *The Objective*

But, my adversary—that is, myself—will again object, can I ignore the lessons of experience? How many historians manage today to share the fratricidal passions of the Spartans and Athenians or even, closer to our own day, of our fathers who fought the Germans from 1914 to 1918? How many historians sing the praises of the Roman Empire, in spite of the methods employed by those conquerors; were not the conquered peoples themselves, after several generations of peace, reconciled to their lot to the point of retaining, through barbarian centuries, a nostalgia for the vanished Empire? Wars to the death between related units within a single zone of civilization or wars of conquest: there is scarcely one example in which the judgment of the spectators, looking back, has coincided with the passions of the actors. Why should it be any different with our conflict and why should we not take this into account?

Indeed, we should take this into account and become conscious of exactly what we are fighting, of what we are fighting for. We have often, in our analysis of the current situation, noted phenomena of *asymmetry*. The West does not outlaw those who openly take the side of the enemy. The West, with a few exceptions, has not let itself be swept, by the logic of competition, into imitating its enemy. It has not imposed on the liberty of its citizens the same restrictions which Soviet regimes regard as normal and indispensable. The West speaks with many voices, the Soviet Union with only one; each country in the West, faced with an international crisis, displays its uncertainties and hesitations; the Soviet Union time and again employs several languages, combines threats and promises: but all its methods are coordinated by a single will.

This asymmetry appears on the highest level, that of the goals of war and of strategy. The leaders of the Soviet bloc, we have no reason to doubt, continue to think according to the Marxist frame of reference, as it has been revised by Lenin and by Mao Tse-tung. The conflict between the two blocs is for them only one aspect and one moment of the worldwide revolution, of the inevitable transition from capitalism to socialism. The United States is the only power capable of balancing the strength of the Soviet Union, but it is also the supreme expression of capitalism, and both the *national* enemy of Russia and the *ideological* enemy of the socialist world.

The rivalry between the two super powers is not, therefore, according to Marxist-Leninist philosophy, comparable to the rivalries between two candidates for the throne or for the empire; it exists within a context of revolutionary transformation of which it is, in one sub-period, the diplomatic expression. The point is not to bring this rivalry to an end by a lasting agreement based on the distribution of zones of influence or the principle of "live and let live." Peaceful coexistence is and can only be a particular mode temporarily assumed by a protracted conflict. The West tends to recognize, albeit unconsciously, the primacy of peace; also, faced with a conflict, it looks for a peaceful solution or settlement. The Marxist-Leninists, on the other hand, until the permanent and total spread of socialism, recognize the (beneficial) inevitability of conflict. The former are ready to be satisfied with a peace without victory. If the Soviets renounce the destruction of the West, the West will gladly let them live as they wish; it will abandon to them without too guilty a conscience those peoples whom the Red army has "liberated" or "conquered." The Soviets, on the other hand, cannot even conceive of what a peace without victory might be. As long as a capitalist bloc remained, peace would not be certain (because capitalism is imperialist by nature) and the struggle would have to continue, not because men desire it but because the laws of history have so decreed. If such is the asymmetry of goals, has not the West lost in advance?

Such is the conviction of an American school, one of whose latest books, by Robert Strausz-Hupé, William R. Kintner and Stefan T. Possony, is entitled *A Forward Strategy for America*.[2] A few quotations suggest the strategic goal which the West, according to these writers, ought to choose for itself. "The first objective of any 'major' American strategy is, by all odds, the preservation and consolidation of our political system rather than keeping the peace. The realization of this objective may or may not require the establishment of systems compatible with ours throughout the entire world, but it does require the continuation or establishment of free systems compatible with ours in *certain* key parts of the world."[3]

The *survival* of the political regime of the United States being the first objective, a strategy of withdrawal to the American fortress is inconceivable because the United States, in a world entirely converted to the Soviet regime or to a totalitarian regime of one kind or another, could not preserve its free institutions.

But must the United States be content with this relative victory: assuring the survival of its government?

"The fundamental decision which faces us is this: must we accept the Communist concept of coexistence in one form or another, or must we bring about the final defeat of communism? If we choose the second line of conduct, we must decide whether we should rely on the defeat of communism as a result of fortuitous circumstances like internal erosion or revolution, or if we should multiply our efforts in order to attain this objective. We must decide whether a passive, wait-and-see strategy does not in fact risk retarding the fall of communism while hastening our own. And, finally, we must decide why we really want to conquer communism. Is it because we hope to replace its "economic order" with another? Or are we trying to overthrow a certain political system, to raze the intellectual concentration camp of communism, and to help the peoples of the Communist bloc to gain the right to

2 New York, 1961.
3 P. 402.

govern themselves? Or do we base our policy on the belief that communism, in spite of its present hostility, might be an adversary less uncompromising than the system which would succeed it, assuming we lived long enough to see this successor? Once all these ideological resonances are eliminated, our policy should be based on the following premise: we cannot tolerate the survival of a political system which has both the increasing capacity and the inexorable desire to destroy us. We have no other choice than to adopt the strategy of Cato."[4]

And elsewhere, in a formulation just as clear:

"We feel that the permanent coexistence of systems as fundamentally opposed as closed and open societies is impossible, that the tightly contracted world of tomorrow will no more be able to tolerate being indefinitely partitioned by iron and bamboo curtains than the American Union in Lincoln's time could continue to live half slave and half free."[5]

In these two quotations all the problems raised by the pursuit of a strategy for the West are at least indicated. It is easy, and it is correct, to establish first of all that the survival of the United States—survival of the regime as well as of the body of the nation—is the first goal. Under what conditions can this goal be attained? Now the writers whom we are quoting, representatives of the offensive school, go on to say that the *indefinite* coexistence of closed and open societies is not possible. Unfortunately (or fortunately) the adjective—indefinite or permanent—makes such a statement utterly meaningless. Probably the American Union would not have been able, *in the long run*, to maintain the coexistence of slave states with free states: the War of Secession was not inevitable at the date when it took place; if it had been postponed, slavery might have been outlawed without war and the slaves would gradually have become free men. But above all, the reference to the situation of the Union in 1861 teaches us nothing about the future of the conflict between the two blocs. The Confederates and the Yankees both belonged to the Union, whose preservation or dissolution was at stake. The two blocs belong to the same international system, not to the same political unit. Now, in the event of ideological conflict, the spokesmen of each regime tend to regard the citizens of the state of the opposing regime as slaves. The corrected formula, an international system cannot endure half slave and half free, would be equivalent to the statement: any bipolar and heterogeneous system inevitably leads to an inexpiable war which eliminates one of the candidates for mastery. We already know that this has been true countless times in the past, but we also know that the lesson we learn from history depends upon our choice of precedents. If we evoke the empires, lasting coexistence has been the rule (Parthians and Romans, Moslems and Christians). If we evoke zones of civilization which were eventually unified, there is generally to be found a Cato to repeat *delenda est Carthago,* and military

---

[4] *Ibid.,* pp. 405–6.
[5] *Ibid.,* pp. 35–36.

leaders to follow these precepts. But which of the two precedents comes closest to the present situation? Obviously neither of the two comparisons teaches us as much as an analysis of the present.

The Soviet bloc and the Western bloc differ in countless respects from empires whose coexistence has been enduring. The peoples of Eastern Europe are temporarily resigned to the institutions in which they live, they are not devoted to them. The official preservation of state sovereignties, the survival of national and even nationalist sentiments prohibit the Kremlin leaders from placing the seal of legitimacy and of permanence on their conquests. The Soviet imperium remains precarious, lacerated by contradictions, held together by a force which neither consent nor law have yet consolidated or replaced. Nor is the American imperium proof against potential crises. How long will the West Germans prefer their liberty and prosperity to an attempt at reunification? After the fall of West Berlin and official acceptance of the partition of Germany and of Europe, would the citizens of the Federal Republic remain faithful to the European and Atlantic community? Will the French and the English, both nostalgic for a vanished greatness, ultimately accept a political status and military organization that stabilize the American imperium?

But the precariousness of the two empires is only one of the reasons for the instability of their coexistence. The two empires do not belong to the same political unit as did the South and the North, but nevertheless they are not as remote from one another as Moslems and Christians. Each of the two ideologies is directly aggressive toward the other. Men living under one of the regimes can imagine what their lives would be like if they belonged to the other. Finally and above all, technology intensifies the dialectic of mutual fear because it eliminates time and space, so to speak.

If one bases the impossibility of a lasting coexistence on the dialectic of fear, one must conclude logically, with Bertrand Russell, that a monopoly of the strategic weapons offers the only way out of the present crisis. That one of the two super powers has an open society and the other a closed society merely constitutes an aggravating circumstance. The fundamental fact is that ballistic missiles and thermonuclear bombs give any state which possesses them in sufficient quantity the means of destroying any other state in a few minutes or hours and that such a danger will eventually become intolerable to the two states, each of which holds this threat over the other. This argument is quite remote from the argument relating to Lincoln's phrase, and it is hopeless, for it would pose the final choice between the capitulation of the West and thermonuclear war.

Under these conditions the soundest argument for the thesis that the coexistence of the two blocs is impossible eventually comes down to the qualitative arms race, to the capacity possessed by each of the duopolists suddenly to inflict intolerable destruction upon the other. But this argument is not compatible with a "Catonian strategy." The destruction imagined—that of the

Soviet Union or that of the Soviet imperium—can be conceived as physical or as political. Conceived as physical, it would imply the use of weapons of mass destruction. Such a Catonian strategy runs too great a risk of resulting in mutual suicide to be adopted in cold blood by men of good will. If the destruction is solely political, then it amounts more or less to the goal we have attributed to American strategy: the survival of American institutions will be assured only when the Kremlin no longer seeks to destroy them. *Each requires that for which the other must necessarily be its enemy.*

Even in this case, the symmetry is more apparent than real or, at any rate, the partial symmetry results from the dialectic of the struggle. The Russian nation has no reason to consider the American nation as an enemy, and conversely the American nation no reason to consider the Russian nation as an enemy—outside of the fact that they are the two super powers in the international system. Given the competition, each of the two more or less rightly imagines that it would be secure, or master of the world, if the other did not exist. What we have here, as we have shown, is at its origin a case of hostility without enmity, or better, of enmity proceeding from hostility.

But the absence of hate between the peoples does not mean an absence of enmity between the governing minorities. Regimes and ideas are opposed, and because of this, those embodying them on one side feel and actually are threatened by those embodying them on the other. The cold war is to a large extent an enterprise of subversion carried on by the so-called popular democracies against the so-called bourgeois democracies and by the latter against the former. Here again, there is no symmetry. But this time it is the appearance of asymmetry that is deceptive. Even when the so-called bourgeois democracies seem to be passive and to submit to the cold war waged by the Marxist-Leninists without answering them in kind, they are in fact agressive by their very existence, by the standard of living and the freedoms which they reserve for individuals.

Can this war of regimes be called a Catonian strategy? The answer must be a categorical negative. *The formula of a Catonian strategy makes no sense insofar as the West aims to destroy not the Soviet Union or the Soviet imperium but only the regime, and even the regime only insofar as the latter is forced, by ideological logic, to combat all regimes which resist the Marxist-Leninist gospel.* By evoking a Catonian strategy, one implies that in order to win the political or ideological battle against the Soviet Union or the Soviet imperium, the West has no choice but to completely destroy the latter and perhaps even the former. In reality, the West contemplates on the political level the elimination not even of Soviet institutions but only of those ideas and practices which oblige or encourage the Kremlin leaders to make war on the world of heretics, to consider themselves engaged in an enterprise whose end can only be the universal diffusion of what they call socialism. If the Soviets abandon this monopoly of hope, if they stop lying to others and to themselves, if they see their state for what it is—one type among others of modern government—peaceful competition will actually replace the cold war, controversy will replace subversion, and a dialogue of arguments will replace the dialectic of ideologies.

But the advocate of a Catonian strategy will object that dissociation between the rivalry for power and a purely political rivalry is impossible, since each is alternately means and end with respect to the other. To overthrow by subversion a regime favorable to the West is to weaken one side and strengthen the other. In this sense the ideological struggle serves the rivalry for power. But the power acquired by the Soviet bloc increases the spread of ideas and the authority of example. Countries will be converted to the Marxist-Leninist gospel because Moscow is the capital of the state strongest in military terms. All means—military, economic, diplomatic, ideological—are coordinated by Soviet strategists to an end which is inseparably the triumph of a regime and of the state that created it. If such is the end, if such are the means of one of the blocs, how could the other grant the subtle distinctions necessary to combat the universalist claims of the Soviet ideology without seeking to overcome the Soviet Union as such (even if, as men, we desire the fundamental freedoms to be restored to all men, anywhere in the world, who have been deprived of them)? I believe that these distinctions, though contrary to the passions of the struggle, are nevertheless necessary, that in the long run they offer a chance of peace-making without total war, without the total collapse of one of the contenders.

Of course, the West has a political-ideological enemy in the Soviet regime, which has decreed that constitutional-pluralist regimes are condemned to death by the law of history and which is making every effort to hasten the execution of the verdict. *But the West would cease regarding the Soviet regime as its enemy once the latter ceased denying its right to exist.* It will be objected that the Marxist-Leninist ideologists could not grant this right to exist without denying the very principles of their faith. Of course, this is only natural, and in this sense the West desires the death of the Soviet *ideology* just as the latter desires the death of the *West.* But the Soviet ideology, in our eyes, would be dead the day it recognized its own limitation. Whether such recognition is probable or improbable, at hand or remote, is a question of fact which we leave open for the moment. What concerns us here is the determination of the goal that Western strategy should bear in mind; it can be indicated in two words: survival and peace, physical survival by avoiding thermonuclear war, moral survival by the safeguarding of liberal civilization, peace by reciprocal acceptance by each bloc of the other's existence and of its right to existence. Survival in peace would also mean the victory of the West, for the latter would have convinced its enemy to give up the idea of destroying it, a renunciation which in turn is possible only by the conversion of the Marxist-Leninists to a more modest and more truthful self-interpretation. The day this conversion is achieved, we should be victorious without our enemies being therefore conquered: of all victories, the most fruitful, since it would have been obtained without bloodshed and would pave the way for reconciliation.

3. *Assessment of Dangers*

You are living in a fool's paradise, the advocate of the Catonian strategy will reply. Don't you see that the Soviet Union is advancing and the West withdrawing? If things go on this way, it is the West that runs the risk of being conquered without a war, being absorbed by the Soviet imperium as the space available to it diminishes and it loses its sources of supply and its markets.

It is difficult for a contemporary to arrive at an accurate diagnosis of a historical situation which is by nature in flux. The outcome of a crisis, that of Berlin for example, may alter the European climate and hence the relative strength of the two blocs, perhaps for a long period of time. The very nature of the combat in which we are engaged is unprecedented, with the result that a number of judgments of the traditional sort are henceforth meaningless.

The international system, in the mid-twentieth century, is global and bipolar. There is no region in the world which is unaffected by relations between the two super powers, no state which is not or might not be represented in the United Nations. At the same time this system is bipolar since the Big Two possess—and possess exclusively—*in 1965 even more than in 1945,* the physically decisive weapons. Each has the means of devastating the planet, razing cities, exterminating populations. But if the Northern Hemisphere is for the most part covered by the two blocs, the Southern Hemisphere remains outside the area where the two blocs confront one another. It is permissible to claim that the Southern Hemisphere is the stake of this confrontation, but it has not been proved that, even if one of the Big Two were to prevail in the Northern Hemisphere, the rest of mankind would automatically fall under its domination. The military superiority of the two super powers is, in fact, of a unique kind, since it is based on technology, thermonuclear bombs, bombers, ballistic missiles. But up to now these means of destruction are means of power only to a certain extent, since neither of the super powers has utilized its thermonuclear force to terrorize an ally, a satellite or a non-aligned nation. Thermonuclear arsenals, unlike the British fleet in the last century, do not operate against those who do not possess them; they seem for the moment to have no other purpose than to neutralize one another.

The conflict between the United States and the Soviet Union in the Northern Hemisphere is determined by none of the classical causes—space, population, natural resources. Each of the super powers possesses an immense space, retains a margin of growth in extension, produces its food on its own soil and finds under that soil most of the raw materials it needs for its industries. The countries of Western Europe—West Germany, Great Britain, Italy—do not have the same growth potential as the United States. They have an intensive agriculture and must still import a fraction of their food. But for the next few decades at least, continental agriculture—in Germany, France, Italy—will continue to experience the advantages and adversities of the scientific revolution. Overproduction will be more feared than scarcity. The importing countries—Great Britain, Germany—will prefer to buy at the cheapest price on the world market, and countries with a surplus, like France, will be indignant when they cannot find outlets for their surpluses. This kind of crisis does not call for a solution in or by war. These conflicts in which space or resources constitute the determining factors or stakes are today marginal in the Near East (Palestine) or in North Africa (Sahara).

This is not to say that a war to the death, if it were to break out, would necessarily be an absurdity. Each of the super powers may in fact believe, rightly or wrongly, that it would certainly be secure and perhaps master of the world if its rival did not exist. The meaning of the cold war is not the same according to Washington's interpretation or Moscow's, but the meaning of a war to the death, despite the different vocabularies, would be fundamentally the same for both. If the Soviet Union did not exist, it would be possible for Washington to imagine how easy it would be to orient toward constitutional government the legitimate revolution of the masses against colonialism, feudalism and exploitation. If the United States no longer existed, how easy it would be to orient the revolution of peoples toward its logical conclusion, socialism! If the Soviet Union did not exist, the American thermonuclear force would not be continually on the alert, its only function would be to forbid the excessive use of force to the others, the children, those who don't know any better. If the United States no longer existed, the Soviet thermonuclear force would no longer have any function since mankind would be converted to socialism without delay and since peace would be assured between brother states.

The reward of victory, in this duel between giants, would, therefore, in spite of everything people say, be immense, immeasurable. It would justify *almost* every sacrifice because it would apparently be identified with the end of terror, the end of the Hobbesian situation between states. If one of the Big Two is completely eliminated, the ambition of all the Caesars is realized, the dream of madmen and sages alike fulfilled: peace on earth to men even of bad will. The boundaries of the empire would this time coincide with the frontiers of mankind. The sovereignty of force, acquired by victory, would be maintained not by an administration that would soon become odious to the peoples but by the discreet and inexorable control of factories and laboratories.

If neither of the Big Two appears to look upon this supreme struggle as if it were inevitable or even probable, it is not that the stake is too small, it is that the risks are too great. The risks of the final struggle in any international system have always been great. In the days when men killed one another only in hand-to-hand combat, a fight to the death could already mean mutual suicide. The wars waged by industrial societies during the first half of this century did not have this quality; they weakened the first protagonists, favored the rise of peripheral states, allowed the survival of only two or three great powers, ushered in the age of universal history. No one knows if or when the age of universal history will lead to the universal state.

The nature of the weapons still keeps the candidates for empire on this side of the supreme test; it also tends to eliminate and in any case *mitigates the repercussions of the vicissitudes of the cold war upon the relation of forces in the event of a war to the death*. If the United States and the Soviet Union begin to attack one another with thermonuclear bombs, what difference does the location of the frontier between the two empires and the two zones of influence make, or the number of African republics calling themselves popular democracies! Let us imagine the whole of southeast Asia —Laos, Cambodia, South Vietnam, Thailand, Malaysia—converted to communism or conquered by it: the "loss" of these countries, to use the expression popular in the United States, would constitute a defeat for the West. It would add to the prestige of the Soviet side, it would snowball, it would swell the ranks of those rallying out of opportunism to the new faith. "Nothing succeeds like success." When all this has been said, it remains true that the countries of southeast Asia, in shifting from one camp to another, would not substantially alter the relation between the available resources of one side and the other, at least those resources usable for thermonuclear war.

The idea we are trying to suggest might be formulated abstractly in the following terms: *there is no direct, one-to-one relation between the quantity of material and human resources and the military force represented by thermonuclear equipment*. If the balance between thermonuclear capacities is upset, it would be futile for either side, in the present state of the world, to try to restore it by recruiting new allies or by seducing allies from the other side. The relation of thermonuclear forces is a function at any given moment of the striking and retaliatory capability, the active and passive defense of the Big Two. This capacity and this defense, in turn, depend on weapons and organization, that is, on laboratories as well as authorized expenditures. Perhaps the Americans would create difficulties for the Soviets if they increased their national defense budget to eighty billion dollars. For the moment, Soviets and Americans have devoted a more or less equal quantity of resources to armament, research and stockpiling. Whatever the respective development of the gross national product of the United States and the Soviet Union in the course of the next two or three decades, neither of the super powers will be outclassed for lack of material means or money.

Is this to say that there is no common measure between advances and retreats of the two blocs on the one hand, and the relation of forces at grips on the other? Certainly not. But to clarify these relations we should proceed to an abstract analysis. Let us distinguish three concepts: balance of deterrence, relation of thermonuclear forces, relation of total forces in the thermonuclear age. The balance of deterrence is established when each of the possessors[6] has the same capacity as its rival to deter direct aggression or extreme provocation. In fact, this capacity does not depend merely on the instruments which each of the players possesses, but also on the move to resist, the willingness to run risks, the art of making people take an improbable threat seriously. Since deterrence is a relation between two wills, the balance of deterrence is a psycho-technological equilibrium. The spectator observes—not without difficulty—the equality or inequality of the instruments of deterrence, but he cannot know in advance what will happen when it comes to the tests.

The relation of thermonuclear forces results from their confrontation, and the possible consequences for each power of their use of this method. The side which, thanks to the preparations of passive defense, had the best chance of survival would be the strongest. This relation of thermonuclear forces is even more difficult to assess than the relation of military forces was formerly. Fortunately, we lack experience; moreover, the disproportion between crime and punishment may be such that the strongest is automatically the one who strikes first.

Neither the balance of deterrence nor the relation of thermonuclear forces is affected, generally speaking, by the allied or non-aligned countries when they change status, break an alliance to become neutral or go over to one camp or the other after having been neutral. Again, we must stress the reservation *generally speaking* and clarify it by the following commentary: provided the countries under consideration are fundamentally outside the thermonuclear systems of the two super powers. Indeed, the network of military bases around the territory of the Soviet Union is far from being useless to the military force of the United States, even in the event of a war waged with nuclear weapons (the bases facilitate the dispersion of instruments, they are take-off or relay points for bombers, they afford possibilities for observation or surveillance of Soviet frontiers, etc.). The thermonuclear force, withdrawn and concentrated in the American fortress, as the Soviets and certain Americans weary of their international obligations prefer, would be incomparably weaker both in itself and as an instrument of deterrence.

But it remains true that *recourse to allies to re-establish an endangered balance belongs to the past.* The decision of Corinth and of Corcyra controlled the balance of naval forces at the start of the Peloponnesian War; the change of allegiance of the French fleet in 1941 would have been enough to compromise the precarious rule of the British fleet. If one of the Big Two

---

[6] We are entertaining the simple hypothesis of two possessors. If there were several possessors of thermonuclear forces, various combinations would be possible. We will postpone to another occasion the analysis of the thermonuclear game with several players.

gains possession before the other of anti-missile missiles or of a large-scale civil defense, the recruiting of an ally or the seduction of an enemy satellite will not compensate for the setback suffered in the race for progress. In a certain sense the two super powers are alone, face to face, in this duel whose logical outcome would be a draw and whose possible outcome is the death of one or both combatants.

Is the concept of a global balance of military forces or of a global balance of forces therefore devoid of meaning? I do not think so. It is possible to form an approximate idea of the military means at the disposal of each bloc, means of waging a local or a general conflict either with conventional weapons or with all available weapons. But this assessment of the total forces of one side or the other is even more liable to error than in the past because the hypothesis of a war comparable to past wars, in which the belligerents would mobilize all their forces and gradually all engage their weapons, seems improbable (it is difficult to imagine the *broken-back* war, the war that would be waged by countries devastated by thermonuclear bombs).

If this analysis is correct, two kinds of expectations are forbidden us: those based on a comparison of the resources at the disposal of the two sides, and those which would invoke the superiority of one kind of weapon or force. The (very approximate) proportionality between the number of men and machines on one hand and military force on the other characterized the first half of the twentieth century. In the reign of nuclear and electronic industry this proportionality ceases to seem even broadly true. Mobilization after the outbreak of hostilities becomes impossible. Laboratories take over the role of factories, quality triumphs over quantity. The greater size of the American national product would weigh heavily in the balance if the two super powers renounced their mutual suicide pact and concentrated all their efforts to prepare for their survival in the event of thermonuclear war.

General statements on the respective advantages of land and sea have lost their validity at the same time that the law of number—of men and machines—ceased to be applicable to combats in the foreseeable future. Military writers have frequently speculated about the notion of the *decisive weapon*. Which weapon—infantry, cavalry, artillery, then the air force—exercised the major influence on the battlefield, determined either victory or defeat? These speculations have never entirely convinced me because the weapon by which one of the belligerents had been assured of an overwhelming technical or tactical superiority seemed decisive until the moment when, equality having been restored, all weapons became decisive again or another weapon benefited from an innovation.

In the past, when the weapons themselves changed only slowly, a combat instrument like the Roman legion or heavy cavalry ruled the battlefield for centuries. In our age, reigns are short. The combination of tanks and dive bombers constituted the decisive weapon in 1940: two years later defensive tactics had made up for lost time and armored weapons no longer seemed the sovereign ones.

Similarly, Mackinder's books have shown that the outcome of the conflict between the bear and the whale has varied according to the times, that it depended not only on the respective efficiency of the naval or land weapons but also on the relation between the available forces on land or on sea. Naval power has actually exerted considerable influence on the course of modern history, but the circumstances were exceptional: the countries of Europe were of medium dimensions, the coalitions they formed by means of temporary alliances balanced one another approximately, the resources of other continents, used by the state whose fleet ruled the waves, were enormous; outside of the Continent there was no military power of the first rank. The development of land mobility, industrial concentration, the formation of the German Empire, then the Russian Empire, brought the centuries of English hegemony to an end. At the present time the scale of the political units engaged is without precedent. It is the United States— a continental-state—which is the island in relation to the mainland. It is the Soviet imperium—extending to the middle of Germany—that plays the part of the land power.

Both empires have at their disposal land weapons as well as those of the sea, and it would be futile to claim to predict the victory of the sea or that of the land masses, as if such weapons established the supremacy of one element or the other. In fact, the decisive weapon, if there is one, is the combination of air (or of interplanetary space), transmission medium, and nuclear firing power. The Bear is no longer confined to his earthly prison for lack of access to the open sea, the Whale no longer has the protection of distance and the ocean. Neither walls nor security for one or the other. Each is capable of exterminating the rest of mankind. Each risks perishing if it takes the initiative.

If such is the situation, if such is the nature of the competition, is the West in danger as a result of the advances made by the Soviet Union over the past ten years?

From the territorial point of view, it was during the years 1945–50 that the changes so disastrous in the eyes of the West occurred: the Sovietization of Eastern Europe, the victory of the Communist party of China. These two events prematurely upset the relationship between the two blocs. Reduced to a fringe position on the Eurasian land mass, Western Europe lacked the spatial depth necessary for an effective defense. In Asia the establishment of a new regime, of a strong state at Peking, reduced the American presence to islands and beachheads and hung over southeast Asia a threat of domination if not of conquest. If one compares the situation in Europe and in Asia in 1950 and in 1960, after a ten-year interval, what is most surprising is that it has not deteriorated more than it has. The economic recovery of Western Europe has exceeded the most optimistic hopes. The island states—Japan, the Philippines, Taiwan—are more prosperous and stronger today than they were ten years ago. Even the successor states of Indo-China—South Vietnam, Cambodia, Laos—whose survival seemed at least doubtful following the Geneva Convention in 1954, have not yet been swallowed by the Communist or near-Communist forces.

What are the facts that have appeared during the last decade which inspire so much pessimism in so many observers? I discern four: *the technological successes of the Soviet Union and the equalization of deterrence capacities; the end of private hunting grounds and the tendency of many states formerly associated with the West to insist on neutral status; the theoretically or actually greater rate of growth in the Soviet Union than in the United States, in China than in India; and finally the feeling which seems to be spreading throughout the world that the wind of history is blowing toward the East, that the future belongs to the regimes of so-called popular democracy.* In short, the Soviet side is said to have advanced *militarily, politically, economically, morally.*

On the military level the modification in the relation of total forces is incontestable. In 1950 Soviet superiority in conventional weapons was great, but American quantitative and qualitative superiority in the area of atomic weapons, means of delivery (bombers) and bases was apparent.

In 1960 the United States probably possessed a larger and more diversified stock of atomic and thermonuclear weapons, and it had at its disposal more bombers, more numerous and better distributed bases. Does the Soviet Union have a compensatory advantage in the area of ballistic missiles? In 1964 the American experts denied this with the same vehemence with which some of them once affirmed it. Moreover, they maintained that numerical superiority was on the American side and that the detection of Soviet launching sites would, if necessary, permit a counterforce strategy. According to other experts, the Soviets possess more powerful bombs (several dozen megatons) and rockets whose thrust is sufficient to carry these monstrous bombs for thousands of miles. Finally, the United States, because of its type of government, is less capable of taking the initiative. To maintain its equality in deterrence capacity, it must be able to inflict a punishment equal to the crime, that is, must possess a thermonuclear force which after a massive attack would retain means equal to that of the intact enemy force.

To a certain extent, this deterioration of the relation of nuclear forces was inevitable. The Soviet Union is in a position to devote to those goals it considers of highest priority its best scientists and all the material and financial resources the latter require. The transition from unilateral deterrence to the balance of deterrence was therefore inevitable sooner or later. Is the United States mistaken to subscribe to a mutual suicide pact? Can it recapture the advantage by a counterforce strategy? Should it retain plausible first-strike capability? These are questions more technological than political, on which the experts do not agree. Let us say that probably, short of a vertiginous acceleration in the arms race, the equality in reciprocal deterrence capacity is bound to occur sooner or later.[7]

On the political level the elimination of private game preserves and the spread of the cold war to the Near East, Africa and Latin America are the result of two historical movements, the breakdown of colonial empires and the worldwide action henceforth being taken by the Soviet Union. Since the countries formerly subject to the sovereignty of a European country or part of a zone of influence have, as a result of the conflict between the two blocs, acquired a certain freedom of maneuver, since these countries all nourish some resentment against their former master or protector, and since they express or magnify this resentment in words, it is easy to confuse this extension of the zones of the cold war with a defeat for the West: from sovereignty to partnership, from zone of influence to rivalry of blocs, from partnership to non-alignment, from neutrality to active neutralism and from the latter to adherence to the Soviet bloc, such is the path which all peoples, according to the Soviets, must necessarily follow to its very end, such is the nightmare of the defeatists among the Westerners.

But these defeatists do not even realize that they are adopting, with inverted value judgments, their enemy's philosophy of history. It is the Marxist-Leninists who confuse colonial domination and the imperialism which proceeds from capitalism, who imagine that capitalism is doomed the moment it is deprived of its colonies, who claim that all roads lead to Moscow, who believe in an inexorable determinism of which national or bourgeois revolutions are one stage and of which the climax is the triumph of the Communist party. We have no difficulty, in the context of our own philosophy, in explaining why new states and peoples with underdeveloped economies have trouble adopting political institutions similar to those of the United States or Great Britain. But, once again, it is Marxist-Leninist dogmatism which poses the absurd dilemma: either the power of the so-called worker-peasant party or the power of the bourgeois class; it is this dogmatism which lumps together in a single concept all regimes not of the Soviet type and which sees no other solution to all crises, whatever they may be, than a regime of this type. None of the Arab countries, despite their hostility to the West and to Israel, has joined the Soviet bloc or has become a popular democracy. In Africa, even Guinea and Ghana continue to maneuver between the two blocs. In Latin America, Cuba is the only country up to now which has spontaneously achieved a revolution whose leaders, out of anti-American passion or necessity or ideological preference, have officially declared their allegiance to socialism and to the Sino-Russian camp.

[7] Let there be no mistake: I do not mean that this equality is automatic, or that it will be achieved without difficulty, nor that the situation of the two gangsters is inconceivable, nor that either of the two cannot take some advantage or other; I mean that the West can no longer count on a lasting superiority in this kind of rivalry.

It is possible—probable, even—that still other countries, in the course of the next decade, will go over to active neutralism, that is, to "people's republics"; so many defeats for the West, to be sure, since to contain the Soviet Empire is the goal of Western strategy. But if states and peoples are regarded as pawns on a chessboard, as usable instruments in the rivalry for power, if the recruiting of allies or satellites is, for each side, a means of strengthening itself and of weakening its rival, then a great many of these defeats are without grave consequences. Neither Laos nor Guinea strengthen the economic or military potential of either bloc. For the West, a change of allegiance has a military significance, either in the context of the cold war when it snowballs or threatens local capacity to resist, or with regard to the possibility of total war when it takes bases or facilities away from the American thermonuclear force or gives them to the enemy force.

It will be objected that the more the territory of the bloc is enlarged, the greater the increase in its resources. But this is a misleading impression. In certain respects, allied or satellite states are henceforth a burden more than a contribution: they receive from their *grand frère* more than they give. Insofar as they are developing countries, only a slight percentage of their national product is available for diplomatic-strategic use. Economically, it is true, the expansion of the socialist world market and the contraction of the capitalist world market involve advantages for the former, disadvantages for the latter. If we imagine the entire world, except for the United States, changing to the Soviet side, obviously the United States would be defeated politically and militarily as well as economically. But we are far from such a situation. The Soviet bloc has made and will continue to make advances, as regards volume of production as well as relations with the non-aligned nations. But the non-aligned nations continue to have by all odds the most considerable fraction of their commerce with the West. In the course of the foreseeable future—that is, the next few decades—unless the territorial status of the globe is utterly disrupted, the West will not lack for either sources of raw material or markets for manufactured products.

There remains the argument of the disparity in rates of growth. A scientific comparison of rates of growth requires greater precautions than characterized the speeches of Mr. Khruschev or even the articles of most Western economists. It is true, generally speaking, that the Soviet rate of growth during the years 1950–60 was appreciably higher than that of the United States, whether we are dealing with gross national product or with per capita production. For various reasons, the American rate of growth was relatively low during this period, even compared with that of the economies of the European Continent. Polemics on rates of growth (is the Soviet Union's 8 per cent or 6 per cent?), on the present relation of national production (is Russian production equal to approximately a third or a half of the American national product?) make it difficult to arrive at undisputed results, so poorly understood are certain questions of fact, so greatly do these comparisons require conventions (relative to prices) which no one adopts in-contestably. It would be better, therefore, in order to avoid entering a technical argument, to concentrate on general, incontestable facts which are sufficient to our discussion.

Whatever may have been the growth of Soviet consumption for the past ten years, the standard of living and, even more, the comforts and pleasures of existence remain, for the large mass of the population, in-comparably inferior to what they are in the West. Living conditions, inadequate supplies, the organization of trade, as any visitor to the Soviet Union finds them, suffice to confirm the foregoing statement. More than 40 per cent of the manpower continues to be used in agriculture in order to nourish—indifferently—about 210 million persons. Less than 10 per cent, in the United States, produces a surplus which weighs on the budget and is distributed around the world. As long as such a disparity persists between the agricultural productivity not only of the Soviet Union and the United States, but on both sides of the Iron Curtain, the West has nothing to fear from the alleged threat of socialist prosperity. Those who imagined, even some years ago, France or Europe lowering in their turn an iron curtain to prevent com-parison between "capitalist exploitation" and "socialist liberation" did not know what they were talking about. Being statisticians or ideologists, they were led astray by statistics or passions.

On the other hand, the reduction of the relative disparity between the industrial production of the Soviet Union and that of the United States, between that of the Soviet bloc and that of the Atlantic bloc, is in fact probable. Soviet newspapers have proclaimed that the share of the Soviet bloc (including China) in world industrial production was 37 per cent in 1960, that five years from then it would be over half. An increased per-centage is a normal result of the higher Soviet growth rate in industrial pro-duction. That in certain sectors the Soviet bloc will produce by 1970 as much or even more than the Western bloc (United States and Western Europe) is possible. That it will produce by 1970 as much as the Western bloc either with regard to industry as a whole or per capita is out of the question. But, provided the Soviet Union catches up in the area of agricultural productivity, nothing is to prevent it—on paper—from someday catching up with the United States (more likely in the next century than in this one).[8]

If we focus our attention on the next two or three decades, must we say

[8] On July 9, 1961, Mr. Khrushchev gave the following figures: the industrial production of the U.S.S.R. amounted to 60 per cent of that of the United States in 1960. In 1966 it will produce 106 per cent and in 1970 156 per cent of the present American production. Allowing a rate of growth of 2 per cent to the United States, Mr. Khrushchev concluded that the U.S.S.R. will outstrip the United States by 1967, allowing a rate of 3 per cent by 1968. He added: "Approximately the same statistics could be adduced for the development of agriculture in the two countries." This last remark proves that we are dealing here with exercises in propaganda, not statistics.

that the Soviet advance "threatens" the United States or Western Europe?
The statement may be understood in two senses: either the Soviet Union, because of its growth, would have the means to devote more resources to foreign policy (arms and aid), or because of its wealth and prosperity would be
an irresistible example to the West and to the non-aligned nations. Each of
these "dangers" is real, but neither is as serious as Mr. Khrushchev would
have had us believe. The day the United States recognizes the necessity of
spending sixty billion dollars for defense rather than forty-five or fifty billion,
it will in so doing bring about a more rapid increase in the gross national
product and in industrial production. The latter increases less quickly than in
the Soviet Union partly because of the distribution of demand. If the public
does not want to buy more industrial products, if it spends its additional
income on better housing or amusements or travel, industrial production will
advance less rapidly, the rate being determined primarily by that of the other
two advances, that of productivity and that of population.[9] But the capacity
for growth, in the case of the arms race, remains intact in the United States.
The latter runs no risk of being militarily outclassed. As for the economic
weapon, the Soviet Union and its allies will use it more generously tomorrow
than they do today. Psycho-political effectiveness does not depend merely on
sums of dollars or rubles given or loaned.

If there is a danger, it is at the moment, and for many years to come it will
remain, more psychological than material, more political than military. The
growth of the Soviet economy is an argument in the great debate in which
each bloc attempts to persuade the other of the superiority, hence of the
legitimacy, of its institutions. The West has not much to fear from a comparison of the realities: let the non-aligned peoples go to Berlin and compare
the lot of the people and the quality of life and culture on both sides of the
Wall. As a matter of fact, the West has nothing to fear even from the advances which the Soviet Union may make over the next ten years. If the
standard of living rises and the drabness of Soviet life tends to assume a little
color here and there, perhaps the Kremlin leaders will be more sincere in
their desire for peaceful coexistence.

Finally, there remains the last "threat," the threat created by the vague but
powerful feeling in the West and throughout the non-aligned world that
the future belongs to Russia and to regimes of the Soviet type. That this
feeling is already widespread in some quarters I do not doubt. But in France
it is more prevalent among certain intellectual or bourgeois circles than in
the masses. It is far from being universal, it is the product of propaganda
and even more of propagandists, it does not arise spontaneously in the minds
of men considering the spectacle of the world. After all, some twenty years

---

[9] The population of the United States increases as rapidly as that of the Soviet Union.

ago it was another totalitarianism which rallied opportunists to its cause. By definition, such allegiances are never permanent. It is better to combat than to count them.

4. *The Strategy of Peace*

Bearing in mind not only the objectives of Western strategy as I outlined them in the second section, but also the facts of the situation as I just reviewed them in the third, what should be the principles of Western strategy in terms of these two analyses?

The West will never really enjoy security until the day the Soviet bloc no longer seeks the destruction of those regimes it calls capitalist, that is, the destruction of the West itself. Western Europe will never really enjoy security until the day the partition of Germany and of the Continent as a whole has been abolished. As long as the Russian armies are stationed two hundred kilometers from the Rhine, the doors of the temple of Janus will remain open. But these two statements must be supplemented by two others: since the United States was unwilling to take the slightest risk to liberate the nations of Eastern Europe at a time when it was strongest in military terms, it should not logically do so now. More generally, the West, short of being ready to wage a thermonuclear war, has no way of "destroying" the Soviet regime or imperium, and scarcely any way of influencing the internal development of this imperium, or relations between the Soviet Union and Communist China.

These four statements combined will seem characterized by a fundamental contradiction in the eyes of those who put a crude interpretation on the dialectic of antagonism and hope we will pay back with interest the hostility our enemies display toward us. The contradiction disappears the moment that we consider ourselves victorious on the day the Soviets have sincerely abandoned their enterprise. But since this conversion, assuming it someday occurs, is still remote, we must realize that the conflict will be prolonged and that short of a happy accident (the breakup of the Soviet bloc) or an unhappy accident (the breakup of the Atlantic bloc or war) the best we can hope for is a slackening of the Soviet advance in the third world and a gradual stabilization of relation of forces—political and not just military—between the two blocs. Whether we want to or not, we shall live under a military threat as long as there is no agreement on arms control, and under a political threat as long as the Marxist-Leninists remain true to their faith.

It is useless to evoke the strategy of rollback, as did James Burnham on the eve of the Republican return to power in the 1950s, or of *forward strategy*, as do the three writers we quoted above. The West, given its nature, has never had the political capacity for an offensive strategy, nor has it the material capacity for it today. It is not out of the question, however, that the weakened West may be more aggressive or more intransigent than the United States was just after the war, when it alone was intact and powerful. We know that democracies are inclined to make war when they are provoked, not when circumstances are favorable to them.

Granted that we have no way of "forcing" Soviet societies to become open or to "liberate" the countries of Eastern Europe, we must be prepared to live in a world that is "half free and half slave" for a long time to come, without excluding the possibility that the slave half of the world may change of itself. There is no question of subscribing to the simple-minded theory of some Marxists or pseudo-Marxists[10] whereby the Soviet regime will *necessarily* become democratic as the standard of living rises. But neither need we accept as a dogma that the Soviet regime cannot change or that Moscow's diplomacy-strategy is now and forever determined by the *intention* of Lenin or Stalin. Within the context of a philosophy which is for the moment invulnerable to experience, the Kremlin leaders act according to circumstances. The West can have an effect on the circumstances to which Moscow will deem it reasonable to adjust.

This strategy will be called a defensive strategy or a strategy of coexistence. And I do not deny that compared with a strategy whose goal is to destroy the Soviet Union or the Soviet imperium, to eliminate the Soviet threat once and for all, this strategy deserves to be called defensive, since it adopts the slogan of coexistence from the enemy, so to speak, with the difference that it gives it another interpretation. But the choice of a strategy must *also* be governed by an analysis of the relation of forces, and since the aim is to avoid thermonuclear war as well as to preserve liberal civilization, it seems to me preferable not to match the universalist intention of the Soviets with an intention equally universalist. It is by championing the rights of institutional pluralism against the monism of Marxism-Leninism that the West accurately defines its mission against totalitarianism, not by setting up a monism analogous and antagonistic to that we are combating.

Having accepted the fact of coexistence between the two blocs, the first requirement is the preservation of the balance between the global military forces. Or, to express myself more precisely, the major danger is still, for the present time, the military danger and not, as everyone insists, the danger of subversion or infiltration. That the majority of commentators think otherwise springs from the identification of urgency with importance, of visible crises with the unending and fundamental rivalry. It is very true that thermonuclear bombs and ballistic missiles do nothing to check Soviet expansion in southeast Asia and the Near East. It is very true that those—assuming they exist—who have counted on atomic strategy to contain the Soviet Union throughout the world were mistaken and that in this sense it is possible to speak of the failure of atomic strategy. But by definition a strategy of deterrence—politically defensive—can have only a negative success. Since it aims

---

[10] Isaac Deutscher, for example.

no further than the status quo, it seems sterile as soon as one decides retrospectively that the status quo would have been maintained in any event.

The priority I accord to military considerations has the following significance: if the Soviet bloc were to become convinced that it possesses an incontestable superiority either as regards passive or active instruments of deterrence, or as regards military means in general, the danger would risk being fatal; the Kremlin leaders would feel that the time for the final struggle had come or, more probably, they would press their advantage to the point of forcing the West to choose between capitulation and war. Most of the time the struggle between the two blocs is not waged on military terrain, precisely because the balance of forces is maintained. Were the latter to be compromised, everything else would be jeopardized at the same time.

Now military equilibrium, in the probable absence of an agreement on arms control, presupposes a constant and large-scale effort of research and production which is far from being achieved once and for all by a minimum retaliatory capacity. This equilibrium, during the period beginning now, will make it increasingly difficult to tolerate a radical inferiority in any category of means—for example, in the area of conventional weapons. The probable development half a dozen years from now toward thermonuclear weapons which are increasingly terrible and increasingly invulnerable is accompanied by the probability, despite Soviet claims to the contrary, that conventional weapons may be used, even by the two super powers against one another, and without escalation.

The primacy of military considerations is not just the result of the enormity of the risks involved in possible negligence: it has to do with another primacy, itself contrary to the opinion prevalent today—the primacy of Europe or of the theater of operations in which the two blocs confront one another with respect to the third world. Here again, the distinction is between *importance* and *urgency*. During those years which preceded Mr. Khrushchev's revival of the Berlin crisis, nothing seemed to be happening in Europe. Each of the two blocs was organizing: each found its territorial status unsatisfactory but preferable to the cost of a war, which seemed to be the only way to change it. Meanwhile, the war in Indo-China, or the nationalization of the Suez Canal, or the Algerian War, or the breakup of the Belgian Congo, or the revolt in Angola absorbed the attention of the leaders of the United States and of most of the European governments.

But the same is true of the "draw" in Europe as of the "balance of deterrence" on the global level: neither result is attained automatically or definitively. *Success or failure can be decisive only in the area of armaments or on the European Continent.* If the Federal Republic of Germany, in the hope of restoring its unity, were to turn to Moscow, Western Europe would be lost and so would the Atlantic Alliance. As long as Atlantic unity is preserved, all can still be saved; if Atlantic unity were shaken, all the West's other positions would be endangered.

I see still another reason to reduce the importance which Western strategists generally grant to the verbal or actual commitments of the Afro-Asian countries. In the short run, most of these countries, taken separately, would, were they to shift their allegiances, alter only slightly the balance of resources or of power between the blocs. In due time, if most of these countries adhered to one camp or the other, an imbalance would result on a universal scale, but the allegiances of these countries to one bloc or the other are circumstantial, revocable. They have no definitive character since it is obvious that an African or Latin American republic will not choose to be subject to the arbitrary power of Moscow once it ceases to fear European "colonialism" or "Yankee imperialism." If the two centers of force prevail in the Northern Hemisphere, neither will exercise a lasting domination over the Southern Hemisphere, because those countries which constitute stakes in the eyes of Moscow or Washington have above all a desire not to be subject to anyone, and express this desire today by the various modes of non-alignment or neutrality.

If we accept this hierarchy of importance, how can the West improve its diplomacy-strategy? Personally, I believe that the decisive answer, but also the most difficult, would be a tightening of the bonds among the Western countries, the taking of another step in the direction of an authentic Atlantic community. During the postwar phase, Atlantic unity, regarded as a zone of civilization, faced three tasks: the reconstruction of devastated regions (Western Europe), the giving up of colonial empires, and the organization of the community which required the presence of the United States in Europe from now on as indispensable. The first task was accomplished faster and better than anyone dared hope. The second was achieved without any real cooperation between the United States and the colonial states of Europe, the former making every effort to alienate neither its allies on the Continent nor the nationalists revolting against colonial power. It is easy to say in retrospect that with a little more clairvoyance here, a little more courage there, the process of decolonization could have been less costly, could have left less resentment in the hearts of the colonial peoples, less bitterness in the ex-imperial nations. But men—especially statesmen, rulers and citizens —do not always accept the events they foresee. The majority of French ministers foresaw decolonization, but this did not mean that they would have made the first move and, acting upon their accurate foresight, put into effect, in agreement with Washington, a ten- or fifteen-year program of accession to independence for the colonies or protectorates of North Africa. Perhaps the colonial peoples' violence was necessary to force the colonial powers to take seriously those ideas with which they prefer to play without acting upon them.

When all this has been said, it is still true that decolonization has been nearly completed without breaking either the alliance between the colonial powers and the anti-colonialist United States, or the internal unity of those European powers which have been forced to an awareness of something other than themselves and their mission.[11] Once the process of decolonization is over, the West will experience different, almost converse opportunities and problems. On the psychological level, in the war of propaganda, the West will be able to take the offensive and denounce Soviet colonialism. But nowhere will it be any longer in a position to exert an exclusive influence, nowhere will the ideas, the agents, the subversive influence of the Soviet bloc be absent, nowhere can it afford to ignore the new states, with their passions and their injustice, any more than its Marxist-Leninist enemy. The exchange of accusations between French and American public opinion on colonialism and anti-colonialism (what have you done to the Algerians? and what have you done to the Indians?) belong to the past (perhaps the roles are reversed in Latin America). But on the other hand, all those bases outside the countries of the Alliance are now preserved only precariously.

These disadvantages would be more than compensated if, released from the colonial mortgage, the countries of the Atlantic Alliance succeeded in conducting a unified diplomatic strategy, or at least a consistently coordinated one. Now the relative weakening of the United States, in relation to its enemy and its allies, threatens to exert an influence in the opposite direction. The economies of the Common Market countries henceforth do not depend upon the American economy more than it does on them. In military terms, France is trying, after Great Britain, to produce a national nuclear striking force. The Bonn Republic is less impressed than ever by Mr. McNamara's doctrine. Where the latter sees a flexible strategy, his interlocutors in Bonn see the first signs of withdrawal.

The first condition for the Atlantic Pact to last and grow into an Atlantic community is for the leaders in Washington to realize that the time of the American (or Anglo-American) directorate is past (though this does not mean that the time of the *troika* directorate has arrived). In theory, perhaps, it might have been preferable to limit to the United States possession and disposition of the nuclear weapons within the Alliance. But it was contrary to the nature of states and their age-old aspirations to give up these decisive weapons once and for all. Today the problem is less to ascertain what formula would be best in itself than to avoid certain ill-fated consequences of the multiplication of costly national forces, which are of scant effectiveness and quickly outmoded by technological progress.

On the economic level President Kennedy set the tone with the word *partnership*. It is still too early to know how relations between the Common Market, Great Britain, the Commonwealth and the United States will actually be organized, but it is apparent that Europe's spectacular recovery, far from destroying the solidarity between the Western fringe of the Continent and the New World, is destroying the last vestiges of isolationism. The Six

[11] Portugal, if Mr. Salazar remains in power, is in serious danger of effecting its own ruin by fighting to the bitter end to maintain the fiction of the Lusitanian community.

of the Common Market, which together are the leading international exporter and importer, constitute a great economic power, the indispensable partner to the prosperity as to the diplomacy of the United States.

On the military level the goal would be to insure the permanence and gravity of the American commitment while at the same time giving the Europeans a real participation in the strategy of deterrence. The long-term solution, once Great Britain and France have initiated national programs, seems to me the formation of a European force which, without officially depending upon the American deterrent, would act only in cooperation with it. In this way Europe would resume awareness of its responsibilities without the American commitment being thereby weakened. The tightening of bonds among Europeans would attenuate the inequality between *one* great power and *several* small ones. The Alliance would no longer be regarded as a kind of American protectorate, but as a common undertaking.

As regards those zones outside the direct confrontation of the blocs, the analyses in the foregoing section have shown that there was neither an infallible formula, a universally valid priority (of economic aid or of military aid), nor a regime inherently suitable to the joint requirements of economic development and of Western interest. The greater part of what is called the third world—Asia, Africa, Latin America—is going through a phase of revolutionary upheaval whose causes are in variable proportions political, economic, demographic and psychological.

Politically, the traditional powers are almost all weakened. Tradition and the past no longer constitute valid qualifications for the exercise of authority. Legitimacy has become democratic, but the realization of this formula of legitimacy by election generally encounters insurmountable obstacles. Those elected do not respect the decisions of the electorate; these decisions are manipulated or fabricated. Between the two formulas consistent with the idea, that of the constitutional regime with several parties and that of the ideological and monopolistic party, intermediary experiments abound: conservative oligarchy with or without an electoral façade, despots with or without parties, modernists or reactionaries, military leader or junta of officers replacing a discredited or powerless parliament.

Economically, the peoples and, even more, the governing minorities almost all desire not to remain on the margin of development, that is, of industrialization, but whether the conditions necessary to development are or are not given in a country of Asia, Africa or Latin America does not depend on American diplomacy. If necessary, the donor can always build a few factories: such constructions solve none of the problems of underdevelopment, neither the impatience of the elite and the masses nor the disparity between the population and the volume of resources.

Those countries which today are trying to make up for lost time and to achieve the same revolution by which the favored third of mankind has shifted from the agricultural to the industrial stage enjoy one advantage in relation to their elders: the technology to be inherited is not that of one hundred and fifty years ago but that of today. The knowledge available is not only natural but social. We know a little more today than we did yesterday about social constants, the probable consequences of fiscal measures, the requirements of a program of investment, etc. The countries in the process of development are not advancing into unfamiliar territory.

The advantage of coming *after* the West is purchased at a high price. In certain cases the population has tripled or quadrupled (India) before the process of industrialization has got under way. The effectiveness of investments in hygiene and medicine is such that the mortality rate may be lowered without economic progress increasing resources accordingly. Such is the case with the principal countries of Asia (China, India), with the Near East (Egypt) and with Latin America.[12] Economic progress must catch up with demographic growth in order for living conditions to improve; the percentage of investment in relation to national income must reach 10 to 15 per cent in order for the advance to become cumulative, in order to make it increasingly easier to devote to current consumption a growing fraction of a national product which is expanding every year.

In addition to this fundamental difference between the situation of the Europeans in the eighteenth and nineteenth centuries and the situation of the Chinese, Indians and Latin Americans today, there are differences the consequences of which are not so easy to see. The traditional institutions of the political and social order were less weakened in Europe than they are in the countries of the third world in a comparable phase of development. The people were more passive, they were not aware of other possibilities, their demands were not justified by the example of advanced countries. The competition of the two super powers and the two ideologies, so long as the Communist party has not seized the state, sustains uncertainty, exploits the passions, diverts the energy of the elite toward civil strife. It is not just inevitable circumstances such as population pressure, the resistance of former privileged classes, the demands of the masses which favor adoption of the Soviet model of development; it is the Communist party itself wherever, by its opposition, it curbs any development from which its own ambitions would not benefit.

Half or two thirds of mankind would be in revolution even if Moscow and Marxism-Leninism did not exist—a revolution which cannot but accompany the efforts of underdeveloped peoples to achieve the industrial type of society of which the West and the Soviets offer them two rival, but in certain respects similar, versions. The United States has never by itself had the power to control or channel this revolution. Whatever name we give it—revolution or

[12] Greater than the population of the United States right now (around two hundred million), the population of Latin America, at its present rate, will roughly triple between now and the end of the century.

rising expectations (revolution of hope, one might say) or revolution of the masses—we have here a universal phenomenon whose causes are a biological-economic imbalance and a social upheaval, and which will continue for decades if not centuries. To recognize the obvious facts and to impress on strategists the necessary *modesty* in the determination of objectives is the first step toward a reasonable policy.

It is now acknowledged, even in the United States, that certain political institutions (the multi-party system and representative government) and economic institutions (the open market, freedom of entrepreneurs and consumers) are rarely suited to the requirements of initial phases of development. *The West should therefore prefer not those regimes which are closest to its own but those which have the best chance of promoting growth.* Also we must beware of the illusion that successful development will *insure* an attitude favorable, or at least neutral, to the West. No such guarantee exists. There are even circumstances in which economic progress will tend to strengthen the groups which incline toward the Soviet bloc, and thus to exert an influence contrary to our objectives. This could happen each time the West allows itself to be identified with the conservative or reactionary classes, leaving the quasi-monopoly of "progressive" slogans to the Communists or demi-Communists.

When things have reached this point, it would be futile to ask the American government to prefer an anti-Western regime because it accelerates development to a pro-Western regime which paralyzes it. But it is not impossible to convince American strategists first and foremost that no regime—whatever its institutions—need be called Communist as long as a party owing allegiance to Moscow is not in power. Next they must be convinced that even a regime in which the Communist party is in power, in Africa or in Latin America, is not the same as a regime imposed upon a country of Eastern Europe by the Red army; in Asia, in Africa, in Latin America, revolutionary regimes, even if they declare their kinship with Moscow, will have an interest in not breaking with the West, if only to receive aid from both sides. In other words, instead of acting and above all talking as if our security were endangered each time "Ruritania" declares its allegiance to Moscow, it would be better to show detachment and a certain indifference, to expose in advance the Communist blackmail to which incompetent rulers are too frequently prone, wrongly convinced that the Americans would be damaged more than they themselves by a victory for Moscow. On the contrary, we should remember on every occasion that the relation of military forces in our age is not seriously affected by the vicissitudes of the cold war.

These precepts—to isolate the enemy by recognizing as such only the Communist party, to accept any socialist party or regime, to prefer rulers effective in their own countries to those repeating declarations of allegiance, to aid development because such is our human obligation and in the long run our political interest, but to be neither disappointed nor surprised if

India or Brazil become more nationalist and more neutralist in proportion to their acquisition of an industry—will seem to some to be pervaded with the spirit of Munich. But this is a radically inaccurate interpretation. Since, even ninety miles off the coast of Florida, the United States refused to send Marines to put down a regime hostile to it in Cuba, we might better draw conclusions from this refusal to resort to armed force as well as from the dissociation between the vicissitudes of the cold war and the balance of deterrence.

These precepts in no way keep us from waging the cold war on the three battlefronts of economics, subversion and debate. On the first, two changes are desirable, one which is being made, the other scarcely recognized as yet. Since aid is futile if the government is weak and the anachronistic structure of ownership is maintained, it is better to concentrate resources, which will always be limited, where those conditions indispensable to a good return on investment are realized or can be realized as a result of outside pressure. Gifts or long-term loans are and must be an element of an over-all policy by which the West contributes, within its means, to the industrialization of the Southern Hemisphere. But even now, and increasingly during the years to come, it is the whole of the West's commercial policy which adds to or subtracts from the available resources of the third world. It has not been possible to do much about stabilizing the markets of raw materials. Another problem arises, and will arise tomorrow in even more acute form: that of the entry into developed countries of those simple manufactured products (textiles) which countries in the process of development are relying on in order to acquire foreign currency. At the present time, trade is tending to become increasingly free between Western countries, the Common Market having given an additional impetus to a movement which had already started. But since the United States is having increasing difficulty assuring itself the foreign currency necessary to finance gifts or loans, it is probable that aid will increasingly take the form of long-term credit with the obligation to buy in the creditor country. Moreover, in order to avoid the possibility of inter-European or inter-Atlantic free trade having unfavorable consequences on the third world, some measures inspired by a directed economy will probably be inevitable—price guarantees for the purchase of raw materials, the opening of Atlantic markets to the merchandise of countries with cheap labor, loans entailing purchases on a fixed market.

Economic aid needs time to be effective. Where subversion is about to win the day, countersubversion (or counterguerrilla activity) alone is an effective countermeasure. On this point it is prudent to call attention to a few commonplace ideas which are too often forgotten. Subversion has been successful in colonial territories because technological and tactical opposition came up against a decisive fact: the revolutionaries spoke the same language and belonged to the same race as the populations who were the stake in the conflict between subversion and repression. Even in Algeria, where the Moslem population was never unanimously won over to the FLN, the presence of a European minority established by right of conquest and obviously privileged, paralyzed the psychological and political efforts of the French army to pit slogan against slogan, the liberation of individuals against the liberation of Algeria, or a free Algeria in association with France against an independent Algeria. Where circumstances do not assure the forces of subversion such an advantage over those of repression, why should the former have won out in advance?

It is true that a small minority is enough to make repeated attacks and to foster a climate of insecurity. It is true that the Viet-minh commandos from the north raid the villages by night, terrify the villagers and apparently succeed in rallying the population, whereas the latter, had they not been subjected to threats or violence, would incline to the other side. In short, the techniques of subversive warfare not only reveal a pre-existing popular will, they are also capable in many circumstances of creating it. But precisely because this will does not exist, countersubversion—repression or counterguerrilla activity—*provided it uses suitable means*, does not have, *a priori*, less opportunity to succeed than the aggression it opposes. Do these *suitable means* entail, and to what degree, adopting the enemy's methods of leadership, of parallel organization, of inflexible discipline within the insurrectional core, of terror with respect to wavering crowds? It would be hypocritical to deny that almost through necessity adversaries are obliged by their dialectic to imitate one another when they fight. And the Soviet side has a twofold advantage: the spontaneous organization of the Communist party is immediately adaptable to the necessities of underground fighting (Lenin's principles of organization corresponded to these necessities); once in power, the Communists deny their enemies those liberties they have often enjoyed.

Repression is always necessary when subversion has reached the guerrilla state. It is rarely effective against propaganda, infiltration, attempts to seduce intellectuals, to exploit popular unrest, to convince the vacillating of the moral or historical superiority of the Soviet bloc. The fundamental principle which, like all strategic principles, is simple albeit difficult to apply, is that for every weapon there is an appropriate response, that on every kind of terrain the defense must erect an obstacle against the attack, and that one cannot afford to overlook any theater of operation. We are beginning to understand that the thermonuclear threat is no protection for territory liable to conquest by subversion. But we have not yet learned that too pronounced an inferiority in one kind of armament is dangerous and that one does not combat guerrilla forces by economic aid, any more than one combats propaganda by police methods. To be sure, there are cases in which one must also use the police against the enemy's propagandists: after all, the Marxist-Leninists are not above this. But the police force in a totalitarian regime is at the service of an enterprise of indoctrination. The police alone, without the aid of organization and persuasion, are ultimately ineffectual.

To say that we should follow the enemy on all kinds of terrain does not mean that we ought to model ourselves after him. On the contrary, whether we are talking about strategy or tactics, persuasion or subversion, asymmetry is inevitable. We are not trying to destroy the power that wants to destroy us, but to convert that power to tolerance and peace. We do not seek to persuade men that our institutions alone offer hope, but on the contrary to persuade our enemies and the third world too, that mankind, aside from respect for certain principles, has a natural bent toward diversity. Countries with democratic regimes cannot use the same tactics as countries with totalitarian regimes, and when they deny their principles they pay dearly in the end for a temporary advantage. They are neither able nor willing to sow revolution; they are neither able nor willing to forbid nations to seek their salvation, each according to their nature. But as long as the two worlds remain as they are, the freedom the West enjoys will have a subversive meaning on the other side of the Iron Curtain—a revolutionary meaning which Western strategists will never renounce but whose gradual disappearance they themselves desire. The day the Soviets have the same right to read, write, criticize and travel as Western nationals, the competition will have become truly peaceful.

This outline of a strategy will seem disappointing to all, to the school of offensive strategy and the school of peace alike. I am not unaware of the arguments of either school. The real question is to determine to what degree the prince's adviser has the right to conceive of the world as different from what it really is.

Personally, I think that it would have been possible, for several years after 1945, to liberate Eastern Europe without serious risk of war. Even in 1956, at the time of the Polish and Hungarian revolts, the West had an opportunity which it did not know how to take. But the possibility we are asserting without proof was altogether material; it presupposes that the United States and Western Europe were different then than they are now, with different institutions, different leaders, a different state of mind. But what was materially but not politically possible yesterday has for the time being ceased to be materially possible. Given the balance of power, the Kremlin leaders would probably prefer war to the loss of an important part of their imperium. Territorially, the West is in no position to aspire beyond self-defense.

If the West, under the protection of an approximate balance of deterrence capacities and of over-all military strength, keeps abreast in every theater of operations, it can hope not to suffer any serious defeat, but it cannot hope for any spectacular victory, barring either the conversion of the Soviets or a break between the Russians and the Chinese—possibilities it would be just as absurd to count on in the near future as it would to dismiss forever.

To the school of peace, this strategy, which involves a qualitative arms race, a continuation of the cold war with countersubversion and counterpropaganda, will seem warmongering and fraught with immeasurable dangers. How long can the two blocs oppose one another in this way on every continent and by every means, while threatening one another with the worst punishments and without executing their threats?

The first school censures this strategy for running the risk of gradual defeat which it involves, the second the risk of thermonculear war which it sustains. Both these reproaches are justified. The West runs the risk of being gradually smothered by the advance of the totalitarian regimes, buried by the wave of subversion. It could also be devastated by the monstrous weapons which its enemy, like itself, possesses. But the risk of suffocation could not be eliminated or reduced without increasing the risk of the thermonuclear catastrophe. And the risk of the military catastrophe could not be eliminated or reduced without accepting a greater risk of being forced to capitulate.

So the moderate strategy seems to me to offer the best chance of simultaneously averting these two kinds of danger—the danger of suffocation, the danger of violent death. If these two dangers are averted, the West's survival will be assured, a survival which in our time is the best, if not the only expression of victory.[13]

[13] The reader will perhaps be inclined to raise an objection to the analyses in the two foregoing chapters, as to those in the preceding part of the book: Is the international system still bipolar? Assuming that it still is today, will it be so a few years from now?

I. In the West the United States remains *the* dominant power because it alone possesses a thermonuclear force. It has lost a part of the economic lead which assured it an indisputable supremacy within the Western world. The dollar is threatened because of a persistent deficit in external accounts. Temporarily, on the monetary level, the United States depends on the good will of its European allies just as much or more than the latter depend on their American protector. Moreover, the countries of the European Continent have had a higher rate of growth from 1950 to 1960 than the United Kingdom and the United States. To be sure, the national output of the Six is still generally lower than that of the United States, for a population which is almost the same (36 per cent if we use the official rate of exchange, probably half of this by a method of reckoning that takes price systems into account). Nevertheless, the gap since 1945 and especially since 1950 has narrowed. Assuming that growth continues to be more rapid on the European side of the Atlantic and that the Common Market absorbs other European countries, a few years from now the Atlantic community will consist of two great powers which, although not of equal strength, *will no longer belong to two qualitatively distinct categories.*

On the Soviet side, the major fact since 1945 is not economic but political. The economy of Communist China has entered a phase comparable to that of the Russian Five-Year Plans of before the war, with one aggravating circumstance: at the outset, the ratio of space to men, agricultural resources and number of mouths to feed was such that Communist China was condemned, in the event of setbacks similar to those of the Soviet Union in the course of collectivization, to a general food shortage. In 1961 China's purchases of foodstuffs abroad totaled 6.5 million tons, at a value of 360 million dollars. Undernourishment seems to be largely responsible for the slackening in industrial growth, perhaps even for a reduction of industrial production. The China of 1961, with a steel production on the order of 10 million tons, was still not on a scale with the super powers, the Soviet Union or the community of the Six.

This is not the case on the political level. The Soviet Union cannot use methods of force to coerce Peking. The latter is strong not only by virtue of a population of some 700 million people, but also because of the revolutionary dynamism which it maintains and the ideological orthodoxy which it claims to embody. An official break in Sino-Soviet friendship would be a defeat for Khrushchev's successors as well as for Mao Tse-tung. The doctrine does not allow for inter-state conflicts between countries with socialist regimes. Each of the protagonists in the drama would be forced to treat his adversary as a schismatic or a heretic. In an ideological universe, a disagreement between heads of state, even one based on a divergence in national interests, must be translated into a theological dispute.

What effect on relations between the two blocs would a rivalry between Peking and Moscow have? It is difficult to foresee in any detail. It may be that in certain circumstances relations would become more difficult, since the fear of being accused of revisionism would provoke each of the two Communist great powers to outdo one another in their aggressiveness against capitalist imperialism. If this does not happen and if Moscow proves to be more conciliatory at a given point on the planet in order to prevent Chinese expansion, Peking may be in a position to prevent an agreement between Moscow and Washington by not respecting the promises made by Soviet negotiators (it is not out of the question, for example, that North Vietnam may, at Peking's instigation, sabotage Russo-American attempts at peace in Laos).

Of course, a contrary result, that is, a reconciliation between Washington and Moscow as a result of the tension between Moscow and Peking, is also conceivable. In the long run this would be the logical consequence of an open conflict between the two Communist great powers. But in the short run, as long as the Soviet regime chooses to be Marxist-Leninist and therefore cannot publicly acknowledge the possibility of a national hostility between two socialist states, the polyarchy within the Soviet universe involves as many dangers as advantages for the West and for peace. The Soviet Union continues to cover Communist China with regard to the United States and must prevent a collapse of the Chinese regime or an official break of the alliance. Moreover, China, which now receives scarcely any economic aid from the Soviet Union, is no longer obliged to deal tactfully with its Big Brother, since henceforth the latter can threaten it only with a punishment—an open break—which the Kremlin fears no less than Mao Tse-tung.

It would be awkward for the country, the party and the men who were the initiators of the revolution of our time to surrender to others the reputation for doctrinal purity. The Kremlin must fear, in the event that the two capitals ever compete for the title of metropolis of the new faith, that Peking will win out over Moscow in the eyes of the militants of Asia, Africa and Latin America.

II. The United States and the Soviet Union have done nothing to promote the acquisition by their respective allies of a thermonuclear force. The thesis, which is common to all or almost all American writers, is that a deterrence strategy pursued by four or five states would involve more risks than the present strategy pursued by two actors.

In the pages we have devoted to our theoretical and practical analysis of deterrence strategy, we have deliberately utilized simplified models. We have assumed two states armed with thermonuclear weapons (because this is actually the case) and we have generally assumed a symmetrical situation: the advantage, for example, of striking first being hypothetically the same for each. We have not complicated the models by imagining the various asymmetrical situations conceivable between the Soviet Union and the United States, in order not to exceed the bounds of this work. Furthermore, once the mode of argument has been understood, it is not impossible to analyze the consequences of asymmetrical situations. The difficulty is to ascertain in advance the situations which will result from the qualitative arms race and the reactions of governments to these situations.

For example, a question of decisive importance seems to be the following: a few years from now, will the two thermonuclear forces be invulnerable to such a degree that the deterrence of an extreme provocation (that is, of an attack directed against the territory of a state not in possession of nuclear weapons) will cease to be credible? Will the result be an extension of the possible hostilities without recourse to thermonuclear weapons? Or will the rigor of commitments and the magnitude of the improbable risk combined with a program of passive defense give a super power the possibility of insuring its allies against aggression, of convincing the enemy that in certain cases it would take the initiative in resorting to nuclear arms?

The American writers are under an illusion as to the probability that China and Western Europe, and other states after them, will definitively renounce atomic arms. States are not prepared to leave to the two super powers the monopoly of those weapons today regarded as decisive, to delegate to them a power of attorney for mankind, a mission to exercise supervision over these monstrous instruments.

In an abstract model, a world in which four or five states possessed a thermonuclear force would not necessarily be more unstable than a world in which only two such forces exist. Various combinations are possible, depending on whether these five states are all independent of one another or are divided into two or three groups. But in any case the presence, outside the Big Two, of a state (or a bloc or coalition) which also possesses a substantial capacity for nuclear reprisal, would reduce the freedom of action of the present great powers. The elimination of the other would not give a super power control of the universe, even on paper. It would have to use only part of its arsenal against its rival; otherwise, even after a possible victory, it would be at the mercy of a third power, which would have become the *tertius gaudens*. One can argue that even now the presence of the third power—China or all of Asia—even without atomic arms contributes indirectly to preventing the outbreak of total war between the two super powers.

III. The immediate outlook is not that suggested by an abstract model of four or five thermonuclear forces: a few years from now China will probably possess atomic bombs and planes capable of transporting them. Great Britain already possesses thermonuclear bombs and bombers capable of transporting them (but perhaps not capable of penetrating Soviet defenses or of surviving an attack). France will have atomic bombs and Mirage IVs around 1965, perhaps around 1970 will have thermonuclear bombs and ballistic missiles of intermediate range. The foreseeable situation between now and 1965 or 1970 will not resemble a simplified model of five actors endowed with more or less equivalent capacities. The Big Two will still be the leaders, and China, Great Britain and France will possess striking forces, possibly deterrence forces in relation to each other, but will be incapable of withstanding one of the super powers, either because their force could not survive a first attack, or because the disproportion would be too great between the losses they would suffer (almost total destruction for the two European countries) and the reprisals they would be able to make.

Let us go further. Even if the countries of the Continent combined their resources to produce a deterrent together, they would still be in a state of inferiority in relation to the two super powers because of the small extent of European space as compared with Russian and American space. One of the paradoxes of our time is that prosperity no longer requires a vast area of land though military strength still does, since extent of territory is one of the conditions of the capacity to absorb attack. A deterrent produced by the Six together, or better still by the Six plus Great Britain, would not, however, be ineffectual. On the contrary, it would promote Europe to the rank of a principal actor. Indirectly, Europe would continue to be protected by American strength, even if American divisions were no longer stationed in Germany; the Soviet Union would not launch an aggression, even a minor one, against either the United States or Europe without fearing the reaction of the other Western power.

For the immediate future, it is probably the acquisition of a certain atomic capacity by China which would do most to alter the present situation. Communist China would surely derive therefrom an increase in prestige throughout Asia. Moreover, Peking nurses specific grudges: the presence a few miles off her coast, on Quemoy and Matsu, of hostile forces commanded by the survivors of the previous regime, supplied by a foreign power, would be regarded as intolerable by the government of a great state. On the day she possesses some atomic capacity, will China be content with passivity?

chapter XXIII

Beyond Power Politics

I: *Peace through Law*

International politics have always been recognized by all nations for what they are—namely, power politics; except in our time when some jurists are intoxicated by concepts or some idealists confuse their dreams with reality. But such relations have never been openly accepted as such. The jurists deplored being obliged to ignore or to legalize war and the moralists attacked the essence of diplomatic-strategic conduct, and the fact that this conduct, even in peacetime, refers to the possibility of war, that is, to coercion and violence.

The horrors of twentieth-century war and the thermonuclear threat have given the rejection of power politics not only an actuality and an urgency, but also a kind of obviousness. *History must no longer be* a succession of bloody conflicts if humanity is to pursue its adventure. Never has the disproportion appeared so striking, so tragic, between the possible catastrophe and the stakes of inter-state rivalries. All classical strategy—including that which has been sketched in the preceding pages—appears lamentably inadequate, measured by the demands of peace and the dangers of war. It leads to an acknowledgment of impotence, a kind of resignation to the absurd.

I do not protest against these sentiments; I share them. Men aspire to a historical transformation of states and their relations. This aspiration is not unprecedented and it is not universal. There is no lack of fanatics who set the victory of their ideology above all else. Nonetheless this aspiration pertains to transnational society; it rallies millions of individuals as men and not as citizens of a democratic state or militants of a revolutionary party. Perhaps it will help to forge a path to the future, as other protests have done before, against what passed for the immemorial order of collectivities.

At least we should raise the question, at the end of this long inquiry, on what conditions international politics would cease being power politics, that is, developing within the shadow of war, and what is the likelihood of these conditions being realized today or tomorrow.

1. Pacifisms

Max Scheler, in an essay which is the published version of a lecture given at the Ministry of War in January 1927,[1] has distinguished eight kinds of pacifism, whose enumeration will serve us as a point of departure.

1. *Heroic and individual pacifism* of non-resistance to violence by principle.

2. *Christian pacifism*, the semi-pacifism of Catholics—in part inspired by dogma, in part by natural law and ethics—which seeks, in the last analysis, to make the Pope the supreme judge. The Protestant Churches which attempt to unite with a view to eternal peace are inspired by this same pacifism.

3. *Economic pacifism*, that of free trade, whose greatest theoretician has been the English philosopher Herbert Spencer and whose themes are inspired by positivist thought and a system of utilitarian values.

4. *Juridical or legal pacifism*, whose origin is the modern doctrine of natural law and the application of the latter to the *law of nations* (Grotius, Pufendorf) and which reappears in various forms: Abbé de Saint-Pierre, Kant (perpetual peace), Utopian socialism. It has as its ultimate goal general and systematic disarmament on land and sea and the replacement of the *ultima ratio* of states by a supreme tribunal which settles all conflicts by juridical decision, according to a rigorous system of norms.

5. *Semi-pacifism* of communism and Marxist socialism, that seeks to achieve perpetual peace by coercion as a result of the suppression of the class state, beyond a temporary dictatorship of the proletariat. In its Russian form, semi-pacifism is not immediately peaceful: it approves that all wars lead to the goal it announces and exalts.

6. *Imperialist pacifism of universal empire* (Roman pacification of the universal empire, *pax Romana*, Napoleon's attempt, a certain form of Anglo-Saxon pacifism).

7. *International class pacifism of the great capitalist bourgeoisie*, of several great powers in Europe and in America, which fear being the victim of a new war and seek to oppose the Soviet idea of a war leading to world revolution.

8. *Cultural pacifism of cosmopolitanism*, which goes back to stoicism and which, by uniting the intellectual elites of all nations, seeks to achieve perpetual peace by an effort of propaganda, intellectual and moral reform, education.

Such were the eight forms of pacifism which the German philosopher distinguished between the two wars, writing in the same essay: "The idea of an economic and relative political cooperation of the peoples of Europe will

---

[1] *Die Idee des Friedens und der Pazifismus*, posthumous publication, Berlin, 1931.

not disappear again. But if it should, woe to all European culture!"[2] Max Scheler, it seems to me, sought to clarify the various inspirations of the political and spiritual movements for peace. The latter are no different today: pacifism is inspired either by the rejection of violence, or by the traditional faith of the transcendent religions, or by economic utilitarianism, or by the desire for a juridical order, or by the new faith of Marxism-Leninism, or by the secret desire of some to "pacify," to suppress by force the plurality of states or military sovereignties (to which many would be receptive), or by the fear of war on the part of capital and its desire to oppose Marxism's International by one of its own, or finally by the criticism of nationalism and an attachment to the cosmopolitan idea. All reject war—the doctrinaire of non-violence, the Christian, the theoretician of free trade, the advocate of peace by law, of peace by socialism, of peace by universal empire, of peace by the international organization of capitalism, of peace by the action of scientists and the education of the masses. If we compare the inspiration of these various pacifisms, it is the first form alone which, Scheler tells us, is purely spiritual, insofar as the non-violent doctrinaire agrees to submit to violence rather than commit it. The other pacifisms are "ideologies of interests," their objective being peace not as a value in itself but as favorable to the interests of a class or of all humanity (trade is more useful than war). The distinction between the quality of these various pacifisms does not seem to me so simple. Of course, only the man who is ready to sacrifice his life in order not to suppress that of his kind proves that he rejects the heroism of combat because he transcends it. But the man who aspires to peace by law, the victory of the proletariat or of culture, is also animated by an ideal, even if this latter corresponds to the interest of some or of all. Finally, the quality of the inspiration is not compromised by the calculation of causes and effects.

The true distinction between these various forms of pacifism seems to me different. I believe these pacifisms are distributed into two categories: some oppose war, conditionally or unconditionally, without having either a theory of the *causes* of war or a doctrine of the *means* of peace; the others base on a theory of wars a pacific or belligerent action with a view to perpetual peace. In the first category belong the pacifisms of non-violence, religion and culture. The non-violent who refuse to perform their military service believe in the meaning of martyrdom, the long-run effectiveness of individual protest (and they are right). They have no illusion of preventing war in general nor even a particular war. When the non-violent organize, when they undertake spectacular manifestations against the possible use of atomic weapons, they are no longer moralists of conviction but moralists of responsibility, and they must be judged as such, according to the probable consequences of their action, no longer according to their intentions. The rejection of atomic weapons results from a judgment that is more political than ethical. It should

[2] *Ibid.*, p. 28.

be approved, if it is of such a nature that it will reduce the volume of historical violence without compromising the values that should be safeguarded. That it has such consequences is possible, but not incontestable. Similarly, the philosopher or the educator who struggles against national fanaticisms and attempts to spread the awareness of human unity accomplishes a labor good in itself. If he imagines that a reform in education or the millions of dollars spent by UNESCO will assure peace, he is too naïve to be taken seriously.

On the other hand, the advocate of free trade, the jurist, the Marxist, the imperialist and the capitalist have (or at least may have) a theory of war and a doctrine of peace. If they know the causes of wars, they must propose to eliminate them and thereby guarantee perpetual peace. But these five theoreticians, in their turn, are divided into two groups: the advocates of *peace by law* and of *peace by empire* seek to modify the essence of international politics as it has developed down through history. The advocates of peace by free trade, by the global victory of classless societies, finally by the interor supranational organizations of production and exchange have a chance of success precisely to the degree that their sociology of wars is accurate.

These two schools of pacifists correspond, it seems to me, to the two possible types of explanation of war. Either the state of nature between states involves by essence the greater or less frequency of war, in such a way that peace can only result from the substitution of the rule of law for the rule of force, or it involves the substitution of the universal state for the multiplicity of sovereignties. States fight either *for something* (land, men, booty, etc.) or else *because of something or someone* (population pressure, search for markets, despotic or capitalist or Communist regime, ambition of the rich or of the military or of the munitions men). These two types of explanations are neither contradictory nor incompatible, but they involve a fundamental difference. *The explanations of the first type do not exclude the partial truth of the explanations of the second type. Explanations of the second type are false if they are regarded as complete.* In other words, it is true that the multiplicity of military sovereignties implies the *possibility* of armed conflicts, hence power politics and war. Thus any doctrine that counts on the disappearance of certain stakes and the elimination of certain causes in order to *assure* perpetual peace is, as such, erroneous.

The theories and doctrines fashionable in our period are economic. The reasons for this vogue are many, some lasting, others circumstantial. Labor and war are two activities both contrasted and complementary. Man seeks to dominate nature and his kind. Perhaps he desires to dominate his kind in inverse proportion to the success of his manipulation of natural forces. It suffices to add to these common ideas the notion that societies have and can only have a single object in order to arrive at the concrete vision of an evolution of humanity, the positivist and industrial age succeeding the theological and military one. Since, as a matter of fact, modern societies attach more value to production than did the societies of the past, the interpretation of wars by the avarice of trusts, of capitalists, of munitions men, suggested itself as had, in other periods, the interpretation by the desire for glory on the part of kings or the caprices of their favorites. The race for markets, raw materials or profits replaces the monarchic quest for provinces, subjects or strongholds. Liberals estimate that the stakes of conflicts would be devalued in a republic of exchanges and that, consequently, states would no longer have any motive for fighting. Capitalists expect the same result from an inter- or supranational organization; Marxists from the final and worldwide triumph of the proletariat in the socialist regimes.

Among the doctrines of peace by the suppression of the economic stakes which armed conflicts involved, Marxism-Leninism is the most complete. In a capitalist world, monopolies are, by essence, greedy for domestic and foreign profits; the monopolists *must obey* the pitiless coercion of expansion and profit; the objectives of monopolies and states are incompatible. In a regime in which profit has ceased to be the motive, the material and moral development of peoples will be the goal the leaders will set for themselves. There will no longer be antagonistic classes within the regime, no longer a reason for imperialism's "headlong flight," hence no longer causes for wars. In other words, Marxism-Leninism explains modern wars both by the *actors* and by the *stakes*, by the contradictions of the capitalist regime and the ambitions of the monopolies on the one hand, by the incompatibility of objectives which the states subject to monopolies are obliged to seek on the other. The so-called proletarian revolution would change the nature of the actors[3] and would cause the stakes of the conflicts to disappear.

This doctrine of peace, even if we subscribe to the analyses on which it is based, would still not be demonstrable unless we suppose an unprecedented conversion of the *eternal diplomat*. Let us suppose that all states were organized according to Marxist-Leninist conceptions, with a planned economy and a so-called proletarian party in power: Would the states renounce maintaining armies? Would they all be convinced of their security? Would none of them be tempted to defend their interests any longer or to impose their ideas by force or by using the threat of force? To answer such questions affirmatively, we must make two hypotheses: that none of the traditional stakes—land, wealth, men—has kept any meaning; that none of the states has the ambition to dominate or the fear of being dominated.

The first hypothesis involves a degree of truth, in our period, whatever the economic-social regime. Indeed, we have seen that as long as growth and intensity remain possible and the freedom of international trade permits the supplying of men and factories, the domination of underdeveloped nations

[3] The explanation by actors belongs simultaneously to two possible types: explanation by the *intentions* of the actors, explanation by the *forces* which compel the actors without the latter being aware of them or being able to control them.

is more often than not costly to the developed nations.[4] But, even leaving aside the marginal cases of lands whose subsoil is rich and which are sparsely inhabited, ignoring the disputes over terms of trade, this virtual disappearance of economic stakes is not effected definitively. If the Chinese population continues to grow at the present rate, if it exceeds one billion between now and the end of the century, the lack of space will probably be felt by this people and its leaders. Supposing that in economic terms other solutions remain preferable to conquest, the latter could still nonetheless appear to be the best solution. There remain, in Siberia and in southeast Asia, sparsely populated territories.

In order for the state, whose territory is small in relation to the number of mouths to feed, not to be tempted by conquest, for its neighboring states not to feel threatened, it does not suffice for both to have the same kind of regime and to declare themselves brothers. Even the fraternity created by a common hostility to the capitalist world has not prevented the Yugoslav dissidence nor the tensions between Moscow and Peking. *A fortiori*, if we imagine a universe in which the socialist states would no longer have an enemy, it is impossible to exclude conflicts of interests of which the compartmentalization of space will be the occasion, in the future as yesterday. These conflicts will not necessarily provoke war, but if they are not to be settled by arms, we must imagine that a tribunal pronounces the law or that an arbitration is solicited by both sides, or finally that a superior will imposes a solution. The first two hypotheses refer us back to peace by law and the renunciation by states of their right to administer their own justice, the third to universal empire.

Starting from sociological explanations of war by causes or stakes, we reach a doctrine of peace by the submission of state sovereignties to law or to force. An itinerary which cannot surprise us: if states retain the supreme right to render justice, they cannot live within a definitive peace, unless they have changed their very nature or unless the world itself has *essentially* changed. The nature of an industrial society effectively attenuates the economic causes of wars and, if all states had the same regime at the present time, there would probably not be a threat of a major war between the principal actors of the international system. But this pacification, as a result of the possibilities of intensive growth, does not definitively shelter humanity from conflicts for land and wealth: everything depends, in the last analysis, on number, or more precisely still, on the rate at which number increases.

If we started from peace by law or by force, by the indisputable authority of a tribunal or the irresistible will of a single state, would we, in a round-about way, have rediscovered the danger created by economic-social causes of conflicts? In a sense, yes: the inequalities of development provoke, within

---

[4] We have shown above in what sense and with what reservations such a proposition is true.

states, tensions that sometimes explode into revolution. Why should it be different within a universal state or a world federation? But abstract analysis does not permit us to specify what character internal violence in the universal state would assume. It all depends, actually, on the degree of autonomy and the weapons that regions and populations have retained.

The difference between the two ideals of peace is thus, above all, a conceptual one. If we imagine perpetual peace without the disappearance of the Hobbesian situation, we suppose a radical conversion of states and the disappearance of possible stakes of disputes. If we imagine perpetual peace by the rule of law or universal empire without any other hypothesis, the risks will be those which the internal orders of states know today, amplified by the heterogeneity of populations subject to the law and by the foreseeable capacity of resistance to commands coming from above, whether from a tribunal or an empire, of the surviving groups of nationalities or civilizations.

These solutions indicate the path to be followed. A doctrine of peace must not be attached primarily to the stakes and to the actors, but to the basis of the Hobbesian situation: the claim by states on the right to dispense their own justice, hence to reserve for themselves the *ultimo ratio* of a recourse to arms. Our goal is peace: can the rule of law be established among nations?

2. *From the League of Nations Covenant to the United Nations Charter*

We have already considered international law—*jus gentium*—either on the abstract level of theory[5] or on the level of history and practice,[6] by analyzing the present role of the United Nations.

The principal idea of our theoretical analysis coincides with the principle commonly admitted by jurists before 1914, i.e., that international law does not forbid states to resort to force and even that this recourse constitutes an aspect of their sovereignty. I have subsequently discussed what I called the failure of the League of Nations, insofar as the latter's function and effect was to insure peace. This failure had a character both striking and symbolic: the League of Nations, created by the victors, joined, in its preamble, to the acceptance of "certain obligations not to resort to war" and to the establishment "in broad daylight of international relations based on justice and honor," "the rigorous observance of treaty obligations." The conservative tendency of all international law resulting from the will of rival states was accentuated by this intentional confusion between the respect due to international law and the respect due to the territorial status established by the Allied and associated powers. The victors hoped that the treaties would thereby derive a further authority, to which the vanquished retorted that the authority of the League of Nations was weakened by the juridical-moral

[5] Chap. IV, Secs. 3, 4, 5.
[6] Chap. XVIII, Sec. 3.

caution which it gave to the *Diktat* of the Allies, that is, to force. But neither victors nor vanquished could have specified which status would have been just in itself, without reference to the historical right of force. The imperial attempts of Japan, of Italy and of the Third Reich followed the immemorial conduct of politics.

Since 1945 a bipolar and heterogeneous international system has gradually developed. It is determined, in its essential features, by its political and technical conditions (weapons of mass destruction, rivalry of the two super powers, formation of blocs, incessant action of persuasion and subversion, etc.). Would the international system be what it is if the United Nations did not exist? I do not know; I have confined myself to the assertion, obvious to me,[7] that the United Nations has not exercised a major influence on the course of international relations.[8]

That this double failure has been due to facts, not to texts, is indisputable. But it may be of some use to inquire whether and to what degree the texts actually have modified the customary international law, forbidden recourse to arms, and finally introduced an effective organization of collective security.

That the spirit of the League of Nations Covenant and, still more, of the Kellogg-Briand Pact was an innovative one in relation to this customary and traditional law is quite incontestable. Never would kings in the seventeenth and eighteenth centuries have solemnly proclaimed "that they condemn, in the names of their respective peoples, the recourse to war for the solution of international controversies and renounce that recourse as being an instrument of international policy in their relations with one another."[9] Never would they have committed themselves to not resolving conflicts, whatever they were, by other than peaceful means.[10] It remains to be seen whether these texts are a homage paid by vice to virtue, or whether they testify to the authentic progress of individual or collective conscience.

Let us first recall that even the Kellogg-Briand Pact did not make *all wars* illegal. War remained legal if it was waged against an enemy that had not signed the pact or against a signing state which violated it, or in conformity with the obligations of the League of Nations Covenant. (Now, each state maintained, *de jure* and *de facto*, a great latitude in the interpretation of the obligations of the pact.) But, above all, the signers had reserved two escape clauses by which the old practices were still valid: the right of self-defense and the possibility of employing force without declaring war. The right of self-defense was explicity acknowledged by the Kellogg-Briand Pact, and the latter provided no organ to determine and limit the consequences and

---

[7] But those who *want to be* idealists have an almost unlimited capacity for *not seeing* reality.
[8] It is not important to us to measure precisely the advantages and the disadvantages, for both sides, of the effective but limited role played by the United Nations.
[9] Article I of the Covenant.
[10] Article II.

implications of this right. Each state was thus almost always in a position to plead, more or less truthfully, that it was confining itself to exercising this right, as Japan did apropos of Manchuria, and Italy apropos of Ethiopia. It was convenient to employ simultaneously the other escape clause, that is, not to declare war—to refuse to qualify as war, for instance, the "incidents" in China. Further, the so-called peaceful powers, the United States for instance, also provided an innovation with regard to the "equivocal" situation: before December 1941, without declaring war on Germany, the United States took measures favorable to one side and hostile to the other which were not compatible with the customary conception of neutrality. Non-belligerence was a mode of participation, as the incidents in China were a kind of war.

The lacunae of the Covenant were still more evident. The article which was supposed to introduce a kind of collective security, Article 16, paragraph 1, had been written as follows: "Should any member of the League resort to war in disregard of its covenants under Articles 12, 13 or 15, it shall *ipso facto* be deemed to have committed an act of war against all other members of the League. . . ." But in what cases did war constitute a violation of the pact? In Article 12 the members of the League committed themselves not to resort to war within the three months that followed an arbitrary or judiciary decision. In Article 13 they committed themselves not to enter into war with a state, to be party to a dispute, which had conformed to the judgment of an arbiter or to the verdict of a tribunal. Finally, in Article 15 (paragraph 6) they committed themselves not to enter into war with a state which had conformed to the recommendations of a report unanimously voted (the states party to the conflict being excluded) by the Council of the League of Nations.

Of course, the states committed themselves also to submitting their disputes to arbitration or to a decision of the tribunal or, by default, to the Council of the League. But the states remained individually free to decide whether or not a conflict was open to arbitrary or judiciary decision. If the dispute was political and if the Council took it up, the recommendations of the Council had authority only on condition that they were made unanimously. If the Council was not in a position to arrive at a unanimous agreement, "the members of the League reserve to themselves the right to take such action as they shall consider necessary for the maintenance of right and justice" (Article 15, paragraph 7).

In other words, in the case of conflicts subjected to an arbiter or to a tribunal, illegal wars were those launched either *before* the expiration of the three months' period or *against* the state which had submitted to the decisions of the arbiter or of the tribunal. But, since the members of the League had not accepted the *obligation* to submit their differences to an arbiter or to a tribunal, the likelihood was that grave conflicts, capable of provoking war, would be evoked by the Council or by the Assembly of the League of Nations. Now, in this case, war could be illegal only when launched *before* any attempt to resolve it in peaceful terms or *against* a unanimous recommendation of the Council; the principle of collective security—a war launched by a state in violation of the Covenant must be considered by *all* as a war launched against *each*—only applied, therefore, in a case of unanimity. Each member of the League reserved the sovereign right to decide whether a specific war actually violated the Covenant.

If this unanimity was gained, Article 16, paragraph 1 fixed (or seemed to fix) the economic sanctions obligatory for all members of the League, but only authorized the Council to formulate recommendations with regard to the share of each state in the military sanctions.

Theoretically, one could "fill in the lacunae" of the Covenant in three ways. The first would have been to render obligatory the arbitrary, judiciary or political decision (Council or Assembly of the League) for the parties to it. The second would have been to suppress the rule of unanimity so that the Council or Assembly would always be in a position to settle conflicts. The third would have been to deprive the states of the right to determine freely, if the Covenant had been violated, the part they would play in the sanctions. These three reforms were implied in each other. In order to eliminate paragraph 7 of Article 15, the right to take the measures necessary for the maintenance of peace and justice, it would have been necessary to accord the League of Nations the *basic* authority to settle conflicts. But since, in many cases, the unanimity of the members was inconceivable, the Council would have had to be able to settle disputes by a majority decision. Finally, for a majority judgment to be politically effective, it would have been necessary to reinforce and specify the terms of Article 16, paragraphs 1 and 2, the duties of states in case of a violation of the pact and with regard to sanctions.

Article 16, as we know, was invoked against Italy on the occasion of the conflict with Ethiopia. The method was as follows: first the conflict was examined by the Council, which reached a unanimous agreement. This Council vote was not regarded as involving obligations for all members of the League nor even as a collective decision. The President of the Assembly decided that no organ of the League had the right to take a decision that all members were obliged to acknowledge that one of them had violated the pact. Each member of the Assembly was free to manifest its opposition to the opinion expressed unanimously by the members of the Council. Austria, Hungary and Albania exercised this right. The other members, by their silence, joined with the members of the Council. The same freedom of individual decision was granted *de facto* to members of the League with regard to sanctions, despite Article 16, paragraph 1.

The failure of the attempt to oblige Italy to renounce the conquest of Ethiopia, it is easy to discern at this point in time, was not imputable to the "lacunae" of the Covenant, but to the repugnance shown by the leading powers (France and Great Britain at the time) to resort to extreme means.

These extreme means would have involved a (slight) risk of war, but the same would have been true if the Covenant had not contained lacunae. The League of Nations being composed of states that had not alienated their military sovereignty, it was not possible to stop one of them if it had decided to use force, unless force was used. The ambiguities and lacunae of the Covenant, from Article 11 to Article 16, did not paralyze the League's action with regard to Italian aggression in 1935, German aggression in 1938 (Austria and Czechoslovakia) or Soviet aggression in 1940 (Finland). Germany no longer belonged to the League of Nations in 1938 and the Soviet Union was expelled from it in 1940. A reinforcement of the obligations of the Covenant would not have made the slightest impression on either Hitler or Stalin.

If the member states had had the sincere desire to respect the Covenant, the prohibition of war would have sufficed, either before the expiration of the three months' period, or against the state accepting the sentence of the arbiter, the decision of the tribunal or a unanimous agreement of the Council. But Japan had no intention of respecting China's territorial integrity, nor Italy Ethiopia's independence, nor Germany that of Austria or Czechoslovakia. None of these three states would have consented to submit its claims to an "equity tribunal." None regarded itself as bound by the agreements of the League of Nations. None considered the existing territorial status as definitive. None accorded it a dignity superior to that of the past and that of the future. If paragraph 7 of Article 15 had been modified, even if the non-unanimous agreements of the Council had had the force of law, the revisionist states—Italy, Japan, Germany—would not have yielded and would have had to be constrained by force. Now the conservative states did not possess this force, and they themselves would not have agreed to ratify a rule of law which would have deprived them of their free will, whether it was a question of distinguishing between what related to internal legislation and what would be subject to international law, or whether it was a question of a strictly political conflict with another state.

The United Nations Charter is profoundly inspired by the same philosophy as the League of Nations Covenant, that is, by a legalist and pacifist philosophy. According to the preamble, the goal of the new institution is to preserve future generations from the holocaust of war and to insure that force will no longer be employed except in the common interest. Nonetheless, informed by experience, the writers insisted less on the scrupulous respect for treaties, that is, on the status quo, and more on the conditions without which the obligations of international law could not be honored. Respect for the rights of man and the economic and social advancement of peoples are the goals of the United Nations to the same degree as peace.

With regard to the central problem of this peaceful order, the Charter contains vague formulas in Chapter 1, which express either the manner in which the states should behave, or the principles according to which the conflicts must be settled. According to paragraph 4 of Article 2: "All members shall refrain in their international relations from the threat or use of force against the territorial integrity or political independence of any state, or in any other manner inconsistent with the purposes of the United Nations." Similarly, according to paragraph 3 of the same Article 2, all members "shall settle their international disputes by peaceful means in such a manner that international peace and security and justice are not endangered." But, in fact, all the states have, at one moment or another, used the threat of force. Further, if the recourse to peaceful means only is favorable to peace, it is not necessarily favorable to justice. Finally, if the territorial integrity of all the states were to be respected, no state could be fractured or absorbed by another by threat or coercion. But when has a state let itself be mutilated or destroyed if not under threat of coercion? These formulas in Chapter 1, like those of the League of Nations, are inevitably bypassed or ignored by some states. One might say that they express an ideal rather than precise obligations, or that they impose legal obligations upon states only to the degree to which they are specified by Chapters 6 and 7, that is, the chapters relative to the peaceful settlements of conflicts and, further, to actions in relation to threats to peace, to violations of the peace and to acts of aggression.

Chapters 6 and 7 of the Charter tend to a result analogous to Articles 10 to 16 of the Covenant. They are more specific, longer, more detailed, in certain regards more ambitious, and in others less. They are more ambitious in that they give the Security Council authority to take collective decisions, that is, to impose respect upon the parties by all means, peaceful or not. It is actually provided in Chapter 7 that the Security Council possess armed forces put at its disposal by the member states. But the Charter is less ambitious also, since the measures referred to in Chapter 7 cannot be taken by the Security Council except on condition that the five permanent members are in agreement. In other words, the five permanent members possess a veto right with regard to the decisions of the Council and still more with regard to the measures which the latter might take to make them effective. As for the General Assembly, it can vote recommendations on any subject by a two-thirds majority but not act in order to impose the respect for its recommendations. What the Covenant of the League of Nations called sanctions, what the Charter calls "actions relative to the threat to peace, breach of the peace and acts of aggressions," what the Anglo-Saxon jurists call "measures of enforcement" belong to the Security Council, not to the Assembly.

The Charter also contains "escape clauses." It adopts, in paragraph 7 of Article 2, the reservation that figured in paragraph 8 of Article 15 of the Covenant: the United Nations is not authorized to intervene in matters "which are essentially within the domestic jurisdiction of a state." The colonial powers—Holland, France—attempted to utilize this clause to forbid the Security Council or the General Assembly to intervene in the Indonesian and Algerian conflicts. As a matter of fact, the Charter gave the Council the right to intervene (by reference to Chapter 7), insofar as there was a threat to international peace. And each year the Assembly put the Algerian question on its agenda, despite the vain attempt of the French delegation to prevent this move or discussion by a spectacular withdrawal.

Article 107 gives, so to speak, carte blanche with regard to enemy states. The text of the article is so vague that it allows extreme freedom.[11] Probably the authors of the Charter intended here only a precaution with regard to the transitional period. But the article has assumed a major significance since the coalition of the victors has broken up, and the treaties of mutual assistance signed by the states of the Soviet bloc are directed explicitly against the likelihood of a German aggression or of an aggression by states allied with Germany. Measures authorized against the ex-enemy state easily become measures against the ex-ally which, after the breakdown of the coalition, has attempted to reinforce itself by linking itself with the ex-enemy.

The two most important escape clauses are Articles 52 and 53, relative to regional organizations, and Article 51, which contains the expression of self-defense already used by the Kellogg-Briand Pact. But, according to the letter of the text, the two clauses do not seriously limit the rights of the Security Council. The regional organizations that the authors of the Charter were thinking of included the Organization of American States. So that this organization could act autonomously in order to maintain peace or so that the Security Council might act through it, neither of these two eventualities involved "legal violence" without the authorization of the Security Council (with the exception of measures against an ex-enemy state). What, on the other hand, gave a margin of maneuver to the traditional policy was Article 51, which the alliances of the Atlantic bloc have evoked just as the alliances of the Soviet bloc have evoked Article 107. It suffices to add that "collective self-defense" requires preparation and that it cannot be effective if it is improvised precisely when an armed attack is occurring.

Jurists have discussed the legality, according to the Charter, of the Atlantic Alliance. Is it as a result of Article 51 or Articles 52 and 53 (regional organizations) that the latter has been established? The expression "the natural right of individual or collective self-defense" is sufficiently vague to generate endless controversy. But whatever the ingenuity of the exegesis, even if the jurists move that no one has explicitly and openly violated the Charter, the fact remains that the international world today differs essentially from the one conceived and imagined by the American creators of the Charter. The latter were hostile to zones of influence, to the balance of power, to power politics, to the use of force by a state or a group of states in its own

---

[11] "Nothing in the present Charter shall invalidate or preclude action, in relation to any state which during the Second World War has been an enemy of any signatory to the present Charter, taken or authorized as a result of that war by the governments having responsibility for such action."

interest. They counted on the United Nations and, in particular, on the Security Council to maintain peace. No one believes this to be the case today. If the policy of blocs is the logical development or the expression of the Charter, the latter should have been written in terms such as to permit the contrary of what its writers intended.

Without entering into the disputes of jurists over the legality of the action undertaken in Korea (in the absence and without the consent of one of the permanent members of the Security Council), over the article of the Charter that justified the Atlantic Alliance and, further, over the famous resolution "Uniting for Peace," it seems to me that on the historical level the Charter gave the Security Council the task of assuring collective security and peace, and that consequently it counted on the agreement of the permanent members of the Council. This agreement having been revealed to be impossible, the latter has never had the military forces which Articles 45 and following provided, the states have noted that the veto of the permanent members forbade the Council to decide to act, and have concluded therefrom that they must prepare their own legitimate "collective self-defense." That the text of Article 51, broadly interpreted, finally places the system of blocs in agreement with a Charter which was intended to exclude it, is possible. But it seems to me difficult not to yield to the reasoning of Julius Stone[12] when he concludes that "collective self-defense arises not in order to fulfill the Charter but unfortunately because the Charter has not been fulfilled." Collective defense is a substitute for, not a consequence of, collective security. The motion voted in 1950, "Uniting for Peace" in order to legalize "collective action," is also based on the customary right of defense that the charter had allowed to continue rather than on the principle of force put at the service of the international organization.

As the same jurist we have just quoted remarks, the Charter had a double face. Veto right, legitimate defense, and action against ex-enemies constituted the traditional face and made possible the classical interplay of power politics. The authority of the Security Council to impose peace represented the other face and was to have created a world order. The conflict of the two super powers has paralyzed the Security Council and today the traditional face alone appears, in a harsh light.

It would be childish to blame the Charter and to dream of a reform that would restore the hopes of 1945. In the same way as the lacunae of the Covenant were not responsible for Hitler's ambitions, the veto right is not the cause of rivalry between the two super powers.

To sum up, the idea of collective security has never been translated into legal obligations. Either each state preserved the right to decide whether or not there had been a recourse to war in violation of the Covenant—and if there had been, security was compromised, since it rested on the

[12] *Legal Control of International Conflicts,* London, 1954, p. 265.

plurality of individual decisions—or the Security Council had the right to take a collective decision and to impose it, even if there should be recourse to arms. But the decision demanded the agreement of all the permanent members, that is, in theory, of all the great powers of the system. Now, when the great powers are in agreement, with or without collective security, there is no major war.

3. The Essential Imperfection of International Law

What is the source of the failure of international law to exclude the use of force outside the circumstances provided for by law? This is the central question that dominates the controversies over the nature of the *jus gentium.* It is difficult indeed to conceive of a juridical order, conforming to its essence, that does not forbid its subjects to become a law unto themselves, to resort to violence by their own decision and with a view to their own interests. Personally, I find convincing, on the conceptual level, the identification of the juridical order with the pacific order on which H. Lauterpacht concludes his book *The Function of Law and the International Community.*[13] "It is possible that in dealing with questions relative to the place of law and tribunals in international society, international jurists have attached importance to separating the juridical view from any pacifist tendency. But if pacifism is identified with the insistence on the rule of law in international relations, then one may wonder if the jurist conscious of the true nature of his task can hope to achieve a separation of this nature. For peace is not only a moral idea. In a sense (although only in a sense) the idea of peace is morally indifferent, insofar as it may imply the sacrifice of justice on the altar of stability and security. Peace is above all a legal postulate. Juridically it is a metaphor for the postulate of the unity of the legal system. Juridical logic inevitably leads to the condemnation by law of anarchy and of private force."

I believe indeed that in a sense peace is a legal postulate, the principle of the unity of the legal system. Not that human relations, subject to law, do not involve violence, but they involve only violence in the service of law, employed against the violator of prohibitions or by the decision of the legal authority.

The modern jurists who are inspired either by positivist ideas or by neo-Kantianism and the distinction between fact and norm have still more difficulty acknowledging as fully juridical the legal order between states. In fact, since that law is considered a command of the state, the absence of a state superior to the subjects of international law tends to efface the strictly juridical character of the obligations to which the states would be subject. As for the pure theory of law, which defines the juridical order by the control of violence, it asserts the reality of a "juridical community" constituted by in-

[13] Oxford, 1933, p. 438.

ternational law only by interpreting wars and reprisals as acts of coercion, provided for by the rules of international law.[14]

Once wars and reprisals are interpreted as sanctions, brought about by illicit acts, the theoretician of pure law had the illusion of developing, without seeing insurmountable obstacles, a system of norms comparable to the national systems. But this is, it seems to me, an illusion, or, at least, the edifice of norms thus raised, even if logically satisfactory, would be too detached from reality to retain any meaning.

First of all, the interpretation of wars and reprisals as sanctions responding to illicit acts is only a juridical fiction, not in accordance with the meaning that historical figures of the past, be they leaders or soldiers, have attributed to the use of force. Diplomats or soldiers have never thought of themselves as dispensers of justice, responsible for the execution of decrees handed down by tribunals. Of course, given Kelsen's definition of law, there would be no international law if there were no control of violence and legal sanction when certain factual conditions occurred. But the hypothesis according to which the violence between states is either a crime or a punishment is neither evident nor demonstrated, and Kelsen himself sometimes suggests that he prefers this hypothesis to the hypothesis of the legality of any war for political and not for scientific motives.

This is not all. When considering pure theory we must go back to a fundamental norm that is not itself a rule of thumb, but a postulate that governs the whole system. Now, with regard to international law, none of the fundamental norms (*Grundnorm*) to which one may refer is satisfactory. The formula *pacta sunt servanda* is an example in particular, for it justifies the respect for treaties and conventions, is indispensable to international order, but it is difficult to make it that order's logical origin. If, instead of proclaiming that the commitments made must be respected, we proclaim as a fundamental norm that the states must behave as they behaved according to custom, we substitute for the respect for treaties the respect for custom. But if the respect for treaties has too limited a sense, the respect for custom has too vague a sense. Which custom must states respect? The recourse to force constitutes part of the age-old behavior of states: how condemn it in a juridical system which is supposed to be the outcome of custom?

Further, international law offers no perfect process for the determination of facts and the interpretation of norms. As a heretical disciple of Kelsen

[14] "It must be acknowledged that the international juridical order or the community constituted by it is not a state on account of its forced decentralization, insofar as the word state should be applied only to relatively centralized orders or juridical collectivities. But its character as a juridical collectivity is certain so long as war and reprisals can be interpreted as acts of coercion provided for by the rules of international law, that is, where they are the sanction of illicit acts and can be only that." (Hans Kelsen, "Théorie générale du droit international public," *Recueil des cours de l'Académie de droit international*, 42, 1932, p. 134.)

writes,[15] "according to the traditional conception—and according to Kelsen's—each state is the competent organ that freely makes decisions in each particular case without there existing any juridical possibility of control. *There are therefore a great number of parallel processes, processes having the capacity to posit norms and forced, each time there is a conflict, to posit norms contradictory to each other.* According to general international law, the state alone is competent to decide if the concrete norm is juridically valid, if a phenomenon is existent or non-existent, if it must be qualified as war, as intervention, as null and void. . . . If State A takes any one of these decisions, if it asserts a norm, if it describes a fact, etc., it posits a juridical rule, a norm belonging to international law. But State B is also competent to settle these same questions and its decision, too, posits a norm. Every time that there is an international conflict, the norm posited by State A will be contradictory to that posited by B, in the absence of which there would be no conflict. . . . The functioning of a super-state's international law is impossible, it is logically excluded. In this sense, a super-state's international law is non-existent." Or again, "international law, conceived by traditional theory as a sovereign super-state order linking states, is not only ineffectual, but indeed logically impossible because its norms do not constitute a coherent system."

If the pure theory of law fails, unable to produce an originating norm and to guarantee that this system will not be contradicted as the result of a supreme process of interpretation, the other philosophies of law do not succeed any better insofar as they claim to institute the obligatory force of an international law which would be imposed upon states. Let us concede, along with Mr. Gurvitch, to the existence of facts that are in themselves normative, let us posit a pure social law, the expression of non-state communities. Let us concede further that international law is a law of integration and not of subordination. The essential still remains to be done: What are the obligations of the pure, spontaneous law of the international community? Where will the jurist find proof that "social law" forbids or authorizes recourse to force? When the jurist asserts that "the will of the international community must be obeyed," it is too easy to reply that the will common to the sovereign states exists only in the imagination of the theoretician.

Finally, if the theoretician takes as his point of departure the states and the plurality of "sovereign wills," he is thereby reduced to invoking the consent of the subjects of law, under a more or less subtle form such as self-limitation[16] or implicit consent. It is easy to counter theories of this kind by observing that they do not transcend the sovereignty of the states posited at the outset. The obligation that results from consent alone is not imperative.

[15] Panoyis A. Papaligouras, *op. cit.*, p. 174 in French text.
[16] Today jurists often qualify as "absurd" Jellinek's theory of self-limitation. It seems to me much less absurd than many modern theories. It obviously does not establish law's "obligatory force." But it is a formulation of the historical-social reality.

And on what is based the principle that the rules owe their validity to consent alone?

Let us conclude: no theory of international law has ever been satisfactory, either in itself or in relation to reality. Logically, a theory that posited the absolutism of sovereignty did not justify the obligatory character of international law. Politically, such a theory restrained the authority of law and encouraged international anarchy. A theory that posited the authority of a law superior to states was incapable of finding either "normative facts" or an originating norm comparable to these same facts or to this same norm in the case of internal law. Further, the absence of a supreme process for interpretation and of an irresistible force of sanction compromised the logical rigor of the theory of a law superior to the state and rendered it alien to reality.

The permanence of controversies, the valid objections against any theory, taken by itself or in its political bearing, are explained, it seems to me, by the ambiguous and in a sense contradictory character of international law and of "the international society" of which it is the expression. International law, as it exists today, derives from the *jus gentium* as it has been elaborated in Europe, especially since the sixteenth century. The *jus gentium* originally had two aspects or two meanings: it designated the elements common to all national laws on the one hand, the rules that were imposed or ought to be imposed upon the sovereigns in their mutual dealings on the other. The elements common to all national laws passed for *natural*, that is, in conformity with the nature of man, or the commandments of God, or the light of Reason. Now, to the degree that it was natural in this sense, the *jus gentium* applied of itself to the dealings of sovereigns, since the latter could not be subject to a particular set of laws. Hence the employment by analogy of municipal law, that is, of civil law, for the solving of problems raised by the relations between sovereigns, each considered as a supreme and independent will.

But if these relations derived from a natural law, philosophically conceived as superior to the law of the particular state (to what we call a positive law), they also appear on analysis as natural in another sense: they were a "state of nature" anterior to the civil state created by the submission of individual wills to laws issuing from a superior will. The theories of the *jus gentium*, from the sixteenth century to the eighteenth century, have been influenced simultaneously by the conception of a natural law (universal, divine or rational) and by a state of nature. On the decisive point of the legality of war for both sides, the consequences of the state of nature have clearly prevailed over the demands of natural law. War is just if it is the sanction of an illicit act, if it aims at obtaining satisfaction or reparation, if it is a defense against an aggression. But just or not, it is legal for all the belligerents because there is not, between the sovereigns, either a tribunal to express the law or an irresistible force to impose it.

Of course, the philosophers of the seventeenth and eighteenth centuries did not all conceive the state of nature in the same way. If men are peaceful, if they aspire to society, the law valid for the pre-civil state (that is, for relations among the sovereigns) will not fundamentally differ from the natural law of tradition. But the absence of a civil state, of tribunal and police, nonetheless imply that the sovereigns preserved, to a large degree, the right to make their own law in their dealings. The reader will remember the famous description of the state of nature in Chapter XIII of Book I of *Leviathan*:

"But though there had never been any time, wherein particular men were in a condition of war one against another; yet in all times, kings, and persons of sovereign authority, because of their independency, are in continual jealousies, and in the state and posture of gladiators; having their weapons pointing, and their eyes fixed on one another; that is, their forts, garrisons, and guns upon the frontiers of their kingdom; and continual spies upon their neighbors; which is the posture of war."

Hobbes is prepared to accept this state of nature between states, and concludes his description by this remark: "But because they uphold thereby the industry of their subjects, there does not follow from it that misery which accompanies the liberty of particular men."

Similarly, Spinoza in Chapter III of the *Political Treatise* adopts the idea that independent commonwealths[17] are naturally enemies in the same way as men are in a state of nature (paragraph 13), that the right of war belongs to each commonwealth. He censures neither cunning nor bad faith[18] in the relations between commonwealths. Yet he sees no contradiction between the state of nature thus conceived and the "natural appetite men have for the civil state," and as a result the civil state can never be entirely dissolved (Chapter 6, paragraph 1).

But those same philosophers who conceive of the state of nature quite differently from Hobbes acknowledge the essential difference between the internal order of commonwealths and the inter-state order. In the second treatise *On Civil Government*,[19] Locke writes:

"Men living together according to reason, without a common superior on

---

[17] In the most general sense of "politically organized human group."

[18] "Every commonwealth has the right to make its contract whenever it chooses, and cannot be said to act treacherously or perfidiously in breaking its word, as soon as the motive of hope or fear is removed. For every contracting party was on equal terms in this respect, but whichever could first free itself of fear should be independent, and make use of its independence after its own mind; if then a commonwealth complains that it has been deceived, it cannot properly blame the bad faith of another contracting commonwealth, but only its own folly in having entrusted its own welfare to another party, that was independent, and had for its highest law the welfare of its own dominion." (Paragraph 14.) And, still more brutally, "If the supreme authority has promised another to do something which subsequently occasion or reason shows or seems to show is contrary to the welfare of its subjects, it is surely bound to break its word." (Paragraph 17.)

[19] Chap. III, paragraph 19.

earth with authority to judge between them, is properly the state of nature. But force, or a declared design of force, upon the person of another, where there is no common superior on earth to appeal to for relief, is the state of war; and 'tis the want of such an appeal gives a man the right of war even against an aggressor, though he be in society and a fellow subject."

Thus Locke separates conceptually the executive and the federative power.[20] The first has as its function to assure the execution "of the municipal laws of the society within itself upon all that are parts of it"; the second "to assure the management of the security and the interest of the public without, from all those that it may receive benefit or damage from."

As a matter of fact, Locke adds, these powers are confused and cannot help but be so, but they remain in essence different. For the power of peace and war, leagues and alliances "and what is to be done in reference to foreigners, depending much upon their actions and the varieties of designs and interests, precedently established and still valid, must necessarily be left in great part to the prudence and wisdom of those who have this power committed to them, to be managed by the best of their skill for the advantage of the commonwealth." Prudence and wisdom, not legalism, these must be the qualities of federative power.

Is Locke, on this point, merely tributary to Hobbes and more influenced by the latter than he wishes to admit?[21] It is possible but not certain. For the consequences of the state of nature—or if one prefers, of the absence of the civil state—affect even the man who denies the natural hostility between persons, individual or collective. In fact, lacking a judge and lacking police, each man must be prepared to defend himself against the *other* without reason and without scruple. The inter-state order, without the *de jure* and *de facto* supreme legal process, leaves to those in charge of each commonwealth the task of freely determining the measures necessary to legitimate defense.

The modern tendency to deny natural law or, at least, to deny its strictly juridical character should have incited jurists, in the fashion of the philosophers of the seventeenth century, to emphasize the state of nature (absence of tribunal and police) in which states live, hence to emphasize the difference between municipal law and international law, that is, to deny the juridical character *stricto sensu* of what we call international law. However, at least until a recent date, the majority of specialists in international law reasoned quite differently and sought to prove that international law was an authentic law based on premises which, in appearance, suggested the opposite conclusion. Every theory that takes as its point of departure the sovereignty of states and, in one way or another, relates law to this sovereignty, robs international law of certain constituent characteristics of law.

If the specialists of international law have often hesitated to draw such a

---

[20] Chap. XII, paragraph 147.
[21] Cf. Richard Cox, *Locke on War and Peace*, Oxford, 1960.

consequence from their principles and to reduce (or to raise) international law to the level of a positive morality, acknowledged by "civilized societies" but deprived of the rigorous formulation, of the systematization and of the strictly obligatory character of law in the proper sense of the word, I see at least three principal reasons for their doing so.

First of all, international law, as much in theory as in practice, was handled by jurists trained in the disciplines of municipal law. Inevitably, it acquired an increasingly juridical form. Since, until 1914, the European states imposed their own conceptions of law, reserving the freedom to decide which human collectivities deserved to be considered as states and, consequently, to be protected by the *jus gentium;* furthermore, since economic liberalism limited the sphere of state intervention and sanctified private property, it would have been paradoxical to deny the legal character of international law at the very moment that the latter had never before resembled municipal law so closely. How dismiss as positive morality texts and commentaries so visibly inspired by the juridical spirit?

Further, a good share of international law, whatever the general theory of international law, deserved to be considered as law *stricto sensu:* the common use of the wealth that belongs to all or to none (the sea), the relations between states necessitated by transnational society (which, in the period of capitalism, seemed alien to the states), the privileges and obligations of the citizen of one state established in another, all these problems, born from the coexistence on the same planet of territorially organized collectivities, were subject to a constantly elaborated and normally respected regulation. Jurists debated the question as to whether or not municipal law was superior to international law or, inversely, the latter to the former. As a matter of fact, the tribunals almost always maintained the supremacy of national law but, as long as the various legal systems belonged to the same type, as long as most norms of international law could be considered by judges as integrated with municipal law, the question affected public opinion less than it troubled the specialists.[22]

Finally, the theory of a law superior to states, and, after 1918, the League of Nations, seemed to show the way by which the acknowledged imperfection of international law could finally be overcome. International law, it was said, was at the stage of so-called primitive societies, without a supreme tribunal to express the law, without a monopoly of unconditional constraint. The same progress which has caused the appearance in states of a system of jurisdiction and a police organization would gradually contribute to the legal development of the inter-state order.

Nothing justified such optimism either on the level of facts or on the level of theory. On the level of facts it is evident that the use of force against a

[22] Cf. P. E. Corbett, *Law and Society in the Relations of States,* New York, 1951, p. 43.

state would only resemble the use of force within states when no state would any longer have the material means to oppose the "international police"—without which, police action, as was the case in Korea, is no different from a war and runs the risk of ending not by the punishment of the guilty but by a prudent compromise that is scarcely in accord with the spirit of a sanction.

On the level of theory the so-called primitive stage of international law was all the more revealing in that what was in question was the law of so-called civilized states. Now the latter, despite lip-service being paid to the law's sovereignty by one minister or another, have unceasingly acted as if they refused to acknowledge in advance the authority of the tribunals. If states sign a treaty of obligatory arbitration, they hasten to add that the arbitration does not apply to matters of municipal law and that the delimitation of these matters belongs to them (which comes down to reserving the choice of circumstances in which the obligation functions). If they have renounced this first reservation, then they produce another by the distinction between the disputes that involve a juridical settlement, by a tribunal or by an arbiter, and those that do not involve such a settlement. This distinction, as has often been shown,[23] is equivocal. But it has at least two meanings that are politically clear. States do not consent to commit themselves unconditionally, to submit to an arbiter or to a tribunal questions which they regard as being of vital interest. The disputes that are capable of provoking war are called political and thereby are not to be treated by legal procedure. Nor do states agree to being bound unconditionally by existing law, because in certain circumstances treaties and conventions may be or seem unjust, and because they hesitate to confide to judges (who, moreover, hesitate to assume it) the responsibility for judging according to equity. This double refusal is the expression of a desire for autonomy; it implies an element of international anarchy. Whether we censure it or not, it has been and is an element in the unique character of relations among states. It leads logically to what shocks geometrical minds, the status of war in international law.

War is not illegal in the manner of a revolution. One might say that "recourse to war was neither legal nor illegal; international law suffered in a sense an eclipse once the choice of peace and war was made."[24] Or again, elsewhere: "What in the municipal order constitutes a 'legal revolution' operates in international law as a kind of legal pseudo-transaction which, through the principle of efficacity, transmits the international representative capacity. The municipal legal system is broken, the international legal system is not broken: it merely functions."[25]

[23] H. Lauterpacht, *The Function of Law in the International Community*, Oxford, 1953.
[24] Julius Stone, *Legal Control of International Conflicts*, London, 1954, p. 297.
[25] Julius Stone, "Problems Confronting Sociological Inquiries Concerning International Law," *Recueil des cours de l'Académie de droit international*, 1956, 89, Leyden, 1957, p. 133 (73).

As long as war is legal or tolerated, it will remain true that "customary international law differs from municipal law at least in this. It provides for its own destruction by the simple force of its own subjects. By the expedient of its tolerance of war, of the room left for belligerent solutions, of the status attributed to conquest and of the validity of treaties imposed upon the vanquished, one may conceive of a single state imposing its legal authority on all the others."[26]

4. Inter-State War and Intra-State War

Inter-state relations consist of social behavior: diplomats or soldiers, except in extreme cases when the humanity of the "savage" is not acknowledged, do not treat their enemy as an object to be utilized as they please or an animal that they kill at will. Diplomatic-strategic behavior is social in a double sense: it reckons on the reaction of the very person in relation to which it orients itself, and it always attempts to justify itself, thereby admitting the authority of values or rules. Now as we have seen, international law, even in higher civilizations, is marked by an essential imperfection: lacking a tribunal qualified to interpret it, it is likely to break up into as many systems as there are to interpret it: lacking an irresistible force in the service of the law, each subject reserves, in fact, the right of rendering justice for itself. Why this essential imperfection?

To attempt an answer, let us try to distinguish the various categories to which the disputes among states belong. Let us leave aside temporarily the concepts with metaphysical connotations, such as the concept of sovereignty. Let us confine ourselves to positing at the outset the incontestable fact that men are not subject to the same laws all over the globe. There exist various legal systems, each valid over a *fragment of space* or for a *given population*. A first category of disputes results from the possible contradiction between the *territoriality* and the *nationality* of the law. To what obligations is a state qualified to subject the citizens of another state inhabiting its territory? To what degree can a state deprive nationals of another state of their possessions and their liberties by applying its own legislation, even if this latter violates the custom admitted as civilized?

States are not merely related through nationals visiting other nations, they are related also through the international public domain, the sea, and tomorrow perhaps the air above a certain as yet not fixed limit of sovereignty. Certain water routes, though situated within the territory of one state, are so indispensable to others that their utilization is guaranteed to all or to some by international conventions, and conflicts may arise as a result of contradictory interpretations of these conventions or as a result of their pure and simple violation by the state that physically possesses that means to effect such a violation. For example, the Egyptian government does a serious in-

[26] *Ibid.*, p. 132 (72).

jury to Israel by forbidding ships flying the latter's flag to use the Suez
Canal. Is this a conflict of interpretation (a state of war exists between
Egypt and Israel) or a violation of a statute? Jurists debate the matter, but
generally adopt the second alternative.

In the third place, states are related because economic life is increasingly
transnational. By the intermediary of state administrations or private exporters
or importers, merchandise is exchanged across frontiers. Yet, although each
state is entitled to limit its exchanges with the external world in general or
with other states in particular, although it can legally forbid the purchase or
sale of certain goods, a sudden and coordinated refusal of several states to
deal with others is equivalent to a kind of aggression. The blockade of
Yugoslavia by the states of the Soviet bloc offered an example of the disputes
in this third category.[27]

In the fourth place, states can take measures or can tolerate activities
within their territory which tend to the overthrow either of the regime or of
the government established in a neighboring state. The murder at Sarajevo
was the immediate cause of the First World War; it had been conceived in
Serbia, and the Serbian government was accused of having known about,
even though it might not have organized the preparations. Recruiting or stationing of armed groups destined to wage guerrilla warfare on the territory of
the neighboring state figured, between the wars, in the "enumerative" definition of cases of aggression.

Lastly, states are related and potentially in conflict with regard to the
primary object of international law, the distribution of space. They may not
agree as to the possessor of a space, whether empty or half-empty, or whose
occupants are not recognized as "subject of law" by the members of the juridical community of civilized states. Further, they may dispute as to the tracing
of boundaries, invoking arguments alternately strategic (natural frontiers)
or moral (right of self-determination).

Such a classification manifestly covers the majority of, if not all international disputes. In the inverse order of the preceding enumeration, the disputes bear first of all on the compartmentalization of space, that is, on the
very content of any state order. Next they result from the political or economic hostility a state can manifest toward its neighbors on its own territory,
either by organizing subversion or by interrupting normal trade, or by neglecting the legitimate interests of the others in the use it makes of what is
supposed to belong to all states. Lastly, disputes are provoked by the manner
in which one state treats the possessions and nationals of another state.

Disputes relating to possessions and persons are generally settled amicably
or by juridical procedures; that is to say, when the states subscribe to the
same principles. When this juridical community does not exist, but when one

[27] The blockade of Cuba is another example.

state (or a group of states) is stronger, it on occasion imposes respect for its principles. This is what the European states did at the end of the last century and at the beginning of this one, when they sent gunboats to oblige defaulting states to pay their debts or to take over the administration of tariff duties or of justice of a non-European state. When the legal systems of states in conflict are inspired by incompatible ideals, and when neither one has the force or the desire to coerce the other, all that can be done is to conclude a diplomatic compromise or to permit each state to act in its own way on its own territory. The United States could do nothing for the American journalists condemned in Czechoslovakia or in the Soviet Union by reason of acts qualified there as espionage and which would be legal on this side of the Iron Curtain. Fidel Castro has no more intention of "equitably" indemnifying the American corporations than the Soviet Union has of indemnifying the holders of "Russian bonds." A legal settlement of disputes of this kind has as its condition the *rapprochement* of legal systems rather than the progress of international law; it requires the judicial-moral homogeneity of the international system. Now, as we know, the latter, extending to all humanity, has become more heterogeneous than it was in the context of the European Continent.

Disputes of the second category can be submitted, generally, to an arbiter or to a tribunal. They rarely affect the major interests of states. They become serious when they manifest a latent hostility or when the conduct of one state, judged illegal by another, ignored the law because it corresponded to a military necessity (or pseudo-necessity). Such, for example, was the case of the violation of the Soviet air space by the American U-2 plane. Of course, national susceptibilities have sometimes transformed maritime incidents, provoked by an arbitrary interpretation of boarding rights or of the width of territorial waters, into international crises. States have become less sensitive because recourse to arms is henceforth dangerous. If outer space offers pretexts for grave disputes tomorrow, the reason will not be that the states are jealous of their honor, but that they wish to utilize satellites for military purposes.

The practices of economic hostility—refusal without justification to sell or to buy—are in fact linked to political conflicts. They are their expression rather than their cause. Between the two wars a vague fear had spread that the "access to raw materials" would be refused to certain states. There was a confused evocation of two quite different hypotheses: that a state would not have the necessary currency to buy raw materials, or that the sellers of raw materials would be in a position to keep certain countries from acquiring them. We find the echo of these fears in the Atlantic Charter. Perhaps, on the day when the reserves of raw materials will begin to be exhausted, the possessors of the last sources or at least of the last rich sources of supply will be in a position to exercise such blackmail. For the moment, we know cases in which international cartels have exploited "consumers." These detestable practices that have frequently been observed within states are not the causes of conflicts settled by arms.

This brings us to the major rivalries, of which the delimitation and the regime of political units constitute the object and the cause. Such conflicts are those Proudhon refused to submit to a right[28] other than that of force. In certain respects similar to those that fracture political units, they assume, on the inter-state level, a different meaning.

The comparison of ownership and sovereignty is a commonplace. It has been said that a collectivity possesses its soil as the farmer possesses his field. It is conceivable that at the dawn of history, a tribe, while reserving a strip of land for pasture and agriculture, should have created both property and territoriality. But once human collectivities were converted to sedentary life and the greater part of the planet was populated, disputes rarely concerned vacant land. As their object they have either the attachment of a certain population to one state rather than to another, or the right of the population to constitute an independent state. By definition, such conflicts that touch on the very existence of the "political unit" differ essentially from the conflicts between parties, classes or groups, which do not call into question the unit to which they belong.

Of course, states claim they do not act without justification, and they invoke historical ideas comparable to the moral conceptions which animate the reformers of laws, such as the "right of self-determination." But this example indicates the profound difference between the ethical conceptions that contribute to the progress of municipal legislation and the historical ideas to which the moralists choose to submit the conduct of states. That each may choose his nationality seems at first glance an incontestable right. But who chooses? And what is chosen? Is it the population of the province or the population speaking a certain language which will be regarded as the subject of the choice? At what moment will we halt the breakup of the collectivity to which the unreserved application of the right of self-determination might lead? What will become of the minorities that within the "unit of choice" have expressed themselves against the majority? Yet this idea is not a futile one. It does not permit the settlement of all disputes, but it authorizes the condemnation of violence done to certain populations. It cannot be translated into specific norms in the manner in which the prohibition of slavery or the suppression of the orders (of the old regime) had been juridically formulated.

History offers examples, though few, of the peaceful disintegration of a national or imperial state. Sweden and Norway separated without the former offering any resistance to the latter's desire for independence. Following the Second World War, Great Britain granted independence to India, Burma and Ceylon. Contrary examples are nonetheless more frequent, even in our

---

[28] "Right" in the subjective sense, not a system of norms.

period when decolonization corresponds to the rightly understood interest of the metropolitan nations. Holland resigned herself to Indonesia's independence only under the constraint of rebellion and the coercion of the United Nations (or the United States). The Indo-Chinese war lasted eight years; the Algerian rebellion began in the autumn of 1954 and went on until 1962. It is by fighting that nationalists have generally given evidence of their capacity to constitute themselves into a nation. If imperial disintegration is rarely peaceful, national integration, whether Great Britain, Germany or France was involved, has probably never been so. And the shift from one regime to another—the revolution—is always violent, whatever quantity of blood is shed.

Pacifists aspire to a history without violence, but they do not reflect on the relations between revolution and warfare in a world in which the interdependence of peoples is gradually increasing. The Algerian Moslems rebelled against French sovereignty, the Hungarians rebelled against the Communist regime as practiced by Rakosi and his henchmen. Even in theory, what could be the "juridical settlement" of rebellions that affect the interests of other states, since the success of the rebels would have repercussions on the worldwide relation of forces and ideologies? Historically, such conflicts have never been and cannot be submitted to a tribunal, pronouncing a sentence after due process and according to criteria comparable to those of civil and criminal trials. Theoretically, two methods are conceivable to reduce the volume of violence: either to isolate the theater of the rebellion, or else to impose upon both sides the decision of an external and therefore supranational power.

During the last century, international law in the homogeneous European system implicitly recommended the method of isolation, which the customary rules of non-intervention rendered more or less obligatory, in the interest of inter-state society. The American practice of non-recognition of governments coming to power by means of *coups d'état* was criticized in the name of the theory of non-intervention. The governments which effectively exercise power over a territory of sovereignty should be recognized, whatever their origin. If we begin questioning the legality of their accession, what will bring to an end the deadly confusion of recognition, which is a strictly juridical act that should be purely declarative (and not constitutive), with approval, and which is ideological and moral?

But, as we also know, this doctrine of isolation is neither applicable nor applied when the sovereigns—kings or Communist parties—unite against revolutionaries or against counterrevolutionaries, when each of the blocs between which the international system is divided feels obliged to intervene through fear of the victory of the party championing its enemy, in one way or another, in all civil wars. In the last century the isolation was, in certain circumstances, corrected by the concerted intervention of the great powers: international society dictated a solution that was not always equitable, but that did establish peace. In our heterogeneous system, states rarely agree either to abstain or to impose a solution elaborated in common and acceptable to all.

Despite the difficulties created by the heterogeneity of the system and the transnational ideologies, states continue, on every occasion, to resort either to the method of "isolation" or to that of a "common solution." In 1936 neither Fascist Italy nor the Third Reich nor even the democracies respected non-intervention agreements relative to the Spanish Civil War (the democracies violated them less). But, to avoid the internationalization of the conflict, they created at least a façade of non-intervention. By qualifying the divisions of the regular army which they sent to fight in Korea as "volunteers," the leaders of the Chinese People's Republic clearly expressed their rejection of a declaration of war which might have involved the belligerents in escalation. "Volunteers" represent an intermediate formula between a non-intervention agreement (violated by the clandestine delivery of men and matériel) and an official internationalization of an internal conflict that would oblige the great powers, protectors of the rebels or of the legal government, to adopt belligerent measures. All civil wars today involve, to a varying degree, "isolation" and "internationalization."

The conclusion obvious to me but so often misunderstood is that we cannot conceive a non-violent diplomacy so long as we have not eliminated violence from internal politics. What occurs within one of the member states of an international society cannot be a matter of indifference to the other members of that society. The latter declare themselves indifferent when the changes of regime and government do not substantially modify the international actor and the rules of the game, hence when the system is homogeneous. They cannot pretend to indifference when the substitution of one regime for another involves a change of sides. The day when half the states have neither a legitimate regime (that is, a regime admitted to be such by the majority of the people) nor a stable regime (that is, a regime assured of a minimum of continuity and force), internal instability and the precariousness of equilibrium are multiplied by each other, and peace becomes a "cold war."

Peace between states, in a heterogeneous system, excludes the implicit agreement of sovereigns against rebels and heretics, since the heretics of one bloc are the believers of the other. Peace would therefore require, at minimum, reciprocal abstention, but the latter, in its turn, is forbidden by the technological unification of the world and the universal vocation of the ideologies of our century. Peaceful coexistence derives from diplomatic hypocrisy; the cold war designates the true course of international relations. How could it be otherwise, since international law, the regulation of a certain kind of social relations, does not suffice to create order when society itself is anarchic?

5. Progress or Decline of International Law

Should we conclude that international law is making progress or is in decline? Both theses have been sustained by various authors. Personally, I confess I cannot see much progress, whether it is a question of transnational society, of the international system, or of the consciousness of the human community.

Means of transportation and communication are incomparably superior to what they were at any moment in the past. The number of persons who travel abroad is, in the West, considerable. Never have so many men visited so many foreign countries. Never have so many men, without leaving their own country, been capable of seeing, on large or small screens, the images of so many countries they will never visit. But it would be illusory indeed to regard the percentage of persons who have left their own country, or the average number of kilometers covered by certain merchandise before being consumed, or the statistics of world trade in kilometer-tons as a valid criterion of transnational society.

First of all, even with regard to these external and quasi-material signs, there is no lack of contradictory phenomena and divergent lines of evolution. Transnational society is global, whereas it has never been so before. But, by the same token, the intensity of trade, persons and merchandise, great in the context of little Europe, is slight between the Far East and Europe for example. Exchanges across frontiers are, in the Soviet universe, denied to private persons; they have become international and not transnational. Thereby they are less free, more subordinate to the interests of states than in the century of liberalism. The people's democracies, as they are called, consider it in accord with their principles to restrain the rights of citizens to travel abroad. The frontiers of states that call themselves proletarian are guarded with barbed wire, illuminated at night by floodlights—like the concentration camps. It takes ten hours to fly from Moscow to Washington in a jet plane. But what is the percentage of Soviet citizens who have an opportunity of obtaining authorization to make the trip?

The heterogeneity of the system hampers the development of transnational society which material means would make possible. It destroys the moral unity of human community. It keeps individuals from becoming aware of it. The inferior form of solidarity is interaction—what happens at one point of the system has repercussions at all the other points: in this sense, all political units, or almost all of them, are united. A superior form of solidarity, beyond simple interaction, would be the self-regulation or the uniform qualification, by all members of the system, of a given event. Neither of these two varieties is present in the system today.

A multipolar homogeneous system possesses a certain capacity for self-regulation: the chief actors, out of fear of universal monarchy, have a tendency to limit their ambitions, to spare each other on the day of settling accounts, and to replace one defaulting actor with another. But this last formula precisely marks the narrow limits of self-regulation: no actor can, in the long run, rely on it for the maintenance of his own existence. Poland has been erased from the map of Europe without the European system being thereby destroyed. Even this limited self-regulation is at the mercy of a major war or of a rapid development of the resources of one of the protagonists.

A heterogeneous bipolar system, in which many unstable states figure, has no capacity for self-regulation. Each principal actor, that is, each bloc, knows that it would not be spared by its rival if it no longer had the means to defend itself. The powers do not have a common interest in maintaining the approximate balance which has been established between them; each attempts to prevent its enemy from acquiring a superiority of forces at any cost.

Today it is even less true than yesterday that an event receives, around the globe, the same judgment, whether just or unjust, favorable or contrary to liberty. Men react to a *natural* catastrophe as to a misfortune which touches all humanity and the humanity within each man. Floods and famine in China do not awaken, it seems to me, a sense of satisfaction, even in the heart of the most passionate anti-Communist. Similarly, I do not believe that even the most fanatical Communist rejoices over the collapse of a dam constructed by capitalists. But how rare and weak are these shared emotions compared to the national and ideological emotions which unite people or blocs and divide humanity!

I also agree that these emotions are frequently contradictory. The citizen or the statesman sometimes rejoices over the success won by a nation of the other bloc, regardless of diplomatic expedience. The first Soviet cosmonaut was greeted as a representative of all Europe by one chief of state who, in so many other circumstances, has loudly manifested his Atlantic orthodoxy. The British acclamations of the same Soviet hero probably had a certain relation to their resentment of the other English-speaking people. But that these popular emotions were not entirely in agreement with the diplomatic situation does not make them other than human, indeed, purely human. One need merely attend a contest between national teams to realize that the identification of individuals with the group is powerful, the attachment to the human race or to the rules slight.

Never, in any limited system—that of the Greek city-states, that of the Christian community, or that of the European concert—have the values of the common interest controlled the conduct of the actors *in major circumstances*. In peacetime, to settle secondary problems, the semi-consciousness of a common civilization was not without an influence. It was immediately repressed by passions when the call to arms was sounded.

In the global system today, society has more reasons for tearing itself apart and fewer reasons for acting as a unit. Each of the super powers attempts to convince its nationals and non-committed groups that the other regime is hateful. The same fact is detestable according to one ideology, admirable according to another. Free elections, with multiple parties, are merely a camouflage of the tyranny of the monopolists, according to Moscow propaganda. Dictatorship of the proletariat and 99 per cent elections are merely the screen of one-party despotism, according to Washington propaganda. *Communication* between peoples is blocked by contradictory interpretations that are integrated into the messages themselves, although the means of transmitting these messages, in number and in rapidity, are incommensurate with those of the past. In no way is it true to say that the members of transnational or international society desire that humanity should be *one* in the manner of national communities. Men and states are perhaps afraid that humanity will no longer exist, that it will disappear in an apocalyptic catastrophe; they do not conceive of human unity as a reality or as an ideal, in the manner in which they aspire to prosperity, to expansion, to the glory of a people, a bloc, an ideology. The fear of war inspires the combatants to moderation; it does not suffice to reconcile them.

If the social relations to which international laws apply exist, by what miracle would the latter appear to be making progress?

I admit at best that international conventions are increasingly numerous, that the domain of legalized inter-state relations is increasingly large, that the respect for these laws is granted, on the part of an increasing number of states, in an increasing number of circumstances. I am not sure that any of these propositions is true, but even supposing that they were all true, the essentials would not be changed. One does not judge international law by peaceful periods and secondary problems. With regard to crises, that is, international conflicts, one would seek in vain for a symptom of progress. If the goal is peace by law, we are still as far away from it as ever. If the goal is merely the limitation of a war that is legal for both belligerents, we are further from the goal than at any other moment since the end of the wars of religion.

International law, which has become that of the global system, is, in its essentials, the *jus Europaeum*. Its application was limited at first to the Christian nations, then to the European ones; it has subsequently been extended to the nations called civilized, then peaceful. Henceforth the "sovereign equality" formerly reserved for the privileged, that is, the great powers of international society whose center was in Europe, is explicitly granted to all the states, great and small, emerging from the disintegration of the colonial empires. It is the duty of the states that assume responsibility for the "non-self-governing peoples to act with a view to the latters' well-being and development." The time is past when a member of the House of Commons could declare without shame and without restraint that England sought no more than its profit in the government of India. The ideology of the duty of the rich and civilized nations with regard to the peoples who have not yet acceded to modern civilization is more than a homage rendered by vice to virtue; it is the awareness of a historical fact: the global extension of the inter-state system.

But, beyond these facts, nothing indicates progress on the essential points. For the rule of law to be established, states must renounce being a law unto themselves and citizens and governments must regard the submission of states to an impartial judge as morally praiseworthy. Now, Mr. Khrushchev declared that he would not hesitate to oppose any decision taken unanimously in the United Nations if it was contrary to the interest of the Soviet Union. The United States, despite its attachment to the ideology of peace by law, hesitates to leave to others the discrimination of what relates and what does not relate to municipal law.

There are fewer states capable of settling their disputes by the sword, but most of those no longer capable of doing so regret their vanished power. There was scarcely any moral indignation in France against the bombing of Port Said or the operations around Bizerte (July 1961). Public opinion in Great Britain was less hostile to Sir Anthony Eden and to the Suez expedition than the "intellectual party." If law cannot and must not ever precede by too great a gap the values actually felt by the common conscience, the moment has not yet come legally to forbid states to judge for themselves without appeal to a superior authority.

One cannot say that states more often violate the code of international good behavior today than yesterday, but this code exists less than ever. States declare war on each other less often, but many practices that would have implied a declaration of war in good and due form no longer seem incompatible with the maintenance of diplomatic relations.

The conclusion that must *not* be drawn from these remarks is that peace, in our time, depends on the progress of international law or even that such progress could offer a substantial contribution to the cause of peace. It is not impossible to imagine a constitution, inspired by the national constitutions, with an executive power (the Security Council reformed), a legislative power (the United Nations Assembly), a tribunal (the International Court of Justice), and a police force (armed forces obeying the executive power). A detailed plan of such a constitution has even been elaborated by American jurists.[29] As an intellectual experiment, it is not without interest. But it would be a mistake to attach too much importance to these academic exercises. The rivalries of power, the contradictions of interests, the ideological incompatibilities are facts. So long as they exist, the Security Council will not have at its disposal armed forces capable of overcoming all resistance: the major states will not commit themselves to obeying the majority of an Assembly (whatever the mode of representation adopted). The veto is a symbol, not a cause. A great power does not take orders and does not let itself be coerced.

Must we conclude that peace by law is a false idea, contradictory to the

[29] Grenville Clark and Louis B. Sohn, *World Peace through World Law*, Harvard University Press, 1958.

nature of men and societies? Or that it is an *idea of reason* in the Kantian sense of this expression, that is, an idea that can never be entirely realized, but which animates action and indicates a goal?

Law is a regulation of social life, resulting from custom, justified or inspired by a conception of the just and the unjust, consolidated by systematic formulation and jurisdictional system, whose means of constraint normally permit assuring its respect. This regulation derives, to a degree, from the force that has created the state or the regime or the constitution. But within collectivities, the originating role of force is generally effaced, forgotten, camouflaged; the extreme modes of inequality have disappeared or are gradually attenuated. Common values unite those who were originally victors and vanquished.

Of the various kinds of municipal law, it is constitutional law that always remains closest to its violent origins. Hence this is the law that is most difficult to revise peacefully, the one that is the most often interrupted by recourse to arms on one side or another. The law that would establish peace between nations would resemble constitutional law more than any other because it would redistribute power, if not wealth, among the various procedures of the international organization.

What are the conditions by which the functioning of a constitution of the international society would be, in theory, possible? They seem to me to be three in number. For states to agree to submit their external conduct to the rule of law, the leaders must yield to a similar discipline with regard to the peoples. It is truly absurd to imagine that the Communist leaders, who scorn the majority principle and manipulate any election, will respect, spontaneously or by habit, decisions taken by the majority of voters in an international parliament. Let us say, to return to Kantian language, that the constitutions, at least of the principle states, must be *republican*, based on the consent of the citizens and the exercise of power according to strict rules and legal procedures. If this first condition were satisfied, a second would, thereby, have every chance of being so. States would be aware of their kinship, the system would be homogeneous, a community first international and then supranational would begin to exist, and this community would judiciously choose, in case of a local crisis, between "isolation" and "imposed solution."

Nonetheless, if this "international community" is not conceivable without the homogeneity of states, without the kinship of ideals, without the similarity of constitutional practices, this necessary condition is not sufficient. States must also consent to say a "farewell to arms" and must agree without anxiety to submit their disputes to a tribunal, even those disputes whose object is the redistribution of lands and wealth. A homogeneous international society, without an arms race, without territorial or ideological conflicts—is such a thing possible? Again, yes—in the abstract, but under various conditions. The end of the arms race not only requires that states no longer suspect each other of the worst intentions; it also requires that states no longer desire force in order to impose their will upon the others. The will to collective power must disappear or rather be transposed to another field. As for the conflicts of an economic order—which were not the direct or predominant cause of wars in the past, but which make the wars of traditional civilizations appear intelligible to our utilitarian minds—they have become attenuated of themselves in our period: all modern societies can grow more advantageously by intensification than by extension and by conquest.

Let us combine the results of these analyses: homogeneous system, states that no longer suspect each other, respect for the same juridical and moral ideas, attenuation of economic-demographic conflicts. Who could fail to see that all humanities, pacified by law, would resemble those national communities in which the competition of individuals and interests now only rarely assumes a character of violence? But would such a world, in which according to reason the rule of law would assure peace, still be divided into states, or would it unite humanity into a worldwide federation, if not into a universal empire?

Should we, out of love of peace or out of fear of war, desire such a federation or such an empire?

chapter XXIV

Beyond Power Politics

II: *Peace through Empire*

According to historical precedents, the outcome of the present crisis should be universal empire. Each of the empires that are called universal has unified one zone of civilization and set an end to the conflicts of rival sovereignties. Reasoning by analogy suggests that universal empire, in the second half of the twentieth century, will include all of humanity.

We have neither admitted nor rejected this reasoning, which we have encountered in following certain major perspectives opened by Toynbee. For the situation involves differences as striking as are the similarities.

First of all, it is the Northern Hemisphere rather than all of humanity that the wars of this century would destine to imperial unity. National sentiment is so strong that no imperium would be acknowledged as such. Let the Russian and American armies withdraw, one behind the Soviet frontiers, the other beyond the seas, and each of the European states will tend to resume its own autonomy. What is true in Europe is still more so outside of Europe. The states that have just appeared or gained their independence jealously guard a precious possession. The ideological conflict hampers communications among peoples on either side of the Iron Curtain, represses the consciousness of an interest common to all of international society. If Moscow already suffers such difficulty in maintaining the coherence of its bloc in Europe, what would happen if this bloc were extended to the whole of the Northern Hemisphere or to both hemispheres?

Our intention is not to speculate on the chances of imperial unification, but to analyze the requirements of peace by empire as we have analyzed, in the preceding chapter, those of peace by law. The difference between the two points of departure is as follows: the theoreticians of peace by law assume the plurality of states and inquire into the manner by which the latter can be subjected to the rule of law. The theoreticians of peace by empire observe that the plurality of states implies the risk of war and inquire into the manner by which sovereignties might be overcome.

1. *The Ambiguities of Sovereignty*

Hitherto we have occasionally employed the term *sovereignty* without rigorously defining it, because it served to designate the original fact of the international system. Now this fact—political units in competitive relations seek to judge, in the final instance, their own interests and acts—is historically incontestable. But so many juridical and philosophical theories have been elaborated around the concept of sovereignty, the ideal of transfers of sovereignty has been so widespread, that it is impossible to avoid considering disputes between the schools of interpretation.

Sovereignty can be considered as the basis both of inter-state order and of intra-state order. A state is sovereign in the sense that on its territory, with the reservation of the customary rules obligatory for all "civilized states" and of the commitments made by convention or treaty, the legal system it dictates or with which it is identified is the final word. Now, this system is valid only within a limited space; it applies only to men of a certain nationality. If, then, sovereignty is absolute, intra- and inter-state order are essentially different, since the first implies and the second excludes submission to a single authority.

Today jurists, philosophers, theoreticians of international relations emphasize the historical character of the doctrine of sovereignty. From the sixteenth to the eighteenth centuries, thinkers sought an unconditional authority, which would be subordinated to no terrestrial power, to no human law; they asked both where it resided and how it was justified. The universe of Christianity is dissolving. Theorists elaborate the ideology of the historical movement of which absolute monarchies and national states were the result. Absolute sovereignty corresponded to the ambition of kings eager to free themselves from the restriction Church and Empire imposed upon them, medieval residues. At the same time, it permitted condemning the privileges of intermediate bodies: feudal lords, regions, cities, guilds—privileges which no longer had any basis if the sovereign's will was the unique source of rights and duties.

Modern jurists, elaborating "implicitly normative" theories, readily attack the concept of sovereignty, either in the manner of Kelsen and his disciples because they see no difference between juridical order and state order, or, on the contrary, because they reduce the state order to a sector of a larger juridical order. In the first case the concept of sovereignty is useless since in pure theory it has no other meaning than the validity, within a given space, of a certain system of norms. In the second it is harmful because it suggests that the juridical imperatives derived their obligatory force from the will of state powers and that all legal order is an order of command. On the other hand, the realistic theoreticians of foreign policy are inclined to retain the concept of sovereignty in order to recall that each political unit legislates for itself and does not yield to an external authority.

Thus Hans J. Morgenthau qualifies the sovereign authority as *the supreme lawgiving and law-enforcing authority* and regards it as indivisible by essence, a divided sovereign authority being, so to speak, a contradiction *in adjecto*, as a squared circle. Nor can there be two sovereigns within a politically organized collectivity, just as there cannot be two generals at the head of an army. Even within democratic regimes, there exists, despite appearances, one sovereign power. "Since in a democracy that responsibility lies dormant in normal times, barely visible through the network of constitutional arrangements and legal rules, it is widely believed that it does not exist, and that the supreme lawgiving and law-enforcing authority, which was formerly the responsibility of one man, the monarch, is now distributed among the different co-ordinate agencies of the government and that, in consequence, no one of them is supreme."[1] But this is an illusion. In the vain effort to make democracy into a government of laws and not of men, reformers have forgotten that in every state "there must be a man or a group of men assuming ultimate responsibility for the exercise of political authority."

Sovereignty belongs to the authority that is both *legitimate* and *supreme*. Thus the search for sovereignty is, at the same time or alternately, *the search for the conditions in which an authority is legitimate and of the place, men and institutions in which it resides*. The first question, at the highest level is strictly philosophical. It is a fact that, down through history, the basis and extension of the right to command or of the duty to obey have been transformed. In our age, in all modern societies, the leaders claim their inspiration from the *democratic idea*, they do not claim to "possess" territories or peoples in the fashion of monarchs nor to have, by birth or by force, the authority to give orders. But both interpretations of the democratic idea—multiple parties, competitive elections, constitutional rules on the one hand, a single party, proletariat of the avant-garde on the other—restore a duality of fact and of "formulas."[2] The elected, temporary victors in the legal competition of parties, or the members of the Presidium, also temporary victors in the struggle of factions and persons, *legitimately* give orders, if legitimacy refers to the actual *formula* of each regime. Neither the democratic nor the Soviet formula nor even the democratic idea are ultimate answers to the question of legitimate authority (the democratic idea, in its turn, refers to a philosophy for its basis). But we may stop without going beyond these contradictory formulas and the common idea.

Let us leave this first aspect of the search for sovereignty, it being under-

---

[1] Hans J. Morgenthau, *Politics among Nations*, p. 281 in cited edition, p. 328 in third edition.
[2] We here distinguish the *democratic idea*, at the most abstract level, from the *formula* closer to reality, which justifies plurality of parties or a single party.

stood that a philosophy of legitimacy justifies the establishment of a given regime or the rule of certain men. Let us consider the search, within collectivities, for the instance in which the power known as sovereign resides. Here again the search does not lead to unequivocal results, because it bears alternately on the *authority of law* and on the *power of fact.*

In the expression *sovereignty of the people,* the concept does not apply to the actual possessor of the authority, but to the human group from which, according to the logic of the constitution, the authority of laws and leaders derives. At a level closer to reality, one refers to the sovereignty of the Supreme Court in the United States because in a case of conflict between a citizen and the courts, between the federal government and one of the fifty united states, the last word belongs not to the President, to the senators or to the elected officials, but to the judges. The sovereignty of the judges is linked to the primacy of the Constitution, itself established by the original desire of the states that joined in a federation. But the Supreme Court, in the United States, cannot be called sovereign in the sense in which the kings were sovereign in the absolutist regimes. It exercises neither the executive power nor federative power, to employ Locke's terms. Thus it seems to me unwieldy to employ the concept of sovereignty to designate the center or source of the effective power because the latter is, in fact, *divided.*

The proposition that there is in all states, as Morgenthau writes, "a man or a group of men assuming ultimate responsibility for the exercise of power," involves a degree of truth as the sociological theory of oligarchy: in the last analysis the decisions that concern the whole of a collectivity are taken by one or several men. But if, contrary to usage, we attribute sovereignty to this "power elite," the latter cannot be called either absolute or indivisible.

The division of the *de facto* power, in any constitutional-pluralist regime, results both from texts, from customs and from men. For example, in the United States, when it is a question of peace or war, the initiative belongs to the President, the consent or the veto (this latter generally impossible if hostilities have begun) to Congress, without the Constitution—in text or practice—permitting us to foresee what influence will be exercised upon the conduct of foreign policy in a given period by the personality of the President, the influence of his advisers and the action of various pressure groups.

Similarly, in Great Britain, the power belongs to the Cabinet more than to the Parliament, so long as the former possesses a cohesive and disciplined majority in the House of Commons. Custom and practice have swung the balance on the side of the Cabinet without the Cabinet's necessarily being, in case of crisis, the ultimate authority. In June 1940 the Conservative party, despite its majority, could not and did not wish to govern without the collaboration of the Labour party. In this case, did the final authority come from the House of Commons, the Crown, public opinion, the political class? In Great Britain as in the United States, one or several men decide and act in the period of national danger, the President in America, the Cabinet in England, the former chosen by constitutional procedure, the second formally by the Crown, but actually by the majority party in a calm period, by the entire political class or nation at the moment of danger. The "man or group of men" are those who exercise what Locke called the federative power, that is, conduct the relations of the collectivity with other collectivities; they are not necessarily identified with those who possess on paper "the supreme lawgiving or law-enforcing authority."

Is the formula of absolute and indivisible sovereignty false in relation to the actual power within political units, true when applied to the actors on the international stage? *De facto,* it is incontestable that in a given space, one system of norms and only one is generally valid, having for its source one and only one legislating authority, applied by one and only one juridical organization. *De jure,* external sovereignty signifies the same thing as independence, but the insistence on sovereignty suggests a philosophy hostile to the primacy of international law and conforming to the practice of states, the latter reserving the freedom to interpret their obligations and to assure their own defense.

Intermediate situations between independence and the total effacement of sovereignty have existed intermittently in the course of history, particularly during the last century. The European states did not "recognize" the human collectivities of other continents as they recognized each other. The principle of "sovereign equality," inscribed in the United Nations Charter, was applied only to the nations of Europe, in fact only to the great nations of Europe. We have seen the extension to all states (even to collectivities which scarcely deserve this name) of the constitutive principle of the *jus gentium Europaeum.*

During the last century some European states several times withdrew their nationals from local tribunals, instructed their officials to manage the finances or the tariff duties of a state that did not pay its debts and even to assume responsibility for the foreign affairs of a state that had submitted to a protectorate treaty. In all these circumstances the non-European state ceased to be, on its own territory, the supreme lawgiving and law-enforcing authority. At what moment had this state lost sovereignty? No one would assert that Tunisia or Morocco, in 1953, were sovereign states, yet they were states, subjects of international law. Was Cuba sovereign as long as the Platt Amendment, inserted in the Havana Treaty of 1901, granted the United States "the right to intervene for the preservation of Cuban independence, the maintenance of a government adequate for the protection of life, property and individual liberty"?[3]

The answer depends, from all evidence, on which criterion of sovereignty one prefers. Despite "concessions" and the management of tariff duties by foreign officials, China, in the last century, had preserved most of her "fed-

[3] Cf. Morgenthau, *op. cit.,* p. 251.

erative power." She also continued to conduct her foreign relations through her own nationals. On the other hand, in the case of a strict application of protectorate treaties, Tunisia and Morocco, while communicating with other states through the French resident alone, retained in general their internal autonomy; the authority responsible for legislating and enforcing respect for the laws, in the essentials, was Tunisian and Moroccan, not French.

It is incontestable that territorially organized collectivities have, over a more or less long period of time, lost certain attributes of sovereignty, recovered them subsequently or, quite the contrary, lost them altogether by integrating themselves into a larger collectivity. Tunisia and Morocco have recovered the temporarily lost attributes; the Swiss cantons and the American states have renounced sovereignty. The non-European states or semi-states have obtained the abrogation of treaties called unequal and have become free to determine their constitution, their legislation, their foreign policy, the composition of their armed forces, the management of their finances (which does not exclude their being, like all other states, subject to the obligations of international law, treaties, conventions and customs).

Everything seems to occur as if sovereignty, even external sovereignty, was divisible in fact, but as if the division, at least in our times, had a precarious and quasi-contradictory character, so that in the long run external sovereignty is either achieved or effaced. The men who claim to represent a political community, that is, a human group conscious of its uniqueness and determined to obtain recognition of its identity from others, will normally and logically tend to claim equality of rights, that is, the same right as other states to settle "in a sovereign-like manner" their so-called internal affairs.

Let us summarize the results of these analyses. The concept of sovereignty, outside of its strictly juridical sense (the validity of a system of norms in a given space), serves either to justify, internally, an idea (or a formula) of government, the power of certain tribunals (the sovereignty of the Supreme Court in the United States) or of certain men (the sovereignty of the Cabinet or of the Assembly),[4] or, on the contrary, to dissimulate the power of men by emphasizing the authority of a collective sovereign (the people) or an impersonal one (the laws). Externally, sovereignty is identified with non-dependence, but the meaning of this non-dependence is itself subject to contradictory interpretations: if states are sovereign, must we say that they are not subject to the obligations of international law? If they are subject to such obligations, can we still say that they are sovereign, in the sense in which sovereignty implies a supreme authority?

It is in order to avoid the formal difficulties that result from the contradiction between the theory of (absolute) sovereignty and the theory of international law (superior to states) that a school of jurists seeks to eliminate

[4] When jurists spoke, under the Fourth Republic, of parliamentary sovereignty, they meant to condemn and not to justify the latter.

the concept of sovereignty entirely. Personally, I should offer no objection to abandoning this concept, because of the ambiguities it sustains. But jurists also suppose that they have suppressed the facts that cover the concept once they have eliminated the word. It does not suffice to have constructed a theory of international law (superior to states) for states to renounce the "subjective rights" that they have traditionally reserved. It does not suffice to evoke the transfer of sovereignty for so-called supranational organisms to replace national realities and authorities.

2. *Sovereignty and Transfer of Sovereignty*

What is the present juridical and ideological meaning of the expression, employed by the United Nations Charter, of "sovereign equality" of states? These states having traditionally been treated as people, according to the philosophy of natural law, they passed for "equals" in the manner of the individual subjects of municipal law.[5]

Transposed to the international order, this conception inspired the pacifism of Wilson and the League of Nations: if the "collective persons," the nations, are free and equal as are the citizens within the democratic states, if they submit like the citizens to the rule of law, peace will be founded on justice. This transposition was illusory, since there was neither a supreme tribunal to qualify the facts or to interpret the law, nor an irresistible force to impose it, nor a legislative power to revise the law, nor a tribunal to decide according to equity. If the pacifism drawn from the philosophy of "nations free and equal in law" has been tragically refuted, the ideology of "sovereign equality" has nonetheless played, since the Second World War, a historical role: it has justified the recognition of the formal equality of all peoples, the abrogation of unequal treaties, mandates, protectorates, in short *decolonization*. International law, positing the sovereign equality of states, has influenced the course of events in the manner of a morality accepted by the common conscience which gradually suppresses the facts in contradiction to it.

Once states are recognized as members of the United Nations, their governments invoke the ideology of "sovereign equality" in order to reject the interventions either of the other states or even of the international organization itself. Everything that traditionally derives from municipal law does not concern the latter. The measures taken by a state on its own territory with regard to possessions and persons, whether or not they are contrary to the customs of civilized states, are the exclusive concern of "sovereign states."

On the other hand, the same ideology has left intact the distinction be-

---

[5] The equality of men before the law has never excluded inequalities of fact nor even inequalities of "subjective rights" resulting from the redistribution of wealth or power. Birth forbids no one to exercise rights which result from the ownership of the Citroën factories, but he who possesses this ownership, by inheritance or by legal acquisition, has, in fact, "subjective rights" quite different from the wage-earner who sweeps the factory floors.

tween great and small powers, or powers with limited interests and powers with world interests, a distinction of which the veto right granted to the five permanent members of the Security Council remains the symbol. The ideology of "sovereign equality" is invoked by the small states in order to enlarge the sphere of their internal competence, but it does not disturb the privileged position which the great powers have always claimed to occupy.

It will be objected that in the course of the last decade or so, another evolution in the opposite direction has occurred: the European states have, by treaty, consented to transfers of sovereignty which open a prospect of "federal unification" without recourse to violence. What is the juridical status of the Common Market? Here is one answer of the jurists that we can take as a point of departure for our analysis:

"Is the Common Market a sovereign entity? In the sense that it exercises exclusive and ultimate authority with respect to certain important governmental functions within the territory covered by treaty, that it enters into binding relations with states and other supranational entities external to the Common Market, and that it possesses some of the immunities and rights normally considered attributes of sovereignty, it undoubtedly is a sovereign entity. If, on the other hand, one considers sovereignty to imply broad territorial jurisdiction, the Common Market would not be sovereign. Although the areas in which the Common Market exercises ultimate authority are of the greatest importance, it remains primarily a functional rather than a territorial authority."[6]

"Supranationality," to adopt the concept currently employed in such discussions, is characterized, in the European organizations, by three criteria: renunciation of the principle of unanimity, direct relation between the legislative or regulative power of the Common Market and the citizens or enterprises of the various member nations, and finally agreements concluded by the Commission or the High Authority with foreign states.

Renunciation of the veto right, that is, acceptance of the simple or qualified majority rule, under certain conditions and with certain reservations, does not mark a rupture with inter-state rules or practices. In many international organizations—the International Postal Union, the Civil Aviation Organization, the International Monetary Fund—certain majority decisions are taken by an assembly consisting of the representatives of the states, none of the latter possessing the veto right and each vote being weighed according to more or less strict criteria. The field of application of the majority vote, the contrast between the supranational process and the Council of Ministers thus have much less bearing than is suggested by the passions favorable or hostile to "integration," that is, to the High Authority or the Commission which are supposed to act as superior and united entities, not as the expression of multiple and intact sovereignties.

[6] Morton A. Kaplan and Nicholas de B. Katzenbach, *op. cit.*, p. 139.

The supranational organs, it is true, have prerogatives that the states did not traditionally abandon even to organs created by themselves. With regard to coal and steel the supreme legislative power belongs to the High Authority (within the limits traced by the treaty), and this legislation and the regulative measures which result from it apply directly to the individuals and enterprises of the Six. Further, commercial negotiations of the Six will be conducted, once the common tariff is established, by the community itself. Now, the commercial and tariff policy is traditionally a part of "state sovereignty." It escapes or will shortly escape each of the Six powers taken individually.

Is it possible to bring the European communities within the old concepts of municipal or international law? Certainly the ingenuity of the jurists can manage to do so. According to doctrines or preferences, the originality of these "supranational" institutions will be reduced or emphasized. The sovereignty of the member states will seem to be preserved if we assert that the states have simply delegated certain administrative or technical functions to organs whose authority is based on a *ne varietur* treaty, itself emanating from the desires of the states that have signed it. The sovereignty of the states will appear to be reduced if we insist on the role that the High Authority or the Commission plays or can play either in establishing rules comparable to laws or in taking *ad hoc* administrative measures comparable to those taken by national ministers.

Let us leave aside the controversies of juridical conceptualization and ask to what degree there is and is not a "transfer of sovereignty." Let us employ Locke's distinction between the two aspects of the executive power: the execution of municipal laws, the relations with the other states. What the European Community henceforth administers, either by unanimous or by majority decisions, is the execution of laws relative to certain objects and, in the future, trade relations with the non-members. The transfer is the expression of the desire common to the member states of creating among themselves a transnational and in certain regards supranational society, but the essence of national sovereignties is not seriously affected.

Let us call *sovereign* the supreme authority which legislates: none of the assemblies provided for by the three treaties (Coal-Steel, Euratom, Common Market) possesses legislative power. None of the executive organs has the right to elaborate laws, except to interpret the rules posited in the treaty, and to attain the objectives fixed by the latter. As for the functions of the executive organs, they exceed the powers ordinarily delegated to administrative bodies of international organizations, but they do not affect the federative power except in the case of trade negotiations with the foreign states.

Let us call *sovereign* the constitutional organ that, in case of crisis or exceptional circumstances, takes the decisions necessary to the reform of institutions or to public welfare within the framework of existing institutions. In this case, again, none of the European communities implies a transfer of sovereignty. Neither the Atlantic Alliance nor the Common Market has paralyzed the revolutionary capacity of the French, nor even prevented military operations such as those of Suez or Bizerte.

Let us call *sovereign* the man or the men who *effectively* possess the supreme power, who, according to ordinary or exceptional practice, take the decisions that commit the future of the collectivity (the manufacture of the atomic bomb, recognition of Algerian independence): here, too, the sovereignty of each of the Six is intact.

Finally, let us call *sovereign* the organ that possesses the law-enforcing capacity, the capacity of imposing respect for the laws and of punishing their violation: neither the European executive organs nor the Court of Justice have at their disposal means of force. Yet it does not result from this that the decisions of the High Authorities or the decrees of the Court of Justice will not be carried out. In many circumstances, individuals or groups obey the laws because, convinced of their common interest in the legislation, they have acquired the habit of obeying them without the threat of punishment being felt, without its being necessary.

It is not important for us to carry any further the analysis of the relations provided for by the treaties or confirmed by experience between the High Authority or the Commission and the Council of Ministers, on the number and importance of majority decisions, on the respective role of compromises among states and of deference to community interest. It was merely important for us to recall that the transfers, granted that we use this expression, are limited (certain executive and federative functions, particularly of a technical and economic nature) and that, if sovereignty is defined as the supreme power of deciding in a case of crisis, it remains intact within national states.

This analysis does not solve a very different problem, that of the influence the Common Market will ultimately exercise over the relations among the Six. The sovereignties of the member states being progressively dismantled by the "transfers," will a higher sovereignty also be formed at the very time when the elements of the transferred state powers have been gathered together? Will a European nation be born as the national states die away? Will a European nation receive the heritage of the French, German and Italian nations? Will a European Minister of Foreign Affairs emerge, at a still undetermined stage, from the process by which the Common Market is being constituted?

I do not believe that it is possible to give a categorical answer: the formation of a Common Market does not lead, either by juridical necessity or by historical necessity, to an authentic federation. The jurists who hope to separate law from the state and who are convinced that law can be both positive and effective without being the result of a governmental control possessing means of sanction, tend to insist on the originality of the European institutions. On the other hand, the jurists for whom sovereignty is monolithic because in the last analysis it is a will, show the ambiguity of supranationality which is reduced to a delegation of administrative authority if it does not lead to a true federation.

I am not choosing between these implicitly normative theories, but I observe that the second is, for the moment, closer to the reality than the first. The High Authority of the Coal and Steel Community has not yet utilized the so-called supranational powers it possesses on paper, it has not taken the non-unanimous, majority decisions which would be imperative for national governments. The Brussels Commission possesses on paper few of these so-called supranational powers. But this is not the essential point: let us suppose the Common Market were achieved according to the means provided for in the Rome Treaty. Germany, France, Italy would each continue to have a foreign policy, an individual political history, a separate police force and army. To assume that the Common Market *necessarily* leads to a European federation (or to a European federal state) is to assume either that economics, in our period, control and so to speak encompass politics, or that the fall of tariff barriers will of itself cause the fall of the political and military ones. These two suppositions are false.

The Common Market, once completed, would not prevent France or Germany from executing divergent, even opposed, actions in the Arab region or in the Far East. It would not put the army and the police force at the orders of the same men. It would leave the constitutions of these various nations exposed to dangers that would be, for each of them, different. An electoral victory of the Communist party in Italy would compromise Italy's regime, not that of France and Germany, unless the European Assembly had become, for the Six, the equivalent of Congress for the fifty American states, in other words unless a federation had been born.

If we imagine the Six politically united once they are economically united, it is because we have, so to speak, eliminated the political order by the implicitly admitted hypothesis of the Atlantic Alliance and of the rivalry of the two blocs. Within the Atlantic bloc, Germany, France, Italy are supposed to act in common, under the direction of the United States, confronting the Soviet threat. Within this context is set, bounded by the bloc, the economic integration achieved by the Common Market, and from this, by a tap of a magic wand, is produced a united Europe, the European federation! We have, as a matter of fact, lost the essential thing: the community power, animated by a community desire, the state and the nation, the human collectivity, conscious of its uniqueness and determined to assert and affirm it in the face of all other collectivities.

I am not saying that economic unification, such as might be achieved by the Common Market, does not help to create either the "European nation" or the "European state." This unification certainly reinforces transnational society, it creates embryos of "federal administration," it accustoms the states to permit decisions that affect their interests at a "European" level. Certain classical prerogatives of sovereignty may thus escape the national states without the latter even realizing it. But the thesis I should call "clandestine federalism" or "federalism without tears" seems to me illusory. The system of obligations created by the institutions of Europe will surreptitiously absorb neither the authority to take decisions by which a human collectivity asserts itself in opposing others nor the power to resort to the *ultima ratio;* it will not create a common will among French, Germans, Italians to be henceforth autonomous as Europeans and no longer as members of historical nations. A legitimate authority, a *de facto* power, the consciousness of a higher nationality *may* gradually emerge from the economic community, but on condition that the peoples desire it and that the leaders act in accord with this desire, or again on condition that the leaders act with a view to federation and that the peoples consent to it.

The hope that the European federation will gradually and irresistibly emerge from the Common Market is based on a great illusion of our times: the illusion that economic and technological interdependence among the various factions of humanity has definitively devalued the fact of "political sovereignties," the existence of distinct states which wish to be autonomous. Of course, it would in many respects be desirable for the human race to reach an awareness of its unity, to approach certain problems (the exploitation and conservation of natural resources, the population explosion) as if they confronted a single collectivity. But it remains false (unfortunately, perhaps) that prosperity or peace is indivisible (although the contrary is daily affirmed by personages great and small). The poverty of the Indian masses does not compromise the well-being of the average European or American. The well-being of the one is not the cause of the other's poverty. For some decades to come, the planet offers enough resources so that all men, on condition that they are trained and capable of organizing production, can attain an honorable standard of living. But the contrast between the hunger of half of humanity and the agricultural surplus of the Western world would suffice to prove, if there were any need, that on a global scale the equivalent of national communities does not exist.

It is possible that in the long run disparities of wealth are dangerous for the privileged themselves, because of the spread of communism or even, directly, because of the resentments awakened among the dispossessed by the inevitable comparison between the condition of the West and that of the rest of the world. It is appropriate to use this argument in order to bring an enlightened egoism to the aid of pure generosity. But in the short run, the West is more threatened by the weapons of the Soviet bloc (which also belongs to the rich minority) than by the bitterness of the starving millions.

Finally, it takes a strange blindness to claim that "sovereignty" or "independence" no longer means anything. Even within the Soviet bloc the persistence of a Polish state means a great deal to the Polish people, both in idea and in fact, both in the immediate present and in the long run. Between the condition of the Baltic ex-states and that of the satellite states,

Poland, Rumania, Czechoslovakia, the difference is at least substantial: "Russification" (by the system of education and the movements of populations) is possible in one case and not in the other; the gaps, in relation to the orthodox model, which "Polish sovereignty" permits are without any common measure with the gaps existing between the various socialist republics of the Soviet Union. In October 1956 Poland proved that it still had, in the giant's shadow, a political history of its own, whereas neither the Ukraine nor White Russia nor the Baltic states have one any longer.

The widening of the functions of the state, the principle of international law that forbids open interference in the internal affairs of independent states, the nationalization of culture—these three characteristic facts of our century preserve for national independence, despite technical-economic interdependence, despite supranational blocs and transnational ideologies, a meaning which we may deplore but not ignore. Must we, in fact, deplore it?

3. Nations and Federation

We have hitherto omitted one of the meanings of the ideology of sovereignty: that states are comparable to persons. Now, according to many observers, this personification of the state animated by a will of its own, distinct from that of individuals, is false and responsible both for theoretical contradictions and historical disasters.

"The truth is that states are not persons, however convenient it may often be to personify them; they are merely *institutions*, that is to say, organizations which men establish among themselves for securing certain objects, of which the most fundamental is a system of order within which the activities of their common life can be carried on. They have no wills except the wills of the individual human beings who direct their affairs; and they exist not in a political vacuum but in continuous political relations with one another."[7] This radical nominalism, also implicitly normative, seems to me philosophically unsatisfactory. But even if admitted, it would not modify the "essential imperfection" of international law. In ordinary language one would say that states have not renounced their right either to interpret independently their obligations or to be a law unto themselves. In the nominalist language of institutions one would say: the men who claim to speak in the name of an institution commonly called the state invoke "national honor" or "vital interest" in order not to submit to the authority of other men who claim to speak in the name of an international organization. Now, these first men control the behavior of other men generally wearing uniforms and capable of wielding weapons. Thus, in the case of a conflict between two groups of men, each invoking a state incorrectly personified, there is no juridical solution. The doctrinaire theorists of natural law who introduced the notion of the state as person were much closer to the historical reality than the

[7] J. L. Brierly, *The Law of Nations*, fifth edition, Oxford, 1955, pp. 55–56.

positivist doctrinaire theorists who defined the essence of law by the legality of sanction and yet affirmed that there exists an international law *stricto sensu.*

But further, it does not seem to me at all unjustifiable to define nations as "collective personalities." In each man, personality is the synthesis of a biological condition and a conscious will; it is created, through its duration, by the unit's becoming what heredity has transmitted and reflection creates. It participates in nature[8] and in reason. One can, by analogy, evoke "the collective persons" of nations.

"The nation," writes Father Gaston Fessard,[9] "is the people which, conscious of a certain community of origin, of culture, and above all of interest, tends to objectify its unity, that of a personal individuality in the eyes of its members, to represent it to themselves and to others, in order to be able to orient themselves toward their destinies with complete independence." This definition does not apply to all the "political units" among which humanity has been divided down through centuries. But the modern nation in Europe consists precisely of the conjunction of a community of culture[10] and a desire for autonomy. Today's various political units are far from achieving this conjunction uniformly, and another type, in accord with the ideas of the century, is already visible: the federal state in which the communities of culture are multiple and respected, but which preserves a desire for autonomy in confronting other political units.

The collective personality of a nation, like the individual personality, is born and dies in time. It has many conditions of a material, physical or biological order, but it asserts itself only by consciousness, being capable of thought and of choice. Participating both in nature and in reason, these national personalities express the wealth of human possibilities. The diversity of cultures is not a curse to be exorcized but a heritage to be safeguarded.

The national individuality is not visible as human individuals are visible, but it is nonetheless knowable, by observation and analysis. It functions only through the intermediary of persons, but these latter, for themselves as for others, act as interpreters or guides of the collectivity. The formula that the state is an institution established by men is acceptable to the degree that the concept of an institution remains equivocal. It is not true, however, that the exclusive object of this institution is to insure the regular and peaceful exercise of the activities of each and every man. It is neither true nor desirable that collective beings not have an end in themselves.

Of course, in the last analysis, it is the life of people which is the goal of commonwealths. But this life is not a solitary one, it is not achieved outside of the "national communities," each of which tends to promote particular

---

[8] Nature, here, in the naturalistic, biological sense of the term.

[9] *Pax Nostra, Examen de conscience international,* Paris, 1936, p. 422.

[10] This "community of culture" is never entirely one and homogeneous. Even in France, Bretons, Alsatians, Basques and Provençals often speak a first language distinct from French.

values. To efface the distinctions between these communities would be to impoverish humanity, supposing that such an objective were possible to achieve. The ideal of a humanity conscious of its own solidarity does not contradict the fact of a humanity divided into nations conscious of their uniqueness and of the value of their uniqueness.

Further, this fact is also an ideal. For each man, to contribute to the realization of "national values" is a duty and not a servitude. This duty does not suppress duties with regard to all of humanity. Each nation gives a specific content to the ideal, it does not (or should not) deny the universal and formal rules which are imposed upon every man *qua* man. But how could the individual be obligated to all of humanity without being so with regard to the nation that makes him what he is?

Why the nation, it will be objected, rather than any other group? The answer, it seems to me, results from the analysis of the groups to which by necessity each of us belongs. The root of the family is biological, but the unity of families that gather to constitute a people is neither exclusively racial nor strictly territorial. It is the unity of a culture, of a singular grouping of beliefs and behavior. With the shift from archaic societies to historical ones has developed the dialectic of communities of culture and political entities, still occurring in our period. Violence has made empires rise and fall. Armed groups have seized power, kept whole populations or classes in servitude. But, formed down through the centuries by force and by bloodshed, certain modern nations have discovered the secret of the (never perfect) union of culture and politics, history and reason. The nation has its language and its law, which it has received from the past and which express a unique calling. Citizens seek to live together, to establish their own laws in order to make a contribution to the human enterprise which, without them, would not exist. In this sense, the nation, as Father Fessard writes, has a vocation which class does not possess.

Whatever specific definition we make of class, the wage-earners who work with their hands are chiefly characterized by their similar situation with regard to job and pay. They are in contact with matter, they do not earn their livings in and by human relations, they have incomes which, within a nation, are not very different, they manifest a certain similarity of opinions or attitude (or the various attitudes are distributed according to determined percentages), sometimes they are aware of their similar condition and out of this awareness they organize (or many among them organize) with a view to defending what they regard as their common interest. If this common interest is of an economic order, if their organization is a trade union or if it is political and accepts the national unit, the class is subordinated of its own accord to the nation and does not attribute to itself a vocation in the sense in which the nation has one.[11] On the other hand, the ideology that

[11] Cf. Gaston Fessard, *De l'actualité historique,* Paris, 1960; see for instance Vol. II, pp. 228 ff.

denies the nation in order to affirm the class is lost in inextricable contradictions. When the class or the party that claims class as its inspiration has
taken power, does the nation disappear or does the class? If the class disappears, it is because it did not have a permanent vocation beyond the
modification of the economic regime. If the nation disappears, what becomes
of the community of culture, and from whence does the legitimate authority
come?

As a matter of fact, in that part of the world where the doctrine proclaiming the primacy of class over nation has in theory triumphed, the nations
continue with their own vocation of culture, although they are deprived of
a degree of their autonomy by the supremacy of the Russian Communist
party and of the state which it has constructed. Nonetheless, class divisions
remain, characterized by similarity of conditions, although they are reputed
to be no longer antagonistic and no longer have the right to organize into
pressure groups. In other words, political power in terms of material things,
that is to say power attributed to the working classes, disappears with the
revolution for which the doctrine was conceived. This is a strictly ideological
notion in that it offers as an eternal truth a reversal of the hierarchy of values,
an inversion of the essential relations that are explained only by and for one
historical action.

If the nation is an ideal as well as a fact, if a humanity deprived of national heterogeneities would be impoverished, nationalisms—desire for power
or pride of nations, refusal to submit to a law or to a tribunal—are not
thereby justified. Here is, in effect, the final antinomy of man's political
destiny. It is not more satisfying for consciousness to deny than it is to
sanctify nations, to refuse them the right to determine their own destiny
than to grant them the right to determine without appeal their own justice.
The antinomy is not solved by the jurists who reason as if the state were
merely an institution among others, as if human society had the same
cohesion as national societies, as if the normative system of the *jus gentium*
had the same character as the systems of municipal law, as if the prohibition
to resort to war or to the threat of war had, for states, the same positive
charge and the same effectiveness that the prohibition to kill or to steal has
for individuals. This antinomy is real, it has lasted in one form or another
since the dawn of history. It is not necessarily eternal, but it is not yet
resolved, supposing of course that it can be.

The *theoretical* solution is that of federation, a civilized or voluntary version of empire. The community of culture is preserved. It merely renounces
those powers needed by the superior unit in order to insure the protection
and welfare of all. The classical example is that of Switzerland. It is the
Helvetian Confederation that is "sovereign," that desires independence,
that has an army, that is the equivalent of a person on the international
stage: internal freedom for the individuals and for groups to live according
to their ideals and to worship in their own way is nonetheless rigorously

preserved. Why could not all humanity create a global confederation in the image of the Swiss one, entrusted with the mission of solving the problems that could not be solved on a lower level—conservation of natural resources, conditions of trade, reduction or limitation of organized violence?

Two kinds of questions arise concerning the Utopia of the global confederation or federation. The first are historical-sociological: What are, in the abstract, the conditions of such a federation? Do such conditions, in the middle of the twentieth century, appear likely or unlikely? The second are strictly philosophical: is the Utopia contrary to the nature of man? To the nature of human societies? To the essence of politics? Can we conceive of a human society without an enemy?

The answer to the questions of the first order is afforded by the analyses of the preceding chapter. The path to global federation is the same as that of peace by law. The decisive step would be to abandon the state's right of determining justice without appeal, that is, to abandon what has been and what still is the essence of "external sovereignty." But this abandonment, in its turn, that has been neither imposed nor achieved by the Covenant of the League of Nations or by the United Nations Charter, will be vainly demanded by men of good will so long as there have not developed, between members of global society, relations comparable to those that link the members—individuals or groups—of each national society: consciousness of the community, acceptance of a juridical and political regime, monopoly of armed force. Let us repeat once again: none of these three conditions has been realized at the present time, and none promises to be so in the immediate future.

Of course, the philosopher willing to accept the illusion of a rational history can invoke several facts. After the madness of Hitler's racism, the intellectual vogue has turned to the other extreme, and the most fashionable theory is the one which proclaims most noisily the equality of individuals, races, nations and states—to the point of occasionally forgetting that the inequality of individual gifts is the least contestable of all facts. In the United Nations, representatives of some hundred states invoke on every occasion the duties the Charter imposes upon the governments and sometimes upon the authority of the international organization as such. Finally, the obligation of assistance to the so-called underdeveloped peoples, the admission that it is to the common interest of humanity to reduce the gaps in the standard of living between rich collectivities and poor ones, can be interpreted by those who seek motives for optimism as the first seeds of a "human awareness," of man's consciousness of humanity as a single unity.

These arguments are unfortunately weak compared with the arguments in the opposite direction; the indications of a human consciousness are almost invisible compared with the daily renewed proofs of a tribal consciousness or of an ideological fanaticism. The devaluation of national units which some observers emphasize does not mark a weakening of one tribal consciousness in favor of another kind. The "nation," in the Soviet Union or in the United States, is more heterogeneous than the old countries of Europe.[12] The European nations no longer possess the resources necessary to play a leading role; divided between the American and Russian imperial zones, they are morally weakened, the citizens oscillating between "bloc patriotism" and "traditional patriotism," incapable of subscribing entirely to one or the other. "French nationalism" is rent rather than weakened by the fact that some Frenchmen desire the victory of the Soviet bloc, and that those whose adherence goes to the Atlantic bloc maintain a nostalgia for France's independence. The number of Frenchmen who passionately aspire to an international society in which disputes such as those of Suez and Bizerte would be submitted to a tribunal is insignificant.

Neither of the super powers, it is true, admits, in the manner of the Third Reich, the ambition of conquering lands or of subjugating men: we know why. Does the Soviet Union conceive of a humanity converted to communism as united into a single state?[13] It may, although this remote objective, or rather this vision, has in any case little influence on its present behavior. The goal of the Soviet Union is to eliminate the enemy, that is, the United States: the latter is the symbol, in the eyes of the Kremlin leaders, of the capitalist universe that is evil and that must vanish according to the determinism of history and for the good of humanity, but it is also the only center of a force capable of opposing Soviet force. Consisting of ideological hostility at the same time as of state hostility, the rivalry of the two super powers neither prepares nor announces a human reconciliation. The progress of rational organization, in labor and administration, has made neither individuals nor collectivities reasonable.

More than once, intellectuals of humanitarian, that is, pacifist inspiration have expressed a kind of hatred for those who do not share their passions. They declare capitalism bad in itself and socialism good in itself, they preach the class struggle and do not realize that in our period, when each ideology is incarnated in a bloc, they are contributing to war. Do you not do the same in denouncing Sovietism, it will be asked. To a degree, it is true, we all participate in the cold war, and we can only avoid doing so by renouncing ourselves and our values. But there remains a fundamental asymmetry. We know that all regimes are imperfect, and although we regard the Soviet regime as being more imperfect than our own, we have not sworn to bring about its death, we ask it only to renounce its lies and to admit that it is one possibility among the others. If the Soviets accepted themselves for what they are, an authentically pacifist competition could be established. On the other hand, the Marxist-Leninist doctrine, as it is taught

[12] On the other hand, the national consciousness, in the United States and perhaps in the Soviet Union, is inseparable from the political regime, whereas a Frenchman does not assert that France might be inseparable from any political regime.

[13] E. R. Goodman, *The Soviet Design for a World State*, New York, 1961.

in the Soviet Union and preached throughout the world, is essentially bellicose; it excludes the acceptance of a common law, the principle of any world organization.

Impossible today, is a world organization impossible in itself because it is contradictory to the nature of man or to man as a social being? Bergson has suggested as much and C. Schmitt has sought to prove it by positing the alternative of friend and enemy as constituent elements of politics. Both are right, it seems to me, to emphasize the essential difference between the broadening of political units and the *unification* of humanity. The usual argument—that of extrapolation—is tantamount to ignoring this difference. The federation of Western Europe, desirable or not, will contribute to peace or to international tension, but in any case, it will not modify the international order. On the other hand, it does not seem to me feasible to deduce the contradictory character and consequently the impossibility of a world organization from the friend-enemy alternative posited as being the elements of politics.

Either, in effect, one assumes the plurality of "sovereign units": in this case, the friend-enemy alternative is only an expression of the rivalry of power, of reciprocal suspicions, of desires for autonomy. Each, being afraid of all the others, feels threatened sometimes by one, sometimes by another. The formation of common or conflicting fronts results from this situation. But in this hypothesis, the friend-enemy alternative results from the "state of nature" between the units; it does not demonstrate its fatal permanence.

Or else one assumes a collectivity whose members have accepted, in principle, submission to law. In this hypothesis, rivalries exist between individuals or groups. But these rivalries which, according to the norm of the accepted regime, are not settled by force, do not create inexpiable hostilities. Or, in any case, these hostilities do not make impossible a world organization, since they have not been incompatible with national organizations.

There remains a final interpretation, the least fragile of all: hostility is natural among men; it accepts regulation only within a political unit which is based upon opposition and defines itself in its turn by hostilities. In other words, historical dialectic never suppresses the recourse to force, but transposes it to its higher level. If we assume a world organization which, by definition, would no longer have any external enemy, it would dissociate itself, once again, by the action of internal conflicts.

This dialectic is the one, in effect, which we have observed down through history. New powers have surmounted rivalries among the old powers only by assuming or discovering the existence of enemies. It is against the threat of the Soviet Union that the Atlantic bloc has conceived a common will. It is in order to recover a partial independence in relation to the super powers that the European states are trying to unite. If the conflict of the giants should disappear by the stroke of a magic wand, what would remain of European integration or the "Atlantic bloc"?

These same examples confirm and refute the objection. Certain powers, it is true, exist only by and for a certain hostility. The "political persons," the nations organized into states, sometimes require a federative power (in the sense Locke gave to this expression) in order to persevere in their being. The autonomy of these persons is defined only by resistance to external forces. In a humanity hypothetically pacified, perhaps many political units would tend to dissolve; the communities of culture, narrower and closer to individuals, would resume their autonomy, the functions necessary to security and to welfare would be exercised at a level higher than that of the national state.

The question is whether this dissociation of political-cultural units in favor of communities of culture that are narrower and of a universal economic-military organization signifies the resumption of the dialectic of hostilities and alliances. In theory, as long as the human groups have different languages and beliefs, they will have countless occasions to criticize each other, to misunderstand or despise each other. Is it correct to call such mutual misunderstanding hostilities? Would the human groups be more disposed to tolerate each other when neither welfare nor security is any longer endangered? If we assume a monopoly, accepted by all, of the decisive force, if we assume the conditions of the exploitation of global resources fixed by all humanity in agreement, will the various cultures coexist in peace?

The question will seem a futile one, I fear, so remote are these hypotheses from the real world in which we live. I readily grant that these hypotheses would be qualified by some as absurd and by others as Utopian. Such skepticism is nonetheless not entirely justified. The history upon which we are embarking and which will last until a natural or military catastrophe has suppressed the acquisitions of science and technology and returned humanity to the agricultural and artisan stage will be *universal*. It will not be dissociated into "histories of civilizations," to adopt the concept of Spengler and Toynbee. It will include the whole of the human race.

For this history to be less violent than that of nations or empires, three conditions must be realized: *thermonuclear (or equivalent) weapons must not be used, the equitable distribution of resources must be assured, the races, peoples, nations and creeds must accept and respect each other.* None of these three conditions having been realized as yet, it is not false to say that the political order is inseparable from hostilities. If as a hypothesis we eliminate the first two, would friendships and hostilities exist as an expression of the aggression manifested by any human individual with regard to *another*—the other who prevents me from peacefully enjoying the certainty of incarnating absolute truth or supreme values?

The question is not a rhetorical one, but it does not require a categorical answer. A positive answer would be to wager on a conversion of the human race. A negative answer would leave no other hope of peace than the triumph of a race, a people, a Church, hence would enjoin us to sacrifice either peace or the wealth of diversity. But the question must remain posed so that men of good will do not imagine that it is enough to put thermonuclear weapons at the disposal of some United Nations commission or even to confide the task of worldwide economic planning to a committee of experts, so that political hostilities and ideological enmity would disappear simultaneously. Below the level of a global state, groups would not live in peace if, like Hegel's version of consciousness, each seeks the death of the other.

Some years ago I concluded a book by an appeal to skepticism which critics discussed more than they read. The fanaticism I opposed is that of the ideologists of our century, simplifiers and "perfectionists," who believe themselves to possess an infallible formula for prosperity and justice and who will accept any violence in order to attain this luminous goal. To doubt these abstract models has nothing to do with vulgar skepticism. It is, on the contrary, to rely on reasoning that confirms the imperfection of all social orders, accepts the impossibility of knowing the future, condemns the vain pretension of drawing up the schema of an ideal society. It is our knowledge that reveals the limits of our power and recommends that we gradually improve what exists, instead of starting over from zero after having destroyed the work of centuries.

This ideological skepticism differs, in many regards, from the tolerance that was gradually established after the orgies of violence launched by the wars of religion. Catholics and Protestants do not each cease believing in the truth of their interpretation of the Christian message, the authority of their Church, but they have renounced crusades and forced conversions. They have finally acknowledged that only voluntary conversions are meritorious and authentic. Ideally, this renunciation of violence testifies not to an exhausted faith but to a purified one. As a matter of fact, men, being what they are, tolerate the faith of others more often out of indifference than out of respect for freedom.

Ideological skepticism is somewhat similar to religious skepticism: temporal salvation depends less on the liberal or socialist Church than on elements common to all dogmas and all practices. But ideological skepticism is inclined to doubt even the possibility of an exemplary order, whereas true Christians have doubted neither the revelation nor the incarnation nor the sacraments. There should be no crusade where faith is and cannot help being unconditional; there should be no unconditional faith where the preferable cannot be certain and where the objective cannot be perfect; such would be the moral roots of the pacific institution.

4. Federation and Empire

To come back to earth, none of the conditions necessary for the effectiveness of a world organization is realized at present. If we cease to dream of the distant future, then peace in the ordinary run of things, the kind of peace for which those who are still alive can do something, will not be assured by states' *voluntary* renunciation[14] of the rivalry of power and the use of force. Instead of asking if peace is compatible with human nature, it is better to discuss the means of inducing states to behave reasonably, that is, no longer to play with monstrous weapons. The outcome of the present crisis is, in theory, either a world federation gradually established by agreement among the states, or else a world empire imposed by the victory of one of the candidates for supreme power.

How, if they included all humanity, would such a federation and such an empire differ? According to concepts, a confederation (*Staatenbund*) and a federation (*Bundesstaat*) differ essentially. The former permits the existence of the political sovereignty of member states, hence the plurality of armed forces; the latter effaces the external sovereignty of member states and consequently creates a single actor on the national stage who replaces the actors that have become members of the federal state (the German Empire or the United States). As always, intermediate cases make the factual distinction less clear than the conceptual one.

On the worldwide level the organization would reproduce neither federation nor confederation exactly. Whatever the rights which the fifty states reserve, whatever the effectiveness, in the United States, of the appeal to the Supreme Court, the federal state is gradually broadening its attributions, and the powers of the federated states are gradually diminishing to administrative functions. It is difficult if not impossible to imagine in the near or foreseeable future a world government comparable to the Soviet government or that of the United States. It neither could nor should concern itself with so many affairs, nor even impose so many rules common to all men. It would not thereby become confederal, insofar as confederation permits the member states their own armed forces and, with some reservations, the disposal of the latter.

A "world organization" would have to deprive the states of most of their military sovereignty, without depriving them or even attempting to deprive them of the management of their national existence. This is the difficulty, if not the contradiction—one that is provisionally insurmountable. The models of "world constitutions" are all borrowed from the Western constitutional-pluralist regimes.[15] They presuppose either a state of the American type, created by immigrants who had brought with them the heritage of violent history, but who had freed themselves from it by starting all over again on the basis of colonization, or the slow acceptance of a legal discipline by individuals and groups conscious of their community. Since the circumstances in which these constitutions function within states are not to be found on the level of the human race as a whole, two hypotheses seem conceivable: either

[14] Unless there is a catastrophic event, which is not impossible but not foreseeable.
[15] This is the case of the constitutional model constructed by Grenville Clark and Louis B. Sohn, in the book from which we have quoted above, *World Peace through World Law*.

an explicit agreement of the super powers to transfer to a neutral authority the decisive weapons, instead of today's implicit and partial agreement, or the disarmament of all states or blocs by the victory of one of them.

The explicit agreement to transfer the decisive weapons to a so-called non-committed authority (or one composed of representatives of all blocs and states) is not radically inconceivable. It would represent the extreme form of what we are trying to achieve today by various methods of arms control. But unless a common disaster overcame all prudence, it is very unlikely that in the foreseeable future the super powers will manage to "neutralize" the weapons which both assure their superiority and sustain their anxiety.

Must we then hope for universal empire, that is, today, the victory of the Soviet Union? Before for a second time answering such a question which, shocking as it is, is not an idle one (it may come up one day), let us ask if and how the universal empire would differ from a world federation.

A first difference comes to mind immediately: when we evoke a "world organization" or a "peace by law" or a "world federation," we imagine the transition from plurality to unity, from a peace by equilibrium (or balance of terror) to a peace by law or satisfaction, without the intermediary of a death-struggle or a victor. Federation demands a conversion of the will to power, a conversion that is both simultaneous and voluntary. And since we do not suppose that in the foreseeable future the Russians or the Chinese will accept a government that would be neither Communist nor national; since, on the other hand, we do not suppose that short of a defeat the Americans or Europeans will accept a government subject to the Kremlin leaders or in which the latter would participate, the "neutral" world organization (and probably such neutrality would be guaranteed in the eyes of the Soviets only by equitable representation of the blocs) would have to possess an authority absolute in certain respects but strictly limited in its field of application. Its essential function would be less to guarantee disarmament (an effective control of disarmament would require an enormous, costly and pervasive administration) than to maintain an indisputable military superiority of the world power over any state or bloc. Such a formula would not so much tend to forbid hostilities as to prevent their extension. It would formalize, would legalize, would confirm the regime that the optimist attributes as of today to the international system: the agreement of the two super powers not to fight each other and to prevent their allies, the satellites or the non-committed powers, from involving them in a war to the death that they do not wish to wage.

The idea of universal empire is quite different. It supposes that a state or a bloc has eliminated its rivals and stabilized its victory by integrating the vanquished in an order guaranteed by the monopoly of violence. In our epoch this hypothesis is equivalent to that of the defeat or the capitulation of the Western powers. But what would be the imperial world order? Let us imagine that regimes inspired by the same ideology had been established in all nations. The experiences of Yugoslavia and China suffice to remind us, if there were any need, that the Marxist-Leninist world would not necessarily be more united than Christianity. Imperial peace, extended to the dimensions of the entire planet, that is, including peoples of different languages, cultures and standards of living, in order to be lasting would have to belong either to the Roman type or the federal type, or would have to borrow certain features from one or the other. Communities of culture, perhaps narrower than the present nations, would have to retain all the autonomy compatible with the security and welfare of the human race, and at the same time the elite governing the empire would have to be recruited gradually from all nations or ex-nations. An empire that we wish to construct for the ages or the millenniums would resemble a federation on two essential points: the lower level collectivities would retain the freedoms compatible with peacefulness; the career of honors, even political honors, would not be closed to anyone.

But could such an empire result from the military victory of the Soviet Union, the capitulation of the West? In the long run, perhaps. In the short run it would require a robust confidence in the nature of men to imagine victors "surmounting their victory" and sacrificing the pride of triumph to the reconciliation of all. Even if the victors gave evidence of this unpredictable wisdom, they could not fail to eliminate what is, in their eyes, capitalist prejudice or bourgeois vestiges and, in ours, the very meaning of human existence. Further, as long as the Western standard of living—American and Western European—is on the average higher than that of the Soviet nations or that of the third world, the loss of political autonomy would involve an impoverishment of which the only uncertainty would be its degree.

This is not all. We have hitherto examined universal empire by implicitly admitting the technical-economic characteristics of the exceptional period in which we are living, the abundance of raw materials and energy available to any people possessing the necessary knowledge, the importance of investments to initiate industrialization in the third world, the high rate of growth of the national product in all nations already industrialized, the low return of servile labor, the cost of colonial government when it does not go to the extremes of exploitation and inhumanity while reserving all the better jobs to those from the metropolitan power. In this unprecedented period of human history the economic stakes of conflict are less than at any moment of the past. And the Western powers can surrender to an illusion that at the worst, stripped of their power, they would only have to increase their contribution to the development of the third world.

Perhaps this would be the case, if the masters acted according to economic rationality. The standard of living to which all peoples aspire cannot be transferred in the manner of gold and diamonds. No booty, no triumph assures a heavily populated collectivity of what is now called wealth, that is, a high standard of living. But it is possible to transfer the products of effective labor (the Soviet regime facilitates the payment of reparation) and to assure their enjoyment no longer to the idle but to the incapable.

Finally, and above all, the present period—that during which the loss of a colony can be, without being paradox, likened to an economic advantage—is not definitive. Extrapolation, even on the basis of several centuries, is absolutely impossible. Let us consider only the near future. The world's population numbered some three billion human beings as of 1960. According to moderate anticipations, it will double between now and the end of the twentieth century. At the end of the twenty-first century, by extending the curve, we reach figures which perhaps do not exceed the resources of nutrition and raw materials, which humanity can provide by utilizing the knowledge acquired as of now, and *a fortiori* the knowledge acquired between now and the end of the next century, but which, certainly, again jeopardize the balance within nations as well as the balance among nations. No one can foresee with any certainty the economic or political regime of a United States of America populated by five hundred million people—a figure much lower than that which would result, two centuries from now, by the maintenance of the present birth rate, and still less the economic-political regime of a China populated by three billion human beings.

Let us leave these uncertainties aside and keep to the least problematical figures, those relative to an immediate future. According to a modern estimate, between now and 1980, the population of Latin America will have grown from 190 to 340 million, that of the Near East from 50 to 85, that of Africa from 230 to 335, that of the Asian nations (excluding Japan and the Communist nations) from 730 to 1170 million, that of all four of these regions together from 1200 to 1930 million—in other words, an increase of about 60 per cent in twenty years.

The demographic increase is now relatively independent of the economic increase. It is automatic, inevitable, once the birth rate allowed by nature is not reduced by the voluntary and anticipatory action of individuals. The diffusion of medical knowledge and of techniques of hygiene has lowered the death rate in proportions unknown in the course of the past centuries. In Western Europe around 1730, the life expectancy at birth was twenty-five years; today it is seventy-two years for men and seventy-four for women.[16]

Simultaneously, certain facts—for example the rise of the birth rate in the United States (the increase is over 1.5 per cent a year)—have called into question certain generally accepted ideas as to the size of families desired by the majority in prosperous and middle-class societies. It is not impossible that once a certain standard of living is achieved, the education of all the children being guaranteed, parents often prefer four or five children to two or three.

[16] J. Fourastié, *La grande métamorphose du XXe siècle*, Paris, 1961, p. 11.

Between now and the year 2000, despite extreme inequalities of density, humanity will face the problem of number as a function of the problem of development. The present distribution of peoples territorially—eliminating the possibility of a war to the death—will be regarded as a datum from which to calculate the rate of economic growth and the volume of trade necessary for the most underprivileged populations to reach at least an annually higher per capita income. This result will probably be achieved for a part of the third world, but not for all of it. If we grant for the Soviet world and the Western world, until the end of the century, a gross-national-product growth rate of the same order of size as between 1950 and 1960,[17] the gap in per capita income and still more in standard of living between the privileged minority and the mass of humanity will tend to widen, even if a certain fraction of this mass joins the leading group.

This phase is the one we are in at present, whose characteristics specialists have gradually recognized in the course of the last thirty years while public opinion is just beginning to understand them, and whose likely duration both specialists and public opinion often mistakenly overestimate. This phase is that of the construction of an industrial society which is fundamentally changing the immemorial distribution of workers among the various occupations. Yesterday agricultural workers represented three fourths or four fifths of the labor force; they now represent no more than 5 to 10 per cent of that labor force in the most advanced societies. Even the European societies which, for lack of space, practice an intensive agriculture, manage or will manage to feed themselves without keeping more than about 10 per cent of their labor force in the fields.

The political-ideological problems which concern humanity and which the experts attempt to treat objectively have a double origin: various methods are possible in order to shift from agricultural society to industrial society, as various methods are possible in order to administer this society (that is, to make the decisions that control the distribution of resources and revenue); further, all collectivities (at least through their leaders) seek to accomplish the same change; they are unequally advanced on this path, but also unequally endowed for this task. Reduced to its economic-ideological terms, the conflict of blocs is a conflict of two methods. As for the tensions between the West and the third world, colonialism being on the verge of liquidation, they result from the backwardness of the third world and the latter's hesitation concerning the choice of method.

---

[17] From 1952 to 1960 the growth rate of the gross national product was 8.7 per cent in Japan, 8.3 per cent in West Germany, 5.7 per cent in the U.S.S.R. and the Eastern countries, 4.1 per cent in France, 3.5 per cent in the United States. These rates result both from the increase in the labor force and the rise in the value produced by each worker. In France, where the size of her labor force was not appreciably increased, the rate of growth of the gross national product is only slightly higher than the rate of growth of the population's per capita income.

Historically, the two methods do not deserve to be put on a basis of equality. One has served for creation, the other has served only for imitation. An economy planned in detail by an authoritarian administration would never have overturned traditions and would not have taken as its goal to establish innovations, but once the scientific knowledge is acquired, once the techniques are applied by certain countries, it is not impossible that those people who initiate by systematic planning should advance at a greater speed than those who try to take over but leave matters up to the initiative of the individual. At the present time the Soviet societies have the example of the most advanced industrial societies. Scientific research can, in certain sectors, be organized and discoveries depend to a degree on the means enlisted: nothing prevents the spectacular successes of the planned regimes in realms where the latter have concentrated their resources, especially the rarest resource, the best minds.

According to Soviet propaganda, the West fears the successes of socialism and fears them justifiably, since these successes will involve its own ruin. This propaganda is no more than a half-truth. The West fears certain successes, but also certain failures of the so-called socialist countries. The nations that shift by planned imitation to an industrial society succeed better with regard to industry than to agriculture. They acquire the means of power before distributing an even mediocre comfort. In the same speech in which he celebrated the exploit of the second Soviet cosmonaut, Mr. Khrushchev admitted the difficulties of supplying the Soviet cities. The cosmonaut will reach the moon before the kolkhozians are reconciled to collective ownership. Now, just as the mouse or the boxer takes more pleasure in the struggle if he wins each bout, similarly a regime is tempted to make a virtue of necessity, to declare itself indifferent to the activities in which it reveals itself to be mediocre, and to exalt those in which it has testified to its excellence. What does the standard of living matter, if the Hammer and Sickle is the first flag planted on the moon?

Whatever Mr. Khrushchev might have said, there is no chance, unless there is a radical and unforeseeable change on both sides, that the average Soviet citizen's standard of living (comfort of housing, quality of food, means of transportation, public facilities) will equal that of his American equivalent by the end of the century—I mean that of the average American today, *a fortiori* not the higher level of the year 2000. It is not impossible, though it is improbable, that the Soviet Union's industrial production will exceed that of the United States by the end of the century, either *in toto* or per capita. But it is conceivable that with regard to heavy industry, the Soviet Union will be superior to the United States by 1975 or 1980. It is obvious that an absolutist regime has a greater freedom in the use of its resources: with a view to the rivalry of power, it can mobilize more men and more machines.

If the planned imitation of industrial society, combined with the rejection of the West's liberal and humanitarian ideas, runs the risk of leading to the primacy of power over welfare,[18] the radical failure of imitation, planned or not, a rate of economic growth inferior to the rate of demographic increase would multiply—in Africa, in Asia, in Latin America—the despotic regimes hostile to the West (and later, perhaps, to the Soviet bloc). For the time being, the rate of demographic increase of the third world is also accepted as a fact, and the privileged peoples are attempting to influence the rate of economic growth. Certain countries which have suffered from an excessive lowering of the birth rate, certain schools which fear that a lowering of the rate of demographic increase will provoke a more than proportional lowering of the rate of economic growth, certain churches which deny that the problem of number faces the world as a whole say there are some national population problems—overpopulation here, relative depopulation there—there is no world population problem. Nowhere, or almost nowhere, does the increase in the number of mouths to feed *necessarily* involve a diminution of the individual income or even a diminution in the increase of this individual income.

It is in this context that the "rationalized pacifism" of the mid-twentieth century has developed: domination is scarcely profitable, and thermonuclear war would be still less so. Such pacifism does not exclude the risk of war, because the super powers need, both against each other and in relation to the rest of humanity, not to use but to keep in reserve the monstrous weapons. Nor does it exclude colonial wars because the negative balance-sheet for the nation as a unit is not incompatible with the positive balance-sheet for minorities established in the colony or even in the metropolitan nation. The desire to rule over the conquered or to convert them to the civilization or the ideology of the victors outlives the economic benefits of colonial exploitation.

But "rationalized pacifism," contemporary with awareness of industrial society in the period when the latter is in the process of spreading though developed among only a minority of the human race, is not definitive. A half century from now, at the most, it will be *impossible to admit both that the distribution of land among the peoples is a* fait accompli *and that the rate of demographic increase is the concern of each nation taken individually but not of humanity taken as a whole.* As of now, aid should be granted to certain states only on condition that they take measures to reduce their birth rate. But what does "should" mean in this case? In writing this word, I was thinking *reasonably*: given the immediately accessible rate of the increase in resources, the lowering of the birth rate would facilitate the transition to the phase of cumulative growth, desired by all nations outside the two blocs.

At the moment, the application of this "reasonable" policy is difficult for many reasons: some churches persist in opposing it, confusing historically

---

[18] It follows that this risk is still incomparably greater in the case of China than in that of the Soviet Union.

justifiable imperatives with the will of God; biological methods for reducing the birth rate are costly and imperfect; "Malthusian" action is most necessary precisely where it is most difficult, that is, among the poor populations, loyal to tradition, which know no other joys than those of the family and which receive them as a sign of divine favor. But the Marxist-Leninists still refuse to accept the evidence, that is, that there must be a limit to the number of men even in the age when science multiplies our resources, without our being able to say if they are blind to this evidence or if they are consciously refusing to acknowledge it.

But if today passions, ideologies, hostilities prevent our reasonably envisaging the world problem of number, what will it be tomorrow, and what would it be under a universal empire? It would be *reasonable*, if the peoples continue to occupy the space which is theirs today, to encourage the birth rate in France and to discourage it in Algeria, to encourage it in Argentina and to discourage it in India or in China, to leave it as it is in the Soviet Union and in the United States, the two super powers having a reserve of space and a rate of economic growth higher than that of demographic increase. But by the end of the century, when there will be six billion human beings, and at the end of the century following, when there will be three or four times more, the problem of number will be raised, willy-nilly, in absolute terms.

Let us consider the simple and striking figures cited by M. Fourastié[19] in his latest book. Let us suppose that man does not modify the physical geography or climate of the earth: in this hypothesis, the earth has no more than about seven billion hectares that man can inhabit "without feeling in a situation of political deportation or scientific experimentation." This surface will be increased to fifteen billion if we suppose that a part of the seas can be reclaimed, by leveling mountains, etc. The seven billion acres will have, in the year 2000, a population density higher than that of France today (0.9 per hectares as against 0.8). If we assume the density of the population of New York City over seven billion hectares, the earth could sustain 700 billion human beings; over fifteen billion hectares, 1,500,000,000,000. But by doubling in forty years, the first figure will be reached by 2270, and the second in 2310. It would also be easy to show that the rate at which industrial production has been increasing since 1950 cannot be maintained for centuries without the results being physically impossible. "If French industrial production were to continue for 140 years its present increase of 7 per cent a year, we should be producing in the year 2100: 12×2^{14} million tons of steel, a figure close to 100 billion tons, and the world steel production would be on the order of 10 to 15 trillion tons."[20]

The period we are living in is thus exceptional with regard to demographic

[19] Fourastié, *op. cit.*, p. 16.
[20] *Ibid.*, p. 58.

increase as to economic growth. In a few decades, at the latest in one or two centuries, a voluntary regulation must be substituted for the natural mechanisms which slackened the population of the human race. Thereby, the establishment of an economically stationary status would become possible: the distribution of the labor force among the various occupations would not change very much; the effort would bear on the quality of existence rather than on the quantity of goods; the fundamental needs (housing, clothing, transportation, communication) would be considered as fully realized.

If the conscious and voluntary regulation of number is not undertaken, or if the peoples are incapable of agreeing on a regulation in common, the struggle for space will assume a violence unknown in the past. Of course, universal empire would be, in this case, the "rational" solution. But for the one master people free to distribute space and resources according to its choice, the most precious of these would henceforth be space.

Will historical man ultimately be accessible to reason and to equity? If this were to be the case, the nations will organize their coexistence on the planet and will find other domains of rivalry. Will historical man resemble, at least, the wolf that spares its kind, baring its throat as a sign of capitulation? Universal empire itself would be acceptable as a supreme recourse since, in the long run, the masters must grant equality to the slaves. But man does not always obey, like the wolf, the inhibition of pity: he sometimes behaves like the doves, which are merciless to the vanquished: "The day will come when two warring factions will have the possibility of exterminating each other completely. The day may come when all humanity will thus be divided into two opposing camps. Will we then behave like the doves or like the wolves? The answer to this question will settle humanity's fate."[21]

[21] Konrad Z. Lorenz, *op. cit.*, p. 199.

FINAL NOTE

Rational Strategy and Reasonable Policy

A famous economist, Oskar Morgenstern, at the conclusion of a book entitled *The Question of National Defense*, makes a pitiless judgment on the state of political science:

"Political scientists have spent much time and effort to produce a body of knowledge that is singularly unsuited to guide us in the present dilemma of our life—a body of knowledge that is a peculiar mixture of constitutional law, history and description of political institutions of all kinds, everything generously sprinkled by strong opinions and value judgments. Some maxims of behavior occur occasionally, for example, those formulated by Machiavelli. They may or may not be 'good' or 'respectable'; at any rate they were an attempt to formulate rules by which men seek the attainment of their aims in political situations. . . .

"Of the social sciences only economics has so far achieved a modicum of operational value. . . . We know, for example, how to make or stop inflations, how to tax without destroying the taxed source of income, and many other things. We do not yet know how to stabilize employment, how to compare tax burdens placed on different persons, and how to perform other important tasks. Political science may help us to set up a workable constitution but not to know whether it will be applicable to a given country. It certainly contributes little, if anything, it would seem, to resolving the problems the world faces now, the most important of which is how to live with the thermonuclear stalemate, how to get stability and safety for all participants in the most fearful struggle the human race has ever been involved in. And it tells us nothing of how to cope with the growing unbalance in the world due to the increase in population and in the widening gap between poor and rich countries.

"What negotiations are possible with the Communist bloc involve bargaining of the most delicate and difficult nature. As on the military side of the picture, one is here also concerned with the problem of decision-making under uncertainty, where the uncertainty is not of the simple, well-understood kind to be dealt with by probability theory, but is of the highly complex nature arising from the strategic moves of the opponent, who labors under the same difficulty. This is precisely where political science should make its most significant contributions. Nothing is offered except the mathematical techniques associated with the theory of games of strategy, but to this theory political scientists, with a few exceptions, have paid virtually no attention. So far political science has not even abstracted the counsels given by Machiavelli in order to discover whether a consistent system of rules of behavior could be constructed on that basis."[1]

This quotation reveals the mixture of rigor and confusion, of profundity and naïveté characteristic of certain scientific minds at grips with problems external to their discipline, especially political problems. That political science is not *operational,* in the sense in which physics is, or even in the sense in which certain sectors of economics are, is incontestable. It remains to be seen if it is the insufficiency of knowledge and of the experts that is responsible, or the very structure of the object and the activity.

Let us take the constitution as an example. The difficulty—what constitution suits a given people—has been familiar to thinkers for thousands of years. It has never been completely surmounted by philosophers or statesmen, but when the mathematicians or physicists have tried their luck, they have done no better. In the abstract, we determine whether a constitution is "workable" in two ways: either by a formal, abstract analysis comparable to the analysis of a free market or of "planning an economy with a free market of consumer goods," or else by an experimental method (which constitutions have, in fact, worked?). Generally, the two methods are used concurrently. But neither one provides results of any certainty. The enumeration of the variables on which a constitution's functioning depends is never exhaustive. The experiments are few in number, difficult to interpret, and each case offers particular features which jeopardize the validity of the "lessons of history" or the "teachings of science." Even when a "lesson" is probable (let us say the dangers of proportional voting), there will be members of the constituent assembly to cite exceptions to the rule in order to justify their preference, whose origin is strictly selfish (a voting method may conform to the interest of a party, and oppose that of the regime). The behavior of the men who will apply the constitutional law is not foreseeable by reason of the excessive influence that one or several men can exert: we anticipate the frequency of crimes or suicides, not the wisdom of a person chosen by an electoral college, still less the circumstances in which this wisdom will have to function. The first two Presidents of the French Republic will greatly contribute to the success or failure of the French Constitution elaborated in 1958.

Would it be possible to subject to a *scientific* analysis the maxims of

[1] O. Morgenstern, *op. cit.,* pp. 263–65.

Machiavelli—for instance: *it is good for a prince to be feared rather than loved?* There is no need to read Proust and the Marquis de Custine to realize that the sentiments of peoples with regard to their tyrants are often ambivalent. But let us leave this ambiguity aside: is it better, for a state, to have the reputation of despising or respecting international law? From one page to the next, two authors who try to answer this question give the impression of contradicting themselves, indicating alternately the advantages which both practices afford.[2] Lacking quantification, I doubt that science can measure these advantages with any rigor. As for the advice given to a usurper to eliminate all the members of the ruling family, it was followed, a few years ago, in a Near Eastern country, not without favorable results: the new prince is still in power.[3] But without even recalling that "no man can be called happy before his last day" and that the long-run consequences of these murders are not yet visible, such maxims also belong to the realm of the moralist.

As for the indifference which political analysts have apparently shown with regard to games theory, it is far from being as great as is suggested by the co-author of the famous book *Theory of Games and Economic Behavior,* since recently another expert, a physicist, B. M. S. Blackett,[4] on the contrary reproached the American specialists for making excessive use of games theory which, he said, was of virtually no use with regard to strategy, the latter continuing to fall within the exclusive competence of the military. I should not personally subscribe to the opinion of either side in this controversy.

The comparison of war and games does not date from the mathematical theory of games of strategy. Huizinga, in his celebrated work *Homo Ludens,*[5] gives many references to authors who, studying various civilizations, have emphasized the sportive element of war. According to Huizinga, war "may be regarded as a function of culture, as long as it is waged within a circle whose members acknowledge each other as equals or, at least, as equals before the law." When this mutual acknowledgment exists among the combatants,

---

[2] "Churchill understood better than most . . . the importance of the reputation of virtuous behavior. . . . A reputation for principled behavior is highly advantageous for a nation. Its agreements are respected and its offers more acceptable because they can be counted on." (*The Political Foundations of International Law,* by Morton A. Kaplan and Nicholas de B. Katzenback, p. 344.) And a little farther, p. 348: "Since the Soviet Union is both more revolutionary than the United States and more able, politically, to take the measures necessary to exploit the consequences of technological development, either in terms of hard political bargaining or the waging of war, its attitude toward the normative rules is naturally more instrumental than that of the United States. This places a harsh burden upon the United States, for it must now bear most of the costs and much of the burden of maintaining desirable normative rules of international law. . . . Thus, the Soviet Union makes ever increasing demands that the western publics regard as justified because 'one cannot expect the Soviet Union to accept any other position.' "

[3] It was true at the time I wrote this book. Since then he has been assassinated.

[4] "Critique of Some Contemporary Defense Thinking," *Encounter,* April 1961.

[5] *Homo Ludens, A Study of the Play-Element in Culture,* Boston, 1950. First published in Holland in 1938.

war is essentially a contest for a prize, an ordeal in which each side seeks to vanquish the other for the glory of winning rather than for the benefits of victory. And the historian does not hesitate to write: "Even in highly developed cultural relations, and even if the statesmen who are preparing the conflict interpret it as a question of power, the desire for material gain remains, in general, subordinate to motives of pride, glory, prestige and the appearance of superiority or supremacy. The general term *glory* furnishes a much more realistic explanation of all the great wars of conquest from antiquity to the present day, than any ingenious theory of economic forces and political calculations."[6] Wars of chivalry and wars in lace cuffs mark the full development of the simultaneously *ludic* and competitive intention. The place and moment of combat tend to be fixed by a mutual agreement; both sides regard themselves as honor bound not to violate the rules because the victory would have no value if it were won by underhand means. This trial of strength is nonetheless serious and not simulated, and though the enemy's death is not necessary to the victor's glory, it may result from the struggle itself.

Bergson considered—mistakenly, I believe—that wars of chivalry were not true wars, but merely rehearsals for the human race, training for genuine warfare of which pillage and massacre are the result and the confirmation. Personally, I prefer to say with Huizinga that competition, the rivalry for prestige, is one of the human elements of warfare but that the latter also involves an element of brutality pure and simple. In games, sports and chivalry it is the former element which prevails, and the moderation of violence is imposed on each man by the respect for the rules and his own honor. But at all levels of civilization, there is a risk of brutality sweeping away the barriers raised by culture and animal fury stifling the sense of human community in the soul of the combatants.

Huizinga suggests that war tends to depart from games, which are formal and limited, in proportion as the individuals or groups in conflict lose the awareness of their relationship. "If it is a question of a combat against groups which are not, actually, acknowledged as men, or at least as beings possessed of human rights—whether they are called 'barbarians,' 'devils,' 'pagans' or 'heretics'—this combat will remain within the 'limits' of culture only as long as a group which imposes limits on itself for the satisfaction of its own honor."[7] The reality seems more complex. The passion to affirm one's superiority, which is the root of competition, can in certain circumstances provoke an escalation, even when the combatants, like the Greek city-states, continue to obey customs and prohibitions. The spirit of competition is in itself alien to the appetite for booty and murderous fury, but it sometimes provokes the latter as well as the former, because it rejects the mediocrity of compromise or negotiation. Further, however close the social

---

[6] *Ibid.*, p. 90.
[7] *Ibid.*, p. 90.

groups in conflict may appear to the observer, one readily becomes "barbarian" in the other's eyes and each is prompt to seek at the other's expense a satisfaction we may call holy, the proof that fortune favors its own side: war is a game of chance at the same time that it is a competition.

Archaic societies, like historical ones, have known the oscillation between brutality and formalized conflict, between respect for the rules and exclusive desire for victory on any condition, between emulation and greed for power and wealth. The instrumental rationalization of war, whose highest development we are observing today, has not created the danger of cruelty and dehumanization (perhaps, as Huizinga says, the modern-day tendencies to exalt war revive, as a matter of fact, the Assyro-Babylonian conception), but it has rendered it more serious than ever. Weapons themselves, and not the refusal to recognize the enemy, run the risk of effacing all *ludic* survivals of warfare.

Once the thermonuclear exchanges begin, indeed all trace of *game* will have disappeared. But the diplomatic-strategic rivalry, as long as it occurs *in the shadow of the apocalypse,* is, on the contrary, more complex than it has ever been, since it involves, actually or virtually, *all* the elements ordinarily kept separate.

One author[8] has recently distinguished *fight, game* and *debate.* In a fight, the object (if any) is to harm the opponent. In a game, the opponents seek to outwit each other. In a debate, finally, they seek to persuade each other or to persuade the *third men,* noncommitted or neutral in one way or another. The distinction is attractive on the conceptual level, but evidently there is no fight without an element of intelligence, and most games have an element of force: in chess, the rivalry of intelligence appears in the purest state; on the other hand, even in a free-for-all or a weight-lifting contest there is an element of intelligence (of technique). Diplomatic-strategic competition is, by definition, a mixture of *fight and game,* since it brings into competition wills which seek to *outwit* each other but which reserve the recourse to the *ultima ratio.* It is clear, by the same reasoning, that debate is never pure, not only on account of the oscillation between the effort of persuasion and the methods of violation of conscience, but also because, lacking the ability to convince, the masters of the debate do not reject coercion (the Kremlin leaders would have preferred that the Hungarians were convinced of the benefits of "socialism"). The great illusion among the leaders, and even among the American professors, is to suppose that the Russo-American competition for the allegiance of the third world is similar to a tournament of generosity or to a colloquium of economists, the generosity of gifts or the rate of growth constituting a decisive argument in favor of one side or another. It is true only that, according to the time and the circumstances, combat, strategic intelligence or debate dominate inter-

[8] Anatol Rapoport, *Fights, Games and Debates,* University of Michigan Press, 1960.

national relations. Between Cortez's Spaniards and the Aztecs no debate was
possible. Against the Soviet divisions, no intelligence would have saved
the Hungarians. When the atom bombs fell on Hiroshima and Nagasaki, the
Japanese could only suffer.

Strategic intelligence and the effort to persuade are reduced to impotence
only at the extreme moments of the combat, when the warriors' muscles
are strained, when swords clash against shields, or when bombs or shells fall
on soldiers or cities. Normally, whether in peace or in war, whether one
practices strategy (the conduct of operations) or diplomacy (non-violent
means) or both together, intelligence intervenes: each strategist taking a
decision expects a reply from the adversary and the expectation of this reply
controls his decision. The problem is to know in what direction the mathematical theory of games of strategy informs the decisions that statesmen
and war leaders have traditionally taken by intuition, by a clumsy evaluation
of chances and risks.

The matrices of games theory render at least three services to the political
scientists. They oblige them to accept a kind of discipline of thought, to
analyze and enumerate all possible eventualities in a given situation. They
help them to construct ideal types of circumstances of conflict (games with
two players, N players, zero-sum games, non-zero-sum games). They permit
the abstract formulation of the *dialectic of antagonism*: decisions are not
taken with regard to a future about which we know nothing, nor with regard
to a future in which each event is unknown to us, but in which the approximate frequency of the various classes of events is known to us. The
strategic decisions constitute a chain, each decision provokes the following
and the latter tends to counteract the preceding one. The chess player moves
a pawn in response to the movement of an adverse pawn: the strategist opposes his enemy similarly.

But once the nature of diplomatic-strategic conduct is illuminated, the
political scientists have performed a necessary task by focusing on the differences between the simplified models that lent themselves to mathematical
treatment and the concrete situations. Some of these differences, it seems to
me, are of degree, others of kind. Generally, the diplomatic-strategic games
in the historical world are played by N players, and not by two; they are not
zero-sum games (in other words, what I win is not always equal to what my
adversary loses: there is a share of cooperation between the enemies, an
element of competition between the allies); it is rarely possible to enumerate
all the possibilities available to each actor's choice. But, however serious they
are, these classical difficulties do not have the same radical character as the
indeterminacy of the *stakes* and the *limits* of the game. For there to be a
game in the rigorous sense of the word, for a mathematical solution defining
rational conduct to be possible, there must be a beginning and an end, a
finite number of moves for each of the players, a result susceptible of

cardinal or ordinal evaluation for each of the players. None of these conditions is, strictly speaking, fulfilled in the field of international relations.

Can we give a cardinal or ordinal value to the stake of a strategic-diplomatic rivalry? It is in the hope of quantifying this value that the theoreticians have sometimes identified power with utility, the latter being so to speak the universal means of diplomatic ends, as money is the universal means of economic ends. But as we have seen,[9] this identification lends itself to many objections. The means is not, strictly speaking, clearly defined (resources, forces, power); it is not neutral, separated from the true end of action, whereas money is separable from the concrete preferences of each individual; and finally, it is always a relation, since it depends on the configuration of the relation of forces: a unit's power depends on the positions taken by all the units, so that an absolute increase can, in fact, be expressed by a relative diminution.

It is nonetheless conceivable to give an approximate value to a diplomatic-strategic stake: for instance, is it not obvious that Laos, for the United States as for the Soviet Union, is worth less than Berlin? We do not disagree. But the mere notion of more and less does not suffice to permit a mathematically valid solution, hence a rational prescription. Suppose we were to try to compare the following various issues of the Laotian crisis: 1. Laos is entirely communized without the military intervention of the United States; 2. Laos is entirely communized after the military intervention of the United States; 3. Laos is divided between the Communist party and the non-Communist party; 4. Laos is governed by a so-called neutral government in which Communist influence dominates. Does the American government prefer 3 to 4 or 4 to 3? It probably prefers 1 to 2, but can we establish the size of the interval between 1 and 2 on the one hand, and between 3 and 4 on the other? Does the Soviet government, on its side, prefer 1 to 2 or 2 to 3, in other words, does it prefer the United States to reveal its incapacity to defend Laos by a timid intervention or by non-intervention? Does it prefer division to a semi-neutrality? Each of the players, in this relatively simple and isolable crisis, would be hard put to establish his own hierarchy of preference, still more that of his adversary. As for the determination of the cardinal values or the value of the differences, he would regard them as merely an intellectual exercise.

Further: he would object that the value of the stake or the relative value of the various outcomes is transformed in the course of the crisis. The Sovietization of Laos, if two Marine battalions have taken part in the battle, represents a loss much more considerable than the same Sovietization without the official engagement of American soldiers. To advance the Marine pawn thus automatically changes the game and the values of the various outcomes. To return to a structure of a game of strategy, we must eliminate

[9] Cf. above, Chap. III, Sec. 4.

the movement of the pawns which changes the value of the results (payoffs) and reason on two different games, each defined by the values which result from the authorized movements alone (no Marine intervention in one case, Marine intervention in the other). But each of these two games would differ fundamentally from the real strategic-diplomatic game, since this latter has as its *essential* characteristic the eventual recourse to arms and the fact that this recourse, in most cases, involves simultaneously the incalculable risk of the course of operations and the possible transformation of utilities and even of hierarchies of preference, as the result of the military character assumed by the conflict. If one side loses a province following a battle, it loses both battle and province; sometimes a side may accept losing the province, but does not resign itself to losing a battle. Let us not be in haste to insist on the "irrationality" of this attitude. The concern for pride is intrinsically linked to competition. Whether one plays the game of diplomacy, chess or tackle football, not to submit to the adversary's will is one of the objects each player legitimately seeks.

Further, the value of a diplomatic stake changes as a result of the course of the crisis, even without reference to pride: for states, the game is never finished because the final stake, so to speak, is never to be excluded from it. Any isolation of a diplomatic game or stake is artificial: the outcome of one game modifies the terms of the next, the prestige of the super power is shaken or confirmed by the attitude adopted. It was not so much to save South Korea as to save its honor, its reputation for loyalty to commitments, that the United States fought for three years in Korea. The value of a stake is thus not separable from the total context, from the consequences whether foreseeable or not, from the way in which the game will be played and will be concluded. A player cannot evaluate his adversary's loss or gain merely as a function of the physical characteristics of the stake, he is obliged not to accept at face value the evaluation his adversary attempts to suggest to him, but to take it into account. Even for the qualification of the results (the payoff), the psychology of the players is not separable from the mathematics of the decision.

Of course, there are certain *strategic* decisions (not diplomatic-strategic) which offer the equivalent of a game with a mathematically rigorous solution. In a lecture given at the Sorbonne in the second term of 1960–61, Mr. Worms presented the following example: a Japanese convoy was sailing from Rabaul in New Britain to Lae in New Guinea. Two different routes were possible: the northern one, where visibility was relatively poor, and the southern one, where it was better. The number of squadrons available obliged the American commander to concentrate his reconnaissance planes on only one of these routes. Each of the adversaries, therefore, had their choice between two strategies, that is, between the two routes, the Americans by concentrating their squadrons, the Japanese by directing their convoy. If the Americans concentrated their squadrons on the southern route (where visibility was good) and the Japanese chose this route, the convoy would be rapidly sighted and the bombing would last during almost the whole of the voyage, about three days. But if the Japanese chose the northern route, spotting the convoy would be delayed and the bombing would last only one day. On the other hand, if the Americans concentrated their squadrons in the north, they would have two days of bombing in any case, either because the convoy on the northern route would be rapidly sighted or because the few American planes on the southern route, where the visibility was good, would succeed in locating the Japanese ships despite the small number of their own planes. Let A designate the American strategy and J the Japanese strategy. The matrix thus appears as follows:

		J	
		Northern Route b_1	Southern Route b_2
A	Southern Concentration (a_1) . . .	1	3
	Northern Concentration (a_2) . . .	2	2

The Americans concentrated their aviation in the north and found the Japanese convoy there. The Americans had allowed themselves two days of bombing and the Japanese had limited to two the number of days of possible bombing. The two players had adopted the "strategy" of prudence.

This example of pure strategy and not of strategic diplomacy supposes the equivalence between the number of days of bombing and the results of the game (which eliminates hazard from the course of military operations). On the other hand, there was in this case a "saddle point": the prudence of one side encountered the prudence of the other. But it is easy to use the same matrix and change the figures:

		B	
		b_1	b_2
A	a_1 . . .	0	2
	a_2 . . .	3	-1

Having the chance of winning three, A is tempted to choose a_2, but risks losing 1. If it applies the strategy of prudence, it will choose a_1 which will assure it at least a draw. B, on its side, will be tempted to choose b_2, which would permit it to win 1 if A has played a_2 But, fearing to lose 2 if A has played a_1, it would play the prudent game of choosing b_1. Nonetheless, it will play b_2 if it suspects A of having played a_2, in the hope that B, expecting a_1, will have played b_1. Supposing that A will have made this calculation, it outwits the latter by playing b_2. But A, in its turn, may expect this calculation and outwit B, and so on indefinitely. In other words, in the absence of a saddle point and if it is a question of a single move, the game has no "rational" solution, and psychological intuition and the preference for risk or security determine reasonable policy.

Games theory, as we know, has surmounted the obstacle of the absence of a saddle point by the so-called mixed strategy.[10] It is possible that the notion of optimal strategy involves analogous lessons with regard to diplomacy: when the adversary is in a position to assure himself an advantage if he knows in advance our decision in a given circumstance, the best way of preventing this anticipation is to choose one or the other of the possible decisions irregularly, without apparent order. But the best strategy *as a rational solution* supposes the rigorous evaluation of the results which each of the decisions would provide for each of the players at the same time as the delimitation of the game. Generally, recourse to arms (which constitutes one of the possible strategies) introduces a coefficient of uncertainty which widens the gap between the model and reality.

The diplomatic circumstances of the thermonuclear duopoly, of the cold war, of the choice between conventional weapons and atomic weapons have suggested to American authors many analyses of typical situations, an indisputable method provided one does not forget the gap between the scheme and the historical world. Sometimes these calculations are calculations of objective probability based on the performances of weapons (given the acknowledged precision of ballistic missiles, the resistance of bases, how many ballistic missiles would be required to arrive at a probability of 90 per cent or 95 per cent in destroying the fifty American intercontinental bomber bases or the ten launching platforms?). Sometimes the calculations concern

---

[10] Mathematicians demonstrate that the best strategy, in the preceding game, is determined in the following manner: the difference between the cases of the first line is 2, between the cases of the second line is 4. The relation between these two differences, 4 over 2 or 2 over 1, will determine the frequency with which A should choose a_1 and a_2, that is, $66\frac{2}{3}$ and $33\frac{1}{3}$ of the time (A chooses at random each time a_1 or a_2). B's strategy is determined similarly by the relation of differences between the spaces of the columns. Since these differences are the same, B should play b_1 and b_2 as often. The two mixed strategies are the best. Each time B chooses b_1, A wins 0 two out of three times and 3 once out of three times. It thus wins 1 as an average. Each time B plays b_2, A wins two out of three times and loses once out of three times, which again give $(2 \times \frac{2}{3} - 1 \times \frac{1}{3}) = 1$, which is the value of the game. B can improve the situation only by abandoning the optimal strategy, which would lead back to the "psychological circle" we started from.

This model has permitted various applications, with regard to military technique, and it could even be applied to simple strategic problems. It would suffice to modify the problem of the two routes and the two convoys by suppressing the saddle point for the mixed strategy alone to offer a solution—this latter requiring from all evidence that there be a repetition so that each player can choose *at random* one or the other of the decisions available, in a frequency which determines the relation of the differences of values on the two rows or in the two columns.

the probability of a strategist's diplomatic or military reaction, given the importance of the stake (Berlin) and the apparent cost of using either conventional weapons or atomic or thermonuclear weapons.

Calculations of the first type, themselves quite legitimate, must be corrected by a coefficient of uncertainty, which it is impossible to estimate even approximately (how perfect, in other words, is the knowledge of the location and resistance of the bases? To what degree would the actual firing proceed as the exercises do? etc.).

Calculations of the second type seem to me more dangerous than useful: they give an appearance of rigor to decisions which are at best the result of reflection, and above all they falsify the nature and the development of the deliberation. First of all the stake is never definite because it is not separable from the total conflict and because the very stake of the total conflict is not and cannot be known to the strategists. What does the United States risk? Would the Americans, in case of defeat, become the slaves of the Russians? Would millions of Chinese come to live in New York or Chicago as Oskar Morgenstern imagines?[11]

I do not doubt that any member of the Committee for a Sane Nuclear Policy would reply that the famous economist is the victim of his own delusions and that neither Russians nor Chinese have ever imagined such a transfer of population. Probably they have not imagined it, but nothing proves that they would not envisage it on the day the United States, after or without a thermonuclear war, had capitulated. In abstract terms, let us say that the stake between the duopolists depends on the progress of the conflict itself and that neither diplomat-strategist calculates what he risks losing, since neither can know how he will be treated by his potential conqueror. If, further, this conqueror has lost half his cities in the battle, the risk is still greater than in the hypothesis of a capitulation without combat. At the present time all the stakes of the isolated games are more or less according to the repercussions attributed to them with regard to the total game.

---

[11] O. Morgenstern, *op. cit.*, p. 289: "No one can say reliably what the enemy would impose on this country if it were to surrender without fighting. But some lines of this dismal picture can be drawn, and dismal it would be, indeed. The destruction of any vestige of military power would be imminent. Nothing would be easier to accomplish in this time when weapons are becoming smaller and more powerful, yet are concentrated in the hands of the few. The government would go over into the hands of Communist trustees; the well-trained, obedient underdog would take over. The inhabitants of our slums would move into the penthouses and those living there now would wind up in labor camps in Alaska and northern Canada. Motor cars would be produced, not for the United States but for Asia. Perhaps one hundred million or two hundred million Chinese would be moved to this country, taking over the houses we inhabit now. According to their standards, even when crammed together with us, they would be better off than they are now. Our factories would produce 'reparations' for the rest of the world while we would be put on a subsistence level, just good enough to secure the continuing services of the docile new slaves (easily kept docile by the administration of proper amounts of tranquilizers)."

The impossibility of assigning a value to the stake because the isolated game is not the same depending on the strategies adopted combines with the fact that neither the isolated game nor the worldwide game is a zero-sum game. Of course, the American leaders tend to believe that everything would be quite different if the Soviet Union did not exist, and the latter, on its side, sees only a single obstacle in the path of the universal spread of "socialism." But, as long as the Big Two exist, each maintains some common interest with the other. I do not know if, as one author suggests, the American refusal to allow Communist China access to the United Nations is a deliberate or unconscious contribution to the maintenance of the Kremlin's authority over the whole of the socialist universe. But the Big Two act as if they wanted to close the atomic club, as if each had as its object to preserve the duopoly as long as possible. Perhaps in the long run the United States even prefers that there be two socialist great powers rather than one. Perhaps it sees one as a factor of equilibrium against the other or, at least, a possible moderator of the other's extreme ambitions.

The moment absolute antagonism—the zero-sum game—yields to a mixture of hostility and competition, the paradoxes of the mathematicians gradually tend to coincide with the intuitions of the psychologists. A problem classical among games theoreticians, the one called the "paradox of the prisoners," will serve as an illustration.[12] Two suspects are questioned separately by the examining magistrate. They are convicted of a minor felony, suspected of a grave crime. If they both keep silent (a_2 b_2), that is, refuse to admit to the crime, they will receive the slight punishment for the minor felony ($+5$). On the other hand, let us consider what happens if one of the two confesses. If A confesses (a_1) and B does not (b_2), A will escape the punishment ($+10$) and B will receive the severest punishment (-10). If both confess, both will be punished, but somewhat less severely (-5) than the one man who had not confessed (-10). The matrix is thus as follows:

		B			
		b_1*		b_2	
A	a_1 ...	-5	-5	$+10$	-10
	a_2 ...	-10	$+10$	$+5$	$+5$

* The first figure is that of the payoff for A, the second that of the payoff for B.

What is the best solution? It is clear, it seems to me, that there is no "rational" solution. If A or B confesses, convinced that the other, loyal to honor, will not, the solution maximizes his advantage even though he is the more guilty with regard to "average morality." But if, in order to minimize the risk, both confess, the solution for the community (-10) is inferior to

[12] I borrow the formulation from A. Rapoport's study referred to above.

that $(+10)$ which would result from the silence of both. In this case, it would suffice to permit communication between the players for the two suspects to have an advantage in choosing together the solution, best for the community, of silence. But this solution would not, however, be equivalent to a rational imperative. For each man, despite the agreement reached, might suspect the other of deception. Finally, everything would depend on A's idea of B's behavior, and B's of A's. The "most moral" solution (in terms of average morality) and the best for the community (but not the best for each man) is that of common silence. If, instead of two players, we were to assume three and attempted to find a rational distribution of the stakes, we could reach neither *one* solution nor even a unique class of solutions. What share will each player receive of a certain sum to be divided, each player being free to ally himself with either of the two others? Everything depends on the psychological relations which are established between the players, on the implicit agreements between two among them, the promises each of them makes to the other or to one of the other of the adversary-allies, on threats each of them has suffered from the two others. These strictly psychological notions necessarily intervene in a game in which the best solution for the community does not coincide with the best solution for each of the players or in which an explicit understanding among the latter is impossible.

Now these notions are those which the theoreticians of thermonuclear strategy have utilized either spontaneously or starting from simple models of games theory. Any use of thermonuclear weapons being improbable by reason of the risk of reprisal, the strategist can only confer a certain plausibility upon it by manifesting in every way possible the extreme value which he attaches to the stake (Berlin). Thermonuclear strategy does not consist in calculating decisions to be taken, given the result of the non-use of these weapons (the loss of such and such a position), as if this result had a value known in advance. Thermonuclear strategy consists in moving the pawns in order to increase the value of what is at stake, the strategist's prestige being compromised if he accepts losing what he has shown he regards as extremely valuable. One might say that he has given to what is at stake in the isolated game a value commensurable with the cost of a thermonuclear war by proceeding as if the loss of this game has a serious influence on the issue of the total game, that is, on a stake which would be on the scale of thermonuclear war (capitulation, total defeat would not be preferable to the exchange of thermonuclear blows). Yet it would be better not to carry this qualitative formulation too far: for the mathematicians also do not permit calculating the rational decision when the loss risks being "infinite." For the players of the great strategic-diplomatic game, thermonuclear war is the equivalent of an infinite loss. Now the players can emerge from this game only by a capitulation which would not involve fewer risks. In this game in which the players are obliged to accept almost infinite risks, there is no rational strategy; there are strategies which to us seem reasonable and whose implicit rules we urge the adversary to respect.

In the thermonuclear age the objective for each of the players is to avoid escalation without at the same time losing each of the more or less isolated games. To limit his losses without exposing himself to escalation, each player commits himself to defending vital stakes and attempts to convince the other that this commitment is irrevocable, but he does his best to keep this commitment from being unacceptable to the adversary, so that it will involve for the latter neither a loss of important position nor a loss of face. Such a game is essentially historical and psychological, each action modifying the conditions of the initial game, the utility of a stake never being the same for the adversaries, no transfer of utility having a concrete meaning. It does not exclude reasonable behavior, any more than a traditional diplomacy does. It lends itself, no more in our period than in the course of past centuries, to a rational formulation (one which would impress the actor as the truth of a theorem impresses someone who understands the demonstration). Indeed, it seems to me that the strategy of the thermonuclear age is further from the model of rational strategy than that of the ages of pre-nuclear armaments. Before 1955, that is, before the establishment of the thermonuclear duopoly, the game itself did not seem unreasonable, whereas today the players would probably prefer to leave the game or to put an end to it in one way or another.[13] The strategy of commitment, of threats, of bluff, is linked to the "personality" of the player more than any other strategy. Now, the players of the democratic camp, with a free press and a political personnel often unconscious of the nature of the game, have never so little resembled *one* person. The decisions taken run the risk of reflecting non-transitive preferences because they express compromises, within states, among individuals or among groups.

Reasonable and not rational, a diplomatic-strategy, in the thermonuclear age and in the age of ideologies, confronts leaders and mere citizens with moral antinomies still more agonizing than those of the past. What President of the United States would give the Strategic Air Command the order to attack, knowing the cost of a thermonuclear war for the American people themselves? Would the acceptance of risk and the refusal of appeasement that passed for virtues when dealing with a Hitler be the same if we were confronting another Hitler now? Are they virtues, confronting the man who brandishes a hundred-megaton bomb?

The contradiction between morality and politics, says the philosopher who observes past history with the detachment of a sage, is not as Friedrich Meinecke, the analyst of the *raison d'état*, describes it. Morality, too, is born

---

[13] The suppression of the infinite risk by stopping the game or by the monopoly of armaments (which is another way of stopping the game).

in history, has been developed through time. It is the very progress of our moral conceptions which leads us to judge severely the practices of states and gradually to transform them. It is in the concrete morality of collectivities that universal morality is realized—however imperfectly. And it is in and by politics that concrete moralities are achieved.[14]

It is true that the absolute antinomy between morality and diplomatic-strategic action is, in certain doctrines, created by the partial definition we give of both. If there is no other morality than that of the Christian who sacrifices himself without a calculation, of course a chief of state, even a Christian one, will not act as a Christian, *but neither would the director of a corporation.* The individual responsible for a private or public collectivity, who is just to the others, must insist on his due because this due is not his own but that of those for whom he has assumed responsibility and leadership. No prince is entitled to make his nation the Christ among nations. A nation which seeks to live, hence which asserts a will to power among other nations, is not thereby immoral. The pessimism of the American realists often has at its origin a false or excessive idea of what morality requires.

It is nonetheless true that *coercion* is and has always been inseparable from all politics, that coercion among states is expressed by the *threat* or *use of armed force*, and that the individual is obliged by law *to serve his country, whether or not he approves of the cause for which the latter is fighting.*

Of course, coercion is not illegitimate as such. All or almost all nations owe their existence to coercion, and even the American nation, created by civilized individuals on an almost virgin soil, must forget the War between the States in order to believe in its favorite ideology, that of the fundamental opposition of consent and domination, of idealist diplomacy and power politics. Nor has internal politics ever managed fundamentally to eliminate the element of conflicts and violence. Even when the constitutional order is not violated by *coups d'état* or revolutions, which mark the return to a kind of state of nature, the regular functioning of democratic regimes does not keep one or another fraction of those governed from feeling, and sometimes with cause, oppressed, from suffering coercion and therefore from seeing no other hope of avoiding it than rebellion, i.e., violence. At least it is possible to give meaning to the political course of events within states: to establish government by consent, to insure the protection of individual liberties by laws, to create conditions such that all members of the collectivity will share

[14] Eric Weil, apropos of Meinecke's book *Idee der Staatsräson*, in *Critique*, July 1961, pp. 664–65: "... *Pure violence* is no longer possible, and, if it appears, arouses a united opposition and thus aids historical awareness and its moral progress. It would be a paradox only in appearance to assert that the problem of violence in history would not be raised if it were not already transcended by the thought which raises it and if this consciousness lacked more than the courage to understand, to acknowledge itself."

the benefits of culture and the city. Down through the centuries, man has acceded to humanity: the dignity of each is recognized by all, the rule of law permits all to live according to reason.

Among the nations, do we perceive the slightest sign that the course of events has a meaning? That states are disposed to renounce the right of deciding their own law? That the great powers are more inclined in the twentieth century A.D. than B.C. to respect the small and not to abuse their own strength? What is more serious is that the common conscience seems to me even today ready to subscribe to the formula (which we may judge sublime or ignoble) *my country right or wrong* rather than the imperatives without which peace by law or world federation is merely a dangerous Utopia.

How, moreover, would the moralists condemn the citizen who pledges himself to obey the orders of his state, whatever these orders may be? If the historian finds it so difficult, even with the perspective of time, equitably to distribute blame in the armed conflicts where human collectivities are in opposition, how can an individual, besieged by contradictory propaganda, lacking adequate information, claim to settle the matter? Is not his best course, once and for all, to abide by the oath of allegiance which he implicitly made the day when he first enjoyed the privileges and the heritage which the mere fact of his membership in a historical collectivity assured him? We know today what such an oath may oblige us to do. We also know that there are circumstances in which the moralist, like the historian, observes the antinomy, the contradictory choices of each side, and refuses to judge. The German who detested Hitler but served in the German army, the German who detested Hitler and worked for the defeat of the Third Reich found themselves in opposing camps, though deep in their hearts they cherished the same refusals and the same hopes. There is no general rule which permits determining with certainty where the individual right of rebellion begins and where it ends against the state that has fallen into the hands of a usurper, against a regime which betrays the elemental values of the collectivity.

Short of extreme cases, should the citizen who believed the Algerian war more unjust than just have gone into exile and fought beside the Algerian Nationalists? Should he have refused the uniform if he was called to serve? Or obeyed the rage within his heart? What attitude should a member of the opposition take in order to serve his ideas without being disloyal to his country?

Such cases of conscience also appear within states, it will be objected: if the prince is tyrannical, the regime despotic, if the leaders abuse even a legal authority, the individual faces the alternative of submission or revolt. Surely this alternative is inseparable from political existence, since all concrete moralities require submission to laws and to princes, but none forbids revolt against certain laws and certain princes. The alternative, nonetheless, has quite a different bearing when we consider the rivalry of nations.

The state requires that the citizen risk his life for it. When the state's cause is identified, in the eyes of the citizen, with that of the nation, the acceptance of sacrifice appears an integral part of the duties which life and society involve for each man. But the day when a Hitler requires a German of liberal conviction to take the supreme risk, the contradiction is, in the true sense of the word, a tragic one: he must betray his ideas or his country, contribute to the victory of a regime he detests or to the abasement of a collectivity to which he is attached with all his heart. Further, if he wishes to be clear-sighted, he must admit that certain features of the regime which are odious to him are not necessarily contrary to the secular fortune of states. It is sometimes true that *this world* belongs to the violent.

Let us stop a moment to consider this aspect of the dispute over Machiavellianism or of *raison d'état*. Are the nations which prevail in international competition the least just, the most brutal, that is, the most primitive both internally and externally? It is difficult, and it would be false, I believe, to answer with a categorical *yes* or *no*. The thesis of the constant contradiction between what is good for the collectivity and what is in accord with morality is indefensible, even if we wrongly define the *useful* exclusively by reference to the power of the collectivity. When candidates for the exercise of power or those who possess it act contrary to the rules which subjects or citizens spontaneously regard as valid, they weaken the respect for law and morality, which is a source of strength for the collectivity itself, at the same time that they undermine their own credit. A people which thereby comes to despise its own laws and its masters is certainly not a strong people. But when an order has collapsed and must be built anew from nothing, those who have the best chance of prevailing are those who possess the least Christian virtues,[15] the capacity for command, the aptitude for brutality and cunning, fanatic confidence in themselves and in their cause. The victors believe in a government by men, not in government by law.

Externally as well, it is not true that only the Machiavellians, in the vulgar sense of the term, are assured success. On condition that we give force a vague and vast sense, P. J. Proudhon was not entirely wrong to suggest that in the end the right of force tends to coincide with justice or even that force does not give any more than what it deserves to each nation. France's armed force permitted the conquest of Algeria, not the assimilation of the Algerians:

[15] Bruce Lockhart, the British consul general in Russia at the time of the fall of the Tsars, tells how he predicted the success of the Bolsheviks after having observed an edifying scene: Trotsky, by the force of his speech and his personality, restoring to obedience a half-drunken band of soldiers. The other party, the Mensheviks, the revolutionary socialists, had the majority of the Russian people for them. They dreamed of laws, liberties, anarchism. The Bolsheviks re-established army discipline and the death penalty.

because this assimilation exceeded France's forces, the conquest was vain as well as unjust. But to count upon this final reconciliation (when does the end come?) is to believe in fairy tales. Armed force, down through history, has permitted both making and maintaining conquests (social, moral and spiritual) that were not justified by force. It is possible that the Soviet Union will one day pay for the injustice which it has committed, since 1945, with regard to the East Europeans, as France has paid since 1944 for the injustice it committed a century before with regard to the Algerians. We know nothing of such matters, and we have no guarantee that such will be the case.

A regime that reduces the citizens' concrete liberties, that dedicates an important fraction of the national resources to external politics, possesses evident advantages over a regime which leaves to individuals the prerogatives of determining the degree of mobilization or of investment. Certainly if the citizens who enjoyed this prerogative were virtuous, they would prevail over a despotic regime. What the latter obtains by coercion, virtuous citizens would grant out of civic-mindedness. In the real world, voluntary mobilization will remain generally inferior to enforced mobilization. The formula that peoples lose their empire when they lose the desire to rule, a notion borrowed from a British diplomat, expresses only a part of the truth: peoples often lose the desire to rule when they discover the impossibility of retaining their empire. But it remains true that today, as yesterday, the desire to rule is indispensable to secular greatness and that the leaders of the Soviet Union give us proof that compromises with principles are possible.

Thus the essence of international relations remains apparently constant down through the centuries, the concrete characteristics of war and peace being determined by the weapons available, the character of the regimes in conflict and the stakes of those conflicts. Peace is less pacific today than a century ago because the rivalry of states and the competition of ideologies reinforce each other. A major war would be more terrible than at any other period not because men are worse, but because they know more.

Is there no sign of a progress of order among states, comparable to that which it is not impossible to glimpse in the internal order of states?[16] Does not the present result of the history of wars permit us to define the international order which would correspond to the vocation of humanity and at the same time to specify under what conditions it could be realized?

This optimism is not entirely without foundation. Among those who subscribe to it, some emphasize the awareness, by a minority, of humanity as a unit, higher in dignity than all individual collectivities. According to others,

---

[16] I am concerned here neither with a regular progress nor with a certainty for the future. There are regressions. I mean that the philosopher can determine in what would consist the social order desired by moral conscience today and that, in relation to this ideal, political history assumes a meaning and a direction.

it is economic solidarity among all collectivities which is the major phenomenon and which will oblige the nations to transcend nationalisms and to
perfect a reasonable organization of their coexistence. According to still
others, it is the evident absurdity of a war waged with the modern means of
destruction which makes recourse to weapons by the great powers anachronistic. As for wars of liberation, they belong to the epochs which the
peoples of Europe have behind them.

None of these arguments is without its weight. None is convincing. Tribal
consciousness is, on the whole, incomparably stronger than human consciousness. The increasing complexity of relations among political units, the fact
that in the twentieth century history is for the first time universal do not
prevent the breakdown of communications in the face of a totalitarian regime. In a sense, between one ideological universe and the other, more is
spoken but less is understood and less is desired to be understood. Two
thirds of humanity are not contemporary with the privileged minority, but
will they be so tomorrow? When will they be so? Will they accept *not* being
so? The collective wills-to-power and thirsts for glory are there, intact, along
with the thermonuclear bombs at their service. The right to life of communities of culture is perhaps ignored less by today's conquerors (with the
exception of Hitler) than by the barbarians. Would it suffice, if a totalitarian
state should prevail, to preserve the existence of communities which, like
Carthage, would have resisted their conqueror down to the last man?

I dare not assert that we can discover the present effectiveness, the
Wirklichkeit of the idea that would give meaning to the monotonous succession of victories and defeats, of states and empires. I am not sure that men
desire peace on this earth. Certainly they wish to escape the horrors of war,
but do they wish to renounce the joys of collective pride, the triumphs of
those who speak in their name? Can they, from one collectivity to another,
trust each other to the point of doing without the means of force and entrust-
ing to a tribunal the task of settling their conflicts? A century from now, will
they have decided in common on the reasonable limit of world population,
without which they will be confronted by the threat of a virtually absolute
overpopulation or, at least, of an overpopulation that will revive a struggle
for resources, for raw materials, for space itself, a struggle compared to which
the wars of the past will seem insignificant? Finally and above all, will men
be close enough to each other within their systems of beliefs and values to
tolerate differences of culture just as the members of the same political unit
tolerate differences among provinces?

It is difficult for me to answer all of these questions affirmatively. I do
not deny two new factors: the capacity for manipulation of natural forces
for production and for destruction, the germ of a human conscience, both
moral (all men are men) and pragmatic (it is in the interest of all men to
limit conflicts among the fractions of humanity). Are these two new factors

proof of a new phase of the human enterprise? We cannot know, we must desire, we are entitled to hope that it is so.

But we also know, to return to Bertrand Russell's prophecies, that peace and war among nations are capable of leading to various results. Either humanity will forget what it has learned and will return to the pre-industrial age; or humanity will emerge from a belligerent period following the catastrophes, and all peoples will not survive to know the benefits of the post-belligerent phase; or else humanity will continue for some centuries more the tragic game in the shadow of the apocalypse, hygiene being capable of filling within several decades the gaps opened in a few minutes by the thermonuclear exchanges; or else, finally—a preferable but not the most probable hypothesis—the nations will gradually surmount their prejudices and their egoism, fanatics will cease to incarnate their dreams of the absolute in political ideologies, and science will give humanity, grown conscious of itself, the possibility of administering the available resources rationally, in relation to the number of the living. The organization will be universal; the communities of culture will be numerous and small. The so-called *Macht-staaten* having completed their mission, will wither away into a pacified humanity. . . .

Let the reader not smile too quickly. Humanity is still in its childhood, if we refer to the time which it still has to live. "We may believe today, without speaking of the vanished races, that *Homo sapiens* has existed on earth for sixty to a hundred thousand years, and that the present state of the cosmos promises him a posterity of some several million years. Limiting the duration of the *human phenomenon* to a million years, we can estimate that we have lived perhaps a tenth of it and that nine tenths still remain to be experienced. Thus the duration of humanity would be in a relation of 10,-000/1 to that of the individual. Humanity today would be to mature humanity as the child of ten is to the old man. A thousand years of humanity corresponds to a month in individual life. In the life of humanity, we are ten years old. During our first five or six years, without parent or master, we were scarcely able to distinguish ourselves from the other mammals; subsequently we have discovered art, morality, law, religion. We have known how to read and write for less than a year. We built the Parthenon less than three months ago; two months ago, Christ was born. Less than fifteen days ago, we began to identify clearly the experimental scientific method which permits us to know a few realities about the universe; two days ago, we learned how to utilize electricity and build airplanes; we are a little boy of ten, brave, strong and full of promise; as of next year we shall know how to write themes without mistakes in spelling and how to do our arithmetic correctly. In two years we shall enter our last class of school, and we shall then take our first communion. In a hundred thousand years we shall attain our majority."[17]

[17] J. Fourastié, *op. cit.*, pp. 260–61.

It would be shameful to let ourselves be overcome by the woes of our generation and the dangers of the immediate future to the point where we abandon hope. But it would be no less so to abandon ourselves to Utopia and to ignore the wounds of our condition.

Nothing can prevent us from having two duties, duties that are not always compatible, toward our people and toward all peoples: one is to participate in the conflicts that constitute the web of history, and the other is to work for peace. Humanity might be brought to peace and no man speak French any longer. Other collectivities with a national vocation have disappeared without leaving a trace. In a few years or decades from now, it may be that the human race will destroy itself; or that one people may exterminate all others and occupy the planet alone.

Will we be obliged to choose between a return to the pre-industrial age and the advent of the post-belligerent age? Will humanity, in this unknown age, be homogeneous or heterogeneous? Will societies be comparable to an anthill or to a free city? Will the age of wars end in an orgy of violence or in a gradual pacification?

We know that the answers to these questions remain uncertain, but we do know that man will have surmounted the antinomies of action only when he has finished with violence, or with hope.

Let us leave to others with more talent for illusions the privilege of speculating on the conclusion of the adventure, and let us try not to fail either of the obligations ordained for each of us: not to run away from a belligerent history, not to betray the ideal; to think and to act with the firm intention that the absence of war will be prolonged until the day when peace has become possible—supposing it ever will.

Index

deplorable effects of victory for
American side, 29
different goals of allies in, 43–44
national unity of combatants in, 66
political conduct of, on Soviet side,
29
responsibility for, 115–16
victory as goal of, 26–27
Worldwide federation of humanity,
possibilities of 7, 735–36, 755,
757–59, 766, 784–87
Wright, Quincy, 320, 322, 327n.,
328, 329, 333, 352, 364n.

Yalta agreement, 30
Yamamoto, Gombei, 32n.
Yugoslavia:
and Soviet bloc, 501, 508, 510,
534
Soviet Union blockade against, 59,
726

Zero planes, of Japan, 66
Zones of refuge, and limited wars, 38